Jacques Lacan & Co.

Elisabeth Roudinesco

Jacques Lacan & Co.

*A History of Psychoanalysis
in France, 1925–1985*

Translated, with a Foreword, by Jeffrey Mehlman

The University of Chicago Press   *Chicago*

ELISABETH ROUDINESCO is the author or coauthor of several previous books on psychoanalysis.

JEFFREY MEHLMAN is professor of French literature at Boston University. A translator of Lacan, he is the author, most recently, of *Legacies: Of Anti-Semitism in France*.

This book was first published in Paris under the title *La bataille de cent ans: Histoire de la psychanalyse en France, 2*. © Éditions du Seuil, octobre 1986.

The University of Chicago Press, Chicago 60637
Free Association Books, London
© 1990 by The University of Chicago
All rights reserved. Published 1990
Printed in the United States of America
99 98 97 96 95 94 93 92 91 90   5 4 3 2 1

Library of Congress Cataloging-in-Publication Data
Roudinesco, Elisabeth, 1944–
   [Bataille de cent ans. 2. 1925–1985. English]
   Jacques Lacan & Co. : a history of psychoanalysis in France,
1925–1985 / translated with a foreword by Jeffrey Mehlman.
      p. cm.
   Translation of : La bataille de cent ans. 2.
   Includes bibliographical references.
   ISBN 0-226-72997-4
   1. Psychoanalysis—France—History. 2. Lacan, Jacques, 1901–
I. Title. II. Title: Jacques Lacan and Co.
BF175.R67813 1990   89-78164
150.19′5′09—dc20   CIP

To the memory of Laurence Bataille

Concealed in the submission to the rules of a task and the regularity of objectively imposed exigencies there is a possibility for an eroticization of history—a quickening and quickened passion, I might almost say, love itself.

—Michel de Certeau

Contents

Translator's Foreword

Lacan burst into American intellectual awareness some twenty years ago as a baroque tonic to the minimalist imagination.[1] The analytic or "symbolic" efficacy of Poe's "purloined letter," to choose his most celebrated example, was crucially enmeshed in the question of the ultimate irrelevance of that "letter"'s author or contents. Even more than through his tortured syntax, Lacan was—or should have been—associated with Mallarmé by virtue of their common commitment to understanding per se construed as a radical *askesis*. Now it is one measure of the significance of Elisabeth Roudinesco's accomplishment in her history of psychoanalysis in France that Lacan, beyond his affinities with the minimalists Poe and Mallarmé, emerges from it as having his most profound literary bond with the world of the epic. For he figures here as the protagonist of an almost Virgilian narrative of the half-century struggle to effect the establishment—and ultimate intellectual hegemony—of a *gens freudiana,* cast out from Vienna, on French soil.[2] Set between a Viennese Troy and a Parisian Rome, this work is in many ways a tale—or series of tales—of two cities. But in the centrality of Lacan's role in virtually all those tales, it is nothing so much as a Lacaniad.

Paris, of course, was no more than a way station for Freud himself on his path of exile from Vienna to London. And indeed it is one of the fascinations of Roudinesco's work to have situated her history against the broad backdrop of what might be called the westering of psychoanalysis, that general trend which has seen the institutional spread—and success—of the movement find its center of gravity in the English-speaking world. That triumph, like every triumph, was, by definition, a form of repression. And the paradox of every "triumph of psychoanalysis" lies in the fact that psychoanalysis draws its very sustenance from a nurturing—or freeing—of the repressed per se. So that every triumph of psychoanalysis risks, in principle, being a triumph *over* psychoanalysis. The point is, I think, implicit in a number of Lacan's formulations, but finds a particularly telling illustration in Roudinesco's provocative reading of the resonances between the case of Dr. Schreber, in Freud's classic study, and that of the exemplary figure of that West toward which

---

1. The first translations of Lacan to appear in English were Jan Miel's "The Insistence of the Letter in the Unconscious" in *Structuralism, Yale French Studies* 36–37 (1966); Anthony Wilden's "The Function of Language in Psychoanalysis" in *The Language of the Self* (Baltimore: Johns Hopkins University Press, 1968); and my own "Seminar on 'The Purloined Letter'" in *French Freud, Yale French Studies* 48 (1972).

2. The "half-century" refers to the lion's share of the period covered by this volume, which is the second and final one in Roudinesco's history. The complete history covers a full century (1885–1985), from Freud's stay in the Paris of Charcot to the aftermath of Lacan's death, and is entitled *La bataille de cent ans.*

psychoanalysis, already in 1932, seemed destined, Woodrow Wilson, in the post-humous Freud-Bullitt monograph.[3]

Within France itself the most prominent representatives, during Freud's last years, of that Viennese "orthodoxy" that would eventually triumph in the United States were Marie Bonaparte and (Lacan's psychoanalyst) Rudolph Loewenstein. Indeed Loewenstein would go on to be a founder, along with Heinz Hartmann and Ernst Kris, of American ego psychology. Now what is quite remarkable—and unprecedented—in Roudinesco's reading of French psychoanalysis is her delineation of what—and whom—it was that psychoanalysis *triumphans,* in the persons of Bonaparte and Loewenstein, was triumphing over and indeed "repressing." For it turns out that Lacan, in championing an understanding of Freud that had been *repressed* in the course of the westering of psychoanalysis, at times implicitly, at times explicitly, revived the traditions and terminology of that repressed "trend."

Broadly speaking, the trend receives the name "chauvinist" from Roudinesco and finds its exemplary spokesman in Édouard Pichon. In the first volume of her history, we learn that Pichon wore three hats: leading (though conventional) French psychoanalyst and president of the Société psychanalytique de Paris from 1935 to 1937; highly inventive and prolific theorist of French grammar; and militant of the extreme right-wing (royalist) group, Action Française.[4] In that latter capacity, moreover, Pichon may have been the last spokesman of a tradition in French thought on the "unconscious," before World War II and its camps changed the rules of discourse on the subject, which allows Roudinesco, during the first part of her work, to write a history—or prehistory—of French psychoanalysis concomitant with a history of French anti-Semitism.[5] (The pertinent names are Barrès, Drumont, Le Bon, Bertillon, and Léon Daudet, the entire cohort of proto-fascist thinkers wed to a hereditarian-degenerative understanding of what many of them called the "unconscious.")[6] The chauvinist qua racist trend, that is, precisely to the extent that it was an efflorescence of a French political tradition no longer entitled to expression and (for the best reasons) destined to abject oblivion was perhaps on that very account ideally suited to cathexis (and, to be sure, displacement) by the "unconscious" and the innovative discourse—Lacan's own—about to strike out (in both senses of the phrase?) in its behalf.

If the unconscious is, among other things, the conflictual (parental) discourse presiding over the launching of an individual existence and imperfectly grasped by its *subject,* consider in that light the circumstances of Lacan's appointment, in 1938, as a titular member of the Société psychanalytique de Paris. Pichon, eminently distrustful of the cosmopolitan and Viennese cast of the international psychoanalytic movement, dreamed of cleansing French psychoanalysis of such influences and constituting it on the model of a militant "league" of the sort then convulsing French

3. See *La bataille de cent ans,* vol. 1 (Paris: Ramsay, 1982; Seuil, 1986), pp. 143–144.

4. Ibid., vol. 1, "Édouard Pichon: Doctor Jekyll and Mister Hyde," pp. 297–320.

5. Ibid. See in particular the chapters entitled "L'inconscient à la française (de Gustave Le Bon à l'affaire Dreyfus), pp. 181–221, and the subchapter "Judéité, israélisme, antisémitisme," pp. 395–411.

6. Roudinesco makes ample use of the important work of Zeev Sternhell on "the French origins of fascism," *La droite révolutionnaire* (Paris: Seuil, 1978).

national politics.[7] His choice for a potential leader, we learn from Roudinesco, was (after René Laforgue, whose abortive attempts at collaboration with the Germans during World War II are set forth in this volume) Jacques Lacan. Lacan himself enjoyed to a far lesser degree the support and confidence of his own analyst, Rudolph Loewenstein. Indeed Lacan's appointment in 1938 was something of a trade-off. Loewenstein was made to understand that if he expected Pichon to go along with the appointment of Heinz Hartmann, then fleeing Hitlerian persecution, to the French society, he would have to swallow the appointment of Pichon's protégé (and his own analysand), Lacan. Plainly if the conflictual lines of force informing the emergence of a human subjectivity are of the essence in psychoanalysis, the political deal that saw Lacan—who was in no way an anti-Semite—traded off for a Jewish victim of persecution (who would later become his *bête noire!*) cannot but be of central importance.[8]

At the level of Lacan's own theoretical discourse the debt to Pichon is still more curious. At its best, the Lacanian touch in reading lies in a sensitivity to what might be called the conceptual doublet, the realization that a number of crucial Freudian terms are doubly inscribed and that the whole Freudian problematic can be generated (or squandered) in the systematicity of the gaps between those twin valences.[9] The process begins in Freud with the distinction between instinct (*Instinkt*) and drive (*Trieb*) and ramifies productively throughout his work. The most interesting case in the present context is that of *forclusion*. "A *Verdrängung* is something other than a *Verwerfung*," Freud wrote in "The Wolf-Man," and Lacan's theory of psychosis lay in a teasing out of a psychic mode of "foreclosure" or repudiation (*Verwerfung*) other than that of repression (*Verdrängung*).[10] The rejection of a "primordial signifier" (such as the phallus) from the subject's symbolic universe would entail a veritable gap in the unconscious, and a return from without of what had been "foreclosed," as hallucination. Now whatever the (considerable) value of "foreclosure" as clinical and epistemological concept, it has become clear, thanks to Roudinesco, that the term, before being a translation of Freud's German, was a borrowing from Pichon's French. In an essay on "the psychological significance of negation in French," the grammarian Pichon isolated a grammatical instance which he termed the *forclusif* and associated with what his psychoanalytic colleague René Laforgue had been advancing, under the rubric "scotomization," as the motor mechanism of schizophrenia.[11] Both terms—one linguistic, the other psychological— would deal with a wished-for inexistence of something banished from consciousness and to that extent would serve as a matrix (in ways Roudinesco deploys with great

7. See *La bataille de cent ans*, vol. 1, p. 309.

8. On this subject see p. 122 of the present volume.

9. The most illuminating reading of Freud in this light is, no doubt, Jean Laplanche, *Life and Death in Psychoanalysis*, trans. J. Mehlman (Baltimore: Johns Hopkins University Press, 1976).

10. Freud, "From the History of an Infantile Neurosis" in *Three Case Histories* (New York: Collier, 1963), p. 270. Lacan's principal discussions of "forclusion" are to be found in *Écrits* (Paris: Seuil, 1967), "Réponse au commentaire de Jean Hyppolite" and "Du traitement possible de la psychose."

11. Édouard Pichon, "Sur la signification psychologique de la négation en français" in *Journal de psychologie normale et pathologique* (March 1928), p. 245.

adeptness) for Lacan's later "discovery" and isolation of *Verwerfung*. Significantly, Laforgue himself was locked in conflict with Freud over the acceptability of the term and notion of "scotomization," which Freud rejects in an addendum to *The Problem of Anxiety*. He would eventually use the term *Verleugnung* (disavowal) to hold Laforgue's term at bay. What is most significant in the present context is that in this (exemplary) case it was Pichon who allowed Lacan to reopen Freud's debate with Laforgue and settle matters in a way which may indeed be more radically Freudian, but which is no less Pichonian for that. Here as elsewhere, to quote Roudinesco, "the conceptual labor of Pichon serves as a support for Lacan's reelaboration of psychoanalytic doctrine." [12]

Did the debt to the most prominent psychoanalyst in Action Française leave a political mark in Lacan's work? Roudinesco suggests not. Yet consider the exemplary use he made of the myth of Acteon at the end of "La chose freudienne [The Freudian Thing]." On the one hand, the myth is a parable of psychoanalysis properly construed: The analyst, upon confronting the truth of castration (Diana in her nudity) is called on to play Acteon, bearing witness to the violation of the integrity of his ego by his "own" unconscious drives (allegorically, the hounds). On the other, the myth is a somewhat paranoid allegory of the historical tragedy of psychoanalysis—the work of Freud-Acteon, having encountered truth, is torn to shreds by his inferior followers. Now those followers are referred to as a "diaspora" of "emigrants." [13] Lacan's villains, that is, are in this case less Americans than Jews. Freud-Acteon, on the other hand, is said to be inspired by "a properly Christian concern for the soul's movements." [14] In the logic of this reading of the myth, moreover, the role of Diana in her bath falls to none other than the Statue of Liberty, before whom, Lacan notes, Freud and Jung passed en route to Clark University: the emigrant diaspora comprise the "hounds" of Liberty. All of which—the castigation of ego psychology as a Jewish cultural formation, the outlandish identification of Freud with Christianity, and the oblique assimilation of treacherous Diana to the Statue of Liberty—join to revive a Christian typological reading of the myth—Acteon/Christ and the hounds/the Jews—that one suspects the Action Française militant in Pichon might have appreciated. [15]

Freud's own unremitting fidelity to the Jews, if not to their faith, took the form of an identification with Hannibal, the Semite hero of the Second Punic War, who came close to laying Rome low. [16] Lacan, whose fascination with Rome, as Roudinesco observes, was less with the glory of antiquity than with the baroque

12. *La bataille de cent ans,* vol. 1, p. 383. On "the fantastic itinerary of the concept of 'foreclosure,'" see also pp. 314–316 and 384–395.

13. Lacan, *Écrits,* p. 402.

14. Ibid., p. 407.

15. For a discussion of Lacan's affinities with and possible debt to the great Catholic *fin de siècle* writer Léon Bloy, see my "Suture of an Allusion: Lacan with Léon Bloy" in *Legacies: Of Anti-Semitism in France* (Minneapolis: University of Minnesota Press, 1983) and "The Paranoid Style in French Prose," forthcoming in *Oxford Literary Review.*

16. Concerning Freud's identification with Hannibal, see *The Interpretation of Dreams,* trans. J. Strachey (New York: Avon, 1967), pp. 229–230.

Counter-Reformation, nevertheless came to assign himself an imaginary role in the Punic Wars. Toward the end of his life, at the time he decided to place the full brunt of his authority into the dismantling of his own École freudienne, he issued a *Delenda est,* which served as the slogan of the "dissolutionists." [17] In identifying with the fanatical anti-Carthaginianism of the aging Cato, in dissolving the work of his maturity, Lacan may have been seeking to embody Thanatos itself—that is, essaying the most Freudian posture imaginable. Yet for anyone alive to the force of Freud's identification with Hannibal, the recourse to a figure of anti-Carthaginian fanaticism cannot but give pause. Somewhere between those identifications, Hannibal and Cato, Freud and Lacan, in the chiasmus they configure, the extraordinary story told by Roudinesco, with the pivotal role it assigns to Édouard Pichon, looms as a promise of uncommon illumination.

Paris, Vienna; Rome, Carthage: Roudinesco's history, I have suggested, offers more than one tale of two cities. Perhaps it is fitting, then, that this introduction to the University of Chicago Press edition of *Jacques Lacan & Co.* end with one final tale—of Baltimore and Chicago.

In the late 1960s and 1970s, Baltimore was for many American academics the port of entry from which news of what seemed the unprecedented intellectual effervescence in Paris came to be expected. It was there that Lacan made his first appearance in the United States, declaring that "the unconscious was Baltimore in the early hours of the morning." [18] It was there too that Derrida performed the pseudo-gallant gesture, in a much remarked seminar, of restoring to Marie Bonaparte the reading of Poe he erroneously suggested that Lacan had all but purloined from her. [19] And it was also in Baltimore that critic after critic hatched the plan of at last bringing the good (traumatic) news from France home to English. But the unconscious has never respected the logic of (dazzled) perception. Indeed it is the signal quality of the Freudian unconscious to stage its attacks not at all through the perceptual port of entry that Freud (in 1895) called the *phi* system, but by way of reminiscences, from a site—or direction—the ego is least prepared to deal with. [20] I believe something analogous to this will happen to the "Baltimore-bound" American reader of this book. For he will perceive that the Baltimore-Paris story, in so far as the Lacanian venture is concerned, was but a very local formation within an older and larger dialogue that (never) took place between an International Psychoanalytical Association said to be run from Chicago and the Lacanians. "Lacan contre Chicago" was indeed the battle-cry of Lacanianism during what were undoubtedly

17. See below, p. 656.

18. See below, p. 412.

19. See Jacques Derrida, "The Purveyor of Truth," trans. W. Domingo, J. Hulbert, M. Ron, and M.-R. Logan in *Graphesis, Yale French Studies* 52 (1975). In claiming that the "purloined letter" finds its castratory destination in the lap of the Queen, Derrida overlooks Lacan's statement that the letter's "address" is "in the place previously occupied by the King, since it is there that it would re-enter the order of the Law" (p. 69). But in so doing, he stages an allegory of his own would-be gesture of restoring the allegedly purloined argument of Lacan's text to its source (and destination), Marie Bonaparte.

20. See Laplanche, chapters 2 and 3.

its finest years.[21] And if psychoanalysis consists in part in the restoration of a forgotten or repressed past, this work may fulfill just such a function for many a literary intellectual.

Here I shall take the liberty of sharing my personal jolt in discovering—in an appendix to this volume—the table of contents of an English-language collection which, for a variety of reasons, was never published, but which comes close to coinciding with that of the collection *French Freud,* which, some years later, I believed I had the unprecedented idea of publishing in 1972. If the discovery that one's own words are but the quotation of a statement never uttered is one touchstone of analytic success, this volume is one of the very few that has had that effect on me. It is a book of encyclopedic lore and fascinating detail, as close to the intellectual history of several generations of French intellectuals as we are likely to get, but it was above all the hope that it might foster moments of analytic insight in others of the sort I encountered in that appendix, I confess, that led me to translate it.

A word on the notes to this volume: Because the existence of the many French translations of psychoanalytic texts referred to by Roudinesco is itself a significant element in this history, I have retained those references, appending where appropriate references to English-language editions of the same works.

21. See below, p. 334.

Preface to the American Edition

The English-speaking reader of *A History of Psychoanalysis in France* (originally entitled *La bataille de cent ans*, "The Hundred Years' Battle") will have access only to the modern period of this long adventure, that is, to sixty rather than a hundred years. In the French edition, this volume is preceded by an earlier one (called *Bataille* I in the references, see n. 2, chapter 1) that covers the period 1885–1925 and retraces the prehistory of psychoanalysis as well as the period of the pioneers of the French movement in their relations with Freud and with the international psychoanalytic movement. Since that first volume is at present not slated for publication in the United States (although it has already appeared in Spanish and in Portuguese), I shall offer a glimpse of its contents in order to afford readers some information concerning the period prior to the one whose course they are about to follow.

The temporality of "battle" is not that of war, but of a privileged phase of war in which the history of a doctrine merges with that of its crises, in which the crises themselves bear witness to the implantation of a doctrine, to its defeats and triumphs. The author relates the history of psychoanalysis from the perspective of its battles, occasionally resorting to theoretical tools forged by psychoanalysis itself.

The use of the terms French, American, Viennese, or Jewish psychoanalysis is incorrect. I have used them only "metaphorically," or in order to relate them to authors who have defined them in a specific ideological context. There is no *French psychoanalysis,* but a *French situation of psychoanalysis,* as idiosyncratic as that of other countries. Theory, like thought itself, knows neither national boundaries nor homelands, but the conditions under which it is pursued are always national and language-bound.

The first phase of the history of the origins of psychoanalysis in France retraces the discovery of hysteria at the "hospice" of the Salpêtrière, Freud's meeting of Charcot in Paris, the dismembering of the latter's doctrine under the influence of the works of Babinski, and finally the traces left by his teaching in French literary culture, particularly in the work of Guy de Maupassant.

A detour is then taken through Vienna, where, within a specifically Jewish milieu, the first psychoanalytical circle was formed. Then the conflict between Freud, on the one hand, and Jung, and the Zurich school, on the other, is broached, followed by a discussion of the rise of the international psychoanalytic movement, a veritable "conquest of the West" for Freudian doctrine. Against those three backdrops are deployed the reformulations and battles which marked the introduction of psychoanalysis in France.

The return to French territory begins with an historical discussion of the various intellectual currents linked to the theory of heredity and degeneration. That theory was not only a psychiatric doctrine but a mode of thought running through, most notably, the constitution of modern anti-Semitism in the crucible of the Dreyfus Affair and as an extension of the themes of social Darwinism. The chapter closes with the advent of a psychology fundamentally grounded in its hostility to alleged "Freudian pansexualism."

The section of the first volume entitled *Histoire des Douze* ["Story of the Twelve"] relates the fate of the first generation of French psychoanalysts, that of the founders of the Société psychanalytique de Paris (SPP), created in 1926: Marie Bonaparte, René Laforgue, Raymond de Saussure, Edouard Pichon, Charles Odier, Adrien Borel, René Allendy, Georges Parcheminey, Rudolph Loewenstein, Eugénie Sokolnicka, Angelo Hesnard, and Henri Codet. The study of that period brings us to 1939, with incursions, in the course of commenting on certain texts, into the postwar period. In a kind of counterpoint, the reader will also find a history of the first generation of the psychiatrists of the Evolution psychiatrique group, founded in 1925. They represented a new dynamic tendency in psychiatry, and most of them were members of the SPP.

I would like to express my gratitude to Jeffrey Mehlman for his splendid translation and my hope that he will one day have the opportunity to return to the task and bring before the English-speaking world the first part of this hundred-year battle.

Elisabeth Roudinesco
January 1989

Preface to the French Edition

The first volume of the original French edition of this work pursued the history of psychoanalysis in France until 1939. It began in 1885 with the meeting between Freud and Charcot at the Salpêtrière and ended in 1939 with the exploits of the Société psychanalytique de Paris and its twelve founders. But it excluded a crucial phase of that heroic era: the implantation of psychoanalysis by way of the literary imagination. That is why this second volume takes up the story afresh in 1925, in order to deal with the same period (until 1939) from an entirely different perspective.

The first part of this volume thus covers the history of the literary implantation of psychoanalysis until World War II. As opposed to the psychoanalytic movement in the strict sense, writers and poets placed themselves in the service of an unofficial Freudianism, producing an original version of it that was quite far removed from the medical aspirations—either French or internationalist in orientation—of the twelve pioneers. This section is devoted to Surrealism, the *Nouvelle Revue française* group, and André Gide, as well as to Pierre Jean Jouve and a configuration in which the history of the relations between psychoanalysis and the Communist movement, approached by way of the roles played by Henri Wallon and Georges Politzer, begins to be delineated. To illuminate those relations, a detour is taken through Russian (and then Soviet) psychoanalysis, with the birth of Freudo-Marxism providing a counterpoint. This first part ends with an evocation of the youth of Jacques Lacan. He and his work enter upon the French cultural and psychiatric scene and never leave it again in the ensuing fifty years. In that respect, this volume contains the first biography of Jacques Lacan as well as the first overall treatment of the historical and political advance constituted by his doctrine.

Part 2 deals with the dark years of the Occupation and provides a glimpse of psychoanalysis in Germany under the Third Reich. The years of the Liberation and the cold war follow, including a discussion of the prospering of Freudianism in the United States and a study of the mechanisms of power specific to the International Psychoanalytical Association (IPA), which has administered the Freudian empire in all corners of the globe since 1910. In the case of France, the history of that second implantation of Freudianism is accompanied by a meditation on the relations between psychoanalysis and the Communist movement during the 1950s, as well as a study of the introduction of Freudian practice within the Roman Catholic Church.

The history of the two major splits of the French psychoanalytic movement (1953 and 1963–64) is evoked with the help of entirely unpublished archival material and testimony assembled over several years. Those two splits turned on the relations between French psychoanalysis and its Anglo-American counterpart, with the IPA as the pivotal force in negotiations ending in the separation of Lacanianism from the empire founded by Freud. At stake in both splits were Jacques Lacan's analytic practice and training techniques. Given the fact that the evaluation of that practice was at the heart of this history for nearly twenty years, I have undertaken to gather concrete testimony intended to illustrate it. Such testimony, as integrated into the narrative, is documentary and not anecdotal.

The contemporary situation of psychoanalysis in France is related in the third part of this book, which begins with the structuralist configuration specific to the period 1964–74. In this context, the works of Louis Althusser and Jacques Derrida and the personal roles they assumed proved central in that they gave rise to two specific tendencies within Freudianism: theoretical antihumanism in the one case, deconstruction in the other. These tendencies followed those issuing from phenomenology, and Lacanianism intersected with them all. The detailed functioning of the four major institutional components of French Freudianism is evoked in this third part: the École freudienne de Paris (EFP), the Fourth Group (OPLF), the Société psychanalytique de Paris (SPP), and the Association psychanalytique de France (APF). Both within and beyond that space, the second implantation of psychoanalysis in France is shown to have occurred by way of the literary channel. This is set against the history of the women's movement, the events of May 1968, and the introduction of psychoanalysis in the university. The great decline of dynamic psychiatry—whose most valiant representative during the interwar years was Lacan's close friend Henri Ey—began and reached its completion within that period. Part 3 closes with the death of Jacques Lacan, the disbanding of his school, and an evaluation of a hundred years of psychoanalysis in France.

Two important areas are missing from this epic: ethnopsychoanalysis, founded by Georges Devereux, whose work is in large part based in the United States, and the activities of the non-Freudian societies, in particular the Jungian and Adlerian branches. I originally intended to include them in this volume, but later recanted. To write the history of ethnopsychoanalysis, one would first have to study that of "colonial" psychiatry. Together they would deserve a separate volume of the history of French psychoanalysis. As for the implantation of Jungianism in France, it too would merit a separate history, focusing both on microhistory and on psychoanalysis in Zurich. Like Adlerianism, Jungianism failed to take root in French cultural soil. It remained dependent on a foreign movement and marginal in a country dominated exclusively by the great Freudian saga. Since about 1980, the history of psychoanalysis has emerged as an independent field of scholarship, particularly in France. There are currently works under way whose completion I did not want to interfere with: Jean-Marc Giraud's for the history of Jungianism in France, Michel Coddens's for that of psychoanalysis in Belgium, and Mireille Cifali's for psychoanalysis in Switzerland.

Finally, I have not offered any detailed study of Gaston Bachelard's thought. It is a monument unto itself. The psychoanalytic part of his thought emerged from the Surrealist breakthrough. But it owes nothing to the psychoanalytic movement, and that movement does not owe it very much. Moreover, it has already been studied by others: in particular by Georges Canguilhem. With these exceptions, the present history encompasses all aspects of French Freudianism.

Acknowledgments

Copious thanks to Serge Leclaire and Wladimir Granoff: without their memory, their archives, and their eloquence, a central portion of this history could not have been written.

I thank Louis Althusser, Jacques Derrida, Jenny Aubry, René Major, Philippe Sollers, Renée Ey, Françoise Dolto, Jean-Luc Donnet, Marc-François Lacan and Xavier Audouard for their constant assistance in the course of this effort.

Thanks as well to André Green, Serge Lebovici, Juliette Favez-Boutonier, Solange Faladé, Jean Laplanche, Maud Mannoni, and Moustapha Safouan for having shared their personal recollections with me on several occasions.

I thank Professor Didier Anzieu for his collaboration in this work.

More particularly, I would like to express my gratitude to Jacques-Alain Miller, who opened his archives to me, shared his memories, and allowed me to quote unpublished material of Lacan even though we were not always of the same opinion.

My thanks to Pierre Macherey, Bertrand Ogilvie, Bernard Daubigney, Pierre-François Moreau, Paul Henry, and Émile Jalley, who through their advice and efforts have contributed to the execution of this project.

I thank Jenny Aubry, Marianne Saint-Clair, and Michel Plon for their translations from the English and the Italian, and also Geneviève Jestaz, who translated from the German archival material, transmitted to me by Régine Lockot, concerning the Occupation period.

I thank Professor Charles Reagan, Paul Ricœur's biographer, for his patient assistance.

I thank Maître Jean-Pierre Roche for his legal opinions.

I thank Philippe Boyer and Henri Deluy, who were kind enough to read the manuscript, and Jacques Nobécourt, who read the proofs.

Finally I would like to express my gratitude to the following individuals, who brought me their testimony or helped me in the search for information: Jacques Postel, Élisabeth Lagache, Agnès Lagache, Célia Bertin, Anne-Lise Stern, Philippe Marette, Jacques Sédat, Jean-Bertrand Pontalis, André Berge, Georges Mauco, Nina Ivanova, Olivier Jouve, Alain Cuny, Délia Clauzel-Laforgue, Eva Rosenblum, Martine Broda, Michel Coddens, Guy Rosolato, Octave Mannoni, Roger Martelli (of the Institut de recherches marxistes), Michel Collée, Danièle Tartakowsky, François Tingry, Thibaut Lacan, Lucien Bonnafé, Madeleine Lacan-Houlon, Marcel Bleustein-Blanchet, Julien Rouart, Sylvia Lacan, Janine Chasseguet-Smirgel, Albert Plé, Louis Beirnaert (deceased), François Roustang, Patrick Kéchichian (of the documentary service of *Le Monde*), Daniel Widlöcher, Charles Durand, François Dupuigrenet des Roussilles (Bibliothèque nationale), Piera Aulagnier, Georges Pertuiset (wine-steward of Lameloise), Charles Melman, François Wahl, Robert Pujol,

Étienne Balibar, Michel Tort, Jacques Rancière, Paul Ricœur, Jean-Paul Ricœur, Jacques Gagey, Sandra Basch, Francis Hofstein, Ginette Raimbault, Thémouraz Abdoucheli, Robert Lefort, Rosine Lefort, Andrée Bonnier-Lespiaut, Renée Boulay, Jean-Paul Moreigne, Olivier Corpet, Jean-Pierre Salgas, Gérard Pommier, Danièle Arnoux, Antoinette Fouque, Marie-Claude Grumbach, Kostas Axelos, Maria Torok, Alain Didier-Weill, Roland Castro, Geneviève Baurand, Gérard Blès, Marcelin Pleynet, Michèle Montrelay, Claude Prévost, Georges Th. Guilbaud, Odile Rapp, Jean-Paul Valabrega, François Perrier, Jean-Michel Ribettes, Jean Allouch, Jean Clavreul, Jean Szpirko, Patrick Guyomard, François Baudry, Cyrille Koupernik, André Bourguignon, Contardo Calligaris, Georges Canguilhem, Didier Cromphout, Catherine Clément, Michèle Bargues, Anne Levallois, Marc Nacht, Raphaël Brossart, Gisela Pankow, Michel de Certeau (deceased), Victor Fay, Martine Lilamand, Warren Montag, Catherine Guillaume, Blanche Grinbaum, Aissa Melamed, Hubert Bonnier, Thierry Garnier, Martine Bacherich-Granoff, Diane Chauvelot, Helmut Scheffel (of the *Frankfurter Allgemeine Zeitung*), Jean-Pierre Cotten, Jean-José Marchand, Jean-Jacques Lebel, Claude Halmos, Gérard Miller, Florence Prudhomme, Françoise Gadet, Régine Robin, Henri Lefebvre, Henri Roudier, Mireille Cottin, Nata Minor, Jacqueline Rousseau-Dujardin, Michel Plon, Michèle Cadoret, Alain Vanier, Jean-Michel Louka, Gérard Bonnet, Daniel Soulez-Larivière, Muriel Brouquet, Christian Simatos.

Part One

The New Sensibility

I belong to a time in which people will no longer dream, man having become the dream.

Joë Bousquet

1   Surrealism in the Service of Psychoanalysis

I. Day and Night

Paris, July 1925. The traveler recalled his first stay in France. At that time, during the fall of 1885, he was thirty and believed the pronouncements of science. He was writing the history of the discovery of hysteria, had been present at Freud's first meeting with Charcot, and was an enthusiast of the demonstrations at the Salpêtrière. Now there was a war on: the Moroccan crisis had just exploded. For four years already, under the instigation of Abdel-Krim, rebellion had been spreading in the Spanish zone of the Rif mountains. A republic had been constituted and the rebels were occupying the French zone. In the nighttime heat, the traveler pondered the years that had just elapsed. Change was in the air, bearing with it an enigmatic calm. The whole city seemed given over to the impersonal exertion of time. He thought of his country, Germany, which had already waged two wars against France. He feared the pale horse of the cannonades, dreamed of death and future exiles. The Versailles treaty had trampled over the losers. Apocalypse was on the way. Approaching the Closerie des Lilas, he recalled that in former times one could dance there to the accompaniment of Carnaud's orchestra. Beneath the delicate chandeliers, he watched the partisans and adversaries of Latin genius confront each other. The novelist Rachilde had just maintained that a Frenchwoman could not marry a German without dishonoring herself. At those words, André Breton rose, demanding apologies on behalf of his friend Max Ernst.[1]

Although French writers acknowledged Freud's importance before the world of medicine, the notion of the precedence of the "literary channel" over the "medical channel" remains relative. Starting in 1914, in fact, an interest in psychoanalysis could be found in a large sector of French thought. In that sense, precedence is less important than the divergences through which the two modes of implantation of Freud's doctrine contrasted with each other. The literary and medical channels were part of a single process in which resistance to the theories from Vienna was the sign of the effective progress they were making.[2] There was not a priority of one channel over the other, but the concomitance of two processes of introduction. On the literary side, psychoanalysis tended to be advocated as the expression of a genuinely new discovery, whereas, for the physicians, it was adapted to the ideals of an alleged Latin or Cartesian genius. It was thus simultaneously recognized in two contradictory manners. The acceptance it found among some and the resistance it encountered among others were part of a single ideological phenomenon. In both cases, the battle was joined, the terrain occupied, the implantation effected.

There is no such thing as a "proper" assimilation of a doctrine, only "false" recognitions, consisting of distorted visions. When the writers discovered Freud's ideas, they read in them something different from what the doctors or the psychoanalysts had read. The permeability of the literary world to Freud's ideas may be explained by the importance accorded to the status of the writer by French society during the interwar years. At a time when the democratization of education had not been achieved, culture remained an elitist phenomenon. It was transmitted through a variety of journals playing a role which in our own day has fallen to the vehicles of mass communication. Whether he conformed or rebelled, the man of letters was simultaneously herald of his own writing, theoretician of all doctrines, and political militant. He filled the position of a committed writer and an acclaimed or accursed artist.[3]

After the Second World War, a considerable shift was initiated. The intellectual par excellence was no longer the writer, but the philosopher—be he an academic or self-taught. To him was accorded the place formerly occupied by the writer, and the latter withdrew into the shadows of a labor that was more literary and less strictly centered on ideological struggle. He abandoned to the thinkers responsibility for writing committed—or "engagé"—novels. In that context, the artisans of the "new novel" no longer took on Freudianism as a principal issue in their literary battles. Psychoanalysis, moreover, was in a period of considerable expansion, and as a consequence was confronting different problems, a function at times of its relation to the human sciences, at times of its corporatist structure. On the one hand, it attracted the interest of philosophers meditating on the status of man and of freedom; on the other, it was an issue for practitioners of mental health either in the exercise of their profession or in the organization of their institutions.

In an earlier book (see note 2, above), I showed how Freud's ideas were propagated by way of Janet's psychology and Bergson's philosophy. I observed the rise of the French psychoanalytic movement, then of the foundation, in 1926, of the Société psychanalytique de Paris. I examined the oppositions among diverse tendencies: the *chauvinist group* represented by Angelo Hesnard, Edouard Pichon, Adrien Borel, and Henri Codet; the *orthodox faction,* affiliated with the International Psychoanalytic Association under the aegis of Marie Bonaparte, Raymond de Saussure, Rudolph Loewenstein and Charles Odier; the *neutralists,* the partisans of an articulation between psychoanalysis and psychiatry, such as Paul Schiff or Eugène Minkowski on behalf of Évolution psychiatrique; and finally a *dissidence,* represented almost exclusively by René Laforgue. We must now approach the literary side of the implantation of Freudianism on French soil.

Whereas the psychoanalytic movement was organized into an institution of eminent individuals or "notables," among whom the ideals of therapeutic healing reigned supreme, the world of literature on the whole was the vehicle of a *lay* [*Laienanalyse*] or nonmedical representation of psychoanalysis[4]: What enthused the writers was the opening up of a new field of inquiry. If several of them—such as Michel Leiris, Georges Bataille, René Crevel, or Raymond Queneau—did undergo analysis for personal reasons, therapy per se remained for them distinct from the adventure represented by Freud's discovery, which might or might not traverse their writing, independent of any entry into analysis.

Within the literary channel, the Surrealists, more than any other, took their distance from the positions maintaining in the medical world. Chauvinism remained the dominant note of the therapeutic caste at a time when the rejection of all forms of racism, anti-Semitism, and xenophobia was an informing feature of Surrealism.

The "lay" character of Surrealism's adherence to Freudian doctrine is all the more striking in that several members of the group had undertaken medical studies, abandoning them after the war. As a second year medical student during the year 1914–15, Aragon met Breton at the Val-de-Grâce Hospital in the auxiliary medical service that owed its expansion to the scarcity of nursing personnel. Théodore Fraenkel followed the same route: He was to be found at Val-de-Grâce in 1917 before being sent off with three ambulances to the Russian front. As for Philippe Soupault, he was the son of a renowned gastroenterologist and refused to become a physician.

Within the movement there thus existed a doctor's club. For them the transition to a life of creativity went hand in hand with forgoing a medical career. That situation favored both an intimate knowledge of what was therapeutically at stake in Freud's doctrine and a refusal to see it reduced to a curative technique. It will thus be understood why *Révolution surréaliste* published a fragment from *Die Frage der Laienanalyse*. The article bore the title: "The Question of Analysis by non-Physicians." Mention is made in a note that it is a selection from a volume to be published under the same title by the *Nouvelle Revue Française* (*NRF*) in a translation by Marie Bonaparte. The book would in fact appear under the erroneous French title of *Psychanalyse et médecine*. At the time the Surrealists were virtually alone in France in taking the notion of "lay analysis" literally and in waging a merciless fight on its behalf. The note allows one to infer that the book was to appear under its true title, which had been modified at the last moment.[5]

For the Surrealists, the struggle for lay analysis did not have as its objective the recognition of the right of nonphysicians to practice therapy, as was the case for Marie Bonaparte. It was on the contrary a matter of establishing a radical break between psychoanalysis and the ideals of medicine. That authentically separatist attitude did not exist in the prewar French psychoanalytic movement, except, on occasion, for Laforgue. It would not appear until after 1945.

The Surrealists' radicalism, their defence of a sovereign primacy of the unconscious, was located at an opposite extreme from the ideals of a *Gallic unconscious*. The group's poets did not speak the same language as Pichon, Hesnard, or Laforgue. Nor did they belong to the same France. Their Freudianism was not the same Freudianism, and within that opposition was waged a battle of polar opposites.

One consequence of such a split was to create an incommunicability between the psychoanalytic movement and the modernist vanguard. Although they were divided among themselves, none of the twelve founders of the SPP acknowledged the importance of the Surrealist movement in the infiltration of Freudian ideas in France. At the same time, they turned their backs on the entirety of a literary intelligentsia deemed to be dangerous.

The impasse of the first analytic generation concerning Surrealism and, more generally, the literary production of their time would weigh heavily on the destiny of the movement. For which reason the very notion of "verbal form" was absent from their discourse. Whence the mediocrity of their style and the botching of their theoretical efforts. One could say that with the exception of Pichon, these practitioners of the unconscious devoted as little care to matters conceptual as to the language in which they wrote.

The Surrealists challenged the principle of novelistic performance in order to invent new modalities of creative expression. The psychoanalysts, for their part, retreated to positions that were academic. Instead of following Freud's lead in seeking to elucidate the status of poetic creation, they "applied" therapeutic technique to literary works. This gave rise to *psychobiography*, which restricts itself to the study of the classics and treats writers' lives as though they were case histories, making writing the expression of a neurosis or mental illness.

At the time, the ideals of heredity and degeneration had suffered a collapse. The dynamic psychiatry of the 1920s had activated a new manner of perceiving madness, abandoning the antiquated notion of congenital defects, which assimilated genius to crime. It waged a progressivist struggle against the power of the judiciary in order to spare the clinically insane from the guillotine, and claimed madness to be a part of man's condition. But in the realm of art it drew on a concept of madness modeled on the doctrine of degeneration. Psychobiography was the continuation, by other means, of a policy toward madness which thought of creation as a form of pathology and made of the creator a "superior abnormal individual." In that perspective, the artist was a "case," like other neurotics, but he was a "pathological case" since he possessed a hereditary "defect" which the others did not. In order to understand how it works, a pathological diagnosis of the work must be elaborated and related to the author's fate. One thus ends up with a coherent system thinking through "creative madness" by way of a rational body of knowledge that is ultimately substituted for the work itself. Thus it was that the anti-pathological orientation of the 1920s, which permeated the psychoanalytic movement, retained residues of the hereditarian configuration with which it broke, in order to rechannel them into the genre of psychobiography. Charcot, in this respect, was ahead of his time: He had sought a proof of his conception of hysteria among the paintings of the old masters, without perceiving, as Freud later would, that hysteria itself was a distorted work of art. But his clairvoyance had led him to posit a new relation between creation and madness, revealing a neurotic "form" that was at once its own messenger and identical to creative expression.

Whereas French psychoanalysts relegated Charcot's teaching to the shadows, the Surrealists, on the contrary, claimed the legacy of the Salpêtrière as their own and made hysteria a poetic act. In 1928, Aragon and Breton paid homage to the impassioned poses of the notoriously beautiful Augustine: "We Surrealists," they wrote, "are intent on celebrating the fiftieth anniversary of hysteria, the greatest poetic discovery of the latter part of the century, and we do so at a time when the dismemberment of the concept of hysteria appears to be complete. We who love nothing so much as those young hysterics, whose perfect exemplar is provided by the observations concerning the delectable X. L., who entered Dr. Charcot's service at the Salpêtrière on October 21, 1875, at the age of 15 and a half. How could we be affected by the laborious refutation of organic disturbances, which might appear to bear on the case of hysteria solely in the eyes of medical doctors? What a pity! Monsieur Babinski, the most intelligent man to have attacked the question, made bold to write in 1913, 'When an emotion is sincere, profound, and shakes the human soul, there is no longer any room for hysteria.' "

After that lyrical flight, Aragon and Breton recalled Charcot's importance for Freud and then evoked the days when the interns at the Salpêtrière made love with the hysterics. Clovis Vincent is described in passing as the "Raymond Roussel of science." In a few lines the authors paid homage to Galen, Plato, Hippocrates, Bernheim, and the demoniacs of Loudun. Finally, they proposed a new definition of hysteria. "Hysteria," they wrote, "is a more or less irreducible mental state characterized by a subversion of the relations between the subject and the ethical universe in which he believes himself a practical participant, outside of any systematic delirium. This mental state is based on the need for a reciprocal seduction, which explains the hastily accepted miracles of medical suggestion (or counter-suggestion). Hysteria is not a pathological phenomenon and can in every respect be considered a supreme vehicle of expression." [6]

In comparing their text to Freud's in 1893, and above all to Codet and Laforgue's in 1925,[7] one perceives that Aragon and Breton were performing as rigorous theoreticians. Against the official representatives of psychiatro-psychoanalytic science, they did not back the dismembering of Charcot's teaching. They refuted him with a demonstration by the absurd: Babinski and the doctors, they said in substance, may still believe that hysteria does not exist; that does not prevent hysteria from existing.

The authors spoke like Charcot and adopted toward hysteria an attitude similar to Freud's. They thought through the history of its symptoms with the infirm body as their starting point, and reinterpreted the medical gaze within a configuration in which the therapist no longer occupied a position of mastery. For the Surrealists, hysteria was a language, a means of expression, a work of poetry whose subversive form ought to be championed against art itself, against literature. Aragon and Breton chose to ignore suggestion, showing it to be nothing more than a deceptive feat of seduction for the physician. They refused to reduce hysteria to malingering and differentiated it from systematic forms of madness, thus demarcating the boundaries of the phenomenon of psychosis. Finally, they rejected the category of pathology (that is, anomaly) in favor of that of expressive form.

Prior to this celebration of hysteria, the Surrealists published a declaration entitled "Lettre aux médecins-chefs des asiles de fous [Letter to the chief-doctors of the insane asylums]." Inspired by Antonin Artaud, the text was initially drafted by Robert Desnos before appearing in its definitive form. It is a veritable collective manifesto in which no individual hand can be recognized, only the state of mind of the group. The text begins with a violent attack against psychiatry's right to "measure mind": "Your profession's trial has been judged in advance. We don't intend to discuss here either the value of your science or the dubious existence of mental illnesses. But for a hundred pretentious pathogeneses disseminating confusion between mind and matter, for a hundred classifications of which only the vaguest ones are at all usable, how many noble attempts to approach the mental world in which so many of your prisoners live? How many are you, for example, for whom the dream of a sufferer from dementia praecox, the images he is prey to, are anything other than a salad of words?"

Asylums are then compared to barracks or prisons and the authors defend the right of all to the antisocial act par excellence. Finally, the Surrealists demanded the opening of the asylums: "Without insisting on the utter genius of the productions of some of the insane, to the extent that we are able to appreciate them, we affirm the absolute legitimacy of their conception of reality and of all the acts stemming from it." [8]

The manifesto appears to illustrate in advance a conception of madness that would be taken up again by the antipsychiatric movement of the 1960s. Upon closer examination, however, it may be perceived that the text, however "antipsychiatric," does not truly anticipate contemporary antipsychiatry. Moreover, the principal representatives of that movement, which was born not in France but in England and in Italy, drew little inspiration from Surrealism, to which they preferred existentialism, phenomenology, and personality theory.

The 1925 manifesto lashed out at the Tower of Babel constituted by the various classifications of so-called mental illnesses. Yet it did not question either the existence of madness or that of a differentiation between mental states. It did not allege, as the antipsychiatrists later would, that individual madness is the product of social or familial alienation. In other words, for the Surrealists, the individual act is always a form of madness and the madman just as much a creator as the dreamer or the hysteric. In those three conditions are to be found a conception of reality whose legitimacy was to be undividedly acknowledged. The text was contemporaneous with the creation in France of the Évolution psychiatrique group (EP), but it skirted the objectives of *dynamic psychiatry*.[9] With Marie Bonaparte, Paul Schiff, Eugène Minkowski, Adrien Borel, and later Henri Ey, there was a preventive orientation that would wrest madness from the grips of the judiciary. With Surrealism, a different tendency began to emerge, intent on stripping the psychiatric gaze of its right to domination over the mental realm. Whence the notion that madness, like hysteria, is irreducible to reason. Such a conception was "ahead" of the ideals of the new psychiatry, but it was contemporaneous with what it denounced, namely, the subversion effected by Freud within the field of science. When the Surrealists identified with the madwomen of the Salpêtrière or the lunatics of art and literature, they were borrowing their concepts from an epistemological soil on which were to be found pell-mell the classifications of Kraepelin and Charcot, the automatism of the legionnaires of glossolalia, and the structural concepts of Freudian thought.

The psychoanalysts entertained a variety of relations with the writers, which were frequently marked by their psychobiographical conceptions of art. Some, such as Allendy and Borel, gradually became "specialists" in the treatment of creative artists. The former could analyze Anaïs Nin or René Crevel and was interested in Antonin Artaud; the latter accepted Leiris and Bataille on his couch. Both were drawn to artists, in keeping with a classical tradition of the study of mental diseases. Fascinated by occultism, Allendy found in Surrealism resonances with his own concerns. As for Borel, what led him to greet the advent of the movement favorably was the study of dreamers rather than of dreams per se. In 1925, in the first issue of *Évolution psychiatrique,* at the end of an article co-authored with Gilbert Robin, he wrote: "We have just learned of a new movement: Surrealism, as explained and commented on by its creator, André Breton. Without undertaking a critique of his book, *Manifeste du surréalisme,* we feel obliged to take note of the escape from the real the author has attempted in order to enclose himself (or rather expand himself) into an extremely extended imaginary universe toward whose elaboration every means of expression and all that is marvelous or enchanted in the individual join to contribute." [10]

Jean Frois-Wittmann was the only psychoanalyst of the first generation to publish texts in Surrealist journals. In 1929, in *Révolution surréaliste,* he published an article entitled "Mobiles inconscients du suicide [Unconscious motives for suicide]." It contains a variety of judiciously selected clinical details as well as several opinions at odds with the psychoanalytic consensus of the day. Frois-Wittmann thus provided the following definition of a "normal" man: "He is a man who behaves as though he had been psychoanalyzed." He also insisted that "Surrealism, psychoanalysis, and a certain socialism, even if they are unaware of each other, would form a single system of unavoidable consistency." Finally, he noted that *Les Chants de Maldoror* were a veritable "bible of the unconscious, with its associative mode of thought and all its complications." That observation indicates that the author was interested in "literary form" in its own right and was not a practitioner of psychobiography.

In an other article from *Le surréalisme au service de la révolution,* entitled "Les mots d'esprit et l'inconscient [Jokes and the unconscious]," Frois-Wittmann wrote as late as 1930: "Little by little, Freud's books are being translated into French. The eleventh, on jokes, has just appeared thirteen years after the English translation (1917) and twenty-five years after the first edition, all of which gives some idea of the interest in psychoanalysis shared by the French medical public prior to these last few years." [11] The author then provided an accurate, if academic, summary of Freud's book. What is worth observing, in any event, is that he did not hesitate to attack the guild to which he belonged.

No member of the Surrealist group published an article in *La Revue française de psychanalyse.* Among the founders of the SPP, only Angelo Hesnard, after Borel, seemed to take an interest in the group's fate. In a late article, entitled "Freud et la latinité," Hesnard wrote: "There is a French school of art, already dying before the war despite its recent origins and rather strident ambitions, whose common features with the scientific school of psychoanalysis have been noted: Surrealism. But within the realm of artistic innovation, it represented precisely what is least French and most resolutely anarchical. More haughty than constructive, the movement was striking in the sovereign contempt its adepts demonstrated toward all received ideas: dogmas, traditions, and patrimony. It made something of an exception for the doctrine of psychoanalysis, which was pardoned because it seemed to share with Surrealist theory—something that was far from pleasing to all Freud's disciples—profound affinities." [12] Hesnard also explained that the Surrealist occupied in relation to the psychoanalyst a position similar to that of a patient who might reveal irrational productions as enigmatic as messages from the planet Mars. He concluded his article by affirming that Freudian doctrine shared with Surrealism an irrationalist conception of the unconscious, from which French psychology should draw inspiration even as it tempered it.

The Surrealists had no reticence about treating the publications of certain psychoanalysts as nonsense. In a 1933 issue of *Surréalisme au service de la révolution* (*SASDLR*), there are two quotations written in the margin of a text by Pierre Yoyotte entitled "Théorie de la Fontaine." In the first, under the rubric "Predominance of imbecility," a passage from Allendy's *Capitalisme et sexualité* is offered up to the public: "When an old man," wrote Allendy, "has seen his children grow up, leave his house, and found new families; when in turn the children of those children begin to spread out over the world and thus all that remains to him to love is dispersed over the earth; when the companion of his life also approaches the grave, then death, that supreme weaning, in marrying him to universal life, opens to him in a way the gates of infinity and eternity, etc." Then, under the rubric "Predominance of rubbish," a particularly harrowing passage from Laforgue's *Échec de Baudelaire* is ridiculed through mere quotation: "In Baudelaire," wrote Laforgue, we find united all the diverse forms of affective retardation, neurosis, syphilis (a consequence that might have been aggravated by a physical imbalance), opium and even theft, and fraud. . . . The passage concerning the French is naturally best applied to the author himself: "The Frenchman," wrote Baudelaire, " 'is a barnyard animal so well domesticated that he never dares cross any barrier. See, for instance, his tastes in art and literature. He is an animal of the Latin race: Excrement does not displease him. In his home and his literature, he is scatophagous. He is wild about excrement. Barroom *littérateurs* call this Gallic salt. A fine example of French baseness on the part of a nation claiming to be independent before all others.' " From the psychoanalytic point of view, emphasized Laforgue, commenting on Baudelaire's sentence, "it is impossible to be more precise. We shall merely add that at a certain degree of neurosis, such as was the case for Baudelaire, the subject can effectively come to eat his excrement and drink his urine." [13]

With the second generation of the Évolution psychiatrique group, there came a genuine interest in Surrealism. The movement was no longer rejected as part of a "literary channel" or a poetic mystification, but accepted, on the contrary, as an adventure of the unconscious linked to the renewal of psychiatry. Henri Ey published an article to that effect in 1948, in which he distinguished between Surrealist works and the creations of psychotics.[14] He would later say that it was through Surrealism, and not the medical literature, that he discovered the importance of Freudianism.

The first generation of French psychiatrists and psychoanalysts thus participated in a dynamic movement, which was historically contemporaneous with Surrealism. But that contemporaneity prevented it from seeing that Surrealism belonged to the same movement. Ten years later, the second generation would become aware of a history which had escaped its elders. As a result, that generation felt a debt toward Surrealism. Such a change is possible when there is a questioning of a past which had itself been at the origin of the change.

Surrealism thus effected a curious fracture in the history of the French psychiatro-psychoanalytic movement. Contemporaneous with a dynamism whose authority it contested, Surrealism contributed to nothing less than its apotheosis by supplying the weapons needed for its renovation. Without the Surrealist scandal, the second psychoanalytic generation would have spent its energy without hearing any echo of the new battle.

Sarane Alexandrian[15] evokes the recollection of two physicians who participated in the movement during the 1920s. The first, Émile Malespine, an adept of Dada, founded the journal *Manomètre* in Lyon in 1922. He invented a permanent method for "weighing writing": *graphography*. His journal was intent on being polyglot and supranational; it mixed languages, registered ideas, and indicated pressures at every latitude. It published manuscripts through a process of random selection. The second physician, Pierre Mabille, had begun a career in surgery before joining the Surrealist movement in 1934. An astrologer and an occultist, he declared himself a disciple of psychoanalysis. Despite appearances, his theory of the unconscious was no more extravagant than that of the respected Bergson. Mabille defended the thesis of a "visceral unconscious" whose fluctuations could be followed by means of the interpretation of dreams. To this he added a (both personal and social) "unconscious of forgetting," whose uncovering was made possible by a maximal lowering of the threshold of consciousness. Following the exodus of 1940, he went to Guadeloupe, then settled in Tahiti, where he worked to improve the hospital services of the French Asylum. Thanks to his knowledge of the native population, he allowed Breton to attend Voodoo ceremonies. At his death in 1952, the weekly magazine *Arts* paid him elaborate tribute.

In France, such physicians remained marginal to the psychoanalytic movement. Obliged to demonstrate his scientific seriousness, Mabille relinquished the residues of an occultism that was tending to revive, during a time of crisis, in the form of a *hypnotic symptom*.[16] During the interwar period, the Freudian movement's misconstruing of a certain occult version of psychoanalysis promoted by the Surrealists and a very few physicians went together with the advancing of a "Jonesian" political line within the IPA, which tended to exclude from the analytic community the great "madmen" of Freudianism, those who, like Reich, Ferenczi, or Rank, could not manage to submit to the etiquette of the movement's "notables."

To be sure, all those dissidents were not defenders of occultism, but to the extent that their positions aimed at rectifying the rationality of an institution intent on adapting to the ideals of science, it was often through an *occultist crisis* that their break with the mother organization occurred. Moreover, such crises almost invariably resulted in appeals to religiosity or "irrationalism" at the expense of science, deemed to be too "rational": a mystique of the maternal mother for Rank, of the oceanic depths for Ferenczi, and of energy for Reich. All those tendencies bear witness to the form in which crises were experienced in the house of Freud.

In France, things were both similar and different. There did indeed exist among the analysts a diffuse opposition between the scientificity invoked by some and the irrationality appealed to by others. But the old occult tradition—of wizards and magnetizers—was no longer alive within the nation. Above all, it did not achieve any reimplantation within the psychoanalytic movement. While Switzerland played a major role in the penetration of Freudian ideas, Jungianism could not find any support that would allow it to emerge as a major current in France. This was in part a function of the minority situation of French Protestantism, but not merely that, since in Italy Catholicism served as fertile ground for Jungian doctrine. In point of fact, there was no true dissidence of any sort within the SPP prior to World War II. This was no doubt because the only marginal figure in the group, René Laforgue, was also its founder and would never be excluded from the IPA. It may be noted in passing that the *rapprochement* he effected in the 1950s between Catholicism on the one hand, and Oriental religions on the other, had something of the aspect of an attack of occultism.

It was thus Surrealism—that is, a literary movement—which, against official psychoanalysis, brandished the torch of the hypnotists and the miracle workers. But there too, it was not truly a matter of occultism. In its French form, Surrealism bore the blazon of a romanticism turned scientific.[17] It belonged to the occult less through any adherence to the mystical ornaments of occultism than through the way in which it manifested a clandestine, nocturnal, and "accursed" vision of the doctrines it defended. Fundamentally, Breton identified with the Freudian adventure in its most resolutely modern aspects, which is why his spiritism, and that of his friends, was more like a strident demonstration of iconoclasm than an appeal to the crystal ball. Despite his cult for astrologers and fortune-tellers, Breton did not sink into the religion of the beyond. He never surrendered the slightest parcel of Surrealist territory to ghosts or phantoms. Nor did he ever abandon the primacy of sexuality in favor of what Freud called the "black tide" of occultism. For all these reasons, Surrealism did not serve as a means for the implantation of Jungianism. Surrealism's conception of psychoanalysis remained profoundly pagan. It resembled the objects it would construct: Max Ernst's Oedipus, Duchamp's mustachioed Mona Lisa, de Chirico's automaton, Dali's sleeping women, and Benjamin Péret's jumbles.

II. Suicide, Sex, and the Criminal Woman

The history of the Surrealist movement began with the foundation in 1919 of the journal *Littérature,* in which the first three chapters of *Les champs magnétiques* appeared. Written by Philippe Soupault and André Breton, the text was inspired by Janet's definition of automatic writing: "In the course of our research," wrote Soupault, "we did indeed observe that the mind, once freed of all critical pressures and school-bound habits, offered images and not logical propositions; and that if we adopted what the psychiatrist Pierre Janet called a practice of automatic writing, we produced texts in which we found ourselves describing a 'universe' as yet unexplored. We thus decided to give ourselves fifteen days to write in collaboration a work in which we [*sic*] forbade ourselves from correcting or erasing our 'lucubrations.' We had no trouble respecting that time period, and it was with increasing joy that we came to discover the texts."[18]

The notion of automatism was central to the writing of *Les champs magnétiques,* but it was to the *Chants de Maldoror* that the work referred. It evoked the famous book announced by Isidore Ducasse at the threshold of his death and prolonged the notorious slogan: "Poetry must be done by all and not by one." As for the idea of a dictation of thought in the absence of any rational control, it drew as much on the program of the French "alienists" as on Rimbaud's projected: "I is an other." According to Breton, that inaugural text was written in eight days, at the cost of a protracted disordering of the senses. It was dedicated to Jacques Vaché and ended with a simulated suicide.

Since April 1919, the painter Francis Picabia had been living in Paris. Early in January 1920, he was joined by Tristan Tzara, who came from Zurich, where psychoanalysis had rooted in the crosscurrents of Freudianism and its Jungian dissidence. Tzara did not share the enthusiasm of his French friends for the new doctrine and commented in terms similar to those formerly resorted to by Karl Krauss: "Psychoanalysis is a dangerous idea; it deadens man's anti-real tendencies and systematizes the bourgeoisie."

Before long the members of the *Littérature* group rallied to Dadaism, and the technique of automatic writing was abandoned in favor of other procedures drawn from the Dadaist arsenal. And yet, contrary to the process of "words in a hat," it marked the advent of a first Surrealist act, leading to the formation of an autonomous movement that would later break with Dadaism. The birth of that new writing was announced by Breton in terms of a conspiracy. He explained to Tzara that he had studied very little philosophy, but that he was quite familiar with psychiatry. Kraepelin and Freud inspired strong feelings in him. He was astonished that his friend did not answer his questions concerning Jung and Maeder. Tzara, for his part, gave himself over to an astonishing reflection on the nature of modern literature: "One no longer writes today with one's race," he wrote, "but with one's blood (what banality). What for the other literature was a *characteristic* is at present *temperament*. It is more or less equivalent if one writes a poem in Siamese or dances atop a locomotive. It's only normal for the old not to have noticed that a new type of man is being created in all parts. With insignificant variations of race, the intensity is, I think, everywhere the same, and if one were to look for an aspect shared by all those currently producing literature, it would be their antipsychology." [19]

The recourse to automatism separated Dada from Surrealism, but both doctrines had in common a rejection of the ideals of race and fixed characteristics. The antipsychologism specific to the new sensibility rejected a dual tradition: that of the nineteenth-century novel, to which it opposed the nocturnal afflatus of the "accursed" poets; and that of the psychology of the soul, of peoples, and crowds, against which it brandished the principle of a "new man" defined by the free emergence of his desires or the intensity of his utterances.

The ideal of race rejected by Tzara was also denounced by René Crevel in a 1931 article entitled "Le patriotisme de l'inconscient [The patriotism of the unconscious]." He noted the comment of an author from the SPP to the effect that conflicts were the same among blacks as among whites: "But the case analyzed was not conclusive because there was barely any mention of unconscious conflicts." The commentator's sentence was ambiguous, and as was frequently the case at the time, notably on the subject of the Jewish question, did not betray any manifest racism, but rather a repressed variety of it of which the author was unaware. In any event,

Crevel perceived it and hastened to unravel its meaning: If the case was not conclusive, it meant that a study would be needed to demonstrate what was plain to see—to wit, that a black man's skin is worth as much as a paleface's. But if, in the analysis of the black analyzed by our bibliographer, few unconscious conflicts were found, it would follow that a black's unconscious is not of the same nature as a white's and that there might be an unconscious that would vary according to race. At which point Crevel parodied a missionary line and applied it to psychoanalysts: "I hereby baptize you if you do indeed have a soul." And he continued: "The Negro of whom there was no certainty, among ecclesiastics in 1905, that he had a soul, and in a journal of specialized medicine in 1931, that he was vulnerable to conflicts as distinguished as those currently passing muster at the psychoanalytic counter of the mother institution (and note that the French says little in order to allow much to be understood), in cases of forced labor or a little war, will be recognized as a brother—a younger brother, to be sure, and thus one to be led with a firm hand." [20] In this text, one can see how the Surrealist manner succeeded in casting light on one of the major components of the French psychoanalytic movement at a time when the movement itself was still unaware of it. The divergences between official psychoanalysis and Surrealism were theorized by an author at the very time they were being produced.

The first issue of *Révolution surréaliste* opened with a questionnaire: "Is suicide a solution? One lives, one dies. What is the part of will in all that? It appears that one kills oneself the way one dreams. We are not asking a moral question." In the same issue, there is a narrative account of several actual cases of suicide, presented as a kind of geography of human desperation.[21] The question prompted several replies which were published in the next issue.

The Surrealist fascination with death brings us to the person of Jacques Vaché, whose legend would be written by Breton. An overdose of opium would dispatch him to the underworld in 1919. With his cult of derision and his philosophy of humor, he offered the example of a Rimbaldian life anticipatory of the spirit of Dada. As for Jacques Rigaut, another "trumpeter of death," he too was a part of the Surrealist museum. An abuser of drugs, he took his life ten years after Vaché.[22]

Breton never attempted to put an end to his life, but he celebrated in his own way Maiakovsky's suicide in 1930: "As for myself," he wrote, "I am more grateful to Maiakovsky for having placed the immense talent accorded him by Trotsky in the service of the successful Russian Revolution than for having compelled our admiration for his private benefit with the striking images of his 'Cloud in Shorts.' "[23] Breton ended his article with a de rigueur attack on the journalist in *Humanité* who had depicted Maiakovsky as a bourgeois refractory to the ideas of proletarian emancipation.

One senses in this case the opposition between the Surrealist new man and his Communist counterpart. In Surrealism, the invocation of a right to death was the expression of a reasoned apology through which the individual was to rebel against the established order. That shift in attitude with respect to the "passive" status of a suicidal fate brought the Surrealists to transform the desire to die into a willful mode of "acting out." And that slippage was not unrelated to the global context within which Freud was elaborating his new doctrine of the death instinct.

The Surrealists were not "influenced" by the publication in German of *Beyond the Pleasure Principle,* which would be translated into French in 1927. And yet the lure of death, which has traversed the writing of poetry from the time of its inception, constituted an advantageous terrain for the implantation of the Freudian notion of the death instinct. That notion was refused simultaneously by the psychoanalytic movement, by Freudo-Marxism, and by Communist discourse. In the face of that rejection, the Surrealist cult of suicide took on the aspect of a veritable "theory" of morbid energy.

At the time Freud was completing his writing of *Beyond the Pleasure Principle,* he took care to write to Eitingon: "*Beyond* is finally completed. You can confirm that it was already half finished at a time when Sophie was alive and flourishing."[24] That precaution may be explained by the fact that Freud's entourage, in resisting the new doctrine, attributed its genesis not to a discovery, but to a "context" by which the master would have been influenced. Among the elements invoked were the carnage of the war, fear of an incipient cancer, and the twin deaths of a beloved daughter, Sophie, and a close friend, Anton von Freund.

Freud was right to separate the domain of science from that of feeling and to skew things in favor of a primacy of theory. And yet the debate was engaged on slippery grounds that would favor the emergence of "ego psychology" some thirty years later.[25] If it is true that a doctrinal elaboration remains extrinsic to the historical configuration within which it is produced, it is also the case that the existence of that configuration authorizes a new apprehension of reality. Now concerning the evolution of psychoanalytic concepts, the importance of the historical configuration lay less, in 1920, in Sophie's illness or the death of a friend, than in that cultural organization of the European world which had seen the defeat of the middle empires.

For the 1920s put the seal on the second death of the nineteenth century, which was, in its decline, the original home of modernity—that modernity began at once in Darwin's jungles, Nietzsche's madness, and Rimbaud's desert, finally coming to flourish on Surrealist soil.[26] In the field of psychoanalysis, it was achieved a first time with the inaugural gesture of the *Traumdeutung,* and then renewed, two decades later, when the old order was overthrown.

In 1929, the lure of death resulted in Freud's observation of a fundamental discontent in civilization. A certain "golden age" of psychoanalysis had disappeared in the torment of war, but, beyond the disaster, a hope subsisted: The renunciation of murderous instincts could engender sublimation.

It was in his introductory text to *L'âge d'or* that Breton took a stand on the notorious death "drive," as Freud had it, but which he, like his contemporaries, called an instinct. At the time, he had read *Beyond the Pleasure Principle* in translation, but did not yet know Freud's text, *Civilization and Its Discontents,* which would be translated in 1934.[27] Refusing to limit himself to the notion of sublimated energy, he appealed to extravagance for its own sake. According to Breton, a fundamental machination allowed the creator to exist: He was the seat of a struggle between the sexual instinct and the death instinct. Eros itself was subject to anti-Eros, through the passion of love, and that latter tendency played a revolutionary role. He ended his article with an appeal to the frenzy outside of which no form of artistic expression was valid. As for Bunuel's *L'âge d'or*, it symbolized the bird of prey sailing over a waning Western sky.

The invocation of a murderous instinct was thus of the same nature as the cult of suicide. To visit death on oneself was to accept the extravagance of the criminal drive characterizing the authentic poet. Freud situated creation on the side of sublimation and explained cultural mechanisms on the basis of a renunciation of murderous impulses. Breton reversed the problematic, rejected sublimation, and situated art in a morbid machination. He theorized the Freudian material, in the negative, by enlisting it in the Surrealist project, but in so doing, he delineated certain shared intentions: the stakes of childhood, sex, or a golden age lost and regained.

After death and suicide, sex. In 1928, *Révolution surréaliste* published an astonishing report entitled, "Recherches sur la sexualité, part d'objectivité, déterminations individuelles, degré de conscience [Research on Sexuality: The role of objectivity, individual determinations, and degree of consciousness.]" [28] Several poets met around a table and spoke of their sexual experiences. Breton led the discussion in an authoritarian manner, while Benjamin Péret, Raymond Queneau, and others answered him. It was first asked whether men had the means to perceive female erotic fulfillment. Queneau was perplexed, Péret approved his attitude, and Breton, always in control, defended the admirable values of reciprocal trust and subjectivity. Naville, who was no dupe, noted the importance of mental illusions. Then the question was reversed, and Breton announced proudly that in most cases women found the proof of the existence of male sexual fulfillment by proceeding to examine the locale in which their partner deposited it. The discussion then moved to pederasty. Queneau approved of sexual relations between men, which succeeded in exasperating his friends. Pierre Unik declared that representatives of the "accursed race" disgusted him as much as the sight of excrement. Queneau was surprised by the Surrealists' prejudices against homosexuality, and Breton became angry. "I accuse pederasts," he said, "of asking human tolerance for a mental and moral deficiency tending to set itself up as a system and paralyze all the undertakings I respect. I acknowledge exceptions, including one of the first urgency for the case of Sade, and one, which is more surprising for me, for that of Lorrain." [29]

Following a discussion of masturbation and different positions for the sexual act, the friends in the group began a discussion of brothels. Breton suggested that they be closed; Pierre Unik and Benjamin Péret approved his stand; and Queneau confessed to enjoying the company of prostitutes. Religion was attacked, and Péret seized the opportunity to "desecrate wafers and deposit his excrement in the chalice."

The second evening took place in January 1928, in the presence of Aragon, who had been absent from the previous meeting. Queneau questioned him about pederasty. Embarrassed, he put off answering until later on, and, after lengthy statements about the male ejaculation and female vaginal secretions, Breton asked Queneau brutally if he was a pederast. Queneau answered in the negative, and threw the question back to Aragon, who exclaimed: "Pederasty seems to me—just like other sexual habits—to be a sexual habit. This does not entail any moral condemnation on my part, and I don't think this is the time to issue restrictions, concerning certain pederasts, that I could also make concerning certain womanizers." Marcel Duhamel responded that he did not condemn pederasty and envisaged sleeping with a man without any repugnance. Unable to bear it any longer, Breton broke out in a fury. "I am absolutely opposed," he shouted, "to any further discussion of this subject. If this talk turns into an advertisement for pederasty, I shall abandon it immediately." [30] In the face of such violence, the friends preferred to keep their silence, and the conversation was directed quite spiritedly to the subjects of exhibitionism, voyeurism, and fellatio. Aragon declared himself to be a resolute practitioner of fetishism, and maintained that he always carried his favorite sexual objects around with him. With the self-assurance of an inquisitor, Breton criticized acts of sexual perversity, and did not hesitate to state that it was impossible for him to be interested in two women at the same time. No one dared to evoke *Nadja,* an early fragment of which had just been published, and the evening ended with a discussion of infantile sexuality. Each related his dreams or his recollections, and Queneau concluded with these words: "I remember having an erection," he said, "upon seeing two dogs coupling. I also had an ejaculation when I once saw a dancing girl dressed as a page at the Folies-Bergères. There were two on the stage. I was only interested in the one on the left." [31]

Let us imagine the impossible: In 1929, the *Revue française de psychanalyse* (*RFP*) dares to publish a special issue of research devoted to the sexual practices of the founders of the movement. Marie Bonaparte starts things off and asks Pichon if he is a pederast. Furious, Pichon lashes out at feminists, attacks the decadence of current mores, and vaunts the benefits of virginity. Loewenstein in turn queries Borel on the interest of donning a priest's cassock during the sexual act. The latter retorts acidly that he prefers servant girls to princesses. Laforgue attempts to calm everyone down by expatiating on the delights of fellatio and cunnilingus. Allendy confesses his impotence, and Saussure puts him under hypnosis so he can relate his numerous visits to brothels, etc.

To be sure, had such a dialogue been published, it would have meant that psychoanalysis no longer had any existence. Attentiveness to sexuality in therapy presupposes the exclusion of any sexual relation between the analyst and his patient. For the same reasons, psychoanalysts are required to obey an ethic preventing them from publicly recounting their sexual practices. Whence this paradox: They are "listeners" to sex par excellence and are banned from speaking of their sexuality even though it is at the heart of the secret history of their societies.

The Surrealist inquiries into sexuality at present read as parodies of the case histories being published at the same time in the *Revue française de psychanalyse.* They made use of a vocabulary which gave their exchanges a technical cast. It could be said that on the one hand, the poets translated their phantasms into a playful vocabulary—situating themselves in a kind of ongoing therapy allowing them to evolve an impassioned lexicon of love—and on the other, the practitioners of the soul told of sex in medical terms, carefully avoiding any revelation of the erotic reality governing their social relations.

The Surrealists were not satisfied with merely talking about sexuality, death, and suicide. They also invented a new figure of femininity through the celebration of the female criminal. The case of Violette Nozière would provide them with the opportunity.

On the evening of August 21, 1933, Violette Nozière, the daughter of a train mechanic employed by the PLM company, poisoned her parents with a powder of her own preparation. She was eighteen years old. Her mother, Germaine, of peasant origin, had been married previously to a man she did not love. After thirteen months, she separated from her husband: He had brutalized her, deceived her, and gambled at the racetrack. She obtained a divorce and then married decent Baptiste Nozière.

Violette was arrested, then found guilty. Her father had been killed and her mother taken to the hospital—she would survive. No doubt suspecting something, she had not drunk all the potion her daughter had given her.

For a long time, the Nozière couple had been behaving strangely with Violette, who was leading a double life. In the Latin Quarter, among students, she passed as a totally liberated woman. Dressed in black and delicately made up, she presented herself as an employee of an haute couture establishment. She chose her lovers with the flighty humor of a courtesan; then, in the evening, at the family table, she became a studious adolescent again.

But Baptiste and his wife were distrustful of their whimsical daughter. When she came down with syphilis, she succeeded in convincing her parents that it was an hereditary illness and forced them to submit to a treatment of her concoction, which was alleged to be prescribed by a physician. On the evening of the poisoning, the father had his doubts. He decided to go to the pharmacy and determine the composition of the mysterious antisyphilitic powder that so resembled arsenic. The shop was closed. Then, with a single gulp, he swallowed the poison. Did he know what the glass contained? That will never be known.

For some time already, Violette had been seeing Jean Dabin, a young student with bourgeois pretentions. She began to steal for him, perhaps to prostitute herself. She was wildly in love. One day she gave him a ring she had pilfered from her father. The student seemed unaware of the doings of his mistress.

Before the investigating magistrate, Violette affirmed that she had not wanted to kill her mother, but only her father. He had been raping her for months she said. He made her read obscene songs and showed her provocative drawings. As a result she had been frigid until she met Jean Dabin.

In the press and public opinion, there were two adversary camps. One, which was the patriotic and conservative majority, was convinced of Baptiste's probity, and saw him as the victim of a perverse creature. The other, the minority, recommended a certain prudence. In the fall of 1933, all of France was obsessed with the Nozière affair. Street songs were being written on the subject, as for the celebrated criminals Vacher or Landru. The Satanic figure of the sorceress was being invoked, with calls for the stake, punishment, torture. . . . [32]

The psychiatric experts, including Professor Claude, delivered a devastating judgment: In their view, Violette presented no signs of insanity; she was "perverse," and thus fully responsible for her acts. Strangely, she continued to invent weird stories about herself. She claimed, for instance, that she was being kept by a certain Monsieur Émile, who drove a blue Talbot. Thanks to the newspapers, that individual came to fascinate France. Thousands denounced him, attempted to track him down, or thought they recognized him. "Hunting Émile" became a parlor game, stimulating subsequent careers as detective or police informer. That mysterious individual would never be found, but since Violette had not been declared insane, it was not possible to regard her as the victim of her own myth.

Without delivering a judgment or counter-evaluation, the Surrealists were fascinated by the young criminal. In her act, they saluted the dawning of a new era. A booklet bearing her name was published beyond the French border. Max Ernst, Tanguy, Magritte, and Dali celebrated the glory of this Joan of Arc of dishonor, while Breton, Char, Éluard, and Péret placed their pens in the service of her cause. One does not supervise one's daughter the way one does a train, wrote Mesens. "Old man Nozières / In the best of Republics / Drove a locomotive / For the train of many a president / And when he passed in a station / The French army saluted him." [33] A few months later, René Crevel in turn gave vent to his feelings: "Violette Nozière, in the moldiness of the shadow imprisoning her, the bouquet of phosphorescence will not fade. A high black flame dances higher than the horizon and habit. Every storm will echo the voice which cried out in words of sulphur, words of suffering, the condemnation of a world in which everything was against love." [34]

Germaine Nozière started up a civil suit and the trial began in October 1934, at the time the suffragette Louise Weiss was organizing a demonstration on the Champs-Elysées demanding equal rights for men and women.

In court, Germaine defended the memory of Baptiste; she explained that Violette was trying to snatch the household money, but immediately asked for the jury's indulgence. After Jean Dabin's testimony and the prosecutor's speech, the accused fainted. Her attorney, Maître de Vésinne Larue, evoked the recent case of the Papin sisters and took a stand against the archaic practice of psychiatric evaluations, which sent madwomen to jail instead of attempting to treat them. To avoid his client's being sent to the guillotine, he evoked the ravages of syphilis. Overwhelmed with remorse, Violette threw herself on the court's mercy, then thanked her mother for forgiving her. Despite that, the verdict was devastating: According to tradition, the girl would be executed on Place de Grève; she would be brought there barefooted, her faced concealed by a black veil. At the time, however, women were no longer guillotined, and the death penalty was commuted to life imprisonment by President Albert Lebrun.

In 1937, the affair resurfaced. In a public letter, Violette retracted the accusations she had brought against her father. She confirmed that these were odious inventions intended to exculpate her. This did not occur by chance. At that time, the only man Violette had loved, Jean Dabin, died of illness in a hospital. Germaine, who had preferred charges against him, accusing him of stealing Baptiste's ring, was thus rid of the only authentic witness of her daughter's double life, and specifically of her sexual relations. Violette, for her part, rejected her adolescence; her stay in prison had turned her into a mystic. Only her mother could stop her from taking vows, which she succeeded in doing by invoking the pain such a decision would cause her.

Through her letter, Violette dispelled all trace of an incestuous relation with her father, just as through her religious vocation she had renounced a sexual past judged to be shameful. In thus obeying the wishes of her mother, who wanted her virtuous and chaste, she revealed the unconscious motive for her crime, which turned on the realization of a homosexual fusion between the two women. That fusion could be accomplished in reality following a mystical episode and at the time of the death of her former lover from the Latin Quarter. It took concrete form in a letter in which Violette accepted full responsibility for her crime, thus completing the obliteration of her past. The religious conversion had the effect of "curing" her of her murderous passion, while the confession of her responsibility substantiated the opinion of the experts and allowed for a definitive reunion with her mother.

In paying homage to Violette Nozière, the Surrealists once again indicated their attachment to that figure of passionate insanity through which they never stopped proclaiming their revolt against the values of familial happiness. Violette, a parricide and a mythmonger, was cousin to Charcot's Augustine or the tragic Blanche Wittmann of Jules Janet. She was also the twin of the famous Papin sisters who, during that same year, 1933, tore out the eyes of their employers. She was also a counterpart to Breton's Nadja, an errant creature, or Jacques Lacan's celebrated Aimée, a failed criminal. Her fate resembled that of the anonymous Mme Lefèbvre, who was visited in her prison by Marie Bonaparte and whose story served to open the first issue of the *RFP*. It is as though during that era, a new representation of woman was emerging at the center of the intellectual epic of the interwar years. It began with the adventure of Germaine Barton, the female anarchist whose crime was celebrated in 1924 by *Révolution surréaliste,* and ended in the brothel of Madame Edwarda, during the dark years of the Occupation. Edwarda, the mystic and prostitute, heir to the defeated women of years past, then becomes, in Georges Bataille's text, a triumphant madwoman, capable of inscribing the name of God on the "rags" hanging from her scarlet sex.[35]

The female ecstatic—criminal, or mad—was present at the heart of psychiatry in the form of a "clinical case" refractory to traditional diagnoses, but she traversed the Surrealist adventure in the manner of a Valkyrie heralding new twilights. Baudelarian, nocturnal, dangerous, and fragile, a new vision of femininity took shape, bearing witness to a transformation in mores due in part to Freud's discovery but which would not be fully accomplished until after the Second World War. In that sense, Surrealism's representation of woman is contemporaneous with the rise of feminism and the recasting of psychiatry's perspective in the first quarter of the century. The young Lacan was nourished on that vision as much as André Breton was. Both drew sustenance from an epistemic configuration which took concrete form with the forgetting of Charcot's teaching and the transition from the clinical reality of "nervous diseases" to one, which was more psychiatric, of "mental disorders." That was why when Breton and Aragon paid homage to the Augustine of the Salpêtrière, it was already Violette, Aimée, and Nadja whom they were addressing—that is, a rebellious, criminal, paranoid, or homosexual woman, who was no longer the impoverished laundry maid of former times, the slave of her symptoms, but the heroine of a new modernity.

It should be stated that in 1930 a mutation occurred within French society. By the time the storm from Wall Street made its way through Europe, the mythology of the "roaring" 1920s was already part of a distant horizon, and an air of disappointment hovered over the rising intellectual class. The Surrealists were part of the generation that had experienced the War, and they would have a hard time accommodating the events accompanying the change of decade.

Thus does the celebration of the mad woman account for that increased tension through which murder, valorized as an heroic act, announced the decline of a civilization. Through an exacerbated representation of the female, the "generation of refusal" no longer sought the exile of sleep within, but, in the negative idealization of crime, finally discovered the means to struggle against a society reviled from every quarter.

III. André Breton between Freud and Hegel

"Had Breton completed his studies and specialized in psychiatry," Ellenberger has written, "he might very well, given his new methods, have become the founder of a new school of dynamic psychiatry." [36] That judgment should be compared with Babinski's on the subject of his young student. In 1926, Breton attended a performance of a play entitled *Les Détraqués* ["The deranged"], in which the actress Blanche Derval played the role of the very curious Solange. The play's authors, whose true identity would be revealed thirty years later, were named Palau and Paul Thiéry. The latter, a friend of Babinski's, was an established surgeon. The play relates a case of circular-type psychosis, and the two men, lest they commit any errors in transcribing symptoms onto the stage, asked for advice from the illustrious neurologist. When Breton attended the performance in 1926, he was unaware that his former teacher had participated in its elaboration. It was only in 1962, for a reedition of *Nadja,* that he evoked Babinski's memory: "I have always felt honored by the kindness he showed me—even if it misled him into predicting a great medical career for me!—and in my way, I believe I profited from his teaching, to which homage is paid at the end of the first Surrealist manifesto." [37]

André Breton rejected a medical career, but unlike the other members of the group, he retained from his study of psychiatry a taste for doctrinal adventure and the construction of theories. This was why he always attempted to furnish foundations for the Surrealist experiment by reflecting a fusion among various methods of dream interpretation. His identification with Babinski was not unconnected to the position of "chief" which he occupied in the movement, authoritatively presiding over new inclusions, excommunications, and the daily life of the group.

In 1917, Breton was working as a temporary intern in Babinski's service at the Pitié hospital. The previous year, he had been an assistant to Dr. Raoul Leroy at the psychiatric center of the French Second Army division at Saint-Dizier. It was there that he had experimented with the associative methods in use at the time.

At the Saint-Dizier center, soldiers suffering from acute forms of insanity were sent home from the front along with delinquents, for whom a legal-medical report was required. During his stay, Breton had the opportunity to observe a young man of strange behavior, who had distinguished himself in the front lines by acts of extraordinary boldness. Standing on the parapet in the middle of a bombardment, he would direct with his finger the trajectory of shells. To explain why he had not been wounded, he told the doctors that the "alleged" war he was participating in was only a simulacrum and that "false" bombshells could not hurt anyone. He also maintained that the "apparent" wounds of his companions in arms were the result of skillfully applied makeup, and that the war dead were nothing but corpses borrowed from the medical schools and strewn over fake battlefields.[38]

Quite impressed by the insane but logical argument, Breton had compared it to the speculations of Fichte and the radical doubt invoked by Pascal. It was thus on the basis of a genuine clinical experience that he conceived the idea of "surreality." Subsequently he sought to attain it through automatic writing.

While he was staying at Saint-Dizier, Breton, who did not know German, learned of the existence of Freud's works through Régis and Hesnard's book *La psychanalyse des névroses et des psychoses* (Paris: Alcan, 1929). He only began reading them in 1922 with the first translations of the *Introduction to Psychoanalysis* and the *Psychopathology of Everyday Life.* On the other hand, he had already read the works of Janet, Myers, Richet, and had familiarized himself with the texts of the great predecessors, Alfred Maury and Hervey de Saint-Denys. He was particularly fond of Flournoy's book, *Des Indes à la planète Mars,* and the name of Hélène Smith, a spiritualist, would constantly crop up in his writing, specifically in *Nadja,* where he confuses it with that of a wandering girl.

It will thus be perceived that Breton's conception of the unconscious was not part of the same field of knowledge as Freud's. For the poet, the unconscious was not a structure organized topographically into agencies or instances, but a psychical site conforming to those automatisms described by psychologists, magnetizers, spiritualists, and occultists. Although the young Breton was nourished on German literature and philosophy, and although his anti-chauvinism was as radical as his opposition to any form of inegalitarianism, his theoretical training had a quite French cast to it. Breton was a classical psychiatrist, an admirer of Nerval and Hegel, but also of Taine and Barrès. He read Kraepelin before Freud and studied Babinski's neurology before knowing of the psychoanalytic method. Although he did not consider Janet an intellectual master, his training owed a lot to the kind of diffuse influence of Janet's thought that presided over the introduction of Freudianism in France. And yet it was indeed Freudian doctrine which would be an object of unabating inquiry for him.

One day in October 1921, he knocked on Freud's door, quite excited at the idea of meeting the great innovator to whom he had sent an enthusiastic letter. Freud received him in his afternoon consulting room and had him wait with his patients. The poet had the time to contemplate several allegorical engravings decorating the walls and to pause before a photo of the master surrounded by his disciples. When his turn came, he found himself facing a not particularly engaging old man with no interest in the Dada movement. Breton tried to animate the conversation, spoke of Charcot and Babinski, but Freud responded with commonplaces. At the end, he bid him a friendly farewell with the words, "Fortunately we are counting a lot on the young."

Breton would spend years recovering from the disappointment he felt. In an enraged and laudatory account, he told of his encounter in violently Dadaist terms: "To the young and the imaginatively inclined," he wrote, "who, because the fashion this winter is with psychoanalysis, need to have a sense of one of the more prosperous and mercenary agencies of contemporary flashiness, the office of Dr. Freud— with its devices for transforming rabbits into hats and a blue determinism serving as sole blotter—it causes me no anger to say that the greatest psychologist of our time lives in a house of mediocre appearance in an out-of-the-way neighborhood in Vienna." [39]

It was from a similar (but far more virulent) perspective that Aragon, in his *Traité du style,* published in 1928, would ridicule the same Gallic spirit and its need for the fashionable: "It was then," he wrote, "that the idea of having Freud blow his nose and drinking of his head cold occurred simultaneously to several bookstore hags who were expecting that magical operation to cure them of their perivascular swelling. Monsieur Paul Bourget, always in a certain relation to his era, preferred to restrict himself to the dejections of Monsieur le professeur français Janet, may his senility preserve him in his wheelchair!" And further on, "All that the Psychiatrist from Austria is lacking is consecration by the Pope." [40] Never would Aragon have imagined that one day a certain Jacques Lacan would request an audience with the Holy Father!

The misunderstanding between Breton and Freud rested on a double misperception that was the result less of Freud's hostility to the new ideas than of the two men's respective positions. At the time, Breton came to Freud in search of the figure of a rebellious master that he himself dreamed of becoming. He asked him for a measure of recognition which Freud could not bestow on him. He was mistaken about Freud because he thought him capable of understanding the nature of Dadaism. As for Freud, he was wrong about Breton because he thought he was dealing with the representative of a new literary school and not the leader of a movement of cultural negation.

It was thus not out of antimodernism that Freud remained deaf to Breton's initiative, but because he took it for something other than it was. An analogous situation would occur in the writer's relations with the Communist movement. Toward Freud, as with the Marxists, Breton was prepared to make numerous concessions, except for one on which he would never compromise: allowing himself to be locked into the status of an artist, that is, of a "specialist in objective awareness." [41] Because of that refusal, he would reject (against Tzara) the Sartrean notion of commitment, even though his participation in the political life of the 1950s would be as intense as Sartre's.

In 1921, Freud's indifference to Breton was a sign of the specific atmosphere of the decade. During the same period, the scientist received quite warmly a popular and rather mediocre society novelist, Henri Lenormand, who brought him a box of chocolates.[42] Against a France hostile to psychoanalysis, or inclined to celebrate it as a fashion, Freud preferred to give his backing to official institutions: medicine, on the one hand, provided that it recognized his discovery, and edifying literature on the other. That attitude was not a function of any concerted strategy, but of Freud's ignorance of avant-garde activity. One might say that the history of the relations between psychoanalysis and Surrealism is not part of the same history as that of Freud with France. There was a disjunction between the two principal modalities of Freudianism's penetration in France, even though they were concomitant in time. The encounter between Vienna and the new sensibility would bear its fruits after the fact because it would have eluded Freud's perception as well as the official organization of psychoanalysis.

The technique of automatic messages employed in *Les champs magnétiques* had a long history behind it. If we are to believe Ellenberger, the adventure of "spirits" began, in modern times, in the state of New York around 1847. Alarmed by strange noises one evening, a man decided to leave his house and entrust it to a family of peasants. They settled in and it was not long before they too heard the ill-famed sounds. There was no doubt possible; the house was haunted. The new tenant's wife, who was quite curious, decided to converse with the intruders. With the help of her daughters, she questioned the noises, which began to respond in an easily decipherable code. The peasant woman thus learned that the house had formerly been the site of a horrendous murder. The news spread, and their reputation was established: The farmer's wife and her daughters were specialists in communicating with the beyond.

It should be stated that the invention of the telegraph did much to perturb febrile imaginations. For ghosts, it was a unique opportunity to get their second wind: They emerged from their dens, invaded the American territory, perfected their noises.

Around 1852, the vogue of spiritualism crossed the Atlantic, swept through England, and then triumphed in Germany and France. Spirits appeared in private seances; some of their adepts succeeded in photographing them, others in exhibiting their hand or foot prints. Only a few rare and privileged individuals, called "mediums," could serve as intermediaries between the living and the dead. Touched by grace, they "wrote automatically" at the dictation of spirits. Occasionally, they received a fluid allowing them to play pianos at a distance or activate harps and accordions in the clouds. Serious witnesses claimed to have seen mediums grasp flames without burning themselves, leave simultaneously through several windows, then return by the roof or the fireplace without the slightest difficulty. Men of science joined in and began using automatic writing to explore the unconscious.

In 1882, Frederick Myers founded a society for psychical research and began collecting a vast amount of "parapsychological" information. He accepted the hypothesis of survival after death and the possibility of communication with the souls of the deceased; Flournoy, on the contrary, felt that medium-related phenomena were to be explained by cryptomnesia.[43] Janet in turn made use of automatic writing for therapeutic ends and combined it with hypnosis. This practice led quite naturally to automatic drawing, and before long, mediums and spiritualists resorted to it as well.

Breton drew on this tradition in its entirety. But with Surrealism, automatic writing changed ideological ground. In the first place, its practice was emptied of all therapeutic content. Then the spiritualistic point of view was abandoned: "As far as I am concerned," wrote Breton, "I categorically refuse to admit that communication between the living and the dead exists." [44] Fundamentally, the Surrealist utilization of automatic writing was part of a vast project aimed at liberating the forces of unconscious desire. It was not spirit that manifested itself in the writings of the poets, but the spontaneity of a language-bound thought common to all men. As a result, automatic writing was also doomed to failure since it was impossible not to invoke a qualitative choice that thus restored differences between talented texts and mere messages, obtained through the same method, but without interest. In vain did Breton condemn poetic rivalry as execrable; he himself came to observe that the history of the relations between automatic writing and Surrealism was one of unabating misfortune. [45]

With the exception of *Les champs magnétiques* and a few texts of Aragon and Desnos, the device was scarcely used as such in the sum total of the Surrealists' works. In point of fact, its interest lay less in any concrete achievement than in a program to "definitively clean out the stables of literature." [46] Its value was as a slogan and it remained in the service of a cultural project whose aim was to open the individual to a Rimbaldian "elsewhere." From that point of view, it was combined with the experimental use of hypnotic trances, which would also be abandoned in short order. One evening in September 1922, at René Crevel's suggestion, a few friends decided to sleep over at the studio on rue Fontaine to which Breton had just moved. Before long, the trappings of a seance were improvised: The guests sat in a circle around a table, fingers spread. Crevel began banging his head on the wood of the table and launched into a long spoken improvisation. Very quickly, Desnos showed himself to be a fantastic sleeper: He engaged in monologues, wrote, drew, then entered into all sorts of dialogues. His companions questioned him on the future of the world, and when Éluard asked him what he thought of Péret, he answered, "He will die in a train full of people." Only Philippe Soupault remained skeptical.

A year later, Breton decided to put an end to the twin experiments of hypnotic sleep and automatic writing. He observed that he himself was subject to hallucinations and that certain of his friends were suffering from disturbances. One evening, after a session of table-turning, several persons attempted to hang themselves from a coatrack in their sleep—the idea had come from Crevel. On another evening, after dinner, Desnos, in a fit of somnambulism, chased Éluard through the garden and almost killed him with a knife.

As an enlightened psychiatrist, Breton realized that the experiment was becoming dangerous. He then relinquished automatic writing, somewhat in the manner in which Freud abandoned hypnosis. Nevertheless, in 1924, in his definition of Surrealism, he retained the idea of a dictation of thought beyond any control by reason. Thus, without automatic writing and without hypnotically induced sleep, Surrealism would not have become an authentic cultural movement; but at the same time, without that abandonment and without that reconversion of automatic writing into a genuine mode of writing, Surrealism would have remained an adventure without a future, something of an infantile malady of the new sensibility. It was as a kind of residue or effective phantom that automatic writing would continue to function within the movement, giving it the requisite energy to avoid becoming academic.

Automatism according to Breton referred to a notion of the subconscious prior to the concept of the Freudian unconscious, but to the extent that it liberated an anonymous form of universal expression, it dissolved the "Cartesian" notion according to which language would be the property of a thinking subject. The automatism of the Surrealists appeared as an instrument of the decentering or destabilization of the subject, who no longer recognized himself with any self-certainty. Through it, poetry was no longer a representation of reality or a site of inspiration, but language itself, objectivized as a form of being. Thus did Surrealism, in France, find itself in the service of psychoanalysis, because it accompanied the adventure of the Freudian unconscious for which it offered a mode of expression that was not *theoretical* but *analogical*. With automatic writing, the Surrealists functioned philosophically as though consciousness had disappeared. That, moreover, is what Georges Bataille would reproach them with later on.[47]

In a 1968 article entitled "Freud, Myers, Breton," Jean Starobinski, thinking of the work of Lacan, wrote: "The frigid Orphics of a 'structuralist'-inspired literature (for which the subject has been supplanted by language itself, for which *I* do not speak, but *it* speaks in me) approaches the automatic writing of the Surrealists in rather different ways; Breton, in order to endorse it would have begun by requiring a supplementary dose of warmth! And to say that 'the unconscious is language' is in no way to reconcile Freud and automatic writing, since the Freudian unconscious was language only in the mode of the impossibility of speaking: It was language only for the interpreter who made it speak."[48] If it is true that the structural conception of language, from which Lacan borrowed his argument after World War II, has little to do with automatic messages, it remains the case that the Surrealist experiment brought to light, for the first time in France, an encounter between the Freudian unconscious, language, and the decentering of the subject, which would broadly inspire the young Lacan in his formative years. Even if later on he would be inclined to criticize Surrealism, he drew from it in his youth nourishment that would prove essential for his later course.

"Who am I? If, exceptionally, I resorted to an adage: for indeed is not the whole question a matter of determining whom it is I haunt?"[49] Thus begins *Nadja,* the narrative published by Breton in 1928. The book is offered as a "novelistic" continuation of the twin experiments of automatic writing and hypnotic sleep. After commenting on the performance of Blanche Derval in the role of Solange, the murderess of *Les détraqués,* the narrator relates his encounter with another figure of womanhood, Nadja. This was no longer an actress in black silk stockings, but an errant and mad soul whose name evokes in Russian the beginning of a hope that fails to reach fruition. In the manner of Hélène Smith, the girl believes she had lived in the past under the reign of Marie Antoinette. She had been hypnotized on several occasions by a man she calls her "great friend" and whom she has told in detail all the moments of her life. One evening, she in turn hypnotizes a waiter who breaks his plates and spills his wine on the table. Since she is in debt, Breton gives her money, then attempts to help her by having her draw sketches whose meaning he interprets. The experiment fails, and a few months later, Nadja is interned at the Vaucluse asylum for having indulged in certain "eccentricities" in the corridor of her hotel. The narrator then devotes several pages of his story to a denunciation of arbitrary confinement: "I know that if I were mad, I would take advantage of a remission accorded me by my insanity to murder in cold blood one of those, preferably the physician, who might fall into my hands." And further on: "The contempt I feel for psychiatry, its rituals and works, is such that I did not dare inquire into what became of Nadja." [50] The tale ends with a final act of homage to the hysterics of the Salpêtrière: "Beauty will be CONVULSIVE or it will not be." [51]

Freud had often noted that his case histories resembled novels. Now *Nadja* is the story of a therapy in which a narrator occupies the position of a psychiatrist who cannot manage to cure his patient. He then renounces psychiatry in violent terms and identifies with the madwoman: She becomes the subject of an autobiographical narrative through which the narrator accedes to his identity. *Nadja* is a novel of initiation in the manner of the famous *Bildungsroman* of the German Romantics. Through it, Breton describes his refusal of psychiatry in terms of a defiance hurled at Satan—he literally gave up the "rituals and works" of mad-doctoring as he would a temptation. The madwoman allowed him to attain his desire to write and to achieve that convulsive beauty of which he dreamed while contemplating the iconography of the Salpêtrière. It is interesting to note that it was only in 1962 that Breton added to his text the note concerning his relations with Babinski. Thirty-five years after the publication of *Nadja,* the author thus felt the need to underscore his attachment to a medical tradition in which his writing had been tempered. He did so within a work signifying the abandonment of that tradition and the emergence of a new narrative style. *Nadja* is not only the tale of a "failed" therapy; it is also the story of the "successful" analysis of a narrator who finds in the insanity of a woman the modalities of a new novelistic genre.

The fiction so resembled reality that the "alienists" of the day took Nadja's adventure for an authentic case history. In November 1929, the book was commented on by Paul Abély during a meeting of the Société médico-psychologique. That worthy representative of the medical guild did not hesitate to accuse Breton of wanting to incite the mad to murder their psychiatrists. He related that a dangerous maniac he was treating had underlined in blue the poet's insults against psychiatry, thus causing a considerable commotion in the asylum. Without the slightest irony, Abély demanded sanctions against the publisher who had dared bring out such an incitement to murder.

The lecture was followed by a truly extravagant discussion. The celebrated Pierre Janet and the illustrious Gaëtan Gatian de Clérambault buried the dangerous Surrealists with opprobium.

The former affirmed that their works were "the confessions of doubters and the obsessed," while the latter lashed out at the "haughty indolence and gimmickry of these pretentious upstarts of French thought." Then Janet returned to the attack, recalling that the Surrealist techniques consisted of fabricating words "with chance" and in constructing stories out of "turkeys" and "top hats." Clérambault upped the stakes and invited the authorities to protect the institution of psychiatry from the odious slander it had received.

To be sure, by the following day, the press latched onto the affair and exploited it to comic ends. Janet was singled out for his blunders, but Clérambault's declaration went unmentioned. Whereupon Breton selected his finest pen and published an article entitled "La médecine mentale devant le surréalisme": "It is clear," he wrote, "that psychiatrists, accustomed to treating the mad like dogs, are astonished at not being authorized, even outside their clinical service, to slaughter them." [52] He then lashed out at medico-legal evaluations, referring in passing to the notorious case of Mme Lefèbvre. After that he took apart Article 64 of the Penal Code on the irresponsibility of the insane, maintaining that it was "philosophically incomprehensible." Finally, he demonstrated that the Bleulerian idea of autism had been abused by psychiatrists in order to condemn everything in man that was not adaptation, pure and simple, to external conditions: "We insist here on the honor of being the first," he concluded, "to indicate the peril and to rise up against the intolerable and growing abuse of power on the part of those we are inclined to see less as physicians than as jailers and even more so as purveyors of cells and scaffolds. *Because they are physicians*, they seem to us still less excusable than others for assuming the base tasks of the executioner. However surreal or 'gimmicky' we may be in their eyes, it is impossible for us to recommend any more forcefully to them, even if certain of them should accidentally fall under the blows of those they seek arbitrarily to diminish, to have the decency to keep their silence." [53]

It was thus in the name of a true practice of medicine that Breton condemned the psychiatric science haunting his own endeavor. In 1930, he published without commentary the declarations of Janet, Abély, and Clérambault at the beginning of the *Second Surrealist Manifesto*. A few pages later, he wrote: "The most simple Surrealist act consists, revolver in hand, of going into the street and shooting at random as often as possible into the crowd. Whoever has not, at least once, felt like putting an end in such manner to the petty system of degradation and cretinization currently in effect has his place already marked in that crowd, his stomach at gun-level." [54]

Pierre Janet, France's most influential psychologist during the first half of the century, had little luck with the creators. His deafness to literary talent was equalled only by the stylistic platitude of his clinical narratives. For several years, he graced Raymond Roussel, suffering from chronic depression, with his treatment, without ever realizing that he was dealing with one of the most important French writers of the century. It should be stated, however, that at the time only the Surrealists, whom

Janet detested, recognized the genius of that odd, solitary, and somewhat archaic writer, whose ways disconcerted literature's official representatives. The man spent fortunes to publish his poems in author-subsidized journals or books. He rented out theaters for the performance of his plays, which no one understood, and personally paid actors, stage designers, directors, and occasionally even members of the audience. The Surrealists organized demonstrations on his behalf, declared his genius, all to no effect; Roussel was regarded as a worldly mystifier, a lunatic, an eccentric, or an imbecile. . . . The strangeness of his behavior was so much grist for the mill of his detractors. Whenever he could, he manifested an exaggerated fury against changes in style or sexual exhibitions. He organized his life the way he conceived his books, midst reclusive rituals, adopting as his major rule of conduct to wear his collars only once since he was horrified by anything washed. At his mother's death, he caused a scandal by arranging for the coffin to have a window allowing the corpse to be observed.[55]

When *Locus Solus* was published, François Mauriac wrote: "A millionaire can treat himself to anything: a Gallipaux theater, costumes by Poiret, Signoret, and above all the right to deride his audience. Monsieur Roussel decided to write a play about madmen and has succeeded all too well. For the truly mad are not at all gay, and his play is indeed sinister." [56]

During a performance of *L'Etoile au front,* in 1924, the Surrealists showed up *en masse* to acclaim their idol. During the second act, a resentful member of the audience shot out at Robert Desnos, "The hired clappers [*la claque*] have their nerve tonight." Desnos, furious, shot back, "We're the smack [*claque*] and you're the cheek [*la joue*]!" As for Roussel, he rushed in with his own punning comment, "We're the *claque* and you're *jaloux* [jealous]." By the third act, the tumult was such that the performance had to be interrupted.[57]

In 1928, Janet reported the case of his patient in *De l'angoisse à l'extase.*[58] He called him Martial, after the character in *Locus Solus,* and described his state under the rubric "The psychological characteristics of ecstasy." A sad, solitary, and megalomaniacal individual, Martial devoted the best part of his life to the elaboration of literary works without achieving the success he had hoped for. And yet at no point did he ever have doubts about himself. He identified with Victor Hugo, Napoleon, and Wagner and knew that he bore within himself an immense glory, a "formidable bombshell that has yet to explode." Janet compared his patient to his beloved Madeleine, to Plotinus, to Jean-Jacques Rousseau. He observed that he was neither haughty, nor mentally deficient, nor agitated—merely a neuropath. His behavior was characterized by ecstatic crises; his life was constructed like his work, which seemed to refer to an extra-human world containing nothing real, only imaginary combinations. At bottom, Janet was not far from thinking that if Martial were to "try a little harder," he would obtain the recognition he wanted, even though his works did not appear intended for a large audience.

After Roussel's death, Michel Leiris paid a visit to the psychologist to ask him not to destroy his personal notes concerning the case of Martial. Janet refused, calling Roussel a "pathetic little patient." Furious, Leiris stormed out, slamming the door.

Janet's attitude, and particularly his lack of understanding concerning literary creation in general, has often been criticized. But that is not enough. It was not Janet's deafness to Roussel's literary talent that posed the real problem, but rather the frivolity of a therapeutic practice consisting of mechanically noting down a patient's declarations and appending a moral judgment stripped of all interpretation. Consider two examples: Allendy did no better than Janet in his treatment of Artaud or Anaïs Nin; and yet he was perfectly aware of the former's genius and the latter's talent.[59] On the other hand, Freud was in no need of understanding artistic gifts in order to attend to the dreams, memories, and stories of any individual, whether a neurotic, a painter, a musician, a talented inventor, an unrecognized genius, or a "failed" writer. It is known that he did not like to accept creators, whom he regarded as adepts of the pleasure principle, for analysis. And yet, in 1910, he made an exception for Gustav Mahler, who came to consult him because of sexual impotence. In the course of a four-hour walk in the streets of Leyden, he revealed to the composer an infantile fixation which caused him to drag one foot because his mother limped. Then he brought to his attention a matter involving first names and interpreted the meaning of the repetition of a musical phrase heard in childhood. That therapeutic episode was recounted by Jones, who erred on the date, and probably deformed the reality. And yet through his account, it becomes clear that Freud, who was not a music lover, was not interested in Mahler's talent. He simply listened to what the composer said and offered him interpretations which were "wild" but adequate to his discourse.[60]

Janet was not a psychoanalyst, and he should not be reproached for not being Freudian in his conduct of therapy. But one is obliged to observe that his therapy partook of a theoretical position based on a notion of instrumentality. For him, discourse was always the reflection of sociological reality from which fantasy was excluded. He thus could neither recognize Roussel's literary genius, since that would presuppose an ability to distinguish between words and things, nor bestow a meaning on Martial's ritualized and megalomaniacal insanity, since that would necessitate its being related to a structure and not a mode of behavior. Janet's attitude toward Surrealism was of the same sort as his verdict on Roussel: If he took the Surrealists' works as "confessions," it was because his conception of art was an exact reflection of his practice of therapy. For him, the man and his work were transparent in relation to a reality whose content was prior to any formal considerations. We may note in passing that Clérambault's judgment was different from Janet's. The psychiatrist was able to characterize Surrealist style and techniques by linking them to a form of "gimmickry."

It appears that Roussel was also treated by Ludwig Binswanger, but the case history he assembled of his patient has not survived. According to Michel Leiris, the writer, on the eve of his death and at the urging of his friend Charlotte Dufrène, decided to go to the clinic in Kreutlingen to effect a detoxification. At the time he was no longer writing and moved into a boarding house frequented by drug addicts and homosexuals. During the night of July 13–14, 1933, he ended his life by taking an overdose of sleeping pills. The incident occurred in Palermo, in a hotel whose decor evoked the enigmatic beauty of *Impressions d'Afrique,* one of his most innovative works. A police investigation was conducted, and, through a skillful bit of tampering, the functionaries of fascist Italy concluded that the death had been a murder: Under the "idyllic" reign of Benito Mussolini, a suicide would be inconceivable.

In 1954, Michel Leiris gave an excellent clinical description of the Martial "case": "He died at his own hand," wrote Leiris, "on the very threshold of that *communication* he had recognized as impossible, at least in his own lifetime, and with his eyes turned toward the only person (Charlotte, it seems) who might have shared somewhat (but only somewhat) his intimate concerns." [61] As for Raymond Roussel, it was with cruel irony that he consigned Janet's commentary on him to his *Comment j'ai écrit certains de mes livres* ["How I wrote some of my books"], a posthumous work conceived in the manner of a glorious mausoleum.

At the end of 1932, André Breton sent Freud a copy of *Les vases communicates*. On the very first page, the Viennese master came upon an impertinence he could not have appreciated. For the poet reproached him with referring to a book by Hervey de Saint-Denys without having read it. Further on, he added: "Freud himself, who on the subject of the symbolic interpretation of dreams, appears to have done no more than take over the ideas of Volkelt, an author concerning whom the bibliography at the end of his book remains rather significantly silent; Freud, for whom the entire substance of dreams is all the same caught up in real life, could not resist the temptation of declaring that the inner nature of the unconscious is as unknown to us as the reality of the external world, thus providing arms to those whom his method had almost vanquished." [62] Piqued, Freud initiated a rather absurd quarrel with Breton on the subject of the omission of precursors. It was not Johannes Volkelt, he said in essence, but Karl Albert Scherner who discovered the symbolics of dream interpretation. He then added that Volkelt's name did not appear in the French edition of *The Interpretation of Dreams*. There followed a second letter from Freud explaining the omission by the fact that the French translation of the *Traumdeutung* had been prepared from the seventh German edition, in which Volkelt's name no longer appeared. Stung to the quick, Breton responded by saying that the affair was really a tempest in a teapot. He nonetheless pursued the quarrel, reproaching Freud with not having pressed the analysis of the sexual content of dreams sufficiently far. Wounded, the old man answered that it was not timidity but a limit he had set for himself concerning his relations with his father. Then he added: "And now a confession that you must receive with due tolerance! Although I have received much evidence of the interest that you and your friends have for my research, I myself cannot manage to perceive very clearly what precisely Surrealism is and what it wants. Perhaps I am in no way made to understand it, I who am so far removed from the arts." [63]

Thirteen years after Breton's journey to Vienna, the misunderstanding between the two men took a new turn. In 1921, the Frenchman had found himself politely dismissed. By 1932, he had won a few stripes. He still looked on Freud as a respected elder, but he in turn had become the leader of a movement in which he occupied the position of master. He thus allowed himself to speak to the man of science as an equal. As for Freud, he did not understand the objectives of Surrealism any more than he did those of Dada, but he now addressed Breton with respect and modesty. He apparently saw him as an authentic thinker, significant for his era and for the future of culture. This time the misunderstanding concerned less a divergent conception of art and literature than the entirety of a theoretical position. Freud did not have the better role and he knew it. The ardor he brought to the dispute betrayed his inability to read the Surrealist texts.

He was unable to grasp the conception Breton had of his own doctrine. The quarrel concerning proper names in fact concealed a philosophical divergence. The writer asked Freud to acknowledge that the psychoanalytic theory of dreams was insufficient to explain the material life of men and that it had to be completed by "something else," by a conceptuality allowing for a passage to be opened between the world of the imaginary and that of objective existence. Naturally, Freud did not grasp Breton's demands: His own conception of the unconscious remained based on a metapsychology which separated psychical reality from material reality and structured one and the other in a hierarchy incompatible with the notion of "communicating vessels."

"Freud is Hegelian in me," Breton declared one day.[64] In his eyes the communication thus seemed possible. In order to achieve it, it would be enough to annex to Freudian doctrine a kind of Hegelian philosophy which would be able to effect an encounter between the imaginary and reality. The writer had a privileged relation to Hegel. Once again, as in the case of Freud, it was a nocturnal and occult version of the philosopher's work that retained his attention. Breton had "intuited" Hegel in a philosophy class. He impregnated himself with his texts "convulsively," in the manner of a hysteric: "Any specialist," he declared in 1952, "would be able to show me up so far as exegesis is concerned, on his subject, but it remains no less true that since I have known Hegel, indeed since I intuited him through the sarcasms heaped upon him in or around 1912 by my philosophy teacher, a positivist, André Cresson, I have impregnated myself with his views and for me his method reduces all others to indigence. Where the Hegelian dialectic does not function, there is for me no thought, no hope of truth." [65]

Breton's plunge into active Hegelianism was contemporaneous with a political change within the Surrealist movement. The *Second Manifesto* had announced the quest for a "point in the mind" that would allow one to surpass antinomies and discover the means to effect their fusion. Through that philosophical monism, Hegelian dialectic seemed capable of resolving the contradiction artificially pitting dreams and material life against each other. Breton's Hegelianism thus became the weapon par excellence for a transformation of Surrealist revolt into social revolution.

In 1930, Crevel, Aragon, Éluard, and Breton had already joined the ranks of the French Communist Party. *Révolution surréaliste* changed its title to become *Le Surréalisme au service de la révolution*. In opposition, Leiris, Desnos, Queneau, Morise, Limbour, and Simone Kahn oriented their work elsewhere. Regrouping around Bataille and the journal *Documents*, they did not hesitate to publish a brochure of unprecedented violence in which they called Breton a cadaver. Under the title *Thomas l'imposteur*, Desnos wrote these words: "You have guessed that I was André Breton. I regaled myself with the flesh of corpses: Vaché, Rigaut, and Nadja, whom I claimed to love. Crevel, on whose death I was counting for the use I could make of it, buried me with his own hands and shat, with a sense of justice and tranquillity, on my carcass and my memory. I hated pederasty because I was no more than a big-time trickster. I thought I was God, etc." [66] For Breton, the loss of the companions of his early years was offset by the arrival of Dali, René Char, Sadoul, Buñuel, and Thirion, who would contribute to Surrealism's second wind. On the horizon, there was already the break with Aragon.

Through his secret Hegelianism, Breton adhered to Marxism. By means of it, he attempted in vain to give a philosophical basis to what he called Freud's "metaphysic." Thanks to it as well, he attempted to transport Surrealism into the revolution. With it, finally, he tried to bring dreams into creative reality. *Les vases communicants* recounts from beginning to end that interminable quest which did not end in the elaboration of a philosophical doctrine but in the realization of a new literary genre, already there in *Nadja*. In refusing to write novels or poems, Breton invented a narrative style in which an encounter between the Freudian technique of dream interpretation and the old tradition of the intitiatic dream, inherited from German romanticism, was effected. "What makes his case fascinating," wrote Julien Gracq, "was that in spite of his poetic gifts, he was first of all a theoretician and a writer of ideas, and yet a poet as such; and that he attempted to resolve within the domain of pure ideas the problem of sense-laden communication, and he succeeded there in obtaining that quality of intimacy in one's belief which has passed for the exclusive privilege of the poetic image." [67]

Other more "modern" Surrealists—Leiris for prose, Péret, Artaud, or Desnos for poetry—were affected by the excitement of the Freudian adventure, but Breton was alone in inventing a syntax capable, in a single narrative gesture, of theorizing that adventure and exploring that stratum of it which was itself a dream.

In December 1937, the poet proposed to Freud that he join the group in their publication of an anthology entitled *Trajectoire du rêve*. Still mystified as to the interest the Surrealists took in his person and his doctrine, Freud sent a polite refusal: "An anthology of dreams," he wrote, "without the associations connected with it, without any knowledge of the circumstances in which the dream was dreamt—such an anthology does not have any meaning for me and I am hard put to imagine what it might mean for others." Breton did not respond, but at the time he was sending the manuscript to the printer's, he learned that Freud had just been arrested by the Nazis in Vienna. The following day, a correction in the newspapers informed readers that the scientist was merely being "kept under surveillance." Breton then decided to add a passage to the first page of the work to which Freud had decided not to collaborate: "The illustrious master," he wrote, "the mind in whom the 'More light' called for by Goethe has found its true incarnation, he who has given so many in the world our reasons for being and acting, Freud, at the age of 82, falling into the hands of a wretched troop of soldiers, finding himself specifically marked for the fury of imbeciles and dogs!" [68]

Six months later, in a letter to Stefan Zweig, Freud expressed himself for the last time about the Surrealists, after a visit from Salvador Dali, who had just painted his portrait: "I must really thank you," he wrote, "for the word of introduction which brought me yesterday's visitors. For until then, it seems, I had been tempted to regard the Surrealists, who have apparently chosen me as their patron saint, as complete madmen (let us say 95 percent, like "absolute" alcohol). The young Spaniard, with his candid fanatic's eyes and his undeniable technical mastery, has impelled me to reconsider my opinion. It would in fact be quite interesting to study the genesis of a painting of this kind analytically. From the critical point of view, it might, however, always be said that the notion of art should not be extended when the quantitative relation between unconscious material and preconscious elaboration is not kept within fixed limits. We are faced there, in any event, with serious psychological problems." [69]

Once again, Freud showed himself intent on not establishing a connection between heterogeneous domains and restricting himself to a notion of art which would not use his theory as an instrument of transgression. But on the threshold of death, he was traversed by a doubt. The Surrealists were perhaps less insane than he believed, since the craziest of all, a young Spaniard, had succeeded in convincing Freud to reconsider, if only for a moment, an opinion he was not, all the same, about to compromise.

2 Marxism, Psychoanalysis, Psychology

I. Pavlovianism and Freudo-Marxism

Around 1909, during a stay in Vienna, Leon Trotsky frequented the meetings of certain psychoanalysts and read the works of Freud. He published a Russian newspaper, *Pravda,* with the collaboration of Adolphe Yoffe, who would become his friend and faithful partisan. Yoffe suffered from a "nervous disease" and was undergoing an analysis with Adler that would end in 1912. In 1923, Trotsky wrote to Ivan Pavlov, explaining to him that psychoanalysis, despite its "literary" aspect, had ceased believing in the primacy of the soul's abyss and that Freudian theory could be encompassed by a materialist psychology as a specific case of the doctrine of conditioned reflexes. Four years later, in the context of a lecture on "socialism and culture," the organizer of the Red Army pursued his reflections on Freudianism. For him the study of reflexes was situated entirely within the scope of materialism because it did away with the barrier between psychology and physiology. As for the Viennese school, Trotsky also situated it within materialism although he took his distance from the primacy accorded to sexuality. He believed Pavlovian experimentation superior to Freudian speculation, which he deemed overly "fantastic": "The attempt to declare psychoanalysis incompatible with Marxism and to turn one's back without further ado on Freudianism is too simple, and even simple-minded. We are under no obligation to adopt Freudianism. It is a working hypothesis which may give—and which indisputably does give—hypotheses and conclusions which are entirely in line with materialist psychology." [1]

Trotsky's position accounts elliptically but precisely for the situation of psychoanalysis in the Soviet Union at the time. To grasp how Pavlovianism gradually became a standard for materialism in the field of psychology, one must establish the relation between the introduction of Freudianism in Russia and the doctrine of reflexes as conceived by Bolshevik ideology in the context of the ongoing struggles between 1920 and 1935 on the subjects of philosophy, the sciences, and Marxism. In taking that twofold adventure as one's bearing, one can then attempt to grasp the grounds on which the relations between Marxism, psychology, and psychoanalysis evolved during that period as well as in the years following.

From the point of view of the history of ideas, the works of Ivan Petrovich Pavlov were contemporaneous with those of Freud and Janet. Born in 1849 to a poor family, he initially intended to follow the path of his father and enter the priesthood. Then, at the age of 21, he left the seminary for the University of Saint Petersburg, where he became assistant to a renowned physiologist and then a doctor of medicine. In 1904, he won the Novel Prize for his work on digestion. His research in that field led him to concentrate on the phenomenon of "psychical secretion," which would serve as the basis for his hypotheses on the higher functions of the nerve centers. It was thus through physiology that Pavlov was led, despite his antipsychologistic bias, to lay the grounds for a new psychology based on the study of conditioned reflexes.

The story of the fox terrier and his ration of meat is well known. If one introduces into a dog's mouth a morsel of deliciously cooked beef stew, the animal behaves like a gourmet and produces a certain quantity of saliva. That saliva can be collected through a fistula and measured. Whether named Buck, like Jack London's hero, whether a hound, a bulldog, or a Pekinese, the dog reacts to the experiment whatever his age or the external conditions of the experiment itself. He is not interested in the texture of the serving receptacle, whether earthenware or porcelain, nor in the color of the experimenter's apron. For that reason the salivation of the gentle mammal during his lunch is called an *unconditioned, innate,* or *instinctual* reflex. If one starts the experiment anew, this time cruelly substituting the sound of a plate or the odor of a sauce, one triggers in the animal's gland a salivation identical to that provoked by the actual introduction of nourishment. The resultant process is referred to as *psychic salivation* or a *conditioned reflex*.[2] A conditioned reflex is nothing more than a scientific explanation of the well-known human and animal phenomenon of "making one's mouth water." Such was, schematically, the discovery of Ivan Petrovich Pavlov, a colorful scientist, endowed with colossal vitality and an extraordinary reserve of political naïveté.

Despite its name, psychic salivation is not a psychological phenomenon. Pavlov's central project attempted to provide a description of higher neurological activity formulated in terms of excitations and inhibitions. On the basis of his research into reflexes, he constructed an animal typology that would lead him, during the last years of his life, to a rapprochement with human psychology. He divided temperaments into four types: melancholic, choleric, phlegmatic, and sanguine. He then placed them in relation to the phenomenon he called "experimental neurosis": When one activates, in rapid-fire succession, processes of excitation and inhibition and brings them closer and closer to sources of excitement to be differentiated, the animal lapses into a state of neurotic agitation. He becomes depressive, maniacal, or hysterical. At the end of some time, the acquired differentiations disappear and the animal returns to his normal state. Pavlov observed that the strong (or choleric) type shared with the weak (or melancholic) type a greater propensity to acquire an experimental neurosis.

The Pavlovian conception of the experimental neurosis was perfectly adapted to the theory of reflexes. For if a neurosis were not a structure inherent to the psyche, it was assimilable to a form of conditioning and could be produced or made to disappear experimentally. Because he was above all a physiologist and an observer of animals, Pavlov was not the founder of a new psychology; but his doctrine, which could be applied to human physiology, entailed a psychological representation of human behavior that excluded the notion of the unconscious, or, rather, dissolved it in a neurophysiological system. That is why, despite profound divergences, the notion of conditioning, in its psychological extension, was not alien to the Janetian notion of behavior and, more generally, to a typology of characters based on a hierarchy of strong and weak states. Pavlov did not err on this score and sent an open letter to Janet in 1933 in which he proposed to interpret in physiological terms the phenomena of persecution and mastery described by the French psychologist.[3]

Along with Pavlov's works, there emerged in Russia, at the beginning of the century, a school of objective psychology, led by Vladimir Bekhterev and also based on the study of reflexes.[4] Pavlov had scant affection for such reflexology, which belonged to the field of behaviorist psychology and for which psychical activity was an epiphenomenon of physiological activity. Nevertheless, in association with Pavlovianism, reflexology, first as applied to individuals, then to collectivities, would become, after the October Revolution, something of a diffuse official doctrine, charged with spreading the thematic of the "new man." For if the human subject can be defined in terms of conditioned (as opposed to instinctual) reflexes, it means that there is no "eternal human nature." And in that case, any theory of "psychical structure"—and that is what Freudianism was—risked being assimilated to a pessimistic ideology of instinctual "conservation." By virtue of its fundamental law, which consisted in assuring the satisfaction of man's material and cultural needs, socialist society was able to find in Pavlovianism the confirmation of its revolutionary ideals, through which the individual was to be changed or "conditioned" so as to learn new ways of living. If, as has already been demonstrated for the cases of hypnotism and behaviorism,[5] every psychology carries within it a politics (and vice versa), it is a safe bet that Pavlovian reflexology, as it took concrete form in Soviet society, was the psychological translation of the ideals of Communist happiness. It will never be repeated too often that the story of the dog and his stew found a new meaning in the splendor of the storming of the Winter Palace and that it ended in the nightmare of Stakhanovism, a final and ludicrous version of the doctrine of conditioning.

To be sure, from a strictly scientific point of view, the theory of reflexes was not limited to that Pavlovian psychology partially constructed by Pavlov himself. And yet the scientist's political attitude was not foreign to the fusion that occurred between his works and the ideals of Communism. Pavlov never considered himself either a materialist or a Marxist. For a long while, he fought the Soviet regime, which sponsored his research and entertained a fervent cult in his honor. When religion was attacked, he defended it publicly. When the sons of priests were removed from schools, he tendered his own resignation as a professor and let it be known that he himself was a priest's son. But gradually his attitude mellowed and on the eve of his death, in 1935, during a banquet offered by workers' organizations, he declared enthusiastically: "Formerly, science was separated from life and detached from the people, but now I see that things are different—I see that the entire nation respects and appreciates science. I raise my glass and drink to the sole government capable of bringing this about and which esteems science so highly and assists it with such fervor—to the government of my country."[6] In 1949, the celebration of the centenary of Pavlov's birth had something of a holiday air about it. Psychoanalysis was definitively devastated as a reactionary ideology and the name of the physiologist was associated with that of Michurin. There were strident declarations to the effect that "Pavlov had destroyed Freud's house of cards."[7]

It will thus be better understood why, in 1923 and 1927, Trotsky posed the question of Freudianism in terms of a Pavlovianism serving to measure the materialism of psychology in general. If psychoanalysis seemed a particular case of a materialist psychology of which the theory of conditioning would provide the absolute model, it meant that any theory of the psyche failing to give proof of its connection to a physiological trace should be consigned to the inferno of spiritualism. Because of that presupposition, Trotsky eliminated the Freudian thesis of the primacy of sexuality. For him, in fact, sexuality could not be inscribed within the framework of Pavlovian experimentation since it did not partake of conditioning but of an organization independent from the physiological, in which sex was separated from its anatomical substratum.

Despite its dogmatic character, Trotsky's position was not sectarian for that era; it was, on the contrary, "liberal" in its politics. Instead of condemning Freudianism, as the true adversaries of Freudianism desired, Trotsky maintained that it was compatible with Marxism. Scientifically, that affirmation was extravagant, but politically, it bespoke a will (which was also Lenin's) not to reduce cultural debates to pure and simple condemnations. Like most of the Marxists of his time, Trotsky was blinded by his own conception of materialism. If he came to accept Pavlovianism as the standard of materialism in the field of psychology and that led him to posit the problem of a possible compatibility between Marxism and psychoanalysis, it was because his conception of materialism rested on the idea that there was a single science of the brain whose task was to account for the unity of body and mind. Pavlovianism served as a model for him to the extent that the doctrine of conditioning also presupposed the existence of that single science and sought to effect a fusion of the three domains of psychology, neurology, and physiology.

It may thus be said that from the very beginning of the century, in Russia Pavlovianism constituted the principal archaic soil in which psychoanalysis took root. The Bolshevik government would only systematize the values of that configuration, which was already present, by bringing to it the nourishment of a unifying Marxist perspective. Just as in France, Freudianism was implanted in terrain shot through with Bergsonianism, Janetism, and the concept of hereditary degeneration, similarly in Russia, then in the Soviet Union, it was introduced by way of a diffuse Pavlovianism, which functioned as a resistance, leaving its mark on all discussions of psychoanalysis.[8]

Freud's discovery was made possible, as is known, by a gradual autonomization of the psychical and by the shattering of the very notion of a single science of the brain. There was thus a radical contradiction, not between the doctrine of the conditioned reflex and psychoanalysis, but between Pavlovianism, which tended to effect a fusion of psychology, neurology, and physiology, and the new theory of the unconscious, which tended, on the contrary toward a decentering of any unitary orientation. In that perspective, the debate which began in 1920 on the compatibility of Marxism and psychoanalysis and which drew on the ideal of a fusion-oriented approach could only end in disaster; and that was all the more the case in that the fratricidal struggles among the various political movements emergent from the revolution gave an increasingly dogmatic cast to discussions about the sciences and culture.[9]

As of 1914, Freudianism was known to the Russian intelligentsia.[10] In 1909, Moshe Wulff, from Odessa, who had worked in Berlin, participated with other collaborators in founding the journal *Psychotherapia,* edited by Dr. Wyrubov. At the same time, Nicolas Ossipov, chief physician at the clinic of the University of Moscow, created a therapeutic ambulance and disseminated psychoanalytic ideas. Several of Freud's texts were translated into Russian up until 1927, specifically the *Three Essays on the Theory of Sexuality, The Interpretation of Dreams, The Introduction to Psychoanalysis,* and *Beyond the Pleasure Principle.* In 1921, Ermakov joined Wulff in setting up in Moscow a Psychoanalytic Association for Research on Artistic Creation. It had eight members, only three of whom were physicians. Among them was the mathematician Otto Schmidt, who was director of State Publications and thus made possible the dissemination of works of Freudian inspiration. Dr. Ermakov was named president of the association and gave courses in aesthetics at the Moscow Neuropsychological Institute. Along with Wulff, he directed an educational center which was also founded in 1921, through the initiative of Vera Schmidt,[11] and which took on the name of the "Experimental Home for Children." This was a pedagogical hostel, holding about thirty children, in which methods of child rearing based on Marxist and psychoanalytic principles were applied. The traditional system of humiliations and corporeal punishments was abolished. The ideal of the patriarchal family was severely criticized to the benefit of pedagogical values privileging collective needs. Demonstrations of affection such as kisses or caresses were replaced by more "rational" exchanges and children, raised without religion, were authorized to satisfy their sexual curiosity. Finally (and this was the supreme scandal) the educators themselves received training encouraging them not to suppress masturbation and to establish relations of equality with the children. Today, the pedagogical ideal promoted by Vera Schmidt may provoke smiles, but in its own time, it was the living (and even excessive) manifestation of that new spirit emergent in the 1920s through which, in the Soviet Union as elsewhere, the impossible dream of a fusion between the liberatory values of social revolution and those of a sexuality at last rediscovered was concretized.

In 1924, Vera Schmidt, who was neither a physician nor a psychoanalyst, published an evaluation of her experiment in a brochure entitled *Psychoanalytic Education in Russia.*[12] To be sure, the creation of the Home aroused the distrust not only of the local authorities but above all of the international psychoanalytic movement, which did not want to combine the chaff of Bolshevism and the wheat of Freudianism at whatever price. It was during that period that a conflict emerged over the status of the psychoanalysis of children which would last for several years and which pitted the theses of Anna Freud against those of Melanie Klein.[13] In the context of that debate the experiment of the Slavic hostel could only perturb the notables of psychoanalysis. They were too conservative to grasp what was at stake in that far-off adventure and too orthodox to understand that its contradictions were part of the very history of the development of Freudian ideas in the Soviet

Union. Ignored by the psychoanalytic movement and increasingly criticized by the local authorities, Vera Schmidt's experiment was doomed to extinction. Very early on, in Moscow, there were rumors. The educators were accused of corrupting youth and of stimulating sexual practices in the children. A committee of specialists was formed to investigate, and a majority of psychologists condemned the Home. The new director of the Neuropsychological Institute cut funds and withdrew his support from the institution, which closed down in 1924, after nine years of operation and internal quarrels.

The leadership of the IPA was as distrustful of the Home as the Soviet psychoanalytic movement. As of 1922, a Psychoanalytic Association had been created in Moscow, whose members were for the most part nonphysicians. These included Vera and Otto Schmidt, Ermakov, Wulff, as well as the psychiatrist I. W. Kannabich, and then the psychologist Alexander Riom Luria. Most of the members of the association were either Marxists or followers of the Communist Party. At the same time, there was founded in Kazan, at Luria's instigation, another association in which physicians were far more numerous than in the Moscow group. At the Berlin congress of 1922, Freud supported the Moscow group's incorporation into the IPA. But Jones invoked "administrative reasons" to delay it. In point of fact he was "playing" Kazan against Moscow in order to promote a balance between physicians and nonphysicians, on the one hand, and Marxists and non-Marxists, on the other. In September 1923, Vera and Otto Schmidt traveled to Berlin to request Abraham's backing for the group's admission. A compromise was hammered out resulting in the creation of a Pan-Russian Psychoanalytic Union comprised of the Freudian circles of Kazan, Odessa, Kiev, and Rostov, presided over by Ermakov, then Wulff, who resigned in 1927 to return to Berlin and then subsequently emigrate to Palestine. Between 1922 and 1930, that union contained about thirty members.

Within the IPA, the Soviet psychoanalytic movement thus found itself isolated for both political and geographical reasons. But inside the Soviet Union, Freudian doctrine was the subject of a debate of considerable importance and unprecedented violence. More general discussions took place in the context of the building of socialism on the subject of literature and philosophy in which the partisans and adversaries of socialist realism, on the one hand, and "liquidationists," "mechanicists," "Deborinians," and "Bolshevizers," on the other, confronted each other.[14] It was a time when the whole of the Soviet intelligentsia was invited by the party to mobilize along a new front in the class struggle in order to unify Marxist theory, purify it of the "residues" of the old idealism, and train new generations in the spirit of militant materialism. In the field of psychology, the debate over the status of psychoanalysis was pursued on the terrain of a triumphant Pavlovianism and gathered representatives of the psychoanalytic movement, psychiatrists, philosophers, linguists, and Trotsky himself before the liquidation of Trotskyism.

Two principal tendencies emerged: On the one hand, the "Freudo-Marxists" sought to demonstrate that Freudian doctrine was compatible with the principles of a materialist or "Pavlovian" psychology on condition it be freed of its sexual theory, which was regarded as too "bestial," of the death instinct (too "pessimistic"), and of its alleged philosophical monism (too "idealist"). Among the representatives of that tendency, despite their divergences, were men such as Luria, Zalkind, Kanna-bich, Fridman, or Bykhovski, who published articles to that effect and criticized the old "literary" orientation represented by Wulff, Ossipov, or Ermakov. On the other hand, authentic anti-Freudians were opposed to the Freudo-Marxists: They argued the absolute incompatibility between Marxism and psychoanalysis and relegated Freudian doctrine to the idealist attic. This was the case of the psychologist Jurinetz and above all of Voloshinov, Bakhtin's student, who, in the name of his master, published in 1924 and 1927 two particularly well-documented attacks on both Freudian spiritualism and the "reflexological Freudianism" of Freud's Soviet parti-sans.[15]

From the outset, the debate over the theory of the unconscious was thus falsified, because both partisans and adversaries of Freudianism situated themselves on the absurd grounds of a Marxist evaluation of psychoanalysis, and remained convinced the amount of materialism in a doctrine could be "measured," much as one might dissect a brain. In neutralizing each other, the two tendencies participated in the gradual stifling of the psychoanalytic movement, which would cease all activ-ity around 1930. That was the year of the first Soviet Congress for the Study of Human Behavior, in which the party intervened officially to take charge of the new orientation toward a dialectical psychology.

In all countries, the resistance to Freudianism occurred by way of a rejection of the theory of sexuality. In the Soviet Union the effort was not to destroy the thesis of pansexualism, but rather to reproach psychoanalysis for maintaining, against the possibilities of conditioning, the pessimistic notion of a human instinctual nature of which the theory of the libido would be a reflection. In the face of the ideals of Communism, the notion of sexuality seemed dangerous because it was deemed to be "asocial," that is, carrying with it an anarchical order that might lead the masses to debauchery and prevent them from directing their efforts toward collective hap-piness.

That representation of sexual theory authorized the claim at times that Freudianism was a spiritualistic philosophy that failed to take into account the so-cial existence of men, and at others that it was a biological doctrine that excluded history in favor of the permanence of the instincts. All the discussions between Freudo-Marxists and anti-Freudians were pursued on those grounds, for which Pav-lovianism served as a diffuse point of reference, at times without the protagonists, who were often anti-Pavlovian, realizing it. In that perspective, and according to shifts in political orientation, it became possible either to condemn psychoanalysis or to assimilate it, on the condition that it be "reevaluated" in terms of two systems alien in nature to Freudian theory and practice: Marxism, on the one hand, and the single science of the brain, or organicism, on the other.

Between 1920 and 1930, psychoanalysis continued its development in the Soviet Union, the subject of violent debates. After that date, the Communist Party sought guidance from the pedagogical achievements of Anton Semionovitch Mak-arenko, who in1920 had founded a colony for education through work. Within the school apparatus a thesis of the voluntaristic primacy of consciousness was intro-duced; Freudianism was judged to be too biologistic. Work therapy seemed a means of eradicating neuroses, which were considered to be the result of capitalist exploitation.

After World War II, there was a new shift linked to reconstruction and the affirmation of the triumph of socialism in a single country. At the time, Freudianism no longer existed, the psychoanalytic movement having been buried since 1930. In the Zhdanovist framework, psychoanalysis had become an "American" ideology or a "bourgeois science." [16] It could then be condemned not for its biologism, as was previously the case, but for its reactionary or idealist character. It was claimed that socialism had vanquished neurosis and psychosis. But since neurotics and madmen or deviants had not disappeared from Soviet society and the origin of their affliction could not be traced to capitalism, which no longer existed, or socialism, which created the happiness of all, science—that is, a still active Pavlovianism—was called on to discover the organic or physiological causes of so-called "mental" illnesses. During that period, "special" psychiatric hospitals were created to deal with dissidents judged to be "mad" because of their failure to adapt to the ideals of Communist happiness. A general doctrine of prevention and eradication flourished in all institutions, on the basis of a newly reconquered unity between brain and soul in which Freudianism had no place.

Toward the end of the summer of 1919, Freud confessed humorously to Jones and Ferenczi that he had "half" converted to Bolshevism since his meeting with an ardent Communist. That individual had predicted to him that the revolution would bring a few years of hardship and chaos, but that thereafter peace, prosperity, and happiness would prevail. Freud added the line: "I answered him that I believed in the first half of his program." [17] For numerous militants that comment would seem to confirm the opinion of Paul Roazen, for whom Freud was a reactionary suspect for his sympathy with the old regime. In point of fact, things did not happen that way. On several occasions, Freud spoke about Marxism in moderate terms, taking care to emphasize his incompetence. He criticized neither Marxist theory nor the Soviet economic system, but the psychological postulate on which the Communist ideal was based. "The Communists," he wrote in 1929, "think they have discovered the path of deliverance from evil. According to them, man is solely good and wants only the well-being of his neighbor, but the institution of private property has corrupted his nature. The possession of goods confers power on a single individual and gives rise to the temptation to mistreat his fellow-man; whoever is stripped of property should thus be hostile to his oppressor and rise up against him. . . . The economic criticism of the Communist system is not my business and it is not possible for me to examine whether the elimination of private property is opportune and advantageous. As far as its psychological postulate is concerned, I nevertheless feel authorized to see in it an illusion without the slightest consistency. In abolishing private property, one is certainly withdrawing from human aggressiveness and the pleasure it brings one of its instruments and no doubt a powerful instrument, but not the most powerful one. On the other hand, one has changed neither the differences in power which aggressiveness abuses, nor the nature of aggressiveness itself." [18]

In 1932, in a lecture entitled "Of a Conception of the Universe," Freud returned to the subject without alluding to the ongoing debates in the Soviet Union about his doctrine. "At the very time," he said, "that the great nations are claiming to await salvation from their loyalty to the Christian faith, the revolution in Russia—despite all its painful episodes—appears to be a harbinger of better days. Unfortunately, neither our skepticism nor the fanaticism of the others allows us to intuit the results of that attempt." [19] That position led Freud to oppose the notion of aggressiveness to that of the class struggle, which was judged to be too obscure. He attempted to show that destructive impulses were part of "civilization" because they were inherent in human nature.[20] He avoided any simple-minded assimilation of Marxist theory to a religious doctrine, but he reproached Bolshevism for having transformed Marxism into a state religion. "Marx's works," he said, "have replaced the Bible and the Koran as sources of revelation even though they offer as many contradictions and obscurities as the old sacred books. And even while pitilessly banning every idealistic system and illusion, Marxism, in practice, has itself created new chimeras which are no less dubious and no less undemonstrable than the old ones." [21] It will be seen that Freud's critique of Marxism was neither conservative nor obscurantist, as is frequently claimed. On the contrary, it situated itself on the terrain of a thoroughgoing materialism since it took as its target the religious illusion, traces of which it detected in Marxist practice itself. In that perspective the nodal point of Freud's opposition to the ideals of Communism lay in the affirmation of the existence of a death "drive" disruptive of any belief not only in the primacy of consciousness over the unconscious but also in a possible conditioning of man by human "reason." Put differently, all the discussions of that era between Freudians, Marxists, anti-Freudians, and Freudo-Marxists were part of a single theoretical debate that concerned, on the one hand, the status of the unconscious in relation to consciousness and, on the other, the acceptance or refusal of the hypothesis of the death drive. Within that debate, Pavlovianism in the larger sense joined with the Reichian project of a "libertarian" psychology through a shared condemnation of Freudian pessimism.

The itinerary of Wilhelm Reich in the history of the psychoanalytic movement shows, however, that the Freudo-Marxism which developed in Austria and Germany had nothing in common with its Soviet counterpart. Reich's opposition to Freudianism was based on a rejection of the death drive and the idea of a possible happiness for humanity, but it did not take Pavlovianism as the materialist standard in the domain of psychology. In that sense Reich was indeed the founder of an authentic Freudo-Marxism, that is, of a theoretical current intent less on gauging the measure of materialism in Freudian doctrine than on uniting, in a libertarian project, Marx's hypotheses on social revolution and Freud's on the subject of sexuality.

Reich committed a "fruitful error": He was convinced that the discovery of the unconscious should allow man to become cognizant of the constraints inhibiting the free exercise of his sexuality. On this score, he was not at all wrong since the massive extension of psychoanalysis contributed considerably to a transformation of sexual habits and practices. But the error in Reich's project consisted in believing that the subject might be free to exercise his sexuality however he wished once it was no longer subject to the devastating effects of social puritanism. For Freud showed that precisely such liberty was a utopia since sex was itself a source of constraints that did not come solely from social repression but from the organization of the psyche. In other words, psychoanalysis brought a new understanding of the libido that favored changes in sexual habits, but it also showed that the ego was not free to administer its sexuality as it wished. To shore up his thesis of a "liberated" sexuality, Reich had genitality replace sexuality and made libidinal power an equivalent of social happiness outside of alienated labor. Whereas Jung desexualized sex to the benefit of a kind of vital energy, Reich proceeded to a desexualization of the libido to the benefit of a biological genitality based on the hope of a possible orgiastic fulfillment of man from which the death drive would of necessity have been eliminated. Once again it was on the subject of the Freudian doctrine of sexuality that a battle royal within the psychoanalytic movement was fought. Writing to Lou Andreas-Salomé in 1928, Freud commented on Reich's position in these terms: "We have here a Dr. Reich, a decent but impetuous mounter of battle horses who now venerates genital orgasms as the antidote for all neurosis."[22]

Born in 1897 in Galicia to an assimilated Jewish family, Wilhelm Reich was raised outside of any religious tradition. At the age of fourteen, he played a crucial role in his mother's suicide by revealing to his father her affair with one of his preceptors. Three years later, Leon Reich died of pneumonia and his son succeeded him as head of the family farm and cattle ranch.[23] He nevertheless pursued his studies, and then, upon returning from the war, registered at the Vienna medical school. In 1919, he was admitted to the Vienna Psychoanalytic Society, and the following year he presented his first paper, entitled "Libido Conflicts and Psychotic Formations in Ibsen's *Peer Gynt*." The Norwegian hero wandering in search of an unfindable identity and getting himself named emperor of Egypt in a lunatic asylum symbolized tragicomically the post-Romantic malaise of the end of the nineteenth century with which Reich identified in his quest for a marginal fate.

In 1921, he began practicing psychoanalysis without having served time on an analytic couch and conducted a seminar on sexology. During that period, he was already orienting his work toward an energeticist perspective that fitted poorly with the new Freudian orientation. Later he would maintain that the death drive was the result of a depression Freud had undergone, caused by the orthodox evolution of the analytic movement following World War I. By 1924, Reich was interested in the works of Marx and Engels and sought to demonstrate the social origin of mental illnesses. In that perspective, he attempted to reconcile Marxist concepts with those of psychoanalysis.

In 1927, he published two fundamental works, *The Function of the Orgasm* and *Character Analysis*,[24] in which the essential elements of his theoretical and therapeutic differences with Freudianism were broached. He accused psychoanalysts of wanting to domesticate sex and participate in its suppression by accepting the principle of individual adaptation to the ideals of bourgeois capitalism. Like Rank and Ferenczi, he abandoned the role of passive therapist and intervened actively in analyses; but his practice and theory remained influenced by a medicalizing point of view that was attuned to his increasingly pronounced energeticist perspective. Because of that, he was opposed to the partisans of lay analysis, believing the scientificity of psychoanalysis could best be maintained through such a policy.

In 1928, disappointed by the Austrian Social Democrats, Reich joined the Communist Party and participated in the construction of a worker-oriented mythology according to which proletarian genitality would be exempt from the bourgeois "microbe." He did not hesitate to claim that neuroses were rarer in the working class than in the higher strata of society. That did not prevent him from creating a Socialist Society for Sexual Information and Research or from opening the first sexual hygiene clinics intended for the care and information of paid employees. At the same time, he pursued his own research and published in the Moscow journal *Under the Banner of Marxism* what was virtually a Freudo-Marxist manifesto, entitled "Dialectical Materialism and Psychoanalysis."[25] Fascinated by the Bolshevik revolution, he arranged a stay in the Soviet Union where he furthered his knowledge of the debates between Freudo-Marxists and anti-Freudians. At the time, he was the only intellectual in Western Europe who was informed on the subject of the Russian debates over psychoanalysis and who was at the center of the internal conflicts of both the IPA and the international Communist movement. With his Soviet colleagues, he organized a lecture tour throughout the country, visited nursery schools and pedagogical centers, then met with Vera Schmidt, whom he reproached for her concessions to psychoanalytic ideas, specifically to the ideal of adaptation.[26]

Upon returning from his trip, he left Vienna for Berlin, where he underwent analysis with Sandor Rado. There, too, he was a member of both the Berlin Psychoanalytic Society and the German Communist Party (KPD). He founded the Association for Proletarian Sexual Politics, or SEXPOL, which tended to assimilate the sexual struggle of workers to the class struggle. Before long, he became a subject of mistrust. The KPD had begun to follow a sectarian political line, designating Social Democrats as the principal enemies of the working class. The militants feared that the activities of SEXPOL in favor of a free sexuality would weaken the revolutionary ardor of the masses. Reich was accused of wanting to transform gymnasiums into brothels and of failing to give priority to the economic struggle. It was also claimed that problems with orgasm were the province of the bourgeoisie and that it behooved the people to demonstrate its morality. At the time Hitler took power, Reich was excluded from the Communist Party and in March 1933, he left Berlin for Vienna. But there he met with the opposition of psychoanalysts, who wanted to exclude him from the movement less for his divergences from Freudianism than for his Bolshevik opinions. He then emigrated to Denmark, and in August of 1934, at the Lucerne congress, was excluded from the international psychoanalytic movement thanks to the collaborative action of Jones, Eitingon, and Anna Freud, and despite the opposition of the Scandinavian group.[27]

Reich then directed his activities toward a therapeutic method which no longer had anything to do with psychoanalysis. He spoke in favor of an almost delirious biologism. Before long, he was being called a "charlatan," a "pornographic

Jew," or a "psychopath." In 1939 he left Norway, where he had taken refuge, to move to the United States. In his adopted land, he constructed orgon boxes, intended to measure sexual energy, and ended his days in a penitentiary.

Thus concluded the European destiny of this tragic Peer Gynt of psycho-analysis—persecuted by the Communists because of his Freudianism, and by the Freudians because of his Bolshevism.

The Freudo-Marxist phenomenon emerged in the Soviet Union in the context of a quarrel over Pavlovianism. In the Germanic world, on the contrary, under Reich's impetus, it emerged as the result of a practice attempting to fuse the concepts and the experience issuing from both doctrines without any reference to the need for an extrinsic domain. If one compares that twofold situation to the French one, one fact seems clear: At the time the infiltration of psychoanalysis was at its most intense, between 1922 and 1935, the Freudo-Marxist configuration did not enjoy any life in that country, and that for a variety of reasons. On the side of official psychoanalysis, where political conservatism and the ideals of "Latinate genius" were in the ascendant, the Bolshevik debates were unknown, and even if thy were not, a priori they would have aroused great suspicion. In that context, Allendy's espousal of socialism took on an eccentric character, as we have already observed. As for Reich's works, they interested no one, and if they had aroused any interest, they would have fallen under a triple anathema: as communistic, "Teutonic," and nonorthodox. In the *RFP*, there appeared only a single review of a publication by Reich, a technical and painstaking piece on *Character Analysis* by Saussure.[28] He did not at all allude to the political positions of the author or to his divergences from Freudianism. It may thus be said that on the whole, French psychoanalysts of the first generation were completely ignorant of the Freudo-Marxist phenomenon be-cause they had kept their distance from anything having to do with Marxist theory or the Communist movement.

For its part, the party of the working class was not interested in Freudianism and did not attempt to develop any discussion of the materialist or idealist character of psychoanalysis. In France at the time, Pavlov's works were known to specialists, who occasionally attempted an articulation between the doctrine of reflexes and that of the unconscious. But that orientation remained strictly scientific. In that perspec-tive, Pavlovianism could not be used as an ideological substrate, either in the French Communist Party (PCF) or elsewhere, to serve as a counterweight to psychoanalysis. That terrain, moreover, was already occupied by Bergsonism or Janetism. Marxist intellectuals were no better informed of the ongoing debates in the Soviet Union than psychoanalysts were. Those who might have taken an interest could not read Russian and were thus unable to grasp the import of a discussion which eluded them in as much as it was alien to the French cultural situation.

Moreover, it is clear that the Bolshevik party was not looking to transform the debate over psychoanalysis into an international affair, as would be the case in 1949 when the PCF officially condemned Freudianism in the context of the cold war. It was only at that point that a discussion occurred in France identical to that which had taken place in the Soviet Union twenty years earlier.[29]

The adventure of Georges Sadoul and Louis Aragon in 1930, during the writers' congress at Kharkov, bears witness to the divergent situation in the two countries. Aragon had no idea at the time of what the vast machinery of that meeting organized by the Soviet party might represent. He was quite prepared to imagine that quarrels among writers were conducted—much as in the Surrealist group—through diatribe and incendiary metaphor. From the podium, he declared his love for the people and paid homage to the spontaneity of the workers. Convinced that Surrealism would be received as the vanguard of the poetic revolution, he attacked the novelist Henry Barbusse for lagging behind the exigencies of the day, then sent a telegram to Breton to inform him of his triumph. Before long, the two Frenchmen were obliged to change their tune. They received a visit from official emissaries who presented them with a letter of self-criticism in which they were to confess their guilt for having been unworthy militants and having wrongly insulted Barbusse and the Communist press. In addition they were constrained to renounce Surrealism and to condemn Freudianism and Trotskyism.

Upon his return, Aragon complained to Breton that his signature had been extorted from him, but refused to publish a correction. He affirmed his support for Surrealism and published a manifesto entitled *Aux intellectuels révolutionnaires* ["To the revolutionary intellectuals"], in which he defended psychoanalysis in terms close to those of Freudo-Marxism: "Certain revolutionary intellectuals, and particularly the Surrealists," he wrote, "have been led to use the psychoanalytic method as a weapon against the bourgeoisie. That weapon, in the hands of men grounded in historical materialism and who are intent on using it, allows one specifically to attack the family—despite the defensive barriers the bourgeoisie has erected around it. Psychoanalysis has served the Surrealists in studying the mechanism of inspiration and in subjecting themselves to it. It has helped them to abandon any individualist positions. Psychoanalysis cannot be legitimately held responsible for the applications that various individuals invoking it have made of it." [30]

At the time Aragon signed his letter of self-criticism at Kharkov, the Soviet Communist Party was embarked on an increasingly sectarian political line. The year 1928 saw the collapse of the united opposition represented by Trotsky, Kamenev, and Zinoviev. In various sections of the Internationale, the fight against left-wing opponents took the form of a witch-hunt. Whereas Kamenev and Zinoviev capitulated and were then reintegrated into the party, Trotsky, unyielding, opted for the path of exile. Within the alliance in power, conflicts were beginning to surface between Stalin and Bukharin. The latter denounced the regime of police terror descending on the country and compared the Georgian to an Oriental despot. But his influence was waning and in July 1929, he was relieved of his political responsibilities and his functions as an officer of the Internationale. The reality of personality cults was exposed with the elaborate pomp that characterized the celebration of Stalin's fiftieth birthday; his advance toward absolute power was underway. Forced collectivization resulted in an economic catastrophe as significant as the one affecting the capitalist world. Famine spread through numerous regions of the vast Soviet land mass. On the political level, voluntarism prevailed: Failures were transformed into triumphs and the victory of the socialist paradise was proclaimed. [31]

It will be understood in this context why Aragon felt "obliged" to condemn

Trotskyism and Surrealism. In the Soviet Union and the French party, which was more than ever the French section of the Communist Internationale, the Surrealists were regarded as troublemakers. Their political positions were not in harmony with those of the workers' movement to the extent that they appeared to be "ultrarevolutionary." Breton and his friends sought to get others to acknowledge the subversive import of Surrealism, but the party could not accept that a revolution in language might be regarded as being as significant and "political" as the proletarian revolution. It was less concerned with the ideological rigor of intellectuals interested in joining its ranks than in their ability to serve or enlighten the masses. Given that situation, it preferred to gather to its cause traditional writers, pacifists, or adepts of the Enlightenment rather than representatives of an avant-garde that might outflank it on its own left by combining Marxist theory, poetry, and revolution.

Every vanguard group which raised the question of adhering to Communism after 1927 had an intellectual approach to Marxism that did not correspond to the pragmatic orientation of the French workers' movement. In addition, they all contested the humanist current appealed to by the Association of Revolutionary Writers and Artists, which was supported by the party and the Internationale. In 1933, those Surrealists who were excluded from the party would direct their attacks against it in the name of a Marxism they felt had been betrayed. For the same reasons, Breton warmed to Trotskyism. There too, he was not following a political current but an intellectual Trotskyism that was no more than a denunciation of Stalinism. For their part, the members of the journal *Philosophies* sought to construct, from within the party, a Marxism breaking with the dominant mode in the workers' movement.[32] Thus Henri Lefebvre drew on the works of the young Marx to make the thesis of alienation the nodal point of his research.

As far as psychoanalysis was concerned, things went differently. Aragon signed his condemnation of Freudianism at Kharkov at a time when, within the Soviet Union, the quarrel over Pavlovianism was resulting in the snuffing out of the Russian psychoanalytic movement. But in France that condemnation made no sense since there was no debate on the subject within the party, where there reigned no more than a pronounced distrust of psychoanalysis. For that reason, the poet's declaration on the materialist character of psychoanalysis did not provoke a discussion echoing the one taking place in the Soviet Union. Since he was not personally involved in a battle for the defense of Freudianism, that battle—given Breton's departure from the party—did not take place.

Two great theorists, Georges Politzer, on the one hand, and Henri Wallon, on the other, might have enabled a debate between Marxists and psychoanalysts or even engendered a French variant of Freudo-Marxism. But the former renounced any discussion with the members of the SPP and repudiated his interest in Freudianism at the time he became a Marxist. As for the latter, he remained prudent and did not associate with the psychoanalytic movement. Moreover, he made a radical distinction between his activity as a psychologist, in the course of which he commented on Freud's texts, and his attachment to a dialectic, which was more Hegelian than Marxist. Thus, in the interwar years, the conditions were not present for psychoanalysis to be introduced within the French Communist movement, either in the form of a Freudo-Marxism, or through a discussion between Marxists and Freudians, or in terms of an explicit rejection.

Between 1933 and 1936, a Cercle de la Russie neuve was constituted and enjoyed the participation of several intellectuals who were either Communists or close to the party. Among them were Henri Wallon, René Maublanc, Marcel Prenant, Jean Langevin, Georges Friedmann, et al. The circle had given itself the objective of informing the French public, at times with undeniable naïveté, of the reality of research conducted in the Soviet Union. It also proposed to be an organ for reflection on the articulation between sciences and historical and dialectical materialism. Several talks of a high theoretical caliber were given on the subjects of philosophy, mathematics, biology, linguistics, and Marxism, but there was no work on psychoanalysis, as revealed by the two volumes published by Éditions sociales internationales (ESI) under the title *A la lumière du marxisme* ["By the light of Marxism,"].[33]

The same Éditions sociales internationales brought out in 1934 a book by Reich entitled *La crise sexuelle*. The volume, translated by a medical student named Ténine, in fact grouped together three texts only two of which were by Wilhelm Reich. The first, called "La crise sexuelle," was an extract from the first version of *The Sexual Revolution,* published in Germany in 1930. The second, entitled "Matérialisme dialectique et psychanalyse," was an expurgated reproduction of the article that had appeared under the same name in *Under the Banner of Marxism.* Finally, the third was the translation of a long presentation by the Russian sociologist I. Sapir, entitled "Freudisme, sociologie, et psychanalyse." The author attacked Reich quite vehemently, adopting the theses of the Soviet anti-Freudians, notably those of Jurinetz. The preface to that first French edition of a work by Reich was written by an author who went by the pseudonym of Arthur Manet.

The initiative for that publication came from Victor Fay, who was involved with (among other projects) the "Problèmes" series at ESI. Although that publishing house was subject, as its name indicated, to the dictates of the Internationale, Fay had achieved a certain autonomy in relation to Moscow. But to publish a book by Reich at a time when the Internationale was rather seeking to stifle everything partaking of psychoanalysis, a certain determination and a good "cover" were needed. Concessions were indispensable, a circumstance accounting for Sapir's text and the amputations inflicted on Reich's essay.[34]

In Germany, the debates pursued in the Moscow journal *Under the Banner of Marxism* were translated and published under the identical title: *Unter dem Bannen des Marxismus.* Sapir was a student of Deborine, who had condemned psychoanalysis before himself being accused of dualism by the "Bolshevizing" group of Marc Borisovich Mitine. Sapir had published his text in 1929 in the same issue of *Under the Banner of Marxism* that had contained Reich's. There was thus a German and a Russian version of the two articles. It was the German version which was adopted by the ESI since the Soviet discussions had not been translated.

Arthur Manet interpreted Reich's work in a somewhat restricted sense, showing that it consisted in refuting bourgeois conceptions of marriage and conjugal fidelity. Then he lashed out at Freudo-Marxism, deemed to be too "biological," and opposed it to Sapir's more "proletarian" theses. Ultimately, he concluded in these terms: "Despite the reservations we have felt obliged to formulate—and we are far from having exhausted the subject—Reich's book deserves to be read by as broad an audience as possible, since, in a vigorous and clear manner, it exposes the ravages visited by the capitalist regime on the sexual life of humanity." [35] Naturally, Manet mentioned neither the Soviet debates nor Reich's conflicts with Freudianism and the German Communist Party. Since there had not been any discussion of psychoanalysis in the French party, the ESI felt "obliged," in presenting Reich without causing displeasure to the Internationale, to assign to a foreign author, Sapir, the task of rectifying those of Reich's opinions that were judged to be contestable.

Beyond that publication, everything transpired as though the hostility of the French Communists toward psychoanalysis could become manifest only through a rejection of a Freudo-Marxism they knew nothing of and occur only at a distance from the genuine debates being held in other countries. The party thus came to condemn Freudian doctrine implicitly, through reference to a battle whose stakes it could only suspect and which it was not capable of waging on its own.

In the original version of "Matérialisme dialectique et psychanalyse," Reich attempted to delineate the bonds that might exist between the two doctrines. In his view, psychoanalysis did not complete the Marxist theory of history because it was a "natural science" having as its object the psychical life of man in his social evolution. For Reich, Freudianism was "sufficiently materialist" not to contradict the principles of socialism. In that perspective, the assimilation of psychoanalysis to a "phenomenon of decomposition emergent from bourgeois decadence" had to be rejected. Reich thus attacked the anti-Freudianism of the Soviet psychologist Jurinetz, whom he reproached with not having understood anything of the hypothesis of the death drive and of Freudian theory in general. Now the passages concerning that Germano-Russian polemic were eliminated from the French adaptation of 1934. Jurinetz's name appeared only once in Reich's text in a passage in which his diatribe becomes incomprehensible.

The censorship exercised by the ESI bore on a corpus containing the essential formulations of the debate between Freudo-Marxists and anti-Freudians. On the other hand, it did not intervene on the issue of Reich's defense of the materialist character of psychoanalysis. The French publisher thus gave the impression of spontaneously rallying to the positions which were then triumphing in the Soviet Union without knowing anything of the conditions under which that triumph had been achieved. Sapir's text was published at a time when its author was victim of the repression coming down on Deborine and his students and which ensured the victory of Bolshevization in the field of philosophy. [36] The French version of Reich's book thus sinned by omission.

It was thus Sapir and not Jurinetz who appeared in the book as sole representative of an anti-Freudianism concerning which it could not be told whether it had come from Russia, Germany, or the planet Mars. The censors seemed so preoccupied with Reich's text that they forgot to eliminate from Sapir's the passages concerning Deborine and Jurinetz through which the author demolished Reich's positions. It was thus difficult for the French public to understand the polemic between

Sapir and Reich, as they were hard put to determine what the two authors were in disagreement about. All the more so in that Sapir wrote: "Reich acknowledges the accuracy of the critique through which Jurinetz and Deborine responded to those 'scientists' (that is: the primitive anti-Bolsheviks), but he warns against the dangers that might lurk in extending his critique to all of Freud's doctrine, that is, to the logical bases of those anti-Bolshevik attacks. We should say right off that Reich's attitude is perfect." [37]

Sapir was a true anti-Freudian, as thoroughgoing a one as Jurinetz or Voloshinov, even though he did not attack the Soviet Freudo-Marxians. His text was directed solely against Reich, in whom he saw "a faithful student of Freud's." Confusing Reichianism and Freudianism, he accused psychoanalysis of being a biologism. He mixed up instincts, sexual desires, and drives, declaring that the "atmosphere of sated idleness characteristic of bourgeois society favored the appearance of psychoneuroses." But he recognized that psychoanalysis had the merit of shedding light on the decomposition of capitalism, even if it did not allow for a critique of it. He situated himself quite interestingly in relation to Pavlovianism: "It is not the theory of conditioned reflexes which shows the path to psychoanalysis, but rather psychoanalysis which reveals to the theory of conditioned reflexes dozens of problems which by virtue of the very nature of that theory elude its horizon." [38]

It can thus be seen that the French edition of 1934 presented the debate between the Freudo-Marxists and the anti-Freudians in a Manichaean context that did not respect the extremely complex hierarchy of the opposing positions. One has the impression that the discussion over the materialist character of psychoanalysis pitted the partisans of an absolute anti-Freudianism, represented, through Sapir, by unknowns, against those of a coherent Freudianism whose sole representative would have been Reich.

The latent hostility of the French Communists toward psychoanalysis was thus pursued by way of an overt opposition to Freudo-Marxism. This is an indication that during the interwar period, in a rather confused way, a debate was emerging that was identical to the one in the Soviet Union. With a certain delay, what was already at issue was the compatibility between Freudianism and materialism, and not any genuine consideration of Freud's theses per se. This explains why, in 1949, the discussion would surface explicitly in terms of a Pavlovian evaluation of psychoanalysis.

Another oblique attack against Freudianism was produced by Politzer in 1933 in an article published in the journal *Commune* and entitled "Psychanalyse et marxisme: un faux contre-révolutionnaire: le freudo-marxisme." [39] The author lashed out violently at the "delirious" Freudo-Marxism of the Surrealists, then at Jean Bernier, accused of being a Souvarinian,[40] and finally at Jean Audard, a young philosopher who had just published a quite interesting article in *Les Cahiers du Sud* on the materialist character of psychoanalysis." [41] The text was unique in the annals of that period in attempting to show that psychoanalysis was more materialist than Marxism, whose idealist failings it could "correct," and that the Communists of Moscow were not defending the same Marxism as those of Paris. In addition, Audard indicated quite clearly that the dispute between those affirming and those de-

nying the materialist nature of psychoanalysis was less a debate over Freudianism
than a quarrel between two opposing currents within Marxism. That argument dis-
pleased Politzer; forgoing a direct attack against psychoanalysis, he criticized
Freudo-Marxism and reproached Audard with "bootlegging Bergsonianism."
The talented philosopher in this case revealed a total ignorance of the reality of
Freudo-Marxism, which he envisaged as no more than an erroneous conception of
Marxism.

The circumstances of that polemic are worth relating because they were not
merely academic. In point of fact, the article published by Politzer contained the
greater part of a lecture given at the Mutualité in Paris, in the presence of the Surrealists, who were ardent supporters of Audard's work. As at the dinner at the Closerie des Lilas a few years earlier, the meeting turned into a free-for-all. While Politzer
lashed out at his adversary and sought to humiliate him, rotten eggs and tomatoes
were flying through the auditorium. Amidst the general confusion, one could hear
insults against the Stalinists, on the one hand, and the valets of imperialism, on the
other. A woman claimed that a Surrealist dagger had scratched her cheek. In fact, it
turned out to have been a harmless ring.

In 1939, the same Politzer published in *La Pensée* an article entitled "La fin
de la psychanalyse [The end of psychoanalysis],"[42] in which he took on the pen
name Th. W. Morris, in homage to Maurice Thorez. In that text, which appeared in
an official journal of the French Communist Party, the author accused Freud of being
philosophically confused and especially criticized "analytic sociology," the method
attempting to "apply" psychoanalysis to social history. It seems clear that at the
time Politzer had read *Group Psychology and the Analysis of the Ego* as well as
Civilization and its Discontents. Perhaps he also knew *The Mass Psychology of
Fascism*,[43] which had been published by Reich in Germany in 1933. He was certainly aware of developments in psychobiography, but undoubtedly did not know
Moses and Monotheism, which had appeared in London in 1938. He reproached
orthodox psychoanalysis for its obscurantism and its "psychologistic" conception
of history.

Without quoting anyone, he conflated, in a deceptive amalgam, the Jungian
current of collective psychology, the Reichian current of mass psychology, and the
various psychoanalytic theories attempting to transform history into a domain amenable to psychobiography. Against the notorious "analytic sociology," of which
there was no certainty as to what it in fact included, Politzer used the same argument
he had resorted to six years earlier against Freudo-Marxism. He denounced, to be
sure, the "reactionary" character of psychoanalysis. Whereupon he took one step
further down the path of abusive amalgamations by committing the implicit error
of reducing Freud's position to that of the right-wing "crowd-psychologist," Gustave
Le Bon. Without mentioning the latter, he reinterpreted the Freudian theory of the
unconscious in terms of the old doctrine of race. Being a connoisseur of Freudianism, German philosophy, and Nazi theories, he did not dare assimilate psychoanalytic obscurantism directly to a form of racism. But he remained convinced that
Nazism's hostility toward psychoanalysis was more in the order of a "tactic" than
a function of any radical incompatibility. As a result, he lapsed into a grotesque

argument that consisted of viewing certain elements from Jung as containing the essence of Freudianism and consigning the whole of psychoanalytic doctrine to the inferno of anti-Semitic theory: "It is true," he wrote, "that much has been made, in psychoanalytic circles, of Freud's exile, taken as a symbol of the condemnation of psychoanalysis by the Nazis. To be sure, there have been Nazi speeches against psychoanalysis. It is no less true, however, that psychoanalysis and psychoanalysts have furnished quite a few themes to Nazi theorists, beginning with that of the unconscious. In taking on iconoclastic airs, psychoanalysts have profoundly jostled the feelings of the middle-class masses. Such is the specialty of petit-bourgeois anarchism. In addition to the racial question, it was in order to exploit that fact that Nazism issued something of a denunciation of Freudianism. But that did not prevent it from integrating psychoanalysts into its personnel or from borrowing themes from Freudian doctrine." [44]

That affirmation was made by Politzer at a time when Freud had already, in his lifetime, through the publication of *Moses and Monothesus* consecrated the definitive break of his theories with the concepts of race and degeneracy.

Beyond Politzer's personal settling of scores with psychoanalysis, the 1939 text calls for comment. At the time, one could observe within the ranks of the Communist movement the confused beginnings of an argument that would be taken up ten years later. Indeed, in 1949, it was also in the name of a hostility to analytic sociology that Freudianism would be condemned by the French party. This time, the enemy was not the defeated Nazi, but the victorious American. Freud was not cast into the flames of Hitlerianism, but psychoanalysis was accused of being a reactionary ideology in the service of imperialism. In the interwar period, that thematic of tracing effect to cause surfaced in the form of an implicit critique of Freudo-Marxism and by way of a courageous publication that did not enjoy any great success, but which was the only one to make Reich's work known in France.

Given the way in which psychoanalysis took hold in the country, through the twofold channels of medical conservatism and literature, one is hard put to see what place it might have won for itself within the workers' movement. For a true encounter to have occurred, what would have been needed, beyond the authorization of the Internationale, would have been an interest on the part of Communist physicians in psychoanalysis. But at the time, the party recruited its members in the working class, among artisans, teachers, minor functionaries, and certain eminent intellectuals. Medical doctors, and particularly psychiatrists, were absent from its ranks. As for writers interested in both Freud and the revolution—essentially, the Surrealists—they had been excluded from the party without any debate. After World War II, the situation would change as a result of the massive arrival of new militants in the Communist movement and the shift in their social origins.

In the Soviet Union, between 1920 and 1930, all discussion of literature, philosophy, and the sciences took Marxism as its point of reference to the extent that the Bolshevik party was the governing body in the country. In that context, the Pan-Russian psychoanalytic movement did not escape the obligation of having to situate itself compatibly between Freudianism and materialism. That was in effect the only way in which it could attempt to survive. Even if Pavlovianism had not served as a standard, another doctrine would have been used to similar ends, as would later be the case for biology or linguistics.

In France, where the party was not only removed from any exercise of power but also fought by reactionary forces, there was no reason for such a discussion to occur with comparable amplitude. Moreover, at the time, there was no political current outside the party prepared to welcome Freudo-Marxism or another doctrine of the same type. Under those conditions only publishing houses of Communist affiliation were in a position to accord Reichianism any measure of space, and that with the restrictions we have seen. This explains why Reich's works would not be translated in France until the events of May 1968. After that date, there emerged a libertarian current violently hostile to the party and to the psychoanalytic movement and which served as a forum for an in-depth reexamination of Reich's aims and specifically of the notions of sexual freedom or politics. It should also be stated that Reich's American career, marked by its extravagant biologism, did not allow for his works to be understood in France before a return to their German origins.[45]

Georges Politzer regarded Breton and his friends as "Freudo-Marxists." Now although Surrealism situated Freud's discovery within the field of the revolution, it did not adopt the theses generally accepted by Reichian or Soviet Freudo-Marxism. In *Les vases communicants,* Breton tried to effect the entry of the dreamworld into reality by means of the Hegelian dialectic, but in no case did he lend his support to Reich's aims any more than he did to Jung's. The Surrealists were probably the only representatives of what might be called a "Gallic Freudo-Marxism," on the condition that it be acknowledged that the movement was exempt of all the principal ingredients normally considered part of that current. Surrealism posited the principle of a revolution through language, excluding biologism and hostile to any medical appropriation of Freud's discovery. At the same time, it championed the death drive and regarded only the metapsychological sector of psychoanalytic doctrine as "idealist." Thus the only common point between Freudo-Marxism in general and Surrealism in particular was the linking of the notion of social revolution to that of sexual revolution.

Within that configuration, René Crevel was the most Freudo-Marxian of the Surrealists. His commitment to the party was at once more political than Aragon's and less reserved than Breton's. He was also the only one in the group to undergo analysis, which he did for reasons that were both therapeutic and guided by the desire to turn Freudianism into an instrument of revolt against bourgeois conventions. In *Le clavecin de Diderot* ["Diderot's harpsichord"], published in 1932, in which he recounted his own analysis, he did not hesitate to demolish the "socialist" views of his analyst: "Dr. Allendy," he wrote, "in his last book, *Capitalisme et sexualité,* dares to pretend he is involved in combatting prejudices; he nonetheless does not fail to hasten and take pleasure in affirming that *women have adapted to a role of social parasite and are bound to capital. Woman,* Allendy concludes, *is not only, as in the symbolism of the poets, the cup which receives the seed and preserves it. She is also the cash-box that keeps the coins.* In response to all this gallantry," Crevel continues, "it should really be asked of this doctor whether his medical practice is not also *bound to capital.* And so here comes my little question: How does Dr.

Allendy conceive of *his* psychoanalysis after the building of socialism? In his view, if I recall properly, analysis, in order to bear fruit, has to impose on the patient, among other sacrifices, a monetary sacrifice. One can already see the therapist, out of scientific probity, saying to the therapized: 'You receive two thousand francs per month. If you want me to cure you, let me have a thousand.' Facetiousness reclaims its rights (which, by the way, it never lost). King Ubu invites psychoanalysis to mount his 'phynancial chariot.' "[46]

Throughout his life, René Crevel was dominated by contradictory situations. He became a pederast without being able to affirm his homosexuality, which would have been widely disapproved of by his best friends. In 1923, at the time of the break with Dada, he adopted an ambiguous attitude, performing a role in Tzara's play *Le Coeur à gaz,* and receiving a slap in the face from Éluard. In 1932, he participated in the work of the review *Paillasse,* which marked the Surrealists' break with Aragon. He was excluded from the party, then reentered its ranks in an attempt to bring his friends closer to the Communist movement. That did not stop him from signing a petition protesting Trotsky's expulsion from French territory in 1934. Finally, in 1935, he committed suicide, without his psychoanalysis, sadly conducted by Allendy, having succeeded in sparing him the tragic fate of his father, who had hung himself twenty years before.

It was in an article entitled "Notes en vue d'une psychodialectique" and published in 1933 in *Le Surréalisme au service de la révolution* that Crevel attacked the idealist character of Freudianism and the inability of analysts to dialecticize the relation between the social and the individual. He reproached them for not bestowing an historical dimension on the clinical cases they studied. From the same perspective, he criticized the Freudian conception of culture because it refused to take into account differences existing between social classes and ways of life. Crevel's materialism consisted of defending the concrete against the abstract and existence against any putative essence. In his view, only a genuine "science of personality" would allow psychoanalysis to emerge from the rut of an idealism that could only generate abstractions. Crevel waged a fierce battle against that "French psychoanalysis" which dominated the first generation members of the SPP. Now Crevel discovered the emerging lineaments of the science of personality he was calling for in Lacan's thesis, *De la psychose paranoïaque dans ses rapports avec la personnalité,* which had been published a year before. After presenting and commenting on the "case of Aimée," Crevel defined what he called a psycho-dialectic: "For failure to conduct sufficiently close clinical examinations of certain social types, as Lacan has done in the case of Aimée," he wrote, "for failure to situate patients socially (since the patient had been so pertinently situated in his family), for failure to study the relations of a specific family with society in general, and thus, more or less distorted by complicity with the parents or in reaction against them, the relations between the individual and the species, psychoanalysis or, rather, psychoanalysts have not given what might have been expected of them. Materialist science will need detailed, precise, and complete monographs for its psycho-dialectic." [47]

Crevel's "Freudo-Marxism" did not aim at reconciling the principles of Marxism with those of psychoanalysis, but rather at drawing psychoanalysis toward a dialectical perspective based on a *concrete theory of personality*. Despite certain divergences, this position is not that far removed from Politzer's. Crevel was an ardent defender of the Soviet Union, and he reproached Freud for pretending not to realize that the homeland of socialism was in danger, like a fortress besieged by enemies. Then he paid homage to the old man: "He [Freud] is tired enough to want no more than to busy himself with his trinkets. We can excuse that. But which young psychoanalyst will speak up?"[48]

That bit of incentive would not fall on deaf ears, and Jacques Lacan would frequently evoke with tenderness the memory of his "dear Crevel."

One day in June 1935, André Breton encountered Ilya Grigorievich Ehrenburg walking on the boulevard Montparnasse. The latter was part of the Soviet delegation to the International Congress for the Defense of Culture that was to be held in Paris during the following days. He had recently accused the Surrealists of being adepts of pederasty, sodomy, and onanism. Without any fuss, the Frenchman grabbed him by the lapel and slapped him vigorously in the face. The following day, the Russians threatened to boycott the congress if Breton were allowed to speak. At a total loss, René Crevel attempted to reconcile his Communist comrades and his Surrealist friends. His initiative failed. After a long walk at night, he committed suicide.

Ten years earlier, he had written these words: "No effort will ever be able to counter that mysterious surge or *élan*, which is not an *élan vital*, but its marvelous opposite, the *élan mortel*."[49]

II. Georges Politzer and Henri Wallon as Readers of Freud

In 1924, a group of young philosophers was formed in Paris. Their taste for new modes of thought was combined with a pronounced predilection for spirituality, a cult of the "other" and the human individual, and a desperate effort to shatter the structures of the very sacred and very secular French university.[50] The journal *Philosophies,* which assembled the talents of Pierre Morhange, Norbert Guterman, Georges Friedmann, Henri Lefebvre, Georges Politzer, and occasionally Paul Nizan, took political positions as clear as those of the Surrealists: hatred of war and patriotism; pronounced hostility toward chauvinism, middle-class values, and colonialism. The "philosophers," as they were called, were intent on both distinguishing themselves from and allying themselves with other vanguard groups, even as they maintained the imperative of making their journal into the expression of the new literary movement. Soupault, Jacob, Drieu la Rochelle, and Crevel collaborated on the second issue of *Philosophies,* but a few years later the break would be consummated. Breton would insult the philosophers, while Politzer would call the Surrealists Trotskyites and counter-revolutionaries.

In 1924, no member of the group adhered to Marxism. But the horror they all felt toward the traditional academic "French-style" philosophy, as represented by Brunschvicg or Bergson, inevitably led to the idea that philosophy no longer had a raison d'être and that by proclaiming its "end," the authentic philosopher could turn toward genuine political action (to which Marxism was giving a new meaning), or toward poetic creation, the symbol of the contemporary era's modernity. There was thus elaborated a theory of "fertile moments," which brought the philosophers to join the concrete struggle alongside the Communist Party. In its marginal, arrogant, and suicidal aspect, that fragile school offered an anticipation of the various recastings which would subsequently be effected in the structure of French philosophy. Ten years later, through the teaching of Kojève (who also professed the "end" of philosophy), Hegelianism, which was still banned from the universities, made its entry into the École pratique des hautes études. Bataille, Queneau, Lacan, Breton, and others participated in the event, while the names of the "philosophers" were to be found in the Party's publications. And yet their "spiritual" revolt prepared the ground for the emergence of a new way of conceiving of the philosopher's relation to history and politics. After the war, the advent of existentialism gave concrete form to a thematics of marginality, freedom, individual adventure, and the primacy of the individual, that was not foreign to the concerns of the philosophers.

The poet Pierre Morhange gave the group its mystical dimension. Believing frenetically—and in an inquisitorial mode—in God, he invented the slogan of the "trust [in English] of faith" to designate the elite individuals capable of transcending their conflicts in order to place themselves in the service of an idea. He called these "new men" of philosophy and action *refined brutes*. He classified Lenin among them for his daring and his faith in revolution. He wanted to be the heir to Christ and to Marx and announced the project of a vast opinion poll on the subject of God. The content of the journal *Philosophies,* moreover, led Henri Daniel-Rops to establish a parallel between the mysticism proclaimed by the group and the neo-Thomism being restored to currency by Jacques Maritain. In passing, he noted that the intellectual training of the philosophers tended to be more Jewish than Christian, which was his explanation for the fact that they seemed less tempted by Catholicism than by the elaboration of a personal mystique.[51]

With the exception of Henri Lefebvre, all the members of the *Philosophies* group were Jewish. But among them Pierre Morhange was alone in laying claim to his Jewish identity at a time when assimilationism prevailed in France. He would be persistently tormented by the anti-Zionist positions of the French Communist movement.

During those years, a renewal of spirituality was on the agenda in all intellectual circles, and specifically among Catholics, who were undergoing an anxiety attack caused by the divorce between faith and science, progress and obscurantism. The mysticism defended by Morhange and the group of philosophers was part of an intellectual tendency marked by the rise of Marxism and the emergence of new literary forms.

In 1925, Pius XI declared that the greatest scandal of the nineteenth century lay in the fact that the Church had lost the working class. It is true that at the time in France the Communist Party was emerging as a power and the command posts of the government were held by anticlerical republicans. Christians were all the more a minority in that religion was a value of the bourgeoisie or one appealed to fanatically by Action française. The need for a modern form of spirituality was thus omnipresent. If the working class had been "lost" for the clergy, the religious spirit, nevertheless, was triumphant in the ranks of the party. Most of the active militants during the interwar years came from Catholic—or occasionally Protestant—families. Their break with the "religion of the exploiters" or the conservative ideals of the Church did not bring them (far from it!) to any authentic atheism. On the contrary, during the 1930s, joining the Communists functioned as a religious—if not a mystical—conversion. The militant abandoned a belief, an upbringing, and ancestral values in order to conquer a new identity. He literally changed identity to become an initiate of the revolution. He replaced his individual history with that of a collectivity whose monuments were called the Bastille, the Commune, or the Winter Palace.

For the numerous reasons already mentioned, there was no true theoretical work with the masses that might have allowed becoming a Communist *not* to be experienced as a religious engagement: belief in or submission to a bureaucratic authority. Vassalage to the Comintern, gradual Stalinization, the establishment of a personality cult, and finally the inevitable fanaticism of the antifascist struggle contributed to the image of a simplistic Communism stripped of the theoretical complexity or that philosophical culture which Marx and Lenin had bestowed on it. The mechanism of conversion, renunciation, and disappointment, through which a subject abandons his personal history to adopt the identity of a class or a sect, is religious in its essence. It functions in the manner of a descent of grace or a revelation.

To be sure, that mechanism does not entirely explain the functioning of an institution, but only certain processes of idealization and identification. We have seen that it played a central role in the history of the psychoanalytic movement and that it was at the heart of the contradictions within the Viennese Jewish community at the end of the nineteenth century and, more generally, within Jewish communities in the face of the rise of anti-Semitism, on the one hand, and Zionism, on the other.[52] It was in part because Freud was not caught in the infernal cycle of conversions and repudiations that he was able to describe with such lucidity what are normally described as religious "patterns of behavior" or "attitudes." He did so without managing to avoid a situation in which psychoanalysis itself became a new religion for its adepts and in which the IPA turned into a kind of Comintern.

Within the spiritual renewal that occurred in France between 1925 and 1935, that mechanism functioned perfectly.

The importance taken on by the Communist movement provoked transformations within the Catholic world. Pius XI remained violently anti-Communist, but that did not prevent him from issuing a decree condemning Action française in December 1926. To the great regret of Édouard Pichon, Action française would not recover from that blow, and neither would the program for a "Gallicization" of psychoanalysis. Numerous Catholics, including Jacques Maritain, took their leave from Maurras at that point, and the domination of fundamentalists in ecclesiastical circles receded.

The banning of Action française by Rome opened up to French thought a new field of Christian inspiration. From it the journal *Esprit* would emerge in 1932, under the impetus of Emmanuel Mounier and with the covert participation of Maritain.[53] The spirituality proposed by that journal did not resemble the one put forth by the philosophers in 1924. At its base lay a primacy accorded to the spiritual as well as the theme of the quest of the other and the values of the individual, all of which would flourish in Mounier's doctrine of "personalism," which was so admired by the phenomenologist Eugène Minkowski. But unlike the philosophers, the founders of the journal *Esprit* did not seek to create a "trust of faith" or inquire into the consequences of the "end of philosophy." From the outset, they wanted to effect a gathering of Christians of every stripe as well as free spirits coming from every horizon in order to initiate a break between the Church, which had compromised itself too often, and an eternal Christianity which they wanted to see open up to the values of modernity.

The anxiety of the philosophers and their mystical revolt were part of the same configuration as the one that ended in the creation and success of the journal *Esprit,* but it did not lead to the same political commitments. At bottom, each in his way, the liberal Mounier and the doctrinaire Maritain were humanists. Within the Christian faith they never repudiated, they found the wherewithal to lay the grounds for an antifundamentalist and antinationalist spirituality that would give French Catholicism a new, progressive, liberal, and socializing energy. For their part, the philosophers, who did not belong to any church and were the exiles of thought, preferred God to religion and mysticism to humanism; they would have no other choice, when the time came, than to "convert" to a Marxism that was all the more flamboyant in their eyes in that it came with the prestige of a successful revolution.

The restructuring that occurred within Christian thought with the creation of *Esprit* did not lead to an interest in psychoanalysis, which did not have any roots in progressive Catholic circles. We have already seen that the case of *abbé* Paul Jury, who practiced analysis before renouncing the Christian faith, was an exception in the climate of the interwar period.[54] The same holds for that of Jules Monchanin, a nonconformist priest from Lyon and a sympathizer with Mounin, who wrote Surrealist poems, was interested in Freud and Romain Rolland, and in 1929 delivered a lecture devoted to sexual morality.[55]

The founders of *Esprit* did not misperceive Freud's discovery, but adopted toward it Dalbiez's separatist point of view, which consisted in accepting the therapeutic value of psychoanalysis while rejecting its "philosophy," which was described as pansexualist. The new spirituality they were initiating was pursued above all through an evaluation of Marxist thought, toward which they also adopted a separatist position: They accepted the "young Marx," his humanism and his critique of superstructures, but refused his materialism as well as the notion of a "primacy of class struggle." Obsessed by the idea of commitment, turning their backs on the bourgeois Church, which had betrayed the essence of Christianity and supported capitalism, they looked toward the ideals of Communism, either to reflect on its errors and successes or to see how they themselves measured up to its militant energy. That permanent confrontation between progressive Christians and Marxism took on the appearance of an act of defiance. The Communist "religion" fascinated them all the more in that it came with a mystique of the chosen class that was not foreign to their own spirituality. But it repelled them because it was theoretically based on the absence of God. That act of defiance remained inscribed in black and white in the journal's title: In 1932, the word "esprit" leapt out of the founders' collective head after a long night's work, and Mounier commented on the event as follows, "Imagine a Communist journal that would have the courage to call itself *Matière!*" [56]

Because he was interested in Marxism, Mounier preferred Adler's work to Freud's. It corresponded to both his inquiries into individual will and his socializing preoccupations.

Under those conditions, it was only after World War II that progressive Christian circles would take an interest in psychoanalysis. The psychoanalysts, for their part, would extend a hand to Christians of every tendency.

"As of a specific date (1925, I think)," wrote Henri Lefebvre, "we reached an agreement about certain formulas. The preceding generations had abandoned the absolute for the relative. It befell us to make the transition from the relative to the absolute, given the bankruptcy of relativism. . . . In the name of philosophical thought, we wanted to put an end to intellectualism, some through the transcendental imagination (the 'surreal'), others through psychology (psychoanalysis), and finally others through a new metaphysic endowed with modern means of penetration and application." [57]

Psychology was the private domain of the impetuous Georges Politzer. Born in 1903 to a Jewish family in Nagyvarad, in Hungary, [58] he had read the principal texts of Freud early on. At the same time, he was witness to the crushing of the Budapest Commune, in which his father, a physician, had been rather active. Politzer arrived in Paris in 1922, after a period in Vienna during which he had attended the seminars of the Psychoanalytic Society. There he had met Freud and Ferenczi. The "wildman of the Carpathians," as his friend Henri Lefebvre called him, was a tall and awkward young man with a shock of red hair whose waves augured an unprecedented ardor for philosophical battle. Like numerous Jewish intellectuals of that period, he was an assimilationist, scarcely spoke of his Jewish background, and chose twice to marry a non-Jewish woman. Violent and jealous, he did not hesitate to insult and even strike his own friends when their writings or actions displeased him. In his harsh voice, he prophesied the coming of a spiritual dictatorship or endorsed the mission of leaders in theoretical matters. He took to Freudianism with incredible sectarianism, choosing a furious course of self-analysis for himself. Not only was Politzer an authentic reader of Freud, but he had the stature of a great theorist. The French language attained an incomparable measure of verve and refinement in his writing. He was a Hungarian who respected nothing, neither celebrities, whom he considered empty vessels, nor that famous "French intelligence" whose ludicrousness he lashed out at time and again.

In the fourth issue of the journal *Philosophies,* he wrote a remarkable review of Laforgue and Allendy's book (prefaced by Henri Claude), *La psychanalyse et les névroses.* While recognizing the honesty of the publication, Politzer took positions which can be found in most of his subsequent writings. First, he refused the notion of Latinate genius and treated as "demonic pathos" and worthy of a "philosophical flea market" the "theoretical" arguments of the two colleagues. He then denounced the book's moralizing content, its "philanthropic" side. He reproached the authors for presenting Freudian theory with a simplemindedness bordering on stupidity.

From an identical perspective, he lashed out violently at Charles Blondel in an article entitled "Le mythe de l'anti-psychanalyse," which was also published in *Philoso-phies*.[59]

The journal ceased publication after one year and five issues, soon replaced by another entitled *L'Esprit*, which first appeared in May 1926. That publication was intent on being more strictly philosophical and less open to literature, book reviews, and thus the pluralism that had characterized its predecessor. Its duration was brief.

In France, it was still thought that dreams of adventure resembled adventure itself. In obeying, no doubt unwittingly, that tradition, our philosophers came to confuse Lord Jim with Emma Bovary. Following a collective reading of Spinoza, they entertained the project of "rehabilitating wisdom."[60] The idea took concrete form when Georges Friedmann received a small fortune as an inheritance and placed it at the disposition of his friends. The group immediately decided to use the sum to purchase a piece of a peninsula in the Morbihan gulf. A realtor was contacted in Vannes, who proposed to our would-be Robinson Crusoes the acquisition, in the middle of the ocean, of a dilapidated building surrounded by arable land. Full of grand hopes, they baptized the ruin the "Isle of Wisdom." They planned to live there and meditate on the world's disorders.

Things, however, soon became complicated. An ardent Spinozan, Friedmann believed that money was a curse. He could not manage either to accept the inheritance of his banker father or to devote it to philosophical projects. Morhange made fun of him and Politzer waited impatiently for the matter to lead to concrete propositions. Finally, Friedmann refused to resolve the difficult question of being and having, and after several extended negotiations, decided to withdraw his purse. The journal *L'Esprit* closed down and the adventurers joined the ranks of the Communist Party. The money from then on could be invested in revolutionary endeavors favorable to the proletariat. There was talk of a new journal, a publishing house. . . . It appears, however, that the negotiations with the party leadership were not as simple as had been hoped. They nevertheless resulted, in 1929, in the twinned creation of the *Revue marxiste*, on which Morhange, Friedmann, and others collaborated, and the *Revue de psychologie concrète*, through which Politzer planned to launch his project of a revolutionary psychology. The two journals were financed by Friedmann's money, but enjoyed little success.

At this point a curious character enters on stage, a kind of confidence man, issuing from the Parisian corridors of the Comintern. He claimed to be interested in the future of philosophy and proposed to Morhange the chance to double his investment. Quite excited, Morhange persuaded Friedmann to entrust his inheritance to the adventurer. The man was all the more captivating in that he was thought to have connections in "high spheres." Nobody knew exactly what the phrase referred to, but it exuded an odor of alcoves and conspiracy that the two heroes found hard to resist. Morhange and Friedmann went with him to the Monte-Carlo casino. The adventurer took the fortune and asked his friends to wait for him outside. To win at roulette and double his bet he needed the solitude required for concentration. Naturally, he disappeared and Friedmann never saw his money again.[61] Furious, Politzer

told the story to agents of the Comintern. Before long the affair took on the appearance of a scandal, and Breton took advantage of it to drag the philosophers, whom
he detested, through the mud. Morhange, in turn, would accuse Politzer of betrayal.

Was the man a run-of-the-mill swindler? Was he, as Lefebvre suggested, an
agent of the Internationale sent by Moscow to torpedo adversarial publishing enterprises? In any event, the two journals were shipwrecked along with Friedmann's
fortune.[62]

At the time he published his *Critique des fondements de la psychologie*,[63]
Politzer was unaware that it would be his sole contribution to the vast field of "concrete psychology" whose founder he wanted to be and for which he foresaw a dazzling future. The aim of Politzer's experiment was not to reform psychology, but
rather to demolish it. He hoped not to transform a scintillating ruin into a construct
built over a swamp, but rather to destroy the entire edifice. Basically, Politzer, like
the Surrealists, was part of the Rimbaldian adventure of conquering the "other
scene." He called on psychology to effect a radical break, to risk losing the empire
whose mistress it believed itself to be.

Oddly enough, his work is reminiscent of Michelet's version of "la Grande
Histoire." Politzer was not an historian, but the editorial form in which he conceived
his project was similar to the romantic dream of a "total restitution" of the field
studied. Consider: the *Critique des fondements,* his only published book, takes as
its object psychoanalysis and more precisely the theory of dreams and the unconscious, that is, the inaugural phase of Freud's discovery. The book was presented as
the first volume of a work whose title was to be *Matériaux pour la critique des
fondements de la psychologie* and which was to include two more volumes, one
dealing with *Gestalttheorie* and phenomenology, the other with behaviorism. Politzer presented his already gigantic project as preliminary to a critical study in the
strict sense, to be entitled *Essai critique sur les fondements de la psychologie.* Like
the two final volumes of the *Matériaux,* that essay was never written.

Between an aborted fantasy of total restitution and a successful dream leading nowhere, Georges Politzer's psychological work is no more than a third of what
was intended. If we limit ourselves to the philosopher's statement on the resolutely
provisional character of the *Matériaux,* of which we have only the first part, it must
be concluded that Politzer's project of a *new psychology* had no chance of coming
into existence.

It has often been claimed that Georges Politzer had abandoned his research
in psychology "on orders from the party" after he joined in 1929.[64] At the time,
psychoanalysis was not particularly appreciated in the ranks of the Communist
movement and Politzer, like other intellectuals, was invited to devote his energies to
political economy, which represented the promised land of Marxism. But the young
philosopher's decision to become an active militant was like a conversion. Politzer
repudiated psychoanalysis with as much ardor as he had defended it. He did still
more—he proceeded to admire Stalin as he had never admired Freud. Moreover, he
found in Marxism a doctrine that seemed to him more solid than the Freudianism
toward which he had always kept a critical distance.

The extravagant hatred he evidenced toward psychoanalysis after 1929 had nothing in common with the latent hostility manifested by the Communist Party during the same period. Even if he was "acting on orders," Politzer did not produce a single text on political economy. On the other hand, in his excesses, he proved far more sectarian with respect to Freudianism than the French Communist movement. His militantism did not prevent him from continuing to write philosophical texts. In hiding in 1941, he wrote a polemical piece on Rosenberg, the Hitlerian philosopher, in which he dissected racial ideals[65] with such intelligence that one wonders if indeed it was the same man who had written two years earlier accusing Freudianism of serving the interests of Nazism. The fact that Politzer was Jewish was no doubt not unrelated to that ambivalence. It was as though the philosopher's "Jewish self-hatred" revealed itself in a fanatical rejection of Freud, while his horror of anti-Semitism led him to a struggle against Nazism in which he would find an heroic death.

It is thus absurd to attribute the "conversion" of 1929 to orders received "from above." If there was an imperative, it stemmed "from below," that is from Politzer's project itself. It was not because he had "received orders" that Politzer abandoned his research, but, on the contrary, because his research had led to an impasse that he repudiated psychoanalysis and adhered to Marxist doctrine, which offered him a measure of certainty he had been unable to find in Freudianism. With Marxism, he left the "ghetto" of psychology at the cost of renouncing a project that had no future. The request for submission worked when the ground was prepared for it, and that ground, in 1929, was the anticipated failure of a new psychology.

Dead at an early age, Politzer did not have time to assess the full measure of his renunciation of psychoanalysis. Who can say today what his position would have been in 1949 at the time of Zhdanov's condemnation of psychoanalysis? What words would he have uttered about his own Jewishness in the wake of Auschwitz and Treblinka?

It was certainly not by chance that Politzer's fanatical attitude toward psychoanalysis went together with a kind of ambivalence toward the question of his Jewish identity. The philosopher was obsessed with the theories of Rosenberg, against which he waged an unrelenting battle. Against that anti-Semitic ideologue, he did not invoke his own Jewish identity, but resorted rather to the weapons of Marxism and Leninism. In other words, he did not fight Nazism in the name of his position as a Jew, but on strictly political and philosophical grounds. Moreover, in a 1939 article on "the end of psychoanalysis,"[66] Politzer also spoke of racism and anti-Semitism. Because of the ban on Communist publications after the Soviet-German pact, the article was written under a pseudonym and was not attributed to Politzer until much later.

In the case of numerous Jewish *émigrés* during that period, assimilationism worked its way out through a fusion with the ideal of French nationalism. For Politzer, it was realized through adherence to Communism. The party was an adoptive family, a land of refuge in which the ideals of race had been eliminated in favor of those of a people and a nation. In that respect, the Thorezian policy of unifying French Communism under the aegis of Stalinist internationalism was perfectly suited to the philosopher. Moreover, in June 1939, he published an article in rhapsodic praise of Maurice Thorez, ascribing to him the merit of having been able to distinguish between the ideals of race and of nation.

Suffering and drama were there at the heart of the adventure of the "Isle of Wisdom." Whoever the figure of the confidence man may have been, the philosophers themselves participated in the liquidation of their publishing endeavors with a sense of failure that did not exist as such for the Surrealists. It was as though they found themselves caught in a dilemma that brought them to deny their own identities. Whence that quest for a heroism which might function as a constant form of defiance. There was in Politzer a taste for the absolute, for defiance, and for suicide that accounted for the talent of his prescriptions and the disappointment of their realization.

What remains is a book unique in the annals of psychology, posing to psychologists the question of the scientific and philosophical status of their object. Between physics, an "objective" third-person science, and psychology, a science of the first person, there was no room for an additional scientific domain capable of studying first-person data in the third person. And yet psychology had the pretention of fulfilling that role, and if it failed to do so, it was because of its abstractions. Under that rubric, Politzer classified psychology, of whatever tendency, which he reproached for its impersonal point of view, stripped of meaning, and above all for its rigid conception of human behavior. Against it, he pitted the principle of a "concrete psychology" that would take the person itself as its object of study: man in his desires and his actions. The *person,* for Politzer, was not an object of consciousness, endowed with affects and behavioral patterns, but the individual in his historical "becoming." The object of concrete psychology was the personal drama of a desiring human being, the drama of his existence. Politzer thus rejected the perspective of a subject fully master of his actions as well as the reverse configuration of somnambulistic states or automatic forms of behavior.

Because it took personal drama as its subject, concrete psychology attempted to shatter the framework of psychology itself. At bottom, Politzer's method had the effect of linking a structure to a history, a subjectivity to an evolving dynamic. Although he was not a Marxist when he became interested in the problem, the philosopher approached a Marxist conception of historicity: a position, that is, which would lead to materialism. For the contradiction he brought to light between the abstract and the concrete was not far from coinciding with that pitting idealism against materialism. That is the reason the project of a concrete psychology contained elements hidden within it that would lead Politzer to convert to dialectical and historical materialism. And yet the way in which the philosopher approached the subject of psychology had few links with the attempt to elaborate a materialist psychology such as the one that can be observed in the cases of Reichian Freudo-Marxism or the Soviet psychologists. Politzer was above all criticizing the foundations of psychology and taking Freudianism as an instrument of that critique.

With respect to the French situation, Politzer remained an innovator. He was the only one of the psychologists of his time to have understood what was at stake for psychology in the discovery from Vienna and to completely accept the Freudian notions of the unconscious, desire, and sexuality. Perhaps he was able to accomplish as much because he was not truly a psychologist. His project of a concrete psychology could not come to fruition since its sole object was to reveal the impasses of psychology itself. That is why Politzer substituted a new doctrine for the Freudian instrument, which he deemed to be no longer useful. In his conversion to Marxism, he threw out the baby with the bath water, psychoanalysis with psychology. Freudo-Marxism would become for him an enemy to strike down, just like any other attempt to construct a materialist psychology drawing on psychoanalysis. For Politzer, becoming a Marxist gradually led to two repudiations: of concrete psychology, whose realization proved impossible, and of Freudianism, which was no longer needed as a critical instrument.

Between the time he definitively abandoned his psychological work and the time he became a Communist, Politzer was able to write a polemical text against the leading French figures of psychoanalysis, whom he reproached for having denatured Freudian doctrine and delivered it over to its adversaries to do with as they pleased. In the editorial of the first issue of the *Revue de psychologie concrète*, which appeared in 1929, the philosopher announced his intention of working, along with all those who wished to join him, on the elaboration of a new psychology. He noted the existence of a "psychoanalytic crisis" and invited psychoanalysts to abandon the abstract schemes of the old psychology. Moreover, he granted space to dissidents, and particularly to Adlerians, in order to make known non-Freudian tendencies. He himself published an interesting article on individual psychology in the second issue of the journal. In the first, he reprinted Hesnard and Pichon's article, "Aperçu historique du mouvement psychanalytique français," which had first appeared in 1925 in *Évolution psychiatrique*.[68] On this occasion, he initiated a violent polemic against Hesnard.

Hesnard himself was rather unlucky in his dealings with Hungarian Jews. In 1915, Ferenczi had administered a formidable theoretical dressing down to him, and now Politzer was joining in the sport.[69] The philosopher did not proceed with kid gloves. He ridiculed all concerned: Bergson's honeyed discourse, Janet's monarchical pretentions, the doctrinal vacuity of the founders of the SPP, and their compromising of principles as well. He did not spare the ladies and mocked Bonaparte's "stupidity" as much as Sokolnicka's "blunders". "Dominated almost exclusively by proselytism," he wrote, "the tactic of French psychoanalysts has been one of an opportunism—and thus a timidity—which has been excessive. Instead of openly accepting their battle with classical psychiatry, the French psychoanalysts have opted to accommodate feelings as much as possible and have simply agreed to live under a regime of tolerance. Never at any moment, even facing the most violent and least scientific of attacks, have they been willing to seize the opportunity thus extended and demonstrate that their adversary was enthroned atop what was no more than a house of cards. That is how they proceeded with Professor Janet, and even more so with an individual [Charles Blondel], who having no other scientific credentials than his famous thesis—which was no more than a philosophical farce performed for doctors and a medical farce performed for philosophers—decided to appeal to every trace of offended Latinity and interested false modesty in France in order to defend against the attacks of psychoanalysis the Champs Élysées of French psychology and psychiatry. Instead of undertaking a labor of scientific renaissance, the French psychoanalysts have preferred to dream up excuses in order to accommodate every interest." [70]

In his critique of the psychoanalytic situation in France, Politzer thus resorted to the same tone as the Surrealists. His discourse was genuinely *new* because it formulated the *negative* of the psychoanalytic discourse of the time, that of the other France—anti-Germanophobic, anti-racist, hostile to conservative values.

In 1942, while participating in the Resistance in the clandestine publication of *Lettres françaises,* Politzer was arrested by the Gestapo along with his comrades Jacques Decour and Jacques Salomon. Tortured terribly, he defied his oppressors, who dragged him, dying, to his execution. He was not yet forty years old. His wife, Maïe Politzer, was deported to Auschwitz and died of typhus.

Four years later, at the Bonneval Colloquium, Jacques Lacan spoke to Henri Ey about the status of the object of psychology. He recalled the aborted project of concrete psychology whose imprint would remain on his work. "It was with such feelings, I know," he said, "that Politzer's great mind gave up the theoretical mode of expression on which he was to leave his indelible mark to dedicate himself to an activity that was to deprive us of him irreparably." [71]

As much as Politzer's work in psychology was marked by failure, Wallon's was to a similar extent characterized by such flourishing prosperity as to qualify as one of the most copious achievements—in terms of quantity of publications—of modern times. From the talk he gave in 1903 at a lycée prize ceremony in Bar-le-Duc to his final article, interrupted by his death in 1962, Wallon's discourse never suffered the slightest retreat. His bibliography included almost three hundred titles, including some ten books, numerous prefaces, and a number of important lectures—such was Wallon's contribution to that science of the human whose legitimacy he never questioned.

Unlike Piaget's achievement, Wallon's has remained for the most part unknown to the Anglo-Saxon scientific world. This was a function not of its character or any particularly Gallic cast, but of other factors. First of all, the man's political activism was not of a sort to please a scientific community priding itself on being above the political melee. In addition, the seeming confusion emanated by his style did not allow for a clarification of his positions in a domain in which an illusory systematicity was generally demanded. Finally, Wallon never looked on psychoanalysis with the mixture of distrust and fascination that might have intrigued the international community of psychologists. In a word, he remained French even though he had never been, like Janet, the representative of any sort of putatively French mentality. [72]

Wallon's course did, however, resemble Janet's. Born in 1879 to a family of intellectuals, by age he might have belonged to the generation of the founders of the SPP. But in his innovative position in the field of psychology, he was closer to Jacques Lacan or Henri Ey, who were twenty years his junior. His grandfather had been a brilliant republican academic, a disciple of Michelet's, who turned to the right toward the end of his life out of hostility to the Commune. Faithful to his family tradition, Henri Wallon entered the École normale supérieure and became an *agrégé* in philosophy in 1902, all the while following the incidents of the Dreyfus Affair with rapt fascination. On the advice of Georges Dumas, he opted for the field of psychology, which he entered by way of medical school. Unlike most of the psychologists of his generation, he was active in politics and militated in the ranks of the Socialist Party among the hard-line followers of Jules Guesde. Hostile to Jaurès, he left the party shortly before 1914 out of disgust with what he perceived to be the triumph of electoral politics. For that reason, after the Tours Congress, he became a Communist fellow traveler. It was only in 1942 that Wallon joined the Communist Party, and it appears that the heroic death of Politzer and his friends played a fundamental role in that decision.

Even before becoming a member of the party, Wallon showed a deep attachment to it. His attitude was close to Aragon's in the kind of ethic of loyalty which he would never compromise, but differed from it in the prudence of the positions he adopted. Thus, during the 1950s, Wallon remained faithful to the pro-Soviet orthodoxy without taking a stand one way or the other concerning the Lyssenko Affair or Zhdanov's condemnation of psychoanalysis.[73] He praised Pavlov without affirming that Pavlovianism might serve as an antidote to bourgeois psychology.

Prudence and loyalty: such was Wallon's orientation within the Communist ideal to which he adhered from the time of his youth. He was not interested in Freudo-Marxism or in any other attempts to reconcile psychoanalysis and materialism. He would also manifest the same prudence in his relations with the French psychoanalytic movement. Trained early in German philosophy, he was unaware of the anti-Freudianism of the 1930s and never opted for Latinate genius against an alleged Teutonic cast of mind. He kept abreast of new ideas without any excessive passion and with a comprehending distance never marred by intolerance. For all these reasons, Wallon's joining the Communist Party in no way resembled a conversion. It was part of the normal development of a young intellectual raised in the traditions of French Jacobinism. Unlike Politzer, he did not repudiate a religion or a doctrine in order to worship new idols. On the contrary, he remained quite balanced in his orientations and kept his activities as a militant separate from his scientific work.

And yet his adherence to communism drew on a theoretical choice in favor of dialectical materialism that would serve as a basis for his conception of psychology. Wallon grounded that conception on a dualism in which the notion of development played a central role. The biological factor, linked to the maturation of the nervous system, remained inseparable from the social factor constituted by man's interactions with his entourage. In according priority to a dialectic of transformations, Wallon envisaged the whole of psychology beginning with childhood. It was the discontinuous succession of stages, then their restructuring in terms of crises, which gave the key to the transition from childhood to adulthood. In his own field, Wallon's position was not far removed from the scheme elaborated by Gaston Bachelard for the history of science.

Wallon defined the object of psychology as a dialectical transition between two situations. He was not interested in the concrete drama of the individual, was not concerned with constitutional fixities, and did not bring into play the flow of conditioning factors. That is why his doctrine was refractory to experimentalism, subjectivism, and organicism. But there too Wallon attempted to avoid the trap of an unconscious that might float like a phantom between the biological and the social. His perspective consisted rather in constructing a psychobiology—that is, a theory of mentalities—taking into account culture, on the one hand, and heredity, on the other. To that extent he participated in the new movement of ideas in a way different from the Surrealists or the "philosophers." Even if he recognized the importance of Freud's discovery, he rejected the idea of an absolute primacy of the unconscious and did not impose on psychology the question of its status. He attempted, rather, to articulate it within a new field of inquiry which had arisen in the interwar years through the impetus of Marc Bloch and Lucien Febvre, both founders of the *Annales d'histoire économique et sociale*.

Contrary to the entire French tradition of psychology, Wallon situated himself on the same terrain as that of the historians of mentalities, who were fighting for a history based on an "intermethodology" of the sciences of man. These historians rejected scholarly chronologies dealing with individuals or events and promoted the development of a "total" history situated at the crossroads of the social sciences. Wallon's notion of the unconscious was inseparable from their renewal of the study of mentalities. Even if it did not correspond to Freud's, it escaped the Jungian definition of the collective unconscious and did not fit into the tradition of the ideologues of a Gallic unconscious. In point of fact, Wallon introduced into the field of psychology a certain number of concepts that would be used by the second generation of psychoanalysts, and particularly by Jacques Lacan, in the context of a "French" recasting of Freudian doctrine.

Wallon's position thus remains quite eccentric in the French psychiatro-psychoanalytic configuration of the interwar period, since, in an initial phase, it was part of the introduction of Freudianism in the country, and in a second one, part of its reinterpretation.

A philosopher become physician, Wallon, like Janet, was concerned with psychiatry. In 1908, he defended his thesis in medicine on chronic interpretative disorders, and then became an assistant to Jean Nageotte at Bicêtre and the Salpêtrière. At the same time, he opened a consulting service for retarded or abnormal children. During World War I, he was assigned to the psychiatric center of Tours where he took care of disturbed cases among the wounded. In 1921, he was appointed to a teaching position at the newly created Institut de psychologie of the University of Paris. He served with several medico-pedagogical clinics, and opened his own private practice in the XVIth arrondissement. It was during this period that he became seriously interested in Freud's works. In a text entitled "La conscience et la vie subconsciente," he implicitly reproached Janet for his excessive attachment to the old associationism, to which he opposed the Viennese discovery. "It is progress, however," he wrote, "to have affirmed, in the face of conscious representations, the existence of psychical states which are not conscious. In decomposing mental life into systems of images and perfectly clear concepts, associationist and intellectualist doctrines allowed nothing of psychical spontaneity to subsist; they substituted the crude imprint of objective realities for the processes and laws of an activity which, although adapting to the external world, is never a simple response to it. This was a fortunate and necessary turn of events. As a result the previously established opposition between consciousness and the unconscious has changed its meaning." [74]

Wallon reproached Freud for his excess of symbolism and often considered psychoanalysis to be a branch of philosophy. He was wary of the notion of the libido, which he found chimerical, and accepted repression without wanting to situate it in the unconscious. But he considered Freudian theory to be a genuine theory that objective psychology should make use of. With that point of view, he avoided the trap of classical anti-Freudianism. In a study of *The Interpretation of Dreams*, published in 1927, he noted the Viennese doctrine's indebtedness to German culture, but did not reproach it for its "Teutonic cast." "Its essential themes," he wrote, "are plainly more romantic than scientific in origin. German poetry and philosophy of the last century are full of conflicts between the elementary, primitive, passionate, and anarchical powers of the earliest days, and the order, reason, and reflective action whose final triumph does not prevent them from being perpetually unsettled by the latent insurrection and ruses of their prisoners. If one encounters certain particularly gripping formulations in Freud, they are no doubt the result of his genius. But their first contact with objective and scientific psychology must be to be gathered, verified, and used by it." [75]

In 1931, six years after being named Professor at the Collège de France, and three years before the publication of his celebrated work, *Les origines du caractère chez l'enfant*, Henri Wallon wrote an astonishing text on the experience of the mirror and the notion of the body proper, whose principal elements would serve as the basis for Lacan's elaboration of two concepts fundamental to his teaching: the imaginary and the symbolic. [76]

The famous mirror adventure begins like a novel by Lewis Carroll. One finds stories of dogs, cats, ducks, and infants in their cradle who make their way through looking glasses, then observe in delight or repugnance their scintillating trappings. Wallon, a great pedagogue, would never know the joys of paternity, but, during the 1930s, he could not resist the pleasures of polymorphous perversity, happy as a king in his gallery of mirrors. Yet the ordeal of the mirror was presented with all the seriousness of a scientific laboratory. Consider: if one deprives a drake of his female and locks him into a chamber lined with mirrors, he takes his own image for that of his absent mate. In identical circumstances, a dog has a reaction of avoidance. He responds to caresses, but refuses his reflection, and turns toward the experimenter. The monkey, for his part, reveals himself to be shrewder and stupider. In the presence of the mirror, he stretches his hand behind it. Furious at not finding anything, he becomes as agitated as a caged lion.

In comparing the reactions of children with those of animals, Wallon observed different responses according to age. Until the end of the third month, the human infant remains insensitive to his mirror image, but in the course of the fourth month, changes occur. The gaze becomes steady and the child observes his reflection as though it were foreign to his person. Yet the beginning of a smile appears. Two months later, he still smiles at his image as well as that of his father, when seen in the mirror. But when he hears his father's voice behind him, he turns around in surprise: He has not yet succeeded in making a reflection and an actual presence coincide in time and space. He does indeed perceive the relation of concomitance between image and model, but does not grasp the relation of dependence between them. He is content to attribute an independent reality to each of them.

At the tenth month, things develop still further. The child extends his arms toward his image and looks at it if he is called by his name. He perceives the self outside of himself as the complement of his natural figuration. With that, he imagines his own body in fragments and at the end of a long process of externalization. To unify his ego in space, the child has to obey a dual necessity. First he has to accept the existence of images that have no more than the appearance of reality; then, he has to affirm the reality of an existence that eludes perception. He then finds himself caught in two contradictory modalities of representation. On the one hand, he encounters sensory images that are not real, and, on the other, real images unavailable to sensory apprehension. To accept the fact of his spatio-temporal existence, the child must gradually subordinate the data of immediate experience to pure representation. The mirror ordeal serves him to introduce an increasingly differentiated play of distinctions and equivalences. Through it, the notion of the body proper, which in turn leads to the unity of the self or ego, is formed. During an initial phase, that ordeal is situated in the domain of specularity: No relation is established between the reflected image and the real image. During a second phase, however, a relation is instituted, allowing for the constitution of a unified self within an imaginary space escaping the specular effect. Wallon compared that second stage to a prelude. It is the anticipated form of a third—symbolic—stage, which will give the child the means to organize his sensory experience.

Around one year of age, another threshold is crossed in the structuring of the symbolic. Wallon placed an attractive little girl before a mirror. She proceeded to admire the flowery hat she was wearing on her head; the reflection was at that point experienced as a veritable system of references allowing her to orient her gestures toward parts of her body. That reflection remained distinct from the other system of images through which the child identified her body and her self within a more abstract space. The ability to establish distinctions in space defines the symbolic function and that function opens the field to a veritable apprenticeship of subjective and objective reality. At that stage, the child is no longer satisfied, as in the tenth month, with establishing a relation between the reflected image and the real one. He renews the ordeal of the sixth month in a different register: Instead of radically separating the reflection from the actual person, he recognizes the existence of a duality between the two; he sees that one is subordinated to the other and thus gains access to a kind of symbolic comprehension of that imaginary space within which his ego or self has been forged.

At fifteen months, the mirror ordeal takes a new turn. Invited to point to his mother, the child first designates her in the mirror, then turns toward her while smiling. In that way, he indicates that he has mastered the previously acknowledged duality. He plays with his existence. "Slyly," Wallon writes, "he pretends to accord preponderance to the image precisely because he has just clearly recognized its unreality and purely symbolic character." [77]

At the time he wrote his text on the psychogenesis of the body proper and the unity of the self, Wallon did not establish any relation between his own method and Freud's. He situated his experiment in the context of a psychology centered on the primacy of a dialectical consciousness in which the unconscious barely had a role. He was not aware that the notions he had forged would play a fundamental role in the modern history of the French psychoanalytic movement. At the time, Lacan had not yet defended his thesis on paranoia and was only beginning to discover the work of Freud. The encounter between the psychologist and the young psychiatrist would not take place until several years later, and that through the ordeal of a mirror so extravagant that even Lewis Carroll might have lost his bearings in the process.

3 Writers, Literati, Dream-Devourers

I. Verdurin and Guermantes

We have seen that the notion of a priority of the literary over the medical channel was not admissible in explaining the various modes through which Freudian ideas came to be introduced in France. The two channels had coexisted since 1913, and transmitted, according to the time and place, divergent and frequently opposite versions of psychoanalysis. While the Surrealists were alone in implementing in their poetic inventions a kind of appeal to a language-based form of the unconscious, there were other writers who took Freud's discovery into account. But there too we would do well to make distinctions and establish hierarchies between authentic writers and "dream-devourers," between those, like Romain Rolland, André Gide, Pierre Jean Jouve, Jacques Rivière, or Albert Thibaudet, who were genuinely challenged by Freudian theories and those, like Henri Lenormand and before him Paul Bourget, who used the data of psychoanalysis as a bit of gimmickry or in order to pretty up a fading novelistic style.

Starting in 1922, the "Freud season" was upon Paris. There occurred with psychoanalysis something identical to what transpired around the theory of relativity during Einstein's stay in the French capital.[1] Stylish salons hurriedly began to comment on the Viennese works much as when Mesmer's tub had been a source of excitement among the city's courtesans. Elegant ladies became fascinated with the alchemy of dreams and thought they detected in the complicitous eyelid of their neighbor at table the ultimate explanation of a repressed tendency, slip of the tongue, silence, or pun. From receptions to alcoves, a variety of charlatans dismantled the figures of a sexuality whose perversions they flaunted with as much delight as their ancestors had elicited voices from tables. Couches invaded boudoirs to which exalted souls fallen prey to their own dereliction hurried. All recounted their fantasies while devouring petits fours, and conversations waned beneath the weight of their own insipidity or jargon.

Literary and cosmopolitan journals played a leading role in the explosion of Paris's infatuation with Freudianism. It is difficult to determine whether they served as its echo or if, with the help of rumor, they channeled an already existent spread of enthusiasm. In any event, they participated substantially in the recognition of the writings from Vienna. Besides the *Nouvelle Revue française,* in which numerous articles were published on the subject, *La Revue de Genève, Le Disque vert, La Revue européenne,* and *Europe* contributed to the rise of psychoanalysis.[2]

Founded in 1920 by Robert de Traz, *La Revue de Genève* supported the renewal of European awareness by assembling writers of various countries. It promoted the idea of a comparatism between literature and various fields of knowledge, notably psychology. De Traz considered himself a fervent Freudian, and at the end of 1920, he published the first French translation of a text by Freud. This was the

Five Case Histories, which appeared under the title *Origine et développement de la psychanalyse.* It was that publication which Freud waved triumphantly at Breton when the latter visited him. De Traz also made a trip to Vienna and recounted his meeting with the scientist in *Les Nouvelles littéraires.* "I told him," he wrote, "that French writers in growing numbers were interested in his discoveries. At first he was amused: 'Really? But there are so few translations of me in French! So, you don't say, in literary circles?' He liked the idea." [3]

La Revue européenne was created in 1922. At that time, Maurice Martin du Gard left the editorship of *Écrits nouveaux* to found *Les Nouvelles littéraires* with Frédéric Lefèvre. André Germain, who financed *Écrits nouveaux,* then suggested to Philippe Soupault that he take charge of the journal, which took on the name of *Revue européenne.* Its first issue came out in March 1923. Edmond Jaloux gave it its truly European dimension. He was interested in the Swiss psychoanalytic movement, and particularly in Jung's work. In 1931, he prefaced Yves Le Hay's translation of the latter's *Essays in Analytic Psychology.* Downplaying the doctrine of sexuality, he attempted to effect a fusion of Jungian and Adlerian theories. *La Revue européenne* did not have a large readership and did not devote any major article to psychoanalysis. Gilbert Robin, who was a founding member of the Evolution psychiatrique group, participated in the activities of the journal as well as in those of *La Revue de Genève.*

Europe published its first issue in January 1923 with the sponsorship of Romain Rolland. In its cosmopolitan orientation, it attempted to do battle against chauvinism and played an important role in the difficult matter of bringing French and German cultures closer. In October 1923, an article by J. Robert-France appeared, entitled "Le conflit de Freud et du freudisme," in which the author opposed the favorable impact enjoyed by the *Introduction to Psychoanalysis* to the poor reception given the *Three Essays on the Theory of Sexuality.* He seized the opportunity to put writers back in their place and support the point of view of a psychoanalysis reserved solely for medical practitioners. In the May 1924 issue, Félicien Challaye listed the various French translations of Freud's works. He observed that the famous argument about the country's resistance to psychoanalysis was not at all convincing since Freud's name was referred to as often in intellectual circles as Einstein's and Bergson's. In 1938, *Europe* protested strenuously the disgraceful treatment Freud was given at the hands of the Nazis. [4]

In 1925, Jean Dandieu launched a large-scale opinion poll on Freudianism in *Information universitaire.* Two questions were asked, one on the psychological value of the Viennese theses, the other on the fortunate or baneful influence psychoanalysis might have in the domain of literature. The answers were scaled and were characteristic of the polemical climate of the period. A certain Critias, a journalist, used terms that even Léon Daudet dared not use a year later in his article for *Action française.* "The fact that in Vienna," wrote Critias, "a Jewish brain, obsessed with the sexual hallucinations of his race, and docile to the elementary pseudo-science of old sawbones, has conceived an entire system of man resting solely on sexual desire, solely on libido, is nothing astonishing for the historian. . . . But where his stupefaction begins is where he sees serious thinkers, respectable groups, grow infatuated with this pretentious and hypocritical pornography and pay it the honor of an in-depth study. . . . Freund [sic] is not merely a charlatan or a nut (both at once, it seems to us); he is already bespattered with the blood of the weakest of his victims."

Pierre Janet, for his part, did not hesitate to play Piaget off against Freud. He explained that psychoanalysis enjoyed no respect in France and that its practitioners were young physicians short of patients. In another response, F. Dinchit lashed out at *Totem and Taboo* and opposed Freud to Durkheim and his works. As for Gau-delette, he replied energetically to Critias that the French university should hasten the triumph of Freudianism, which was renewing human psychology and giving writers excellent novelistic material. Finally Allendy defended dream symbolism with admirable honesty.[5]

It was in the same spirit that the journal *Le Disque vert* launched a major opinion poll in 1924 on psychoanalysis. Founded in Brussels in 1922, that publica-tion was a sequel to *Signaux de France et de Belgique*. Among those on the editorial committee were Jean Paulhan, André Salmon, Melot du Dy, O.-J. Perier, and Paul Fierens. As for its director, Franz Hellens, he also collaborated on *La Revue de Genève* and *La Nouvelle Revue française*. For him, the interest in Freudianism went together with the great questions preoccupying a considerable portion of France's young intellectuals, among which were suicide, the case of Lautréamont, and the adventure of Rimbaud.[6]

The special issue of *Le Disque vert* devoted to psychoanalysis enjoyed a lively success to the extent that Hellens managed to assemble between the same covers prestigious names from the fields of literature and medicine. For once, writers and doctors were seated alongside each other.

The issue began with a letter from Freud paying homage to Charcot. Then came articles by Hesnard, Laforgue, Allendy, Clarapède, Henri Claude, Lenormand, Valéry Larbaud, Jean Paulhan, Ramon Fernandez, Marcel Arland, then testimony from Georges Duhamel, Philippe Soupault, Jacques de Lacretelle, and Albert Thi-baudet. Considered in its entirety, the issue expressed rather well what was at stake in the 1920s battle over Freudianism. Some condemned an ephemeral fad or de-fended the seriousness of a genuine doctrine; others opted for therapeutics against science; still others continued to affirm commonplaces about the unconscious or the Teutonic spirit. All the authors spoke abundantly about sexuality.

We should take note of two original articles by Edmond Jaloux and René Crevel. Adapting for his own use the theses of national psychology, Jaloux at-tempted to demonstrate the causes for French resistance to psychoanalysis. He ex-plained that his compatriots manifested their unconscious productions rather less frequently than Slavs, Scandinavians, or Anglo-Saxons. He then added that Protes-tantism was favorable to the expressiveness of the unconscious and that the cases described by Havelock Ellis would have been inadmissible in the country of Des-cartes. Jaloux situated antipansexualism identically: In his view, the French liked pleasure too much to experience "that profound straying of the individual under the pressure of sexual instincts characterizing the illnesses studied by foreign neurolo-gists."[7]

The text shows that the medical world was not alone in France in situating the unconscious in terms of racial ideals. Unlike Henry Claude or Hesnard, Jaloux did not maintain the thesis of a superiority of Latinate genius, but preached on the contrary an opening of French culture to foreign cultures. Within his antichauvinism, he remained indebted to a conception of the unconscious alien to Freud's.

René Crevel, for his part, wrote a superb text in praise of Freudianism, capable, in his view, of bringing man back to his true sexual instinct. He noted that the modern era tended to speak of love in terms of sexuality, thus issuing a challenge to the grandiloquence of the romantics. By way of Gide and Socrates, the poet paid homage to homosexuality and implied that he too, like the Jews, belonged to an "accursed race," destined perpetually to invert the laws of normality. "What was most imperious in us was forgotten," he wrote, "and for that negligent omission the influence of Christianity, which is in this case the influence of Judaism itself, must be blamed. The Jewish race was always afraid of the violence of its appetites, of its animal odor; but the fragrance of incense has never been able to conceal the odor of the sexes. That is why Jesus vomited up the lukewarm and said of Mary Magdalene: 'She will be forgiven much for much has she loved.' For him greatness alone was holy, and therein lay his divinity. . . . As for Freud, he is not doing anything more than recognizing the force of that path of Love when, speaking the daily idiom of a man of science, he establishes the undeniable influence of the sexual impulses. Ethically, his conclusion is thus that every individual, after having discovered his norm, ought to accept it always." [8]

Three months later, in the heat of a summer train ride, André Gide was browsing through an issue of *Le Disque vert*. No doubt he was thinking of the poet's curious praise of Freud when he wrote in his journal a sentence destined to become famous: "Ah! How irritating Freud is. . . . What he brings us above all is having accustomed readers to hearing certain subjects discussed without having to blush. What he brings us above all is his daring, or, more precisely, what he relieves us of is a certain false and irritating modesty. But how many absurd things there are in that imbecile of genius!" [9]

The notion of a priority of the literary channel was defended by the writers themselves around 1920. Most of them bragged of being first to have discovered Freud's work. It will thus be seen that historians of the analytic movement were not alone in espousing that questionable notion. They merely repeated, after the fact, what men of letters were elaborating at the time of the introduction of Freudianism in France. That claim should be understood as symptomatic of the conflicts emerging between various writers, on the one hand, and between the literary and medical channels, on the other.

Generally speaking, the world of French literature was somewhat ahead of its medical counterpart in its idea of Freud's discovery. During the same period, there emerged two ways of apprehending Freudianism, one of which expressed better than the other, as if in anticipation, what psychoanalysis would become after 1945. Within that literary world, the Surrealists themselves were in advance of other conceptualizations of Freudianism; they found themselves, that is, in the vanguard of a movement that would only bear its fruits much later in the psychoanalytic community.

    While the medical milieu of the 1920s remained attached to the epistemolog-
ical ideals of the end of the nineteenth century, the literary milieu was, on the contrary, traversed by that current of new thinking that made it well suited—even if
only out of "snobbery"—to detect the loci of modernity within Freud's discovery.
That discovery belonged to the two centuries it happened to straddle. In being
rooted in the romantic tradition, it remained marked by its origins, but in its theoretical advances, it was located at the center of the great inquiries haunting the
cultural domain of the 1920s. Following the interwar period, it reappeared as a
major phenomenon in the spread of whatever was most crucially at stake in modernity.

    There was thus a gap between the literary and the medical channel. In that
perspective, a discontinuity should be noted between the "medical" generation of
the founders of the SPP and the literary milieu, on the one hand, then another between the second generation (to which Jacques Lacan belonged) and the first. One
sees then that within that second generation there coexisted representations of
Freudianism as divergent as those existing between the generation of the founders
and the literary channel. In other words, the conflicts that opposed the writers to
the founders would create opposition among the psychoanalysts of the second generation, notably Sacha Nacht, Daniel Lagache, and Jacques Lacan. There would
thus emerge around 1947 two antagonistic representations of Freudianism, one centered on lay analysis, the other on medical practice. The stakes of that new battle
will be comprehensible only if they are related to the interwar period—that is, to
the conceptions of Freudianism which were already dividing the founders, on the
one side, from the literati, on the other.

    From a strictly chronological point of view, it would seem that the honor of
having mentioned Freud for the first time in a literary journal falls to Guillaume
Apollinaire.

    In 1914, in his column for the *Mercure de France,* Apollinaire included an
observation about the Otto Gross affair.[10] The poet learned of the episode from his
friend Blaise Cendrars, who had discovered psychoanalysis in the course of his travels in Austria, Germany, and Switzerland.[11] Before becoming a writer, Cendrars had
been enrolled as a student at the medical school of the University of Berne. Although
he abandoned his medical studies, he nonetheless continued to be interested in questions of psychology and sexuality. His knowledge of psychiatry was sufficiently extensive to allow him to keep Apollinaire informed of work in that field. He himself
rejected psychoanalysis, which he accused of "hairsplitting," and which he also reproached for its acrobatic recourse to symbolism. In *L'homme foudroyé* ["Thunder-
struck man"], he wrote: "If psychoanalysis had interested me, I could have written
a major essay or a brochure to popularize that theory in France. But I didn't believe
in it. Upon my return from Germany, where I had been able to observe myself the
ravages it had caused among the intellectuals of Vienna and Munich . . . , I said just
enough on the subject to Guillaume Apollinaire to furnish him with material for a
copious echo." [12] Cendrars' position here joined that of the "French majority," which
reproached Freud for his excessive symbolism and the ill effects of his therapy.

    Like Cendrars or Romain Rolland, Paul Morand boasted of having been the first in France to have discovered psychoanalysis. "My wife's brother," he said in 1964, "had been treated in Basel in 1915. I was the first Frenchman to know what psychoanalysis was. Long before Jules Romains spoke of it in the *NRF* in 1922, we were a small group in London who made frequent use at the time of the new words: extroverted, introverted, complex, etc., around 1917." [13] Assigned to the embassy in London between 1912 and 1916, Morand claimed he had applied the lessons of the new psychology in his first book, *Tendre Stocks* [*Fancy Goods*], published in 1921. Concerning this point, David Steel has remarked that the author's tales of worldliness belong more to the neurasthenic taste of the end of the nineteenth century than to the Freudian epic.

Paul Bourget, on the other hand, was truly interested in psychoanalysis. A writer of considerable mediocrity, but quite famous in his day, he was enamored of psychiatry. In his youth he had dreamed of studying medicine, and Apollinaire mocked him in his column, "I learned that this important writer was passionately involved with the insane." The poet related how Bourget would go to an asylum and meticulously observe the deranged, while taking notes. [14] Connected with numerous psychologists and a friend of the psychiatrist Ernest Dupré, he quickly familiarized himself with psychoanalysis and introduced the name of Freud into his novel *Némésis* in 1918. He labeled him a "psychiatrist," forgetting his training as a neurologist. Concerning a heroine whose husband had just died, he wrote, "The young woman had received one of those blows for which one of the most original of modern psychiatrists, the Viennese Freud, has created the barbarous but expressive term: trauma." [15] Speaking as well from the perspective of precedence, Henri Daniel-Rops observed in 1926 that Bourget was one of the first French writers to recognize Freud's work. "It does not seem useless on this occasion," he wrote, "to inform those youngsters who rather unjustly suspect Monsieur Bourget that that novelist was aware of the theses of Dr. Freud and paid homage to them at a time when one was not a Freudian out of snobbery." [16]

Two years after the publication of *Némésis*, Bourget again made use of Freudian theses to explain the behavior of one of his characters. In an anthology of short stories whose title, *Anomalies*, evoked the heyday of heredity-degeneration there is a tale entitled "La maison de Saint-Cloud." Much as Maupassant had done in the past, Bourget has a case history recounted by a psychiatrist, here named Courriolles. A pathetic tailor succumbs to a state of sleepwalking after having visited a strange residence endowed with demonic powers. Following that episode, he traverses the city in search of objects to furnish the house of his dreams. Before long he lapses into a madness which Bourget calls "cerebral arteriosclerosis." After what appears to be an initial recovery, he attempts to murder his psychiatrist. Here is the style with which the unfortunate Bourget invokes the "Viennese theories": "Just how long did that sort of psychic ictus last? Dupin was aware of it only since the evening chill had set in. I have just used a rather pedantic term. Excuse me for using two more in order to make myself clear to Professor Freud, the Viennese psychiatrist. . . ." [17]

The most amusing aspect of the whole business was that before submitting his manuscript to the publisher, Bourget felt the irresistible need for scientific endorsement. He asked his friend Dupré to add a few clinical commentaries to the volume. The psychiatrist obliged him, and the novelist incorporated his observations at the end of the collection. The result of that operation was both comic and disastrous. What may be retained from the adventure is that Bourget's sole contribution to the spread of Freudian ideas in France was the one that allowed Eugenie Sokolnicka to meet Professor Heuyer.[18]

Like Paul Morand, Henri Lenormand discovered psychoanalysis thanks to his travels. Stricken with tuberculosis, he was treated in the famous sanatorium at Davos, where periodically a large number of intellectuals, notably René Crevel, would meet. There, he was taken with the actress Rose Vallerest, who became his mistress. She found it difficult to tolerate their relationship and went to consult with a "psychologist from Kusnacht" who was remarkably similar to C. G. Jung.[19] Her therapy ended in the separation of the lovers. Jealous, Lenormand drew on the incident to write a sentimental drama entitled *Le Mangeur de rêves* ["The dream-devourer"]. The play was produced in Geneva in 1922, then revived in Paris a few months later. Its resounding success turned Lenormand into the traveling salesman of the Freudian fashion.

The plot involves a jazz-age charlatan named Luc de Bronte and his mistress, Miss Fearon, a compulsively deluded Englishwoman out of a Charles Morgan novel. Bronte takes care of a fragile young girl, Jeanine, who lost her parents in childhood during an ambush by Moroccan thieves. Naturally, he falls for her and she does not resist the ardor of a transferential love that fills her with joy. As a result, a repressed memory emerges from the shadows: The girl worshiped her father and detested her mother. The jealous Fearon learns of this and slips a loaded pistol into her rival's hand. The melodrama ends with the suicide of the poor patient and the damnation of the dream-devourer.

In Geneva and Paris, the story caused quite a sensation. But the reactions were not the same. The Swiss insisted on the play's contents, while the French were more sensitive to the problem of the "influence" of psychoanalysis on literature. Journalists felt that they had found in the play the final word on the relations between Freud's ideas and artistic creation. The odor of scandal stemmed from the fact that the play recounted something more than a mere sentimental adventure; it revealed in broad daylight behavior that the psychoanalytic movement was accustomed to concealing and which concerned the twofold question of suicide and love relations between a therapist and his patient.

Henri Lenormand, Édouard Claparède, and Sabina Spielrein were not wrong. The play's program contained a declaration asking the audience not to confuse Freudian doctrine and the errors of a practitioner. "It would be a mistake," we read, "to interpret this work as a demonstration or a refutation of the famous doctrine. The failure of an individual is not that of a method which has already proved its worth."[21]

Claparède presented the play as a new and audacious undertaking. In his address, he paid homage to the late Flournoy, who had died two years before, and underscored France's backwardness compared to Switzerland on the subject of psychoanalysis. Finally, he went directly to his subject and issued a defense of "true psychology" against charlatanism: "At bottom," he said, "I am not too sure what I want to accomplish here. (Psychology is an extremely honorable profession.) For I am forced to admit that Monsieur Lenormand has done an admirable job of drama-tizing psychoanalysis, and after reading his play, I felt like writing a scene for him, that is, adding a tenth scene to the *Mangeur de reves* in which psychology and psychologists would be rehabilitated." [22]

Echoing Claparède's sentiments, Spielrein published an article in *Le Journal de Genève* entitled "Qui est l'auteur du crime?" [23] in which she offered an allegedly psychoanalytic reading of the play. In her view, Fearon revealed Luc's unconscious, that is, the unbound instincts he could no longer master. She compared "true" psy-chologists with "bad" cure-mongers and emphasized the playwright's talent. Was it that the story awakened a memory for Sabina? She had found herself in an identical situation when she became Jung's mistress during her analysis. And "good" Freud saved her from the "nasty" seducer. [24] For her, as for Claparède, the drama was a chance to denounce, through denial, practices that existed in all analytic communi-ties.

In Paris, things took a different turn. The play was performed four years prior to the foundation of the SPP, at a time when ethical problems were not raised at an institutional level. *Le Mangeur de rêves* was received above all as a literary event. François Mauriac treated Lenormand with the same scorn he reserved for Raymond Roussel, and hastened to observe that the playwright had given a perfect illustration of the ideas of a "German man of science." "Throughout these nine scenes," he wrote, "he forces reality to conform to the views of a German scientist. The artifi-ciality of it all is so flagrant that the entire drama, which might have had pathos, seems icy." [25] Jacques Rivière, for his part, knew that Austria was not Germany, and that true literature belongs to those able to write it. He subtly denigrated the play and explained what a true relation between literature and psychoanalysis ought to be: "Monsieur Lenormand's *Le Mangeur de rêves* by itself does not demonstrate that influence. Moreover, should it ever be exercised . . . , it would be, I believe, in a far less literal manner—simply by giving a new orientation to the writer or nov-elist's attention." [26]

Lenormand did not distinguish himself through any predilection for the in-novative. No doubt he recognized Freud's genius, but his attitude toward Dada and the Surrealists was always quite foolish. In 1920, he called the Dadaists neurotics and proposed that they undergo psychoanalysis. Breton and Picabia, of course, im-mediately replied by calling the author an imbecile and a malevolent one at that. [27]

In 1927, he paid a visit to Freud on the occasion of the performance of a new play in Vienna. He brought him a box of chocolates on behalf of a disciple of his from Zurich. Later on, Lenormand recounted the meeting and observed that the scientist did not fail to recognize the meaning of *Le Mangeur de rêves:* " 'It's a play. . . . Hmmm. . . . Oh! how witty!' he said." Freud then escorted him into his library to show him volumes of Shakespeare and the Greek tragedians. " 'These are my masters,' he exclaimed. 'These are my references!' " [28] Freud received Lenormand far more amiably than he had Breton, as though he were constantly fearful of con-fronting true poets. At no point did he take the minor author seriously, and that because he did not disturb the organization of his identifications. In Lenormand's presence, he did not hesitate to see himself as the Sophocles of modern times, but facing a talented poet, even a Dadaist, he was seized by a feeling of fear and strangeness. With Breton, as previously with Schnitzler, he feared seeing his double, the dangerous image of an "other" capable of robbing his ideas or surpassing them.

II. Love Letters

While Freud avoided responding to Breton's advances and could not have cared less about Lenormand, he sought to establish a relation with Romain Rolland. Everything would seem to separate the two men, who would nonetheless fall for each other. Rolland was as much of a music lover as Freud was insensitive to that art. He was as mystical as his friend was irreligious. Finally, he preferred heroes of the heart to great theorists. The Viennese's delight in him was of a strange nature. Freud did not admire Rolland as a master or a conqueror; what he was attracted to in him was above all the ideologue, the pacifist, the celebrity, the generous author of the articles collected under the title *Au-dessus de la mêlée* and published in 1915 [published in English as *Above the Battle* (1916)].

In the middle of the war, while Freud was meditating on death and the destructive drives, Rolland attempted to give the voice of love, justice, tolerance, and the reconciliation of peoples a hearing. He preached friendship among nations and was scornful of Germanophobia. For that reason he was abundantly detested by French public opinion, but attracted much sympathy among the intelligentsia. Awarded the Nobel prize in 1916, he was already fascinated by Indian thought, whose wisdom seemed to him to contrast with what he considered the bankruptcy of European civilization. His passion for eastern religions did not prevent him from being drawn to Soviet Russia. After condemning the revolution, he then rallied to its glories. In 1930, he declared his support for the Communist movement, which he would defend, through the struggle against fascism, until his death.

Freud's love for Rolland was accompanied by a certain unconscious rivalry. The writer was ten years younger than the analyst. He had received the celebrated Nobel prize that Freud, despite the maneuvers of Marie Bonaparte, would never get. Somewhat in spite of himself, the Viennese admired the celebrities of his day. He loved Rolland in the same way as he would have a soft spot for his dear princess. Whence the thrust of the incredible letter he sent to Monod-Herzen, one day in 1923: "Since you are a friend of Romain Rolland," he wrote, "may I ask you to pass on to him a word of respect from an unknown admirer?"[29]

The illustrious unknown admirer angled his line in such manner that the fish bit the bait. Rolland sent Freud a letter in which he boasted of being one of the first Frenchmen to know his works. He compared Freud to Christopher Columbus and noted that psychology and literature were better suited than medicine to profit from the conquests of psychoanalysis.[30] Like the crow in the La Fontaine fable, Freud could not resist the flattery and dropped his cheese. "Until the end of my life," he wrote, "I will remember the joy of having entered into relations with you, for your name is linked for me to the most beautiful of illusions: the joining of all the children of men in a common love. I belong, of course, to a race that the Middle Ages made responsible for every national epidemic and that the modern world has accused of having led the Austrian Empire to its decline and Germany to defeat. Such experiences are sobering and make one little inclined to believe in illusions. In addition, throughout my life (I am ten years your senior), an important part of my work has consisted in destroying my own illusions and those of humanity." [31]

Thus was their moving correspondence launched. Following their first exchange, the two men decided to meet. In Vienna, at 9:00 P.M., on a Thursday in May 1924, Freud and Rolland sipped a China tea and sampled chocolate pastries in the presence of the ladies of the house, Anna and the rest. The two friends would never see each other again, but would continue to send each other affectionate letters and to exchange their books. Some time later, Freud would confess a great sadness and his wish "to take leave of life." He again declared his passion to his friend: "You are unforgettable. At the cost of how much pain and what suffering have you succeeded in rising to such a height of humanity! In you I had revered the artist and the apostle of human love. . . ." [32] Three months later, Rolland responded to Freud in comparable terms: "May the light of your mind pierce the night of life! And for you, peace of body and joy of thought!" [33]

The word "unforgettable" would be much commented on. Theodor Reik would resent the passion binding the two men and reproached Freud for having written in the *Neue Freie Presse* that Rolland was incomparable [*unvergleichlicher*] and thus that he had no equal in the master's heart. In a letter dated February 1926, Freud set things straight. Not without humor he remarked to Reik that he had not used the term "incomparable," but the word "unforgettable" [*unvergesslicher*], which sounds similar in German. Then he added, "Despite your own admission of propensities toward vengefulness, I regard you as a man of good will and disposition, and it is for that reason that I dare entrust to your indulgence my weaknesses and shortcomings." [34]

The correspondence between Freud and Rolland was not limited to the expression of their mutual love. It also dealt with their divergences on the subject of religion. Freud had recourse to certain of Rolland's remarks in shading his critique of illusions. In 1927, he sent the writer a copy of *The Future of an Illusion*. After reading it, Rolland wrote to him: "Your analysis of religions is correct. But I would have liked to see you undertake the analysis of the spontaneous religious sentiment, or more exactly of the religious sensation, which is something quite different from religions in the strict sense and is much more durable." [35] The writer called that religious sensation, which existed in the great Asiatic mystics and in various Christian doctrines, the "oceanic feeling." In his view, it could regenerate a humanity entered into decadence if it were not captured and dessicated by churches from which true religiosity had disappeared.

Freud answered his friend that the notion of an oceanic sensation left him "restless." At the time, he was working on *Civilization and Its Discontents* and asked Rolland permission to allude to their private correspondence. [36] Flattered by the attention, the writer gave his assent, "It is entirely within your right to bring these questions before a broad public, and I by no means have any thought of evading my responsibility in the matter." [37] In addition, he informed Freud of his forthcoming book on the subject,[38] whereupon Freud shot back: "I learned with pleasure that your book is to appear before my little work, which it will not be possible to publish before February or March. But don't expect any assessment of the 'oceanic feeling.' I am doing my best, on the contrary, to distance myself from the feeling by analyzing it. I have removed it, so to speak, from my path. How foreign the worlds in which you travel are to me! Mysticism is as closed to me as music."[39] Rolland reproached Freud for distrusting music the better to keep his critical faculty intact. Finally, *Civilization and Its Discontents* appeared before the writer's three volumes and Freud, without mentioning Rolland's name, spoke of an "honored friend" and the discomfort he felt at the notion of an oceanic feeling. He claimed never to have discovered such a sensation in himself and a few lines later quoted a book by Grabbe on Hannibal in which the poet has his hero say: "Plainly we shall never fall outside this world. If we are here, it is once and for all."[40]

Then Freud launched into a long digression on the status of the ego followed by considerations on the city of Rome—its archeological strata, its great emperors. Returning to "his friend," he demolished the thesis of an oceanic feeling by demonstrating that that feeling was rooted in an infantile desire for paternal protection which took the form of a quest for the great whole of things. He confessed to being "uneasy" and quoted "another friend" who assured him that in practicing yoga one could manage to arouse a sense of universality within oneself. At the conclusion of his first chapter, he wrote: "It would be appropriate at this point to compare these phenomena to other obscure modifications of the soul, such as trances or ecstasy, but I myself am rather inclined to shout out along with Schiller's diver, 'Let him rejoice who breathes up here in the roseate light.'"[41] Hannibal, Schiller, Nero, Jupiter, Hadrian, etc., such are the figures appearing in the text. On the other hand, we do not know who the "other friend" was—someone whose name went as unmentioned by Freud as Rolland's. In any event, in the letter of July 1929, in which Rolland authorized Freud to quote him, he wrote, "Since 1927, I have been able to pursue in depth the oceanic feeling, which I have not only found in innumerable examples among hundreds of our contemporaries, but as well in the (if I may use the words) ritualized and centuries-old physiology codified in treatises of yoga."[42]

The love correspondence came to an end with the publication of Freud's "little work." In January 1930, the analyst cordially thanked the writer for having sent him the three volumes of his great work on Indian mysticism. "Contrary to my calculations," he wrote, "my little work *Civilization and Its Discontents* has preceded it by a few weeks. Under your guidance, I am now trying to penetrate the Hindu jungle, from which until now a certain combination of Hellenic love of proportion, Jewish sobriety, and philistine anxiety had kept me at a distance." A few lines later, he moved to his central concern, Rolland's polemic against "rationalist extremists." After which he added, "The fact that you have called me 'great' I have been able to tolerate; I find it impossible to be offended by your irony when it comes infused with so much amiability."[43]

A fine dialogue indeed! A famous writer uses the words "great man" to refer to a man of science pretending to believe himself less illustrious than the writer and claiming to have wished his own brief text might appear before the major work of his friend, who is not mentioned in the short work even though he had given his authorization to be quoted!

We continue our reading of the correspondence. As in his letters to Breton concerning "precursors," Freud pursued a theoretical argument with Rolland. He attempted to shift the transferential relation onto ground less uncertain for himself and more dangerous for the Frenchman. He reproached Rolland with being a Jungian and Jung with being a mystic. He then explained to his friend that his use of psychoanalytic terminology was inadequate and that the distinction he proposed between the terms "extrovert" and "introvert" was not orthodox. This was followed by solid definitions of narcissism, regression, and several other terms. Freud ended his letter with these words, in which a certain irony toward the notion of reincarnation may be sensed: "If we should ever meet again in this lifetime, it would be extremely interesting to discuss all this. At a distance, a cordial greeting is preferable to a polemic. One thing more. I am not a skeptic. I am completely sure of one thing: that there absolutely do exist certain things which we cannot know at the present time." [44]

Rolland was not fooled by Freud's unconscious rivalry and preferred a theoretical debate to transferential disputes. In March 1930, he asked Charles Baudoin to reproduce in his bulletin his exchanges with Freud on mysticism. "He resisted," he wrote, "condemning either one of the two forms—centripetal or centrifugal—of the mystic spirit. He has displaced the fault onto Jung. . . . That smells of excommunication." [45]

Two months later, Rolland put an end to hostilities, even if it meant erroneously implying that his name had appeared in the "little work." "And allow me to tell you," he wrote to Freud, "(thanking you for having been willing to associate my name with your recent book, *Das Unbehagen in der Kultur*), that it is in its last words ["without desire, without hope, and without fear"] that I feel morally closest to you! Your friendly dedication opposes with an affectionate irony the *Landtier* [land creature] to his "oceanic" friend. That opposition has not only been achieved between two men, but within the same man: myself. I too am a *Landtier* of the French countryside, of the heartland of old France, which seems supremely protected from the breezes of the sea. And I am also an old Frenchman, who sees things without illusion, and who is none the worse off for making do without them. . . . Since the appearance of my three "oceanic" books, I have received from *Landtiere* in every quarter (including your Austria) as though a fount of repressed waters. I have a whole file of letters. And that is why, in history and in practical action, one should always count on those invisible and secretly effective forces when they do not in fact explode in broad daylight." [46]

Touched to the quick by that dispatch, Freud allowed himself to indulge in the mysterious attraction he felt for Rolland: "You have answered my pleasantry," he wrote, "with the most valuable information about your own person. I thank you deeply for it. Rather close to the inevitable end of my life, as a recent operation has reminded me, and knowing I will probably never see you again, I can confess to you that I have rarely felt the enigmatic attraction of one human being for another more vividly than I have in your case. Perhaps it is linked, in a way, to the awareness we have of our differences. Stay well." [47]

It was on those words that the epistolary relation came to an end. In 1936, Freud celebrated Rolland's birthday by writing as a letter his famous text, "A Disturbance of Memory on the Acropolis." It contains a subtle analysis of the problems of transcending the paternal figure and of rivalry between brothers. Athens, Rome, the conquerors, cultural differences, and Judaism are all present, and this time the name of Romain Rolland is in fact featured: "I have long sought a subject that was in some way worthy of you, that might express my admiration for your love of truth, for your courage as a thinker, your humanity, your succoring nature. Or that even might bear witness to my gratitude to the poet to whom I owe so many elevated joys. It was in vain. I am ten years your senior; my production is waning. Finally, all I can offer you is the gift of an impoverished man, who once knew 'better days.' " [48]

"Knowing better days": such were the words Jakob Freud had used when he lost his fur hat and compared former times to the present. At the end of his life, Sigmund would see himself in the features of a father—not deficient, but diminished, despite the glory he had finally attained. [49] Some time later, and following two exchanges of birthday greetings, Madame Rolland wrote to Freud, requesting a manuscript of his for an auction to benefit the Spanish Republicans. The unknown admirer of years past replied in these words, "Attached are two samples of my handwritten work, but do you really think anyone would give money for this?" [50]

III. André Gide and *La Nouvelle Revue française*

Upon arriving in Paris in 1940, Otto Abetz declared that there were three powers in the city: the major banks, the Freemasons, and *La Nouvelle Revue française*. That opinion of the German ambassador gives some notion of the importance taken on by the *NRF* since its founding in 1908. At the time of the collapse of France, literary and cosmopolitan publications were beginning to lose their readership and to be replaced by weeklies giving priority to current events at the expense of creative texts and in-depth articles. But during the entire first half of the century, the name of the *NRF* symbolized the intensity of Parisian cultural life. The journal's success was a function of a particular climate, in which writers enjoyed a measure of recognition they would later lose with the expansion of the human sciences. Paradoxically, in becoming the stars of a system centered on the progress of audiovisual techniques, writers today have lost in elitist prestige what they have gained in media-spawned fame.

Prior to 1940, men of letters were endowed with an omnipotence that was often extravagant. The figures of Voltaire and Zola still haunted the popular mind, and when the nation's affairs turned sour, writers were accused of concealing the plague in their sentences. Thus in *Le Figaro,* which had retreated to Lyon during the summer of 1940, there is a cartoon by Sennep in which a citizen sporting a Basque beret and decorated with a collaborationist *francisque* explains to two agricultural workers the causes for the defeat: "What do you expect? You were reading too much André Gide and Marcel Proust." It was quite conceivable for a peasant in the 1930s to propose Gide's candidacy to replace Léon Blum in representing the masses as head of state. Simultaneously, the *Figaro*'s choice was not innocuous, since it cast the blame on two writers known for their homosexuality. Once again, the "accursed race," like the "Jewish race," was made responsible for the fatherland's disgrace.

In 1911, three years after the founding of the *NRF*, Gaston Gallimard gave his name to the publishing house that emerged from the journal. The logo, designed by Jean Schlumberger, adorned each book and the journal's authors were published by the new house. Starting with the 1920s, the enterprise enjoyed considerable success. The *NRF* and Éditions Gallimard modified French literary life either by imposing new values or following fashions, although these remained both classical and modernist. Bernard Grasset, on the other hand, was already at that time introducing editorial policies that would triumph after the war and would radically transform the status of men of letters. Until his intervention, it was assumed that success naturally accrued to those works whose qualities were recognized by a competent reading public or by the critics. Grasset changed that perspective by breaking with the wait-and-see attitude. His was a policy intended to manufacture the literary event. Considering a book to be a product of the mind like any other piece of merchandise, he created a public relations network replete with dinner parties and house visits in order to ensure the promotion of his publications. The traditional pact between publisher and author was supplanted by a new kind of relation in which the author was not simply content with royalties but insisted that he be attended to, that both his image and his production be a subject of the publisher's attentions. Although his own house was in competition with that of his neighbor, Grasset did not try to found a journal identical to the *NRF*, and it was with Gallimard that he published a book on his conception of the publishing market in 1929.[51]

It may be noted, if only out of anecdotal interest, that psychoanalysis also traversed the literary life of the time: René Laforgue accepted both Bernard Grasset and Marc Schlumberger, the writer's son, in analysis. The latter would become a psychoanalyst and would play a role in the second generation of the SPP.

The *NRF* group's interest in psychoanalysis was as significant as that of the Surrealists. And yet the stakes were entirely different in the two cases. For the writers of the *NRF*, it was less a matter of implementing the Freudian revolution through acts of writing than of reflecting critically on the relations between literature and psychoanalysis. It all began with the extraordinary imbroglio of a lost correspondence between Freud and Gide.

According to Jones, the Frenchman wrote to the Viennese to ask him for permission to translate his works for *NRF* publications. The letter found its way to the addressee, since the historiographer attests to it, but it did not appear in the writer's correspondence, which was published after his death. According to Anna Freud, the letter would have been destroyed at the time the Freud family went into exile in England.[52] What is rather astonishing is that no one knows what became of Freud's reply to Gide, which appears to have disappeared without leaving a trace. During that very year, 1921, Henri Lenormand made a curious declaration to André Lang. He affirmed that Gide was the only writer to manifest an interest in Freud's writings in his work. Gide did not share his colleague's opinion and hastened to issue a denial to Lang. Out of intellectual honesty, he refused to enter into the race for priority so dear to French writers: "I heard of Freud for the first time," he wrote, "last spring. I don't read German with sufficient fluency to have dared approach him in the original, and it was only thanks to the articles of his published in *La Revue de Genève* that I have been able to enter into contact with his thought. I have not yet finished reading his long book [*An Introduction to Psychoanalysis*], the translation of which I awaited impatiently and which no psychologist has the right to overlook."[53] Davis Steel has ascertained that the letter was dated December 26, 1921.

André Gide, moreover, had a protracted correspondence with Dorothy Bussy, the sister of James Strachey, who translated Freud into English and periodically went to Vienna for his analysis.[54] The author met the young woman for the first time during a trip to England in 1918, at a time when he knew nothing of psychoanalysis. But in April 1921, he wrote to her conveying his violent desire to meet Freud: "Your brother knows him, isn't it so, and would not refuse to introduce me to him? There is no hurry by the way, and we'll have time to discuss it again at our next meeting. I am already dreaming of a preface by him for the German translation of *Corydon*, which might well precede the French edition. All this has to be studied. After all, I might well present my book as "translated from the German." That's an idea that just came to me and which I haven't yet examined. The preface by Freud might underscore the book's usefulness and opportuneness."[55]

Dorothy Bussy's reply was not long in coming. The very next day, she wrote: "Freud, how well chosen his name seems this evening! . . . Needless to say, it will be quite easy for you to enter into contact with him. My brother James is in the process of translating one of his books and happens to be in Vienna at this very moment. Nothing would be easier for him than to give you an introduction should you wish it. But how strange it is that you did not discover him sooner—and how amusing! Confirmations one did not expect are the only satisfying ones."[56] Dorothy so admired the two men that she failed to understand Gide's hesitation waltz and could not for a moment conceive of Freud refusing to offer his endorsement of a book that was an apology for pederasty. The writer was both perplexed and impassioned, and on May 2, 1921, he confided his anxiety to one of his friends, Mme Mayrisch. "Do you read Freud?," he wrote to her. "I know only very little of his work at this point and I am quite fearful that his writings may be diffuse and full of redundancies."[57]

After that confession, he requested Dorothy Bussy to ask her brother which book of Freud's was deserving of translation for the *NRF*. In his letter, he no longer spoke of his suggestion of a preface. On June 17, the affair resurfaced: Dorothy transmitted a letter to Gide which her brother had sent to him. The writer thanked her, "Your brother James is exquisite for having replied so explicitly and at such length on the subject of Freud."[58] Nothing more. Strachey's letter seems to have disappeared since it does not figure in the Gide manuscripts deposited at the Bibliothèque nationale.[59] Will the mystery of that strange exchange be clarified some day? In any event, it was on that date, after receiving Strachey's reply, that Gide sent Freud the lost letter mentioned by Jones.

There is good reason to suppose that that reply did not reflect the same enthusiasm as Dorothy had evidenced and that after having read it, Gide limited himself to asking Freud for permission to publish his works in the *NRF*. Even if that hypothesis should prove false, the facts show that after 1921, the Frenchman no longer sought to meet the Viennese. Freud, for his part, was scarcely interested in the literary productions of his phantom interlocutor. Between an epistolary exchange that disappeared and the dream of an impossible preface, Freud's relation with Gide might well resemble a tale by Poe or Maupassant. And yet *Corydon* owed nothing to the genre of the fantastic. Published in 1911 anonymously and in a limited edition, the work was republished in 1920, still anonymously, then a second time in 1924, accompanied by the author's signature.

At the time he was dreaming of a preface by Freud, Gide was still fearful of public shame and hesitated to emerge from the closet. *Corydon* is in the form of a Platonic dialogue between an intellectual who makes no secret of his tastes and one of his former friends wanting to write a book on homosexuality. By way of syllogism and scientific argument, Corydon champions the civilizing virtues of pederasty and rises up against its detractors. The book today has aged a good deal, because the author did not succeed in taking his distance from an apologetic style that impeded any genuine literary innovations. Through his hero, he pretended to erect a hierarchy of homosexualities. In point of fact, he accorded priority to pederasty (the love of children or adolescents) at the expense of "inversion" and sodomy in which he saw a parody of the conjugal relation. In his life as in his work, Gide refused anal sexual intercourse with his partners and defended mutual masturbation, symbolized by the love of the teacher and his disciple. In banishing Sodomites and inverts from his kingdom, he reestablished a norm separating "good" —angelic or pederastic—homosexuality from the "bad" variety, judged to be barbarous. He thus remained attached to a less intolerant conception than that of the traditional "alienists," but one that was almost as normative in its etiological characteristics. He drew, moreover, on the work of physicians of the end of the nineteenth century who classified the entirety of the perversions in the register of degeneration and heredity. Gide's opening consisted in demanding a less hostile look by society at the dark continent of homosexuality.

When Gide addressed his letter to Dorothy Bussy, the *NRF* had already published the first volume of *Sodome et Gomorrhe*. Now Gide did not share Proust's conception of the "accursed race." The author of the *Recherche* constructed a more innovative theory of homosexuality than Gide's, although he too referred to the work of the old "alienists." Proust did not propose any norms and did not establish any hierarchy; he did not preach the civilizing value of homosexuality. He gave, on the contrary, a clinical description of the fate of all inverts: "A race on which there weighs a curse and which must live in mendacity and perjury, since it regards as punishable and shameful, as unspeakable, its desire, which for every creature is life's greatest sweetness." [60]

The narrator compares homosexuality to a Freemasonry and describes its rites and customs at length. He distinguishes the *gregarious,* whose habits are like those of politicians, the *solitary,* a kind of elegant monkey of melancholy gaze, the *zealous,* who preach the usefulness of their practice the way others adhere to anarchism or Zionism, the *philogynous,* who seek the company of women, the *affected,* draped in gowns and made up, the *poorly recovered,* ashamed of their vice, and finally the *gerontophiles,* whose predilection is for elderly gentlemen. Proust ended his presentation with two principal references, one to ancient Greece and the Platonic doctrine of hermaphrodism, the other to Sodom and the posterity of those who fled it.

Gide was not the first in Europe to attempt to lead a struggle against the persecution experienced by homosexuals. Although Krafft-Ebbing and Moebius considered inversion a form of degeneracy or defect, they nevertheless were in favor of a certain juridical impunity. For them, homosexuality was to be condemned when accompanied by rape, public acts of indecency, or the perversion of minors. For what they were essentially against was pedophilia, various forms of sexual violence, and exhibitionism. In 1903, Magnus Hirschfeld, who practiced medicine in Charlottenberg, organized a movement to aid homosexuals and sought to secure a number of reforms of repressive legislation. He based his argument on theoretical writings and published several articles on "intermediary states," in which he attempted to demonstrate the bisexual nature of human anatomy. Ferenczi, before meeting Freud, had courageously supported that effort. He too demanded a reform of the penal code and authored an article drawing on a theory close to Hirschfeld's.[61]

Most generally, and by way of a complex nosology, the various classifications at the time tended to list under a common rubric domains which are presently differentiated. Disturbances relating to sexual identity, such as transsexualism, were poorly distinguished from those involving homosexuality, such as uranism, pederasty, and transvestism.[62] In addition, all sexual "aberrations" were categorized as perversions without any genuine structure being elaborated other than a listing of pathological symptoms. In publishing his *Three Essays* in 1905, Freud attempted to bring some order to those classifications. He gave a structural description of perversion in its relation to neurosis and classified homosexuality among the deviations relating to the sexual object. He then classified those deviations under the rubric of the perversions, showing that the perverse element was part of the very form of human sexuality. The Freudian definition of "normality" or "deviation" excluded all blame or moral judgment. Even if Freud did not participate aggressively in the struggle against the oppression of homosexualities, his doctrine furnished the theoretical means allowing for the development of that struggle.

In *Corydon,* Gide adapted as his own Magnus Hirschfeld's theses on intermediate states and bisexuality. Proust, for his part, drew on an identical conception, even if he did not put it to the same use. The author of the *Recherche* never read a line of Freud's works, just as the latter knew nothing of Proust's novel. Proust, however, made use of a vocabulary and a descriptive style closely linked with the medical discourse of the end of the century. The writer belonged to a family that distinguished itself through its contribution to the clinical knowledge of the era.

Dr. Adrien Proust, Marcel's father and a student of Charcot's, practiced hypnosis and was interested in hygienically preventive techniques. In 1897, he published, in collaboration with Gilbert Ballet, a work on the treatment of neurasthenia, in which he gave a rather astonishing description of the negative effects of social life. Borrowing from Spencer his evolutionist conception of pedagogy, he advocated the establishment of a kind of code of physical morality. He recommended that the "nervous" treat themselves by taking walks, running races, playing "prisoner's base," and jumping rope. On the subject of individual upbringing, Adrien Proust regarded the apprenticeship of the heart as more important than that of the intelligence. He would spend his life traveling and organizing the struggle against various epidemics, work-related diseases, pollution, and diverse forms of intoxication. His son Robert also chose a medical career. Abandoning preventive techniques and social reforms, he became a surgeon, then specialized in research relating to sexuality and the genital apparatus. In 1901, he performed the first successful prostate operation in France. He then moved on to andrology, then gynecology, and treated the celebrities of the day, while frequenting the salons his brother would describe in his book. An assistant to the celebrated Dr. Pozzi, he became interested early on in sexual anomalies and, by 1912, had reported on several cases of hermaphroditism.[63]

The manner in which Marcel Proust depicted homosexuality was not foreign to this family tradition in which preventive medicine and sexual ambiguity formed the two poles of a thematic present in *La recherche du temps perdu*. The hygienic-preventive ideal of Dr. Adrien turns into its opposite in the narrator's fascination at recounting the splendors and miseries of social life. As for Robert's discourse on hermaphroditism, it becomes in Marcel's writing a nonbiological vision of the different forms of sexual inversion.

In the course of three lectures delivered at the Théâtre du Vieux-Colombier, Jacques Rivière compared at length Proust's work to that of Freud. He noted that the scientist and the writer had each discovered the unconscious in his own way and that their two doctrines allowed for a new orientation in the study of psychology. Without discussing homosexuality, he observed that Proust's writing effected a novelistic translation of Freudian discourse. He confirmed the fact that the two men had not known each other. "There is, first of all," he said, "the ignorance in which they both lived of each other. Even if Freud at present (something I am far from sure of) has read Proust, it is quite clear that he could in no way have been influenced by him in his discoveries. In addition, I know that Proust was aware of no more than Freud's name and perhaps the general thrust of his doctrine. But he had only come to be informed of them quite recently, and I can state that it did not result in any influence on his work."[64]

According to Rivière, Proust invented a "Freudian" theory of desire by advocating a psychology of love rooted in the polymorphous and a method of analysis centered on a complete reconstruction of psychical life. The lecturer compared the concept of repression to the "intermittences of the heart," and situated Proust's scientific appetite in terms of Kepler, Claude Bernard, and Auguste Comte. Rivière's voluminous talk showed to what an extent the publication of the *Recherche* had provoked a rift in the cultural ideals of the period. Rivière avoided any comparison between Proust's work and Bergson's endeavors. In his eyes, Freud and Proust had taken an identical scene as their object: the soul, time, memory, sex, etc.

Within *La recherche,* homosexuality occupies as important a place as the

Dreyfus Affair. But unlike Gide, Proust did not conceive of literature as the transparent expression of the author's biography. He did not transcribe his life in his work; he transformed his life into a literary work. Whereas Proust was both Jewish and a homosexual, the narrator was Christian and courted women. Both were Dreyfusards, but the book was ultimately not concerned with the question of the captain's innocence or guilt. It described the positions of characters and their coteries in relation to the Affair in a world in which belonging to a caste was more important than the search for truth. It was the same with homosexuality. Proust did not write a plea on behalf of inverts; he related the fate of a group and the ruses it resorted to in order to survive in a hostile society. He did not freeze homosexuality in a catalogue of instincts, but organized it around the proliferation of its desires.

Gide, on the contrary, remained attached to an instinctual conception of homosexuality and of sexuality in general. In publishing *Corydon,* he sought desperately for a scientific endorsement, as though the literary value of a work were not sufficient in itself. In dreaming of a preface by Freud, he thus adopted a particularly perverse pose: Under the guise of a book, he was offering his "case" to the examination of psychoanalysis, all in order to advance what he took to be a militant struggle on behalf of pederasty and which was no more than the expression of his own exhibitionism. The matter did not stop there. Instead of contacting Freud—who never neglected to reply to celebrities—directly, he proceeded indirectly. By way of two women, in fact, who might serve as intermediaries—one because she was the sister of James Strachey, the other because she was his confidant. The inquiry concerning the phantom preface thus occurred in inverted form and negative syntax. To Dorothy Bussy, Gide explained that *Corydon* could be presented to the French public as "translated from the German"—that is, as coming from a foreign place and an unknown author. To Mme Mayrisch, he wrote the following astonishing sentence, "Certain passages [in Freud] had led me to suspect that he would not be averse to my asking him for a preface." In its positive version, the utterance meant: "led me to suppose that he would accept my asking him. . . ." Gide made frequent use of formulas of that sort, but this is particularly strained in its complication. Did the writer doubt that Freud would accept, as his hesitation waltz leads one to believe, or did he expect that his interlocutor would answer favorably, as he appears to have believed? In either case, Gide's sentence seems to anticipate, in its very form, the refusal of the scientist—to whom a request would never in fact have been made. A negative hallucination? disavowal? denial? denegation? Whichever is of little import. The letters have disappeared, bearing witness through their loss to the impossible request of the sender and the negative response of the addressee.

A letter was indeed received by Freud, according to Jones. At present, we do not know the answer, which might have informed us as to the contents of the request. But one thing is clear: Freud always refused to analyze artists and would certainly not have accepted to give his backing to a work of Gide's. Not out of puritanism, but in order not to transform a living writer into an object of clinical inspection. It may be hypothesized that Strachey's letter to Dorothy was to that effect and that Gide as a result simply asked Freud for permission to have his works translated for the *NRF.*

The sequel to those events is quite interesting. In 1923, Gallimard published the *Three Essays on the Theory of Sexuality* in a translation by Blanche Reverchon-Jouve, with whom Bernard Groethuysen had collaborated. Who was it that chose that work? Freud, Gide, Reverchon-Jouve, or chance? In any event, it opened with Freud's presentation of the psychoanalytic doctrine on homosexuality which Gide had dreamed of having as a preface for *Corydon*.

In 1922, the publication of the text was announced in a note by Ramon Fernandez in the *NRF*. "It is impossible after Freud," he wrote, "to implicate . . . perversions and inverts in a crusade against nature . . . , perversion being the normal state of the most natural age. Normal love, on the contrary, the result of a difficult integration of sexual tendencies, marks the always chance success of a fragile equilibrium perpetually in need of being reestablished." [65] The French press gave the book an unfavorable reception, quite unlike the one reserved for the *Introduction* two years earlier. Infantile sexuality, the perversions, and the transformations of puberty offered the image of a dark realm which only the literary milieu of the period could embrace with any enthusiasm. It is a commonplace to note that homosexuals are more common among creative individuals than elsewhere and that childhood courses through various forms of inventive writing. In any event, with the works of Proust, Gide, and Crevel, there began to emerge in France a new representation of homosexuality which coincided with the exacerbated vision of femininity appealed to by the Surrealists.

Unlike Gide, and without taking up the idea of an "accursed race," Freud offered a description of the continent of homosexualities as broad and as innovative as the period could dream of. A year later, Gide finally dared to publish the definitive version of *Corydon* with a preface of his own vintage. "A number of books," he wrote, "those of Proust in particular, have accustomed the public to take less offense and to dare consider calmly what it pretended not to notice or at first preferred not to notice. . . . And I can see today that one of the great faults of my book is precisely not to deal with them [sodomy and inversion]—which turn out to be far more common than I had first thought." [66]

Gide's personal interest in Freudian doctrine coincided with that of the *NRF* group for psychoanalysis. In April 1921, Albert Thibaudet published in the pages of the journal a rather interesting article in which he took a positive view of the relations between Freudianism and literary criticism. In 1922, Jules Romains, for his part, denounced in humorous terms and with a certain nastiness the "Freud season" in Paris and salon psychoanalysis. As for Jean Paulhan, it was only in 1924, in *Le Disque vert,* that he expressed certain reservations about the theory from Vienna, a year before succeeding Jacques Rivière at the head of the *NRF.*[67]

In the fall of 1921, the group welcomed Eugénie Sokolnicka with genuine fervor. She organized her teaching in a series of weekly sessions held at her home. André Gide, Jacques Rivière, Roger Martin du Gard, Gaston Gallimard, and Jean Schlumberger attended those meetings, taking an active role in the clinical and theoretical discussions. The group was nicknamed (on the model of the *Salon des refusés*) the "Club des refoulés [Club of the repressed]," and Eugénie, who was known as "la Doctoresse," personified the Unconscious and Psychoanalysis. Gide began an analysis with her. During the sixth session, he found the work involved bothersome and abandoned it. But the Polish woman would serve as a model, in 1925, for a character in *Les faux-monnayeurs!*[68]

In its technique of infinite regression, the book anticipated the procedures of the "new novel." It consisted of an objective narrative and a first-person journal written by a novelist, Édouard, who was attempting to write a novel entitled *Les faux-monnayeurs*. A certain "doctoress" named Sophroniska is treating young Boris de la Pérouse during a summer stay in Saas-Fée. Raised by a quite authoritarian Russian mother, the child believes that his masturbatory practices have caused the death of his father. For two years, he carries around with him a bit of parchment enclosed in a bag, on which are written five talismanic words serving as a magical entry to a sexual paradise. When the story begins, Boris is thirteen years old. He entrusts Sophroniska with his talisman, and she is convinced of her therapeutic success. In the narrative of the treatment, Gide drew on the famous case presented by Sokolnicka to the *NRF* group and already published in 1920 in the *IZP* [Internationale Zeitschrift für ärztliche Psychoanalyse].[69]

In treating a child's obsessional neurosis, Sokolnicka had used the technique of confession and shortened therapy. Gide, however, transformed her therapeutic success into a failure and displaced the case history onto his own childhood. He had once been expelled from the École alsacienne for his "shameful" practices. His parents brought him to consult Brouardel, a disciple of Charcot's, who threatened him quite ludicrously with castration. Later on, he again encountered the field of medicine in less traumatic circumstances when a practitioner counseled him to marry as a cure for his "vices." In *Les faux-monnayeurs,* Sophroniska occupies the place of that terrifying, consoling and fascinating medical science against which the novelist deployed his fierce irony. The "doctoress" commits grave errors. Not only does she believe in Boris's cure, but she allows herself to be misled by the sinister Strouvilhou, an infernal member of the Confraternity of the Strong, to whom she confides the child's talisman. When Boris sees that his fetish is in the hands of the sect, he attempts to save his honor by playing Russian roulette. Only Ghéridanisol, another member of the band, knows that the pistol contains a bullet. When the moment comes, Boris aims the weapon at his forehead and falls dead on the floor.

Sophroniska, as a character, is quite moving. She loses two children: her daughter Bronja, who dies of tuberculosis, and the young La Pérouse, whom she accepts for treatment. Gide ended the analysis he failed to undertake with a novel, just as he had admitted, through *Corydon,* the "failure" of a book on homosexuality and the "success" of his pederasty. But *Les faux-monayeurs* is a book marked by the seal of failure; it presents an author who cannot manage to write a novel and who is satisfied to write a journal. The Gidean novel was the "completed novel of a failed novel." [70] It was also the writer's sole attempt at a novel. Gide's therapy was thus related to the elaboration of a book whose theme was the implementation of a death sentence. In killing Boris, the author eliminated not the phantasmal childhood which reigned within him, but the child he had been in his sad existence. At the same time, he also killed off Bronja, *alias* Madeleine Rondeaux, the young cousin with whom, as an adult, he had contracted a marriage that was never to be consummated. Symbolically, Sophroniska underwent the same fate: Despite her talents, she is defeated by Boris's therapy. The actual Sokolnicka had received from Gide, in the course of their six sessions, an admission, a talisman, a secret concerning childhood and sex. In the book, the writer ended his simulacrum of an analysis by "liquidating" the recipient of his confidences through the failure of the "doctoress."

Two children died in the novel while an actual child was born in reality. In July 1922, at the time Gide was beginning his imaginary initiatives to secure a preface from Freud, he asked Elizabeth Van Rysselberghe, the daughter of the "petite Dame," for permission to impregnate her. One more attempt to get backing for another project, relating to origins, to proof, to traces. The young woman accepted the proposition and gave birth the following year to a daughter who was named Catherine. She would be recognized by her father in 1938, after Madeleine's death. Gide thus simultaneously preserved his pederasty, his Platonic love for his wife, and his paternal position. The gain was not unaccompanied by loss, whence the three deaths in a novel that itself marked the birth of a new form of writing, distinct from the *sotie* or the journal.

Following the publication of *Les faux-monnayeurs,* a polemic irrupted, and in the appendix to the *Journal des faux-monnayeurs,* Gide reproduced the letter of an indignant reader who accused him of plagiarizing Saint-Simon in describing the illness of the aged La Pérouse, Boris's grandfather. The writer responded with mockery. "I add with a blush," he wrote, "that I did not yet know the passage from Saint-Simon and I take the greatest pleasure in reading it. . . . I fail to understand how the merit of a work of art can be diminished because it is based on reality. That is why I thought it useful to give the incidents that served as points of departure for my book in an appendix to the *Journal des faux-monnayeurs.*"[71] One more confession. . . .

Gide made numerous pronouncements on the sources he drew on in writing his novel, but he said nothing of his borrowings from the "doctoress." She, for her part, abstained from claiming "paternity" for young Boris even though his story resembled in detail the case history published in the *IZP.* She would have had all the more reason to protest in that Gide had made into a failure what had been presented as an exceptional success. She no doubt understood that the writer was using a book to confess the secret of his analysis, even while pretending to transpose the actual case history of a case of childhood neurosis. This time, the talisman did not disappear since we know nothing of Gide's therapy with Sokolnicka except that he began "cutting" sessions he judged to be too "tedious." We would merely venture that the failure of that novelistic analysis did not play any role in Eugénie Sokolnicka's subsequent suicide.[72]

In 1956, the year of the centenary of Freud's birth, Professor Jean Delay published an enormous work in two volumes devoted to the youth of André Gide. The author of *Corydon* was thus to have his dream realized: Posthumously, he had become an object of clinical inspection. Jacques Lacan was not wrong. Paying tribute to Delay's talent, he wrote: "The work of Proust himself does not authorize one to challenge the fact that it is in his life that the poet finds the material for his message. But precisely, the operation constituted by that message reduces the data of the life to their use as raw material. . . . Let us say that in allowing Jean Delay to write *in his place* about his fugitive papers, Gide was not unaware that Jean Delay knew how to write, and also that he was not Ackermann. But he also knew that Jean Delay was an eminent psychiatrist and that, in the last analysis, it was with the psychobiographer that those papers were to find the destination that had always been theirs." [73]

Lost letters—in the idiom of Lacan's seminar on Poe—always reach their addressee!

IV. Pierre Jean Jouve and the Ladies' Chamber

Unlike the Surrealists and the *NRF* group, Pierre Jean Jouve's appeal was to a mystical vision of Freud's discovery. Blood, death, and culpable desire were the emblematic signs of a spiritual quest in which passionate love combined with the elaboration of a distinctive mode of writing. The encounter with psychoanalysis took place under the sign of conversion and repudiation. In 1924, Jouve decided to erase the traces of his previous work and did so in such manner that his gesture would be retained by posterity. At present, there is little mention of his "accursed" characters and the poet still remains master of their posthumous fate. In his will, he required of his heirs that his repudiated texts remain unknown. "To be sure," he wrote in 1954, "I have within me an implacable judge, something of an executioner." [74] The conversion also bore witness to an adventure with a woman—Blanche Reverchon, his companion and doctor, a protective mother and a deeply Christian psychoanalyst. Before and after: The break cut across his life much as the life betrayed the course of a work, in the manner of a death sentence.

Born in Arras in 1887, Jouve began legal studies well suited to the lawyerly posture he would later adopt in relation to his texts. At the age of twenty-two, he underwent an operation in which he came close to dying. Convalescing in Switzerland, he lapsed into deep depression, then met a vigorous Protestant woman who welcomed him into her home. Before long, he married his benefactor's daughter, a young woman of culture and a militant suffragette. Some time later, she gave birth to a son they named Olivier.

In the spring of 1921, Jouve made the acquaintance of a friend of his wife, Blanche Reverchon. The meeting took place in Florence and the liaison between the two lovers officially began in Salzburg the following year. Storm, mist, and tragedy: The new passion ended in a double break. Rolland and his friends took the side of the abandoned spouse and the poet abandoned his pacifist ideals for those of inner experience. He moved to Paris with Blanche and, in 1923, cast a glance at the translation of the *Three Essays*. Raised as a Catholic, he needed no "conversion" to remain so, but his development toward mysticism nonetheless followed the principle of a conversion. In repudiating his former writings, Jouve discovered psychoanalysis through a woman and it was Woman as such that would become the principal subject of a novelistic career cut short in 1935. He read the texts of Freud along with those of the great mystics, Theresa of Avila, Catherine of Siena, John of the Cross. Within a Christian itinerary, it was a matter of repudiating the earthly Church and replacing it with a religion of soul and spirituality. In his crisis, Jouve vituperated against the literary movements of his day, denouncing the falsities of the world. "As for the contemporary movement," he wrote in 1954, "I felt separated from it as by a thick clay wall. I saw them without their seeing me. It was the beginning of a general triumph: Gide, Valéry, Joyce, Sade, and several lesser lights. Against all that falsity, I felt, I said, the need for a religious content in poetry." [75]

If Breton, Rolland, and others prided themselves on having been first in France to know of Freud's work, Jouve imitated them: Not only did he claim chronological priority, but he maintained that his way of proceeding was "truer" than that of his contemporaries. Like them, he felt himself to be the most Freudian poet in France. In 1954, he did not hesitate to affirm that the preface to *Sueur de sang* ["Blood Sweat"], published in 1935, was the first text developing a poetic derived from unconscious values. At the same time, he attacked Surrealism, which he regarded as guilty of fabricating phantoms or dealing with the devil: "It will be seen what it was at that time which pitted me against the productions of the Surrealists. I accepted neither the use of the mechanism of automatic writing for its own sake, nor the fabrication of phantoms more grotesque than they were real, nor the exploitation—for purposes of publicity—of the unconscious." [76]

Although Jouve had no appreciation for the methods of the Surrealists, he had no more luck than Breton in his epistolary relations with Freud. In 1931, he sent him his novel *Vagadu*, which recounted the therapy of one Catherine Crachat, a singularly well-named heroine. A rather laconic letter arrived: "Copious thanks for sending your engaging books which I read in a single sitting, not without some protest from my sober side." [77] Despite that elegant evasion, the poet was hooked. He sent the scientist a long commentary on *Vagadu* concerning the novelistic transposition of the psychoanalytic method. At that point Freud sent back a postcard picturing the thermal hotel of Salzburg: "I write to confirm receipt of your commentary on *Vagadu*." [78] Nothing more. . . .

At the time she first met Jouve, Blanche Reverchon practiced psychiatry in Geneva. She had studied medicine in France and been trained in neurology by Babinski. In 1922, she moved to Paris with her lover and, in 1922, she married him. It was at that point that she underwent analysis with Eugénie Sokolnicka. Later on she paid a visit to Freud, who advised her, it seems, to practice psychoanalysis. She pursued her training with a control supervised by Loewenstein, then, in 1928, was accepted as a titular member of the SPP. While Jouve discovered Freudianism through his wife's therapy, she "espoused" psychoanalysis upon marrying a poet. That complex fusion was not foreign to the way in which Jouve appropriated the Viennese doctrine for his work. On all questions, his wife served as his interpreter. He did not speak any foreign language and it was she who accomplished the word-to-word task needed for his translations.

Born in 1879, Blanche belonged to the circle of the founders of the SPP without participating directly in its creation. Very early on, she became an influential psychoanalyst who was all the more respected because she had medical credentials. Less fragile than Sokolnicka and more committed than Marie Bonaparte, she nonetheless shared with the latter a capacity for authority that led to her prominence in the world of Paris. She preferred her patients rich, in order to keep her husband happy: He enjoyed luxury, courted other women, and had no financial resources. As a result, she did not train any analysts—at the time, training analyses were less profitable than personal therapy.

Blanche Reverchon watched over her husband's career the way he kept watch over his wife's clients. The couple frequently stayed in sumptuous hotels during their travels, and were accompanied by analysands organized as a coterie around the beloved poet, and who soon became adepts of his salon. Madame herself did not have the clinical talent of a Laforgue and her professional scruples were no more rigorous than those of her colleagues in the SPP. Her tendency to mix registers was not limited to the creation of a circle of initiates. Between 1929 and 1933, she had a young ballerina on her couch who later found herself unemployed. Some years after that she advised Olivier Jouve to pay a visit to the young lady. He fell in love and wanted to elope with her. But Blanche wanted to stop him and issued a diagnosis of "dementia praecox" for the dancer. Olivier was not to be stopped and did not hesitate to break off with his father and stepmother.[79]

Written in its entirety between 1925 and 1935, Jouve's prose work[80] coincided in time with Blanche's becoming an analyst. At the time he met her, she was only a psychiatrist, and when he stopped writing fiction, she was a renowned analyst. It was as though the poet's novelistic universe owed its existence to the experience of a woman who left behind no written work. She supplied him with a female substance, which he transformed into narrative, in the manner of a vampire.

In inventing the troubling adventure of *Pauline 1880,* Jouve drew on a tale borrowed from the Reverchon family archives. Blanche told him the story of one of her great-aunts who had killed her lover. In *Hécate,* published the same year as *Nadja,* he described the case of a depressive heroine, Catherine Crachat, who disseminated death around her. The text was written in the first person, as though emanating from the pen of the heroine. The name Hécate came from Greek mythology. It designated a mysterious three-headed goddess who guided travelers through the shadows. She resembled a lunar star, waxing and waning periodically. *Vagadu* was a sequel to *Hécate* and related a second episode in Catherine's adventures. According to an African legend, the term referred to the living strength of the human soul. To draw it out, Jouve dispatched his heroine to the couch of a Jewish psychoanalyst who resembled a demon: "'Monsieur Leuven is Jewish, moreover,'" she exclaimed "'He is not handsome. His red lips emerge from his beard. Seeing him, one senses something thick and enigmatic, poorly concealed by his ruddy coloring. . . . His ears are pointy like those of mythological creatures, his curly mane is already balding; behind a flowery vest, the forty-year old gentleman spreads his paunch, and his clothes, made of fine fabric, have been spoiled by poor care.'"[81]

Contrary to Gide, who settled his score with Sokolnicka, and Breton, who adopted the position of a dreamer, Jouve used the raw material of psychoanalysis to construct a novelistic vision inherited simultaneously from Stendhal and ecstatic mysticism. His fictions are entirely derived from the relation of fusion he entertained with Woman, assumed to be guilty of murder and capable of reaching paradise through her redemption. Whence the necessary interruption of a prose organized on the model of a magical obsession. Freud interpreted feelings of guilt, but he did not think that human existence could be confused with a natural history of sin. He described the mechanism of sublimation without regarding the drive toward divine love as a reality. Jouve, however, introduced an aim alien to Freudianism by integrating God into the problem of archaic desire.[82]

For *Vagadu,* he used his wife's therapy with Eugenie Sokolnicka, her control with Loewenstein, and finally a document she furnished herself, *Le cas de Mademoiselle H.,* whose trace may be found in the pages of the *NRF.* We shall return to it. In this novel, the second installment of the Adventures of Catherine Crachat, the analysis is related from the point of view of the heroine and without the intervention of an external point of view. Jouve describes the transferential experience of his feminine character, who pours out the most impassioned forms of her sexuality to a Dionysian Jew. The name "Leuven," derived from Loewenstein, is transformed into *leuvre* [from *couleuvre,* serpent], then *lèvres* [lips]. It is then associated with the figure of a devil adept in cunnilingus and accused of "looking under his patient's skirt."

Rather uncharacteristically for the period, *Vagadu* earned a review in the pages of the *RFP.* It was written by René Spitz, who took care to warn his readers of the dangers of using psychoanalysis for literary ends. He did not quote anyone and it was plain that he had no special affection for the writings of Gide, Breton, Crevel, or Lenormand. "It is quite clear that in most cases," he wrote, "this reconciliation [of modern literature] with psychoanalysis, and even its recognition, are superficial phenomena, matters of fashion, and involve for us a new, more subtle, and more hidden form of resistance. It is thus with a certain distrust that we approach works claiming to have been influenced by psychoanalysis. But the work we shall be discussing is completely different from literary productions of this type."[83] Given the platitude of the article, it may be doubted whether Spitz was capable of recognizing in *Vagadu* the existence of an authentic talent. No doubt he was particularly attentive to Jouve, but he was less interested in the style of his prose than in the respect due his wife.

Generally speaking, one can understand why the leading personalities of psychoanalysis were more sensitive to Jouve's approach than to that of other writers of the period. The poet did not attack—and for good reason—the medical ideal of his wife's colleagues. He did not participate in the fashion of salons, since they had created together his own poetico-psychoanalytic circle. Moreover, his religious commitment, although nonorthodox in its relation to the Catholic church, was not regarded by them as being as dangerous as the absolute atheism of a Gide or a Breton, who, in addition, were sympathetic to Communism. Finally, Jouve did not find in Freudianism that politics of subversion of the established order that was so dear to the Surrealists. As a result, his position in the epic of the new sensibility was both isolated and acknowledged. We may note in passing that the female figures haunting his prose belong to that exacerbated vision of femininity also present in the writings of Bataille, Lacan, and Breton.

After *Hécate* and *Vagadu,* there was a break in Jouve's prose production. In his final novels, the poet disdained the narrative domain previously opened up by

Blanche and returned to the feminine universe of his adolescence. *La scène capitale,* published in 1935, consisted of two tales turning around an enigmatic character named Hélène. She in fact fused three feminine figures, among whom Jouve placed Lisbé, *alias* Elisabeth, one of his former mistresses. Here again it was Woman that allowed the existence of his fiction. In 1909, in Paris, the poet had met the notorious Lisbé, "a creature with dark gold hair," with whom he fell in love.[84] After a few innocuous frolics, the creature returned to her province. Jouve had subsequently known other women, and had then married twice, while forgetting her. Twenty years later, he rediscovered her walking on Boulevard Raspail on a radiant April day. She had become the respectable wife of an officer and her life was being lived out uneventfully. A stormy affair between the poet and the lady ensued. Jouve felt guilty for deceiving his wife, and Lisbé discovered that she was pregnant, for the first time, after fifteen years of marriage. Before long, she gave birth to a stillborn child. The two lovers continued to meet in secret, but Lisbé fell sick, stricken with incurable cancer. Jouve retreated in solitude and wrote a narrative entitled *Dans les années profondes,* which he included in *La scène capitale.* Two years later he sent the novel to his mistress, saw her again, and was present at her decline and death. He then decided to abandon writing prose definitively, admitting that he "had conjured up Lisbé when his work needed her." [85]

If *Vagadu* put an end to a narrative universe dependent on Blanche's evolution, *La scène capitale* signified the death knell of prose itself. At every stage of his novelistic career, Jouve thus appropriated the body and story of a woman in order to make of them the mythical site of his writing. Jouve's fiction in its entirety was engulfed in that problematic: No fiction possible without the ladies' chamber.

In addition there was the poetry, in which women did not have the same status. When Jouve completed his last work in prose, he published *Sueur de sang,* preceded by a preface, "Inconscient, spiritualité, et catastrophe," in which he announced "good news": the reconciliation of mysticism and Freudian theory. *Exeunt* Woman and clinical reality! Poetry was sufficient unto itself, and individual catastrophe was transformed into a universal cataclysm. The poet was to fuse the death instinct with literary creation in order to exorcise the "world's psychoneurosis," to wit, "the Nazi catastrophe." Like the Surrealists, Jouve claimed to be part of the tradition of visionaries. "For we are," he wrote, "as Freud says, masses of unconsciousness slightly elucidated on the surface by the light of the sun; and that is something the poets said before Freud: Lautréamont, Rimbaud, Mallarmé, Baudelaire. In its present state, poetry is in the presence of numerous condensations through which it succeeds in attaining the symbol—no longer controlled by the intelligence, but surging, formidable, real. . . . May poetry advance by way of the 'absurd,' as is said." [86]

In that text, Jouve did not oppose the Surrealists, and it was only in 1954, in *En miroir,* that he took his distance from that movement in order to arrogate to himself the role of a precursor. Already in 1925, he had created a free line of verse woven with rhythmic shocks and charged with expressing the archaic respiration of the unconscious.[87]

The preface to *Sueur de sang* was written in 1933. That was the year Jouve published jointly with Blanche Reverchon a clinical study entitled *Moments d'une analyse*. In it, he recounted the case history of Mademoiselle H., whose fate was strangely reminiscent of that of the heroines of his novels. She consulted a doctor in the hope of freeing herself from a "vampire," a compulsion to reverie "devouring" her days. She incessantly saw a cortege of Czars descending the Champs-Élysées with much noise of stomping boots and fanfare. The troop stopped at the corner of the rue de Berri, where anarchists were hurling bombs. On each occasion, the explosive charge boomeranged against the terrorist, sparing the czar, but killing his son. Mademoiselle H. intervened to resuscitate one of the two individuals. She applied rouge to the face of the chosen one while a cloak, which was also red, was thrown over the body of the deceased, who was not to awaken. After that operation, the cortege continued its procession back to its starting point. The women were eliminated and replaced by masked men playing their role. The czar was involved in incestuous relations with his son. At times, he died and left him his place; at others, he transmitted his illness to him in order to continue his reign. Certain grotesque episodes impede the advance of the procession: thus, at the corner of the rue de Berri, the czar breaks a few eggs and makes an omelette. In such cases, the attacks do not take place.[88]

Jouve and Reverchon interpreted the reverie in terms of catastrophe and discovered in it the struggle between the life and death instincts. They noted that the omelette corresponded to a desire to emasculate men and that the "curly-haired" czars were an erotic symbol.

After several months of therapy, Mademoiselle H. replaced that reverie with a new one. She saw a "repulsive" couple emerge and indulge in "obscene" acts before her eyes. The man sodomized the woman, and then both together proceeded to play at housekeeping. Jouve and Reverchon immediately interpreted that fantasy as the unveiling of a sexual repression: "Mademoiselle H." they wrote, "saw the woman in the couple lie down alongside her to help her fight off the fear of dying. The woman in the couple thus became the analyst herself. As a result, for Mademoiselle H.'s conscious mind, and then for a part of her unconscious, to speak of the couple to her analyst became first dangerous, then obscene."[89] The authors noted that the patient manifested a marked resistance to analysis and accused her therapist of being obsessed. After two years of therapy, the reverie about the couple disappeared and the following year, Mademoiselle H. was rid of her vampire.

The young woman probably existed, but, in reading the article, one has the feeling that the case was entirely invented by a gifted fraud. The impression of strangeness stems from the fact that the tale is told by a couple taking itself for the object of the narrative and seeking its identity through a gallery of mirrors infinitely reflecting the image of a stroller lost in a labyrinth. If the girl so resembles a novelistic heroine, it is because the conditions of therapy allowed Jouve and Reverchon to transform analytic practice into a tale of devouring. The *Moments d'une analyse* was totally unlike the case histories published during the same period in the *RFP*. It functioned as the *negative* of a novelistic world: On the one hand, Jouve created fictions out of clinical reality, and on the other, he bestowed his literary talents on an actual case of therapy, thus seeking to establish a bridge between the two domains of the feminine—that of Blanche, and that of the novels. When he finally revealed the source of his inspiration, he put an end to the novel itself. A prelude to *La scène capitale,* the article in the *NRF* marked the definitive transition from prose to poetry and the abandonment of a mode of writing entirely dependent on the feminine.

It will thus be understood why Jouve's career as a writer was at once infused with Freud's discovery and yet marginalized at the core of the French adventure absorbing psychoanalysis into literature. Jouve was as fanatically interested in analysis as the Surrealists, but unlike them, he supported a medical (and even orthodox) vision of the Viennese doctrine. In the course of his poetic career, he cultivated the traditional ideal of the creator as demiurge, the agent of human consciousness. It did not occur to him, as it did to Breton or Rivière, that Freud's discovery was a revelation for the history of sciences. His inclination, instead, was to turn it into a religion capable of bringing the world a new spirituality. In that perspective, he would evolve toward a certain Jungianism. Jouve did not contest the established order, and his aesthetic of catastrophe was translated into a political itinerary. Having abandoned pacifism for mysticism, he would subsequently find in Charles de Gaulle, the Christian savior of the nation, the providential man dear to his poet's heart. In May 1968, he would demand that the street be swept clean of all the demonstrating scum.

4 Jacques Lacan: A Novel of His Youth

I. From Alfred to Gaëtan

At this point in our story, the author might relate a number of piquant details from the youth of a protagonist who the reader already knows will effect a new introduction of Freudianism in France. She might inquire into a distant past and call up scenes at which she could not have been present: the child being nursed by his mother, his penchant for hot chocolate, rivalry with a younger brother, or whimsies concerning a map. With a measure of novelistic craft, she might drape a princely mantle over the dinosaur skeleton and flesh out in words the empty spaces within the beast. She might be convincing as to the violence of a scene, the exquisiteness of a gown, the reality of an encounter that never took place, or even the sulfur-like aroma of a particular glazed chestnut chosen for the beauty of its hue. The author might invent a fiction truer than history itself. But would she not have the impression of deceiving either herself or her readers with an illusion sustained by the sheer pleasure of writing? In order to break with the imaginary, she would then reverse her stance and invest in a technique modeled on the photographer's: police investigation, raw data, telegraphic concision. There too she would be disappointed and forced to admit that a hatred of language has won out over the imaginary. To escape such a dilemma, she would have to delve into archives, testimony, recollections, the collective memory, and then forge out of it all something of a novel, halfway between a complete reconstitution of the facts and the necessary invention of a story. Between the precision snatched from a document and the transformation of a dinosaur into a circus animal, there is a way of imagining the truth without yielding to the false transparency of an archival entry.

Unlike Sigmund Freud, Jacques Lacan did not have to prove the existence of the unconscious on his own. He was not obliged to interpret his own dreams or publish the catalogue of his fantasies. He did not make known the chronology of his life. Nor did he write a *Selbstdarstellung* [self-portrayal], as the German has it. Few men have displayed as clearly as he a desire to keep secret (if not intact) the part of his life relating to his childhood and family origins. He did not falsify anything, but neither did he take into account in his teaching or the evocation of his career the adventures of his private diary. A historian is not obliged to respect that attitude, but if she wants to understand the importance assumed by the individual at the threshold of the 1930s, she ought to ponder the meaning to be attributed to the will not to establish any linear correspondence between the itinerary of a life and the elaboration of a theoretical enterprise. It is in the man's style, in his ways of writing and quoting, that we are accorded a chance of grasping what is essential in a history that eludes one's eyes because it is articulated in the weave of a text which itself prophesies the hero's trajectory. It speaks within the work, conveyed by metaphors, enigmas, ellipses. May the narrator know how to read!

His thesis in medicine on paranoid psychosis is dedicated to a woman, MTB, Marie-Thérèse, his first mistress. A quotation in Greek indicates what the author owes her: "I would not have become what I am without her assistance." On the following page, in a second dedication, Lacan addresses his brother, Marc-François, a Benedictine monk of the Congregation of France. He then thanks his father and mother, in filial gratitude for their example and beneficence, along with his sister and brother-in-law. He adds words of homage to all those who taught him psychiatry: Claude, Heuyer, Toulouse, Logre, Trénel, Alajouanine, Guillain, Dumas, et al. He mentions a renowned senior, Édouard Pichon. Finally, he offers warm salutations to his friends and colleagues during his years as an intern: Henri Ey, Pierre Mâle, Pierre Mareschal.[1] The first would become as famous as he did, and would remain his friend, despite substantial differences. The second, analyzed by Loewenstein and then Marie Bonaparte, would choose the SPP at the time of the first split. As for the third, he caused quite a splash in 1931 in the emergency ward of the Hôpital Sainte-Anne while delighting in the conflicts among his colleagues.[2]

A year after his defense, in 1933, Lacan drew up a general statement of his scientific efforts. He paid tribute to the originality of his thesis, which established, for the first time in France, an authentic interpretation of the paranoid personality.[3] As the starting point of his personal history, he thus seized on the emergence of a new clinical perspective, whose initiator he claimed to be. At age 32, let us say, he did not take himself for just anybody. He was not completely wrong, his talent had just been recognized in literary circles as well as within the Évolution psychiatrique group. It was only the psychoanalytic community that failed to perceive the amplitude of the event.

Thirty-three years later, at the age of sixty-five, Lacan published an anthology of his principal articles. He called the book quite simply *Écrits*.[4] At the heart of his vast 900-page past, we find a brief entry proudly entitled "Of Our Antecedents." Father, mother, former teachers and colleagues are dismissed. On the other hand, the name of Gaëtan Gatien de Clérambault is accorded pride of place. That man, criticized in 1932 and absent from the acknowledgments, is now recognized by Lacan as his "sole master in psychiatry."[5] Similarly, the names of René Crevel and Salvador Dali, who were not mentioned in 1932 and 1933, are evoked. Lacan speaks of Surrealism as the "new relay station" at which his thesis was welcomed. Finally he emphasizes that Clérambault's teaching led him to the discovery of Freud's work. Two pages later, he writes: "Current generations of psychiatrists will find it hard to imagine that we were, at our age as interns, some three to commit ourselves to psychoanalysis, and without any ingratitude toward the Évolution psychiatrique group, we may say that the fact that it was among its talents that psychoanalysis came to light, does not imply that it in any way received thereby a radical calling into question. . . . In truth no teaching other than of the accelerated routine variety emerged before we inaugurated our own, privately, in 1951."[6]

Once again Lacan did not take himself for just anyone. And again, he was not completely wrong: In 1966, adulated by numerous disciples, he founded a school over which he reigned like an enlightened monarch. His doctrine was taught there. Better still, the irreversible error of reading Freud's work in the light of Lacan's words was commonly committed there, as if the first had had no history and could receive its prestige only through a confrontation with the second.

Lacan's texts were sacralized, his person was imitated; he was made into the sole founder of the French psychoanalytic movement. Subdued, an army of barons spoke like Lacan, taught like Lacan, smoked Lacan's cigars, without perceiving that nothing is more fatal than forgetting the past. If that army had been able, it would, like Lacan, have carried its head inclined to the left or had the cartilage of its ears stretched in order to have them, like his, stand out.

The Lacan of 1966 was no longer the Lacan of 1932. He was treated like Lacan and played the role with a certain derision, like the madman who claimed he was king while realizing that the king was as mad as he was. "Of Our Antecedents" reflects that situation: In that text, one no longer finds the Lacan of the 1930s, but a legendary character, the son of no man, without parents or family, having had as his sole master a solitary psychiatrist and as fellow travelers a famous painter and a poet who had committed suicide. Where do his "seniors" fit in this version of the story? Where are the twelve pioneers of 1926? Where are René Laforgue, Marie Bonaparte, Édouard Pichon? Where is Rudolph Loewenstein, Lacan's analyst, to whom the same Lacan does not accord any space in his history? Who are the two unknowns emergent from the ranks of Evolution psychiatrique and committing themselves toward 1930 to psychoanalysis? Is the reference to Daniel Lagache, an intern at Sainte-Anne at the time, or Sacha Nacht, who was also a consultant at Sainte-Anne? Is it to Pierre Mâle or to any number of others?

And yet if the legend does not give us the truth, it is not for all that mendacious. Lacan did not present his itinerary in the same way in 1932 and in 1966, but between the two opposing versions, names, events, and filiations need to be added. Without draping our dinosaur skeleton with a princely mantle, it is possible to show that the contradictory statements bear witness, at thirty years' interval, to a truth that is not univocal, but dialectical, itself traversed by the history of its own recastings; at which point the fable will appear at its true worth—as a fragment of a novel.

Born on April 13, 1901 to a Parisian middle-class Catholic family, Jacques-Marie Émile Lacan spent part of his childhood reading atlases and winning each year first prize in German. He slept little, worked a lot, tyrannized those around him with his incessant requests, and appeared not to suffer from an emaciation which his mother's cooking did not succeed in remedying. Very early, he revealed himself to be a bibliophile, a collector of various objects, and desirous of earning money. Alfred Lacan was a thrifty father, with roots in the Auvergne, who was not concerned with matters intellectual. His profession was trade representative for oil and soap manufacturers. Without any particular intensity of faith, he attended mass like everyone else. In contrast, his wife, Émilie Baudry, was heir to an elaborate Christian culture and an ardent streak of mysticism. Born of a devout mother and a father who was a gold beater, she assisted her husband in his business and in raising their children. After the birth of Jacques-Marie, she gave birth to a second son who soon succumbed to illness. Then came Madeleine, in 1903, born on Christmas day, followed by Marc-François in 1908, who was also born on December 25.

The children spent their first years in an apartment on the boulevard Beaumarchais, after which the family moved to the rue de Montparnasse, facing the Collège Stanislas, where the two sons would pursue their studies. In 1924, Alfred and his wife left Paris for Boulogne to live in a house that they had had built for themselves.

Toward 1916, Jacques-Marie, against his father's advice, was hoping to become a doctor. During the same period, he began to be interested in philosophy, and above all Spinoza. On the wall of his room, he hung up a huge diagram on which he traced the outline of the *Ethics* with colored arrows—a veritable topography of the book, designed on the model of the atlases of years past. There soon ensued a break with religious faith. The young Lacan did not renounce the religious culture he had received, but abandoned all belief in God and all affiliation with Christian practice. That would not prevent him from getting married in church and having his children baptized. But his renunciation was accompanied by the sign of dropping the name Marie, which had been attached to Jacques. From the time of his earliest publications, in 1926, he would sign Jacques Lacan, and sometimes Jacques-M. Lacan. In 1919, at the exit of the Collège Stanislas, he definitively decided to embark on a medical career and, in 1921, he was discharged from military service because of his thinness.[7]

The break with religious faith was accompanied by an opening to the world of modernity. Jacques Lacan frequented Adrienne Monnier's bookstore, was interested in Dadaism, in the theories coming out of Vienna, and the ideas of Charles Maurras. He met the man on several occasions and admired in him a master of the language.[8] Without adhering to any principles of anti-Semitism, he occasionally participated in meetings of the Action francaise and found in monarchism the wherewithal to nourish his abandonment of God. Essentially political, Maurrassian Catholicism sought support in clerical tradition less for reasons of faith than because of the crusade it authorized on behalf of a renewal of rationalism and the genius of Rome. Maurras and Spinoza are thus the two eminently contradictory figures who interested Lacan during the jazz age.

Alfred and Émilie were worried by their son's atheism. He had affirmed his independence and was living in what were formerly maid's quarters in Montmartre. Beneath its rooftops, he contemplated Paris and played at being Balzac's Rastignac. Insofar as his love life was concerned, he was closer to a Regency aristocrat than a nineteenth-century man of science. He would always have numerous mistresses. Lacan preferred slightly androgynous women, with narrow hips, flat breasts, and long legs. Extremely seductive, he dressed like a dandy, and gaily squandered the little money given him by his parents. Lacan had contempt for the middle class into which he was born, and was eager to acquire wealth, distinction, and celebrity. Soon he would take on princely manners, and would appear to his contemporaries as he wanted to: indifferent to his roots without having to conceal them.

If the elder brother had abandoned God, the younger one trod a very different path, which also led him to abandon his family. As early as 1926, he had decided to enter a monastery. Three years later, he left for the Abbaye de Hautecombe, a monument of an earlier age stuck right in the middle of Lamartine's elegiacal lake. On that day, on a station platform, a man watched a train plow through the city's black snow. Protectively wrapped in a fur-collared grey overcoat, he carried his head at an angle and walked with elegance. His short hair slicked back, his clear complexion, and his fine oval face did not succeed in hiding the sadness clouding his eyes. Overwhelmed, Jacques Lacan watched as the friend with whom he still shared the memories of a comfortable childhood fled into the winter landscape. A fragment of his story floated off toward the horizon, toward an unknown site cradled by the gentle slopes of a mountain range. Bitterly, he reproached himself for not having prevented his brother, a philosopher like himself and soon to be a theologian, from choosing the path of perpetual confinement. Had he been hoping for the impossible in wanting his junior to embrace the career of tax inspector?

His medical career followed a normal, traditional course. Between 1926 and 1930, Lacan published several articles in collaboration with Trénel, Alajouanine, Marchand, Courtois, Heuyer. . . . From the study of pseudo-bulbar disturbances to that of general paralysis, by way of analyses of chronic hallucinatory psychosis, he received the neuropsychiatric training prevalent at the time. He attended the courses of Henri Claude on the clinical treatment of mental illness and encephalitis, and spent a year at the special Infirmary for the Insane of the Police Prefecture. There the vagrant mad, picked up from the street, were brought and authorities were granted permits allowing them to intern them in the various asylums of the city. It was there that Gaëtan Gatian de Clérambault—a celebrated psychiatrist, theoretician of "erotomania," expert in the mechanics of paranoia, and devotee of Roman togas and drapings—reigned as master. Gatian de Clérambault was his patronymic, Gaëtan his first name. He was called Monsieur de Clérambault for short. He traced his descent to the poet Vigny on his mother's side and to Descartes on his father's.

This aristocrat of another age was born in 1872 to an extremely Catholic family with close ties to the land. The year of Freud's meeting with Charcot he donned the uniform of students of the Collège Stanislas. A devotee of literature and music, he studied law before opting for medicine. During the Great War, he joined the Moroccan army, where he began his study of Arab draping, the art and manner of pleating and folding fabrics, knotting them, causing them to fall voluptuously alongside the body, according to ancestral custom. Upon returning to Paris, he was named chief physician of the special Infirmary, and he occupied that post until 1934, the year of his suicide. During the fourteen years of his reign, he fascinated his entourage with the elaboration of an unfinished body of work and with a clinical practice in which the cult of the gaze was pressed to a paroxysmal extreme. In Cléramault, the art of observation merged with a "story of the eye" as revised by Charcot and corrected by Roussel. Such was this formalist of clairvoyance whom Lacan was to meet one fine morning in the year 1928.

As opposed to Claude and his disciples, who favored a Bleulerian vision of schizophrenia and of madness in general, Clérambault, like Kraepelin, sought to furnish a coherent and systematic classification within the field of the psychoses. He proposed to define them in terms of a single shared element, "the syndrome of mental automatism." That phrase was used to indicate the insane essence of the illness beyond the diversity of its manifestations. It was based on psychical and sensory disturbances, which were always the same, and which were imposed on the subject's mind in a brutal way, that is, "automatically." Such disturbances erupt from outside and have nothing to do with the ideas formulated by the subject. As for the syndrome itself, its origin remained entirely organic. With that definition of "automatism," Clérambault distanced himself from Janet and his followers; he opted for organizational structure as opposed to mental deficiency. In this, his position was not far removed from Freud's, who himself preferred Kraepelin's doctrine to Bleuler's to the extent that it seemed adequate to his own style of classification, despite the organicist core underlying it.[9] An anachronistic and marginal thinker, Clérambault was simultaneously behind his time (since he favored a narrow constitutionalism to the detriment of a dynamic perspective) and ahead of his contemporaries (since he grasped the pertinence of structural theses necessary to a new organization of knowledge). Whence the paradox of his position: Supremely unaware of the Viennese theses, he elaborated a doctrine of psychosis that was apparently more "Freudian" than "Bleulerian." He thus opted for the field of paranoia over and against that of schizophrenia.

Freud had taken his distance from the rigid constitutionalism of the German tradition by integrating an experience of dynamism into his structural perspective. Now on that point Clérambault remained Kraepelin's heir: Not only did he retain his organicist bias, but he refused all reform in matters of therapy. Conservative and tyrannical, he sought first of all to ferret out the symptom or to prove the coherence of his doctrine before worrying about the patient. Violently hostile to the reforms proposed by Édouard Toulouse and quite marginal in relation to the new psychiatry of the twenties, he belonged to that category of alienist who took it upon themselves to confine the insane at a time when efforts were being made above all to treat them. He was a superb emblem of the repressive function of a state apparatus and his position as chief physician of the special Infirmary reflected his doctrinal stance. Without any private practice, he spent his life perfecting his eagle-eye gaze; he manipulated and observed his patients without ever listening to them, did not judge, but noted and obtained admissions in the manner of a confessor of genius. He composed his certificates of internment in a telegraphic style, resorting profusely to visual notations, capital letters, theatrical strokes seeming to emerge from the stock of ancient tragedy. Here, for instance, is his summary of the case of a poor fellow brought to his office: "Chronic alcoholic. Acute attack. State of confusion. Monotonous and ceaseless microactivity. Incomplete memories of anxious dreams. At present euphoric. Denounced and caused the arrest of his pursuers: four men and four women of whom the youngest wanted to castrate him and replace his organs with a bouquet of roses. Penchant for the dramatic. Will be reduced to pudding the following day at 7 o'clock. Slackness. Suggestibility. Pick-ups. Tremors. Dysarthria. Embolalia."[10]

The syndrome of mental automatism allowed Clérambault to classify, on the one hand, the hallucinatory psychoses, and on the other, delusional passions, among which, between jealousy and revindication, pride of place is accorded to erotomania. The term traditionally designates the madness of chaste love. A subject believes herself to be loved Platonically by the object she is pursuing, who is normally a famous individual. Clérambault's contribution consisted first in categorizing ero-tomania among the delusional disorders, which became a clinical entity, then in introducing a sexual theme into the description of the phenomenon. That renunci-ation of the Platonic dimension makes of erotomania a kind of hysterical psychosis described by way of its formal properties. It becomes a delusion in which sexual pride dominates, since the object is superior to the subject. That pride is structured around an obsession, which develops in three phases: hope, chagrin, and rancor.

Thus, for example, a woman believes herself loved by the King of England. He has made advances to her and all the members of his court are eager to be present at the culmination of his passion. The lady "hopes." She then crosses the Channel and moves through the waiting rooms of the railway stations in which the King has arranged meetings with her. Since he fails to come, she believes she has been de-ceived. All the more so since he persists in playing tricks on her. Whereupon she begs his pardon: She is "chagrined." Upon returning from London, dissatisfied with her trip, she slaps a policeman, and finds herself in Clérambault's office, where he interns her after extorting whatever confessions are needed for his doctrine. She now believes that the King of England is the cause of her confinement; she feels "rancor" toward him, and has, moreover, blamed the policeman, whom she holds responsible for her misadventures. For Clérambault the patient is incurable. From the perspec-tive of this description, erotomania appears as an assuredly "mad" vision of reality, but also one that is as "true" in its structure as "normal" thought. He thus shared with Freud and the Surrealists the conviction that there exists a great proximity between madness and truth.[11]

It would, however, be a bit excessive to classify Clérambault as one of the watchdogs of the established order. For the young interns of the 1930s completing their studies under the aegis of Henri Claude, the august chief of the Infirmary was a psychiatrist of genius, as Henri Ey put it. Paradoxically, it may have been because of his mechanistic orientation that he was able to be an innovator in the study of delusional passions, as though a blindness to dynamics and psychogenesis allowed him to take into account the vestiges of an object whose value had escaped the prevailing mode of knowledge.

In order to gauge the importance of his efforts, his ethnographic endeavors should be associated with his accomplishments in psychiatry. The passion for fab-rics, hems, pleats, ruffles, in a word the fetishized love of the adorned body of the (preferably Arab) female illuminates in retrospect the other passion, the one Clér-ambault bore for erotomania, that is, for that madness of an insane love which he himself had lived in secretly "marrying" the wax figurines that served as his models in his study of the art of draping. At a time when French clinical practice was com-pleting its dismemberment of Charcot's teaching, Clérambault rechanneled the ar-chaic passion of hysteria into the psychotic register, thus participating in that ten-dency of modernity through which the—exacerbated—feminine was to regain its patents of nobility. Before Lacan, before Breton, before Bataille, Gaëtan the bache-lor, Gaëtan the paranoid, Gaëtan the cop, Gaëtan the misogynist remade contact with the world of the Salpêtrière and transposed into the colonial universe of the first third of the century a vision of woman that his contemporaries had abandoned. Whether it took the name of "delusional love" or a "love of draping," it was no less sexualized through and through.

While Lacan was a student of Clérambault's at the special Infirmary, the latter went blind. Stricken with a cataract, the master of the gaze could not bear to lose his sense of relief, color, and perspective. He decided to be operated on by a Spanish surgeon whose method consisted of removing the lense while holding it fast through suction. After the surgery Clérambault never regained a perception of relief.

On the morning of November 17, 1934, he wrote up a will in which he accused himself of stealing a painting he had in fact purchased from a dealer shortly before. Then he withdrew from his family and his friends the right to partake of his inheritance. Finally, a few minutes later, he tried out his pistol in the garden of his house at Montrouge. His servant was alarmed at seeing him climb up to his room as though he were attacking a fortress. There he placed an armchair in front of a mirror and a bed, transversally, behind it. He sat down, leaned his elbow on the arm of the chair and fired a bullet into his mouth. The weapon fell to his left and his spectacles to his right as the projectile exited through the back of his head. The next day the press held forth and did not hesitate to announce the tragic end of a new Caligari living alone with his wax dolls draped in bizarre fabrics. There remained a sentence discovered in a posthumous text in which Clérambault recounted his operation in detail. The presentation ends with these words: "We maintain our eyes at the disposition of any colleague wishing to examine them." [12]

Questioned by his brother about the spectacular suicide of his former master, Jacques Lacan commented, "He didn't miss his shot and it doesn't surprise me. . . . It's like Nero's line: What an artist I am. . . ."[13] In 1973, evoking Montherlant's suicide, which occurred under similar circumstances, he declared: "You should know that I have on several occasions seen hope, a taste for what is called a brighter tomorrow, bring individuals for whom I have as much esteem as I have for you to nothing other than suicide. Why not? Suicide is the only deed capable of undivided success." [14]

What did Lacan retain of the instruction he received from Clérambault during the academic year 1928–29? A vestige of it is to be found in a 1931 article entitled "Structures des psychoses paranoïaques" and published in *La Semaine des hôpitaux de Paris*.[15] The author studies consecutively three types of paranoid psychosis: constitutional; interpretative delusions; and delusions of love. He adapts for his own uses the notion of a constitutive paranoia with its three themes of pathological self-aggrandizement, distrust, and false judgment. The study concludes with the author advocating a systematic internment of the insane, who are perceived to be agitators: "Within the asylum, all protests should be communicated without exception to the competent administrative authorities." And further on: "Similarly, in cases of youthful insubordination in military service, it is advisable, given the inevitable failure of the rising ladder of disciplinary measures, to refer such patients to military justice, which can then in turn refer them to a psychiatrist." It may be wondered what Benjamin Péret and René Crevel would have thought upon reading such a passage! Concerning a borrowing from Clérambault, he adds a footnote: "This image is borrowed from the oral teaching of our master M. G. de Clérambault to whom we are indebted for the entirety of our method and material, and to whom, to avoid plagiarism, we would be obliged to pay homage for every one of our terms."

In point of fact, he laid claim to his master's teaching, but in order to transform it, since he replaced the concept of "syndrome of mental automatism" with that of "structure," and absorbed delusions of love within the general framework of paranoia. Moreover, in speaking of plagiarism, he knew exactly what he was doing. The august head of the special Infirmary had always manifested a certain distrust of his entourage; he was convinced that "his ideas were being stolen." After the publication of Lacan's article, he threw a fit and broke into a session of the Société médico-psychologique. He hurled dedicated copies of his work in Lacan's face and accused him of plagiarism.[16]

II. Aimée or Rudolph

If Lacan initially adopted the method and material of this master's teaching, he would soon channel his efforts in a quite different direction. After the article that triggered the storm, he published another one, in collaboration with Pierre Migault and J. Lévy-Valensi (who were both students of Claude), on " 'Inspired' Writings." [17] The authors presented the case of one Marcelle, a 34-year-old school teacher, suffering from erotomania and paranoia. She took herself for Joan of Arc and believed she was destined to regenerate the morals of France. The pretext of her delusion was one of her hierarchical superiors, who had died the previous year. Clérambault had her interned because she demanded that the state pay her 20,000 francs in damages for deprivation of intellectual and sexual satisfactions. The originality of the analysis lay in the fact that the authors studied their case through the patient's written language. They defined the structure of her paranoia on the basis of semantic, stylistic, and grammatical disturbances found in her letters. Linking those disturbances to a syndrome of mental automatism, they modified the term by introducing a measure of intentionality. At the same time, they demonstrated that the states of inspiration by which she was visited were in no way spiritualistic, but rather an automatic phenomenon understandable in the context of the Surrealist experiment of the same name: "Nevertheless, not everything in these texts need be attributed to the degenerative verbal formulation of affective tendencies. There is an aspect of play that is apparent, concerning which it is imperative to overlook neither the inventive nor the automatic aspects. The experiments conducted by certain writers in a writing style they have called Surrealist and whose method they have described quite scientifically show what a remarkable degree of automatism written automatisms, outside of any hypnosis, can achieve." [18] The authors do not speak of "paranoid constitution," nor do they emit any repressive opinions on the dangerousness of madness or the necessity of interning patients. On the contrary, they call attention to a link between the syndrome of mental automatism and a Surrealist experiment.

It will thus be seen that the year 1931 was a watershed in the development

of the young Lacan's thought. He was intent on being both a theoretician of paranoid structure, the doctrinal heir of Clérambault, and the servant of a modernity he
was beginning to confront. At Sainte-Anne he had already been observing for some
time a certain Aimée, whose writing revealed more talent than Marcelle's. He frequented the Surrealists, became a friend of René Crevel, met André Breton, and
became a fervent reader of the works of Pichon, in whom he admired a new master
of the language. He discovered the works of Freud in German and took an interest
in the entire range of work in German on psychosis: first Kraepelin's, then Kretschmer's and that of the criminologists. In his intern's room, he engaged his friends
Henri Ey and Pierre Mâle in discussions of psychoanalysis and the Russian Revolution; of Lenin, in whom he saw a new aspect of Hegel's system; of contemporary
literature, in which his seniors showed little interest, but which was quite important
for the second generation of young French psychiatrists. Soon Lacan was to take up
with Pierre Drieu la Rochelle, as dandified a lady's man as he himself was. The
novelist had just left his second wife, Olga Sienkiewicz, nicknamed "Eau fraiche
[Fresh water]," whose father, a banker, had just succumbed in the economic crisis.
He loaned his friend his apartment on the Ile Saint-Louis so that he might work
calmly on his thesis. Lacan was smitten briefly with Olga, then chose to clarify
matters to Drieu in "long obscure sentences." [19]

One day, he telephoned Salvador Dali to discuss with him a text the latter
had just published under the eloquent title L'âne pourri. ["The rotten donkey"].[20]
The painter agreed to meet with him and received the psychiatrist in his home. As a
provocation, he wore an adhesive plaster on his nose and expected a surprised reaction from his visitor. Lacan did not flinch, and the two spoke together of Dali's
thought. Upon reading L'âne pourri, Lacan realized that the phase of automatic
writing had already passed, and that Dali was giving Surrealism its second wind
with his notion of "paranoia-criticism." This consisted, in the wake of automatism,
of delivering a final blow to the world of reality. For Dali, paranoia was the equivalent of a hallucination, since it consisted in delusional interpretation of reality, but
it was also the opposite of a hallucination, since it sustained itself through a coherent
critical method, possessing meanings and a phenomenological dimension. In other
words, Dali recognized that the paranoid phenomenon was "pseudo-hallucinatory"
in nature. He illustrated his argument through the appearance of double images: for
example, in painting, the image of a horse that is simultaneously the image of a
woman. "It is through a plainly paranoid process," he wrote, "that it has been
possible to obtain a double image, that is, the representation of an object that (without the slightest anatomical or figurative distortion) is simultaneously the representation of another object, similarly bereft of any deformation or abnormality that
might reveal any arrangement." [21]

That position of Dali's served to confirm a second one: delusion is part and
parcel of interpretation. Indeed, the existence of double images disqualified the classical psychiatric conception according to which the paranoid would commit errors
of judgment whose corollary would be a rationalistic mode of insanity. There would
be no interpretation followed by delusion, but rather the simultaneous appearance
of a mode of delusion and an interpretation; in other words, the delusion is already
an interpretation of reality and paranoia a creative activity which does not depend,

like hysteria, on deformation, but on logic. Consequently, the madman would not be a man bereft of reason, but the herald of an act in which the coherence of a dream attains objectivity. As Freud had already understood at the beginning of the century.

The first Surrealist generation had seen in mental illness a creative resource and announced with Breton that beauty would be convulsive. It defined hysteria in terms of passion and crime which lead to a new representation of femininity. In 1930, Dali abandoned the notions of convulsion and automatic writing in order to systematize, under the rubric of paranoia, a coherent method of knowledge and of creative interpretation of reality. He received from Lacan the scientific seal which his endeavors had lacked until then and would salute the publication of the latter's thesis enthusiastically. "To this thesis," he wrote in 1933, "we are indebted for giving us, for the first time, a global and homogeneous idea of the [paranoid] phenomenon, beyond any of the abject notions in which psychiatry at present is mired." [22]

And yet Lacan met Dali at the fertile pass of his own itinerary in which he was himself effecting a synthesis of the teachings of the Surrealists, of Freud, of Clérambault, and of the entire tradition of psychiatric doctrine concerning paranoia. That synthesis is confirmed in the title of his thesis: *De la psychose paranoïaque dans ses rapports avec la personnalité*. Paranoia is classified, as in Freud, under the category of psychosis; it is "structural" without being "constitutional" or "innate," and to that extent affects the entirety of the subject's personality without being determined by an organic origin.

In order to understand the coherence of that structure, the *human meaning* of the phenomena specific to it must be interpreted, that is, the full range of elements characterizing a "psychogenius" of the personality must be defined. Lacan uses that term rather than *psychogenesis* in order to show that the etiology of psychosis is expressed as a function of phenomenological mechanisms deriving entirely from the concrete history of the subject. The author thus emphasized the genesis of the psychosis as a reaction-formation while opposing, on the one hand, the theoreticians of a "constitutive nature" of the illness, and, on the other, the partisans of a "core" of delusional conviction. In other words, and in the same perspective as Dali, Lacan rejected the *folie raisonnante* of Sérieux and Capgras as well as the syndrome of mental automatism dear to Clérambault.[23] Against that dual lineage, he opted for "concrete psychology:" It allowed for an analysis of the subject's entire personality, the evolution of a consciousness, the events of a personal history, and the confrontation between a private drama and the social milieu. Beyond any borrowing from Politzer, Lacan sought support in Freud's discovery, affirming that psychoanalysis alone offered the technique required for an experimental study of the subject. On that basis, he defined a method of "directed psychotherapy" which he applied to the case of Aimée. Against all the specialists in the field, he thus posed a prognosis, if not of total cure, of treatability.

It will thus be understood why he took the side of Henri Claude against Clérambault. At the time, he was unable to make the connection between the concept of mental automatism and that of unconscious structure in the Freudian sense: founding a scientific approach to psychosis entailed bypassing constitutionalism and allying oneself with dynamism, without which no "psychogenius" is acceptable.[24] It would be only after the fact that Lacan would acknowledge his antecedents and accord Clérambault's theory a structural value. But in order to do so, he would have to conduct a rereading of Freud in the light of the concept of "foreclosure," which was itself borrowed from Pichon. We have already seen that that effort occurred in two distinct phases: first in 1954, on the occasion of a confrontation with Jean Hippolyte on the notion of "denial"; then in 1956, in the course of a seminar devoted to the psychoses.[25]

In 1932, Lacan thus threw out the baby with the bath water, automatism along with constitutionalism. He preferred paranoia-criticism, concrete psychology, and a clinical practice rooted in dynamics. Since he was defending a thesis in medicine, he avoided mentioning the names of Politzer and Dali in his bibliography. He would pay homage to them only later on. He nevertheless retained that segment of Clérambault's teaching concerning the observation of patients and the description of erotomania. If he made use essentially of psychoanalytic method, he would never give precedence to the ear at the expense of the eye. His tendency was rather to integrate a listening to the subject and a visual observation of his person. Ever the accomplished student of his master, he was *still* a psychiatrist, but *already* a psychoanalyst; whence the emergence in his practice of a hybrid method, "directed psychotherapy," which consisted in gathering information about the patient, searching into his past, inquiring of family and witnesses, all things which Freud had renounced in order to grant exclusive privilege to the utterance of fantasy and a "talking cure." Lacan, moreover, retained from Clérambault the notion of erotomania and added to it the Freudian theme of repressed homosexuality, specific, according to that author, to the structure of paranoia.

The young psychiatrist was not satisfied with effecting a brilliant critical synthesis among several trends of French thought; he also proposed a *writing* of madness which was as innovative at the time as that of Breton or Bataille. Instead of a traditional case history, we find in the 1932 thesis a novel 150 pages in length, in the style of Flaubert, that is, in a literary language irreducible to the wooden prose of psychiatric discourse. Lacan recounts his heroine's adventures with the pen of an authentic writer, displacing onto the character of Aimée the misfortunes of a contemporary Emma Bovary. That in fact is the greatest originality of this innovative book, which is as readable as a serialized novel!

The story begins as follows: "On 10 April 193 . . . at eight o'clock in the evening, Mme Z., one of the most admired actresses of Paris, arrived at the theater where she was to perform that evening. She was approached, on the threshold of the actors' entrance, by an unknown woman who asked her the following question: 'Are you indeed Madame Z.?' The questioner was attired quite appropriately in a coat whose collar and sleeves were fur-lined; she wore gloves and a handbag; nothing in the tone of the question aroused the actress's suspicion. Accustomed to the adulation of a public intent on approaching its idols, she answered in the affirmative, and, eager to be done with the matter, attempted to move on. The unknown woman at that point, according to the actress, changed her expression, quickly removed an open knife from her bag, and with a face glowing with hatred, raised her arm against her. In order to block the blow, Mme Z. seized the blade with her bare hand

and cut through two flexor tendons of her fingers. Already two assistants had gained control of the perpetrator of the attack." [26]

The actress was named Huguette Duflos and Aimée's first name was that of a flower. It was Lacan who invented for her one of love. He recounts that the actress did not press charges, but that her attacker was sent to Sainte-Anne with an official report that read as follows: "Persecutory insanity based on interpretation and with megalomaniac tendencies and an erotomanic substrate." For several weeks, Lacan devoted an extraordinary amount of energy to her case. He accumulated a variety of documents relating to it, going even so far as to read the books she read in order to better understand the novelistic characters with whom she was identifying. Thirty-eight years old, and employed by a railway company, Aimée had always dreamed of being a writer. She produced literary texts, both poetry and prose, and admired well-known women of letters of her day. She was also convinced that the actress was mocking and threatening her, in complicity with a novelist intent on exposing her own intimate life in his books. She accused the actress of wanting the death of her child. In addition, she feared the K.G.B. and was chastely in love with the Prince of Wales, to whom she sent poems and letters.

Instead of preparing a catalogue of the patient's symptoms, Lacan sought to grasp the unconscious meaning of the paranoid motif. To do so, he deciphered Aimée's family romance. On the basis of a series of interpretations, he gradually came to realize that the figures of persecutory females were surrogates for a feminine imago. For Aimée had in fact had an elder sister who early on had taken the role of a maternal authority. The mother of the two women was herself stricken with a type of persecutory insanity. The sister was a participant in a *délire à deux*. Lacan realized as much when she confessed to him that she feared Aimée's eventual release, as though the murderous deed might well fix on her as its object. He soon discovered as well that the patient's paranoia had erupted in earlier years, at the time she had lost a baby in childbirth. Aimée at first accused her sister of having stolen her baby from her, then displaced the deluded motif onto other women, first a friend, then Mme Z.

Lacan demonstrated that in her case, erotomania went hand in hand with a homosexual dimension. Aimée became attached to famous women because they represented her *ego ideal*. Moreover, she was smitten with the Prince of Wales. That passion allowed her to satisfy her limited inclination toward heterosexuality while permitting her to misperceive her suppressed drives toward her own sex. Thus did her delusion receive a "Dalian" or "Lacanian" meaning, taken to be an interpretative activity of the unconscious, as opposed to dreams, which received their interpretation from without. In other words, Aimée may have been insane, but her insanity, or her paranoia, functioned in a register that was not alien to the logical universe of creators, builders of empires, or theoreticians of psychiatry.

In that perspective, Lacan isolated, within the same group, plaintive paranoia and self-punitive paranoia. They were determined not by the obsessive mechanism of erotomania, but by a stoppage in personality development at the phase of the ego ideal. Put otherwise, Aimée transformed a complaint into self-punishment by dint of her interpretation of the act. She was thus free to be spontaneously "cured" of her delusion without the psychotic structure at the core of her personality disappearing. The cure occurred when the patient realized, with the help of her therapist, that in striking the actress, she was striking herself. "Aimée thus strikes in her victim," Lacan wrote, "her externalized ideal, just as the *passionnelle* strikes the sole object of her hatred and her love. But the object attacked by Aimée had no more than a purely symbolic value, and her deed brought her no sense of relief. And yet with the same blow which had made her guilty before the law, Aimée had struck herself, and when she understood as much, she experienced the satisfaction of a wish fulfilled. The delusion, no longer serving any purpose, disappeared. The nature of her cure demonstrates, we believe, the nature of her illness."[27]

From a penal perspective, Lacan adopted a position opposed to the one he had recommended two years previously when he was still an adept of Clérambault's doctrine. He criticized the repressiveness of prison and opposed to it the tolerance characterizing isolation in an asylum as apt to bring to fruition the prognosis of treatability appropriate to Aimée's case. He thus allied himself with the partisans of dynamic psychiatry, while contributing to it an innovative point of view. Lacan in fact emphasized that psychoanalysis was not to serve as an auxiliary technique of use to psychiatry; it could, on the contrary, radically transform any approach to madness, on the condition that it not be used in a purely pragmatic fashion. In other words, Lacan was unwittingly effecting a new introduction of Freudianism into France. Before him, the first psychiatro-psychoanalytical generation had implanted the Viennese doctrine in the context of a psychiatric perspective resulting from a recasting of the theories of heredity and degeneration; it had provoked a "dynamic" modification of that perspective by confronting it with an "alien entity." But with the publication of the case history of Aimée, what we have is the emergence of an unprecedented encounter between the older dynamism and Freudianism: something of an encounter to the second degree. It was characterized by a liquidation of the notion of an *integration* of psychoanalysis into psychiatry. Lacan did not seek to force Freud's theory into the pre-existent mode of a diagnostic tradition; on the contrary, he reversed matters by introducing the primacy of the unconscious into clinical understanding.

If the nature of the cure demonstrated the nature of the illness, it was because nature itself vanished and was supplanted by culture or structure. Illness no longer partook of an essence or an "idealism," but an existence or a "materialism." As for any diagnosis, it was to conform to the concrete or historical existence of the subject, that is, to a phenomenology. Lacan dubbed that practice a "science of personality." He was thus not strictly Freudian, but rediscovered Freud's work in the light of Spinoza's philosophy, in a specifically French cultural context and on clinical terrain that was strictly psychiatric. To be sure, he had read the case history of Dr. Schreber,[28] knew the specific place Freud accorded to paranoia, and was acquainted with his classics; his monograph is thus strangely reminiscent of Freud's five case histories. And yet, within the history of the French movement, it played the role of a founding text. It took on the importance that had previously been accorded the *Studies on Hysteria* in the rise of the international movement. Just as Freud had given hysteria its patents of nobility in endowing it with full-fledged existence as an illness, so Lacan, forty years later, gave paranoia, and more generally psychosis, an analogous place within the French movement. It was no longer a matter of turning it into an authentic illness, but, on the contrary, of designating a proximity between two realities, that of madness, and that of reason. Better yet, it was a matter of dissolving the world of reason and of granting coherence or expressibility—in its very form—to that of the imaginary.

The reader may perhaps begin to realize why the publication of an obscure monograph might make its author famous. It was writers and young psychiatrists, before psychoanalysts, who intuited that Lacan's argument had broken with the prevalent norms of accepted doctrine. Dali and Crevel saluted the event in their fashion, but so did Henri Ey, Lacan's classmate, and others as well. In *La critique sociale,* Jean Bernier attacked Lacan violently for his poverty as a therapeutist, but located the *place* of the young psychiatrist within the French context: "It is not without a distinct sense of satisfaction that we observe a representative of our very bourgeois world of psychiatry illustrate the Marxist conception of human person-ality and demonstrate that in psychiatry, as in psychology and all the other sciences having man as their object, everything currently impels one to found that realist humanism (which is realist in the biological, economical, and sociological senses) in whose name historical materialism declared war on bourgeois civilization. *To be sure, Dr. Lacan seems, to read him, as yet far from suspecting where his views can and should lead him."* [29]

Surrealists and Marxists of the opposition were not alone in noticing the event. For his part, Paul Nizan published an article in *Humanité* in which he too spoke of the materialist nature of Lacan's hypotheses: "Note should be taken of a book which, against the tendencies of official science, and despite the precautions that need be taken by the author of a university thesis, betrays an extremely sure and conscious influence of dialectical materialism. Dr. Lacan has not yet clarified all of his theoretical positions, but he is reacting against the various idealisms which presently corrupt all research in psychology and psychiatry. . . . *A book such as this announces a significant scientific battle."* [30]

Despite their differences, Salvador Dali, René Crevel, Paul Nizan, and Jean Bernier were in agreement on two points. First, they recognized the materialist tenor of Lacan's hypotheses and opposed it to the idealism of the psychiatric tradition. Of a sudden our hero became the victorious warrior of a kind of Leninism applied to the field of psychiatry. In the case of a former admirer of Maurras, emerging from the Catholic middle class, the idea is rather amusing. But a man and his work, as tradition has it, never quite mesh. . . . In addition, our four commentators attributed to the author of the monograph a position of the first importance in the history of the 1930s. They announced the beginnings of a new scientific battle and the arrival of a new doctrinal leader. They were anticipating the course of events.

If "materialism" there be in the young Lacan's argument, it is the fruit of an antimechanistic and an anticonstitutionalist perspective. To refuse the older clinical doctrine was not to adhere to Marxism, but to accept the primacy of the uncon-scious over the conscious. In 1932, such an understanding was "revolutionary" since it amounted to advocating a historicity or an "ethnography" of mental illness as alone capable of accounting for the universality of the madness in every individual. It was thus by way of a new philosophical stance toward psychoanalysis and psychiatry that Lacan made his entry, in advance, into the history of the French psychoanalytic movement. For the while, he himself did not perceive the place he occupied and that had been granted to him from without by a number of writers. It was only after the event that he would acknowledge the breach brought about by his hypotheses within the field of psychiatry. As proof, should it be necessary, the following presentation of his scientific works, written in 1933, may be adduced: "The originality of our study is that it is the first, at least in France, to have attempted an exhaustive interpretation of the mental phenomena of a typical delusion as a function of the concrete history of the subject as reconstituted through as complete an inquest as possible." [31]

Why should a literary and artistic vanguard accord a young psychiatrist a founding role that he himself did not yet attribute to himself? At this juncture, a further historical detour is necessary.

Like Sacha Nacht, Daniel Lagache, Pierre Mâle, Marc Schlumberger, John Leuba, and many others, Jacques Lacan belonged to the second generation of psychoanalysts of the SPP. For reasons that have been explained at length, [32] a number of these initially forged their arms within the Évolution psychiatrique group, which was less nationalistic and more liberal than the Société psychanalytique. The practitioners emerging from their ranks tended to choose their analysts from among the orthodox faction of the SPP, a faction that considered itself legitimately as more "Freudian" than the minority group. In those conditions, Rudolph Loewenstein became the most popular training analyst of the 1930s. During the fifteen years of his Parisian existence, he undertook the training of those who would emerge as the intellectual leaders of the postwar period.

The younger analysts were barely distinguishable from their seniors; through them, however, a new channel for the integration of psychoanalysis in France was being elaborated, which coexisted in part with that of the pioneers. Three elements entered into the relations affiliating the first and the second generations. On the one hand, Pichon had already potentially lost his battle for a "French psychoanalysis," which did not mean particularly much to the new contingent, which was in its majority antinationalist and faithful to the cause of orthodoxy. On the other hand, René Laforgue, despite his clinical genius and the importance of his private practice, was not received as a master. To that extent, his was the strange position of a thinker without doctrine and a founder without disciples. Finally, Marie Bonaparte represented only herself, and her authoritarianism, together with a remarkably impoverished theoretical sense, did not succeed in satisfying the aspirations of those who may well have begun wondering whether the celebrated Viennese ear had not been definitively lost under the couch of this princess from another age.

If the second generation respected its seniors, it did not always adhere to the principles guiding their endeavors. It tended to be nonnationalist and more open to certain tendencies of the aesthetic vanguard. For its members, Freud was an ancestor admired and known through his written work, so distant had his physical presence become.

The men of that generation were born with the century and joined the SPP between 1928 and 1938. They brought with them new stakes, new quarrels, and new rivalries. They did not participate in the bloody battles of the Great War and knew Douaumont and Verdun only from maps and the tales of veterans. Confronted with a prevailing Germanophobia, but not having had to safeguard the spirit of France, they benefited from a certain distance. They were able not to reject their masters and not to yield to their prejudices. Thus certain of them, like Lagache and Lacan, would seek out a measure of rigor in their orientation and effect a kind of return to sources representative of a perturbed period.

Whether French, Jewish immigrants, or Swiss, the members of the first generation had all been analyzed either by each other or by Freud or by his immediate disciples. Those who had never met the "great leader" could have known him at one period or another of their lives. These pioneers were witnesses of a period in which therapy was not yet institutionalized in the form of an obligatory training curriculum. The practitioners of the second generation, on the contrary, joined a society governed by the rules of the IPA and were all analyzed by training analysts of the first generation. The younger generation was confronted with contradicatory transferential situations: On the one hand, it found itself subject to the authority of pioneers enjoying the aura of founding members, but none of whom was, in theory, a true disciple of Freud's; on the other hand, it perceived that no one was actually occupying the position of a master thinker, for the reason, as we have seen, that that position remained empty. For the new generation, the SPP thus resembled an institution in which the kings did not reign, the princesses were errant empresses, the clinical practitioners were not the founders, and Vienna resided at light-years from psychoanalysis. There were nevertheless two points which the two generations had in common. Both were dominated by relations of fraternal complicity, and neither one nor the other practiced a true policy in favor of lay analysis.

We are thus forced to the conclusion that in the fall of 1932, the French psychoanalytic community was unwittingly in search of a doctrinal master it could not find. His name was Jacques Lacan, and he was nothing more at the time than a young director of a clinic, in the process of becoming famous in the world of literature. Jean Bernier, René Creval, Salvador Dali, Paul Nizan, and others observed, along with Henri Ey, the importance of Lacan's thesis because they were outside the analytic movement. That exteriority allowed them to take note in advance of what the movement itself would take several years to acknowledge.

Although it is impossible to date precisely the beginning of Lacan's analysis with Loewenstein, it may be inferred that it began toward the middle of 1932, perhaps a few months prior to the publication of the thesis on paranoia. If we restrict ourselves to his written work, it is impossible to locate any moment of break that might indicate what came "before" and what "after" therapy. Lacan discovered psychoanalytic doctrine through a reading of Freud's texts, not through an experience of the couch. His approach was characterized from the beginning by a personal appropriation of the Viennese theory, outside of any relation of transference to the training analysts of the first generation. Lacan followed a traditional itinerary insofar as his training was concerned, but beneath the cloak of that classical progress, his was the position of a free-lancer within the domain of theory. Within the second generation and in relation to the first, he was not only the first but the only one to effect a synthesis of some scope among all the doctrinal tendencies of the interwar years, between dynamic psychiatry and psychoanalysis, on the one hand, between German philosophy and the theory of the unconscious on the other, and finally, between Surrealism and anthropology.

Lacan's genius was quite unlike Freud's. It lay less in an ability to forge a new mode of knowledge, than in a capacity to join together, in a subtle exercise in what Lévi-Strauss was to call *bricolage,* the essence of the knowledge of an era. Lacan did indeed contribute an innovative reading of Freud's texts, but he constructed his concepts out of a heterogeneous cultural context. The intellectual masters of the young Lacan were first of all Spinoza for philosophy, Maurras for his love of the language, Clérambault for his observation of patients, Édouard Pichon for the conceptualization of his theoretical tools, René Crevel and Salvador Dali for their Surrealist experience of language, Henri Ey for the friendship of an interlocutor, and finally Freud for his texts and his distant role as founding father. Later, his new masters would be named Henri Wallon for the mirror phase and Alexandre Kojève for the genius of his insight into Hegel's discourse. Within that family romance, the eminently decent Rudolph Loewenstein had no place. Despite his competence, that training analyst would remain for several years the analyst of a man who would never be his student, and of whom it may even be wondered whether he was in fact analyzed by him.

Loewenstein has remained quite discreet on the subject of the contents of Lacan's analysis, and the latter never revealed his feelings about the progress of his therapy. Nevertheless, it is known that their relations were conflictual over a period of six years. On those grounds, it is possible to risk a few hypotheses and to reconstitute what may have been Lacan's psychoanalytic "education."

When Lacan arrived on Loewenstein's couch, the latter seemed destined to enjoy a brilliant career. Naturalized a French citizen upon his arrival in Paris,[33] he had the firm intention of not emigrating again. He felt at home in the land of Voltaire and Diderot, and hoped to pursue the career of an acknowledged master. For this he possessed the technical, if not the theoretical, means. Crowned with the prestige that his years in Berlin had earned him and admirably supported by Marie Bonaparte, whose lover he was,[34] he possessed all the qualities needed to become the leader of the French group. Born in 1898, he was in fact the youngest member of the first generation, and thus the near contemporary of the future practitioners of the second generation. By his position and by his age, he was ideally situated to effect a bond between the founders and their disciples. In 1932, no one could imagine what France would be in 1939. No one knew that a new emigration would shatter the French career of Rudolph Loewenstein.

It may thus be suspected that as soon as he accepted Lacan in analysis, he perceived that his student might become his greatest rival. No doubt he was quick to recognize the man's theoretical genius, his capacity for work, his immense intellectual curiosity, the undeniable charm of his personality. He admired him and envied him. Nevertheless, as a rigorous technician, he attempted to subject his patient to the rules of analytic practice as he himself formulated them in his articles: a measure of tact, the interpretation of resistances, a fixed number of sessions, a fixed length of each session, a refusal to combine theoretical thought with the transferential relation, an attempt to diminish narcissism or to deflate megalomania, in brief, everything characterizing orthodox therapeutic technique. In other words, Loewenstein was certainly intent on analyzing Lacan according to the classical directives of the IPA.

The adventure undoubtedly ended in failure. Not that Lacan was unanalyzable, as frequently has been subsequently said, but at that time, and in that context, such therapy could not succeed even if it were to go on indefinitely. What was at play in that analysis would be reactivated on a vaster scale during the splits of 1953 and, later, 1963. What was at stake in the latent dispute between the two men was therapeutic technique: In Loewenstein's eyes, psychoanalysis was first of all a medical method for curing symptoms and understanding resistances, whereas for Lacan, it was above all an intellectual epic, a discovery of the mind, a theoretical journey. Thus the therapy of the young psychiatrist by the future founder of "ego psychology" already bore within it the seeds of the conflict that would break out twenty years later and would oppose, on the one side, the defenders of a psychoanalysis tending to see itself as a therapeutic or a training technique, and, on the other, the partisans of a philosophical adventure that might renew the great message from Vienna.

In the course of his analysis, Lacan probably began to realize that his seniors, with the exception of Pichon, were not valid interlocutors for him. Ambitious, arrogant, disdainful, and rebellious, he elaborated a personal doctrine in the margins of the SPP, which he used as a springboard in order to acquire the necessary training for his career as a private practitioner. Much touted in the world of literature, he exasperated the movement's establishment. He was already reproached for his style, his airs, his fits of anger, his difficult personality, his desire to ingratiate himself, and the excesses of his utterances. In a word, he irritated his colleagues, but all were in agreement in acknowledging the importance of his contributions. He was simply required to undergo a "classical" analysis like everybody else. For his part, he submitted to the rules. Perhaps out of *arrivisme,* but above all because he did not have any choice. He was aware that fame and a practice were to be attained only by way of submission to the norms of a society. Lacan had a certain affection for Loewenstein; he admired Paul Schiff, liked Laforgue, respected Odier, who would be his supervisor,[35] and had friendly dealings with Sacha Nacht and Daniel Lagache. And yet he felt more comfortable in the Évolution psychiatrique group, where Henry Ey now held sway, than in the ranks of the SPP.

Very early on, Marie Bonaparte feared the gradual advance of Lacan in the French movement. Obsessed by her sexual misfortune, lost in the contemplation of her biologistic schemes, invested by Freud with a masculine omnipotence, she could only fear the doctrinal event that was transpiring before her eyes. Now, however ignorant Loewenstein may have been of it, the Princess's attitude must have weighed heavily on the young psychiatrist's analysis. Despite his decency, the training analyst could not have been invulnerable to the passions of his mistress. It was a heavy burden to receive on one's couch the near totality of the members of a society in which each one knew the other and considered him his rival.

We may risk a hypothesis: The analysis, which was not truly taking place on Loewenstein's couch, occurred for Lacan elsewhere—and with a woman. Aimée the criminal, Aimee the paranoid played a fundamental role in Lacan's itinerary. She gave him her words, her story, her writing, her madness, allowing him to become the artisan of a new introduction of Freudian thought in France. With Clérambault, Lacan learned how to observe the insane. With Aimée, he renounced becoming Clérambault. At Sainte-Anne, he began to write, transformed himself, and acquired an identity as a theorist and a psychoanalyst. If Clérambault was for Lacan what Charcot had been for Freud, Aimée was for Lacan what Fliess had been for Freud. Hers was the position of an analyst whose particularity it was to resemble Dr. Schreber as much as she did Anna O. There is always a woman behind the emergence of a master, and it was with this one that Lacan underwent something in the order of a spontaneous self-analysis that would prevent his lying down for real on the couch of a man.

Rather astonishingly, Aimée's son, whom she so feared was threatened by the actress, would become a psychoanalyst after being analyzed by Lacan.

In this superb episode, reality seems composed of the stuff of novels. In 1941, the authorities decided no longer to feed the inmates of asylums, who were judged to be too expensive in war time. Hundreds of madmen were thrown into the streets without any resources. Aimée shared their fate. Dismissed from Sainte-Anne, where she had held a post as assistant librarian, she was received in the countryside by her second sister. After the Liberation, she made the acquaintance of some wealthy Parisians who kept a country home in the village where she was staying. She became their cook, and since they appreciated her talents, they invited her to follow them to their home in Boulogne. Beside her stove, she continued to write under the impetus of a religious inspiration. At the end of her life, she would plan to write an essay on the women of the Bible. At times, she would experience mystical crises in which she felt persecuted. Despite her madness, she would not commit another violent act and would never be reincarcerated.

Didier Anzieu, Aimée's son, suffered his mother's madness from childhood on. An only child, he came to occupy the place of his deceased little sister. Aimée also bore the name of a deceased sister, who had been born before her. Soon Didier was entrusted to an aunt who was also his godmother. After dreaming of becoming an actor, then a writer, he entered the École normale supérieure and received the agregation diploma in philosophy in 1948. His mother's memory led him to an interest in psychology. Four years later, he undertook an analysis with Lacan, without realizing that his mother had preceded him in other circumstances. For his part, Lacan did not recognize the son of the former inmate of Sainte-Anne. Anzieu learned the truth in the course of a conversation with his mother, who spoke to him of her recollections and her relations with the psychiatrists of her day. Whereupon he rushed to the library and discovered in a state of febrility a past which belonged to him and of which he was for the most part ignorant. Questioned as to the fact that he had not recognized the identity of his patient, Lacan confessed to Anzieu that he himself had managed to reconstitute the truth in the course of the analysis. He had been unaware, he said, of Aimée's married name, since she had been admitted to Sainte-Anne under her maiden name. As for Aimée, she told her son that she had never wanted to read her case history. She reproached Lacan bitterly with his refusal to return the manuscripts she had confided to him and that she had intended to publish.

In 1953, Anzieu completed his analysis and became a therapist. During the same period, Aimée continued to frequent the kitchens of Boulogne. Eventually, she was hired by Alfred Lacan, who was looking for a replacement for his governess. His wife, Émilie, had died in 1948 following an operation performed at the Hartmann Clinic in Neuilly. Living alone, Alfred appreciated the culinary talents of Aimée, who would serve him for ten years. One day, Jacques paid a visit to his father and encountered the woman who had made his fortune. She continued to demand the return of her manuscripts and he refused to listen to her. She observed that the father and the son had nothing to say to each other and told Anzieu that Jacques resorted to playing the buffoon in order to mask the silence.[36]

One detail deserves commentary. At the beginning of the analysis, Lacan was unable to identify his patient. Now he could not have failed to know the name Anzieu. In his thesis, he mentions the initial and calls Aimée "Mme A." Furthermore, in the course of his questioning of her family, he could not have failed to hear the name Anzieu. Aimée spoke frequently of her son, invoking his name Didier. Even though she was known at Sainte-Anne by her maiden name, it is impossible that the word "Anzieu" had been erased from her story to the point of not being remembered by Lacan. No doubt he once knew it but forgot it. We may thus be tempted to hypothesize that in his analysis, Anzieu was confronting an act of repression on Lacan's part that concerned the transference the latter entertained with the married name of a woman whose first name, invented by him, had become mythic in the formation of Lacan's thought.

Throughout the duration of Lacan's analysis, Loewenstein cultivated an interest at times in theoretical objects close to those chosen by his patient, at times in themes favored by the Princess. In 1932, after an article devoted to a case of pathological jealousy, he published an article of ten pages on a self-punitive mechanism, then another one on the notion of "constitution."[37] In 1934, he pondered the question of sexual impotence. During a meeting of the SPP, at which Lacan was present for the first time as a member, he examined different types of sexual intercourse characterizing different populations. Marie Bonaparte was all the more exultant in that Malinowski was present and she had asked him to clock the act of intercourse among the Trobriand Islanders.[38] Three years later, Loewenstein made another presentation in which he called into question the death instinct. Lacan intervened politely but at length against him, in order to affirm what he regarded as the correctness of the Freudian position on the problem: "It strikes me as extraordinary to hear some claim that in the subject of the death instincts, Freud had elaborated a speculative construct and was far removed from the facts. It is more speculative to want everything that we encounter in our domain to have a biological meaning than, following man's concrete experience (and no one more than Freud in this century did), to evolve this stupefying bastardized notion. It matters little that it constitutes a biological enigma; what is certain is that within the realm of biology, man is distinguished as a being who commits suicide, who has a superego." Irritated, Loewenstein answered his patient curtly, perhaps forgetting that the latter had been the disciple of a master who had killed himself with consummate flair: "Monsieur Lacan is attacking biologism; but we can't make do without it. It's inevitable; we even mustn't make do without it." [39] To the conflict of the transference was added the major doctrinal opposition separating the first from the second French analytic generation, bearing on the integration of Freud's notion of the death instinct. [40]

Some time later, after he had just been named titular member of the SPP, Lacan made a presentation entitled: "De l'impulsion au complexe. [From impulse to complex]" Concerning two clinical cases, he applied the theoretical positions stated in his "Stade du Miroir [Mirror stage]" in 1936 and his text on the family, which Wallon had published in the *Encyclopédie française*. In the course of the discussion, Odier reproached him with the excessive length of his discourse as well as his propensity to prefer theory to the study of clinical material. Borel, Parcheminey, Cénac, and Laforgue intervened in the debate, and in retrospect it may be seen that they were not treating the lecturer as an equal, but rather commenting on the doctrine of a man they were considering, without realizing it, as their intellectual master. At that date, they did not exchange diverging or converging opinions with Lacan; they rather discussed his theses as though they already had an existence extrinsic to him. Loewenstein intervened on the subject of the self-punitive drive, and as a response, Lacan invoked the late hour, then spoke briefly in the manner of a theorist refusing all discussion. [41]

We know today, thanks to a letter from Loewenstein to Marie Bonaparte, dated February 22, 1953, and quoted by Célia Bertin, that Lacan's election to the ranks of the titular members had been the subject of violent conflict within the SPP. Against the advice of his analyst and thanks to pressure from Pichon, Lacan received his nomination to compensate for that of Heinz Hartmann, who had taken refuge in Paris. The latter, fleeing the Nazis once again, would emigrate, like Loewenstein, to the United States to become a founder of "ego psychology." In exchange for his full affiliation, Lacan promised his analyst to continue his interminable analysis, which was becoming increasingly difficult. Naturally, as soon as he secured his appointment, he abandoned Loewenstein's couch. Furious at being betrayed, Loewenstein regarded Lacan as a cheater and was to comment on the event in 1953 in a letter to the Princess: "What you tell me of Lacan is depressing. He always constituted for me a source of conflict: on the one hand, his lack of character, on the other, his intellectual value, which I prize highly though not without violent disagreement. But the problem is that even though we had agreed that he would continue his analysis after his election, he did not come back. One does not cheat on so important a point without dire consequences (let this remain between us). I hope that his trainees who have been analyzed in a rush, that is, not analyzed at all, will not be accepted." [42] Two points may be noted in passing that indicate the link between Lacan's analysis and his later practice of shortened sessions. With Loewenstein, he could bear neither the length of the therapy nor probably that of the individual sessions, which were about fifty minutes long. For it was over a question of temporality that the conflicts culminating in the split would arise—concerning students analyzed "in a rush, that is, not analyzed at all" according to the criteria of the IPA.

For Pichon in 1938, Lacan was the man called for by the situation. To be sure he found our dandy too Hegelian for his tastes, too Spinozan, too Marxist; above all he begrudged him his style, his manners, ambitions, and Surrealist connections. But in his eyes he was best placed to occupy the position of master which had been deserted by Laforgue. The tempestuous grammarian observed the edifice of his ideals collapse and awaited his death with lucidity, though not resignation. In that context, Lacan seemed to him the only one capable of representing that "French psychoanalysis" for which he had fought and which he feared would go under with the war. This "son" he loved was not Jewish; he spoke the beautiful language of the genius of Latinity; knew how to write like Flaubert; in a word, he was profoundly French, ancestrally attached to the soil of the country Pichon felt he was defending against the forces of barbarism. In him perhaps might reside the hope of bringing to fruition, beyond the troubled history of Europe, a doctrinal project that was anti-German, antiforeign, soon to be anti-American. . . . In brief, Pichon chose his camp and assured the appointment of "his" student under conditions that were terrible for him. To be a token in a negotiation, exchanged for an émigré persecuted by the Nazis, was not an enviable fate for a psychiatrist arriving at the threshold of his doctrinal maturity, the very year of the Munich accords. Lacan was to disappoint his analyst, but he would never adopt as his own the ideals of "Frenchness" in whose name Pichon had "traded" him for a foreigner.

Lacan's doctrine is formulated in French; it is a form of Freudianism that is *culturally* French in its origins and its mode of integration. But it was not linked to any of those diverse branches of "knowledge" that sadly disfigured the first wave of the introduction of psychoanalysis in France. In his life, in his thought, in his love of Spinoza and German philosophy, Lacan would never be either a Germanophobe or a theorist of race. If Pichon's project of a French school of psychoanalysis was to be partially realized through him, that school was founded on a scientific universalism akin to Freud's. When Lacan would lash out against what has been incorrectly called "American psychoanalysis," it would be to criticize the aims of a practice cut off, he felt, from Freud's true message. He would never be "anti-American," since at no point in his life did he adhere to the chauvinistic ideals of the psychology of nations. Had he done so, he would not have been an authentic theoretician. Perhaps in France, for reason of the historical and political circumstances surrounding the implantation of Freudianism, only a non-Jew—an atheist, but culturally a Catholic—could occupy the place of a founder analogous to Freud's in the first Viennese Society. That does not mean that Lacan was alone, in the second generation, in exercising the functions of the head of a school. We shall see that alongside him Sacha Nacht and Daniel Lagache had a project equivalent to his, without managing to give their orientation a specifically psychoanalytic dimension. One thing was common, in any event, to Freud and to Lacan and in part determined their position with respect to the universality of the unconscious: Neither one renounced the religion of his ancestors, but in taking his distance from the faith that religion mediated, each sought sustenance in a culture capable of nourishing his doctrine. Freud partook of the Talmud as Lacan partook of the Gospels: nothing more, nothing less.

III. Christine and Léa

Let us return to the year 1933. Jacques Lacan was beginning to realize that he bore within him a doctrine whose principal underpinnings he had set out in his thesis on paranoia. He was a collaborator of the magazine *Minotaure,* where he published an article on the problem of style in its relation to the psychiatric conception of paranoid forms of experience.[43] His writing had changed, becoming lighter, more elliptical, less "novelistic." Lacan spoke of the "original syntax resulting from lived paranoid experience" and predicted an anthropology capable of freeing itself from a naive realism of the object.

That same year, in the good city of Le Mans, one rainy afternoon in February 1933, Mme Lancelin, the wife of an honorable attorney, and her daughter Geneviève were returning to their family home. They had bought a few items at a charity sale and were in a hurry to set down their packages. During their absence Christine and Léa, their maids, had been assigned to complete their ironing, which had been interrupted the previous day by a stoppage of electricity. The two girls, aged 27 and 22, were model employees, diligent workers and little inclined to frequent the opposite sex. Stemming from poor peasant stock, they had passed their childhood in the Bon-Pasteur orphanage and wanted to be placed together, with a common master. Their mother never stopped requesting money of them. In order to escape that imposition, Christine had tried in vain to emancipate her sister at the local city hall. On that occasion, the two servants had complained of being "persecuted" and the police superintendent had not failed to inform Monsieur Lancelin of the incident, which was deemed not to be serious. No one appeared to know that the Papin sisters' grandfather had died an epileptic, that one of their cousins had gone mad, and that an uncle had hanged himself in his barn. As for their father, he had been the lover of his elder daughter.[44]

On February 2, an electric breakdown had prevented Christine and Léa from attending to their laundry duties. Toward six o'clock in the evening, at the moment the Lancelin women were entering their house, they noticed the elder sister going up to her room with a candle in her hand. She immediately turned around to tell her employer of the breakdown. Irritated, Mme Lancelin reacted with hostility. Whereupon, as though in response, Christine attacked her with a pewter pitcher standing in the cupboard. Upon hearing a shriek, Geneviève ran in to help her mother and in turn was to receive the pitcher in her face. Grabbing on to the head of her murderess, she pulled out a tuft of hair that would remain stuck between her tensed fingers. Soon the carnage was to increase: Christine, in her excitement, ordered her younger sister to finish off Mme Lancelin and pull out her eyes. Léa obeyed: In a moment of furor, she dislodged the gelatinous balls from their orbits and hurled them against the staircase wall. Christine in turn seized Geneviève's left eye as her victim screamed in pain before fainting. With growing fury, the two sisters grabbed one a knife, the other a hammer, and used them to hack away at the bodies of their victims. During these terrible maneuvers, they stripped Geneviève's sex bare, splattering the quarters with blood and brain. Calmed by their act, they bolted the entrance door shut, carefully washed their hands, and then got rid of their filthy clothes. A half-hour later, the police discovered them huddled against each other in the same bed and dressed in a simple robe. They confessed their crime, which had no other motive than the incident of their interrupted ironing.

Summoned as expert witnesses, three psychiatrists, Schutzemberger of Le Mans, Baruk of Angers, and Truelle of Paris, examined the suspects and declared them of sound mind and body, that is, fully responsible for their acts. They were then found guilty of unpremeditated murder and faced, in one case, a death sentence, and, in the other, a life sentence in prison.

After five months of incarceration, Christine found herself subject to fainting spells and hallucinations. She indulged in erotic exhibitions, began to pray, or attempted to rip out her eyes. On occasion she would announce that in another life, she would be her sister's husband and occasionally she could still see Léa in a dream, her legs cut off, hanging from a tree. Her severe agitation necessitated a straitjacket and isolation in a cell. When her lawyer asked her why she had undressed Mlle Lancelin, Christine responded: "I was looking for something whose possession would have made me stronger."

Summoned anew, Dr. Schutzemberger offered an extravagant judgment: He regarded Christine as a malingerer and sent her back to stand trial. The courageous psychiatrist Benjamin Logre rallied to the defense and declared the Papin sisters insane without having had the right to examine them. He represented his diagnosis of mental anomaly engendered by hystero-epilepsy, with sexual perversion and ideas of persecution.[45]

The criminal court of La Sarthe opened its doors on September 29, 1933, as an early winter settled in over the region. There were a variety of conflicting opinions. For the plaintiff and the public prosecutor, the Papin sisters appeared to be blood-thirsty beasts, bereft of all humanity. For others, they were the expiatory victims of bourgeois ferocity. Péret and Éluard sang the glory of these heroines "sprung fully armed from one of Maldoror's chants": "Six years, in perfect submission, they endured criticism, demands, insults. Fear, fatigue, and humiliation slowly gave birth within them to hatred, that very sweet *liqueur* which offers secret solace since it promises violence to grant it sooner or later physical force. When the day came, Léa and Christine paid evil back—in coins of red-hot iron."[46]

While bar president Houlières pleaded responsibility and attempted, in the name of the Lancelin family, to gain acceptance for the thesis of a kind of "semi-premeditation," Maître Germaine Brière tried to demonstrate the insanity of the accused. As in the earlier trial of Joseph Vacher, as more recently in that of Mme Lefèbvre, the advocates of dynamic psychiatry were opposed to the partisans of the older doctrines of heredity, constitution, and malingering. In the midst of the battle, in which once again the adepts of the guillotine were to triumph, the two sisters, locked in silence, confessed that they had nothing to reproach their victims. They used words unknown to their public, half in dialect, half in some primordial language, thus expressing the secret significance of an act whose meaning they themselves were ignorant of, so much was the crime growing unreal in an imaginary world foreign to the world of reason and yet so close to it in its logic. For the incisions made on the women's bodies, Christine used the word *encisures,* as though she wanted to remind her audience of her taste for embroidery and lace. And then, concerning the murder she declared that she had *alourdi* [weighed down] her mistress and caused her eyes to pop out. A strange trial indeed in which the presiding magistrate was named Monsieur Boucher![47]

Christine received the death sentence kneeling. Her sentence was immediately commuted to a life's term in prison. In 1934, again subject to fits of delusion, she was interned at the psychiatric hospital of Le Mans where she would die three years later of vesanic cachexia, thus punishing herself for her own crime. As for Léa, she would rediscover her mother after a few years of incarceration.

In *Le Minotaure,* Lacan commented on the Papin sisters' crime.[48] He compared their story to that of Aimée. He paid homage to Benjamin Logre's courage, but rejected his diagnosis of hysterical epilepsy in favor of paranoia, which alone, he felt, was capable of accounting for the strangeness of the murder. It would appear that Lacan was correct, but since he had not had the opportunity of examining the patients, he avoided pressing his interpretation of their act unduly. He nevertheless noted a number of details that allowed one to classify the crime under the category of paranoia. For example, the insane episode erupted on the occasion of a seemingly banal incident. Now that incident must surely have had an unconscious meaning for the two sisters whose behavior had always been so "normal." Lacan offered the hypothesis that the darkness, which ensued on February 2 on the occasion of the breakdown in electricity, may have conjured up a different—more symbolic—*darkness* into which the protagonists of the drama may have been plunged. From one group to the other, between the servants and the mistresses, "the current was not flowing" since they "didn't speak to each other": "That silence, however, could not have been empty, even if it was obscure to the eyes of the actors." [49]

The latent homosexuality informing the two sisters' fate also bore witness to the acting out of a criminal attitude. Its meaning was uttered retroactively by Christine, who took herself for Léa's husband, thus revealing the phenomenon of a *délire à deux* as well as the characteristics of a drive directed toward two other women, one of whom was the other's mother or "elder." If Aimée had attacked the actress because she represented her ego ideal, the Papin servants killed the Lancelin women for a reason that was probably identical, in a "specular" strategy. Whence the need for self-punishment that appeared five months after the crime, when Christine tried to tear her own eyes out, then, at the time of the verdict when she knelt to hear the death sentence. There remained the question of castration. The sisters bared Geneviève Lancelin's sex in order, as Christine put it, to "possess" something that did not exist but that would bear the trace of a phallic omnipotence. Thus in their distress they tore out the eyes of the women they admired, both to destroy the unhappiness of their lives and to contribute, in reality, a bloody solution to the enigma of female castration.

Beyond that series of interpretations through which Lacan elaborated his doctrine, the originality of a position tending to forge a new conception of the relations between psychiatry, criminology, and penal justice may be seen to emerge. Faced with the partisans of dynamic psychiatry attempting to save the insane from the guillotine as well as with the official experts who had become the executioner's accomplices, Lacan emitted, for the first time in France, the hypothesis of a third path which would bear its fruits only in 1968. He sent packing, back to back, the adepts of both responsibility and irresponsibility. For him to explain a crime was neither to forgive nor condemn it, neither to punish nor accept it. It was, on the contrary, to "derealize" it, that is, to restore to it its imaginary, then symbolic dimension. In that perspective, if the criminal is mad, he is not for all that a monster reduced to his murderous instincts. If madness is to man what language is to humanity, than there is no "nature" or "instinct," nothing "sub-human" or "super-human" which is not already in man himself. It is well known, moreover, that animals, acting out of innate or instinctual behavior patterns, do not kill out of sadism but out of need or by nature. Torture, sexual perversions, horror museums, and concentration camps belong solely to the realm of the human, and if the obscene beast springs from the womb of mothers, it is by way of human metaphor, as Freud demonstrated in the theory of drives so dear to the young Lacan.

In other terms, as a consummate dynamic-psychiatrist, our hero rejected the entire range of doctrines stemming from considerations of race and degeneration. But he went further still. He also criticized the dynamic perspective, that junior branch of the theory of heredity,[50] by showing that the madman was not without responsibility for his acts, since madness was the alienated reality of man and not the reverse side of an illusory reason. With Freud's message, Lacan *thus de-realized the crime without dehumanizing the criminal*. At the same time, he emphasized that psychoanalysis resolved the principal enigma of criminology, which remained stymied by the dilemma of a symmetry endlessly pitting reason and madness, man and beast, God and Satan against each other. And yet all crimes are not identical, even if all criminals are human. Thus the paranoid's crime is not caused by class hatred or the warrior's desire for revenge, but by the psychotic structure through which the murderer strikes the ideal of the master he bears within himself, obeying (without realizing it) the imperative of that "alienated reality" defined by the Hegelian dialectic of the master and the slave.

Against Marie Bonaparte, Paul Schiff, Édouard Toulouse, Benjamin Logre, and even Henri Ey, Lacan refused the very notion of expert psychiatric testimony to the extent that such expertise had no other alternative than to submit the madman to the categories of reason or madness. He did not subscribe to that progressive tradition of dynamism, under whose auspices he had all the same forged his doctrine, but allied himself with the Freudian position intent on separating psychoanalysis and psychiatry. Since he remained a psychiatrist, Lacan transposed the art of psychoanalytic listening to the field of psychiatric observation. He would never give expert testimony, but would always preserve that ethic of visual observation he had learned from Clérambault. It would find its concrete form in the maintenance of a clinical morality centered on the presentation of patients. "Analyzed" at Sainte-Anne by a female paranoiac, Lacan would remain, throughout his life, faithful to the inmates of his first "residence."

That new way of thinking of criminal insanity (and of insanity itself) would not find expression in Lacan's work during the 1930s, even though it was implicit in his thesis and in the article on the Papin sisters. It was only twenty years later that it would come to doctrinal fruition in an address to the Thirteenth Conference of French-language Psychoanalysts on the Function of Psychoanalysis in Criminology.[51] On that occasion, Lacan evoked the Nuremberg trials and the cruelty specific to humanity, then returned to the Papin sisters' crime: "That last case," he wrote, "proved that the analyst alone is able to demonstrate, against prevalent opinion, the alienation of the criminal's reality in a case in which the crime gives the illusion of a response to its social context."[52]

And yet even before that communication, which dates from 1950, it is possible to surmise Lacan's positions concerning expert psychiatric testimony and in opposition to his colleagues of the psychoanalytic community. In 1935, during a scientific session of the SPP, Paul Schiff presented the case of a young woman who had murdered the aunt with whom she had lived since birth. One morning, the victim was handling a tear-gas dispensing pen which her niece had given her, and emitted some gas into her eyes, thus provoking in short order an inflammation of the cornea. Immediately, matters turned violent: The girl struck her relative with a kitchen knife and, regretting her act, proceeded to nurse her, then struck her again before double-locking herself in the bathroom. The aunt died, in a manner poorly explained, of gas poisoning. Upon examination, the experts uncovered a long-standing hatred between the criminal and her victim. Unable to understand the motives of the paranoid crime, they decided to subject the young woman to psychoanalytic therapy. The affair was entrusted to Schiff, who, after five months, discovered the unconscious causes of the murderous act. Acting in a kind of homosexual delusion, the niece and the aunt were engaged in a fierce battle for the exercise of an illusory family power. The girl confessed that she had previously attempted to poison her aunt, a fact that allowed Schiff to reveal the slip leading to the final tragedy: The niece had quite simply "forgotten" to turn off the gas spigot in the bathroom.

In accordance with the principles he had always espoused, Paul Schiff was intent on enlisting psychoanalysis to assist in reforming the judicial apparatus. Now in the debate, Lacan intervened in a rather different register. He first noted the triggering significance of an apparently absurd incident, as in the case of the Papin sisters. Then he insisted on the importance a corneal inflammation might take on in the case of these two masculine women. Marie Bonaparte then spoke to state peremptorily that the criminals should either go to jail if they were responsible or be treated if they were curable, that is, not responsible. Lacan retorted that society ought not simply defend itself against murderers, and that it was psychiatry's obligation to lay the grounds of a coherent doctrine of personality without compromising itself in court testimony. It was only on that condition that it might eventually give the collectivity a valid account of the meaning of criminal insanity.[53]

IV. Henri, Sigmund

Toward 1933, Lacan was taken with Marie-Louise Blondin, the sister of his friend Sylvain, a practicing surgeon. Her slender gazelle-like beauty was pleasing to our hero: He gave her a small gold chain that she would long wear around her ankle. The Catholic marriage took place January 29, 1934. For the occasion, Lacan invited the reverend abbot of the Hautecombe Monastery to give his blessing to the new-lyweds. Yet Marie-Louise, who was nicknamed Malou, belonged to a world that was agnostic. With his marriage, Lacan became part of the Parisian upper bour-geoisie. His wife gave him three children: Caroline in January 1934, Thibaut in August 1939, and finally Sibylle, on November 26, 1940. Lacan resided first on the rue de la Pompe, then on boulevard Malesherbes. In 1936, he set up his private practice as a psychoanalyst even though he had just been named a physician of the state psychiatric hospitals; he continued, nevertheless, to see patients at Sainte-Anne. The previous year, on May 1, 1935, he had traveled to Hautecombe to attend the sacerdotal ordination of his brother Marc-François; he never again returned.[54]

While Lacan was brilliantly pursuing his career, Henry Ey was far from in-active. Born with the century, that warm and uncommonly intelligent individual played a role within the history of the French psychiatric movement that was anal-ogous to the one played by his classmate within the psychoanalytic venture. Thanks to his influence, his rigor, and his extreme tolerance, the treatment and study of the insane in France would, over fifty years, present an aspect that was more humane and generous than elsewhere.

Henri Ey was born in 1900, in his family house at Banyuls-des-Aspres, facing an ancestral pine tree that he would love all his life and that would wither, almost in mourning, after he died. His grandfather was a physician and a fervent Catholic; his aunt belonged to Action française; and his father, a pure-blooded Catalan, was a wine grower. After schooling with the Dominicans, Henri pursued his medical studies at the University of Toulouse. He soon moved to Paris to become the student of Claude, Capgras, and Guiraud. He respected Clérambault's genius without adopting his doctrinal positions, then did his internship at Sainte-Anne along with Lacan, Mâle, and Mareschal. Like them, he rejected the constitutionalist doctrine, manifested an interest in a variety of avant-garde enterprises, and devoted to Proust an admiration that knew no bounds. In 1922, he attended the author's funeral. The *Recherche* would remain a fundamental point of reference for him.

When René Laforgue withdrew from the directorship of the Évolution psy-chiatrique group, Henri Ey gave the journal—which began to appear thrice yearly—a new impetus. His policy consisted in staging confrontations between psychiatry and psychoanalysis and in requiring of each a more rigorous orientation—to be achieved by way of the other.[55]

During that period, he met Renée Schlouch, a Jewish woman of Algerian origin through her father, but who was raised by her mother as a Catholic. As handsome as a Manet canvas, that splendid woman seemed to incarnate Spain. She loved Henri Ey all her life and would second him in his efforts, assisted by another woman with the same first name, Renée Boulay. The latter took up her secretarial functions at the Bonneval hospital when Ey joined the staff and served him faithfully until his retirement in 1970. Even today, she alone is able to decipher his handwriting. Ey himself had always been an accomplished gourmet, a lover of bullfights, a bridge enthusiast, and a great cigar smoker. His wife was nevertheless sharper at cards than he, and, with her culinary gifts, was able to give every evening the atmosphere of a gastronomic event. Ey preferred the country to the city, farming to society gatherings, and local wines to exotic beverages. An artisan of the organodynamic school, he was intent on being the heir to that progressive tradition which had been the greatness of the new psychiatry. And yet by virtue of his clinical gaze and the exceptional relation he maintained with his patients and his students, he was also the last practitioner of the earlier school of "alienism."

A right-winger in his political opinions, a disciple of Maritain, Henri Ey was hostile to the Popular Front and during the Spanish Civil War opted for Franco. For that reason he was not part of the emerging journal *Esprit*. His faithfulness to the caudillo would not, however, prevent him from becoming a Gaullist after 1940, and later from accepting a number of Communists within the Évolution psychiatrique group. In particular, he would count Lucien Bonnafé as one of his foremost disciples.[56]

At the time that Lacan was defending his medical thesis, the director of the antiquated psychiatric hospital of Bonneval asked Henry Ey to take charge of the 750 inmates of the former Benedictine monastery dating from the tenth century. The psychiatrist accepted all the more willingly in that he was eager to live in the country while maintaining his teaching career at Sainte-Anne. Each Wednesday he presented patients to an attentive audience. In 1933, he moved into Bonneval with his wife and set up his office in the former monks' kitchen. It was there that he gradually realized his organo-dynamist conceptions and inaugurated a new approach to mental illness. Without ever abandoning the division between the normal and the pathological, and even while accepting the principle of expert psychiatric testimony in cases of criminal insanity, he promoted a reform of the world of asylums that would result, years later, in that recasting of the art of clinical observation commonly known as the "policy of sectorization." It consists, in the spirit of the dynamic perspective, in no longer isolating the insane from the community of the living, but in attempting, on the contrary, to reintegrate them into society by making use of all possible therapeutic techniques, including psychoanalysis. Ey's experiment at Bonneval thus marked the first stage of a project aimed at opening up the world of the mad to that of the citizens of reason, beginning with the very space of the hospital. In that sense, the project partook of the bi-polar representation of madness which Lacan was calling into question at the same time and that may be found in the division suggested by Ey between the "organic" and the "dynamic." And yet it was part of a movement identical to the one authorizing a challenge to it. In 1946, at a colloquium at Bonneval, the same issues could be found tendentially dividing the advocates of a "biological unconscious" and the partisans of a more "linguistic" unconscious.

In 1934, Henri Ey published a study entitled *Hallucinations et délires*,[57] which constituted something of a summation of his early positions on the structural singularity of "mental" illness. Taking up anew Séglas's work, he criticized, like Lacan, Clérambault's automatism and maintained that the essence of chronic hallucinatory delusions lay in a pathology of belief that disturbed the relation between the subject and the living world. In that perspective, the madman defends his own reality as the expression of an authentic objectivity. Ey called into question the classical distinction between actual and pseudo- hallucinations in order to classify hallucinations within mental structures and delusional patterns of behavior. In so doing, he sought support not in any pre-established diagnostic scheme, but in an attentiveness to the discourse of the mad. Like the entirety of the second French psychiatro-psychoanalytical generation, he integrated Freud's message into his conception of madness. It will thus be understood why Lacan authored an article for *Evolution psychiatrique* in praise of his friend's book. He took advantage of the occasion to show that the latter's hypotheses were aligned with his own, which was indeed entirely the case. He did, however, reproach him for not paying sufficient attention to either the creative mechanism of hallucinations or the notion of personality structure, which governed, he claimed, the unity of all chronic delusions. Once again Lacan "historicized" his own doctrine by situating the dynamic movement within conceptual categories he himself had formulated.[58] One might think that he feared not so much being "plagiarized" as being insufficiently recognized by his peers.

In 1936 Henri Ey began his elaboration of what has since become the classic notion of "organo-dynamism."[59] Inspired by Jacksonian neurology, from which Freud had borrowed certain of his theoretical tools, the doctrine posits a primacy of the *hierarchy* of functions over their static organization. It considers psychical functions as mutually interdependent, from higher to lower. Thus the dissolution of higher nervous activities brings about a *freeing* or unbinding of lower activities previously controlled by them. From the anticonstitutionalist perspective of the 1930s, the Jacksonian model, already introduced in France by Ribot, was for Henri Ey what the Freudian model was for Lacan. If Jackson had shorn neurology of its mechanist presuppositions, Lacan abandoned neurology in order to found the theory of the unconscious and contribute to psychiatry a new conception of madness. According to Henri Ey, it was now the time to unite neurology and psychiatry in order to endow the latter with a true theory, accommodating Freudianism. From Lacan's point of view, what was needed, on the contrary, was to renew Freud's separatist gesture, even if it entailed rethinking psychiatric knowledge on the model of the Freudian unconscious. In other words, Lacan did not oppose a "psychogenesis" of the psychoses to their "organogenesis," all of which would have maintained the original symmetry of the organic and the psychic; he substituted *psychogenius* [*psychogénie*] for both psychogenesis and organogenesis, thus granting priority to a "mental structure," that is, a purely psychic organization of personality. Organic causality did not drop out of the clinical picture; it was simply secondary.

Henry Ey opted for a second orientation. He chose the camp of a "hierarchized dualism" and maintained that there was no pure psychogenesis of mental disturbances since their origin lay in a dissolution of organic functions determining psychical activity. In that perspective, psychosis resulted from an "energy deficiency" perturbing the subject's balance and "releasing" within him instinctual tendencies escaping from conscious control.

It will thus be seen that the notion of structure did not take on the same meaning in Ey's work as in Lacan's. The organo-dynamist doctrine in part reintegrated the old mechanist orientation within a kind of structural (that is, hierarchized) phenomenology of morbid thought. To that extent it retained the principle of a psychophysiological dualism. Lacan's theory, on the contrary, removed itself from such a dualism by having psychogenius rest on a "dialectic of the unconscious personality," which would alone be capable of isolating a "psychical causality," without, however, eliminating the organic substrate which would simply be dissociated from the psyche. Ey's doctrine was based on a theory of "personality involution," in which the unconscious becomes the expression of the involuted instances of human personality. Through it there appear morbid entities ranging from neurosis, the most superficial, to dementia, the deepest, and passing through the "intermediate states" of paranoia, mania, and schizophrenia. Lacan's thought, on the contrary, presupposed a *structural* theory of personality irreducible to any notion of deficiency or involution, but granting to the unconscious the position of psychical structure itself. The morbid entities thus flow, as with Freud, from the unconscious organization of the subject.

During the 1930s, Henri Ey shared with Lacan the conviction that psychoanalysis should not be used as an auxiliary technique of traditional psychiatry. For the two friends, Freud's discovery restored a meaning to psychiatry to the extent that it refuted the idea of a nosology that might be separated from the human dimension of madness. In other words, psychoanalysis was for them a modern rebellion against the meaninglessness of a clinical tradition that deprived the madman of the utterance of his insanity in order to replace it with a classification written in jargon.

And yet for Henri Ey psychoanalysis remained the child of psychiatry since the former saved the latter from its original sin. They were thus complementary and formed a structural whole within the history of medicine. The organo-dynamist doctrine found its political translation at this juncture in the form of a refusal of lay analysis. Whereas Marie Bonaparte defended the cause of psychoanalysts who were not physicians while transplanting the ideals of medicine and biology within the psychoanalytic movement, Henry Ey, as early as 1932, was putting into practice a quite different policy that may be regarded as a continuation of the efforts of Minkowski. For him, there was no such thing as lay analysis, and psychoanalysts would have to be physicians in order to practice therapy. But it was not a matter of importing medical ideals into analytic practice. What was needed, on the contrary, was, through Freud's discovery, to bring new vigor to the practice of mental medicine by endowing it with the philosophical charge and the doctrinal power that it had been lacking before the Viennese venture. In that manner, Ey was to manifest a hostility toward *Laienanalyse* without for all that participating in the struggle to maintain the pressure of medical tradition weighing on psychoanalysis. As opposed to the Princess, who sought to transform psychoanalysis into a branch of medicine, and in contrast to Laforgue, the sole advocate of lay analysis during the interwar period, Henri Ey elaborated a policy destined to maintain Freudian practice under the aegis of a medical ethic that would itself be revised and rectified by that practice. For this intellectual master of the organo-dynamist school, psychoanalysis ran the risk of religion or madness if it attempted to pass itself off as the "science of sciences," while forgetting to measure itself against man himself in the concrete reality of his illness.[60] That position, in its exemplary antidogmatism, would not manage to prevail within the psychoanalytic movement, but would endow the science of psychiatry with a new impetus.

For his part, Lacan directed his efforts in a different channel; during the interwar period, he did not participate (and for good reason) in the conflicts pitting the "false" partisans of "lay analysis" against the "true" adepts of complete medicalization. And yet his doctrine bore the seeds of elements that might authorize the emergence of an authentically separatist policy. Because he refused organodynamism while remaining, like Henri Ey, the advocate of a recasting of the art of psychiatric observation, Jacques Lacan was laying, without realizing it, the grounds of a politics of *Laienanalyse* that would take concrete form thirty years later after two organizational splits. Having been a psychiatrist from the beginning, he did not dream, like Marie Bonaparte, of becoming what he had always been, but neither was he, like Sacha Nacht, intent on remaining what medical practice had made of him.

In 1936, Lacan went for the first time to a congress of the IPA, at Marienbad. Freud, who was ill, stayed in Vienna. The thermal city, which was near Austria, was chosen so that Anna Freud might return hastily to her father's side should there be need of it. Marie Bonaparte and René Spitz were also representing the French group. As for Lacan, he presented his ideas on the "mirror stage," a term borrowed from Henri Wallon to which he gave a new interpretation. After ten minutes, he was interrupted by Jones. Displeased, the Frenchman vented his rancor at the Welshman. Which may be the reason why he "forgot" to submit his communication—which does not appear in the proceedings of the congress—to the competent authorities. The larger part of his presentation appeared in an article published in 1938, at Wallon's request, in the *Encyclopédie française*. At the congress, Lacan met the members of the Vienna Society, who, he claimed, received his ideas warmly. In 1949, at Zurich, he would take up the theme of the mirror stage anew and thus produce the definitive version of the historic text, whose origins go back to 1936, which constituted a turning point in his thought. On his return from Marienbad, he passed through Berlin and attended the famous Olympics at which the Nazi esthetic was intended to triumph. Anguished by the rise of Hitlerian violence, he expressed his fears at the military weakness of the Western democracies.[61]

It will perhaps never be known whether Lacan wanted to pay Freud a visit. No doubt he was disappointed: He had sent off his thesis to the master, who had sent him a curious postcard, partially crossed out, in response. Freud wavered, writing two addresses: Alfred Lacan's at Boulogne and his son's on the rue de la Pompe. He acknowledged his receipt of Lacan's gift with polite indifference: "Thank you for sending your thesis." The psychiatrist kept the card for a number of years, then entrusted it to one of his analysands, who held on to it. After Lacan's death, the patient found himself on the couch of an analyst who had himself been trained by Lacan. He mentioned the precious correspondence. The therapist pricked up his ears and urged his client to show it to him. After a few hesitations, the patient did so. At which juncture the document was published in the journal *Ornicar?*. A striking parable indeed: The story of a letter sent, distributed, rediscovered, then returned by way of transference seems like a tale by Edgar Allan Poe.

Freud treated Lacan like Pierre Jean Jouve. Worse yet—in his eyes, the psychiatrist was not as interesting an individual as the writer. At that time, Freud did not read the productions coming out of France. He was no more interested in Aimée's adventure than he was in *Vagadu*. For his part, Lacan did not adopt the same attitude throughout his development. In 1932, it was his wish that Freud understand what he was writing or be interested in him. Four years later in Marienbad, he was no longer the same. He felt himself to be the bearer of a personal theory and received Jones's intervention as though it were an act of censorship. On the other hand, he had the impression of having been understood by the Viennese. Beyond any interpretation he gave of his first encounter with the international movement, the position he sought to occupy in France, at a time when the gradual victory of the new world over central Europe was coming to pass, may be intuited. Lacan was already dreaming of a "Freudian France" capable under his authority of founding a kingdom similar to the Vienna of the Habsburgs.

In 1938, he changed still again. When Marie Bonaparte received Freud on his road to exile, Lacan did not attend the gathering she organized in Freud's honor. He would later say that he did not want to pay homage to the Princess. In six years, which correspond to the duration of his analysis and the formation of his thinking, he thus went, in relation to Freud, from a request for recognition to an acceptance of reality. At the end of the novel of his youth, he knew that he was letting his last chance to meet the founding father escape. Had he decided to pay a visit to Freud, it would have been an error. The confrontation would have culminated at best in a misunderstanding, at worst in a disaster. Lacan identified far more with Freud's texts than with his person, and it was in the written work of the Viennese master that he discovered the theoretical tools needed for the elaboration of his own doctrine. Thus was there established a new transferential bond between a text and a reader, at a distance from any personal or didactic relation. Lacan had done his best not to restore with the ancestor a bond that had already been broken with the first generation.[62]

V. Alexandre

Since 1933, a mysterious guru, with the manners of a prophet, had been fascinating the Parisian intelligentsia. At each session of his seminar at the École pratique des hautes études, he would interpret a few lines of *The Phenomenology of Mind* in diction unlike any other. As commentary, he proposed a highly idiosyncratic translation, midway between fiction and speculation. Combining an intonation laden with meaning and the charm of a Slavic accent, he spoke in impeccable French without notes. Through the discourse of Alexandre Kojève (his real name was Kojevnikov), an entire intellectual generation discovered the key terms of Hegel's philosophy. The auditors of his closed seminar learned with delight of Desire, Recognition, Praxis, Negativity, Self-Consciousness, the End of History, and Satisfaction or Wisdom. For a period of six years, the man's speech became the very language of modernity, the quintessence of the intellectual vanguard, in which each was free to intuit the outlines of the End. Lacan could not get over it. Eager for philosophical nourishment, he borrowed from the seductive master not only his concepts but a teaching style evocative, as if in reverse, of Clérambault's own flamboyant manner. For Kojève was, in his way, a clinical observer, an artisan of the capital letter, a formalist of discourse, a mesmerizer of students, a legendary commentator on texts.

Seated alongside Lacan, Raymond Queneau was similarly responsive. Day by day, he polished his notes, thus allowing for a written transcription of this jewel of oral teaching. Further off, Georges Bataille felt suffocated, crushed, shattered, killed ten times over, nailed to his place.[63] As for Raymond Aron, who was more of a rationalist, he could not stop wondering why this thinker of genius defined himself as a "Stalinist of the strictest obedience." Forty-five years later, he would still be seeking an answer to that vain query, without realizing that it is contained in its entirety in Kojève's approach.[64] Other initiates attended the seminar and debated every week around the café tables of the place de la Sorbonne. One could find there Maurice Merleau-Ponty, Eric Weil, the Reverend Father Fessard, Pierre Klossowski, Alexandre Koyré, and André Breton, who would make fugitive appearances.

Born in 1902 to a well-off family of the Moscow bourgeoisie, Alexandre Kojève was the same age as the majority of his pupils. He had seen his father die during the Russo-Japanese War and his first step-father in a fight with thieves. As a young student in 1919, he was forced to leave his country as he was not authorized to pursue his studies because of his class origins. One evening, he decided to cross the border clandestinely. Despite the cold, he crossed through Poland and took refuge in Germany with an uncle. He quickly learned the language and studied philosophy at the university of Heidelberg, where he initiated himself in Hegel's thinking. Thanks to a friend, he succeeded in retrieving the family jewels, which allowed him to provide for his needs; armed with his small fortune, he arrived in Paris in 1928. He remained faithful to the ideals of a revolution which had, all the same, chased him out of his own country, and each year he would return to the Soviet Union. A naturalized French citizen, he invested his money in a business that went bankrupt and soon found himself constrained to earn his living, a circumstance that distracted him from his philosophical conception of Wisdom. He nevertheless accepted a proposition from his friend, Alexandre Koyré, to conduct a seminar under the auspices of the chair of philosophy of religions at the École pratique des hautes études. Thus began, in 1933, the famous course on the various chapters of *The Phenomenology of Mind*.[65]

The history of the implantation of Hegelianism in France bears the same features as that of the introduction of Freudianism. In both cases, we find identical phenomena of resistance, which functioned as the active symptom of the progress registered by the two doctrines. If the penetration of Freudianism began at the beginning of the twentieth century and ended around 1950, thus mobilizing two generations of thinkers, the diffusion of Hegelianism lasted about 150 years and came to an end around 1945. In the 1930s, a new interpretation of Hegelian doctrine was to encounter a new representation of Freudian theory.

The first stage in the formation of a French Hegelianism took place during Hegel's lifetime. It was dominated by the relations maintained by the German philosopher with his French counterpart, Victor Cousin. A child of the Revolution, in 1810 Cousin graduated first in the first graduating class of the École normale supérieure. Interested very early on by philosophy beyond the Rhine, he saw in it a way of compensating for the theoretical void prevailing in French universities.[66] Without knowing German, he made several trips to Frankfurt, Jena, and then Heidelberg, where he met, successively, Schlegel, Goethe, and Hegel. Shortly thereafter, in his course for 1818, he was to become the spokesman for a kind of rationalist Hegelianism opposed to the romantic vision of German culture to be found, for example, in Mme de Staël's celebrated work. Just as the introducers of psychoanalysis in France would do a hundred years later, Cousin sought to give an allegedly "French" cast to a system of thought alleged to be "German." The Hegelian system was to be assimilated to the ideals of a moderate liberalism. If the French resistance to psychoanalysis took the form of a constant attempt to sever Freudian doctrine from its theory of sexuality, the resistance to Hegelianism consisted (through Cousin) in stripping the Hegelian system of the essential figure of dialectic in its aspect as negativity. Made "positive" and less "barbarous," the Hegelian model thus became more acceptable to the land of Descartes. In a first phase, and in accordance with his liberal orientation, Cousin implemented (on Hegelian grounds) a policy of modernizing the teaching of philosophy, centered on a nonsensualist theory of the objectivity of the forms of knowledge, in which Reason was to be opposed to God, and pantheism to religion.

Subsequently attacked by the clerical right and the "ultra" extremists, Cousin saw his right to teach suspended. During a stay in Dresden, he was arrested by the Prussian police, who accused him of maintaining relations with the political opposition. Hegel and Schelling intervened. At which point the Frenchman was transferred to a prison in Berlin and then freed in 1825. Starting in 1828, the victory of the moderates over the conservatives permitted him to reign as absolute master over the French university and to elaborate the official philosophy he dreamed of. Thus it was that *eclecticism* took shape, a doctrine inspired by Hegelianism, but cleansed of its "Germanic" defects. That first implantation of Hegelianism in French soil consisted in effecting the *recognition* of a philosophy in a deformed state, and without effecting its *cognition*. "Eclecticism," Pierre Macherey has emphasized, "was Hegel's philosophy without negativity, without dialectic, and without contradiction." [67] With the publication in 1837 of his famous work, *Du Vrai, du Beau, et du Bien* ["Of truth, beauty, and goodness"], Cousin removed from his teaching whatever traces may have subsisted of his previous Hegelianism. He even went so far as to substitute the term "spiritualism" for that of "eclecticism."

As of 1850 and for nearly a century thereafter, Hegelian thought vanished from the French academic scene. The philosopher was regarded as the spiritual father of "pan-Germanism," and German theorists fell victim to the nationalist prejudices that unfurled after the war of 1870. And yet Hegelianism was taken up in an almost clandestine manner by a variety of autodidacts, political exiles, socialists, and poets. Hegel remained hidden, but his philosophy gained ground in France in the form of a subterranean "rumination." It began with Villiers de l'Isle-Adam, Mallarmé, and Lucien Herr, and was continued by the Surrealists and particularly André Breton. "Kojèvism" belongs to that tendency by which Hegelianism resurfaced in an initiatic context.

During the interwar period, the situation changed. In 1929, Jean Wahl became interested in the texts of the young Hegel; in 1932, Alain contributed a study of his method, and in 1938, Henri Lefebvre published Lenin's *Notebooks* on Hegelian dialectic. With Kojève's teaching, the ruminative tradition took on a new aspect. The man was neither a writer nor a political figure, but a true philosopher. Despite his marginality, he introduced Hegelianism into the heart of the university, by way of the École pratique des hautes études and under the aegis of the *philosophy of religon.* Thus did a connection begin to be forged between the hidden and official currents of Hegelianism. Against Kojève and thanks to him, intellectual France would be Hegelian until the 1960s. By way of Jean Hippolyte, who translated the *Phenomenology* in 1939. By way of Georges Canguilhem, who pointed out in 1948 the almost delirious nature of Hegelianism as interpreted by Kojève. By way of Alexandre Koyré, who observed in 1961 a radical shift concerning Hegel. By way of Merleau-Ponty, finally, who declared in 1966 that Freud, Nietzsche, and Marx owed everything to his philosophy.[68]

Those attending Kojève's seminar had the impression of living in a period of chaos that forced them to reflect on the past. The idea of an "end of history" made its way into the minds of those men who were thirty at the time of the Depression and a few years older when Hitler came to power. "At a time of world revolution, of world war," wrote Georges Canguilhem, "France discovered in the literal sense a philosophy contemporaneous with the French Revolution and whose crisis of awareness it in many ways was."[69] The resurgence of a Hegelianism centered on atheism and on a violent (then, "naturalist") vision of historical evolution meant two contradictory things. On the one hand, French intellectuals no longer felt themselves capable of "making history," like their revolutionary ancestors, but on the other, they gained awareness of their power to reflect on history and specifically on the meaning of revolutions. All of Kojève's thought was inscribed in that double gesture bent on thinking "the history of the end of history" based on the observation of the potential end of history. In other terms, if history stopped in 1806 when Hegel saw Napoleon, that "soul of the world," passing beneath his window, it stopped a second time when the Bolshevik revolution produced its greatest tyrant, Joseph Stalin. If the thought of the end of history was made possible by the publication in 1807 of the *Phenomenology of Mind,* the history of the end of history reached its culmination in Kojève's commentary on that *Phenomenology.* Man's obligatory transit through negativity authorizes his becoming creative, his *being for death,* and, finally, his attaining of wisdom. Through that process, he becomes no longer a "hero," but a simple visitor of battlefields. Whence the novels of Queneau, in which irony wins out over seriousness, and atheism borders on a ludicrous anthropology of everyday life; whence the idea of a sacred terror or of the primacy of the unconscious, which inspired a number of Bataille's most splendid pages; whence finally the prevalence Lacan attributed to the desiring subject, generator of recognition and bondsman of the desire of the other. Those figures were inspired by Kojève's vision of Hegelianism.

If we restrict ourselves to the actual texts, Kojève was no more "Hegelian" than Breton. But the problem is not one of determining in what ways a commentator betrays or respects a master's doctrine. It should rather be said that the break-up of Hegel's philosophy belongs to the history of Hegelianism in the same way that the dissident trends of Freudianism belong to the history of the psychoanalytic movement. No philosophy is prior to its historical actualization, and the actualization is part and parcel of the philosophical reality from which it draws its history. On the basis of that observation, it is possible to set up a comparison between original doctrines and the interpretations produced by their break-up. In that perspective, it may be said that Hyppolite is closer than Kojève to Hegel's text.

And yet Kojève's teaching may be regarded as part of an innovative implantation of Hegelianism in France once one acknowledges that such a Hegelianism does not restore the integral truth of Hegel's text but rather casts it in an original light. Specifically, that teaching dispelled any notion of "Gallicizing" Hegel. It was a matter of reading a text and interpreting it, and not of building a philosophy in agreement with an alleged national spirit. It was not by chance that Lacan discovered in Kojève's discourse the wherewithal to effect a new interpretation of an original body of thought. At Kojève's side, he learned how to make Freud's text say what it does not say. He endowed Freudianism with a philosophical system in which subjectivity escaped from the psychology of the self. And he retained two central notions: the *belle âme* or "beautiful soul" [*schöne Seele*], through which the subject projects its own disorder onto the world in order to wax indignant at it, and the *dialectic of master and slave,* whose versions he would proliferate without end.

Twenty years later, Lacan would "call" Hyppolite to his seminar in order to learn what a Hegelian might say about Freud, and would then dismiss Hegelianism from his concerns.[70] But between the wars, through the discourses of Kojève and Lacan, the styles of implanting Hegelianism and Freudianism overlapped in the project of advocating an "initiatic" return to the text.

Kojève interpreted the *Phenomenology of Mind* in an anthropological and Marxist direction. He fascinated his audience by giving Hegelianism a concrete aspect, in which philosophy takes to the streets in order to come to terms with tyranny. If there is no difference between a philosopher and a tyrant, every history is the illustration of a certain terrorism. Kojève did not issue an apology for "totalitarianism," but he encompassed within his discourse the unreasonable materiality of reason itself: massacres, struggles to the death, the folly of the great. He attempted to reconcile "the Sunday of life" with "the working days of the week," the sacred functions of existence with its secular aspects. Between Hegel and Kojève, the Bolshevik revolution had occurred, as well as a new philosophical art. Between Napoleon and Kojève's audience in 1933, there came Lenin and Heidegger. Kojève thus began by criticizing theology, showing that it was a humanism unaware of its own existence. When it spoke of God, it was speaking of man without realizing it.[71] Thus the place within theology accorded the kingdom of heaven was to become, in atheism, one reserved for the universal State whose actualization was Absolute Knowledge. In that sense Kojève was being quite rigorous when he defined himself as "a Stalinist of strict obedience." Without being an adherent of Stalinism, he assigned himself the role of commentator on the history of a tyranny, just as Hegel had commented on the history of the "Great Corsican." He did no more than reflect on the famous line by Victor Hugo, which so fascinated Lacan: "Déjà Napoléon perçait sous Bonaparte [Already Napoleon was piercing through beneath Bonaparte . . .]."

In order to think through the relation between the religious illusion as "superstructure," and actual history, as "infrastructure," Kojève made use not only of a Marxist vocabulary, but of the notion of the "inverted form of an image," which would be taken up by Lacan. If every religion gives an inverted image of the Real, then the passage from Representation to Concept translates that from the kingdom of heaven to the earthly State. Theology thinks the End of History in apocalyptic terms and Hegelianism, according to Kojève, also thinks the end of history, but in humanist terms. For indeed, Absolute Mind was incarnated in Napoleon, who was revealed by the Sage, *alias* Hegel, who was himself commented on by another Sage, Kojève, who gave expression to the position of philosophy in its confrontation with the new tyrants. Therein may be found a translation of the Christian trinity: if Absolute Mind is God, Napoleon is Christ and Hegel the Holy Ghost, charged with bringing family affairs to light. The "Great Man" acts in ignorance of the labors he is accomplishing and the Sage has nothing else to do than repeat tirelessly Hegelian discourse. At the end of the cycle, history disappears and man can become an animal again and live like a Sage, that is, like a "leisurely loafer" having reconciled his Sundays and his weekdays.

In characterizing his ontology, Kojève made use of a dualism. For him, dialectic does not exist in nature, which obeys solely the principle of positivity. Negativity, on the contrary, defines every human phenomenon, and Being is revealed through Desire, Discourse, and Speech. Discourse reveals Man in his totality whereas man and nature do not partake of the same ontological principle. Nature is not "dialectical," but its transformation by human knowledge obeys a dialectical process. Dialectic, which is negative, is divided into two instances: man's relation to the transformation of things and relations between men, which are governed by the relation of Master and Slave.

Kojève transcribes Hegel's fable in the style of a serialized novel. He dramatizes the abstract entities in order to turn them into living characters. He thus grants a privilege to a dialectic of praxis at the expense of a dialectic of consciousness. Whence the extravagant extension he gives the concept of Desire, *Begierde* in German, defined as "the manifest presence of the absence of a reality." Desire is Desire of Recognition; it is the desire not of an object but of another desire. To want to be recognized in a struggle between master and slave is above all to want to be desired; it entails risking one's life in a dual interaction for the sake of something that exists only in the imaginary. Thus reality is social insofar as it is the *totality of desires mutually desiring each other*. Human desire, which is anthropogenic, thus differs from animal desire by virtue of the fact that it does not bear on a real object but on another desire. Kojève thus defines the sexual relation between a man and a woman: Desire is human only if one desires not the other's body, but the other's Desire. Human history is the history of desired Desires.

Desire passes through Negativity, and that latter dimension defines human freedom, that is, wherein men differ from animals. Freedom is thus the power to negate what is, through the struggle for recognition. This theme joins up with that of the validity of state terrorism since what is politically at stake is causing *what is* to yield to *what should be*. Kojève interprets history as the history of a struggle for recognition through class struggle. In wars and revolutions, blood flows, and slaves rebel in order to become masters. In the dialectic of recognition, on the contrary, there is an equality of adversaries, and the master returns to his inferiority because he was unable to be scornful of death. For the philosopher, revolution is impossible once the Desire of the other's Desire is fully satisfied. At that stage of history, class and national differences disappear, and man can evolve toward the positivity of his animal existence. But things are not that simple, since Desire never stops desiring. Kojève is thus "condemned" to read Marx into Hegel and Hegel with Heidegger. As a philosopher, he refused to give advice to princes. Hegel was not Napoleon's minister; Kojève would not be Stalin's commissar. But in order to attain Wisdom, the philosopher had to be a man of action. That explains why Kojève, in 1945, accepted an official French position in Foreign Trade. Preferring the role of gray eminence to that of official intellectual, he entered the administration and was an enthusiastic participant in the "play" of international negotiations, through which he fulfilled his philosophical conception of wisdom.

The importance of Kojève to the intellectual generation of the years 1933–55 may be easily imagined. The problematic of sacred terror was central to the founding (by Bataille and Caillois among others) of the Collège de sociologie. The themes of tyranny, nothingness, terrorism, atheist humanism, and "commitment" impregnated the philosophical positions of Sartre and Merleau-Ponty. As for the notions of desire, negativity, recognition, and the end of history, they ran through Lacan's rereading of Freud: from the *Stade du miroir* ["The mirror stage"] in 1936 all the way to the seminar on *L'envers de la psychanalyse* ["The reverse side of psychoanalysis"] in 1970.[72]

Kojève's teaching exercised an "influence" on Lacan in the literal sense of the word. Every time he confronted a text of Hegel, he reintroduced the spark of a Kojèvian reading. Thus did he activate the fruitful phase of Kojèvian thought under the category of "Hegelianism." He would never contribute anything on the subject of Hegel that was not drawn from Kojève, as though that teaching had penetrated him to the point of being indistinguishable from his own later reading of Hegel's text.

With the exception of Clérambault, Lacan never actually laid claim to the name of a master or, better, to the *name of a father*. When he called himself a Freudian, it was in order to situate himself as the *interpreter* of a text and not as the disciple of a theorist. When he borrowed from Lévi-Strauss or Jakobson, he quoted his sources and paid them homage. As with Merleau-Ponty. When he referred to Koyré and took him as his guide in matters of epistemology, it was in order to note in passing that his works had not been appreciated as they deserved. He mentioned his attachment to Clérambault moreover, first in 1946, then in 1966, when the latter was no longer in a position to accuse him—wrongly, as it happens—of plagiarism. The heir's debt to his master, or that of the "son" to his "father," was expressed when the son had already become a founding father.

When we come to Kojève, matters are simultaneously similar and different. Although the philosopher's name is not mentioned in the *Écrits*, on several occasions Lacan acknowledges that he had been "trained in Hegel" on the benches of the seminar at the École pratique des hautes études. "Let us recall at this juncture," he wrote in the first issue of *Scilicet*, "the irrationality of a knowledge such as that forged by the humor of a Queneau, by virtue of his having been trained, on the same benches as I was, in Hegel, namely his *Dimanche de la vie* ["Life's Sunday"], or the advent of the do-nothing and the rotter, demonstrating in their absolute lethargy the knowledge capable of satisfying animals. Or merely the wisdom authenticated by the sardonic laughter of Kojève, who was master to us both." [73] Lacan acknowledged his debt after the fact, when he had himself become a personality as important (if not more so) than his former master.

Gradually, Lacan reached his theoretical maturity by undergoing an analysis with Loewenstein with whom he did not learn anything and in attending Kojève's seminar, at which he learned as much as he had with Aimée or Clérambault.

The philosopher was the same age as Lacan and initiated him to the art of commenting on the text of a master—preferably orally. Lacan shared with this "twin brother" a certain taste for provocation and mystery as well as a profound hostility toward publication, which he would later call "poubellication" [from the French *poubelle,* garbage can]. Like Kojève, he would benefit from the services of a scribe in "interpreting" or "transcribing" his teaching and, again like him, he would be simultaneously marginal and perfectly well installed within the university system. Nevertheless, unlike the philosopher, he would not become the sage of an absurd *polis,* but the monarch of a psychoanalytic community in need of a master. Lacan was fascinated by "Napoleon piercing beneath Bonaparte," in Hugo's phrase, that is, by the power of tyrants, by Pericles, Themistocles, the pope.... He identified with the position occupied by Kojève during the six years of his reading of Hegel's text and would assume, in his school, that position of command which the philosopher refused to take in order to become a government employee.... Lacan was to Freud what Kojève was to Hegel; he was the interpreter of a text, but, if Freud identified with Hannibal, Bonaparte, and then Moses in order to occupy the position of a "master without command," [74] Lacan identified with the "role" of Kojève in order to revive psychoanalysis's "Hannibalian impact," a subversive and initiatic vision of the Viennese discovery.

Through his doctrine and through the relations he entertained with his disciples and with the psychoanalytic community, Lacan put into effect the essence of that negative dialectic of human Desire and the Struggle for Recognition, as Kojève formulated them out of Hegel's discourse. He put it into effect in order to rediscover a "Hannibalian" vocation of psychoanalysis, a vocation of reconquest based on the primacy of the unconscious.

It was no doubt no accident that on the occasion of Kojève's death in 1968, Lacan rushed to his apartment in order to take possession of a copy of the *Phenomenology of Mind* annotated in Kojève's own hand.[75]

VI. Family Chains

After the elections of 1932 and the defeat of the parties of the "national Union," Édouard Herriot formed a cabinet in which Anatole de Monzie was named Minister of National Education. That designation was thereafter to replace the more traditional one of "Public Instruction." In the course of the month of July, the new minister entered into discussions with Julien Cain about a projected *Encyclopédie française,* destined to bear witness, in the spirit of the Enlightenment, to the state of contemporary civilization. Soon a committee headed by eminent personalities and charged with financing the project through a subscription campaign was set up. Toward the end of the year, the historian Lucien Febvre was awarded the position of director of the project; he forwarded a plan to Monzie, who approved it. The labors of composition began immediately, and the first volume appeared in 1935.

The *Encyclopédie française* was conceived as an inventory of human knowledge and its real object was ultimately no other than man himself, stationed at the center of the universe and attempting to master matter. That idea of recentering man within his habitat is as far from Freud's approach as a duck is from an elephant, but in his conception of a "total history," Lucien Febvre evinced an interest in psychology and particularly in the work of Wallon. His plan was to have Wallon draw up something in the order of a catalogue of affective life that would take its place within the framework of a "psychical paleontology." Wallon soon accepted the historian's proposal and started work in 1934 on volume 8 of the *Encyclopédie,* which he entitled *La vie mentale.* He would end up personally writing a good quarter of the volume. Nevertheless, he called on numerous collaborators of various tendencies. On the one hand, he assembled the leaders of the French school in psychology, Pierre Janet, Charles Blondel, and Georges Dumas, and on the other, representatives of the dynamic trend: Eugène Minkowski, Paul Schiff, Édouard Pichon, and Benjamin Logre. Finally, he tapped two "youngsters," Daniel Lagache and Jacques Lacan. While Pichon took charge of the article on psychoanalysis, Lagache covered the field of sexuality. As for Lacan, he received an impressive slice of the pie since he was solely responsible for section A of the second part of the work. That section bore the title *La famille,* and it was under that name—Family—that the article which Lacan had in fact entitled "Les complexes familiaux dans la formation de l'individu" was to appear.[76] The text, published in 1938, constitutes the last contribution written by Lacan during the interwar period. He remained silent throughout the entire Occupation and only picked up his pen again in 1945 to publish in *Cahiers d'art,* an article quite new in its tone, entitled "Le temps logique et l'assertion de certitude anticipée. Un nouveau sophisme."[77]

It was at the Société de psychiatrie that Jacques Lacan and Henri Wallon had met on several occasions between 1928 and 1934. During that period, the young psychiatrist became acquainted for the first time with Wallon's *Origines du caractère chez l'enfant*,[78] in which the famous mirror experiment had been formulated for the second time. Drawing on Wallon's original work, Lacan presented his thesis on the mirror stage at Marienbad. Since he had "forgotten" to submit his text to the competent authorities, he expressed the core of his position on the subject in his text on the family, which had been requested by Wallon. In comparing Wallon's point of view with Lacan's, one perceives that Lacan radically transformed a psychological experiment into a theory of the imaginary organization of the human subject. Whence the change in terminology: "Ordeal" [*épreuve*] became "stage" [*stade*], and a transition was thus effected from the description of a concrete experiment to the elaboration of a doctrine.

Already in 1931, Wallon had demonstrated how the child moves from the imaginary to the symbolic. If the psychologist was a Hegelian, he was not a Kojèvian. He adhered to the idea according to which the transformation of an individual into a subject passes through the defiles of a "natural dialectic" conceived in terms of the resolution of contradictions and conflicts. Wallon thought of psychology under the category of a Hegelian consciousness, unlike the French tradition which viewed it statically and made of consciousness the visible portion of the subconscious. In Wallon, the mirror experience specified the dialectical transition from the specular to the imaginary, then from the imaginary to the symbolic. Taking up that formulation in 1938, but without yet defining the nature of the symbolic, Lacan conceptualized Wallon's experiment in order to complete the theory of the Oedipus complex, which, he believed, did not allow for an explanation of the way in which the subject projected itself into a specular image in order to construct for itself an imaginary ego dominated by a narcissistic structure. Lacan distanced himself from Wallon by describing the process from the perspective, no longer of the conscious, but of the unconscious, and by affirming that the specular world in which the primordial identity of the ego is expressed does not contain any *others*. Lacan retained the notion of the imaginary, but defined it under the category of negativity. In so doing, he showed himself to be more "Kojèvian" than Wallon. Against the idea of a natural dialectic, he adopted the negativist version of the Struggle for Recognition and introduced the "presence-absence" of an "other" or of "others." And he attributed to Hegel the formula according to which an individual who does not struggle to be recognized outside of the family group never achieves his personality before his death.

The text of *La vie mentale* thus represents a crucial phase in the elaboration of Lacan's doctrine. He put in place the elements of a vast—and for the moment blurred and elliptical—synthesis, in which Wallonism was reinterpreted from the perspective of a Freudianism which was itself elaborated in terms borrowed from Kojève. To this was added a theory of psychoses and personality that emerged from his thesis of 1932. That brilliant synthesis might be summarized as follows: Family complexes, as they achieve expression in the contemporary form of the conjugal family, lie at the heart of the formation of human personality. That personality is structured in a purely negative manner, through a series of unconscious representations or *imagos*, which define an identificatory modality of "recognition" or "misprision." In an initial phase there appears a "weening complex" expressive, in the infant, of a primordial need of parasitism and leaving its imprint in the psyche to the point of inspiring in every individual a nostalgia for the Whole and for fusion with the imago of the maternal breast. In a second phase the "mirror stage" appears, corresponding to the decline of the weening process and allowing the subject to achieve a specular or anticipatory unity of the ego, in which the "other" or "others" have no place. Finally, in a third phase, the "other" appears, constituted in the drama of (typically, fraternal) jealousy and the struggle for recognition. It is only then that the Oedipus complex, as described by Freud, ensues.

In the second part of his presentation, Lacan brings into play a notion of "pathology" and interprets the psychoses and neuroses dominated by familial themes as a function of the synthesis elaborated in the first part and with emphasis on the point of view he had already developed in his thesis of 1932. The text on the family thus constitutes a veritable "revision" of the classic doctrine of the Oedipus complex. In the manner of Melanie Klein and with support drawn from Wallon and Kojève, Lacan drew theoretical conclusions from what psychiatry had taught him. It was by way of the notion of misprision, drawn from the logic of paranoia and inspired by the case of Aimée, that he completed Freudian doctrine in the sense of a better interpretation of the archaic dimension specific to the structuring of the human subject.

The conceptual epic of the notions of "mirror stage," "recognition," and the "desire of the other" did not end in 1938. In 1946, at the Bonneval Colloquium, Lacan delivered a lecture entitled "Propos sur la causalité psychique [Remarks on psychical causality]," [79] in which he criticized Henry Ey's organo-dynamism while at the same time evoking such figures of the past as Clérambault and Aimée. He had just read the work of Ferdinand de Saussure, which he had learned of from Claude Lévi-Strauss, and he was in the process of rethinking the Freudian theory of the unconscious in the light of structural linguistics. Nevertheless, Kojève's teaching had not disappeared and Lacan took up the theme of the mirror from a perspective that was still more phenomenological than had previously been the case. Without referring to Wallon, he noted that the notion he (sic) had introduced had already made its way and had been taken up by numerous researchers. Once again our hero did not take himself for just anyone. He evoked Hegel and emphasized that the human subject constitutes an identity by identifying with the image of the other, which in turn holds captive his feeling of selfhood. He then gave his definition of Desire and attributed it to Hegel: "Man's desire is constituted [Hegel tells us] under the sign of mediation; it is the desire to have one's desire recognized. It has as its object a desire, that of the other, in the sense that man has no object which is constituted for his desire without a measure of mediation, a circumstance that appears in his most primitive needs, in this, for example, that even his food has to be prepared—and in what may be rediscovered in the entire evolution of his satisfactions, by way of the conflict between master and slave, through the entire dialectic of labor." [80]

In 1949, Lacan traveled to the IPA congress in Zurich and presented a paper entitled "The Mirror Stage as Formative of the *I* Function as Revealed to Us by Psychoanalytic Experience." [81] Once again he recalled that it was he who had introduced the notion and that it was widely used by the French group. Playing Hegel against Descartes, he was in fact playing Freud against psychology by emphasizing that the psychoanalytic experience of the subject is opposed to every philosophy emerging from the *Cogito*. Lacan was not referring to the Cartesian theory of the subject so much as to the neo-Cartesianism that allowed psychology to recenter the unconscious on consciousness by granting priority to the latter over the former. He drove a wedge into the Freudian notion of *Ich* [ego] and opposed the *imaginary ego,* alienated in the figure of the other, to a *subject of the unconscious,* restored through language to its symbolic matrix. Beyond that new reference to linguistics, the notion of *the desire of the other,* borrowed from Hegel via Kojève, was retained. That notion allowed an articulation of the dialectical modalities of the subject's identification with the other in the non-Freudian terms of *"recognition," "alienation,"* and *"misprision."* It is through his rival that the subject grasps himself as an ego; he desires the desire of the other, in such manner that man's desire may be defined as the desire of the other through the mediation of language.

There are three words in German designating the notion of what the French calls *désir.* The term *Begierde* is used by Hegel to define the tendency, appetite, or lust through which consciousness's relation to itself is expressed. If consciousness attempts to know its object, that object is apprehended not through an act of cognition [*erkennen*], but of recognition [*anerkennen*]. In other words, consciousness, in the Hegelian and nonpsychological sense, recognizes the other to the extent that it rediscovers itself therein. The relation to the other occurs by way of desire [*Begierde*]: Consciousness recognizes itself in an other (that is, in an imaginary object), only to the extent that, through recognition, it posits that other as an object of desire. The other is the object of desire which consciousness desires in a negative relation allowing it to recognize itself therein. But as a consequence, once the negative relation to the object of desire surfaces, consciousness, become self-consciousness, discovers that its object of desire is not outside of itself but rather within. Consciousness was obliged to transit through the other in order to return to itself in the form of the other. Such is the Hegelian definition of the movement of *Begierde* concerning the self-certainty of consciousness or satisfaction [*Befriedigung* in German]. Consciousness can say *I* only in relation to an other who serves as support for the process of recognition in a dialectic of domination and servitude: I recognize myself in the other to the extent that I deny him as an other. Kojève, as we have seen, adopts this position by emphasizing consciousness in the sense of the characteristically human, by endowing consciousness, that is, with an anthropological or historical aspect.

Alongside the term *Begierde,* there exists in German the word *Wunsch,* meaning *wish,* without any connotation of envy or recognition. Moreover, we also find *Lust,* in the sense of *passion* or *penchant.* Neglecting *Begierde,* Freud used the word *Wunsch* to designate the *unconscious wish* [rendered in French as unconscious desire, *désir*] and *Lust* to define the *pleasure principle* [*Lustprinzip*]. In Freud, the *Wunsch* is an unconscious desire tending to seek accomplishment [*accomplissement,* but the standard English is *fulfillment*] rather than satisfaction [*Befriedigung*]. It tends toward accomplishment or fulfillment by restoring the *signs* linked to the first experience of satisfaction, particularly in dreams, then in the symptoms in which it appears in compromise formations.[82] Even if he did not take the notion of recognition into account, Freud did not identify desire [or wish] with *need*. Need in fact finds actual satisfaction through adequate objects (food, for example). Desire, on the contrary, is linked to memory traces and finds its fulfillment in a simultaneously unconscious and hallucinatory reproduction of perceptions, which have become *signs* of satisfaction. Naturally, such signs have a sexual character, and unconscious desire always entails that what is at stake is a sexual desire.

It may thus be seen what teaching Lacan drew from the Kojèvian reading of the *Phenomenology of Mind*. With Kojève, he "anthropologized" desire, but without (or against) him he put the Freudian unconscious in the place of Hegelian consciousness. It may be noted in passing that he would distance himself from Kojève's humanism not through a return to Hegel, but through a Saussurian reinterpretation of Freudian doctrine, allowing him to play "science" against "man" and to make of psychoanalysis a "conjectural science." Before that, and at a time when the French psychoanalytic movement tended to biologize Freud's theory, by failing to distinguish, for example, between drive and instinct, or desire and need,[83] Lacan refocused the Viennese discovery on a notion of unconscious desire revised and corrected from a Hegelian-Kojèvian perspective. He did not pit a "philosophy" against a "biologism"; he made use of philosophical discourse in order to restore its adequate meaning to Freud's endeavor. He thus effected a merger between *Begierde,* that is, desire founded on recognition or the "desire of the desire of the other" and a *Wunsch* unconscious in nature and bound to signs. He introduced the Freudian unconscious into the Hegelian-Kojèvian definition of *Begierde* and the "struggle for recognition" into the Freudian definition of *Wunsch*. In the process, he restored the Freudian distinction between desire and need, which was tending to disappear within the history of the French psychoanalytic movement. Through the notion of recognition, between 1953 and 1957, he subsequently introduced a third term, which he called *demande*. This last dimension is addressed to an other, but even though it bears on an object, that object remains inessential, since the demand [or request] is a *demand for love*. Otherwise put, need, which is biological in nature, is satisfied with a real object (food . . .), whereas desire [*Wunsch-Begierde*] is born of the discontinuity between need and demand. Irreducible to need, it does not bear on an object but on a phantasm, an "imaginary other." It is a desire of the other's desire to the extent that it seeks to be recognized absolutely by that other, be it at the cost of a struggle to the death.

Starting in 1936 from Wallon's notion of the mirror experience, Lacan transformed it into a concept allowing him to revise the doctrine of the Oedipus complex toward a superior understanding of the archaic dimension of the unconscious as it was revealed in the experience of psychosis. But in order for that "experience" to become a phase in a nonbiological sense, Lacan rethought it with the assistance of a philosophical discourse—whence the synthesis of 1938. Then, taking up the notion of *Begierde,* he gave a new definition of the Freudian concept of desire. Finally, later on, he split the system by introducing the notion of demand. Then, in order to crown his entire project, he rethought the whole of his argument in the light of structural linguistics. He would then take up Wallon's notions of the specular, the imaginary, and the symbolic, while endowing them with new contents. To be continued. . . .

In 1939, Lacan fell in love with Sylvia Bataille, whom he would marry in 1953. They had met as friends in 1934 and then again in 1936. Sylvia had separated from Georges Bataille in 1933, but had not divorced him. She had become, under his name, a well-known actress, playing notably in two films of Jean Renoir, *La Partie de campagne* (in which Bataille appears as a priest) and *Le Crime de monsieur Lange*. A Jewish woman of Romanian origin, Sylvia Maklès would have her career shattered by the war. She had long frequented the vanguard of the French intelligentsia, among whom she counted her closest friends.[84] Sprightly in temperament, she possessed, aside from her slenderness, a charm and a sense of humor that attracted Lacan. With her he was to accede to a more Bohemian existence than he had known with Marie-Louise Blondin. In 1942, he rented an apartment at 5 rue de Lille, where he remained until his death. Sylvia had had a first daughter by Bataille, Laurence, who would become a psychoanalyst; she then had a second daughter, Judith, by Lacan. When Marie-Louise Blondin learned that her husband's mistress was pregnant, she decided (with the encouragement of her brother Sylvain) to request a divorce. The separation was not to be announced until the end of hostilities with the result that when Judith was born, in 1941, she was given the surname Bataille.[85]

Jacques Lacan and Georges Bataille had come to know each other, independently of Sylvia, at Kojève's seminar and perhaps a bit before 1933. The two men respected and admired each other without sharing the same opinions. Both discovered Hegel through the same master and both nurtured an identical vision of the feminine, which may be detected in their respective writings. Bataille pressured Lacan to publish, specifically in 1939, when he had little desire to write. Mobilized like Loewenstein for a period of several months, the psychiatrist subsequently returned to Paris in order to continue practicing psychoanalysis. For a while, he maintained his psychiatric activities at Sainte-Anne, and then restricted himself to his private practice. Overwhelmed by the Nazi occupation, he did not write a line during the war and ceased all publication. He studied Chinese and obtained a degree from the École des langues orientales.

As of 1940, Sylvia, who was pregnant with Judith, was living in the unoccupied zone. After a stay in Auvergne, she moved to Cagnes-sur-Mer, where Lacan joined her every two weeks. The Maklès family was harassed endlessly, by the French authorities, who were soon to force Sylvia's mother to declare her Jewish identity. Learning of this, Lacan rushed to the police headquarters of Cagnes, accompanied by his mistress, and demanded the family papers, which were carefully arranged in a file on a shelf. Losing patience, Lacan climbed on a stool, took the documents with him and ripped them up as soon as he was outside the door. Naturally, he had "promised" the police superintendent to bring them back in due time. Without participating in the Resistance, he undertook, in Vichy, to obtain official papers for Jewish friends seeking refuge in the unoccupied zone or in Paris. It was thus that Sylvia managed to leave Cagnes, after paying a visit one day to René Laforgue at his home in Provence.[86]

Part Two

Cold Wars, Hot Wars

Fate will say if anything will remain of the future that is in the hands of those I have trained.

—Jacques Lacan

5   The Situation of Psychoanalysis at Midcentury

I. Chronicle of the Brown Years

I described in another volume how the Nazification of psychoanalysis occurred in Germany, under the aegis of the sinister Matthias Heinrich Göring, the war-marshall's cousin. A former assistant of Kraepelin's, he had been interested in hypnosis before becoming a physician. Analyzed by two disciples of Adler, he was a convinced pietist and a fearsome Nazi, but was not regarded as dangerous by his adversaries because of his seeming timidity, his long beard, and his childlike good nature. He was nicknamed "Papi." In 1928, he began to consolidate his power in the Allgemeine Ärztliche Gesellschaft für Psychotherapie (AAGP), the German society composed of psychiatrists and psychoanalysts. With Hitler's accession to power, Ernst Krestschmer was forced to resign from the AAGP in order to yield his place to Jung. That same year, believing they were "saving" psychoanalysis and depriving the Nazis of the pretext of banning it, the non-Jewish members of the Deutsche Psychoanalytische Gesellschaft (DPG), founded in 1910, opted to accept the "resignation" of all Jews from their society. Max Eitingon, Otto Fenichel, and others left in exile while Felix Boehm and Carl Müller-Braunschwig, both advocates of the plan to rescue analysis, were propelled to the leadership of the DPG.[1] As of that date, Freud did not conceal his pessimism but chose not to intervene in German affairs. "My father," wrote Anna Freud, "did not want to do anything that would complicate the affairs of the Berliners. As for being in agreement with their procedure, to be sure, we were not."[2]

In December 1935, during a meeting of the DPG presided over by Jones, the Jewish training analysts of the Society were obliged to take the initiative in excluding themselves from their group. John Rittmeister, Karl Landauer, and several others would pay for the alleged rescue project with their lives. Edith Jakobson and Maria Langer managed to emigrate. A single non-Jew had the courage to refuse the procedure and to choose exile. His name was Bernard Kamm. A year later Matthias Göring founded the Deutsche Institut für Psychologische Forschung, destined to regroup the "Aryanized" societies. In conjunction with all this, the Gestapo in Leipzig liquidated the holdings of the International Psychoanalytic Editions. In July 1936, negotiations took place in Basel between Jones, Brill, Göring, Müller-Braunschweig, and Boehm with the aim of merging the DPG with the pro-Nazi society. The Berlin Institute was then converted into the Aryan Center for Psychotherapy. Four months later, the DPG withdrew from the IPA, once again in the name of the "rescue" thesis. In January 1938, just prior to the Anschluss, Felix Boehm met Freud in Vienna in the presence of Jones and Jeanne Lampl de Groot. After listening to Boehm for two hours, Freud left the premises quite brusquely without forbidding anything but making clear his contempt for the procedure. Soon the Viennese Psychoanalytic Editions was liquidated, its books burnt or confiscated. The black apocalypse was unfurling

151

over Europe. The DPG was dissolved after having been "rescued." During the war, activities continued, and Aryanization took the form of absolute suppression of all reference to Freudian concepts. All the concessions had served no purpose, and later generations were to be the primary victims of the errors of their elders.

In 1946, the DPG was reconstituted, then readmitted to the IPA at its Zurich congress. In 1950, a split ensued, which resulted in the creation of a Deutsche Psychoanalytische Vereinigung (DPV), which was in turn recognized by the IPA at its Amsterdam congress. Emerging from the former Nazified DPG, the two societies immediately began an apologetic reinterpretation of the past. The first continued to maintain the validity of the rescue thesis, and the second spoke of a liquidation necessary for a subsequent reorganization. It was not until 1985, in Hamburg, that the first IPA congress on German soil, subsequent to a decision reached at Jerusalem in 1977, was held. Toward 1984, the French were beginning to grow acquainted with the period of the "brown years" without having previously paid serious attention to psychoanalysis's German or French past. In Germany, on the other hand, the labor of memory occurred gradually, when the war was over, in part outside the organizational framework of the IPA.[3]

In occupied France, events did not transpire as in Germany. The war came at a time when the political and theoretical landscape of the psychoanalytic movement had already shifted. By 1940, the nationalist faction had ceased to exist. Pichon and Codet had died; Borel was ripe for retirement; and Hesnard was asail on his ship before weighing anchor at Bizerte where he would write a notorious text on Freud's "Hebraism."[4] Upon his return, although he was the most nationalistic of the nationalist group, he adapted to the new situation. He pursued his career in the south of France without bending to the imperatives concerning obligatory therapy. Despite his opportunism, he no longer played any role within the SPP and profited from his role as a pioneer. Similarly diminished by the beginning of the war, the orthodox group was no better off than its rival. Most of its members opted for exile. The princess left France; Odier returned to Switzerland; and Loewenstein, Hartmann, and Spitz arranged to have themselves transferred to the Psychoanalytic Society of New York.

Upon the arrival of German troops in Paris, the SPP closed its doors, the *RFP* suspended publication, and the members of the EP group disbanded. The practice of psychoanalysis was not forbidden by the authorities, but Freudianism fell into disfavor. The Jews who had not emigrated began hiding while the non-Jews continued to receive private patients, though in smaller number than previously. Assigned by Professor Laignel-Lavastine to reorganize the psychoanalytic section of the Sainte-Anne Hospital, Georges Parcheminey, in his inaugural lecture, offered ringing praise of his master Sigmund Freud. The result was the exit of the German officers present from the auditorium. John Leuba and Philippe Marette gave consultations, and soon Jean Delay served as interim occupant of the chair in psychiatry, keeping the group intact despite the disapproval of the Germans. The *Annales médico-psychologiques* continued to be published, and the word "psychoanalysis" appeared once in a text by Michel Cénac, without however appearing in the table of contents.[5]

The very fact of interrupting all public activity in itself constituted an act of opposition to Nazism that held for the entirety of the French psychoanalytic movement. In this regard, Marie Bonaparte's attitude was not only exemplary but decisive: There would be no "rescue" operation. Through her exile and her immediate support for the Jews, the princess precluded any possibility of reconstituting an "Aryanized" society. Since she was no longer there and the EP group, under Henri Ey's direction, was also missing, no negotiations could be broached with leaders of the psychoanalytic movement, who had either died, emigrated, or fled—to private resistance or passivity. In other words, the French psychoanalytic situation in June 1940 was such that it would not lend itself to the creation of a Nazified society on the model of that of Berlin. Which is why the evaluation of acts of resistance or collaborationism by the movement ought to be conducted on the basis of individual acts, and generation by generation. Only Laforgue indulged in a collaborationist attitude: He attempted, with Göring's help, to set up a local section of the Nazi institute in Paris, but failed for lack of members.

Relatively few psychoanalysts of the SPP participated as individuals in resistance efforts. A majority of the founders were not free to—they were either dead or in exile. From their ranks only Paul Schiff can be considered an authentic hero of the anti-Nazi struggle. Rather astonishingly, his deeds would be forgotten by the official historians of his own society. I have dealt with his adventure in another volume[6] and shall confine myself here to the resistance activities of the psychoanalysts of the second generation. They were rare and I shall recount them in the course of evoking individual histories. Such an evaluation is not applicable to the practitioners of the third generation. None of its members was as yet a part of the psychoanalytic movement at the time of the Occupation. Nevertheless, they were more numerous than their elders in their heroism—or simply commitment to the struggle. A few names may be noted: Jean-Paul Valabréga, Guy Rosolato, Jean-Claude Lavie, Jenny Aubry, Léon Chertok, Louis Beirnaert. Their activities will be recounted individually, without being related to the collective saga of the movement during the period 1940–45.

Fleeing the occupying troops, Marie Bonaparte took refuge in her house in Brittany, where she sheltered Loewenstein and his family. Then, reversing direction, she moved into her residence at Saint-Cloud, which had been pillaged. Shortly thereafter, she decided to leave for her villa at Saint-Tropez, where she again received Loewenstein. At the end of December 1940, no longer having any professional activity, she opted for exile. She obtained the necessary visas from the Vichy government and sought refuge in Athens in February 1941. From there, anticipating the German offensive, she left for Alexandria with the royal family of Greece. Finally, in July 1941, she set sail for South Africa, where she arranged to teach Freud's doctrine to psychiatrists. She wrote long letters to Anna Freud, while all the while dreaming sadly of her house on the rue Adolphe-Yvon, which had been requisitioned. After the battle of Stalingrad, she became a supporter of the Soviet Union and planned to return to France. At the beginning of the autumn of 1944, she moved to London where she remained until February 1945, at which point she returned to Paris, fearful of the new conflicts emerging within the SPP.[7]

Aside from Leuba, Parcheminey, and Lacan, several other psychoanalysts practiced their profession during the Occupation. Whereas Nacht was forced to go into hiding and Lagache retained his position as professor at Clermont-Ferrand, where the University of Strasbourg had retreated, Marc Schlumberger, Juliette Boutonier, and Françoise Marette practiced in Paris. Starting out as an oil driller, Schlumberger was named titular member in 1937, after undertaking medical studies with the sole intention of becoming a psychoanalyst. The orphan of an English mother, he had difficulty tolerating his father's homosexuality and openly declared that the future of psychoanalysis lay with women who were not physicians. A dashing aesthete, he was an admirer of the feminine, but suffered a certain inhibition in his writing that he never succeeded in overcoming. Considering his analysis with Laforgue a failure, he quickly undertook a second period of analysis with Nacht. Later he would accept on his couch a number of psychoanalysts of the third generation, in particular Wladimir Granoff, Moustapha Safouan, and Joyce Mac Dougall.[8] Also analysed by Laforgue, Juliette Boutonier, Françoise Marette, and Philippe Marette became members of the SPP on the eve of the war. Trained as a philosopher, Juliette studied medicine during the thirties, after corresponding with Freud, and then became the friend of Paul Schiff, Daniel Lagache, André Berge, and Gaston Bachelard.

Born in Lausanne in 1902, Georges Favez defended his thesis in Protestant theology (on Luther) before becoming a pastor in the Evangelical Church. A student of the Clarapède Institute, he became a psychopedagogue and a psychotherapist. Toward 1936, he entered analysis with Hartmann in Paris, then continued his therapy in Lausanne, where he did his military duty. After the war, he undertook a period of analysis with Nacht, while dividing his time between Paris and Lausanne. On the eve of the first split of the SPP, he married Juliette Boutonier, and he never left the SPP despite joining the SFP, then the APF.[9]

Unlike Saussure and Odier, John Leuba did not return to Switzerland. A Swiss national, he had participated in France in the fighting of World War I as a hospital volunteer. In 1918, he was awarded the official *médaille des épidémies* and six years later he went to work at Éditions Armand Colin, where he published a book on a subject that was a passion of his—geology. He cooked splendid fondues for his friends, and for his pleasure, he cultivated a miniature kitchen-garden on his balcony. Analyzed by Loewenstein, he became part of the first generation. During the Occupation, he took up service anew in passive defense and played an important role at the emergency station of the XVIth arrondissement town hall. He treated all sorts of wounds. One day, he returned home with a trophy: the skull of a German soldier, adorned with a brain fragment. He placed the skull in front of his couch. This veteran of another war did not like the "Krauts."[10]

For her part, the "little Marette woman," as Pichon gently called her, studied medicine and published a thesis in 1939 on the relations between psychoanalysis and pediatrics. Born in 1908 to a family of graduates of the École polytechnique, she is at present, under the name of Françoise Dolto, the most popular individual in the French psychoanalytic community. Gifted with a prodigious clinical sense, she is the marvelous embodiment of a kind of spontaneous spiritualism within psychoanalysis and continues to speak, without the slightest chauvinism, the splendid French she inherited from Pichon.

Suzanne Demler, Françoise's mother, was the daughter of a graduate of the Polytechnique whose father had been a preceptor at the Court of Wurtemberg. She had married Henri Marette, also of the Polytechnique, who worked in his father-in-law's factory. In the Marette family, traditional methods of upbringing prevailed. Girls were allowed to like music, to learn how to cook or do housework. But only boys had the right to pursue a higher education. Prevented from registering in medical school, Françoise early on opted to be a nurse. She planned on a career as a "doctor of education" and was in a rush to pay for her studies with the money she was earning. Every Sunday, the members of her family would meet to play chamber music. An excellent violinist, Françoise accompanied them. Soon her parents obliged her to accept an *agrégé* in Greek as her *fiancé*. Unable either to break off relations or to marry, Françoise, who did not like the boy, decided to enter into analysis. Schlumberger sent her to see Laforgue some time in 1932. In the beginning, her parents agreed to finance their daughter's therapy, then, when she seemed better, they cut off all funds. Laforgue proposed that she pay half price. Some time later, in 1936, she cut short her therapy with the declaration, "All of your interpretations I apply to your own story." Whereupon Laforgue began to address her in the familiar *tu* form and allowed his disappointment to surface: "I have never worked as well as with you." [11]

Françoise Marette began a practice as an analyst, specializing in children and psychotics. Still poor, she did not have the wherewithal for a waiting room. Patients were thus obliged to wait outside the door on the landing. In between sessions, she raced down the stairs, walked around the block while declaiming alexandrines, then returned to her chair for fifty-five minutes of attentive listening . . . and immobility. Around this time, she went to a Surrealist exhibition that so disturbed her that she slept for forty-eight hours and woke only when the morning's first patient rang the doorbell. Laforgue introduced her to Alain Cluny, then urged her to join the SPP. She followed his advice and undertook control analyses under the supervision of Nacht and Lagache.

A nonresident in 1934 in the service of Professor Heuyer, Françoise, on his advice, applied for residency in psychiatric hospitals. One day, Pichon proposed that she come work with Odette Codet at the Bretonneau Hospital. Under his direction, she defended a magnificent medical thesis, *Psychanalyse et pédiatrie,*[12] whose innovative nature was not immediately noticed. It would be republished at the author's expense several times in the course of thirty years before being published, thanks to Paul Flamand, by Éditions du Seuil in 1971. After Pichon's death, Françoise Marette took charge of a consulting room at the Trousseau Hospital, where her success would cause a sensation. In 1938, she discovered Lacan's work while reading *Les complexes familiaux*. Later, she followed his teaching at Sainte-Anne and quickly became, not a student, but a friend. If Lacan was the artisan of a new integration of Freudianism in France, Dolto was the founder of a new understanding of child psychoanalysis, centered not on the a priori study of psychoses, but on that of the

psychopathology of everyday life. Before her teaching, that field had been represented in France by Eugénie Sokolnicka and Sophie Morgenstern, both of whom
had committed suicide.

On the eve of the war, she thus laid the ground for a psychoanalytic method
of child therapy centered on a listening to the unconscious and freed of the psychiatrist's gaze. Wanting to be a pedagogical physician, Françoise Marette was at once
more of a pedagogue than Melanie Klein and less of a conformist than Anna Freud.
She did not conceive the field of child psychoanalysis in terms of a morality of
upbringing, but integrated the parental position into her treatment. Addressing a
large audience from the outset, she made use of a concrete vocabulary without for
all that yielding to the lures of popularization. Above all, she "invented" a practice
that did not stem from any theoretical a priori. She abandoned the play method and
attempted to isolate the suggestive bond of the transference in its effectuation of
therapy. She thus used the same words as the child without giving any direct interpretation of his drawings. As soon as her thesis was published, Françoise received a
letter from Jean Rostand congratulating her on her work. It was at a dinner at his
home that she met an émigré Russian physician, born in the Crimea, near the Sea of
Azov. She married him shortly thereafter. His name was Boris Dolto. He would
found a new method of massage therapy and a school of podology.

As early as 1939, René Laforgue entered into contact with Matthias Göring
in an effort to retrieve copies of one of his books, which had been published in
Vienna at the author's expense and had been confiscated by the Nazis.[13] He was
asked to prove that he was a foreign national.[14] Twenty months later, Göring announced his visit to Paris and invited Laforgue to enter into discussion with him
about the International Society for Psychotherapy. He informed him that his mail
came to him through the intermediary of one Dr. Dillenburger, a doctor to the General Staff at the Luftwaffe Hospital in Clichy. Laforgue wanted to be accepted as
sole member of the society with the avowed intent of founding a French branch in
Paris.[15]

Between those two letters, Laforgue had been mobilized near Saint-Brieuc.
Lost in his failure neurosis, and prepared to do anything to be recognized, he behaved as he had always done before the war, with a kind of blind ambivalence.
Incapable of choosing his camp, he was convinced that Germany's victory was permanent and that it was imperative to "come to an arrangement" with the enemy in
order to "salvage" something. Not only did he act as one of the defeated, but he
feared, as an Alsatian, being obliged to wear a German uniform. At Saint-Brieuc,
under the aegis of the Petainist prefect of the Côtes-du-Nord, he was thus delighted
to be able to demonstrate his effectiveness and his linguistic competence. Upon returning to civilian life, during the summer, he accepted the position of chief physician of municipal hygiene services. He eluded a number of imposed requisitions,
distributed medical certificates, and was responsible for the liberation of several
prisoners interned in camps surrounding the city.[16]

Upon returning to Paris, Laforgue attended, in October 1940, the final meeting of the EP group, which decided to cease all activities. Since, unknown to the

others, he had already made contact with Göring, he proposed that the journal reappear under German sponsorship.[17] This shocked his colleagues, who were unaware of his contacts, but who had contempt for his attitude. Laforgue, at the time, was in an impossible situation. Still a member of the administrative committee of the International League against Anti-Semitism, he feared being harassed by the Gestapo even as he was attempting to found a Nazified institute. In 1939, he destroyed the pages devoted to Hitler in an essay on great men and replaced them with a study of Napoleon. Imperiled on every front because of his inconsistencies, he entrusted his correspondence with Freud and various documents to Juliette Boutonier. Without asking any explanation, she kept the precious texts until the Liberation.[18]

Around November 15, Göring arrived in Paris for a brief visit. He did not meet Laforgue, but asked one Dr. Knapp, a functionary in the Reich's medical society, to see the Alsatian and to transmit a report on the individual to him. It appears that Göring had his doubts about the possibility of creating a French section of his society. Laforgue did not wait for Knapp to get in touch with him and telephoned him the following day to arrange a meeting. Knapp then transmitted to Göring a detailed account of their meeting: "Dr. Laforgue believes he can assemble without difficulty French physicians to join the International Society for Psychotherapy. He believes he can exclude Jews and the declared friends of Jews. . . . It would appear that he has belonged for years to the Dauriot [sic] group, with which Germany is presently collaborating. . . . Laforgue's membership in that group shows, however, that he is not a political dreamer, but is trying seriously to put himself in the service of the collectivity. He said that he was a follower of the national-socialist movement and that, not understanding its position on the Jewish problem, he had for a while been a member of the suspect International League against Anti-Semitism. Nevertheless, Laforgue told me in detail how he had come—in pursuing his own observations and on the basis of personal experiences—to understand the point of view of German anti-Semitism. By 1936, he would thus have resigned from the League and since then would have been an open anti-Semite. These explanations were given and justified quite plausibly, but I will try, if possible, to verify them through other sources. My impression is that we should not allow the energy he represents to escape, and above all that we should accept his offer to assemble important researchers and physicians in the French group in order to have them affiliated with the international association you are directing. In the process, we would have an opportunity to observe Laforgue and to decide how to use him later on. . . . Dillenburger has already met Laforgue and has the same impression as I, namely, that we ought to try to have him participate in our work. Heil Hitler."[19]

The letter demonstrates that Laforgue was attempting to get the Nazis to believe that he was capable of grouping a majority of French psychoanalysts around him. But this was by no means the case. Not only did he not attract anyone, but there was no one willing to accept his leadership. Moreover, he did not attempt to inform his colleagues of his intentions. For their part, the Nazis distrusted him. But since they had no other contact in Paris, they opted both to extend him their confidence and to keep him under surveillance.

On December 9, Laforgue wrote to Göring to ask him once again to allow him personally to join the International Society for Psychotherapy. He then promised to devote all his energy to the creation of a group and to the promotion of active collaboration between France and Germany.[20] In order to reassure him of his prominent position in Paris, he sent him an implausible list of potential members of a future Aryanized society. It included nearly all SPP therapists—from Lagache to Lacan, and including Schlumberger and Juliette Boutonier—who were neither Jewish nor exiled nor foreigners. Göring recopied it in his hand, apparently with the intention of proceeding to a number of verifications. He added the annotation "Psychotherap. zum Laforgue."[21] Aware of impending difficulties, he nevertheless responded to his interlocutor that in no event should he rush into the creation of a local section. Then he assured Laforgue that the membership he desired would not be long in coming.[22] In February 1941, he asked him for a list of psychological or psychiatric journals in which it would be possible to publish articles favorable to German psychotherapy.[23] On March 11, Laforgue responded that the two most interesting journals were *Évolution psychiatrique,* which had been founded by himself and by Hesnard, and *Encéphale,* which was edited by Professor Claude. Whereupon he announced his next visit to Berlin, scheduled for March 19.[24]

The meeting took place. In May, Laforgue intervened with the Nazis on behalf of the medical clinic at the Château de Garches, which was partially occupied by the Luftwaffe. He succeeded in liberating it. He then left once again for Berlin in order to negotiate with Göring the setting up of the notorious local section, whose status was becoming increasingly illusory. He was above all interested in the publication of his manuscript, *L'homme au service de sa destinée,*[25] a copy of which he had transmitted to Göring so that it might be read by the censorship committee of the International Society. He stated that the publication of the book would allow the French therapists to regroup. He also proposed to organize a meeting in Paris between Dillenburger, Knapp, Professor Claude, and several other physicians.[26] Dillenburger attended the session and transmitted his impressions to Göring: "It appears set that with their support, the local group of psychoanalysts will be constituted by the end of the year at the latest. We also debated whether it would not be preferable to replace the designations psychoanalysis and psychotherapy by others. No solution was found that satisfied everyone."[27]

Fifteen days later, Laforgue sent Göring the chapters of his book on Rousseau and Robespierre. He was planning to add another one on Napoleon without saying that he had destroyed the one on Hitler. He then told his interlocutor that he was fighting for the same cause as he.[28] In September, Dillenburger announced to Göring that Laforgue was worthy of their trust and that they should depend on him in all circumstances. "Laforgue," he wrote, "mentioned to me the names of several Parisian personalities who, he thought, represent a grave danger for the *rapprochement* of our two peoples. He thought that there was still time, but that there should be no delay in eliminating the nefarious influence of certain individuals by expelling them. It was his opinion that I should inform Minister Goebbels. I am now going to see the "general" of the aviators stationed in Paris to speak about all this with him, then with the Gestapo. That is the opinion of my chief physician whom I asked if I could take charge of this matter. His inclination was to be quite positive."[29]

Toward the end of December 1941, the research department of the Institute of Psychotherapy reached its verdict on Laforgue's manuscript and decided not to publish it: "From the scientific point of view, it [the manuscript] does not contribute anything new. It is, on the contrary, a noncritical repetition of the concepts of Freud, which have long been obsolete. It is thus one or two decades behind in relation to the present state of depth psychology." [30] The decision was transmitted to Laforgue, who went into a veritable fury. In order to calm him, Dillenburger intervened with the authorities in charge. But they did not hesitate to confirm their judgment, adding that the work was also guilty of Jungianism and nonracism: "I fear that this effort is not only indefensible (for example, in maintaining that it would not be race that would make the Jew, but environmental influences), but that in addition it is deficient at the scientific level." [31] Toward the beginning of the year 1942, the "collaborationist activities" of the French psychoanalytic movement amounted to no more than a fool's bargain, two meetings between Laforgue and Göring, and a meeting—that was to have no sequel—between Professor Claude, a few French physicians, and two pitiful functionaries of the Reich.

In the summer of 1942, Laforgue moved to the unoccupied zone and took refuge in his estate Les Chabert at Garéoult, near La Roquebrussane. There he began to "redeem" his prior conduct without, however, breaking off his correspondence with Göring. In the neighboring village of Tourtour, he took on the responsibility of protecting the house of his Jewish friend Bernard Steele, who had emigrated to the United States. He spent 100,000 francs to rebuild the chicken coop, renovated the sheep-pen, and transformed the site into a reception center for the victims of persecution of every stripe: Jews, members of the Resistance, dodgers of obligatory work duty (STO) in Germany, and Communist militants.[32] In September, Laforgue renewed contact with Göring to ask him to intervene on his behalf so that he might obtain a travel pass; he wanted to return to the occupied zone and then go to Berlin.[33] Göring wrote to Knapp and let him know that he wanted to meet Laforgue. He was desirous of speaking to him about the criticism his manuscript had encountered and then of recommissioning him for collaborationist activities.[34] In the meanwhile the South was now occupied. Laforgue returned to Paris and informed Göring of his next visit to Berlin.[35] Thus ended the relations between Laforgue and the Nazis. We know nothing more except that there would never be a local section of the Institute. Beyond that no other trace of any exchange between Göring and a French psychoanalyst has come to my attention.

Upon returning to Les Chabert, Laforgue continued to protect the oppressed. He facilitated the flight abroad of Oliver Freud, Sigmund's son, and his wife, who had sought refuge in France before the Occupation. Simultaneously, he supervised the therapy of their daughter, Eva Freud, who refused to leave French territory. Since she lived in Nice, he entrusted her to Henri Stern, who lived in the same city. Stern had studied psychiatry in Germany, his native land, where he had been a member of the Communist Party. A Jew and a Marxist (although not a Reichian), Stern had emigrated in 1933 and subsequently became foreign intern at the asylum of Blois.

Between 1935 and 1938, the date of his naturalization, he underwent therapy, intermittently, with Laforgue.

Henri Stern could not concern himself with Eva Freud for very long. A police raid soon forced him to seek refuge at Les Chabert, where he stayed for a certain time. As for Eva, she died of blood-poisoning without ever having seen Laforgue again; it was he who took responsibility for her burial. For his part, Stern joined the rural resistance of the Albi region. Once integrated into the Resistance, he was in charge of the wounded.

Anne-Lise Stern, Henri's daughter, did not have the opportunity to meet Laforgue, but she became Eva Freud's friend and left her her job as secretary in a theater. After the girl's death, she was arrested in the course of a police raid and on April 15, 1944, she was deported to Birkenau. From there she was sent to Bergen-Belsen, then to Theresienstadt, from which she was liberated by advancing Soviet troops. Upon returning to Paris, she rediscovered her father, who was preparing to make the trip in the opposite direction. Appointed as an army doctor, Henri Stern did in fact visit several concentration—and extermination—camps. When he came back, he wrote an astonishing report on the behavior of deportees toward their executioners.[36] Two years later he applied for membership in the SPP, but John Leuba, the new president, informed him that his analysis with Laforgue was insufficient. He advised him to resume his analysis with Nacht or Schlumberger.[37] He did not have time to. Stricken with cancer, he died the following year at the age of 55. Anne-Lise assisted him in confronting his fate, as Max Schur had done with Freud. She would become a psychoanalyst after an initial period of therapy with Bouvet, then a second on Lacan's couch. A woman with a bibliography, she embodies, in all its splendor, the impassioned adventure—bereft of homeland and of borders—of psychoanalysis.

After Henri Stern's departure for the *maquis,* Laforgue ended "his" war in the south of France. He no longer had any epistolary contact with Nazi Germany.

With the end of the Occupation, the judicial purge extended to every sector of French economic and cultural life. Lesser and greater affairs of collaborationism were judged before tribunals presided over by titled magistrates and composed of ordinary jurors, Resistance members, *maquisards,* or the notoriously insubordinate. The unions, which had been banned by Vichy, were reconstituted, and the principle of an Order of Physicians was maintained despite its Petainist origin. In January 1945, temporary administrative entities were assigned responsibility for effecting a purge of the profession in order to allow the reconstruction of a new Order of Physicians cleansed of the blemishes of its association with Vichy.

A twofold system of legislation was in function: one concerned with unspecialized penalization (courts of law, civil chambers) to which were sent collaborationists of all professions, and one internal to the medical profession, designed to judge practitioners denounced by their colleagues or by victims they might have had. The temporary entities were structured on the three-tiered model of the old Order, and it was the middle level, the regional council of physicians, that was placed in charge of cases to be purged. Its members were to elect from their ranks a president, a vice-president, and a secretary along with a purge committee to be composed of half of its members. That committee was presided over by a magistrate, who was himself appointed by the presiding magistrate of the appeals court under whose jurisdiction the region's principal town fell. Three types of accusation were delineated, to which there corresponded three types of punishment, from mere censuring to definitive exclusion from the profession. National disgrace could be officially visited on the accused if he or she were recognized to be guilty of denunciation, failure to assist the wounded or sick of the FFI [Forces françaises de l'interieur—part of the French Resistance], destruction of republican freedoms, or cooperation in the deportation of workers.[38]

At the time the purges were being conducted, no one in France knew of the collaboration activities of René Laforgue. The author of the present book was unaware of them at the time of the publication of the previous volume of this history. Three years of research were necessary to exhume both his correspondence with Göring and the files of the purgation tribunal assigned to pass judgment on Laforgue. All those documents are presented here for the first time.

Around 1945, the rumor began circulating in the psychoanalytic world that Laforgue had perhaps behaved poorly during the Occupation. Mention was made of a German uniform that he may have worn at Saint-Brieuc, of gasoline coupons obtained with strange ease, of an official trip to Germany. Laforgue, it was said, had met Arno Breker or Marshall Göring. All those reports were false, and the rumor was based not on the ascertainment of any facts, but on Laforgue's ambivalences during the brown years. Elected president of the SPP, John Leuba, who detested the Alsatian, took advantage of the occasion to accuse him of collaborationism. Claiming to represent the group at Évolution psychiatrique, he issued a complaint against him and brought him before the purgation committee of the Paris council of the Order of Physicians. To be sure, he was unaware of the activities of the man he was accusing, both of his relations with Göring and of his efforts in southern France. Forced to defend himself, Laforgue assembled a great deal of favorable testimony about his time passed at Saint-Brieuc and his stay at Les Chabert. Jean Rostand, Juliette Boutonier, Henri Stern and numerous others, all of whom knew nothing, testified on his behalf to the impeccable nature of his record. "He sheltered me and my wife," wrote Henri Stern. "I am all the more grateful to him in that he took responsibility for his act of courageous generosity with full knowledge of what was at stake." [39]

Jacques Feschotte, the former prefect of Côtes-du-Nord, and Alain Cuny were called as witnesses for the defense, while Adrien Borel and Françoise Dolto were called on by Leuba as witnesses for the prosecution without knowing what exactly was expected of them. Might they perhaps at some point have transmitted a rumor without any malicious intent? In any event, the case against Laforgue fell apart. Françoise Dolto delivered a ringing speech of homage to Laforgue and Berge refused to plead either innocence or guilt.[40]

On March 27, 1946, the purgation committee convened at the First Chamber of the Paris Court of Appeal under the direction of presiding magistrate Janvier, a judge by profession. He observed that no evidence had been presented by the prosecution, which based its case on rumors. He emphasized, on the other hand, that the defense was able to demonstrate that Laforgue had protected victims of Nazism after 1942. The accused had also succeeded in proving that his trip to Germany had been motivated by family reasons. As a result, he was discharged on all counts, the documents of the case were ordered classified, and the case itself was dismissed. "Nothing precise could be proved against him," Marie Bonaparte wrote to Loewenstein, "and no witness—with the exception of Leuba, chairman of the EP—appeared. Under such circumstances, nothing can be done against him in our group; that is also the opinion of Anna Freud, to whom I explained the case. I have seen the accused myself. He had talked of starting up a suit for defamation of character, but has given up the idea. I think that Borel did a lot to calm him. All these group stories disgust me, and I am eager to go to Saint-Tropez and work and not to see any more colleagues." [41]

The purge trial drummed up without any evidence by Leuba is as lamentable as Laforgue's collaborationist attitude during the Occupation. As for the tribunal's verdict, it was just. No one should be condemned without evidence or tried on the basis of rumors.

Discharged by the Paris Court of Appeal, Laforgue was neither excluded from the IPA nor expelled from the Order of Physicians. Nevertheless, he felt guilty and did not publish the fact that the charges were dropped. A month after the trial, he was struck by misfortune, losing his granddaughter in particularly painful circumstances. As a result, he became increasingly inclined to direct his attention to spiritual concerns. He began making overtures to the Maryse Choisy group, and in 1950, intervened violently at the World Congress of Psychiatry to denounce the fanaticism of psychoanalytical societies. Finally, in the fall of 1953, he joined the ranks of the SFP after having sent the president of the SPP a letter of resignation that would never be made public. [42]

Fleeing the quarrels of Paris, he packed his bags and settled in Casablanca, in a house he had bought a short time before. Morocco was rebelling against colonization at the time Laforgue was founding a psychoanalytic circle in which he held the position of a fallen master, split between his love of exile and his nostalgia for a lost homeland. He became a student of the mentality of the native populations, and took an interest in the problem of redemption. Five years later, suffering from a bizarre series of grippes, he returned to Paris and assembled around him a group of loyalists. In 1962, overwhelmed by fatigue, he died in a state of near insanity as the result of complications from an operation.

The official historians of the French psychoanalytic movement are not particularly scrupulous. Not only were they unaware of the actual relations between Laforgue and Göring, but they list Paul Schiff, the only Resistance member of the first generation, as having died in 1940 [he died in 1947]. In addition, they were quick to forget that the principal founder of their society was found innocent in the spring of 1946, and that no man should be tried for the same offense twice. Ilse and Robert Barande restrict themselves to writing that Laforgue was accused of collaborationism by his colleagues. They do not take sides, but consider as a given that there was a basis for the accusation. As for Paul Denis, he embarks on the wrong train and believes that Laforgue accompanied Vlaminck, Derain, and Van Dongen in their lamentable "cultural" journey to Nazi Germany. Alain de Mijolla is alone in demonstrating a degree of honesty when he writes: "René Laforgue's role seems difficult to assess, and although, in recent years, criticism against him has been less virulent, he continues to be reproached for his pro-German tendencies. His friends assure that his house in the South was a refuge for numerous members of the Resistance, that he sent food to his Jewish friends hidden in Paris. His adversaries accuse him of having participated (aside from other indulgences) in one of the trips for French intellectuals to Germany organized by Hitler's favorite sculptor, Arno Breker." [43]

It appears clear that the French psychoanalytic community felt the need, after Auschwitz, to strip René Laforgue of his symbolic position as founding father. He had become a burden, he who never succeeded in reigning. It also appears clear that this founding father always behaved as a defeated man: in relation to Nazi Germany, to which he told his fables; in relation to his community, which would preserve only the memory of his ambivalence, if not his clinical genius. No doubt this murder was necessary for the French movement so that it might bestow on itself the self-image it wished to have after the war: more orthodox, more Freudian, more internationalist, and more forgetful of its chauvinist past. Paradoxically, Laforgue would thus have paid quite dearly for the Maurrassian policies of Pichon, whom he had never supported.

With the return of the deportees, the French history of psychoanalysis ceased being written in its earlier idiom. The movement no longer dreamed of a Freudianism rooted in its soil and adapted to the ideals of an alleged Latinate genius; it turned to a more doctrinal apprehension of mental phenomena. The dynamic endeavors had born their fruit: In the context of the Liberation, the confinement of the insane tended to be seen as a symbol of exclusion, even of genocide. Psychiatry took its distance from any affiliation with the vestiges of the heredity-degeneration theory, and hostility to Jews became less verbal, more guilt-ridden, and still more repressed. Auschwitz revealed to those who had wanted to ignore it the true face of Nazism. The earlier Germanophobia tended to disappear and be replaced by hostility to what was already being called totalitarianism. France was less chauvinist and more antifascist. It began to realize that xenophobia and anti-Semitism are the two breasts from which ordinary racism draws its nourishment. It strained not to confuse Hegel with Hitler and Kant with Göring.

Starting with 1945, the history of the implantation of Freudianism is a closed book. The historian leaves the terrain of the grandiose adventure of the pioneers for the less heroic turf of the negotiation of conflicts. We shall now look at the mores of the psychoanalytic community from the point of view of its internal quarrels. But before approaching this new episode in the hundred years' battle, a new view of the horizon is called for. The period about to begin was marked by a dual movement. On the international scene, dominated by America's triumph, one observes a formidable expansion of an adaptative version of psychoanalysis, assimilated to the ideals of mental hygiene. Within France, the ball changes court. The world of literature no longer plays a vanguard role, and Freudian doctrine becomes a matter of interest to Communist discourse, which condemns Freud in the name of Coca-Cola, and to the Catholic world, in which there occurs, despite the hostility of Rome, an implantation that had not taken place before the war. Philosophy joins the fray. Each in its own manner, the works of Sartre, of Bachelard, and of Merleau-Ponty inquire into the Freudian status of the subject, the primacy of the unconscious, or the poetic path to be followed by a depth psychology. As for the psychoanalytic community, it forgot its chauvinist errors. Therapists began to proliferate in great number, and that quantitative transformation brought about a better adaptation of teaching to its new circumstances. More solid in its foundations, the movement could now tolerate a concatenation of internal splits. The multiplication of practitioners led to the creation of rival societies, which would—or would not—discover a fictive unity by seeking affiliation with the IPA.

II. From East to West

In an earlier book, I showed how the migration of Jewish psychoanalysts from central and eastern Europe led to the victory of the West over the East and to a radical transformation of the ideals of the international movement. During the interwar period, the IPA, successively directed by Eitingon and Jones, came gradually under Anglo-Saxon, then American control, with a pragmatic and medical orientation quite distant from the lay perspective recommended by Freud. Nonetheless, that loss of the older Viennese ethic was accompanied by a triumph: America enthusiastically adopted the theory come from old Europe. Jones kept the empire's affairs moving apace at a difficult time during which the American Psychoanalytic Association (APA) took on growing importance through the impetus of A. A. Brill.

On the morrow of World War II, a variety of problems of all sorts, linked to the expansion of the national societies, began to crop up in the international movement. The implantation of Freud's doctrine had been accomplished in all quarters, and henceforth the empire would be wracked by internal quarrels. Psychoanalysts continued, of course, to face resistance from without, but after Freud's death, they no longer hesitated to dispute a complex legacy, which was, moreover, opening up to the progress achieved by medical science. Simultaneously, differences centered on the preparation of training analysts began to surface.

In order to understand the French antagonisms of the 1950s, it is imperative to make a detour through the world of American psychoanalysis, which in part governed the evolution of the international scene.

The American movement was all the more hostile to the practice of lay analysis in that the psychiatric tradition was less strong—even nonexistent—on the continent. Already at the time of the initial penetration of Freudian ideas, neurologists, psychiatrists, and psychologists did not share the European notion according to which the phenomena of sexuality belonged to the register of instinct or degeneration. They retained the idea that every therapist of the soul should be a practitioner of medicine, but their conception of medical knowledge was from the outset dynamic and removed from any hereditarian configuration.[44] Thoroughly pragmatic, the American vision of psychoanalysis granted priority to the ego at the expense of the unconscious to the extent that it found in Freudian doctrine the wherewithal to adapt its subjects to a society alleged not to suffer from the decadence attributed to old Europe.

For that reason the integration of psychoanalysis into psychiatry was achieved without resistance; in their majority, the American therapists understood neither the meaning of the term *Laienanalyse* nor Freud's bitter struggle on its behalf. For them, psychoanalysis was above all a therapeutic technique which was not to be separated from its medical context. It subverted that context by transforming itself into a "global" medicine of body and soul. After World War II, that integration accelerated as a result of the progress registered in the fields of pharmacology, chemotherapy, and biological research. In France, the conflicts revolved around a reevaluation of Freud's work tending toward a more pronounced separatism in relation to the ideals of medicine. In the United States, on the contrary, none of the great trends born of the break-up of Freudianism split from the medical context. A biological vision of the subject, unified through its twofold (social and somatic) roots, was accorded priority. Whence the tendential rejection of the sexual problematic in favor of sublimation, of the unconscious in favor of the ego, of the destructive drive in favor of culture.

Starting in 1945, Hollywood affirmed its rights to the Freudian epic and presented a different image of it from the one maintaining in the American school (if we may temporarily merge its various tendencies) of psychoanalysis. One aspect nevertheless was common to the therapists and moviemakers of the New World who were interested in Freudian doctrine. With the exception of John Huston, who was born an American, and later moved to Ireland, the directors attracted to psychoanalysis had virtually all come from Europe. The Freudian vision allowed them, in Hollywood, to undertake a critique of the ideals of American society. In that sense, their position concerning psychoanalysis was radically different from that of the practitioners, who had also emigrated. Which is why, in the films of Alfred Hitchcock, Charlie Chaplin, Elia Kazan, Vincent Minelli, and Nicholas Ray, one finds a representation of Freudianism diametrically opposed to that put forth by the psychoanalytic institutes and more generally by the IPA: something of a return to the origins of Freudian thought.

Alfred Hitchcock was the first to attempt the venture with his adaptation of a popular novel, *Spellbound*. The book tells the story of a psychopath who becomes the director of a clinic in order to act out his insane fantasies. The filmmaker turned it into a love story, which is also a mystery centered on the hero's amnesia. He commissioned Salvador Dali to design a series of extraordinary dream sequences. Nineteen years later, with *Marnie*, he achieved a masterpiece. In a modern, hygienic America, amid the hues of autumn, he nostalgically rediscovered the atmosphere of Freud's first analyses. A female robber, frigid and dispossessed by her mother of the secret of a crime committed in her childhood, manages to be cured by virtue of the perverse gaze of the man who has married her in order to play psychoanalyst. The ending is a jewel: Marnie removes the veil of secrecy in the course of a storm sequence during which she relives her criminal act while adopting the voice of the little girl she used to be.

With *Limelight*, which was made in 1952, Charlie Chaplin reconstructed the old London of his childhood for the story of a clown who succeeds in curing a dancer of her hysterical paralysis. In the character of Calvero, played by himself, he reenacts Freud at the discovery of the transference. The clown is loved by the dancer with a "false" love linked to her miraculous cure. Calvero forces her to realize that her love is for a different man. He dies as a result after a last stage comeback during which he rediscovers for a brief instant the omnipotence of his youth. As for Elia Kazan, he was responsible for one of the finest Freudian films of the period, *Splendor in the Grass,* which recreates the years of the Depression, by way of the initiation of two adolescents constrained by their families to internalize the sexual taboos of puritanical America. The heroine emerges from a therapy in which she renounces her lost youth. In the film, the Freudianism of the 1930s, the period of the great pioneers, is depicted as the vehicle of an incredible freedom. Kazan thus returned to the origins of an effort at implantation which had not as yet been normalized.

It was in this context that John Huston went a step further by deciding, in 1958, to make a film about the life of the young Freud, who represented for him the prototype of the true adventurer. Huston asked Jean-Paul Sartre to write a summary of a projected scenario. The French philosopher accepted. He considered Freud to be a narrow-minded ideologue, but in reading Jones's biography, discovered a neurotic hero quite close to himself. He even envisaged the prospect of taking to the couch. At the end of the year, he submitted a synopsis of ninety-five pages, which earned him a contract. Then, a few months later, he completed a first version which was far too long. If filmed, it would have lasted seven hours. Huston suggested cuts, and Sartre sent a second version that was still longer. In October 1959, he spent a few weeks in the director's house in Ireland working on the scenario. The two men soon fell to quarreling. The philosopher reproached the filmmaker with not understanding anything of the unconscious and of wanting to abolish it. Huston accused Sartre of being stubborn and of not wanting to listen to anyone. He attempted—in vain—to get him to undergo hypnosis. Finally Sartre accepted a handsome sum, and withdrew his name from the film's credits.

Shot with Montgomery Clift in the role of Freud, Fernand Ledoux in that of Charcot, and Susannah York as a composite of various hysterical patients, the film appeared in the United States, with huge cuts imposed by the producer and a ridiculous title, *Freud, the Secret Passion.* It did not have any success. And yet the black and white photography of Douglas Slocombe recaptures superbly the baroque universe of fin de siècle Vienna. As for Montgomery Clift, he portrays an anguished, somber, and fragile Freud, closer to the James Dean of *Rebel without a Cause* than to the mummified figure imposed by the official historians of psychoanalysis: a character, in any event, more Sartrean than Jonesian. The work was distributed to the movie houses of Paris at the beginning of June 1964, two weeks before Lacan's foundation of the École freudienne de Paris. It went completely unnoticed by the psychoanalysts of Paris, who failed to find in it the hero of their imagination. Sartre's scenario would be published twenty years later, posthumously, and upon its appearance, *Le Nouvel observateur* would dedicate its cover page to the event. Even Lacan would never receive such acknowledgment on ground that was, all the same, very much his for fifty years.[45]

There were numerous divergences in the modes of implantation of Freudianism in Europe and in the New World. But it would be erroneous to believe in the existence of a single, sovereign "American" mode of psychoanalysis. Unity was not to be found in ideological tendencies, but rather in a technique imposed by the empire on all its member societies. In order to grasp the specificity of psychoanalysis's situation in America, the vastness of the continent should be taken into account. In America, differences between local societies are as important as those separating the societies of Europe. The American psychoanalytic situation was characterized from its inception by a proliferation of numerous tendencies and a profusion of conflicts.

Three main tendencies held sway. Their common denominator lay in a definition of the ego alien to the Freudian conception of the subject and centered on the predominance of the notion of the *individual*. Born of the work of Malinowski, *culturalism* attracted thinkers as different as Abram Kardiner, Ruth Benedict, Erich Fromm, Margaret Mead, and Karen Horney. The movement criticized Freudianism by reducing the structural theory of the Oedipus complex to an anthropological model. It attempted to adapt the principles of therapy to patterns of social behavior and to psychological characteristics. It was around Karen Horney that a series of splits occurred, during the war, within the New York Psychoanalytic Society.

The second trend was represented by Franz Alexander, the founder of the *Chicago School*. His aim was to transform classical analysis into a therapy of the entirety of the individual's personality. Concentrating on the problem of gastroduodenal ulcers, Alexander was struck by their frequent appearance in active persons. From there, he demonstrated that the source of the illness lay in a need for tenderness dating from childhood; that need is opposed to the adult ego and manifests itself as the emergence of intense aggressiveness. The more activity increases, the more the unconscious infantile feeling grows. It is then expressed as a demand for food, which entails an excessive secretion of gastric juices and the development of an ulcer. Confronted with such symptoms, Alexander recommended the association of two modes of therapy: One, which was psychoanalytic, involved an exploration of the unconscious and gave priority to speech; the other, which was organic, treated the ulcer. His position led to an assimilation of psychoanalysis to a form of psychosomatic medicine. It was characterized by a questioning of the canonical length of analysis and of its sessions and by a revision of the Freudian theory of sexuality.

The third trend, *ego psychology*, lay closer to Freud's classic doctrine, but entailed a complete revision of the second topographical model. We have already seen that Freud, in 1923, had reaffirmed the primacy of the unconscious over the ego, and the death drive over the other drives; he had renewed the inaugural gesture of his discovery at the beginning of the century. The ego, the repressive instance, was inscribed within the id and expressed the literal idea of an *Unbewusste*, an unknown force acting without the knowledge of the subject.[46] Now the partisans of ego psychology, Rudolph Loewenstein, Ernst Kris, David Rapaport, Erik Erikson, and above all Heinz Hartmann, maintained a position whose tendency was diametrically opposed to Freud's decentering. Instead of granting priority to the unconscious, they reconceived metapsychology on the model of psychology by according a preponderant role to the ego. In part because of her rivalry with Melanie Klein, Anna Freud supported the ego-psychological tendency within the IPA, where it also received the approbation of Jeanne Lampl de Groot, whose power was linked to the

fact that she had been analyzed by Freud. The struggle for the preservation of the
ego thus was to know its first surge in 1936, when Anna extended the notion of
defence to the very principle of adaptative therapy.

Viennese by origin, Hartmann, like Kris, belonged to that central European
tribe of Jews that had been forced to flee pogroms and change languages, diplomas,
and cultures numerous times. Initially analyzed by Sandor Rado, then (without pay)
by Freud, he spent some time in Paris before landing permanently in America, where
he published his works. There, he joined up with Loewenstein, who had himself
been exiled from Poland, Berlin, and Paris. David Rapaport, for his part, had traveled a similarly tumultuous route. A Hungarian Jew, he had led a Zionist group at
age twenty and pursued studies of mathematics and physics at the University of
Budapest. Like Eitingon, he emigrated to Palestine, where he remained for two
years, before returning home to lead a youth group. He took advantage of the occasion to undergo analysis (without becoming a physician), and in 1938, chose exile
in the United States. He allied himself with the partisans of ego psychology by elaborating a methodology for adaptative tests.

It would be false to reduce ego psychology to a mere ideology for adapting
subjects to capitalist society. If the notion of adaptation is one of the ideals of American life, it also informs the dreams of a certain Diaspora intent on ending its wanderings. From that perspective, there was a link between the theory of ego autonomy
and the private history of each of its founders.

In order to extricate his discovery from the ghetto and avoid the stupid rubric
"Jewish science," Freud in 1910 forwent assuming the directorship of the IPA. He
preferred placing a Swiss Protestant at the head of the empire while reserving for
himself the idiosyncratic role of "master without command." [47] Later, with the elaboration of the second topographical model and his declared hostility to the "Americanization" of the movement, he tended to underscore his Spinozan situation as an
isolated Jew; at the same time, he endowed his theory of the ego with a singular
lack of all narcissistic mastery. For years, he had refused to leave Austria and abandon Vienna, the motherland of new ideas. He preferred internal exile to migration,
the Diaspora to the promised land, a loss of self to effective command, the division
of being to its reunification, and, ultimately, knowing how to die to any immortality
of the soul. Within the doctrine of ego psychology an opposite tendency took shape.
Invented by immigrant Jews, ego psychology accomplished in reverse the Freudian
dream of leaving the ghetto. It replaced the division of being by a sovereign reconquest of man's unity, at the cost of liquidating the vestiges of internal exile. Ego
psychology was not a "Jewish science," for such a science does not exist, but it
reflected the ideals of the great victims of the East, forced to plant the flag of their
ego on the finally conquered soil of a promised land.

David Rapaport illustrated the notion of ego autonomy with a Jewish anecdote. A king of the Orient, contemplating a portrait of Moses, asked his astrologers
their opinion. In their opinion, the man was vain, cruel, venal, and a glutton. In his
dissatisfaction, the king paid Moses a visit and found him to have numerous qualities. He was preparing to denounce the incompetence of his wise men, but the

prophet prevented him: "Your astrologers are right," he said. "They know who I was without understanding who I have become."[48]

In the eyes of the theorists of ego psychology, the fable signifies that the ego *grows autonomous* by controlling its primitive drives. It acquires its independence in relation to external reality. And yet the autonomy remains relative. From the drives, the ego looks for a guarantee against bondage to the environment. From the environment, it demands the same guarantee against the exigencies of the id. The adaptation of the ego to the twofold constraints of id and reality occurs by way of a golden mean underwriting the balance necessary for the flourishing of human life. But if the ego tends to adjust in order to achieve its autonomy, identification is no longer an unconscious process but rather an imitative mode of behavior. The theory of sexuality undergoes a distortion as remarkable as the concept of identification. Channeled toward sublimation, libido ensures a *desexualization* or *neutralization* of aggressive drives. The "stronger" the ego is, the more it reinforces its quantum of neutralized energy. The weaker it is, the less its neutralization accomplishes. Ego psychology is thus based on a fundamental rejection of the death instinct, accompanied by a recentering of the unconscious on consciousness and of sexuality on its derivatives. Through the transference, the therapist fulfills the role of the strong ego the patient would like to resemble in order to attain the autonomy of an ego related to the narcissistic forms of a "self." Within therapy, such a revision takes the form of a priority granted to the analysis of resistances at the expense of the interpretation of contents.

To these three tendencies may be added one represented by the Kleinian school, whose significance we have situated in a previous volume. Skillfully backed by Jones, Kleinianism brought an innovative reading of Freud's work, close in certain respects to that undertaken by the young Lacan. Despite her quarrel with Anna Freud, Melanie Klein did not leave the British Society, which pulled off the virtuoso exploit of combining under the same roof three rival chapels: the Anna-Freudians, the Middel Group, which was independent, and the Kleinians. Across substantial divergences, the British retained grounds of agreement allowing them to maintain a single training curriculum for the three tendencies and to remain in the IPA. The Kleinian school did not in fact succeed in taking root in the United States, but it was recognized in all quarters and particularly in Latin America, which was thus able to manifest its difference (if not hostility) in relation to a community deemed imperialistic.[49]

All these tendencies were part of the history of the break-up and progress of Freudian doctrine. If some claimed to be more "orthodox" than others, they all were oriented toward a better adjustment of theory to national conditions of psychoanalytic practice. And yet they were the bearers of a genuine conceptualization that was by no means the mere reflection of a fixed ideology. Some of the trends succeeded in taking root within the IPA; others, on the contrary, were obliged to leave the empire in order to create the kind of organization required for their expansion. Quarrels tended invariably to focus on the role of intellectual masters considered "charismatic" and deemed nefarious by some for that very reason. The charisma of the leaders was opposed to the "normative" progress of an institution exclusively oriented toward the production of competent therapists, and governed in accordance with high-level technical rules. Whenever there erupted doctrinal reformulations calling into question the technical orientation of the IPA, the crisis ended by shattering the principles of peaceful coexistence. In such cases, what was at stake in every split was a recasting of doctrine in the form of a reevaluation of the accepted modes of its transmission. The conflict then focused on technique, but in fact bore on the theory authorizing that technique.

After World War II, the bureaucratic leviathan of the IPA played a dominant role in the Old World, imposing its technocratic reign on the societies of Europe. The international association comprises or is empowered to recognize five kinds of organization: regional associations; member societies which may (or may not) be organized as federations; provisional societies; study groups; and associated organisms. A *regional association* combines a certain number of societies located in a continent, a subcontinent, or a large national territory. It is responsible, once it exists, for the development and recognition of new societies. A *member society* of the IPA is an organism directly affiliated independent of any regional association. It is authorized to train and license therapists for clinical and training practice, in accordance with extremely strict criteria. Before obtaining that status, the highest in the administrative hierarchy, a society is first a provisional society, and in order to become a member, it must undergo evaluation, for a fixed period of time, by a *consulting committee* or a *visiting committee,* named by the executive council of the IPA and charged with determining the group's capacity for producing therapists.

Below the provisional society in status is the *study group*. Such an entity may be sponsored by a member society or, if possible, by the council itself. It is authorized, with the supervision of a consulting committee and under certain conditions, to train analysts. Finally, an *associated organism* is a society not authorized to license training analysts, but allowed to maintain close relations with the IPA.

In addition to the status of the different collective entities governed by the IPA, individual membership in the association is simultaneously dependent on and independent of belonging to a society. Two categories of membership are recognized: *members* and *associates*. In general, the rank of member or associate is automatically granted to members (any category) of a member or provisional society. It may be lost by resigning from one of those societies and is not automatically accorded to members of study groups. That is why an individual appointment of member at large for three or four members is necessary to obtain the sponsorship of a group changing status from provisional to affiliated society. Alongside the societies, there are federations, thanks to which, on an individual basis, the rank of member may in some cases not be lost in the event of withdrawal from a society.

The various societies closely supervised by the IPA have as their principal tasks producing training analysts and selecting students in accordance with normative criteria we shall have ample occasion to discuss. The IPA is directed by a president who is elected every two years at each congress by a general assembly of members, constituted for the occasion as an administrative assembly. The president is assisted by a council, composed of honorary members, a secretary, a treasurer, former presidents, six vice-presidents, and associate secretaries. Each vice-president is intended to represent a different geographic region. The IPA divides the world into three huge kingdoms corresponding to the might of its empire: North America, the countries of South America along with Mexico, and the rest of the world—which means principally Europe, in which Great Britain has de facto a privileged position.

In North America, the APA counterbalances the power of the IPA insofar as it is the largest and most individualistic federative member of the international movement. In the 1940s, it obtained a special status according it the right to grant official approval to the training programs offered by local societies, which normally comprise one or several institutes connected with a university or a medical society. The APA thus oversees the totality of psychoanalytic training in America. Under those circumstances, the IPA serves largely to ensure the cohesion of European, Latin-American, or other societies, under the domination of a centralized power. The major instrument of psychoanalytic training in America is called the Board of Professional Standards. A true agent of normalization, the Board defines criteria of selection and supervises the educational curricula in use at all institutes. In addition, it serves as a model for the administrative organ of the IPA, which governs psychoanalytic training throughout the world on the basis of its different categories of societies.[50]

The societies of Europe are arrayed beneath the banner of the IPA and define themselves as members of the international movement. Whenever an organizational split seems on the horizon, in particular in France, the problem is raised, for societies born of a schism, of being immediately, recognized by the IPA, lest (should that validation be lacking) they no longer exist on the world scene. We will have to wait for Lacan's break and the establishment of a tendency bearing his name, along with its international expansion, for nonmembership in the Freudian empire no longer to be experienced as a particularly dramatic development by those considering resignation from member societies.

Within North America, the presence of the APA limits the importance of the IPA, which remains, in any event, under American domination, whatever the nationality of its president or secretary. Kleinianism, Anna-Freudianism, and ego psychology, in the 1950s, represented the majority tendencies within the IPA. The organization thus was in large measure under Anglo-American "influence." Despite the expansion of the Latin-American societies, the power of the IPA grew with the victory of the Allies, which occasioned a new preponderance of English in the face of a defeated Germany and an isolated France. Within the history of the psychoanalytic movement, the two world wars had the effect of ensuring the triumph of the West over the East and of recentering control of the empire's affairs onto an increasingly Anglophonic scene, which was itself more and more an American-dominated fiefdom. There was thus, by 1945, something of a psychoanalytic Yalta, but no Stalin had been invited to the banquet because of the extinction of Freudianism in the Soviet Union and in eastern Europe. The dividing up of territories concerned three major powers: France, in which the Lacanian movement was to emerge; the New World, in which the Anglo-American influence reigned; and England, in which a peaceful coexistence among several tendencies flourished.

Within the APA, the New York Psychoanalytic Society plays a principal role. The major organizational split of the American movement occurred within its ranks, centering on Karen Horney. As early as the 1920s, that society served as a turntable for struggles intent on weakening the power of Europe. In 1931, the Society created a training institute, the New York Psychoanalytic Institute, inspired by its counterpart in Berlin, and in 1932, it published a journal, the *Psychoanalytic Quarterly*, which ensured a large audience for its activities. With the influx of Jewish emigrants, who tended to settle massively in New York, the Society further strengthened its position at the heart of the IPA empire. As for the Institute, which was first directed by Monroe Meyer, then by Dorothy Ross, it expanded its instruction to large sectors of the population: magistrates, policemen, social workers, teachers, and so forth. It effected the infiltration of neo-Freudian ideas into the nonmedical community on the basis of its predominantly medical orientation.

In 1946, the influence of the Society extended further with the creation of a Treatment Center, affiliated with the Institute, which received veterans suffering from war traumas, then civilians and children. In the 1950s, the flourishing of the doctrine of ego psychology reinforced the new importance of the New York Society.

The break-up of Freudianism led to a series of splits. Already in 1941, the Society condemned Karen Horney's positions and disqualified her teaching, which it accused of being troublesome to the minds of her students. Born in 1885 to a Protestant family of Hamburg, she nevertheless followed a classic route. She received her doctorate at Berlin and underwent therapy with Karl Abraham and Hanns Sachs. In 1932, she joined Alexander in Chicago, where she directed the Institute before becoming a member of the New York Society. Very early on, Karen Horney called into question what she called "Freudian orthodoxy," particularly in the domain of female sexuality. She attempted an elucidation of the castration complex in women centered on the bisexual origin of the anatomical difference of the sexes and on a critique of phallocentrism, understood as the expression of male superiority. A participant in the culturalist movement, she did not reject psychic determinism, but described neuroses from the perspective of their assimilation to cultural differences.[51]

Forced to resign from the New York Society, Karen Horney took along with her five members and fourteen students in training. Simultaneously, the dissidents left the APA and consequently the IPA, but immediately founded the American Association for the Advancement of Psychoanalysis (AAAP), which would become the APA's rival. Among those who resigned were Harry Stack Sullivan, Erich Fromm, and William Silverberg. They formed a training institute, the American Institute of Psychoanalysis, and attempted to regroup around it the disaffected of other cities. But soon new conflicts surfaced within the AAAP. Partisans of the very jealous Karen Horney contested the privileges granted the powerful Erich Fromm, who felt persecuted and left the group in 1943, taking his friends along with him. Whereupon a second dispute erupted in the ranks of the AAAP. Several members, including Sullivan, sought to enlarge the Institute's psychiatry department and envisaged an affiliation with New York Medical College. Fearing her eminence might suffer from such an arrangement, Karen Horney expressed her disagreement. As a result, her adversaries resigned, and the group, which was intent on being eclectic, returned to square one. It became a sect organized around the teachings of a doctrinal master exercising undivided influence over her disciples.

As opposed to the New York Society, the Chicago Institute for Psychoanalysis, founded in 1932 by Franz Alexander, managed to surmount its conflicts without falling prey to any secessionist compulsion. Organized on the Berlin model, the Chicago school specialized in psychosomatic medicine and counted a significant number of women among its members. It organized numerous lectures, revealed itself to be open to doctrinal winds from abroad and managed to separate radically the activities of the Society from those of the Institute.

In the Washington area, a series of investigations into the notion of mental hygiene prevailed.[52] Founded by Adolf Meyer in 1914, the Washington Psychoanalytic Society (WPS) very quickly situated psychoanalysis under the banner of psychiatry. In 1924, a rival society, the Washington Psychoanalytic Association, was founded. In order to avoid confusion, the first group changed its name and became the Washington Psychopathological Society. The two were in a state of war, each claiming to be the legitimate representative of psychoanalysis in the region. They also attempted to win recognition by the APA, and Brill ended up opting for the WPS, directed by Sullivan, who was later to move to New York. The WPS was eventually replaced by a far larger organization, the Washington-Baltimore Psychoanalytic Society, which was to group psychoanalysts from Virginia and Maryland, outside of any European lineage. During World War II, that society was to seem too huge to its members. They chose to split up and form two groups, each capable of representing the interests of a single city.

In 1947, Henri Ey proposed the creation of an international association charged with periodically organizing world congresses of psychiatry. An initial discussion took place under the leadership of Jean Lhermitte, Laignel-Lavastine, Jean Delay, and Pierre Janet. Twenty-five societies accepted the proposal.[53] Three years later, in the fall of 1950, the first congress assembled in Paris representatives of some ten countries and about forty societies. There were more than 1,500 participants. All the leading names of the French movement figured among the speakers, from the first to the third generation: Marie Bonaparte, Adrien Borel, René Laforgue, Louis Angelo Hesnard, Blanche Reverchon-Jouve, Jacques Lacan, Sacha Nacht, Daniel Lagache, Françoise Dolto, Marc Schlumberger, Juliette Boutonier, Pierre Mâle, André Berge, Maurice Bouvet, and finally René Diatkine, Francis Pasche, Serge Lebovici, Georges Favez, Robert Pujol, Jenny Roudinesco, and Serge Leclaire. Despite the opposition of the SPP, Ey invited representatives of the Adlerian and Jungian movements.

In the interest of representing recent trends in psychoanalysis, Henry Ey invited Franz Alexander, president of the American Psychiatric Association, to open the proceedings. He had recommended inviting Anna Freud, who agreed to come. But Ey also was intent on having Melanie Klein present. He consequently asked Juliette Boutonier to write to her. She refused by return mail, unhappy that priority had been accorded Freud's daughter. In order to have Melanie in spite of everything,

Ey resorted to a ruse. He had the lady informed that it was Alexander who had recommended inviting Anna. Then, he pledged to have the two rivals speak at noncompetitive hours. Melanie accepted.[54]

Gala festivities accompanied the gigantic assemblage of celebrities. One evening, the participants could be found on the highest floor of the Eiffel Tower, savoring petits fours. Another evening, they attended a gala performance by Roland Petit, Madeleine Renaud, and Jean-Louis Barrault. At the end of their sessions, they were received at the Élysée Palace by Vincent Auriol, president of the Republic, who wished psychiatry a long and healthy existence, even as he evoked the drama of the Korean War. Finally, they attended a sumptuous banquet at the Palais de Chaillot, where they danced until dawn. While the men debated neo-Freudianism, psychosomatics, and Kleinianism, their spouses, abandoned, visited the studios of leading couturiers and bought ankle-length skirts or strapless evening gowns, studded with sequins.

Alexander opened hostilities with a speech in which he described to perfection the American and international psychoanalytic situation: "I once declared that the heroic phase of psychoanalysis belongs to a past in which it had to struggle against the prejudices of a world minimally prepared to view it objectively. Today psychiatrists as well as a large number of physicians fully recognize the significance of Freud's fundamental discoveries. . . . That shift in our relations toward other disciplines requires a modification of our own attitude lest we become victims of sclerosis, reacting with old reflexes to a world that has evolved. The attitude of splendid isolation is a bit antiquated and, more important still, the insistence on agreement among ourselves is equally superseded. During a certain time, when we constituted a small group surrounded by a world incapable of understanding our work, internal unity, demanding agreement on scientific matters, on theory itself, was indispensable. Today we can afford the luxury of diverging from each other because scientific inquiry and progress are possible only in a climate of freedom of thought in which emancipation from traditional points of view, and even from those of great value, is encouraged when new experiments demand such revision."[55]

Alexander presented in detail the hypotheses and methods of the Chicago school. Against him, Raymond de Saussure defended a rather curious notion of "prelogical mentality." By way of the case of a thirteen-year-old boy, he distinguished two forms of emotion: *assimilated emotion,* which is part of conscious memory; and *hallucinated* or *isolated emotion,* which gets repeated stereotypically without approaching the scene as originally experienced. Such hallucinated emotions created in the neurotic individual sectors of prelogical thought functioning on the model of an affective realism in which adaptation—once again—cannot be accomplished through assimilation of reality. At the conclusion of his implausible jumble, Saussure substituted a "prelogical sector" for the Freudian id. He transformed the ego into an "adapted"—or rational—ego, and concluded that neurotic conflict occurred between the prelogical sectors and the rational ego. The physician was to "convince" his patient to be cured, to the extent that the latter transferred onto the former his hallucinated affects and the mechanism serving to disguise them.

He added that it would be valuable to have precise transcripts of analytic sessions in order to verity the therapeutic results.[56]

Quite dissatisfied, Francis Pasche ridiculed Raymond de Saussure's presentation. He emphasized that the notion of prelogical thought had been abandoned by Lévy-Bruhl, because of its tendency to institute inadequate distinctions between "civilized" mentalities and other "primitive" ones. He denounced the Genevan's amalgamation of Piaget's theses with Freud's and affirmed the unacceptability of the opposition between an alleged normal psychology and one applicable to pathology. He added: "Yesterday Charles Odier reproached myself and several others with what he calls our 'misoneism,' our refusal of new ideas. I am inclined to judge that charge as paradoxical and to happily maintain that Freud's thinking in the 1920s, which it is our intention to defend, is newer than the thoughts that are being opposed to him today, and is even ahead of our own time." [57]

Francis Pasche was not alone in supporting a return to the rigor of the second topographical model. Daniel Lagache in turn thanked Alexander for underscoring at the outset that the therapeutic model from Chicago was more strategic than tactical. "Eminently adroit," he said, "such therapy commits its practitioner to acting out and almost to psychodrama. The spacing out and shortening of the analytic sessions make contact rather precarious. But Mr. Alexander is admirably aware of all this; he has written quite pertinent pages on the danger of acting out and the benefits of interpretation." [58] Whereupon Lagache defended the perspective of a merger between psychology and psychoanalysis.

Jacques Lacan intervened in turn. He reproached Saussure for his lack of a sense of humor, his outmoded etiological schemes, and his blunders concerning the amalgamation of Freud and Piaget. "What interest can there in fact be," he said, "in translating our experience into the categories through which Monsieur Piaget, with his questionnaires, separates child psychology from an ideal adult psychology alleged to be the philosopher's in the exercise of his functions . . . ? Why seek to found upon such fallacious objectifications of structure what we discover by way of a method so utterly opposed to it: to wit, through a familiar dialectic, at the level of the idiosyncratic interests of the subject, in which the mere virtue of the meanings comprised within language mobilizes the very images which unwittingly inform his conduct and may be revealed to regulate even his organic functions." [59] To the notion of a prelogical mentality, Lacan thus opposed for the first time, the concept of a language structure borrowed from Saussurean linguistics. Finally, in an act of homage to Claude Lévi-Strauss, he emphasized that the adults of "primitive" societies believe that their own children participate in mental forms specific to civilized man. In closing his diatribe, he hurled at Saussure the magic name of Roman Jakobson.[60]

Lacan then attacked ego psychology and designated the ego as the "syndic of the most mobile functions through which man adapts to reality." Following which he showed that Alexander's conception of sexuality reversed Freud's doctrine by turning the sexual function into an "itch" or an excess born of the ego at the extreme limit of its effectiveness. According to him, such a psychological science had been affected by the ideals of the society in which it was produced. Without making any link to any alleged American manifestations of sex, Lacan reproached the therapists of the New World with reducing man to a mechanical animal. He prophesied, not without a certain facetiousness, the advent of an era in which those "animals" would manifest a new desire to make love, then expressed his happiness at seeing certain American colleagues share his point of view and denounce the danger threatening Freudian doctrine.

In his address on current tendencies of psychoanalysis, Sacha Nacht, in his way, also took a stand for a return to the meaning of the Viennese discovery. He observed that the current situation was characterized by an importance attributed to the ego and the aggressive drives. Without attacking American revisionism, he emphasized that analysis had turned away from the elucidation of the repressed in order to focus on the agency of repression. In the face of that state of things, he proposed his own version of a "new psychoanalysis," which would consist of taking into account both the reinforcement of the ego and the adaptative integration of the aggressive drives. He thus managed to be opposed, on the one hand, to ego psychology, on the other, to the opening invited by Lagache, and in addition, to Lacan's reelaboration.[61] We shall later see the three tendencies evolve within the SPP.

Through this congress, it is possible to perceive the outline of the major opposition that was to divide the masters of the SPP. Running through his critique of the theses of Alexander and Raymond de Saussure is Lacan's will to puncture the "new psychoanalysis" intent on recentering the theory of the unconscious on a psychology of consciousness while reducing the experience of therapy to the labor of adaptation, desire to need, and the psychical to the biological. Now at the time he was not alone in France in denouncing this "New Deal." All the psychoanalysts of the second generation were opposed to the revisionist interpretation rampant in the American societies. To that extent, there may be found as of 1950 a confrontation between a *French school* of psychoanalysis, desirous of recapturing the élan of Freud's message, and a more pragmatic *American school,* seeking to liquidate the residues of the teaching from Vienna. Within that configuration, Lacan occupied a vanguard position by virtue of the fact that the writings of his youth were already responsible for a split within the history of the French movement. As he approached his fiftieth birthday, our hero was alone in forging the theoretical tools necessary for a truly "Freudian" reelaboration of Freud's work. Whence the following paradox: He became "Lacanian" because he was Freudian, and because, instead of opening Freud's teaching to an alleged modernity, he drew support from his Surrealist past, from Hegelian philosophy, and, in short order, from linguistics, in order to rethink the entirety of a discovery in the light of his own history.

To be sure, Lacan was sustained by the French movement, which was overwhelmingly opposed to revisionism, but he was the first to bestow upon that opposition a coherent theoretical tool. He criticized the adaptative ideals of American society, not out of chauvinism, but to the degree that they offered support for an ideology of the ego concerning which he himself would later say that it might be summarized as a theology in the service of free enterprise. Lacan did not take up as his own the ideal of a "French psychoanalysis" opposed to an "American psychoanalysis," but, in order to criticize the situation overseas, he waged a political battle against a certain "imperialism" whose implantation seemed underway in the IPA. In the course of his struggles, he would not exclude his cause's assuming a form of anti-Americanism and would occasionally employ the words "American psychoanalysis" to designate the entirety of a configuration centered on ego psychology.

There thus emerged a new divide: conflicting tendencies, bereft of homogeneity, in which national situations appeared to be at stake, at a time when "nationalism" was no longer a point of reference, within a struggle in which it was first of all a matter of reflecting on the history of the split-up of Freudianism. That contradiction between a theoretical reflection and the political forms traversing it would weigh heavily on the elaboration of Lacanianism, which would erroneously be experienced, by both its partisans and its adversaries, as a typically French—and even antiforeign—doctrine.

An anecdote bears witness to Lacan's position concerning the American psychoanalytic situation. During a lecture at the Neuropsychiatric Society of Vienna, in 1955, Lacan claimed to have from Jung's own mouth a curious item of information. Approaching the American continent in 1909, Freud was alleged to have said to his disciple; "They don't know that we're bringing them the plague." [62] Jung, however, appears to have reserved for Lacan alone the revelation of that secret. In his memoirs, he makes no mention of a plague. [63] For his part, Freud never uses the word. As for the historians of the psychoanalytic movement, from Jones to Schur, and including Ellenberger, Clarence Oberdorf, Vincent Brome, and Paul Roazen, they have no knowledge of any "scourge." Freud simply said, "They'll be surprised when they find out what we have to tell them." [64]

The parable of the black death traverses the psychoanalytic movement. On the one hand, the English-language historians know nothing of the existence of an imaginary utterance that does not correspond to their representation of the Freudian saga, and on the other, Lacan invents a fiction that seems truer than life in order to restore to the international community the "Hannibalian truth" of the message from Vienna. Simultaneously he underscores the fact that Freud had erred in believing that psychoanalysis might take hold as a scourge on the American continent. What occurred was the opposite: The Viennese doctrine was devoured by America, but at the cost of seeing itself cured of its subversive cultural ideals. During the 1950s, Lacan thus relaunched the thematic of an "analytic plague" in order to combat the "illness" from across the Atlantic. He simultaneously represented the history of the analytic movement in terms of a "true legend" and took himself for the plague-ridden traveler of Freudian memory. His message was received rather curiously. Today in France everyone uses the word "plague" to designate the Viennese discovery. Abroad, on the contrary, only the partisans of Lacan employ that term. The French thus attribute to Freud a sentence transmitted by Lacan without perceiving that Freud never uttered it nor did Jung confirm it. Thus progress the rumors that give rise to legends and end up becoming history itself. . . .

Whereas in the West, psychoanalysis enjoyed significant renown, in the Soviet Union, the celebration of the centenary of the birth of Pavlov foreboded a new condemnation of Freudianism. The psychoanalytic movement had not existed in the country since 1930, but with the advent of the cold war, Freudian doctrine continued to seem dangerous by virtue of its expansion on the American continent. In 1950, at the Moscow Conference on Pavlov, a critique was broached of prior "deviations" from Pavlovian thought. What was at stake was no longer using Pavlovianism as the standard of materialism within the field of psychology, but rather rehabilitating it as a full science in its own right, capable of explaining man in his totality. It was believed that a "true" science of human behavior was at hand and that it was no longer necessary to denounce the idealist nature of psychoanalysis as had previously been customary. If analysis was not a science, it was nothing more than a reactionary ideology in the service of American imperialism. Whence the new turn given to its condemnation: For the Soviets, Freud was to be found hidden within Truman's skull, and his doctrine distilled in a glass of Coke.

The crusade began at the end of the 1940s with the recycling of the theory of "two sciences" elaborated at the start of the century by Bogdanov and subsequently criticized by Lenin.[65] During the interwar years, the theory had become—by way of the thematic of socialist realism—one of the principal components of Stalinist ideology on literary matters. After the war, it resurfaced and served to impose Lyssenko's theses in biology and Zhdanov's in the field of culture in general.

According to Alexander Bogdanov, a science may be "bourgeois" or "proletarian" in its very nature, and specifically in its origins, methods, and ends. To that extent, all the social sciences, including logic and mathematics, may and indeed do have a class character.

The massive promotion of that thesis may be explained in part by the economic situation of the Soviet Union and by the division of the world into two antagonistic camps. While a witch-hunt mentality was already visible on the horizon in the United States, Communist discourse congealed as of 1946–47 into an exaggerated denunciation of the horrors of capitalism. In Zhdanov's perspective, the world was divided into two camps: One, under American domination, had as its aim the reinforcing of imperialism; the other, powerfully enlightened by the Soviet Union, sought to combat the first by contributing its support to the colonized nations struggling for independence. The division of the world into two camps found a favored mode of expression in the domain of the sciences and culture. In 1934, Zhdanov had affirmed that Soviet literature was optimistic because it conveyed the ideals of a rising class,[66] but in 1946, he did an about-face and declared that literature and culture are the product not of a single class, but of the Soviet nation as a whole. The struggle between a workers' vanguard and the residues of a declining bourgeoisie was over; what was now needed was to liquidate the enemies of the nation, that is, the foreign cultural forms that were alien to Soviet ideology, which represented the triumphant ideas of the victorious proletariat.[67] Culture and science obeyed the principle of the division into two camps, with the exception that the Soviet camp escaped the principle of a division into classes. There were no classes in the Soviet Union since the Soviet state satisfied the interests of proletarian science and culture, whereas the imperialists and their lackeys sang the praise of bourgeois culture by slandering socialism. If any residues of the past existed, they would have to be eliminated in order to consolidate the moral unity of the people. Such, schematically, were the theses of Zhdanovism.

Within that context, the academic agronomist Trofim Denisovitch Lyssenko published in 1948 a report in which he summarized theses he had elaborated as early as 1934. Drawing for support on the works of Michurin, another agronomist who had grafted "pear trees onto apple trees" and transformed autumn wheat into spring wheat, Lyssenko recounted in his own way the history of Darwinism. In his view, the doctrine of *The Origin of Species* was divided into two parts: One was "materialist," since it admitted, through the idea of natural selection, the possibility of modifying heredity through the environment; the other was "idealist," because it alleged a struggle for existence. According to the agronomist, that split was perpetuated within the work deriving from Darwinism, giving rise to two lines of research. The first, which was "fully materialist," was represented by the Soviet school and maintained the principle of a *proletarian biology* in which man had the power to transform the animal and vegetable worlds; the second, which was deeply "reactionary," was inspired by the works of modern genetics and concerned the biologists of the capitalist world.

Before long Lyssenko's insane theses had won the support of Stalin and Michurin's biology was saluted by Communist discourse as the great discovery of the century. Two years later, the same Stalin went the other way on the subject of linguistics. He refuted the theories of Nicolai Yakovlevich Marr, founder of an allegedly supranational language destined to ensure communication among peoples. Marrian theory attended to the division of societies into antagonistic classes and considered languages as their reflection. In addition, it refuted the Indo-Europeanists' concept of a mother tongue in order to replace it with the utopia of a single language, both archaic and yet to come, capable of achieving Communist happiness in a classless society. After the death of their master in 1934, Marr's partisans transformed his doctrine. They abandoned the thesis on the origin of languages in order to retain the notion of "reflection" and impose the idea of a supranational language. The posthumous Marrism of the 1950s was thus an edulcorated version of that of the 1930s. It rejected the outlandish aspects of the doctrine and kept its rational aspect. And within the new conjuncture, Stalin rejected Marrism, which he reproached for not having taken into account the question of nationalities.[68]

In point of fact, the condemnation of Marrism went hand in hand with the defense of Lyssenkism. It was a matter, on the one hand, of uniting the people while respecting the diversity of languages and cultures, and on the other, of showing that that same people had the power, in accordance with its will, of modifying animal and vegetable nature in the direction of a primacy of acquired traits over heredity. For a variety of reasons, no actual "scandal" erupted in the domain of psychology. Being neither a science like biology, nor a theory like linguistics, psychology had no object. It partook of the dogma of two sciences only by dint of its capacity to give expression to a behavioral ideal. Since there was no longer a psychoanalytic movement in the Soviet Union, it was no longer necessary to oppose a materialist standard to Freudianism. The affair had been judged years before. But despite that, it was still imperative to condemn psychoanalysis as a reactionary ideology since it represented, beyond the national borders, the interests of the capitalist camp. The new denunciation came at a time when the principal Soviet Jewish writers were being murdered and the last Yiddish schools were being closed.[69] Although it was never said, it is not out of the question that psychoanalysis was also felt to be, at the time, a "Zionist science" apt to serve the State of Israel during a period in which it was swinging into the American camp.

In 1949, the renewal of Pavlovianism was able to serve, in the form of a "Michurinian psychology," as a scientific guarantee for a conception of happiness centered on the primacy of man's conditioning by man: Thanks to it, one could transform the "mad" into well-adapted individuals. The new-style Pavlovianism served to affirm that madness (psychoses and neuroses together) had disappeared from Soviet territory with the liquidation of "pathogenic" capitalism, and that, if it did subsist, its cause was physiological or organic and thus fell into the province of "Michurinian medicine." That logic notwithstanding, it was nonetheless observed that certain of the "mad" remained beyond rehabilitation. In order to treat them, special psychiatric hospitals were set up under the aegis of the Ministry of the Interior and charged with defining a bizarre mental affliction that would later be named "torpid schizophrenia" in order not to use the term "dissidence." Thanks to that partially unconscious reasoning, a *Michurinian Pavlovianism* emerged without being named as such and without provoking the same international scandal as the Lyssenko affair.

In the French Communist Party, in which there had been no anti-Freudian battle prior to the war, it was a matter of condemning psychoanalysis as a reactionary ideology while countering it with "something else" that would be the perfected form of an alleged materialist psychology. There is indeed a relation between Zhdanovism and its Gallic counterpart, but the difference bears on the fact that the French Communists were a battle behind in their understanding of the recycling of Pavlovianism in the Soviet Union. Unable to consecrate as proletarian a Pavlovian science they knew nothing about since it had not taken root in France as a dominant psychology, they made use of a Pavlovianism served with a 1930s-style Soviet sauce and used it both as a standard of materialism in the field of psychical phenomena and as a "Michurinian medicine" opposed to a psychoanalysis deemed to be reactionary. Thus they did not have the theoretical means to distinguish Freudian doctrine from its "deformed" or "revised" use in a country in which the psychoanalytic movement itself was traversed by currents hostile to "Americanization." In the Soviet Union, the liquidation of Freudianism took place in the interwar years in the course of conflicts between opposing anti-Freudians and Freudo-Marxists. In the PCF, nothing analogous transpired, so that in 1949, the French Communists did not know what they were talking about. They did not know whether they should condemn reactionary psychoanalysis, allied with imperialism, or Freudian doctrine, as irrationalist and antimaterialist. In the absence of any theoretical discussion, they would kill two birds with a single stone, refuting simultaneously Vienna and Coca-Cola. And at that point the "extravagances" of Politzer were recycled in order to underwrite an antipsychoanalytic war dominated at times by anti-Americanism, at others by an amalgamation of Freudianism and Nazism, and at still others by a hastily patched together "Michurino-Pavlovian" synthesis.

The rather primitive anti-Communism of the international psychiatro-psychoanalytic movement made matters even more difficult. At the time, a massive hostility toward dictatorships had led the World Health Organization to concern itself with the insanity of heads of state. Naturally, all Western eyes were fixed on Stalin, who became the most celebrated paranoiac of the 1950s. At the Congress on Mental Hygiene in London (1948), numerous therapists proposed submitting great men to therapy in order to diminish their "aggressive instincts" and preserve world peace. Confronted by the stinging attacks of Benjamin Logre, who did not hesitate to declare that the only remedy to war would be the extension of the analytic couch to the entire planet, *L'Humanité* organized an anti-Freudian campaign. The tone was established in an article by Guy Leclerc, entitled "La psychanalyse idéologie de basse police et d'espionnage [Psychoanalysis as the ideology of police abjection and spying]." The author distinguished sincere therapists from the mystifiers and lackeys of imperialism. He dismissed the latter brutally and warned the former of the urgency of condemning Freud's thought as such. "Thus it is," he wrote, "that some psychoanalysts of good faith try to persuade themselves that the psychoanalysis of the others is, of course, to be condemned, but their own is something quite excellent. But the facts speak for themselves. . . . There is the body of irrationalist doctrine juggling its entities (the ego, libido, the superego, Eros . . .); the idealism manipulating essences assumed to be immanent to the human condition; the idea of an anxiety forever linked to man, of a perpetual renewal of conflicts branded with the seal of fate (is not the Oedipus complex accorded a veritably eternal aspect, thus entailing a dismissal of the ideas of evolution, progress, and human liberation?). There is the notion of guilt, which connects so well with the myth of original sin. And the recourse to a savior: the father, God, or for an entire people, a father-substitute: Hitler, for example. . . . There is above all the ultra-reactionary, conscious and deliberate use made of psychoanalysis in the context of a general offensive on the part of obscurantism, destined to undermine man's trust in science. The general offensive of an imperialism on the ropes attempting to shatter the momentum of the democratic movement the world over. Such is the 'psychoanalytic reality' in 1949. It is that and nothing else. Some prefer to replace it with what they think psychoanalysis should be. They bring to mind those left-wing intellectuals who declare gravely: 'I am a socialist but I deny the socialism of the U.S.S.R.' There is none other outside of their beclouded minds. In the same way psychoanalysis is psychoanalysis American-style. Are you a socialist? Then you are for Soviet socialism. Are you for psychoanalysis? They you are for Yankee-style psychoanalysis. Because what you have to choose between are real things and not the ideas you entertain yourself with about things."[70]

The article, with it clichés, reveals clearly that for official Communist discourse Freudian doctrine was of the same nature as the "reactionary" or "American" use made of it. And indeed, according to the principle of the division of sciences into two camps, it was impossible to separate a theory from its concrete utilization, since that utilization was the very expression of the class nature of the theory in question.

That official line did not reflect the minority positions of those within the party in the 1950s who were interested in the Freudian venture. With the surge of the Liberation and the expansion of dynamic psychiatry, numerous therapists joined the ranks of the Communists and participated in the elaboration of a new form of mental medicine. Instead of favoring the virtues of adaptation and submitting to the progress of pharmacological therapy, they attempted to take into account social and political factors in their elucidation of the phenomenon of madness. Such progressive therapists resisted the Anglo-American vogue of mental hygiene and criticized what they called "American psychoanalysis." For them, Freud's lesson, in the authenticity of its message, conveyed neither a reactionary ideology nor an idealist theory. On the contrary, it was the bearer of a subversive vision of human nature that was capable of serving the interests of a "social" psychiatry in part inspired by the works of Henri Ey. The latter, moreover, supported the efforts of Communist psychiatrists, all the while avoiding any reduction of madness to a class phenomenon. Alongside the official Communist line, there thus developed, within the party ranks, a resistance to the dogma of the two sciences. It attempted to *separate* Freudian doctrine from the American or "reactionary" psychoanalytic position, at the risk of rejecting the latter for the sake of the former.

But working within the Zhdanovist perspective, the party leadership, through the persons of Jean Kanapa and Laurent Casanova, insisted on a condemnation pure and simple of Freudianism. Simultaneously, it demanded of biologists adhesion to the principles of Michurinian genetics. Victor Leduc, a philosopher with responsibilities among the intellectuals, received the mission of initiating discussions with Communist psychiatrists and psychoanalysts and proposing that they sign a text of "self-criticism." It was in fact not enough for the party to condemn psychoanalysis officially; in addition, that condemnation had to be ratified by those who drew inspiration from it in the exercise of their profession. Whence the trap and the conflict, since the condemnation would be all the more persuasive in that it would emanate from the interested parties themselves, thus forced to denounce the bread on which they lived.

Naturally, Leduc shared the official point of view and considered psychoanalysis to be a reactionary ideology. He quickly drafted a working document and contacted three kinds of analysts: psychoanalysts hostile to the condemnation and members, for the third generation, of the SPP (Serge Lebovici, Salem Shentoub, Evelyne and Jean Kestemberg); nonanalytic psychiatrists who were equally hostile to the condemnation (Lucien Bonnafé, Louise Le Guilland); and finally two psychiatrists hostile to the condemnation (Émile Monnerot and Sven Follin). The psychoanalysts were Jewish and the psychiatrists weren't. None refused his or her signature, but none accepted the self-criticism without an argument. Serge Lebovici turned out to be the most rebellious and experienced the event as a humiliation. Jean Kestemberg showed his comrades the troubled countenance of an authentic militant, a former member of the International Brigades, brutally confronted with the horror of Stalinism. As for Lucien Bonnafé, he attempted in vain to speak in praise of Freud's lesson.

Today, the testimony varies, memories deviate, and recollections are dulled. All agree that Lebovici was the most rebellious, Kestemberg the most torn, and Follin the most fanatical, but each attempts to assign responsibility to his neighbor for the text that was signed by all and published in 1949 in *La Nouvelle Critique*.[71] According to Bonnafé, Victor Leduc would have been the craftsman behind the final version, which itself was the result of a compromise among several texts, some emanating from the signatories, others from the leadership, that is, from Leduc himself. The definitive version would have been an attenuation of the violently dogmatic original, but since no one can remember the contents of that first text, it is difficult to ascertain how it differed from the others and from the final one. Leduc rejects Bonnafé's comments and maintains that the signatories accepted spontaneously their mission and composed on their own, unconstrained, the texts of self-criticism, after several sessions of discussion. Furious at their own submission, they would then have projected onto Leduc the paternity of a text which he had no knowledge of since it never existed. He recalls that things transpired quite rapidly, on already conquered territory.[72]

As for Serge Lebovici, he acknowledges having yielded to the ambient pressure. But his sense of revolt and of humiliation was soon to exclude him from the party. In conversation with me, he evoked the scenes of a painful past. The son of Solo Lebovici and Caroline Rosenfeld, he was thirty years old in 1945 and adhered to communism in the wake of the Liberation and an analysis with Sacha Nacht. Without being a Marxist, he had felt indebted to Communist militants who had hidden him after his father's arrest.

The story of Solo Lebovici is the most moving of those encountered in the course of this saga. A Rumanian emigrant, he had passed time in the trenches of Verdun in the company of Alexandre Roudinesco, a physician like himself, of Bucharest. He had lived happily and tranquilly on French soil until the spring of 1942 when the Gestapo descended on his home. With admirable calm, he managed to pass his wife off as one of his numerous mistresses. The stratagem saved Caroline's life, but the heroic Solo was deported—first to Pithiviers, with war veterans, then to Auschwitz and the horrors awaiting him there. He never returned.

Despite the Nazi presence, his son took over his father's practice, moving about from address to address under a pseudonym. During the anti-Freudian crusade, he found himself one day in the office of Henri Wallon, who advised him icily to denounce the reactionary character of psychoanalysis. He obeyed and delivered a lecture at party headquarters, declaring the doctrine to be infiltrated with bourgeois ideas, but maintaining that in practice one might avoid them. Deemed too indulgent, his text nonetheless served as a point of departure for the fabrication of a document, which apparently led to Leduc's mission to the other comrades. Like Bonnafé, Lebovici recalls the endless discussions, mitigations, and contortions, the thousand and one ways of nuancing a word in order to pass off an insolent act of condemnation as a biting critique. The signing took place at his home on the rue Campagne-Première. He was "screamed at" by Nacht, and contracted jaundice shortly thereafter. . . . [73]

Sacha Nacht did not indeed appreciate the political ideas of his former patient. In February 1950, without either mentioning the "Self-Criticism" or succumbing to any primitive anti-Communist reflex, he lashed out at Lebovici, who delivered a lecture to the SPP entitled "The Value of Psychoanalysis." Nacht responded harshly and published in the pages of the RFP the text of his intervention. "Dr. Lebovici," he wrote, "seems to have attempted to delineate above all the 'insufficiency of psychoanalysis.' That insufficiency, in his view, would be manifest in an alleged ignorance of the role of social and economic realities on the part of 'psychoanalysts' in the genesis and cure of psychopathological problems, on the one hand, and, on the other, in the doctrinal weakness of psychoanalysis. The ignorance graciously bestowed on 'psychoanalysts' by the author (he doesn't mention any names!) in fact exists only in his own mind, since the entirety of the literature of psychoanalysis testifies to the contrary. I myself, some time ago, emphasized in certain of my writings (*Pathologie de la vie amoureuse, La thérapeutique psychanalytique*) the importance of social and economic difficulties on psychoanalytic therapy. But above all, I cannot believe that Dr. Lebovici is unaware of *Civilization and Its Discontents* by Freud himself. . . . Finally, since Dr. Lebovici brings us nothing new on this score, may I at least ask him what is the incidence of the economic factors on which he insists at such length upon his psychoanalytic activities? How in fact does he integrate social and economic realities into psychoanalytic therapy?" [74]

Thus began, under the sign of a double humiliation, the long career of Serge Lebovici. He would end up defending, after having fought it, an adaptive version of psychoanalysis, would become the personal enemy of Jacques Lacan, and would be the sole Frenchman to accede to the presidency of the IPA.

Victor Leduc's memory is defective. The text entitled "Autocritique, la psychanalyse, idéologie réactionnaire [Self-criticism, psychanalysis as a reactionary ideology]" was not composed without violent conflicts on the part of certain of its signatories. Two tendencies were at work in the spring of 1949. One represented Zhdanovism and aimed at a unilateral condemnation; the other sought, without knowing how, to separate the "mystifications" from the doctrine itself. The text reflects that antagonism. When read today, and compared with others of the same vein, it appears to be rather moderate. To be sure, it conveyed the habitual hostility to the notion of a death instinct, recycled Politzer's "errors," attacked the "bourgeois" practice of therapists, the Anglo-American vogue of mental hygiene, and even the "superficiality" of Lacan's critique of familial ideals, but, on the whole, *partial* condemnation won out over simple-mindedness, and the partisans of the moderate tendency pulled off the exploit of presenting a refutation not of Freudianism and psychoanalysis, but of their "pernicious" or "mystified" misuse. Dare we say: despite its title and certain obligatory passages on Viennese decadence, the article pays homage, in the negative mode, to Freud's discovery.

Compared to the "official" texts of *L'Humanité* and later on of *La Nouvelle Critique,* it bears witness to the harsh battle waged by the majority of its signatories against the directives from above. But that sad victory was accompanied by a bitter failure. For the content of the text finally mattered little; what counted for the party in the spring of 1949 was that the therapists accepted a condemnation, however mitigated. The latter submitted because they were Communists and did not possess the theoretical means to criticize the absurd hypothesis of the "two sciences." Since psychoanalysis was not a science in the sense of genetics, and psychology was in this context but the pseudo-scientific expression of a power-oriented ideal, one is hard put to see how the signatories, in the absence of any reflection on the role played by Pavlovianism in this inextricable debate, might have been able to disengage themselves from their belief in the virtue of an alleged materialism in the domain of psychology. And in that case, the article in *La Nouvelle Critique* could serve, *without being read,* as the starting point of an extraordinary anti-Freudian crusade. In that perspective, the dogmatic tendency triumphed and the rebel signatories, caught in the trap of their confession, had no other choice than to accept the reality of Stalinism or to desert the ranks of the Communist movement.

In an unsigned article in *L'Humanité,* the "leadership" offered an account in their own manner, in June 1949, of the self-critique published by *La Nouvelle Critique.* Between the lines, what was at stake in the conflict could be clearly seen. The anonymous author drew the text in the direction of a condemnation and admitted that the party had "helped" recalcitrant comrades to shuck off their illusions and to cease distinguishing between Freudian theory and its practice. "The signatories," he wrote, "psychoanalysts, psychiatrists, technicians and intellectuals, had their attention drawn to these problems by the reaction's offensive. *In this they were aided by the party* (we recall specifically Guy Leclerc's articles published in *L'Humanité* on January 27 and February 17, 1949). *They were thus brought to examine afresh the question of psychoanalysis from the critical and self-critical point of view while stationed on the solid ground of the principles and positions of the party.* They first analyzed the class content of psychoanalytic doctrine and practice and *came to recognize* that psychoanalysis, envisioned in all its aspects, is a weapon of the bourgeoisie and *that it would be false to distinguish, as did some comrades during the first stage of the discussion, between psychoanalytic theory and technique.* Thus for the first time, practitioners of psychoanalysis *themselves denounce* the mystifications contained in the doctrine of Freud and of his disciples. They show how and why psychoanalysis in 1949, with the enormous publicity it derives from literature, the movies, radio, and journalism, is used even within the state apparatuses of reactionary governments to ends of social conservatism and preparation for war." [75]

From then on, there appeared numerous texts denouncing the "infiltration" of Freudianism into the arts and state apparatuses. The theme of an invasion of microbes combined, as formerly the accusation of "German—*boche*—science," with the accusation of irrationalism and occultism, thus authorizing a frenetic condemnation of Hollywood movies and the shady operations of the Freudian police. Truman was consecrated chief barker of the bellicose nations and psychoanalysis became the symbol of the growing exploitation of man by man, blacks by Americans, workers by bosses, and Communists by capitalists.

Propaganda was not enough. If Freudian doctrine was not a science, it be-

came imperative to oppose to it "something else," namely a Pavlovianism quickly
fabricated for the needs of the cause. Always prudent, Henri Wallon did not pronounce any public anathema, but founded with Louis Le Guilland, in 1950, a journal pompously baptized *La Raison,* which devoted itself fervently to the elaboration
of a "scientific psychopathology." In the first issue an interesting article by Bonnafé
was to be found that was free of any anti-Freudian polemic. The author drew up a
balance sheet of "social psychiatry" and emphasized the necessity for the French to
effect a radical critique of the doctrinal weaknesses of psychiatry in the course of
the half-century. A few pages later, Victor Lafitte published his contribution to a
Michurinian-inspired psychopathology which, by transforming Anglo-Saxons into
blacks and vice versa, would allow one to avoid biological "fatality" and to combat
hereditary predispositions to mental illnesses. Finally Sven Follin drew up a catalogue of the conceivable benefits of an application of Pavlovianism to psychiatry.
The following extravagant statement is to be found in his text: "Although Pavlov
did not, to our knowledge, comment on Clérambault's ideas on hallucinatory madness, it seems to us that the conceptions of that author might be quite significantly
renewed in a manner that would extricate them from the atomism and the mechan-
icism whose imprint they have perhaps retained." [76]

In November 1951, Henri Ey agreed with good humor to participate in the
journal's efforts. "I accept all the more gladly," he wrote, "in that this is for me an
opportunity to apply a principle quite dear to me: the separation of my scientific
activities from my political and philosophical activities." Our Catholic Catalan then
affirmed his support for the theses of a social psychiatry that refused to be the righter
of wrongs born of the disorder of nations. Thereafter he defined mental illness as an
actual illness, as irreducible to its social aspects as to its individual factors. He then
distinguished a veritable Pavlovian reflexology from Pavlovianism, showing that the
former did not in any way shed light on neurotic disorders. Finally, he took his
distance from Communist discourse on the subject of psychoanalysis: "As for the
critique of psychoanalysis, I have engaged in it often enough myself, on the ideological level, to understand that you might combat it from your own point of view. But
it remains nonetheless the case that the practice and theory of psychiatry have been
completely renewed by it and that it seems to me, as to you I believe, impossible not
to derive from it the greatest benefit in our conduct of therapy as in the study of
dreams and the 'mental illnesses' which are their reflection." [77]

In 1953, at the culmination of *La Raison's* defense of Pavlovianism and Mi-
churinism, Lucien Sève set pen to paper to denounce the dangers of using reflexology
to ideological ends. His article was published in December 1954, at a time at which
the party's anti-Freudian crusade was beginning to wane. Under the title "Pavlov,
Lenin, and Psychology," [78] Sève demonstrated that the French comrades were lagging
behind Soviet efforts, which had abandoned former deviations in order to reactivate
a scientific Pavlovianism. In that perspective, he criticized the illusion according to
which physiology would allow one to solve the problems of psychology. He did not
speak of psychoanalysis and merely proposed to French Communists that they reset
their clocks by reading the Russian texts. In the process, he did not analyze how in
the Soviet Union "neo-Pavlovianism" continued to serve as a standard for the con-

demnation of Freudian doctrine at a time when the psychoanalytic movement no longer existed in that country. Ahead of the party's discourse, Sève did not succeed, despite the intelligence of his position, in initiating a genuine critique of the utilization of Pavlovianism in the domain of psychology. In that sense, he was "already" behind in relation to a new situation whose effects would be felt ten years later with Louis Althusser's publication of an article devoted to Freud and Lacan. To be continued. . . .

While *La Raison* was oriented, between 1950 and 1954, toward the development of a Pavlovianism and a Michurinianism *à la francaise, La Nouvelle Critique,* the official organ of Communist intellectuals, participated in a more distinctly anti-Freudian crusade. Once again Sven Follin mounted the battlements and offered in 1951 his "balance sheet" of psychoanalysis. After a bit of fanfare, he explained that the scientific value of Freudianism is a "problem that has long been resolved." Then, forgetting the existence of Auschwitz, he took himself for Politzer and did not hesitate to write: "Thus the circle is closed: Idealist in its method, psychoanalysis is openly mystical in its content. Psychoanalysis joins that family of ideologies founded on the irrational, up until and including the ideology of the Nazis. Hitler did nothing else in cultivating the myths of race and blood, the Nazi version of the irrationality of the instincts." [79]

During the national "study days" of Communist intellectuals, which were held at Ivry in March 1953, Victor Lafitte denounced Freudian irrationalism and American-inspired psychosomatics, then went on to praise "a Pavlovian conception of illness" of which he affirmed that it was supported by fantastic therapeutic results. "Thus," he emphasized, "it is only in the light of a dialectical materialism advanced and enriched by Stalin that a scientific theory of medicine, the reflection of the objective laws of reality, is in the process of being elaborated." Another physician, Émile Baulieu, proclaimed his love of Marxism by explaining that psychoses had disappeared in the Soviet Union. "But we should not simplify," he added. "Illnesses still exist in the Soviet Union. A 'fundamental' thing has disappeared: the pathogenic influence of the social conditions of current capitalism. Every day on the contrary, new social relations exercise their influence on human physiology, on biological phenomena, in a direction favorable to man." [80] Without realizing it, Baulieu bore witness to the actual situation of Pavlovianism in the Soviet Union. In the land of Stalin, it was indeed proclaimed that madness did not exist; but since the deranged, the crazed, the demented, the maladapted and the neurotic were as frequently visible as in the vast capitalist world, Pavlovianism was reactivated in order to prove that madness did not derive from social causes, but from an organic or physiological substrate; that dimension would have to be treated in "Michurinian" fashion in order to transform the insane into worshippers of the Soviet paradise.

With Khrushchev's denunciation of Stalin's crimes, a new era opened in the relations between psychoanalysis and the PCF. The abandonment of the crusade, which had already begun in 1954, did not lead to any genuine critique of Pavlovianism or to a reevaluation of the meaning of Freud's doctrine. The pitched battles of the cold war were replaced by a certain silence and occasionally by repentance. *La Nouvelle Critique* did not budge, but in 1956 the editors of *La Raison* revised their former position and criticized the dogmatism of former days. Timidly, they attempted to separate Freudian doctrine from its deformed use, an effort which brought them, at the same time, to distinguish between Pavlovian reflexology and "Michurinian" Pavlovianism.[81]

The following year the advent of something of a peaceful coexistence could be observed. The journal published a collective account of what was itself a collective volume published under the auspices of Sacha Nacht and entitled *La psychanalyse d'aujourd'hui* ["Psychoanalysis today"].[82] The lengthy work in two volumes emanated from the psychoanalysts of the SPP and attempted to assess the situation of psychoanalysis on the occasion of the centenary of Freud's birth. It consisted of a number of articles on neurobiology, psychosomatic medicine, therapy for psychotics, sexology, clinical practice, etc., and expressed rather well the political and doctrinal "line" towed by the SPP three years after the first split.

The review published by *La Raison* was signed by two former Zhdanovists, Follin and Lafitte, and by a number of distinctly more liberal comrades. The discussion opens with an ambiguous statement: "Praiseworthy efforts are courageously being deployed in an effort to extricate 'psychoanalysis today' from its too frequently esoteric and occasionally nebulous character."[83] In general, the authors evoked the boring book in a boring manner and their obsession with technical aspects was contrary to the flamboyant perspective of the 1950s. Follin and Lafitte forgot their Michurinian passion and, as a result, their opinions appeared for what they were—nugatory. Reading the measured praise bestowed by our marmoreal heroes on their colleagues of the SPP, one begins to miss the days in which extravagance bore witness to the madness of a world fallen prey to the spectacle of its own insanity.

In 1968, over the grave of Louis Le Guilland, an unfortunate signatory of the 1949 text, Henri Ey evoked the career of his old friend, who had devoted his life to taking care of "housemaids" and *déclassés* of various sorts: "For us who knew him well, it was for having suffered the passion of the Papin sisters that Louis Le Guilland, among all the great services he rendered to his patients and to psychiatry in general, took on in our eyes the prestige of a truly moving discovery. . . . What would it have been without you [the emergency room of Sainte-Anne] and for each of us, that youth which we shared? It is indeed a part of each of us—Mareschal, Mâle, Lacan, Masquian, Dublineau, Nacht, Rouart . . . and still many others—who formed the corps of that youth which, for all of us, was our own, and has never stopped, until death, enlivening and uniting us."[84]

A generation behind in the implantation of Freudianism in their country, the French Communists spoke of psychoanalysis at midcentury in terms strangely reminiscent of the chauvinistic France of the 1920s. And yet, as could be seen at the World Congress of Psychiatry in 1950, they were not alone in denouncing the "new psychoanalysis" come from the other side of the Atlantic. It was in that sense that the rebellious signatories of the text of self-criticism had allowed themselves to be trapped: While succeeding in expressing their disagreement with the leadership, they did not manage to bring off a critique of the adaptative ideals of Michurinian Pavlovianism. For that reason, their condemnation of the American psychoanalytic situation fell completely flat, even if it was aimed, in a distorted manner, at an actual process.

In 1945, four years before the *Nouvelle Critique* affair and three before the notorious Congress on Mental Hygiene that triggered the polemic, Lacan journeyed to London, where he spent five weeks. During his stay, he sought to acquaint himself with the state of psychiatry and paid a visit to the Hartfield residence where former prisoners and veterans of overseas combat awaited reclassification. He particularly admired the principles of group therapy and psychodrama and concluded that the war had turned out to be a midwife to progress in the field of mental care.

A year later, he delivered a lecture on the subject to the Évolution psychiatrique group. Among those gathered for the occasion were Lucien Bonnafé, Paul Schiff, Adrien Borel, Eugène Minkowski, Henri Ey, Gregorio Bermann, the Argentine delegate to the medical division of the United Nations,[85] and finally Pierre Turquet, a major in the British army. Descending from Anjou stock, the last mentioned individual was an impassioned admirer of France and of fine cars. During the war, he had been a star of the Intelligence Service and, drawing inspiration from the works of Wilfried Bion had Melanie Klein, had reorganized the army's psychiatric service along Freudian and democratic lines.[86] Lacan referred to him as "my friend" and paid homage to his accomplishments. Similarly, he shared certain of the options of Lucien Bonnafé on social psychiatry. He appreciated the taste in films of that loyal Communist with whom he frequented movie houses, all the while chatting about the future of Freudian France.[87]

Lacan paid homage to England in the tones of a man who had lived the war years as a terrible humiliation. In 1939, the British psychiatrists decided to put to some use laggards, malingerers, dullards, and delinquents by assigning them to various tasks in the rear of the army. Without any segregationist intent, they grouped together misfits and separated them from their comrades who had been assigned to combat. Thus purged, the fighting units were no longer subjects to the neurotic shock born of contact with perturbing elements. As for the others, they became all the more effective in that they were deemed useful and organized into autonomous subgroups. The subgroups each defined the object of their work under the aegis of a therapist supportive of everyone, but refusing to occupy the position of a leader or an "authoritarian father." Lacan emphasized that the ability to modify human relations in wartime stemmed from the massive diffusion of Freudian concepts in the British psychiatric world.

It is as though one were dreaming! Our hero was speaking in praise of an adaptative group psychology whose Freudian inspiration he vaunts, whereas four years later he would be denouncing the adaptative ideals of the "new psychoanalysis." In point of fact, Lacan's interest in the English psychiatric situation was as much a function of his admiration of its reformist pragmatism as of his desire to take stock of his own development as the century approached its midpoint. With his customary genius, he noted that the British experience had invalidated the doctrine of constitutions, which he himself had criticized in 1932, and that it bore witness to the decline of the paternal imago, whose course he had also noted in his text on the family. And indeed, if an organization in small groups presupposes the identification of all with the therapist's ideal ego, it leaves empty the place of the virile leader, the recruiting sergeant, and the stirrer of crowds.

Thus in 1945, a Frenchman crossed the Channel in order to discover on British soil, devastated by the war but never subject to the horrors of a foreign occupation, the mirror image of his own works. Once again he was not one to take himself for just anyone. After Freud, who identified with Copernicus, Lacan evoked the figure of Galileo and ended his discussion with these words: "I insist on affirming anew the unitary conception which is mine in anthropology. To the objections on principle that have been raised against the role befalling psychiatry during the war, I respond with a "E pur si muove [And yet it moves!]," refusing that my talk be given any other meaning or any other merit." [88]

Under Vichy, no comparable experiment had taken place, but within the Lozère region, the war revealed itself to be a source of progress. Toward 1932, at Reus, in Catalonia, a diminutive moustached gentleman named François Tosquelles attended enthusiastically the lectures of Professor Mira i Lopez. The latter was in charge of the Pere Mata hospital, founded by his student's uncle, and was interested in a dynamic reelaboration of child psychiatry, group psychology, and pedagogy. An energetic militant of the left, Tosquelles quickly devoured Lacan's thesis, along with the works of Freud, Marx, Reich, and Politzer. At the same time, he was in therapy with a Viennese Jew who had emigrated to Spain. Aware of the necessity of introducing into the institutional world a couchless variant of Freudianism, he reflected on the principles of a community psychiatry that would allow for a transformation of relations between caregivers and the insane and thus open up the world of madness. During the Spanish Civil War, he took part in fierce fighting on the Aragon front, then reorganized the psychiatric service of the Republican Army. He realized that numerous psychotics had been spontaneously cured of their delusions and symptoms by becoming, through the fight against fascism, useful to their comrades. In a world given over to death and the forces of destruction, both the mad and the soldiers lost their bearings, and every man took part in the ordeal of his own madness. In 1939, fleeing the Falangists, Tosquelles clandestinely crossed the Pyrenees. In Luchon, he tended to his bruised feet in a mountain hotel, then met a gendarme who advised him to join the Foreign Legion. In his inimitable jargon, he replied in these words: "If you want to lose the war, you can lose it on your own; I am not a foreigner."

Near Toulouse, Tosquelles took care of Spanish political prisoners grouped at the Saint-Fonds camp, then, in January 1940, at the request of the prefect, he accepted a position at a psychiatric hospital in Saint-Alban. That institution was directed by a Catholic psychiatrist, Paul Balvet, who was attempting to reform the hospital in the direction of a communitarian society. In 1942, Lucien Bonnafé succeeded him, effecting a fusion between Communist-inspired positions and more libertarian ones born of the Catalan experience. There thus began, in a mythical site radiating the prestige of the anti-Fascist struggle, the long history of French-style institutional psychotherapy. A man of action, Tosquelles did not realize that he was inventing the tendency to which Georges Daumezon would give a name ten years later.[89]

There could be found at Saint-Alban a mix of Resistance-fighters, madmen, and therapists. Paul Éluard and Georges Sadoul hid there and read the texts of the mad. Upon leaving the Resistance in July 1944, Georges Canguilhem spent a few days in residence and treated the injured on neighboring farms.[90]

In its insertion into the French dynamic tendency and its refusal of a rigidified asylum, institutional psychotherapy was part of the vast mental hygiene movement born of the pragmatic integration of psychoanalysis into psychiatry. But since it arose in a country in which the German occupation was lived as a kind of "great confinement," it was not (at least at its inception) the bearer of the same adaptative ideals as its American counterpart. Whereas in England the reorganization took place within a fighting army, in France, it occurred outside of the reigning institutional framework, and in a context in which the heroism of the Resistance played a preponderant role.

After 1945, the "disalienation" movement continued its work, but without resulting, as the Surrealists had once wanted, in the disappearance of medical authority and the affirmation of an absolute legitimacy of the discourse of madness. Quite to the contrary, in France as elsewhere, new biological therapies were spreading, allowing one to keep the expression of madness under psychiatric control. In that sense, institutional psychotherapy was located at an intersection of contradictory ideas. On the one hand, using Freud it challenged a hospital organization centered on the doctrine of constitutions, and, on the other, it bestowed on the medical authorities modern techniques of surveillance that did not have very much in common with the ethic of psychoanalysis.

Between 1933 and 1938, several varieties of treatment appeared to replace the traditional "straitjacket." Invented by the Austrian Manfred Sakel, insulin therapy served to treat schizophrenia, as did electroshock, which came from Italy, and would soon be replaced by electronarcosis. These therapies were being used by the artisans of communitarian psychiatry, who discovered as of 1952 neuroleptics, tranquilizers, and antidepressants, all of which became the symbol of a new form of appropriation of madness by psychiatry.[91]

The process of hospital reform and the reelaboration of psychiatric knowledge affected the evolution of the psychoanalytic movement profoundly. Starting with the split of 1953, which divided the SPP and resulted in the formation of a new group around Lacan and Lagache, several types of experiment flourished, each of which was linked with the tendencies born of the break-up of the Freudian community. Institutional psychotherapy found its second wind with the establishment, around 1953, of a private clinic in the department of Loir-et-Cher. Jean Oury, an analysand of Lacan's and formerly of Saint-Alban, bought with his own funds the chateau of La Borde, located at Cour-Cheverny, in order to welcome marginal elements of every stripe. He attempted a pragmatic synthesis between a utopian Lacanianism and a psychiatric militancy stripped of its Resistance connection. To be sure, the La Borde experiment did not eliminate drug-based or electronarcotic therapies.

In 1965, it too got a second wind with the founding of a federation of study groups and institutional research efforts and the adoption of certain theses of the Anglo-Saxon antipsychiatry movement.[92]

In a more "American" vein, Philippe Paumelle founded in 1954 a mental hygiene dispensary in the XIIIth arrondissement of Paris. The experiment became systematized with the proliferation of sections and subsections, one of which, that of child psychiatry, was entrusted to Serge Lebovici. What was at stake was providing a possibility other than the classical psychiatric hospital, through outpatient treatment, group therapy, and home hospitalization. In that framework, the medicalizing line defended by the SPP during the reign of Sacha Nacht was well suited to the project, which aimed at the integration of psychoanalysis with a "reformed" psychiatry. In 1959, an association governed by the statute of 1901 became the enterprise's base of support, enabling both its generous financing and innovative style of functioning in comparison with that of the public psychiatric services. With the circular of March 15, 1960, in part at the behest of Henri Ey, a mental health policy given the name of "sectorization" took shape. The word designates a dividing up of territory. Each segment constitutes a sector, which was to receive a full institutional spread of services destined to ensure the prevention and treatment of mental illnesses, alcoholism, and drug addiction. In the context of an "advanced psychiatric society" as thus conceived, the dispensary of the XIIIth arrondissement merged in 1963 with the services of an open hospital situated at Soisy-sur-Seine and itself directed by the training analysts of the SPP. The La Borde clinic also profited from the benefits of sectorization, while retaining an idiosyncratic status linked to the fact that its physician-director was also owner of the property and was free to choose his collaborators without prior authorization from Social Security.

By liberating the madman from the asylum and from constitutionalism, the open psychiatry of the 1950s, communitarian or otherwise, benefited from a more humane model of confinement. That novel configuration fulfilled a dream shared by Pinel and Charcot. Set loose from his chains, the madman took refuge in a chemical straitjacket and adapted to the society of normal citizens at the cost of renouncing his madness.

The expansion of an adaptative psychoanalysis and a reformist psychiatry went together with the renewal of a certain crisis of occultism. After his trial, René Laforgue converted definitively to spiritualism and participated in the efforts of the journal *Psyché,* founded in 1946 by Maryse Choisy. Baptized an "International Review of Psychoanalysis and the Human Sciences," the publication was intent on being open to all problems of the contemporary world. It was part of a revisionist effort regarding Freud's teachings, of an occultist, meditative, or Orientalist tendency, through which a rather diffuse fidelity to the ideals of the Roman Catholic Church was affirmed.

Analyzed by Charles Odier, then by Laforgue, Maryse Choisy practiced psychoanalysis. She dreamed of making *Psyché* the rival of the *RFP* and of dethroning Marie Bonaparte by pitting against Freudian atheism a synthesis between Rome and the Bhagavad Gita. There can be little doubt that beautiful Maryse was in search of

God, but before finding him, she made, it appears, a detour through Vienna by way of Freud's couch. A journalist at *L'Intransigeante*, a friend of the novelist Rachilde, and the tumultuous mistress of Joseph Delteil, she had begun training as an aviator and an animal tamer. Soon she was to travel the world collecting the confessions of the "great." Stalin and Mussolini were her preferred interlocutors. Around 1936, the quest for adventure turned into mystical anguish and our heroine converted to Catholicism. Teilhard de Chardin took charge of the conversion, explaining to the new recruit that science does not contradict the principles of faith. Thereafter, "la Choisy," as she was known, repudiated her previous works, renounced Satan, and plunged into an unprecedented struggle to inform the Pope of the benefits of Freud's doctrine.

Maryse Choisy was not alone during the cold war years in taking an interest in the relations between psychoanalysis and the Vatican. At the same time, Marc Oraison, an affable priest, broached the difficult question of the relation between sexuality and religion. He began his studies in surgery around 1933 and entered a seminary in 1942. Three years later, he joined Leclerc's expeditionary corps for Far Eastern operations. In Saigon, he was director of a urological service and in 1946 he returned to Paris, exhausted by his Indochinese adventure. He attended the lectures of Father Tesson, who advised him to read Hesnard's writings. Through them, Oraison had the revelation of the importance of Freud's discovery and decided to devote his life to the transformation of Christian morality.[93] To that end he wrote his doctoral thesis in theology, which he defended in 1952.

Unlike Maryse Choisy, Oraison was neither a convert nor someone who had repudiated his past. Without any interest in the traditions of the occult, he made no ecumenical attempt at unifying all forms of spirituality. His meditation bore less on the idea of a conceivable compatibility of Freudian doctrine with theology than on the concrete problem of the sexuality of the Christian and the priest. Yet his intervention and Maryse Choisy's would combine and issue in a dialogue—sometimes positive, sometimes negative—with the Catholic Church. Another priest played a considerable role as of 1949—Father Bruno de Jésus Marie. He incited Christians to ask themselves questions and opened his journal, *Études carmélitaines*, to psychoanalysts. For her part, Maryse Choisy founded along with Father Leycester King of Oxford, the International Association of Psychotherapy and Clinical Psychology, and attempted to obtain from Pius XII something on the order of a Christian status for psychoanalysis.

In Italy, psychoanalysis took root during the first quarter of the century in the city of Trieste, which had belonged to the Austro-Hungarian Empire until 1919. An odd situation indeed: The history of the Italian psychoanalytic movement begins not in Italy, but in a port similar to baroque Vienna, at the intersection of a number of contradictory cultures.[94] Two individuals contributed to making Freud known in the Trieste milieu and then throughout the country: Edoardo Weiss and Italo Svevo. The first was a physician, the second a writer. Both were Jewish. With the publication in 1923 of *The Conscience of Zeno*, largely inspired by an experience of analysis, Svevo played in Italy the role of a Proust who had read Freud. As for Weiss, who was analyzed by Paul Federn, he traveled between Vienna and Trieste and remained for almost twenty years the sole representative of Freudianism on Italian soil. In 1925, at the behest of a Venetian Jew, Marco Levi-Bianchini, the Società Italiana di Psicoanalisi was created. Not sharing the views of Levi-Bianchini, Weiss emigrated to Rome where he constituted in 1932 a different society which was admitted to the IPA three years later.[95]

A Jungian tendency enjoyed a sizable audience as of 1936, but was not better received by the Church than its Freudian counterpart, with which, moreover, it maintained peaceful relations. If the spread of Jungianism was facilitated by the reign of Catholicism, it was not the Vatican per se that furnished the best weapons for resisting psychoanalysis. In this case as elsewhere, Freud's alleged pansexualism was rejected, but the refusal was ratified under the sway of two contradictory tendencies, experimental psychology on the one hand and idealist philosophy on the other, the latter being on the rise during the first quarter of the century. To this may be added fascism, which "materially" prevented the expansion of the movement. The racial laws of 1938 and anti-Semitic attacks forced the analysts, who were all Jewish, to emigrate or to go into hiding. Edoardo Weiss left Italy in 1939 and rejoined Alexander in Chicago.

Founded in 1921 by Agnostino Gemelli, a priest, the School of Experimental Psychology was organized within the framework of the Catholic University of the Sacred-Heart of Milan. It promoted a resistance to psychoanalysis as strong as the school of Janet in France, and there too, it was a "charismatic" personality who played a major role. Gemelli's adherence to fascism did not make matters easier for Freudians. A student of Kraepelin and a Franciscan monk, he began his medical career at the turn of the century. His works of experimental psychology were integrated into the neoscholastic movement he himself was promoting.[96] That theologico-philosophical doctrine was characterized by an attempted reevaluation of the philosophies of the Middle Ages in the light of the data of modern science. It was based on a dualism that accorded as much place to the body as to the mind and led to an ontological metaphysic. In that sense, neoscholasticism was opposed both to classical idealism and to contemporary materialism. It tended to infuse Catholicism with a realist theory of consciousness, directly inspired by the labors of psychology. Gemelli's "supple" hostility to Freud will thus be understood, as well as his choice of the school of Janet in the face of a discovery centered on the primacy of the unconscious and of sexuality.

It was not in Italy but in France that a postwar shift in Catholic discourse on psychoanalysis was initiated. The interest in psychoanalysis emanated neither from Rome nor from the cardinals, but from the "base," that is, from French priests confronted by the expansion of the analytic world. Now at that time the Church was struggling with the reality of the proletarian world. Since the Liberation, France had seen—animated essentially by the Jesuits—the famous experiment of worker-priests. Fearing that contact with Marxism would result in voluntary defrocking, the Holy Office condemned by decree in 1949 Catholic membership in and collaboration with the Communist Party.[97] Three years later, a crisis erupted, and in May 1953, the archbishop of Marseille asked the worker-priests of his diocese to withdraw. Rome forbade French seminarians to serve apprenticeships in factories, and shortly thereafter Cardinal Liénart would close down the seminary of the French mission in Limoges. The following month, the new papal nuncio summoned the bishops and superiors responsible for the worker-priests to tell them the Pope's decision. The latter declared that the experiment was a subject of scandal and should not be supported by the Church of France. He reaffirmed that communism was the scourge of the modern world and condemned the worker-priests without appeal. Cardinal Liénart observed that the evangelization of the working world would be severely compromised by that decision and Feltin emphasized that the experiment was at last changing the image of a Church compromised by capitalism. Nothing worked: In November 1953, Pius XII vigorously denounced French communism.[98] At the time the Holy Office was governed by the terrible Cardinal Alfredo Ottaviani, who rejected pell-mell feminism, Marxism, liberalism, Freudianism, and atheism in all its forms.

In order to grasp the ambiguous but nonetheless hostile attitude adopted by the Church in relation to the French psycho-analytic situation, it should be related to the context of the anti-Communist crusade conducted by Rome in the face of the worker-priest experiment. For the Pope as for the Holy Office, Freudianism was as dangerous a malady as Marxism. But on the political level, there was a certain urgency in condemning communism, a mass phenomenon directly inspired by the Soviet Union. On the subject of psychoanalysis, on the contrary, it was sufficient to remain attentive or severe according to whether the experiment affected vocations or faith.

In relation to Freud's work, the Church found itself in a difficult position. In 1949, a campaign to revalorize Jewish culture had begun. Anti-Semitism was condemned and Catholics were asked to no longer consider the "Zionist" Jews of their day as guilty of the death of Christ. Not only was it recalled that Jesus was a Jew and descended from the great line of the prophets of Israel, but the faithful were counseled to avoid any assimilation between the "bad Jews" of years gone by, belonging to a deicidal people, and the Jews of the current day, living in Palestine or in the Diaspora. In the pages of *La documentation catholique,* the priest Paul Demann recalled the following precept: "Avoid first of all expressions which, without explanation, might engender dangerous generalizations: 'the Jews' condemned, 'the Jews' crucified Christ. . . . One says 'the Jews' and the child will oftentimes understand 'all Jews'. Today's boyhood chum is one; tomorrow's rival will be another. . . . Those actually responsible for the death of Jesus were only a handful of unworthy leaders, creatures of the pagan occupant and hated by the people, conjointly with the Roman, representing the 'Gentiles' in the drama. . . . Do we then have the right to imprint on the souls of Christian children the image of a 'deicidal people,' deicidal in all its people and in all countries in all ages?"[99] In such a context, after Auschwitz, it was difficult for the Church to reject officially the work of a Jew, even if he were unfaithful to his own religion.

In France, the denunciation of materialism, atheism, and sexuality was expressed in the condemnation of certain literary or philosophical works, written for the most part by non-Jews. In 1949, a decree from the Holy Office placed all of Sartre's books on the Index. The chronicler of the *Osservatore romano* took care to note that the Communists rejected existentialism, which nonetheless drew on Marxism for its inspiration. He added these words: "The 'Sartre case' is a symptom of the perilous hour humanity is currently passing through, when all values appear to founder (and the recent war gave us a terrifying example of it) with a violence compared to which the declamations of Zarathustra are of mere archeological interest. Pornography, violence, and degeneracy are not inventions of Sartre; Sartre has merely demonstrated that they are the necessary consequence of the apostasy of the Absolute and that the cosmetics supplied by culture are but hypocritical lies concealing nothing. Sartre's heroes achieve their enormities without passion, coolly, without fervor, without reason, without even that scrap of humanity invariably possessed by every passion and which leaves open a path toward goodness and redemption." [100]

Three years later André Gide received, postmortem, the same treatment. Without uttering the word "homosexuality," the chronicler of *Osservatore romano* commented on the Holy Office's decision as follows, "A writer gifted with a fine expressive talent and among the most renowned, his art itself smacks of a lasciviousness eager to be of service, much like a chamber maid dressing and adorning her mistress." [101]

Two kinds of problems confronted the Catholic progressives seeking to introduce Freudianism within the confines of the Church. On the one hand, it would be necessary to demonstrate that the interpersonal relation binding man to man and man to God escapes—even the most scientific—psychological analysis, because it mediates a supplementary dimension that cannot be explained by reason. That dimension could not fall under the category of sublimation, but of faith and revelation, and would be irreducible to analytic investigation. Such an argument would allow one to "save" religion, at least in appearance, by making it extrinsic to every form of neurosis. But it had the disadvantage of eliminating, without acknowledging as much, the primacy of sexuality and of reducing Freudianism to a rationalism without an unconscious. The second attitude consisted, as previously with Dalbiez, in separating theory from practice by making the latter "compatible" with Christian spirituality. It was toward that dual and apparently pragmatic program that Catholic therapists turned their efforts. Thanks to an ambiguity which in ways recalls Soviet Freudo-Marxism, they actually succeeding in having Freudianism penetrate to the heart of the Church while avoiding the wrath of the Holy Office and obtaining from the Pope his "benevolent neutrality." Should tempests or experiments deemed provocative occur, the Vatican was free to denounce them.

Rome and Paris confronted each other in a war pitting cassock against lacework. In 1949, Gemelli criticized those responsible for the French opening. He attacked *Études carmélitaines, Cahiers Laennec,* founded by Catholic psychiatrists, and, to be sure, Maryse Choisy. "A Catholic cannot adhere to psychoanalytic doctrine," he declared with a certain sharpness. "He absolutely cannot accept it and should not submit to treatment. . . . Psychoanalysis is a danger because it is the sick fruit of Freud's crude materialism." [102] Gemelli abandoned his former flexibility, but the prudent Maryse Choisy named him in 1951 honorary member of her association of therapists. In addition, she invited him to debate with her in the pages of the journal *Psyché*.[103] At the time, the necessity of a papal stand on the issue seemed clear.

Before Pius XII's first intervention, Msgr. Felici, a member of the Roman Curia, hastened to attack psychoanalysis. His article appeared in a bulletin restricted to the Roman clergy and was not reproduced in *Documentation catholique,* the official organ of the Church of France. "From the moral point of view," he wrote, "the psychoanalytic method readily becomes a school of corruption." [104] The author then lashed out at Freudian doctrine, judged inadmissible by Christian morality, and after that denounced the misdoings of therapy.

During an international congress on the histopathology of the nervous system, the Holy Father specified the limitations of psychoanalytic treatment from the point of view of Christian morality. Sparing psychotherapy, he attacked Freudian "pansexualism" without mentioning the name of Freud: "In order to free himself of repressions, inhibitions, psychic complexes, man is not free to awaken within himself, to therapeutic ends, each and every one of his appetites in the sexual sphere. . . . It is not proven, it is even untrue that the pansexual method of a certain school of psychoanalysis is an integral and indispensable part of any serious psychotherapy worthy of the name." [105] Six months later, in Rome, on April 15, 1953, he delivered a speech to the members of Maryse Choisy's association, who were gathered for their fifth congress.[106]

Pius XII defined still another Christian attitude to matters psychotherapeutic. He reaffirmed the integration of psychology within metaphysics and maintained that no physical dynamism could affect the Thomist dogma of the unity of being. According to that orientation, the physician of souls ought to accept three rules. In the first place, he should exclude from his method the search for sexual causes, preferring to psychoanalytic investigation an "indirect" treatment centered on consciousness and respectful of "self-mastery." In addition, he should avoid violating the confidentiality of confessions and safeguard the resistance of patients who refuse to "tell all." Finally, he should accept the existence of sin or error, which elude the category of guilt and can be absolved only through contrition and sacramental pardon.

In the simplemindedness of its contents, Pius XII's discourse conveyed a hostility to Freudianism as radical as the more official variety of the Communists. And yet, his address ought to be read less for what it contained than for what it implied. In the Pope's voice, the Church condemned neither Freudianism nor psychoanalysis. It sought on the contrary to assign a status to psychotherapy in which Freudians would have their place on the condition they respect the rules of Christian morality. It mattered little that those rules contradicted the essence of a discovery and a practice; it would suffice, in the worst of cases, to maintain appearances, and in the best, to feign belief in a possible compatibility between a discourse and its opposite. In that sense, the Pope's words authorized a number of openings. As of 1953, Marc Oraison was to pay the price for that confusing policy.

In 1952, the French priest published his thesis in theology on Christian life and the problems of sexuality.[107] The book received a *nihil obstat* and achieved such remarkable success that it attracted the attention of the Holy Office. For some time already, Oraison had been frequenting two remarkable priests who were involved in introducing psychoanalysis into the ecclesiastical world. Father Albert Plé, a journalist and a Dominican, a friend of Bruno de Marie Jésus, founded in 1947 the *Supplément* to *Vie spirituelle,* in which he published articles on Freud. He became known, and some "cases" were even directed to him, even though he was neither a doctor nor a psychologist.

For his part, Father Louis Beirnaert, a Jesuit, began practicing psychoanalysis. Born at the beginning of the century, he had been a student of philosophy and theology. In November 1940, while a chaplain at the École des sciences politiques, he defended students who had demonstrated their hostility to the occupying forces. Because of that, he was incarcerated for two months at the Santé prison. After being freed, he was denounced and only barely escaped the Gestapo. At that point, he went into hiding and joined the Gaullist network "Defense of France" in which he waged doctrinal war against Nazism. In Paris, he met Robert Desoilles, the inventor of the waking-dream technique and a Communist militant, and later associated with Françoise Dolto and André Berge. He was initially interested in Jung's writings, but as soon as the war was over requested authorization from his superior to undergo— for didactic purposes—psychoanalytic training. As a good Jesuit, he wanted to understand the reality of things and to participate in a spiritual fight for the transformation of the Church. He went to Zurich to meet Jung, whom he found too religious, and turned finally to the study of Freud's writings. After an epistolary exchange concerning an article of his in the journal *Études* on jealousy, he entered into therapy in 1946 with Daniel Lagache. His analysis lasted four years and Beirnaert completed his training with three supervisory analyses undertaken with Nacht, Pasche, and Lacan, whom he would follow in the two splits. Forced to work under a medical cover, he became friends with Granoff, who generously opened the doors of his splendid home in Neuilly to him.[108]

Oraison joined Beirnaert and Plé in a congress in Holland, during which a number of fascinating debates occurred. Oraison was treating distressed priests or believers suffering from the rigidity of dogma. He practiced therapy without having been analyzed. In his thesis he confronted directly the threefold question of chastity, the discernment of vocations, and sexuality "without sin." The book's interest resided less in its (rather feeble) theoretical content than in the newness of the problems it envisaged. At the time, Oraison read Freud's works in the light of Hesnard's sexology and made nonpsychoanalytic use of the data of psychoanalysis. His procedure, characterized by great honesty, consisted in a courageous reevalution of Christian morality in the light of the discovery from Vienna. Through the analysis of several cases, revealing a clear fascination with homosexuality, Oraison relativized the notion of "sin." According to him, sexuality is pathogenic and a correlative of human existence. To that extent, it is not assimilable to a mortal sin but rather to a venial sin. Christian morality should take that observation into account or run the risk of sinking into dogmatism. From there, Oraison goes on to distinguish between true and false vocations. A true vocation rests on both divine grace and sublimation, which allows the priest, according to Thomist ethics, to "freely choose" his life of chastity. On the contrary, false vocations stem from a terror of sexuality and lead postulants to commit themselves to lives of renunciation that are in fact evasions and end in catastrophe.

Oraison's gesture was potentially scandalous: Without adhering to acknowledged psychiatric principles, he had shown that the Church should eliminate candidates who were "dangerous" for themselves and for religious life—psychotics, perverts, the "sexually sick." All those individuals who had chosen a life of religion in order to escape their own mental disturbances were to be treated rather than integrated into sacerdotal life. In addition, Oraison maintained the necessity of an orientation in one's vocation. Candidates were to be assisted in selecting the order best suited to their personality.

In 1952, the Church was not prepared to receive such a message "officially". Five years would be needed for it to implement a procedure for discerning vocations based on medical criteria. That would result in the creation of various assistance organizations for anguished ecclesiastics. By virtue of his courage, Oraison thus appeared to be something of a provocateur. On the theological level, his reasoning was weak. It is in fact hard to see how a vocation might be stripped of its neurotic content without disappearing altogether. From a Freudian point of view, every mystical, religious, or fanatical belief has a neurotic—and even a psychotic—source. What remained, however, was the "real" problem of discernment, that of avoiding a candidate's entry into an order unsuited to his mental structure.

A week before his address of April 15, Pius XII had made a decision apparently opposed to his policy of openness. He confirmed a decree of the Holy Office, dated March 18, which placed Oraison's thesis on the Index. The event occurred at the very time the priest was at Rome, along with Plé and Beirnaert, participating in Maryse Choisy's colloquium. Cardinal Ottaviani summoned him and explained to him that the tribunal, out of indulgence, had consented not to make its judgment public. Only bishops and those responsible for training for the priesthood would be informed. The book would silently disappear from circulation and a second edition would be envisaged if the offender consented to "correct his errors." Upon returning from Rome, Oraison went to see Cardinal Feltin, who informed him of his indignation. Father Tesson had received a punitive letter for his preface and the Faculté de Théologie a letter of blame for its irresponsibility. As for Father Plé, who had signed the *nihil obstat,* he once again saw his career shattered.[109]

Oraison accepted the verdict and began to censor his book. Two years later, when he was preparing to send his new manuscript off to Rome, the Holy Office made public its decree of interdiction. The priest received his notification as a humiliation, but submitted once again. In February 1955, he wrote for *Le Monde* a letter of self-criticism on the subject of an article concerning him. "As a priest of the Roman Catholic Church, I acknowledge the Holy Office's higher right to decide in the last analysis on the legitimacy of my publications. It is inevitable that the perspective of a group of individuals accustomed to a somewhat idiosyncratic mode of discourse will not always concord with that of a Church organism universal in its purport. And it is quite evident that the latter perspective alone allows one to discern whether a book is dangerous or not for the greater public of the world at large. . . . The 'dangerous errors' referred to in the commentary of *Osservatore romano* are

opposed to my personal thought. But it is undeniable that without certain information my text lent itself to interpretations compatible with those errors. How could I
have perceived as much without the measure of the Holy Office? The Holy Office
merely did its work and I subscribe to it fully. I interpret it logically as an invitation
to work henceforth in such manner that these confusions be avoided." [110]

Not only did the condemnation not prevent the continuation of the struggle,
but it bore witness to the effective progress of Freudian ideas in ecclesiastical circles.
With the publication of Oraison's book, and despite its banning, numerous priests
could now frequent the analytic couch. Some chose defrocking in order to become
psychoanalysts; others exercised psychoanalysis without being defrocked; and still
others began living with women or secretly practicing homosexuality. Certain of
them, nevertheless, remained open to Freudianism without losing faith or breaking
their vow of chastity. Despite the hope kindled by a possible compatibility between
Christian morality and the discovery of the unconscious, the penetration of psychoanalysis into religious life ran the constant risk of resulting in priests breaking with
religion. In that sense, Freudianism was a real danger for the Church, and the Holy
Office was right to distrust all psychoanalytic experiments. But since the crisis of
vocations had become a pressing reality, it was difficult to resist the advances of a
theory regarded by some as capable of ameliorating true faith.

In 1954, the publication of Hesnard's book *Morale sans péché* ["Morality
without sin"][111] renewed the debate and stirred up sentiment in the small Catholic
community concerned with the problem. Undergoing a spiritual renewal, our pioneer maintained that a new morality of social action should be substituted for the
former Judeo-Christian taboo founded on sin. Against the notion of "guilty
thoughts" he pitted the benefits of mental hygiene and affirmed that every sexual
manifestation was a matter of prophylaxis and not error. The journal *Recherches et
Débats* organized an elaborate exchange on the book. Father Beirnaert subtly criticized Hesnard's point of view by showing that there was a good chance that the new
rational morality would be no different from what it believed it was denouncing.
Jean Lacroix, for his part, contributed a philosopher's perspective and recalled that
Mounier, before dying, had read with fascination *L'univers morbide de la faute*
["The morbid world of sin"]. Then Marcel Eck paid absurd tribute to Hesnard's
qualities while emphasizing that it was dangerous to analyze "normal cases" on the
basis of "abnormal" ones. Finally, Canon Jacques Leclerq bypassed the book in
order to broach the general problem of a theology of sin.[112]

That same year, Agostino Gemelli entered the fray and published in Italy an
ardent critique of the book in which he recalled with brio that Hesnard had completely deformed Freud's thought. He was as interested in the admiral's theses as in
the situation of French Catholics, whom he reproached with wanting to shatter
Christian morality. He did not forgo commenting on Beirnaert's article and ended
his remarks with a moderate conclusion: "Dr. Hesnard's book is fundamentally in
error and should be read with caution; but we can derive from it a motif and an
opportunity to recall that certain forms of spirituality, certain ascetic paths, and also
certain norms of moral life should be reviewed, corrected, and allowed to achieve a
new equilibrium." [113]

Plainly, Gemelli had recovered his earlier flexibility, but the Holy Office did not take it into account, and decreed in January 1956 that three of Hesnard's books, including *Morale sans péché* and *L'univers morbide de la faute,* be placed on the Index. Through that new act of condemnation, what was being aimed at was the French experiment, as may be seen from the commentary in *Oservatore romano:* "The condemnation of the doctrine contained, not only in these three books, but also in other volumes of the same Dr. Hesnard as well as by other Catholic authors following the Freudian tendency, undoubtedly constitutes a warning and an invitation addressed particularly to all Catholic writers and publishers. From all that we have just said, a very simple conclusion follows: One cannot distance oneself with impunity from the fundamental principles of Christian moral doctrine, nor can one yield with impunity to the suggestion of the so-called 'new morality,' which seeks thoroughly vacillating support in fundamentally anti-rational and anti-Christian tendencies." [114]

The new assignment to the Index was testimony of the Vatican's paradoxical attitude. Concerned lest it condemn the works of a universally recognized thinker, who was Jewish to boot, the Roman Catholic Church opted to turn against its own. In the voice of the Holy Office, it denounced French priests who were themselves a generation behind when it came to the acceptance of Freudianism in their country. The priests sought initiation to psychoanalysis through the writings of a notorious chauvinist, at a time when he himself no longer represented anything in the psychoanalytic community. Kept at a distance by the SPP and poorly tolerated within the SFP, Hesnard was interested in sin and "mythic morality" to the extent that he had converted his chauvinism into a simplistic critique of Judeo-Christianity. It may be noted in passing that the priests were not fooled: They never assumed as their own Hesnard's former ideals and used his work in order to understand Freud's.

Under John XXIII's pontificate, a period of détente ensued. Until the opening of Vatican Council II, the Holy Office did not publish any decrees against psychoanalysis. For his part, the Pope abstained from all commentary, either favorable or hostile. And yet the interest aroused by psychology and psychiatry would be translated into a number of concrete acts.

In 1957, a year before the death of Pius XII, the Sacred Congregation published its new constitution, *Sedes Sapientiae,* concerning apostolic training. Article 33, devoted to the admission of candidates to the noviciate, calls for obligatory psychiatric evaluation with the aim of removing from the priesthood postulants suffering from congenital defects or mental illnesses: "The specific signs of an authentic vocation as well as it motives must be pondered attentively, according to the age and condition of those desiring admission to the noviciate. The moral and intellectual qualities of candidates will be examined carefully and from every point of view; in addition inquiry will be made into their physical and psychical aptitudes, with recourse to the diagnostic and anamnestic judgment of an experienced physician, even as concerns hereditary—and above all—mental defects; the physician's opinion will be marked on the individual's card." [115]

For the Freudian priests, that normative measure opened the way to its opposite. It allowed a more significant integration of psychoanalysis within ecclesiastical circles. Indeed, by skirting the psychiatric character of the legislation, it was possible to set up psychologically oriented organisms charged with the discernment of vocations. Through their intermediary, a practice that had been clandestine or individual until then was able to attain official status. In 1959 AMAR, the Medico-Psychological Association for Aid to Priests, was founded, largely at the behest of Plé and Beirnaert. It was charged with responsibility for the regular clergy. Without "testing the Holy Ghost" or touching on the notion of "divine grace," it attempted rather to orient candidates for the priesthood to the orders suiting their personalities. The founding staff was to consist of two ecclesiastics, an educational psychologist, and five psychoanalysts, preferably psychiatrists. Among them, three were students of Lacan (Beirnaert, Daniel Widlöcher, Claude Dumézil). Soon the founding staff proved insufficient and other specialists were recruited to form juries of three members each: a priest, a psychiatrist-psychoanalyst, and a psychologist. Rejecting the evaluation requested by the Roman document, Plé and Beirnaert offered candidates a guarantee of medical confidentiality and made submission to examination optional. The official conclusions were sent to the principal superior of the priestly house with the agreement of the postulant and without any specifications about his personality. No more than a favorable or an unfavorable opinion was to be indicated. Candidates deemed "unsuited" for religious life were invited to seek treatment and frequently ended up on the couch of a member of the association.[116] The sexual question was obviously of the greatest importance. The staff in fact was to judge the novice's capacity for accepting a life of chastity. Father Plé offered a rather amusing criterion: "The more a man seems normal and capable of being a good husband, the better he can renounce conjugal life by becoming a normal priest, that is, a man like everyone else." [117]

Father Pohier, a Dominican, was not satisfied with so pragmatic a judgment. During a colloquium devoted to priestly celibacy in 1965, he did not hesitate to declare that chastity was a virtue of desire itself in which it was a matter of desiring according to the spirit. It was as an authentic desire, which would be all the more chaste in that it would discover its pleasure and its happiness in desiring according to the spirit.[118]

Beirnaert, for his part, situated the debate on more doctrinal grounds. Relying on a Lacanian conceptualization, he recalled that the role of the psychoanalyst in discerning vocations consisted in helping the subject to clarify the circuit of his demands: the one the Church makes of him, the one he addresses to the Church, and the one he addresses to the psychoanalyst. From there it was to awaken an authentic desire leading the candidate to examine on his own the nature of his vocation. If it was true, it would come from God; if it was deceptive, it would have to be reexamined by a specialist.[119]

Aware of the need for a more theoretical work on the relations or incompatibilities between Christian spiritualism and Freudian materialism, Beirnaert created a Teaching Center, affiliated with AMAR, in which candidates for pastoral training could be initiated to the principles of psychoanalysis under the supervision of competent therapists. Open to foreigners, the center received numerous priests from a variety of countries, and specifically from Latin America. After a few years it was obliged to scuttle its operations, since Church superiors had become afraid and recruitment was dropping off.

Given the unprecedented paradox constituted by the functioning of psychoanalysis under such conditions, it is hard to determine whether the AMAR experiment had allowed for a genuine discernment of vocations or if it merely promoted disbelief. Two things, in any event, are sure: Faith is no longer the same after an adventure with psychoanalysis, and, if it remains, it is transformed by an attentiveness to the unconscious. In addition, it may be supposed that the experiment rid the religious community of a large number of perverts, paranoiacs, and maniacs of various stripe. But what was the status of those "normal" priests who had entered a life of religion after the ritual examination? How many priests observed their vow of chastity after analysis? How many remained within the Church's faith without transgressing its interdictions? The question remains open. . . .

Perceiving the danger, the Holy Office made public in July 1961 a Monitum forbidding priests from consulting a psychoanalyst without the authorization of their bishop and without serious reason. It was specified, moreover, that analytic training was absolutely not necessary for priestly ordination.[120] Once again, the diktat was ambiguous. It avoided condemning Freudianism and attacked the excesses of a number of experiments. A year later, Cardinal Feltin, who had defended Oraison, delivered an address on respect for the person in which he reaffirmed the Roman position: "The progress registered by psychology is no less dangerous for the person. Depth psychology and its therapeutic use, for example psychoanalysis, pose a certain number of grave problems. The risks it raises for freedom and the unity of the self, the limits it places on responsibility, on the secrecy of conscience, constitute so many dangers for the individual, which account for the Church's reservations and its calls for greater prudence."[121]

All the warnings did not prevent Freudian priests and Catholic therapists from holding congresses and officially continuing their experiments. It would appear that the Holy Office's strength lay in the simplemindedness of its positions and the permissiveness it demonstrated in relation to its own diktats. The more it manifested its authority, the more psychoanalysis attracted significant sectors of the clergy. At that point, there occurred an event without precedent in the history of the Church, beside which French affairs seemed like a drop in the ocean.

At the Benedictine monastery of the Resurrection, located in the heart of the ancestral village of Santa Maria de Ahuacatitlan, near Cuernavaca in Mexico, a prior of Belgian origin, Father Grégoire Lemercier, decided to expedite his monks to the analytic couch.[122] The oldest refused, but sixty of them agreed and entered into group therapy conducted by two non-Catholic psychoanalysts, who were members of the IPA. One, Gustavo Quevedo, was Mexican; the other, Frida Zmund, was an Argentine woman. She would be the first woman in the world to penetrate the masculine mysteries of monastic life. The participants paid for their therapy collectively through additional labor. After a year, twenty monks chose to be defrocked, and two years later, twenty more. Lemercier, who was pursuing his own therapy with Quevedo, did not hesitate to affirm that the experiment had strengthened authentic vocations. Nevertheless, a few years later, he would shed his habit and marry.

This unique epic, conducted in a missionary country, does not prove that analytic investigation, even reduced to group therapy, always leads to a dissolution of faith or a baring of the neurotic underpinnings of religious vocations. Although he claimed not to, Lemercier had constrained his monks to follow him in his quest of the unconscious: At the least he had made use of his transferential authority. Despite its spectacular side, the Mexican adventure was less innovative than the French experiment, which demonstrated that it was preferable to discern the meaning of a vocation before a postulant's entry into a specific order.

In November 1962, an anonymous document, probably prepared by Lemercier, circulated in the corridors of the Council. It emphasized the necessity for priests to undergo analysis and for initiating broad discussions with the international analytic community.[123] A theologian advised the prior that the experiment was too recent not to provoke a polemic and that it should be pursued in silence. It was true that the Sacred Congregation had not remained indifferent and had studied the Mexican dossier. Three years later the scandal erupted and the international press began recounting the adventure. The Sacred Congregation was then dispossessed of the file, which was removed to the Holy Office, which would in turn have the affair removed from its purview. . . . In September 1965, the bishop of Cuernavaca, Mendez Arceo, intervened in the Council in support of Lemercier. He denounced Schema XIII, devoted to the Church in the world, which he reproached for its silence on the subject of psychoanalysis: "Psychoanalysis presents itself to us," he declared, "as an authentic science. . . . Analytic discourse is part of human culture; it imposes a renewal of the concept of man and raises problems of which we did not have the slightest idea before. The Church, because of the anti-Christian dogmatism of certain analysts, has taken a position which recalls the case of Galileo; but there is not a single area of pastoral life in which we are not obliged to take account of psychoanalysis."[124]

As rigid and prudent as Pius XII, Paul VI gently disavowed the experiment in an ambiguous address giving rise to numerous interpretations.[125] Four years later, in a sermon, he declared that psychoanalysis stirred the troubled depths of the human mind, but it deserved the Church's attention.[126] Finally, in 1973, he expressed his esteem and his reservations regarding it: "We cannot silence our pained astonishment in the face of the indulgence, and even the publicity and propaganda so ignobly disseminated at present for all that troubles and infects minds: pornography, immoral spectacles, and licentious exhibitions. . . . We esteem that sector [psychoanalysis] of anthropological studies now famous, although we do not always find it to be coherent with itself, nor always confirmed by satisfying and salutary experiences, nor in agreement with that science of the heart which we have drawn from the school of Catholic spirituality."[127]

The works of the Council provoked widespread satisfaction among the Freudian priests of France, who showed no irritation with the Church's immobility on the questions of contraception, sexuality, and the celibacy of priests. Moreover, the infusion of psychoanalysis was proceeding briskly through numerous Catholic colloquia on the benefits of psychotherapy. In 1966, Father Bouchard of Saint-Sulpice founded, on the model of AMAR, a Medico-Psychological Association for

Aid to the Clergy. The efforts of Beirnaert and Plé had thus borne fruit among the secular clergy. And yet the same year, despite the reform allowing authors faced with having their books on the Index to defend themselves, Oraison was denied authorization for a reedition of his book.[128]

For some, an interest in psychoanalysis was in fact favoring an advance of unbelief under guise of a better evaluation of one's sense of faith or vocation. In 1964, Father François Roustang, a Jesuit, was named director of the journal *Christus*. Simultaneously, he joined Beirnaert and Father Michel de Certeau, also a Jesuit, in creating the École freudienne de Paris, founded by Lacan after the second split. Shortly thereafter he began therapy with Serge Leclaire. In 1966, he published an article entitled "Le troisième homme [The third man]" on the decline of belief in the Church within the Catholic world and among the clergy. To all appearances, the text had nothing to do with Freudianism. And yet the reflections it contained were the direct consequence of the shifts effected by psychoanalysis in the author's thinking. The Congregation was not fooled, and relieved Roustang of his functions. Some time later, he broke with the faith, shed his habit, married, and became a psychoanalyst.[129] We shall examine later on the reasons that led numerous Freudian priests to choose Lacanianism.

III. Two New Masters: Sacha Nacht and Daniel Lagache

Sacha Nacht's face in no way evokes the gentle slopes of the Romanian countryside. Slit-eyed, dull of complexion, high cheekboned, exuding authoritarianism, he might be thought the descendent of a vaivode come directly from his Walachian castle. Nacht was born the same year as Lacan, deep in the Moldavian forest, of a family of Jewish peasants converted to Christianity. His father grew grain and decided one day to start up business as a woodcutter. His mother read French novels, and hoped that her son would one day be a physician. Bearing a Russian first name and a German patronymic, Sacha Nacht flaunted his love of France in the face of Ottoman barbarism.

At the age of six, he dreamed of a medical career. His family abandoned the countryside where he was born and settled in a suburb of Bucharest. A fire ravaged the area and the Nachts were ruined. Sacha began his medical studies in Romania before emigrating to Paris in 1919. He easily obtained equivalency credits and discovered Freudianism one evening in 1922 while attending a performance of Lenormand's play.[130]

An assimilationist, he did not reject his Jewish identity, but rejected belief and turned to scientific positivism. Unlike Polish, Hungarian, or Austrian emigrants, he was infused with a sense of Latinity by upbringing and remained a peasant by origin. In this ambitious man whose grandparents had converted to escape anti-Semitic persecution, medicine was the bearer of an adaptative ideal that functioned as surrogate for every form of fulfillment. In his long love affair with medicine, he wanted to make psychoanalysis into a noble therapeutic mode, shorn of any philosophical message and set on an organicist pedestal. The opposite of Lacan and Henri Ey, the inverse of Freud. He was neither a theoretician nor a discoverer, nor a stylist of language, but an Oriental despot gifted with a superb clinical talent. A boyar and a landholder, he reigned in splendor, while demanding of his own an undivided ardor. He dreamed of an authoritarian association based on the artisanal presence of its therapists and on a de Gaulle-like humanism that would be more conservative than Jacobin. He preferred the solid competence of bourgeois values to speculation and would leave his students with the enduring imprint of a fine attentiveness to the transference. He would never be able to tolerate any questioning of his intransigence.

On his analytic couch would pass a number of psychoanalysts of the second and above all of the third generation, in particular Serge Lebovici, Evelyne Kestemberg, Bela Grunberger, Serge Viderman, as well as Marc Schlumberger and Jenny Roudinesco for their second analyses, followed by Conrad Stein for his third, and many more. . . .

Besides Nacht, the postwar SPP counted five "titular" members active as training analysts. Schlumberger was perhaps the most admired, with an impressive list of students, including Safouan, Granoff, Yves Dalibard, and Julien Rouart for his second analysis, Conrad Stein for his first, Pierre Marty and Ruth Lebovici. The aged Parcheminey, who had analyzed Bouvet, also trained Francis Pasche and Margaret Williams-Clark. As for Leuba, he accepted Jean Favreau and Pierre Luquet in therapy. Maurice Bouvet, for his part, was the analyst of André Green, François Perrier, Michel de M'Uzan, and Daniel Lagache for his second psychoanalysis. Finally Lacan had as students Jean Kestemberg and René Diatkine, as well as all those who followed him in the first split.

Before the great expansion of the SPP, Nacht participated as did Lacan in the rise of dynamic psychiatry. Despite a classic itinerary which brought him in 1933 to the psychiatric hospital competition, he remained attached to the old ideals of neurology. In 1926, he defended a thesis of no special brilliance on the anatomical and pathological study of syphilitic myelitis.[131] By 1925, he had chosen Loewenstein as his training analyst. His therapy lasted two-and-a-half years and Nacht became a member of the SPP in 1927. The following year, he went into private practice and, in 1929, became a titular member of the Society. At the age of 28, he thus became the youngest of the masters of the second generation to obtain that title. Already before the war, his reputation as a clinician was greater than Lacan's, but outside the walls of the SPP, Nacht was little known. Head of the Psychoanalytic Laboratory of Sainte-Anne in 1931, he remained at a distance from the French intellectual epic. He saw frequently several creative artists such as Marcel Duhamel and above all Yves Tanguy, but separated his clinical activity from the Surrealist venture. In 1933, he dreamed of meeting Freud, as though in search of an "aristocratic affiliation." Two years later, he married Lydie Farman, the daughter of an airplane manufacturer of English origin. She had studied nursing and had undergone analysis with Sophie Morgenstern. In 1936, he attended the Marienbad congress, where he did not speak. From there he went to Vienna: Since May 20 of the previous year he had had an appointment with Freud to begin an analysis at a hundred dollars per session.[132]

Nacht barely spoke German, and at the time, Freud could no longer express himself in French. He thus advised his patient to continue his work with Hartmann. Nacht obeyed, then returned to France in November 1937 for the birth of his son.

At that time, Freud recommended him to a French patient for his clinical competence.[133] Radiating the prestige of his Viennese adventure, he wrote a book on masochism.[134] At a French-British meeting, he presented his first important contribution on the role of the ego in therapeutic technique. He would take up that theme again in various ways during the 1950s, first refusing, then accepting the tendency represented by ego psychology.

The German invasion imposed some harsh decisions on him. Contrary to Loewenstein, he was not a polyglot and could thus not envisage, even if constrained, a career on the other side of the Atlantic. Moreover, having broken all his links to Jewish tradition, and not being a veteran of the Great War, he did not idealize, as did Minkowski, the homeland of the rights of man. He thus refused both emigration and the wearing of a yellow star. On November 13, 1940, an inspector named Georges Brun notified Nacht of the order to cease his activities. Ashamed no doubt at having to execute an order he disapproved of, the functionary committed an unbelievable blunder. Instead of writing out the interdiction correctly, he wrote a sentence meaning the opposite of what he intended. He enjoined Nacht "to exercise his profession within a period of one month." [135] The slip was considerable, but the doctor was not misled. He immediately asked Claude and Heuyer to support him. Nevertheless, in 1942, the Office of Jewish Affairs sent him a new summons. At that point he left Paris and joined a Resistance network with the rank of lieutenant. A year later, he accomplished a mission in England via Spain. In the course of that trip, he was arrested by the Gestapo and interned at Compiègne. Lydie Farman and her mother intervened, bringing the authorities proof of the "Aryan" origins of the prisoner. With documents in hand, they invoked the burial of Romanian grandparents in an orthodox cemetery, and Sacha's baptism at age two. Upon being freed, he worked as a farmer while hiding in Saint-Tropez. Beneath that cover, he pursued his Resistance activities in collaboration with the Maures brigade.[136]

After the Liberation, his notoriety made him the most visible member of the SPP. Marie Bonaparte had no affection for this rival, who had managed to win Freud's trust. Exasperated by his increasing authority, she called him the "rug merchant." And yet the princess and he both shared a love for the world of medicine. Marie ardently defended the cause of nonphysicians while Nacht dreamed of denying them access to titular membership. She wanted to transform psychoanalysis into a form of medical therapy exercised by lay practitioners, and he sought to maintain medical degrees and prerequisites within a society dominated by an ethos of healing. Each one's struggle was different, but what was at stake was identical: On both sides, it was a matter, as in the United States, of submitting Freud's legacy to a medical ethic and anchoring the unconscious in organicism. It would be enough for the storm to threaten for both to find themselves in agreement in opposition to the rising tide of Lacanianism and the academic liberalism represented by Daniel Lagache.

In January 1949, Sacha Nacht succeeded John Leuba at the head of the SPP. He modified the principal statutes and presided over a commission on instruction, created by him, and whose rules and doctrinal content were drawn up by Lacan. Three years later, he bestowed upon himself, after a hand vote, the directorship of the new Institute of Psychoanalysis. That organism's function was to unburden the SPP of its teaching tasks, and its existence was made possible by a gift from Central-European Jewish emigrants settled in the United States. An appeal for funds allowed for that sum to be supplemented and for the purchase of a building. Until 1952, when the problems leading to the split began to surface, Nacht had in fact monopolized the totality of directorial positions opened up after the war. Gently squeezed out, but strong with her symbolic position, Marie Bonaparte still held a position on the commission in 1949. In 1951, her name appeared only as honorary president of the SPP. In December 1950, Nacht proposed the creation of a Syndicate of Psychoanalytic Physicians. Despite its anti-lay aspect, the proposal was adopted unanimously. Parcheminey was named president, Lacan and Lagache vice-presidents, and Maurice Benassy treasurer.

Although femininity constituted a fundamental object of theoretical reflection in French psychoanalytic writings between the wars, that did not mean that female practitioners found a favorable reception within the SPP. The question of *Laienanalyse* coincided in part with that of the access of women to the profession of psychoanalyst and more specifically to that of training analyst. There was little misogyny in the ranks of the SPP, but to the extent that women found it difficult to undertake medical studies during the first half of the century, they encountered more obstacles than men in a society that granted privileges to those with medical degrees. That explains why the fight on behalf of lay analysis was an issue of particular concern to women, who tended to be more organicist in orientation than their male colleagues by virtue of the fact that they had not had access to medical training. Doctrinal differences did not, for that matter, always coincide with anatomical ones. The first women to pursue careers in the second generation were all physicians and less organicist than the lay pioneer women of the first generation. This was the case for Juliette Boutonier, who had undertaken her medical studies in order to be able to practice psychoanalysis, for Françoise Dolto, who wanted to be a "pedagogical physician," and finally for Jenny Roudinesco, whose itinerary was quite different. Initially a neurologist, and then a neuro-psychiatrist, she was the second woman in France to obtain in 1939 the title of hospital doctor [*médecin des hôpitaux*]. It was only in 1948, at the age of 45, that she discovered the importance of psychoanalysis and began her "visits" to titular members for a training analysis. As opposed to Dolto and Boutonier, she thus practiced medicine for twenty years without knowing anything of psychoanalysis.

In 1950, there erupted around a woman who was not a physician—a foreigner—an appalling affair that was to reveal the divisions within the psychoanalytic community and pit Sacha Nacht against Marie Bonaparte. In 1945, at the behest of Georges Mauco and with the support of Bonnafé and Le Guilland, a psychopedagogical center had been founded under the auspices of the Lycée Claude-Bernard. André Berge had participated in its creation along with Juliette Boutonier, who became its medical director. The center welcomed children encountering difficulties in making the transition from the first to the second cycle at school. The founders deliberately rejected medical terminology and situated their efforts under the aegis of psychology. If they were all physicians, they were also psychoanalysts;

they hired nonphysicians to conduct—under their supervision, or with their agreement—therapy privately or in public. In that context, a certain Margaret Williams-Clark practiced the profession of child analyst. An American citizen, she had been analyzed by Raymond de Saussure and had pursued her training with Georges Parcheminey. In 1950, she was elected an "adhering" member of the SPP. Shortly thereafter several discontented parents brought a complaint against her involving two cases: one of enuresis, the other of digestive problems. They brought the matter to the Ordre des médecins, which agreed to be party in a civil suit against her for the illegal practice of medicine.

In order to grasp what then transpired, some consideration of the legislation of 1945 is called for. Since the time of the Penal Code, punishment in such matters had passed through three successive phases. Until 1892, the legislative concern was to protect the sick from charlatans. After that date, the interest was rather in shielding physicians from individuals capable of diminishing their practices.[137] That shift in attitude reveals the transformations that had occurred within medical knowledge as well as in the status accorded to practitioners. Charlatans were no longer condemned because they exploited the sick but because they endangered a profession protected by university degrees. The postwar system effected a synthesis of the previous legislations. "Paramedical" professions were recognized, but the law envisaged a series of practices that were to be reserved for physicians. "Auxiliary" activities remained legitimate if they were supervised by a physician and thus controlled by the "Order" of medical practitioners. Only a physician had the right to perform a diagnosis and to prescribe a treatment, although he was free to have it executed by a nonphysician with auxiliary status. The practice of analysis fell under the provisions of that ordinance: No therapist could have recourse to it if he were not protected by the legitimacy of medical authority. That meant that the titles of "adhering" or "titular" member awarded by the SPP were of no value in the eyes of the law, even though they conferred on their possessors moral qualities or competencies that might be recognized by a court of law.

Naturally, history did not conform to the legislation, which was amply contradicted by reality. Nonphysicians at midcentury were practicing psychoanalysis without any recourse to the direct authority of a physician. They were shielded "morally" by their membership in the SPP, but were subject to being sued should a complaint be lodged. In that case, the SPP would use its institutional muscle to protect its member, even if it had to argue that his practice was in fact under the auspices of a physician. With the expansion of the movement, psychoanalysts enjoyed a greater renown than their healing colleagues, be they chiropracters, sorcerers, or hypnotists. . . . Even though the courts occasionally delivered verdicts as absurd as the law authorizing them, several trials for illegal practice ended with acquittals. The judgments, however, had no other meaning than that of the legislation. Thus a simple mesmerizer found himself condemned by an appeals court, whereas a genuine charlatan was acquitted by a tribunal. In Nice, a vertebrotherapist was persecuted for his elongations while verdicts of innocence were handed down to bizarre individuals who measured the electromagnetism of the human body by capturing, with the help of a catalyzer, the forty-four fundamental metals of the organism. In each case the acquittal or condemnation was a function of the presence or absence of a diagnosis or a treatment. From that point of view, the law would protect Cagliostro and pursue a genuine therapist, and vice versa.

The trial began at the end of 1951. Officially, the Claude-Bernard Center did not recognize psychoanalysis. What it undertook was reeducation therapy and other pedagogical counseling validated by official diplomas. In that context, Margaret Williams-Clark was admitted as a benevolent foreign visitor, and it was as a "liberal" psychoanalyst that she was dragged before the courts. The lawyer engaged by the Order assured all that he had no desire to attack the Center, a respectable institution, which did not stop Juliette Boutonier and André Berge from insisting on the competence of their colleague. She herself, moreover, appealed to the cover offered her by Francis Pasche for the private therapy undertaken in her home. Soon the press got wind of the affair and public opinion became interested. Marie Bonaparte delivered a vibrant speech in favor of *Laienanalyse* and her rival, Maryse Choisy, waxed indignant at the thought that Freud's dream might be swallowed up in Hippocrates' belly. As for the defense attorney, she maintained that her client's activities did not fall under the category of medicine but of pedagogy.

After a request for additional information, the trial was postponed. Finally, on March 21, 1952, after hearing the testimony of several eminent individuals of the medical and academic worlds, the 16th Correctional Chamber acquitted Margaret Williams-Clark and dismissed the case of the Order's Council.[138]

The judgment was commensurate with the extravagance of the situation. For in fact, the partisans of lay analysis could hardly defend a point of view that would amount to officializing a practice that had until then been entirely informal: the fact that nonphysicians were conducting therapy without any real medical cover. Were they to admit it publicly, the accused would have been found guilty. Vis-à-vis the law it was thus imperative to demonstrate something and its opposite: the "theoretical" validity of the lay project and the existence of a "cover" they knew to be fictitious. On their side, the advocates of integration did not come down hard on the accused; not only was she a member of the SPP, but she could also appeal to her prestigious (French-Swiss and French-American) training. In the curriculum she had pursued, she was heir to the celebrated orthodox and medicalizing tendency to which both Nacht and the princess belonged despite their divergences. Had she been Turkish and analyzed by an obscure Bulgarian emigrant, her fate would have been different. Nacht, in fact, testified on her behalf with such ambivalence that he unleashed the fury of Bonaparte. She believed firmly, upon hearing the verdict, that the victory of *Laienanalyse* in France was now an accomplished fact. To Loewenstein she wrote as follows: "At last the question of lay analysis is established in France. We shall have to have a statute. Let us hope it is not too narrow. Nacht has demonstrated remarkable cowardice. Obsequiousness toward the Ordre des médecins. He's disappointed in the acquittal. He had been hoping for an official position at the University in exchange for his support of the Order's Council."[139]

On the one hand, the acquittal maintained that Margaret Williams-Clark possessed qualifications requisite for practicing, without being a doctor, a nonmedical discipline, and, on the other, it annulled that affirmation by emphasizing that in her home she was acting as a pedagogue and not a psychoanalyst. In other words, if she were practicing psychoanalysis, she would have fallen under the provisions of the law since she was producing diagnoses and presiding over therapy. But since the court maintained that she was a pedagogue, thanks to the arguments by the defense, it also admitted that she required the authority of a physician. Thereafter, it stipulated that that authority had not been exercised since she had omitted reporting on her work to her supervisor. There too, she should have been found guilty. But the court found that auxiliaries were indispensable to mental health. There was thus neither an illegal practice of medicine on the part of a suspect of whom it was no longer clear what profession she was exercising, nor complicity of the physician who had nevertheless violated the statute since he was "covering" for a practice without supervising the results. To be sure, the judgment did not hold up and reflected both the contradictions of the psychoanalytic movement in search of its identity and those of a law that could not manage to be applied because of its incoherence.

This explains why in July 1953, the 11th Chamber of the Court of Appeal reversed the tribunal's judgment and retained against Williams-Clark the crime of illegal exercise of medicine, punishable by a fine of one hundred francs, which was suspended (a symbolic franc). But in order to maintain the previous judgment, it declared the punishment purely one of principle, in view of the impeccable ethics of the lady and because of her expertise in psychoanalysis, which eliminated all suspicion of fraud.[140] Naturally, the Court of Appeal showed itself to be more coherent than the correctional tribunal and maintained, by virtue of the law, that the infraction pertained to the conduct of a treatment and not the utterance of a diagnosis. Implicitly, it thus recognized that the practice of psychoanalysis ought to remain a medical prerogative, even if there were neither medication nor physical intervention.

In order to apply the law, the court based itself less on current jurisdiction than on an article of the rules of the Commission on Instruction drawn up by Lacan in 1949. In point of fact, it repeated word for word the terms of that text in which the following may be read: "It is agreed, moreover, that psychoanalysis is essentially a medical technique for which the neuroses are merely the field of its exercise, but which extends its grasp perpetually further, along with the field of psychosomatics. That is why medical qualifications—diplomas and practice—and among them a specialization in psychiatry, which the modern movement orients perpetually further in the direction of analysis, are most recommendable for psychoanalytic training. We can thus not prevail too much upon candidates to obtain them." [141]

They were no fools in the Court of Appeal! In order to rectify the judgment of a tribunal, they threw the ball back into the opponent's court, appealing to principles formulated by the Freudian movement itself. The Court was thus playing a double game: that of enforcement, on the one hand, and on the other, that of a society which in reality reserved analytic practice solely for physicians. The 16th Correctional Chamber, moreover, did not wait for the review of its decision in order to conform. In July 1952, it condemned another woman, on her own this time, who did not benefit from the support of the SPP. She was Hungarian and her medical degree was judged unacceptable by French law.[142] It should be noted in passing that the two condemnations involved foreign nationals. It may be wondered whether, through them, what was occurring was not, in a repressed manner, a reactivation of the former chauvinistic problematic. To be sure, Freudianism was admitted as a "French science" on the condition that its practitioners submit to an order ratifying that Frenchness.

On the morrow of the new verdict, Professor Heuyer spoke in favor of a complete integration of psychoanalysis within medicine. According to him, analysis was to be practiced exclusively by psychiatrists and fall under the authority of the University. Nacht reacted with moderation: "If what is wanted is for the Faculty of Medicine to take complete charge of the training of future analysts, the question should be examined at length, since it would present some grave disadvantages. . . . First of all, the theoretical teaching of analysis, as the medical school would be qualified to dispense it, cannot suffice for training in conformity with the very essence of psychoanalysis. . . . Finally, theoretical instruction is not enough for training an analyst. The essential condition of his education remains a training analysis, since no one can honestly claim to psychoanalyze another if he has not himself undergone an analysis, that being the sole means of acceding to the unconscious. . . . As far as the practice of psychoanalysis is concerned, all measures capable of eliminating incompetent psychoanalysts would be more than desirable; I would even say that they are imperative. But at this point a further complication arises: the absence of a status for psychoanalytic auxiliaries (psychoanalysts who are not physicians)." [143]

Through the trial, the oppositions dividing the psychoanalytic community at midcentury may be intuited. Against the integrationist policy of the patrons of the university, intent on annexing the training of therapists within the framework of academic "disinterestedness," Nacht defended a policy of independence based on privatization. The configuration resembled the quarrel between religious and secular schools. Nacht wanted to preserve the financial and ideological autonomy of the SPP while reorganizing it on the model of medical tradition. In that perspective, his hostility to *Laienanalyse* was not of the same stripe as that of the Ordre des médecins. It was not for him a matter of constraining candidates to pursue medical studies in order to have the right to practice, but of reserving for physicians alone the rank of titular member or training analyst, even if one ended up making the other members function as auxiliaries. Training presupposed a personal analysis, on the condition, however, that the therapist be assigned to the candidate by the Institute created to that end. That was tantamount to distinguishing between two modes of practice: one, which was therapeutic, oriented toward the sick, and accessible to all members, and another which was didactic, and reserved only for titular members, that is, for physicians, and dispensed according to criteria defined by the new Institute. The training function included that of supervisor, which conferred on the rank of titular member extraordinary importance. In fact, Nacht organized the community of the 1950s on the model of the American societies, thus redeeming France's tardiness in that domain. Previously, the Institute had an artisan-like air about it and functioned thanks to the contributions of the princess; in 1952, it was juridically independent of the SPP, which became a scholarly society. It had its own statutes and was entrusted with the task of delivering to all practitioners a diploma that might be recognized by the university and the public powers to the extent that it was authenticated by physicians. Even before the split, and without adhering to any precise doctrinal tendency, Nacht was thus in complete agreement with the dominant ideals of the IPA.

If one compares that policy with the one recommended by Lacan in the notorious rules of the Commission, considerable differences may be seen. At first sight, the Lacanian project appears to be hostile to lay analysis. Not only did the author maintain that a lay individual not undertake any therapy without medical cover, but he recommended that candidates commit themselves to a psychiatric career, preferably in hospitals. In addition, everyone knew that Lacan would pressure his students down the path of medicine, even when he would be, through his school, the promoter of a genuinely lay policy. In 1949, he went so far as to affirm the necessity of eliminating from careers practitioners deemed to be psychotic, unduly awkward, epileptic, or feebleminded: "We ought to categorize as such in principle," he wrote, "those states of disgrace apt to ruin at their core the imaginary support which the analyst's person gives to the transferential identifications through the generic homeomorphism of the imago of the body: shocking deformities, visible mutations, or manifest malfunctions." [144] One would almost think these the words of an advocate of eugenics or of a timid esthete stricken with a serious phobia.

Nevertheless, his position was distinguished from Nacht's. For Lacan, the acquisition of medical knowledge did not function as a substitute for an adaptative ideal. Psychiatric specialization was recommended not for organicist or pragmatic reasons, but for epistemological ones. It was to be accompanied by literary, philosophical, and anthropological training. Lacan took into account, in the instruction of candidates, the French adventure of the interwar years, his own, through which psychoanalysis interrogated psychiatry in the direction of a "modernization" of Freud's conceptualizations. In 1949, his project was closer to Henri Ey's than to Nacht's. That is why it would become the vehicle for a lay policy that was not yet apparent.

Despite their divergences, Nacht and Lacan had close relations. One admired the other for his doctrinal talent, and the latter acknowledged the former's remarkable clinical competence. Even after the split, he would not hesitate to send him patients. Both had a pronounced taste for money, which was linked to the way in which they lived out their ambitions. In July 1952, in the village of Le Tholonet, Nacht took as his second wife Edmée Schemla, a Jewish woman of Tunisian origin, previously married to Tedesco, an industrialist and friend of Laforgue. The wedding took place in the residence of the painter André Masson, Sylvia Bataille's brother-in-law. She herself was Edmée's witness, while Lacan fulfilled the same role for Sacha Nacht, even as he filmed the couple's happiness against a landscape beloved by Cézanne. Toward 1960, Edmée would convert to Catholicism after having led a study group on problems of religion.

In 1956, Nacht lost his authority in the wake of a terrible accident. One winter's morning, he was riding his favorite horse on an ice-covered path. The animal slipped: The rider fell head first and was unable to get up. Stricken with double vision, Nacht could no longer manage to direct as he had previously the notorious

Institute for which he had fought so hard. His taste for power disappeared but his analytic ear remained as attentive as ever. Gradually, Nacht was replaced by Serge Lebovici, whose more flexible policy allowed certain nonphysicians to attain the rank of titular member. When Lacan published his *Écrits,* Nacht did not read the book and acted as if the EFP did not exist. He may have remembered Cézanne's mountain on which were kindled the last embers of a friendship destined for disaster. In May 1968, he could not bear the barricades, and watched the collapse of all the symbols of his own authority. Eight years later, suffering from a cancer of the prostate, he died in unbearable agony.

In December 1967, Marcel Bleustein-Blanchet lost his daughter in an automobile accident. In utter despair, he left for Megève where he attempted in vain to find some repose. His friend Sacha Nacht joined him there. He dragged him on a long walk through paths of snow. Marcel spoke in asides, and Sacha hurried his pace in silence. Occasionally he would disturb the mountain calm with an inspired comment: balm for the wound. Marcel asked his companion if psychoanalysis could cure human suffering. The latter did not answer and continued walking, like Freud with Mahler in the streets of Leyden. That peripatetic therapy lasted three days through forests and on icy paths. When evening came, the two friends took refuge beside a fire. Then each returned to his occupations.[145]

Léon Gorodiche was a man of a type no longer found. A Lithuanian Jew, he emigrated to Switzerland around 1876 and lived three years in the circle of Plekhanov. His populist ardor led him to neurology. He liked to treat the poor and practiced hypnosis. When the time came, he supported the Bolsheviks. After settling in France, he made several trips to the United States in order to take care of his abundant Jewish practice. He raised his daughter Hélène to be independent. When she met Daniel Lagache, a third of the way into the century, she knew that her marriage would be nonreligious: Léon Gorodiche was proud of his Jewishness, but uncompromising toward religious tradition. A militant of the finest stripe![146]

Louis Lagache, Daniel's father, came from a different world. A lawyer of Picard origin and a "good Frenchman" for as long as could be remembered, he admired his homeland, protected the oppressed, and recited lines of Corneille to his sons. No one challenged his reputation as a rigid moralist and educator. At home, he preferred Daniel, his elder son, and his younger one suffered for it. When the venerable father died from the aftereffects of a protracted illness, Daniel was thirteen years old. He already loved military music, honor, and La Bruyère's *Les Caractères.* He ardently wished to be an object of interest. Contrary to her deceased husband, Marthe Lagache preferred her younger son. Out of jealousy, Daniel turned to his nurse, Ernestine, than to his maternal grandmother who saw in him the reincarnation of her late husband. Ferreting through drawers, he one day came across a portrait of his grandfather in school uniform. He kept it as something precious. At school he took to protecting young girls, all the while discouraging their seduction attempts. He played leader with his friends and one night dreamed that he had saved a geometry manual after a cataclysm. He competed with his brother. Soon he fell in love with his cousin, who wore a cloche hat and predicted a brilliant future for him. She was right. Daniel Lagache would be one of the finest adornments of the French university. As a professor, and heir to Janet, Binet, and Ribot, all he lacked was a chair at the Collège de France.[147]

Daniel Lagache's itinerary was pursued under the sign of the "French unconscious." It was as though a fairy had designated him when still in his cradle to establish him on the home ground of the most illustrious adversaries of psychoanalysis. In his youth, he had read Janet's *L'automatisme psychologique* before the *Introduction to Psychoanalysis*. A short time later, he was oriented by the formidable Georges Dumas toward a medical career. Upon reaching maturity, he succeeded Georges Blondel in his chair at the University of Strasbourg. Finally, on the threshold of old age, he left his position of professor at the Sorbonne to a confirmed disciple of Janet. Whatever the phase of his reign, Daniel Lagache's place was on the psychologists' bench, leaving it to Lacan to occupy the throne of psychoanalysis.

He entered the École normale supérieure in 1924, the same year as Paul Nizan, Jean-Paul Sartre, Raymond Aron, and Georges Canguilhem. With the exception of the last mentioned, the others attended the presentation of patients by Georges Dumas. Aron, Nizan, and Sartre went through a third of the first-year medical curriculum without intending a medical career. It was a prerequisite to register for the *agrégation* in philosophy. A pupil of Alain's, Canguilhem had had little tenderness for psychology and no admiration at all for Dumas. He would undertake medical studies ten years later in Toulouse in order to complete his training as an historian of science. In that celebrated class, Lagache was thus alone in engaging that French tradition of psychological medicine whose history I traced in a previous volume. An *agrégé* of philosophy, an intern of the psychiatric hospitals, then head of a clinic for the mentally ill and for encephalitis, he spent time in the service of Henri Claude, and attended Clérambault's demonstration at the Special Infirmary. Finally, in 1934, he defended his medical thesis on verbal hallucinations of speech.[148]

Like all clinicians of his generation, he participated in the reconceptualization issuing from dynamic psychiatry and focused his first works on affective psychoses and paranoia. At the same time as Lacan, who was his junior by two years, he became acquainted with German texts, grew interested in madwomen and criminology, devoured Jaspers and phenomenology, challenged the chauvinist perspective of his seniors, and discovered with ardor the importance of language in the structuring of personality. Unfortunately for him, Lacan overtook him when it came to constructing a coherent synthesis. A world separated the two men, who shared the project of giving Freudian doctrine the place it deserved within the domain of science. Lacan started from psychiatry, reconceptualized Wallon in the light of Freud, and traversed Kojève and the Surrealist epic while Lagache chose an impossible integration of psychoanalysis into psychology. Appointed professor at Strasbourg in 1937, he began his labor of unification by creating the first certificates of psychopathology and social psychology.

A gifted orator, Lagache was a pioneer regarding the integration of psychoanalysis into the university. From the height of his erudition, he knew how to speak to students and was quite impressive in a style of teaching oriented toward commentary on texts. For that reason, his written work resembles a vast scholastic exercise. It allows for the inclusion of new elements without ever exploiting them in a synthesis of broad scope. Being neither a stylist of language, nor an authentic innovator, nor a grand clinician, Lagache would remain throughout his life an excellent teacher.

In 1932, he married Hélène Gorodiche, whom he admired for her intelligence and for being Jewish. She gave him twin girls, then another daughter named Élisabeth. Surrounded by four women, he was to find in his home the maternal love he had missed in childhood. In the middle of the war, Hélène died prematurely from the aftereffects of a poorly treated case of diphtheria. Lagache did not recover from this loss. Despite two subsequent marriages and the birth of a fourth daughter, Agnès, he remained faithful to his first wife, the only one who was Jewish. On the eve of his death, he asked to be buried beside her and bequeathed his library to the University of Tel Aviv.

As opposed to Nacht and Lacan, Lagache recounted his analysis in a curious article published in English in 1966.[149] It began in 1933 and was completed at the end of 1936, with a few weeks of interruption. Analyzing a lawyer's son who is proud of his intellectual success and marked by an obsessive jealousy of a younger brother is not an easy business when one occupies, within the transference, the place of a prestigious rival. In search of recognition, Lagache saw Loewenstein as a double of himself. He attributed to him the role of older brother which had been his in childhood. Quite quickly, he identified with his protector, but declared he felt superior because of his degrees and his medical career. He applied himself meticulously to discovering his analyst's weak points, suspected him of sleeping during their sessions, and reproached him for reading detective novels which he himself admired. At the end of three years, Loewenstein forced his patient to end his analysis following a dream in which he had compared himself to Freud. Nevertheless, he urged him to publish the story of his therapy and arranged his appointment to the rank of titular member. Thus was the good student recognized by his peers. Dissatisfied and delighted, Lagache begrudged his therapist the decision to replace him with a new patient.

On the couch, he was haunted by bell-shaped fantasies. He delighted in recounting them in order to interest his analyst in "something that played a role in his distant past."[150] Lagache discovered a banal recollection: One day he spied his father's penis, the organ of a prestigious individual in his eyes, who happened still to be dressed in a frock-coat and high hat. Later during his medical studies, he was struck by the expression "a cock like a bell clapper." He associated the term with the phenomenon of paraphimosis observed in certain patients. He then recalled having believed, during his childhood, that his mother had a masculine organ. Hearing her urinate, he made a connection between the presence of a loud noise and that of a large penis. The business of the bell did not stop there. In his adolescence, Daniel had fallen in love with a cousin. They went out together, but soon their meetings came to an end. Daniel decided not to marry and to continue his studies. The girl attributed that resolution to the money her cousin had spent during one of their outings. On the couch, Lagache realized that he had interrupted their relationship because she was wearing a cloche hat that he did not like. Obsessed by the image, he thought one evening of his cradle: The piece of furniture seemed like a bell with its shaft around which muslin curtains floated. Questioned by her son, Marthe specified that as an infant, his first toy was a legless doll mounted on a stick and called a "folie." The object resembled a bell. The author concluded with these words: "I will not risk the hypothesis that the name of my first toy sufficed—almost twenty years later, and through an almost instantaneous decision, opposed to the plans I had envisaged, but not without relation to still earlier projects—to make me a specialist in madness [folie]. That would be to overestimate the determining power of words. It is also possible that the toy had already disappeared from my universe by the time language had made its entry into it. I have, nevertheless, retained a pronounced taste for the word and its various uses, as in designating, in the eighteenth century, small country houses where one retired for pleasure; but "little houses" [petites maisons] were also mad houses and certain of them, with their pointed roofs, still had, thirty years ago, the form of a bell." [151]

Reading that conclusion, one has the impression that the author still believed, in 1966, that objects, not words, fashioned unconscious destinies. His discourse functions a bit in the mode of what Freud termed denial. If the taste for little bell-shaped houses derived from the word "folie," designating a doll, it was because the word had priority over the thing. Language does not enter into the subject's world when the object disappears. On the contrary: Language is first, so that the object exists solely by virtue of its being named. The bell-shaped fictions resembled each other within significant variations. They bore witness to the subjective quest for a sexual and symbolic identity, and not, as Lagache seemed to believe, to the simple reproduction of a mnemic experience attempting to construct the object outside of language. It might be said that the revelation of a fundamental term did not permit the patient to unravel a transferential relationship in which an Oedipal relation was repeated. Enclosed in his elegant silence, the therapist occupied the position of an all-powerful person. Simultaneously mother-father, older brother and protective rival, Loewenstein kept the analysis in a relation of stagnation. At that point, the patient began uttering words in order not to say anything, as though the purpose of the representations evoked was to fuel the analysis instead of being served by it. "Today still," wrote Lagache more that thirty years after his therapy, "through the choice of bell-shaped fictions and through a certain insistence in interesting my analyst in them, I reproduce what came to light at the end of my training analysis. That transferential repetition was itself the return of the first objects, cradle and doll, which, since the beginning of my life and at least in the course of my first year, had structured the framework of my life and given 'form' to very archaic experiences of communication and exchange." [152]

That account is quite precious. Compared to those of Abram Kardiner and Marie Bonaparte, it bears witness to the manner in which Loewenstein trained the future masters of the second generation, according to the orthodox criteria of the IPA. Contrary to Freud, Loewenstein remained silent, did not intervene in "the real," and interpreted neither the meaning of dreams nor the "buttress" of the transference nor the problematic of castration. He gave priority to the ego at the expense of the unconscious and attempted to reduce resistances. With Lacan, he was tilting against windmills by prolonging an analysis in which, by his own admission, nothing was happening. With Lagache he played big brother and interrupted their work the moment the patient dreamed he was identifying with Freud. Finally, with Nacht, we do not know what he did except that the patient went to Vienna to complete his training. One cannot overemphasize the fact that the adherence of this brilliant trainer of analysts to the principles of ego psychology began, as if by anticipation, during his Parisian career. Lagache must have perceived what was inadequate in his analysis since, after a supervisory period with Odier, he felt the need for a second analysis with Bouvet, about which he would never speak publicly.

After a first address to the SPP on the work of mourning, Lagache wrote several articles for the *Encyclopédie française,* and later met Freud at the famous reception organized by the princess. In 1939, he was mobilized as a forensic physician. A prisoner at Meursault, he escaped and took up anew, after being demobilized, his position at the University of Strasbourg, which had retreated to Clermont-Ferrand. There he rediscovered his friend Canguilhem. Refusing to serve Pétain, Canguilhem had quit his teaching post, then reassumed his position, at the advice of Cavaillès, while joining in 1940 the active Resistance. Without participating in combat, Lagache assisted certain Jews in hiding or in crossing the line of demarcation. Soon he became director of medico-psychological consultation at the city's general hospital.[153] He organized student apprenticeships, introduced the Rorschach and other tests in his teaching, and revived the term "clinical psychology." Alongside him, Marianne Hossenlop, who would be his third wife, pursued her work in social psychology, concentrating on delinquent gangs which were flourishing in the region. During the year 1941–42, Canguilhem attended Lagache's course and followed his presentations of patients. On a small maroon-colored spiral pad, he took a number of notes. In them may be found the name of Kurt Goldstein, a German neurologist who had emigrated to the United States. Before Merleau-Ponty, Lagache was the first person in France to publicize the works of that eminent specialist. Canguilhem would remember it when he wrote his thesis on the normal and the pathological.[154]

The term "clinical psychology" was used a single time by Freud, in a letter to Fliess on January 30, 1899. "Now," he wrote, "the connection with psychology as presented in the *Studies* [*on Hysteria*] emerges from chaos. I perceive relations with conflict, with life, all that I would like to call clinical psychology." [155] If the psychoanalytic method is based on clinical practice, that practice forgoes direct observation of the patient and interprets symptoms according to what it hears of unconscious discourse. In the context of the pathway blazed by Freud in *Traumdeutung,* no "clinical psychology" could be sustained. Freud did not conceptualize the term, which did not exist in his doctrine. Moreover, the field was being constituted without him under the name of "clinique psychologique." Janet adopted the formula for strategic reasons: It was a matter of withdrawing from medicine the privilege of the doctor's celebrated bedside gaze and of endowing psychological "science" with a "clinical" competence. Based on inquiries and the study of behavior, Janet's analysis refused any attentiveness to the unconscious and rejected structure in favor of functions. In that perspective, hysteria was a toxic illness of hereditary nature and the subject a "psycho-social" totality open to all the winds of eclecticism. Without prejudging the issue, Lacan accepted his principle with a sort of pragmatic naïveté.

Wanting to promote *Laienanalyse*, by way of the University, Lagache proceeded according to the same strategy as his illustrious predecessor: transferring clinical practice into psychology. But unlike Janet and the psychologists of the French tradition, he had come by way of the couch. He was thus obliged to accept the unconscious, sexuality, analytic therapy, repression, etc. And yet he did not make very much of them. Instead of benefiting from the teaching from Vienna and demonstrating, for example, the irreducibility of any psychology to the primacy of unconscious determination, he proceeded along the path of an impossible integration. Since he could not remain a mere disciple of Janet's (for times had changed and that would entail his not being a psychoanalyst), he came to think that the theory of behavior might be adapted to psychoanalytic experience. He then invented a definition of the personality which consists of excluding any unconscious dimension: "In sum," he wrote, "if we strip this definition of its esoteric apparatus, we may provisionally say that psychoanalysis has as its object the total personality in its relations with the world and with itself. Those relations being nothing other than modes of behavior, we may conclude from it that in its spirit, this definition includes psychoanalysis within psychology conceived as the science of the behavior of living beings." [156]

That integration of Freudianism into Janetism, under the umbrella of a vast psychology, sheds light on Lagache's definition of clinical psychology: "In presenting our conception of clinical psychology," he wrote, "we are not merely intent on defining a term whose use has little currency and precision. Our ambition is to show that, in achieving the program of a psychology that is both scientific and applied, clinical psychology reveals itself to be the best instrument, in the human sphere, for a coordination and verification of the various psychological disciplines." [157]

In other words, clinical practice ought to become the instrument of a superior scientificity for psychology in order to ensure the latter's domination over the totality of fields of the "human mind," all tendencies merged. It is the in-depth study of "individual cases," a statement which, theoretically, does not mean anything. Its method rests on three postulates: dynamics, totality, and genesis. The first aims at the investigation of conflicts; the second envisages the unfinished totality of the individual on a Sartrian model; the third seeks to grasp a subject's history in terms of evolution and equilibrium. From those three postulates practical aims are derived. The clinical psychologist cures the sick, teaches children, advises adults, and reclassifies the maladjusted.

Upon returning to Strasbourg in 1945, Lagache participated in the reconstruction of the university, then left for Paris, two years later, to succeed Paul Guillaume to the chair in social psychology at the Sorbonne. He undertook his state doctoral thesis on a subject dear to his heart, *La jalousie amoureuse* ["Jealousy in love"],[158] but did not succeed in writing the third section of the work, which was to be devoted to the psychoanalytic interpretation of the phenomenon. Another sign of his ambivalence: At the Presses universitaires de France he founded a collection destined to bring out Freud's unpublished works and the major texts of the psychoanalytic movement. He first called it "Bibliothèque de psychanalyse et de psychologie clinique," then eliminated the second term, leaving the title "Bibliotheque de psychanalyse." It was at that time that he introduced the notion of "personnologie" in order to designate the "science" resulting from clinical psychology. Its aim was to grasp the interaction among the essential elements of the personality and its overall configuration. Which is to suggest that it would not grasp anything since that "overall configuration" did not exist. This did not prevent him from relying on tests, interviews, prognoses, orientation, all things having nothing to do with either clinical practice or a theory of personality.

In order to complete his strategy, Lagache devoted his inaugural lecture in 1949 to the *Unity of Psychology*.[159] The project would result in a disaster. The author categorized "psychologies" into two tendencies. One he called "naturalist"; it included behaviorism and learning theories, with statistics and experimentalism as their methodological base. The other was related to the "human" and was medical in its clinical practice and phenomenological in its theory. Clinical psychology was part of it and psychoanalysis could find its way within it since it was, according to the author, "ultra-clinical." According to which it has as its object the transference as it appears in the study of behavior.

That curious observation went directly counter to what Freud advanced. Moreover, it pretended to "go beyond" the battles waged for years among the various psychological schools, who had felt harassed by the discovery from Vienna. Lagache worked for peaceful coexistence at a time when there was occurring in France a formidable expansion of psychoanalysis, which precipitated psychology's crisis by accentuating its internal divisions. Was it possible to choose a worse warhorse in a country in which the powerful psychologizing tradition, inspired by neo-Cartesianism, was the principal obstacle to the penetration of Freudian ideas? The question is worth asking. Unfortunately, Lagache did not. In the face of Nacht's policy and against that of the medical schools, he believed he was participating, in the name of psychology, in a major advance of the cause of lay analysis. He was wrong. We have seen that the resistance of medical circles functioned as a symptom of the effective progress of Freud's discovery. Through the Évolution psychiatrique group and thanks to the reconceptualization effected by Henri Ey, Freudianism had taken root in France under the dominance of a medical ethic. Associated with the orthodox tendency of the SPP, that ethic had contributed to the penetration of psychoanalysis at the cost of pitting it against lay analysis. Freud had understood this and supported, against the chauvinist tendency, a policy which he elsewhere had fought. Now the French psychiatrists of the first and second generation revered Janet's person the better to turn away from his teaching. They played "medicine" against psychology. Of Janet's orientation, they retained the psychiatric side while accepting the clinical practice without the psychology. Since Janet had borrowed the term from medicine, they were merely restoring a diagnostic program belonging to them. Lagache reversed the course of events. Against the dynamism to which he in part owed his training, he rethought the unity of psychology under the category of a philosophy of consciousness—one less Hegelian than Sartrian, more Janetian than Politzerian, and less "German" than French.

Instead of separating psychoanalysis from the ideals of medicine, he replaced them with a body of knowledge stemming from psychology. In that perspective, he advised his students not to study medicine and to opt rather for a degree in psychology. He believed he was thus promoting lay analysis. Despite appearances, Lagache's system does not resemble the model of ego psychology. It did not constitute a *revision* of the Viennese theory centered on the primacy of the ego, but an integration of Freudianism into an earlier doctrine. For that reason, his efforts did not give birth to any "dissident" or "orthodox" tendency within the psychoanalytic movement.

Drawing on the works of Kurt Lewin, Lagache infused into social psychology a dose of blue blood. As of 1951, he created a laboratory of the same name whose purpose was the renewal of the former "psychology of social life." Two years later, he promoted the return to experimentalism by assuming the directorship of the Institute of Psychology of the University of Paris. The two tendencies would never be done liquidating the unitary project and rejecting clinical psychology, judged to be too close to psychoanalysis and not "scientific" enough in the sight of the neophysiological or neo-biological model. Thus Lagache gradually lost the unitary battle the more famous he became; in analytic circles he remained a psychologist and among psychologists, he cut the figure of a psychoanalyst.

In 1956, Georges Canguilhem delivered to the Collège philosophique an admirable lecture on psychology, which would be republished ten years later in *Les cahiers pour l'analyse*. While paying homage to his friend Lagache, he torpedoed the whole of his edifice and thus opened the way, for future young Lacanians, to the possibility of an antipsychologizing fight that would reduce Lagache's enterprise to a theoretical naught. He referred to psychology as philosophy less its rigor, ethics less its demands, and medicine without verification. He ended up with the following superb sentence, which would become famous: "It is thus with all due vulgarity that philosophy asks psychology the question: Tell me what you tend toward so that I may know what you are. But the philosopher can also address the psychologist in the form—once does not make a habit—of advice on orientation, and say: When one leaves the Sorbonne by the rue Saint-Jacques, one can climb either up or down; if one climbs up, one approaches the Pantheon, which is the Conservatory of a few great men, but if one climbs down, there is no doubt that one will be heading toward the Prefecture of Police." [160]

Around 1958, starting with a project originating with UNESCO, Lagache launched the vast enterprise of preparing an inventory of Freudian concepts. He drew up a list and devoted his seminar to the question. Two of Lacan's analysands, Jean-Bertrand Pontalis and Jean Laplanche, became interested in the matter. They worked with Lagache, preparing each week the necessary "copy" on which the professor delivered his enlightened opinion. Gradually, they brought to completion the monumental work entitled *Vocabulaire de la psychanalyse,* which would be translated into numerous languages and admired, quite properly, as a model of epistemological rigor.

But at the time of its publication, a conflict erupted between the master and his students. Lagache wanted to have his name alone appear on the cover. The two friends refused and agreed that they were the actual authors of the book. Lagache then demanded a preface and the phrase "under the direction of." He obtained both. "I undertook with Pontalis," Laplanche declared later, "the *Vocabulaire de la psychanalyse* at the behest of Lagache. We read him our articles which he criticized and amended at times, but it was we who furnished the lion's share of the work. Lagache had in fact had the initiative of the project, and in the field of medicine many sponsoring professors sign before their students. . . . Lagache was a great professor without students. It was really dramatic. He had great clinical intuition along with an unabating intellectual rigor and an introverted sensibility." [161]

6   The Great Divide

I. Disagreements

The respective positions of the three masters of the second generation, all analyzed by Loewenstein, reveal the opposing tendencies within the SPP of the 1950s. Favoring an assimilation of Freud's teaching to the ideals of medicine, Nacht recommended the creation of a hierarchical Institute with a rigid pedagogical curriculum. He sought to introduce psychoanalysis into the university while preserving its juridical and moral autonomy. He supported candidates who were physicians and encouraged research into psychosomatic disturbances, but refused to allow the "grand masters" of psychiatry responsibility for running the affairs of the movement. Although he was not the advocate of any doctrinal tendency, neither Kleinianism nor ego psychology, he adopted an attitude in conformity with the internationalist line whose history I have retraced in an earlier volume. His project was thus bound to a classical orthodoxy. He represented an "American-style" defense of a "psychoanalysis of notables" and sustained it with an authoritarian politics suited, in the transference, to his person.

Lagache, for his part, was the promoter of a democratic integration of psychoanalysis into psychology. In his system, which aimed at the integration of Freudianism by way of the university, psychological knowledge occupied the same place as the medical ideal did for Nacht. The two men had in common a respect for the established order, a cult of adaptation, and a submission to institutional models alien to the Freudian ethic. Little influenced by the tradition of the hospitals, Lagache remained above all a professor. As a good moralist, he preferred, to any authoritarian project, a politics of tolerance based on communication between professors and students. He thus represented within the SPP a liberal tendency hostile to Nacht's autocratic trend. That liberalism did not go so far as to call into question the rules imposed by the IPA. He aimed at adapting them to the new French situation. The antagonism between the two tendencies bore on the mode of institutionalization of psychoanalysis. It did not allow for a redefinition of the strictly Freudian conditions of an improved instruction. At most, it was a matter, in the two cases, of organizing a mass society in conformity with already existent orders and without taking into account a politics of psychoanalysis articulated with a theory of the unconscious.

Freud had approached that thorny problem when, in 1907, he dissolved the first Viennese group. He then founded a "psychoanalytic society" and not an "association of psychoanalysts." In other words, psychoanalysts were to organize around a "common cause." The bond uniting them was based on an ethic that neglected the imaginary relations among members of the group. The society's purpose was the defense of a theory, that of the unconscious, and not the support of a group of therapists in their professional demands. They recognized each other because they were working for a "cause," but the society's function was not to facilitate a lateral recognition among members of a clan in order to better guarantee the exercise of their egos. Such was the program of a politics of psychoanalysis centered on the theory of the unconscious. The position was not false in itself, but it led to the disastrous results with which we are familiar. Moreover, Freud accepted the position of founding father, but refused that of political leader. Whence his situation as a "master without command," which led him to leave the management of the affairs of the empire to his disciples.

The history of psychoanalytic societies reveals something unprecedented: The more one favors the emergence of a democratic power founded on a respect for the ideas of individuals, the more one tends to eradicate the work of the unconscious. One ends up supporting a guarantee for the ego, that is, an associative guild mentality, to the detriment of a theoretical struggle intent on decentering the position of the subject. In point of fact, democracy is bound to a concept of freedom in eminent contradiction with Freud's discovery, which maintains that men are subject to a destiny that eludes them and which therapy allows them only partially to uncover. If one restricts oneself to that theory, it is impossible to create an association of psychoanalysts, respectful of the ego's "freedom," without simultaneously liquidating the doctrine it is supposed to be defending. At the other extreme, one should not yield to autocracy. Indeed, the more one is absorbed by the passion for a cause, the greater the risks of dogmatism, and the less one ends up favoring new experiences. Against a guarantee for the ego, one then ends up with a cult of the master, or with the ardor of a mystic, which amounts to replacing the illusory freedom of individual speech with a religious adherence to the imaginary person of a leader or a cause. To date, no psychoanalytic society has managed to resolve that insoluble contradiction, but neither has any conceded that the contradiction is insoluble from the perspective of the discovery of the unconscious.

In France, only Lacan would succeed in implementing, for sixteen years, an institution entirely democratic in its modes of functioning, but nonetheless centered on a quasi-"religious" relation to his person and his doctrine. The ephemeral character of that experiment, which would end with the death of its master, well demonstrates the existence of that contradiction, since it required a "great leader" to dare to run the risk of true democracy and to attempt, in spite of everything, to avoid the illusions connected with the "freedom" of the self. But at what a cost!

After Freud's death, the IPA took on increasingly the aspect of a mass organization that was both tolerant, since it admitted diverging tendencies, and autocratic, since it submitted their coexistence to respect for a common rule based on adhesion to a single mode of "technical" training. In order to avoid chaos, and to protect against secessionism and dissidence, the IPA resolved the insoluble contradiction born of Freud's discovery by promoting, at the cost of a frenzied insistence on technique, an imaginary democracy of guilds and an illusory autocracy of local leaders. The barons of the movement had the right to give their approval to a tendency on the condition that it not jeopardize the pragmatic unity of the empire—that is, the principles of didactic training, the only site of its centralizing power. Since it was impossible to do truly innovative work while sparing the sacrosanct technique, the empire created by Freud resembled in the 1950s a paper tiger in a porcelain shop.

In that context, Lagache's academic liberalism was as acceptable to the leadership of the IPA as Nacht's medical autocratism. The first agreed with something of an "English line," the second was better adapted to American positions. Thus the first split, in which those two policies were pitted against each other, did not result in an actual break of the French community with the international movement. There was room within the latter for the two tendencies, even if the masters representing them did not give their name to any coherent doctrine.

Lacan's position was quite different. Having broached before the war an implicit return to Freud, our hero became aware of the need for an organization of the training experience that would conform to the principles of Freud's discovery. He rejected neither the university nor the medical channel, but insisted that each be dependent on the primacy of a politics of psychoanalysis. He did not hesitate to take the role of a legislator or a commander in chief, thus confronting the contradictory reality of a democracy and an autocracy.

Freud suffered from the complexes of a Viennese Jew. He sought to "surpass his father" in order to accede to a different culture, while remaining faithful to his origins. His personal history traverses that of his theory. Lacan was quite different. Emerging from a narrowly Catholic tradition, he fashioned for himself, in conformity with his aspirations, the aspect of a *grand bourgeois*. He bought his clothes from the best tailors of the Right Bank, addressed certain of his intimates in the formal— *vous*—mode, had his hair cut at home, and stayed in the most luxurious hotels when traveling. He wanted to be his own master, being in his own eyes the son of no one. No biographical instance traverses his written work, which is entirely oriented toward a quest for unconscious truth. From the outset, Lacan held the position of command which Freud had lacked: Themistocles at Salamis.

Two texts of juridical inspiration express the Lacanian position within the SPP: One deals with the preparation of training analysts, the other with counseling of children.[1] Lacan recognized the value of medical studies and university degrees, but maintained that a psychoanalyst ought to be an *"honnête homme,"* a gentleman in the French classical sense—a cultivated bourgeois, elegant, sympathetic, well educated, curious, and above all not psychotic. He considered the training analysis to be a "personal ordeal," required that therapy last a minimum of four years, and affirmed the necessity of two supervisory or control analyses, to be conducted by titular members other than the training analyst. In addition, he established a theoretical (and not merely hierarchical) distinction between "adhering" and "titular" members. The first was one who had satisfied the requisites of training; the second had shown himself capable of transmitting the experience of therapy in the course of a training analysis. Lacan made access to "titular" rank dependent on a supplement, an *"en plus,"* namely, a doctrinal function that would not be extrinsic to the transferential relation but delimited by it. Acquisition of diplomas and recognition by universities were necessary but not sufficient from the perspective of a teaching defined by the Freudian criterion of personal dependence. Titular rank would be that through which psychoanalytic knowledge was transmitted. The training analyst would be a theoretician of therapy since technical training governs theoretical intelligence.

Through that rule, the SPP was tending to become authentically a *psychoanalytic society* ruling an *association of psychoanalysts*. It guaranteed a right to the exercise of a profession on the basis of an ability to acquire or transmit an expertise, without that right having priority over that ability: The ego was not master in the Freudian household.

On the subject of men and women counseling children, Lacan's procedure was identical. He included in their training a curriculum of Lagache's type without integrating Freudian doctrine into psychology: "If psychoanalysis," he wrote, "is neither the only psychotherapy, nor applicable to all cases, it alone has brought a general theory of psychotherapies and ensures the psychotherapist satisfactory preparation whose basis is the training analysis. What is true of psychotherapy in general is no less the case for the psychotherapy of children. All those who choose that path should thus be analyzed as completely as possible, by a qualified analyst and under the conditions of a didactic or training analysis." [2]

Under the program urgently defined by that regulation, counselors had every chance of one day becoming child analysts. Lacan took the occasion to recall the impropriety of the term, even as he retained its use: "It was in adults that the meaning-laden relations which have revolutionized our idea of the child were discovered, before being verified by new observations and by therapeutic and even pedagogical applications of unexpected extent. In order to maintain in its accuracy the fruitful path of Freud's thought, one need barely modify a sentence of Aristotle's, who says that it is not necessary to question how the child's soul takes pity, learns, or thinks, but rather man *with* the soul of the child." [3]

It was thus to a new orthodoxy different from Nacht's that Lacan's project was bound. In principle, that project partook neither of a defense of the eminent (the "notables") nor of a politics of autocracy, but of the relation of a theory to a "pure technique" (the training analysis), which respected the register of personality while dodging none of its antinomies. In that perspective, the training analysis took on new value at the expense of the therapeutic analysis without the problem of their unity or difference being raised.

Lacan was thus the first master of the second generation to bestow on the French movement a *politics of psychoanalysis* articulated with a theory of training. His procedure was of the same order as Henri Ey's in the organization of the field of psychiatry: a militant commitment combined with a doctrinal reconceptualization. And yet things were not that simple.

Until 1952, the Commission on Instruction had played the role that would subsequently fall to the Institute. It unburdened the SPP of its teaching function, selected candidates, chose a program, defined titles and attributions, and was responsible for the naming of adhering and titular members. It was not an organism independent of the Society, but allowed for a separation between a legislative power, which was its province, and an executive power, conferred upon the titular members of the SPP. What was at stake was an organization of the movement in which the administrative apparatus was not confused with the teaching institution that gave it its orientation. That organization respected—without resolving—the contradiction born of Freud's discovery: The executive guaranteed the free association of individuals and their professional recognition, while the commission ensured the reign of an unconscious determinism based on a transferential relation which prevented the ego from believing itself master in its own household.

In December 1949, Nacht brought a modification of the statutes of the SPP to a vote. He acknowledged the creation of the commission and of its legislative existence. He emphasized that the SPP "has delegated its authority to a commission on instruction which is responsible for a selection of candidates, which defines, according to the classical technical norms, the conditions of regular training and supervises their implementation in each case. This commission functions in accordance with the forms registered by an internal regulation."[4]

In 1926, the commission on instruction did not exist. The recruitment of members occurred through a secret vote by the founders. A candidate for titular rank had to have completed his training analysis whereas an adhering member was under no such obligation. One could be named titular member without having been an adhering member. Nevertheless, and with the exception of Lagache, most of the therapists of the second generation had been adhering members before becoming titular, and had been analyzed for at least six months before becoming adherents. The creation of an Institute in 1934 did not transform that situation. Financed by Marie Bonaparte, it functioned parallel to the SPP and no modification of the statutes was necessary.

The 1949 change rectified all this. Nacht introduced the status of "associate member" that had previously been rejected by Pichon. The existence of that rank made any new "Hartmann affair" impossible. The society could welcome to its midst foreign colleagues on the condition that they were members of an association affiliated with the IPA. The recruitment of titular and adhering members was also transformed. The former were chosen from among the latter, and the latter were obliged, in order to be elected, to have received training from a titular member. Naturally, only titular members had the right to vote for the election of another titular member or a new adhering member.

Nacht's modifications ratified the creation of the commission and received the approbation of the body of titular members. Through them, approval had been accorded to psychoanalysis in its modern form, that is, with a theoretical separation between the training analysis and therapeutic treatment.

Before the war, things had proceeded in an artisan-like way. The pioneers of the movement had aimed as much at a career as at an adventure. They chose their analysts on the basis of a personal affinity and among a limited number of therapists, all titular members or in the process of becoming so. The difference between therapeutic and didactic or training analyses did not have a theoretical status—all "patients" were potential analysts and all analysts were former "patients." The SPP resembled a madhouse, for one had to be mad to want to become a psychoanalyst.

After the new regulations, which ratified an expanding situation, only the training analysis was recognized as a formative instrument. Each candidate to the rank of adhering member was obliged to receive the commission's approval in order to have the right to enter treatment that was "valid as training." In order to obtain that approval, he paid visits to the members of the commission, who met and decided whether or not to accept his candidacy. If the applicant was deemed to be severely neurotic, a pervert, or a psychotic, that is, really "sick," there was a considerable chance that the response would be negative. If it was positive—without, however, it being revealed on what basis—the candidate's duty was to select an analyst from among the titular members of the SPP. The commission thereupon consigned responsibility for the requested training to the titular member. He in turn encouraged his patient to take the course and seminars recommended by the commission and the patient committed himself to not taking the title of psychoanalyst before being authorized by his election as an adhering member. The training analyst would allow him at the proper time to conduct a first analysis under supervision, then a second one, on the condition that his permission be ratified by the members of the commission. The future adherent then became a *stagiaire,* a probationer. He had the right to present his candidacy to the SPP by writing an original work on a clinical subject—a kind of master's thesis. After having heard the opinion of his three tutors (the training analyst and two supervisors), the society voted on the admission of the candidate at the rank of adhering member. At the end of a more or less long period, he would be recruited as a titular member by the other titular members.

Let us translate the regulation into its underlying absurdity: Anyone has the right to be analyzed by an adhering member. But since an adhering member does not have the right to conduct training analyses without being named a titular member, the patient who chooses him has the right only to be sick. Should the idea occur to him to become an analyst, he must leave the adhering member's couch for that of a titular member (with the approval of the commission). In other words, adhering members are condemned to analyze the "sick," and titular members future adhering members judged not to be sick by the commission. In theory, the situation was insane since it is clear that the value of therapy is not amenable to such a criterion. But in practice, it favored a controlled rise of the analytic profession, a veritable policy of birth control.

The regulations drafted by Lacan in the context of a reorganization of the SPP thus responded to Nacht's intention and integrated the principles in force in all the societies run by the IPA. Even if he reestablished the primacy of a Freudian ethic at the cost of a guild organization, he ran the risk of making the former dependent on the latter through a meshing of their roles. In reality, the separation between the commission and the SPP, that is, between teaching and administration, remained a pure illusion. Moreover, the distinction in rank between adhering and titular members tended to coincide with hierarchical functions unrelated to theoretical attributions. Under such a system, it was always the same individuals, titular members and physicians, who everywhere occupied the same leadership roles. This is testified to, if testimony be needed, by the distribution of tasks and titles in 1951. In the SPP, we find Marie Bonaparte (honorary president), Nacht (president), Lacan (vice-president), Lagache (assessor), Bouvet (treasurer), Pasche (secretary), and, for the commission, Nacht (president), as well as Bouvet, Lacan, Parcheminey, Lagache, Schlumberger, Pasche. A remarkable case of centralization!

The disagreement among the masters erupted at a time when the long-cherished project of an Institute of Psychoanalysis, whose function was to absorb the former commission, had reached fruition. Since it was to have its own statutes, independent of those of the society, the inevitable problem of the autonomy of the new commission in the face of the new administrative power arose.

For some time already, a rumor had been circulating among the ranks of the SPP: Lacan refused to comply with the prevailing rules on technique. Without practicing as yet what would later be called the *short session,* he would interrupt in his own manner his patients' discourse. He was implementing a kind of technique called the *session of variable length.* Some of his patients were stretched out longer than others, and certain others found themselves dismissed after ten or fifteen minutes.

In the regulations of 1949, no mention is made of a therapist's obligation to respect a fixed span of time for his sessions. And yet it had been agreed for twenty years in the IPA that training analyses should last at least four years, with three, four, or five sessions of at least fifty minutes each week. That practice applied to therapeutic as well as training analyses, but since the formation of therapists was the object of rigorous regulation, it was through the training analysis that the society's control over its members was exercised. Training analysts adhered to an implicit, though never theorized rule, which fixed the length of each session at three-quarters of an hour. Pressed to the extreme, that tradition gives the following result: At the agreed hour, the therapist springs from his seat like a Jack-in-the-box and interrupts the patient in the middle of a sentence or a silence. Such an act is without interpretative meaning, and such a technique runs the risk of totalitarianism. In point of fact, it takes no account of human differences or of clinical realities. A chatterbox is not the same as a taciturn individual: an hysteric is not an obsessive; a pervert is not a psychotic, and even if everything is connected with everything else, each subject entertains with the temporality of his discourse an idiosyncratic relation that is a function of his psychic structure or simply of his way of being. A rule is necessary, but if it functions in order to maintain the rule, it becomes incongruous.

And yet the tradition has its reasons for being. After the era of the movement's pioneers, what was at stake was limiting the imaginary omnipotence of clinical practitioners within a framework both technical and transferential. The rule's purpose was to oblige the masters to think of being nothing more than "notables," eminent practitioners. The patient paid and had a right to a fixed span of discourse, even if he spent the time speaking in order not to say anything or in remaining silent. So much for technique. On the analytic level, matters were unclear. It was thought that by reducing the imaginary omnipotence of training analysts, one would allow the negative transference to become a positive one and vice versa. Thus analysis would come to an end in the best conditions possible. The reductive will was translated in the medium of facts by actual limitations. If the proper functioning of a society required that the training analysts be equals among themselves, that meant that no titular member had the right to train more students than his neighbor. Otherwise, he would become the leader of a school and would no longer be a (mere) notable. A second variant: if no titular member had the right to exploit an adhering member by earning more money than any other titular member, that meant that all training analysts had the obligation to enrich themselves in accordance with their competence, degrees, and curriculum vitae: for equal work, equal fees. It did not work, to be sure, but such was the rule.

I described in a previous volume how Freud trained his first disciples, and thereafter the "foreigners" who came to Vienna after 1920. Not only did he make no distinction between training and therapeutic analyses, but he was unaware of the very principle of such a difference. And quite properly so. In general, his analyses were short and his sessions long: six months for some, an hour for others, at a rate of five or six per week. Freud did not bend to comply to any of the technical rules that would be formulated by his successors. He did not hesitate to give expression to the difficulties of his counter-transference, played the fortune teller, did not separate his clinical position from his theoretical ear and his place as founding father. Like an aged Jewish matchmaker, he adored marrying off, unmarrying, remarrying, or serving as witness at the wedding. He accepted couples in analysis, suggesting that one member replace the other if the first had missed a session. He prescribed contraceptives, loaned books, gave and received gifts, recommended theatrical performances, gave compliments on attire, and did not hesitate to leave the room if he felt the need to urinate. Not a trace of frivolous seductiveness, but a passion for the unconscious. Countless paradoxes: In his view, lasting therapeutic successes were based on the confidence the patient continued to have in his analyst, beyond the span of his therapy, or in other words, on an unresolved positive transference. Another matter on which he insisted: He thought that the best conditions for analysis are to be found precisely where it is unnecessary—in an individual in good health. And yet Freud healed, analyzed, removed symptoms, invested his genius in clinical practice.[5]

On certain points, Lacan's technique resembled Freud's, but the historical situation of the man in the French movement was not the same as that of the Viennese in the IPA. In the eyes of his colleagues of the second generation, Lacan was not a founder nor an innovator nor the leader of a school. At the very most, he was a brilliant theoretician. In any event, an equal. He did not have the right, as Freud did previously, to be an exception and was expected to conform to the common rule. Lacan did not see matters in that light and thought himself different from the others. Without yet taking himself for Lacan, he knew he was superior to the men of his generation. In order to benefit from the actual status of a master, he would have to create an audience for himself by training students won over to his cause. In other words, he sought less to turn out "notables" than to infuse new blood into an experiment whose guide he would be. He thus insisted on the difference between "pure technique," or the training analysis, and therapeutic treatment. In his eyes, the renewal of Freudianism would take place by way of a new importance attributed to the training analysis, the sole means of creating a circle of disciples in the image of the Vienna of years gone by.

By temperament as well as by doctrinal impulse, he had a sovereign contempt for the standard rule. Lacan behaved like a monarch constrained to obey in spite of himself an egalitarian principle unsuited to himself. His own way of questioning routine and conformity lay in practicing the variable-length session. On three occasions, he spoke on the subject before the SPP. The first lecture dated from December 1951, the second from June 1952, and the third from February 1953. All three remain unpublished. According to witnesses, Lacan justified the liberties he had been taking by maintaining that analytic material in therapy acted as a system of defense. According to him, the reduction of the length of sessions as well as their less frequent rhythm had an effect of frustration and interruption whose action was beneficial for the patient. It was a matter of dialecticizing the transferential relation by cutting it short on selected significant words in such manner as to restimulate the expression of unconscious desire.[6]

Such a technique is perfectly valid if it is not transformed into a rule of short sessions. It implies a break with the deadening and congealing effect of a fixed ritual of timed sessions. And yet a love for money and social ambition played a considerable role in the reduction of the length of sessions. The more students came to him, the more Lacan wanted to have students; the richer he got, the more he liked the sight of cash. In that respect, he was no different from Nacht, who also liked having students and money, and who, while respecting the standard time restriction, asked exorbitant fees of his patients. Both men, moreover, gradually became as rich as each other. Lagache was the exception, without for all that being a better clinical practitioner than they. Belonging to the academic guild, he did not have the financial ambitions of the representatives of the liberal professions. Money was not for him a medium through which to gain recognition, he himself having emerged from a bourgeois family of the provinces. He was not fearful of lacking, like Lacan, nor did he come, like Nacht, from a world of ruined peasants. There was thus in Lacan's way of proceeding a fusion between an individual temperament and a theory of therapy. Lacan reduced the length of sessions because he liked money and recognition, but he also reduced them because he thought that such mobility responded to a doctrinal necessity of the first importance.

The time reduction was not the only source of strain. There was to be found in Lacan's practice a freedom that characterized Freud's own. It did not focus on the same objects, but betrayed the same refusal to conform. Lacan received people at any hour, occasionally without appointment. At midnight, he was capable of picking up his phone and complaining to a patient of the harshness of his colleagues. At the same hour, he might listen at exaggerated length to a sufferer from anxiety whom he would dismiss the next day after fifteen minutes. He could eat an entire meal during a session, make a show of being rushed, pace back and forth, emit a few grunts, utter an enigmatic comment or sit down at his desk to finish off an article. He intervened in divorces and marriages; took families in analysis; recommended psychiatric internment if he detected a danger of suicide; visited a patient convalescing from an operation; asked for addresses he was in need of; asked people to perform chores for him; demanded that all be present at his seminar, where their therapy continued; and occasionally measured a patient's blood pressure without anyone knowing why. If a student protested, he would reply in an inimitable voice, "But, *mon cher,* it doesn't interfere with my listening in the slightest." It was impossible to distinguish in his case the transferential role from the public one. Lacan mixed every register and spoke at his seminar as he spoke in private. Same words, same punctuation, same intonation.

Between 1947 and 1960, he trained the finest exemplars of the third French analytic generation. Some would remain his disciples, others would leave him with the violence demanded by their own personal needs. During that period, sessions lasted between ten and forty minutes, supervisory sessions a bit longer.

Let us record at this point the words of a few witnesses.

Didier Anzieu: "I was analyzed in order to become a psychoanalyst. I wanted to choose Lagache, but I was preparing my thesis on Freud's self-analysis under his direction, so it wasn't possible. I had heard Lacan at the École normale supérieure. He had come to deliver a curious lecture on identification. He had brought two glass tubes in each one of which was a migratory locust, one living alone, the other in a collective cloud. He showed us the morphological changes effected in the animal by life in common. He already possessed an instinctive sense of group effects and their production. I began my analysis with him on January 1, 1949. When he learned I was a Normalien, he immediately accepted me. I paid a very low fee and went to him three times a week for sessions lasting between thirty and forty minutes each. I engaged him in a positive and intense paternal transference, which allowed me to speak to him at length and with relief of things I had never told anyone. After two years of work, the analytic framework began to unravel. The length of sessions dropped to twenty minutes. The waiting room was full of persons worried at whether or not they would be received. Lacan opened the door, designated the chosen one, who returned to cross the room ten or fifteen minutes later on his way out. . . . When my turn came, at times he would signal me to come, at others he would take me by the arm and ask me to come back later. Emitting a deep sigh, he would confess to me, as to a friend, that he was overwhelmed, that he had been obliged to make an unexpected appointment, confront a difficult case, leading me to believe that such was not my case, that I could thus come by later and he was sure I understood. All this reinforced my narcissism, which really didn't need it, and made it difficult for me to formulate my criticism, that is, a negative transference without which a psychoanalysis is not complete. In the beginning I was flattered to be thus put on equal footing; then I regressed. At a lecture at the SPP, it was said that he suffered from verbosity. I mentioned this in a session, and he asked me for names. I refused to answer, but I did give one. He answered that coming from that person, it was no surprise. Then he asked me to come to his seminar although I did not want to. I was about to suggest that mixing instruction and therapy was perhaps counterindicated, but he anticipated my objection, emphasizing that at my stage, the problem no longer existed. "I ended my analysis during the summer of 1953 with a last disillusionment. He invited me to have my training analysis validated by the commission on instruction. Then he warned me that when I went to see it, I should be careful about what I told them. I looked at him in perplexity and he told me that it was in my interest not to say anything about the shortening of sessions. He added that I had regressed and that it had done me the greatest good. I hadn't noticed anything at all, and the sky came crashing down on my head. My treatment had been an analysis, but there had been too much seduction. My fear of hereditary psychopathology had been dissipated. I was able to write and to be a father. But my angers were not analyzed. The complexity of my relation to a maternal imago split into an ideal mother and a persecutory mother remained untouched. A more psychoanalytic meditation on my self led me to discover, with the help of Anna Freud's book, *The Ego and the Mechanisms of Defence,* which had just appeared in French, that a whole series of defense mechanisms had lost their force and that I now had at my disposal a surplus of freed-up energy. Lacan believed that I owed him that self-awareness acquired in extremis. He asked me for my notes: He wanted to publish them. In making him the false promise of sending them to him once I had drawn them up in final form, for the first and last time, I found myself inwardly laughing at him. "It was in my second analysis with Georges Favez that I was able to 'work through' all that. His Swiss robustness, his great inner availability, his firmness in putting his finger on my errors in self-understanding, the abundance and the pertinence of his interpretations concerning my early Oedipal conflicts reconciled me with my mother's love and allowed me to forge the few new ideas with which I believe I have enriched the field of psychoanalysis. In the meanwhile, I had chosen to become a psychologist. It was necessary for me, in a certain solitude, to assume the fact of being one. The third or fourth version of my perpetually unfinished autobiography then began as follows: 'I am one of the unloved, a son of unloved parents. . . .'"

Xavier Audouard: "I had a first period of analysis with Lacan from 1958 to 1962. I had been a Jesuit since 1943. The sessions lasted about twenty minutes. Few interpretations, but interventions which led to decisions. When I decided to leave the Company of Jesus, Lacan did everything he could to stop me. He said that in marriage, my superego would be worse than in the Church. That allowed me to abandon my robe and to make a decision on my own. Lacan taught me that actions taken tend to go unrecognized. The shorter sessions allowed me to avoid obsessionalizing my therapy. I resumed my analysis with him from 1965 to 1969."

Robert Pujol: "It was Hesnard who advised me to come do my analysis in Paris, since he knew that if I had done it with him, it would not be deemed valid. He entrusted me with a letter of recommendation for Nacht, Lacan, and Ey. During my round of visits, it was Lacan who attracted me the most. He asked me what I was reading and I spoke to him of a book by Mariani about the limits of the notion of the object. He told me that I interested him. I had been told that he charged ten francs, and he charged me twenty, declaring that given my position, it was not expensive.

"The sessions lasted about a quarter of an hour. I didn't have to wait and there were few in his waiting room. I absolutely did not have the impression that the sessions were long or short. They suited me well. My analysis made a different man of me. I was transformed. Lacan had an exceptional presence, a devoted, attentive, and sustained manner of listening. He sat at first in an armchair behind me, then to the left in front of the window.

"At the end of my analysis in 1953, when the institutional problems arose, his sessions lasted a half-hour. Then he began to intervene about reality. One day I dreamed that I was hooked to a facade and he told me that it was the facade of the rue Saint-Jacques. I obeyed his wishes and the whole question for me during the splits was that of loyalty to Lacan. At the Rome congress, I decided to stop my analysis. I told him about it. He didn't answer. I conducted an analysis under his supervision."

Jean-Paul Valabrega: "I began an analysis with Lacan after Parcheminey's death. My sessions lasted about a half hour and my therapy about seven years. Lacan moved about, did not sit in a chair, at times gazed at me. The analysis took place on a level that was more initiatic than technical. Lacan would not tolerate my not coming to his seminar. I don't have the feeling of having undergone analysis with him, but he had an extraordinary gift: the capacity to listen in the other to something *other*. I did not approve of the sessions of variable length. After that experience, I underwent several other analyses, since I believe like Freud that an analyst ought to be in permanent training."

Octave Mannoni: I spent twenty years in Madagascar, from 1925 to 1945, as an ethnologist and the director general of the information service. In 1947, I was trying to undergo analysis, and I chose Lacan's couch on the advice of the brother of Jacques Baron. At the first session, Lacan took my blood pressure. At the time, sessions lasted three quarters of an hour. He remained silent, but occasionally made some good interventions. He should be compared to Dali or Buñuel. He had the same ambition of becoming rich and famous. I had the impression that he was playing at being an analyst. Then the sessions began being less long. After an interruption, I began again in 1952. Everything had changed. There was a domestic. The sessions became shorter. Lacan didn't prevent me from undergoing psychoanalysis, but I wasn't interested in it since, in Madagascar, I had cured myself of an obsessional neurosis. I understood, moreover, why Rimbaud had cured himself in the desert. Dislocation can do the job of analysis. Being a white man among the blacks is like being an analyst among the whites."

Anne-Lise Stern: "I did an analysis with Lacan, the third time around, after a first one with Bouvet, then with Dolto. At the time it was apparently quite difficult to speak of the extermination camps in analysis since I was obliged to dream simultaneously of the 'camps' and of 'Lacan.' Lacan alone was capable of hearing about it, and of the German language as well. As a result, I immediately stopped dreaming about them. When I brought letters, photos, objects, tales of deportation, or texts of my father, Lacan took them and was interested in them. I told him of my previous analyses. Very quickly, he said, 'What you need is a disanalysis.' I ended my analysis by dreaming that I was throwing all the books and objects in Lacan's office out the window. At the very end, there was only myself. I said that it was a dream of the end of analysis and he said that he agreed."

Rosine Lefort: "I began my analysis with Lacan around Easter in 1950, sent by Jenny Aubry. I had spent several years in a sanatorium, away from the world. I had read a lot, but was no longer capable of leading my life. Lacan took in all that. I knew neither his thesis nor his articles and I learned everything in my analysis and in my practice at Parent-de-Rosan. I went to Lacan's place six times a week. He modulated time and space; the sessions were of variable length, and above all, he was willing to tolerate my not saying a word, that is, a burden of reality. I insisted that he speak since I was horrified at not being able to speak; but he said to me, 'If I speak, you won't tolerate it, and if I don't speak, you won't either.' In point of fact, he spoke a lot. One day, in a state of distress, I told him I had died layer by layer, and he answered me, 'Well, what do you need!'

"That difficult period lasted eight months. Lacan was not there as Lacan; what he said came from elsewhere as happened for me with children, and what I did with them had nothing to do with an 'ego.' At one point I could no longer go to my sessions. Analysis with children had taken the place of my horror in the transference. Children for me were not children, but subjects: There was no 'child psychoanalysis.' I left several transcripts of sessions with the 'wolf child' to Gloria, who conveyed them to Lacan. But in my sessions we never spoke of them.

"One of the most forceful moments of my analysis came when I recounted a visual hallucination in which there appeared a silhouette with a cap framed by a window in my bedroom. It brought me to a childhood memory. Lacan asked me, 'Do you see through it?' I realized, thirty years later, the importance those three signifiers had for me. The 'you' referred me to the Other that I was in Nadia's analysis and to the alleged knowledge of that Other in which I learned that the fall of the object between the signifying pair S1-S2, 'Nadia-Mama,' constituted a subject. The 'see' had to do with the scopophilia of the wolf child when he confused himself with the object he gave me to see. The 'through' was opposed to the opaqueness of the real object which was a double for Marie-Françoise.

"In 1952, I went to join Robert in the United States, where I worked at a center at which I observed, not without astonishment, how a young obese person under treatment was given a dozen slices of toast in order not to frustrate him. In my analysis with Lacan, and with Nadia, I had learned the role of lack as an essential axis for every analysis.

"I subsequently resumed therapy with Lacan in 1976 for personal reasons. I had the same rhythm, without any 'flash sessions.' I said to him, 'Tell me something,' and he answered, 'Give me some time.' I derived from the experience the fact that the ego is very little in the face of the destitution of the subject. To the very end, Lacan's manner of listening remained the same. He was tired, but never 'non-speaking,' and always present. I went to see him three times a week, and I had an appointment in September 1981 when he died. I brought him at that time the case of Marie-Françoise in order to ask him whether I could use the term 'double' in speaking of her relation to objects, as I had previously; he answered me, 'In those days, you could not have been wrong.' "[7]

So much for the rumors about sessions of varying lengths, which the members of the SPP called "short sessions."

The technique pleased no one. In the eyes of his colleagues, Lacan was accepting too many training analyses and making students out of his patients. It was feared lest he become a master, without any inquiry into what motivated so many students to rush to his couch. His theoretical and clinical position was reduced to a "charismatic power" that was deemed to be nefarious. Thus within the battle waged by the partisans of Lagache and those of Nacht, Lacan's practice was an object of permanent contestation. It was not the focus of the principal conflict, but it played a preponderant role in the distribution of alliances. In 1951, the commission on instruction demanded of Lacan a solemn promise to regularize his situation. He gave his assurance, but continued to make use of his technique. When Nacht invited him to explain matters before the titular members, he interpreted that request as freeing him from his previous vow. Finally, a promise was extricated from him in which he agreed to conform to the norms: a minimum of twelve months for treatment; three sessions per week of three-quarters of an hour each. Lacan promised and urged his analysands to "lie" to the commission. Whence the irritation of some of them, their revulsion both at the questions asked them and the bluff expected of them. No one paid any attention to the theoretical reasons invoked by Lacan and no one accepted the "role" he enjoyed playing. Lagache wrote that everyone was in agreement in rejecting his technique, but as a good liberal, he defended the right of anyone to innovate. Whence his hesitation waltz: At times he accepted Lacan's practice, in the name of the novelty of experimentation, and at times he defended the point of view of normalization. In point of fact, he could not tolerate the growing influence of a man whose renown he envied.

Nacht was much clearer. He sought to impose the submission of all to his authority and to the established rules. As for Marie Bonaparte, she reasoned like a brigadier general leading her troops on with a whip. Her hostility toward Lacan had turned into hatred. In 1945, in a letter to Loewenstein, she called him paranoid,[8] and in 1953, she rejected outright the request to the commission by three of his students for supervision.[9] Lacan, for his part, did not spare the princess, and transmitted his opinion to Loewenstein. "To be sure," he wrote, "it may be thought that the activities of the individual have always been deleterious in our group. The social prestige she represents can but falsify relations. What she derives from her role with Freud allows her to be listened to by all with a patience that takes on the appearance of approval. The respect due an old lady brings with it a tolerance for her opinions which is demoralizing the young in whose eyes we appear to be in a state of ridiculous subjection."[10] He was not wrong, but when one knows what Loewenstein thought of his former analysand, and when one is apprised of his relations with Marie, it becomes clear that his task was not an easy one. He was receiving by letter, in New York, the griefs of two adversaries of which one was incapable of announcing her retirement and the other was on the verge of becoming the scapegoat of the entire society. Lacan paid homage to Lagache's courage and honesty (it would not last) and revealed a certain clairvoyance on the subject of Nacht: "I should render Nacht the fairness of observing that he has never diverged nor flinched in the pursuit of his design. And that if he continues to group around him a majority of our former colleagues, he owes it to a consistency in his policies that would be worthy of respect had it not been pursued no less consistently by the most unscrupulous means."[11]

On the evening of June 17, 1952, Nacht launched the first wave of an offensive that would last a year and end with a clamorous split. With the support of his lieutenants, he proposed to elect for a term of five years a directorial committee responsible for the affairs of the new Institute of Psychoanalysis. He immediately offered his own candidacy for the presidency, and brought off, by a hand vote, the election of Maurice Benassy and Serge Lebovici as scientific secretaries. One more roll of the drum, and Henry Sauguet was chosen for the position of administrative secretary. Sauguet was not yet an adhering member, but he was entirely devoted to his patron's cause. By then, Nacht had hoarded all of the leadership functions: He reigned at the head of a phantom SPP and at the summit of an Institute which was about to receive full power.

In November 1952, the titular members, feeling duped, awakened and perceived the coup d'état. Nacht distributed the new statutes as well as the anticipated curriculum of instruction. Everything was to be voted on, then discussed with due rapidity in order to assure the committee's control over the Institute and the commission functioning under it. The announced ambition was to obtain official recognition for a diploma of psychoanalysis reserved for physicians, categorized under the rubric of "neurobiology" and defined as a branch of scientific activity useful to medicine.[12] The administrative secretary introduced the idea that in order to facilitate negotiations with the state, it would be advisable to extend Nacht's term as president of the SPP. Clamorous protestation. Lebovici read the program of courses and invited the members of the administrative council to approve it. They objected that they had been trapped by not having been given the relevant documents sufficiently in advance. Nacht declared himself prepared to discuss matters, but refused to answer questions.

The program assigned him the role of king. Three annual cycles were planned: "General Theory of Psychoanalysis," "Clinical Practice of Psychoanalysis," and "Psychoanalytic Technique." Nacht reserved for himself the terminal cycle, arrogating to himself alone the activities of the third year. Lacan's seminar was reserved for the first year and scheduled at the same time as Lagache's, which was also recommended for the first year.[13] As a protector of nonphysicians, Marie Bonaparte saw red. With Odette Codet and Parcheminey, she sided with the liberal faction, in which Lagache had assembled Berge, Françoise Dolto, Juliette Boutonier, who had just married Georges Favez, and Blanche Reverchon-Jouve. Maurice Bouvet joined them in order to slow down the resistible rise of the "dictator." They disposed of the majority. On December, during an open meeting of the SPP, Lagache denounced on parliamentary grounds the hand vote of June 17. Nacht and his lieutenants resigned, but the former was returned to office on a temporary basis. To Lacan's great regret, the medical core had crystallized around the minority group. Nacht had his partisans sign "commitments" in his favor, and behaved like the leader of a faction. Refusing to yield to Lagache's demands, he insisted on managing in his own name the movement's affairs. He wanted to be both president of the commission on instruction and director of the Institute. Against him, Lacan maintained the principle of separatism. The minority then brandished a threat of secession. Infuriated, the princess ran to the telephone. She asked Anna Freud whether the IPA would grant recognition to Nacht's partisans in the event of a split. She responded in the affirmative, and Marie called her adversaries gangsters.

The adversaries were not particularly benign toward each other. If Lacan was judged to be "paranoid" by his enemies or suffering from verbosity, he himself called Lebovici a "bad rabbit," Benassy an "adjutant," and Sauguet "mediocre." The last mentioned, moreover, was described as an "irresponsible agent" by Lagache,[14] who was accused by others of being jealous and without clinical talent.

At the open meeting of December 16, Nacht attempted to obtain a vote in favor of his statutes before the election of the new board. Lagache refused. Nacht then proposed that only the contestable articles be submitted to a vote. The majority coalition rejected the compromise, forcing the executive committee effectively to resign. Lacan volunteered himself as temporary director. Elected in the second round by a vote of nine to eight with one abstention, he retained Sauguet in his position.

Hostile to every form of secessionism, he presented in January 1953 a proposed amendment to Nacht's statutes. "If you will allow me at present," he wrote, "in the spirit of a wish for the new year and the ritual license connected with it in all traditions, to make use of a private joke, I would say that I present here to our fragmented body of members the instrument of a mirror in which, heaven willing, it may anticipate its unity."[15] Lacan reaffirmed the regulations of 1949, proposing that the bonds uniting the officers of the Institute to the commission be conceived in such manner as to ensure the primacy of teaching over management and the autonomy of the one in relation to the other. In addition, he emphasized that psychoanalysis was reducible to neither neurobiology, nor medicine, nor pedagogy, nor psychology, nor sociology, nor the study of institutions, nor ethnology, nor mythology, nor the science of communication, nor linguistics. "Its dissident forms," he added, "identify themselves as doing all those things which it is not."[16]

In the active negativity of that formula, Lacan was focusing on a *Freudian* position of the movement in the face of the medical path chosen by Nacht and the psychologistic one opted for by Lagache. The previous statutes had privileged organization, reinstated the simple hierarchy of titular and adhering members, and made of the SPP an annex of the Institute. Lacan's, on the contrary, established specific ranks according to the stage and career of candidates in order to distinguish clearly the Society from the Institute, and the Institute from the commission. In that context, the Institute could award two titles: that of *agréé* recognized the right of candidates to practice psychoanalysis; that of *assistant* acknowledged eminent collaboration in the works of the Institute without reference to "professional" qualification. The 1949 rules retained their full validity in the functioning of the commission and the relations of the Institute with the SPP.

In the statutes proposed by Nacht, the director of the Institute and the president of the SPP had regular seats on the commission on instruction, which automatically moved under the authority of the head of the Institute. The three secretaries could be members of the same commission, which became the tool of an executive committee elected for an exorbitant term of five years. Although he was an excellent lawmaker, Lacan betrayed a certain lack of seriousness in the way he settled his difference with Nacht. His amendment forbade the secretaries from having any function on the commission and did not allow the director to be a member of it without a specific election. But the author did not spell out the precise modalities of a genuine separation of powers, leaving it to a general assembly to ratify the proposed modifications. In addition, he committed the blunder of not granting the princess any honorary title. Lacan drew up his text as a disciplined democrat, forgetful of all protocol.

Bonaparte continued to detest the man, whom she called paranoid, abundantly. Despite her friendship for Lagache, she could not overlook the fact that the biological ideals for which she had always fought were better represented by the authoritarian group than by the liberals. She had, moreover, proposed an amendment tending to strengthen the autocratic tendency by allowing the scientific secretaries to sit on the commission. Nacht was not fooled by the princess's whims. He exploited the situation in order to negotiate a splendid compromise which resulted in a dislocation of the fragile majority coalition. He yielded on the reduction of the executive committee's term to three years, accepted that the commission not be automatically presided over by the director of the Institute, and gratified the princess with the honorary title forgotten by Lacan. On the other hand, he insisted that the scientific secretaries be members of the commission. Return to square one: If Nacht's statutes were voted through, the executive committee would have accorded itself effective control over psychoanalytic training.

In order to reinforce his position, Nacht charged full speed ahead, through the intermediary of the commission. That organism extracted from Lacan a promise to submit to the rules. That strange battle further divided the liberal group. Attacked by his own and censured by his adversaries, Lacan committed himself to normalizing his technique. Which he in no way did.

The date for voting on the statutes and electing a new president of the SPP was set for the evening of January 20. That afternoon, Nacht began an offensive with the aim of charming Her Majesty, who was already shaken by the extent of her own contradictions. He helped her to see, quite accurately, that Lacan was for her the worst of dangers, since he threatened her position as commander in chief of the French movement. The princess's love for the liberal faction yielded before that argument and Nacht carried off his prize. He "turned" Bonaparte "around," for she was now prepared to return to the fold of those of the medical tendency. With that, there was an immediate reversal of alliances: The minority troops became the majority, and the members of the former majority sounded the retreat. The princess recruited Cénac, who offered his candidacy against Lacan's for the presidency of the SPP. Nacht's statutes were voted through, but at dawn on the twenty-first, lightning struck: Lacan obtained a majority in his favor. Bonaparte's about-face had not yet produced the results hoped for. The new president designated a moderate slate: Daniel Lagache, vice-president; Pierre Mâle, assessor; Pierre Marty, secretary; and Maurice Bouvet, treasurer.

The Pyrrhic victory accelerated the dismemberment of the liberal coalition and favored the process leading to the split. On February 3, Lacan's technique was again a subject of attack. The president of the SPP attempted to justify his innovations, but the commission, under the influence of the authoritarian clan, rejected his candidates. Marie Bonaparte requested additional information; Parcheminey emphasized the necessity of a firm position; Pierre Mâle insisted on respect for the analytic contract, and the director of the Institute managed to get a unanimous vote for the preservation of the established norms. Only Lagache intervened in favor of the accused. The curtain fell on the spectacle of the masters in discord.[17]

Thus ended the victorious offensive waged by Nacht against the introduction of liberalism into the French psychoanalytic movement. At the heart of the battle, Lacan played the roles of both mediator and scapegoat, according to whether he functioned as legislator or training analyst. Facing him, Lagache was already dreaming of a society conforming to his academic aspirations within the university. The alliance between the two would take on more precise shape with the entry on the scene of the masses: the *stagiaires.*

Jenny Weiss was twenty-three years old when she met Lacan for the first time in a salon of the Parisian *haute bourgeoisie.* She noticed his brilliant eyes, his thinness, his dandyism, and the ambitious seductiveness he seemed to emanate.

In the Weiss family, women did not conceal their frequently extreme opinions. They flaunted with a certain pride the twin Jewish and Protestant lineage of their ancestors. Her father was Alsatian and a brilliant graduate of the Polytechnique. He cultivated secular ideals, but felt that his daughters ought to prefer housework to their studies. An *agrégée de lettres* at the age of twenty, Louise blazed the path of protest by taking to the street with the suffragettes. Following her example, Jenny also took up the challenge and began medical school. In 1928, she married Alexandre Roudinesco. Urged on by him, she did her first training as a neurologist with Clovis Vincent, who would be the godfather of her daughter, then stayed on in Professor Heuyer's service where she worked alongside Sophie Morgenstern. Named a hospital physician on the eve of the war, she assumed the following year the duties of an *agrégée* at the Salpêtrière, under the direction of the aged Guillain, Charcot's biographer.

At the beginning of the Occupation, she slapped an assistant who had called her a half-breed and intimated that Hitler was the one to straighten her out. Then, after a stay at the hospice in Brévannes, she became chief consultant at the Enfants-Malades hospital. Thanks to a forged certificate of baptism, drawn up by an indulgent chaplain, she received the ignoble certificate of "non-belonging to the Jewish race," which allowed her to pursue her clandestine and medical activities.[18] In collaboration with a Communist network, in which Victor Lafitte participated, she daily sabotaged the functioning of STO—the service deporting Frenchmen for work in Germany. A complex system of tampering with X-rays and laboratory tests allowed for the certification, with accompanying documentation, of tubercular lesions in recalcitrant candidates.

At the Liberation, she became chief of pediatrics at the Ambroise-Paré hospital, to which the Fondation Parent-de-Rosan was attached. In that public welfare warehouse were deposited young children who had been abandoned by their mothers. They tended to be prostrate, did not speak, and would stare at others with an air of suffering. Jenny Roudinesco did not enjoy the sight, and she began a new crusade. Formerly she had fought diphtheria, then the "brown plague" of the Nazis; hereafter she would be launched in a merciless struggle against the deprivation of maternal care. The objective was clear: preventing psychosis and introducing psychoanalysis into the world of the hospital. Shortly thereafter, at the request of her sister Louise, she hired for the service Rosine Lefort, a daughter of the journalist Geneviève Tabouis. In her benevolence, Lefort would work wonders among the infants. She thus took care of Nadia, the "wolf child," and Marie-Françoise. At the time, Jenny Roudinesco was still ignorant of Freud's writings, but she had observed the powerlessness of medicine and began to read works on autism. Eventually, she traveled to London, to the first Congress on Child Neuropsychiatry, where she met Anna Freud, who encouraged her to undergo analysis.

Upon her return, Professor Debré, who was director of the International Childhood Center, proposed to fund her for a collaboration with John Bowlby and James Robertson of the Tavistock Clinic. Two years later, she received a fellowship from the Rockefeller Foundation for a trip to study the organization of child neuropsychiatry in the United States. Upon arriving, she was brutally confronted with the spectacle of psychoanalysis in a phase of unremitting expansion. Both fascinated and terrified, she visited several guidance centers, then went to Princeton University, where she met Albert Einstein, who seemed moved by her Parisian hat. The scientist lived in a white house surrounded by a green lawn. He asked her why she had come to see him, adding, "Just to see the animal?" He was a great practical joker. One day, his bust, which sat in the library, was mysteriously moved in front of a window, facing a field. The culprit was sought. The director of the library apologized to Einstein, who, beside himself with laughter, confessed: It was he who had displaced the statue, fearing lest it be bored. He wanted it to get a breath of fresh air. Near the university, there was a modern dairy at which cows were milked automatically by machine. When their production diminished, they were sent off to the slaughterhouse. Einstein observed to Roudinesco that the scientists at Princeton were like those cows. After a few years of intensive research, their faculties dulled. They then became useless beasts, and a new emigration occurred.

Her head aswim with the American dream, Jenny Roudinesco returned to France and began her tour of visits to the titular members. Lacan insisted on having her on his couch. She refused categorically. Her brother had begun treatment with him, and she did not want her analysis to be mixed up with family affairs. She met Nacht, Schlumberger, Bouvet, Cénac, and Bonaparte. Since she was a hospital doctor, they all agreed to supervise her training.[19] She found the first too brutal, the second too Protestant, the third too obsessive, and so chose the fourth. In point of fact, Nacht was the only one to tell her the truth without flattering her. He explained that an analysis turns a life "upside-down" and occasionally leads patients to divorce. Frightened, Roudinesco sought refuge with Cénac. Two years later, she provoked him. Instead of interpreting her aggressiveness as an act of transference, Cénac asked her to leave. She then returned to Nacht, who immediately reserved a place for her on his couch. He had perceived things well: In 1952, she would divorce in order to marry Pierre Aubry, an *agrégé* in mathematics. Under her new name, she would publish a book relating her experience at Parent-de-Rosan.[20]

In 1951, after a congress in Mexico, she made a detour through New York in order to meet Margaret Mead. Invited to her house for a reception, she spoke with Hartmann and Kris, who asked her for news of the Parisian scene. They wanted to know what Lacan was up to and where his relations stood with the SPP. She was unable to respond.

By her training, Jenny Roudinesco belonged to the third French psychoanalytic generation. Accustomed to rebellion, she unwittingly provoked a huge uproar in the SPP by sending Nacht and Lacan an open letter that triggered an explosion in the ranks of the students. Among them, Wladimir Granoff, Serge Leclaire, and Robert Pujol were already to all eyes among the most active.

The Institute opened its doors on March 5, 1953. The new regulations obliged candidates to renew their vow not to take the title of psychoanalyst without the authorization of the commission. But these statutes were unknown to them, and a number of them were already practicing the profession with the permission of the Society. The registration procedure for the Institute was thus felt to be an instrument of dissuasion that would annul work they had already done. In addition, tuition was fixed at an exorbitant rate: 15,000 per "cycle," from 500 to 1,000 francs per seminar, and 1,500 francs per collective supervision. Excellent pay for an excellent ear: Such seemed to be the motto of the new Nachtian school. . . . The students had the impression they were being treated like children. They were uneasy in the face of the discord rampant among the masters and, although their rebellion was spontaneous, they tended to look toward the liberal group. A third of them were in therapy with Lacan, and all of them were favorable to a less authoritarian mode of instruction that conformed to Lagache's aspirations. That sympathy of the "base" with the minority clan would immediately be exploited by the Nacht group, who accused Lacan of being a "leader." In point of fact, the students' revolt followed the masters' disarray according to a classic process: The malaise of those in power results in the masses taking to the streets to demand a new regime in which the leaders of a progressive coalition might exercise power by managing the interests of the people more effectively.

"It happens," wrote Jenny Roudinesco, "that my personal situation is not affected. My analysis was begun because I realized the impossibility of conducting child psychotherapy correctly without knowing the discipline of psychoanalysis. It has allowed me, even though it was not the most serene of processes because of my age and my situation, to resolve my personal problems to my satisfaction and to yours. . . . That is why I take the liberty of telling you that there is a malaise reigning among the young candidates in psychoanalysis, and that in my opinion that malaise can be dissipated only if the society transmits the statutes and internal regulations to them so that they can study them and formulate their criticisms and their opinions in complete freedom." [21]

On May 17, the fifty-one psychoanalysts in training met, learned of the letter, and decided to put off provisionally any new commitments. They were waiting to receive the regulations. Nacht replied curtly that the problems Roudinesco had raised were not the province of either the SPP or its president. He was right. She had written simultaneously to her analyst and to her supervisor in order to inform them of a "malaise" without concern for "juridical propriety." Nacht thus challenged her right to address Lacan, given the fact that the problems of the Institute did not concern the Society. Embarrassed, Lacan drafted a response which he did not send. "So here I am," he wrote, "impelled to join to my answer the question of knowing what authorizes me to give it to you and what sort of status you might grant it among those who have taken you as their interpreter."[22] He addressed his interlocutor as a member of the SPP and authorized her to transmit his letter to the candidates by virtue of his office as president. But since he did not mail it, his words would not be conveyed. With customary irony, he explained the juridical functioning of the Institute and showed how Nacht and the princess had managed to effect a fusion of the executive and the legislative.

Juliette Favez-Boutonier, for her part, wrote to Françoise Dolto in order to propose that the titular members support the student uprising against Nacht's dictatorship.[23] A new meeting was scheduled for May 31. On that occasion, and following Juliette's letter, Françoise marshalled her finest prose and wrote to the students. After congratulating them for their rebellion, she wrote, "The *lupic* attitude (from *lupus-lupi*, wolf), if I may allude to the etymologies dear to my master Pichon, is no more that of psychoanalysts with their patients than with their students. For in relation to you, we are not masters but witnesses who have worked a few years longer than you, and our teaching has value and is utilizable by you only if we transmit to you the fruit of our personal experience. We should be urging you to confront that experience with that of others who have also worked with all their personality and have conveyed their testimony of it to you."[24]

In an interview with Irène Roubleff published in 1978, Françoise Dolto told of having received, on the eve of the meeting, a telephone call from Serge Lebovici, advising her not to attend a student meeting the following day which did not concern the titular members. Since she had answered by letter, she decided to take off for the country. On Sunday, because of the grayness of the day, she decided to stay in Paris. Around 11 o'clock, she received a phone call from Madame Guiton: "Come over to the Institute. Lebovici, Diatkine, and other titular members are there, saying they were invited by the Institute. They have come to attack us as though we were a bunch of vulgar schoolkids rebelling. Come support our position, I beg you." Fifteen minutes later, Françoise Dolto was there and heard Lebovici say the following words, "This is unacceptable; I came believing that I was summoned to a regular meeting of the Institute of Psychoanalysis, and I fall into a mutiny hatched by these kids." Dolto claims she responded, "I am surprised that Lebovici came after having advised me not to come, since this is not an official meeting, which is, moreover, beyond doubt. In that case, who is lying?" He did not answer, but the howls from the auditorium, according to Dolto, were like a reduced version of May 1968. "From that day on, I knew he was going to hate me."[25]

That testimony is confirmed by Juliette Favez-Boutonier: "Upon returning from Strasbourg on May 30, I consulted my schedule, which was kept by my housekeeper, and I learned that Dr. Lebovici had telephoned. I wondered why, but it was too late to call back. I went to bed and fell asleep after having found in my mail a call to a meeting of students at the Institute on May 31. I was intent on being there. I arrived late, around 10:30, without any information and quite calm. I approached Lebovici and asked why he had called me. Quite uncomfortable, he told me that he had wanted to inform me that there was no need for me to go to the trouble of attending. I observed to him that he himself had come. A moment later, I encountered Françoise and told her of my conversation. She told me he had tried the same thing with her. That day marked a shift in the trust I had in Lebovici, whom I had regarded until then as an unenigmatic friend." [26]

Serge Lebovici does not remember having telephoned Françoise Dolto. But he does not deny the affirmation. "What I know," he writes, "is that Jenny Roudinesco played an important role in everything surrounding that meeting and that it was probably she who roused the students of the Institute to attend. I don't believe I said that I was in the presence of kids. It is possible that I spoke of the inconsequentiality of their demonstration, which was more in favor of Lacan than against Nacht. I know I told the students that Lacan had not kept his promises: specifically, to furnish the Institute with the names of the students he had in training analyses, and to give them the sessions of normal length he had promised to give them. Jenny Roudinesco attempted to turn the situation around by complaining of the abusive powers which Nacht had arrogated during the affair. She asked me questions on the subject, and I defended the project, which I thought good at the time. The discussion was confused and came to blows. In particular, Serge Leclaire, who had a different name at the time, more or less attacked me physically, although not seriously, of course. There was thus a certain agitation and confusion as well as a success on the part of Jenny Roudinesco in the affair. It is quite possible that Françoise Dolto came that day, but she did not play an important part. When she is made to say, or when she says that I must have detested her from that day on, it is, of course, quite false, since I reserve my hatred for more interesting causes." [27]

Lebovici attended the student meeting along with Sauguet, Marty, Benassy, Dolto, Favez-Boutonier, and Lagache. Shortly thereafter, he would accuse Jenny Roudinesco of conspiring with Lacan. In his "Memorandum," Lagache gives the following summary: "Drs. Françoise Dolto, Juliette Favez-Buotonier, Lagache, and Lacan answered the students' motion by letter, each in his or her style, and only the first three attended the meeting. It was so plainly not a conspiracy that one of the opponents was astonished by the presence of several teachers, among whom the secretaries of the Institute and the secretary of the SPP. No one could say that—since the meeting was public—the students had been urged to rebel. For my part, my concern was not to betray the administrative council of which I was a member and not to use the student protest for personal ends; even as I insisted on the necessity of a liberal climate conducive to the spirit of psychoanalysis, I urged the students to resume contact with the executive committee." [28] In the notorious "black book" in which he kept minutes of the meetings of that period, Pierre Marty did not mention the session of May 31. It was not for the secretary of the SPP to give an account of a meeting that concerned the Institute, even if he was present at it.

After becoming acquainted with the statutes and internal regulations, the students formulated three demands. They wanted the administrative council to be separate from the commission, a change in the composition of the commission, and finally a nonvoting representative of nonphysicians on the council, for purposes of consultation. The motion was passed with a large majority.[29]

Meanwhile, Lacan hopped into a taxi and arrived on the sidewalk of the rue

Saint-Jacques toward the end of the meeting. There, he chatted with the mutineers and warned them against the despotism of the majority group. The mood turned violent. Certain of the students expected a shoot-out worthy of *High Noon,* but since no one wanted to play the part of Gary Cooper, nothing serious transpired. Shortly thereafter, Lacan would be accused of again violating the rules and of using his transferential power to sow seeds of rebellion in the student ranks.

Crisis was inevitable.

On June 2, a terrible administrative meeting was held. Cénac reproached Lacan for his presence among the students and his contempt for his twofold role as titular member and president. He recalled that it was in order to avoid the current difficulties that he had proposed his candidacy for the presidency of the SPP. Lacan responded that he had received a telephone call during the May 31 meeting informing him that he had been attacked. Upon arriving, he had transmitted a slip of paper to Jenny Roudinesco asking whether or not he should participate in the discussion. Nacht interrupted in order to launch a new offensive against short sessions. Pasche and Cénac intervened in chorus on the perils of such a practice while Nacht reiterated his attack. He emphasized that Lacan's analysands constituted a third of the Institute's students and were finding themselves in an inextricable situation in relation to the commission, which refused to validate their therapy. When his turn came, Lebovici attributed to Pujol principal responsibility for the mutiny. The rebellious student, he said, had physically opposed regulation by his colleagues of the rights of the Institute.

Pasche then declared that certain students were demanding permission to begin supervised analyses without authorization from the commission. Lacan answered to all that his analyses, with the exception of a single one, were all in conformity with the fixed-length rule. Concerning rhythm, he claimed never to have made any commitments. Nacht retorted that twelve training analyses may have been normalized, but the letter acknowledging that fact had been submitted to the commission only fifteen days before. Wanting to avoid a break, Lacan acknowledged his imprudences and qualified as dangerous the freedoms he had taken with the rule. Lagache took the floor: In his opinion, nothing demonstrated that there was any relation between the present malaise and the question of short sessions.

In order to counter him, Nacht denounced the existence of a "collusion" between Jenny Roudinesco and Jacques Lacan. At the end of the meeting of May 31, she challenged the commission's authority and the value of its decisions on the regulation of training analyses. According to Nacht, those words proved she was in cahoots with Lacan. Lebovici, in turn, adopted the tone of a prosecutor. The proof of "collusion," in his opinion, lay in the exchange of the famous slip of paper. Nacht went on: He accused Roudinesco of having one day declared that the question of short sessions lay at the heart of the conflict and that Lacan had never promised to obey the rules. . . . His analysand, he said, was astonished that Lacan's analyses had been rejected after they had been judged satisfactory. He claimed to have answered that Lacan's practice had never been accepted by his colleagues.

Lacan rejected the notion of "collusion." He emphasized that it would have been insanely imprudent of him to have used Jenny Roudinesco with the students.

Not only had he not acted in such manner, but he never said that he had not given his word to the commission.[30] That affirmation is confirmed by the facts and by testimony. At the time, indeed, Lacan did not "lie" in that manner. He told his analysands, "See how I'm obeying the rules; I'm lengthening my sessions, and you can testify to it," then he continued practicing the length that suited him.

There was, in fact, no "collusion" between Jenny Roudinesco and Jacques Lacan. She had put the president of the SPP in an embarrassing position by obliging him to respond personally in a letter he did not even send. Moreover, there was no manipulation of the students by the liberal instructors since it was the former who called on the latter to support them. In such a situation, it was normal for the struggling mutineers to find themselves in the same camp as those who were fighting for the same ideas. Nacht's strategy was thus based on an absurdity, but it was extremely effective. He wanted to exploit the growing uproar in order to oblige his adversaries to abandon Lacan on the subject of a technique that everyone disapproved of. In that manner, he would be able to force his removal from office while avoiding all discussion of the student demands. He was proceeding without risk, for indeed, Lagache was already dreaming of founding a new institution whereas Lacan remained hostile to every kind of secession.

In order to prove "collusion" and turn the titular members against Lacan and the liberal clan, Nacht made use of a conversation he had had with Roudinesco a few months earlier. Already in February 1953, she had denounced the despotism of the authoritarian clan and accused Nacht of hypocrisy. She had told him she could not understand why he remained Lacan's friend while denouncing his practice. At the time she was in analysis with the one, under supervision with the other, and had just completed another supervised analysis with Lebovici. Nacht had answered her that Lacan's practice was inadmissible. In addition, he could not tolerate Roudinesco's challenging his authority in public. He had thus made her, in the form of an interpretation, a proposition she could not refuse. "You are in the process of getting a divorce," he had said, "and in that confrontation with reality, you are no longer in need of continuing therapy." Dismissed by Cénac a first time, Jenny Roudinesco had thus been expelled by Nacht at a time when she would have needed to continue her training.[31]

It was nonetheless the case that by June 2, Lacan had come to understand the maneuvers of Nacht and his troops. That is why he in turn attempted to divert the debate in a direction advantageous to the liberal clan. He played the martyr and asked for the indulgence of his peers. "Dr. Lacan," Marty noted, "is appealing to the comprehension of the assembly. For five years he says he has given the best of himself in the interest of psychoanalysis; he has also given the worst; he has acted with a passion which, to be sure, may occasionally have been clumsy. If he is slow to submit to discipline (this is still Lacan speaking), he desires but one thing, which is to work with all of his friendship for his colleagues; he wants the Institute to live and he wants to work in it. He asks for a vote of confidence, since the malaise is not that serious. He commits himself to doing whatever he can."[32]

The soliloquy did not convince anyone. Francis Pasche went as far as to say that even if Lacan did not inspire the conflict, he was responsible for it by virtue of his mere existence.[33] The liberal group attempted in vain to start up the debate anew on the subject of the malaise in the institution. Dolto and Favez-Boutonier emphasized that the difficulties resulted from the poor initial welcome the candidates received and the changes that had occurred in the composition of the commission, which assigned too much power to the director. Lacan added that the students did not need to be indoctrinated in order to rebel. Confronting Benassy's offensive, he proposed the creation, by lots, of an arbitration commission. The suggestion was rejected without a vote. Françoise Dolto immediately asked for the Society to begin its anticipated vacation. An identical refusal. Several titular members insisted on tabling the motion of confidence desired by Odette Codet and supported by Cénac since the beginning of the meeting. After a negative vote, the motion was accepted. It was to be on the agenda for the meeting of June 16, 1953. The debacle of the liberal group was complete: Only Favez-Boutonier, Lagache, and Dolto were opposed to the repudiation ratified by fifteen titular members. "I shall remember all my life," wrote Lacan, "through the comments of that Robespierre [Pasche] which retained a certain decorum in their madness, the convulsed faces of those participating in that bizarre manhunt. It was not a pretty sight and, resisting their howls, I accorded myself the luxury of contemplating it a second time."[34]

In the face of the dissensions splitting the masters, the student leadership summoned all the *stagiaires* to a new meeting in order to set forth demands to be discussed at a subsequent gathering of the titular members. For their part, five clumsy colleagues—Pasche, Lebovici, Benassy, Diatkine, and Cénac—requested that the revocation of Lacan's presidential mandate be put on the agenda for June 16. They sent their letter off to Marty, and claimed their position was based on Article 35 of the statutes. Lacan in turn, asked for the text, then invited the board to meet at his house on June 12. Marie Bonaparte, Lagache, Mâle, Bouvet, and Marty were present. They all perceived that the version of the statutes transmitted by Pasche to Marty, then sent by the latter to Lagache and Lacan, contained some bizarre anomalies. The offices of the SPP were switched to the address of the Institute and Article 35 was added. It had appeared neither in the historic statutes of 1927 nor in the revised version of 1949. Nacht seemed unaware of the source of that pathological document. In addition, the motion was sent to the secretary's home and not to the (changed) address of the SPP's offices. That extravagance made the motion all the more inadmissible in that the precise location of the society in question could not be determined. Confronting disaster, the board wisely opted unanimously not to include the motion of revocation on the agenda of the forthcoming meeting.[35]

In that poisoned atmosphere, a break was inevitable, and Lagache decided to create a free institute, inspired by academic norms. He mentioned it to Juliette Favez-Boutonier, André Berge, and Georges Favez, whose candidacy for titular membership had just been rejected. Favez-Boutonier found it hard to tolerate the chastening of the recalcitrants and complained of a threat to bring her before a "disciplinary board." In Strasbourg, where she had taken over Lagache's position, she had created a "psychoanalytic study group," judged to be suspect by the authoritarian clan. Françoise Dolto, for her part, supported the project while helping Lacan emerge from his isolation among the titular members. Extremely depressed, the latter felt he was living a nightmare. Attacked on his right by the Nacht group, he was gently rejected on his left by the liberal faction. Despite his dominant position among the students, he felt persecuted and seemed to be as yet incapable of breaking with a society that represented the established order. At bottom, he would have preferred, rather than an alliance with Lagache's psychologism, an agreement based on trust with those advocating a medical ethos. Lagache was aware of this, and was in no way eager to introduce a wolf into his manger. His attitude rested on an act of denial: He did not want Lacan to participate in the founding of the new society lest it be believed that the society was the work of Lacan.[36]

On the eve of the June 16 meeting, Lacan was wondering which faction would devour him and what place he might have in the new group. Thereafter he would have no choice and supported Lagache's project without being part of it. One day, he showed up at the home of Jenny Roudinesco, who was lunching with Pierre Aubry, her future husband, and her daughters. Refusing to eat, he paced back and forth. Annoyed, Aubry said to him: "Why don't you found your own society? You could call it the 'Société française de psychanalyse.' It wouldn't be limited to the city of Paris, but could extend throughout the land." Originally from Poitou, Pierre Aubry had not forgotten the rights of the provinces, which had been neglected in the Parisian quarrels. Lacan stood still and said: "What a good idea."[37]

Lagache had the same one and chose the same name. Quite quickly, he drew up statutes, registered them at the Prefecture, and got ready for the day of reckoning. Along with Favez-Boutonier and Dolto, he wrote a circular of unprecedented violence, which was distributed on June 16. Its authors denounced the institutional inconsistencies of which the authoritarian clan, through its machinations, was guilty: "If President Nacht considered Lacan incompetent or guilty," they wrote, "why cloak the matter in mystery? Why allow him to be nominated to speak at the Rome congress? Why agree to propose him for president only to attack him (or allow him to be attacked) later on and fuel his adversaries with retroactive arguments? There are other inconsistencies: Three years ago, the Society, in administrative session, refused to consider a candidacy for adhering membership because the individual in question had signed a manifesto, 'Psychanalyse, idéologie réactionnaire,' which appeared in La Nouvelle Critique in June 1949. But that manifesto was also signed by one of the titular members of the Society, who after keeping his silence during the session, when his cosignatory was attacked, never clarified his position on the subject. And that titular member has been subsequently not only tolerated but assigned important functions, demonstrating the trust he enjoys. Is this an inconsistency or is it an encouragement to duplicity?"[38]

The allusion was clear and the accusation tremendous: In 1950, Jean Kestemberg's candidacy for titular membership had indeed been refused, whereas Lebovici, a titular member since 1946, had signed the same text in La Nouvelle Critique. The former had been in analysis with Lacan, and the latter had completed his analysis with Nacht. The authors of the circular did not say why they had not themselves asked Lebovici for an explanation of his silence and his signature.

The diatribe ended with these words: "It seems impossible for us to collaborate usefully with a group whose authoritarian tendencies create a climate that is incompatible with respect for others and fatal for all scientific thought. That climate is not a threat but a reality. It is that of the Société psychanalytique de Paris at present, as we have demonstrated. That society, moreover, is no more than what the Institute will want it to be. It is not the Institute which is in its service; it is the servant of the Institute." [39]

On the eve of the historic meeting, Lagache officially informed Lacan of the coup d'état he was planning for the following day. The latter prepared once again to confront his accusers.

After a turbulent discussion in which Lagache reproached Benassy for having spoken ill of him to a student, and in which Lacan contested certain comments that had been attributed to him at the previous meeting, the administrative session of June 16 took a dramatic turn. Supported by Marie Bonaparte, Odette Codet read her motion: "The general assembly of the SPP, meeting in administrative session, noting its profound disagreement with its president, Jacques Lacan, as appeared in the course of the session of June 2, can no longer accord him its confidence and requests its vice-president to assume the tasks of the presidency until the election of a new slate, as provided by the statutes." All the titular members were present with the exception of Laforgue and Hesnard. Forewarned by Lacan, the latter had sent him a letter authorizing him to vote in his place in all circumstances.

André Berge called on the participants to manifest a measure of unity, then asked for the creation of an arbitration committee. He forgot that that same proposal had been rejected at the preceding meeting.

Lacan said that he had accepted the presidency in order to expose himself to the judgment of his colleagues on the value of his teaching and his views on the statutes of the Institute. He did not contest the legitimacy of the motion of nonconfidence but emphasized that what was reproached him concerned more the Institute than his activities as president. He thought that a phase in the evolution of the Society had come to an end on that day and saw no statutory obstacle to the motion's being decided by a hand vote. Marie Bonaparte was categorically opposed to such a procedure, with Lagache close behind her, answering that the will of a single titular member was sufficient to make a secret ballot obligatory. The secretary then indicated that a "yes" meant approval of the motion, which was immediately passed with twelve of the eighteen members present voting in favor.

Upon the announcement of the results, Lacan tendered his resignation, then relinquished his tasks at the Institute. In point of fact, he had been removed. Lagache, as vice-president, immediately assumed his place and forthwith violated the limits of legitimacy. He emphasized the existence of a chronic malaise among the titular members and finally read the decision leading to the split: "The undersigned, Lagache, Favez-Boutonier, and Dolto hereby resign from the SPP." Mesmerized, the assembly remained silent. Lagache rose, flanked by his two companions, as Blanche Reverchon-Jouve followed them and similarly tendered her resignation. The notorious manifesto was circulated in the room, which was presided over by Pierre Mâle. Erect amid his adversaries, Lacan soon announced his break with the SPP. He joined those who had resigned, who reassembled at the home of Françoise Dolto in order to celebrate their departure in the presence of Granoff, Leclaire, and Perrier.

Impressed by the dramatic aspect of the historic moment, Mâle proposed that Georges Parcheminey, the most senior member of the Society, be named president. The vote was by hand and was unanimously in favor of the old founder, who would die two months later. Nacht seized the opportunity to suggest that the statutes of the Society be adapted to those of the Institute and that a reform commission, composed of Cénac, Bonaparte, Bouvet, Berge, Mâle, and Marty, be elected. Their election was unanimous with the exception of Berge, who abstained and requested a stay of two weeks before making his position known. Finally Parcheminey underscored the fact that any resignation from the SPP automatically entailed resignation from the Institute.⁴⁰ Georges Favez would not run the risk of resigning and would remain an adhering member of the SPP until his death, despite his role in the APF.

Thus ended the second act of the first split of the French psychoanalytic movement.

Oddly enough, those who had resigned did not realize that in leaving the SPP, they were effecting their own exclusion from the IPA. And yet, when Marie Bonaparte still belonged to the liberal group, she had telephoned Anna Freud in their presence in order to raise the question of affiliation in the event the authoritarian clan seceded. Anna had responded that the dissidents would be immediately recognized. She was wrong. She was probably thinking of crises in America, where the situation was idiosyncratic. In the United States, each society belonged to the APA, which in turn belonged to the IPA. When a group broke with its original society, it continued to be part of the APA, whose function was to group all societies on American territory. In the event of a break, the dissidents remained members of the IPA to the extent that they could retain their affiliation with the APA. In Europe, there was no federative movement. When one seceded from a society, one automatically lost one's membership in the IPA. In order to hold on to it, those who had resigned would have had to found a lateral society without leaving the mother group, and to have subsequently presented to a congress the disagreement which pitted them against their rivals. On that condition alone would they have been able to make their griefs known without losing their status as members of the IPA. In his haste, Lagache had not thought of this juridical problem, which was of the highest importance.

Whence the letter sent on July 6 by Ruth S. Eissler, secretary on the central executive committee of the IPA, to Jacques Lacan. It read as follows: "We are convinced that you are aware of the fact that your decision entails as well the loss of your status as a member of the IPA. Nevertheless, if you are desirous of attending as a guest the scientific sessions of the XVIIIth International Congress of Psychoanalysis in London, kindly inform us to that effect. Unfortunately, we cannot invite you to the administrative session, given the fact that, as you know, that session is open solely to members of the IPA."⁴¹

Marie Bonaparte had started her maneuvers in the month of June. In the blindness of her passion, she went so far as to attribute the split to Lacan, forgetting that he had followed Lagache's lead. "In these conditions," she wrote to Loewenstein, "the Institute and the journal remain ours—although they will be able to found others with what remains of the poorly-analyzed students of Lacan, who will follow them perhaps—I should say, for sure. But the question of affiliation with the IPA will be raised at the next congress, and they will be there. I have written to Hartmann on this score, informing him of everything. Also to Jeanne Lampl de Groot and to Sarasin. Anna Freud I prefer to call by telephone." The first mentioned had just been elected president of the IPA, and the three others were vice-presidents. The princess knew whereof she spoke. "It seems to me," she continued, "that those who have resigned cannot be recognized by the IPA until whatever technique they employ to train candidates is examined. That is, the question should be raised only in two years' time and not in London; for there is a risk that Lacanianism will spread. . . . I find it most regrettable that Lagache followed that madman." [42]

Bonaparte did indeed write to Hartmann. She shrewdly reminded her addressee that he himself had been at the origin of Lacan's admission to the ranks of titular members: "Elected at the urging of Pichon, the chauvinist, in counterpoint to your appointment." [43] In other words, she was asking the president of the IPA for the agitator's head, by reviving the memory of a painful past. Hartmann would not be long in letting his opinion of Lacan be known.

Meanwhile, on June 18, the SFP group published an official communiqué, written by Lagache. It defined the authoritarian group as a "faction without principles" which had used Lacan as a scapegoat. It emphasized that the conflict was ethical, not doctrinal, then affirmed that there was no obstacle to IPA recognition of the new group. It was wrong. Finally, it ended with these words: "Our fight is for the freedom of science and for Humanism. Humanism is without any strength if it is not militant." [44] After announcing the creation of a study group, the temporary board of the SFP published a list of its analysands in training as of June 23: They were thirty-four in number, more than a third of them on Lacan's couch. Others would follow.

Taken by surprise by the central executive committee's decision, Lagache and Lacan attempted in turn to justify themselves to the competent authorities. The former wrote his "Memorandum" and the latter his long letter to Loewenstein. Each retraced his "subjective" version of events. Lacan, for his part, wrote two more letters, one to Professor Nicolo Perrotti, organizer of the XVIth Conference of Psychoanalysts of the Romance Languages, which was to be held in September in Rome, and the other to Michael Balint. In an address of 1947 to the British Society, the latter had mocked training institutes and their sclerotic rituals, recalling his master Ferenczi's formula: "A training analysis is simply an analysis." Lacan had given the text extensive distribution in the SPP, but had not always taken account of all its implications in drawing up the statutes of 1949.

Lacan thought he would find support within the IPA and proposed to Balint that they meet in London two days prior to the congress. He wanted to set forth the situation of the French movement for him. A week later, he wrote to Hartmann: "You know, I believe, that I did not initiate the secession. . . . If they now reproach me with alleged freedoms of technique, they were always in a position to control their effects, and did not judge them to be unfavorable. And it is at the very time that I have for months been in conformity with the common rule on the accepted principle of professional supervision that they make use of it as a weapon against me. . . . I am not speaking of Nacht, and will never speak of him again. . . ."[45]

Trapped in his desire for recognition, Lacan believed he could convince his interlocutors that he had submitted to a rule whose principle he never stopped opposing in practice. At the time, he thus continued to pretend he was obeying orders. Now the history of that feint would weigh heavily on what was to follow. Lacan's situation was comparable to that of the scorpion asking the tortoise to help him cross the river. If the scorpion bites the tortoise, he drowns along with him, but if he behaves well, he is no longer a scorpion. In an analogous fool's bargain, Lacan was playing a difficult game: If he refused to obey the common rule and bit the tortoise, he risked losing his membership in the society of tortoises. On the other hand, if he accepted, he would no longer be Lacan. It would take him ten years to understand that a scorpion ought not to cross a river on a tortoise's back, but build a bridge for all the animals of his species. At the end of that period of maturing, which would bring him to the threshold of old age, he would take the initiative of founding his own school. In the meanwhile, he remained on the riverbank promising not to bite the tortoise. The problem in the story is that the tortoise did not believe the scorpion, etc.

On July 26, 1953, at the London congress, Hartmann announced the creation of a committee consisting of Winnicott, Lampl de Groot, Greenacre, Eissler, and Hoffer. Its charge was to examine the SFP's request for affiliation and to pass judgment on the notorious "deviations" in training analyses. Thereupon Loewenstein was quick to plead for tolerance and to compare the split to a divorce of parents, eminently dangerous for the students. Without naming Lacan, Marie Bonaparte insisted on the necessity of studying closely the technique of the members of the new group. Nacht, for his part, declared his intention of coming to an agreement with Lagache in order to spare students in training the disastrous consequences of strife between their masters. Anna Freud supported him and Zilboorg proposed that the dissidents remain members of the IPA throughout the duration of the inquiry. Hartmann refused, supported by Anna, who blamed the French for airing their divergences in public. Balint attempted a reconciliation and requested that the dissidents be named members of the IPA on an individual basis. Marie Bonaparte created an obstruction to that and mired the debate in the problem of deviations. Loewenstein then intervened to regret the absence of the individuals concerned, but Hartmann took advantage of the disorder in order to cut discussion short and entrust the committee with the task of deciding.[46] The motion was voted for by all but two of those present.

From that day on, the fate of the French psychoanalytic movement became— by dint of the error of those who resigned—the special business of the apparatus of the IPA. The France of Lacan and Lagache had given itself over to Pontius Pilate, and Pilate entrusted the fate of the SFP to the bureaucrats of his empire. At the center of negotiations, which promised to be difficult, the parable of the tortoise and the scorpion was already tearing apart the veil of a peaceful coexistence in which an expanding kingdom had believed it could forge its own unity.

II. Rome in September: A Baroque Overture

Freud had gone to Rome in order to take up the challenge of Hannibal's oath, conquer an empire, and gain access to a different culture. He had gone to Athens in the footsteps of Sophocles, then, moving from one ancient world to another, had turned to Moses, ferreting out the secret of a family romance in the process. In Pompei, he had contemplated the immobile memories of bodies suddenly petrified in the middle of their lives: ruined inanimate objects. In Rome too, he had visited the splendor of the arenas, dreaming of gladiators before the madness of Caesar. Freud's Rome was a city of the past, a dead city, a moment recaptured in the interpretation of a dream. Rome-Hollywood.

It had nothing in common with Lacan's Rome.

Having lived more than fifty years, the master prepared to travel. He did not like the same historical artifacts as Freud. Lacan's Rome resembled rather the ceilings of the Galleria Farnese, the archangels of Andrea Pozzo, or the facades of Francesco Borromini. From His Majesty's pen there issued forth a monumental style: sophims, successions of mirrors inserted into each other, the infinite delight of language. Occasionally, antiquity would revive in the form of philosophical references or famous battles, but never ruins. The unconscious discovered by Freud was to be started up anew as a Counter-Reformation, sumptuously draped in the folds of Clérambault. Rome would be his palace, the French language his garden.

One could almost say the classical age at that moment when the baroque congealed into a last incandescence. Lacan's Rome began with Ignatius of Loyola and ended in rococo madness. As founder of a new orthodoxy, the master spawned a flamboyant theory in which the transverberation of Saint Theresa fused with the alexandrine poetry of Racine. Rome emigrated to Versailles and the Holy See to the rue de Lille. Lacan's Rome was that of the Roman Catholic empire, a city in which the Pope was no longer a preacher but a commander in chief. The Rome dreamt of over maps in childhood; the Rome of adolescence and the Collège Stanislas: everything in the realm of religion, nothing accorded to faith.

In July, Lacan assumed first place in a society he did not found by opening the inaugural meeting of the SFP, in the large amphitheater of the Saint-Anne hospital. There he had treated Aimée, and there he began his teaching anew under the aegis of the Faculté de Médecine. Lagache presided over the session and announced that he had chosen freedom. Then he gave the floor to his comrade, calling attention to his "minor faults." The latter then delivered "Le Symbolique, l'Imaginaire, et le Réel." [47]

In the history of the elaboration of Lacan's doctrine, that presentation marked the first phase of the introduction of a topographical model which would become more explicit over a period of thirty years. Lacan, in that presentation, can be observed fabricating his concepts like a goldsmith. He restored palaces, stripping facades, commenting with gold-tipped pen on the twist of the slightest fringe, never halting a definition so much as pursuing it. He did not freeze words but adorned them with a thousand turns, endlessly seeking the essential detail of a function or an articulation. Coloration, ornament, and amplification were the characteristics of a style at once overly subtle in its appearance and carefully crafted in its foundations.

The baroque Lacan of the mature years was an impassioned reader of Saussure's *Course on General Linguistics,* Heidegger's philosophy, and Lévi-Strauss's *Elementary Structures of Kinship.* He was beginning to delve into Freud's texts from the perspective of a system of language conceived as a *structure* and composed of *signs,* which were themselves defined according to their *value,* by way of the *symbolic* relation joining a signified to a signifier. If the structure of language was situated within linguistic reality without ever being reducible to an instrument of communication, since subjects were not "free" to use according to whim the system determining them, speech [*parole*] was distinguished from language [*langue*] as the individual from the social, and the accidental from the essential. Before conceptualizing the Freudian unconscious under the category of language [*langage*] and the symbol under that of the *signifier,* Lacan rethought the position of the subject in treatment from the perspective of speech. It would be a matter henceforth of founding a doctrinal tendency and of making of the SFP the political seat of the new Freudian orthodoxy: a Counter-Reformation movement in the face of the ascendancy of the adaptative ideals from across the Atlantic. "Orthodoxy" was to be taken in the noble sense of a dialectical renewal: a relay that would not destroy what it was replacing, a reading that would not denature, a veritable science of man and not a narrowly technical orientation in the service of the illusions of the ego. In other words, Lacan presented his adversaries with an argument they could not answer. By way of the detour of a theoretical argument, he seized on the subject of technique, the weak link on which he had been forced to pretend to yield. The *Rome Discourse* and the lecture preceding it constituted a first step toward the elaboration of a theory of therapy, of its conduct, temporality, and punctuation.

In the mirror adventure, Wallon differentiated three phases in the elaboration of the psychogenesis of the body proper: the specular, the imaginary, and finally the symbolic, which gave the child the wherewithal to organize his sensory experience. Without mentioning the psychologist, Lacan borrowed the term from him and transformed it completely by drawing on a personal interpretation of Saussurean linguistics. We have seen that the imaginary refers to the dual relation in which a self-image takes shape, in the other, according to a kind of *captation.* Now the symbolic introduces into that space a *mediation* comparable to that of the signifier or symbol in the register of language. In other words, if words name things by eliminating them through the existence of a sign which conceptualizes or *symbolizes* them, the *symbolic order,* as opposed to the *imaginary order,* allows the speaking subject to distance himself from his relation of captation to the other, by naming the space of the dual relation. That process is called a symbolization. In therapy, the mediation occurs through the third person of the analyst. Through the transference, he occupies simultaneously the position of an *imaginary other,* since he is invested with an illusory omnipotence, and that of a *symbolic other,* since he interprets the subject's words by restoring a meaning to them. In that perspective, the temporality of therapy is defined according to a Hegelian-Kojèvian dialectic. The subject imaginarily attributes to the analyst a knowledge about himself while at the same time conferring symbolic authority on him. Later on, Lacan would designate that place as that of the *sujet supposé savoir,* the subject alleged to know, or additionally as that of *l'Autre*—the Other—with an upper-case A, in order to distinguish it from the *imaginary other* [*autre*] with a lower-case a.

Therapy "progresses" according to a series of dialectical reversals. The analysand seeks recognition from the analyst. To that end he constructs resistances which are deployed in a negative transference. But he also imagines symbols by producing dreams, that is, *symbolized images.* At the other end, the analyst symbolizes the image by interpreting not resistances but dreams. In his *Rome Discourse,* Lacan would say that the analyst is a *practitioner of the symbolic function* and not a mere healer of symptoms. He would also emphasize that an act of language constitutes a communication in which the sender receives his message from the receiver in reverse form. At the end of the interpretative reversal, the subject can adapt to a *real* [*un réel*]. Lacan here introduced the third term of his topographical model, by revising the Freudian notion of *psychical reality.* For Freud that term designated unconscious desire and its associated phantasms. For the subject, that reality presents a coherence comparable to material reality. In fact, it takes on the value of a reality as powerful as external reality, to the point of even replacing it. In psychosis, it can take on a hallucinatory aspect. The Lacanian concept of the *Real* refers to that formulation and designates something in the order of the subject's desiring reality. The subject's adaptation to a real or to the Real means that he recognizes the reality of his unconscious desire and allows it to be recognized by his fellows through his success in symbolizing it. It will be perceived how Lacan was running contrary to an adaptative version of psychoanalysis. In 1950, at the World Congress of Psychiatry, he had fought the battle against Alexander. Three years later, he implemented—to resort to a Hegelianism—an *orthodox sublation of the doctrine* which no longer had anything in common with a modernist transcendence of the ideas from Vienna. It might be said that the orthodoxy of the sublation was more resolutely "modern" than the modernism of any transcendence.

If therapy consists in bringing about the subject's recognition of his desire for himself as well as for the other, it does not provoke any triumph of self-awareness, any recovery of the unconscious by consciousness, or of the id by the ego. It uncovers, on the contrary, a process of decentering, in which the subject delves, through speech, into the loss of his mastery, that is, into his Oedipal state. As a result, the analyst again reverses the situation through a labor of "symbolization of the symbol." He interprets the superego, symbol par excellence of all symbols. In Freud's second topographical model, that term characterizes the judge's position in relation to the ego, and refers specifically to the subject's internalization of parental interdictions. Now Lacan, before the war, had revealed himself to be the most sensitive clinical observer of his day when it came to self-punitive paranoia. He had emphasized repeatedly that paranoid-type crimes stemmed from the superego and were versions, for the criminal, of the realization of his own punishment. It may be said that the mature Lacan revived that function in order to make of it the ne plus ultra of a possible end of therapy. In symbolizing the superego, the analyst allows the subject to name the constraining—and occasionally murderous—force through which the concatenation of interdictions is internalized. Since he himself, through the transference, is the symbol of that interdiction, he has no difficulty in translating its meaning. His so-called "benevolent" neutrality prevents him from making choices in the subject's place, and the subject himself is freed, through the act of naming, from the *unreal* situation of therapy. But such therapy also resembles the experience of an organized variety of insanity or a controlled paranoia, since the subject delivers himself over to a real that may shift into madness.

Lacan was not "paranoid" as Marie Bonaparte naively believed, but his theory of therapy presupposed, at the core of every subject, the existence of a paranoid structure of cognition. On the subject of the case of Dr. Schreber, Freud emphasized that the paranoiac reconstructs the universe through the labors of his madness, and that such labors are, in fact, an attempt at achieving a cure, at reconstruction. As a theorist par excellence of paranoia, Lacan developed the ultimate consequences of that proposition by introducing into his conception of therapy the principle of a controlled paranoia. Lacan did not identify neurosis with psychosis, since he would introduce in 1956 the concept of "foreclosure," which is alien to Freud's argument, in order to think through the latter category. But he rethought the entire edifice by displacing psychoanalysis from the epistemological terrain of hysteria to that of paranoia: from the mad servant to the master-builder of doctrines. That process, already broached before the war, was pursued later on in new ways, and Hegelian philosophy served as a pivot for the displacement. It was in 1951, in his *Intervention sur le transfert* ["Intervention on the transference"], that Lacan, in the context of a discussion of the Dora case, attributed to Freud a Hegelian vision of therapy: "It is striking," he wrote, "that no one until now has underscored the fact that the Dora case is presented by Freud in the form of a series of dialectical reversals. It is not a matter here of an artifice of exposition for material concerning which Freud formulates decisively that its surfacing is abandoned to the whim of the patient. What is at stake is rather a scansion of the structures through which truth is transmuted for the patient, and which not only affect his comprehension of things, but his very position as a subject of which his "objects" are a function. This is to say that the concept of the presentation is *identical* to the subject's progress, namely, to the reality of analysis." [48]

In other words, Lacan was transporting a logic onto the terrain of an experience. From the evolution of therapy, he deduced the concept of analysis according to an argument evocative of the constructions of paranoia.

There is in that fascination for paranoia, as well as in the predominance accorded to the figure of the master and the slave, the memory of a mode of servitude which recaptures the man's intellectual itinerary. Lacan loved slaves or disciples in the manner of the *grands bourgeois* with whom he identified in his youth: Maurras, Clérambault, Kojève. It is hard not to intuit, in that dialectic of reversals characterizing for him the essence of therapy and of his theory, the reemergence of an hysterical fantasy in which Aimée would teach Freud's commentator the phases of the master by way of the furors of the servant.

To that theory two elements were added, which had already been elaborated on the morrow of the war. In a difficult article, to all appearances unrelated to psychoanalytic doctrine, Lacan had attempted to solve, with a sophism, the question of the *logical time* specific to subjectivity and of the *assertion of anticipated certainty.*[49]

A prison warden summons three detainees to appear before him and proposes a test to them in exchange for their freedom: "Here are five discs," he says, "three are white, and two black. I am going to affix one of those discs to the back of each of you without saying which disc I am choosing. You are to remain silent, but you are free to look at each other, although without having any sort of mirror at hand. The first one who manages to guess his color will leave the room on the condition that he can explain the logical motivation leading to his result." The prisoners accept and the director places a white disc on each of their backs. After having looked at each other for rather little time, they simultaneously leave the prison courtyard. Each one had separately understood that he was the bearer of a white disc at the conclusion of an identical bit of reasoning.

Three configurations are possible: (1) If A sees two blacks (on B and C), he deduces that he is white and leaves immediately. (2) If A sees a black and a white, he reasons as follows: If I were C (who is white) and I saw two blacks (A and B), I would leave. (3) If A sees two whites, he reasons as follows: If I were black, B and C would each see a black and a white. Each of them would say to himself: If I were black, the other white (B or C) would see two blacks. They would thus deduce that they were white and leave. But since they are not leaving, I deduce that I, A, am white.

That third argument is employed simultaneously by the three prisoners and that is why, separately, they explain their exit in the same way. In the first case, the argument functions in terms of logical exclusion. The *time for understanding* is reduced to the clarity of an observation: B and C are black. In the second case, a time for understanding is necessary prior to the *moment for concluding*. A ought to put himself in C's position and perform a deduction. The third case is more flawed since A must make a deduction in two phases (which will be the same for B and C). In a first phase, he assumes he is black and puts himself in place of B imputing a deduction to C and vice versa. Then in a second phase, he concludes, by the negative, that he is white. Since all three proceed with the same argument, each one simultaneously precipitates his judgment and his departure. The "time for understanding" is reduced to the "moment for concluding," which merges with the "instant of the gaze." Indeed, each one recognizes that he is white by watching the others hesitate to leave. Lacan named the *haste* characterizing this phenomenon of decision-making the "assertion of anticipated certainty."

In his *Rome Discourse,* which he entitled *Fonction et Champ de la parole et du langage en psychanalyse* ["The function and field of speech and language in psychoanalysis"],[50] he explicitly took up the two terms of "time for understanding" and "moment for concluding" in order to define the notion of a session of variable length or a "punctuated" session. One might reformulate the sophism as follows: In therapy, the analyst occupies the position of a penitentiary warden. He promises the analysand "freedom" by inviting him to solve the riddle of his condition. The latter individual speaks to an interlocutor who is to discover what his discourse is not saying, since by definition, the unconscious fails to be at the disposition of the subject. Now the warden is fooled on his own grounds. He has promised freedom to a single prisoner, but finds himself constrained to grant it to all three. In other words, the analyst is indeed master of that truth whose progress is the discourse of the subject, but that mastery is limited by two boundaries. On the one hand, he can never predict what will be the time for understanding of each subject, and, on the other, he is himself prisoner of a symbolic order fixing the law for all partners in the form of a law of language. Man does indeed speak because symbols have made him a man. The analyst is thus but an alleged master acting in the manner of a scribe. He deciphers and punctuates a discourse as a commentator "adds" punctuation to a sacred text.

It is here that the function of haste intervenes. In order for the analysand to be led onto the terrain of a "true decision," without taking as a reference point any preconceived span of time which might serve as an escape, the analyst must precede him, at least in deed. In that manner, he acts like any of the prisoners allowing another prisoner to deduce his decision from what he supposes to be that of his neighbor. Lacan thus theorized the principle behind the variable-length session and answered his accusers: It is better, he was saying in substance, to conclude too soon than to let the patient conclude too late and get mired in vain and "empty speech." From that point of view, punctuation aims at delivering the subject of true utterance by reducing the time for understanding to the moment for concluding. "We would not have said as much," wrote Lacan, "had we not been convinced that in once experimenting with what has been called our short sessions, we succeeded in bringing to light in a male subject fantasies of anal pregnancy with a dream of resolution through a Caesarian, at a time at which we would otherwise still be listening to his speculations on Dostoyevsky's art." [51]

In order to specify the nature of the procedure, Lacan made reference to a passage from the analysis of the *Wolf Man*. Freud observed that his patient, aged twenty-five, imbued his impressions from age four with an intensity he would have been incapable of imagining at the time. He concluded that that manner of reasoning constituted a deferred (*nachträglich*) effect functioning in two phases. The analysand was one-and-a-half years old when he received a first impression to which he was incapable of reacting. Later the first effect of deferment was produced: At the age of four, the child underwent, without understanding, the revivification of that impression and succeeded only twenty years later in describing consciously what had happened then. He did not take into account the three temporal phases and situated his present ego in the long-resolved situation. Freud emphasized that the analyst should follow him on that terrain, since a correct observation of oneself and an adequate interpretation result from one's negligence of the distance separating the second and third temporal phases. In other words, Freud gave priority to the second phase of deferred action to the extent that the analyst did not have any means of describing the processes produced in the second phase. [52]

Lacan commented on that observation, stating that Freud "annulled the *time for understanding* to the benefit of the *moments for concluding* that precipitate the subject's meditation toward the meaning to be assigned to the original event." And he added: "We should note that *time for understanding* and *moment for concluding* are functions that we have defined in a purely logical theorem and which are familiar to our students for having been shown to be quite propitious to the dialectical analysis through which we guide them in the process of a psychoanalysis." [53]

To be sure, Freud did not invent a theory of the variable-length session on the basis of the effect of deferred action. But we may observe in this case, in detail, how Lacan's return to Freud functioned. Lacan exploits the "resonances" of the Freudian text, listens attentively to what it does not say. His adversaries would have an easy time accusing him of attributing to Freud statements which were but the product of his over-refined or even "paranoid" wit, in the sense that paranoia designates for psychiatrists a "falsity of judgment." His dogmatic students would have the tendency to read Freud in the light of Lacan, believing that the latter's concepts were already to be found in the former. As for less hostile and partisan commentators, they would simply say that every innovative thought is characterized by an idiosyncratic, and even "paranoid," way of displacing the accepted meaning of a text or a discovery. What remains is the question: Why did Lacan need to conjure up Hegel, Freud, Prajāpati, Zen, and a prison warden in order to fight the overly technical orientation that was reducing the principle of therapy to a matter of clockwork? Would it not have been worthwhile to formulate all those matters more simply? Apparently not. But it should also be asked whether that theory—for it is one—did not serve to justify the extremely personal manner in which Lacan conducted his analyses: ceaseless agitation, an inability to remain seated too long in his armchair; a taste for money; surprise interventions in real life; and finally, at the threshold of old age, a dissolution of the time of the session, which could merge with the moment of a gaze and the gesture of payment. We have already answered that question: At stake was both a genuine theory of therapy and the authentic expression of a temperament.

Both were unacceptable for the partisans of the "classic" conception as established by the standards of the IPA. Those standards subordinated every theory of analysis, were it training or nontraining, to a technical imperative whose essential function was to analyze resistances and limit the therapist's imaginary omnipotence in the transference. But Lacan bypassed resistances in order to listen to speech, and placed the boundary of omnipotence in the symbolic order, that is, "elsewhere" than in technique and in conformity with the demands of the unconscious. Lacan's technique had the advantage of laying bare the various forms assumed by an obsession with technique whose function was to hide a theoretical void. But the gain was accompanied by a certain loss: It had the fault of allowing therapists to gnaw away at the time of the session and to transform the creative function of haste into a ritual of zero-degree duration.

During the summer of 1953, Lacan hastily put together the 150 type-written pages of his immense *Rome Discourse*. He ended the presentation with an invocation drawn from the Upanishads. At the end of their noviciate, men, the Devas (heavenly divinities) and the Asuras (earthly divinities) asked Prajāpati, the god of thunder, to speak to them. To each group, he answered by the word: "Da." The Devas understood: "Tame yourselves (*Damyata*)," since the sacred text says that the powers from above yield to the law of speech. The men understood: "Give (*Datta*)," since the sacred text says that they will recognize each other by the gift of speech. Finally, the Asuras understood: "Give thanks (*Dayadhvam*)," since the sacred text says that the powers from below resonate at the invocation of speech. The reference was not chosen randomly. Originally, the Upanishad word designated an initiatic rite through which a student sat at the foot of a master in order to receive wisdom. The teaching establishes a bond among objects partaking of the cosmos, of sacrifice, and of the human psyche. In the course of its transmission, none of the terms can be reduced to its mere meaning, since each of them takes on all possible resonances.

On August 8, François Perrier announced through a circular that the founding meetings of the SFP would be held in Rome on September 26 and 27.[54] Lacan's presentation, originally scheduled for the Conference of Psychoanalysts of the Romance Languages, was maintained. Perrier specified that the members of the SPP had not waited for the constitution of a commission of inquiry to ask in London for the exclusion from membership of those who had resigned. He forgot to specify that they had committed the error of neglecting the international regulation, and characterized the current situation as "surprising," while abstaining from searching out its causes. But he emphasized that the new society had received the sympathy of numerous foreigners, promising it a brilliant future.

Despite the general enthusiasm, Lacan was not happy with his fate. He felt isolated and could not tolerate the break with the mother society. In fact, he found it hard to bear not having founded the new group himself. He feared not being recognized as well as the consequences of splitting away from the medical world and the international community. Anguished and at times panicked, he sought to propagate his doctrine on the market of existing institutions. Like Lagache, he wanted an implantation of psychoanalysis in the university, but in a perspective in which it would find its allies on the side of philosophy and not psychology. Aware of the expanding situation of Freudian ideas, he directed his attention to two institutions that seemed important to him for the future, the Catholic Church and the Communist Party.

At the beginning of September, he sent Lucian Bonnafé a copy of his Rome address without asking him in any way for his opinion of the text. "I am sure," Bonnafé explains, "that the gesture was intended to attract the party leadership's attention to his doctrine. Lacan was quite attentive to what the party thought of his work."[55] To be sure, with the exception of a few psychiatrists, no Communist was yet interested in the ideas of Lacan, whose name was still unknown to the general public. But he was betting on the future. He no doubt thought that a day would come in which a new generation of Marxists would be capable of rediscovering Freud in the light of his own theory.

Toward the Church, Lacan's position was far clearer. At the time he sent his discourse to Bonnafé, he sent a long letter to his brother Marc-François. He informed him that he had founded (*sic*) with Lagache a new society which had brought a majority of the students with it. He found it all quite bracing, and was delighted to be able at last to diffuse his teaching on clinical matters. In his opinion, the crux was in Rome where he was about to deliver an address on language in psychoanalysis. In addition, Lacan informed his brother that his wisest students were urging him to obtain an audience with the Holy Father, and he himself felt rather inclined to do so. In his eyes, it would not be without interest for the future of psychoanalysis for His Majesty to pay homage to the "Common Father." He thus asked his brother Marc-François to assist him in obtaining an audience with the Pope.[56]

The summit meeting would not take place. Pius XII refused to grant Lacan the desired interview and his successors would do the same. In 1953, Marc-François did not know anyone in the Roman Curia to whom to recommend his brother, who was obliged to give up his plan after having unsuccessfully attempted to arrange things through the French embassy. Despite the failure, he could not stop himself, after the congress, from traveling to Castel Gandolfo to attend a public audience in the company of Serge Leclaire and Maryse Choisy.

Normally, it is maniacs, melancholics, or paranoiacs who impose their delirious complaints on the great figures of the world. Artaud wrote to the pontiff calling him a dog and recommending the Dalai Lama as an acceptable pope. President Wilson took himself for Gladstone and assigned himself a divine mission. As for Aimée, she was satisfied sending her manuscripts to the Prince of Wales, then, not receiving any answer, she botched her assassination attempt. Sovereigns and celebrities also have pride of place in the discourse of psychotics. At the heart of the Aeropagus, the Pope enjoyed exemplary fame. Not only was he unique in reigning over the planet while governing the smallest state in the world, but he was incomparable in not engendering any descendents. Being the father of no one, he was the patriarch of all, irremovable in his temporal power, inaccessible in his renunciation of procreation, eternal in his mission of divulging to men a revealed world which was its own sequel. The person of the Holy Father fascinates the insane as well as those doctrinal masters interested in becoming popes. It is not clear why, given that principle, Lacan would not be received by the Vatican. It remains, of course, open to speculation who would have played the role of Prajāpati.

Lacan was never mad, although he was occasionally a megalomaniac. His desire to meet the Pope was based on a coherent political position. At the time, as we have seen, the future of psychoanalysis was a challenge to the Church, and the future of the Church was of interest to psychoanalysis. In other words, a priest wanting to be a therapist had a better chance of pursuing a career in the SFP than in the SPP, where nonphysicians were scarcely ever admitted to the ranks of titular members. That is why the defrocked, priests, and Christians who had not studied medicine, tended to prefer the new society to the old one. But several other reasons explain that attraction. Lacan's doctrine, on the one hand, and Lagache's academic orientation, on the other, were better attuned to Christian aspirations than the medical ideal of Nacht's partisans. The first because it revived certain theological themes, the second because it was in continuity with the teaching function characterizing religious schools. In point of fact, it was essentially Lacan's doctrine which attracted Catholic intellectuals, and particularly the Jesuits, insofar as it allowed for an ac-

ceptable assumption of Freudian *doxa*. The existence of such an attraction was tendential: It did not characterize the totality of Christians or priests interested in psychoanalysis.

In his concern to privilege a subject constituted by the desire of the other, in
his references to the mystical tradition, in his manifold winks at the technique of
directing consciences, and finally in his quest of a Trinitarian order opening, through
the symbolic, onto the prevalence of a divine word, Lacan translated Freudian discourse into a language familiar to Catholic tradition. In following his own discourse, men accustomed to theological debates were apt to rediscover the Rome of
the Vatican or the spiritual exercises of Ignatius of Loyola. All that was easier to
digest for them than Freud's apparent positivism, his excessively radical critique of
religious illusions, the remains of his biologism, and finally his violent affirmation
of the primacy of sexuality. In brief, Lacan charmed the priests, but did not fool
them as to the atheistic character of what he was up to. He was interested in the
Pope without seeking God, and in religion without rekindling faith. His dream was
that a two-thousand-year-old institution could serve as a source of support for the
recognition of his doctrine and his person. That is why he encouraged his disciples
who were priests not to leave their orders, just as he had advised others to study
medicine, and still others not to break with the restrictive superego of existent institutions. There developed in his orbit, starting with the *Rome Discourse,* a veritable
"current" of Catholic inspiration.

For the history of the French psychoanalytic community, that current came
to occupy a place left vacant by the turmoil of the postwar purges. Previously, when
priests were as yet unfamiliar with Freudianism, a Christian inspiration could be
heard at the SPP, on the one hand, in Laforgue's spiritualism and, on the other, in
Pichon's Maurrassian Catholicism. The latter tendency was shot through with both
chauvinism and a separatism borrowed from the works of Dalbiez.[57] Now the new
configuration at midcentury ratified the liquidation of that legacy. On its terrain,
there developed a new current of Christian inspiration that was plainly Catholic and
stripped of all chauvinism. It arose in the SFP and would truly flourish in the circle
of the EFP. It was divided into two modalities. One drew its nourishment strictly
from the Lacanian recasting of psychoanalysis, the other from the sensuous discourse of Françoise Dolto, sole heir to Laforgue's spiritualism and to a certain Pichonian sense of Frenchness. Lacan's Catholic students did not appeal to the same
Church as Dolto's did, even if they all assembled beneath the banner of that flamboyant pair. The former entertained philosophical inquiries and sought to build
bridges between psychoanalysis and theology, whereas the latter tended rather to
cultivate a faith that was populist in inspiration. In brief, some were theoreticians
of the soul and the mind, and the others clinicians of the family, childhood, or the
maternal body. The SFP presented an attractive aspect to all of them. Not only did
it respect nonphysicians and university academics, but it was especially generous in
its treatment of provincials.

As opposed to the SPP, which was essentially composed of Parisian *grands
bourgeois,* the SFP appealed to a certain Gallic pride. It was proud of being more
"French" than its rival, that is, more open and more "national." It did not have a

choice: In order to be recognized by the IPA, it had to prove that its existence was not factitious and justify the reality of its influence. Its youth, its enthusiasm, the soundness of its claims were not enough to demonstrate its strength. In that context, the reactivation of a Parisian-provincial axis was not exempt from a certain chauvinism. After World War II, chauvinism disappeared from the French psychoanalytic community as a doctrinal component of the movement. The "chauvinism" which resurfaced during the split, with its implicit privileging of a French character of the SFP, was thus not of the same nature as the chauvinism of years gone by. It was not the affirmation of some superiority of the French mind, but partook rather of the actual situation at the time. The masters of the SFP were all "good Frenchmen," of Catholic culture, raised in the harem of national intelligence. They were neither Jews, not emigrants, nor among the "assimilated." Even if they did not overtly appeal to their French identity, and even if, for the most part, they were agnostics or atheists, they were felt to be more Latin, more Gallic, and more "Christian" than the masters of the SPP. That is why the rebirth of a Parisian-provincial axis and the twofold emergence of a Catholic and an academic current was accompanied, in the SFP, by a sentiment of "non-Jewishness."

If one restricts oneself to the sociological composition of each group, one sees that the opposition Jew/non-Jew has no relevance to the problem under consideration. Indeed there were as many Jews as non-Jews in each group, and anti-Semitism was absent from the one as much as from the other as a doctrinal component. The feeling of Jewishness or non-Jewishness does not respond to a sociological analysis so much as to the comprehension of a phenomenon of belonging or an "identificatory bond."

Because it identified with non-Jewish masters and implemented a policy of national resurgence, the SFP gave its adherents the impression of being a "less Jewish" society than the SPP. But the SPP, for its part, saw itself as "more Jewish" than its rival insofar as it remained affiliated with the IPA under the banner of a master who was both Jewish and an emigrant. In other words, the two societies looked at each other like porcelain dogs. The SFP sought to incarnate a French school of psychoanalysis issuing forth from the Declaration of the Rights of Man, and the SPP tended to represent an internationalist legitimacy stemming directly from the great Austro-Hungarian diaspora. In relation to the IPA, the former wanted a national, democratic, and republican identity conforming to the ideals of the French Revolution, whereas within the IPA, the latter drew its authority from a community without borders, in which being Jewish was symbolically part of the glorious Freudian epic. As a result of that polarization, the "Jewish question" reappeared in the French psychoanalytic movement in the form of a feeling of belonging or not belonging. That phenomenon occasionally led to unconscious displays of Judaeophobia or anti-internationalism, particularly in the cases of Berge, Mauco, or the two Favezes, who incarnated the mood of the SFP at its most "French," but it did not have much to do with the prewar conflicts where what was at stake, beneath the categories of the opposition between a "French" psychoanalysis and a "German" psychoanalysis, was in fact anti-Semitism and anti-egalitarianism.

Thus the Christian current found its identity within a group defining itself by

its feeling of non-Jewishness, that is, by its quest for a French school of psychoanalysis unrelated to the ideals of a "French psychoanalysis". In Rome, in September, the
Church became the elder daughter of a new Freudian France.

"That evening," François Perrier has written, "the goodnatured cadence of
cabbies throughout Rome provided the rhythmic accompaniment to a procession of
psychoanalysts." [58] If the SFP's adherents had a bit the impression of participating in
a student rebellion, the masters made no secret of their enthusiasm, even as they
maintained a certain reserve. They realized that future negotiations presented less
than optimal prospects, and could already sense the Roman sky clouding over.
Nevertheless, they lingered in the city's taverns, sampled (in abundance) Orvieto
wine, and treated themselves to Severino's celebrated *saltimbocca*.

Proud of their legitimacy, the representatives of the SPP spoke first. Francis
Pasche, overseer of an "orthodoxy" which would be the drawing card of the new
Institute, dealt with anxiety and the Freudian theory of drives, while Lebovici and
Diatkine presented a study of childhood fantasies. They would become the specialists of a variety of child analysis attached to the ideals of psychiatry. Barely had they
packed their bags than the "others," the SFP team, burst into the large lecture hall
of the Istituto di Psicologia dell 'Università, in order to hear the much awaited address. Professor Canastrelli opened the discussion by declaring that psychology
brought to psychoanalysis an incomparable guarantee of scientificity. Then Lagache
took the floor to express his regret that Lacan's address could not be delivered, as
planned, in the context of the XVIth Conference of Psychoanalysts of the Romance
Languages. Negotiations to that end had failed.

Too long to be read out loud, Lacan's address had been distributed to participants. In Rome, the speaker thus limited himself to "translating" his address into
an idiom accessible to his audience. He insisted on the symbolic order and affirmed
that the ego was only half a subject. In addition, he took a shot at Lagache by saying
that psychoanalysis was not commensurate with psychology. Vexed, the latter realized that Lacan was pulling the rug out from under his feet. He had hoped to serve
as mediator between the text and its audience, but the lecturer was doing that himself in an idiom in which "for once there was nothing Mallarméan." [59] Before offering his reaction, he read a letter from Juliette Favez-Boutonier, who was unable to
make the trip and who had charged him with reading her commentary to the members of the congress.

Whereupon Lagache gave himself the floor.

Instead of stating clearly that his position diverged from Lacan's, he presented his objections in so allusive and sinuous a manner that they seemed like
corrections noted in the margin of a brilliant student paper: "I will begin by specifying and commenting on what the author says of the literary genre in which he has
expressed himself; this is certainly not a 'report' as normally conceived; I find myself
a bit frustrated in my admittedly dusty academic expectations: I don't find any
methodic division of the subject, nor any history of it, nor a bibliography, nor any
of those objectivizing aids which are so agreeable. Shall we call this an essay? We
shall say with the author that it is a 'discourse' which ends with Prajāpati's dialogue
with the Devas, the Asuras, and men." [60] After that introduction, Lagache observed

that Lacan "was not attacking a technique, but rather a distortion of technique," which reduces technique to a series of "reifying devices." In other words, he attempted to bring his partner back into the fold by emphasizing that his innovations were acceptable insofar as they entailed a critique of distortions and not a rejection of the technique which authorized them. Now the Lacanian position was far more extreme. It did indeed attribute distortion to a technique serving as a smokescreen for the abandonment of theory. It thus rejected any possible rectification of that technique, to which it opposed a rereading of Freudian doctrine and a rediscovery of the technique that would issue from it. After pretending to submit, Lacan announced that he would never yield on the subject of *his* desire, that is, of *his* technique, which he considered to be authentically Freudian. In the face of that imperative, Lagache remained ambiguous since he failed to say what a technique without distortion and without Lacan would be.

Lagache then reproached the speaker with the malicious use he made of quotations. He observed that Lacan did not hesitate to make texts say the opposite of what they meant. Then he defended his beloved unity of psychology by defending the proposition that one can articulate different fields without giving up their specificity. Finally, he returned to the question of technique, only to underscore his refusal to take a stand: "Lacan alludes," he said, "to the problem of the length of sessions. And at this point I will not be very precise, since no one knows very much about this subject. I think Lacan is not wrong in saying that it is unreasonable to consider the length of the session as fixed, once and for all, at fifty or fifty-five minutes. But neither do I think that the short session is the only possible consequence of that doubt. In certain cases, a speeding up of the rhythm, a greater frequency of sessions of normal length, brings about the advent of what Lacan calls authentic or true speech [*la parole vraie*]." [61] We should note in passing that Lacan included in his theory an increase in the number of sessions or the speeding up of their rhythm, and that Lagache did not manage to define what "normal length" might be. Was it the standard of fifty minutes or a length whose characteristic would be not being short? In either case, one would have to determine where precisely the "norm" was located and whether its principle was acceptable. Deep down, Lagache did not dare say publicly that the theory of sessions of variable length ran the risk of turning into a "technique of the shortened session." He limited himself to "allusions."

After a brief but remarkable intervention by Granoff on the subject of object relations, Françoise Dolto mounted the podium. Superb in her guru-like eloquence, she announced that she had come to Rome for the first time in her life. Then she told a tale about a fountain and dragons: "I think that I am here playing the little dragon contributing what she can to the encounter with what has been given to us by the big dragon Lacan, accompanied by the other big dragon Lagache. I am speaking so that there will be harmony." [62] She then reproached the principal speaker for his discrediting of the mythology of instinctual maturation and for not perceiving that mythology is itself constructed like a language whose meaning is translated by the analyst. After paying vibrant homage to the role of women in psychoanalysis, judged to be more capable than men, through their sense of "nesting," of climbing the rungs of intrasubjective exchange, Françoise Dolto recalled for her audience that she herself had demonstrated through her clinical experience, that language existed with or without words. She then evoked the famous story of the "flower doll."

In 1949, "the little Marette girl," having become "Madame" Dolto, had presented to her colleagues of the SPP two cases that would create quite a stir. What was at stake was drawing two young girls, Bernadette and Nicole, out of their psychotic state. One would often scream without managing to make herself understood; the other remained mute even though she was not deaf. Bernadette tended to reify human beings and to humanize plants in order to destroy herself, whereas Nicole remained petrified or reified in her muteness. For the first case, Françoise had the idea of asking the mother to construct something like a Surrealist object which would play the role of a scapegoat for the child. Bernadette would thus be able to rout out her destructive tendencies on her own. The "flower doll" was born: a stem wrapped in a green fabric, in place of limbs, and an artificial daisy for a face. Bernadette projected her negative attitudes onto the "thing" and soon began to talk. With that excellent result, Françoise decided to try again. She tried the doll on Nicole, who abandoned her silence and rediscovered words. At the Trousseau hospital, her students imitated the mother-goddess without realizing that the "miracle" had been more a function of their teacher's clinical genius than of the doll itself. And yet the experiment was extraordinary: It revealed that a symbol could play a mediating role in the restoration of speech. When Lacan heard of her adventure, he reacted with true enthusiasm. He informed Françoise that the flower doll fit in well with his own research on the image of the body proper, the mirror stage, and the fragmented body. He also told her that he hoped someday to contribute a theoretical commentary to her experiments. Thereafter they became the best of friends.[63]

In Rome, Lacan did not comment on Dolto's works, but it was she who brought her contribution to the big dragon's discourse. On that day, she fulfilled a function that would remain hers for thirty years and would allow the Lacanian movement to soar as prodigiously as it did.

Taken with his friend's words, Lacan rushed toward her and embraced her. He announced that a "divine voice" had been heard through her mouth. "But what did I do? I was so moved at having to speak that I was no longer thinking of what I might say." "By God, Françoise-little-dragon," Lacan answered, "you no longer needed to think of it in order to make us the gift of your speech, and even in order to speak very well about it."[64]

Didier Anzieu, who had ended his therapy with Lacan two months earlier, then took the floor in a rather combative manner. He reproached the Lacanian position for its excessive systemization, which stemmed, he thought, from the way in which the speaker sought to identify language with the entirety of the psychoanalytic domain and the totality of human praxis. He observed that a simple Cartesian theory of language-signs would have been able to account for the phenomena described. Then he emphasized that alongside phenomenology and even existentialism, there existed another current of thought which privileged the power of speech and produced illuminism and Surrealism. "That current," he said, "was hardly referred to in the speaker's presentation, but it is perhaps more or less unconsciously at the origin of the themes he has proposed to us; in the effort to make of language the center of a system accounting for the field of psychoanalytic experience, there perhaps remain several residues of enigmatic adoration before the surprising power sung by poets and which Surrealism was the last to renew." After those two remarks, Anzieu spoke in praise of Lacan's work and emphasized that he allowed for a demystification of the analyst's position in therapy: "When I began my psychoanalytic studies, there were a certain number of problems I expected psychoanalysis to be the first to attack, and which I feared, for a while, that analysis would be the first to recoil from in fear: the problem of the ends of analysis, the problem of the cultural character of those ends, the problem of the idolatry that might reign over this new modern myth. Assuredly, the report we have here reassures us. Its demystification of the analyst-idol, its way of positing the ends of analysis correspond precisely with what most of us here, myself included, have been living these last months." [65]

That intervention was no doubt the most interesting one in the colloquium. Not only was it the only one to inquire into the historical foundations of Lacanian doctrine, but it came from a man who did not hesitate to ask his analyst to account for his Surrealist past. Now that past belonged to him as well, since it bore witness to the period in which Lacan was Aimée's therapist.

On Tuesday, September 27, after an intervention by Professor Perrotti and a long commentary by Leclaire, Lacan answered his interlocutors point by point.

He began by thanking Lagache for having commented on his report with the solemnity of a thesis director. Then he elaborated on his use of the theory of the signifier. He rejected the notion of language-signs, reproaching Anzieu with falsely ascribing to him a magical conception of language. Finally, he appealed to Lévi-Strauss and responded further to Lagache that he did not share his enthusiasm for freedom: "Things have even reached the point that certain enthusiasms, however approving they may be, are apt to inspire greater reservations on my part: That the liberatory effects my remarks have aroused are applauded is fine, but let it happen just quickly enough for the applause to die down along with the euphoria of that sentiment." [66] Toward the end of his discourse, he made use of a metaphor to define his technique of precipitous or hasty punctuation. He compared language to a "barrier" whose "sound" must be traversed in order to anticipate the subject's resistances and provoke the *bang-bang* [in English] *of true interpretation*. An admirable formula!

The heart of the response was constituted by a diatribe against Anzieu, whom Lacan called his "student." He quite properly rejected the notion that Surrealism was part of a "magical" tradition in order to retain its most modern aspect: the uncovering of man's relations to the symbolic order. But he added immediately: "If it is indeed in the power that I accord to language that Anzieu is intent on seeing the meaning of my remarks, let him renounce tricking me out with Romantic sponsors. Without repudiating my Surrealist friendships, or disavowing the Marat-like style of their discourse, it is rather under the aegis of Monsieur de Tocqueville that I would situate my own. And in this, at least, that I indicate that language, in freeing itself from the human mediations which have masked it until now, reveals a power in relation to which the old-regime pretentions of those mediations to the absolute, will appear to be ludicrous attenuations." [67]

In 1953, Lacan wanted to be spokesman for a reading of Freud based on Hegel (still), but also on Heidegger, Saussure, and anthropology. Implicitly he did not "disavow" his Surrealist past, but neither did he refer to it any more, whereas later on, in 1966, he would come back to it.

Since the war, he had forged a new face for himself and felt, perhaps unwittingly, that transformation to be a disavowal of the past. In his policy of rekindling orthodoxy and negotiating with the institution, he was "playing" Tocqueville against Marat, that is, the intransigence of an enlightened conservatism against the follies of the Revolution. At the time, moreover, the Surrealist movement was producing only epigones. It was consequently a question of wiping clean the slate of a past that had become inconvenient in order to turn Lacanianism into something of a Phoenix born of its own ashes or engendered through internal mutations unrelated to its external environment. Its founder could thus present himself as the *first* founder of a French school of Freudianism, a unique enterprise bereft of links with any other past than the one it ascribed to itself.

Lacan was horrified at being reminded of his origins and projected that attitude onto his conception of history by choosing to see himself as a reader of Freud and a son of no one. That tendency—to denial—would lead the third and fourth generations of the master's disciples to declare that their doctrine owed nothing to the France of the interwar years; nor to the twelve founders, whose names they would forget; nor to Wallon; nor to Surrealism. Those disciples would live their history as a family romance, attributing a prestigious ancestry to Lacan: Freud without Pichon, Hegel without Kojève. And simultaneously, they would make the French history of psychoanalysis begin with the postwar years, that is, with that rosy period in which they were themselves the analysands of an adored monarch. That reversal, in a legend, of a disavowed origin, had its inception in Rome.

Toward 2 p.m., Lagache bestowed laurels on the man who was already his greatest rival. "I am satisfied," he said, "and we can congratulate each other that this conference took place, reserving a very special bouquet for our friend Jacques Lacan, not only for his address, and comments which are the most idiosyncratic expression of his own genius, but also because of all his material efforts, in what he has undertaken, and because of his spirit of enterprise, which bear witness for us not only to his genius, but also to his virtues." [68]

III. Maurice Bouvet or French Neo-Freudianism

Too old to be part of the third generation, and as yet too young, before the war, to fit into the second, Maurice Bouvet occupied the strange place in the expanding SPP of a junior among the masters and an elder brother among the students. Analyzed by Parcheminey, then supervised in his controls by Nacht and Leuba, he accepted Lagache on his couch shortly before the split, a circumstance which demanded certain precautions on his part.

A graduate of the École polytechnique near the head of his class, Maurice's father embarked on a career as an artillery officer. Garrisoned at Clermont-Ferrand, he married a girl from that region, and it was in that city that their son studied classics at the Collège Massillon. In 1932, Bouvet finished his internship and became a student of Jean Castaignac before being drawn to mental pathology. Following the classic itinerary, he defended his thesis on disturbances of nitrogenous metabolism and nervous lesions, then became chief of a clinic in Professor Laignel-Lavastine's service. Very early on, he was stricken with meningitis, which was gradually to make him blind and to spare him military service—a painful fate for the son of a career officer. This infirmed clinician was a calm man who loved hunting, fishing, gastronomy, and perhaps women. He always arranged to conceal his secret passions from those around him. He did not marry and his friends did not know where he lived. When they drove him home, they would always drop him off a few blocks from his place and watch him take off on foot for his inner sanctum. In 1946, Bouvet was elected an adhering member of the SPP, and two years later he was promoted to titular rank. Selected by his elder colleagues, he was called on in 1949 to sit on the commission on instruction, then on the Society's board, where he fulfilled the tasks of treasurer until 1953.

Without personal ambition, he resembled not Lacan, nor Nacht, nor Lagache. He had no project for psychoanalysis other than to exercise it in the best possible manner, rigorously, and even ritualistically. If his illness prevented him from adopting combative positions, his ethics forbade him from using his analysands in a conflict in his interest. That is why he was respected by the masters and admired by the students, who appreciated his neutrality. He preferred the calm of his office to the noise of a society in crisis, and received his patients in a bizarre apartment on the rue Jean-Mermoz which he shared with a gynecologist. The place was ugly, impersonal, without any attention to appearances, and rendered a bit less sad by the sole added touch of sumptuous flowers, which were changed regularly.[69] As for the law books decorating his library, they did not really bespeak their owner's interests. Perhaps they were there to signify the exalted morality of the man, dressed in his dark suits, as dark, perhaps, as the blackness into which his blindness had plunged him.

When the split came, Bouvet hesitated and abstained several times in the voting. Torn between a genuine attachment to the ideals of medicine and profound sympathy for the progressive tendency, he finally opted for the Nacht clan without ever holding Lacan up to obloquy. He did not follow the latter in his interest in language, and was hard put to accept the twists he was imposing on a technique Bouvet assumed to be established once and for all. He remained sensitive to the notion of the imaginary, appreciated the clinical talents of the psychiatrist, rejected his audacities and overall preferred the author of *The Mirror Stage* to the flamboyant monarch of the *Rome Discourse*. Too honest to allow himself to be carried away by the passions of rivalry, Bouvet did not accuse his neighbor of plotting, condemned no one, and revealed himself to be open to numerous influences. If he swung toward the authoritarian group, it was because he opted to adhere completely to the principles of a medical psychoanalysis, defined by standard criteria and confined to a specialization. That did not mean he was hostile to *Laienanalyse*. He simply considered Freudianism to be a medical discipline and not a philosophical revolution.

Influenced by the phenomenological tradition of the prewar years and closer to Claude on schizophrenia than to Schiff or Lacan on paranoia, he did not possess a good knowledge of Freud's writings, to which he preferred the revisionist version of Fenichel. He had a lively curiosity for the Anglo-Saxon and American movement even though ego psychology and Kleinianism were alien to him. Nevertheless, like all the neo-Freudians of the period of expansion, Bouvet built his work on a vision of the second topographical model which privileged the ego at the expense of the unconscious. He thus remained the representative of an adaptive ideal conforming to the principal aspirations of the IPA. Whereas Nacht organized the Institute as a function of his personal power and did not produce any genuinely new body of work, Bouvet attempted to endow the group with a real theory of therapy, in the face of the Lacanian advance. He behaved like a benevolent father toward those students progressing on the other bank. How ought one to act when one has been the supervisee of an authoritarian master, the analyst of a dissident master, and the elder brother of a generation in the throes of rebellion? Bouvet always chose rigor without hatred, orthodoxy without transcendence, and finally conservatism against new ideas. No doubt that suited the temperament of an army officer's son. The infirm clinician was not a happy man. Today his work is no longer read and his name is known only within the walls of the house of Freud. In 1953, his choice of neutrality meant the loss of an important ally for the dissidents and the gain for the Institute of a witness who refused to howl with the pack.

Lacan knew Bouvet's attitudes. With the advent of the split, he began choosing him as his target. Through the mediation of Henri Ey, who was pursuing a policy of confrontation, the two were pitted against each other a first time through their texts for the *Encyclopédie médico-chirurgicale*. Henri Ey had asked each of them for an article on the theory of therapy. What was in question was explaining to physicians the concrete reality of listening to the unconscious. Bouvet dealt with standard therapy and Lacan with its variants. Neither of them knew in advance what the other would write. The result was edifying.[70]

Bouvet wrote a weighty piece, as long as the *Rome Discourse*, a classic expression of the reigning orthodoxy. Analysands were referred to as "patients" and analysts were labeled "physicians." As for treatment, it was entirely centered on an analysis of the ego by means of a desirable reduction of resistances. "So much so," observed the author, "that it is at present possible to speak of an 'analysis of the ego,' and one of my teachers told me just recently that the word 'unconscious' had almost disappeared from contemporary analytic works. He was, of course, being ironic, but his statement nevertheless is quite revealing of that dominant concern of analysts these days to obviate the important deficiencies of the ego which, until the contemporary period, had seemed to constitute the limit of analysis."

He was not being ironic: During that post-Freudian period, the concept of the unconscious did indeed tend to "disappear" from psychoanalytic texts. Like most therapists in the international community, Bouvet maintained that the aim of analytic psychotherapy had always been to reinforce the ego's strength and to render conscious what had been unconscious. Implicitly, he translated "Wo Es war, soll Ich werden"[71] as "le Moi doit déloger le Ça [the ego ought to dislodge or supplant the id]," and derived from it a series of precepts which were the spontaneous theorization of the standard criteria: fixed fees, number of sessions determined in advance, length of sessions clocked to the minute, color of therapist's attire, odorless neutrality, recommendations of prudence, etc. All these were accepted as established values, unquestionable and unquestioned. The article defined quite remarkably the medical and essentially technical conception of psychoanalysis through which, right up to the present in the SPP, the principle of an analytic *profession* has been affirmed.

Reading it, one understands why the author, despite his hesitations, could not follow the dissidents. His Freud was a pure physician, without any desire for universality and without any philosophical or cultural vocation. To that extent, Bouvet was indeed the chief theoretician of a French neo-Freudianism which was less adventurous than the American variety.

Obliged to speak of "variants," Lacan was not happy with the task assigned him by Henri Ey. He saw himself as representing an orthodoxy, and considered his— American and French—adversaries to be revisionists or deviationists. He too sought support in the second topographical model, but in order to derive hypotheses that were radically opposed to those of Bouvet and the entirety of the neo-Freudian movement. Despite his reluctance, he gave Ey the requested contribution; what was at stake for him was reconquering the medical "market," which seemed lost for those who had seceded. In 1966, he would retain for his *Écrits* the title "Variantes de la cure-type [Variants of standard therapy]," but would add the following commentary: "Let us say that we regarded it as abject. What our throat has just emitted allows us to rewrite with a certain lightness our first chapter."[72]

Instead of defining standard therapy with its variants, Lacan continued to promote his own procedures. He dealt with three terms, "defense," "resistance," and "ego," and attempted to reinscribe them in philosophical terms. In the history of Freudian thought, the notions of resistance and defense had evolved in parallel manner. If defenses are the sum total of "military" operations destined to maintain the ego's integrity, by eliminating any possibility of modification or "conquest" from without, resistance is a process specific to therapy. We have historicized the term in order to designate the symptom through which a doctrine effects its implantation by a "negative" path. But in therapy, it is the analysand's words which oppose the assaults of the unconscious even as they bear witness to their dangerousness. In other words, resistance is quite simply the "true" symptom of the labor through which the repressed emerges. To that extent, it arouses a defensive function whose agent is the ego.

Freud originally sought to overcome resistance through persuasion, before perceiving in it a means of gaining access to the repressed. In his second topographical model, in which he asserted that the ego was in large part unconscious, he observed that resistance was not the sole privilege of the ego. There existed a resistance stemming from the id, just as the defensive aspect of the ego could be attributed to an unconscious process. Defense mechanisms are entirely complicitous with resistance since the former return in therapy in the form of a resistance to treatment.

As of 1920, Freud thus ascribed extravagant importance to the ego, but simultaneously integrated that agency into a metapsychology in which the unconscious has priority over consciousness. That new definition authorized the theoreticians of the ego, through a confusion of tendencies, to grant a privilege to the ego at the expense of the unconscious and to center therapy on the possibility of reinforcing it. Thus did the analysis of resistances become the spearhead of a therapeutic orthodoxy: In order to cure a subject, one has to attack his defense mechanisms, which return in his resistance, in order to "rebuild" the ego on the basis of its most solid functions. Nonetheless, two interpretations of the famous topographical model remain possible, to the extent that Freud's doctrine contains within it the antagonistic conditions of its own rupture. The first interpretation moves in the direction of a recentering of the ego on itself and leads to a series of techniques in the service of adaptation, and the second, which was Lacan's, implements an opposite procedure.

In that sense, the thrust of Lacan's thought is no more "Freudian" than his adversaries', since, in order to show that the Viennese conception had nothing in common with its psychologistic revision, Lacan too was obliged to "revise" the second topographical model. He did so by way of a philosophical perspective that emphasized not a reinforcement of the ego, but its decentering.

In his article, Lacan observed that post-Freudians regarded the ego as constituted by resistance and made of it the only subject which the analyst addressed. He emphasized that such a perspective lead them to conflate resistance with the ego's defense and to transform the ego into an objectivized subject. Against that confusion, which, in his opinion, limited therapy to the analysis of resistances, and reduced the subject to his ego, he opposed a dialectical process, once again, allowing the analyst to bypass the mirage-like effects of the dual relation. With remarkable stubbornness, he continued his progress toward the elaboration of a "Hegelian" return to Freud. Only the introduction of a third position, he said in substance, authorized the development of therapy in accordance with authentic speech. That position, in order to be symbolizable, and to avoid all narcissistic complicity between the analyst's ego and the subject's, must be constituted around the figure of death, absolute master of human destiny. "It is thus indeed there," he wrote, "that the analysis of the ego finds its ideal term, there where the subject, having rediscovered the origins of his ego in an imaginary regression, touches, through the progression of remembrance his end in analysis: to wit, the subjectivization of his death." [73]

The analyst was a *porte-parole*, less a "spokesperson" than the bearer of speech: He answered the subject from a "being for death" without wanting anything for him of what determined his place. Through that affirmation, Lacan transposed into Hegelian terms the drive of the same name and gave it a more symbolic and less biologizing turn. Finally, he concluded his text by paying homage to Balint, Freud, and Pichon. Without mentioning that last figure by name, he wrote: "A hundred mediocre psychoanalysts won't enable a single step further in one's knowledge, whereas a physician, by virtue of being the author of an ingenious work on grammar (and let no one imagine at this point some agreeable production of medical humanism), preserved, throughout his life, the style of *communication* among a group of analysts against the winds of discord and the tides of its servitudes." [74]

That act of homage to Pichon, in an article which Lacan knew took a stand opposed to Bouvet's, had not been placed there by accident. The master was "playing" the card of the austere grammarian, and a physician to boot, against that of a French-style neo-Freudianism, even if his shots were aimed point blank at Anglo-American revisionism. In brief, he attacked the principal enemy in order to ridicule the secondary enemy and to restore currency to a forgotten past. We shall see later how he would use certain of Pichon's ideas in his new theory of the subject.

Judged too "difficult," the article was soon withdrawn from the *Encyclopédie*. It would remain a source of bitterness for Lacan.

The second skirmish between Bouvet and Lacan occurred in 1956 on the occasion of the publication of the collective volume *La Psychanalyse d'aujourd'hui* ["Psychoanalysis today"].[75] The anthology, which celebrated the centenary of Freud's birth, assembled the principal names of the SPP. Bouvet was charged with "the clinical practice of psychoanalysis," and presented his hypothesis on "object relations."

That term had been used by Freud on several occasions without receiving any conceptual definition. What interested the founder was the *object* and not the *relation*. A correlative of the drive, the object designated a person as well as a partial, real, or phantasmatic object. Although the drive seeks satisfaction through it, the object remains eminently variable and is structured around a *loss*: It is not to be found, is lacking in its place, and may be rediscovered through substitutes. In the post-Freudian literature, the notion of object relations took on considerable importance, on the one hand, because it emphasized the relation at the expense of the object and thus seemed to specify the very principle of the analytic relation, and, on the other hand, because it set the stage for a definition of personality centered on the defense of the ego. The extension of the term accompanied the expansion of psychoanalysis. In becoming a mass doctrine, Freudianism found itself obliged to rethink its relational organization through a meditation on the subject's relations with his entourage. The preponderant importance accorded that question in the course of the 1960s defines the very evolution of the psychoanalytic movement.

For Maurice Bouvet, object relations constituted a cornerstone of clinical analytic practice. He adopted the term uncritically as though it had been part of Freudian doctrine from time immemorial. Bouvet thus confused the Freudian point of view with its various "revisions." As a result, he was unable to define correctly the concepts he advanced. In his discourse, the theory was like a totality without history, a dogma without internal shifts, a corpus of texts without origins.

Within that perspective, object relations were described through a diagnostic prism featuring the three classic structures of neurosis, psychosis, and perversion. Drawing on the second topographical model, Bouvet gave precedence to the relation over the object, conceived the relation in terms of the ego, and defined it as a compromise between the internal world and external reality. Corresponding to the three structures were three organizational types of object relation, characterizing three stages of human development: oral, anal-sadistic, and genital. Bouvet translated the notion of *stage* into the "modern" concept of object relation. The oral type corresponds to the first months of life, in which the infant is concerned solely with nursing. The anal-sadistic type concerns the third year with its constraints of cleanliness, and the genital phase develops thereafter by way of Oedipal conflicts.

In adulthood, individuals are classified into two categories: pregenital and genital. The former are divided into oral and anal types, whereas the latter succeed in moving beyond those archaic modes of relation. Plainly Bouvet was not embarrassed by aesthetic considerations: He used the most horrendous words without the slightest concern for how ridiculous they might sound—and too bad for the whimsical reader. Anal and oral types are ascribed a weak ego, apt to lapse into pathology or "depersonalization," depending on whether the subject is neurotic, psychotic, or a pervert. Such individuals entertain with their objects, that is, their entourage, relations of possessiveness, jealously, and dependence. In the case of anal types, the relation is stable and favorable to obsessional ritualization, whereas in that of oral types, it is mobile and implies a certain hysterical agitation. As for genital types, Bouvet endows them with a strong ego, only slightly dependent on its object relations. They are individuals without undue "complication" who have attained a high degree of instinctual and relational maturity. In brief, they are "normal" and completely "Oedipalized" subjects. To be sure, the distinctions neurosis/psychosis/perversion retain their relevance, since a "weak" or "strong" form characterizes the variants of the ego according to a hierarchical scheme. Nevertheless, Bouvet situated the psychotic ego on the side of the weak form and the neurotic or perverse ego on that of the strong one. His classification is so muddled that it allows one to infer that pregenital types are always psychotic and genital ones necessarily perverse or neurotic.

In order to grasp the internal variability of an object relation, Bouvet proposed that we consider the "instruments of the distanced relation." Such instruments designate the arrangements intervening within the object relation, and particularly in therapy, when the ego abandons its defenses. As for the dimension of distance, it refers to the separation between object relations experienced consciously by a given subject at a given moment and what they would be if the unconscious fantasy underlying them swept away defense mechanisms and became conscious. In other words, if the ego is constituted by its defenses, and if the analysis of resistances leads straight to their reduction, there is a good chance that the distance will diminish in the course of therapy. According to Bouvet, therapy tends to make conscious what is unconscious and consequently to reduce the separation between conscious experience and the unconscious fantasy determining it. When the defense is worn down, it is easy to take the measure of the pregenital or genital modes structuring the states of the ego.

At the conclusion of this argument, Bouvet arrived at a stupefying affirmation. In his view, therapy could bring harmonious genitality to a pregenital individual, but it could not succeed in modifying Oedipal neuroses of genital origin, which tend to disappear since they pose no problem for the therapist. When one learns, in the same text, that the author, as he naively declares, never had a pervert on his couch, one wonders why he devoted some eighty solemn pages of small print to such a subject.

This time, Lacan answered Bouvet directly by entitling his seminar for the year 1956–57 *Object Relations and Freudian Structures*.[76] He spared neither sarcasm nor irony nor downright nastiness in devoting two opening sessions to the collective publication by the leading figures of the Institute. He did not, of course, bother to mention Bouvet's name—the better to endow the hypotheses of the individual he regarded as his most dangerous French adversary with still greater anonymity. Disappointed by the defection of a man he hoped would leave the medical clan, Lacan avenged himself in the worst possible manner—through ellipsis and contempt.

The strategy was all the more shrewd in that Bouvet was an obscure clinical practitioner who would never found a school. In that regard, Lacan always divided the texts he referred to into two categories: on the one hand, a "noble lineage," and on the other, an "unmentionable heritage." When a doctrine, in his opinion, had been sufficiently recognized or when a master, even if unknown to the public, had been assigned special value by him, Lacan gave names. In the case of ego psychology or Kleinianism, for example, he cited his sources and named individuals. On the contrary, when he wanted to bury an individual deemed to be "contemptible" or little known, he was quick to eliminate all names. In similar manner, he did not mention his borrowings from certain authors if their position was insufficiently "luminous" in relation to the "greatness" of Freud's accomplishment.

That unpleasant habit did not prevent his effort in this case from being quite remarkable. The seminar on object relations was spread over eight hundred typed pages in the course of which Lacan commented on the Little Hans case, the childhood memory of Leonardo da Vinci, the problematic of castration, the question of the father, and finally that of artificial insemination, which was a novelty at the time. A monument of words—most often luminous, on occasion boring.

The author undertook to criticize the importance taken on by object relations in post-Freudian thought, and then attempted to restore the notion to a conceptual, rather than clinical, framework. He rediscovered the ideas of lack and loss, accorded as much importance to the relation as to the object's *place* and translated the Oedipus complex into terms of acceding to castration. In point of fact, he presented a veritable "geometry" of object relations, without "stages" or "maturation" or "diagnosis." There intervened, by way of that geometry, three relational modalities: "deprivation," "frustration," and "castration," hierarchically ordered according to the three registers of the imaginary, the real, and the symbolic. Lacan defined deprivation as the real lack of a symbolic object (something significant is missing from its place), frustration as the imaginary lack of a real object (a never satisfied demand), and castration as the symbolic lack of an imaginary object (the solution to the enigma of sexual difference).

Naturally, that theorization was radically opposed to Bouvet's, even though it took into account the post-Freudian notion of "relation." It was no longer a matter of describing a "pathology" of relational attitudes, but of defining a general conception of the relations between subject and object from which clinical practice might be deduced.

Bouvet was not at all happy with the attacks of his overbearing adversary, and wanted to respond. But orders had been given at the SPP to pay no attention to Lacan. Bouvet would consequently remain silent.

Stricken in mid-life with arterial hypertension, he agreed to follow a draconian diet, which deprived him of life's pleasures. One day, while hunting, he found himself shooting way off target and came to a first diagnosis of his physical state. A short time thereafter, in 1960, he suffered a stroke. At the moment of succumbing, he himself identified the cause of his death. But for his lack of genius, the man resembled Édouard Pichon: the same relation to chronic illness, the same complicity with the inevitable, the same assent to fate's decrees. And a passion for medicine.[77]

7   Life and Death of the Société Française de Psychanalyse

I. Our Finest Years

Ten years elapsed between the strife of 1953 and the extravagant maneuvers that culminated in the break-up of the Société française de psychanalyse and the creation by Lacan and his disciples of the École freudienne de Paris. During those ten years the emergence of the third French psychoanalytic generation changed the face of the country's Freudian community. "Our finest years," the veterans of the struggle would say—a group in crisis, a hoard without an identity, a movement in search of recognition. Paradoxically, it was the strife and the turmoil that would make of the SFP an active, seething, and prosperous society, open to every form of modernism. It is as though nothing were more favorable to the ascent of psychoanalysis than a state of permanent battle and an unsatisfied desire for recognition.

After the penury of the Liberation years and despite the defeat in Indochina, France was entering the age of consumption. The return of abundance benefited the middle classes and new strata of the population were gaining access to psychological treatment or to the profession of psychoanalysis. The Algerian conflict proved favorable to the rise of a new non-Communist left, whose humanistic aspirations brought it into contact with the house of Freud. Sartre was interested in the unconscious. The phenomenology of the "in-itself," the "for-itself," and the "sign" reigned sovereign over a philosophy that was still Hegelian, and psychoanalysts remained reluctant to commit themselves politically despite their interest in a more "existential" and less "medical" psychoanalysis. Only two of them, Maud Mannoni and Jean-Bertrand Pontalis, signed the "Manifesto of the 121" on the right to insubordination in Algeria, and one would have to wait for the fourth and even fifth generations in order to see the rise of anti-imperialist, Marxist, libertarian, or *gauchiste* concerns in the psychoanalytic community. Between 1958 and 1963, the psychoanalytic milieu remained ensconced in a certain comfort, discovering in Gaullism the expression of an expansionist ideal well suited to its ways of representing power.

From its inception, the SFP belonged to the men of the third generation. Despite the numerical importance assumed by women, it was still the males in the movement who occupied the leading positions. Students at the SPP, then witnesses while in analysis, they observed the strife of their masters while playing their own part in the adventure. The new liberal society responded to their ambitions: They would be its spearhead, each in his own way. What was at stake in the second split was reintegration into the IPA, against which—so normal did the return appear—no voices were raised. There was no psychoanalysis possible in France at the time without affiliation with the great Freudian empire, whatever its demands. The third generation was called [in English] the *juniors,* in opposition to the *seniors,* who were their teachers in the SFP and who were given nicknames: "le grand Jacques" for Lacan, "Oncle Dany" for Lagache, "Juju," "Jojo," and "Bouliette Jutonier" for the

Favezes. To those names, Granoff added a few of his own invention: "Dany-Caca" for Lagache, in memory of a private joke, and "Zipa" for the IPA, among others. The juniors played at the October Revolution while dreaming of America. They borrowed its legend and its vocabulary. They spoke of "soviets" and "troikas" and often amused themselves by resorting to a somewhat parodic Franco-Russian idiom, calling each other "tchouffanalystes," "Wona Gravoff," "Lagachinian doctrinaires," or "Lacanov." A superb folklore against the backdrop of a genuine battle.

That young generation reached the age of 40 in the middle of the 1960s. It no longer knew anything of the activity of the twelve pioneers whose works it found disappointing and whose memory had faded with the postwar purges and the first split. In sum, it was cut off from the French history of psychoanalysis. Trained in a period of renaissance, it forgot the heroic era and preferred reading the Anglo-Saxons or the Viennese to the texts of Pichon or Allendy. Prior to that generation, the teachers of the previous one had effaced the memory of origins, turning their students into history's orphans. For the majority of the juniors, the French adventure in psychoanalysis began in 1948 with the teaching of Bouvet, Lacan, Dolto, and Lagache. In their eyes, the leaders of the SFP seemed like the true founders of the movement. Facing the seniors, they had the impression of being heirs to a doctrine that had every right to demand its patents of nobility from the normalizing apparatus that the IPA had become. That is why they would end up wanting to be part of the great Anglo-American empire, the symbol of seriousness and competitiveness. They were urged on in this by their teachers, who had nevertheless dragged them into the break by resigning from the SPP, and by two other juniors who had advanced further in their careers: Wladimir Granoff and Serge Leclaire. Both were passionately devoted to the great cause of a Lacanianism integrated into the empire.

The juniors were Lacanians out of love for psychoanalysis, internationalists out of a desire for recognition, therapists out of cultural ambition, and "French" out of their demand for a patrimony at last regained. Children of the war, they forged their arms in a strife-torn society, and dreamed of one day rediscovering peace, occasionally at the price of servitude, disappointment, careerism, or mere drifting. Despite an intellectual success of great stature, and a theoretical output that remains unequaled, they would be among those defeated by history, some torn apart by their break with Lacan and their limited sympathy for Lagache or the Favezes, others by their entry into a voluntary servitude inherent in the failure of negotiations.

At the heart of this splendid golden age of psychoanalysis, a group of seven juniors played a role of major importance. Some of them, like Moustapha Safouan, Didier Anzieu, Jean-Bertrand Pontalis, and Jean Laplanche were university academics, students of Lagache, analysands or disciples of Lacan. The others, like Serge Leclaire, François Perrier, and Wladimir Granoff, were physicians: They were called the "troika." To that group may be added other physicians who were analysands of Lacan: Daniel Widlöcher, the youngest of the juniors, Jean-Claude Lavie, the eldest, and Victor Smirnoff, Robert Pujol, Guy Rosolato, and Piera Aulagnier. Like those previously mentioned, they came to play a part in the conflict pitting the SFP against the IPA. In a general way, that third generation was more innovative than its rival contemporaries in the SPP, to the extent that it benefited from the formidable advance constituted by Lacan's teaching. It published texts revealing a certain taste for theoretical and stylistic research without yet yielding to a servile imitation of Lacan's prose. It would produce the most accomplished works of the new French psychoanalysis. At present it plays for the fourth and fifth generations the role that Dolto, Lagache, and Lacan had previously played for it.

It should also be said that from the very inception of the SFP, Lacan pursued his own political agenda, refusing to feel personally guilty for the collective resignation. In order to outwit Nacht, on the one side, and fight Lagache's psychologism on the other, he chose to endow Freudianism with a theory of the subject grounded in philosophy without ever forgetting medical science. He thus surrounded himself with brilliant physicians, possessing titled positions in hospitals, whom he advised to read Saussure, Heidegger, and Merleau-Ponty, and brilliant philosophers, graduates of the École normale supérieure, *agrégés* and priests, whom he encouraged to begin medical school. Parallel to that, he urged his three "favorites," Leclaire, Granoff, and Perrier, to embark on the path of negotiation. He too was intent on sacrosanct recognition in order to export his doctrine abroad.

Within the group of seven, Wladimir Granoff cut an exceptional figure. He was neither a student of Lagache nor an analysand of Lacan. In addition, he possessed a splendid knowledge of the history of the French and international movements. Trained on Schlumberger's couch, supervised in his controls by Pasche and Bouvet, he had first dreamed of being an actor or an architect before discovering Freud's works in the municipal library of Nîmes, where his parents had taken refuge during the Occupation. He was in no way predestined to the career of psychoanalyst, except perhaps through his contradictory rearing, which was at once puritanical and enlightened, Jewish and agnostic, liberal and impassioned.

In the Granoff family, much pride was invested in an exalted genealogy, and the novel of origins was evoked with pride. The first to bear the name lived in Odessa after having received from Catherine the Great the privilege of possessing lands and thus enriching himself through trade. From cloth merchants to barristers, from philanthropists to artists, and from physicians to aristocrats, the tribe's heirs admired freedom without sacrificing the soul's passions. They exalted love to the status of supreme truth, and the appetite for sex never served as a pretext for obscene jokes. At birth, little Wova was given his paternal grandfather's first name. The senior Wladimir had been a lawyer. He defended the oppressed and did not hesitate to give away his best suits to friends in distress. He died of a heart attack while rejoicing at the fall of the Czarist state. One of his brothers was a physician and the other had the famous Katia as his daughter. As for the great-grandfather, Constantin Granoff, he had achieved recognition in his day for his work in linguistics.[1]

With his double-breasted jacket, his habit of kissing hands, and a discreet carnation in his lapel, young Volodia, second in the line, was raised in Alsace amidst the Russian *émigré* intelligentsia. Seductive, generous, and an accomplished gourmet, he made use in his cooking of excellent recipes, admired such collectors' cars as Bugattis or Hispano-Suizas, and exuded a fin-de-siècle dandyism. In his charm, he resembled John Barrymore; in his gift for living, Charles Swann; and in his taste for staged effects, Erich von Stroheim. Always prepared to lose his investment, he cultivated intrigue in the manner of the Czar's officers: with a baroque sense of truth bordering on the ludicrous. Every deed was for him a question of life or death. If a weapon was loaded, it had to be aimed at either himself or another, whether the best of his friends or the most formidable of his adversaries. No morality for Wladimir, rather an ethic in which the drama of a destiny—with the richness of its pleasures and the bleakness of its despair—was to flourish.

Too much the player to confess his inner rift, too tender not to reveal the passions of his soul, and too much the rigorist to relinquish his gentleman's armor, he had the gift of being able to evoke all the heart's intermittences in a sustained style of exquisite elegance. A magnificent correspondent, he wielded the pen of a Saint-Simon when he sketched in a single stroke the essence of a situation or the value of a secret imparted. Wladimir always found the words to say everything, from the most ferocious to the most sprightly. Fearful of stupidity, he tracked it down with all his resources, to the point of invariably squandering his energy in the process. He adored telling tales, making use of lies to impart the truth, feigning betrayal, or pretending to conspire. He combined with wondrous talent the nobility of a warrior of the Fronde and the fragility of a Chekhov character. An admirable polyglot, a Jew among Jews, he bore within the lines of his exile's face the whole saga of a sublime and triumphant diaspora: The world was his.

As a student at the SPP, he encouraged its young members to rebel and identified with the Freudian adventure of origins to the point of becoming an actor in a history relived with the features of a collective memory. Volodia was intent on resuming contact with the tempest of a family romance. He wanted to make of the SFP the site of a grand reunion between a vanquished East and a conquering West, between German, seen as a symbol of the past, and English, symptom of the new expansion. His project was at once mythic and pragmatic. And in order to achieve his striking dream, he sought support in the brilliant generation of young Lacanians. He consequently favored a group-based political orientation: men with their master. When the debacle approached, he chose, out of faithfulness to his strategy, the IPA camp, in which he had made friendships, for better or for worse. He did not hesitate at that time to write up in his own hand the supreme verdict: the expulsion of Lacan. He obtained the signatures of the Favezes and of Lagache in support. Having performed that terrible deed, he confronted his French allies, who had no real sympathy for him, and succeeded single-handedly, against all obstacles, in obtaining the much desired affiliation. That would be his sole triumph and he fell sick as a result of it. He thus lost all his battles, with the exception of that of the history of psychoanalysis, whose most talented narrator he remains.

Lacan liked and feared this St. Petersburg prince, who by birth possessed what he himself had had to create for himself: an art of polished living, an aristocracy of the mind. Lacan was a master surrounded by disciples; Granoff was a samurai in love with every aestheticism. There developed between the two a story of men linked by the privileged bond of the analytic couch: Lacan had Wladimir's wife in analysis and conducted a successful therapy with her, in which he helped her through a period dangerous for her health.

Before the first split, when the young Russian was making his tour of visits, Lacan had told him, "Whatever your decision, come see me, we have things to say to each other." Later on, at the time of the first conflict, he put him on guard against the intentions of the masters of the SPP. Finally when the student began his first control, Lacan added, "Have you analyzed your relation with me?"[2] As soon as Granoff had joined Leclaire in the battle for recognition, Lacan supported him and listened to him, addressing him as a sovereign might his most trusted general. He was able to see that Wladimir needed neither a surrogate father nor an abusive mother, and he drew on Granoff's immense culture and skill as a negotiator in order to promote all his attempts at affiliation.

The entire political history of the SFP may be reduced to a matter of negotiations with the IPA in which what was at stake for the troika was managing to win acceptance for Lacanianism abroad. Although, by virtue of his teaching and his clinical genius, he occupied the principal place in that history, Lacan did not always understand the meaning of the IPA's demands. He was quite familiar with the intentions of the major "charismatic" figures, could not have been more distrustful of Bonaparte, whom he called "the Ionescan corpse," knew that Hartmann would never be favorable to him, feared Gillespie and Anna Freud, and thought that Jones was a "little Welshman" who was protecting Melanie Klein while wreaking revenge on the founding father. But he was not always aware of the normalizing contraption that the IPA had become, an organization far more dangerous in its anonymity than in the effective power of its leaders.

Granoff, on the contrary, was familiar with the terrain, a diplomat without homeland or national boundaries. He had neither flatterers nor servants, and when he attracted sympathizers, he made friends of them and gave them the best of himself with a generosity that made him seem a traveler from some past age. Imbued through and through with the very history of psychoanalysis, he knew better than Lacan the movement's transformations, its anecdotes, its cultural recesses. Which would not stop him from being deluded . . .

In 1956, he published in English, in a collective volume on perversions, a text cosigned by Lacan and intended to make the French doctrine known abroad.[3] Nevertheless, he refused to conflate a master's teaching with the manner in which that master exercised his power: "From the moment," in his words, " the bearer of a teaching allows himself to be assisted in his daily life, a confusion has taken place. The first day he asks a student to bring him a drink because he's suffering from rheumatism; the next day, he asks him to go down and buy him cigarettes, and the day after, he orders him to polish his boots."[4] Wladimir accepted the master without the master's follies, the father's theory without allegiance to the father. He had no need to: He was not the son of no one, but simply himself, Granoff, from father to son, with the romance of his origins perpetually fresh.

It was in Strasbourg, before the war, that Wova came across Serge Liebschutz for the first time. Without knowing each other, the two adolescents were students in the same program at the Lycée Fustel-de-Coulanges. Although both were Alsatian, they did not share any common culture or tradition. Jewish circles in Strasbourg remained closed to the Russian emigration. Serge's father, Henri Liebschutz, had a Germanic name. Born in occupied Alsace, he fought alongside Laforgue in the ranks of the Kaiser's army, then founded a textile factory with his brother. Love (*Lieb*) and protection (*schutz*): The two words were well suited to this family of agnostics, who were nevertheless observant of the Jewish high holidays and of the rite of circumcision. Toward 1936, an extravagant uncle predicted in his hallucinations the coming of the apocalypse. He announced the camps, the war, the persecution. Henri listened to him, and as soon as the Munich accords were signed, decided to leave Alsace for Saint-German-en-Laye. Some time later, in flight from the Nazis in Bordeaux, young Serge dreamed of a trip to America. At dockside, he watched the departure of the cargo ships. He would not choose exile.

In Paris, during the Occupation, he took his *baccalauréat* exams; then, in 1942, the family migrated south. In Lyon, Serge joined a Catholic chorus, and had a brief career with the boy scouts, eventually occupying a position as counselor in a vacation camp—strange vacation indeed! In the Marseille city hall, his father acquired false papers under the name of Leclaire. Upon returning to Paris, toward the end of the war, he managed to support his family by working in an aluminum shop. At the time of the Liberation, the son was interested in Hindu philosophy, but without forgetting his imaginary galleons. He had changed his name back to Liebschutz and was studying medicine. During that period, the father was taking the necessary measures to legalize the second name. Everything might begin again, he thought; it was best to shield the family from future hatred, best to break with the signifiers of Teutonic oppression. Leclaire was a fine name, suffused with Mediterranean light, a symbol of freedom regained. Despite a certain disagreement, Leclaire refused to disavow his father; he accepted the procedure, then adopted in turn the family name, less out of a taste for assimilation than of a desire to affirm Alsatian Frenchness. In 1949, he married Geneviève Marion, a woman of great intelligence with whom he had four children. He would have them baptized.

He soon became acquainted with a Hindu monk, serving as cultural envoy in Paris, who spoke to him for the first time about Freud and psychoanalysis. The scholar frequented the Catholic circuit, and was familiar with Bruno de Jésus Marie and *Les Études carmélitaines*. He advised the young Liebschutz to go see Françoise Dolto, to become a psychoanalyst, and to realize his philosophical dreams. In the meanwhile, Liebschutz had reencountered his schoolmate Granoff in Henri Mondor's service at the Salpêtrière. The association this time was to be permanent: The Russian prince and the dreamer of the Indies became inseparable, sharing with each other their Alsatian childhoods.

In 1948, Serge did his tour of the SPP, then asked Françoise Dolto for advice. They spoke of their affinities for Hinduism, but, with her customary brutality, Françoise launched into a bit of uncontrolled interpretation. "The attraction you feel," she said, "for Hindu culture and mysticism corresponds to an anal character, it seems; it's quite typical."[5] At the Rome congress, without naming Françoise, Leclaire recounted the episode in public: "I was not prepared. That answer left me somewhat speechless. I have subsequently been able to gauge the accuracy of that evaluation—I was about to say its perfect exactitude. That is how I came into contact with the language of psychoanalysis. No doubt, that remark, despite its pertinence, had ruffled me a bit, for since that time, I have never been able to consider the language of psychoanalysis without a bit of distrust." [6]

Dolto sent Leclaire to Lacan, and his analysis, which was explicitly conceived as a training experience, took place between 1949 and 1953. The sessions lasted about twenty minutes, then began dwindling with the passage of time. Lacan remained silent. He did not make an interventions on the subject of the name change, although it was a subject of hesitation and anxiety for Leclaire, who spoke to his friends about it. For three years he told his story without understanding what was going on. Then, in 1952, the process was reversed. Lacan broke a thigh-bone in a skiing accident. Immobilized in the American Hospital, he invited Leclaire to continue his sessions in his hospital room. The analysand sat in an armchair and observed the clinician stretched out on his bed. A spark was set off by the broken leg, even though the student still did not have the impression of undergoing analysis. The analysis would be accomplished through the deferred temporality of the movement of history, in partially autobiographical writings or texts written in common with friends such as Anne-Lise Stern and Jean Laplanche, themselves in therapy with Lacan.[7] Serge Leclaire loved the silent master and became his disciple without kowtowing or descending to obsequiousness: history's first Lacanian.

At the SPP, he had conducted a control supervised by Pasche and joined Granoff in the student rebellion. Together they participated enthusiastically in the Rome congress and convinced each other of the necessity of having the new society recognized by the IPA. In their opinion, it was not sufficiently strong to exist on its own in France without international backing. As much as the Russian was a cosmopolite, with his passport always in his jacket pocket, just as much was the Alsatian the great servant of the policies of his prince. He never hid his origin but did not view his Jewish roots to be symptomatic of the history of psychoanalysis. His project was not quite the same as Granoff's. For Leclaire, it was less a question of hitching the Lacanian wagon to the resplendent epic of a dream-diaspora than of having the IPA admit the existence of a French master of psychoanalysis, even as the latter would be obliged to accept certain limits to his power.

With his bushy eyebrows, dark intense eyes, shortness of breath, and openly derisive laughter, Leclaire seemed to step out of a novel by Stendhal: something on the order of Count Mosca. Without succumbing to extravagance, he dressed tastefully, injected a measure of *politesse* in his relations and revealed an extreme of tolerance in dealing with his adversaries. Loyal in friendship, he accorded special importance to intellectual exchanges with women, and did not conceal his lucid love for Lacan, his sole sovereign.

As secretary of the SFP between 1959 and 1962, president the following year, and member at large of the IPA between 1961 and 1965, he occupied a difficult and tormented position in the crisis-laden village. It was on him that the burden of the secret negotiation, through which the SFP requested admission to the empire, fell. In that position he revealed himself to be alternately courageous, shrewd, tireless, and faithful to his commitments. Thus did he, like Granoff and Perrier, devote the finest years of his life to a policy that ended in bitter defeat. It was a terrible fate for this first disciple of a master who adored him but did not hesitate to accuse him occasionally of betrayal or to besiege him with anguished confidences. Leclaire was superbly cast as actor in a major drama; simultaneously secretive and tortured, he negotiated the truth with a series of imperturbable silences, perpetually in search of an elusive assurance to which he had attached all his desires. He would be desperate at the break between Lacan and the IPA and at the breakup of the SFP, which would lead to the ruin of all his projects. Having become one of the most celebrated and authentic clinical practitioners in France, he would never stop converting his defeat into a dream of reconquest. A thoroughly engaging individual, perpetually in search of a formidable elsewhere . . .

Leclaire encountered the name of Françoise Perrier for the first time while studying the anatomy of the nervous system in a manual which the latter had devoted to the subject before becoming interested in psychoanalysis. Martial, François's father, was a journalist and did not conceal a certain Judaeophobia, which was linked to private quarrels he had had. He wrote poems in verse on syphilis in the morning, the lugubrious color of the moon, and the ashen complexion of young ladies. . . . [8] Martial died in 1935, leaving his son an orphan at the age of thirteen. Raised by women, he would spend his life trying to find a father again—to the point of publishing, in his middle years, a book introduced in these terms: "Martial, the son of François Perrier, lost his father before learning how to read. He was only two at the time. Later on he would decipher on the tombstone of a suburban cemetery the first name of his deceased and legitimate progenitor. In 1922 he entered the name of his son at the registry office as François Perrier. He came to him from his wife Marcelle and Jules Logier, Printer. He died a poet, a writer, and a journalist, in 1935, near the 'fortifications,' in the desire that his son fortify himself through his taste for reading and writing." And further on: "My father set his suicide to verse during his lifetime before dying at an early age of what was called natural death and without cremation." [9]

François studied piano, became an excellent soloist, and wrote songs. His mother did not work and he was constrained to earn a living. Before undertaking, medical studies as a vocation, he tried himself out at several jobs. He repaired fountain pens and worked as a cocktail pianist, interpreting excellently a repertory worthy of the Closerie des Lilas. In 1940, the happy performer did not know whether to opt for de Gaulle or Pétain. He would understand too late and would always suffer, in relation to his Jewish colleagues, from the torments of the petty Frenchman: "Thank God," he wrote in 1982, "our Pope is Polish, but unfortunately the French are as cynical as in 1940. The difference from those days, when Hitler's war was on, is that today torture and killing go on in the name of three monotheisms: the Arab, the Christian, and the Jewish. The most realistic and the best informed of the three are the people of Jerusalem." [10]

After the war, he did his tour of visits at the SPP and began therapy with Maurice Bouvet. As a competent clinician, he ascribed an hystero-phobic syndrome to himself, then perceived that his therapist was "applying" to him his theory of the object, trying to get his "superego to internalize the maternal phallus." Perrier, who was already familiar with the refrain, soon had had enough of that analysis, which brought him no solution to his enigmas. He decided to stop. At the last session, he cried out in an inimitable voice: "There it is, I can feel my mother's big prick in my ass. I've finally introjected the psychoanalytic superego." Bouvet could not get over it.

In 1956, Perrier found himself on Lacan's couch at the time that the latter was competing with Bouvet on the theory of the object. He remained there for three months. The master listened attentively and sought to find out in what way Bouvet had been unable to analyze his patient. The relation between the two men ended in catastrophe: "In point of fact, what interested the master was less the analysis of a typical hystero-phobic than the manner in which his predecessor had treated me, making me a hypochondriac and impotent." [11]

Perrier did not speak the same idiom as his friends. If he was as capable as any of employing a scientific vocabulary in his texts, he was also the only one of his generation to make public display of his moods—and bile—in a vocabulary, reminiscent of Léon Daudet, bordering on the vulgar. He blithely mixed analytic couch and private life, alcohol and theory, sex and science, in order to exhibit the anguished adventure of his body, as though, from as far back as could be recalled, he had been devouring Freudiana out of the recesses of a tentacular placenta. The turbulent child of a psychoanalysis he preferred to call Francophonic in order to distinguish it from its unpleasant "Frenchness," he will remain forever the wandering troubadour of Lacanianism, naive and passionate, as whimsical as his master (whose genius he lacked), but a prodigious theorist of female sexuality, hysteria, and love.

Obsessed by his father complex, he suffered early on from bearing the same name as a celebrity, as well as the last name of a bottled beverage scorned by lovers of fine wines: "At school I was already called 'Monsieur Pschitt' as in the mineral water source. . . . François Perrier, the well-known actor, was already on the stage; he had just married Jacqueline Porel, Réjane's daughter, and I read the newspapers. I was in the provinces and, before my baccalaureate, chastely in love with a quite young girl who was also named Jacqueline Porel. And my buddies would laugh and joke about it. . . . In the world of advertising it was worse. The Pschitt company had commissioned a sketch from Jean Effel. The text read as follows: 'Perrier-vous à boire? [Payeriez-vous, would you pay to drink?] Better get pschittanalyzed instead.' I have often wondered to what extent my psychoanalytic couch was chosen rather than another's simply because the word père [father] is in Perrier." [12]

Along with Serge and Wova, the troubador would be third in the trio. Gypsy violin, goyish piano, and Alsatian memories: a notorious troika for a failed negotiation. They were impetuous, ardent, and full of hope; their heads were crammed with Lacan and America. A Parisian from Montmartre, Perrier had no internationalist project. He took himself for another Lacan, made fun of the IPA, and dreamed of becoming the head of a Francophonic school of psychoanalysis. He would never succeed in doing so. Between presumptuousness and aimlessness, he consumed the incompleteness of his story too soon. In his hexagonal fixations and his tormented

love for a master, he already anticipated the adventure of a new generation of Lacanians, the scarred and triumphant generation of the great structuralist springtime
which would never dream of joining the IPA, because Lacanianism would have become for it, for better or for worse, the sole Freudian school of the modern world.

Upon Lacan's death, Perrier would write these superb lines: "He was a 'trub-
lion,' a troublemaker of genius. And without him, everyone is bored silly. Only many
don't yet realize it. Little groups and little texts come into existence and fade away.
At the performances, and various intermissions of the theater of psychoanalysis,
what is lacking is a gatherer rather than a leader. . . . Someone possessing the impertinent and difficult talent of angling a joke or a retort. One of life's aristocrats." [13]

In the famous group of seven, the "students" of Lagache analyzed by Lacan
were to all appearances less interested than the men of the troika in the international
negotiations. It should be noted that their university training allowed them access
as equals to intellectual movements centered either on philosophy or psychology. At
bottom, they were in no need of recognition by the IPA in order to have careers in
France. But in choosing that path, they ran the risks of a confinement that would
exclude them from dialogue with foreign colleagues. That is why, like members of
the troika, but for different reasons, they too aspired to sacrosanct recognition. In
order to obtain it, they were prepared, not to "betray" their Lacanian training, but
to demand of Lacan submission to the standard rules. If Granoff and Leclaire had a
genuine internationalist project, based in one case on a dream of reunion with the
diaspora, and in the other on loyalty to a doctrine and a master, if Perrier dreamed
of becoming a "great Francophone leader," the university academics, to which certain physicians may be added, had the impression of wagering their future by wreaking legitimate revenge on a history from which they felt excluded since the split in
1953. They reproached their masters for having resigned from the IPA without realizing the consequences of such an act. In addition, they entertained complex transferential relations with Lacan, which went from excessive idealization to equally
excessive disillusionment and which would reach their resolution in rejoining the
empire.

In a general manner, that feeling of exclusion was aggravated by the fact that
a good number of juniors had never been students at the SPP, either because of the
lateness of their training or for other reasons. They belonged to the same generation
in age as the members of the troika (born between 1922 and 1925) but tended to be
less far along in their careers. Deprived simultaneously of a revolt and an affiliation,
they believed they had a right to recognition. Anzieu, as we have seen, did not have
the same itinerary. As of July 1953, he no longer felt himself to be a "Lacanian" in
either training or doctrine and thus had nothing more to demand of his former
analyst. He supported the position of Lagache and the Favezes from the beginning.
As for Robert Pujol, he too had finished his analysis with Lacan in July 1953, but
would break with him later on grounds more or less identical to those of the other
juniors.

Like Leclaire and Anzieu, Moustapha Safouan received his training at the
SPP before the first split, but did not participate in the student uprising. As a result

he maintained with Lacan relations of loyalty of a rather idiosyncratic sort. Born in Alexandria, this young philosopher was the quintessential man of letters. Sensual, cultivated, and doctrinaire, he was in search of a rigorous theory. His father was a person of stature who taught rhetoric and fought illiteracy. A militant nationalist, he had been first secretary of the first Egyptian workers' union and frequented Henri Curiel's circle. He had been imprisoned for his ideas, and his son suffered from his absence at home.

Brought up as an atheist, Moustapha dreamed, from adolescence on, of going to Cambridge. He studied Greek, Latin, French, English, and classical Arabic, and was an enthusiast of Frege and Koyré. In 1940, he discovered Freud through the teaching of Ziwar, a member of the SPP and a professor at the University of Alexandria. Ziwar advised him to accompany him to France and to undergo a training analysis. Since Safouan had not received any answer from Cambridge, he booked passage and made his way to Paris in 1945, whereupon he lapsed into a something of a torpor. At that point he sought therapy. Ziwar sent him to Nacht, who directed him to Schlumberger with whom he underwent a therapeutic analysis. Soon, he was able to resume his intellectual activity, but came up against the question of the father, which had not been resolved for him by that analysis. He did not know that Schlumberger had suffered from a relation with a famous homosexual father. When he asked him how to resolve his paternal problem, the analyst answered him that one had to "kill" the father. Safouan had the impression of an evasion and remained unsatisfied with Schlumberger's maneuver. Nonetheless, the analyst deemed him "trainable," and sent him before the commission for a control.

Moustapha chose Lacan, who asked him where he came from. He told Lacan that he had been raised by women while his father had been in prison. The student then began speaking about his uncles. The supervision had begun: "The sessions lasted about a quarter of an hour with varying lengths. I did not have the impression that they were short. Lacan allowed the analyst to take risks and helped him to discover his own qualities. I learned with him to forget what I knew in order the better to listen and not to interpret with a ready-made theory. Lacan was a very fine clinician who accepted the reflections of classical moralists and did not reject gratitude. He taught me the vanity of 'knowing about' and of infatuation. He prevented self-assurance and attempts at eliminating guilt. He was attentive to the analyst's deafness. In 1950, he sent me an hysterical patient abandoned by his father at the age of four. I could not understand why the analysis was invaded by paternal material, whereas the father did not exist in reality. I wanted to interrupt. Lacan then proposed that I participate in a seminar at his place at which I met Anzieu, Aubry, Amado Lévy-Valensi, Leclaire, Beirnaert, and Octave Mannoni. He spoke of the real, symbolic, and imaginary father. That orientation toward the notion of a non-natural father marked the beginning of my transference with Lacan."[14] Subsequently Safouan would remain fifteen years in control under Lacan's supervision.

In December 1953, he had to return to Egypt because of the expiration of his study grant. There he began to exercise his profession, but above all he spent his time preparing the first and only translation into Arabic of *The Interpretation of Dreams*. For that, he drew on the German, English, and French editions. The volume is stupefying in its beauty. Twenty years later, Safouan would take on the first part of *The Phenomenology of Mind*. In 1958, he returned to France and two years later, in the context of the decentralization requested by the IPA, he was sent by Leclaire to Strasbourg in order to pursue, in the wake of Lagache, Favez-Boutonier, and Anzieu, the implantation of psychoanalysis in the provinces. There he met the psychiatrist Lucien Israël, who had himself begun to direct the interns of Professor Kammerer's service to various local or Parisian couches. The Arab student of letters and the Strasbourg Jew became the best of friends, each of them aficionados of gastronomy and champagne. From Alsace to Burgundy, the story of individual destinies follows its course. . . .

Meursault, Volnay, Vosne-Romanée, Chambolle-Musigny: a profusion of names, evoking in the disparity of their images a history and geography of places. Côte de Beaune in blue on local maps, Côte de Nuits in red—one might almost say the whim of a Burgundy architect seconded by the grip of a descendant of Charles the Bold. In its lacework of vines shielded by a border of poplars, the Laplanche property is located at Pommard amid a thicket of dark trees. The house seems to take its distance from the village, like a bird from its shadow, proudly exhibiting its elaborate hearths, its windows inaccessible to the wind, and its grey stone steps. Since the reign of Louis XV, the members of the family have gathered in the fall at harvest time. Sometimes, when an early frost seems in the offing, they sleep beneath the branches in order to keep watch, as soon as dawn comes, over the changing color of the precious vines.

Jean-Louis for the Château of Pommard, Jean for psychoanalysis, such is at present the divided existence of twice-blessed Laplanche, vintner on Sundays, intellectual during the week. At Beaune, in his stately residence, he lives with the rhythm of the seasons; in Paris, from his apartment on the rude de Varennes, he watches ministries fall. The man is quite similar to his land and his commitments—as hardworking as a landowner, as thrifty as a rural lord. At times acting as though he had been flayed alive, but always honest, he teaches superbly, from the height of his excellent Germanic culture, the principal fermentations of Freudian conceptuality.

Raised in a Catholic ambience, in which independence of mind was highly prized, a liberal if not a libertarian, and emphatically pacifist, he made the transition at the age of eighteen from the student movement Action catholique to the Resistance. Hostile to Stalinism, he inclined at the time of the Liberation toward Trotskyism and participated in the founding of the group Socialisme et Barbarie. A student of Jean Hyppolite's at the École normale supérieure, he received a travel grant to Harvard and visited Rudolph Loewenstein. Upon returning to Paris, he was intent on entering into analysis in order to resolve problems of a personal order and consulted with the philosopher Alquié, who often spoke of his own therapy. He saw Lacan for the first time during a lecture, then began his analysis with him, without knowing anything about the movement. After earning his *agrégé* degree in philosophy, he thought of becoming an analyst, and Lacan advised him to begin studying medicine, an undertaking for which he felt a priori no particular attraction. "I was eligible for skipping the preparatory year of medical school," he said, "because of my activities in the Resistance. Lacan asked me for my papers in order to submit them to the offices of the medical school and then lost them. Because of that slip, I never received my Resistance card, which is rather droll when one considers what 'resistance' means for an analyst. My sessions were on the lengthy side, between twenty and thirty minutes. My analysis was going on during the first split. I knew nothing of the psychoanalytic movement and I was never part of the SPP. But Lacan, overwhelmed by events, would step out of his neutral position in order to complain bitterly about his conflicts with the Institute. The analysis seemed to be moving backwards. . . . In 1961, when the commission of inquiry was hearing Lacan's students, he said to me, 'You won't have to lie, because from now on your sessions will last 45 minutes.' I was augmented, but my sessions remained the same length. All this is merely anecdotal, and one can't speak of one's analysis in just a few words. I greatly benefited from a long analysis with Lacan and I remain quite grateful to him for it, even if I have subsequently seen its shortcomings. Despite all the criticisms, many of which are cogent, his memory remains dear to me."[15]

After a brilliant academic career, Laplanche became part of a department of psychopathology in which psychoanalysis was taught. Like André Green, he aspired to a chair at the Collège de France and would resent not receiving it.

Related to Louis Renault, Jean-Bertrand Lefebvre-Pontalis, "Jibé" for his friends, enjoyed the privileges of being born rich into a family of the Parisian upper bourgeoisie. Committed to the left very early on, he became an *agrégé* of philosophy, a professor, and chose Pontalis as his pen name. Following Merleau-Ponty's teachings, he became interested in problems of language. By 1945, he was publishing reviews in the second issue of *Les Temps modernes*. A bit later, he wrote up the testimony of a soldier in Indochina. He was not alone among psychoanalysts of the new generation in writing for Sartre's journal. Writing from the perspective of the SPP, Francis Pasche published in the first issue a text on war psychoses, then another, in 1948, on sublimation.[16] A year later, Claude Lévi-Strauss also brought out an important text entitled "The Sorcerer and his Magic."[17] While endorsing the project of a history of the "symbolic function" capable of accounting for man's intellectual condition, he reproached psychoanalysis for reducing the patient's universe to the therapist's interpretations. He opposed to it the sorcerer's technique, which allows the patient to abreact on his own, outside any transference. Pasche replied to him by defending a "psychoanalysis without magic."[18]

As of 1953, Pasche's by-line disappeared and it was Pontalis who thereafter represented psychoanalysis in the pages of *Les Temps modernes*. The journal thus became an organ for the expression of the new nonmedical orientation. The young professor took a vigorous stand on behalf of the SFP by publishing, in 1954, an article entitled "Psychoanalysis in Question," in which he categorized Lagache's work as a "molar behaviorism" and situated Lacan's as part of modern phenomenology.[19] He observed that the SFP was a source of encouragement to all those who wanted to develop a philosophical perspective on Freud's discovery. That stance earned him a stinging reply from Récamier, who, in the name of the SPP, defended the medical status of analysis by citing the notorious regulations of 1949.[20]

After the first split, Pontalis did his tour of the titular members with the intention of beginning a training analysis. Lagache recommended Bouvet, but he chose Lacan, who told him: "Go nowhere else, *mon cher.*" His treatment began in 1953 with sessions lasting an average of thirty minutes. Lacan often remained silent, moved about in his chair, paced back and forth, took notes and also meals. When his patient protested, he assured him that it did not interfere with his listening. Soon he urged Pontalis to attend his seminar and begin medical studies. The latter went no further than the preparatory curriculum. He began writing up, for the *Bulletin de psychologie,* excellent summarized transcriptions of the master's words. That effort, approved by Lacan, lasted from 1956 to 1959 and involved three seminars: *La relation d'objet et les structures freudiennes, Les formations de l'inconscient, and Le désir et son interprétation.*[21]

While undergoing a first collective control with Lagache, then a second individual one with Perrier, Pontalis continued to publish numerous articles in *Les Temps modernes.* Although he was closer to Merleau-Ponty than to Sartre, he did not leave the journal at the time of the break between the two. In 1962, he became a member of the editorial committee. Through his impetus, several psychoanalysts of the third generation published significant texts in the journal: Widlöcher, Berge, Anzieu, Octave Mannoni, and Jean Clavreul. In 1964, Pontalis collaborated with Laplanche in writing a text that would become a classic study in the history of science: "Fantasme originaire, fantasme des origines, origines du fantasme [Fantasy and the Origins of Sexuality]."[22]

At the time he signed the Manifesto of the 121, Pontalis had a research position at the CNRS [Centre national de la recherche scientifique]. Summoned to appear before a mixed commission to be censured, he was present at Merleau-Ponty's speech in his defense. Quite shrewdly, the philosopher emphasized that he had not come to defend the content of a text but the right for an intellectual to affix his signature to a petition which in no way involved his status as a government functionary.[23]

In 1963, Pontalis adopted the same positions as his friends of the third generation. He left Lacan and participated in the foundation of the Association psychanalytique de France, along with Anzieu, Widlöcher, Laplanche, Granoff, Pujol, and Smirnoff. He would thus become the serene baron of an unadventurous brand of psychoanalysis, at last recognized by the IPA, and—the supreme gratification— accepted as an equal in the most prestigious fortress of French publishing: Gallimard. There he would preside over a prospering journal and series with an intelligence for compromise unequaled in the history of psychoanalysis in France. Talented and witty, Jean-Bertrand Pontalis is at present a past master in the art of publishing acknowledged classics—works that are barely polemical and already recognized abroad—as well as manuscripts that are elegant in style, risk-free in content, and unassailable in scholarship: a distinguished administrator of Freudian culture.

From the time of its founding, and thanks to Lagache's position with the Presses universitaires de France, the SFP published a journal, *La Psychanalyse,* which would have eight issues. Jean-Paul Valabrega was in charge of editorial matters. The son of an Italian emigrant, he had been part of the anti-Nazi struggle as early as 1940. Two years later, he went clandestine, then joined the underground network of the Montagne Noire where he associated with Jean Cassou. During the Liberation, he worked with the journal *Wort und Tat* ["Word and deed"], which was intended for Germans and Austrians. He designed the dummies and was in charge of page make-up, assisted by his friend Jean Picart Le Doux, who would put his talents in the service of *La Psychanalyse*. The first issue, put together by Lacan, dealt with problems of speech and language. To be sure, the *Rome Discourse* was there, as well as a text by Heidegger. Hegel was still in favor thanks to a discussion on the subject of *Verneinung* [negation].[24] On the linguistic side, Émile Benveniste contributed a fundamental text on the function of language in Freud's discovery. In their introduction, the officers of the SFP announced their colors, ones in which Lacan's version of Freudianism was accorded pride of place at the expense of La-gache's: "If psychoanalysis inhabits language, it ought to open up to dialogue. . . . And in giving space here to authors who are not psychoanalysts, we are but extending the confrontations that took place in the framework of our society under the auspices of the Clinique de la Faculté during the year 1954–55. . . . This opening of psychoanalysis to the human sciences is an act which puts an end to the extraterritoriality which psychoanalysis has long claimed for itself by using the pretext of the ambiguity of its loyalties to cast them all off."[25]

The second issue was called *Mélanges cliniques*. It contained Lacan's famous seminar on Poe's "The Purloined Letter," as well as texts by Lagache, Perrier, Leclaire, Granoff, and Rosine Lefort. In addition, there were contributions from abroad. The third issue, dated 1957, confirmed the opening toward the human sciences, with an additional text by Lacan, a quite fine article by Louis Beirnaert on Ignatius of Loyola, another by Favez-Boutonier on criminology, and finally a contribution by Hyppolite on Hegel's phenomenology in its relation to psychoanalysis. In the fourth issue, psychosis was the principal focus, with Lacan's commentary on the Dr. Schreber case, in which the concept of foreclosure [*forclusion*] was introduced. Serge Leclaire recounted skillfully a psychotic episode in *The Wolf Man*, while Gisela Pankow spoke of a case of chronic hallucinatory psychosis. The sixth edition was devoted to the International Colloquium at Royaumont, organized in 1958 under the auspices of the SFP. It opened with a famous debate between Lagache and Lacan, in which their deeply divergent views on the question of the individual emerged. In the seventh issue, the SFP published research conducted in the course of the year 1959–60 on the subject of psychoanalytic theories of female sexuality. Once again Lacan had pride of place, alongside Camille Laurin, Dolto, and Perrier. Finally, in an eighth edition, in which Lagache had top billing and Lacan did not publish anything, it was above all the Lacanians who contributed their approaches to the subject of fantasy, dream, and reality.

While the French school of psychoanalysis was in a phase of major expansion, and the return to Freud was inducing therapists to inquire into the original texts in German, efforts at translation remained quite fragmentary. Never had Freud been so little translated as in the period between 1953 and 1963. In that respect, there was a formidable contradiction between the prewar and postwar periods. In the 1920s and 1930s, during which the greatest resistance to psychoanalysis in

France held sway, translating activity enjoyed an unprecedented expansion. The pioneers of the movement did not build authentic doctrines. They wrote a lot but did not leave any lasting imprint on the movement. On the other had, and no doubt because they were pioneers without personal theories, they were quite active when it came to establishing themselves in the world of publishing. It was the princess who had the distinction of undertaking the first major translation of the Viennese works. Even if her labors left something to be desired, they were genuine and undebatable. After 1945, the opposite tendency emerged, and a slowing down of translating activities can be perceived both at the SPP and the SFP.

Consider: six original translations of works by Freud appeared between 1945 and 1963: *Moses and Monotheism* by Gallimard in 1948; *An Outline of Psychoanalysis* by Presses universitaires de France a year later; *The Problem of Anxiety,* by the same publisher in 1951, followed by *Psychoanalytic Technique* in 1951 and *Studies on Hysteria* in 1956. Finally the article "Screen Memories" was translated in 1959 by Didier Anzieu as part of his book *L'auto-analyse de Freud.* To that may be added four reeditions of texts translated before the war, only two of which, *The Interpretation of Dreams* and the *Three Essays,* were significantly revised, the former by D. Berger in 1950, the latter by Laplanche and Pontalis in 1962. The two other reeditions, *Madness and Dreams in Jensen's "Gradiva"* (Gallimard, 1949) and five case histories (*Cinq psychanalyses,* PUF, 1954) were reprinted in their original version. The most significant publishing event of the period consisted in the appearance of Jones' monumental work on the life of Freud, which included numerous unpublished letters, as well as the letters to Fliess, in 1956, under the title *La Naissance de la psychanalyse* [*The Origins of Psycho-Analysis*].[26] Compared to the renewal in theoretical activity, such labors of translation were clearly extremely limited in scope.

There are several explanations for this phenomenon. Although Lacan never stopped criticizing the extant translations, he himself never participated in the establishment of a new team of translators. He was concerned above all with his own doctrine and asked his students to read Freud in German. On the other hand, Lagache, whose theoretical endeavors left much to be desired, proved far more active than Lacan when it came to translation, with respect to the works not only of Freud, but of others. There were thus university academics—and specifically Laplanche and Pontalis—to be found around him, gearing up for a long-range project that would bear fruit after 1963, by which time the SFP had already broken up.

During the period 1955–60, there was discussion of a translation of Freud's complete works similar to that accomplished by James Strachey for the Anglo-American world. Nonetheless, it was not until 1966 that three publishers, Gallimard, P.U.F., and Payot managed to reach an agreement allowing for the sale of the *opus magnum.* But the agreement was not enough: Because of quarrels internal to the psychoanalytic movement as well as other more personal conflicts, the translators would be secretly at each others' throats.[27] At present, the psychiatrist André Bourguignon is in charge of the as yet tenuous project of a complete edition. Assisted by Pierre Cotet, a distinguished Germanist, the amicable professor, with his fascination for history, has succeeded, in spite of the disputes dividing Pontalis, Laplanche, Marthe Robert, and Roger Lewinter, in bringing together a competent team capable of completing this gigantic project. A century after the historic encounter in the Salpêtrière, a standard French edition will finally see the light of day: a hundred years' battle.

Between 1953 and 1963, one thus observes a certain waning in the French-language publication of texts by Freud, whereas starting in 1966, such activity resumed with an intensity equal to that of the interwar period. The publication of *Vocabulaire de la psychanalyse* in 1967 constitutes, in this respect, a turning point in both the translation and the comprehension of Freudian concepts. For in order to be able to translate scientific or philosophical texts, it is imperative to know *how* to translate and what *words* to employ in order to unify the conceptual terminology.

Although Lacan was not part of that effort, for which the credit accrues to others, he had a significant investment in the venture. During the finest years of the SFP, he had not settled into any publishing fiefdom nor did he have any clout in the university; he was "camping" in the facilities of the Sainte-Anne hospital. Nevertheless, by virtue of his demand for a renewed orthodoxy, he played a role of the first importance in the manner in which Freud was read and in which attempts were made to translate him—more rigorously than previously. It is clear that without Lacan's teaching, the psychoanalysts of the third generation would never have apprehended Freud's texts as they did during the years of the SFP. In that regard, for example, the entire *Vocabulaire* is shot through with a Lacanian perspective of Freud's conceptual system. Reading it, one perceives that the return to Freud's meaning bore its fruit in the manner in which its authors "revised" the history of notions or translated several terms. Lagache's influence was also present, if only in the idea of a lexicon capable of uniting a Viennese-inspired Freudianism with an Anglo-Saxon-style post-Freudianism. Finally, it should not be forgotten that work for the project was done in part at a time when both Laplanche and Pontalis were spending time on Lacan's couch and actively participating in his seminar. In losing them, he would lose the best of himself, and they the best of themselves.

Among the therapists of the SFP, an important place was occupied by Gisela Pankow, whose rank was "associate." Raised in Berlin after World War I by parents who were democrats, she arrived in France in 1950, invited to present her work to the First World Congress of Psychiatry. In 1956, she joined the SFP, then worked in Australia, and finally in Baltimore after having undergone three controls with Lacan, Dolto, and Lagache. Her seminar began in 1958 and dealt with the psychotherapy of psychoses. An original theoretician, Gisela Pankow's teaching was centered on a conception of madness inherited from both Freud and Kretschmer. It made therapeutic use of modeling in clay and defined a notion of the symbolic order differing from Lacan's but based on linguistic experience. In 1959, as the result of a misprint, her seminar was dropped from the bulletin of instruction and replaced by Lacan's. She took offense and sent a letter of resignation to Lagache: "My current situation makes it intolerable for me that my name be effaced without explanation from the society's activities concerning the psychotherapy of psychoses. Given the list of my scientific publications, herewith appended, and my international reputation, to which seventy-two reviews of my book bear witness, it is unacceptable that

I be excluded for no reason from all official activities of the society. Kindly confirm the fact of my resignation." [28] Lagache called her in and observed to her that a psychoanalytic society was not the same as a society of scientists, and that she was insufficiently respectful of the neurosis of her students.[29] He then offered to consider her letter of resignation as unofficial and to wait. In June 1960, she resigned definitively, having been appointed to a position at the medical school of Bonn.

II. The Birth of Lacanianism

At the beginning of the Occupation, Georges Bataille, who lived at 3 rue de Lille, informed Lacan that an apartment was about to be vacated at no. 5 of the same street. Lacan rented it and Sylvia Bataille joined him there when the Germans crossed the line of demarcation. At the Liberation, Bataille moved, and left his own apartment to his former wife, who still bore his last name. During that period, Judith, Laurence, and their grandmother came to live there, while Jacques and Sylvia stayed at 5. That is where the master received his analysands. He directed his control groups and began his first seminars in the living room of 3, which was more spacious than the rather cramped rooms of 5. His disciples were thus accustomed to meeting Lacan in one building or the other.

Judith and Laurence witnessed the rise of Lacan's doctrine and were themselves raised in the movement's inner sanctum. Sylvia, for her part, was quite sympathetic to the emerging group. Soon the couple would buy a charming country home, located in Guitrancourt, near Mantes-la-Jolie. It was called "La Prévôté" [the Provostry]. Lacan would escape there for weekends to work. In a large construction facing the garden and crowned with a glass roof, he set up a library and an office filled with objets d'art. The place was known as his "studio" or "atelier." In a loggia overlooking the single room, a strange dyptich dominated the premises: a "double" painting whose recessed component was a Courbet canvas representing a female sexual organ and which was hidden by a wooden screen constructed by Masson in which the elements of the first painting were reproduced in abstract fashion. A concealed mechanism allowed one to slide the wooden screen in order to reveal the Courbet canvas.

Around 1948, Lacan hired for his service a Spanish girl named Gloria Gonzalez. Having served as a domestic from the age of thirteen, she was accustomed to hard work. While offering first Sylvia, then Lacan, her undivided loyalty, she proved able to serve the great man without responding to his endless requests. She never cooked. Gradually, she grew attached to the family, and became the master's private secretary. She resisted him, loved him, admired him, and obeyed him with a combination of enthusiasm and discretion. For his part, he developed a special bond with this willful, muscular, and voluble woman, who understood his projects, intuited his disappointment, and embraced his passion for psychoanalysis. When he received patients, it was she who opened the door, then observed the movements of each out of the corner of her eye. She calmed the agitated, consoled the distressed, and accompanied would-be victims of depression down the stairs. In the "Doctor's" shadow, she reigned like a Velasquez lady-in-waiting replete with the virtues of Proust's Céleste Albaret.

Although Lacan himself was not directly involved in any political struggle, his family played its role in the fight against colonialism. In 1954, Laurence Bataille traveled to Algeria where she had a part in a theater company, along with Alain Cuny. Upon her return, she became a member of the Communist Party. Lacan found the idea grotesque and compared the party to a church, but in the face of his step-daughter's will, he did not insist and accepted her decision. When the Communist deputies voted to delegate special powers to the government, Laurence handed in her card, and in the spring of 1958, she joined her cousin Diego Masson in a network directed by Robert Davezies for aiding the FLN [Front de Libération Nationale]. She was involved in collecting funds at the same time as she was pursuing her medical studies. On May 10, 1960, she was arrested by two policemen. At the Roquette prison, where she was kept for six weeks, Lacan brought her pages from the typescript of his seminar on the "Ethics of Psychoanalysis." The passage was carefully chosen: a commentary on Antigone's revolt against Creon. Laurence's attorney, Roland Dumas, managed to get the charges dismissed and, on that occasion, came to know Lacan: He would subsequently become his lawyer.

Three years later Laurence entered into analysis with Conrad Stein. She chose a member of the SPP in order not to find herself on the couch of one of her stepfather's students. Previously, she had enlisted Judith in the anticolonialist cause. After the emancipation of Algeria, Judith taught philosophy for two years at the Faculté d'Alger, then received her *agrégé* degree with distinction, a source of great satisfaction to her father. Lacan was, moreover, as proud of Judith's academic achievements as of the political activities of Bataille's daughter. In a letter to Winnicott, in response to the latter's suggestion that he visit London, Lacan did not hesitate to convey his feelings. "I am here with my wife and my young daughter," he wrote from Saint-Tropez in August of 1960. "The other one, Laurence, my wife's daughter . . . has given up much torment (of which we are proud), having been arrested for her political relations. She is free now, but we nevertheless remain preoccupied with a matter that is not yet over. We also have a nephew, who lived in my home during his studies as though he were a son, who has just been sentenced to two years in prison for his resistance to the Algerian war." [30]

From 1951 to 1953, the seminar was held in Sylvia's home. Each Wednesday, Lacan commented on major Freudian texts: *The Wolf Man* and *The Rat Man*. He gave up his British suits for more extravagant garb. Thereafter he dressed in a manner similar to his baroque syntax. Shortly after the first split, he moved to the amphitheater at Sainte-Anne, which had been loaned to him by Jean Delay. There, over a period of ten years, he held forth in a vacillating voice, alternately faltering and thunderous, laced with sighs and hesitations. He would note down in advance what he would say, and then, in the presence of his audience, improvise like an actor from the Royal Shakespeare Company who might have had Greta Garbo as diction coach and Arturo Toscanini as spiritual guide. Lacan played false because he was speaking true, as though through the rigor of a voice perpetually on the verge of cracking, he was, like some ventriloquist, effecting the resurgence of the secret mirror of the unconscious, the symptom of a mastery endlessly on the brink of collapse. A sorcerer without magic, a guru without hypnosis, a prophet without god, he fascinated his audience in an admirable language effecting, in the margins of desire, the revival of a century of enlightenment.

Lacan did not analyze; he associated. Nor did he expatiate; he produced resonances. At every session of that exercise in collective therapy, his students had the impression that the master was speaking of them and for them, in a coded message secretly addressed to each of them alone. They consequently would rush to the best bookstores to acquire such and such a book he had referred to or to devour a passage from an unknown text. For ten years, then for twenty more, His Majesty commanded the labors of Freudian France.

Along with the seminar, he pursued his presentation of patients at Sainte-Anne with a clairvoyance inherited from Clérambault and an art of commentary borrowed from Kojève. Lacan questioned the mad and did not hesitate to affix to their bodies the labels of traditional nosology as reviewed and corrected by Freudian clinical practice: Aimée once again, Aimée returned to life.

The parable of the tortoise and the scorpion[31] reveals the dilemma facing a thinker once he is constrained to identify with the authority of an institution. If the scorpion crosses the river on the tortoise's back, he runs the risk of biting it and dying along with his host. On the other hand, if he decides to build a bridge, he runs a far more serious risk: that of turning himself into a tortoise and shifting from the position of a "master without command" to that of leader of a school. We have seen how Freud had escaped that alternative by entrusting the running of the empire to his disciples. So long as Lacan remained a scorpion, he was a Hegelian. He knew that "being-for-death" was the ultimate figure of "being-an-analyst." But if he built a bridge, he also knew that sooner or later he would be obliged to found an institution destined to be the reflection of his own doctrine. Secure in his sense of Freudian experience, this great reader of Machiavelli understood early on the incompatibility between an authentic exercise of institutional power and the position of doctrinal master. It was not for nothing that he had written up the famous regulations of 1949.

At the SFP, Lacan sought to implement that politics of the unconscious whose inadequate founder Freud had been. Yet he was not safe from the paradoxes of his own temperament. He could thus not stop himself from fusing the doctrine with his own person by asking his students to love or serve him. But since he was neither a dictator nor a dangerous paranoiac, he was perfectly aware of the limits of such a reign: He knew he was king of an imaginary monarchy based on voluntary servitude. That is why, for ten years, his hope was affiliation with the empire. In deciding to leave it, he ran the risk not only of having to abandon any expansionist project, but above all, of being obliged to create a school in his own image, thus effecting a permanent fusion of the master's doctrine and his person. It was clear that belonging to the IPA would allow Lacan to remain a thinker and avoid having to implement policies "in his name." On the contrary, any definitive break would inevitably lead to his identification with a political authority that would make of him not only an emitter of signifiers but the leader of a school.

More or less consciously, he knew that such a fusion was untenable: better indeed the difficult situation of the saboteur than the comfortable one of a tortoise rid of all scorpions. It may thus be hypothesized that Lacan's quest for integration into the empire functioned as the symptom of a master's will not to become the director of an institution. In keeping with that perspective, it should be admitted that Lacan would found his school only when forced to, when he would perceive that he could no longer either escape the rules or have his position as master accepted by the IPA. But simultaneously, in losing all hope of being part of the empire, he would run the risk of losing himself in a sovereign identification with his own name or more precisely with the name of a leader. During the ten years of the strange existence of the SFP, Lacan had the leisure of reigning like a prince without as yet having a prince's obligations.

It was no doubt no accident that he elaborated the essential part of his work while he, like his colleagues, was in the position of an exile in search of recognition. In ten years, he founded what is presently known as *Lacanianism* and which should be known more simply as Freudianism. The baroque Lacan of his maturity constructed an *orthodox rearticulation of Freudianism* that possessed a feature unique in the history of psychoanalysis, that of not being separable *in theory* from the original work whose commentary it claimed to be. Because he attempted to turn Freudian theory into veritable "human science," beyond all known forms of "neo-Freudianism," Kleinianism, or the transcendence of Freudianism, Lacan would always refuse to affix his name to an undertaking that he wanted to remain separate from any reference to a nation, a sect, or a religion. If he symbolized the name of Freud, by naming his rearticulation of matters "Freudian," it was in order to become himself the instrument of a renewal of the Viennese discovery. Whence this unprecedented paradox: Lacanianism existed to the extent that it did not exist. It existed because it constituted itself *historically* at the heart of the post-Freudian adventure and in part against it, but it did not exist because it thought of itself in its entirety as a Freudianism and even more as the sole theoretical path for the completion of the Freudian project.

As a second hypothesis, it may be shown that Lacan effected two successive readings of Saussure's work. The first occurred before 1953 and took its place simultaneously in the philosophical landscape created by the reception of Heidegger's thought in France and in that of the discovery of *Les structures élémentaires de la parenté,* while the second took the form of a structuralist and quasi-Cartesian recasting of Freud's conceptual system. The texts of that period reveal that Lacan did not read the same Saussure before and after 1953. For the *Rome Discourse* and the preceding lecture on "The Symbolic, the Imaginary, and the Real," he read Saussure with Lévi-Strauss on the one side and Heidegger on the other. On the one hand, he gave emphasis to the notion of symbolic thought and, on the other, he insisted on the question of the meaning of being through the "true" unveiling of speech and language. When Lacan spoke in Rome of the signifier, what he was referring to was a conception of the "logos" and "utterance" as well as to a Lévi-Straussian conception of the symbol. But he had not yet elaborated an authentic theory of signifying determination. In order to reach that point, between 1953 and 1963, he would have to reread Saussure from a Jakobsonian perspective while dreaming of a possible connection between the second topographical model and the Genevan discovery.

Stated in other terms, for ten years, Lacan rethought psychoanalytic doctrine on the basis of a productive (and no longer passive) reading of Saussure's achievement.

It is always difficult to determine whether or not Lacan was aware, within the overall rearticulation he was proposing, of his different and successive readings. His utterances seem simply to indicate the pursuit of an endeavor, whence the impression of excessive continuity, and even repetition, emanating from his work. That continuity is all the more deceptive in that Lacan never effected a clear break or "transcendence" vis-à-vis a prior stage of his thought. In other words, he still continued to use Hegelian terminology when Hegelianism was no longer a principal point of reference, just as he perpetuated his dependence on Lévi-Straussian terms even after he had already elaborated a theory of the symbolic that no longer owed anything to the anthropologist. Everything was always "already there," still there, and yet to come in Lacan's immense corpus, in which essential revisions were often manifest as apparently futile inflections and permanent returns to earlier formulations.

Lacan's first encounter with Heidegger occurred in 1950, which of course does not mean anything as to Heidegger's contribution to Lacanian thought. As always, friendships and relations are one thing, and conceptual borrowings another. Thus, for example, Lévi-Strauss and Lacan would remain good friends, but the former would not support the latter's doctrine in any manner, and would even confess that he did not understand it, whereas the latter would endlessly draw nourishment from the former's thought, even as he was already formulating something quite different from it.

In 1950, then, the philosopher Jean Beaufret, one of the principal introducers of Heideggerian thought in France, spent some time on Lacan's couch. The two men had friendly relations. One day, irritated by his analyst's silence, Beaufret decided to make him speak, whatever it might cost. "Two or three days ago," he said, "I was in Heidegger's home in Fribourg and he spoke to me about you." Lacan reacted immediately and, bursting with anticipation, asked: "What did he say to you?" The trap had worked.[32]

Lacan journeyed to Freiburg during that period when Heidegger was still forbidden to teach because of his support for the Nazi regime before the war. He would be readmitted as a professor a year later. In France, he was already celebrated by the left-wing intelligentsia as the greatest modern master of philosophy. Heidegger and Lacan did not communicate much in Freiburg. The former did not speak French, and the latter could not express himself in German. Nevertheless, they exchanged a few words of philosophy: probably a mixture of ancient Greek and old Germanic etymologies. It was nonetheless the case that Lacan had already read *Sein und Zeit* [*Being and Time*] and Heidegger had never heard of Lacan. Moreover, he was not interested at all in psychoanalysis and very little in Freud. Lacan was transfixed by Heideggerian philosophy, by its style, its problematic of being and the unveiling of truth. All that is clear from the *Rome Discourse*. But he did not borrow from Heidegger what he borrowed from Hegel, Lévi-Strauss, Saussure, or Jakobson. There were echoes, a certain sonority, a tendency to imitation, and a fascination—not much more.[33]

Some time after his visit to Freiburg, he translated the 1951 article "Logos" with the assistance of an eminent scholar of German. He read into the text—or discovered in it—his own preoccupations with the categories of utterance and truth. The philosopher learned of the translation, gave it his approval, and Lacan published it in the first issue of *La Psychanalyse*.

Heidegger made his first trip to France during the latter half of August 1955, in order to participate in the colloquium at Cerisy-la-Salle, where he delivered his lecture "Was ist die Philosophie?" Jean Beaufret and Kostas Axelos had organized the occasion. The former had joined the Resistance during the earliest stages of the Occupation, and the latter had been condemned to death in Greece for having borne arms against the Nazis. Axelos had arrived in France in 1945, entered into analysis with Ziwar, and met Lacan in 1950. Like Beaufret he had no guilt complex to impede him from receiving Heidegger, who also met Lucien Goldmann, Maurice de Gandillac, Paul Ricoeur, and others at Cerisy. Sartre and Merleau-Ponty, who had barely participated in the Resistance, nonetheless refused to attend the meeting in order to indicate their hostility toward Heidegger's pre-War political engagement.[34]

At Guitrancourt, Lacan organized a small gathering in honor of the philosopher and his wife. He invited Beaufret and Axelos. The latter, who spoke German, served as a mediator for an unrestrained discussion in which Lacan and Heidegger exchanged ideas while taking in the fragrances of the last evenings of summer. Heidegger stayed at La Prévôté, then visited the cathedral at Chartres. Lacan drove his car with the same speed as his psychoanalytic sessions. Seated in front, Heidegger did not flinch, but his wife could not stop complaining. Sylvia conveyed her dissatisfaction to Lacan. But to no effect: The master drove faster and faster. On the way back, Heidegger continued to keep his silence while his wife's protests grew louder and Lacan pressed down still harder on the gas-pedal. The trip came to an end, and each of the passengers went his or her own way.[35]

The more influential of the articles of the SFP's glory days would make Lacan, during the 1960s, into the founder of a "structuralist," "antihumanist," and "scientific" conception of psychoanalysis. That Lacan would be the most famous, the most commented on, and the most caricatured—to the point of ridicule. With his fertile reading of Saussure's work, perpetuating the return to Freud, he became, along with others, the leader of a new school of thought centered on a break with the ideals of phenomenology. The celebrated quintet of Althusser, Barthes, Foucault, Lévi-Strauss, and Lacan is all too well known. We shall return to it in due course.

It is not impossible that the second (and far more important reading of Saussure) was inspired by the teaching of Merleau-Ponty. The two men knew and liked each other, but, of course, that does not prove a thing. It should be noted, however, that Merleau-Ponty was the first in France to appeal to a philosophy drawn from the *Course on General Linguistics*. In his inaugural lecture at the Collège de France in 1953, he announced the news. "The theory of the sign," he said, "as elaborated by linguistics, may imply a theory of historical meaning going beyond the alternative of *things* and *minds*. . . . Saussure may well have sketched out a new philosophy of history."[36]

In 1951, to be sure, the philosopher had suggested that psychoanalysts should give up the concept of the unconscious and convert to *Gestalttheorie*. He had in a sense advised them to make of the unconscious an *other side* of consciousness, and not its *other scene*. But as Vincent Descombes has remarked, Merleau-Ponty marshalled in the service of his phenomenological project a structuralist authority which would subsequently be invoked against every phenomenology.[37]

Now it was precisely that structuralist authority which Lacan was appealing to in his double rearticulation of the unconscious and the second topographical model. Yet when he invoked the name of Merleau-Ponty, he referred to neither the 1953 lecture nor to his famous behavioral dialectic. In his seminar of 1963–64, he paid homage to the deceased philosopher by emphasizing—with reference to his posthumous work *Le visible et l'invisible*—that it had succeeded in forcing the very limits of phenomenology.[38] But Lacan did not allude to any of his other works.

Between the *Rome Discourse* and the lecture on "The Purloined Letter," which marked the productive entry of linguistics into the Freudian domain, an extraordinary event occurred. During a session held on February 10, 1954, a strange dialogue took place between Lacan and the philosopher Jean Hyppolite,[39] an exchange which led the former to "dismiss" philosophy in the name of a Freudian theory capable of ensuring a transcendence and absorption of philosophy itself. In a remarkable text entitled *Le leurre hégélien* ["The Hegelian lure"], Pierre Macherey has shown that in the course of that memorable exchange—in which, through Hyppolite's commentary on *Verneinung* [negation], the first lineaments of the notion of "foreclosure" were sketched—Lacan came to an awareness of a divergence between Hegelianism and Freudianism, based on their common reference to dialectics.[40] In other words, it was a question for him, through the intercession of Hyppolite, of "stepping out" of Hegelian philosophy, and indeed of philosophy itself, in order to gain access to structuralism. That operation did not lead to a break with the reading of Hegel's work. It was simply that once it had occurred, Lacan no longer read the same Hegel. In between, Heideggerianism had worked its effects, allowing for a translation of the unconscious as a discourse and a language.

If, twenty years earlier, Kojève had produced the spark allowing a young psychiatrist to be a "Hegelian in Freud," Jean Hyppolite in turn, in relation to the mature Lacan, played the role of a new Kojève. However, the new Kojève did not occupy the position of an intitiator for the master of 1954. He had more the role of a partner, and even a student. The eminently sympathetic Hyppolite attended Lacan's seminar as he might a totemic feast in which Lacan "devoured" philosophy while repudiating the loves of his youth. Lacan abandoned Hegel for Saussure and phenomenology for psychoanalysis—a final way of remaining Hegelian through Freud and Heidegger while fulfilling Merleau-Ponty's prophecy. A year later, after a new debate with Hyppolite, he wrote his commentary on Poe's tale, "The Purloined Letter." On that occasion, the fertile reading of Saussure produced its first effects.[41]

On several occasions, Lacan observed that Freud's second topographical model posed certain problems. In May 1954, he emphasized that in the theory of the ego elaborated by Kris, Hartmann, and Loewenstein, the ego continued to play "the problematic role that it already has in the writings of Freud's third period."[42] In other words, he allowed it to be inferred that the second topographical model would authorize, in its ambivalences, the psychologizing rearticulation inherent in Freud's period of great renewal. He "allowed to be inferred," but did not state openly, that Freud's hypotheses may be read in two divergent manners. He chose instead to fight the process leading to the egological revision. That is why, in all his other commentaries, he did not hesitate to affirm that the theoreticians of ego psychology had misunderstood the second topographical model in making the ego the center of an adaptative psychoanalysis. He was not wrong concerning the results, but he was not completely right concerning Freud's propositions, which are indeed rather ambiguous. Returning to Freud from a perspective opposite that of ego psychology would consequently consist in *reinventing* the unconscious, in rediscovering the id, and in endowing them with their full weight. In order for that to be achieved, it would be necessary to complete or "sublate" the Viennese doctrine through a theory of the subject that would make any recovery of the unconscious by consciousness an impossibility: Linguistics would serve that end. In Rome, Lacan had said that the ego was half a subject; thereafter, he would delve further into the dialectic of divisions.

He thus introduced a separation, which does not exist in Freud, between the *ego* and the *I* [*je*], between an *imaginary ego* and a *subject of the unconscious*. In order to do so, he had recourse to the resources of the French language which allows one to cleave the Freudian *Ich* into an *ego* (*moi*) and an *I* [*je*], a move that would be impossible as such in German. That split had already been effected before Lacan by Édouard Pichon.

In 1926, the grammarian noted that the *Ich* designated an inner world and that *moi* in French was opposed to *non-moi*. Consequently, he said, *moi* cannot render the conceptual content of *Ich,* which would have to be translated as *je* [I] or *ego*. Nevertheless, the word *moi* prevailed against Pichon in the official translations, and the grammarian returned to the subject in 1938, in an article in which he differentiated *moi* and *je* according to the subject's modes of expression in representing the self. Pichon split the notion of the personal pronoun, dividing it into an *attenuated person* [*je, tu, il*] and an *ample person* [*moi, toi, lui*]. The first is strictly grammatical whereas the second expresses a concrete personality.[43]

Imbued with Pichon's teaching, Lacan took up the distinction afresh in 1960 in *Subversion du sujet et dialectique du désir.*[44] Well before that date, however, he had divided the concept of *Ich* in a manner different from that of the splitting of the ego (*Ichspaltung*) proposed by Freud. In point of fact, he reworked in a personal manner Pichon's observation by adding to it a notion of division which was not actually present in the grammarian's work. In order to effect that epistemological operation, literature was conjured up in the form of Poe's tale: "It appears to us more and more clearly," he stated in March 1955, "that this subject which speaks is a dimension *beyond* the ego."[45]

The story is well known: It takes place in France during the Restoration. Detective Auguste Dupin is to solve a mystery. At the request of the prefect of police, he succeeds in retrieving a compromising letter stolen from the queen and hidden by the minister. The letter is placed in full view among the vaults of the fireplace. Visible to whoever *wants* to see it. But the police do not find it because they are caught up in the deceptions of psychology. Instead of observing the evidence before their eyes, they ascribe intentions to the thief. Dupin proceeds differently. He politely requests an audience with the minister, and, while speaking to him, observes the room with an alert eye. His gaze is concealed by dark glasses. He immediately locates the object, snatches it without the thief realizing as much, and replaces it with an identical one. The minister thus remains unaware that his secret has been penetrated. He persists in believing he is master of the game and of the queen, since to possess the letter is to exercise a power over its addressee. The minister does not know that he no longer has it, while the queen knows that her blackmailer no longer has any power over her in relation to the king. Only possession—and not use—of the letter creates that ascendancy.

In order to explain his discovery to the narrator, Dupin himself has recourse to a fiction. He relates the anecdote of a boy and a game of evens and odds: "I knew a child eight years old," he says, "whose success at guessing in the game of 'evens and odds' attracted universal admiration. The game is simple, and is played with marbles. One player holds in his hand a number of these toys and demands of another whether that number is even or odd. If the guess is right, the guesser wins one; if wrong, he loses one. The boy to whom I allude won all the marbles of the school. Of course he had some principle of guessing; and this lay in mere observation and admeasurement of the astuteness of his opponents." [46]

At his seminar, Lacan asked the participants to play at evens and odds, and then commented on the fable. Four characters are on stage: the king, the queen, the minister, and the letter. The whole affair is similar to the famous prisoner sophism through which he had introduced his theory of therapy: once again a game, and once again a gaze. . . . But this time, Lacan emphasized that the central character was the letter, since, for each, it *was* his or her unconscious, something which seizes the subject and drags it in its train. [47]

A month later he began the actual writing of the text and completed it in August in San Casciano, the village of Machiavelli's birth. He visited the house, then the tavern selling souvenir ashtrays of the great man. In his article, which would serve eleven years later as the opening text of the *Écrits*, he gave testimony of this fertile reading of Saussure. Like Dupin, he no longer theorized merely a symbolic function, but a *logic of the signifier,* which was a "political" logic. A letter always arrives at its destination because the letter (or the signifier)—like *fortuna*—determines the subject in its itinerary. It was under the sign of that structuralism inflected by the presence of Machiavelli that Lacan envisaged himself as a founding father.

He was, of course, obliged to explain his procedure—why the letter (of the signifier) now prevailed over speech; why the change had occurred since the *Rome Discourse*. Two lectures followed, which should be related (as always) to the Seminar, the site of oral formulation. Over a period of two years, between 1957 and 1959, Lacan took as the theme of his teaching *Unconscious Formations* and *Desire and Its Interpretation*. In counterpoint, he wrote up two lectures delivered in chosen locations, one in the Descartes Amphitheater of the Sorbonne, on May 9, 1959, at the request of the Fédération des étudiants en lettres, the other at Royaumont, in

September 1960, at a colloquium on dialectic organized by Jean Wahl. Literature on the one hand, where the importance of linguistics was beginning to be felt, and philosophy on the other, where the decline of phenomenology was clear to all. The first presentation was entitled *L'instance de la lettre dans l'inconscient ou la raison depuis Freud* and the second *Subversion du sujet et dialectique du désir dans l'inconscient freudien.*[48]

Ferdinand de Saussure gave the name *signifier* to the component of the sign which was the acoustic image of a concept, which he called the *signified*. The *linguistic sign* was thus defined as the relation between a signified and a signifier within a system of values. A sign's *value* resulted negatively from the simultaneous presence of all the other signs in the language, whereas its signification was deduced from the bond between a signified and a signifier. In order to interpret the second topographical model in the light of linguistics, Lacan began by shattering the problematic of the sign. Saussure placed the signified over the signifier and separated the two by a bar indicative of signification. Lacan inverted that configuration and placed the signified beneath the signifier, which is accorded a primordial position. Then, taking up the notion of value, he emphasized that each signification refers to another one. Whereby he inferred as a consequence that the signifier was separable from the signified, which slid endlessly beneath the signifier. He gave the name of *letter* to the signifier and compared it to a *word-symbol* bereft of immediate signification, but determinant for the unconscious destiny of the subject. As for the subject himself, not assimilable to an (imaginary) ego, he was first of all a *subject of the unconscious*. And for that reason, he was divided, as required by the Freudian principle of *Spaltung*.[49]

In that perspective, the subject's existence was not that of any plenitude: He was, on the contrary, represented by the signifier, that is, by a *letter* which was nothing other than the linguistic inscription of the unconscious. Lacan thus drew a first philosophical conclusion from the Freudian notion that the subject is not master in his own home, but inhabited by the id. That divided subject is represented by a chain of signifiers in which the level of the message uttered [*énoncé*] does not coincide with that of the utterance [*énonciation*] itself. Thus did Lacan translate into linguistic terms the division and the sliding. But it was not enough for that subject to be divided or represented. He is represented *by* a signifier *for* another signifier within a chain: Man is determined by words in the form of a language speaking in his place.

That is why Lacan replaced Descartes's *je pense* [I think] with a Freudian *ça parle* (it—or the id—speaks). But the Cogito was a fundamental moment in human history since it divided the subject into reflexive knowledge and repressed truth. From that Lacan derived the consequence that the unconscious was in some way an effect of language. But why, after renouncing Hegelianism, did he summon up an old Cartesianism? Why did he fish out the aberrant term "subject of the unconscious," where Freud had carefully avoided it? Lacan's inference in fact was that Freud had neither invented nor eliminated the subject but rather seized on it there where he found it, namely among the aftereffects of the Cartesian perspective, which had inaugurated, after Galileo, modern science. If Freud chose to be Copernican, Lacan took it upon himself to be Galilean, by deriving the logical consequences of the second topographical model.

The notion of the subject surfaces in the *Méditations*. The concept claims to describe man as escaping all extrinsic determination. "The subject," Bertrand Ogilvie has written, "as author and responsible agent of his thought and behavior, initiator of all meaning, and, in Kant, of all morality, gives the keystone of a future-oriented ideology, an ideology of law, or humanism, at the foundation of industrial societies."[50] Exploiting that situation, Lacan thus produced, by way of Freud, the theory of the "modern ego," namely of the "paranoid" subject of scientific civilization. Thus the Freudian experiment radically reversed the philosophy resulting from the Cogito. But in summoning up Descartes alongside Freud, that is, the subject founded by science, Lacan also summoned up the subject of doubt, an "I-know-not-what-I-am." He could thus bestow on the unconscious, by way of Descartes, a subject divided in itself.

The Freudian concept of *Ichspaltung* must thus be translated in order to demonstrate that the human subject is divided twice over. A first instance separates the imaginary ego from the subject of the unconscious, and a second is inscribed within the subject of the unconscious itself, representing an originary division: Lacan called this *la refente* [the splitting]. That division is impossible to unite since the (divided) subject is always represented by a signifier for another one. Along with *refente*, the term *fading*, which Lacan borrowed from the English, is defined as a kind of flickering: the appearance or disappearance of the subject in the chain.

To be sure, the three registers of the Symbolic, the Imaginary, and the Real are to be found in this new logic of the signifier. As are the three previously defined levels of demand, need, and desire: *Demand* is addressed to someone; *need* is a biological appetite; and *desire* is the desire for an absolute recognition of desire. What Lacan had called *objet a* (site of the imaginary) was now distinguished clearly from the *grand A* (site of the symbolic). From the unconscious as discourse of the other the transition had been made to the unconscious as discourse of the Other, inscribed in a language in terms of letters or signifiers. "The unconscious received from Freud," Lacan wrote, "is a chain of signifiers which somewhere (on another scene, he put it) repeats and insists in order to interfere in the breaks afforded it by the effective speech and cogitation which it informs. In that formula, which is our own only in conforming to Freud's text and to the experience it inaugurated, the crucial term is the signifier, revived from ancient rhetoric by modern linguistics, in a doctrine whose major phases are all we can allude to in this context, but whose dawn and present culmination will be indicated by the names of Ferdinand de Saussure and Roman Jakobson, recalling that the pilot science of structuralism in the West has its roots in the Russia which witnessed the flourishing of formalism. Geneva 1910, Petrograd 1920 say with sufficient clarity why Freud lacked the necessary instrument."[51]

Saussure was in fact not sufficient for Lacan's "Cartesian" operation. Very early on he understood that the Genevan's work would have to be reinterpreted in the light of Freud and as a function of the work of post-Saussureans, specifically of Roman Jakobson.

Born in Russia in 1897 and a member at age 18 of the formalist group, Jakobson had discovered the *Course on General Linguistics* in 1920. After the Bolshevik revolution, he left for Czechoslovakia to become the founder with Troubetzkoy of the Prague Linguistic Circle. After emigrating to the United States, he became friends, during the 1940s, with Claude Lévi-Strauss, who had fled France after the Nazi invasion. In the course of their impassioned discussions, the two persuaded each other that there existed a link between linguistics and social anthropology. Shortly thereafter, Jakobson taught at Harvard University, then at the Massachusetts Institute of Technology. It was in 1950 that he met Lacan for the first time during a trip to France. Subsequently, he would habitually stay at Sylvia's home during his visits to France.[52]

Thus Lacan had heard of Saussure's work through numerous channels: Lévi-Strauss, Merleau-Ponty, Jakobson. In addition, he had probably discussed the subject with Pichon in years past.

A few months before delivering his lecture on *L'instance de la lettre,* he discovered with amazement *Fundamentals of Language,* published by Jakobson and Morris Halle in the Hague. The book contained an article entitled "Two Aspects of Language and Two Types of Aphasia,"[53] which would allow him to polish his hypothesis of a language-unconscious. With that text, Lacan was able to accomplish a fertile reading of the *Traumdeutung.*

Jakobson brought to light a bipolar structure of language. Speakers unwittingly perform two types of activity: One involves *similarity* and concerns the *selection* of paradigms or language units, and the other entails *contiguity* and concerns the syntagmatic *combination* of the same units. In the act of selection, one chooses or substitutes one word for another. One uses, for instance, the word "bonnet" to designate a particular hat, rather than "beret" or "fedora." In the act of combination, on the contrary, one establishes a relation between two words forming a continuity. To describe the way an individual dresses, one chooses, for example, to associate a skirt with a blouse, then a blouse with shoes, etc. In taking up the works of J. H. Jackson to his own end, Roman Jakobson showed that the language disturbances resulting from aphasia deprive the individual at times of the capacity for selection, and at others of that for combination. In disturbances of similarity, the affected subject has trouble finding his words. The loss bears on the selective function whereas the combining function remains intact. On the contrary, in problems of contiguity, the individual is affected by a breakdown of grammar. He speaks telegraphically and cannot manage to associate; he replaces a sentence by a *heap* of words, at which point his statement, in French, resembles a certificate of psychiatric internment drawn up by Clérambault.

Pursuing his argument, Jakobson invoked the traditions of rhetoric as made use of by linguistics and noted that the selective activity in language consisted of a *metaphorical* function whereas the combining activity resembled the device of *metonomy.* Metaphor, as is known, is the most elaborate of tropes, particularly in poetry, since the transition through substitution from one word to another is based on a veritable interpretation of linguistic meaning. Metonymy, on the other hand, is more novelistic, prosaic, and realistic to the extent that it allows one to designate something by the name of another element in the same totality, by virtue of a clearly defined relation.

That association of linguistics and rhetoric led Jakobson to identify metaphoric activity with the selective function and metonymic activity with the combining function. Disturbances of the former prevent the subject from having recourse to metaphor and those of the latter deprive him of all metonymic activity. The linguist observed that the two devices were to be found in the functioning of dreams as described by Freud. He categorized symbolism as a metaphoric activity and condensation and displacement as metonymic activities.

Freud separated the dream's *manifest content* from its *latent content*. The first term designates the dream as it appears to the dreamer recounting it. The second refers to the set of meanings at which the dream analysis arrives. In other words, the latent content is the complete translation of the manifest content, the adequate expression of the dreamer's desire. That process of translation defines the dreamwork. On the one hand, the manifest content is produced by dreamwork, and on the other, the latent content is also produced by work in the opposite direction. In the unconscious operation which consists in transforming the latent content into the manifest content, two principal mechanisms need be considered: *displacement* (*Verschiebung*) and *condensation* (*Verdichtung*). Displacement allows the primordial elements of the latent content to be transformed, through an associative sliding, into minimal details of the manifest content. This kind of translation is related to the trope named *synecdoche:* The whole is represented by the part, the boat by its sail. Condensation is different in nature; it allows the latent content to be translated into an abridged or abbreviated manifest content. In this case, each element of the manifest content is determined by several latent meanings. This kind of transformation is related to metonymy since several features come to be "condensed" or "united" in the same figure, as in the creation of composite characters or puns. One sees why Jakobson attaches these two mechanisms to the activity of contiguity—one refers to synecdoche and the other to metonymy in the strict sense.

Taking up that demonstration on his own, Lacan transcribed the Freudian conception of dreamwork—which was the key to the linguistic functioning of the unconscious—somewhat differently. If the dream in general is characterized by the activity of transposition, that activity may be translated, in the light of Saussure, as an endless sliding of the signified beneath the signifier. There are thus two dimensions to the signifier's incidence on the signified: One is defined as *condensation* and refers to a structure of superimposition of signifiers (puns, composite characters); the other relates to a swerving of meaning (the part for the whole or contiguity) and designates *displacement*. Contrary to Jakobson, Lacan thus assimilated the Freudian notion of condensation to a metaphorical procedure and displacement to a metonymical one. In metaphor the symptom is determined as the substitution of a corporeal signifier for another repressed signifier, whereas in metonymy unconscious desire comes to be caught as the "desire of desire."

From there, Lacan integrated the structure of the subject into a logic of the signifier: "Is the place I occupy as subject of the signifier concentric or ex-centric in relation to that which I occupy as subject of the signified?" Ex-centric was his reply, in accordance with the subversion he visited upon the Cogito, "I think there where I am not, therefore I am there where I do not think."[54] The new Lacanian topographical model thus consisted in ascribing to the unconscious the structure of a language in which the *I* [*je*] is defined as an effect of the signifier. That I-subject resembles a shifter, in Jakobson's terminology, that is, a grammatical unit whose meaning is referentially dependent on the message. The shifter designates the subject of the speech act without signifying it. That subject was represented by Lacan through a negative signifier, specifically the expletive *ne* as defined by Pichon in an article on negation.[55]

If the unconscious as developed from Freud could be formulated as a "chain of signifiers," it meant that Freud was ahead of the formalizations of linguistics even though he was unaware of Saussure's work. As a result, Lacan came to think of himself as the deferred mediator of an encounter that never took place. It was I, he would later say as an ironic provocation, who discovered the unconscious. In the meanwhile, his topographical model could be formulated as an algebra conforming to the principle of the signifier's incidence on the signified. Three formulas were obtained in the process: The general formula describes the signifier's function in relation to the bar—or barrier—of resistance to signification. The metonymic formula translates the signifying function of *connecting* signifiers, in which the eliding of the signified refers to the object of desire as missing in the chain. Finally the metaphoric formula transcribes the signifying function of substituting one signifier for another, through which the subject is always represented. Using the terminology of sewing, Lacan then named *point de capiton* [the cap or boss between tufts or buttons] the moment through which, at certain privileged spots in the chain, the signifier is bound to the signified in order to give rise to a meaning. In analysis, such a "cap" is translated as punctuation.

Such, schematically, is the sum total of the theoretical operation allowing Lacan to endow psychoanalytic doctrine with a non-Freudian theory of the subject. It should be noted that that theory claimed to be "philosophically" Freudian, since, transcending Hegelianism and Cartesianism, it derived consequences unconsidered by Freud from his own doctrine. Thus a return to the unconscious . . .

III. An Autumn in Bonneval

Around 1956, Henri Ey decided to devote the Bonneval Colloquium of 1960 to the theme of the "unconscious." Always alert to the shifting winds of contemporaneity, the amiable Catalan realized the significance of the debate taking place between psychoanalysis and philosophy concerning the status of the Freudian unconscious. In keeping with his conception of psychiatry, he was aware that such a discussion raised the problem of the training of therapists and the elucidation of the nature of madness. Since he adored large-scale theoretical jousts, he invited to the colloquium both renowned philosophers and psychoanalysts of both tendencies, SPP and SFP. Among the latter, he chose significantly not to invite any of the magisterial figures of the second generation. He made an exception for Lacan, who was not invited to deliver a paper, but merely to participate in the discussions. The principal names featured at the meeting were those of the third generation. Henri Ey proposed a triple confrontation—psychiatric, philosophical, and psychoanalytic— while excluding psychology, that is, the tendency represented by Lagache.

The SFP was represented by Serge Leclaire, François Perrier, Jean Laplanche, and J.-B. Pontalis, while the SPP was present in the persons of Serge Lebovici, René Diatkine, André Green, and Conrad Stein. Among the philosophers in attendance were Paul Ricoeur, Maurice Merleau-Ponty, Henri Lefebvre, Alphonse de Waelhens, and Jean Hyppolite. As for psychiatry, its positions were conveyed through the contributions of Georges Lantéri-Laura, Sven Follin, Claude Blanc, François Tosquelles, and René Angelergues.

Superb in the almost abbot-like figure he cut, Henri Ey took great delight in receiving his guests on his own turf. He warmly moderated the discussions which ran over into the gardens of the hospital or amid the arcades of the cloister. Despite the somewhat cheerless autumn weather, the atmosphere was exceptional: a combination of intellectual excitement, conviviality, and ferocity in the pursuit of personal polemics. On one side as on the other, the psychoanalysts came forth in dispersed order. The SFP was represented almost exclusively by Lacan's students, who were not all in agreement with each other. In the SPP camp, two tendencies were expressed: one, which was plainly medical and Nachtian, in a contribution cosigned by Diatkine and Lebovici, and the other, which was far closer to Lacanian hypotheses, with the presentations of two "young Turks," Conrad Stein and André Green, who revealed their hostility to the orthodoxy of their own group.

Henri Ey had thus brought about a genuine tour de force. Thanks to his intervention, psychoanalysts of the two rival societies met without either one forming a united front against its competitor. Speaking of their work, the "Lacanians" were as divided among themselves as the members of the SPP. Now the discussions were organized around Lacan's teaching. Lacan himself was not unaware of this and used the occasion to reaffirm the importance of his position. He did so all the more eagerly in that his situation in relation to the IPA at the time was far from enviable. In the refectory, the cloister, or the lecture hall, he would multiply his provocations, calling his absent colleagues from the SPP "caricatures of analysts," or using less than honorific epithets to describe them.[56] Fearing lest his forum degenerate into a circus, Ey called his old accomplice to order even as he acknowledged the importance of his doctrine.

For Lacan, what was at stake at Bonneval was considerable. It was a question of demonstrating in France, in the teeth of the IPA, that Freudianism as revised and corrected by linguistics had the full status of a science. If philosophy wanted to escape its rut, it would have to interrogate psychoanalysis and admit that the Freudian unconscious placed the certitudes of consciousness in jeopardy. On this score, the colloquium was a success: All the philosophers present testified to the importance of the Viennese discovery for their own work. Yet that victory of psychoanalysis was only partially accompanied by a triumph of Lacanian doctrine. All the philosophers paid homage to the works of Freud, but not all accepted Lacan's reconceptualization. Such was the case, in particular, of Merleau-Ponty, who declared, "It makes me uneasy to see the category of language occupy the entire field." [57]

The psychiatric battle was as important as the philosophical struggle. Henri Ey more or less assisted Lacan in shoring up the strategic position of psychoanalysis in psychiatric circles. He allowed him to conquer the vast audience of interns who attended the jousts. It amused him to see the two societies competing in his abbey, but in so doing he also allowed the triumph of a policy that tended in a direction contrary to his own. His colloquium, in fact, was of greater benefit to psychoanalysis than to psychiatry since it attracted young physicians drawn by the brilliance of Lacan's discourse to the analytic couch.

Henri Ey wanted to integrate psychoanalysis into a psychiatry which was itself open to Freudian experience, but at Bonneval, he found himself, on the contrary, furthering the omnipotence of psychoanalysis at the expense of psychiatry— and this was an omnipotence whose principal beneficiary was Lacan. Ey's strategy turned out to be all the more favorable to Lacanianism in that a year after the colloquium, an unknown author was to publish a volume whose fate would be monumental: Michel Foucault's *Histoire de la folie à l'âge classique*.[58] Supported by Canguilhem against Lagache in the course of a memorable thesis defense at the Sorbonne, the young philosopher's demonstrations inflicted a fatal blow on the modern science of psychiatry, to wit, on the already waning school of dynamism whose final artisan, against all obstacles, Ey was intent on being. Even though he skirted Freud's discovery, Michel Foucault favored the emergence of a new perspective on madness which would benefit the Lacanian reconceptualization for some ten years. In reducing the notion of "progress" in psychiatry to nought, the philosopher-historian returned to madness as Lacan did to Freud: a return to madness against mental illness, a return to the madness at the core of a logos decked out in the finery of reason, and finally a return to the madman at the expense of a conception of man as entirely inhabited by the certitudes of consciousness. A rout, then, of psychiatric science and, simultaneously, of the "medical tendency" represented by the SPP. Henceforth, after Bonneval, interns would head toward (preferably Lacanian) couches, while reading *Histoire de la folie*. The breach had been made in France that would lead to a new organization of psychiatry: between its liquidation, pure and simple, by anti-psychiatry and its triumphant but dehumanized reemergence by way of pharmacology.

Even as he remained a psychiatrist, Lacan, at every turn, made his move at the right moment. In 1946, he rejected organo-dynamism. Ten years later he forged a psychoanalytic appreciation of psychosis. Finally in 1960, he integrated his teaching into the Saussurian structuralism which had become the nourishment of a new generation of thinkers. In his way, he took up Henri Ey's torch by making of psychoanalysis the "extramural" heir to the old psychiatry, even as he made the transition from a triumphant humanism to a theoretical antihumanism.

The colloquium was principally concerned with the relations between the unconscious and language. Leclaire and Laplanche in collaboration presented a communication divided into chapters signed individually by each author. The two friends were in fact not in agreement on Lacan's hypotheses. While writing a draft one evening in the country, Leclaire felt quite uncomfortable. He suddenly fainted and then entered a "labyrinthine" state. Urgently called to his bed, Lacan and Lhermitte comforted him, then, after a moment of panic, he resumed his work in a climate of combined good humor and passion.[59] The presentation was in the image of the storm on the horizon—as tumultuous as a Turner seascape. Whereas Leclaire defended the thesis of a language-unconscious through a stunning clinical example, Laplanche, on the contrary, took his distance from the Lacanian hypothesis by affirming that the unconscious would be the condition of language. The entire text is of a fine theoretical cast, and Lacan, after the second split, would never again find in his disciples a discursive tone so little marked by the ungainly style to whose prevalence he himself would contribute.

Leclaire recounted the dream of a young Jewish analysand named Philippe-Georges Elhyani, suffering from obsessional neurosis and about thirty years old: "The deserted square of a small city; it's weird, I'm looking for something. Liliane—whom I don't know—appears barefoot and says to me: A long time ago I saw sand as fine as this. We are in a forest and the trees seem curiously colored in striking and simple shades; I think there are a lot of animals in the forest and as I prepare to say so a unicorn crosses our path; the three of us walk to a clearing which we sense down below." [60] From the dream, which was itself associated with various tales and memories of the patient, Leclaire deduced that the name *Liliane* referred to Lili, Philippe's mother's cousin, with whom he had once spent a vacation on an Atlantic beach, and to Anne, his niece with whom he had been walking in the forest the previous day. At dinner, Philippe had eaten Baltic herring and late at night, after the dream, he had awakened with a burning thirst. Armed with all these elements and several others, Leclaire explained that the dream's manifest content did not express any desire to drink, but that on the other hand, the thirst caused by eating herring had furnished the subject the means of appeasing a desire to drink that was different from the real need. The desire referred to the memory of Lili, since, following a walk on the beach during which Philippe had not stopped talking about an intense thirst caused by the heat, she had nicknamed him *Philippe-I'm-thirsty*. The name had become inscribed in the young man's unconscious like a veritable signifier. Leclaire observed that the name *Lili* was embedded in the world *Li-corne* [unicorn] which contains *Li* and *corne*. That word is related to Lili's bare feet—to the sole or *corne* of her feet. Now *corne* refers as well to another of Philippe's dreams in which a child falls into a hole and knocks against a kind of billhook [*serpe*], which wounds him on the heel. Thus a dream of castration . . .

As he listened to his analysand, Leclaire reconstructed a signifying chain composed of the words Lili, feet, sand, *corne,* wound, trace, billhook [*serpe*], unicorn [*licorne*]. . . . Then he interpreted the entire set in terms of metaphor and metonymy. Thus in the dream text, the signifier *place* [square] was substituted for the signifier *plage* [beach], which had been repressed. The metaphor of the square both designated and masked the former scene of the beach through an act of condensation. As for the signifier *licorne* [unicorn], it serves, according to Leclaire, as the metonymy of Philippe's desire: a phallic position represented by the *corne* [horn], which also refers back to the scar on the heel, the wound, the billhook but also to Lili's desire, to her *lit* [bed], to the extent that the young woman formed with her husband a couple whose relations contrasted with the more difficult ones entertained by the analysand's parents, etc.

That evocation of cascading signifiers is not unrelated to the manner in which Jacques Derrida, a few years later, would conceive of his return to a *mythos*—a letter or writing prior to *logos*--through the allegory of "Plato's Pharmacy." [61] In that respect, Serge Leclaire was tendentially taking a distance from Lacanian theory in the strict sense. He was doing so through "excessive" diligence or a certain love for the letter. There is something of the mystic in this Jewish atheist who invested his entire soul in the great Lacanian struggle. Intent on proving the signifier's inscription on and in the body, he came to regard the signifier as the very formula for the engendering of language. There thus surfaced at Bonneval for the first time a genuine debate internal to Lacanianism and bearing not only on Lacan's interpretation of Freudianism but on the legitimacy of that interpretation. In the discussion following the presentation, Leclaire found himself obliged to provide answers and to elucidate the case of Philippe still further. André Green and Conrad Stein asked him questions. Henri Lefebvre, for his part, challenged the validity of the interpretation, claiming that psychoanalytic discourse believed itself authorized to dump just about anything it wanted on the backs of its subjects. Leclaire explained. . . . Quite brilliantly.

He confided to his audience the family name of the unicorn man, while deforming it just enough to preserve professional secrecy. Then he emphasized the relation between a primordial unconscious fantasy and Philippe's name. That connection is represented by a signifying sequence which itself refers to the nickname the subject gave himself: "POOR (d) J'e-LI or Poordjeli." In that literal sequence, one finds the full set of the unconscious signifiers of Philippe-Georges Elhyani. One sees the "O" and the "Je" of Georges, the "corps" or body of the subject, the "Li" of Lili and Philippe, and finally a certain "Jacques," indicating the first name of a deceased uncle as well as that of Lili's husband. At the conclusion, Leclaire falls upon the unicorn and the feet. But whose feet? Philippe's or Serge's? Surely both of them, since he makes much of the patient's evocation of the first name Serge while speaking of a Lifar ballet. In 1968, he ended the story by publishing, in his first book, the definitive version of the clinical and self-analytic tale.[62] He would make a film of it for television.

With that case, Leclaire inaugurated a new way of thinking of therapy in which the primacy accorded the signifier may be observed. Contrary to the "classical" anamneses published by the *RFP*, this narrative does not "retell" anything and appears not to open onto any therapeutic result. In brief, what was related in this case was not the history of an analysis nor the biography of a patient, but simply the epic of a "cipher" revealed through a series of interpretations—a considerable break with the customary style of presenting cases. The Lacanian analyst is less concerned with curing a patient than with "producing therapy" through the work of the unconscious. That quest for truth has the effect of mobilizing the therapist and his analysand in the adventure of rediscovering a continent. In that sense, it would be an error to believe that Lacanianism is but a philosophy of language bereft of any therapeutic incidence. As opposed to practices based on a voluntarism of the reeducation of the ego, it allows for patients to be treated "otherwise," with a therapeutic benefit that is all the more effective in that it is less intentional. In that sense, Lacanian clinical practice *is* different and reactivates the omnipotence of unconscious determination to the detriment of an immediate curing of the ego.

If Leclaire remained within what could be directly deduced from Lacan's hypotheses, Laplanche quite plainly took his distance from them. It was by way of pure theory that he angled his discussion of the status of language in the unconscious. He attempted to read Lacan in the light of Freud, or more precisely he delved into the difference between the Freudian conception of language and its reformulation by Lacan. Beginning by paying homage to Politzer, Laplanche raised the question of determining whether the unconscious is in the order of a *meaning* or of a *letter*. In the first case, according to a Politzerian perspective, the unconscious would have but a single content and would bear witness to the truth of a first-person subject, whereas in the second case, from a Freudian point of view, it would be a distinct entity interpolated into the gaps of conscious speech. The author chose the Viennese option, then, with the help of a simple calculation of fractions, applied the Lacanian formula for metaphor to the process of repression.

Freud called the physical representation of the drive *Triebrepräsentanz,* and the representation of that representation, in so far as it is constitutive of a primordial unconscious, *Vorstellungsrepräsentanz*. If the drive is thus inscribed in the human psyche through an act of "delegation," such *delegation* or *representation* is divided into two categories. Freud called the direct cathexis of things in memory traces *thing-representations,* and things associated with verbal images *word-representations*. The thing-representation is *visual* and is inscribed in the unconscious, while the word-representation is *auditory* and concerns the preconscious-conscious system. Whereas primal repression bears on a first-phase representation, constitutive of the unconscious itself, secondary repression bears on more stable and better controlled representations. In other words, it may be said that in the primary process, psychical energy passes without obstacle from one representation to another, whereas in the secondary process, the energy is bound and unable to flow freely. There is thus a *double inscription* of representations: in the unconscious, on the one hand, and in the preconscious-conscious system on the other. But Freud then notes that there are two coexistent hypotheses concerning the transposition from the unconscious system to the preconscious-conscious. From a topographical point of view, one would have to admit the existence of a second inscription or registration of the representation alongside which the unconscious inscription would persist. On the contrary, from a functional point of view, the transposition would consist in a change of state affecting the same material; in such manner would there be a "passage" between the unconscious and the conscious. The topographical hypothesis tends to keep the two instances radically separate, whereas the functional hypothesis tends to join them.

With his logic of the signifier, which was more topographical than functional, Lacan accentuated the idea of a separation. For him, the unconscious was a discourse structured like a language and distinctly separate from conscious utterance.

And yet a bond did exist between the two realms, to the extent that the formula for metaphor substitutes one signifier for another. In that case, the first signifier would be repressed in the unconscious while remaining conscious in a form different from its unconscious counterpart. For example, when the name of an animal is substituted for a paternal figure, the signifier *father* remains inscribed in the unconscious through repression, but it is equally present in conscious discourse with a different function. Lacan made the unconscious a *second structure*, that is, a signifying chain always already inscribed in a language, whatever form that language might take. The chain cohabits with conscious speech in accordance with the model of the twisted surface of a Möbius strip: One passes without interruption from one surface to another without any impression of change. In implicitly positing the primacy of language over the unconscious, Lacan attempted to offer a solution to the Freudian alternative of the transposition of representations. Through language, the unconscious inscription was simultaneously present and absent. On the one hand, it promoted the symbolic existence of the subject; on the other, it was not at his disposal. The unconscious was thus an "other" text to be read with the help of certain indices. Prior to the Bonneval Colloquium, Lacan had not said anything more about either the relations between the unconscious and language or the modalities of double inscription as conceived by Freud.

Laplanche took up the formula for metaphor in order to show that it conveyed the general scheme of both primal and secondary repression. Drawing on Freud's distinctions between thing-representations and word-representations, on the one hand and, on the other, between primary and secondary processes, he divided the engendering of the unconscious into two phases. At a first mythical level of symbolization, the network of meaningful oppositions is cast over the subject's world, while at a second level primal repression intervenes in the form of metaphor. It is that repression which creates the unconscious and allows the subject to be anchored in a symbolic world. Correlative with the first level of symbolization is nonverbal language, that of thing-representations. Corresponding to the second is verbal language, that of word-representations. From Laplanche's perspective, the unconscious was thus the enabling condition of language, since certain key signifiers fixated the drive without capturing in their mesh any signifieds. In other words, Laplanche reproached Lacan for reversing the Freudian proposition and identifying the primary process with a language conforming to the strict laws of linguistics whereas Freud had thought of language as strictly verbal, that is, as secondary in relation to the unconscious. Thus did Laplanche propose to reverse Lacan's formula and to reinterpret it in terms of the Freudian perspective.

Master and student were less in disagreement on the reading of Freud's text than on the conditions of its reelaboration. Laplanche emphasized that Freud did not have a modern or semiological conception of language since in thinking the field of representation, he retained the old division between the verbal and the preverbal. Now the linguistic experience appealed to by Lacan rejected precisely such a division in order to interpret all forms of "symbolic" thought in semiological terms. From that point of view, the symbol was not the enabling condition of a language-universe, but, on the contrary, its consequence. The human was construed as language, from linguistic structure to culture, on the condition that language no longer be considered as an instrument of (verbal or nonverbal) communication, but as the general precondition of all forms of symbolic exchange. Lacan inscribed Freud's discovery within that epistemological project without any concern for the Freudian definition of language. From the point of view of linguistics, that definition was both inadequate to its object and ahead of certain perspectives of semiology. Lacan subjected Freud's conceptualization to a distortion that was all the more irreverent in that it resulted in a reinterpretation of the whole of his system. He was Freudian not in his respect for the text but in his disrespect for it.

Laplanche, on the contrary, was faithful to the text. But his critique of Lacanianism was impeded by the fact that he wanted to read Freud not in the light of linguistics, but under the banner of Lacan's concepts. Since it was difficult to be anti-Lacanian on Lacanianism's own theoretical ground, the student found himself in a difficult position. There were two possibilities: Either the thesis of the linguistic unconscious was not adequate to Freud's conceptuality, in which case it would have to be rejected in its foundations, or that thesis possessed epistemological coherence, and it was impossible to identify metaphor with primary repression. The Lacanian definition of metaphor adapted by Laplanche presupposes the existence of language, which determines the processes of symbolization in the unconscious.

In the fall of 1960, Lacan refused to discuss Laplanche's theses. He simply tugged the blanket back to his side and contented himself with observing the prominence enjoyed by his doctrine. Bonneval was a political event for him. The success with which his students' presentation was met had to be made to benefit Lacanianism. "We were flag-bearers," Laplanche has written. "I was rather disappointed at the time not to see Lacan entering into dialogue with me on precise criticisms. . . . I had always indicated quite clearly our points of disagreement, even as I indicated no less clearly in what way I was using and prolonging certain of Lacan's ideas (the formula for metaphor, for example). The specificity of a living body of thought is to take up problems on its own and not to prolong a 'master's' thought." [63]

For the publication of the proceedings of the colloquium in 1966, Lacan transformed his rather unbridled remarks into a programmatic text which was quite different from what he had originally said. He entitled the article *Position de l'inconscient* and inserted it into the *Écrits* with a commentary in which the thrust of his modifications is explained. [64] All participants had been invited to rework their contributions, but Lacan was alone in transposing oral comments into a text taking the form of an exposition. Between 1960 and 1964, the date when manuscripts were due, the split had worked its effects. Lacan was no longer intent on protecting the fragile unity of the SFP and consequently seized the opportunity to accuse Pontalis, without naming him, of having posthumously transcribed Merleau-Ponty's remarks inaccurately: "It would not be without interest," he wrote, "if only for historians, to have the notes in which were gathered the words actually spoken, even without the lacks left within them by the defects of the mechanical recorders. They underscore the shortcomings of the person whom those services designated to accentuate with a maximum of tact and faithfulness the intricacies of a moment of struggle in a place of exchange, when his knots, his culture, even his worldly wisdom allowed him to grasp better than any other what was heard and with what intonation." [65]

When the final editing of the proceedings took place, Pontalis had indeed accepted the task of summarizing Merleau-Ponty's comments. He took care to observe that the transcription did not render the tenor of his remarks in their entirety. Nonetheless, the transcription had been authenticated by Henri Ey and the philosopher's wife. Merleau-Ponty expressed his reservations concerning the linguistic unconscious and offered a point of disagreement with Laplanche's reading of Politzer.

Out of friendship for Pontalis, Laplanche threatened not to allow his text to appear if Lacan did not withdraw his attack. But Leclaire, always the subtle mediator, observed to his partner that he would be the first victim of such a retaliation. Laplanche thus decided to maintain his contribution, and thus Leclaire's as well, while adding an enigmatic note. "How might one be surprised," he wrote, "to see the analyst himself occasionally reveal a blindness going as far as to allow him to assimilate the misadventures of his person and the misfortunes of his ego with the progress of his thought and even with the destiny of truth. His 'good conscience' will in such cases not hesitate to conflate theoretical exposition with settling of scores (Oh! Chicago thy disgrace!)." [66]

After that direct allusion to the break between Lacan and the IPA, Laplanche took a still clearer stand in the debate pitting himself against his former teacher. He underscored his complete disagreement with the thesis of the linguistic unconscious, thus invalidating his previous proposition, which tended to secure a place for Lacan's concerns at the heart of Freud's conceptual scheme. Lacan's maneuver against Pontalis would at least have allowed Laplanche to free himself from a hypothesis which he only half accepted. In the note written in 1964, he admitted implicitly that it was impossible to ascribe a linguistic reality to the unconscious while maintaining the idea that the unconscious was language's enabling condition. Either the unconscious was structured like a language and language was its enabling condition, or the unconscious was not structured like a language and in that case none of its mechanisms could be transcribed in terms of metaphor and metonymy since those terms are linguistic figures.

In a lecture delivered at the École normale supérieure, during the year the proceedings of the Bonneval Colloquium were published, Lacan came back to the question of double inscription, insisting on the topographical hypothesis. Remaining within the linguistic perspective, he there made the transition from topography to topology: An inscription is double in that it does not register on the same side of the parchment coming out of the printing press [la planche à imprimer] of truth or of knowledge. A direct answer, then, to a student become dissident.[67]

It was only in 1969, at the request of a Belgian academic, Anika Lemaire, who had just devoted the first French-language thesis to his work, that Lacan finally deigned to answer his former analysand. While situating the debate on theoretical grounds, he allowed himself to lapse into a diatribe of astonishing vulgarity against Laplanche. He called him his "little chick wing" [aile or "L" de poussin], then confessed that he did not expect much from his university-trained followers. "I have to admit it; in my naïveté, at a difficult turn when I despaired in psychoanalysts, I invested some hope, not in academic discourse, which I was as yet unable to gauge, but in a kind of true opinion which I assumed to be lodged in its body. . . . I saw a few members of that body drawn to my fodder. I awaited their approbation. But all they were doing was copywork." [68]

Naturally, in the interview summarized by Anika Lemaire, as well as in his preface, Lacan avoided implicating Leclaire's contribution, with which, after all, he might have had a few problems. The entire polemic was directed against Laplanche and, on the theoretical level, it was entirely rigorous. It allowed him, moreover, to progress a bit further in the formulation of his own hypotheses and to invent a formula to which he had not subscribed previously: *Language is the condition of the unconscious*. That maxim followed logically from the primacy ascribed to language and led in 1970 to a further theoretical proposition, uttered on Belgian radio: *The unconscious is the condition of linguistics*. [69]

It was nonetheless the case that Lacan's tone against Laplanche was extraordinarily crude. It bears witness, if need be, to the transformation that had taken place in a few years in a man deeply humiliated by two splits that had made of him something of a scapegoat. From that date on, Lacan began resembling a solitary and disillusioned idol, adulated by disciples more intent on mimicking his style and his person than on giving themselves over, like Laplanche and Leclaire, to genuine research.

Anika Lemaire's thesis offers a rather good reflection of the new Lacan's style: "Whoever is not with me is against me." The author studied the Bonneval presentation in detail, but did not hesitate to call Laplanche a deviationist. She reproached him, among other sins, with "pillaging" his master's ideas. Too intelligent for that, Lacan took care not to resort to such terms. And yet he gave his support to the enterprise. Should we say that he found the success *Le vocabulaire de la psychanalyse* had been enjoying for two years unbearable? If he found it hard to tolerate the fact that authors of renown alien to psychoanalysis did not back him in his struggle, he was even less prepared to accept that a work from "within" and written by two disciples might be remarkable and much admired. He would thus spend his days criticizing the book, both in private and in public. Either because of a legitimate disagreement concerning the translation of a concept or because the work did not pay sufficient attention to his own hypotheses. In that respect, he was not entirely coherent: The *Vocabulaire* claimed to be strictly Freudian, and within its own Freudianism, to be inspired by Lacan's rearticulation. It made no difference—although Lacan said he was Freudian, he wanted his students to be Lacanian. And when they took their distance from his person, they were treated as traitors to a cause one is hard put to name. The judgment against the *Vocabulaire* would not prevent generations of Lacanians from purchasing the book and making frenetic use of it in their own works.

For some third-generation members of the SPP, Bonneval was an opportunity to establish contacts within the rival society. Since the time of the great divide, and specifically in relation to Lacanianism, the representatives of Nacht's policies had fallen into a deep silence. But such willful silence was not the sign of any great doctrinal leap forward. Despite its proud steadfastness, the SPP could not shield itself from the aftereffects provoked by the great theoretical tempest issuing from the SFP. Cracks and rifts began to be sensed within the new generation. Nacht's authoritarianism irritated everyone: as much his students, who wanted to be petty academics, as the paltry battalion of his adversaries, who nursed identical ambitions. From that point of view, the SPP was not at all similar to its rival. Composed of technicians and practitioners, it was not at all divided into doctrinal tendencies. Its sole objective was to survive or to produce heirs. Having become the only official representative of the IPA, it tended to be organized into different adversarial clans more inclined to argue with each other than to undertake any theoretical reelaboration. The premature death of Bouvet and the disappearance of the princess in 1962 would allow for an acceleration of the Society's reorganization on increasingly oligarchical premises. Nacht himself, having all too long affirmed a position of unmitigated autocracy, would be its first victim.

Around 1960, Serge Lebovici was the man of the hour. A shrewd politician, he struggled to gain control of the Institute, which had become the principal organ of the SPP. In overthrowing the Nachtian monarchy, he gave the SPP the IPA-oriented physiognomy which it retains to this day. This explains why he would be the sole Frenchman to become president of the IPA. Lebovici devoted the best years of his life to the pursuit of the crudest and most vigorous anti-Lacanian policies and to an undivided submission to the ideals of the IPA empire. He would garner numerous laurels as a result.

Invited to the Bonneval Colloquium, Conrad Stein and André Green represented, each in his own way, the "liberal" aspirations of the new generation. One was in charge of debates and the other, who had waded through the texts, delivered an impressively rigorous introductory address. Green's senior in his psychoanalytic career, Stein had been analyzed by Schlumberger, then by Nacht, before gaining easy access to the rank of titular member. At the SPP, he earned a reputation early on as a rebel known for the immoderate love he bore his own person. The colloquium allowed him to shine at his brilliant best, but not to take into account, in either his practice or his texts, the theoretical innovations emerging from the SFP. He was an early participant in Lacan's seminar and dispensed—as a kind of counterpart in his own society—a teaching imitative of the master's. That small open seminar would play an important role at the Institute. The adversaries of the "orthodox" line would meet there to cultivate a certain iconoclasm.

The itinerary of André Green, who had begun his career later than Stein, was quite different. At the time of Bonneval, he was in search of an authentic intellectual adventure. Curious about everything and self-taught, endowed with an extraordinary talent for mimicry, he experienced the doctrinal feebleness of the society he belonged to as a protracted defeat. That is why, that fall, he was impatient to meet his brothers of the other camp. . . . He would not found a school, would obey the majority discipline of his society, and would produce a series of works of genuine interest.

As an adolescent, after spending his entire childhood in the Jewish community of Cairo, he had dreamed of taking a boat to France. His family had long since emigrated, from Spain on his mother's side, and from Portugal on his father's. The name was originally Ashkenazi and Anglicized through the addition of an *e* by a distant cousin who preferred Queen Victoria to Chancellor Bismarck. . . . A middle-class businessman, his father observed Yom Kippur without manifesting any intensity of belief. But two years before his death, knowing he was ill, he summoned the rabbi to teach him Hebrew. In his family, there was little memory of either Bonaparte or the Mamelukes, but French and Arabic were spoken. English was the government language; André did not learn it. He would do so later on. Once his studies were over, he took advantage of the second boat joining Africa to Europe to leave Egypt. One day in 1946, he discovered the City of Light. He strolled around Saint-Germain-des-Prés, read works by Sartre, and became an enthusiast of new ideas. He was soon to lose his illusions. Paris was a city that did not take kindly to foreigners. Green lived in a modest hotel room and suffered from loneliness. It took him three years to be received into a family, still more to receive citizenship. During that harsh crossing of the wilderness, he often saw a young woman who let him know that her parents would not allow her to go out with a stranger. He immediately suggested that he meet her family. But the girl replied politely that he was a Jew. Thus did he receive for the first time the full brunt of an anti-Semitic remark. Everything changed when he took his entry exams. At Sainte-Anne he made real friends, particularly with Rosolato, who had spent his childhood in Turkey before joining the Catroux army, at age twenty, to fight the Nazis. A young psychiatrist like Green, he had just begun his analysis with Lacan, and it was with enthusiasm that he suggested Green join the juniors at the SFP.[70]

But Green refused and chose the other camp. For lack of a doctrinal master, he discovered at the SPP artisans capable of instructing him in their craft. Hostile to Nacht's authoritarianism, he was drawn to Bouvet's couch even as he took the prospect of a career in psychiatry quite seriously. He became Henri Ey's student quite early on, attended his seminar assiduously, and appreciated his paternal warmth. At Bonneval Lacan perceived the intelligence of the young Middle Easterner, appreciated his elegance, and invited him to join the ranks of the SFP. Not at all attracted by Lagache, Green also distrusted the lure of Lacan. He nonetheless attended his seminar and as a result occupied the difficult position at the SPP of a Lacanian in the sheepfold. It would take him a good deal of time to be received as a titular member. Called upon to choose his camp, he answered that he had already chosen, then, toward 1961, he took the initiative of forming an intersociety group composed of the most brilliant "juniors" of both sides. Fruitful discussion took place, but the experiment was soon compromised by the second split. Lacan hardened his positions, demanding a clear-cut choice on the part of his partisans. He thus asked Green to put an end to his meetings. The latter complied, but was wrong to do so. Subsequently he would cease attending Lacan's seminar and would orient his options toward clinical work of Anglo-Saxon inspiration.[71]

IV. The Grand Maneuver

With the creation of the SFP, the evaluation of Lacan's technique became the business of the international movement. Juniors and seniors would together struggle for a common recognition, even though they were divided among themselves. At the London congress of 1953, the central executive of the IPA, presided over by Hartmann, had refused affiliation to those who had resigned and entrusted consideration of their candidacy to a consulting committee which turned into an investigatory board. Led by the celebrated Donald W. Winnicott, who was himself associated, within the British society, with the independent group, the committee was additionally composed of Phyllis Greenacre, W. Hoffer, and J. Lampl de Groot, the last named representing the orthodox position. The board began work in the fall, interrogating the juniors who had rebelled. "In that series of interviews," Granoff has written, "an equitable division of labor had been arranged. To the most hardline, if I may be pardoned the word, and to Mme Lampl de Groot in particular—the direct spokesperson of the central power—was assigned the task of interrogating the most hardboiled—and above all the leaders of the uprising at what was called the 'student' level."

The commission was also interested in the seniors. Winnicott took it upon himself to question Françoise Dolto. He asked her how, with the abandoned children she was treating at the Trousseau hospital, she managed to analyze oral and anal components without arousing their aggressive drives. She replied that she made use of fantasies and not drawing techniques. She also avoided any kind of reparative assistance, preferring to evoke memories from before their separation so that the children might acknowledge a break without remaining prisoners of any deleterious nostalgia. Winnicott told her that her work was extremely interesting, that it was thirty years ahead of the field, and that it should be retained within the framework of the SFP. But he immediately appended a three-part verdict: First, that her patients and students were entering into an uncontrolled—and consequently harmful—transference with her; then, that she had too much intuition and not enough method to be a training analyst; and finally, that she ought to be kept at a distance from the young lest she "influence" them.[72] Winnicott demonstrated thereby what the IPA expected from any "normalization." What was at stake was rejecting the "charisma" of the leaders in favor of the technique of the artisans. Whence his proposal, which claimed it wanted to preserve a teaching, but on the condition that its author be deprived of any outlet for it.

After a year of investigation, the commission refused the principle of affiliation. Triumphantly, the SPP published the news in the *RFP*: "A careful study of the facts and the report of an international commission specially appointed in accordance with an administrative decision of the international congress of 1953 have led the IPA to formulate the following conclusions, which have just been conveyed to us. 'The unanimous decision of the central executive board is as follows: Given the present teaching conditions in the SFP, recognition of that society as a member of the IPA cannot be granted.'"[73]

Two worlds and two cultures were confronting each other: on the one hand, a neo-Freudianism of Anglo-American inspiration, which conceived the unity of the movement from a narrowly technical point of view; on the other, the French psychoanalytic situation, with which we are already familiar.

In 1954, an exchange of letters between Lagache, Juliette Favez-Boutonier, and Heinz Hartmann occurred. Lagache was attempting to understand the reasons for the negative decision, and Hartmann, initially, allowed him some hope while remaining deliberately vague. "Quite frankly, I must say," he wrote, "that your letter has unfortunately not afforded me any significant increase in understanding. I know the members of the committee to be scrupulously honest and competent to pass judgment. I think that on that score you are in agreement with me. But that also means that their report is not the rationalization of a basically political decision, whereas, according to your letter, that is precisely what you think. I thus still think that any new request for admission should be preceded by an account of changes that have taken place since last year."[74]

Six months before the congress in Geneva, where the commission's refusal was to be ratified, Lagache sent a letter to Hartmann, informing him of his perplexity. He did not understand the criticisms addressed by the representatives of the IPA to the training procedures of the SFP. Nonetheless, he inferred that the principal obstacle was constituted by Lacan. And he immediately sprang to his defense, affirming that the two candidates he had analyzed who had applied to the commission on instruction for admission to the supervisory or control phase had not had any problems. Then he added that the technical criticism addressed to Lacan had been exploited to political ends. Finally, he asked Hartmann to let the SFP know if the IPA had any other griefs against it than the practice of short sessions.[75] Whereupon Hartmann replied in the manner of a high comintern official casting a steely gaze on European affairs: "That Lacan counts for something in all this, as you say, is true. But Lacan is not just any member of your society. He is, through his special gifts, his verve, because he's convincing—gifts I have no intention of disputing—a figure of the first importance. I don't know to what extent you yourself, who are the only one up to it, succeed in counterbalancing him. But I do know, from a considerable number of sources, that his teaching carries great weight with the students. What will happen to the analysts trained by him?" [76] Hartmann did not limit himself to announcing that the battle for affiliation had been lost in advance because of Lacan's unacceptable practice; he also emphasized that the influence of Jean Delay, "a violently anti-analytic man," appeared to loom formidably in the SFP.

Once again, one can see the objectives of the IPA, whoever its officers might be. It was first of all a matter of forcing the French dissidents to "normalize" and submit unconditionally to the rules of the empire: no "charismatic" leader, and no professor of psychiatry whose hypothetical evil intentions might be suspect. To be sure, the actors caught up in the formidable struggle would underestimate the power of the normalizing machine and believe that their cause could still win. From Lacan himself, who was the first to push the troika into the arena, to Lagache and Favez-Boutonier, who began by supporting Lacan only to bend subsequently to the empire's iron law.

At the Geneva congress of 1955, the leaders of the SFP did not deem it opportune, under prevailing conditions, to renew their request for the Paris congress, which was scheduled to take place two years later. In June 1956, Juliette Favez-Boutonier, who was president of the SFP, took pen to paper, after Lagache, to convince Hartmann to accept the Society with Lacan. She pointed out that none of the students trained by him practiced short sessions, and praised the quality of the master's teaching and his personality. Then she underlined the fact that the SFP was not inferior to the SPP when it came to training. Finally she assured Hartmann that Delay did not intervene in any way in the conduct of the Society's business.[77]

Following that letter, Hartmann sent others to Lagache and Favez-Boutonier, while refraining from any commentary on the French situation. But since his interlocutors brought up the subject, he responded with extraordinary cynicism: "Dear Madame, you too speak to me again of Lacan. I almost fear that we are participants in the creation of a myth. And I hope you will agree, despite your admiration for him (I am well aware that he is a brilliant man) that that is more than he deserves. Can it really be suspected that analysts consider him dangerous because he comments on Freud's works with the same rigorous methods as are used for the texts of thinkers every word of whom counts? Such word-by-word commentaries are, moreover, done in many courses on psychoanalysis. Is it correct to explain that what is begrudged him is that he has a lot of personality?"[78]

At the Paris congress, William Gillespie, an Englishman, succeeded Hartmann to the presidency of the IPA. Power had gone European, without changing an iota its normalizing orientation. Nevertheless, the French nursed the hope that English leadership would be more favorable to them than the American one. They were wrong. Gillespie was not as ferocious as his predecessor toward Lacan, but he would implement the same policy.

Two years later, in July 1959, the SFP began its charge anew. The congress was to take place in Copenhagen. The president of the Society, Hesnard, sent Pearl King, secretary of the IPA, a new request for affiliation. Serge Leclaire, for his part, gave himself over entirely to the difficult task of negotiation. He gave the authorities in charge a report discussing the scientific and didactic activities of the SFP.[79] The Society was organized on the model of the SPP. It comprised *titular* members, entitled to conduct training analyses, *associate* members, who were beginning their professional practice, and *trainees* [*stagiaires*]. A year later, a special category would be created, *guest members,* which yoked together students in analysis not yet admitted to the rank of trainee as well as persons outside the movement but participating on a regular basis in the works of the Society. Organizationally, the SFP consisted of an administrative board, a secretariat, a library (run by Granoff), a board of study groups, and a commission on instruction, which accepted candidates for training. The Society had bimonthly meetings or "Provincial Days" intended to complete the training of regional groups.

All that information was insufficient for the executive board. On July 11, Pearl King sent Lagache a letter in which she requested supplementary data of a technical nature: minimum required for a personal analysis, length of sessions, number of weekly sessions for training analyses, number of hours of seminar attendance required for each candidate, list of trainees with detailed information about each, personal cases, counterindications, etc. Hastily and a bit grudgingly, Lagache transmitted the requested information. He then confided his impression to Leclaire: "Nothing has changed, either on their side or on ours."[80] Indeed . . .

The specifics forwarded by Lagache served no purpose. At the Copenhagen congress, on July 28, 1959, the executive board ordered the formation of a new committee charged with evaluating the French candidacy. That committee also was transformed into an investigatory body. In December, a general assembly of the members of the SFP approved the steps that had been taken toward affiliation. Then, on March 21, 1960, Gillespie, the president, announced to Hesnard the committee's imminent visit to Paris. The SFP would be asked to submit the entirety of its archives to its guests.

The new committee was quite different from the previous one. Composed of three members from England, two of whom were women, and one from the Netherlands, it was split into two tendencies. Of the English, Pierre Turquet and Paula Heimann were favorable to affiliation from the outset. The former, who resembled the actor Philippe Noiret, was intimately acquainted with the French situation. A man of intelligence and culture, he was aware that Lacanianism constituted a significant source of renewal for the movement. The latter, a Jewish woman originally from Berlin, was a friend of Lagache. She had been Turquet's analyst and, like him, she revealed herself to be open to negotiation. Both stipulated as a condition for membership Lacan's obedience to the standard rules and a "normalization" of training within the SFP. In that sense, and like all their colleagues in all societies, they adhered to the narrowly technical ideals ensuring the empire's cohesion. They thus separated Lacan's "person" from Lacanian doctrine, and did not in any way take into account the technical innovations of a man whom they considered to be an authentic theorist, but a lamentable therapist. In relation to her two compatriots, Ilse Hellman, a Jewish woman of Hungarian origin, proved to be distinctly more orthodox. She had little sympathy for the French rebels, and shared the point of view of Pieter Jan Van der Leeuw, a "training specialist," who would subsequently become president of the IPA. All four spoke excellent French.

Functioning as four partners and two tendencies, neither one of which was a majority or minority, the committee could swing at any given moment from one direction to the other. As opposed to the executive, and thanks to the bonds that were established among Leclaire, Turquet, and Granoff, the committee would for a while recommend a genuine policy of openness toward the French scene. It was on that recommendation that the secretary of the SFP, supported by Lacan, was wagering. Lacan knew Turquet quite well, and called him his friend. The fight was a difficult one. At every stage of the negotiations, Leclaire kept Lacan informed of developments, while the latter attempted to maintain the cohesion of his students in training. Granoff, for his part, expended a considerable amount of energy in order to bring the negotiations to fruition. He wrote tens of administrative or personal letters and spent his every weekend in London.

Lacan was walking on burning embers. Since the split, he had changed nothing in his technique. He had accentuated the principle of the "*bang-bang* of true interpretation," and tended to reduce still further the length of his sessions. It should be stated that in 1959 the SFP was in a period of theoretical and quantitative expansion. Along with fourteen titular members, the figure for associates and trainees reached a record number of eighty-nine individuals, to which a large number of guests may be added. In all, there were two-and-a-half times as many members as in the SPP, a circumstance which the IPA viewed as sufficient grounds for insisting on normalization. With professionalization, the SFP would become a genuine rival of the SPP, and not a hoard of individuals trained with unseemly haste. At the center of the burgeoning phenomenon, Lacan set himself virtually no limits: In 1959, he had about twenty analysands on his couch, and in 1962, at least thirty. Plus controls and his private practice. In addition, it was clear to all that he could not respect the norm of four weekly sessions of forty-five minutes. Since he was the only theorist of stature in his generation, his fellow training analysts suffered on every count. They had neither a doctrine nor a sufficient number of students.

Not only was Lacan not satisfied with "filching" disciples from his partners; he knowingly violated the technical rules and moral principles of the IPA. He combined the couch with the seminar room, defied every consideration of length, and behaved in all circumstances like a master. Moreover, in the corridors, he was accused of disguising his training analyses as "private" therapy. He could not do otherwise, given the number of his analysands. Such therapy came to be called "clandestine analysis." The "wild" patients who came to Lacan, as well as those whom Lacan lured to his couch, were not recognized by the commission on instruction, and as a result their therapy had no acknowledged value as training. There thus emerged a first phase of a process which tended quite simply to distinguish no longer between therapeutic and training aims, and to consider the preparation of analysts from a new point of view. The process would become a commonplace four years later in the École freudienne de Paris. But at the time it was unacceptable from the standard perspective. Leclaire knew this and tried to convince Lacan, if not to submit to the rules, at least to make an effort not to increase the number of his patients. He counted on the juniors in training as a group to support the master before the investigatory board and thus to avoid any divisions within the Society. In a first period, Lacan accepted the proposition in good faith.

If Leclaire upheld the wager of bringing a difficult negotiation to a successful conclusion, Granoff, for his part, sought to introduce into the IPA a "Trojan horse" consisting of the French juniors with Lacanianism as a bonus. The role of Ulysses was superbly suited to the Russian "prince." At times, he thought that Lacan could at least pretend to respect the rules, and at others, he realized that such a dream was utopian. That is why he spent most of his energy in either supporting Leclaire or criticizing him. Both were agreed to make use of Lagache as a "coating" allowing the empire to swallow the "Lacan pill." To that end, Granoff translated a number of French works into English, and drew up with Smirnoff a first history of psychoanalysis in France, intended for use by the IPA—a hundred typed pages. The translation effort would end up unpublished, and the pages of the history would remain a dead letter.

Allied with Leclaire and a member of the admissions committee, Granoff, between 1960 and 1963, was pursuing an extraordinary two-phased policy, whose aim was to "sell" the SFP to the IPA under the umbrella provided by Lagache, even as it attempted to shatter any possibility of an alliance between the latter and the Favezes. It was a matter of marginalizing all three, and furthering the flourishing of a French school of psychoanalysis centered on Lacan, the juniors, and the students.

Lagache, who had the support of Balint and the bureaucrats of the IPA, entered willingly into Granoff's maneuvers without realizing what role he was being made to play. He had contempt for the Favezes, and Granoff's position thus served his own interests. He did not see that Leclaire and Granoff were playing a different card. Georges Favez had no part in the affair even though he was recognized to be a good training analyst. As for Juliette, she was important to the French strategy because of her academic position. Nonetheless, in the eyes of the IPA, neither she nor her husband represented a doctrinal tendency. Nor did they understand in what direction the grand maneuver was being made. Only Lagache, Lacan, and the juniors were representative of the French scene, the first because he embodied the hoary tradition of Janet (along with a genuine interest in foreign cultures), the second because he was an intellectual master, and the last because they were the future of psychoanalysis in France.

Feverishly Leclaire prepared the commission's work. Week after week, he forwarded to Turquet a monument of archives and confidential files concerning the life of the group and the itinerary of each of its members. With frankness and obstinacy, he played the card of negotiation, with the support of Granoff, who meticulously kept a record of the most important events. Together they implemented a splendid strategy in which each had his role to play. The gambit was pursued on a split stage: the Anglo-American world, on the one hand, regarded as imperialistic but experienced as a necessary evil, and the French continent, on the other, on which was elaborated a drama played out by four partners—the troika with Lacan, the juniors, the two Favezes, and Lagache.

Soon the Algerian war became a factor. In April 1961, the generals' rebellion delayed the committee's visit to Paris. Private discussions nevertheless continued between Leclaire and Turquet. The latter asked the Frenchman for the names of two physicians, who were not psychoanalysts, on whom the committee might call for some sense of the credibility enjoyed by psychoanalysis in France. Granoff and Leclaire immediately deduced that this was the result of pressure on the executive council exercised by influential members of the SPP, all too happy to discredit the SFP while exploiting the delay caused by events in Algeria. Their intuition would turn out to be accurate.[81]

Toward the middle of May, the committee in its entirety landed in Paris, and moved into an apartment in the Hotel Westminster on the rue de la Paix. A splendid symbol! Training analysts and juniors in training all submitted to questioning. Urged forward by Leclaire, Daniel Widlöcher was the first of his generation to answer the questions of the commission.

Stemming from modest origins, this intelligent, likable, and diligent young man had begun his analysis in 1953 after a period in Jenny Aubry's service. Just prior to the first split, he had completed his tour of visits in the SPP, then reserved a place with Lacan before leaving to perform his military service. An aficionado of painting and the visual arts, open to philosophical culture, Widlöcher appreciated the analyst's Surrealist past. In addition, he was disappointed by French psychoanalytic literature, and upon learning of the split, had invested a great deal of hope in the future of the SFP. He was interested in Wallon, in child psychology and psychoanalysis, and had studied medicine in order to become a psychiatrist. Raised as a Catholic, he had lost his faith at the age of fifteen, but upon meeting Father Beirnaert at the time of his analysis, had hesitated, had looked into the evaluation of ecclesiastical callings, and had then opted definitively for atheism.

He was at first astonished by Lacan's technique, not only by the session of varying length, but by the general air of commotion that tended to prevail in the course of therapy. The master moved about the room, and did not offer any interpretations. "I had the impression of being in analysis," Widlöcher has emphasized. "Lacan didn't say anything, but there was an alternation between his listening and an absence of listening. On occasion, there was acting out. For instance, when I mentioned a rivalry with a member of my generation, Lacan said, 'Do not believe that he is more loved by me than you are.'"

Before long, Widlöcher found it hard to tolerate the irregularities in his analysis, the hours of waiting, the presence in the waiting room of four or five individuals, and the unexpected dismissals. When he had problems with money, he asked Lacan to interrupt work. The latter accepted, then pressured him into coming back without any of the reasons for the break being analyzed. Widlöcher perceived the contamination that was taking place between couch and seminar. One day, in a session, he spoke of a painting, and the next day Lacan made public use of what he had been told. On another occasion, an event occurred that would cause him to enter into the opposition. Lacan was receiving a friend of Widlöcher's for therapy and made him wait for two hours. The young man did not return. During an analytic session, Lacan asked his patient to intervene so that his friend would not stand on ceremony and return to the rue de Lille.

Things began to go to pieces around 1959 when Widlöcher came before the SFP commission on instruction to ask for his controls. Lacan on that occasion asked him not to mention his sessions, explaining to him that the members of the commission did not understand anything of his theory of therapy. Shortly thereafter Widlöcher underwent Lagache's notorious collective control along with Laplanche and Pontalis. They exchanged thoughts about their respective analyses and in 1962, the student seized the opportunity to end his analysis by telling Lacan that it had been the chance of his lifetime to have met him. It should be noted that he maintained friendly relations with Lacan, dining with him in the company of Bataille and Jakobson, and appreciating on each session the charm of his conversation.

When Widlöcher came before the commission, he was thus already in conflict with Lacan on the subject of his therapy. He told the English that under no circumstances would he want the SFP to be reunited with the SPP. They replied that there was no chance of such an occurrence, then asked him if he was informed as to recent trends in psychoanalysis abroad. Widlöcher was not. Questioned about Lacan, he rejected the practice and defended the doctrine.[82]

Juliette Favez-Boutonier, for her part, was also summoned to the Hotel Westminster. Turquet asked her if she knew the number of analysts being trained on the rue de Lille. She proposed the reasonable figure of twelve and the Englishman thundered back: nineteen. Whereupon he deduced that the sessions lasted ten minutes. Juliette responded that the commission should ask Lacan himself. Facing the committee, Xavier Audouard and Octave Mannoni praised their analyst's technique, while attempting to block the difficult question of the number of minutes per session.[83]

One day Turquet betook himself to Jenny Aubry's service in order to question her about her control with Lacan and her own practice. He asked not a single question about child analysis and Jenny had the impression that he was challenging her because of her adult therapy. She found his tone inquisitorial and quickly concluded that she was not speaking the same language as her interrogators, who were solely concerned with positive or negative transferences, and without any attention to the archaic bond with the mother in adult analyses or the bringing to light of the unconscious. She explained to Turquet the benefits she had derived from her control with Lacan. For him, everything was centered on the countertransference, which he called the analyst's transference. Lacan always asked her why she had proposed one interpretation rather than another, never gave advice, but often predicted the effect that one utterance or another would produce in the subsequent course of an analysis. She added that she had learned her craft with him whereas with Lebovici she had above all learned what should not be done.[84]

Interrogated as well, Jean-Paul Valabrega thought that the commission was acting in a ridiculous manner. Nonetheless he said that he disapproved of Lacan's technique. As did Didier Anzieu: "I answered their questions concerning the short sessions I had had with Lacan precisely and without complexes (without complexes since they were plainly aware of them). I also indicated that Lacan had advised me against speaking about his short sessions when I had made my tour of visits as a candidate at the SPP. The commission also asked me to speak of one of my psychoanalytic cases. I presented the most difficult one. . . . They asked me my opinion of Lacan's psychoanalytic technique. I replied that my experience was that it sinned in three ways: an almost total absence of interpretation; an inability to tolerate a negative transference; and a misperception of the specifics of the early relation to the maternal image.[85]

In analysis with Lacan, Ginette Raimbault was questioned by Turquet as a friend. She had known him well in London while working with Balint at the Tavistock Clinic. She announced that her sessions lasted thirty minutes, and Turquet wanted to know whether she was telling the truth and what sort of "power" Lacan exercised over his pupils. In response, she did not limit herself to defending Lacan's doctrine. She was among those who approved of his innovations in technique and benefited the most from them. She explained Lacan's conception of therapy to the Englishman, the avoidance of resistances and defenses, the recentering on the unconscious, and the value of scansions and interruptions based on an attentiveness to the signifier. In addition, she attempted to demonstrate to him that Lacan's students had not submitted to a passive transference since they had shown themselves capable of taking their distance—and freedom—from him. From her point of view, his technique proved that Lacan was an excellent clinical practitioner, who never avoided a negative transference. Turquet did not ask Raimbault any questions about child analysis, even though he knew that she had been working for years with Jenny Aubry in a clinic near the porte de Clignancourt, where an important experiment was being conducted in collaboration with nursery schools. Raimbault had the impression that Turquet appreciated her frankness but that it was difficult for him to grasp the meaning of Lacan's innovations.[86]

At the time he was scheduled to be heard at the Hotel Westminster, Jean Laplanche found himself in a complicated situation since Lacan had proposed (without doing so) increasing the length of his sessions, which were then thirty minutes. In conflict with his analyst, he thought that the latter ought to make the sacrifices necessary for the SFP's integration into the empire. Nevertheless, before the commission, the question of length of sessions was not a problem for him.[87]

The committee then decided to question Lacan and Dolto. Both immediately adopted a clear position, deciding not to yield on the most extreme implications of the points under discussion. Dolto defended her conception of child analysis, and Lacan justified his variable-length sessions on theoretical grounds. Each had the impression of being understood by the commission. Nonetheless, their testimony would be interpreted negatively.[88]

Once the interviews were over, the commission communicated its observations to Leclaire and Granoff. It was quite severe concerning the training of analysts in the provinces, particularly in Strasbourg and Marseille. But it left the possibility of a genuine opening. "In sum," wrote Granoff, "the prevalent feeling had been that on the whole, the society had not behaved poorly. Thanks to the courtesy of the investigators, thanks to the rather fortunate choice of students questioned, things had not gone badly. There was a mood of trust between Leclaire and Turquet. The groups in the provinces and Dolto's activities constituted points of friction. Concerning Dr. Lacan, nothing had occurred. The French were reduced to conjecturing—either pessimistically or optimistically according to whatever tenuous clues they had." [89]

In 1961, on the French side, opinions were divided within the SFP as to the value of Lacan's technique. Some approved and benefited from it; others rejected it. Now Turquet and his colleagues were neither uninformed nor unintelligent. All were in favor of normalization. Little by little, they perceived that a majority of the French group disapproved of Lacan's practice even though they wanted to retain his teaching. That realization allowed them to deliver a first fatal blow to Leclaire's strategy. Initially, Turquet insisted that Lacan accept no additional training analyses. The latter accepted the proposition. But as the Englishman gradually gained a better understanding of the Parisian scene, he came to think that it would be necessary to withdraw a number of his current training analyses from Lacan and assign them to other titular members. The master would thus be obliged to "normalize" in spite of himself since his work time would be calculated according to accepted standards. Since Turquet derived his argument from the observation of conflicts within the SFP, it was not difficult for him to affirm that the hostility to Lacan came from the majority of the French group. He could thus favor the marginalization of that cumbersome figure without seeming to be obeying the orders of the central executive. In the face of that argument, Leclaire's position was impossible: He could neither demand of Lacan the requested concessions nor truly support Turquet in his negotiations. Yet he attempted the impossible, and started things up anew, seeking to profit from the contradictions each side was harboring. Had the French group succeeded in projecting the image Leclaire had wanted, the central executive would have been forced to swallow Lacan along with the rest. Only things did not transpire in that manner since no one was willing to pretend: neither Lacan, who refused to go any further in his concessions, nor his analysands, who, in the majority, did not accept a technique whose principal victims they felt themselves to be.

While the French group was making preparations for the trip to the next congress, in Edinburgh, Leclaire committed a serious error. He voiced the opinion that Anna Freud's influence would be crucial in any deliberations and that a meeting would be desirable. He thus suggested to Lagache that he write to that effect to Freud's daughter. Granoff immediately dashed off the draft of a letter and, despite a certain reticence, Lagache copied it and sent it. Naturally, the missive had a disastrous effect on Anna, who received the request as an intolerable exercise of pressure. Granoff was then ordered by the commission not to attempt any secret "maneuvers" at the congress. As a result, he made the temporary decision to cease all correspondence outside France. He received a letter from Balint confirming the disaster produced by the intervention with Anna Freud. Ten days later, Anna Freud herself replied that she would receive Lagache after the meeting of the executive—thus thwarting the French plan.[90]

At the end of July, Lacan vacationed in Rome. He stayed, as always, at the Hotel Hassler, where Sylvia accompanied him. Not far from there, Vera, Granoff's wife (from whom he was separated), was staying. She was in analysis with Lacan, and the two of them strolled while speaking of the recent events. At the other end of Europe, in Edinburgh, arrangements were being made for the new IPA congress. Leclaire, Perrier, Granoff, Jean-Claude Lavie, Lagache, Smirnoff and his wife made the trip. They opted for the Learmonth Hotel, whereas the eminences of the IPA, headed by Anna Freud and Marie Bonaparte, stayed at the George. In each camp, the negotiators prepared for a formidable joust. Rumors abounded, and all knew that the lengthy report written about his investigation by Turquet, which had remained secret until that day, was not favorable to the advocates of Lacan. Discussions would soon begin. . . .

Six days before the official beginning of the congress, Granoff received a sumptuous letter from Lacan, dated July 24, containing eight pages of reflections on the past, the first split, and the policies of the IPA. In tone and style, the letter was quite different from those addressed to Leclaire. With Granoff, Lacan did not complain. He revealed neither his anxieties nor his intimate feelings; he presented his strategy and gave directives with the ferocity of a Bonaparte and the tenderness of a protective father. He began by warning his interlocutor about the manipulative abilities of the Princess, to whom he imputed all responsibility for the first split. He then sketched vitriolic portraits of the dignitaries of the empire, calling Anna a woman "grown stiff under the weight of her father's name," and the power elite "avid crabs." He advised Granoff to play off the "unfortunates"—members of the second rank on the executive chessboard—against them. Lacan's hope was that the troika, strengthened by the splendid mission that was theirs, would win their sympathy. He also declared that a battle, once begun, can always be lost, but that the important thing was to know who one was. Finally, he ended his letter in the manner of the emperor addressing Murat: "Charge! . . ."[91] Five days later he sent a telegram asking that he be telephoned person-to-person in Rome should there be any need, then another letter replete with a quotation from Montaigne on the omnipotence of ladies and even the weakest of women in the affairs of the kingdom.

That superb missive revealed what was already known—Lacan was thoroughly supportive not only of Leclaire's political efforts, but also of Granoff's. Better still, he supervised the development of matters, elaborating with one the daily course to be followed and with the other, more dramatically, the organization of the fray. But it also showed that Lacan overestimated the power of the dignitaries of the realm, and was a bit too neglectful of the anonymous power of the normalizing apparatus which the IPA had become and which weighed on the fate of all its members. In other words, he made a poor assessment of the practical implications of the technical ideals presiding over the unity of the empire and attributed too great a power of decision to its leaders, as though they themselves were not creatures of the apparatus. In addition, on the eve of the congress, he misperceived his own situation in the movement. He did not realize that the committee, like the IPA, did not object to his doctrine, but to his position as a master. Moreover, he did not perceive that a number of students were playing the same game before the committee by not supporting innovations in technique whose first victims they felt themselves to be.

The executive took quick cognizance of the Turquet report and rejected the request for affiliation. For the French negotiators, it was a bitter defeat. At the Edinburgh congress, on August 2, 1961, Gillespie congratulated Turquet, but the SFP was forced to withdraw its candidacy as a member society and accept the more modest rank of "study group under the sponsorship of an *ad hoc* committee." It was additionally invited to favor a "healthy" development of psychoanalysis by correcting its training principles. In order to attain that objective, Lagache, Leclaire, and Favez-Boutonier were made members at large of the IPA. Those appointments had statutory reasons. In point of fact, membership in the IPA was always in one's own name, even if such appointments occurred through the intermediary of affiliated societies. In order for a study group to be recognized, three of its members had to be part of the IPA. The executive board renewed the investigatory commission's charge, but added to it an Austrian analyst, Wilhelm Solms, whose personal sympathies were with the orthodox tendency. Through him the IPA leadership was able to invoke the prestige of Viennese origins on its behalf, even as it introduced a measure of discord in a committee which had until then been quite evenly balanced.

Finally, nineteen "Recommendations" were formulated to the end of effecting the normalization of the French group. Among them were to be found technical rules and ethical considerations. Concerning technique, the executive board required four sessions per week lasting forty-five minutes, with permission, in the case of the provinces, to spread the sessions over fewer than four days on condition that two nights be included. In addition, the prolongation of therapy was considered obligatory for a period of at least one year after the acceptance of a first case. On ethical matters, the executive ordered that students be forbidden from attending the seminars of their analysts without prior authorization from the study commission.

In order to grasp the meaning of these recommendations, it should be recalled that the technical rules were respected by all the affiliated societies of the IPA and thus by their members. As we have seen above, their aim was at once to ensure the cohesion of the empire on professional grounds and to prevent any innovators from becoming doctrinal masters. The IPA feared above all what it called in a poorly chosen word the "charisma" of leaders and preferred the insistence on technique prevalent among its barons. It will be perceived how that representation of power within the psychoanalytic movement was born. Freud's heirs forbade themselves from imitating the practice of the founding father, not only because they found it unsuited to the modern expansion of a normalized psychoanalysis, but because, by definition, a founder is unique and ought not to be imitated. As for the notion of "charisma," it referred to a reality, but its systematic use tended to function tautologically once, instead of circumscribing the notion of the phenomenon, it was used *itself* as an explanation of the phenomenon. Yet that is what the IPA did. In its discourse, the term always carried weight as a substitute for any interpretation of the phenomenon. The refusal of the notion of an intellectual master and its masking by that of a "charisma" judged to be nefarious allowed the IPA to embrace in its ranks all doctrinal divergences on the condition that the technical norms for training were accepted. The respect for divergent doctrines took place against a background of loyalty to a common system. From which it followed that any doctrine calling in to question the accepted training principles was considered suspect. One was thus faced with the following unprecedented paradox: The more innovative the doctrine, the more it was obliged to forgo any new theory of training. But since it was apparent that any innovative doctrine would affect training, it meant that sooner or later it would be rejected by the empire. For that reason, the internal conflicts of the analytic movement always have problems related to the training analysis as their *manifest* subject and questions of doctrine as their *latent* core.

Whereas technical rules were respected once and for all, such was not the case for rules of ethics. The former defined a profession, while the latter partook of a moral code more or less internalized by each society. Those latter rules were almost always given rather rough treatment since analysts were people like everyone else: neurotics, madmen, charmers, egomaniacs, etc. But they had to play a role and pretend they respected ethical considerations. In other words, technique functioned "for real" and ethics as "make believe." Nevertheless, the force of that pretense should not be underestimated; it too served to maintain the unity of the empire. The code of unrespected ethical rules and completely accepted technical rules constituted a formal set necessary to the survival of analytic societies. "For the IPA," wrote Granoff, "it was necessary to respect forms; everyone knew that so and so was a psychotic or a homosexual, but the forms had to be respected." [92]

Such a formalism combined the ideals of the Protestant ethic, dominant in the Anglo-American world, and the residues of a Jewish culture issuing from *Mitteleuropa*. On the American continent, it was accompanied by an adaptative ideal, which served as a counterweight against the violence of a society perpetually threatened by the formidable image of its own conquests. On British soil, on the other hand, a respect for forms was grounded in Victorian tradition. A cult of formalism was almost natural, and any public transgression fell prey to Puritan opprobrium.

Lacan, of course, respected none of this. His ideals came to him from a baroque Rome and his politics were dreamed up in the court of the Sun King. At a time when the IPA rejected charisma in order to avoid all reflection on the notion of an initiator, Lacan, on the contrary, rekindled the torch of the Hegelian master in order to take on his operative functions. On the one hand, he was relentless in insisting that his technical innovations be recognized, and on the other, he advised his disciples not to imitate his practice, which he believed himself alone able to master. At the SPP, he had promised in vain to submit to the rules; at the SFP, he gradually gave up that pretense: He promised less, cast himself as a founding father, and believed he was being protected by his own through the policies of the troika. He hoped that, against the Anglo-American world, his students would defend not only his doctrine, but his position as master and training analyst. He was wrong.

Two other paragraphs of the "Recommendations" bear witness to the IPA's aims. One concerned the "nonexistence" of child analysis within the SFP and was addressed to Françoise Dolto, and the other was directed against foreigners: "The study commission should exercise the greatest circumspection when inclined to give a positive response to a candidate of foreign nationality and particularly when such a candidate will be called on, after his return to his country of origin, to fulfill an isolated position or perform as a pioneer." [93]

Ah! how times had changed since the heroic days when Marie Bonaparte, Abram Kardiner, and James Strachey had taken train or boat to come stretch out on Freud's couch! Did she, Marie, remember, and what did she think of the "Recommendations"? She approved of them, of course. . . . She who had been the most terrible of pioneers would die in her bed as she had lived, overcome by a single raging bout of leukemia. Upon leaving the scene, on September 21, 1962, she refused the presence of a priest and uttered the words, "Will I see another summer?" [94] No, Princess, the sight of Lacan's defeat would be denied you. You would remain in history for your formidable role as *pasionaria* and for having written a magnificent diary of your analysis with Freud—an analysis, it should be said, in which the sacrosanct norms of technique were given short shrift. . . .

In Edinburgh, on August 2, 1961, during an administrative session, Serge Lebovici ascended the battlements. Quite calmly, he attacked Françoise Dolto and Jacques Lacan, proposing that the "good elements" be separated from the "undesirables." He played the card of the divisions within the SFP and was counting on a future alliance with Lagache, the two Favezes, and the juniors, who, he foresaw, would abandon Lacan. In addition, he used the occasion to demand that Hesnard and Laforgue, deemed to be incompetent, be stricken from the list of training analysts. That tactic was all the shrewder in that the presence of the two ancestors was an embarrassment for the SFP in its negotiations. [95] On that day, in the corridors of the congress, Lebovici approached Lagache and proposed that he abandon Lacan and return to the fold of the IPA. Shocked, the professor replied, "Thank you very much, but whom do you take me for?" [96]

In order for a grup to claim affiliation as a member society, four personal memberships, not three, were necessary. In Edinburgh, Granoff should have been that fourth party. He was better suited for it than Perrier, who was too uninformed of events and too close to Lacan's couch. Now, from the wings, Serge Lebovici and Marie Bonaparte were able to stop his appointment, using as arguments his alleged problems with the physicians' guild (*Ordre des médecins*). During that period, Granoff had indeed put two rooms of his home in Neuilly at the disposal of Father Beirnaert so that he might receive his analysands. Beirnaert was not a physician and received difficult cases sent to him by his religious superiors. In that context, he had treated a young—and plainly paranoid—man, who had flooded the Ordre des médecins with persecutory letters. The affair ended without any trial and Granoff, in agreement with the Ordre, did not expel Beirnaert from his house. But it sparked several rumors which were communicated to the executive with the aim of eliminating a fourth candidacy. Naturally, Lagache tried to support Granoff, but he proceeded ineptly and without results. In September, in order to mollify things, Beirnaert sent Turquet a long letter explaining the affair to him and exonerating Granoff of all suspicion. He was too late and would have to await the next congress.[97]

The first round of the battle for affiliation had thus been lost. With the appointment of Solms to the committee, the advocates of openness would be in the minority. In the plane taking them back to London, Lagache, Perrier, Granoff, and Leclaire encountered Turquet. Over drinks, he told them of the existence of a secret thirteenth clause of the "Recommendations" which followed the line advocated by Lebovici: "That the current custom of excluding Drs. Hesnard and Laforgue from training activities be maintained. As far as Dr. Hesnard's students are concerned, they will either enter into regular analytic training or they will not be accepted as students of the Society. That Drs. Dolto and Lacan gradually take their distance from the training program and that no further cases of analysis or control be directed to them. That any modification in the status of the candidates of Drs. Lacan and Dolto, presently in analysis or under supervision, be discussed with the consulting committee before any initiative concerning them be taken. That their analyses and controls presently under way proceed in accordance with all the other present recommendations." [98] Turquet himself had not expected such an ambush.

In September, Pearl King wrote to Lagache informing him of the decisions of the executive and the addition of Solms to the committee. A discussion ensued in the group of French negotiators on the subject of the precise meaning of the English word *requirement*. Did it refer to a "recommendation" or an "imperative"? Granoff composed a sybilline letter intended to calm tempers and to make the balance tilt in the direction of "recommendations": "It appears, he wrote, "that *requirement* has a strong meaning that might be translated by the French *exigence*. The French word *recommandation* may be used since, like the English *recommendation,* its first meaning is to express that it is imperative to satisfy certain conditions. The second meaning, although more customary, expresses the idea of an invitation to satisfy such conditions." [99]

Granoff derived a strange message from the "Recommendations." He was set on believing that the battle had been won and transformed the defeat of Edinburgh into the victory of Austerlitz. Not only did he misperceive the strength of the IPA apparatus, but he thought he could neutralize both Lagache, who had the support of the IPA, and the two Favezes, who did not represent anything at the international level. He thought the students of the SPP could return to the Lacanian fold. Shortly thereafter he presented the outline of his brilliant strategy in a splendid letter to Leclaire, which would become famous: "If one eliminated the vagabonds, long-beards, and Hottentots from Lacan's teaching, if it were *closed,* it would take on a different aspect, a different attraction, and all the repentant would be seen streaming to it. A more general theme which I invite you to meditate: Considering matters now from a greater distance, without taking into account personal bitterness or prejudicing in any way the future, one is forced to conclude that we brought off a success of major proportions. . . . A Lacanian study group without any organic con-nection to one or the other society, but grouping the most thoughtful students. That's important in that it will bring us an atmosphere of peace in two or four years while the relations of force with respect to Lacan's teaching change. . . . It is imper-ative to gather the reins in our hands, a difficult business that can be brought off only by duping Lagache. It follows from all this that our sense of things was accu-rate. And there too no one helped us. No one. Consider that fact carefully. . . . But above all that ZIPA [IPA nickname] is not a homogeneous block. It's shot through with numerous tendencies going in every direction, with unresolved tensions, mul-tiple struggles, and that as a result the more sheepish the project, the less a chance it has to succeed. The crazier it seems, the more it finds ZIPA unprepared to counter it. . . . Kindly don't destroy this letter. So that I may have a witness, a date, in brief, some bearings." [100]

Without realizing it, Leclaire would not forget that request. At the time of the SFP's disbanding, he would accidentally slip the letter into the official documents transmitted to Georges Favez, who would not fail to take cognizance, through it, of Granoff's intentions—which were in any event quite visible, but which he preferred to ignore.

The reaction of the officers of the SFP was not long in coming. Elected pres-ident, Juliette Favez-Boutonier wrote to Maxwell Gitelson, who had just succeeded Gillespie as head of the IPA. Favorably disposed to the "Recommendations," she unconditionally rejected Article 13, which she read as unduly *ad hominem* in its formulation. "Only the application of principles," she wrote, "can justify criticisms or measures to be taken with respect to individuals, and such action is our prerog-ative in agreement with the advisory committee. In addition, we have already been obliged to take measures in order to avoid the polemical use being made of Article 13 here in circles informed by rumors whose origin I need not specify." In other words, the board of the SFP made clear its intention of managing its own internal affairs itself. If heads were to fall, they would not fall by order of a foreign power but in "agreement" with it.

Rumors were rife. Not only did Lacan begin talking of the "Edinburgh plot," but he accused Leclaire of treason. Fortunately, he calmed down rather quickly, and his tenderness won out. In order to make clear that he still supported the troika, he held a gathering of his partisans, titular and associate members, in his home so·that they might formulate plans that would not be construed as criticism. Then, not without a sense of humor, he underscored the fact that the negotiators could not refuse to get on the airplane. Despite that, Gitelson's appointment as head of the IPA was partially responsible for the emergence of a slogan, "Lacan against Chicago," which tended to present the negotiation as a kind of *film noir:* Al Capone, on the one side, with his nasty gangsters, King Arthur on the other, surrounded by his valiant knights.

An American Jew, trained in the inner sanctum of the Chicago school, Maxwell Gitelson defended the orthodoxy in accordance with a tradition fusing a Wilson-like conservatism and a Roosevelt-like pragmatism. Having participated in the fights of his own institute, he was well acquainted with the quarrels endemic to psychoanalytic societies, but he looked on the commotion in France with little indulgence and did not understand very much of the significance of Lacan's reelaborations. Favorable to nonphysicians, he remained a company man entirely devoted to the survival of neo-Freudianism. First analyzed by Alexander, whose practice included short sessions and analyses of six months' duration, he subsequently made the transition to the couch of one of Alexander's pupils without ever becoming an issue in their reciprocal conflicts. Through his administrative skill, he had succeeded in preserving the Chicago Society from any splits. He did not know Lacan, and Lacan knew nothing of him. . . . [101]

In October 1961, Leclaire informed Turquet of the French situation: "After numerous discussions with Lacan, I have the feeling that we (Granoff, Perrier, and myself) are going to be able to be completely and objectively informed concerning all aspects of his training activities. It is agreed that for the present he renounces all new obligations in this domain, but that he quite properly intends to honor all commitments contracted prior to August 1961. It has even been explicitly agreed that he will take into account recommendations 1 and 2 (length and number of sessions). It seems to me that our position on the subject of his training activity in the future will depend on the manner in which we will be able to bring off this first phase of our action. I take it that you will agree with us that to the extent that the formal requirements have been satisfied, it will be ours to reconsider with utter independence of mind the substance of questions of analytic training." [102]

Leclaire had to do battle on several fronts, both inside and outside the SFP. Exploiting the Edinburgh defeat, the most conservative members of the SPP were spreading tendentious rumors concerning the group's situation. They proclaimed that the SFP had suffered a dislocation, that Lagache and Lacan had quarreled, that Lacan and Dolto had been definitively excluded, and Granoff and Perrier marginalized. With the intent of arranging a scientific exchange, Leclaire paid a visit to Francis Pasche, president of the SPP, who responded by raising an obstacle. "He objected," wrote Leclaire, "that a reciprocal exchange would unfortunately not be possible! If the Paris Society were to transmit scientific information to the secretariat of our group, it would be according *de facto* recognition of our society as an analytic group. He displayed great surprise at the fact that the central executive board had granted us the status of study group under the aegis of your committee. He confirmed that he had been informed in the sense indicated in the preceding paragraph. (I should specify that Dr. Green, who is one of the informers, has assured me that he had transmitted in their totality the decisions taken by the executive as they had been presented to the business meeting by Dr. Gillespie.) The frequency with which such imprecise notions are repeated leads me to fear lasting and extremely prejudicial consequences for some of us and for the group in its entirety, a result which goes far beyond that of any commonplace polemic." [103]

The maneuvering was started up afresh.

In order to prove its solidarity with the new "pariahs," the board of the SFP named Lacan president and Dolto vice-president. But immediately thereafter Leclaire strained to reassure the advisory committee, asking Dolto not to accept any additional training analyses. "It is quite evident," he wrote, "that such a position, adopted by a majority of our group, corresponds to the feeling that your practice (like Lacan's) activates resources that are not part of the analytic field as construed in its limited obsessional sense. By virtue of that fact alone, the question raised by any particular case (I am thinking of the way in which you welcomed N.'s demand and responded to it as you did) ought to be examined within the framework of the study commission." [104] No doubt Leclaire recalled the reception Dolto had reserved for him some twelve years before.

That injunction put her in an absurd situation. She consequently immediately sent off a response to Leclaire: "As for the exclusion aimed at Lacan, which you do me the signal honor of associating with the exclusion aimed at myself, everyone knows that they are totally unrelated in their justification, since I never work for fewer than fifty minutes, either with adults or children. Yet concerning Lacan, I'm told, we're dealing with a matter of a taxi meter." [105] Then she simultaneously addressed Favez-Boutonier, Lagache, and Lacan, in order to ask them (as well as Leclaire) three questions: "Do I have the right to conduct a training analysis or a control? Am I authorized to dispense training only in special cases? Are those who might be trained by me, with the exception of special authorization, to be denied the title of trainee of the SFP?" Dolto, of course, did not receive any precise answer from her interlocutors, but each did his best to stretch her patience, affirming that the measure was only temporary. In point of fact, the leading members of the SFP were prepared to sacrifice Dolto: some in order to obtain recognition, and the others, like Leclaire, in order to save Lacan. There would always be time later on, they thought, to retrieve her for the organization. A poor calculation. . . .

Why did the central executive make an issue of Dolto's practice even though, in formal terms, it remained in agreement with the standard rules? She yielded to norms of length less out of obedience than out of personal convenience. Her training was not Lacanian in spirit, and in so far as child analysis was concerned, her clinical practice was attuned to the Freudian heritage. Nevertheless, several elements contributed to make her suspect in the eyes of the IPA. First of all, she had become the personal friend of Lacan, thus participating in the ascent of Lacanianism in France. Then, her practice could be situated in terms of a legacy drawing on Laforgue and Pichon. Now the tendency toward a "French psychoanalysis" had already been condemned several times by the champions of orthodoxy. Finally Dolto, like Lacan, was regarded as a "charismatic figure" and thus a dangerous "guru." In addition, she was neither Kleinian nor Anna-Freudian: Her teaching did not correspond to any of the accepted categories catalogued by the IPA, whence an added dose of suspicion.

On May 2, 1962, the board of the SFP, with Favez-Boutonier presiding, informed the members of the SFP of the state of negotiations. In its report, it acknowledged the validity of the nineteen recommendations, but emphasized that Article 13 was unacceptable. In a peacemaking gesture, Granoff and Leclaire wrote a letter to President Gitelson. They demanded certain explanations: A rumor was circulating that the status granted in Edinburgh might be subject to revision at the next congress. The crisis was by that point confirmed.

In August, Lacan vacationed on the Amalfi Coast. He worked a great deal, slept little, and appreciated the warm isolation that allowed him to reflect on his doctrine. From the Villa Cimbrone, where he was staying in Ravello, and whose address he kept secret, he informed Leclaire that Turquet had asked him for an article for the *International Journal of Psychoanalysis,* the international association's official organ. He was delighted by that sign of interest and decided not to let it go unanswered. Sylvia typed up a note to the Englishman, and Lacan informed his disciple that he had reread his seminar on Hamlet the night before. "There is in it the wherewithal to intrigue you," he wrote, "if I am for you what I believe." Relations between the two men were at their zenith.[106]

In September, in order to put an end to rumors and resolve the crisis, Leclaire entered into new discussions with the advisory committee. He felt he had come up with a revolutionary solution to the problem with the negotiations. He met Turquet in London and upon his return sent him a confidential list of the members of the SFP, on which the names of the most interesting elements in the group were checked.[107] The Turquet commission was preparing to question a new round of candidates and Leclaire thought he could still bring pressure to bear on Lacan through his best students. That last-chance effort did not produce any positive results since, in the interim, the committee had shifted its orientation.

On November 1, Turquet informed Leclaire that things were going poorly: Solms had succeeded in shattering the fragile equilibrium among the four partners. He made use of one woman against the other, running the risk of forcing Turquet to resign out of solidarity with Paula Heimann.[108] In July, the Englishman had thought that "things would work out for Lacan," but this time he was more evasive. Leclaire informed Lacan of the news, still hoping that Gitelson would agree to receive the troika in Chicago. Shortly thereafter they received a favorable response from the president of the IPA. For Granoff, Leclaire, and Perrier, the meeting would allow them both to explain to the American the correctness of the line they were following and to convince him that Lacan could be made to stay in his rightful place within the French group. "One of the major elements of the problem facing us," they wrote, "is that of the relations of the French analytic group as a whole with an exceptional individual. It seems to us that after calmly defining the nature of the elements in question in this old conflict, one can clearly derive the shape of the outcome to be desired. The realistic and fruitful solution seems to us to succeed in granting such an individual his proper place. Such is the place that we must now define in a genuine and mutual agreement.[109]

The signers of the letter proposed that they go to Chicago during the month of March 1963. At the time, Leclaire still felt that with the support of Granoff he could maintain the cohesion of the juniors around the master. As for Perrier, who was still in analysis with Lacan, he found himself in a situation close to that of the majority of juniors in training: He could not bear Lacan's technique any more than they could.

The "revolutionary solution" envisaged by Leclaire and Granoff consisted of turning the SFP into a two-tiered society: one public, intended to pull the wool over the eyes of those on the outside, and the other private, in which Lacan would retain his privileges even while submitting to the "control" of the group. Naturally, the project was not viable: Communication between the two tiers would occur by way of the students, who would not pretend to conceal Lacan's practice, and Lacan, in any event, had no intention of hiding. Always prepared to resort to clandestine solutions, provided they were sufficiently elegant, Granoff selected Versailles as the location for perfecting the new statutes. He rented a sumptuous suite in the Hotel Trianon: an icy weekend for a meeting without results in which Pujol, Aulagnier, and Perrier participated.

At Christmas, Lacan sensed that the scales were tipping against him. More decided than ever to reject a normalization which contradicted the whole of his doctrine and practice, he nonetheless hoped to persuade his students to support him before the committee and thus reverse the momentum toward a rupture. "I don't want to speak of my own feelings," he wrote to Leclaire, "nor of yours, which I know. I mean that you can count on my steadfastness and my strength. . . . For ten years I have done everything to build up, out of its elements, a new form of analytic training, a training that would not be a lie. Who among our students will be the strong ones is something you cannot yet know. But it is imperative to continue our work and keep them together. I can do so, whatever the difficulty it entails. I've been proving as much to you, I think, for a year now. Come review with me the course of action now to be pursued."[110]

Lacan was wrong, and Leclaire knew it. Which is why he decided to disabuse him. In a letter, he informed him that the committee's balance of power had been broken and the negotiations all but shut down. He added that there were murmurs of rebellion in the French camp. Not only did the investigation reveal to the students the importance of a recognition they had worried little about before then, but it reinforced their will to emancipation from their master-analyst. At the beginning of the new year, Lacan thus observed with bitterness that his splendid strategy had in fact backfired.

As of January, the feelings of rebellion grew. A majority of the students began to manifest overtly their hostility to Lacan's technique, just as the men of the second generation had ten years earlier. But within that majority two tendencies emerged: Some were intent on recognition and were prepared, in order to obtain it, to demand of Lacan that he submit to the rules, and others, on the contrary, wanted to force the IPA into a global acceptance of the SFP without any exclusionary clause affecting a master whose authority they in any event challenged. The first tendency was represented by the academic or university group along with Smirnoff, Pujol, and Widlöcher, while the second was formulated rather well by Valabrega. "This is *our society*," he wrote to Leclaire, "as we wished to constitute it and as it has become, and not an *other* society obtained through the removal of its constituent members, through restrictions on its essential prerogatives, and elimination even of its fundamental principles." [111]

Unfortunately for Leclaire, that second tendency remained a minority in the group of the leading juniors, which was moving increasingly toward a contestation that would allow each to obtain recognition and to consummate a difficult break with Lacan. Aware of that contentious mood, Granoff would gradually come to choose the path of the IPA. He went to Chicago and became friends with Gitelson, thus weaving the fabric of his internationalist plan. Our irresistible Ulysses displaced his Trojan horse toward a different fortress: Anticipating the inevitable storm, he consolidated his alliance with Lagache, who continued to be unaware of the role he was being made to play.

At the beginning of January, the committee resumed its interviews at the Hotel Westminster. On this occasion, Piera Aulagnier came before the commission. Originally from Milan, she had lived in Egypt during the war before the study of psychiatry, in Rome, brought her to psychoanalysis. She spoke several languages and had traveled a good deal. A remarkable clinician, gifted with a strong theoretical intelligence, she had taken an early interest in psychosis, having been trained on Lacan's couch between 1955 and 1961. Like Valabrega, she thought that the SFP should be recognized in its entirety. Although she feared that Lacan's technique might be imitated in the future by unscrupulous therapists, she considered the man a genuine educator of his students. During her therapy, he had avoided mixing registers and the sessions lasted about fifteen minutes. She had the impression that Turquet was confining himself to purely formal considerations without any concern for the content of analytic experience. He spoke to her solely about problems relating to length of sessions. She answered that she found it aberrant that Lacan's analysands should be admitted to the list of titular members and that their analyst should not. The Englishman emphasized that things would work out very well for the students, but that under no circumstances would Lacan retain his training functions. After the questioning, he met her again by the elevator and attempted to convince her.

The members of the commission also asked Robert Pujol to testify. They did not question him, but allowed him to speak. He told them a parable in the form of a dream: He was listening to a patient while Granoff whispered a few words in his ear. Then he realized that those words were preventing him from hearing the discourse of his analysand. Pujol implored the committee to come to a quick decision since his hearing might continue to remain blocked. The English were stunned. Paula Heimann would long remember the dream and seize every opportunity to ask Pujol: "Is your hearing problem cleared up now?"

On two occasions, Moustapha Safouan was questioned at the Hotel Westminster, the first time on his practice and the second on Lacan's. Turquet asked him

whether he had a hospital practice and how many times a week he went to Strasbourg. He replied that he went there twice—from Monday morning to Tuesday
evening and from Thursday to Friday. Paula Heimann wanted to know whether this
distance had not aroused reactions of anxiety in his patients. Safouan retorted, humorously, that his patients were big boys and that for the while he had not noticed
anything to that effect. He added that despite the admissions procedures, candidates
succeeded in concealing their symptoms from the study commission and began their
therapy with the sentence: "I must confess that . . ." Then, the English group questioned the junior on his theoretical options. At the second meeting, they asked him
point blank what he thought of Lacan's practice and of short sessions. Safouan then
explained that the duration of a session had to be judged on internal criteria, from
the results it produced in therapy." [112]

It is difficult to offer an inventory of the differences and similarities between
the interviews of May 1961 and those of January 1963; in most cases, the protagonists of the story have forgotten on which date they appeared before the commission. Nevertheless, judging from both archival material and personal testimony, it
appears clear that Turquet's attitude had changed in the interim. Before Edinburgh,
he had still hoped to get Lacan to yield, whereas before Stockholm, his mind was
made up: His prediction was that Lacan would be dropped. From that point on, he
no longer spoke to the candidates in the same manner, and the differences among
the participants in the negotiation grew. The more a majority of students contested
Lacan's technique, the more the commission sought support in their statements for
marginalizing Lacan.

On January 17, Widlöcher informed Leclaire straight out of his position:
"Nonrecognition seems to me to be regrettable at present and catastrophic for the
future. The least bad solution . . . appears to me to be distinguishing between a basic
curriculum, with an official 'primary' training analysis, and a second phase of optional training (an analysis or a control with Lacan). That solution, I believe, will
be hard for Lacan to accept to the extent that he is convinced that his technique in
training analyses is theoretically grounded. Personally, I think that if he is capable
of proceeding in such a manner, it can only be a function of aspects linked to his
personality, his role, and so forth. . . . In the case of a break, the dogmatism and
intransigence of the neologism-lovers may take us very far afield indeed." [113]

Leclaire's answer was to advise Widlöcher to see Pujol. He still hoped that
the group of students would be able, in concert, simultaneously to apply pressure
on Lacan and support him. Widlöcher met Pujol at the seminar and had the impression that he shared his opinion about their analyst's technique. In point of fact, the
young native of Marseille was beginning to think that the negotiation would not
succeed. He too was looking for a way to take leave of a difficult relation with Lacan
by replacing the master's position with some symbolic "elsewhere" that might transcend it. Before long all the students in the group discovered that they more or less
had the same opinion. Instead of remaining isolated, they formed a common front,
thus delivering a new blow to Leclaire's strategy. Pujol conveyed his impressions.
"Do everything," he wrote, "to prevent them from withdrawing our provisional
recognition, and thus pay particular care to overvaluing the 'signs of good will'

emanating from the committee. . . . I saw Lagache Monday afternoon; he let me know his plans, which you ought to be apprised of. On the whole, I agree with him; I nevertheless brought to his attention the fact that what he was proposing was implicit in the "Recommendations" (the 'time for understanding'). I proposed an idea to him which he did not retain—having all those who had been analyzed by Lacan undergo a supplementary phase of analysis with a non-Lacanian." [114] Pujol recalled for Lacan's benefit that in 1910 Freud had refused to assume the presidency of the IPA.

In the face of the insurrection, Leclaire decided to have the board pass a motion shielding Lacan from any arbitrary measures. At the same time, he advised Lacan to assume a position of independence in relation to the group, which could then confirm and recognize his exceptional status: "This solution," he wrote, "corresponds to the will of virtually the entire group, but it will be valid only if the initiative comes from Lacan." [115] The "maneuver" was intended to allow the board to reassume its leadership role in operations while seeming to obey the "Recommendations." But at the same time it ran the risk of ratifying the process of Lacan's marginalization.

Favez-Boutonier informed Leclaire that she would be absent from the board meeting for the vote of January 21. She reminded him of her position: "We have always maintained that it was not our intention to defend Lacan's right to do absolutely anything, nor to defend Lacan above all, but rather a certain liberal and honest atmosphere which no longer existed in the SPP, where power-thirsty clans were resorting to every conceivable weapon in their efforts to get ahead." [116] The next day, Leclaire was elected president of the SFP and his motion was passed: "The board affirms that no exclusionary measure against a founding member of the society can for any reason be entertained. By exclusionary measure, the board understands discrimination resulting from any criteria other than scientific objectivity and simple justice." [117] Naturally, this last-resort measure did not protect Lacan. Ten days later, Leclaire drafted a letter to Paula Heimann in which he explained that the committee should allow the SFP to settle its own differences. Then he sent the draft to Lagache, who suggested that a current list of training analysts be prepared. He stated, in addition, that he had no faith in any surface displays of unanimity.

Given the imminence of the storm, Leclaire cancelled the trip the troika was scheduled to make to Chicago and asked Gitelson for a new meeting. Then he informed Lagache that negotiations had been all but shut down. Lagache immediately demanded a strict application of the "Recommendations." A new step had been taken in the reversal of alliances between the IPA and the French scene. Knowing that recognition had been projected for 1965, Lagache hoped to avoid any internal rupture by getting Lacan to yield. It was at this point that Turquet requested additional information. He wanted to know the names and the number of members of the SFP who had entered into a second period of analysis. To that end, he wrote to Leclaire, observing that the habit of second analyses had become quite common in the British society. Leclaire forwarded the requested information and came up on that occasion with three supplementary analyses for Lacan's couch.

From this point on Lagache began intervening directly in the contest.

In order to further the application of the "Recommendations" and secure Lacan's allegiance, he drew up a report on the preparation and relation of training analysts with the admissions committee. It was a matter of demonstrating to the IPA that the SFP did not need any overseeing in order to normalize itself. On the subject of "clandestine analyses," Lagache wrote, "Such a practice, if it exists, is incompatible with an analyst's commitments to the society and to the admissions committee. In the event that its existence should be established, it would result in the admissions committee's automatic refusal to grant those analyses official status." He then added: "In training analyses as in personal analyses, it appears not at all desirable for an analyst to treat persons well acquainted with each other and seeing each other from the outset (friends, parents, spouses, colleagues working together). To be sure, in an institute of psychoanalysis, it is inevitable that the students of the same analyst will come to know each other, meet, and even become friends. Although the analyst should not intervene in any authoritarian manner, he should not, however, neglect the interference such circumstances occasion in the progress of therapy, circumstances which in the final analysis are always regrettable." [118]

Thus did Lagache denounce Lacan's procedures without mentioning his rival's name. And he simultaneously made public his adherence to the ethical and technical rules of the IPA. Distributed at the SFP, the text allowed the juniors to learn that the majority of the seniors supported their cause. A new failure for Leclaire.

In the spring, Turquet crossed the Channel to inform the officers of the SFP of the conclusions reached in the report that would be presented to the forthcoming congress in Stockholm. François Perrier took careful notes. That second report of the investigatory commission has remained, to this day, as secret as the first, but the comments recorded by Perrier bear witness to the rapt attentiveness of the five partners on the committee. Divided among themselves, they managed quite shrewdly to exploit the internal divisions of the French scene. They perceived the alternation between what was said and unsaid during the interviews and summarized it in this brilliant formula: "There is within the society a desire to exclude [Lacan] without excluding him." Turquet saw that the board of the SFP was intent on not seeing that Lacan remained unacceptable in the eyes of the IPA. Then he paid homage to the troika's efforts even while affirming that the French studied Freud's texts like medieval clerics. He added that they had no knowledge of the negative transference, gave priority to theory over experience, and were uninterested in fantasy. Finally he emphasized that Lacan's analysands had not been analyzed and that they were passive in relation to a master who saw himself as sole dispenser of rewards and punishment. In conclusion, he asked that Lacan, Berge, and Dolto be stricken from the list of training analysts. To all this the report added a terrible clause: Lacan's training activity was to be forever banned from the realm of psychoanalysis and the commission on instruction was to veto the presence of students at his seminar. Lacan would call this decree his "major excommunication." To which we shall return.[119]

With the exception of the fine formula on the "desire to exclude him without excluding him," the Turquet report, in what we know of it, gave a singularly tendentious version of the results of its investigation. It showed in particular that the elimination of Lacan had been decided upon before the last hearings and that they had served as a pretext for justifying the executive's thesis. Not only had Turquet "shifted" in the course of negotiations, granting priority to negative testimony, but he never took account of the unconscious aspect of things. He judged Lacan's technique from an anecdotal point of view without concern for the unconscious effects it might produce on subjects. Put differently, he was acting more as a functionary of the IPA or a sociologist than as an analyst. If it was correct to claim that Lacan could not tolerate a negative transference, it was false to maintain that his students imitated him passively or broke their chains in anger. If such had been the case, they would not have been capable of disavowing clearly and lucidly a practice to which they were hostile. Most of the time they did so without anger and without hatred. Like all important clinicians and like all innovators, Lacan attracted several kinds of disciples: rebels, imitators, the faithful, etc. Now in the SFP, the rebels held power. It was Lacan who flew into a rage and they who tolerated his negative transference—which was not too bad for the end of an analysis. Worship, mimicry, and ridicule came later, when Lacan was constrained to found his own school.

In the face of this, the committee reacted in a normalizing manner. In brutally striking Lacan's name from the list of training analysts, it refused all risk and forced him to merge his doctrine with his person for good. That decision shows the vanity of analyzing the mechanisms of political and analytic power in terms of "charisma." Technical rules were necessary for a psychoanalytic society since they placed limits, within therapy, on the transferential omnipotence of analysts. But in no case could they prevent a master from remaining a master since the position of master was a symbolic value irreducible to any technical sanction. In keeping Lacan within the empire without requiring technical concessions from him, the representatives of the IPA would have given their acceptance an interpretative status forcing the master to define his own place as a function of an unconditionally imposed limit. But in order for such a decision to have been possible, the IPA would have had to change radically its ways of representing power. *That* was impossible by virtue of the IPA's transformation into a normalizing machine. In humorous terms, one could say that if the members of the commission had been capable of understanding both Freud's message and Lacan's, they would have had fewer misunderstandings not only of the history of the French scene, but also of their own movement. At the same time they would have identified the phenomenon of "charisma" without thinking they could eradicate it by "technical" means.

If Lacan, in his daily dealings, could not help identifying his person with his position as master, his relentless pursuit of recognition by the IPA was also the symptom of a will to avoid a fusion that would have dramatic consequences for the future. After all, had he wanted to effect a complete merger of his person, his place as master, and a lawgiving power, he could have refused to negotiate. It was not only out of a wish to export his doctrine abroad that he had not burned his bridges; he had underestimated the normalizing situation of the IPA and thought he could convince its organizers of the necessity of a teaching whose master would still have an initiatic function. In acting thus, he did all he could to avoid founding a school in his name, as though he himself feared being delivered over to an absolute power.

In addition, the members of the committee refused to take account of the subtleties and contradictions of the testimony they heard. Had they wanted to be objective and to take their distances from appearances, they could, for example, have perceived a simple fact—the women analyzed by or in control with Lacan did not speak of their therapy in the same manner as the men. As much as the male disciples felt irritated by the man's intellectual superiority, and could not bear his abusive side, the women encountered in their transference a feminine side of his character. Lacan had learned everything with Aimée, who was psychotic, and nothing with Loewenstein, who was in competition with him. Now Lacan was always a mother for men and often a father for women. He compared himself to a she-wolf in his relations with his disciples: He brooded over them, protected them, and never wanted to let them go. His way of listening resembled simultaneously Freud's with hysterics and that of hysterics themselves. It was entirely invested in neurosis and never in psychosis as has at times been said. "Psychosis is an attempt at rigor," he would say one day. "In that sense I would say I am psychotic . . . for the sole reason that I have always attempted to be rigorous. . . . As for psychotic, it's what I try as little as possible to be! But I can't say it does me any good. If I were more psychotic, I would probably be a better analyst." [120] The "masculine" rigor of a theory builder, the feminine fragility of a mother or a courtesan, such was the authentic clinical genius of the man.

The English did not want to retain anything of the idiosyncrasies of a technique and an individual. They made use of a crude argument attuned to the ideals of a normalization carried to the limit. For them the man was dangerous and irresponsible—a thoroughly negative "guru." It is, nevertheless, curious and hardly analytic to attribute such power to a man without inquiring into the reasons why he interested his audience.

In addition, the French scene was evoked in the report in an almost touristic and superficial manner. It was a bit frivolous, to say the least, and even chauvinistic, to reduce the formidable clinical and theoretical activity of the SFP to a labor of dogmatic clerics. If dogmatism and ethnocentrism existed in 1961, they were not the dominant values of the Society. Quite the contrary. Despite their professional competence, the English observed the continental affair with extraordinary contempt and studied ignorance. The matter was all the more terrible in that two members of the committee were well acquainted with the situation and had become aware of the importance of its ascendancy. Turquet himself, who was passionately committed to the cause of affiliation, had been caught up in the gears of the maneuver in which no one managed either to feign or to obtain sufficient reciprocal concessions. He would have a hard time recovering from the failure of negotiations and from the game he had been obliged to play between the executive's tribunal and the commotion in France. He would die at the steering wheel of a car. . . . Some day we will perhaps know more, when the IPA is willing to open its archives. In the meanwhile, one has to make do with Perrier's notes and the reports of witnesses.

Despite the insistence of certain of his colleagues, Leclaire decided not to disseminate the report's conclusions. He was attempting to gain time and avoid the emotional outbursts that would inevitably shatter the unity of the SFP. Turquet, for his part, tried his best to urge the juniors down the path of breaking with Lacan. Until that date, the French participants in the affair had hoped that Lacan would yield to the common rule. But starting in May, they would be forced to endorse the committee's decision and *themselves* execute the requested exclusion. They thus passed from an aspiration toward normalization to an act of elimination.

On May 23, at the urgent request of the advisory committee, Leclaire called a meeting of the board of the study commission in order to revise the list of training analysts, in conformity with the report to be transmitted to the executive. Discussions took place in the sumptuous terrace of the Pavillon Henri IV in Saint-Germain-en-Laye. It was there, facing the Seine, that Alexandre Dumas had written *The Three Musketeers,* while savoring poached eggs in pastry shells.

Lagache, Dolto, the two Favezes, and the troika participated in the debate. As always, Granoff took meticulous notes on all that was said. As for Leclaire, he directed operations in accordance with his habitual tactics. Against the outside threat, he attempted to maintain the cohesion of the group for as long as possible. That is why, instead of opening discussion of Turquet's demands, he requested each person present to speak on his respective students, on transference, and on the end of analysis. In thus gaining time, he put off the time for making a decision, hoping that Lacan would take a step forward that might lead Turquet to take a step back. In the course of the discussion, Juliette Favez-Boutonier abstained from taking a stand on the requirements of the committee, Georges Favez said he favored Berge's exclusion, and Lagache vacillated between his revulsion at submitting and his hostility to Lacan. Dolto, for her part, declared that it was hard to exclude a man while keeping the students he had trained. As for Lacan, sovereign and contemptuous, he presented the theory of his practice and announced that the SFP was nothing without him since it owed him everything. In addition he defended his students with ardor, even the most contested ones, and mocked Favez, asking him if he had in fact liquidated his transference with Hartmann. In a furor, Favez replied that it would never occur to him to ask whether Lacan had liquidated his transference with his students. Lacan riposted more mordantly still, "I don't see why you would deprive yourself of it." Such was the mood of the theoretical debate that took place that fine spring afternoon.

In desperation, Granoff wrote a lucid report on the situation of psychoanalysis in France on the eve of the Stockholm congress. He knew that the game was over for the troika and could not bear Lacan's intransigence, which was ruining his internationalist projects. Resigned to a break, he thought the master's students would join the ranks of the IPA and swing definitively into the Anglo-American camp. "In speaking of loyalty and treason," he wrote, "as is more and more the case, how can one avoid evoking the central Western figure of Iscariot, whose obsession seems to weigh on Judeo-Christians. Pressing the parallel further, I would say that if proximity to Judas can be intuited in protestations of loyalty, the master, for his part, feels abandoned not by his father, but by his apostles. Whose repudiation of him the Nazarene knew in advance. In addition, his zealots seem to have no desire to assemble in catacombs, but are demanding as their due access to the temple of the established faith—the proof being their dealings with the IPA."

At the end of the month, Leclaire informed Turquet that the report would be made public on June 10. He also apprised him of the meeting at Saint-Germain. "We have attempted," in his words, "to broach the problem of defining a didactic perspective in psychoanalysis." Then he added a personal opinion: "It seems to me that we are observing developments that could have been foreseen at the time of the crisis of last July. I note that intentions which you translated by such formulas as 'having so-and-so's skin' or 'heads will fall' have already done their work. To be sure, I deplore it, as you do no doubt, since such formulas seem to be more in the order of fantasy than its analysis; but it was predictable. All this recalls to me the words D. spoke to me one day when I was his driver, 'Believe me, my dear Leclaire, that Lacan is a dangerous individual.' The situation thus continues to be critical. I nonetheless do not feel inclined to abandon the fray and continue to believe that with a little prescience and a lot of patience it would be possible to bring our plan to a successful end.'[121]

Decidedly, Leclaire was not laying down his arms. His optimism in the circumstance did not prevent Turquet from strengthening his positions. In a few well-turned sentences, he demanded Lacan's elimination pure and simple and made clear the committee's intention of normalizing any cases left in suspension: Lacan's analysands would be redirected to other couches in order to receive training according to the rules.

During the weekend of June 22–23, a final meeting took place at the Hotel Westminster between the members of the committee and the most important representatives of the French camp: Anzieu, Dolto, the two Favezes, Granoff, Lacan, Leclaire, and Perrier. Against Turquet's advice, the French insisted that Lacan attend the debate devoted to the evaluation of his practice. As always, Granoff took careful notes on all that was said. His thoughts were with a future historian. Turquet demanded that all candidates in analysis with Lacan be transferred elsewhere and proposed a fifteen-month plan for accomplishing the task. Leclaire declared his opposition even as he stated that the operation, were it to take place, would require the agreement of the interested party. "We are worried," Turquet emphasized, "about a society having twelve candidates analyzed by him under the present conditions. . . . A society dominated by Lacan constitutes for the IPA quite a different problem from the one we envisaged, that of a society requesting affiliation." Leclaire replied that progress had been made and that Lacan had agreed that his practice be controlled by the group. But Turquet resumed the offensive, demanding a *banishment without return*: "What plan do you have in mind for his exclusion from training in perpetuity?" To which Leclaire answered, "If we are recognized as a member society, it will mean that that problem will have been solved of itself. It's clear that we will not have the recognition before having solved that problem." Turquet tried to convince Leclaire to accept the banishment in order to avoid the executive's having to impose it. Leclaire replied that external pressure already existed. Then he tried to change the subject by observing that the IPA required less of the SPP than of the SFP. The attendance of Lacan's analysands at his seminar provoked a lively discussion, as did the poor implantation of the SFP in Marseille and Strasbourg. Moustapha Safouan was raked over the coals. His answers and affirmations were considered offensive and inadequate, and the committee required that he not take on any new training analyses.

On Sunday the twenty-third, called on by Georges Favez to clarify matters, Lacan took the floor: "If I'm not speaking, it's because I don't see what interest there can be in doing so with interlocutors who are not even capable of being interested in what I might have to tell them. Last year I tried to tell them certain things. The little attention I received is a sufficient sign for me. If I was present yesterday and if I took the trouble to come today, it's out of solidarity with the struggle the group is waging. My presence attests to that. I know that I have not been attacked within the group. To defer to their request would be once again to undergo failure since, whatever one says about it, each time they win, they win a bit for us." Lacan was right not to want to yield to the English, but he was cruelly in error concerning the solidity of the group and the support his students might bring him.

In the face of the committee, Leclaire and Perrier refused to submit, while Lagache swung to the other side by insisting on obedience to the requirements of Edinburgh. "For my part," Leclaire emphasized, "I believe it is completely impossible to accede to their request. Yielding to an uncourteous and insulting request would mean that we could never open our mouths again. My position on this point is unrelenting. I suggest that we give them a refusal without explanation." Lagache refused Leclaire's position and Lacan supported his disciple, stating that he had shown himself to be loyal for two years, aiming only at preserving the quality of his teaching. The break between Lagache and Lacan was from then on complete and definitive.

Shortly thereafter, Lagache, Leclaire, and Granoff met alone with the committee. They had been charged with negotiating the affiliation at the Stockholm congress. "We see a danger," Turquet emphasized, "in the influence Lacan exercises on you all and we cannot pursue this discussion *ad vitam aeternam.* At Stockholm the discussion will depend on the central executive. In the report we present to it, we will underscore the problem posed by Lacan's position. Last night we were struck by a lack of sincerity in your attitude toward the committee." Then the discussion drifted to the practices of Georges Favez and Moustapha Safouan, which were judged to be out of line. Before long, Lagache yielded to most of the committee's demands. He abandoned Leclaire, even while announcing that Lacan was an old friend whose culture and originality he appreciated. Leclaire attempted once again to save the situation: "This is all the same the first time an analytic society has obtained relative control over Lacan's activities. . . . The problem is plainly complex. The question of his lack of attention or his distractions raises the question of attention in general. Even without any positive distractions, do we ourselves possess the attentiveness necessary in all circumstances? When we don't know, we are wrong, but when we know, aren't we also wrong? Lacan's greatest wrong, in my eyes what is intolerable and what perhaps should not be tolerated, is that he embodies the psychoanalyst's bad conscience. But it seems to me that a good conscience in a psychoanalyst is no less dangerous." In conclusion, Granoff attempted to warn the committee of how dangerous it would be for the negotiations to fail. In order to illustrate his idea, he read from an old letter of Loewenstein's, dealing with the worries he experienced on the subject of the fate of psychoanalysis in France, given the existent custom in the country of "quickie" analyses, whose extension and prolongation might well create an irreversible situation. Granoff added that given what passed for the beginnings of psychoanalysis in France, the SFP was the true site of the first implantation of Freudianism in France, whence the necessary return to the texts recommended by Lacan. As a result, the Society was reexperiencing the eternal problem of origins, namely: students who had been better analyzed than their masters. If the leadership were to fail, he added, "quickie" analyses would flourish and an irreversible situation would be created. The future would show that Granoff was right. But the IPA would bear the guilt of never having taken into account the reality of the French situation. It was satisfied with trashing, without any willingness to understand them, the practices of two clinicians of genius, Dolto and Lacan.[122]

A few days after that final meeting, Lacan resurfaced and performed a theatrical act befitting his role. He informed Leclaire of his decision to go to Stockholm in order to try to convince the IPA of the soundness of his doctrine and technique. He was not lacking in courage, but sorely deluded as to the intentions of his adversaries and his own power of persuasion. Aware of the folly of such an act, Leclaire warned him in terms as sublime as they were friendly, "You are marching toward catastrophe under the banner of dignity. But I am loyal and I know what I owe you. I will go with you."[123] Overwhelmed by the response, Lacan had trouble holding back tears, "I am undone at receiving so unique an act of faith, honor of my life . . . my friend. . . . My dignity, you are right, played its role. It will rivet me to this task which has already taken my life from me." Late at night, he sent still another letter to his beloved disciple to announce to him that he could not sleep, that he was writing and telephoning and felt himself prepared to account for his projects: "I shall arrive in Stockholm differently than as the guest who owes you his trip. . . . Struggle along with me and hold on, you are the president. . . . At present I cannot conceive of my line of action in any other terms."[124]

In reality, Lacan was at once enraged, depressed, and full of contempt for his judges and the colleagues of his generation. Like all the protagonists of this story, he played out his role and felt betrayed, defeated, humiliated, and dishonored. In a letter to Paula Heimann, written in English, he challenged the report's conclusions and did not hesitate to accuse Lagache of stealing his ideas. The affirmation was as moving as it was lucid and venomous. It bears witness in any event to the fever that had gripped the man on the morrow of what he knew to be a supreme punishment: banishment without hope of return. "I don't know what your feelings are on the subject of this horrendous story . . . nor why your signature served as a cover for this cynical report. But truly, it would interest me to know if you have understood what is going on under your nose. . . . My work of ten years, devoted solely to the members of the group and intended to form honest thinking in our field, a soul for their practice, will be stolen by a man concerning whom I prefer not to say just how he is listened to by the students. A society of Lacanians under the flag of that dolly from the Sorbonne, will live as a body of the IPA, at the price of my moral and social ruin. . . . Are you yourself ready to let your name be attached to the example of my tragedy for future memory."[125] Lacan wrote that terrible letter on June 27, following his seminar. He transmitted it to Leclaire, who filed it in his archives and immediately informed Paula Heimann that Lacan insisted on participating in a seminar at the Stockholm congress.

On July 1 a meeting of the board was held to make arrangements for the general assembly to be held the following day, at which trainees, for the first time, would have the opportunity of attending, although in a nonvoting capacity. At dawn on July 2, Leclaire warned Lacan, "Yesterday we laid the Society in a coffin and we shall bury it tonight. Thus end ten years." In the course of the general assembly, he presented only part of the commission's report and announced that negotiations had broken off. Then he added that the board had not found either means or reasons to scratch Lacan from the list of training analysts. Finally he observed that if the SFP did not satisfy the executive's demand, it was the Society itself that would be provoking the break and that must shoulder the consequences. Embarrassed, those who chose to intervene in the discussion did not quite know what to say. They were poorly informed as to the state of the negotiations. Only Piera Aulagnier attempted an analysis of the situation, emphasizing that the representatives of the IPA were not villains, but that they had seen the problem from the outside. She also observed that if London's answer was negative, the Society would be forced to take cognizance of its errors on its own, a circumstance that would be constructive for it. Although he was certain he was headed for failure, Leclaire revived his agenda once again and got a motion passed maintaining the request for affiliation.[126]

On the following day he informed Lagache that he had sought in vain to obtain further concessions from Lacan, and then announced his imminent resignation, "If a different policy is to be pursued, it will have to be by someone other than myself." He began to lose hope seriously when he received a new demonstration of the failure of his strategy. Turquet announced to him that Lacan was not authorized to participate in any seminar in Stockholm. Nonetheless he could speak at the precongress meeting to be held in London in July.[127] Leclaire composed a disabused reply: "As French notaries have the custom of saying, one cannot simultaneously cede and retain. So long as the possibility had been offered to members of the study group to participate in the precongress meeting, it was anyone's right to sign up for it. Political expediency—which I understand perfectly well—in this case, by introducing a discrimination, takes on a meaning that will elude no one."[128]

During this period, Granoff and Favez-Boutonier were encouraging the juniors to make public their opinions on Lacan's practice. Urged to take a stand, Widlöcher decided to write a moderate text. Like his friends, he still thought he could convince Lacan to make concessions. On July 11, a motion to that effect was signed by six persons: Aulagnier, Lang, Laplanche, Pontalis, Smirnoff, and Widlöcher. It came to be called the *motion des motionnaires* [the movers' motion] and was aimed at playing down the dramatic aspect of things by indicating that there was no contradiction between Lacan's teaching and normalization.[129] The signatories wanted to avoid at all costs a dogmatic polarization of the situation that would turn Lacan into a "charismatic" leader and the IPA into a police tribunal. At their request, Granoff informed Anzieu of the existence of the motion, and the latter gave his unconditional approval. Nevertheless, he preferred not to sign it, since his hostility to Lacan was known, and the mention of his name might work against the moderate character of the joint position.[130] The movers apprised Lacan of their deed and transmitted the text to Leclaire, allowing him to decide on how best to make it public.

In point of fact, at the juncture to which matters had come, the motion had no other value than as subjective truth. It could no longer modify the course of events, and its content would take on a different meaning than that of its text. The signatories, however, did not know this since they were unaware of the reality of the situation. They were proclaiming their pacifism at a time when tanks had already crossed the border. Leclaire knew as much, which is why he decided both to approve the initiative and not to present the motion to the members of the board. He kept it for himself and would not make use of it two weeks later in Stockholm. In brief, he thought it was too early to admit to himself that he had been definitively defeated and too late to progress any further. Widlöcher accepted Leclaire's decision, while Laplanche opposed it. Confusion reigned.

At the center of the fray, the rebellious juniors had the feeling of being duped by all sides: by Leclaire's "double game," by Lacan's refusal to budge, by Granoff's "false plots," and finally by the committee, whose true intentions they did not grasp. They wanted more information and still thought Lacan might yield. This is why, despite its pacifist air, their motion gave concrete form to the first phase of an official break that would simultaneously serve the interests of the executive and those of the Lagache clan (by way of Granoff's mediation). In the fall, once the Turquet report and the Stockholm decision were known, each individual would be obliged to choose his or her camp: Lacan or the IPA. The motion would thus be used in a manner opposed to what it advocated.

In mid-July, Leclaire had a positive meeting with Sacha Nacht, who assured him that the executive wanted the affiliation and that he himself would not oppose it.[131] Lebovici, for his part, let Favez-Boutonier know, in the course of a colloquium in Milan, that he was giving up all action against the SFP. In Stockholm, he would not vote. He said he was sure that affiliation would be granted. She immediately informed Leclaire: "[He said] . . . that what counted was the future of psychoanalysis, both for himself and for us, he thought. There are perhaps among *us,* he said, then, correcting himself, among *you* (a nice slip!) and (he continued) also among *us* individuals who are more or less interesting, more or less worthy, but that should not stop us. That's not what counts, it's the future that's in question, that of psychoanalysis in France. The past is over." [132]

At that date it was thus established that Lacan would be excluded from training, both by France and by the IPA. What remained to be seen was how it would happen. At that point, Lebovici rushed to propose to the "good elements" an alliance for the future, in order to weld a new anti-Lacanian unity in France.

Jacques Lacan landed in London for the precongress meeting at the beginning of July. He was accompanied by Solange Faladé, an African of the Yarouba people of Dahomey. A student of the SFP, she was his analysand and had worked for the World Health Organization after working briefly in Jenny Aubry's service. She had followed the development of the negotiations closely, offering Lacan her advice. Before Edinburgh, she had thought that the contest was unwinnable and that it would have been preferable to strengthen the SFP's position in France before negotiating. In London, Lacan spoke English. He tried to explain the division of the subject and the *objet a,* but could not manage to find an English term for *reste* [residue]. He thus asked his audience to help him out. No one deigned to respond. Isolated, with his dignity intact, he left the lecture room soon after and took a stroll on the lawn. Solange approached him along with other students who had come to hear him, and he took the group out to lunch at a pub frequented by the royal family. He still hoped to be recognized, and paid visits to Pearl King and Masud Kahn. But both avoided him. . . . [133]

On July 31, at the Stockholm congress, Gitelson announced that the study group status was being maintained for the SFP and that the committee would continue to represent the group in its dealings with the executive. Then he added that Granoff had been made a member at large. The statutes of the IPA had just changed, raising to four the number of members needed to grant group status. Henceforth five would be needed for affiliation, and that battle was far from won, even for the future Association psychanalytique de France, without Lacan. In point of fact, the executive was banking in advance on a split while pretending to back a policy of unity.

That subtle strategy was illustrated in a directive of August 2 that avoided taking into account certain conclusions of the Turquet report, which was not yet known within the SFP. The executive offered its congratulations to Leclaire for the results obtained. Then it insisted on the strict application of the Edinburgh "Recommendations." Finally it added a veritable ultimatum consisting of three points: "(a) All associate members, trainees, and candidates must be informed that Dr. Lacan is no longer recognized as a training analyst. Such notification must be effected by October 31, 1963, at the latest. (b) All candidates in training with Dr. Lacan are requested to inform the study commission whether or not they wish to continue their training, it being understood that they will be required to submit to a supplementary period of training analysis with an analyst approved by the study commission. Such notification must be effected by December 31, 1963, at the latest. (c) The study commission, in agreement with the advisory committee, will interview candidates who have expressed the wish to continue training in order to determine their aptitude. Such interviews should be completed by March 31, 1964. On all these questions the advisory committee will voice its opinion, whether concerning the aptitude of candidates or the choice of a second analyst." [134]

On that day, surrounded by Dolto, Perrier, and Leclaire, Lacan went walking through the Swedish countryside. His daughter Judith accompanied him. In a tavern, Perrier asked in vain for whiskey, while Leclaire barely managed to conceal his despair. Deep in his thoughts, Lacan finished off a glass of wine, and Dolto, quite happy, grew interested in the countryside. Soon, the group arrived on the banks of Lake Mälar for a visit to the famous Gripsholm Castle, located on an island facing the city of Mariefred. The region had always had considerable importance, because of a strategic placement assuring it superior communications by water as far as the Baltic. For the Swedes, the castle was associated with the memory of the German writer Kurt Tucholsky, who committed suicide there in 1935. A popular film was adapted from a novel of his, with the castle as backdrop. Upon leaving the site, Lacan saw the village's name inscribed on a milestone. Still deep in his thoughts, he had not realized that he had visited the castle with his friends. He immediately forced the group to do an about-face, and knocked on the trellis to enter. But the guard refused to open for him and did not yield to his imprecations.[135]

Compared to the second Turquet report, or what we know of it, the Stockholm "directive" revealed both a retreat and an escalation. It did not mention the names of Berge and Dolto, and did not pass judgment on the internal situation of the SFP. In brief all its firepower was directed at a single target: Jacques Lacan. The executive no longer demanded his banishment *without return,* as envisaged by Turquet, but a simple elimination from the list of training analysts. It no longer asked for Dolto's head, because it knew that it had won and that all further action would be in relation to its ultimatum. Finally, it carefully avoided criticizing the efforts of the French group and restricted itself to the training orientation of its members.

Toward the middle of September, the expanded board took cognizance of the executive's minutes. The dissemination of their contents immediately provoked a chain reaction. The situation evolved toward a division of the Society into two parts. One, which was the majority, decided above all to pursue the implementation of the policy of affiliation. The other (the minority) was above all concerned with preserving Lacan's contribution. There remained a policy of unity which revealed itself to be extremely fragile to the extent that the two camps were themselves internally divided as to what course of action to follow. In the minority group, some stiffened their stand and envisaged a break with the IPA, whereas others still hoped to save the SFP. In the majority clan, the "movers" still wanted to promote a middling line, while Granoff and Lagache were determined to break with Lacan. Leclaire steered a tangential course, drawing support from the moderates in each camp—neither for the IPA as a block nor frenetically against Lacan.

Resigned to a break since Stockholm, Lacan demanded of his partisans—of whatever tendency—a definitive choice. He could not do otherwise. With remarkable speed, he wrote a book in two parts, which would fall into oblivion, then oscillated between fury, appeals to dignity, threats of suicide, and acceptance of the debacle. Xavier Audouard was first to affront His Majesty's ire.

He suggested to Leclaire that they sign a joint text asking Lacan to accept his elimination in order to save the SFP. His argument was based on the idea that the rank of training analyst was so ludicrous in itself that any master worthy of the name should be able to make do without it. Audouard demonstrated remarkable naïveté. Had Lacan agreed to endorse his own dismissal, he would have lost on all fronts. He would have been the spearhead of a society capable of sinking into the ridicule of excluding from its training its most brilliant representative. And then no man can "abjure" in such manner unless he is threatened by torture or the stake. And that was not the case. Lacan had wanted integration at any price, but not at the price fixed by the IPA: The entire problem was there.

Leclaire supported Audouard's initiative, but refused to sign the text. He hoped that the letter would convince Lacan, not to yield, but to give supplementary reassurances allowing for a reopening of negotiations. In point of fact, he himself no longer believed in his own strategy. "Why would you wish at all costs," wrote Audouard to Lacan, "to conserve the 'little residue' as if to save the honor of Lacan-as-subject and wishing to remain such? Of what consequences can it be that you feel 'shunted' by the IPA, given what we know—through you—of the position of the analyst and his desire? We worked all last year at avoiding raising our standard and defending with the 'swords of paradise' the sacred values transmitted to us by Lacan. Are we now to see that it was all bluff and that we are consecrated to defend until death the training analyses of Jacques Lacan? That Jacques Lacan in person will force us to save them for him? That instead of tolerating division with its 'residue,' we are to 'grab the spoils' in a struggle whose only end can be a profound division of the SFP against itself?" [136]

An answer was not long in coming. Lacan told his analysand that his letter had arrived in time to confirm the intolerable nature of what was being imposed on him. Summoned urgently to the rue de Lille, Audouard was witness to an outburst of Lacan's fury: "You are aware that I am composing a book in two parts," he told him, "unless I don't have the time to complete the second one. One way or another, that second part will be completed, but the notes are usable only by me. If by chance—such things happen—an accident were to occur (I am on lithotrypsie), people would think it was a suicide, and I wouldn't deny it. I must tell you that the motion I know you are aware of and the letter (from you) which I received this morning will appear as prefaces to my book. Someone will come remove from your home the tapes you recorded at my seminar. Rest assured that it's a good thing you are in my house, for that alone keeps me from following my wish to throw you the hell out. In any event, I want to convey to you my contempt. Now get the hell out." [137]

That scene transcribed by Audouard shows, if necessary, that Lacan had no desire to commit suicide, but that he was as outraged by the defection of his followers as by the decision in Stockholm. He too had let himself be fooled. He had believed firmly in Leclaire's strategy, and had erred as to the wishes of the majority of his analysands. Thereafter, he would harvest the fruit of his errors.

Four days later, Audouard returned to the rue de Lille. Lacan consented to hear him out: "What I sent you was a letter from one analyst to another. I sacrificed all personal interest, all subjective attachment, all demonstration of man-to-man affection in favor of an objective analysis of the state and the interest of the SFP. . . . That earned me a kind of ridicule in some quarters. . . . Do you have a line of conduct for defending yourself to recommend?" Lacan, for good reason, did not answer the question, but told Audouard that he understood better the intentions behind his letter. Then he added that he had decided to abandon his persecutory interpretations.[138]

Within the SFP, the Stockholm "directive" was beginning to poison the atmosphere of collective work. If proof be needed, there is the tragiocomic dispute which broke out shortly thereafter between Maud Mannoni and Jean-Paul Valabrega on the subject of an issue of the journal on child analysis. In a control with

Lacan and an impassioned militant of his cause, Maud Mannoni, who was Flemish by origin, had been trained at the Association des psychanalystes de Belgique. That group had been created in 1946 under the aegis of Fernand Lechat and Maurice Dugautiez with the support of Marie Bonaparte and John Leuba. The following year it was integrated into the IPA, and then, in 1960, took the name of the Société belge de psychanalyse (SBP).[139] Maud Mannoni practiced in France while retaining her membership in the IPA through her affiliation with the SBP. In 1962, she had taken the initiative of preparing an issue of *La Psychanalyse* devoted to child therapies. The board had given its consent, but in 1963 the texts were not yet completed. Since Maud was fearful that the conflict with the IPA might put an end to the existence of the journal, she accused Valabrega of robbing her of first place and of allowing two issues to appear before her own. On the same occasion, she lodged something of an attack against Leclaire in which she accused him both of playing the IPA's game and of killing the SFP. The president immediately responded, not without a touch of humor: "If this is a trial, so be it. I should have done this or not done that. . . . If it's a project, I am not yet sufficiently Gaullist to believe that institutional reform would be a remedy. For what, moreover? You will no longer need the journal, nor us, nor the others in their majority, nor the society for that matter. What can I do about it?" As for Valabrega, he answered with a public clarification in which he specified that issues appeared when they were ready and that no one had been either neglected or favored.[140]

It was in that conflictual atmosphere that the "movers" decided to request a private meeting with Turquet without informing either the board or its president. They wanted to find out about the future of the SFP and the place that would be reserved for Lacan. They did not yet know the contents of the notes taken by Perrier and limited themselves to the "directive." Turquet accepted the proposition and announced to Leclaire that he would be at the Hotel Westminster on Sunday, October 11. Dissatisfied, Leclaire realized quickly enough that the meeting would be used by the Englishman to accelerate the marginalization of Lacan. With the support of Perrier, he protested against the decision to have a meeting to both the committee and the board. But his complaint ended up being used against him. Not only did the petitioners stick to their decision, but Turquet disavowed the maneuver of his partner, thus fueling the desire for a break in the ranks of the "movers."

Widlöcher then protested in the name of the juniors, observing to Leclaire that it was he who was casting a private meeting in a divisive light.[141] Encouraged by Lacan, Piera Aulagnier understood that the motion she had signed was taking on a new meaning. She thus refused to go to the Hotel Westminster and politely took her distance from the juniors. Informed by Leclaire's official communiqué, Lagache sent him a vengeful and laconic letter: "Since the meeting you apprised me of is to take place despite your reservations, it seems more intelligent to me to accept what cannot be avoided. Your invitation to meet with Dr. Turquet seems prompted by a proper and courteous attitude. It is up to you to act in a similar manner." Leclaire reacted immediately: "Would not the 'proper and courteous' attitude you credit Dr. Turquet with have consisted, in all rigor, in informing the board of the SFP before agreeing to meet with the six petitioners? I should like, if you will do me this service, to have your opinion on that precise point before deciding on my own course of action for next Sunday. . . . It happens that for the moment, I regard Turquet's attitude in a manner diametrically opposed to yours: as uncourteous and improper." [142]

In the interim, Jean Clavreul intervened in the fray in the name of the study commission. As a partisan of those completely rejecting the "directive," and a hardcore Lacanian militant, he rejected Widlöcher's initiative, and insisted on being present, as an observer, at the meeting on the rue de la Paix. He would not be there, and neither would Leclaire. Behind the backs of the protagonists, a merger had taken place between the "movers" and the majority of the board with the aim of implementing the IPA's demands within the time period established in the ultimatum.

On the morning of Sunday, October 13, the split went into effect within the SFP. While the "movers" definitively accepted the Stockholm "directive" and envisaged with Turquet the future of a society in which Lacan would be stripped of his prerogatives as a training analyst, the Englishman warned Granoff by telephone that he had to take a 3 o'clock plane and that if he did not bring back with him a statement of exclusion duly signed by the study commission, the executive would refuse the principle of affiliation. Wladimir proceeded straightaway to write in his own hand a "motion": "The undersigned submit to the study commission for a vote on the following decision: Dr. Lacan no longer figures in the list of titular members capable of performing training analyses and controls as of this date. As a result, the present composition of the study commission is open to question." [143]

Armed with his text, he went to see Lagache, who signed without any misgivings. Then he went to the home of the Favezes, fearing all the while that they would be reluctant or would retract. Georges signed first and Juliette after him. She sensed Granoff's fear. But her decision had been made: She would not change her mind. Wladimir bid the couple good-bye, got into his splendid car, and brought the motion to the Westminster. After supporting Lacan for ten years with the hope of ensuring the establishment of a Lacanian school of psychoanalysis abroad, he was the first to break with his own strategy and draw up the implacable sentence. From then on, the game was over for Leclaire.

A few days later, Favez-Boutonier commented on her deed in these terms: "In no longer mentioning Lacan among the training analysts and retiring him from the study commission, I am recognizing what has in fact been going on since the time he stopped accepting new training analyses. I am proposing an anticipatory measure which should, I believe, intervene (and should already have done so) to demonstrate that we really do want to take the "Recommendations" into account. Lacan's absence from the study commission is the only way for that commission to discuss the problem of his students freely, without our being accused of being incapable (and without him being accused of being incapable). I don't see where anyone actually thought of implementing, in Lacan's absence, the decisions recommended by the IPA: first the withdrawal of his students, formal notification, etc. But if a satisfactory arrangement of these dispositions is possible, it will be on condition that no one have the impression that Lacan is intimidating or governing us." [144]

It will be seen that the subjective experience of the protagonists in this story is always *other* than the story being played out without their knowledge. No one in the SFP was thinking of implementing the IPA's decisions as a bloc, but, by signing two contradictory motions, the juniors, on the one hand, and the seniors on the other were unwittingly endorsing a directive that went much further than their own intentions. In its majority, the SFP wanted to make Lacan yield without *really* excluding him, whereas the IPA was intent on excluding him without *really* trying to make him yield. The nuance was considerable. At the middle of the battlefield, the committee was playing the role of a scale, tipping one way until July 1962, then the other during the fall of that year. Only Turquet, Granoff, and Leclaire grasped the true movement of a sequence that remained hidden from the others, but that lucidity did not allow them to master in any way the workings of a fate whose lucid witnesses and blind subjects they were. As such they each played their part one step ahead of their reciprocal partners: Such is the teaching to be derived from this great game of loser wins.

When he learned of the motion, Leclaire did not hesitate to evoke the situation of the Jews persecuted by their oppressors. For which reason Granoff sent him a rather mordant reply: "Need I remind you," he wrote, "that the anti-Semitic acts of exclusion were accompanied by the destruction of books and of their authors. And that they were an end in themselves. That they were inspired by no other consideration than their own destructiveness. It seems to me coherent with my sense of things that the reference chosen should be found in so radically destructive a register. And in addition that that reference should have occurred precisely to you. For indeed it may happen that the Jews become gripped by so great a fear of that anti-Semitic destructiveness that they refuse to perceive anti-Semitism, or that in order not to see it and to avoid their children's seeing it with their own eyes (as the parents did) they change their name." [145] To each his own way of being a Jew: Despite their disagreement, the two friends would remain on good terms, though they saw a bit less of each other. . . .

Two bits of testimony, written in the heat of events, prove that it is always possible to observe the history of one's time with a certain distance. The first comes from a woman, Eliane Amado Lévy-Valensi, who was residing in Israel at the time of the events, and the second from Louis Beirnaert, a great observer of institutional ways. Upon returning from Jerusalem at the end of October, Eliane went through her mail from the SFP, to which she belonged as a *stagiaire* and a student of Lagache. After congratulating Leclaire on his actions, she emphasized that she did not belong to the clan of the "Lacanized". "For many," she wrote, "Lacanianism has replaced all culture and (the eminently cultured) Lacan's system of references has been substituted for all efforts of assimilation and has engendered a kind of parrotry." She then noted that it was childish to insist to such an extent on an act of recognition: "In a hundred years everyone will be judged according to his works, and who will know if he was or wasn't affiliated with the IPA?" Finally, in order to illustrate her point, she commented on a passage from the Talmud: "If a city is under siege and in danger of perishing, and the besieger offers to lift his siege if a single man is delivered over to him, the city ought to perish rather than deliver the man. Even if that man is a criminal, even if he is to be executed the following day. These are extreme images: We are not in danger of death, and our designated victim is not guilty of any crime. The moral scheme nevertheless is the same." [146]

Twenty years later, that judgment has not at all aged and captures admirably the situation at the time.

On October 15, Louis Beirnaert sent Leclaire a dense text, written before he knew of Granoff's motion. Like Eliane Amado Lévy-Valensi, he mobilized the signifiers of his culture in order to analyze the situation. He was Christian and she Jewish, but their positions resembled each other in the perspective they brought to current history and in their common effort to interpret it. Instead of evoking "charisma," Beirnaert proposed a meditation on the status of psychoanalytic societies. In his view, their functioning implied the necessary existence of an articulation between an *initiatic* mode of knowledge, represented by the master's function, and a *scientific* mode determined by the orientation of research. Each mode imposes its limitation on the other. When the division is not respected, the society lapses at times into *ritual,* through an excess of initiation, at times into constituted knowledge, through an excess of scientificity. Beirnaert observed that in the SFP, the initiatic function was winning out over the other. But he added that instead of relegating the initiator to the shadows, it would be preferable to establish a structure allowing the two functions to operate simultaneously. "It will be seen," he wrote, "that these thoughts are neither Lacanian nor anti-Lacanian." [147] At bottom the author was recommending a solution which could not occur to the executive and which consisted not in fearing the "demon" of charisma but in limiting the master's omnipotence through an acknowledgment of his initiatic position. We need not be surprised that a Jesuit who had chosen to remain faithful to the Church should find it within himself, under such circumstances, to reassert the Freudian function of the master.

At the beginning of November, the notes taken by Perrier were distributed to the rank and file of the SFP. To his astonishment, André Berge discovered his name mentioned alongside those of Dolto and Lacan. Within the international joust, his situation had nothing to do with that of a "charismatic leader." Beyond his training by Laforgue, which was judged negatively, Berge represented only himself. He was a man of the past no longer participating in the rise of any psychoanalytic tendency whatever. He thus demanded an explanation from Turquet, who was quick to ascribe responsibility for the unfortunate incident to Leclaire. "Concerning Berge," he wrote, "you continue to err. Berge's name is not mentioned in our report and you have no right to quote us as having mentioned him. His name had been uttered on May 19, as part of your plan, but in order to exclude him from the list of training analysts. We offer no commentary on that plan, which comprised your wish to add Berge to the exclusion of Dolto and Lacan. . . . It is because we are aware that listening is an arduous task that we regret your circulation of documents in your society before verifying the facts. . . . It seems to us that you have made use of that report as a principal element in your polemics against us." Accused of betraying everyone, Leclaire responded sadly: "Leclaire is a convenient scapegoat; you are not the only ones attacking him. I realize this and I accept it without surprise. I simply think that nothing could be more natural and that it entered into the logic of my responsibility and of the action I have undertaken for me to become a target some day so that a change might take place." [148]

Not only did Turquet accuse Leclaire of wanting an additional head to fall, but he reproached him for asking himself for the exclusion of Lacan and Dolto. He could thus demonstrate that the wish for the elimination of all three had been shrewdly orchestrated by the president of the SFP, in agreement with the committee. In point of fact, the Berge affair was of a different nature from those involving Lacan and Dolto and was based on a misunderstanding. Prior to Edinburgh, and in the context of a reorganization of training procedures, Leclaire had asked Berge to normalize his technique and to make the transition to the standard four sessions per week. The latter informed him that he would in no way change his habits. Subsequently, Leclaire evoked the issue with the committee, which understood that the president was asking for the therapist's exclusion. That unfortunate incident offers eloquent evidence of the reciprocally duplicitous conditions under which the contest was played out.[149]

On November 1, Laplanche cut short his therapy, informing Lacan politely that he would remain his loyal disciple despite the positions he had taken in the motion. In a furor, Lacan reacted as with Audouard, accusing his student of exploiting him. At the time, Leclaire was preparing for a general meeting to be held November 10, in which all opinions were to be voiced. On the morning of the meeting, Lacan decided not to leave Guitrancourt: "My mere presence, in fact—I have weighed what I am about to say—would require the society's disavowal of the motion of so-called reprimand of October 14." [150]

On that day, Jean Laplanche took the floor on behalf of the five "movers" of July in order to explain at length the action they had taken: "We were struck," he said, "by the extent of the agreement . . . on the incompatibility between the functioning of a society of analysts and the maintenance as such of Lacan's position in our group. In order to ground such a judgment in truth, an analysis—which would not be 'wild,' and in which one would not find oneself dancing a ludicrous waltz with the murder-of-the-father, the society-of-brothers, and the liquidation-of-the-transference—is necessary. For it to be more than a mere approximation, it would have to go quite far—to the point of uncovering what a passionately assumed function of mastery signifies at the level of desire. . . ."[151] In concluding, the speaker announced the decisions he wished to submit to the following general meeting (scheduled for November 19), which was to take action on Lacan's future. He requested the collective resignation of the board, the election of a temporary commission charged with pursuing the dialogue with the committee, and finally the election of a new board representative of the majority. In addition, he implicitly accepted the motion of reprimand since he asked the study commission to remove Lacan's name from the list to be given future candidates for their training. It will thus be understood why Laplanche would become Lacan's preferred target for several years: He was the last of the dissidents to leave the couch on the rue de Lille and the first to endorse publicly the decision to exclude him.

The next day, with the backing of a majority of the board, Leclaire proposed a vote, to be held at the meeting of the nineteenth, on a text requesting that the motion of reprimand not be ratified. He knew that the game was over and that a majority of the members of the SFP would reject his proposal. Despite that fact, he participated in a meeting between the movers of the July motion and those of the October one, in the course of which a group was formed with the charge of reopening negotiations with Lacan. At stake was defining the conditions under which he could be reintegrated into the SFP, once his elimination from the training list had been accepted. Widlöcher was chosen for that delicate—and impossible—task. He contacted Lacan and the two examined together the list of SFP members who might succeed in so curious an enterprise. Lacan offered the name of two loyalists, while Widlöcher did not choose anyone. The two men decided to meet again, then, during their third encounter, Lacan allowed his fury full reign: "What do you want? To exclude me? For me not to undertake any more training analyses? You're absolutely insane, *mon cher*, to leave me at a time when I am about to become famous. Have you taken a good look at whom you are leaving? You are a boy without money and you are going to join up with a group of young fellows who are loaded, *sybarites* of psychoanalysis. I am not surprised by the attitude you all have: You are all physicians, and one can't do anything with physicians. In addition you are not Jews, and I made the mistake of betting on non-Jews. You all have problems with your fathers and that's why you're joining together against me. You should know that in the future my blows will not be directed against Lagache and the Favezes but against all of you who have profited from my teaching and betrayed me. The day you receive them, have no doubts as to where they are coming from. And now we have nothing further to say to each other." [152] Left breathless by that reply, but also freed from whatever remained of his fascination with the master, Widlöcher left the premises. Thereafter, he could allow his break to take political and juridical form.

On November 19, the motion proposed by Leclaire was rejected by a vote of 27 to 16 with one abstention. Irritated by Lacan's outbursts and by the pressures he was bringing to bear on his students, Jenny Aubry nevertheless chose the minority camp. As soon as the result was known, Leclaire informed Lacan of his defeat.

Banished from training, Lacan could have continued his teaching in the framework of the SFP. He chose, however, the path of exile, and on November 20, spoke for the last time at the amphitheater of the Hôpital Sainte-Anne. To consecrate the break, he prepared a lecture bearing the title of the seminar that had been scheduled for the following year, "The Names of the Father." Written in a febrile state, the text offers a singular contrast with the flamboyant statements the master customarily uttered at the decisive moments of his life. It reveals an abandonment of the baroque style of his maturity, which gives way to a syntax inspired by formal logic, a style that would come to dominate in the works of his old age—works that were essentially "oral." On that day Lacan was overwhelmed by defeat. He did not yet know either where he would find refuge or what society he would found. He thus began his address with a superb act of denial, announcing to his audience that he had no intention of doing anything theatrical. After once again dismissing Hegelian dialectic, and proclaiming the advent of a perspective grounded in formal logic, he took up anew, in theoretical terms, the themes of his diatribe against Widlöcher. Before the "falsity" of the Hegelian revolution, and in the face of a medical order from which he no longer expected anything, he effected a return to Freud's *Moses*, showing that psychoanalysis was in confrontation with the institution of the *Church:* an Augustinian tradition, on the one hand, and a Judaic or Biblical one on the other. In other words, he wanted to be the "leader" of a "new alliance" or "covenant" between a Christian identity and a Jewish identity, both of them "dissident" in relation to their respective Churches. Lacan was appealing to the Christians already present in the ranks of the SFP, and was reinitiating contact with that "Judaic" side of psychoanalysis which he had tended to forsake since the split of 1953. Then he ended his parable with a second act of denial which allowed him to situate his position within the split: "I am not here in a plea for myself. I should, however, say that—having, for two years, entirely confided to others the execution, within a group, of a policy, in order to leave to what I had to tell you its space and its purity—I have never, at any moment, given any pretext for believing that there was not, for me, any difference between yes and no." [153]

Against the democracy of the "barons" represented by Lagache and the rebellious juniors, Lacan mobilized around himself the still loyal minority, with its lack of academic and medical connections. Then he set out in search of a new site for his seminar. From Ferdinand Braudel, he received an invitation to the École pratique des hautes études, thus harking back to his experience with Kojève, and from Louis Althusser came the possibility of disseminating his teaching at the École normale supérieure, where a number of young politicized philosophers had been studying his texts for several months without any thought of belonging to the psychoanalytic guild. At the same time, he gave up on his notorious book in two parts and accepted, at the invitation of François Wahl, to have the essential part of his written works published by Éditions du Seuil. At the very moment of his greatest defeat, Lacan was harvesting the fruits of his finest triumph. Thirty years of labor devoted to psychoanalysis would henceforth make of him an established thinker: He was sixty-two years old.

The day after the assassination of President Kennedy, Gitelson learned of the board's collective resignation. Immediately thereafter, and in order to avoid repeating the errors of 1953, Leclaire specified that those who had just resigned would remain members of the SFP. Two weeks later, the majority party took power and elected Juliette Favez-Boutonier president, Lagache and Berge vice-presidents, Granoff secretary, Land scientific secretary, and Anzieu treasurer.

V. Guerrilla War and "Excommunication"

As of December 1963 a new force emerged within the third generation. In what was as yet a confused way, it tended to call itself the "Lacanian movement." Alongside the dissident juniors, on the one hand, and the simple loyalists, on the other, Lacanianism constituted itself "politically" in order to ensure an orthodox perpetuation of Freudianism. For the SFP, this movement played the role which had fallen in 1953 to the rebellious students. Composed of the mass of *stagiaires* and guest members, all of them without voting rights, it turned out to be numerically a majority and aimed at affirming the singularity of a practice and a doctrine centered on a master and a cause. Gradually, this Lacanian movement would contest the entirety of the negotiation process, then reject both Lagache's liberalism and the organizational principles of the IPA in order to pit against them an institutional model directly inspired by the first Viennese society. For it, the return to Freud had to be accompanied by a revaluation of the transferential and initiatic function of the master, and that at the expense of the oligarchy of the barons. In that perspective, affiliation with the IPA ceased being a major objective and an opening toward the world outside France was dictated by the self-recognition of a "Lacanian"—that is, "Freudian"—identity of psychoanalysis. Thus every arbitrary distinction between technique and doctrine, between personal therapy and training analysis, between the teaching and practice of an author was rejected in the name of a symbolic iden-tification with a living father, the incarnation of the law and the vehicle of a glorious reconquest. To the eyes of the young movement, the IPA seemed like a strange de-mon born out of Freud's embarrassments. Not only would it have to be fought, but its edicts would have to be rejected in order to promote a subversive force capable of transmitting, in its purity, the scandal of Freud's discovery as reinvented by Lacan.

At the very time Lacan was moving his pawns onto a larger chessboard, the Lacanian movement was constructing its political and ideological identity in a guer-rilla struggle that would lead to the definitive break-up of the SFP. Against the tra-ditional alliances, it mobilized the mass of nonvoters in order to destabilize the institution in its entirety. Militants of the cause, baggage carriers, semi-clandestine meetings, the denial of "the politics of the politicians," anonymous post boxes and underground friendships—such were the principal elements of the wintertime bar-ricade of December 11, which took on the name of the Groupe d'études de la psy-choanalyse (GEP). Jean Clavreul, a Breton and fanatic of boating, was its first offi-cial representative. We shall allow him to speak: "I underwent analysis with Lacan between 1948 and 1953 after a bout of pulmonary tuberculosis. That therapy saved me. Lacan came for sessions at my home or in the hospital when I was ill. Then I did a collective control with him, and after that a second period of analysis. With Lagache and Favez-Boutonier, I learned what psychoanalysis was not. I knew from the beginning that the negotiations could not succeed and, moreover, Lacan told me he didn't believe in them and simply let Leclaire do as he wished. In December 1963, I was designated secretary of the GEP because I was not compromised by any polit-ical deals. After the creation of the GEP, Lacan wrote these words to me: 'You are a residue; you know the value I attach to that word; this is your chance; seize it.'" [154]

At the time, Lacan was indeed banking on the "residues" of the SFP, that is, on the *stagiaires* in training and the students who had not rallied to any of the motions. He had no other choice. On those grounds, Piera Aulagnier, Audouard, Beirnaert and others participated with Leclaire and Perrier in the creation of the GEP. But their positions did not necessarily reflect those of Clavreul and the "base." On the whole, and like Lacan, they were favorable to negotiations and hostile to a break of which they knew it would reduce to naught the fruits of ten years of work. They had opted for a complete rupture at the time of the Stockholm directive, when they were forced to choose sides. They thus created the GEP to the extent that the division of the SFP into two extremist tendencies forced everyone to strengthen his position.

On December 17, as a Siberian coldwave continued its descent on Europe, Clavreul made public a program in which he announced that the GEP had already set up several work groups and was prepared to welcome all members of the SFP wishing to join it. The new majority board of the SFP immediately reacted by accusing the GEP of divisiveness and anonymous maneuvering: "What we have is a group constituting itself as the embryo of a society, organizing itself as such and already tending to impose a choice and a competition between its own activities and those of the SFP. Under the guise of a so-called nonpolitical and even antipolitical, 'purely psychoanalytic' project, we find an enterprise aimed at restoring definitively a factional dispute within our society and at posing all questions in terms of a struggle for power." [155]

The state of crisis continued through the Christmas vacation. Lacan was actively preparing his new seminar on "The Four Fundamental Concepts of Psycho-Analysis," reading Colerus's biography of Spinoza, and polishing the inaugural address he was to deliver January 15 at the Ecole ńormale śupérieure. After the vacation, Granoff announced to all the authors concerned that the texts chosen for the collective publication in English had finally been translated and were about to be submitted to the publisher. He himself had worked at length on that important effort. More intent than ever on a break, Lacan responded negatively to the project and withdrew his texts from the volume. Immediately thereafter, Leclaire, who had approved of the project enthusiastically, asked Laplanche to come to a decision concerning the withdrawal of their jointly written article on the unconscious. The latter complied out of friendship and withdrew in turn his text, followed by Lagache, Dolto, and Valabrega. "Under these conditions," wrote J.-L. Lang, "the board, at its meeting of January 13, has decided not to pursue any further a project a large majority of whose authors do not deem it desirable to complete in the present circumstances." [156] Thus did a project requiring years of effort come to ruin in a single week. On this score, the split ended in catastrophe. Granoff retains a bitter memory of it all, "I worked with Laplanche at translating what Lacan had published and it all had a scandalous end." [157]

In order to make his change of course more striking, and find, in the very impasse of his situation, the strength for a new intervention, Lacan invited a number of notables to the inaugural session. Among them Claude Lévi-Strauss and Henri Ey. The former symbolized the golden age of French structuralism, a period to which Lacan had just attached ten years of his teaching, and the latter bore witness, not only to a loyal friendship, but to the presence of psychiatry, which had always been inscribed at the heart of the relations between the two men. The Dussane lecture hall, where Lacan's *coup de théâtre* took place, bears the name of an actress who had once given diction lessons to the École's students. Standing behind his desk, Lacan declaimed in grave tones slightly reminiscent of de Gaulle. Without mentioning Althusser, to whom he owed this new connection, he thanked Robert Flacelière, the director of the ENS, and Fernand Braudel, whose absence he regretted. Then he paid homage to Lévi-Strauss and Ey. In that connection, he evoked the publication of his text, *La Cure-type:* "It will be all the more easy, since he is present, for me to evoke the veritable relentlessness with which that article was removed from the encyclopedia, so extreme that he himself, concerning whom the sympathy he bears me is common knowledge, was, in the end, impotent to put a halt to that operation by an editorial committee on which were to be found, precisely, a number of psychoanalysts." [158]

The old lion's last battle had thus begun. Thereafter, he would transform his defeat into a victory and direct his blows against the entirety of a community which had signed the order banishing him. The room was silent. In the first row sat the court of the faithful along with members of the family. Further back, spread out through whatever seats were available, the militants of the GEP. At the back, the students of the ENS, impatient to hear the man whose texts they had begun to decipher. A few society ladies, draped in furs and silk scarves, prepared to take notes on personalized stationery. They stared at the others, who also looked at them. From that day on, over a period of five years, the Salle Dussane would be the privileged meeting place of a new Freudian France, one more cultured, more philosophical, and more influential than the previous one, a formidable theoretical hotbed open to the intellectual youth of the country.

Quite surprised, Claude Lévi-Strauss attended his first session of the seminar. He would not get over it: "What was striking was the kind of radiant influence emanating from both Lacan's physical person and from his diction, his gestures. I have seen quite a few shamans functioning in exotic societies, and I rediscovered there a kind of equivalent of the shaman's power. I confess that, as far as what I heard went, I didn't understand. And I found myself in the middle of an audience that seemed to understand. . . ." [159]

Before moving to matters theoretical, Lacan situated his place in the psychoanalytic movement for his listeners. In superbly turned phrases, he compared himself to Spinoza, thus renewing his bond with a philosopher who had influenced his adolescence and early works. Yet he did not evoke Spinoza's thought, but rather the events of July 27, 1656, the date on which the philosopher was excluded from the Jewish community of Amsterdam. Lacan affirmed that Spinoza was *excommunicated* from the synagogue, being made the object of a *herem* or *major excommunication,* then of a *schamatta* or exclusion *without possibility of return.* According to the speaker, that double ordeal would correspond precisely to the banishment pronounced against him by the IPA and ratified by the SFP: "I am not telling you—but it would not be impossible—that the psychoanalytic community is a Church. And yet, uncontestably, the question arises of what within it offers a kind of echo of religious practice." [160] Lacan also said that within the whole affair, his role was that of someone who had been "dealt out" and that the "comic" aspect of that role did not belong to the register of excommunication.

In order to appreciate the significance of that magisterial analogy and gauge the status of Lacan's exclusion for the history of psychoanalysis, one ought first to retrace the matter of young Baruch Spinoza's "excommunication." Recent scholarship, published long after the year 1963, has established that the philosopher's

1 Jenny Roudinesco in Professor Heuyer's clinic

2 Henri Ey, Montreal 1951

3 Sacha Nacht, 1944

4 Daniel Lagache

5 Wladimir Granoff, 1960

6   Serge Leclaire

7   Georges Politzer

8   Françoise Dolto with her family

(9) Jacques Lacan, about 1907, with Emile, Alfred, and Madeleine. (10) Jacques Lacan as an adolescent, with Madeleine and Marc-François. (11) Jacques Lacan about 1925.

12

13

(12) The interns' common room at Sainte-Anne in 1932: Jacques Lacan,
Henri Ey, Pierre Mâle, Julien Rouart.   (13) Guitrancourt, 1955:
Martin Heidegger, Kostas Axelos, Jacques Lacan, Jean Beaufret,
Mrs. Heidegger, Sylvia.

14   Jacques Lacan and Sylvia

15   Stockholm, summer of 1963: Jacques Lacan, Serge Leclaire,
François Perrier

16   Leaving the seminar: Jacques Lacan and Philippe Sollers

herem was the work of the "Mahamad," the *lay* authority governing the Jewish community of Amsterdam. It was subsequently ratified by the rabbinate. The Mahamad's agents were called *parnassim,* and Spinoza's father was a *parna* until his death in 1654. In the Old Testament, *herem* is used to doom a being or object to annihilation or destruction. Between the second and fifth centuries, it became a punishment graduated in accordance with the seriousness of the sin committed and could be carried to its extreme degree as *schamatta.* In no way was the *herem* comparable to Catholic excommunication, which was a prerogative of the sovereign pontiff, that is, of canon law. Formerly *major excommunication,* such as that aimed at Luther, for example, was a simple exclusion from the Catholic community, while *minor excommunication* forbade or condemned certain activities. No punishment *without return* was ever pronounced, since repentance has always been inscribed at the heart of Christian tradition. After 1917, because of a reform in canon law, the distinction between the two forms of castigation was abolished and only the case of excommunication as exclusion remained.

Although he was born a Jew and never converted, Spinoza was linked, through his origins, to that Marrano community which had fled the Iberian peninsula to escape the Inquisition. The Marranos were *conversos,* both "new Christians" and "new Jews." In Spain and Portugal, they had become Catholic under duress even as they continued to practice their faith in secret. Upon emigration to Amsterdam, they converted to Judaism, but remained culturally former Christians. It was within that ideological and religious melting-pot that Spinozan deism, which would lead to atheism, was born. In that respect, Marranoism symbolized the transition from the old faith to the new philosophy. The subject of endless conversions, the Marrano subject was everywhere a foreigner, in search of identity, breaking with himself and prisoner simultaneously of his Christian past and his Jewish future. In certain respects, Freudianism is similar to Spinozanism. It was constituted as a universalism on cultural soil in which the quest for identity played a catalytic role within a system of repudiations and conversions. At bottom, the fate of a Karl Krauss or an Otto Weininger is not far from resembling that of a Juan de Prado or an Uriel da Costa: the same laceration of conscience, the same fascination with the destruction and renewal of the world, the same suicidal aspirations, etc.[161] At a distance of two centuries, all the ingredients were reassembled for an unprecedented philosophical explosion. Freud's definitive abandonment of the Jewish religion evokes Spinoza's dissidence; neither the philosopher nor the neurologist were converts, fanatics, missionaries, or ascetics, but both discovered, within the ideals of their age, the conditions for a kind of universal dissidence. Both were marked, in their upbringing, by the practice of a "hidden language," of allusions and feints.

The *herem* came at a time when Spinoza had not yet published anything. Yet the young man was already contesting the soul's immortality, the divine character of Scripture, and the existence of Providence. In brief, he rejected the fundamental principles of the Jewish and Christian faith. In order to avoid a scandal, the *parnassim* proposed two kinds of accommodation to him: "If Spinoza had wanted to," Henri Méchoulan has written, "he could have retired to a small neighboring city, endowed with a nest egg furnished by the community, or he could have continued pretending to practice a faith he no longer possessed. But Spinoza refused to compromise. In breaking with the religion of his fathers, Spinoza wanted to undertake a labor of universal import." [162]

Because he refused to pretend, Spinoza himself implemented the break that would lead him to Spinozanism. Put differently, he accepted and ratified his own exclusion in order to establish thereby the conditions for a future elaboration of his doctrine. That is why the *herem* implied a *nonreturn* on both sides. For the judges, it was accompanied by violent maledictions which are found in no other *herem* of the period: "With the aid of the judgment of the holy and the angels, we exclude, banish, curse, and execrate Baruch Spinoza with the consent of the entire holy community, in the presence of our holy books. . . . May he be accursed by day; may he be accursed by night. May he be accursed during his sleep and during his wakefulness. . . . May the Eternal never forgive him. . . . May his name be effaced from this world forever. . . . Know that you are to have with Spinoza neither written nor verbal communication. No service is to be rendered him, and no man is to approach within four cubits of him. Let no man remain under the same roof with him and no man read any of his writings." [163]

In comparing his exclusion to Spinoza's *herem*, Lacan made use, without mentioning his sources, of Pastor Colerus's biography, published in 1705, twenty-eight years after the philosopher's death. In the 1960s that work was a major reference for students of Spinoza. Lacan was thus well-informed by the standards of the day and adapted to his own use the anecdotes found in the biography. Now that work was at the origin of the legend which transformed Spinoza's (lay) *herem* into a (religious) "excommunication." Colerus, in fact, gives a Catholic version of the philosopher's exclusion by attributing the sentence to the rabbis and not to the Mahamad. In addition, he makes use of the term *schamatta* in order to circumscribe the notion of an excommunication *without possibility of return*—which, in fact, exists in neither the *herem* nor the Christian tradition. If we restrict ourselves to the facts that have been established at present, we may say that Spinoza was excluded from the Jewish community without being "excommunicated." He was not the victim of the *schamatta*, since that punishment was not invoked in his case. As for the notion of *without return* appended to the *herem*, it did not stem from a supplementary punishment, but from a concrete situation in which the exclusion was both desired by the Mahamad and implicitly accepted by the philosopher.

In 1963, Lacan could not have had access to these subtleties. Through Colerus, he took a fable for historical reality and invoked for his own use a Spinozan metaphor of excommunication. If Colerus's interpretation is accepted, Lacan's exclusion is not similar to Spinoza's *herem*. The Edinburgh "Recommendations," the Stockholm "directive," and the October motion were the only official sentences in the entire affair. And they contain no penalty resembling an excommunication without return. They dealt with Lacan's training and not his teaching. He was excluded from all training activity without ever being excluded from the psychoanalytic community. He was invited to remain a member of the SFP and to pursue his teaching there on the condition that it not be validated as part of formal training. The notions of *without return, perpetuity,* and *danger* were contained in the second Turquet report, which was not published, and in the discussions at the Hotel Westminster. They were not part of any "official" document. In other words, the IPA carefully avoided placing Lacan in the position of a martyr or an object of excommunication. It hoped that while remaining a recognized theoretician, he would agree on his own, and without any unseemliness, to give up his training functions. For that reason, the executive was embarrassed by the dissemination of Perrier's notes, for they betrayed a process of excommunication.

Lacan outfoxed the IPA. He used for his own benefit an unofficial truth: the discussions at the Hotel Westminster and Perrier's notes. He could thus identify with Colerus's Spinoza and claim that he had been the victim not of mere banishment, but of an exclusion without possibility of return from the psychoanalytic community. In order to transform his defeat into a victory, he announced that *he had been dealt out*. He could thus conceal his participation in Leclaire's political efforts from his audience and appear as a pure theorist, exempt from all compromise with his oppressors. Since everyone at the SFP knew that he had not wanted to yield to all the demands of the IPA, the congruity with Spinoza's case was acceptable: The philosopher, after all, had also refused the compromises offered him.

Ten years after the *Rome Discourse,* Lacan thus replaced the adventure of a baroque reconquest with the metaphor of Spinoza's excommunication. Through it, and beyond the SFP's "Christian" identity, he renewed contact with the great Freudian dimension of a Jewish dissidence. The orthodox sovereign became a rebel leader, and the rebel leader, from the height of his isolated universalism, could then proclaim himself sovereign of a new Diaspora in conformity with the militant ideals of psychoanalysis at its inception. In 1953, Lacan had regretfully left an internationalist society marked by its belonging to the "Jewish" identity of psychoanalysis; a decade later, he summoned dissidents of every stripe back to his side in order to start out in search of new conquests. Christians dissenting from their church, Marxists dissenting from their party, Jews dissenting from their synagogue, and students dissenting from the IPA: All would join in the fight against "official religion," the symptom of every "deviation." All were called on to become "Lacanians," for better or for worse.

In that sense, the use of the metaphor of excommunication went beyond Colerus's text. Without knowing more recent scholarship on Spinoza's *herem*, Lacan interpreted *in Spinozan terms* his historic break with the international community. He was neither excommunicated nor excluded from his society, but constrained to make an unacceptable choice. The IPA wanted to transform him into a master without students, without legacy, and without the right to participate in training. In response, he himself activated a process of excommunication and a dissidence without possibility of return. Thus he founded Lacanianism "politically," in the same manner that Spinoza opened the field of Spinozan philosophy.

In the fall of 1963, three solutions were available to Lacan: changing his practice, accepting his exclusion, or becoming a dissident. If he had chosen the first, he would have pretended to submit by repudiating his theory of therapy. If he had opted for the second, he would have signed his death certificate by acknowledging his own inadequacy for training. In choosing the third path, he was obliged to found a "Lacanian" school of psychoanalysis. But on precisely that score a contradiction emerged that would be aggravated throughout the period that followed. As we know, the originality of Lacan's reading of Freud lay in the affirmation of its Freudian orthodoxy and in its rejection of all post-Freudian "deviations." From that perspective, it was possible to become a dissident only on condition that one reinvent the Freudian breakthrough (and no other one than that). Now in creating a school in his own name, Lacan found himself constrained to admit that he was Lacanian, or at least to accredit the political existence of something called "Lacanianism." Through that gesture of self-recognition, the movement entered into contradiction with the doctrine sustaining it, which claimed to be Freudian. The movement would take sixteen years to realize that this contradiction was inscribed at the heart of its founding gesture. At the end of that journey, and of the "time needed to understand," the movement would opt for its own dissolution.

Barely had Lacan finished uttering his last sentence than a rather singular voice was raised in the shadows of the Salle Dussane. It came from a young man of rosy complexion and rather childlike bearing. He challenged the master in a tone of grandiloquent and arrogant preciosity, but tinged with fragility. The voice was erudite; it inquired into the philosophical destiny of Lacan's work and contrasted with the customary comments of auditors at the seminar. The young man still had a long way to go. His name was Jacques-Alain Miller.

After the inaugural seminar of January 15, the members of the GEP pursued their divisive tactics. The members of the majority, for their part, felt compelled to react, and when Clavreul presented his candidacy for the rank of titular member, it was denied categorically by the board. Lacan, Leclaire, Perrier, Reverchon-Jouve, Dolto, Aubry, Safouan, and Aulagnier immediately protested the decision and requested that their declaration be included in the official minutes of the Society. During this period, without informing Valabrega, Pontalis assumed the directorship of the journal *La Psychanalyse*. Armed with a note from Favez-Boutonier, he showed up at the offices of the Presses universitaires de France and asked for the galley sheets of the issue about to be published. Valabrega protested vehemently: "Allow me to inform you," he wrote to Juliette, "that if there is to be a change of editorial leadership (in the event it should be decided by the board) this way of proceeding in no way accommodates the interests of our society. The most elementary prudence dictates that we not make our publisher witness to our internal strife and that confusion not be created in the services with which we have been working for years in an atmosphere of trust." [164]

That letter remained without response and did not prevent Pontalis from succeeding in his maneuver. Behind the back of the editor, he introduced spelling changes in the eighth issue, entitled *Phantasme, rêve, réalité*. Valabrega had chosen the spelling "phantasme" in order to specify a strictly psychoanalytic use of the term. But since there was disagreement within the SFP over which spelling to retain, he had written a note with Perrier explaining the editors' decision: "The problem of the spelling of the word *phantasme* remains irreducible in the literature of psychoanalysis in France. . . . We have thus decided to allow each author his preferred spelling." [165] In June, a circular distributed by the majority tendency of the SFP announced that issue no. 8 would appear in its initial form with the table of contents agreed on in December 1963. At the time of publication, however (October 1964), Valabrega noticed two changes. The cover bore the title *Fantasme, rêve, réalité*. In the note he had written with Perrier, the word "phantasme" had been replaced by "fantasme." Outraged at this denial of his freedom of speech, he dashed off an official communiqué in which he specified that the modifications had been effected without consultation of the signatories. Then he sent a personal letter to Pontalis, accusing him of violating traditional editorial norms and the respect due texts written by others. He requested that his protests be made known to the members of the SFP subscribing to the journal. That appeal would not be honored and *La Psychanalyse* would cease publication after its eighth issue.

Thereafter Granoff would devote all his energy to wresting affiliation from the IPA bureaucracy. And for him the match was far from being won. In a letter to Turquet, he foresaw the future with the hopelessness of a defeated man. Instead of analyzing the situation lucidly, he calculated the intentions of his adversaries and believed that the GEP would succeed in bringing the "movers" back into the Lacanian fold if there was any delay in the granting of affiliation. And with that, he began reasoning in the manner he ascribed to his rivals, believing himself that the members of the GEP would return to the IPA if the executive were to give them any assurances. He consequently asked Turquet to rush through the procedures for affiliating. "We have done the undoable for France," he wrote, "the unforgivable: Try for once to double up and feel like a Frenchman. The only way to save the situation is through unabashed cynicism. It's horrible, but it works. For once, 'crime' must pay. Quickly and with a huge dividend. The feeling in the GEP is now quite overt: Those who follow Granoff do so because they think they will be affiliated. If Granoff doesn't succeed, they'll come back to us. They're virtually deserters. This is a hundred per cent true. . . . If the Lagache group gains affiliation, and does so immediately, the GEP (Lacan's group) will be dismantled within a year and all that will survive from it will be Lacan and a few supporters." [166] At this juncture, Wladimir turned out to be completely wrong. Not only did the GEP not dream of restoring representatives of the rival camp to its ranks, but it viewed itself as the expression of a Lacanianism at last rid of all compromise with the IPA. In that sense, no affiliation, however precipitous, could cause it to retreat, since its existence as a group was the result of the gradual constitution of a Lacanian movement within the SFP. As the new year dawned, no act of recognition could any longer affect the historical fate of Lacanianism. Lacan had been wrong once about his students and the IPA. He had thought that the former would support him and that the latter would listen to him, but with the GEP he had no further opportunity to err. While he was losing his American battle, he had already won his campaign in France. And he owed that handsome victory not only to himself, but to the innovative force of his teaching and the students it had drawn to him.

Soon intrigues began to proliferate in both camps. While the Lacanian movement consolidated its base in France, the "expanded" board met in London with the committee in order to work out the conditions of a new affiliation that would, in practice, exclude the Lacanians. In April, Clavreul made public a letter from the president and informed students of the extant situation. Each group wanted the society's name for itself. In order to resolve the juridico-political imbroglio, Gitelson proposed to the majority that the status of "study group" be withdrawn from the SFP and a new "French Study Group" (FSG) be formed grouping the partisans of the IPA. These included six titular members and sixteen associates. On May 10, the agreement was finalized and the FSG officially created. On May 26, in complete secrecy, it took on the title "Association psychanalytique de France" (APF). From that date on, the SFP's existence was no more than a formality, and the split had been declared *de facto* by the majority members. "The move toward the APF," Granoff has written, "constituted a double maneuver. On the one hand, it meant *not* giving oneself a master, not becoming a disciple of Lacan, and, on the other, it was possible to entertain the thought that gradually one was moving toward Freud, who was not quite as dead and buried as the other—non-Lacanian—society would have it. . . . For Lacan's ex-disciples who joined the APF, things might be formulated as follows: 'Analysis is greater than Lacan, who was my analyst, and who no longer counts for me. Only psychoanalysis counts.' For how could one not take into consideration the fact that the Association was in the last analysis invented by disciples of Lacan, who was their analyst one and all, with the exception of the individual who underwrote the whole operation, Lagache, and of the one who brought it off, that is, myself?" [167]

At the general meeting of June 9, Daniel Widlöcher took the floor in his capacity as Parisian correspondent of the FSG. He recalled the activities of the SFP, and announced that the executive had withdrawn its recognition of it on May 10. Without mentioning the (still clandestine) existence of the AFP, he made official the creation of the FSG. On that occasion he put his name to the last deed consecrating his break with Lacan. Beside himself, Lacan rose and exclaimed: "I now know that the hot line between Chicago and Paris passes by way of Widlöcher." [166] Then he left the room, taking his loyalists with him. Three days later, Jean Clavreul denounced the plots hatched by his adversaries: "I believe I can deduce the reason for which this individual [Widlöcher] was chosen as our mentor from a bit of information I received from Dr. Widlöcher himself. This winter he gave a course on the psychology of business. . . . It was then that our Widlöcher, moving from the psychoanalysis of dealing to a dealing (away) of psychoanalysis, managed to do what certain businessmen do when a company is in trouble. Its bankruptcy is precipitated at the same time that another company is constituted that takes over all the assets of the first one." [169] Naturally the author of those attacks did not mention the fact that Lacan was in the process of drawing up statutes for his new school. But was it possible for him to be unaware of them?

Piera Aulagnier, for her part, injected a note of humor into her diatribe against her colleague. "Monsieur Widlöcher," she wrote, "during the reading of the manifesto announcing the creation of this new body, assured us that it was open to anyone desiring to participate in it; all candidacies, of course, being subject to approval from Chicago." [170]

On June 21, 1964, at the home of François Perrier, near the Closerie des Lilas, Lacan read in the presence of a crowd of his disciples the manifesto through

which he founded—"alone and as alone as he had always been"—the École française de psychanalyse. Lacan was not alone and his school would later take the name
"École freudienne de Paris." We will see why and under what conditions. It was with
that gesture, Spinozan in its will to dissidence and de Gaulle–like in its sense of
theater, that the history of the second split in the French psychoanalytic movement
came to an end.

On October 1, without consulting each other, Granoff and Leclaire each sent
Juliette Favez-Boutonier an official letter requesting that the SFP be juridically dissolved. This was officially accomplished in January 1965. At the time of liquidation
and nostalgia, the two veterans of the troika became anew the accomplices they had
once been and closed up shop with all due serenity. Six months later, at the Amsterdam congress, the APF was officially integrated into the empire amidst an avalanche
of applause. Gitelson had died, and Gillespie had replaced him. The IPA's wheel
continued to turn. Before sipping his champagne, the Englishman addressed the last
word to those assembled: "Really wonderful." [171]

In the fall, Rudolph Loewenstein crossed the Atlantic to attend the Congress
of Romance Language Psychoanalysts. One festive evening, he was chatting with
the veterans of the second generation, Pierre Mâle, Daniel Lagache, Sacha Nacht.
They all thought he had aged somewhat, but that he remained as jovial and irresistible as ever. Together they evoked memories of the heroic days: the Princess's furors,
Pichon's eloquence, Raymond de Saussure's seductiveness. . . . All were delighted at
the new alliance which was being formed after ten years of struggle, the return of so
many lost sheep to the fold. But where, then, had Lacan gone, so late at night? The
story does not say. . . .

Part Three

Freudian France in Full Array

Theories and schools, like microbes and globules, devour each other
and, through their struggle, ensure the continuation of life.

Marcel Proust

8 The École Freudienne de Paris: The Reconquest

I. The New French Intellectual Landscape

Until the Bonneval Colloquium of 1960, the French psychoanalytic movement transformed itself from within without modifying the intellectual landscape of the country. But soon, such transformation would leave its imprint on the soil of a newly Freudian France in which psychoanalysis tended to become a major component of the national culture. With the development of the so-called "human" sciences, the ideals of Frenchness seemed to have been definitively supplanted by a dream of scientificity which affected every therapeutic institution. The aspiration to mental health became an increasingly ramifying phenomenon. The growth of dispensaries, outpatient treatment, and different medico-psycho-pedagogical centers forced the psychoanalytic movement to organize on institutional bases that were broader, more "juridical," more anonymous, and less elitist. Psychoanalysis was by then a mass practice, and the societies taking that expansion into account were constrained to adapt to the new norms. For better or for worse, Freud's work was tolerated, if not accepted, and the notions of sex and the unconscious were no longer objects of scandal. Psychoanalytic collections, books, and journals proliferated, allowing Freudianism and neo-Freudianism to become established by means of a variety of publishing channels. There began, as well, to be much talk of the "Freudian revolution," as may be seen from Marthe Robert's beautiful book of that name, published by Payot, in which, for the first time in French, as the result of a series of radio broadcasts, the Judeo-Viennese psychoanalytic situation was evoked as such. In the universities, students were reading Freud's texts and professors quoting them to fit the themes of the day: youth liberation, contraception, sex education, etc.

Paradoxically, the psychoanalysts remained in something of a guild-oriented ghetto, and it was under the aegis of the medical ideal on the one side and psychology on the other that the official movement achieved establishment. Forced to catch up in relation to the organizational norms of the IPA, psychoanalytic France during the second half of the century sought to recruit qualified therapists. In that respect, the two splits occurring at an interval of ten years and pivoting on questions of training marked the advance of a modernist evolution of psychoanalysis: Expansion and anonymity were the two traits of that development. At the center of this context, Lacan's role was simultaneously that of an unavoidable monument and a symbol of dissidence. Not only was he the only theorist of stature psychoanalytic France could lay claim to, but over the years his name tended to replace Freud's as the symptom of both a resistance to and validation of psychoanalysis per se. With Lacanianism, the Viennese discovery again became a theoretical scandal at a time when such was no longer the case for Freudianism. And that scandal took on all the greater value in that it allowed the new psychoanalytic generations and the country's intellectual elite to take up arms against obscurantism and the established order. It was as though the baroque orthodoxy of Lacan's doctrine allowed for a sudden reengagement of the battle for implantation on philosophical, literary, and political grounds: an anti-imperialist, anti-psychologizing, and anti-medical battle.

As far as personal destinies are concerned, the fate of the minor masters of psychoanalysis varied according to generation and individual talent. In the face of the monument Lacan had become, Nacht and Lagache were the principal losers in this story, since they had no confirmed place within French culture. Their written work began to be read less, and the trace of their role in the saga was commensurate with whatever a collective memory chose to recall. In addition, within the new conjuncture of the 1960s, they were both marginalized within their respective societies, one of which, the APF, was for the most part composed of former Lacanians who had broken with their leader, and the other of which, the SPP, was organized as a social-democratic party embracing a gamut of tendencies ranging from liberalism to conservatism. Generally speaking, it may be said that at a time when Lacan had achieved a striking position at the heart of French culture, the two societies recognized by the IPA withdrew into a certain academicism and shut themselves off, at least until 1968, from the questionings of the country's intellectual youth. Both were about to undergo—like the EFP—significant institutional crises. Only Henry Ey continued to play, within his field, a role comparable to Lacan's. These two men who had traversed the epic of Surrealism together would each in his own way leave an indelible mark on the psychiatric science of their era. At their deaths, a splendid conception of clinical practice would go under, lock, stock, and barrel, beneath the weight of the alleged pharmacological revolution, after having been significantly undermined by the challenges of the antipsychiatric movement. Through their symbolic presence and their severity toward libertarian attitudes, they were able to delay in France the unfurling of the ideals of neurobiology, the modern form assumed by an old obscurantism.

Surrealism had introduced psychoanalysis by way of literature against the prevailing Germanophobia. The structuralist discourse of the years 1962–67 seized Freudianism in a context in which the Algerian war had caused a large segment of the intelligentsia to join the struggle against colonialism. Through its general openness to the Third World, its revolutions and its oppressed of every stripe, psychoanalysis appeared at times as a science of the universal capable of explaining the unconscious functioning of societies, and at others as a theory of a "decentered" subject assimilable to the militant values of a proletariat bereft of—or "ex-centric" to—culture. From then on, it could supplant Sartrean commitment by advocating, against a humanism of guilty consciences, the revelation of a structural truth whose incidences were universal.

Since that new way of apprehending the Viennese discovery was occurring at a time in which Lacanianism was constituting itself as an institutional movement, the former resistance to Freudianism was transformed into a resistance to Lacanianism through which the contradictory issues at stake in psychoanalysis's final expansion were polarized. Put differently, in the French context of structuralism, it gradually became impossible to speak of Freud without referring to Lacan. And even when the prevailing philosophical, literary, and psychoanalystic discourses skirted

Lacan's work, that avoidance itself was an allusion to the permanent presence of Lacanianism at the heart of French culture. By virtue of that principle, the École freudienne de Paris was doomed from its inception to being oversized, for its very existence bore witness to the effective progress registered by Lacan's orthodox re-elaboration. Now that progress tended to represent the entirety of a process of expansion affecting the other societies, even when they sought to resist it in order to preserve their appearance of unity or their identity as a guild. Thus, starting in 1964, the history of psychoanalysis in France became subordinate to that of Lacanianism, understood as a symptom of a final rooting of Freudianism in French soil. This does not mean that the non-Lacanian societies did not possess their specific internal history; but that history must be interpreted through that of the Lacanian movement, which occupied thereafter the motor position in relation to which the other movements were obliged to determine their course, occasionally at the price of silence.

In the middle of this great expansion, which unfurled right through the end of the 1970s, the student uprising of May 1968 took place. It was the harbinger of structuralism's decline even as it favored a new golden age of French variants of Freudianism and anti-Freudianism by way of feminism, antipsychiatry, Freudo-Marxism, and a libertarian Maoism. The wave of contestation did not prevent the expansionism; on the contrary, it opened new doors in the universities to psychoanalysis. But in traversing both the Lacanian movement as well as other psychoanalytic institutions, it provoked a crisis that resulted in a generalized splintering of the realms of Freudianism along with a redistribution of the territories it occupied: dissolution and dispersion for the EFP, conflicts and defensive explosions for the other societies.

During the four years preceding the barricades of the rue Gay-Lussac, the light of Austerlitz still shone on a Freudian France enjoying its triumph. But during the twelve years following that event, against the expanding horizon, the somber plain of a psychoanalytic Waterloo could be intuited. It was made all the more sad by the tragic death throes of Lacan and his school.

Expelled from the international psychoanalytic movement, Lacan's work came to occupy a central place in the French structuralist adventure. Ten years after the most fertile phase of its principal elaboration, the return to Freud encountered the preoccupations of something of a "structuralist" philosophy born of the inquiries of Saussurean linguistics and itself became the spearhead of an antiphenomenological revolt. The doctrinal effervescence of the 1960s, which crystallized around the works of Louis Althusser, Roland Barthes, Michel Foucault, and Jacques Derrida, and which took as its object of study the primacy of language, antihumanism, deconstruction, or archaeology, resembled in certain respects the Surrealist explosion of the interwar years. But instead of situating itself initially within the framework of avant-garde literary journals, it took shape within the institution of a university preparing the grounds for the student rebellion of May 1968.

There was no true unity of structuralist thought, but rather an intellectual tendency. In France, Lévi-Strauss, Lacan, Benveniste, and Dumézil were the first, in age and in date of publication, to draw inspiration from the structural method. Although he repeatedly referred to Lévi-Straussian anthropology, Lacan used linguistics in a less mediated manner than Lévi-Strauss, who merely borrowed a model. After them, Foucault, Derrida, and Althusser also made use of the notions of sign, language, system, and structure, but in a quite different manner. The history of French structuralism may thus be summarized in terms of two fertile theoretical moments. In a first phase, linguistics served as a pilot science in the fields of psychoanalysis and ethnology, and in a second, there emerged a whole barrage of works, quite different from each other, which shared the common concerns of evaluating philosophically the status of the "human sciences" and of positing the primacy of language over thought, system over experience, sign or letter over subject, and unconscious synchrony over diachronic action. Within that second configuration, in which the structuralist phenomenon took concrete form, Lacanian doctrine appeared as a *scientific* opening to Freud's discovery. "The point of rupture," wrote Foucault, "came the day that Lévi-Strauss for societies and Lacan for the unconscious showed us that 'meaning' was probably a mere surface effect, a shimmering froth, and that what traversed us in the depths, what came before us, what sustained us in time and space, was system." [1]

It was no doubt no accident that within the antiphenomenological fracas, the interest in Lacanianism first came from Marxist thought, in the person of Louis Althusser. A philosopher raised as a Catholic, he began his discovery of Freud's work at the end of the war, after five years of captivity. During the same period, he joined the Communist Party and met Hélène Ritmann, a woman of Russian-Jewish origin. She was eight years his senior and became his lifelong companion. Together they lived at the École normale supérieure (ENS). He was an *agrégé* and *répétiteur,* she a sociologist.

Hélène had been in the Resistance under the name of Legotien. Because of a sinister and trivial matter involving silk stockings and the whims of Elsa Triolet, she was cast out of the party by Aragon. During the Occupation, at Nice, she had known Lacan and told him her life story beneath the palm trees of the Promenade des Anglais. He decided to convince her to become a psychoanalyst. She declined the invitation. . . . [2]

At a time when the anti-Freudian campaign was moving full blast through the Communist movement, Louis Althusser encountered the psychoanalytic adventure by way of the mirror of his own madness. At times he suffered from depression, at others he felt prey to bouts of feverish exaltation. In search of treatment, he went to Pierre Mâle, who had him interned at Sainte-Anne with a diagnosis of dementia praecox. Unnoticed by all his overseers, Hélène came to see him—she was accustomed to clandestine practices. After a few days, Ajuriaguerra contradicted Mâle's diagnosis and spoke for the first time of manic-depressive psychosis. Althusser underwent electro-shock treatment, then submitted to narcotherapy for a period of sixteen years. On twenty occasions he would be confronted with the saga of the "great confinement," as Foucault called it: from Sainte-Anne to Meudon, from Saint-Mandé to Épinay, from the Vallée-aux-Loups to Soisy. Injections, drugs, white coats—such was his routine, his refrain. [3] "In our philosopher's memory," he wrote concerning the Zhdanov years, "this period remains that of armed intellectuals, tracking down error in all its lairs, a time of philosophers without works, which we were, but making politics out of every work, and cutting their way though the world with a single blade—the arts, literatures, philosophies, and sciences—with the pitiless incision of class division; a time which is still epitomized in caricature by a slogan, its banner flapping in the void: 'bourgeois science, proletarian science.' "[4]

Contemporaneous with the de-Stalinization initiated by the Khrushchev era, the works of Louis Althusser and his students may be situated in the framework of the Soviet-Chinese controversy and the division of the Communist movement into two camps. According to the philosopher, a student of Bachelard, Marx's thought constituted an unprecedented discovery. It opened up a new continent to human knowledge, the continent of history. In order to grasp the meaning of that discovery, *a symptomatic reading* of Marx's texts would have to be elaborated, allowing for the extrication of their unarticulated or untranslatable dimension. The notion of a symptomatic reading was related both to Brechtian distancing and to Freudian clinical practice. It effected a dialectical choice within an irreducible virtual structural set. It denounced the illusion of essence, depth, or completeness in favor of the reality of division, breaking-points, and maturation. In that sense, it was opposed to *literal reading,* which claimed to be innocent or free of bias, and to *interpretative* or *hermeneutic reading,* which pretended to reveal the hidden essence of a text—its "subconscious." Louis Althusser thus took his distance from both the fetishism of the letter and the magic of the signature, that modern form taken by the personality cult.

There was thus an obvious analogy between the return to Freud theorized by Lacan in the 1950s and Althusser's reading of Marx, which was elaborated ten years later. Each in his respective realm entertained an impassioned relation with the notions of symbolic father and founding text. Each occupied a specific place within an internationalist movement, one that went from belonging to marginality, and from isolation to dissidence. The encounter between Althusser's undertaking and Lacan's took place at a time at which the latter was reaching the outer threshold of its own maturity. It took place between two masters and through the interposition of their students and might be characterized as follows: An aged psychiatrist, banished and isolated, found refuge and a new audience by grace of a Communist philosopher educating, from behind the trellis of France's most prestigious school, the intellectual elite of the nation. It was a strange affair indeed, and the singularity of the intersection of two destinies is worth recounting.

Seeking to free himself from the theoretical void into which French communism had locked itself, Louis Althusser attempted afresh, but in a critical manner, the gesture of Georges Politzer. In the Hungarian's footsteps, he took as his target the "pitiful history of French philosophy,"[5] but contrary to Politzer, he situated Freud's discovery at the heart of the historic continent opened up by Marx. Whence this verdict, written in the past perfect, with its striking congruity with what Lacan had written twenty years earlier: "Such is the reality which we had to learn to spell out, and to do so on our own. Alone—since we did not have in our midst, within Marxist philosophy, any genuine great teachers to guide our steps. Politzer, who could have been one had he not sacrificed the major work of philosophy he bore within to urgent economic imperatives, had left us only the ingenious errors of his

Critique des fondements de la psychologie. He had died murdered by the Nazis. We had no masters." [6]

A few years after the creation of the SFP, Althusser discovered Lacan's principal articles in various issues of *La Psychanalyse.* At the same time, he read the texts of Freud's disciples, and, during the academic year 1962–63, had his students working on "the origins of structuralist thought." He himself spoke on Lévi-Strauss, Foucault, and Montesquieu; Jacques-Alain Miller on the archaeology of knowledge in Descartes; and Pierre Macherey on the origins of language. Jacques Rancière, Étienne Balibar, and Jean-Claude Milner also participated in the seminar, in which a presentation by Michel Tort on Lacan was scheduled. Collaterally, Miller joined Milner in attending Roland Barthes's seminar at the École pratique des hautes études, where they heard a lecture by André Green on Lacan. [7]

In Althusser's eyes, Lacan's work occupied a strategic position of the first importance. Not only did it allow for a critique of the Pavlovian grid through which the Communist movement had denounced Freudianism as a "bourgeois science," but it also challenged the adaptive ideals of the American school. Now that dual polemic suited the Althusserian project of a renewal of Marxist thought capable of taking account of a nonpsychological notion of the subject. That is why, toward the spring of 1963, the philosopher was closely following the evolution of the French psychoanalytic movement. He was aware of Lacan's difficulties and seriously thought of proposing that he transplant his seminar to a room of the ENS, where candidates for the *agrégation* might profit from his teaching. In order to lay the groundwork for a meeting, he published an article in *La Revue de l'enseignement philosophique,* thus writing a first text in praise of Lacan's work. "Marx based his theory on a rejection of *homo œconomicus,*" he wrote. "Freud based his on a rejection of *homo psychologicus.* Lacan has seen and understood Freud's liberating rupture. He has comprehended it in the full sense of the word, taking it in its full rigor and constraining it to generate—without reservation—its own consequences. Like anyone, he may err in details, or even in his choice of philosophical bearings. What we owe him is the *essential.*" [8]

That sentence did not fall on deaf ears. His Majesty thus hastened to invite the ENS instructor—or "caïman"—to dinner. Lacan arrived at the restaurant with a cigar hanging from his lips, and Althusser muttered, "So you've twisted it." [9] The two men had several meetings, but remained silent on the subject of an eventual transplantation of the seminar to the ENS. The one was not yet banished from the SFP, and the other was waiting for the right moment. Nevertheless, the former understood the intentions of the latter, and in 1963, when the break with the IPA was finalized, he asked him to find a solution to his problem. The rest is well known. . . .

At the beginning of the school year, Althusser placed Lacan's work on the reading list for his courses and proposed to the students of the ENS that they study the question of the foundations of psychoanalysis. Thus for the first time, Lacanian texts were read from a philosophical perspective that amply exceeded the framework of clinical practice. Michel Tort was chosen to inaugurate the series of lectures since he had already received Freudian training. With Étienne Balibar, he had attended Laplanche's course in 1962 and participated in the translation collaborative led by André Bourguignon. During his vacation, he had worked on the first issue of *La Psychanalyse,* which Althusser had loaned to him.

Tort addressed his classmates on several occasions. He presented Freud's principal concepts, criticized the ideals of "American" psychoanalysis, and explained Lacan's innovations.[10] Étienne Balibar, for his part, presented a study of the seminar on the psychoses, comparing Freud's concepts with Lacan's. Yves Duroux, in turn, studied the different definitions of the word "structure" in texts by Husserl, Lacan, and Merleau-Ponty. Finally, Jean Mosconi devoted his lecture to the relations between psychoanalysis and anthropology. As for Louis Althusser, he spoke on one occasion on the Lacanian conception of desire, and on another, on the status of psychology in the face of the Freudian revolution.[11]

The most symptomatic presentation of that period of theoretical speculation was Jacques-Alain Miller's. Younger than his colleagues, this son of a Polish-Jewish physician was nineteen years old at the time and had not yet read a line of Lacan. "I read him," he would say twenty years later, "at Althusser's invitation. . . . I had not yet read a line by Lacan at the time and was planning to attend the seminar only as an auditor. I completed my *licence* in philosophy. Louis Althusser called me into his office to tell me I would do well to read Lacan, that I would certainly like him, and that I should prepare to take his seminar." Miller followed the advice. He went to the PUF bookstore, and bought all the issues of *La Psychanalyse.* Then he went off to the country to make his way through the texts, accompanied by a friend preparing for the *agrégation.* "I remember quite well beginning my reading of the *Rome Discourse* on the second floor and then coming downstairs at lunchtime to tell my friend, who had spent the morning reading Spinoza, that I had just read something unprecedented." [12]

From the outset, Jacques-Alain Miller's presentation was different from the others.[13] For this young student, soon to occupy a crucial position in the history of psychoanalysis, Lacan's work no longer needed to be read with reference to Freud. It was constructed as a totality and, as such, possessed its own history and its own internal logic. The Lacan read by Miller in 1963 was a Lacan "in the present tense," a Lacan symbolizing scientificity, removed from his Surrealist, Kojèvian, Wallonian, or even French past. Miller's Lacan was the structuralist Lacan of the *Rome Discourse,* and the *Instance de la Lettre,* a Lacan whose return to Freud consisted in a formal operation. At the time, as we have seen, Miller was not alone in reading Lacan in that manner. At the center of the structuralist explosion, the whole of the intelligentsia was discovering precisely that Lacan: scientific, theoretical, antipsychological, hostile to "American" psychoanalysis. But Miller added a note to that apprehension of Lacanianism, since he read Lacan without Freud in order to understand Freud on the basis of an *already* Lacanian Lacan.

Miller's way of proceeding traversed the Lacanian venture at a crucial point of its development and at an historical juncture in which the whole of French thought was tending toward a certain preoccupation with theory as such—or *théoricisme.* At the time the young students of the ENS discovered Lacan through Althusser's teaching, the new structuralist configuration had bestowed on psychoanalysis a scientific status it had not previously managed to achieve. Under those conditions, Freudian theory was studied for its own sake, outside the institutions of psychoanalysis and as a scientific field separate from medicine and psychology. The *théoricisme* of the years 1960–65 thus revived the *universalist* character of Freudian thought by extricating it from obscurantism, spiritualism, and psychologism. That is why, during an initial phase, such theoretical speculation was fruitful, even if it tended to present Freudian doctrine through an almost exclusively Lacanian grid.

For Lacan, the turning point constituted by the years 1960–65 resulted in unprecedented recognition. On the one hand, the master was able to found a school with the residues of a movement whose most worthy representatives had just escaped him, and, on the other, in order to fill the void, he had the possibility of drawing on new and more doctrinaire disciples, who had not been obliged to participate in the institutional quarrels of the psychoanalytic world. That theoretical reemergence, moreover, was part of a political battle. With the decline of French colonialism and the beginning of the American war in Vietnam, the young theorists of the time found in Lacanianism the wherewithal to struggle philosophically against an imperialism which was being attacked on all fronts for its adaptative ideals and its expansionism. With the creation of the EFP, there thus begins the history of what was for Lacan his great revenge. Forced into dissidence and surrounded by "residues," the old lion became the leader of a French school of *universalist* aspect, which would reign supreme for sixteen years thanks to the mobilization of a new intellectual elite. For the "symbolic" launching of that mobilization which would occupy a far larger stage than the ENS, Lacan owed everything to Althusser.

As Lacan was becoming aware, starting January 15, 1964, of the changing vista, Louis Althusser dashed off an article entitled "Freud and Lacan," in which he developed his positions. He revealed his cards from the outset. The author denounced both the "revisionism" of the American school, which fueled the exploitation of psychoanalysis, and the advocates of Zhdanovism, who were victims of the ideology they rejected by confusing it with Freud's discovery. Next he evoked the three great accursed figures of the end of the nineteenth century, Freud, Marx, and Nietzsche, who were forced into solitude, misery, or madness for having invented on their own theories that violated the rules of legitimate filiation: "For when [Freud] wanted to think through—that is, express in the form of a rigorous system of abstract concepts—the extraordinary discovery he encountered anew every day in his practice, he sought out theoretical precedents, fathers in theory, in vain. He could barely find any. He had to submit to and make do with the following theoretical situation: being his own father, constructing with his own artisan's hands the theoretical space in which to situate his discovery, weaving out of cord borrowed left and right the great knotted net in which to catch the redundant fish of the unconscious, which men called mute because it spoke even as they slept." [14] The rest of the article was devoted to Lacan's return to Freud. Althusser did not restrict himself to demonstrating that Lacan was alone in having undertaken a genuine epistemological elucidation of Freud's work. He paid ringing homage to the man, as though wanting himself to identify with the Spinozan solitude of an individual banished from his community. Instead of being "fascinated" by the master's seductive-ness, he drew a portrait in which an understanding of his weaknesses and sufferings exceeded any appreciation of his "charisma". "Whence the contained passion," he wrote, "the impassioned exertion of Lacan's language, which can thrive and survive only in a state of alert and defensiveness, the language of a man already under siege and condemned by the crushing weight of structures and guilds to anticipate their blows, to pretend at least to return them before receiving them, thus discouraging the adversary from crushing him beneath its own. . . . Obliged to teach the theory of the unconscious to physicians, analysts, or analysands, Lacan gives them, through the rhetoric of his words, the imitative equivalent of the language of the uncon-scious, which, as is known, in its ultimate essence, is *Witz*, pun, failed—or success-ful—metaphor." [15]

No doubt Louis Althusser was better shielded than others from the ravaging effects of a neurotic relation to Lacan's person. When the two met, the master did not deploy for him his habitual array of compliments or requests. He did not pro-pose that he attend his seminar, enter into analysis with him, or change his thera-peutic technique. He found something of a barrier to the omnipotence of his reign in the radical alterity presented to him by a man who had been able to discern the human truth of the role he found himself playing.

In order to put a clearly delineated end to the Zhdanov period, Althusser decided to publish his article in *La Nouvelle Critique*. He offered it to Jacques Ar-naud, who accepted it, and the text appeared in December 1964, a year after it was written. At the time, it did not provoke any reaction within the Communist Party, for the abandonment of Zhdanovism had been taking its course quietly since 1956 and had not been followed by any critical movement, in particular relating to psy-choanalysis. That same year, Louis Althusser devoted his seminar at the ENS to a collective reading of *Capital* in which his students Roger Establet, Pierre Macherey, Jacques Rancière, and Étienne Balibar participated. With them, he elaborated the notion of a "symptom-oriented reading" and, with the help of the Bachelardian concept of an "epistemological break," separated a mature—and fully Marxist—Marx from a young—and residually Hegelian—Marx. The work was published in 1965 under the title *Lire le Capital* ["*Reading Capital*"], along with Althusser's first book, a collection of articles entitled *Pour Marx*. ["For Marx"]. The two works served as something of a pediment to the *Théorie* collection published by Francois Maspéro. From that point on Althusser's works were to become famous and take their place at the heart of the structuralist project. They were taken up by a broad intellectual audience, who linked them with those of Roland Barthes, Claude Lévi-Strauss, Michel Foucault, and Jacques Lacan.

That very year, Louis Althusser changed his method of treatment. He aban-doned drug therapy and entered into analysis with René Diatkine, who was himself a former analysand of Lacan's and, with Serge Lebovici, a representative of medical psychoanalysis. With that choice, the philosopher established a separation between his status as an analysand and his theoretical commitment. On the one hand, he criticized the adaptive ideals of psychoanalysis, and on the other, he remained faithful, as in politics, to the prevailing institutional order.

Within the party, Althusser's positions had been the object in 1963 of a violent critique on the part of official philosophers Guy Besse and Roger Garaudy. But with the publication of the two books in the "Théorie" series, things became more open. Althusser's interest in classical Leninism and above all in the theses of Mao Zedong were viewed as Zhdanovian by orthodox Communists, at a time when the party was undergoing the repercussions of the Sino-Soviet split and preparing (for the meeting of the central committee at Argenteuil in 1966) to draw up a charter guaranteeing freedom of speech to writers and researchers. While remaining attached to the humanist ideals of Soviet Marxism, the PCF was moving toward a pragmatic-style liberalism, without any attempt at a "theoretical" critique of Stalinism or Zhdanovism. Seen from that perspective, Althusser's positions seemed all the more dangerous in that they appeared to bring theoretical support to Maoism and ran the risk of influencing a part of the student population.

Around 1963–64, the Union des étudiants communistes (UEC) was traversed by several currents, one of which, the "Italian" tendency, was inspired by the weekly, *Rinascita*. Through the newspaper *Clarté*, it sought to open itself to the great problems of the day: sexual "liberation," contraception, travel, and the new channels of communication open to the young. Among the leaders of that tendency were Yves Buin and Pierre Kahn, who would both have their links with the Freudian adventure. The former would become a psychiatrist and a writer and would publish a splendid book on Wilhelm Reich, and the latter would become a psychoanalyst and a member of the EFP. As opposed to the "Italians," the UEC circle at the rue d'Ulm, led by the Althusserian contingent under the aegis of Robert Linhart, was opposed to that "bourgeois" openness and advocated the primacy of a solid theoretical formation. "The intervention of the delegate from Ulm at the VIIth Congress of the UEC in March 1964," Jacques Rancière has written, "which marked the entry of the Althusserians into the political battle, was expressed in carefully chosen terms: The UEC was to have its own specific practice in the student world. It was not its business to discuss the atomic bomb or the Sino-Soviet conflict. It must first secure for itself the grounds allowing for a debate over such problems. We were to *support* the party's positions, but we were not to base that support on hastily patched together analyses. It would first be necessary to acquire theoretical training. . . . Whence the pressure the circle brought to bear on the newspaper *Clarté*. The motion passed by the congress at its suggestion requested that the paper regularly devote space to commentary on major texts and current theoretical issues. In doing so, *Clarté* was to call on 'comrades competent in those fields.' We, of course, were those comrades." [16]

In a first phase, then, the Althusserian circle of the rue d'Ulm supported the party leadership in the elimination of the Italian tendency, which did not fail to occur in 1965. But a year later, Waldeck-Rochet initiated an attack against Althusser's reformulations by connecting theoretical antihumanism with Chinese sectarianism. He contested the idea that Marx's discovery was essentially scientific, and retained the traditional definition of philosophical Marxism as a humanist ideology centered on the notion of the person or the full subject. [17]

Attacked by the party, Althusser began to be challenged by his students, who reproached him for his political—if not theoretical—loyalty to what would from then on be called *revisionism*. The term, which forms part of the history of the Marxist lexicon, designates the doctrine elaborated by Eduard Bernstein after Engels's death. That doctrine was based on the legalization of communism in the European democracies and criticized the original tenets of Marxism on a variety of points, ending up, politically, by endorsing a reformist strategy. Refuted by Lenin, revisionism was criticized as a form of opportunism and pragmatism for its abandonment of founding principles and its adaptation to the situation of the day. The return of the term, which was applied by Mao to the Soviet situation, resulted, in the 1960s, in a general critique of the Western parties, which were at once accused of entering into compromise with bourgeois democracy and of remaining captive of a Khrushchevian orientation, itself considered a revision of Marxism. Against such revisionism, Maoism laid claim not only to the heritage of Marxism-Leninism, but also to that of Stalinism.

In France, Maoism was organized around that postulate, and the term "revisionism" tended to symbolize in a general way the abandonment of theoretical principles in favor of a pragmatic adaptation to world realities. Now for the young readers of Lacan's work, practiced in the teachings of Althusser, "American" psychoanalysis, and more generally "adaptative" psychoanalysis, were comparable to a revisionism, since they separated themselves from Freud's discovery the better to assimilate it to the ideals of medicine and psychology. Lacan, for his part, used the word "deviation" to circumscribe the doctrinal positions of neo-Freudianism. Thus, on the eve of the Chinese cultural revolution, his orthodox rearticulation could appear as a radical form of antirevisionism. And for that reason a theoretical "encounter" could be envisioned, within the French structuralist context, between Lacanianism and the principles of Maoism, even if such Maoism should be the bearer of the sectarian ideals of the old Zhdanovism on matters of art and the human sciences.

Within the theoretical vanguard, an antirevisionist consensus was thus forged, which resulted, during 1965 and 1966, in the creation of three mimeographed journals, printed by the same publisher and centered on the teaching of three masters: Charles Bettelheim for *Études de planification socialiste*, Louis Althusser for *Cahiers marxistes-léninistes,* and finally Jacques Lacan for *Cahiers pour l'analyse*. Naturally, each of the journals had its own orientation, but all three, despite their divergences, shared a return to the founding principles of theoretical combat—in economics for the first, in politico-philosophical Marxism for the second, and in science and logic for the third.

In June 1964, most of Althusser's students joined the École freudienne de Paris to form a "cartel" devoted to the "theory of discourse." Among the more active members were Jacques-Alain Miller, Jean-Claude Milner, and Yves Duroux. The others, who were not in Paris, participated irregularly, forming a group of eight: Étienne Balibar, Alain Grosrichard, Pierre Macherey, Jean Mathiot, Jean Mosconi, Jacques Rancière, François Regnault, and Jean-Marie Villegier. Fearful of Lacan's seductiveness, Michel Tort did not join the EFP and prepared a degree under the supervision of Lagache. One day, while lunching with the old master, he brought him his thesis, but forgot to leave it with him. Analyzed by Granoff, he would remain neither truly Althusserian nor genuinely Lacanian, refusing both Marxist *théoricisme* and Lacanian *logicisme*.[18] In December 1964, while Althusser was beginning his course on *Capital,* Lacan delivered a lecture before a small group of students at the École normale, thus indicating the importance he attached, beyond his public seminar, to their work on his texts. On that occasion, he chose to comment on the Cartesian formula *I think therefore I am,* which he rewrote *I think: therefore I am.*[19]

In April 1966, with the beginning of the Chinese cultural revolution, a pro-Chinese split took place within the Ulm circle of the UEC, which resulted in the creation of the Union des jeunesses communistes marxistes-léninistes (UJCML). That break scattered Althusser's students into several tendencies. Some chose the Maoist path of "proletarian" struggle; others remained in the party in order to wage theoretical combat; and still others, who had participated in the founding of *Cahiers pour l'analyse,* remained members of the UJCML. A number of the followers of the UJCML would find themselves, after the events of 1968, in the ranks of the Gauche prolétarienne (GP).

Althusser's students were not the only ones during the heyday of structuralism to approach Freud's work by way of Lacan's reelaboration. Before them, and through a less theoretical and more "Third-World" orientation, the philosopher Lucien Sebag, a student of Lévi-Strauss, had discovered the adventure of the unconscious in texts published in *Les Temps modernes* and *La Psychanalyse.* Born in 1933, he belonged to a generation older than that of the Marxist-Leninist circles and *Cahiers pour l'analyse.* Prior to the creation of the UEC, he had participated in the emergence of a Communist opposition, then got himself excluded from the party and allied himself with various extreme-left movements. In 1961, he left on a field expedition among the Guayaki of Paraguay and the Ayoreo of Bolivia. Upon returning, he dreamed of effecting a vast theoretical synthesis between a history of societies written in terms of their economic infrastructure and individual history understood in terms of unconscious determination. Bypassing Freudo-Marxism, he published in 1964 a poignant volume, *Marxisme et structuralisme,* which begins with these words, "Only the first step is decisive: Discourse or violence, effective chaos or reason, which ought I to choose? Once that initial question has been answered—and it has been, since I am writing—what follows may be formulated clearly: There is now no existence possible for me other than one conforming to reason." The book was dedicated to Judith Lacan.[20]

For several years, Sebag had been spending time on Lacan's couch. The analyst entertained a privileged relation with the young ethnologist. He appreciated his intellectual qualities and was counting on him to give his doctrine its second wind. In January 1965, however, matters took a dramatic turn: Sebag committed suicide by shooting a bullet into his face. On his table, he left a personal letter and the telephone number of a woman friend who had given him shelter during a period of depression. Overwhelmed by the violence of an act he was unable to prevent, Jacques Lacan confided his distress to his intimates. To some, he asked that they not tell anything, and to others he explained that he had done all he could to avoid what had happened.[21] "With him gone," Claude Lévi-Strauss wrote of his student, "ethnology will no longer be the same." [22] And not only ethnology. If Lucien Sebag had lived, Lacanianism would undoubtedly have known a different fate.

During that period, in which philosophy began interrogating psychoanalysis from a structural perspective, Freud's work was also the subject of readings other than Lacan's. In 1965, Jacques Derrida, a teacher at the ENS, but Althusser's junior, published in the journal *Critique* an article that would develop into a book: *De la grammatologie*.[23] The term, borrowed from Littré, designates a treatise of letters, alphabets, syllabification, reading, and writing. Derrida employed it to define the conceivable emergence of a "science of the letter" whose truth would have been repressed, since Plato, by the Western *logos*. This repression would have been effected through a primacy accorded to a mystique of "full" speech or phonetic writing. In this perspective, there would have existed a logocentrism construed as the "debasement" of writing which, until the advent of Saussurean linguistics, would have served to conceal the letter's "presence." In the face of that observation, Derrida proposed replacing *semiology* with *grammatology* in the *Cours de linguistique générale*. That substitution would allow for a freeing of the semiological project from the reign of a linguistics based on the logos or phonologism.

In the history of French structuralism, and within the configuration it created, that gesture constituted the first philosophical challenge to the use of linguistics in the human sciences: "When I spoke of Saussure or of Lacan," Derrida emphasized, "I was criticizing less their texts than the role those texts were playing on the French intellectual scene." [24] And yet that critique was effected on linguistic grounds since Derrida took Saussure's discovery as the point of reference for his rejection of phonologism. There was thus no real discontinuity between what he was saying and the totality of a discourse centered on Saussurean negativity. Nonetheless, that absence of discontinuity did not prevent the reversal of a problematic within the consensus according to which the subject remained subordinate to the law of structure: be it signifier, letter, or symbol. Derrida's project attacked Lévi-Straussian ethnology because of the latter's attachment to a Rousseauian conception of the origin of language. In Rousseau, language does indeed derive from a cry or an utterance. But Derrida also implicitly criticized the Lacanian reading of Freud for its adherence to a primacy of the signifier, intuited as the "*telos* of full speech." In the second part of his book, he explained at length his position with regard to the works of Lévi-Strauss, as he had done two years earlier with regard to Michel Foucault's *Histoire de la folie*. To the former, he reproached his ethnocentrism, and in the latter he had contested an overly restrictive—and even overly rational—interpretation of the Cartesian *Cogito*.[25] On the subject of Lacan's work, Derrida kept his silence.

In a footnote, however, he lashed out at the notion of the primacy of the signifier: "The 'primacy' or priority of the signifier," he wrote, "would be an untenable and absurd position by virtue of being formulated illogically within the very logic it is—no doubt legitimately—intent on destroying. A signifer can never in theory precede a signified, without which it would no longer be a signifier, and the signifier 'signifier' would no longer have any possible signified. The thought emergent in that impossible formula (without succeeding in lodging within it) ought thus to be formulated differently: It will no doubt be able to do so only by suspecting the very notion of sign, 'sign of,' which will always remain attached to the very thing which is here being called into question."[26] At the time, Jacques Derrida had reread "L'instance de la lettre," but Lacan's essays were not yet bound as a book, and the philosopher abstained from polemicizing against a theory he would later contest. It would, moreover, not be until the publication of the *Écrits,* then the events of May 1968, that Lacan's work would be both taken into account and criticized by the entirety of French thought. On that score, Althusser was a pioneer.

Aware of the importance of the structuralist juncture, and in order to open the SPP to contemporary ideas, André Green decided to devote an annual seminar to the works of Michel Serres, René Girard, and Jean-Pierre Vernant. Within that framework, he also invited Jacques Derrida to deliver a lecture on Freud at the library of the Institut de psychanalyse. Several practitioners attended the meetings, along with a few persons from outside the movement. Serres spoke on translation, Girard on the Oedipus complex, and Vernant on ancient societies. As for Derrida, in March 1966, he developed his reading of Freud's discovery in the light of grammatology: "Our ambition is quite limited: to recognize in Freud's text several points of bearing and to isolate, at the threshold of an organized meditation, what it is in psychoanalysis which can be but poorly contained within the logocentric enclosure, as it has come to limit not only the history of philosophy, but the movement of the 'human sciences,' and specifically a certain linguistics. If the Freudian breakthrough has an historical originality, it does not derive it from its peaceful coexistence with that linguistics, at least in its congenital phonologism."[27] Never before had the premises of the SPP been the scene of so brilliant a theoretical debate. Philippe Sollers and Serge Leclaire attended the lecture, and Marguerite Derrida, the philosopher's wife, was also present. She was undergoing a training analysis at the Institute and beginning to translate the works of Melanie Klein.

Instead of interpreting the unconscious under the category of the signifier, Derrida drew on the notion of *Bahnung*—"facilitation" or "fraying"—to think through the conscious/unconscious opposition in terms of *differance* and its *effaced proto-trace*. In 1895, in his *Project for a Scientific Psychology,*[28] Freud used the word *Bahnung*—almost a path-breaking—to designate the site of passage from one neuron to another when an excitation succeeded in diminishing resistance between the two. There was *Bahnung* to the extent that the excitation had followed and broken one path rather than another.[29] Thirty years later, in an amusing note, Freud took an interest in a small invention that seems to have anticipated the computer age, the "mystic writing pad" [*Wunderblock*]. This was a child's toy consisting of a wax slate covered by a sheet of wax paper and a sheet of celluloid. On its surface, one could inscribe and then erase signs, but the object retained both an invisible permanence of the trace and a virginity of the receptive surface. Freud compared the mystic writing pad to the psychical apparatus, which did indeed receive traces without retaining them, and retained them even as it erased them. The celluloid sheet and wax paper represented the preconscious system and the wax slate the unconscious.[30]

Starting from *Bahnung* and the "mystic writing pad," Derrida showed that the structure of the psychical apparatus was represented by a writing machine whose metaphorical use cast light on the trace in general. From there, the unconscious was seen to partake of a nonverbal and hieroglyphic writing, which restored through difference (or *différance*) a proto-trace that was prior to speech but effaced in its historical origin: "It is with a graphematics still to come rather than with a linguistics dominated by an old phonologism that psychoanalysis is called on to collaborate."[31] Derrida's move here was radically opposed to the Lacanian perspective, which did not establish any difference between "phonological" signifiers and "archaic" letters. For Lacan, the trace was always already linguistic to the extent that the distinction between language and speech was posited on the basis of a division of the subject and according to a Heideggerian conception of truth. At a certain level, Derrida was criticizing the Lacanian version of the signifier in a manner similar to Laplanche, but one which had the advantage of opening the Freudian problematic to a new field of inquiry—*the becoming literary of the literal*. "For despite several attempts by Freud and certain of his successors, a psychoanalysis of literature respectful of the *originality of the literary signifier* has not yet begun, and that is no doubt not an accident. Until now, what has been accomplished is the analysis of literary—that is, nonliterary—signifieds. But such considerations refer us to the whole history of literary forms themselves and of everything in them which was precisely destined to authorize that misunderstanding."[32]

Compared to the "orthodox renewal" inaugurated by Lacan, and the "symptom-oriented reading" proposed by Althusser, Derrida's method defined itself as a discourse of "deconstruction." A deconstruction of philosophy in general and of Freudian theory in particular, since what was at stake was locating in both the traces of an alleged phonologism or logocentrism as well as the dangers they were exposed to thereby. Deconstructive reading attempted to displace philosophical discourse toward the literary text, even if it entailed the effacement of the reciprocal boundaries separating them. Its plea was for the duplicity of meaning—its ambiguity and its dissemination against the imperialism of the single hegemonic commentary.

Within the history of psychoanalysis in France, the Derridian project was in part a renewal of the Surrealist gesture. We have seen that in opposition to the institutions of psychoanalysis, the Surrealists had introduced Freud's discovery through a philosophico-literary channel in which a latent Hegelianism and a nocturnal vision of the unconscious—particularly in Breton—were combined. That problematic exists in Derrida, but in a different manner, and reemerged during a period when active Surrealism had disappeared from the French intellectual scene. Breton sought his references in and around Flournoy, while turning away from the hereditarian ideal, whereas Derrida seems to have rediscovered the Genevan source through an interpretation of the Freudian unconscious in terms of "trace." Yet he had not read the works of Flournoy, nor did he draw on any Surrealist source. But it is as though his project, in the crisscrossings of its inquiries, came to occupy the place left vacant by Surrealist contestation. Whence that other analogy with Breton's work, which consists in having avoided the path of Jungianism. For the young philosopher, indeed, the conception of an unconscious in the form of a "crypt" did not have its origin in any epistemological ground prior to Freud's discovery. It took shape, on the contrary, in a dialogue with the thought of Husserl and Heidegger, asking philosophy the question of literature, and more generally, of writing. The Freudian unconscious formulated under the category of a mythography would therefore underwrite the existence of a philosophy of trace without subject or writing without consciousness.

The discourse of deconstruction thus opened the path to three kinds of "poststructuralist" inquiries. The first traversed the institutions of psychoanalysis and resulted in a new apprehension of hypnotic symptoms—from crypts to telepathy, by ways of the "margins" of Freud's work; the second renewed the debate on the literary object on the basis of its signifying forms; and the third ended in a generalized critique of logocentrism, along with—as an appendix—a feminist-style attack against the "phallocentrism" of the thought from Vienna.

On the subject of the literary object, Jacques Derrida put his finger on a crucial problem of the structuralist years: that of the critical approach to texts. Before the war, writers and poets had laid claim to Freud's discovery, outside of any academic discourse, in literary journals, whereas the psychoanalysts had limited themselves, in the orbit of René Laforgue and Marie Bonaparte, to psychobiography. Among literary critics, and with the exception of an article by Albert Thibaudet, the notion of the unconscious had encountered the same resistance as in the world of medicine. Nonetheless, during the years following, Freudian theses gradually took hold, leading to a new apprehension of texts. During the 1960s, the old configuration was thus modified. With the advent of a generalized interrogation into language, the practitioners of the unconscious, whether trained in Lacanianism or not, began to call into question the sacrosanct genre of psychobiography which they inherited from the founders. In this context, the most important work of the third analytic generation was Jean Laplanche's study of Hölderlin.[33] Other approaches were attempted by Pontalis, Anzieu, Octave Mannoni, Rosolato, and Green. As far as literary criticism was concerned, it too was gradually transformed as psychoanalysis made its way into the universities. Whence a complex situation, consisting of the coexistence of the old psychobiography, a new psychoanalytic interpretation of texts, and two other innovative methods: *psychocriticism* and *structural analysis*.

It was in 1938 that Charles Mauron, working from a reading of Mallarmé, began to elaborate the notion of "obsessive metaphors." Sixteen years later, on the subject of Racine, he formulated the hypothesis of an objectively definable *personal myth* specific to each author. Psychocriticism was born. It would barely have any descendants after its author's death, but paradoxically, it would have given psychobiographical readings a new impetus. The method was concerned with the reading of texts outside of all reference to an author's neurosis or "psyche." It also distinguished itself from the Jungian option, illustrated by the works of the Genevan Charles Baudouin, since it was concerned less with delineating a collective mythology than with illuminating the specificity of an individual's writing.[34] It consisted in bringing to light networks of images whose combination resulted in the emergence of a personal myth specific to each author. That myth was then interpreted as the expression of an unconscious personality, and then confronted, in the last analysis, with biographical data. It will thus be perceived that despite its originality, psychocriticism entailed a "reverse" return of the principles of psychobiography. In one case, it was a matter of reconstructing, from the work, a mythical and unconscious self, and in the other, of discovering in that work a reflection of representations of the self. To that extent, all psychoanalytically inspired criticism partook of an unacknowledged project, the edification of an aesthetics in which the figure of the "double" would fulfill the role of a theory of the imaginary.[35]

The structural perspective inaugurated by Roland Barthes in 1953 with *Le degré zéro de l'écriture* [*Writing Degree Zero*] and taken up anew seven years later in his celebrated *Sur Racine* was quite different.[36] Although he acknowledged his debt to Mauron, Barthes made use of the Freudian lexicon from a perspective as alien to psychobiography as it was to psychocriticism. Abandoning the one as well as the other, he avoided all cross-references from the man to the work and the work to the man, and situated himself within a mythic, formal, and historical "Racinian world." "What I have attempted to reconstitute," he wrote, "is a Racinian anthropology which is simultaneously structural and analytic: structural in substance because tragedy is treated here as a system of units (or 'figures') and functions; analytic in form because only a language prepared to encompass a fear of the world (as psychoanalysis, I believe, is) seemed suitable to me for an encounter with sequestered man."[37] In taking on a work that symbolized French values *par excellence,* Barthes stirred up a formidable storm among the partisans of classical academic criticism. Over night, his *Sur Racine* became the major work of a structuralism that was both glorious and charged with all the defects of a reviled modernity. In 1964, the polemic exploded and prewar arguments against Freud surfaced anew in the pages of Raymond Picard. "As for psychoanalysis," he wrote in an article for *Le Monde,* "Barthes's application of it to Racine is not encouraging. The psychoanalytic accoutrements with which he adorns the tragedies add up to a rather sad carnival from which Racine emerges travestied."[38]

A year later, the same Raymond Picard published a booklet of uncommon stupidity entitled *Nouvelle critique ou nouvelle imposture,*[39] which had the merit of imposing—as a backlash—the reign of structuralism on the French intellectual and academic scene. Barthes produced a humorous response, in which he seized the opportunity to situate his own relation to psychobiography. He rejected it, but circumscribed the ignorance of the old criticism in relation to psychoanalysis, demonstrating that it had the density and tenacity of a myth. "It is not a refusal," he emphasized, speaking of that ignorance, "it is a disposition destined imperturbably to traverse the ages." Then, to put Picard's discourse in its proper place, Barthes quoted a sentence of Julien Benda: " 'Shall I mention the assiduousness of an entire literature these last fifty years, and particularly in France, in proclaiming the primacy of instinct, of the unconscious, of will in the German sense, that is, in opposition to intelligence?' The sentence was not written in 1965 by Raymond Picard but in 1927 by Julien Benda."[40]

Barthes did not entertain the same relation to Freud's works as did Louis Althusser and Jacques Derrida. In his approach to literary texts, which was contemporary with Lacan's reelaboration, psychoanalytic discourse intervened as a point of reference. Barthes activated it as one language among others. There is no theory of the unconscious or critique of psychologism to be found in his work, but something of a permanent presence of Freudian vocabulary. The author of *Mythologies* understood better than anyone in 1965 how much traditional literary criticism remained attached to the ideals of a "French unconscious,"[41] that is, to the discourse emergent from the theses on heredity and degeneracy which never stopped opposing Cartesian "intelligence" to Germanic "barbarity." Thus, in comparing Picard to Julien Benda, Barthes revived quite splendidly the Surrealist attacks against alleged French "clarity." In that manner, following the path of structure, he participated in the great universalizing implantation of psychoanalysis, not only within literary criticism, but within the totality of the realms of French thought.

II. Intermezzo

I described in a previous volume how Freud one day came to be caught up in an affair involving the "theft of ideas." At the beginning of the century, Fliess reproached him for having pilfered the notion of bisexuality and transmitted it to one of his patients, Swoboda, who subsequently confided the "secret" to Weininger. The story quickly took an insane turn and almost ended up before a court. But Freud had a prodigious sense of humor, and was not mad enough to confuse *plagiarism,* a deliberate and fraudulent act of copying, with the *theft of ideas,* a phenomenon involving belief in an alleged possession of thoughts. As a good materialist and man of science, he did not fail to realize that ideas belong to no one. And yet in his role as innovator, he remained haunted by the theme, and felt guilty for harboring an unconscious wish to appropriate what was not his.

Lacan, in his mature years had no guilt of that sort; his was rather the tendency of endlessly taking himself for the owner of his ideas. Feeling himself to be charged with a mission, he entertained an ambivalent relation with his own discourse. The more he revealed that the subject was not master in its own home, the more he believed his ideas belonged to him alone. He borrowed his concepts from different bodies of work, without always citing his sources, but he dispensed his teaching in a public place, thus running the risk that others might be inspired by it or might draw from it. When he became interested in someone, he invited the individual to his seminar, as though to an open house, since he needed to be seen and heard. Although dispensing his words quite lavishly, he could turn quite fierce if he had the impression that his "priority" was being undermined. He thus broadcast his work even while pretending to keep it in reserve. In point of fact, Lacan was not capable of facing, in his solitude, the hostility of his fellow men. He was a fragile individual who had a genius for grasping the unconscious of others, but was invariably wrong when it come to their manifest intentions. He could not do without public recognition, and in order to secure it, he was prepared to resort to every form of seduction, and even to lapse into ardent bouts of bad faith when disabused.

We have seen that at the Bonneval Colloquium in 1960, his tactic was to promote the unity of the group and that he thus avoided discussing the contents of the lectures delivered there. On the other hand, he crossed swords privately with his adversaries of the SPP and did not hesitate to resort to insult. Unhappy with the positions taken by Merleau-Ponty concerning his structuralist reelaboration, he desperately sought a different source of philosophical support. To that end, he approached Paul Ricoeur, believing or pretending to believe that the latter's work converged with his own.

A student of Dalbiez, the philosopher was in all respects the opposite of Lacan. He was an academic who joked neither about God nor about religion. His intellectual probity was deeply grounded in an infinite submission to the Protestant ethic. He brandished the spirit of the Reformation much as Lacan did that of the Reconquest. Born in 1913, he discovered Freud's work before the war and encountered in the thought of the Jewish atheist a privileged arena for his own thought over a period of several years.[42] At the time he began writing his book on Freud, he enjoyed great prestige. He was one of the few professors at the Sorbonne willing to direct dissertations on Marx and Freud, and his positions in favor of Algerian independence were well known. In 1960, Paul Ricoeur was a man respected for his tolerance, his political courage, and his exalted moral integrity. At the Bonneval Colloquium, he presented his principal thesis on Freud, which would remain unchanged five years later when he published his book *De l'interprétation*.[43]

Taking the opposite tack from Dalbiez, Ricoeur refused to separate the Viennese doctrine from its method and considered Freud to be a thinker of "suspicion" in the same way that Marx and Nietzsche were. From the perspective of "philosophical anthropology," which drew its inspiration broadly from post-Hegelian phenomenology, he proposed defining the unconscious as an object constituted by the totality of hermeneutic procedures used to decipher it. Ricoeur thus yoked a Christian tradition of deciphering texts to a modern philosophy of existence—it being understood that hermeneutics was not a "reading" or a "return" to texts, but an attempt to "interpret" them. According to that procedure, the unconscious was not a reality thinking in the place of the ego, but a site arrived at through a totalizing interpretation. Such interpretation was twofold in nature: It was oriented, on the one hand, toward new symbols, and, on the other, toward the resurgence of archaic symbols. The dialectic of those two hermeneutics allowed light to be cast, according to Ricoeur, on a different dialectical process, that of consciousness and the unconscious. To all appearances, each of those realms corresponds to a hermeneutic, one of which explains the diurnal side of man and the other the nocturnal side. But in reality, the two hermeneutics are one and the same: a symbolics of man or a semantics of desire.

Ricoeur's method consisted in linking Freud and Hegel without adding them together, in order to transcend, through hermeneutics, both metapsychological realism and the phenomenology of consciousness. "Consciousness," he wrote, "whose other the unconscious is, is not self-presence or a perception of contents, but a capacity to travel the itinerary of the mind's figures anew. The hermeneutic of those figures, through the symbols out of which they are born, appeared to us as the true counterpart of the progressive hermeneutic of the phenomenology of mind. It is as the other of its other that the unconscious is revealed at this juncture, that is, as a destiny, opposed to a progressive history oriented toward the future totality of mind. What ultimately remains in question is the deepseated identity of those two herme-

neutics, an identity which leads us to say: A phenomenology of mind and an archaeology of the unconscious do not speak of half of man, but each of man's totality." [44]

At the Bonneval Colloquium, Ricoeur thus proposed an interpretation of the
Freudian unconscious that went counter not only to Lacan's reelaboration, but to
the whole of the structuralist advance of the years 1960–65. For the hermeneutic
philosopher, Freud's discovery partook of a phenomenology which was not of consciousness. The unconscious remained interpretable as an *other of the other* and not
as a site of radical strangeness. That being the case, Ricoeur took only partially into
account the primacy of Freud's act of decentering. If, in speaking of Freud, he made
use of the vocabulary of Christian phenomenology, he simultaneously invoked that
of structural linguistics for purposes of illustration. Whence his constant references
to such notions as "signifying chain," "signifier," "signifying for the other," or "key
signifiers of the unconscious." Through those terms, Ricoeur evoked a conceptual
reality that had nothing to do with the work of Lacan, Barthes, or Foucault, but
which simply bore witness to an intellectual climate in which the apprehension of
structuralism tended to occur in terms of phenomenological categories.

In 1960, philosophers and Lacanian psychoanalysts were reading the same
linguistic texts, but drawing different inspiration from them. Lacan was alone in
having already effected a reading of structural linguistics that was fertile and innovative for psychoanalysis. In that sense, Ricoeur had not read the same Freud as
Lacan, did not owe anything to his teaching, and was more inclined to read Benveniste than Saussure and Jakobson. The hermeneutic project was part of an effort to
transcend phenomenology, and not of a reelaboration of Freudianism.

Nevertheless, at Bonneval, and for strategic reasons, Lacan had the impression, or pretended to believe, that Ricoeur's approach to Freud and his own were
tending toward the same sort of reevaluation. Since he was looking for recognition,
he sought out the philosopher and told him that he had at last found a discourse
suited to his teaching. He brought him back to Paris in his car, invited him to dinner,
and proposed that he come to his seminar.[45] Ricoeur accepted all the more willingly
in that he was preparing his major work on Freud and felt he could benefit from
Lacan's teaching. Without having read a single one of Lacan's texts, he began coming each week to hear him speak. During the same period, along with Yves Bertherat, a Catholic psychiatrist and a student of Ey and Lacan, he attended the case
presentations at Sainte-Anne. At the same time, he had psychoanalytic technique
explained to him by members of the other camp: Serge Lebovici and René Diatkine.
In a word, he immersed himself deeply in the Freudian adventure. Despite all his
efforts, he found himself unable to understand a word of Lacan. He found his discourse "uselessly difficult and perverse in its proclivity toward suspension." [46] Nonetheless, with all his characteristic good will, he continued to attend the seminar and
had Lacan's words explained to him by his Christian friends, Alphonse de Waelhens
and Antoine Vergote, who were also phenomenologists, but nevertheless Lacanians.
On several occasions, Moustapha Safouan joined in, but nothing seemed to work—
Ricoeur remained closed to a teaching he judged to be hermetic.

Lacan, for his part, deployed all his charms with the philosopher and was firmly convinced of his enthusiasm. He hoped to see his teaching figure prominently in the forthcoming work whose great success seemed already certain. Ricoeur was a recognized figure and Lacan was as yet not. . . . During the two or three years that this curious set of cross-purposes persisted, the misunderstanding between the two men was total. Ricoeur did not know what to say to Lacan, and Lacan was convinced that Ricoeur understood what he was saying. Soon the philosopher's son began to accompany his father to the seminar. Jean-Paul Ricoeur was studying medicine. No sooner did he hear Lacan than he had the opposite reaction to his father's. He had already begun to read Freud, understood the message, and rather quickly decided to direct himself toward a Lacanian couch in order to complete his training. At the end of each seminar, he would discuss matters with his father. Without yet enunciating any specific disagreement, he found in Lacan's words an access to a personal meditation on psychoanalysis. Like all those of his generation, he was passionately interested in structuralist reelaborations. Jean-Paul listened, Paul resisted, and Jacques waited. . . .

It is probable that fragments of three different seminars were heard by the two protagonists of this story: *Transference, Anxiety,* and *Identification.* Three key phases in the elaboration of Lacan's thought. Even as he persisted in attending the show, Ricoeur continued to work on his book. No doubt he found it hard to bear the direction his son was taking: a lively interest in Lacan and in a Freud different from his own. In the fall of 1961, the father delivered the Terry Lectures at Yale University; then, in 1962, he traveled to Louvain for a series of eight lectures devoted to Freud. At the same time, he continued to teach his course at the Sorbonne. Finally, in 1964, his book was completed. He gave the manuscript to François Wahl, his codirector at Éditions du Seuil of the series "L'Ordre philosophique." That same year, Jean-Paul moved to Marseille to prepare his CES [*certificat d'études supérieures*] in psychiatry. Four years later, he began his first analysis with Jenny Aubry, who had just established herself in the region. Shortly thereafter, he became a member of the EFP.

At the end of 1963, Paul Ricoeur was preparing to participate in a congress in Rome organized by Professor Enrico Castelli. Returning from still one more session of the seminar, he told himself once again that he could not understand anything of what Lacan was saying. At the very moment he was indulging in that reflection, the telephone rang and Lacan asked, "What do you think, *mon cher,* of what I enunciated today?" Ricoeur answered abruptly, "I was just in the process of telling myself that I find what you say impenetrable." In a fury Lacan hung up. He realized that he had misjudged the other at the very moment he had undergone—at the hands of the IPA—his most stinging defeat. He reacted like a mistress deceived by her lover.

The colloquium took place from January 7 to January 12, 1964. Its theme was "Technique and Casuistry." Before making the trip, Ricoeur read for the first time the *Rome Discourse.* Lacan was also invited. On a day of icy cold, he rediscovered the foreign city where he had felt so at home, the city of Bernini and the Reconquest. He stayed again at the Hotel Hassler. No doubt he had not prepared anything, so busy was he writing up his famous statement on "excommunication" for January 15. He informed Castelli that he would not deliver his lecture on "the Freudian *Trieb* [drive]," lest his ideas be "stolen by Ricoeur." Later he would write, "We refrained from giving over too early [at the colloquium] to a dissemination beyond our control what we have since articulated on the drive in our lectures at the École normale supérieure, which began a few days later."[47]

In Rome, then, Lacan did not give any presentation, but intervened in the discussion. Ricoeur wanted to know to what extent the psychoanalyst's desire caused psychoanalytic technique to enter into the realm of the technical. Lacan responded that they were two heterogeneous domains. Ricoeur took the offensive in his response by questioning his interlocutor on metaphor, metonymy, the bar between signifier and signified, and the distinction between those two terms. Then he spoke of the violence of linguistic operations. Lacan shot back that they were not violent but characteristic. The discussion stagnated. Ricoeur evoked the relations of force in language and Lacan the relations of persuasion. Finally, he declared that the esoteric aspect of an experience could not be invoked, since every approach partook of a cleavage.[48] Misunderstanding or significant dialogue? The two men in any event exchanged a few decorous words on their reciprocal situations. As in the case of Bonneval, Lacan subsequently summarized his interventions. He called the piece "Du 'Trieb' de Freud et du désir du psychanalyste [On Freud's 'drive' and the psychoanalyst's desire]." In Rome, a joke made its way through the lecture room: "Will we ever know what the psychoanalyst's desire is?"

One evening, Lacan said to Ricoeur and his wife, "Come, let's have some fun." They took a taxi and had dinner in Trastevere. The restaurant was rather sinister. At meal's end, Lacan exclaimed, "Go ahead and pay, Ricoeur. You remember I invited you to a 'queer' restaurant at Bonneval." Ricoeur was dumbfounded, but did as he was told after having already paid for the taxi. Another car ride, another stop: Lacan had the couple get out on the banks of the Tiber, telling them he had to pay a visit to an old friend. The philosopher and his wife waited after again paying the taxi fare. Then Lacan returned and decided to walk back to his hotel. The following day, he confessed to Simone Ricoeur that he had behaved quite boorishly. To say the least. . . .

De l'interprétation appeared in May 1965. The book quickly achieved considerable success. It was at once well received, because it was the first book of its kind, and highly criticized because phenomenology had gone out of style. It was 528 pages long and divided into three consecutive books: a problematic, an analytic, and a dialectic. The first was devoted to Freud's situation, that is, to a definition of hermeneutics; the second to a more neutral reading of the Freudian *corpus;* and the third to an interpretation of Freudianism. All the themes developed at Bonneval were present without any change in theoretical order. Freudian epistemology was characterized as the combination of a hermeneutics of meaning and an energetics of drives. The author affirmed that his was an essay on Freud, in which two elements were lacking: analytic experience and a consideration of post-Freudian schools. An evaluation of Lacan's teaching would thus be absent from the work, but Ricoeur did not refrain from commenting on Lacan's theses concerning language.

On the subject of *Fonction et Champ de la parole et du langage* [*The Function of Language in Psychoanalysis*], Ricoeur emphasized that his critique of behaviorist reformulations was quite close to what Lacan had said. He then said that Lacan had "eliminated energetics to the benefit of linguistics." Finally, he quoted *L'Instance de la lettre* and *Propos sur la causalité psychique*. Further on, he ascribed to Lacan and the Lacanians a "linguistic conception of the unconscious," and discussed at some length the article by Benveniste that had been published in the first issue of *La Psychanalyse*.[49] Plainly, he knew how to read that article, just as he was able to interpret in his way Freud's work or the theses of ego psychology. But he erred fundamentally when it came to what Lacan was up to. Had he succeeded in understanding Lacan's use of structural concepts, he would never have written that the latter had "eliminated energetics to the benefit of linguistics" or proposed a "linguistic conception of the unconscious." On the other hand, without understanding him, he was able to affirm that his own critique of behaviorism converged with Lacan's since such an observation did not depend on a serious reading of the texts but on "common sense" or "current opinion."

As far as the use of linguistics was concerned, Lacan did nothing of what Ricoeur claimed. He employed certain concepts from linguistics to effect a rearticulation of Freud's text, but never did he implement the slightest "linguistic conception of the unconscious." As for the "elimination of energetics," it was not part of Lacan's project since that project was concerned with neither energetics nor linguistics as such, nor with any other "elimination." Not only did Ricoeur not "steal Lacan's ideas," but so little did he "steal" them that he misconstrued them completely. He invented a Lacan he was unable to read and whom he tried in vain to confront.

Lacan, for his part, felt offended. When he became acquainted with the book, he went into a rage. He had expected to be glorified and found himself misunderstood by a celebrated philosopher who had attended his seminar. Already in Rome he had extorted payment of his bills; thereafter he would turn positively odious, complaining to his entourage that he was the victim of a "plagiarist." The "rumor" began to spread: Credulous disciples were firmly convinced that Ricoeur had pilfered Lacan's ideas. If proof were needed, he was there at the seminar.[50]

The discussion turned venomous when Valabrega independently published in *Critique* an article in which he emphasized the point that Ricoeur had not rendered unto Caesar what was Caesar's, whereas as a good Christian, he had rendered unto God what was God's. Valabrega used the word "plagiarism" in accusing certain former disciples of Lacan of *paraphrasing* their master's style. But he reproached Ricoeur simply with failing to acknowledge that Lacan was first in France to have introduced the study of language in the field of psychoanalytic research. Then, he added, "In proceeding in that manner, Ricoeur has made his own many ideas which originally did not belong to him. He allows the impression that the theses he developed from his reading were the fruit of his own solitary meditation, which would be a tremendous and admirable thing, to be sure, but which is not true."[51]

Instead of observing that there were parallel concerns being pursued in the discourses of Ricoeur and Lacan, Valabrega assumed that Ricoeur had drawn on Lacan's teaching without acknowledging it.[52] He did not see that if the philosopher had actually understood the meaning of Lacan's reelaboration, he would undoubtedly not have written the same book. The entire business of this fantasy of stolen ideas and "non-plagiary" should be examined in reverse. What is problematic is the misapprehension of Lacan's work in Ricoeur's book and not any alleged theft. In other words, it may be wondered why regular attendance at Lacan's seminar had not had any effect on Ricoeur's investigation: neither on his reading of Freud, which was already complete by 1960, nor on his apprehension of Lacan's texts. What one is confronted with is less a case of *borrowing* than of *resistance.* The debate is thus less a matter of philosophy than of the circumstances of its protagonists.

Although he had not been accused of plagiarism, Paul Ricoeur was indignant at Valabrega's article. In a reply published by *Critique,* at the request of Michel Foucault, he gave free reign to his fury. He emphasized that coming from a psychoanalyst, statements such as Valabrega's were unbelievable, and then recalled that the outline of his interpretation of Freud had been completed before he had ever read Lacan or attended his seminar. Concerning that attendance and that reading, he said no more than was already to be found in his book. Finally, he concluded with these words, "What a proprietary mentality! Doesn't Freud also say important things on the subject of having and devouring, on money and excrement? Are ideas distinct things that one can possess and be robbed of? As though what counted was not the thought activating them and concerning which no one can say that he 'has' it." [53]

While Ricoeur was publishing his reply in *Critique* a long article on *De l'interprétation* by Michel Tort appeared in *Les Temps modernes.*[54] It was a superbly documented and withering attack which situated the debate on philosophical grounds. Tort did not know Ricoeur. He was not aware that he had attended the seminar; he knew nothing of Lacan's fantasies and had not read Valabrega's article.[55] He criticized the book's contents, which he found obscurantist, reactionary, and clerical. Michel Tort was part of that "radical" generation of the 1960s which discovered Lacan's work under the banner of materialism. He gave the article to J.-B. Pontalis, who did not impede its publication in any way, and even confessed his satisfaction with it.

Tort distinguished between a *reading* and an *interpretation,* and showed that a hermeneutic of Christian and phenomenological inspiration contributed nothing to a grasp of the texts because it was obsolete. Without invoking the theme of "stolen ideas," which never occurred to him, he noted the existence of a similarity in the works of Lacan and Ricoeur. Then he emphasized that Lacan had extricated psychoanalysis from the conceptual swamp in which psychologists and philosophers had kept it. "Thus," he wrote, "when Paul Ricoeur declares in a note that a critique 'quite close' to his own in situating the site and object of psychoanalysis might be derived from the *Rome Discourse,* his comment, it should be confessed, falls a bit short of the truth. For—no doubt he would not be averse to admitting it—it would be rendering justice to psychoanalysis itself to observe that all the concepts *without exception* used by Ricoeur to define the specific problematic of Freudianism are concepts elaborated on the basis of that *Discourse* by J. Lacan. . . . And it is possible to gauge just how much the absence of such bearings would have compromised P.

Ricoeur's analysis once one consults a copy of the chapters written by him on the Freudian unconscious in *Le volontaire et l'involontaire* (1950). It in fact appears that he was not at that time able to draw on his own intellectual stock for the wherewithal to delineate with as much assurance as in *De l'interprétation* the domain of psychoanalysis in relation to psychology, since—without being impeded by subtleties—he did not hesitate to write: 'The unconscious signifies in me that not only my body but my psyche is available to objective treatment: There is a psyche-object just as there is a body-object. *Mental physics* is inexpugnable in this case. The object *par excellence* of psychology as a science is the unconscious. . . .' It will be seen from this all too brief retrospective just what advantage a philosophical meditation has derived from replacing its references to candid Dalbiez with others to J. Lacan." [56]

In that passage, Tort showed himself to be more subtle than Valabrega. He did not reproach Ricoeur with appropriating concepts elaborated by Lacan without acknowledgment, but proposed an analysis of the historical situation of his undertaking. He emphasized that if Ricoeur had not been aware of Lacanian coordinates, his interpretation of Freud would have been compromised, since in 1950 he took the unconscious to be the object of psychology. In other words, Tort attempted to show that the dissemination and the existence of Lacanian thought had modified the French intellectual landscape, to an extent allowing thinkers to modify their methods or to imagine theirs were converging with Lacan's.

The argument was interesting, since it attempted to explain theoretically the presence in Ricoeur's book of a problematic shared by all those who at the time were interested in the relation between the unconscious and language. In that sense, it mattered little who had read what when, or who had had "priority," since Lacan's teaching had been part of the intellectual climate since 1953. It might be said, but Tort did not say so, that Ricoeur, like others, had been influenced unwittingly by Lacan's investigations and that he had confronted them by way of his own misunderstandings. We are thus quite far from the absurd debate over a "theft of ideas."

And yet the very existence of such a discussion, on the subject of an act of "non-plagiary" or a "false theft of ideas," bears its own lesson. It reveals that every doctrine is always apprehended "off the mark" in relation to what it is saying. And that is all the more the case when an author believes himself possessor of the sole truth of a text. Lacan erred in the affair in thinking that his teaching was being stolen from him. Ricoeur was not quite right in saying that Valabrega had accused him of plagiarism, and Valabrega did not see that in order to render unto Caesar what is Caesar's, one first has to know who Caesar is. Texts, like intentions, are always misread, and every interpretation bears with it the very history of the possibilities of a plural reading, the active symptom of knowledge's advance. It is, moreover, remarkable to realize that Michel Tort's presentation fueled the polemic over the "theft" of ideas, whereas its author was speaking of something entirely different and was even unaware of that polemic.

In 1969, Paul Ricoeur was elected dean of the Faculté des Lettres at Nanterre. During that troubled period, he courageously agreed to take on a responsibility that others had fled. In the exercise of his functions, he had to deal with disturbed youths who had infiltrated student ranks and crowned him with a garbage pail top. That act of violence aroused a feeling of horror and repulsion in public opinion with respect to the ongoing confrontation. On that occasion, Jean-Paul Valabrega sent a letter to Paul Ricoeur asking him not to consider his past polemic as in any way implying approval of the methods whose victim he had just been. He maintained his criticism of the book, but expressed disapproval of all forms of brutality and total-itarianism.[57]

On that day, at Nanterre, among those hurling garbage cans, a young man seriously pondered recourse to armed struggle. Some time later, he would find him-self, like a number of others, on Lacan's couch, an experience that would stop him from drifting toward terrorism.

III. Recourse to Formal Logic

At the very time the structuralist adventure was in its heyday, there appeared, in January 1966, the first issue of *Cahiers pour l'analyse* ["Notebooks for analysis"]. The title had been chosen by Miller, alluding to the *pour* [for] in *Problèmes cruciaux "pour" la psychanalyse* and *Pour Marx*. The word *analyse* was retained, on the one hand, because of Condillac, and on the other, because of psychoanalysis. The jour-nal was published by the epistemological circle of the ENS. The names of Grosri-chard, Miller, Milner, and Regnault, all of whom belonged to the EFP, could be found on the editorial board. A quotation from Georges Canguilhem served as an epigraph and established the tone: "To work a concept is to vary its extension and comprehension, to generalize it through the incorporation of features outside it, to export it outside its region of origin, to take it as a model or inversely to find a model for it, in brief, to confer on it gradually, through regulated transformations, the function of a form."[58] Signed by J.-A. Miller, an editor's introduction also re-vealed its colors. For Althusser's former students, reassembled under the banner of Lacanianism, it was to be a matter of presenting texts dealing with logic, linguistics, psychoanalysis, and the sciences of analysis in order to contribute to the constitution of a theory of discourse: "Epistemology, from our point of view, may be defined as the history and theory of the discourse of *science* (its birth justifies the singular). By discourse, we mean a linguistic process constrained by truth. As for what that aim implies in our eyes, to wit, a suture, it will be seen from the texts composing this first issue. Finally, we call *analytic* any discourse insofar as it is restricted to putting into place units which are produced and repeated, whatever the principle it assigns to the transformations in its system. Analysis in the strict sense, the theory that treats as such the concepts of element and combinatorial. Who can doubt that such research is of the first importance to dialectical materialism in view of the import ascribed to it by Louis Althusser and of its present day state? . . . There is nothing in our project redolent of the specificity of a doctrine; for us, it is solely a matter of training ourselves, following our masters, in conceptual rigor."[59]

Despite the homage paid to Althusser and Canguilhem, the first issue of *Ca-hiers pour l'analyse* effected without any ado a break with the teachings of those two masters. The announcement of an epistemology centered on the primacy of the discourse of science—in the singular—tended to give validity to a logic-dominated project at the expense of a history of sciences based on the recognition of a plurality of continents. As opposed to the tradition of a history of sciences in the manner of Althusser or of Canguilhem, the editors of the *Cahiers* proposed that analytic discourse serve as a model for a theory of science itself. Now that development also affected the Lacanian position, as though it were a matter for Lacan of stepping outside classical structuralism and achieving a possible reintroduction of the subject into science by the nonpsychological route of a *logic of the signifier.*

After the meditation centered on the foundations of psychoanalysis during the academic year 1963–64, Lacan devoted his seminar of the following year to "crucial problems for psychoanalysis." [60] At the same time, he set up the institutional structures of his school, still seeking to reopen the battle against neo-Freudian ideals, as represented in France by the SPP and by the course Lagache had taken. Strong in the support he had found at the ENS, he wanted to endow his theory with a formalization that might spare him the ordeal of undergoing revisions of the sort Freud had. Within the perspective of such a "scientifization," he proceeded to a reelaboration of his own doctrine while referring implicitly to the efforts of the epistemological circle. He thus invited both Yves Duroux and Jacques-Alain Miller to make presentations to his seminar on the foundations of Frege's logic. At the same time, at the request of students at the ENS, Serge Leclaire devoted a seminar at the rue d'Ulm to the relation between analytic experience and its theorization. Thanks to that exchange, links began to be established between the Salle Dussane, the Epistemological Circle, and the nascent EFP. Still faithful to his role as history's first Lacanian, Leclaire slowly forgot his terrible defeat and plunged into the new hypertheoretical orientation. He became friends with the philosophers of the ENS who thereafter would be part of the Lacanian family.

In order to grasp the decisive evolution that occurred in Lacan's thought between the winter of 1964 and the winter of the following year, and whose repercussions affected the organization of the EFP, comparisons should be made between two lectures delivered by Lacan at the seminar and the two presentations by Duroux and Miller, which also took place at the seminar. The first lecture by Lacan dealt with Chomsky and opened the seminar on "crucial problems." The second was entitled "La science et la vérité [Science and Truth]" and was the opening session of the 1965–66 seminar on "the object of psychoanalysis." As for the two student presentations, they were delivered in February 1965 and reproduced—as "La science et la vérité"—in the first issue of *Cahiers pour l'analyse.* [61]

A contemporary of Freud's, the German mathematician and philosopher Gottlob Frege worked in isolation for thirty years before being recognized by Bertrand Russell as the founder of modern symbolic logic. As opposed to Leibniz, he sought to construct not a language representing thought, but a script that might ground representation. He delineated the essential elements of an *ideography,* that is, a logical language liberated from spoken language. He advanced that notion in his first work, *Die Begriffschrift,* which passed almost unnoticed by his contemporaries. [62] Then, with the *Foundations of Arithmetic,* published in 1884, he criticized the empiricist and psychologizing prejudices of the thinkers of his day. To his mind, the construction of a symbolic language should have enabled a grounding of arithmetic in purely logical notions, purifying it of any appeal to intuition, that is, to a subject of unmediated consciousness. Whence this definition: "The logical may be defined as that which is thought or constructed outside of any intuition, that which is general to the point of belonging to every language and such that no language would be conceivable without it." [63]

Whereas arithmeticians had not conducted their inquiries beyond cardinal numbers and had drawn inspiration from the intuitive idea of number, Frege undertook to define cardinal numbers in terms transcending experience, as *an extension of the concept:* that which succeeds in freeing the concept of number from its psychological determination. This reduction of the psychological took place in two stages. Frege began by distinguishing two kinds of representation. On one side, he located subjective representations, and on the other those partaking of objectivity. The move had the aim of eliminating any reference to a subject and of treating objective representations as logical phenomena. In a second stage, Frege related number to the realm of objective representation, that is, to concepts. The diversity of enumerations thus became the index of a substitution of concepts on which number registered its effect. Numbers were linked to an identity relation allowing for objects or concepts to be ordered in a biunivocal manner. Through that identity relation, all relations of identity or *equivalence* of the concept of number were determined and different numbers isolated. That last operation amounted to defining zero and the successor. Zero was defined by the concept of being nonidentical to itself, that is, by a logical contradiction which itself guaranteed the nonexistence of the object. As for the notion of *successor,* Frege founded it on a double contradiction in the transition from zero to one: He gave himself a concept "equal to zero" and inferred from it that the object falling under that concept was the object zero. As a result, *one* followed *zero* to the extent that *one* was attributed to the concept *equal to zero.*

Part of Frege's operation thus consisted in excluding the psychological subject from operations of thought, which were then ascribed to a formal or symbolic logic. In 1965, the works of Frege and his followers were scarcely known to an intelligentsia working in a different tradition so far as the history of sciences was concerned. Nevertheless, with the structuralist explosion a new interest in logic had emerged, to the extent that the study of linguistic structures tended to lead to a consideration of the most general phenomena of thought and language. That interest was itself contemporaneous with an inquiry into Saussure's legacy. Indeed at the time structuralism was becoming a dominant phenomenon on the intellectual scene, French linguists were becoming acquainted with the research of Noam Chomsky, reading his inaugural work *Syntactic Structures* (1957).[64]

A student of Roman Jakobson, the American linguist was working at the time in collaboration with Morris Halle at M.I.T. In his critique of classical structuralism, he started from the idea that modern science ought to abandon the classification of facts in favor of hypothetical models capable of predicting and explaining language's *creativity.* Instead of defining language in terms of signs, Chomsky circumscribed it in terms of its syntax as a set of sentences. It followed that the aim of linguistics was to elaborate the *grammar* of a language, as the explicit model of that language, by separating "grammatical" sequences from "agrammatical" ones. In order to bring off such an undertaking, it was necessary to reintroduce into language the notion of an intuitive subject there where Saussure had relegated it to the realm of speech [*parole*]. Chomsky called the innate aptitude of a speaking subject *competence,* and *performance* the manner in which competence was implemented in discursive acts. In order to account for the phenomenon of language, outside of any taxonomy, the new linguistics was to construct a model or *grammar of competence,* associated with another model, a *grammar of performance,* which itself comprised two models: that of *emission* (the speaker) and that of *reception* (the listener). Thus, according to Chomsky, might the creative aspect of language be revealed.[65] To be sure, Chomsky did not assimilate the notion of grammaticality to that of meaning and distinguished between the two with the help of two English sentences concerning which he emphasized that they had no meaning. The first was said to be "grammatical," while the second was said to be "agrammatical":

1. Colorless green ideas sleep furiously.
2. Furiously sleep ideas green colorless.[66]

If Chomsky's undertaking represented the first attempt in the history of linguistics to delineate the grammatical and the agrammatical on the basis of the opposition between meaning and nonmeaning, it ran two principal risks. The first consisted in "muzzling" metaphoricity and the second in reviving the notion of a psychological subject by way of the innate.[67]

In 1959, Jakobson subjected Chomsky to a rather harsh critique. Concerning the example of "colorless green ideas," he showed that "colorless green" was synonymous with "pale green" and that a person's ideas might very well be benumbed by frenetic sleep. In sum, he reproached his student for neglecting the metaphorical power of language and called *Syntactic Structures* a proof by the absurd of the impossibility of constructing a nonsemantic theory of grammatical structure. Against Chomsky, he proposed limiting the notion of grammaticality to cases in which all possibility of semantic information had disappeared.[68]

When he in turn commented on Chomsky's example, in December 1964,[69] Lacan took up Jakobson's critique on his own. As a worthy heir to Surrealism, he emphasized that every grammatical sentence is of necessity endowed with "absolutely any" meaning, which escaped the subject's consciousness. Thus the example can afford access to the very image of the unconscious: "Thoughts exhausted in their greenness [or crudity] sleep a slumber accompanied by furor."

Criticizing Chomsky's effort amounted for Lacan to avoiding a rejection, pure and simple, of structuralism. But the question put to the new linguistics of syntax was itself inspired by a need to reaffirm the presence of the subject of the unconscious in the language chain. Lacan thus opposed a *formal theory of the signifier* to a grammatical model. In so doing, he reproached Chomskyan formalization with forgetting "being" and its "rift" for the sake of confining the subject in grammar. In brief, against the risk of a return to intuitionism, Lacan played the card of Fregean logic whose importance he had just discovered. Through it he would be able to define an "ex-centric" status of the subject in its relation no longer to consciousness but to science. The transition from a theory of the signifier to its logic thus occurred for him by way of J.-A. Miller's presentation.

Duroux and Miller had worked their way through *The Foundations of Arithmetic* together. They each perceived the benefit Freudian theory might derive from it, and they both saw as well how Lacanian doctrine might in turn make use of it to strengthen its polemic against psychology. But whereas Duroux was satisfied with simply presenting Frege's theses, Miller thought through the Lacanian theory of the signifier afresh in the context of Frege's logic. First he issued a provocative declaration to the seminar audience. Speaking as an avid Fregean, he situated himself, in relation to psychoanalysts, in the position of an "ex-centered subject," daring to deal with "the thing" without having arrived at it by way of the couch. Pursuing that angle, he challenged Lacan's disciples as to their situation in the movement: "He who has not acquired, through a personal analysis, the precise notions which it alone is capable of bestowing has no right to be concerned with psychoanalysis. The rigor of that interdiction, uttered by Freud in his *New Lectures on Psychoanalysis,* no doubt, ladies and gentleman, is the object of your respect. If, transgressing those limits, psychoanalysis is what I am about to speak about, listening to someone of whom you know he is incapable of producing the credentials that might authorize your confidence, *what are you doing here?* Or, on the other hand, if my subject is not psychoanalysis, to you who so faithfully direct your steps to this auditorium in order to be addressed on problems relating to the Freudian field, I say: *What indeed are you doing here?*[70]

After that introduction, Miller articulated Frege's conception of zero and its successors with the Lacanian theory of the signifier. He called the subject's relation to the chain one of *suture,* adding that the subject figures in it in place of zero as the *marker replacing a lack.* In passing, he observed that the concept of *suture* was not present as such in Lacanian doctrine. But he affirmed immediately thereafter that Lacan, like Frege, excluded consciousness from any definition of the subject. The Millerian interpretation of the theory of the signifier led to a rearticulation of Lacanianism which was to have two immediate consequences, one theoretical and the other political.

On the theoretical level, it consisted in making of Lacanianism the model *par excellence* of a Freudianism capable of escaping *in itself* the ideals of psychology: as though, thanks to the good graces of logic, any theory could succeed in freeing itself from the contingencies of its environment, history, or mode of implantation by virtue of its utter scientificity. On the political level, the rearticulation allowed one to designate qualified adversaries as "deviationists" in relation to a doctrine representing normalization per se in its all-powerful singularity. Miller, moreover, had no compunctions about putting Lacanian theory thus rectified by Fregean logic to work. He courteously referred to an article by Piera Aulagnier, published in the last issue of *La Psychanalyse,*[71] and accused it of constituting a "Lagachian deviation from Lacanianism." Lacan, who had approved the text at the time of its publication, then suggested to Aulagnier that she respond to Miller at the following session. But she abstained, judging the accusation to be without clinical basis. The attack would be withdrawn from the version of the presentation ("La Suture") published in *Cahiers pour l'analyse*.

In his 1964 article, "Freud et Lacan," Althusser had used the term *revisionism* to refer to the "American" school in an attempt to show that Lacan had inaugurated a reading of Freud capable of freeing psychoanalysis from the ideals of psychology. Never was that revisionism defined as a *deviationism* in Althusser's conception of science. For the Althusserians, the hypertheoretical phase of their work was to lead to an antirevisionist struggle, but for the Lacanians of *Cahiers pour l'analyse* and especially for Miller, it tended to lead to a use of formal logic and science in terms of antideviationism. The two words are not identical, even if they belonged, in the context of the 1960s, to a common stem. Deviation always entails the existence of a pathology in relation to a norm, whereas revision designated a perpetually present process within a doctrine subject to continuous transformation. Since the days of his baroque reelaboration, Lacan had come to prefer the term "deviation" to situate neo-Freudianism in opposition to his theory, which he dubbed "scientific" in the belief that it might spare it the "revisions" Freud's had undergone. At the time of Miller's presentation, he had never referred to the manner in which his disciples applied his doctrine as a *deviation*. He tended to reproach them, and others, for using his teaching. And it was Anika Lemaire, we have seen, who, with reference to Laplanche, would play the role of protector of the dogma.

In 1965, Miller's discourse *radicalized* Lacan's. In theory, that discourse pretended to be strictly Lacanian, but in practice, it brought to Lacanianism the pressure of a combative militantism. In that sense there thus existed, already at that time, a *Millerian representation* of Lacanianism which was not a mere translation of Lacanian doctrine. Whereas Lacan produced concepts open to a certain ambiguity, Miller tended to clarify or rationalize Lacanian conceptuality so as to make it more uniform and occasionally more coherent. The slippage is all the more difficult to grasp in that it was frequently not perceived as such by the two men. Miller was intent on being the loyal commentator of the master and did not notice that on occasion he was borrowing from the master reformulations elaborated from his own doctrine. Between the style of the brilliant young man, in a rush to act, and the utterances of the old master, subject to multiple interpretations, so powerful an osmosis occurred that one has the impression that the former was giving up his own writing in order to submit to the pronouncements of the latter, and that the latter was borrowing his statements from the former in the belief that they were his own. In Miller, Lacan met up with that reader—at once mirror and adversary to himself—whom he had spent his life looking for: a mixture of Corneille's Rodrigue and the historical Saint-Just.

During those years, the young Normalien dreamed of Hugo's *La légende des siècles* [*The Legend of the Centuries*]. He identified with the character of Aymerillot. It is a lovely tale with a certain anticipatory force. It goes as follows: Charlemagne was sad upon returning from Roncevaux. He had lost Roland and wanted to conquer Narbonne. He addressed his barons, his old comrades in arms, but none was willing to take up the challenge. All were mortified and stared at the ground. Suddenly Aymerillot stepped out of the ranks. He was wan and frail, "I have come to ask you for what no man wants, the honor of being, oh my King!, if God does not forsake me, the man of whom it will be said: It was he who took Narbonne. . . . I will enter Narbonne and I will be its conqueror. Later, I will punish scoffers, should any remain." More radiant than an archangel, Charlemagne said to Aymerillot, "You will be a count paladin." The following day the youth took the city.[72]

Miller would indeed "take Narbonne" and the barons would lose their kingdom.

If Lacan found in Miller the man of action his theory needed, Miller found in Lacanianism the theory of his politics. His hyperlogical interpretation of Lacanian doctrine had several functions. First of all, it provided support for the commanding position Lacan held in his school. Through it, Lacan sought to avoid the errors of neo-Freudianism by proposing a model of teaching in which a reference to science would rectify any institutional pragmatism. In addition, it justified the decentering of the seminar outside the psychiatric and psychoanalytic community and thus Lacan's policy of expansion. Finally, it situated Miller's position of extraterritoriality, the result of his self-coronation, through the suture and against the practitioners of the unconscious, as an "extra-therapeutic" subject, that is, as chief spokesman for Lacanianism's "scientific" truth. The young man would retain that position for more than ten years before becoming, by way of the couch, the great leader's legitimate heir.

The psychoanalysts reacted to the hyperlogical orientation much as Piera Aulagnier had. They behaved like "notables," refused to debate, and gave a rather icy reception to this "agitator" who had penetrated their circle in order to dictate the master's law to them. In their eyes, the newcomer was a spoilsport. They were all the more jealous of him in that they did not understand very much of the new logical discourse whose acuteness they feared and whose rigor they envied. They were therapists and stood accused of ignorance; he was a philosopher scorned for his arrogance and clinical inexperience. A mutual distrust thus settled over the seminar and the EFP, between the clan of Normaliens without couch and the troop of therapists, suddenly deprived of a master and a doctrine. It was a distrust that was pernicious for all concerned, since it risked leading to a deeper and deeper split between the hypertheoretical orientation of the one group and the pragmatism of the other.

For the while, Serge Leclaire was alone in accepting a direct confrontation, using his personal prestige to bring about a link between the Cercle d'épistemologie and clinical teaching. With his characteristic taste for adventure, he responded to Miller on the suture. Instead of reproaching him for his lack of clinical training, he politely attacked him on theoretical grounds. He situated the young man in the position of a logician allied with a suturing function and pitted him against the impossible localization of the psychoanalyst, whose passion would consist in preventing suture. That move—out of cat's cradle—showed that Leclaire had understood perfectly well the logic of deviation on which Miller's discourse on the suture was based. Against it, he chose, as always, the median path of negotiation.[73]

If Miller conducted a reading of Lacanian doctrine in the light of Frege's logic, Lacan would have implicit recourse to that reading when he wrote up, in November 1965, the opening session of his seminar on "the object of psychoanalysis." He called it "La science et la vérité," and published it *in extenso* in *Cahiers pour l'analyse*. To be sure, he had read *The Foundations of Arithmetic* before hearing Miller, and he had already used at least once the notion of suture. But Miller himself had commented that the conceptualization of that notion was absent from Lacan's writing. Without mentioning Miller's presentation, Lacan proceeded to recycle the truly Millerian concept of suture in order to underwrite a hyperlogical reelaboration of his theory of the signifier.

On the basis of the minimal logic evolved from Frege, Miller called for a concept of "structural causality" able to account for the suture, that is, for that place of the subject as surrogate of a lack. Lacan responded to that question on both Miller's ground and on Leclaire's. If the subject is the effect of the signifier, he does indeed occupy the place of a lack: He appears and disappears in a repetitive pulsation. But how ought one to proceed so that the analyst is neither a logician of the suture nor an unlocalizable ear? To avoid that contradiction, which would result in splitting theory from practice, in the form of a tendential cleavage between *théoricisme* and pragmatism, Lacan effected a hyperlogical rearticulation of structuralism on the model of his rearticulation of Freudianism. Without abandoning the reference to structuralism, he summoned Alexandre Koyré and Kurt Gödel to his aid. From the one, he took the idea that modern science—from which the *Cogito* emerged—had entailed a dramatic devaluation of being, and from the other borrowed nothing less than his second theorem on incompleteness, pertaining to the fact that the notion of truth cannot be completely formalized. Lacan noted that the failure of such formalization was symptomatic of the general failure of science as such in its quest for suture. From that astonishing bit of conceptual tinkering, he inferred that the experience of Cartesian doubt marked the subject's being with a division between knowledge and truth.

Lacan had already appealed to Descartes in order to construct a notion of the "subject of the unconscious" alien to the Freudian problematic. But Gödel's theorem and Koyré's works, assembled as he chose, allowed him to advance a step further. Instead of calling the subject's relation to the chain "suture" and privileging its "closure" over its "opening," he reworked the term to affirm that science *as such* fails to suture—or to effect a complete formalization of—the subject. And he invoked Gödel's theorem and Chomsky's research as evidence. For Lacan, the (divided, split, foreclosed, etc.) subject is the correlate of science and that correlate is called the *subject of science*. If classical structuralism had allowed for a decentering of the subject, as Freud had done through his own discovery, it ran the risk, in serving the ideal of the human sciences, of unwittingly reconstructing a humanism of the "full" (psychological, etc.) subject; and it might do so all the more to the extent that it neglected the position of the unconscious. Consequently only inclusion in a logic might allow psychoanalysis to step out of its status as a human science. But that logic, according to Lacan, was a *logic of incompleteness,* a science of the fallen subject, a science of the unsutured correlate; in sum, it was the science of the *subject of science*. It listened to the suture without suturing, heard the paranoid subject, and pricked up its ear before the "ex-centered" subject of modern scientific civilization.

Against the ascendancy of a hyperlogical formal logic, Lacan was banking on the paradox of a logic of the symbolic function. And with that, instead of invoking the Freudian break as he had until then, he appealed to the founding father's scientistic tendencies. That appeal to "scientism" allowed him to give fresh currency to an ideal of scientificity, that is, a universalism, which he translated into a logic of the signifier or a *science of structural causality*. Psychoanalysis would thereafter have the subject of science (which was itself an effect of the signifier) as its subject. In that context, it rejected magic, on the one hand, and religion on the other. The first because it included the subject within the natural order of the world while excluding it from science, and the second because it forced the subject to ascribe the cause of its desire to God. Both one and the other were paths to obscurantism.

In the name of that ideal of scientificity, Lacan was intent on fighting any psychologizing rearticulation of psychoanalysis in terms of the human sciences. But he also reaffirmed his hostility to what we have called the "hypnotic symptom"— that originary site toward which an experience of the unconscious slips when it is not articulated with the primacy of a theory.[74] As a result, he proposed the constitution of a transmissible mode of knowledge, grounded in logic, and capable of respecting the division of the subject. That knowledge would have to be articulated with a style of training which, instead of being based on prevailing institutional models, would combine in a common equilibrium the styles of teaching emergent from therapy with those elaborated by science.

That programmatic text announced the major "clean-up" Lacan was about to embark on. First of all, within his school, through the introduction of the *passe* as the "logical" principle informing valid training. Then in his doctrine, through the establishment of a psychoanalytic *matheme* capable of conveying clinical knowledge in the Leibnizian form of a universal language. It will be perceived how Lacan used—even as he rectified them—concepts contributed by the works of the Cercle d'épistémologie and particularly by Miller. The Lacanian notion of the "subject of science" was a partial revision of the Millerian concept of suture, moving it in the direction of an avoidance of a completed logic. The hypothesis may be entertained that that revision reflected a more or less conscious will to prevent the split of the EFP between a hypertheoretical tendency, represented by the epistemologists without couches, and a pragmatic tendency, borne by therapists suffering from an "obscurantist" fascination with a pure transferential relation. Lacan would do all he could to maintain around himself that dialectical balance between indispensable theoretical research and a praxis perpetually threatened by the danger of magic. He would not succeed since he himself would remain caught up in the chimerical ideal of scientificity which he had invoked. But the experiment thus inaugurated would indicate to psychoanalysis the sole path susceptible of justifying the existence of the entire struggle.

IV. Jacques Lacan Himself . . .

A few months after the appearance of the first issue of *Cahiers pour l'analyse,* in which the texts of the new hyperlogical elaboration were gathered, Lacan was invited to Baltimore for a structuralist celebration. René Girard, who taught at the Johns Hopkins University, had initiated the festival along with Eugenio Donato, subsequently a professor at the University of Montreal and a specialist in the human sciences. Richard Macksey, who had published works on number theory and French and American literature, was a member, along with others, of the Sponsoring Committee. The symposium took place in October 1966 under the auspices of the Humanities Center of the Johns Hopkins University.

For American academics, the occasion was a considerable one. It was in fact the first time that structuralist thought was viewed in the United States as an interdisciplinary phenomenon. The organizers sought to compare the problems it touched on with those concerning other fields of inquiry. They thus invited representatives of a variety of fields: Jean Hyppolite for phenomenology, Lucien Goldmann and Georges Poulet for sociological literary criticism, and finally Roland Barthes, Tzvetan Todorov, and Nicholas Ruwet for structuralism. Jacques Derrida, whose work on Lévi-Strauss interested Girard, was also invited, along with Guy Rosolato for his literary articles. In that context, Jacques Lacan was invited for his structural reelaboration of Freud's work and not as the representative of a psychoanalytic movement. Moreover, in the United States, universities did not "mix" with psychoanalytic societies, and the acceptance of Freudianism, however broad, did not impinge on college campuses as such.

The image of psychoanalysis entertained by academics in the New World was the one analysis had given of itself. In their eyes, Freud's discovery was part of a medical and therapeutic domain cut off from any philosophical concerns. That is why, at the Baltimore symposium, Lacan found himself facing an audience which was not the same as his own in France and which, in addition, was unknown to the IPA. No American psychoanalyst was invited to the colloquium, and no French psychoanalyst participated in it under that label. What was at stake was investigating structuralism in its relation to philosophy and literature.

Now Lacan was going to America for the first time in his life, at a time when, rejected by the IPA, he was beginning to become famous outside the world of psychoanalysis. That recognition accorded him from without repeated that which he had been granted by the Surrealists thirty years earlier. The old master's destiny resembled that of the young seducer of years past, who had been celebrated for his impassioned relation to Aimée's madness. But Baltimore was not Sainte-Anne or Rome either, and His Majesty had packed his bags with a certain misunderstanding. Always uncomfortable when abroad, and above all in a country so far removed from Latin culture, Lacan traveled that day in tremendous loneliness. Without family, mistress, or members of his court, our hero had to manage on his own in a world whose spoken language he did not know. It was impossible to give one of his seminars in Baltimore. Yet he considered doing so. And in the jet that took him over the ocean, he no doubt thought of the sentence Jung had confided to him and whose mythology he himself had spread. The plague unfortunately would not be there to meet him. In Baltimore, Lacan would be one of the acknowledged stars of the Parisian structuralist scene. It was not much and it was a lot, but it was still too little. The master adulated by his followers would need still more to forget the stinging defeat at Stockholm or to efface from his memory the sad dash through a Swedish castle.

During the same period, in France, the publication of Michel Foucault's *Les mots et les choses* [*The Order of Things*][75] had just given structuralism something of a new aspect. Until then, structuralism had been defined as a method, but the evaluation of its meaning remained a matter for specialists. Starting in April 1966, however, the mass media latched on to the phenomenon as though it were some frightening—but also frivolous—fashion. To the general astonishment, *Les mots et les choses* became a best seller. Many began speculating on the death of man and the author, and his interment, assisted in their concerns by the polemic spreading through university literary studies between the partisans of Barthes and the adepts of Picard. Through an incredible bit of ideological sleight of hand, the Chinese cultural revolution also became journalistically fashionable (in a way that had little to do with its actual content) and all of a sudden, the press became interested as much in the Bachelardo-Althusserian "break" as in the banning of *La Religieuse* or the Ben Barka Affair.

The danger at this point was that the power of the media, whose influence had grown with the development of audiovisual techniques, might intervene in the structualist quarrels. That entry of the mass media on the stage of theory was a new phenomenon at the time. It not only meant the end of the "heroic" phase of structuralism, but forbode a radical transformation of the status of thought, which would gradually be obliged to bend to the constraints of the communications market. Journalists would soon feel authorized to transform structuralist intellectuals into charismatic stars, glorifying—or stigmatizing—the complexity of discourses they in any event referred to as "esoteric"—meaning, in brief, resistant to sacrosanct "communication." It was indeed easier to compare Foucault to a prophet, Derrida to a pope, Lacan to a guru, Althusser to an idol, and Barthes to a sorcerer than to delve into the specific place occupied by language in their spoken or written work. The path was thus blazed for what would subsequently be called the phenomenon of *new philosophy,* and which would consecrate the triumph of media ignorance over academic knowledge. A triumph brought off thanks to the support the philosophers of the post-structuralist period would themselves bring to the liquidation of their thought.

The transition from structuralism to its sad caricature explains in part the importance for both America and France of the Baltimore symposium. On one side of the ocean, an interested gaze was focused on a method that was already known but rather brutally celebrated as a folkloric phenomenon; and on the other, a world which until then had offered rather few openings to "Continental" thought was being observed, with the hope of establishing contacts and arranging fruitful exchanges. The occasion marked the beginning of a migration which would bring more and more French philosophers to teach in American university departments. In that international contest, Derrida and Ricoeur would fare better than Lacan.

Lacan had an acute understanding of the internal shift that was occurring in French structuralism. Moreover, his inaugural lecture on "science and truth" had been both a premonitory sign of that change and a defensive maneuver against it. At the time he was going to Baltimore, he was impatiently awaiting the publication of his *Écrits* by Éditions du Seuil. Furious at the unchallenged success enjoyed by Ricoeur's book, and still prey to his belief in "stolen ideas," he thought that collecting the major portion of his writings in a volume might "fix" his doctrine and ward off any revision of the sort Freud's work had undergone. That will to impede in advance any "deviations" was part of his "hyperlogical rearticulation," since Lacan invoked an ideal of scientificity both out of fascination for the history of mathematics, in which identical problems were raised, and in order to give his movement a unified base. In addition, he still suffered, and properly so, at not being sufficiently recognized as a thinker of stature: either by the masters whom he admired and from whom he borrowed or by the rest, with whom his relations were poor. It should be noted that in the fall of 1966, Lacan was respected by the most prominent figures in modern thought without his work being truly understood. Lévi-Strauss liked him but compared him to a shaman. Braudel supported him, but did not express any judgment about his work. Dumézil and Canguilhem both kept their silence. And Jakobson, who had become his friend, seemed not to grasp the distortions he had imposed on the concepts of metaphor and metonymy. As for Foucault, he understood the meaning of Lacan's work, but opted to bypass the question of Freud's discovery. After May 1968, he would side with Deleuze, without, however, rejecting Lacan.

Lacan, for his part, behaved capriciously with the thinkers whose paths he crossed. To be sure, he did not want to be part of the "structuralist bandwagon," as the press was beginning to call it. He misconstrued Barthes's work, although he found his lecture at Baltimore excellent, and treated the young Derrida as poorly as he had Ricoeur, without perceiving that this new interlocutor offered him the possibility for an exchange which Ricoeur had always fled. If he neglected those who might have offered him an opening, he paid homage to those who neglected him. In brief, he courted all, but not in the same manner. He admired those who were sparing in the compliments they paid him and whom he judged his equals, and did not recognize those who were ready—with or without loyalty—to give him a great part of themselves. He loved his person and wanted his person to be loved by all. It was a curious attitude for a man who never stopped declaring that the ego was not master of the world. But after all, why would Lacan have escaped the rule of that imaginary realm whose deceptive illusions he had delineated so well?

In the fall of 1966, Jacques Derrida had not yet met Lacan. The latter had, nonetheless, devoured *La grammatologie* as soon as it appeared in *Critique* and let the philosopher know, through Miller and François Wahl, how highly he thought of the text. No doubt he expected to see him come to his seminar, taking up the place that had gone vacant since his dispute with Ricoeur. But Derrida was distrustful, and hesitated to throw himself into the seducer's arms. Jealous of his independence, he experienced Lacan's interest in him as a threat. He thus took his time to address Lacan on the philosophical questions he regarded as essential: the place of the subject and the status of the unconscious. It did not, however, prevent him from publishing in *Cahiers pour l'analyse* a rather nasty text on Lévi-Strauss, which earned him the honor of being called a "bear" by the annoyed ethnologist. The text was again concerned with phonologism and the degradation of writing.[76] For the symposium, he opted to be less violent and spent fifteen days preparing a vintage lecture entitled "La structure, le signe, et le jeu dans le discours des sciences humaines [Structure, sign, and play in the discourse of the human sciences]." "There are two heterogeneous manners," he wrote, "of effacing the difference between the signifier and the signified: One, more classic, consists in reducing or deriving the signifier, that is, ultimately in submitting the sign to thought; the other, which is the one we are here pitting against the preceding one, consists in calling into question the system within which the preceding reduction functioned."[77] Lévi-Strauss was again being cross-examined, and Lacan, implicitly, as well.

The America Derrida was visiting was not the same as the one Lacan was dreaming of. The young philosopher had no revenge to exact against the past and no reconquest to accomplish against a hostile continent. When he took the plane with Barthes, Todorov, and Ruwet, he was ill from his vaccinations, but did not suffer from any great isolation or feeling of rejection. He understood English and was not afraid to travel. For him, the invitation was homage paid to his thought during a phase of particular effervescence. Upon arriving, he was amazed to learn from Girard that Lacan had asked for a deluxe hotel room to be reserved for him. Exhausted by jet lag, he put down his bags only to hear the old *maître* exclaim: "So! I had to come all the way here to finally meet you!"

The following evening, at a dinner hosted by the organizers, Derrida raised the questions which concerned him about the Cartesian subject, substance, and the signifier. Standing as he sampled a plate of cole slaw, Lacan replied that *his* subject was the same as the one his interlocutor had opposed to the theory of the subject. In itself, the remark was not false. But Lacan then added, "You can't bear my having already said what you want to say." Once again, the thematic of "stolen ideas," the fantasy of owning concepts, the narcissism of priority. It proved too much. Derrida refused to go along, and retorted sharply, "*That* is not my problem." Lacan was being made to pay for his remark. Later in the evening, he approached the philosopher and placed his hand gently on his shoulder, "Ah! Derrida, we must speak together, we must speak." They would not speak. . . . [78]

A year after Baltimore another dinner took place in Paris, at the home of Jean Piel. Lacan clasped Derrida's hand warmly in his oily palms and asked him what he was working on. Plato, the pharmakon, letter, origins, *logos* and *mythos:* He was preparing a text for *Tel quel.* That journal, under the talented leadership of Philippe Sollers, was becoming the site of a new combination of the old structuralist themes reviewed and rectified in the light of the new "textuality." Derrida had just joined the editorial committee of the journal *Critique,* while publishing *Grammatologie.* Lacan, since the publication of *Écrits,* had been editing a series at Éditions du Seuil. Once again, he announced how curious it was that he too had already spoken of the same themes. His students could vouch for it. Derrida spoke to the psychoanalyst and told him the following anecdote. One evening, as his son Pierre was beginning to fall asleep in his mother's presence, he asked his father why he was looking at him. "Because you're handsome."

The child reacted immediately by saying that the compliment made him want to die. Somewhat troubled, Derrida tried to figure out what the story meant.

"I don't like myself," the child said.

"And since when?"

"Since I've known how to talk."

Marguerite took him in her arms, "Don't worry, we love you."

Then Pierre broke out laughing, "No, all that isn't true; I'm a cheater for life." [79]

Lacan did not react. Some time later, Derrida was dumbfounded to read the anecdote in the text of a lecture by his interlocutor delivered at the French Institute in Naples in December 1967. Lacan recounted it as follows: "I'm a cheater for life, said a four-year-old kid while curling up in the arms of his genitrix before his father, who had just answered, 'You're handsome' to his question, 'Why are you looking at me?' And the father didn't recognize (even when the child in the interim pretended he had lost all taste for himself the day he learned to speak) the impasse he himself was foisting on the Other, by playing dead. It's up to the father, who told it to me, to hear me from where I speak or not." [80]

A father working on the metaphysics of "full" speech, a son playing with his father's words and his own, a master taking himself for the great Other [grand Autre] and making anonymous use of an anecdote in order to accuse a recalcitrant philosopher of not submitting to his imaginary justice: quite an imbroglio! Lacan's role in the affair was not a good one, and Derrida felt wounded. Understandably so. Perhaps Lacan was settling unconscious scores with the name of the father or more trivially with all the Alfreds of the world. Whatever the case, the episode put an end to relations between the two men. A pity for the historian!

At Baltimore, French dominated the symposium. The Americans thrilled to the sharply Gallic flavor of the exchanges, and the French guests were flattered at being so honored. The structuralist feast remained Latinate—a Continental dispute staged as a Western, the local press would say. The term "poststructuralism," unknown in France, would even be coined in English to designate what was emerging from the colloquium. [81] Making little effort to adapt to his surroundings, Lacan spoke in Baltimore as at his seminar, even though his audience was not the one he was accustomed to. But he added a grotesque note to the occasion by delivering his remarks in English. Since all the guests spoke French and he, Lacan, was unskilled in English, the organizers were at a loss. They consequently brought him a young philosopher named Anthony Wilden to polish his style. Wilden was interested in Lacanianism and would subsequently translate several of Lacan's texts. [82] But at the time he was literally overwhelmed by the commotion caused by this Renaissance prince for whom he was to serve as interpreter, guide, tutor in diction, and courtier. After much ado, the lecture was finally ready. On the page, it was a small masterpiece, but hearing it delivered was another kettle of fish. First of all, it was given an extravagant title: "Of Structure as an Inmixing of an Otherness Prerequisite to Any Subject Whatever." [83] One sympathizes with the plight of Wilden, who referred to himself, in the middle of the symposium, as the "unfortunate translator!" Then, the lecture, whose text seemed rather short, was delivered by its author in an idiom midway between Franco-English and Anglo-French, which made it seem endless to his audience.

Plainly, when Lacan spoke for free, he lengthened his sessions, and when he was paid to listen, he never stopped shortening them! Quite an individual! He drove his cars in the opposite direction of his discourse and at the same speed as his analyses—according to the "bang-bang" of genuine interpretation. Even if he did not always succeed in avoiding accidents, he never harmed himself and miraculously spared his passengers as well. Whenever he could, he would speed between the truck coming down the opposite side of the road and the vehicle he had just passed, without any concern as to whether either would use its brakes. Such, for him, was logical time: No sooner had the prisoner solved the mystery than he had to decide. All of Lacan's private and public life was in the image of his doctrine, which never relinquished anything, and was apt to exploit whatever came its way: the speed of the eagle joined to the slow obstinacy of the ant.

In Baltimore, then, Lacan presented himself as he had become. The man of genius, who had devoted thirty-five years of relentless work to the psychoanalytic movement, watched success come his way too late. To be sure, he still had his health, but, above all since Bonneval, he experienced the fact that he had waited so long for recognition—and was still awaiting it—as an injustice. Worn out by the conflicts of the SPP, which were inflicted on him in the fullness of his years, then defeated in his negotiation with the IPA, he recovered only partially from his struggles, and even if his school was bringing him numerous satisfactions, he tended increasingly to neglect those truly loyal to him and to surround himself with courtiers. The old monarch was fragile, and that fragility was visible in the capriciousness of his whims as he advanced toward glory, but also toward death. At the symposium, the French knew, at least by hearsay, the master's habits, but the Americans, who had read his texts carefully, found Lacan's discourse quite strange. The lecture lasted so long that Rosolato was obliged to postpone his own for a day. The only Lacanian disciple on American soil at the time, he could hardly have confronted his own analyst under such circumstances.

Two passages attracted attention. Concerning the subject, Lacan recounted that at dawn, he found himself looking out his window at the neon lights and the traffic, which made him think of *Dasein,* that is, the intermittent and blurred spectacle of "thought thinking itself without knowing it." Whereupon, he uttered the Surrealist sentence, "The most synthetic image I can give you of the unconscious is Baltimore in the very early morning." The second superb moment: Lacan spoke of his forthcoming seminar on the "logic of unconscious fantasy," and said, "I'm late with something I'm supposed to develop before I disappear myself and I'm having trouble progressing." [84] Time once again!

Aware of the effect Lacan's speech was having on his scholarly audience,

Wilden rushed to his assistance. He observed that in approaching his doctrine by way of the notion of *méconnaissance*—misunderstanding—the speaker had plunged his audience into just such a state of misprision. But he immediately added that the Americans should read Freud in order to realize that Lacan had not misunderstood him. After an interesting discussion in which Goldmann and Poulet intervened, Richard Macksey challenged Lacan on his use of Frege's logic. He said he was troubled that Gödel's theorem had been interpreted in *La science et la vérité* as a mere limitation on the power of symbolism. Then he added that such a position brought with it the risk of leading the speaker into a nominalist or conceptualist structuralism, since instead of connecting numbers among themselves, it tended to posit an equivalence between numbers and entities. Lacan replied that he had never denied the structural aspect of numbers. Indeed, his hyperlogical reelaboration remained structural, even if it ran the risk of nominalism or logical formalism. Macksey's question was pertinent, but unfortunately it was not pursued in the discussion. Never would Lacan have an audience as curious about "genuine" questions. . . .

The American trip of 1966 did not allow him (for good reason) to wreak any revenge on the IPA. But paradoxically, his discourse was better understood in Baltimore than in Paris to the extent that the academics at the colloquium, who were neither psychoanalysts nor young Lacanians, were accustomed to theoretical debates and did not allow themselves to be mystified by the strange words of their guest. They debated and criticized the content of his work. Nonetheless, a certain misunderstanding did remain, since on American soil Lacanianism was considered a typically French structuralist doctrine. It would remain so for a long time in certain American universities and for certain feminists without actually receiving the imprimatur of any psychoanalytic movement. In other words, Lacanianism would not take root on the far side of the Atlantic as a school or a reelaboration of Freudianism. There would be no Far West for Dr. Lacan—merely campuses. Back to Paris . . .

Despite pressure from François Wahl since June 1963, Lacan had to be begged to gather his collected writings in a volume. To be sure, he wanted to "fix" his doctrine and bring it to the attention of a broad public, but he was repelled by what he would later call *poubellication* [a pun on *poubelle*—garbage can—and publication]. Yet Wahl's supportive insistence did finally have its effect, and the success enjoyed by Ricoeur's book triggered the final decision. A philosopher by training, Wahl thought that Lacan's teaching occupied a place corresponding to the "real" for the new generation. For him, the master's calling was to act as the analyst of contemporary culture. When he asked him to gather his texts, Lacan proposed several of his disciples to do the job. But nothing worked out.

Toward the end of the winter of 1966, Wahl set to work full-time on the project, taking a month's leave to read, classify, and repunctuate the texts. When he failed to understand the meaning of certain sentences, he would lunch with the master at Calvet's; Lacan would answer all his questions and rework his style himself. It was a huge publishing project and a remarkable collaboration. Early on, Wahl decided to eliminate the text on the family, which he found insufficiently "Lacanian," and Lacan chose to open the book with his "Seminar on 'The Purloined

Letter.' " Wahl did not agree. Lacan insisted and would not yield. Finally, the publisher asked the author to write a postface to the famous seminar in which he would explain retroactively its inaugural position.[85] Lacan then wrote "La parenthèse des parenthèses," a veritable reformulation—in terms of logic—of his piece. Then he ended the unit with a chapter entitled "De nos antécédents," in which he imagined his own itinerary for himself. He spoke of the welcome his thesis had received from the Surrealists, laid claim to Clérambault's teaching, thus forgetting he had leaned toward Claude, and situated *Évolution psychiatrique* in terms of the hearing it gave him. He did not mention Henri Ey, but sent him a copy with the dedication, "For Renée, for Henri, for the youth that still unites us." Naturally, he did not refer to either Wallon or Kojève and presented himself as the inventor of the notion of a "mirror stage." These were the days of the antipsychologistic battle, and Lacan, who was himself so sensitive about issues of intellectual priority, hesitated to evoke a precursor whose name remained linked to the field of psychology and a philosopher whose Hegelian teachings were no longer in fashion during the structuralist years.

He thus commented on his *Écrits* in the future perfect tense, proposing to his readers that they study his work as a totality whose history would lie entirely within itself. In presenting his major work, he thus opted for the path of his hyperlogical reelaboration. He interpreted the past history of his texts in the light of his present doctrine, retroactively imposing on them a conception of history which overdetermined them. "It happens," he wrote, "that our students err in finding 'already there' in our writings what our teaching only brought us to later. But is it not enough that what *is* there did not block the way?"[86] With that ambiguous sentence, Lacan laid claim to the illusory dimension of what was "already there": A work was to be read in terms of what it subsequently became. In sum, the introduction to *Écrits* incited the reader in 1966 to read the prewar Lacan in the light of the *Rome Discourse,* and the Lacan of the *Rome Discourse* in the light of *La science et la vérité.* That conception of history was suited to the manner in which Lacan worked, but it would prove disastrous for the Lacanian movement which, on such grounds, would tend to forget Lacan's borrowings from others, to read Freud without ever separating him from Lacan, and finally to ascribe to Freud himself—through what magic lantern one can only wonder—an anticipatory reading of the *Écrits.* In addition it would implicitly validate, within the Lacanian movement, a whole wave of unreadable prose, not from the philosophers of the Cercle d'epistémologie, whose works would remain quite original, but among the psychoanalysts of future generations, who were too ignorant to follow the master in his pursuit of science *per se*, but too fanatical not to follow him. In resorting to such prose, they would sacrifice whatever writing style they might have had, no longer merely to imitate Lacan's person, but retroactively to fuse with the style of the *Écrits* in a drive to anonymity. As a result they would tend to take on pseudonyms or not to sign their texts.

If Lacan was intially seconded by Wahl in the publishing endeavor, it was Miller who soon took over for him by taking responsibility for preparing a methodical subject index. He drew on the presentation of 1963 at the ENS and confirmed the presentation in the future perfect that Lacan had proposed. Instead of listing concepts in order of their intial appearance and then specifying their successive transformations, he situated the structural position of each in its relation to the totality. He thus proceeded retroactively from the final state of the theory, dividing the body of Lacan's work into five "orders." Finally, he emphasized that certain particularly dense texts were resistant to such a division, and affirmed that the book's organization constituted his own interpretation of Lacanianism. Miller invoked it, moreover, in the name of a better understanding of the *Écrits*. "According to our own concept of these *Écrits*," he wrote, "one gains by studying them as forming a system, despite those ellipses of style necessary, says Lacan, for training analysts. As for us, not having to be preoccupied with the effectiveness of the theory in that domain, we encourage the reader by advancing that there is no outer limit (that is, which the functioning of thought under the constraint of structure does not produce) to the expansion of formalization in the field of discourse, in that there is no place its power fails whose contours cannot be delineated—reducing the gap by changing syntax. At the risk of seeing its negative form anew elsewhere. We refer the reader to Boole, Carnap, and M. Guéroult's studies of Berkeley." [87]

That interpretation of the work corresponds to the Lacanian perspective of 1966, even while radicalizing it in the direction of that integral formalization which Lacan had rejected by invoking Gödel's theorem. He had rectified the notion of suture, pressing toward a lesser formalization, and Miller in turn reinterpreted it—in a kind of pendular movement—by separating the field of clinical training from that of discourse.

As soon as the *Écrits* appeared, in November, Lacan received the consecration he had awaited. He immediately became one of the great thinkers of the structuralist era, even though he had just broached his reelaboration in terms of formal logic. The book was well launched and constituted an "event." On November 30, *Le Nouvel observateur* announced that the publisher had reprinted "the nine hundred pages of Lacan's *Écrits*, which cost fifty francs, and five thousand copies of which have been sold before it has been reviewed." In point of fact, the work was not an immediate best-seller like *Les mots et les choses*, and for a while was selling less well than Ricoeur's book. But gradually, the curve reversed itself. By 1984, 36,643 volumes had been sold and counting from 1970, the paperback sales would set a new record for works of comparable difficulty: 94,000 copies for the first volume and 65,000 for the second.[88] Lacan had thus won his difficult battle for the recognition he deserved. He would thereafter be the "French Freud," and not merely a structuralist author. As a result, he would be the object of even more attacks. But his *Écrits* would be quoted everywhere and his doctrine broadly commented on beyond the world of psychoanalysis. Silence would remain the golden rule at the Institut de psychanalyse, since there would never be a review of the *Écrits* in the *RFP*, in which Lacan's very name would be banned from published texts. But the new analytic generation trained elsewhere than in the ranks of Lacanianism would not hesitate to speak out. A subject to which we shall return.

Naturally, Lacan was sharply criticized in several weeklies. In *Arts*, for example, Jacques Brosse wrote these words: "The whole—let us say so immediately—is overwhelmingly oppressive, because impenetrable. No doubt Lacan wants to select his audience. . . . It is above all to be feared that in the face of an obscurity this aggressive, intellectual snobs, who are masochistic by nature, will forge a success for J. Lacan without having read him." [89] In *L'Express*, Jean-François Revel distinguished between philosophy and psychoanalysis. "It is possible," he wrote, "that Lacan's philosophy is very important, but it seems debatable to me that it constitutes either a return to Freud or a continuation of Freud." [90] As for André Robinet, writing for *Les Nouvelles littéraires,* he merely revived the commonplaces of the old anti-Freudian struggle: "When Lacan's publishers will have brought out an accessible translation of these *re-writings* (which were once written so as to be readable), we will recommend them to our readers so that they too can harken to the lamentable Freud."

In *La Quinzaine littéraire,* Didier Anzieu was quite aggressive in his treatment. He did not hesitate to call Lacan a heretic and to predict the shipwreck of captains destined to be great had they not strayed off course. He compared his former analyst to Jung, Adler, Reich, Rank, and Karen Horney, the better to defend an orthodoxy whose contours he was unable to delineate. Finally, he said that Lacan's texts were not unpublished in order to take a swipe at Miller, referred to as a young philosopher without clinical experience. In a neighboring column, Charles Melman defended Lacan in an article characterized by its dogmatism. Plainly, the master had lost his best students, and those he had were no longer able to criticize him as they had at Rome or at Bonneval. [91]

It was in *Les Lettres françaises* on the left and *Le Figaro littéraire* on the right that Lacan was hailed in terms worthy of him by Pierre Daix, on the one hand, and Gilles Lapouge, on the other. [92] In two interviews displaying remarkable qualities of clarity and intelligence on the part of the journalists, Lacan expatiated at length on his sense of science and the return to Freud. Evoking the famous line quoted by Jung, Lapouge did not hesitate to caption his piece, "Jacques Lacan wants psychoanalysis to become the plague again." As for Lacan, he was somewhat cavalier in dismissing his own affinities with Hegelianism. "I should like to affirm from the beginning," he told Daix, "that everything I have written is entirely determined by Freud's work. That is the first title I lay claim to: I am the one who has read Freud. I've also read a few others, to be sure, but in a manner that is not in any way comparable: Hegel, for example. How has it been possible to read me and reach the conclusion that I remain faithful to his system when for me it is no more than a machine for countering the various forms of madness resulting from identification?" [93]

Jean-Paul Sartre was troubled by the commotion the press was making about structuralism. He thus answered questions from Bernard Pingaud in an issue of *L'Arc* dedicated to him and which appeared a few days after Lacan's interview in *Le Figaro littéraire*. He reproached Foucault, Althusser, and Lacan jointly for their concerted refusal of history in the name of structure, and their rejection of man in the name of a decentering of the subject. He accused them of taking aim at Marxism and of erecting the last obstacle the bourgeoisie was able to build against the author of *Capital*. He was not completely wrong, since those three authors, each in his own way, were sounding the knell of that old-fashioned—*gauchiste* or dogmatic—Marxism which Sartre would serve courageously until he died. Nevertheless, he excluded from his condemnation those "genuine" specialists of structure whom he identified as Lévi-Strauss, Benveniste, and Saussure. He forgot Dumézil and acknowledged that Lacan was a faithful reader of Freud. "Trapped between the id and the super-ego," he wrote, "the psychoanalyst's subject is a bit like de Gaulle between the Soviet Union and the United States. The ego has no existence in itself; it is a construct and its role remains purely passive." [94]

The occasion offered an opportunity for the press to pit two "charismatic leaders" against one another. *Le Figaro littéraire* thus rushed to prolong and reverse matters by announcing on its front page, in a striking headline, "Lacan judges Sartre." In a second interview, Lacan underscored the absurdity of such a notion. He responded to Sartre on the subject of history, and to the press in general on the place he had been made to occupy: "I find it hard to believe that all this is intended to win fresh currency for Sartre. Sartre indeed remains the most popular represent-ative of French thought. But to suppose for that reason that everything that is not Sartrian need first define itself as not being Sartrian is more than debatable. . . . There are those who want me to be something of a successor to Sartre. Allow me to tell you that that is a rather comical idea of what is capable of interesting me. Sartre has had a very precise function, which it is possible to gauge, but which has no relation with the work I am doing. Sartre is younger than I am and I followed his rise with a great deal of sympathy and interest. I do not situate myself in relation to him." In passing, Lacan rejected the press's amalgamation of the "captains" of struc-turalism, and then, for the only time in his life, paid (limited) homage to Althusser's work: "Lévi-Strauss, whom I know well, is not very interested in psychoanalysis. I have found Althusser quite alive to my work, and quite enlivening among those in his orbit. I believe that his manner of dividing up Marx can be regarded as definitive. But who can believe that we act in concert? As for Foucault, he follows what I do and I like his work, but I don't see him as very concerned with Freud's position. So what bond can there be among those four?" [95]

Just as Lacan was savoring his consecration, his daughter Judith married Jacques-Alain Miller. Through that marriage, the history of the Lacanian movement also became a family affair.

V. Had Versailles Been Told Me

The founding act pronounced by Lacan at the summer solstice of 1964 was not without recalling de Gaulle's celebrated speech of June 18, 1940: majestic in tone, splendid in style, impeccable in its legislation. [96] Lacan spoke in the first person, denounced "deviations" and "compromises" and presented himself as the absolute head of a great movement of reconquest. Rediscovering all at once his baroque inflections, he mobilized the signifiers of his culture and was intent on being the savior of a Freudian France gone decadent. He was not alone, to be sure, but the evocation of his "solitude" in relation to the psychoanalytic cause functioned sym-bolically. As opposed to Freud, Lacan agreed to be a master who politically and juridically occupied the position of a master. Sovereign, emperor, or pope? I would suggest, rather, legislator or founding father. Against the empire, he raised his head anew to avenge his ancestor and reestablish the might of the Carthaginian cause, the symbol of that Hannibalian situation which Freud had dreamed for psycho-analysis. He had not wanted to govern, but the defeat of 1963 forced his hand: He no longer had any alternative.

Thus, in order to spare his school the errors of the past, he attempted the impossible. Instead of refusing, like the IPA, the notion of a "charismatic leader," he displaced it and invested it with the results of a reconciliation between the initiatic function specific to the teaching of psychoanalysis and the administrative function characterizing all institutions. He would be simultaneously *director* of his school, *master* through his doctrine, and *legislator* of a new mode of training. Through his seminar and the reduction of the length of his sessions, he would also be the *analyst* of all concerned.

Drawing on theses formulated in *La psychologie des foules* ["The psychology of crowds"], he achieved an original form of power based on the prevalence of the notion of the "great man." The reference to the de Gaulle context was clear, and no doubt Lacan, when issuing his call of June 21, remembered the horror he had felt, a quarter of a century earlier, at the collapse of the French army. Visceral hatred for Pétainist collaboration, revulsion at a democracy which had failed to honor its com-mitments, and finally a cult of the providential man. In 1964, Lacan was not a dictator, but rather something of an enlightened monarch seeking to restore the risks of a Freudian republic—a politics of the unconscious and desire against institutional politics, a "man" against the "parties."

In order to prevent the constitution of oligarchies, he initially assumed all powers. He himself named the elites, was part of all juries, and demanded the obe-dience of those around him, almost as revenge against the past. Three disciples re-mained his "favorites": Serge Leclaire, whom he continued to love passionately; Moustapha Safouan, whom he considered a superb clinician and whose address he gave whenever he recommended therapy to a close associate; Solange Faladé, who was his confidant. A Jew, an Arab, and an African: the choice illustrates nicely Lacan's universalism.

Lacan's place in the EFP was strange from the outset. Being a monarch, he entertained with all—that is, with his people and his courtiers—a privileged relation that escaped any institutional hierarchy. As a result, and despite the autocratic na-ture of his power, he also played the role of an old liberal sage, whom anyone in search of orientation on questions of work or career could come consult in the privacy of his alcove. During almost the entire existence of the EFP, the door at the rue de Lille was open to anyone and without appointment: to members and non-members, to analysands and the "sick," to robbers, thugs, psychotics, and the troubled. Lacan was never afraid of anything and dispensed intelligent advice to all. In sum, anyone could show up at his home to discuss absolutely anything. The Doctor was protected by no Praetorian guard; no security team or secretarial staff separated the monarch from his people. Only Gloria Gonzalez, the faithful Span-iard, received visitors without preventing them from meeting their interlocutor.

There was thus gradually established between Lacan and his "subjects" a kind of direct monarchy in which voluntary servitude combined with the exercise of individual freedoms. That mode of power tended to transform Lacan's practice.

From the moment he created his school, there was no longer any control being exercised over the length of his sessions or the number of his analysands, whose ranks swelled visibly. The former analysands, trained at the SFP, continued to come, and the young, belonging to the fourth and above all to the fifth generations, came *en masse,* so much did the adventure of Lacanianism speak to their own theoretical and anti-institutional aspirations. Very early on, Lacan contracted the habit of no longer giving appointments at fixed times. He was unable to refuse anyone and anyone could come to his sessions according to his whim or need. The Doctor's house was an immense asylum in which one could move about freely, its doors open from morning to night, among first editions, artistic masterpieces, and piles of manuscripts.

Free of all institutional constraints, Lacan established over a period of sixteen years a true *laboratory* of psychoanalysis. He devoted his entire life to it—his strength and his love, without ever giving up. He mixed every approach and wrote off all the rules of classical practice with a genius of intervention rarely equaled in the history of Freudianism. Like some great libertine, he explored with consummate refinement every possible figure of therapy, control, the "passe," the seminar, case presentation, as though always wanting to know still more about the mysteries of the transferential relation, endless analysis, "passage," or identification. He played with the most extreme postures of time, space, and the object. Thus, for example, he was capable of accepting in analysis a patient already at work on another therapist's couch, or another patient whose practice he was controlling regarding a patient whose practice he was also (and at the same time) supervising. The length of his sessions and the time between them underwent infinite variation: from a minute to an hour and from one session per week to ten per day. Analysands were made to move from their chair or couch, then from room to room, changing the symbolic frame of their utterances. It was as though he were acting relentlessly *against* his theory, as if to put it to the test of its shortcomings. The more he denounced the omnipotence of the ego, the more he affirmed the prevalence of his own ego in therapy. The more he mocked philanthropic utopias, the more he assisted all with his humanitarian advice.

In general, the length of sessions tended to grow shorter and when such was not the case, the time allotted was a function of the relation that had been established between the master and the analysand. Lacan was always in a rush, as though death itself were at his coattails. He did not sit in his chair, paced back and forth, turned his back to his patient, ate, drank, and laughed even as he offered a fabulous ear to certain signifiers of his patients' discourse. He did not analyze his patients' transference in relation to him, and even if he intervened to give them instructions, he allowed them to build their own interpretations of his attitude. As a result, he activated in all a permanent "freedom" to serve, reject, and love him—or to actually pursue an analysis. At the end of his life, when he was ill, he continued his practice and exhibited his lapses without concealing his physical or mental state. Some noticed his absences; others saw nothing and retained a flamboyant image of him. Still others accompanied him through his death throes with tenderness or violence.

Concerning money, Lacan, over the years, had become more and more avid.

But if his requests were often exorbitant, no one was obliged to yield to them. There too, the principle of direct monarchy, voluntary servitude, or experimentation was in force. Lacan, on the whole, exploited only the rich or those who were willing to let themselves be exploited. He revealed himself to be different with each patient—always multiple, always diversified at the bidding of an art of listening that was never the same for all.

Having become the head of a school and an intellectual master, he was thereafter obliged to take into account his public *persona*. Numerous militants, addicts, delinquents, or candidates for suicide came to him in search of a father or a savior. He did not refuse their requests and never rejected his position as a "great leader." On the contrary, he accepted it and would allow a portion of the *gauchiste* youth of France not to sink into terrorism, death, or madness. He would only be attacked physically once. Like Charcot at the Salpêtrière, and like Freud in Viennese society, Lacan, as of 1969, became the iconoclastic doctor of a society sick with its symptoms, its *mores,* and its modernity. He took upon himself both its miseries and its splendors. No doubt on occasion he would train therapists who seemed more like merchants than psychoanalysts. But if such were the case, they were not numerous and existed in other institutions as well. The history of psychoanalytic societies can never be summarized as the case of their minorities, and, all things considered, the Lacanian adventure was culturally more interesting than other experiments conducted in Freudian France. Here is additional testimony concerning Lacan's practice after 1964.[97]

Francis Hofstein: "I began my analysis in 1964. During my medical studies in Strasbourg, I had read Freud, and it made me want to become an analyst. I believed, moreover, not without naïveté, that psychiatry and psychoanalysis were one and the same thing. When I landed in Paris, I telephoned the only person I knew to have an analyst's address. He gave me Lacan's, without any explanation. I thus telephoned Lacan, who suggested an appointment a week later. Since I was only there for three days, I asked him to receive me earlier. He agreed and for two hours I told him my life. He listened to me quite attentively and advised me also to see other analysts. Since I didn't know any others, I didn't do so and returned to Strasbourg. When I came back to Paris in January 1965, I called Lacan back, saw him again, but he again told me to look elsewhere. I refused to. And since I did not understand why he wasn't accepting me in analysis, I insisted and asked him for an explanation. He evaded the question, then ended up giving in.

"The sessions lasted between fifteen and thirty minutes and often seemed long to me. Once, at the beginning, he forgot me in his library and, when I finally came to knock on his office door, he became quite upset and almost yelled at me for not having made my presence felt sooner. I ended up setting up my own appointments so as not to wait. He mixed registers only twice. Once, I told him about a film and he asked me to write what I had said. I did it, gave him the manuscript, but didn't get any reaction. On another occasion, I refused and told him that when I would write, I would do it for myself. Much later, I would ask him to verify if I had not misused one of his concepts in an article I had just written about music. While letting me know that music was not his strong suit, he agreed, but upon getting my text back, I noticed that he had made an error in a correction. I called him up, read to him what he had written, and told him what I thought. He laughed and recognized his error.

"In general, I had the impression of doing a normal analysis with him. He intervened, punctuated, and interpreted my dreams. He never appeared disdainful. He effaced himself before my words and did not create any obstacles to analysis. I discovered who he was when the *Écrits* were published. Everyone began speaking about him, and I heard things said about his practice that did not correspond with what I was experiencing on the couch. I spoke to him about it and one day told him a particularly venomous story about himself. That isn't true, he said. From that I concluded in his presence that there was some truth to what was being said. When I didn't yield on certain things, he didn't insist. It was the analyst who was present and not Lacan's 'I.' And he could be made to return to his positions as analyst when he strayed from it. That was something I learned with him. Like a technique. That and keeping an analytic distance from oneself. When it occurred to me to situate Freud's concepts within my therapy, he gave me his opinion. But he never proposed a control to me or asked me to come to his seminar. I ended my analysis in 1972. He was less present, as though, as an analyst, I had worn him down. He allowed me to leave without really holding on to me."

Gérard Pommier: "When I decided to ask for an appointment with Jacques Lacan, I was of the opinion I had already completed my analysis. I had already come to the end of therapy that I considered relatively complete with Raymonde Bargues, whose membership in the EFP I did not know of at the time. I was finishing my *certificat d'etudes supérieures* in psychiatry. I had acquired a copy of the *Écrits,* but the style of his writing seemed obscure. And then one day, despite my militant anti-psychiatric stance at the time, I went to a case presentation at Sainte-Anne. Lacan's presence and his style made a considerable impression on me. I went to his seminar, then asked him for an appointment. I was, at the time, in control with Piera Aulagnier, and the problems I might encounter with patients led me to think that I should continue with my own analysis.

"When I think back on it, I am still surprised at the difference I perceived between the public man, who was a brilliant speaker and somewhat distant, and the man who was so close, who spoke in so individualized and almost violent a manner to his interlocutor, discovering in appearances themselves the point of leverage for the transference. 'Do you know,' he told me during one of our first meetings, 'that you resemble the wounded Gaul?' That proximity also allowed one to speak to him, I mean that his commitment, his attachment also exposed him, laid him bare. He was not, for instance, beyond committing slips such as that of twice giving me appointments at times when it was well known that he would be elsewhere, reserving the right to send me a telegram an hour later or to scream into the phone, 'But where do I have my head today?'

"I thus came over a period of several months, pursuing those interviews which seemed very long to me, long and slow in a way I found trying, and which contrasted with what happened when my analysis proper began. To say that the sessions were short is hardly adequate; they were like flashes, at times no longer than a minute. I remember that it happened that I needed three sessions to recount a single particularly important dream and that I worked with an intensity which a 'standard' session would never have allowed. What I found there was a merciless experience which gave the analytic task an extension that had repercussions on one's entire existence. No doubt it taught me, for my own practice, that time was only a variable of the transference—and thus of undecidable duration. And that consequently it requires that the analyst assume a risk with regard to it. What was hardest was perhaps that with that intensity, prompted by form, I had the feeling that what I was saying was not being understood, that I was speaking to a deaf man entirely preoccupied with writing, reading, and cutting pieces of string. And then, abruptly, concerning an incongruous and barely murmured detail, a few words came there where I least expected them, words coming from afar, for example condensing a sentence uttered without any further attention to it during our preliminary meetings: 'It's hatred of the mothering woman,' words suddenly falling into place with relation to a seemingly unconnected symptom which suddenly came unhinged.

"In 1974, during a session in which I had said that frankly my analysis was enough for orienting me in my practice and that I didn't see what a control could add to it, Lacan didn't let me finish my sentence and announced to me that my control, I could rest assured, would begin the following week. And that is how my supervision with him began; it was to last until July 1981. Around 1978, I considered entering the procedure known as the *passe*, but I hesitated. One day, while I was speaking to him about something quite different, a dream about my daughter, who had just been born, I described a sequence in which I was to pass through a door. It was with that sequence, which proved relevant only after the fact, that I entered that experiment. That new ordeal lasted a long time, two years, and I can attest that it brings an analyst invaluable material. The jury that was to deliberate on my work was scheduled to meet on January 8, 1980. The École was dissolved on the fifth."

Antoinette Fouque: "Before 1968, I had wanted to do an analysis with Lacan. I was a reader for Seuil and I had read Lacan before Freud. I had a passion for analysis. Then there was Serge Leclaire's *Psychanalyser.* There I found technique—concrete material. Finally François Wahl recommended René Tostain to me. He was an excellent analyst, but not what I wanted. I didn't get the transference with him that I did with Lacan.

"Toward the beginning of 1969, I thus went to see Lacan. On the telephone, he asked me, 'Who are you?' I answered that I wasn't recommended by anyone and I explained my activities. 'Come tomorrow,' he said. I stayed twelve minutes. I went for five years after that, at times regularly, at others not. The sessions never lasted more than a quarter of an hour and were not fixed. From the moment one found oneself before his eyes—or his ears—one was his. He carried you, sustained you. He didn't recruit, but impelled one to work. He never intervened on the subject of my physical illness, and I never had to furnish him proof of it, but without that analysis, I would have been paralyzed earlier. Lacan didn't yield to any ideology and he allowed me not to yield to the feminist illusion. He made me avoid the idea that a woman can only be a failed man. He allowed me to criticize Sartre and Beauvoir. I asked him endlessly why he said that she who did not exist had to become an hysteric and why he made the real possible in life even as he stated that the real was impossible. I also said: 'You say the hysteric is looking for a man who knows how to make love, but such a thing doesn't exist, so it can only be a woman,' and 'For you the phallus is an obstacle. Once the erection is over and you've lost your sperm, what happens, you don't even know?' He burst out laughing. Sometimes he approved and sometimes he disagreed. But I am certain he changed his relation to hysteria in light of the feminist question.

"At the same time, I was doing a period of analysis with Luce Iragaray. Lacan knew it. It was a matter for me of investigating fantasmatic partners connected with my childhood. One day, I came very aggressive to my session, with a small knife hidden away, and didn't hang my cape on the rack as usual. As soon as Lacan saw me, he drew me toward him and said to me: 'You haven't taken off your cape. There is something. . . .' Then he took it off himself and went to hang it on the rack. After that I told him I had hidden the little knife. He took all the aggressiveness upon himself.

"I stopped my analysis in 1975. He was becoming deaf, was limping a bit, and was beginning to be interested above all in his cubes and strings. For my part, I was having trouble walking on the cobblestones and climbing the stairs. From 1978 to 1982, I was in analysis with Bela Grunberger. I did not want to end my analytic life without having tried a non-Lacanian couch. There was an aroma of basil in the house, a sense of humor, wisdom, and orthodoxy. Grunberger was quite misogynistic and the sessions were timed. He never expressed any hostility toward Lacan. He helped me to free myself from my transference with Lacan and allowed me to understand, without hatred, where Lacanianism was headed. Lacan was my grandfather, who was called Jacques, and Grunberger was my Freudian analyst. My father was named Alexis Grugnardi and he was a shepherd [berger]. When I had read the Bucolics, handsome [le bel] Alexis had questioned me about my father's homosexuality. I went to see Grunberger and said to him, 'My father was named Alexis, you are Bela le bel Alexis, you are Grün and you are Berger—so it's you.' He laughed and said, 'I too am a shepherd [berger]."

Roland Castro: "I began my analysis with Lacan in 1972 after the dissolution of Vive la révolution [the gauchiste group]. I was a political leader and wanted to see a leader. Brassens and Ferré had aged; Pompidou was in power; Godard was stricken with aphasia; and Sartre had faltered. He was fascinated by May '68 and thus ineffective. In that shitpile, only Lacan continued to think. He was a snob, greedy, and a socialite, but he thought. 'I wait but I don't expect anything,' he had said, and 'Revolution is made in order to maintain order.' The concept of the proletariat was collapsing and Lacan was a truth that was still afloat.

"At the end of 1971, the movement was declining and getting radicalized. The question of forcing destiny was being raised—the question of terrorism. Lacan's discourse, which was in the air, offered me a buoy. The choice was drugs, the couch, or suicide—not yet cynicism. I stormed over to the idol and then gradually secularized my relation to Lacan's thought. When I came to see him, I was on a bad drug trip. I had taken acid. At the first session, he said, 'We won't get there in one try. ' I was furious. I had given up architecture and wanted to take it up again. One of my first discoveries was that analysis excludes the artist. The cost of the sessions was astronomical. I protested, then I ended up paying.

"Lacan intervened on individual words, and one could have spent the night with what he said. I didn't have time to do a 'pipi-caca' analysis, but with Lacan it was a philosophy class, a detour by way of a form of knowledge I had forbidden myself. I didn't stop wanting to commit suicide every day and feeling lousy. I had the feeling of a spiral returning to its starting point, but a notch higher. I bore Lacan's ill health, and when Heidegger died, I told him he had lost his last interlocutor. I knew he had driven him around at 300 km/hr. I stopped because I was tired of paying and I did a period of analysis with a Lacanian woman, where I could speak of ass and mommy-daddy."

Danièle Arnoux: "I began my analysis with Lacan in October 1968, encouraged by a lucky encounter in May. Unaware of who Lacan was, I had introduced to the IMP, where I had just been hired as a psychologist, an enthusiastic group of young psychoanalysts interested in founding an outpatient clinic. I was not long in discovering that whatever inspiration they had came from the man they called 'God the Father.' They were all in analysis with him.

"Abandoning psychotherapy, which was leaving me ashamed and anxious, I decided to go there myself, thinking it was better to deal with God than his saints. Lacan laughed a lot at that. From our first meetings, I experienced a great sense of trust. He showed a sharp interest in me, which removed all shame at my eccentricities. He delivered a diagnosis, formulated a prognosis, allowing me quite quickly to recover enough narcissism to be able to love. When, after several sessions, he announced his exorbitant fee—all that I had to live on for a month—I broke down in tears. He then asked me what I thought I could give and fixed a fee higher than the one I proposed. I was prepared to do the impossible. Was it in order to wipe away the effects of my psychotherapy that he kept me at a standoff until January, saying to me enigmatically one day at the entrance to his apartment, 'You are on the threshold'? I laugh about it today. . . . I had the feeling that once I was on the couch the sessions became shorter and was always surprised when he suspended them with a 'That's it,' or 'That's very nice,' or a heavy sigh, 'Eh oui.' With that one my whole edifice would collapse and I was invited to move on to something else. Or even, 'Excellent,' or the repetition of a word I had said and which suddenly began to shimmer in other unperceived contexts. A very subtle observation from him triggered intense elaborations in every direction. I emerged spellbound, perplexed, astonished, laughing, crying, speaking out loud to myself. I occasionally crossed other analysands on the rue de Lille and we exchanged greetings, bits of therapy, in an ambiguous fraternity.

"By 1970, the symptoms which had brought me to him had disappeared and

I asked to be a member of his school. Starting in 1977, I went to Lacan's place every day. He frequently made me repeat what I had said. I repeated things differently and it seemed to me that my confidence was no longer in Lacan but in analysis. Was he becoming deaf? 'You speak so softly,' he said. Then, during a session in 1978, he asked me for my husband's telephone number. Quite surprised, I said, 'Which husband?' Lacan then named someone else. In a hollow voice, I told him my name. Furious and disoriented, I challenged him violently at my next session. He had fallen from his pedestal and dragged me along with him in his fall. He then humbly excused himself with an 'I don't know why,' which made me confront an eminently fallible Lacan, subject to the unconscious. *Felix culpa!* I could bear no longer dealing with God the Father, but knew that we were still bound by a transference. On October 30, 1979, I was feeling fine and no longer had any reason to see him. I told him so. 'In that case, don't come,' he said. I was moved at leaving him and said so. 'In that case, come tomorrow,' he said. When I said no, I received a magisterial slap in the face. I knew I would never come back. Is that all he could come up with to get me to leave? I experienced a strange feeling of respect as a result, the weight of a reality which made me mourn for him. After that, I began to work on his texts."

Jean-Michel Ribettes: "Starting in 1968, at the age of seventeen, I was part of *ultragauchisme* [the extreme left]. I had begun to read Lacan in school because of a Maoist teacher, a member of the PCMLF [Parti communiste marxiste-léniniste français]. I was part of the first generation of 'autonomous' groups, whose tendencies were close to those of the 'situationists': radicalism, aestheticism, provocation, suicidal activism. . . . We had decided that our aims were to allow for the role of desire in daily life, share luxuries with the masses, live intensely, impose guerrilla war in the cities, break everything. . . . For instance, we caused demonstrations to degenerate into a pillaging of armories. With arrogance and fanaticism, we wanted to be the vanguard of the new world. Our direct enemies were the *gaucho-flics* [leftist cops], Communist Stalinists, Maoists, Trotskyists—above all the security services. We aspired to revolutionary clandestinity and had even shielded members of the Red Army Fraction. But since terrorism didn't catch on in France, some around me quickly drifted toward common criminality: thievery, armed attacks. In point of fact, an aestheticism of provocation was my only political line. What amused me was to find myself on the fist page of the newspapers the next day with a photograph of our last 'action' figuring prominently.

"In 1973, I had a serious car accident. I could no longer walk and knew I would not be able to bear that handicap. I was thinking only of suicide at the time, when it occurred to me that Lacan was the only person to whom I could speak. I had to speak to an historic individual, as befitted the hysterical dimension of *gauchisme*. The symbolic power of the man counterbalanced the deathly character of *gauchisme*. I wrote him a long letter: He had to understand me, it was vital. Lacan received me immediately, without delay. The first time I went to see him I could not yet remain standing. I told him of the idea I already had of becoming a psychoanalyst. For an hour, he spoke very little, but picked up a phobia I had, saying, 'It's a fact: Animals that have your name don't make you laugh.' He questioned me, deliberately making me repeat my sentences several times. For a few weeks, he literally made me yell my request for analysis—as though he wanted me to rediscover my tone of voice at *gauchiste* open meetings!

"It is true that Lacan never made me pay exorbitant fees: He made me give my voice, but not much money. To be sure, he gradually allowed me to assume a more intimate tone. I went to see him two or three times a week, at a time I myself chose once the day arrived. As a matter of fact, I had the habit of coming late in the afternoon and for several years, I was the last patient of the day. The sessions lasted between a minute and an hour—with an average of ten minutes. I could speak seated or, for that matter, standing as well. When he was at his desk, Lacan turned his back to me and read, wrote, clipped together piles of papers or made Borromean knots. He was capable of shifting symbolic backdrops quite brutally. For example, we might be speaking about an academic or a publishing problem. Then, with no transition, he started the session: 'Now, I'm listening to you.' I told him about my friends: suicides, psychotics, or common-law criminals—the result of our fascination with terrorism. In allowing me to elevate my political activity to the level of analytic material and thus to define it in terms of pathology, he did a lot to encourage me to burn my bridges to that chapter of my life quite quickly.

"It should be said, in a general way, that Lacan's impatience and the violence of his short sessions favored the progress of one's discourse. Lacan did not hesitate to cut short the narration of a dream definitively on a single word, to challenge a 'free' association, or to correct a grammatical error—the demand that one 'speak well,' which can be deduced from an ethic of psychoanalysis, being as stimulating as the passion for truth induced by his conception of therapy. Nor did Lacan hesitate to speak with me when we would meet at a party or at the house of friends. He did not hesitate to come—unannounced—to the defense of my thesis, which was directed by Julia Kristeva. That circumstance was all the more unexpected in that the defense took place at a time at which he normally received numerous patients. When I told him that his presence had given me a great deal of pleasure, he answered me, 'But that's why I did it!' I have always thought that in my case, those encounters outside the analytic framework were quite positive for my analysis.

"My break with *gauchisme* occurred in three stages: first, the feeling that I had just barely escaped, then the analysis of its neurotic motivation, finally the discovery of the unconscious fantasy underlying my activism. As for the short sessions, I can distinguish three modalities. A first kind, aiming at the truth of the symptom, effected an interpretative break. A second, which was accorded to the dimension of *jouissance* (the object beyond the signifier), thwarted discourse even as it opened an access to the cause of desire. (During his last years, Lacan plainly conceived of therapy as a limit-experience tending to bring the real—the impossible to signify, a dimension beyond meaning—into the framework of the session. Whence a still shorter kind of session, in which it was less a matter of interpreting a signifier than of causing the eruption of the object 'ex-sisting' beyond the signifier.) A third, which was the analysand's responsibility, and which signified a positive result on my part: several months of analysis which I might condense into a single sentence, a kind of discursive lightning bolt."

Colette Soler: "I was always interested in the recollections of analysands. It's a fact that they frequently take pleasure in speaking of their analyst, if not of their analysis, and it is always quite instructive. But I gradually came to realize that all that never told one anything about the practice at work, unless one were already informed from elsewhere. There is a structural reason for that, which is that testimony—and even more so when it is not fresh—bears witness only to the person addressed by whoever is speaking. Whatever one does, it's impossible to step out of the apologetic mode, which is always a self-apology, especially when it resorts to counter-apology. If what's at stake here is giving what is called the public an idea of Jacques Lacan's practice, personal testimony is not the proper way, and that's why I have refused you mine.

"Instead, if you are willing, I propose two observations. There is the fact that Lacan's practice caused a lot of tongues to wag. Honorability claims it is offended, but was it suspect? Things should be considered in reverse order. A psychoanalysis attempts to transform through speech a subject who asks for it, generally because he is suffering. Success in that attempt implies that people will hear about it. When an analytic practice doesn't make any waves, as the saying goes, the resultant silence is a sign not of seriousness, but of limited impact. And it was in fact the case that around Freud, yes, there was a lot of talk. Around Melanie Klein as well. It is quite clear that the IPA began to challenge Lacan when unprecedented transferential effects were produced as a function of what people were saying. Now without such effects, there is no psychoanalysis. Where are we headed, you ask? Toward what would be common knowledge were it not for the secrecy of the couch: No one trained so many analysts, and such a diversity of analysts, so little in conformity with any standard model, as Lacan. Your book will bring this to light, I suppose. Wherever Lacan passed—specifically in France—there is a possibility of appeal for the subject suffering from his particularity, that subject which a civilization built on scientific norms annuls more every day. That single fact speaks to the subject of Lacan's practice. But people want to know how he went about it? Well, let them read him; it's all there. Not his technique, which remains untransmissible, but the principles behind his action. As in the La Fontaine fable, 'a treasure is buried therein.' Only there, too, there's no way to make it one's own without working a little."

The Freudian republic founded by Lacan resembled the original Viennese society, but it was more like a large-scale combination of direct monarchy and Athenian democracy. If the monarch held all power, he surrounded himself with a circle of initiates for the purpose of defining a program of rescue and reconquest: King Arthur and the Knights of the Round Table. But Lacan was not a Jew; he was not the founder of psychoanalysis; and he was not the head of a society reduced to a few members. He had hundreds of individuals united around him and mobilized to his ends less the spirit of the ghetto than memories of the traditions of antiquity, Catholicism, and Surrealism. Antiquity, since the word "school" was a reference to Aristotelian philosophy, Catholicism because the EFP was organized like a monastery, Surrealism because the group was to discuss new ideas. At every hierarchical level, Lacanian subjects were called on, through a *working transference,* to rise toward the summit of pure psychoanalysis. Every member of the EFP was the militant of a cause and the representative of a Freudian politics of the unconscious. He might also rediscover in his group the terms of his personal history and identity. Christians found in it the practice of spiritual exercises, Marxists the cell-structure of a party and obedience to a doctrine, physicians a revalorizing of clinical practice, atheists a science, Jews a Diaspora or a Talmudic tradition of textual study, foreigners an antiethnocentrism, Frenchmen a de Gaulle–like Frenchness, and libertarians the winds of protest. In that sense, the EFP was a school of its own time: It responded to all the quests for identity of the intellectual scene of the 1960s and 1970s.

Lacan wrote his founding act, with Leclaire, before his speech of June 21, but it was during the summer that he worked out the structures of the EFP. Very early on, he wrote an Adjoining Note, in which he defined the notion of a didactic or training analysis, and a Preamble in which he announced that he had kept the name of the new group to himself. The EFP retained its acronym, but instead of being called the École française de psychanalyse, it took on the name of École freudienne de Paris. "Let us pass by the site," wrote Lacan, "from which we reclaim, not without being entitled to do so, along with the original shield, the act of defiance already saluted by Freud that it entails: the École affirms itself to be first of all Freudian, for the reason that—if there were ever a truth undoubtedly sustained by a presence patient in its reiteration, but which by dint of that effect has become the conscience, as it were, of the French soil—it is that the Freudian message, in its radical thrust, goes far beyond the use to which it is put by practitioners of Anglophonic obedience." [98]

The first name was inadequate and also bore similarities to the defunct Société française de psychanalyse. We have seen that the SFP title had been chosen more or less deliberately with the intention of favoring the provinces against Paris and "national" identity against the international organization. We also know that a society belonging to the IPA had never called itself a "school," and had never dared lay claim to the name of Freud, since the IPA was itself a creation of the founding father. The words "society" or "association" were standard terms which evoked less a doctrine than an institutional order and were better suited to a group of "notables" than to a mode of psychoanalytic training.

In inventing the name École freudienne de Paris, Lacan thus gave juridical status to his doctrinal break with the IPA. Not only did he dare cast as "Freudian" a society which became a "school," thus endorsing the principle of his baroque phase, but he returned—one time does not a custom make—to the French history of psychoanalysis. He was not exactly playing Paris against the provinces, but a centralizing exile against a federative Frenchness: 1926 against 1953. The first French group to be recognized by Freud had claimed Paris as the original site of its legal existence. Founded by a German-speaking Alsatian, the group was not particularly "French": Jewish *émigrés,* a few Swiss, a princess of Greece, and a Maurrassian who was so "French" that he ended up defeated by that very Frenchness. The history of that word in the "French" destiny of psychoanalysis is known. The Paris of 1964 laid claim to by Lacan was the Paris of 1926, a place of pioneers, the city of the Surrealists, the shelter of the novel that was his youth. Lacan organized a new diaspora on the rue de Lille: The EFP was cosmopolitan like the first SPP, innovative like the first Viennese society, "exiled" like all avant-garde groups. Through its "Freudian" label, it reactivated the universalist aspect of the unconscious, knowing no country or border, but belonged to a city, itself the symbol of all the advances of modernity. Lacan's Paris was thus Freud's Vienna: Mitteleuropa against the Anglo-American empire, a diaspora within Frenchness, an ethic of rehearsing origins against the pragmatism of transcending them.

After the adjoining texts, Lacan drew up statutes that were quite simple, in conformity with the principle of associations governed by the law of 1901. They were the most democratic in the French history of psychoanalysis: a single category of members, election of an administrative board through universal suffrage, the same voting rights for every individual. The "king" thus accepted the risk from the outset that he might be deposed by his people. A member might have a different title from his neighbor, but juridically each had the same rights—guaranteed by elections—concerning the conduct of the institution. For the first year, Lacan named an administrative board presided over by himself and composed of distinguished non-analysts: Jean Piel, Hélène Gratiot-Alphandéry, and Madame Dreyfus (the former wife of Claude Lévi-Strauss). The board was to ensure the administrative existence of the École until a general meeting to be held a year later. On September 25, Lacan submitted his statutes to the Paris Prefecture: It had taken three months to complete his work as a legislator.

Toward the end of August, he sent Henri Ey his founding texts and asked him to join the EFP and support its campaign of reconquest. Ey read the documents and wrote a long letter in which he refused to become a member, paid homage to his old classmate's courage, and prophesied a future for an endeavor so different from his own project of transforming and renewing medical science. "I applaud this foundation," he wrote, "sensitive as I am to the immense effort and the great intellectual courage you exemplify in it. But I don't applaud without reservations, wondering—as I do here out loud in your presence—if for failure to break radically with the adventure of lay analysis, you are not going to end up in a hornet's nest. You will not be able, I fear—given the present state of things and of people—to ensure freedom of thought, of practice, and of criticism for a psychoanalysis which, having escaped the feudal order of medicine, can find no other solution than constituting a new one. To my mind what is needed is to cut the Gordian knot that Freud tied tight as an iron-collar around his work and which has asphyxiated it. Psychoanalysis can be understood only as what it originally was and what it essentially is, a psychotherapeutic method for freeing man insofar as he is enchained to the discourse of the other. The whole question is knowing how the art and training of the psychoanalyst can and should be integrated according to the norms of medicine; of medicine insofar as it does not consist simply in surgical intervention or the prescription of remedies. Had you asked for my advice before founding this school, the affection I have for you would have dissuaded you from it, for to the extent that a school is a master, you have it and you don't need anything else. How does it profit you to found a school on juridico-administrative bases, which are always precarious, whereas your school *exists* in its most striking reality? A school is constituted when a master freely teaches free students; it is not founded on the basis of any official status, but on the *maître*'s prestige. . . . As for the collaboration you ask of me, the form, framework, and organization of what you're trying to set up barely allow me to perceive what place I might be able to occupy in it. I could only envisage the matter in the event we were to envision jointly the constitution of an organism for reflection on all the problems raised by psychoanalysis, one sufficiently heterogeneous for genuine debate to be possible in it." [99]

Reading that letter, the historian finds it difficult not to speculate that the Turquet Commission would have done well to question Henri Ey on the question of wherein the position of a master consists.

Lacan did not heed his friend's warning. Seeking support in every quarter, he turned to the SPP and asked Bela Grunberger, a high dignitary of the orthodoxy, to participate in the creation of his school. A Hungarian Jew by origin, Grunberger had left Transylvania in 1918 when it was united with Romania, then fled the Nazis, by way of Switzerland, before coming to France in 1939, where he did his training on Nacht's couch. During the Occupation, he had lived in Lyon with false papers, frequently passing before Fort Monluc of sinister memory. At the time Lacan invited him to join him, he was in conflict with Nacht, whom he reproached for his authoritarianism. Nevertheless, he had little desire to participate in the adventure and declined the proposal.[100] Lacan, moreover, was unable to win the slightest support from that side. In 1964, his teaching was recognized by numerous members of the SPP, but his school attracted none of its dignitaries, who would have been forced to resign from the IPA to follow him. The master was thus alone with his fellow travelers and newcomers of the fourth generation. Which is why he counted a great deal on nonanalysts, who never had to deal with the crises of analytic societies.

In order to shatter the customary hierarchy of psychoanalytic institutions, Lacan drew up internal rules which carefully defined ranks and types of affiliation. The categories of affiliate, associate, titular member, and *stagiaire* were abolished, along with the various commissions, in favor of a complex three-tiered structure reflecting the cultural aspirations of the movement and referring to the ternary character of the doctrine. A simple *member* of the EFP, or ME, was the equivalent of a *student* in the other societies. Such was the first innovation in the EFP, in which students and individuals outside the profession were accepted as full-fledged members. In order to become a member, one had to pay a visit to Lacan and pass before a liaison committee, called "Cardo," (from the Latin for "hinge"). If the candidate was accepted, he was in no event recognized as an analyst, whatever his professional activity. But he had voting rights and committed himself to a working contract with the École by participating in a *cartel*. That term designated the basic unit of the EFP. It consisted of at least three and at most five members and took on a *plus-one* responsible for directing discussions and selecting themes for work.

Alongside the simple rank of ME, two titles were reserved for members of the EFP who were recognized as analysts: *analyst member of the École* (AME) and *analyst of the École* (AE). Here Lacan effected a second break with traditional organization. He eliminated the distinction between "training" or "didactic" analyses and "therapeutic" analyses, thus retaining the notion of the *personal analysis*. To obtain the ranks of AE and AME one was not obliged, as was the case with other societies, to pass before a selection commission. Every member had the right to enter into therapy with an analyst of his choice, and that private contract was not considered the concern of any commission whatsoever. At the EFP there was no "list" of titular members orienting the selection procedure. A member wanting to obtain the rank of AME, which entailed recognition of his professional competence, requested it himself. Whatever the rank of his analyst, he could obtain that title by presenting his candidacy to an *admissions jury*. Before that jury, the candidate would then enter into a new working contract with the École, whose subject was a request to conduct an analysis "referred to a third party" (a control). That request implied that the subject *authorized at that moment and at that moment only* that his situation be discussed *in secret* by persons of his choice. He chose three members out of five to constitute his admissions jury, which automatically included as well the director of the EFP (Lacan) and his analyst. If accepted, he received the title of AME. After an unspecified number of controls, the AME had the right to apply for his titularization, that is, his promotion to the rank of AE. Under such circumstances, the individuals participating in his training were constituted as a *jury d'agrément* [approval committee] presided over by Lacan, which awarded (or refused) the desired rank.

If the Cardo and the jury constituted the institutional structures of the EFP, the École itself was directed by Lacan, who maintained a personal and privileged relation with each member. He was assisted by a *directorate* [*directoire*] chosen by him from among the AEs. In principle the juries were elected at plenary sessions, but since no such session had taken place at the time of the École's founding, all jury members were designated by the director, who also named an administrative secretary. Since initially, juries were not yet elected, the first holders of the ranks of ME, AME, and AE were appointed by Lacan and his directorate. It will thus be perceived how, in the EFP of 1964, the power of its founder was exercised. Lacan was installed at the head of a completely democratic school, for which he fulfilled the roles of intellectual leader, director, and lawmaker. He sat on all juries, and every appointment was dependent on his opinion.

Lacan was not satisfied with that exorbitant power. Along with two different collaborators, he ran the three teaching sections corresponding to the three hierarchical levels of the École. The first section—the *Section for Pure Psychoanalysis*—was charged with problems of training, effected through a permanent confrontation of AEs and AMEs. Subjects for study were restricted to one domain—Lacan's doctrine. Or more precisely, in his own words, "the characteristics by which I myself break with the promulgated standards of training practice, as well as the effects imputed to my teaching on the course of my analyses when it is the case that, as students, my analysands are in attendance. Included therein, if necessary, will be the sole impasses to be retained from my position in such a school, to wit: those that the very induction toward which my teaching aims would engender in its work." [101] That section contained three subsections: the doctrine of pure psychoanalysis, the internal criticism of its praxis as training, the supervision—or control—of psychoanalysts in training. The second section was called the *Section for Applied Psy-*

choanalysis and was charged with problems relating to therapeutics and clinical practice. It too contained three subsections, through which Lacanian theory was to be studied (1) as a doctrine of therapy and its variations, along with (2) psychiatric information, and (3) casuistry. As for the third section, called the *Section for Taking Inventory of the Freudian Field,* its focus would be the possibility of a "science" of praxis, as opposed to "ineffable" experience. Its point of reference was Lacan's doctrine viewed in terms of its structuralist rearticulation. It too comprised three subsections, recalling Freud's great cultural project: a continuous commentary on the psychoanalytic movement, an articulation with related sciences, and the ethics of psychoanalysis, viewed as the praxis of its theory.

At the apex of that huge pyramid, symbolized by the numeral three, Lacan held all powers. He had already indicated as much in his founding act, where he did not take his future directorate into account: "Admission initially will be decided by myself without taking any account of positions taken by anyone toward my person in the past, sure as I am of those that left me that it is not I who begrudge them it, but they who will begrudge me still more their not being able to come back." [102] Not only did Lacan conflate his doctrine with his person at that point, but he spoke like an abandoned father cursing his sons in the very words with which he denied doing so.

Despite such a program, which Freud would never have dared concoct, Lacan's autocratic position in his own school was impeded by the very fact of its excesses. In arrogating to himself power that absolute, the master was condemning himself not to exercise it and it may paradoxically be wondered whether he had not done so on purpose. Real dictators are the ones who subjugate a people through police and an army. Lacan, however, did not act in such a manner. Fearing the feudal rebellion which he had paid for dearly at the SFP, he transformed *marquis* into courtiers and notables into valets. But since he was a modern monarch, who had learned from Machiavelli or de Gaulle, he knew that a true prince is nothing without the people governed by him. Which was why, within his school, he was a "dictator" only for those courtiers desirous of serving him, never for the others.

At the EFP, in its inception, the power of the barons was thus reduced and that of the people reinstated. That people was represented by the mass of mere members. Even if those members were chosen by Lacan after an interview, in the course of an analysis, or because of some work they had done, they ran their own cartels as they wished, themselves naming their *plus-one.* They did not have to report to anyone, could freely choose an analyst, or remain couchless. In addition, they had the right to be analysts without having to ask the École to underwrite their practice. They were recognized as members solely on the basis of a work they themselves had chosen. They thus enjoyed considerable freedom, even as they were assured of an affiliation at the very least. In other psychoanalytic societies, the notion of a mere member did not exist since an analytic practice was a prerequisite for affiliation. Under those conditions, a student *stagiaire* was no one and was obliged— in order to be someone—to embark on a career. At the EFP, on the contrary, a mere member was *everything* on the condition he forwent established promotion procedures. If he wanted titles, he ran the risk of becoming a valet or a courtier, but if he agreed to remain a full-fledged member, he was simply a subject embarked on the adventure of Lacanianism. The EFP thus had the advantage over other societies of preserving the complete freedom of all concerned, even as it excluded various attempts at aggrandizement from within the ranks. In that sense, it was the only institution based on a genuinely Freudian politics of the unconscious, of desire, and of freedom. The contradiction between the autocratic tempest blowing on high and the libertarian wind spreading through the base reflected the historical situation of the EFP. The school was born of an old master's encounter with the intellectual youth of his country. Excluded by his students, who had become notables, Lacan played his newfound people against his own courtiers: such was the underlying significance of his founding act.

If, in theory, Lacan had organized the EFP in that manner, in practice things went differently. Reality never bends to a master's will. Thus, from the time of its foundation, the EFP was a place of conflict. On the eve of its dissolution, the SFP had 182 members of various rank. After the split, 26 relocated at the APF, along with their students, about thirty disappeared from the scene, and some hundred followed Lacan. At its foundation, the EFP was thus not, in composition, a new society. It comprised 134 members, only a third of whom had never frequented the SFP. Among the newcomers, aside from the group from the ENS, philosophers, psychiatrists, psychologists, and a considerable number of priests and pastors were to be found. Some were analysts, others not. Here, at random, is a list of those who would subsequently play an important role—either through their work or their situation—in this history: François Roustang, Michel de Certeau, Catherine Backès-Clément, Cornélius Castoriadis, Félix Guattari, Yves Bertherat, Luce Irigaray, Michèle Montrelay, and Paul Mathis. With the exception of the last named, all were simple members.

By virtue of its sociological heritage, the EFP tended to fall into old routines, customs, and habits. Thus Lacan named the AEs and AMEs not in accordance with the new rules, but according to his will and on the basis of the prior hierarchy. All the former titular members of the SFP were automatically given the rank of AE.[103] Most of the former associates were also promoted to AE (B. This, O. and M. Mannoni, X. Audouard, P. Aulagnier, J. Clavreul, G. Rosolato) as well as several *stagiaires* (Paul Duquenne, René Bargues, Lucien Israël, Louis Beirnaert, Jacques Schotte, and J.-P. Valabrega). Also included in that promotion were two women who were analysands of Lacan and personally devoted to him, Solange Faladé and Irène Roublef, Perrier's former wife. They had been students at the SFP and the only students to make the transition directly to AE. Both were physicians. As far as the AMEs were concerned, appointments took a similar turn. Generally speaking, the ranks at the SFP were reproduced. Among the AMEs appointed by Lacan were to be found men and women of the fourth French psychoanalytic generation who along with the new members would play a role corresponding to the one played by the third generation for the SFP. Among the most prominent: Charles Melman, Rosine Lefort, Claude Dumézil (Georges's son), Claude Conté, and Christian Simatos.

That distribution shows that the AEs and AMEs, who were the "elite" of the EFP, had on the whole received their training in accordance with criteria in effect at the SFP. In addition, whereas the École tended to privilege the principle of lay anal-ysis, with the creation of the section for pure psychoanalysis, the management did not follow suit. Out of 134 members, only 49 were nonphysicians. That is a good proportion, but there was no increase of lay members among the AEs and AMEs. In general, it may be said that the EFP was in conflict with the organization of its teaching: It reembodied what it proposed to fight against. That was why, for more than a year, the juries were not approached by any candidates; the directorate acted disgruntled; and simple members showed no interest in seeking promotion. They retreated to their cartels. There they were not obliged to deal with an institutional power whose functioning they were hard put to grasp and which did not reflect the reality of the École. If simple members did not want to become AMEs, the AMEs were uninterested in gaining access to titular rank—only one request to constitute a *jury d'agrément* was recorded in September 1966.

As for the massive influx of new members, it was contemporaneous with the hyperlogical reelaboration and the publication of the *Écrits;* between September 1966 and January 1967, the EFP accepted eighty new members. At that time the limit of two hundred had been exceeded, without any appreciable increase in the number of AEs and AMEs. The École at that time began its propensity toward being gigantic by way of a "base" that continued to swell and a "summit" that was in-creasingly immobile.[104] All these figures prove that a majority of the fourth French psychoanalytic generation joined Lacan's École without becoming part of the society of his barons. Against the third generation and in part against the fraction of the fourth in power, it would people the ranks of a movement, which, in its eyes, rep-resented authentic Freudianism. It did not encounter the autocratic bent of a master in that movement, but the formidable effervescence of a cultural adventure. In Jan-uary 1967, Lacan's revenge was ratified by a massive uprising of the psychoanalytic youth of France.

The fourth French psychoanalytic generation, all things considered, is far more difficult to delineate than the third. Born between 1930 and 1940, it remem-bered the Occupation, was squarely faced with the dilemma of decolonization, tra-versed the crisis of the Communist movement, and participated in the ascendance of Lacanianism. For its members, the affairs of the SFP, and even more those relating to the first split, belonged to the past. For that generation, Lacan was a founding father or a theoretician of imposing stature, at once close in his person and better known for his doctrine. If his practice was still criticized, it was no longer subject to the same risks as previously. It might be refused without the entirety of his teaching suffering any consequences. The new generation was less concerned with the IPA, laid claim to its own marginality, and was not ashamed of its French isolation. It was, in any event, cosmopolitan and open to winds from abroad. Whether oriented toward the SPP, the symbol of tradition, or the EFP, it was internationalist out of a taste for travel, contentious by grace of the barricades, and "Lacanian" as a matter of course. In its eyes, Lacan had become a monument.

Given the hugeness which came to characterize the entirety of the French psychoanalytic community after 1965, the fourth generation may be defined first of all by its anonymity. With its advent psychoanalysis truly became a mass practice and no longer the affair of a network of eminent individuals. As a result, the history of psychoanalysis can no longer be written as it had for previous periods. For this new saga, the historian can no longer be concerned with a minority caught up in the throes of a struggle over ideas, but must take account of institutional, juridical, and statutory quarrels born of psychoanalysis's massive expansion. Gradually, those quarrels meshed with theoretical stakes or masked them, allowing them to reappear in different guises. During those years, the three existent societies were having a hard time resolving their internal struggles and questions of organization. Despite a number of splendid theoretical productions, they were mired in administrative conflicts which were the direct consequence of expansion. They all experienced the same difficulties, pertaining to admissions, training, and the organization of a mass movement in which anonymity prevailed.

As far as the EFP was concerned, several orientations could be identified within the fourth generation. There was first of all the fraction of those who had studied in the GEP (Groupe d'études de la psychanalyse) and participated in the split. Either *stagiaires* or guests at the SFP, they gradually became the elite of the new school, rising rather quickly to the rank of AME and less quickly to that of AE. Lacan's "personal guard" was recruited from among them, members he appointed to all the important positions as the protesters of the third generation little by little withdrew. In age they remained quite close to that generation, even though they regarded it as their senior. Not having been in the leadership of the battle for integration into the empire, they looked on their seniors' defeat as Lacan's victory. They thus projected all responsibility onto Perrier and Leclaire, forgetting that Lacan had not only supported the troika's policy, but had been its principal instigator. As a result, they imagined the history of Lacanianism in the form of a hagiography, transforming their master into a hero fallen victim to a horrible betrayal. In addition, in order to favor his policy of expansion, Lacan encouraged doubts as to his real role in the past battle. He took on the air of an intransigent individual who had never accepted the slightest negotiation or compromise. He flattered his new courtiers while frequently disavowing those truly loyal to him. And since the courtiers wanted to hear nothing of their master's defeat, they felt themselves—against their seniors— to be invested with a great mission of reconquest.

In a general manner, that fraction of the fourth generation would be characterized by a sectarianism which would weigh heavily on the future of the EFP. Most of its representatives were anonymous in every sense of the word. They produced no written work, no original thought, and oscillated between the unhappiness of voluntary servitude and the omnipotence they enjoyed in their new functions. They supported the master's decisions without discussion and imitated his manners and his style. It is a remarkable fact that the near totality of books published in the "Champ freudien" series begun at Éditions du Seuil before the appearance of the *Écrits* emanated not from that significant fraction of the fourth generation, but from the third and the second. The majority of the names encountered there were those of influential members of the SFP: Françoise Dolto, Octave and Maud Mannoni, Moustapha Safouan, Serge Leclaire, Jean Clavreul, Ginette Raimbault, et al.

That fraction was thus sacrificed in advance to the policy of expansion. If its members occupied the best positions between 1967 and 1977, they were also the first victims of the man they served. In the end, in fact, Lacan would disavow them the better to support the advance of a fifth generation, born after the war. That last generation would in part find its path by way of the reconquest of the EFP effected by Jacques-Alain Miller, starting from the University of Vincennes.

Charles Melman was certainly the most brilliant and authentic representative of that current to the extent that he agreed from the outset to embody the theoretical ideals of dogmatism. Through that choice, he implemented a program of collective instruction at the EFP that would end in an abortive attempt to elaborate a Lacanian dictionary of psychoanalysis capable of being pitted against Laplanche and Pontalis's work.

His father, Max Melman, was a Jewish cabinetmaker forced to flee Poland in 1929 because of his commitment to the revolution. He sought refuge in France, became a member of the Communist Party, and participated in the construction of the young Jewish republic of Birobidzhan by organizing the departure to that territory of numerous families from all corners of the globe. He lived and worked in Moscow, then, hostile to Stalinism, he returned to France even while refusing to publish his travel memoirs. He had already opted to fight Nazism and did not want to give any ammunition to the anti-Communist cause. Having joined the Resistance in Lyon, where his family resided, he left the party when Soviet tanks entered Budapest. Later, he emigrated to Israel, where he rediscovered Leopold Trepper, who had been his childhood friend. He remained a socialist after having raised his son in a secular manner.

Young Charles began his medical studies in 1948 and remained a Communist until the Algerian war. He prepared his internship with Jean Laplanche, who directed him toward Lacan's couch, on which he remained for several years without undergoing any control. He read Freud's works in their entirety, participated in the GEP, and became friends with Conté, Dumézil, and Simatos, who came to be called the "bande à Moebius" [the Moepius strip or band]. At the EFP, he was named AME, and then, very quickly, AE through a decision of Lacan's. "I don't consider myself a dogmatist," he remarked, "but I have nothing against it. I became the representative of such a tendency in order to show that Lacanian concepts had to be taken seriously." [105]

The representatives of that tendency, moreover, were no worse clinical practitioners than their colleagues from other societies. Physicians or psychologists, they were attached to their titles, diplomas, and prerogatives. They practiced analysis like non-Lacanians with the exception that they did not accept sessions clocked to last forty-five minutes. They thus broke up the patient and training market while making enemies on all sides. Their sessions lasted between ten and twenty-five minutes, and their fees were lower. They thus had great freedom of choice in the sociological gamut of their analysands. In that regard, the EFP opened its doors, not to the underprivileged classes, which were satisfied with institutions, but to a middle class within which the therapists of the future were to be recruited. Directed by a monarch, Lacan's Freudian republic thus tended to be more populist than the two other societies. But in other respects, its rituals were similar. The pioneers having disappeared from the scene, psychoanalysts became corporate men, with the codes, tics, habits, and customs characteristic of corporations. As in all other liberal professions, one could find the good, the bad, and the indifferent. Nonetheless, the dogmatic leaders of the EFP, fourth generation, were caught in a terrible contradiction. Like their neighbors, they constituted small clans around themselves. But since in order to obey their master they ceaselessly derided all aspirations to petty chiefdom, they were condemned to mock what they themselves had become. Whence the appearance of a certain number of rites specific to sectarian Lacanianism: sessions timed to last ten minutes, similar but symmetrically opposite to those of the SPP, a silence bordering on muteness, the habit of not returning change in the interest of interpretation, or of getting paid for all missed sessions, etc.

Concerning ethical principles, these Lacanians resembled their brethren. With the spread of anonymity and the standardizing of session lengths, the new notables no longer acted like their seniors of the second and third generations. They tended to be more respectful of rules of abstinence, mixed couch and bed somewhat less, and tried to avoid analyzing their lovers, mistresses, or members of a same family. But since they did not always succeed in doing so, and prohibition in such matters makes no sense, the results were at times mediocre. In the end, the successful functioning of a society depends more on the remobilization of its theoretical assets than on the policing of its members. In that sense, the expanding EFP was a freer, more modern, and more interesting society than its neighbors. According its members no advance guarantees, while leaving them free to choose a practice, it dealt with deviances and transgressions directly, instead of bypassing them with ineffective rules. It thus accepted in its ranks psychotic and occasionally homosexual therapists, to whom the others had closed their doors. But for all that, it did not always award them a title. Yet in according them a privileged right to interpret madness, it ran the risk of institutionally validating a genuine nonpsychiatric practice of psychosis or "pathology," conforming, it should be said, to Lacan's own trajectory. For that reason, it was alone in the psychoanalytic world in hearing Foucault's message, and, later on, that of antipsychiatry.

As early as 1966, the policy of reorganization by way of the base, which had been instituted by Lacan, was bearing fruit, and resulted in a crisis that would lead to the departure of a number of former associates of the third generation. But at the same time, another orientation surfaced with the entry on stage of a new and younger tendency in the fourth generation. It consisted of the mass of simple members and a few AMEs. As opposed to the dogmatists, these members did not occupy any positions of leadership and would never obtain the slightest parcel of power in the EFP—except through the anonymous force of their works and the vitality of their cartels. In general, they received their training at the École, often in successive analyses and with numerous collective or individual controls. They tended to invoke the names of Lacan, Dolto, Leclaire, or Aubry, to appeal to the experience of psychosis or child analysis and hospital institutions. Having known nothing of earlier struggles and expecting nothing of the honorific functions they disdained, they were the spearhead of anonymous Lacanianism, its finest adornments, most remarkable school, and most undeniable success.

Passionately involved with Freudianism, ardent institutional therapists, voracious consumers of analysis, they took on the whole epic of psychoanalysis and showed themselves capable of faddishness, honesty, independence, and authenticity. They gave their school its finest face because they knew how to give it the best of themselves. From Marseille to Paris and from Strasbourg to Montpellier, they are today—as dissidents or as internal exiles—the true heirs of the history of Lacanianism. They are the most heroic product of that history. Wounded by the ritual of the *passe,* excluded from all titles, influenced by the barricades, sensitive to all forms of rebellion and generosity, they would live Lacan's decline and the dissolution of their movement as a personal tragedy. Once that disbanding was accomplished, they would disperse with a sense of abandonment. To that anonymous tendency, which was quite large and a clear majority for several years, may be added the founding group of *Ordinaire du psychanalyste* as well as a large segment of the members of the fifth generation.

To that division, which separated the EFP into two expansive tendencies, may be added another created by the existence of *Cahiers pour l'analyse,* which represented the hyperlogical, theoretical, and extra-analytic tendency. Over the years, thanks to Miller's policies and the support they received from Lacan, that journal also had grown. Its activities took root at the École and functioned during the crisis of 1967–69 as an index of internal struggles. Pursuing his antipsychologizing battle and promoting the hyperlogical reelaboration, Miller gave the *Cahiers* a rather handsome theoretical cast. Over a period of three years, ten successive issues left the presses, featuring work by the most prestigious contemporary thinkers: Georges Canguilhem, Louis Althusser, Jacques Derrida, Georges Dumézil, and, to be sure, Jacques Lacan. To which may be added some extremely interesting articles as well as debates and a few texts by psychoanalysts. Through his activity there, Jacques-Alain Miller, backed up by Judith and an enlarged team, showed himself to be a remarkable editor. After the tenth issue and without warning his readers, he ceased publication in order to plunge into the clandestine adventure of *Gauche prolétarienne,* where he would not have a position of leadership. He returned to publishing, to the EFP, and to Freudian politics in 1974 upon preparing the first issue of a new journal, *Ornicar?,* in which psychoanalysts of the fifth generation had a louder voice.

While Leclaire became interested in the young theorists of the ENS, Piera Aulagnier was not inactive in the field of publishing. Along with Jean Clavreul she brought out a journal entitled *L'Inconscient* at PUF. In its format and style, it seemed a sequel of *La Psychanalyse.* The first issue appeared in the winter of 1967, centered on a theme enjoying currency at the time: transgression. Intent on maintaining the pluralist spirit that had held sway at the SFP, the editors asked Conrad Stein to join the editorial committee, along with Lucio Covello as secretary. The SPP was thus represented in the journal, which would publish articles by André Green, Francis Pasche, Michel Neyraut, Robert Barande, Jean-Luc Donnet, Dominique Geahchan, Joyce Mac Dougall, Serge Viderman, and Michel de M'Uzan. Most of these authors—third or fourth generation—were part of the "liberal" current of the SPP; against Lebovici, they sought to reform the organization of their institute in the hope of democratizing it. Moreover, if they criticized Lacan's practice, they were not hostile to his doctrine and wanted to establish contacts with a school that was tending to achieve majority status in the country.

Eight issues of *L'Inconscient* appeared, devoted to such themes as clinical practice, perversion, identification, paternity, and the teaching of psychoanalysis. But at the end of a year, the crisis that was provoked at the EFP by *la passe* put an end to the pluralist endeavor. In October 1968, the journal halted its activities as a result of the conflict that had broken out between Piera Aulagnier and Jean Clavreul. As a consequence, the liberals of the SPP were deprived of a publishing medium outside their movement where they could encounter their colleagues of the other group. The cessation of *L'Inconscient* thus left the way open for other initiatives, which would not fail to materialize with the generalized institutional crisis of the 1970s.

The first directorate appointed by Lacan was composed of the most brilliant elements of the third generation of the SFP. These included two former members of the troika, Leclaire and Perrier, as well as Valabrega, Aulagnier, Rosolato, and Clavreul. From its very first meetings, conflicts erupted and disgruntlement threatened. Leclaire had little interest in the meetings and turned to other adventures. Perrier challenged the master's authority; Rosolato and Valabrega found his decisions "dictatorial," and Piera Aulagnier's tendency was to calm everyone down. As for Clavreul, he didn't know which way to turn. Concerning the episode of the first directorate, testimony varies according to individual orientation. Occasionally invited to meetings, Charles Melman had this impression: "I was terrified because the sessions took place in an atmosphere of sarcasm and hostility toward Lacan. I had the feeling of being among young hoods defying their teacher. I emerged as though a steamroller had passed over me. There was a kind of spontaneous insurrection." [106]

It was nonetheless the case that Lacan sought to bestow promotions to AE and AME (and the eminence that went with them), without discussion, on the members of his personal guard. Whence the confusion that interfered with the proper functioning of the EFP. For the more the appointments that were granted by a single individual, the less the influence the directorate had. But in addition, the stronger an agency the directorate became, the less the juries were able to function, since they were normally supposed to preside over the advancement of candidates. Whatever the result, the functioning of the EFP was blocked at every level except for its base. To avoid that situation, it would have been necessary for the internal rules to be respected from the outset, that is, for all members to agree to begin from zero without any rank conferred in advance. But that prospect was impossible since none of the titular members of the SFP was prepared to lose the benefit of a previously acquired promotion. The question, moreover, was not raised, and no plenary session was called to make any such decision.

The members of the directorate were not content with harboring an insurrection or running the École. From the outset, they embarked on a vast program of instruction and publication. In the course of 1965–66, Valabrega, Rosolato, Clavreul, Aulagnier, and Perrier attempted the experiment of a collective work. Before the audience of the EFP, they presented for discussion, in turn, their most recent work on the general theme of perversion. After each presentation, one of the lecturers commented on his or her neighbor's text. The audience participated extensively in the discussion. Rosolato spoke on sexual perversions from the perspective of fetishism, Aulagnier on femininity, Clavreul on the perverse couple, Perrier on erotomania, and Valabrega on fantasy. The whole was of a high clinical level, without any stylistic affectation, and bore witness above all to the personal qualities of each of the authors. That series of lectures and that style of instruction were to enjoy great success at the EFP. Collected as a volume, the articles constituted the second book to appear in Éditions du Seuil's series, "Le Champ freudien."[107]

To be sure, the tendencies and cleavages dividing the EFP were not always experienced as such by its members. Their effective reality did not prevent them from enjoying warm relations with each other. For several years, until 1973, the École remained a large family, indeed, even something of a fortress. Against the other societies, the Lacanians were adamant in defending their identity and offered the adversary a rather united front. That unity was ensured by colloquia, "study days," congresses, and personal friendships that did not reflect theoretical divisions. It was above all Lacan's seminar which gave the kingdom its cohesion. All members met there to listen to the master's voice and then to discuss or digest it over a quick lunch. The general atmosphere was convivial rather than distrustful. But as soon as Lacan was no longer up to controlling the conduct of business, divisions would surface and would lead to the group's dissolution.

Two years after its creation, the EFP knew its first public crisis. On December 1, 1966, François Perrier resigned from the directorate, claiming that the juries were not functioning and that the rank of AE was merely reproducing that of titular member. "Existent models of analytic groups," he would later say, "have been introduced into the besieged École like a Trojan horse for our future analysts."[108] Lacan accepted his resignation, spoke at length with Perrier about the future of the École, then asked other members of the directorate to draw up a plan for modifying the school's structures. They could not manage to come to an agreement. A week after Perrier's resignation, a circular was sent to all members, specifying different ranks. But such a move did not precisely amount to a reform. It completed sections of the house rules that had appeared in the 1965 roster, reducing to naught the role of the Cardo and granting the secretariat the role of an admissions jury. It thus reinforced Lacan's power still further since it made membership in the École depend on the director and his secretary (Jean Clavreul) instead of leaving it to a collective body. The procedure was as follows: "The candidate is to present a request for membership to the director along with a copy to the secretariat. That step does not imply any particular participation in a psychoanalytic experience, nor does it exclude it."[109] The circular announced, in addition, the creation of a new title, *analyste practicien* [practicing analyst] or AP, stipulating that a simple member could, upon request, be included in a list on which his activity as a psychoanalyst would be indicated. Naturally, inclusion in such a list did not mean that the École underwrote the activity of APs in any way; it granted them the right to declare themselves practitioners, or better still, it authorized them to authorize themselves as psychoanalysts.

That formula was not yet employed, but it was already implicit and would be introduced by Lacan ten months later.

The addition of that title and the apparent elimination of the Cardo's role had the immediate result of undermining still further the power of the École's elites and juries. Not only did membership now depend solely on Lacan and his devoted secretary, but the notion of ME (simple member) underwent a split that made it contradictory with the initial project. In the beginning, Lacan wanted the École to be composed of two categories of individuals: analysts and nonanalysts. Without the rank of AP, that division was respected, and only analysts recognized as such by the EFP were subject to hierarchization (AME, AE). As far as they were concerned, analysts or not, the MEs remained undifferentiated. With the title of AP, however, those members now had the right to invoke their practice and to award themselves a supplementary title which "anticipated" that of AME and in affect gnawed away at the power of the juries. As a result, nonanalysts were marginalized, and the status of ME was shattered from within.

The advantage of this innovation was that the notion of AP introduced career concerns back into the ranks of the MEs who did not wish to remain part of the base. They became, in a way, "affiliates." The disadvantage was that it tended, as in the other societies, to cause the principle of personal analysis to swing in the direction of training analyses. Previously, the personal analysis was maintained by virtue of the nondifferentiation of the MEs; but now it risked being accepted in advance as a training analysis, since self-attribution of a title was the key. The introduction of the category of AP was thus Lacan's first response to the crisis affecting his school: a *pragmatic* and not a *theoretical* response. It established a "false" institutional guarantee, which functioned as a "true" act of self-recognition and endorsed a self-authorization to practice analysis. That reintroduction of career concerns at the base would bear fruit: In the course of time, all the MEs who were analysts would register on the list of APs both in order to obtain a "false" endorsement or a "true" title and to differentiate themselves from nonanalysts.

During the entire month of December, the École was aboil. It was preparing its first plenary session, to ratify the new organization, for the beginning of the new year. The date was set for January 13. But in the interim, Jean-Paul Valabrega also resigned from the directorate, criticizing the "dictatorial" character of Lacan's decisions. "The directorate," he would later write, "is a fiction. Its history shows that it was selected or modified with the intent that it contain no discordant voice. It is in a state of permanent crisis, and its members have no other possibility than to leave—one after the other. The study organism called 'cartel devenir analyste [cartel becoming an analyst]' has become an object of ridicule and derision among members of the École."[110]

The general meeting which was held on January 13 revealed the absolute support Lacan's decisions received from the base. It should be said that that plenary session played a curious role. Having never been "constitutive," it could not reject the proposals submitted to it, since it had nothing to propose itself. It was there in order to give its approval, and Lacan walked off with the prize. Since the mass of MEs had joined during 1966, in order to affirm their support for Lacan's adventure, and since the barons themselves had nothing to propose, it was not clear why the plenary session would oppose decisions that appeared attuned to the very reasons of all concerned for participating in the École. For the while, the discord functioned "on high," between the (third generation) members of the directorate, the director, and his personal guard. The meeting would thus vote through all the structural modifications decided on by the master.

The administrative board thereafter counted two additional AEs, Jean Clavreul and Solange Faladé, who were respectively secretary and treasurer of the association. Henceforth the board would be elected at a plenary session, from a slate proposed by the director and composed of different categories of members (AE, AME, AP, ME). Its role consisted of creating research or study "departments" whose leaders were to be named by the director. In addition to the secretariat, those departments were five in number: *Instruction* was given to Piera Aulagnier, *coordination of works and research* to Serge Leclaire, the *Bulletin* and *publications* to Claude Conté, and *finances* to Solange Faladé. The department for the *training of analysts* was not given to anyone, since in order to designate a leadership collective, a new plenary session was necessary to pass new house regulations. To that end, a commission was created by the administrative board (that is, by Lacan) to study the question.

As for the second directorate, which was dominated by the new guard, its role would be to define the orientations of each department. It was convened each trimester by the director and necessarily included the secretary and the leaders of each department: Conté, Faladé, Clavreul, Aulagnier, Leclaire, and Simatos as adjunct secretary. Lacan had additionally the right to invite to meetings of his directorate those members of the École whose presence he deemed necessary for the examination of questions on the agenda. In that way, he acquired *all* powers in accordance with the principle of direct monarchy: He could appeal at will to the "base" in order to squelch any emerging concentrations of power. Those concentrations were in any event thwarted *de facto* by Perrier's resignation, then Valabrega's departure, and by the inclusion on the administrative board and the directorate of members entirely devoted to the master's person. Rosolato had gone off on his own; Leclaire and Aulagnier retained honorific functions; and Clavreul gradually took his distance from his friends of the group on perversions in order to implement the new institutional policy.

Lacan, moreover, proposed that a new short-term juridical status be envisaged allowing the École to be recognized as a public utility. The EFP now had the right to apply for that status to the extent that it satisfied four requisite conditions: more than three years of existence, more than two hundred members, ability to constitute an endowment, and appreciable accomplishments in the field of its specificity.[111] That is why he asked Solange Faladé to draw up a new set of statutes, intended to facilitate the acknowledgment of that status. After numerous maneuvers and attempts, such recognition would be refused.

The plenary session of January 13, 1967 thus sounded the knell of the first École freudienne, agent of triumph and paradise of conflicting loves. What still remained to be accomplished was the business of elaborating a model of analytical training that would not reproduce the criteria of the IPA and would be able to hold up under the pressure of the sheer size of the analytic community: Such would be the proposal of *la passe*. . . . In a letter to the "cartel on becoming an analyst." Octave Mannoni gave an account of the situation on the eve of the new year. "Formerly," he wrote, "we perhaps used to put the cart before the horse: Before deciding whether or not an analysis would be valid for training, we proceeded silently to consult the Order of the World. Today, we have happily put the horses in their rightful place. . . . The fact that the world order is consulted at the end instead of at the beginning has entailed an appreciable change, but also a number of new problems." [112]

VI. *La Passe:* A Reverse Split

The institutional crisis which befell the École from its inception and grew with the first plenary session was contemporaneous with Lacan's hyperlogical reelaboration. If the crisis was not a clear reflection of it, and if that reelaboration was not directly linked to the crisis either, there was nevertheless a relation between that fertile phase of Lacanian doctrine and the institutional solution that would be found to resolve the crisis. During the first period, the master was submerged by a small insurrection of his disciples, and they themselves were active only because they observed with a certain bitterness that their school was not functioning according to their wishes. At times they blamed Lacan, who was ruling (it seemed to them) as a dictator, at times the inertia of an institution which they saw was not bringing any new solution to the age-old problem of criteria for training. All the companions in arms were agreed on at least one point: They did not want to reproduce the kind of instruction and the hierarchy in effect in the societies affiliated with the IPA. They rejected the principle of a study commission, the preselection of candidates, the distinction "in advance" between personal therapy and training analysis, the obligatory controls, the "lists," guarantees, and "normalized" sessions. In brief, they refused a bureaucratized form of psychoanalytic training that they regarded as contrary to the manifestation of an authentic desire to be an analyst. They all wanted to found a Freudian republic that did not resemble an association of notables and functionaries. But they did not know how to make the transition from an organization whose failings they knew to one that would better conform to true Freudian doctrine.

Now on that score, Lacan was hardly more advanced. To be sure, he had shown himself to be an excellent legislator. He had abolished what everyone had wanted to see abolished, but he was unable to keep the new distinctions in rank from being more or less similar to what had prevailed before. Moreover, he had conflated his role as intellectual master with his position as director of the École, thus making the "democratic" exercise of power called for in the statutes an impossibility. Hostile to the constitution of centers of power within the organization, he had eliminated them by Draconian means and with that had done away with those who had been loyal to him in favor of a cohort of epigones devoted to his person. On the eve of the new year, the EFP had thus accomplished no more than a demi-revolution. It had had its night of August 4, but was missing its cannonade at Valmy.

Lacan understood as much and would recruit his soldiers of the Year I from the base, even as he effected, through his hyperlogical reelaboration, a theoretical—and no longer pragmatic—reorganization of training principles.

Two months after the circular announcing the decisions voted through by the plenary session, François Perrier invited the AEs to meet at his home to discuss problems at the École and try to come up with a solution. Appended to his invitation was a lengthy proposal for reform; he requested criticism. The meeting took place on April 22. Perrier began by relating the difficulties that had surfaced within the directorate, then rejected the idea of creating a college of titular members separate from the EFP. For him, such a move would lead to a repetition of the old errors and would make the EFP resemble the SPP with an autonomous training institute. But immediately thereafter, he nonetheless proposed the creation of a training college having its own rules of conduct. That organism would take on clinical practice as its vocation.[113]

The proposal was interesting, because it revealed the author's lack of imagination. Perrier was satisfied with wanting to improve the system in effect in societies recognized by the IPA. If he refused the notion of an autonomous institute, he recycled principles of classical hierarchy and selection by one's peers. Indeed, the creation of the college would have had the aim of bestowing on the AEs the fullness of that oligarchical power refused them by Lacan. With that it would have set things in the familiar groove of the old order. The very fact of having restricted the meeting of April 12 to AEs betrays an orientation toward recycling the past.

In the face of the crisis and confronting the incapacity of the men of the third generation to reflect on the "real" conditions of a new mode of training, Lacan set to work. During the summer, he elaborated a fabulous proposal for reform whose content he made public in an address delivered at the EFP on October 9, 1967. "It is a matter," he wrote, "of founding, in a statute sufficiently durable to be submitted to our experience, the endorsement with which our school may authorize, through its training, a psychoanalyst—and, that being the case, to back them up. To introduce my proposals, there is already my founding act and the preamble of the roster. The autonomy of the psychoanalyst's initiative is posited there in a principle on which we cannot go back." [114]

The text of the proposal was divided into two unequal parts. In the first, which was quite lengthy, Lacan situated his project within a history that went from the founding of the IPA to the concentration camps, and in the second, which was shorter, he presented the principles informing a new set of regulations for the EFP. The whole was of singular beauty and once again revealed the genius of its author. Invoking the perspective of science, Lacan reaffirmed the major lines of his hyperlogical reelaboration. But instead of drawing solely on Frege, he borrowed the terms of "intention"and "extension" from logical positivism in order to apply them to psychoanalysis. He thus distinguished between *psychoanalysis in intention* and *psychoanalysis in extension*. The first term designated psychoanalytic experience itself in its conceptual function, as conveyed by the logical proposition: *All apples are red,* and the second was based on the movement's quantitative value, as in the statement: *an apple, plus an apple, plus an apple. . . .* Through those formulations, Lacan articulated the conceptual with the empirical in such manner as to give the relation between the two an aspect opposite the one usually ascribed to it. For psychoanalytic societies had always had the habit of responding to the question of their expansion with pragmatic or sociological models. In so doing, they based their activities on existent models without attempting to construct a kind of society more attuned to Freudian teaching. Now Lacan reversed the process. Instead of drowning every conceptual experience in a quantitative sociology, he made psychoanalysis in extension dependent on psychoanalysis in intention. In other words, he rethought the institutional order in terms of a primacy accorded to the theoretical order. And he deduced that theoretical order from the experience of therapy in so far as it was a passage by way of castration and the Oedipal myth. "Our point of departure is this," he wrote, "that the root of the experience of the psychoanalytic field considered in its extension, the only possible grounds on which to motivate a school, is to be found in psychoanalytic experience itself, by which we mean taken in its intention: the sole reason worthy of formulation for the necessity of an introductory psychoanalysis in order to operate in that field. In which we are in *de facto* agreement with the generally accepted condition of a so-called didactic or training psychoanalysis." [115]

Lacan thus laid claim to the ultra-orthodox notion of a "training analysis." But he used the term in an unprecedented way. Instead of reintroducing the idea of a preselection, with list, certification, and titularization, he defined the training analysis in terms of a theoretical vision of the personal analysis. One and the other were articulated around the transference, and one and the other each had a beginning and an end. But the training analysis actualized the *passage* of the psychoanalysand to the status of psychoanalyst, and it was that transition which Lacan proposed to isolate in order to make of it the fertile and theorizable phase of a possible end of analytic training. Freud and his successors had often pondered that transition without advancing any actual conceptualization of the process and without attempting to establish any procedure capable of giving it institutional reality. Now Lacan attempted to give it a theoretical content.

How might one account for the passage through an ordeal capable of authenticating one's position in training on the basis of a personal therapy? Such was the question raised in October 1967.[116] In order to answer it, Lacan drew on his teaching. He recalled that in 1956, he himself had criticized the hierarchical models in force in the IPA. At that time, in fact, he had taken a kind of Surrealist pleasure in writing a fierce satire of psychoanalytic societies. He had assigned their members four hierarchical positions dubbed as follows: Sufficiencies, Little Shoes, Quite-Necessaries, and Beatitudes.[117] But eleven years later, it was no longer a time for mockery and Lacan changed his tone. Comparing therapy to a treatise on chess and its conclusion to an "endgame," he redistributed his own concepts within the contemporary psychoanalytic situation. The passage or transition partook of the depressive position, through which the analyst was situated by the analysand on the side of *désêtre* in order to be himself placed in a position of *subjective destitution*. The therapist was gradually situated as a *residue* or as a kind of past participle as the therapy little by little pursued its dialectical course. It was that fall of the *subject*

alleged to know which Lacan opposed to the notion of a liquidation of the transference. Indeed in a perspective in which the term *ego* is refused along with that of an
identification with the analyst's "strong ego," nothing is ever evacuated in therapy:
One "passes," as a subject, from one position to another, without transcendence,
annulment, or liquidation.

Lacan was not satisfied with theorizing that notion of passage; he reintegrated his theorization into the history of the psychoanalytic movement, thus showing that his hyperlogical reelaboration functioned as a mirror of psychoanalysis in
extension.

Three points of reference, distributed over the three registers of the symbolic,
the imaginary, and the real, allowed that history to take concrete form in his critical
"deconstruction." On the first level was the Oedipal myth, the sole founding site of
modern societies. Its role in the economy of psychoanalytic thought was to avoid
any lapsing into a Schreber-like insanity. Then came the Freudian function of identification, as formulated in *Group Psychology and the Analysis of the Ego*. It posed
the limit Freud intended to give his message in constituting psychoanalytic societies
on the model of the army and the Church. Finally there was the advent, in this
century, of the *subject of science,* whose eruption was shown by Nazism. "The rise,"
he wrote, "of a world organized according to every form of segregation: That is
something to which psychoanalysis showed itself to be particularly sensitive, not
leaving a single one of its recognized members in a concentration camp. But there
lies the source of the particular segregation in which it sustains itself, insofar as the
IPA presents itself in that scientific extraterritoriality which we have accentuated
and which makes of it something quite different from analogous associations in
other professions. Properly speaking, an assurance assumed of finding a welcome, a
solidarity against the threat of the camps extending to one of its sectors. . . . The
solidarity of the three major functions we have just delineated finds its point of
concourse in the existence of the Jews. Which is not astonishing when one knows
the importance of their presence in the entirety of its movement. It is impossible to
write off the constitutive segregation of that people with consideration drawn from
Marxism and even less from Sartre. Which is why, particularly why, the religion of
the Jews must be called into question in our midst." [118]

Although Lacan did not take the German psychoanalytic situation between
1933 and 1945 into account in his argument, the vision he proposed of the movement's history remains exemplary in its accuracy. It takes its place in the wake of
Moses and Monotheism, whose gesture it renews. We have seen that that splendid
text, written as a last will, had the aim of uncovering the unconscious roots of anti-
Semitism through a critique of the notion of the chosen people. At the time, it constituted a response to the question of Judaism, which had traversed the history of
the IPA since its creation. If Freud and Jones did not succeed in saving the German
psychoanalytic movement from effectively collaborating with Nazism, the existence
of the IPA nevertheless allowed virtually all its psychoanalysts to escape the concentration camps. And it may even be said that the absence of collaborationism among
French psychoanalysts was the result of the triumph of the orthodox tendency over
the chauvinist line. I have already demonstrated sufficiently how the notion of the

Judaic functioned within the history of the French and international movement to credit Lacan on this point: The IPA always constituted a formidable shield for the psychoanalytic community against the threat of the camps and more generally against that of segregation. If proof be needed, there is the difficult but no less splendid welcome America gave to the persecuted of old Europe.[119] But that protection had the result of consolidating the movement in accordance with a principle of extreme normalization or assimilation for which Lacanianism had to pay a steep price during the ten years of the SFP. In saving the movement, through successive migrations, that rigidification nonetheless brought it into line with certain ideals Lacanianism was intent on combatting.

From a besieged fortress, the IPA had become a segregationist empire: Hannibal had lost his battle, and Carthage was now beholden to a new Roman Empire. The movement turned the persecution whose victim it was into a "persecution" of a different type: normalization; the exclusion of the mad, the marginal, and the nonconformists. The free Diaspora had devoured its members and constituted itself as a synagogue on the American model of adaptation.

In 1963, at the time Lacan himself was acting out his "excommunication," he compared the neo-Freudian community to a church. Six months later, he called his school "Freudian," and attempted the adventure of a new universalism which he called "Reconquest." Finally, in 1967, against the segregating power of science per se, which had allowed the genocide to attain the proportions it did, and against the ideals of normalization in which Carthage was mired, he played the card of a "science" attuned to the "logical" universality of the unconscious. His proposal for a revolution in the internal structures of his school was thus inseparable from an analysis of the historical situation of psychoanalysis in all its states. It took its place within a trajectory through which Lacanianism, as an established movement, achieved its definitive break with an empire that had become segregationist. That on the eve of the barricades of May '68, a non-Jew was able to bring about such a break, at the risk of creating a new empire, was enough to make Freud turn over in his grave—he who had spent his life wanting to de-Judaize his discovery in the name of the tradition of the Enlightenment.

After that extended detour through history, Lacan came to what was properly speaking his proposal. "Our poor school," he wrote, "can be the starting point for a renewal of our experience."[120] He proposed maintaining the title of AME as it was and to extend to the directorate and the admissions jury functions identical to those they already had. The same decision was taken for simple members and APs. The major change concerned the *jury d'agrément* and the naming of AEs. That title would no longer have anything to do with that of the former titular members. As for the *jury d'agrément,* it was no longer to be defined in terms of a teaching commission. It was composed of seven members: the director, three AEs chosen at random, and three simple members also chosen at random. The latter would have to be in therapy with AEs who would designate them to sit on the jury at the time they negotiated their "passage." Such members were called *passeurs,* and their role consisted in receiving testimony from ME, AP, and AME candidates, who were called *passants* because they were applying for the rank of AE by going through an ordeal known as *la passe*. It consisted, for the *passant,* in speaking to two *passeurs* about his training and the end of his analysis. The *passeurs* would then transmit that testimony of passage to the AEs on the *jury d'agrément,* who would reach a negative or positive decision on promotion to the rank of AE.

The purpose of the testimony which was thus conveyed was to clarify the specific act transforming a psychoanalysand into a psychoanalyst. The jury would not judge the candidate's clinical experience, which concerned the rank of AME, but an *en plus,* a supplementary dimension: the ability to theorize the training experience transmitted by way of the couch. In that sense there was no hierarchical distinction introduced between the ranks of AME and AE. An AME might be an excellent clinician without having delved into the experience of passage, and inversely, an ME might have no therapeutic experience and reveal himself capable, when tested, of theorizing the question of training: He would be an AE without being an AME. Absolutely any member of the École could thus submit himself to *la passe,* but not any member could be a *passeur,* since the designation of *passeurs* was a prerogative of the AEs. The jury's decision depended on two out of three of the AEs and the director; the *passeurs* had a merely advisory role. If a *passant* received the title of AE, his analyst, if an AME, was named an AE, and, if an AP or ME, he was named an AME.

Some time after delivering that address, Lacan wrote a second version of his proposal. On the whole, he maintained the contents of the original, but injected a measure of obscurity into his syntax, thus making somewhat difficult the comprehension of a text that was originally quite luminous. He added two elements. First, he recalled that psychoanalytic training was not in the order of any guaranteed certification, and uttered a sentence that would provoke much commentary: "The psychoanalyst derives his authorization solely from himself." [121] Then, he distinguished the notion of *gradus* from that of *hierarchy.* The first concerned the elucidation of the analyst's ego and being, whereas the second involved an institutional model or a profession. Here Lacan rediscovered what he had affirmed since his legislation of 1949: The psychoanalytic order ought to be distinct from the institutional order. But he went still further: He eliminated every hierarchical principle from the training analysis, and chose a name from the realm of education, passage. As for the formula: "The psychoanalyst derives his authorization solely from himself," it was the transcription of the abolition of preselection which had already been achieved in the founding act. It did not mean that anyone could authorize himself to be a psychoanalyst, but simply that, in order to authorize oneself as such, no selection by one's peers was necessary. The formula "derives his authorization from himself" was the logical consequence of the elimination of the hierarchy in favor of the gradus. It respected personal analyses even as it abolished the rule of prior authorization.

After having (in a first phase) removed the false cleavage between "therapeutic" or personal analysis and "didactic" or training analysis, Lacan effected, in a second phase, an orthodox recasting of the experience of the training psychoanalysis. He called it "pure psychoanalysis" and sanctioned it with the ordeal of *la passe.* There was thus a remarkable coherence between the two phases of his doctrine.

Around 1950, the baroque rearticulation went against the grain of neo-Freudian revisionism; seventeen years later, the introduction of the *passe* procedure restored in its splendor a didactic purpose that had been obliterated by administrative routine. But the revalorization of that "orthodoxy" was initially effected by way of the abolition of the artificial cleavage between "therapeutic" and "professional" analyses. The didactic or training analysis, as conceived by Lacan in this recasting, no longer had anything to do with what was formulated under that rubric in the societies of the IPA.

The October proposal undoubtedly constituted one of the most innovative acts, with regard to training, in the history of psychoanalysis. What was at stake was the uncoupling of the training analysis from the models of instruction which had obscured the process of passage specific to analytic therapy. Lacan thus wanted to reintroduce what was taught or transmitted by the couch as the *sole* principle of access to a function which until then tended no longer to have anything in common with the specificity of psychoanalysis. In that respect, the procedure allowed for the implementation of an *other site* for analysis, which was neither control nor couch. Although Lacan did not use the term, it was a matter, at bottom, of institutionalizing a "third site" for psychoanalysis, partaking neither of exams in the academic sense nor of any doctorate or diploma, but rather of a specifically Freudian politics of training. After the barricades, Lacan would say that he had achieved in his school a May '68 before the fact.[122]

In that respect, it is not out of the question that the procedure was partially inspired by an event foreign to the history of Freudianism—the Chinese cultural revolution. At the time Lacan was attempting to contribute a psychoanalytic response to the institutional crisis befalling his school, the effects of that revolution were in fact beginning to be felt on the Parisian intellectual scene and specifically in the ranks of the students of the ENS. Now those students played the role of a "symbolic referent" in that crisis: The psychoanalysts did not hesitate to accuse them of constituting a "network" around Lacan, a network "foreign" to the profession. And we have seen that the idea of introducing nonanalysts within the EFP had been if not refused, at least poorly received by a good number of therapists. Lacan, of course, was not Maoist, Marxist, Leninist, or libertarian, and no doubt he was not even thinking of China when he elaborated his proposal. But there was a certain analogy between the principles formulated by Mao Zedong and those Lacan was articulating. In both cases, it was a matter of triggering a revolution at the base, which would be organized at the summit, under the doctrinal aegis of a "great helmsman." The operation's aim was to shatter routines and force members of the elite to a self-criticism and a questioning of their function. In that sense, Lacan would be right to say that his procedure prefigured the barricades, on the condition that it be added that that procedure did not have any libertarian aspect. It was a matter of effecting a mass uprising of the base, but the operation in no way partook of any "spontaneism" (since it was orchestrated by the master himself). It may also be suggested that Lacan had drawn his conclusions from his experience with the Turquet commission. For it was indeed through the testimony it heard that that commission was able to observe, for the first time in history, a certain process of passage. Before the English observers, who functioned at once as *passeurs* and as jury, therapists in training were able to ponder far-reaching questions concerning the end of analysis and the transformation it worked in their therapies. And Lacan, in that affair, may have latched onto a starting point for a meditation on the experience of passage.

However strong it was, the proposal contained several incoherences. It is not clear, for example, why a candidate's acquisition of the rank of AE should automatically result in the promotion of his analyst to a superior rank. If the titles of AE and AME were heterogeneous, to the point of being able to be held simultaneously, there was no reason to mix them by appointing to the rank of AME an AP whose candidate-*passant* would become an AE. In addition, if any member was free to present his candidacy for *la passe,* it was incoherent to insist that *passeurs* necessarily be appointed by AEs. It would have been preferable for the status of the *passeurs* to be assimilated to that of the *passants* and that they too be free to offer to fulfill their function, whatever the rank of their analyst. Finally there was a residual ambiguity in Lacan's text concerning the concept of *la passe.* If the *passage* or *moment of "la passe"* existed in every analysis, to the extent that the question of becoming an analyst was posed, how ought one to proceed so as to prevent the procedure dealing with that passage from concealing it, in a kind of specious duplication? *La passe* was one thing, which was part of therapy, but the *procedure of la passe* was something else—the institutionalized translation of a concrete experience, and to that extent, something that might very well obliterate it. Whence the idea formulated by some of not awarding any title to the accepted *passant,* in order to keep the procedure in ever closer proximity to the original *passe.* Jacques-Alain Miller would be first, in an article of 1977, to observe the existence of that problematic, which Lacan had not analyzed. Without challenging the principle of awarding a title, he would call the totality constituted by the passage, on the one hand, and the procedure, on the other, *double passe.*[123]

As soon as it was announced, the proposal had the effect of an explosive. Since Lacan was fearful of the opposition of the members of his first directorate, and since he wanted to test the opinion of the leading figures of the École, he asked each to give his views. Then he proceeded to a poll restricted to AEs and AMEs. He retained three possible options: *placet, non placet,* and *placet juxta modum.* The last case was to allow for indication of what modifications should be envisaged in light of the reservations expressed. The balloting resulted in a comfortable majority in favor of the proposal: Out of 66 votes cast, 41 were favorable without further discussion, 5 abstained, 14 invoked *juxta modum,* and 5 were radically hostile. The opposition was represented by François Perrier, Nathalie Zaltzman-Perrier, Piera Aulagnier, Guy Rosolato, and Jean-Paul Valabrega. As for *juxta modum,* it was opted for by Louis Beirnaert, Jean Clavreul, Luce Irigaray, Lucien Israël, Andrée Lehmann, Moustapha Safouan, Bernard This, and a few others.[124] Despite that majority, and although he knew the plenary session would be favorable to him, Lacan decided to put off a formal vote on his project. He was intent on retaining in his school those opponents (as well as the undecided) who were, along with a few newcomers, his former colleagues at the SFP.

Soon feelings began to be vented in written form. The day after the meeting, François Perrier sent an open letter to Lacan to protest the fragmentary character of the EFP statutes. He denounced the absence of a training apparatus and called for the drawing up of new statutes.[125] The letter, addressed to "Mon cher maître," was not what the situation demanded. Perrier did not discuss the October proposal and came up with no positive solution to the École's crisis. Jean-Paul Valabrega, on the contrary, wrote a long manifesto in which he opposed the procedure while criticizing the autocratic structure of the EFP and the dictatorial power of its president. He called the "directorate" a fiction, and rejected Lacan's argument point by point. In his opinion, *la passe* ran the risk of introducing nonanalysts into the very heart of clinical practice and the direction of the École. As for the formula "derives his authorization from himself," it would lead, he claimed, to absolutely anyone being authorized to become an analyst. Valabrega rejected, additionally, the principle of random selection, which he called a "fallacious egalitarianism," and contested the idea of a direct passage to the status of AE, emphasizing that the control was the only context for speaking of one's analysis: "It is impossible to speak of one's analysis to someone who is designated for that function. That's why study commissions have always—and of necessity—failed in that task, which has become a pure fiction or (in another idiom) a joke. The only way to speak of one's analysis is concerning a third object. And the situation readymade for understanding something of all that exists: the control." Valabrega also accused Lacan of maintaining a "network" with the rue d'Ulm whose activity had shown itself to be dangerous for the École. Finally, he proposed as a solution to the crisis a democratization of the EFP, with the creation of a college of AEs: "I thus believe that any project concerning training should be supported if not unanimously, which is an impossibility, at least by a large majority (to be defined) and exempt from any major objection." [126]

Guy Rosolato, for his part, did not voice an opinion and resigned from the EFP in November 1967 without having participated in any discussion on the nature of *la passe*. He limited himself to criticizing, through his action, the "dictatorial" character of Lacan's decisions.[127] In January 1968, he joined the ranks of the APF, where he was accepted as a titular member. His hope had been to provoke a collective resignation through his departure. But he had confused splits and epochs: He would be followed by no one.

As for Piera Aulagnier, she produced no critical text, but resigned from the directorate on December 4 as a sign of her opposition to the procedure.[128] She was immediately replaced by Irène Roublef and Charles Melman. Thereafter the second directorate would actually become a fiction: It was composed exclusively of members of Lacan's personal guard. Although favorable to *la passe*, Leclaire himself was not long in resigning from that colorless body. The last representative of the third generation, Jean Clavreul, continued to stay on. As opposed to Perrier, Valabrega, and Aulagnier, he supported the project after having voted *placet juxta modum*. In order to present his position, he sent a lengthy report to the members of the EFP, where he offered an exhaustive chronicle of the crisis, thus furnishing the future historian a fascinating document on the events of that period. Clavreul found the October project to be inapplicable and proposed, without delay, to prolong the term of members of the *jury d'agrément*. In addition, he criticized the notion of *passeur*, but without advancing any remedy for the ill he was denouncing.[129]

In the face of the disgruntled and the hesitant, Lacan still did not want to face a plebiscite at the plenary session. He would exploit the events of May to mobilize the base, but at the time, he answered protesters in an address delivered December 6, 1967. Plainly, he was troubled, and his lecture, which would be transcribed by Solange Faladé, then rewritten by him, revealed both his disappointment and his annoyance. The address was rambling and needlessly aggressive. Responding to Valabrega, Lacan, punning on "rue d'Ulm," called his "network" a "bout d'oulm," and announced that none of its members was on his couch. Then, he evoked the past in an insulting tone, calling Pierre Turquet a "porc" [pig] and shortly thereafter a "dindon." In the written version, he would retain that second epithet: *Dindon* in English is *turkey*. With that his epigones would forget the Anjou roots of the former major whom Lacan called "my friend" and would believe unshakably that the man had never been the defender of the French policy on the committee. This was one more way the master had of spreading doubt about his participation in Leclaire's negotiation. Nevertheless, he announced two items: the publication by Éditions du Seuil of a journal internal to the École and his decision not to impose the procedure of *la passe* so that debate might continue.[130]

In February 1968, institutions were put in place according to the old regulations. The new *jury d'agrément* was chosen at random and Lacan was to maintain a preponderant voice in its deliberations. Four members were designated: Clavreul, Hesnard, Aubry, and Rosolato. Since the last named had resigned two months earlier, he was immediately replaced by Octave Mannoni. The directorate, moreover, had been modified by Leclaire's resignation. Clavreul announced his intention to leave lest he find himself in the position of performing three functions, but at Lacan's request, he remained with positions on the *jury d'agrément* [approval committee], the *jury d'accueil* [reception committee], and the directorate. Thereafter, this third directorate of the EFP was to pass into Lacan's absolute control. He was able to govern through his guard: Clavreul, Simatos, Roublef, Faladé, Melman, and Conté. Only Solange Faladé dared criticize the master in private. This was frequently the case for the women of the École. Melman's thorny character, his intolerance of others, and his style made the conduct of the directorate's business still more complicated. Lacan valued him, however, and rose to his defense when his colleagues complained about him. The composition of the *jury d'accueil* was considerably more varied. Besides Clavreul, there were Dolto and representatives of the third generation: Beirnaert and Safouan.[131]

Lacan at this point asked each member to state his opinion, and the crisis returned. "If the *jury d'agrément*," Piera Aulagnier wrote, "is to consist purely and simply in stating a yes or a no, I confess that I cannot but refuse to be part of it. For indeed, of five names chosen at random, and unless the last one decides to play one of those eminently possible but extremely rare tricks, what is sure is that there will be at least two colleagues for whom your opinion will be the sole (and exhaustive) point of reference. In that case, the jury's role becomes a formality, and I don't see what use it can have."[132] In order to remedy that situation, Aulagnier proposed three solutions: First, the candidate for the rank of AE should already be an AME; then, he would have to furnish the jury with published or unpublished texts he had authored; finally, he would accept a personal interview with a member of the jury. She added that those clauses should be submitted to a vote of the AEs.

The solutions recommended in her letter went in the same direction as those of Valabrega and Perrier: a criticism of personal power, a revalorization of the hierarchy against the gradus, control of the EFP by "titular" AEs, and above all, opposition to a "base" felt to be dangerous for the future insofar as it might have access to a supreme title. Aulagnier was not alone in her distrust, since Clavreul had also proposed that candidates for *la passe* already be AMEs. In addition, he wanted the last appointed AE automatically to become a member of the *jury d'agrément*.[133] Moustapha Safouan, for his part, attempted to define the status of the AME, which was transformed as a result of the introduction of *la passe*. He emphasized quite properly that access to the title of AME did not depend on the passage, but immediately added that it should be reserved for those who had completed their training with an AE or an AME. That clause did not figure in the old regulations, which, it may be recalled, allowed any member, from whatever couch, to receive the title of AME. As far as the rest was concerned, Safouan did not call for any notable change. Should the procedure of *la passe* not be adopted, he proposed a reinstatement of the training methods in force in the IPA before the war. "As a result," he said, "every AME who will have trained another AME becomes an AE as a consequence."[134]

Despite the divergent positions taken vis-à-vis *la passe,* the criticisms all tended in the same direction. Not only were they regressive in relation to the principles of 1964, but they bore witness to the will of the "seniors" to take back the power Lacan had stripped them of. The monarch had put in place a psychoanalytic insurrection, and his princes pitted against it a reform which would make them the genuine leaders of the École. If *la passe* was a project of genius, as far as training was concerned, the conditions prevailing at the time of its enactment did not allow it to function with due calm. Piera Aulagnier was right to emphasize that despite the random selection, the majority of members on the *jury d'agrément* would always be favorable to Lacan's views, if only because the advent of the fourth generation had totally transformed the situation of the École.

Lacan was so well aware of this that he proposed that he have only an advisory role in deliberations. But since he had contrived to fuse his role as intellectual master with his position as director of the school, he could not prevent his presence on the jury from impeding its normal functioning. In order for the *jury d'agrément* to truly hear testimony on *la passe* in the event the procedure were adopted, the least that would be needed would be for Lacan not to be necessarily part of it. And this was all the more the case in that the majority of those enlisting for the ordeal would be his analysands. Caught up in the coils of his own legislation, however, Lacan's behavior in this matter was inspired by the multidimensional position he had accorded himself. Although he was monarch, psychoanalyst, lawgiver, and training analyst, he also arrogated the right to share the fate of his notables and to be an AE "like everybody else," with the privilege of forgoing random selection. That attitude was contrary to the celebrated direct monarchy governing the school and allowing the sovereign to enjoy a privileged relation with each subject. The contradiction could be posited as follows: Either Lacan was a monarch, an innovator, a psychoanalyst and a trainer of psychoanalysts, and he had to forgo sitting on the jury in order to retain his position as a master, or he was simply an AE and should have been selected randomly, despite his position as director. He chose, however, a strange median path which allowed him to escape the position of ordinary AE, but not to have a preponderant voice. In brief, he condemned himself to pretending not to decide anything even as he maintained without limit the permanence of a purview that was decisive. With such a situation, *la passe* could not function as a psychoanalytic process.

Given that state of affairs, the adversaries of *la passe* never managed to implement a constructive project. From their point of view, the first thing needed in order to extricate themselves from the crisis was to effect a democratic transformation of the EFP, which would then allow for an examination of the new modalities of house regulations. In the winter of 1968, the situation was thus stymied on every side: Lacan loved those who resisted him without being able to tolerate their criticisms, and those who criticized him were in no position to do so in a positive manner. The barricades would bring their own solution. . . .

The discussions took a new turn with the "events" of May. Until that time, hostility to *la passe* emanated largely from the dignitaries of the EFP, who were opposed to an initiative that might lead to the loss of their privileges. The majority of simple members (MEs and APs)—that is, the youngest members of the fourth generation—had not yet had a chance to speak. Now for those members, Lacan's proposal was not unrelated to the protests that were laying low the university. The procedure of *la passe* brought with it a radical critique of the relations between teachers and students in traditional analytic training procedures. That was why, starting in April 1968, the EFP's base began to stir and to reflect on the student movement and the "October Revolution." The École's notables, for their part, were challenged by the students in the course of a number of debates. A rather stormy discussion took place at the Faculté de Médecine before a large audience, and another was organized for members of the EFP at the Magnan Amphitheater: That evening, the psychoanalysts met Daniel Cohn-Bendit and some of his friends from the Mouvement du 22 Mars.

The initiative came from Anne-Lise Stern, who had the idea of suggesting the meeting to Michèle Bargues. The latter had been part of the movement since its creation at Nanterre. Her father, René Bargues, a brilliant student of Lacan's, had been named an AE before his death, at the time of the École's founding, and her mother, Raymonde, had been working at the Hôpital des Enfants-Malades, in the pediatrics division directed by Jenny Aubry since January 1963, after the experiment of the nursery schools at the Polyclinic on Boulevard Ney. There Aubry had created a psychoanalytic consultation service, the first in France to be so called, which was frequented, for the most part, by young Lacanian analysts. Michèle Bargues paid a visit to Lacan, who was enthusiastic about the encounter. It took place the day after the great "unity" demonstration of May 13.

Daniel Cohn-Bendit and his friends were interested in getting their politics and their objectives known, while the psychoanalysts were interested in hearing protesters. In point of fact, the two groups had nothing to say to each other, and Serge Leclaire was alone in asking a remarkable question, which would not be understood by his interlocutors at the time. "What will you do," he asked, "with your former combatants?" A bit surprised, Dany was quick to explain that all soldiers were not the same, that it depended on the war they were fighting, that the Spanish Republicans could not be compared with the *poilus* of Verdun. After an exchange of views on the policies of the Communist Party, the psychoanalysts offered the militants their assistance. The latter took up a collection, then went off to dine at *La Coupole* where, by chance, they happened to run into several of their benefactors, who were distressed to see that their hard-earned income from the couch was going to fill the bellies of the jolly leaders of the student commune.[135]

Lacan had been silent that evening, but the next day he interrupted his seminar on "the psychoanalytic deed" to follow the strike order issued by the Syndicat National de l'enseignement supérieur, and commented, in his manner, on the previous day's meeting. Paying homage to Cohn-Bendit, he lashed out at his own disciples: "I am in the process of killing myself telling you that psychoanalysts should expect something of the insurrection. There are some who reply, What should the insurrection expect of us? The insurrection answers them, What we expect from you is occasionally to give us a hand throwing a few paving stones." [136] Then Lacan announced that paving stones and tear gas were fulfilling the role of *objet 'a.'* Finally, he situated matters on a theoretical level and criticized the ideas of Wilhelm Reich.

If the dignitaries of the EFP did not know what to do with the insurrection intersecting the history of psychoanalysis, the expanding mass of members did not wait for October to express their views. Very early on, simple members began speaking up. They represented some hundred individuals most of whom had joined the EFP between 1966 and 1968. Groups were formed, in which seniors and juniors met. The most active core was constituted by the friends of Pierre Fiszlewicz and Robert Lander. The two were Jewish, psychiatrists, and remarkable clinicians. Both would die prematurely, stricken by illness, after having given the best of themselves to the Lacanian movement.

An analysand of Solange Faladé, Fiszlewicz was the senior member of the band. By age he belonged to the third generation, but his training linked him to the fourth. Having lost the use of his legs to polio, he moved about in a wheel-chair. Since joining the EFP, he gathered young therapists for uninhibited discussions of child analysis, epilepsy, and psychosis. He knew how to listen, to advise, and to show himself to be rigorously tolerant of others' opinions. As for Robert Lander, he was the son of a famous journalist whose name he did not share, and was trained quite young on Leclaire's couch. An aesthete, an afficionado of Proust, and a homosexual, he lived in a superb apartment on Boulevard Malesherbes decorated by his brother, an antique-dealer, where he received his friends each week.

At the beginning, the group had been constituted to give currency to a conception of madness capable of resisting the dominant psychiatric one, and specifically that prevailing in institutional psychotherapy, which was represented in the

EFP by Jean Oury. For these Lacanian *enfants terribles,* who seemed to step out of a Queneau novel or a Godard film, the principal objective was to bring the heady air of Freudian adventure into "ordinary" institutions. Most of them were in analysis with Lacan or Leclaire and were part of the hospital team of Jenny Aubry (whom they called "la Mère Aube.") They were Jewish and atheists, occasionally stateless, invariably bearing the marks of a past of deviance, foreignness, or suffering: concentration camps, marginality, exile, segregation, travel. Their names were Lucien Mélèse, Radmila Zygouris, Francis Hofstein, Huguette Friedman-Lawrence, Pierre Alien, Renaude Gosset. . . . Anne-Lise Stern was part of the group. Along with two others, she would found, in 1969, a Laboratory of Psychoanalysis, intended for low-income patients and financed through the reparations payments her mother received from Germany as the widow of a Jewish physician wronged by the Nazis.

Thanks to the barricades, Robert Lander's living room was soon open to all voices of opinion. While continuing to talk about psychosis and child analysis, the friends in the group discussed both street politics and the intricacies of *la passe.* For them, Lacan's project was relaunching once again the psychoanalytic adventure to which they were so attached. He broke with the traditions of the other societies and represented the Freudianism of modern times. In Lander's apartment, amid precious trinkets, nameless individuals from the École and elsewhere would circulate. The atmosphere was warm and febrile. Without the slightest censorship, the structures of the EFP were called into question, and the school's notables paraded through one by one in an effort to take the temperature of this "base" erupting into the history of Lacanianism.

Lacan was quick to realize that the future of his proposal and his teaching were henceforth in the hands of a new generation: the entirety of the fourth and the fifth as yet to come. With Charles Melman, he called a meeting in the home of Paul and Gennie Lemoine, a couple devoted to him, in which nothing happened. Then, at the beginning of the new session, he urged the Lander group to formulate a counterproposal whose effect would be to allow his own to pass. He had decided to let go of the dissidents and to seek support among the turbulent young in order to implement, at whatever price, his institutional reform. Already then, he foresaw, before anyone else, the retroactive effects of May on the psychoanalytic movement: the return of the ideals of heredity, the rise of racism, the appeal to segregation, and the restoration, through pharmacological therapy, of all the old conservatisms. He thus played the card of a "revolution in order." In the face of a libertarian spirit that risked dragging the psychoanalytic community to ruin and against the archaisms which had resulted in its denaturing, he was intent on imposing a training structure capable, during the decade to follow, of preserving the essence of Freud's message.

In the fall of 1968, the debate over *la passe* was thus reactivated from on high through an appeal to the base. Meeting on December 19 with the directorate and the *jury d'accueil,* Lacan polished the text of the new internal regulations he would submit to the plenary session of the EFP at its meetings of January 11, 12, 25, and 26, 1969. He included several important modifications of his original project. It was clear that he had taken into account Piera Aulagnier's objections about random selection, but not those of Safouan and Clavreul. The former wanted the title of AME to be reserved for candidates trained by an AE or an AME, and the latter that candidate-*passants* already be AMEs. In order not to democratize the procedure unduly and to satisfy both the barons and the base, Lacan removed the *passeurs* from the *jury d'agrément,* while allowing its members to present their candidacy freely for election at plenary sessions. Those members would henceforth be six in number with the director being a seventh. The absurd clause allowing the analyst of a successful *passant* to obtain the rank of AE was eliminated, but it was replaced by one that was equally absurd—AMEs elected to the *jury d'agrément* automatically were to become AEs. That clause contradicted the very principle of the procedure, since the objective of *la passe* was not to allow an individual to rise in the hierarchy, but to bear witness to that specific act of passage whereby one became an analyst. Under those conditions, one was hard put to see why an AME should "pass" to the rank of AE simply because he had been elected to the *jury d'agrément*. Either *la passe* was a genuine training experience or it was not. Since it turned out that those elected to the jury would always be AEs, that ridiculous clause would never be applied.

In the new rules, the jury was to be elected at a plenary session for a term of three years, and to be renewed in thirds, which would allow successful candidate-*passants* to sit on it and to replace old members who had never undertaken *la passe*. As for the rest, Lacan maintained the naming of *passeurs* by AEs and distinguished radically the rank of AME from that of AE. The awarding of the first was to take place without the candidate's intervention, on the advice of his controllers and his analyst, whatever their rank. The status of the AME was social in nature: It indicated professional recognition of clinical competence to be exercised outside the École. That of the AE, however, was specifically internal to the community and didactic in nature. The separation of the two titles allowed them to be held simultaneously—or not. A member could, if successful in *la passe*, be an AE without ever having been an AME, and inversely, a member might hold both titles. On that score, the new regulations were perfectly coherent with the logic of psychoanalysis in extension and in intention: There were "edges" and borders, but also a "Moebius strip" with an outside continuous with its own interior.[137] Lacan retained his presence in all the governing bodies of the EFP: He was president of the administrative board and the directorate and sat on both the *jury d'accueil* and the *jury d'agrément*. If the status of the *passant* was made perfectly clear and the manner of electing the *jury d'agrément* satisfactory, the status of *passeurs* was poorly defined. In the long run, they might end up constituting a caste run by an authentic college of AEs.

The members of the École had been informed that they were to vote at the beginning of the year, but they did not yet know on what. Firm in his decision to let the recalcitrant barons go, Lacan urged the base to discuss his project. He received letters from every quarter, along with requested changes. One of the first came from a third generation AE, Maud Mannoni. She was at the time preparing to create the École expérimentale de Bonneuil, drawing on certain theses of the antipsychiatry movement. An ardent *gauchiste,* she limited herself to denouncing the procedure's "reactionary character." But in order to prove her loyalty to a master whose proposal she rejected, she sent in advance a vote favorable to the project she had just refused.[138] Generally speaking, these new requests for modifications were far more interesting than the preceding set. Their contents revealed that the notion of *la passe* was beginning to be understood by the group and that the spring insurrection had borne fruit. Jean Oury sent a message having nothing to do with *la passe,* in which he acknowledged the good deeds of institutional psychotherapy. Like Maud Mannoni, he was preaching on behalf of his own church, but he did raise a fundamental problem, which had not yet surfaced in this form, although it was at the heart of the procedure endorsed by Lacan: "Can a madman be a psychoanalyst?" he asked. "At present there is nothing to prevent it from happening. And I don't think that a few democratic measures will shield us from such a danger." [139]

All the other proposals more or less requested the creation of specialized commissions in order to test, over a span of four years, the doctrine of *la passe.* Thémouraz Abdoucheli, an AME trained by Lacan, sent the directorate a project to that effect. But he was careful to append a letter in the same envelope specifying that his proposal was not to compete with Lacan's. It was, in his perspective, to serve as an instrument of negotiation if the December 19 project should be refused by the plenary session. Abdoucheli, that is, like a majority of those who intervened, supported the *passe* experiment and merely requested a few modifications. The AP Pierre Benoit, for his part, observed that the contradictions weighing on the École stemmed from the joint position occupied by Lacan; he was alone in saying out loud what all were thinking to themselves.[140]

The most interesting modifications were proposed by the friends of Robert Lander. Having meditated on the subject for several months, they understood that *la passe* was the only procedure capable of extricating the École from its institutional crisis. But they also noticed the inconsistencies in the project and their critique dealt essentially with the status of the *passeurs.* They proposed two modifications: *Passeurs* ought to have a position equivalent to that of *passants* and be able to designate themselves on their own, a circumstance that would reduce the power of AEs and would allow *all members* of the EFP to hear testimony of passage. The Lander group also asked that the *jury d'agrément* be constituted, on the occasion of each *passe,* by the *passeurs* themselves. The procedure would thus be consistent with the phrase, "derives his authorization from himself," even as it agreed with the antibureaucratic spirit desired by Lacan. The text of that modification was written by Pierre Alien, an analysand of Lacan's and a nonmember of the EFP, and signed by Francis Hofstein, Radmila Zygouris, Lucien Mélèse, Robert Lander, Renaude Gosset, Anne-Lise Stern, Huguette Friedman-Lawrence as well as Joseph Attié, Claude This, Jeanine Mouchonnat, Claude Jeangirard, and Pierre Benoit. It represented something of an "ultra-Lacanian" radicalization of the original project to the extent that it sought to make it both more revolutionary and more democratic. Like Abdoucheli's, the Alien-Lander project was not intended by its signatories to enter into competition with the December 19 text.[141]

The discussions lasted about three weeks and allowed Lacan to ascertain that his proposal was massively accepted. Too rushed to test an experiment whose fruits he was intent on culling rather rapidly and too concerned with the unity of his school to yield to an ultra-Lacanianism that would reduce the power of the notables to naught, he resorted to a shrewd institutional maneuver. At the plenary sessions of January 25 and 26, he decided to have the meeting vote on three proposals: his own, unmodified (Project A), and two others, the Lander group's (Project B) and Abdoucheli's (Project C). He thus created a competition, against the advice of the interested parties, between texts that were not designed in opposition to his own, but as a means of modifying it or serving as a negotiating medium in the case negotiations were in fact needed with the true adversaries of *la passe*.

The vote took place at an uneasy meeting in a room at the Hotel Lutétia. While the opposition (Aulagnier, Valabrega, and Perrier) had already tendered its letter of resignation, the signatories of Projects B and C were furious at the maneuver to which they had been subjected. In a rush to bring matters to a conclusion, Lacan threatened Alien, saying to him, "Choose, it's either you or me." [142] There was no response; the master had won. In its address, the *jury d'accueil* adopted a more unaccommodating tone, referring to the version of *la passe* presented in the initial debates as "false" and "fallacious." Then Clavreul read a text by Lacan in which the latter referred to the positions of the protesters as "valabregags." [143] Finally, the adoption of a "preferential" mode of balloting proved a further source of disquiet: "At the suggestion of the director, the meeting will vote by casting a ballot in which from left to right, in order of increasing assent, each of the three projects proposed is to be listed: either A (proposed by the *jury d'accueil*) or B (proposed by the list beginning alphabetically with the name of Alien) or C (proposed by Abdoucheli). This mode of 'preferential' balloting is a test to the extent that it is apt to lead (in 9 percent of cases for a group as large as our own) to the Condorcet effect. As is known, that effect designates the inconsistent result in which, while one choice dominates a second, and that second a third, it nonetheless happens that the third dominates the first, a circumstance that excludes any possibility of concluding. In this case, it would be regrettably indicative of a lack of what we have called the spirit of psychoanalysis. K. J. Arrow, to refer to a different order, namely that of the logical determination of the general interest, has demonstrated that outside of unanimity, such can be determined only through the opinion of a single individual." [144]

Before the ballots were even counted, Perrier, Valabrega, and Aulagnier sent Lacan their letter of resignation from the EFP, thus provoking the third split in the history of the French psychoanalytic movement—a *reverse split*. For the first time, Lacan was not banished from a kingdom, but *left* for having built a kingdom. And for the first time as well, he was abandoned, without any attempt at bargaining, by the very individuals who had refused to yield to the decrees of an empire. In the eyes of the fourth and fifth psychoanalytic generations of the EFP, Perrier's departure took on the appearance of a disaster. It announced the twilight of a particular idea of Lacanianism. With the resignation of that overgrown and turbulent child, there disappeared from the movement a romanticism of origins that would forever after be covered over by an advancing dogmatism. "The turn taken by the meetings of the École and the organization that has resulted," in the words of those who resigned, "have had the consequence of setting up procedures and apparatuses for analytic appointments and promotions that we regard as incompatible with the necessary requirements for the rigorous practice of psychoanalysis. . . . There is no need for long sentences to convey the sadness we feel in making such a decision." [145]

From Lacan's point of view, the choice of a preferential system of balloting had the aim of revealing a coherence of individual preferences not reducible to a collective coherence as implied by a majority vote. In other words, if Project A had been voted on in "classical" terms (for/against/abstention), it would have been adopted by an overwhelming majority and with no other opposition than that of the few who had resigned. It will thus be seen that Lacan wanted to give voice to minority opinions, whence the idea of preferential balloting and the transformation of "criticisms" into proposals. But in resorting to such means, he was favoring a breakup of the École and anticipating a certain indecision: *la passe* might be a failure, a success, or both a once. As for the opposition, it was provoked by the vote and expressed in abstentions which were not counted.

At the meeting in the Hotel Lutétia, approximately two hundred members were present out of a total of about 230. But of those two hundred members, only 117 voted: The dissatisfied of every stripe opted to abstain. With 117 votes cast, Project A was preferred 198 times; Project B, 107 times; and Project C, 46 times. If those figures are converted in terms of a majority vote, the text of December 19 turns out to have been adopted by a majority of 93 votes out of 117, with about 80 abstentions, which means that the opponents and abstainers were about as numerous as the members of the majority. [146] At the time Project A was adopted, half the members of the EFP were, if not hostile, at least reticent, and the other half were not sure whether they had been voting for Lacan or *la passe*. Lacan imposed his procedure through a curiously arbitrary decision, which saved the École from slow death, even as it favored its breakup. Without that winter shootout, the EFP would have lapsed into institutional conflicts similar to those of the IPA societies. It would have pretended to exist, would probably never have been dissolved, and would not have made any innovations in analytic training. But the conditions in which the *passe* was implemented bore witness to the risk of its possible failure. What remained to be determined was whether the game was worth the candle.

On February 9, a circular was distributed by the *jury d'agrément* to the members of the École with the approval of the directorate. [147] It pointed out the utter vagueness with which the procedure had been adopted. Three clauses were added, which it would have been difficult to append to the statutes since they had not been voted on at a plenary session. First, an AE might fail to inform a *passeur* of his appointment, and the *passeur* could decline the offer extended him. Then, the *passant*-candidate was to have the authorization of his analyst. Finally, the idea was again retained that an analyst whose *passant* was appointed automatically became an AE. That absurd proposal had been struck from the December 1969 text. The clauses were not part of the regulations, but since no member of the École, including those of the *jury d'agrément,* knew the exact content of the legal texts, over a period of ten years, no one would know exactly how *la passe* functioned. The jury would thus perpetually hesitate in determining whether an approved *passant* was to become an AE. Similarly, it would never be entirely sure whether or not *la passe* was restricted to members of the École and would not rule on the issue of selecting candidates for the ordeal. Nor would it say whether *passants* had to be in *la passe* at the time of candidacy or if they might present themselves after the fact. No one would be able to delineate with any precision the role of second periods of analysis in the process of *la passe*. As a result, the jury would accept virtually all candidacies, from the most farfetched to the most serious. It will thus be understood why so few were actually appointed.

Let me take a single example from tens of similarly incoherent cases I have encountered. One day in 1971, Laurence Bataille[148] was debating theory with Jacques Lacan. He advised her to undergo *la passe*. Quite surprised, she replied that she had no idea of how to go about it. Nonetheless, following Lacan's counsel, she made an appointment with Jean Clavreul to officialize her candidacy. At the time, she was not yet a member of the École. Somewhat peeved, Clavreul insisted on knowing the rank of the candidate's analyst should she be successful. Might Conrad Stein become an AE even though he was a titular member of the SPP? The official texts were quite clear on this question, but the vagueness introduced by the February circular was such that even a member of the jury was no longer sure of his bearings. At that point Clavreul proposed that Laurence become a member of the EFP without clearly specifying whether or not someone from outside the École could engage in *la passe*. He did not know that she was Lacan's step-daughter and told her that he would consult with the jury, of which he himself was a member, to find out whether or not her candidacy was acceptable. Laurence herself did not feel up to joining the École. But the secretariat sent her her membership. She refused it and informed Simatos that she preferred to think things over for a while. While taking his leave, he advised her to hurry since the École's forthcoming roster was about to be published. Finally, Laurence went through *la passe* without having decided. She was rejected. Shortly thereafter, she felt prepared to join the École, but was then informed that she had waited too long. Eventually she became a member. Long afterwards, in the course of a second period of analysis with a jury member, she was named a *passeuse* and found herself facing a candidate who was not a member of the École but who simply wanted to join the community of AEs. Shocked, Laurence nonetheless heard her testimony and transmitted it. The jury rejected the *passante* without asking whether there should have been an admissions procedure to prevent the kind of candidacy that was turning the entire process into a mockery. It was not at all clear, moreover, how such a procedure might function, given the fact that the jury was dependent on Lacan's decisions and incapable of effectively invoking its own regulations.

VII. Anonymity and the Fourth Group

During the month of March 1969, the EFP changed its statutes and became a more modern, more anonymous, more divided, and more specifically psychoanalytic society. The new rules endorsed the *passe* procedure as a means of gaining access to the rank of AE, even as they validated more classical means for obtaining that of AME. The École still retained a single category of member and four separate ranks: MEs (who were non-analysts or unanalyzed), APs, AMEs, and AEs. As the École increased in size, there tended to be fewer AEs while the ranks of APs swelled visibly. The EFP applied for recognition as being of public utility, a status craved by Lacan which entailed the risk of subjection to governmental authority, but also allowed it to receive inheritances and gifts. The administrative board was expanded and two years after the crisis of *la passe,* the EFP was able not only to compete with the SPP but to become the starting point for a new international organization. Small groups of Lacanians would soon be forming in countries of Latin culture—Italy, Spain, and Argentina. Lacan had won his battle in France. Nevertheless, there remained for him one area in which to exact revenge: the Anglo-American world. He was, however, seventy years old, and the task was too much for him; a second crossing of the Atlantic in 1975 brought few results.

In July 1971, the EFP moved to premises entirely its own; they were small but pleasant, located on the ground floor of a luxury apartment house on the rue Claude-Bernard. The new quarters had been purchased with funds from the wealthier members of the École, with significant contributions from Melman, Lacan, and Dolto. With double its former membership (up to 276), the École radiated its splendor throughout the Parisian intellectual scene as well as in the provinces, where it held its congresses. After five years at the Hôpital des Enfants-Malades, Jenny Aubry moved to Aix-en-Provence, training a number of Lacanian therapists throughout the region. In Strasbourg, Lucien Israël and Moustapha Safouan continued to ensure a Lacanian presence on the German border, while in Montpellier, Jean Faure and Pierre Martin performed similarly.

Despite its remarkable implantation and despite its facade of unity, the EFP had become an internally split institution as a result of its expansion, of the aftereffects of May 1968, and of the ways in which *la passe* had been incorporated. Over the years, the *passeurs,* who were still designated by AEs, came to feel an unabating uneasiness in relation to the *jury d'agrément,* which passed judgment on increasingly significant candidacies by way of the testimony of those it had designated and who frequently became *passants* themselves. Most of the successful *passants* came from Lacan's couch; moreover, he accepted more and more members of his school in analysis. Of the five first candidates to be accepted, three were analyzed by the master and the other two were in control with him. As the anonymous *passes* began to expand, appointments, in the course of time, followed an identical model: a virtually silent jury waiting beneath Lacan's omnipresent gaze; he then giving a nod or an interpretation allowing the others to reach an opinion. A large majority of those accepted came from the rue de Lille, which did not mean that all Lacan's analysands received the imprimatur. Quite to the contrary, they were massively rejected. At the end of eight years of continuous functioning, there would be more than one hundred *passes* and more than two hundred active *passeurs* in the École for only nine appointments. After 1977 and a serious crisis, including the suicide of one *passant,* there would be eight more appointments, before the École was dissolved in 1980, out of a total of almost two hundred *passes* in thirteen years. With those figures, the

EFP would remain the most selective association in France insofar as obtaining the rank of training analyst was concerned, as well as the most democratic insofar as voting rights were granted to mere members. In the other societies, the latter were in fact regarded as students and had no power over the conduct of the institution's affairs.[149] Democratic, selective, internally divided, monarchical, anonymous, and libertarian, such was the contradictory aspect of the extraordinary school at its zenith.

These figures and the functioning of *la passe* show that what was at stake in the latter procedure, over the course of time and without the knowledge of its protagonists, was a putting to the test of Lacan's notorious training practices, which had been at the core of all the conflicts in the history of psychoanalysis in France. It may, moreover, be wondered whether Lacan had not invented the procedure in order to treat himself to the spectacle of the limits of his own training capacities. If such were the case, he would at least have had the courage of pondering—better than all the commissions—the authenticity of his being an analyst, and thereby attempting to elucidate the great enigmas of transmission and passage. But it is too early to determine as much—the archives of *la passe* remain sealed, and the question remains open. However, should that hypothesis one day turn out to be right, it will be easier to understand why in thirteen years of functioning, the *jury d'agrément* approved so few candidates and showed itself to be so incapable of giving an account to the École of the specifically psychoanalytic criteria at play in the rejection or acceptance of candidates.[150]

In 1970, the first report of a *jury d'agrément*—presented by René Tostain to the Paris Congress—bore witness to the malaise created by the implementation of the procedure. The author began by announcing that the jury "was not a high court withdrawn behind the incommunicability of its experience" only to observe subsequently that a true analyst, according to *la passe,* is a subject who can bear being "nobody, absolutely anybody, or even a mask or a personal pronoun."[151] It was a formidable act of denial for a disastrous tally sheet of provisional results. In that perspective, *la passe* was nothing other, in the jury's eyes, than the acceptance by each candidate of his fall into anonymity, which had nothing to do with the destitution of the subject, the reduction of the ego, or the calling into question of the subject-alleged-to-know. But if the jury conceived of *la passe* in such terms, it meant that it itself was functioning in a regime of anonymity from which only Lacan emerged with the right to have a name. Working under the multidimensional gaze of a master who in fact continued to be the analyst of one and all, the members of the jury could neither hear from candidates a "passage" which their function prevented them from elucidating nor refuse to hear the same passage, which was offered to them and referred them to their situation as "nonidentified subjects." Under such conditions, it was impossible to grasp the meaning of the end of an analysis or to pass judgment on what Lacan called *désêtre.* The functioning of *la passe* in the EFP had the effect of reducing the protagonists of the great Lacanian drama to the imaginary relation each entertained with a founding father. As a result, appointments were not based on any of the criteria defined by the procedure, which was not even properly applied by those charged with so doing and who functioned as so many sorcerer's apprentices. But over time, they were exemplary in their constancy, as though the jury felt the need, as years passed, to renew the number of AEs in accordance with a minimal quota: four appointments for each edition of the roster, seventeen in the course of thirteen years for a total membership that would reach 609 members in 1980, of which 38 were AEs and 137 AMEs but not AEs. In all, 175 "certified" analysts. With those figures, the EFP would remain both the most selective and the most democratic association in the French history of psychoanalysis.

As for the rejections, which were as little justified as the acceptances, they became more and more numerous with the expansion of the SFP and the "normal" promotion of AMEs. It is as though the members of the *jury d'agrément* considered themselves, beneath the mask of their anonymity, the only possessors of the rank of AE, even though most of them, who were fanatical partisans of the procedure, would never risk submitting to it, since they had obtained their rank before it was instituted. Invented by Lacan, *la passe* could not work without him, but with him it could not work either. Such is the first lesson to be drawn from the progress of a procedure that was to allow the whole of the École to reflect, with or without jury, on the *actual* institutional conditions entailed in *truly* becoming an analyst. In that sense, the "failed" procedure would have effects that were both regenerative and disastrous on the Lacanian movement. A net result of failure can thus offer a kind of negative testimony of a certain success.

The position of anonymity had something to do with the procedure of *la passe*. But instead of appealing to the psychoanalytic value of a kind of "depersonalization," as Tostain did in 1970, it is more interesting to show how the signifier of subjective destitution—that is, of *la passe*—circulated in the divided institution which the expanding École freudienne had become. Anonymity in all its forms encompassed the publishing endeavors collectively elaborated by the members of the EFP. Among them, three deserve mention: the journal *Scilicet,* whose first issue appeared in the fall of 1968; the project of a *Dictionary,* which took place around 1970; and finally the journal *L'Ordinaire du psychanalyste,* which was conceived after the crisis and which would first appear in 1973. Those three endeavors oscillated between a dogmatic submission to anonymity, which skirted collective depersonalization, and an appeal to the absence of signatures that tended to revalorize the creative function of plural writing.

The appearance of *Scilicet* at Éditions du Seuil was prepared by Lacan over the course of a year. "You can know," he wrote in introducing the journal, "such is the meaning of this title. You can now know that I have failed in a teaching which has been addressed for twelve years solely to psychoanalysts, and which, as a result, for four years now, has encountered what in December 1967, at the ENS where I speak, I paid homage to as to the number. On each of those occasions, I failed to break the evil charm operative through the ongoing order governing existent psychoanalytic societies and on its theoretical production, each solidary with the other." [152]

Scilicet appeared with a confession of failure after the events of May '68 and on the eve of the reverse split of January 1969. It was addressed to an audience of "bacheliers" or "bachelors"—that is, "students" of every stripe. For Lacan, the English "bachelor" symbolized one who was not yet wed to any psychoanalytic society and was attracted to the EFP. But the journal bore witness to the specific relation established in the École between the master and his people. In particular, it brought to the fore Lacan's gradual disavowal of the former members of the SFP even as it gave concrete shape to the entry into the movement of a base traversed by several tendencies. Inspired by the spirit of the mathematical collective "Bourbaki," *Scilicet* in fact functioned as the ideal x-ray image of the EFP in the 1970s: Only Lacan had a right to write as an individual, as opposed to the anonymous subjects who had no more than the duty—in order to receive their lord's words—of commenting on his doctrine. To exhibit his solitude, Lacan decided that articles would be unsigned except those emanating from his own pen. At first, several ideas were advanced. Lacan emphasized that a theoretical endeavor could not be a function of a single author, but rather of a teaching. Moreover, he wanted to favor the publication of case histories without in any way violating the requisite confidentiality. Finally, he wanted certain analysts affiliated with other societies to enter into association with his undertaking. The argument was interesting, but the articles were not "clinical," and the authors all belonged to the Lacanian movement. As a result, the texts took on the appearance of anonymous letters. Lacan, moreover, was intent on the journal's not being truly anonymous, and in the second issue, he published a list of collaborators in order to provide certain bearings. After that issue, however, the task was consigned to Charles Melman, and the notorious list disappeared from the masthead.

Scilicet is closed to no one," wrote Lacan in the first issue, "but *whoever will not have participated in it will not be recognized as one of my students.*" [153] With that introductory declaration, Lacan did not merely impose anonymity on his disciples; he also wanted to draw up a list of the faithful. But since at the time, the number of members of the EFP rose to about 230, and since all thought themselves the students of the master, it was materially impossible for all to figure in the journal. As a result, the École was doomed, behind its façade of unity, to permanent division, with the primacy of a dogmatic discourse on the one side, and a "libertarian"-style appeal on the other, for which Lacanian doctrine no longer served as sole reference. It became all the less so for some in that the dogmatism of the others became increasingly stifling. The breakup of the EFP into two major antagonistic tendencies, which emerged after the crisis of *la passe,* was furthered by protests coming from without. As of 1970, Lacanian therapists of the fourth generation began to discover, somewhat later than in the other societies, the existence of doctrines to which they had previously remained deaf. The work of D. W. Winnicott, for example, which was translated into French around that time, brought a sense of clinical practice capable of serving as a counterweight to dogmatic Lacanianism at a time when a generalized opening toward pluralism was dominating the French psychoanalytic scene. In the face of those circumstances, *Scilicet,* over a period of eight years, established at the heart of the EFP a situation of permanent anonymity functioning as an index of the failure of *la passe* and of the advance of dogmatism within the ranks of the movement. Over the years, the journal became the symbol of that "unreadable" Lacanianism that would be the mockery of an entire intelligentsia increasingly hostile to its original message.

The project of a *Dictionnaire raisonné et critique de la psychanalyse* was part and parcel of that anonymous and spontaneous dogmatism promoted by *Scilicet* at a time when the experiment of *la passe* began to spread throughout the EFP a generalized complex of subjective destitution. At the outset, the idea was excellent. It came from François Wahl, who had brought out at Éditions du Seuil, under the direction of Oswald Ducrot and Tzvetan Todorov, a dictionary of linguistic sciences as well as a remarkable collective volume on structuralism.[154] The project was entrusted to Melman and supported by Lacan. Drawing his inspiration from *Scilicet,* Melman also wanted to address an audience of *bachelors*—that is, to make Lacanian doctrine available to a broad public. But he was also intent on getting the members of the École to work together in order to keep them united in pursuit of a common cause. In point of fact, what was at stake was countering Laplanche and Pontalis's *Vocabulaire,* judged to be "eclectic," with a "Lacanian reading" of Freud's work. Such a reading was to demonstrate that the Lacanian point of view was already intrinsic to Freud's text. Now such a reading of Freud, in the light of an already constituted Lacanianism, was dogmatic *par excellence,* since it tended to obliterate the gradual history of Lacan's reelaborations, replacing it with an illusion through which Freud would already have been Lacanian by virtue of the magic of some transcultural hot line. The proposed reading, however honest in conception, was thus but an attempt to do away with the difference between the two corpuses.

Melman gathered around him several of the faithful, including René Bailly, Claude Conté, Claude Dumézil, and Thérèse Parisot. Moustapha Safouan was also part of the undertaking. A seven-part outline was drawn up, then sent to members of the EFP with a request for articles and assignment of each to one of the registers delineated. The outline proposed nothing less than to evaluate the whole of human knowledge from the perspective of Freud's discovery. The dictionary was thus to begin by describing the state of science, ideology, and politics at the end of the nineteenth century, then to continue with a "companion volume to Freud," containing an inventory of the founder's principal articles, and finally to develop into a world history of the psychoanalytic movement from the time of the first Vienna circle. To this three exploratory efforts were to be appended: a "companion volume to Lacan;" a general lexicon of psychoanalytic concepts (according to a "Lacanian reading"); and an evaluation of "frontiers," to contain in-depth studies of philosophy, linguistics, mathematics, history, literary criticism, and religion. If one inspects the wondrous outline at all closely, one understands why dogmatic Lacanianism could not succeed in building an edifice capable of ensuring its own unity. Even the pharaohs would not have dreamed of defying the gods with such dreams. For in order to construct such a mausoleum, the EFP would have needed a hundred years' existence, and its members a maddening degree of productivity. The mountain was thus doomed to give birth to a molehill, but the molehill contained within it a mine of information about the way in which the dogmatic tendency envisaged the relations between Freudianism and Lacanianism during the 1970s.[155]

The "Lexicon" chapter was divided into three parts. The first, entitled "Le signifiant (la structure) [The signifier (structure)]," had as its subject the interpretation of dreams, the psychopathology of everyday life, and jokes. The second, under the heading "Le sujet (clinique) [The subject (clinical)]," defined thirteen notions borrowed from either the works of Freud or Lacan. Finally, the third dealt with "La pratique [Practice]," and also combined the two bodies of work. Under the rubric "the signifier," almost all Freudian concepts relating to the interpretation of dreams are to be found. But instead of being linked to their site of origin and then examined retrospectively from a Lacanian point of view, they were defined from the outset as though the Freudian corpus had never existed. The "other scene," for example, received the following definition: "Place where the signifier exercises its function in the production of significations that remain unconquered by the subject and which turns out to be separated from the subject by a barrier of resistance." All the other Freudian concepts strung out through the lexicon receive a similar Lacanian stamp in unreadable prose intent on obliterating the difference between the two bodies of thought.

Instead of furthering the unity of the EFP, the dictionary project revealed its divisions. Not only did the work actually accomplished never lead to anything, but the disciples themselves began disputing among themselves before a base hard put to figure out what role was expected of it. Jacques-Alain Miller, for his part, who was still a militant in Gauche prolétarienne at the time and remained somewhat outside the EFP, found the project impossible. "The foundations seemed false to me," he has said; "my break with Melman dates from that time. I proposed a companion volume to Freud and he added a companion volume to Lacan." [156]

To understand the rest of the story and the reasons for which the project could not but end in failure, a comparison should be attempted between the spontaneous dogmatism inherent in the EFP and the Millerian reading of Lacanian doctrine discussed previously. We have seen that that reading brought a radicalization and a rationalism to Lacanianism that were frequently alien to it. In his introduction to the *Écrits,* as in his article on "suture," Miller distinguished the doctrine itself from his interpretation of it and, when he brought the notion of retroactivity to bear in the evaluation of Lacanian concepts, it remained in keeping with Lacan's own image of his productivity. But Miller never proposed an amalgamation of Freudian conceptuality and Lacanian conceptuality. On the contrary, he separated the two in order to reveal their absence of homogeneity. He read Lacan without Freud or with Freud "on the side," thus showing the historical and theoretical autonomy of Lacanianism in order subsequently to radicalize it. There was thus a significant difference between the spontaneous dogmatism presiding over the dictionary project and what we can henceforth call a *Millerian tendency.* The first "obliterated" the return to Freud and condemned itself to an amalgamation whereas the second reactivated it the better to constitute itself within the history of Lacanianism as the coherent attempt at a strict and unswerving Lacanianism based on the hyperlogical reelaboration. What followed would shed light on these two branches of a sectarian Lacanianism as the Millerian tendency grew in importance within the EFP. All these cleavages were not experienced as such by the protagonists at the time they emerged; despite their conflicts, the members of the École, either within a common tendency or not, continued to entertain relations of friendship or analytic practice that would gradually wane in the course of successive crises.

"May 1968: the great talkfest . . . It was then that *la passe* took on reverberations that were felt on analytic couches, that inflected and even shattered a number of analyses, and that above all fascinated analysts of every stripe. But even without the formidable amplification it (like psychoanalysis) received from '68, *la passe,* through its practical and theoretical intervention, was destined to stir up those analysts. The shock of the organizational meeting of January 1969 was for that reason all the harder to take. No more accommodation or arrangements: Threats, manipulations, insults, demands, and resignations punctuated a debate from which the modalities of *la passe* emerged as Lacan had wanted them, but weighted down by a kind of institutional leadenness, whose trace can still be felt on our tongues." [157] Thus spoke, eight years after the vote in Lacan's favor, one of the signatories of Project B. If the signifier "subjective destitution" functioned within the dogmatic tendency, it circulated as well in the rank and file of the EFP among practitioners of the opposite stripe. But it did not take on the same meaning there. The idea of publishing a journal in which articles were not attributed took shape in the fall of 1969 in the Lander group. Francis Hofstein was the first to think of it. A jazz enthusiast, he had played the drums for ten years and reflected on the emulation created between two musicians during improvisations inspired by New Orleans–style bands. He mentioned it to Radmila Zygouris and set out in search of a publisher. Time passed, and one day the two friends paid a visit to Lacan to present their project to him. Delighted, the master suggested that he be part of the editorial board and insisted that the journal appear at Éditions du Seuil with the official endorsement of the EFP. But faced with the refusal of his interlocutors, he shouted: "Why have you come to see me if you don't want anything of what I suggest to you?" Hofstein and Zygouris replied that Lacan might well weigh too heavily on the undertaking. Then, mocking *Scilicet,* they suggested that he publish his own texts anonymously there. Lacan burst out laughing, did not say no, and asked that the first issues of the journal be sent to him as soon as they appeared. The adventure of *L'Ordinaire du psychanalyste* had begun. It would last for five years, enough for twelve issues, ending with an act of self-dismantling anticipatory of the EFP's collapse.

Born in Slovenia, Radmila Zygouris had been given shelter by an uncle with a Greek passport. After a childhood spent in Germany, she went to school in Argentina and Switzerland and eventually became a psychologist at the Hôpital des Enfants-Malades. As for Francis Hofstein, he came—by way of his grandfather—from the Yiddish-speaking East and lived through the Occupation under several borrowed names. He reassumed his own at the end of the war. For those two Lacanian therapists, who would be the only members of the opposition to receive the rank of AE, anonymity brought with it freedom whereas an author's signature became the symbol of inscription in a legitimizing order that inhibited all adventure. As opposed to *Scilicet,* their appeal was to a true anonymity as a kind of plural writing. The choice of title reflected a will to publish something in the order of the *daily* discourse of psychoanalysis at work. "We never published unfathered texts,"

Hofstein has declared. "We didn't want articles sent anonymously. There was always an author behind them."

To avoid any form of censorship, *L'Ordinaire du psychanalyste* was ultimately brought out without a publisher. Hofstein took care of the business end and distributed it to bookstores himself under the trade name "Sigismond." The tone taken was that of a newspaper, and the articles, which came for the most part from analysts and analysands of the Lacanian movement, bore witness to the vitality of a certain ordinary Lacanianism during the glory years of the EFP. There was something Dadaist in the journal's texts, which resembled collages, prose poems, *art brut* manifestos, or private diaries. Over a period of five years, the journal became a sounding board for the movement's divided situation and opposed the reigning dogmatism with the irreverent laughter of its libertarian spirit. Lacan knew this and supported the enterprise all the more in that *Scilicet* and the projected dictionary were a resounding failure. At the Rome congress, at the plenary session of November 1974, he announced as a challenge that *Scilicet* was not working well but that "Ostin's" newspaper was a remarkable success. Immediately, the members of the EFP imagined that René Tostain had just founded a paper. Furious, Hofstein went to see Lacan and reproached him for having violated the pact of anonymity. After replying that everyone knew who was publishing *L'Ordinaire*, Lacan apologized and acknowledged his slip.[158]

Nonetheless, in 1976, Hofstein considered halting his publication, which was too onerous a task to take on without a publisher. For his part, Lacan was no longer interested in *Scilicet* and became dependent on Jacques-Alain Miller, who had just brought out the first issues of *Ornicar?*, thus establishing a new connection with the EFP from another publishing locale. No doubt Hofstein and Zygouris were wrong not to accept Lacan's proposition. If *L'Ordinaire* had appeared at Éditions du Seuil, the fate of the EFP might well have been different. But how is one to go "official" when one's name is Dada?

In April 1978, *L'Ordinaire du psychanalyste* ceased to exist—after occupying an innovative place between the end of *L'Inconscient* and the first years of *Ornicar?*. "Let us not fool ourselves. To take off one's apron and to remain an ordinary analyst cannot be taken as a matter of course. First of all, because by virtue of the very existence of *L'Ordinaire*, we are no longer ordinary analysts. Then, because it's hard to do away with the space it occupied between psychoanalysis and ourselves. A transitional object, I might say, in that in order to hurl oneself into that undertaking one had to love psychoanalysis and believe in it. In that it also marked a waning of that transferential love since it set us apart from 'official' psychoanalysis. . . . *L'Ordinaire* is not stopping so that with its capital a journal, a group, a school, or a war can start; it's stopping, period." [159]

During all that period, the EFP was thus represented in the publishing market by an internal organ, *Les Lettres de l'École,* in which its colloquia, works, and congresses appeared, and by the "Champ freudien" series at Éditions du Seuil. To these were added the journal *Le Coq héron,* created in 1971 by Bernard This. This was a mimeographed newsletter reporting work undertaken in the framework of the Centre Étienne-Marcel. Lacan was no more interested in his collection than in *Scil-*

icet. He did not read the manuscripts proposed by his disciples and left it to François Wahl to deal with authors, correct texts, or refuse manuscripts. He would, however, make one exception in choosing himself to publish Pierre Legendre's beautiful book, *L'amour du censeur* ["Love of the censor"].[160] But that author was a jurist and was neither part of the master's personal guard nor part of the former cohort of the SFP. Almost all the authors of the "Champ freudien" would acknowledge their debt to François Wahl, who taught them their craft. This was particularly the case for Moustapha Safouan and Maud Mannoni. In brief, if Lacan neglected the works of his disciples, even as he supported their initiatives, he always needed someone else to manage his affairs and his teaching. And it was Jacques-Alain Miller who would gradually assume responsibility not only for writing up the seminars, but, along with François Wahl, for the publishing activities of the EFP. In that task, he would be quite effective and would succeed where Lacan's disciples had failed.

At the time of the organizational meetings at the Hotel Lutétia, a naval doctor, Jean-Paul Moreigne, sent Jean Clavreul a letter accompanied by a counterproposal that modified Lacan's own considerably even as it retained the principle of *la passe.* In fact, that project was the only one to be presented to the EFP as a true counterproposal. Its author wanted it to be submitted to a vote against the jury's own. Now Moreigne's letter was sent out to the members of the EFP along with the other texts, but the counterproposal itself was not. And yet it was different from Projects B and C and would have been deserving of the plenary session's consideration. The situation was muddled by the fact that votes were held on texts that were not proposals, whereas the only proposal presented as such was not circulated.

Analyzed by François Perrier, Jean-Paul Moreigne spent two years in Dakar, where he participated in experiments in transcultural psychiatry at the Fann Hospital Center founded by Henri Collomb. There he worked alternately with Edmond and Marie-Cécile Ortigues, themselves members of the EFP since 1964, who had studied the African Oedipus complex from an ethnopsychoanalytic perspective different from Georges Devereux's.[161] When Moreigne returned to France in the fall of 1968, he arrived during the crisis of *la passe* and had the impression that the EFP was a pathogenic institution. He did not write his counterproposal from scratch, but corrected Project A on numerous points before writing a new version of it. The modifications tended to eliminate the theory of *la passe* as an authentification of the experience of passage, replacing it with the more classical notion of peer selection. In that perspective, the AEs were gathered in a *collège* that coopted *passants* after an ordeal resembling more an intergroup dialogue than an authentification of one's being an analyst. In addition, the term *titre* [title or rank], which for Lacan belonged to the register of appointments, was replaced in the counterproposal by a more sociological notion of "function" or "qualification." Not only did Moreigne not retain the distinction between hierarchy and gradus, but he transformed the status of *passeurs:* In the ordeal, only one of them was to be chosen randomly while the second was to be selected from among the members after having elucidated his understanding of his role with an AE who supported him. Furthermore, the AME was considered by Moreigne to be a certified psychoanalyst and, as such, had the right ipso facto to accept future analysts in therapy.

It was on the basis of this counterproposal, emanating from a member of the fourth generation, that the idea of a Fourth Group took concrete shape. That group retained part of the Lacanian heritage, but "rectified" it with a sociological perspective. Instead of "titles" or "ranks" there were "functions," "roles," or "qualifications." In place of "symbolic appointments," what was retained was an imaginary circulation of "situations." And the guise of an ordeal of passage was assumed by a valorization of the group's taking charge of the process whereby individuals became analysts. Through those principles, the Fourth Group [*Quatrième Groupe*] would be the only institution in Freudian France to implement in its very structures a teaching stemming from social psychology and a specific culturalist tradition.[162]

In January 1968, the three AEs who had resigned, Aulagnier, Perrier, and Valabrega, were followed by Moreigne and other members, who were for the most part women and in particular women analysands of Serge Leclaire. Among them were to be found Perrier's second wife, Antoinette Logier-Mitchell, and Nathalie Zaltzman, as well as Evelyne-Anne Gasquères and Gabrielle Dorey. André Missenard, who was also trained by Leclaire, joined the dissidents as well, along with Charles Zygel and Paulette Dubuisson. A "school for women" and a Leclairean lineage—such were at the outset the distinguishing traits of the new society directed by three veterans of Lacan's couch. The Fourth Group retained the imprint of its own style of dissidence: It rejected direct monarchy and gave preference to a certain conviviality in the service of oligarchy.

At the outset, the notion of a Fourth Group stemmed from an obvious fact, the dissident group was the fourth to be created in France after three splits. But since it resulted from a break in which affiliation with the empire played no role, it took on the appearance, in relation to its rivals, of an "other scene" in which neither affiliation with the IPA nor Lacanian orthodoxy were at stake. Whence its somewhat amorphous, open, and sociologizing aspect. Very early on, the label "fourth" proved insufficient. It did not include the word "psychoanalysis," and risked having no meaning outside the movement. Which is why the eleven founders opted to append to it, as a subtitle, the name OPLF (Organisation psychanalytique de langue française). Through it they could take their distance from the terms that had been used in the course of French psychoanalytic history. An *organization* was not a *society,* an *association,* or a *school,* and the reference to the *French language* allowed culture to replace nationalism and distance to be taken from an internationalism experienced as subservient to an Anglo-American sphere of influence. In addition, as opposed to the EFP, from which it emerged, the OPLF refused to call itself "Freudian." It thus indicated the existence of a plurality of references among which no group had the right to invoke the exclusiveness of a heritage. The Fourth Group was thus *plural,* in relation to the various forms of orthodoxy, and *feminine* in its sociological organization and the symbolic role falling to its principal representatives. In that sense, it reflected the principal aspirations of the French intelligentsia of the post-May period: women's liberation, the hope for a new conviviality, primacy of the group over the individual, pluralism, etc.

Refusing both the monarchy of a single individual and the accumulation of power of each (in a kind of transferential aggrandizement), the OPLF was intent on being collegial. The principles guiding it were elaborated collectively without it being possible to ascribe primacy to any of its eleven founders. Nonetheless, it was Jean-Paul Moreigne and Jean-Paul Valabrega who theorized the principal notions based on which the collective functioned. Piera Aulagnier, for her part, took it upon herself to found, at the Presses universitaires de France, a new journal named *Topique,* which took the place of *L'Inconscient.* The first issue appeared in the fall of 1969 with a series of articles dedicated to the foundation of the Fourth Group and more generally to psychoanalytic training. It contained texts by the three former AEs of the EFP as well as an article by Guy Benoit on psychiatry and a study by Robert Castel. The latter was a sociologist whose work was perfectly attuned to the group's point of view. Four years later he would publish a bestselling work, *Le Psychanalysme,*[163] to denounce the sectarian and religious character of psychoanalytic societies in France. As for the choice of the term "Topique," it was not indifferent, since it referred to the various sites of Freudian metapsychology and thus to a "plural" representation of psychoanalysis.

The creation of the OPLF occurred in three stages, corresponding to three fertile phases of its history, even as they indicate the developmental side of a very gradual break with the EFP. As early as February 1969, at a session held in the Pavillon d'Ermenonville, the decision was made to found a fourth organization. On March 17, the group's bylaws were tendered at the Paris Prefecture, with the names of Perrier as president, Aulagnier as secretary, Gasquères as scientific secretary, Moreigne as administrator, and Dorey as treasurer. At the same time, rules were drawn up for training, governance, and external relations. The society contained two sorts of members (titular and adhering members) as well as an institutional structure distributed over three loci of power: an administrative council, an executive board, and ordinary as well as extraordinary plenary sessions. Only titular members had voting rights and enjoyed all institutional prerogatives, as opposed to adhering members whose status remained somewhat subdued. The latter were members acknowledged not to be analysts, who had, in order to obtain that rank, to have experienced a particular analysis. As a result they were "observers" in the position of "petitioners."

As principles of training, the founders (i.e., the titular members) recommended a shapeless system: not *passe,* commission, or preselection, but a notion of "plurireferential psychoanalysis." Therapy remained confidential and was not to be judged by any jury; the training analyst was kept at a distance from all deliberations; and the candidate for the rank of titular member could come from an analyst external to the society—certification would be based on control analyses. "The term 'plurireferential' may be suited," Perrier wrote, "to describe one of the key situations in the training process, once that process can no longer be academically reduced to a mere curriculum. For once a candidate comes to take charge of a first patient, it is no longer his training contract, but also his clinical practice, in its unsuspected aspects, that comes to govern the subject's relation to the unconscious. The patient, who is only discussed indirectly, thus refers three analysts back to the partiality and fragmentariness of their own knowledge: There is the neophyte trying out his own mastery, but there is also the control and the training analyst. . . . The question is no longer one of a single armchair for two desires, or of a single desire between two subjects confronting, mirror-like, a single position. There are three armchairs and a *fourth unconscious,* whose language is not entirely expressed in known dialects. The transition from "therapy" to "training" is not played out in a dual mode, but is an opening onto the polyphony of clinical structures." [164]

On the basis of that polyphony, in which the principle of a "continuous" control prevails, the candidate comes eventually to join the group as an adhering member. During the course of his training, he writes a long paper and engages in discussions "in a small group" with the titular members. The "small group" is composed of supervisors and of a study advisor, also chosen from the ranks of the titular members. After psychoanalytic sessions and the final writing of his paper, the adhering member can become a titular member through cooptation, following a vote held in plenary session.

In 1969, the Fourth Group proceeded to an amalgamation of an IPA-based model, a culturalist reference, and a Lacanian legacy. From the traditional societies, it took its hierarchy, its curriculum, and the idea of peer selection. Social psychology gave it the thematic of effectively active minorities. And from Lacanianism it borrowed the idea of continuous training in terms of a Moebius strip. If Lacan invented, with *la passe,* a "third site" for psychoanalysis, the founders of the OPLF replaced that third site with a "fourth" one corresponding to the historical position of the group, but also to a primacy accorded to the "creative" psychology of the collective. Where the EFP took account of the figure "3" and the Oedipal trilogy, the OPLF shattered that structure and moved from the "family" to the group—no more founding father or uneven member, but a working collective modeled on an expanded cartel. The Fourth Group was thus the implementation of a Freudian counter-*école* that could exist only after breaking with its mother society.

The OPLF, as it was conceived in 1969, would in fact never effectively exist and it may be hypothesized that a labor of mourning in three phases was necessary for the founders to extricate themselves from the impasse of a simple critique of the "October Proposal" and to elaborate an institutional model that would be neither a conformist copy of the IPA societies nor a sterile protest against Lacanianism.

In the initial set of regulations, the notions of *fourth site* and *fourth unconscious* were not rigorously defined. But after April and May 1969, Perrier, Valabrega, and Aulagnier would write articles on the subject of training that would serve as the basis for a reorganization of the Fourth Group that was subsequently endorsed by a plenary session in December 1970. It was Jean-Paul Valabrega who essentially laid the theoretical grounds for the new orientation in an article entitled "Les voies de la formation du psychanalyste [The paths of psychoanalytic training]." [165] Criticizing a certain transferential aggrandizement, Valabrega rejected the Lacanian project of a pure didactic or training analysis and called it a *Catharist psychoanalysis:* "The training system implemented by Lacan," he wrote, "and which became institutionalized early in 1969, is a system productive of analysts— Lacan himself calls them his 'students'—who offer an image of their master pressed to caricatural limits. The image is betrayed particularly by a mimicry, a verbal imitativeness without precedent. Let us simply ask in all serenity this question: Who would pretend that an identification with one's analyst, effected, fixed, and ratified in one's very language might be without—I won't say formative, but rather 'deformative'—bearing on the analytic field in its essence?" [166]

In order to prevent the deforming effects of such an identification within a training program, Valabrega proposed that an analyst not have any power over the certification of his analysands in the institution. Then, instead of a *fourth unconscious* or a *fourth site*, he gave, for the first time, a coherent definition of the notion of a *fourth analysis*. He proposed that the term "control" be replaced by that of "fourth analysis," implying a patient in analysis, a candidate who is that patient's analyst, the candidate's analyst, and an additional (fourth) analyst: "The fourth analysis—which is, it will be seen, something quite different from a 'classical control'—might be said to be a training procedure to the precise extent that, being exercised concurrently on the four points of reference, it would necessarily accord a privilege to the analysis of zones of deafness, tendentious inflections, and would manage as a result to locate and situate the unconscious transferences circulating among the four referents. The word 'plurireferential' is thus not out of place either in this context." [167]

At the plenary session of December 1970, two years after the split, the notion of a *fourth analysis*, as elaborated by Valabrega, became the OPLF's principal reference for certifying candidates.[168] At the same time, the terminology was modified. To avoid traditional nomenclature, the founders decided to call titular members *cotisants* [subscribers] and adhering members *contribuants* [contributors]. What was at stake in the change was a metaphorization of the role of money in psychoanalytic societies, so true was it that the different categories of members were always distinguished from each other by the amount of dues they paid to their respective societies. At the OPLF, as of 1970, subscribers were those who took responsibility for the institution's perpetuation whereas contributors were users who participated in its endeavors. The use of the present participle in the terminology took on meaning to the extent that the group was intent on being mobile and active: "constituting" and "instituting" and not "constituted" or "instituted." To be sure, the status of the two types of members remained unchanged, since only the subscribers had voting rights. Contributors, exactly like the affiliates or adhering members of the SPP or the APF, were not listed as members. They were neither students nor practitioners, but "participants." Their views were consultative and taken into account in the deliberations of the subscribers. In addition, they paid their dues "after the fact." In that sense, the OPLF was not a truly democratic society like the EFP, but it resolved the dilemma of hierarchy with a bit of sleight of hand that assured the reign of an active minority over a no less active majority in terms of "conviviality." It should be said that over the years the contributors were not always analysts in training. Among them were to be found members of other societies with no aspiration to the rank of subscriber, but who paid dues in order to follow the group's work. In that respect, the OPLF, since the second phase of its creation, functioned as an open forum. In the shattered village of the post-May period, then in the twilight period, it occupied a position comparable to the one taken by Confrontation between 1976 and 1980.[169] Moreover it would be the first to use that term to designate certain of its meetings. For several years (and at present as well) it has attracted, in a permanent and plurireferential circulation, malcontents of every stripe who refuse the dogmatisms and orthodoxies of the less "amorphous" societies.

As far as the training of therapists went, the group functioned, from its inception, in a kind of intimately closed circuit, with a restricted number of "real" members (the subscribers) who never turned their quarrels into official splits. Since those quarrels never bore on issues of training they did not lead to any secessions. The notions of "fourth analysis" and its "plurireferential" bearings were at once sufficiently neutral and sufficiently solid to ensure the small group's relative cohesion. And if there were in fact two tendencies at the OPLF—one more libertarian and the other more selective—the two managed to respect each other. The few resignations that did occur were a result of personal rivalries or precise points of disagreement.

In that respect, Perrier's departure was significant. Whereas his resignation from the EFP in 1969 had been experienced by a good number of young Lacanians as a tragedy, his exit from the Fourth Group, at the end of the 1970s, took a comic turn. After having been a founder and president of the OPLF, the great clinician of hysteria continued for ten years to take himself for a leader in a society without masters in which women occupied the position of barons. He thus felt dethroned both by the group, which challenged his right to take himself for what he was not, and by the whole of the female population, which he attacked quite crudely as an "ovarian syndicate." Here is how he recounts his exit in a book of recollections not always trustworthy for the exactitude of its reports: "Females, both friends and enemies, then took the Fourth Group in hand. The group and its journal *Topique* shifted to their second cruising speed—slow. The monotonous hum of empty, hollow meetings settled in. Finally, from what I learned, there was even a request for affiliation with the IPA. My name was carefully silenced. The few interventions I attempted met with the distrust and hostility of the audience. . . . Piera, a masterly woman, did not forgive me my frankness. My friend Valabrega, embittered and alone, showed a will to criticize more often than any critical spirit. Their only common point was their Italian origin. As for me, strong in my notoriety, I believed I no longer had much to risk. I thus resigned from *Topique,* then from the Fourth Group." [170] To be sure, the OPLF did not request affiliation from the IPA, and Perrier's affirmation to that effect was more in the order of one of those fabulous rumors the Parisian psychoanalytic milieu has always known how to bring off.

In fifteen years of operation, and despite that spectacular resignation, the OPLF did not experience any serious crisis. As present, it remains a convivial society, characterized by the primacy of a kind of transculturalism. As opposed to its IPA-affiliated rivals, it does not possess a training institute, and as opposed to the EFP, it has always refused the principle of variable-length sessions. Nonetheless, if the founders stick rigorously to the regulation forty or fifty minutes, the younger members have been more flexible. Moreover, like the EFP, the Fourth Group has always made its archives and the documents informing its history public. The increase in the number of subscribers remains minimal—about one appointment per year. The number of contributors is more significant: 150 in 1985, as opposed to 25 subscribers, of whom 15 were women and 10 men. With that figure, the OPLF is the only society in Freudian France in which women form a majority. It was they who induced the transferential aggrandizement denounced by Valabrega at the outset and which should have been avoided. Founded on the basis of a precise disagreement with Lacan, the Fourth Group did not have to make a dramatic choice between a master and an empire. The founders consequently did not leave a master to gain a kingdom. As a result, they agreed, less reluctantly than the former Lacanians of the APF, to meld into a society in which the very notion of a leader had disappeared from the certification procedure, only to reemerge in the personal entourage of the ladies and their epigones. While completely autonomous, the OPLF between 1969 and 1979 resembled those shattered groups of the EFP and that of *L'Ordinaire,* for example, in which collective creation and an opening to pluralism were winning out over dogmatism. And the residue of that affiliation with Lacanianism may be found everywhere in the articles or texts emanating from members of the group.

This is borne out, insofar as training was concerned, by a presentation by Valabrega at the scientific "day" of December 12, 1976, and entitled: "Le fondement théorique de l'analyse quatrième [The theoretical basis of the fourth analysis]." Seven years after the first formulation of the notion, the author went further in the direction of a formalization which was not foreign to Lacan's own. Without mentioning the article "La Science et la Vérité," and without speaking of the matheme,[171] Valabrega referred to them implicitly and effected a displacement of the Lacanian point of view. He rejected a *mathesis universalis,* located the subject in the position of zero, and situated the "fourth analysis" as centered on a *residue* [reliquat]: "The fourth analysis is the opportunity and experiment of removing the seal bearing down on the residual transference, which becomes available and graspable in the form and guise of a counter-transference. . . . The fourth analysis begins with the taking into consideration of the residual transference." [172]

Theorized in several stages and in strange proximity to the development of Lacan's teaching, the notion of a fourth analysis served as a focal point uniting the OPLF. In 1983, a recasting of training principles was collectively undertaken by Aulagnier, Zaltzman, and Valabrega. It constituted the third historical phase of the institutional existence of the Fourth Group. On that occasion, the certification procedure was specified in less amorphous terms. To become a subscriber, a candidate had to have at least two fourth analyses to his credit, at least one of which was with a subscriber of the Fourth Group, and two or three interanalytic sessions. Personal analyses were retained, as well as doctrinal pluralism: "Thus delineated and given currency," the authors wrote, "our model of analytic training makes no claims to being either perennial or perfect. It would already be splendid if we could apply to it Churchill's line about democracy, 'The worst of regimes with the exception of all the others.' "[173]

Five years after the dissolution of the EFP, the OPLF undertook a new terminological reform. In June 1985, the designations "subscriber" and "contributor" were replaced by those of "member analysts of the Fourth Group" and "participant in the activities of the Fourth Group." The members' status did not change, but through the new names, the group effected a symbolic return to the origins of its break. Against the former title of AE, it called for the notion of an AME in terms virtually identical to those formulated by Lacan: The analyst was to be recognized, on the basis of a control, for his competence. After having set up a kind of Freudian counter-*école*, which lasted as long as the EFP, the Fourth Group became a true post-Lacanian society, like its rivals emergent from the defunct EFP. It thus had its "fourth" historical phase.

9 Sunset Boulevard: The Splendors and Miseries of Protest

I. The Great Decline of Dynamic Psychiatry

Two intellectual currents traversed the May '68 rebellion and subsequently flourished during the period of readjustment following that paradoxical event. The first, which was materialist, was an appeal to Marxism (in either its orthodox or *gauchiste* version) and the second, which was libertarian, drew on various sources extending from Surrealism to anarchism, passing by way of spiritualism. That second tendency accentuated the thematic of a possible liberation of the imaginary, desire, and sexuality, whereas the first remained closer to a conception of the revolution in terms of class struggle. Whether one turned in one direction or the other, the "spirit of May" was characterized by a voluntarism of equality or difference that urged revolt against the major apparatuses of the dominant ideology: family, health, church, army, or, more simply, the state. Norms were contested, at times to the benefit of other norms, at others in the interest of abolishing the very notion of norm. But behind the fragile curtain of that authentic breach, a readaptation of modern thought to a pragmatic space in which the civilization of the book and of writing were being subverted by the ideals of communicative transparency could already be perceived. The priority accorded to the realms of "experience" and of the nonverbal would impose itself with such force that the movement would be devoured by the very individuals who were its artisans.

At the time of the barricades on the rue Gay-Lussac, the structuralist "movement," in its various orientations, was at the height of its fame. In fact, however, so ambiguous was its situation that it had already begun to wane. For it had never proposed a model inspired by the ideal of liberation since, on the contrary, it continued to defend the prevalence of the symbolic function over the realm of the imaginary. And yet there was little doubt that it too had long taken the apparatuses of the dominant ideology as its target.[1] There was thus a genuine encounter staged between the thematic of contestation and that of a structuralism already functioning in the register of subversion. The women's movement and "avant-garde" literary journals were traversed by that encounter. There began to appear a "red front" tending to define a new status of writing on grounds laid by the structuralist elaboration: "gendered" writing for the MLF [Mouvement de libération des femmes—Women's Liberation Movement], "textual" *écriture* for the writers and poets of the journal *Tel quel*. The French Communist Party was also traversed by the great red tide to the extent that with the Argenteuil congress of 1966, the question of freedom of research and creation became the principal issue in a liberal policy that resulted in 1972 in the establishment of a Common Program.

The problem of psychoanalysis was on the agenda and a "review" of past errors became imperative as numerous psychiatrists joined the party's ranks. Two channels of implantation were deployed: One was literary and was based on the developing links between the intellectual vanguard and the workers' bastion; the other was "Politzerian" and was focussed on the debate over humanism. The prevalent doctrines of the pre-May period thus continued for some time to enjoy their full prestige, while the new left emerging from the streets did not succeed either in establishing its unity or in translating its aspirations into a political movement. As a result, the French intellectual scene was not long in swinging toward a restoration of the values that had been the most hotly contested. As of 1975, the red front split up after having followed the paths of a Gallicized Maoism, while the Communist Party evolved toward a renewal of its own sectarianism. A new internal order prevailed at the universities, where psychoanalysis was taking root by way of Lacanianism on the one hand, and by way of psychology on the other.

During the ten years following the May revolt, Lacanianism, as the French form of the Freudian venture, dominated the scene with a brilliance it would never know again. But already the restoration of the former values was beginning to exercise its negative effects. At the threshold of the 1980s there reappeared, for the first time since Auschwitz, the old refrain concerning heredity-degeneracy and inegalitarianism. It developed on political ground mined with racism and in an ideological field marked by the triumphal return of biologism, obscurantism, and the religious ideal. Always ahead of his time, Lacan, in 1974, had uttered the prophetic words: "Should God come to regain sufficient force finally to ex-sist, it would harbor nothing better than a return of his sinister past."[2]

In ten years, the sociological situation of psychoanalysis changed completely. Despite the Lacanian adventure, which gave the country's youth for a while the savor of an authentic Freudianism, the massive arrival of the fourth and fifth generations sounded the knell of the last heroic epoch of psychoanalysis, a period in which it still had an elitist—if not a confidential—character. The men of the first three generations were marginal figures, adventurers, self-taught men, or cultured members of the bourgeoisie. Even if the profession of psychoanalysis was for them related, in terms of social hierarchy, to the other liberal professions, choosing that path until 1960 still meant demonstrating a certain nonconformity, originality, culture, or oddity. Up until the third generation, and despite the violence of their conflicts, the members of the community knew and socialized with each other. They had a common history, linked to the battle over the IPA, and shared the same psychoanalytic references. They belonged to the same world. In the face of adversity, they could, should the opportunity present itself, favor alliances or share an abundance of patients. Beyond doctrinal divergences, they entertained personal relations among themselves.

The two new generations reaching maturity after May 1968, however, were confronted with a formidable anonymity which was as much a function of the expansion of the profession as of the cloistered existence of its societies. The fourth and fifth analytic generations belonged to an era in which psychoanalysis and its teaching had been democratized. The men and women who were part of them no longer had the same aspirations as their immediate teachers or their ancestors. They were less scholarly, more inclined toward consumption, less heroic, and more sectarian. Their ideals were those of a middle class, lacking in firmness in its commitments, untrustworthy in its choices and capable of numerous intellectual fluctuations. The expansion of psychoanalytic societies and the rivalry that ensued entailed, moreover, that each would close in on itself. Thus, as of 1965, a student admitted into a society no longer had as many contacts as he formerly might have had with his neighbor from a rival society. He adhered to a cause, a doctrine, a leader, or a system, and found himself condemned to pursue a career within the walls of his institution. Whence a certain fanaticism, a combativeness, an *arrivisme,* an incommunicability, a lack of culture, and above all, an absence of common references from one institution to another. In sum, the therapists of the new generations were no longer the novelistic characters of a golden age of psychoanalysis, but the subjects of an ideological apparatus bearing an acronym or a trademark.

Institutional crises came to ravage psychoanalytic societies at the very time the great alliance between dynamic psychiatry and psychoanalysis, which had permitted the establishment of Freudianism in France, was coming undone. The psychoanalytic community was splitting into a number of shattered realms. Contested from within by the new generations, the three principal societies sought outlets—at times within the universities, and at others in various "confrontations" that allowed their members to emerge from their sorry isolation. The EFP was the first to resolve its internal crisis by establishing the procedure of *la passe,* while the SPP and the APF made use of methods conforming to their juridical rules. One evolved slowly toward sclerosis, in which fratricidal struggles gradually won out over pacification, and the other, on the contrary, managed to establish an "entente cordiale," at the cost of giving up any policy of expansion.

Starting in 1968, the last survivors of the first generation disappeared one after the other. In 1969, Louis Angelo Marie Hesnard died in his bed. The only founder of the SPP never to have spent time on a couch, he was also the one who had most changed his orientation according to historical circumstances: from his initial fidelity to the Gallic principles of *francité* to his circumstantial Lacanianism. Eugène Minkowski was next to leave the scene, taking with him to the grave the last glimmerings of the glory days. Then, it was Rudolph Lowenstein's turn, on the other side of the Atlantic. . . .

At the same time, the hecatomb also began for the second generation. Daniel Lagache disappeared first in 1972, defeated by illness and forgotten by most of his students. The press did not pay him homage commensurate with his position. His work was no longer read except by specialists. Four years later, death struck several new blows: Pierre Mâle, Marc Schlumberger, Georges Daumézon, and Sacha Nacht. Alone in his isolation, the authoritarian *maître* confronted his destiny amid intense suffering from cancer and senility. Finally, Henri Ey succumbed gently in Banyuls, near his Aleppo pine. When he learned of the death of his old friend, Jacques Lacan hurriedly penned a few words to Renée: "I have learned that Henri has died. I am appalled." [3] He was afraid for himself. He had only four more years to live and could already feel his vitality slipping away. He was growing deaf, spent long periods before cubes and bits of string, seeking, like some errant logician, the formal order that would allow psychoanalysis never to sink into the black mire of occultism; the founder's last struggle. He looked on the past with bitterness, increasingly came to misjudge his own entourage, and entrusted his doctrine's fate to his family circle. He was horrified by old age and afraid of death. Quite the opposite of Freud. "No doubt I have won," he wrote in 1976 for the preface to a volume of *Ornicar?* on the 1953 split, "since I have succeeded in conveying what I thought of the unconscious, the principle of practice. I won't say it here. Because everything published here, particularly coming from my own hand, horrifies me. To the extent that I thought I had forgotten it, as he who publishes me can attest. To no longer want to think of something is not, however, to forget it, alas! The feeble individual subject to psychoanalysis always becomes a scoundrel. Let it be known." [4]

For the French history of psychoanalysis, the barricades of May played the role of the advent of talkies onto the great Hollywood scene: *Sunset Boulevard.* . . .

As far as the study of psychiatry was concerned, the student rebellion had as an immediate effect not only the imposition of reforms which had been demanded since 1965, but the dismantling, through a kind of historical acceleration, of the entire tradition represented by Ey for dynamic aspects and by Daumézon for institutional psychotherapy. The gradual defeat followed the apparent victory of the twofold establishment in France of the themes of the antipsychiatric movement and of a diffuse Reichianism.

In a first phase, the introduction of that double problematic did not modify the organization of the study of psychiatry, but the reference to the mythical figure of Reich, a persecuted psychoanalyst who was mad to boot, served as a nodal point for a global contestation of the psychiatro-psychoanalytic movement. Through the antipsychiatric figure of the "schizo," Reich's grandiose insanity was invoked as the powerful symbol of a revolution rediscovered.

It was no accident that the journal *Arguments* was the first in France after the war to speak of Freudo-Marxism and Reichian dissidence, thirty years after the publication by ESI of the famous expurgated text.[5] Created in 1956 by Kostas Axelos, Edgar Morin, Roland Barthes, François Feitjö, Pierre Fougeyrollas and several others, the publication surfaced during the period of de-Stalinization that marked (for the PCF) the end of the Zhdanovian crusade against psychoanalysis and so-called "bourgeois" science. Now the founders of the journal, and particularly Edgar Morin, situated their work in the context of a vast movement attempting to revise Marxism in a humanist direction. Whence a reexamination of established bodies of knowledge, pursued in terms both libertarian and anthropological. Between 1956 and 1962, the journal revealed the thought of Heidegger, Marcuse, and Jakobson to France, even as it opened the path to a meditation on dissidence that was different from that of *Les Temps modernes*. The themes thus activated would course through the May revolt. The journal halted publication, for lack of subscribers, when there appeared on the horizon a contrary movement promising a radical critique of humanism and revisionism whose thematic would also encounter the May revolt. In 1983, Edgar Morin used the phrase "intellectual freeze" to refer to the structuralist explosion that put an end, in his opinion, to an experiment of which the least that can be said is that it was not foreign to that explosion, if only through its publication of the works of Roman Jakobson. "What strikes me today," he said, "is the brutality and the rapidity of the intellectual freeze at the beginning of the 1960s. All the great inquiries whose bearers we were were swept away. Marxism was reconstituted in one of its most rigid and authoritarian forms: that of Althusser. . . . The century entered into a new obscurantist tunnel until the explosion of May 1968." [6] To each his own barricade!

In a 1960 issue of *Arguments* devoted to "the problem: man" and bearing as a subtitle "Anthropologie, marxisme, et psychanalyse," there is an article by Kostas Axelos on *Civilization and its Discontents,* another by Joseph Gabel on the "Crisis of Marxism in Its Relation with Psychology," and still another on "Reich and Sexual Economy." Those three texts were more interested in delineating the meaning of Reichian doctrine than in the double exclusion its author had fallen victim to. And the journal's appeal was to an anthropological vision of Freudianism in its critique of Stalinist Marxism and psychoanalytic orthodoxy. A fourth article by Herbert Marcuse contained themes he had developed the previous year in a seminar at the École pratique des hautes études. [7]

Unlike Reich, Marcuse was not a clinician and his work does not belong to the internal history of the psychoanalytic movement. Nevertheless, the man's geographic trajectory partook of the same migration from east to west that brought many a European therapist to the territories of the New World. A German Jew, Marcuse collaborated with the Frankfurt School before fleeing Nazism in 1933. In the United States, he was affiliated with such universities as Columbia, Brandeis, and the University of California at San Diego. If Marcuse was not a Reichian in the strict sense, his appeal to the Marxo-Freudian heritage led him to a radical critique of the very revisionism placed in the docket by Lacan during the same period. But Marcuse did not effect any orthodox reelaboration of Freudianism. On the contrary, he proposed a new "revision" of the Viennese doctrine, capable, through a kind of reverse symmetry, of opposing the old revisionism, which was attacked as adaptive. To do so, he above all attacked culturalism in an inaugural volume published in 1955 and entitled *Eros and Civilization.* Like Reich, he called into question the notion of the death instinct, reproached Freud for his pessimism, and opened the 1970s to an entire libertarian thematic centered on the prevalence of the imaginary. In 1964, *Eros and Civilization* was translated into French. Four years later, *One Dimensional Man,* which was written at the time of the translation of the preceding book, appeared. [8] The two works enjoyed considerable success, allowing intellectual France to discover, forty years late, the hoary epic of Freudo-Marxism. In a few years the major works of Wilhelm Reich were not only translated but received commentaries and introductions outside the channels formerly opened up by Victor Fay and in the margins of "official" psychoanalysis, whether Lacanian or orthodox. The effervescence would be followed in short order by a reinterment.

Just as the expanding psychoanalytic societies underwent institutional crises linked to the increase in the number of clinical practitioners, so the French psychiatric movement found itself since 1950 in a state of permanent malaise as a result of the increasingly marked specialization of the various medical fields. The arrival of the pharmaceutical straitjacket, the gradual development of community-oriented therapies emergent from the experiments of Bonneval and Saint-Alban, and the ever greater impact of psychoanalysis led to a profound shattering of the former dynamic edifice. The French history of that breakup is long-term in duration. It began in 1949 with the creation of the entity of "neuropsychiatry" and continued until 1969 with the abolition of that same entity. Between those two dates, the rise of sectorization occurred, and the contradiction between psychiatry, neurology, and psychoanalysis became more pronounced as institutional practice obliged the professional psychiatrist—private or state—to define his identity.

In 1949, the French government insisted, through the Social Security bureaucracy, on a specialized definition of the psychiatric function in order to reimburse patients. In response to that request, the psychiatric guild, against the advice of EP, invented the term of "neuropsychiatry." Through it, psychiatry, which until then had been a marginal (albeit medical) field, received official recognition. But at the same time, it found itself subject to that neurology from which it had achieved independence in the course of its long struggle for the recognition of the autonomy of "mental"—as opposed to "nervous"—diseases. The latter were at times regarded as the province of psychoanalysis, at others as that of neurology.

Ten years after the creation of a specialization in neuropsychiatry came the medical reform uniting university teaching and clinical practice with the creation of "centres hospitalo-universitaires" (CHU). In that reform, psychiatry as such was forgotten, since it was absorbed by neurology. It thus benefited from neither autonomous teaching nor a distinct specialty.[9] Forced, in the face of neurology, to defend its autonomy, it was threatened on another flank by the expansion of psychoanalysis, both medical and lay. Now that threat materialized at a time when the progress of pharmacology demonstrated the bond between mental reality and physico-chemical structure, that is, at a moment when, logically, psychiatry should have been mending its fences with neurology in order not to be confused with a psychoanalytic science that tended rigorously to separate the organic from the psychic. Whence this paradox: in order to obtain legitimate status and institutional power, psychiatry had to take its distance from a field toward which it was drawn but which dominated it, without being able truly to ally itself with another that imperiled it. A crisis was inevitable and would lead to the dissolution of the celebrated dynamic tradition which had facilitated the implantation of psychoanalysis.

The only place in which that tradition persisted was that of sectorization. Ever since the circular of March 1960, the policy of geographic division, which concretized the end of the "alienist" tradition and the emergence from a segregationist universe, had been implemented by the government. But since it had been done with extreme slowness and was not followed by a reform of psychiatric study capable of eliminating the dominance of neurology, it had few effects. When it did produce some, it caused psychiatry to evolve toward a new form of segregation, since its result was to promote the extension of a medico-administrative system in which madness became the systematic object of obligatory treatment by way of tracking and preventive measures.

Given that situation of enduring malaise, the EP group, under the leadership of Henri Ey, decided to devote a few days each year to a general redefinition of the

field of psychiatry. Three great themes were on the agenda: the training of psychiatrists, the reform of the 1838 law and of juridical criteria of evaluation, and finally
the problem of the separation of neurology and psychiatry with a possible redefinition of the field of child psychiatry. All the stars of the movement participated in the
council, with every tendency represented: Georges Daumézon, Lucien Bonnafé, Jean
Ayme, Roger Misès, Serge Leclaire, André Green, and many others. Numerous papers were presented with opinion polls and statistics, and the discussion continued
the following year. In 1967 "days" of conclusion were held. All the documents were
gathered in a *Livre blanc de la psychiatrie française* ["White book of French psychiatry"] published in three volumes.[10]

   At the same time, Henri Ey wrote a *Plan d'organisation du champ de la
psychiatrie* [*Organizational Plan for the Field of Psychiatry*][11] in which he proposed
a series of reforms reflecting his doctrine. Faithful to organo-dynamism, he defended
the integration of psychoanalysis into medicine on the condition that both be permanently revivified thanks to their reciprocal relations. Envisaged from that point
of view, the integration was to allow psychoanalysis not to sink into an academic
dogmatism and medicine not to conceal the status of the subject. In the organodynamic conception, that first integration was inseparable from the maintenance of
a connection between psychiatry and neurology. Although he did not accept the
creation of a neuropsychiatric specialization, Ey always affirmed the *theoretical* necessity of not separating psychiatry from neurology. At that stage of his thought, he
was thus caught in a contradiction between a theoretical position, which supported
integration, and an institutional point of view which rejected it. That is why, in
1966, he attempted for the last time to save their unity. In the name of organo-
dynamism, he proposed simultaneously to integrate psychoanalysis into a renewed
medicine (as much in the training of therapists as in the knowledge dispensed) and
to maintain the link between psychiatry and neurology. He thus couched the problem epistemologically, even though he realized that the institutional—and even doctrinal—history of those specializations was evolving toward separatism. That is
how matters stood for him when, over a period of three years, the *Livre blanc*
"days" were held.

   There were several tendencies within EP, of which the least that can be said
is that they furthered reflection on organizational issues at the expense of theoretical
elucidation. Through such a position, the group showed that it had itself evolved
toward the perspective of the breakup imposed by the institutional situation of psychiatry. Some proposed a narrow separatism, whereas others advocated an accommodation with neuropsychiatry. Still others were happy to observe the splintering
of the field of psychiatry without proposing any remedy. All were in agreement on
two points: the necessity of psychiatry's autonomy, both for the training of therapists and for the conquest of the university, and the elimination of the 1838 law,
which had long been rendered archaic by the transition from a segregationist school
of "alienism" to "open" psychiatry. In the discussions, no one was interested in the
status of psychoanalysis, with the exception of Serge Leclaire, who proposed to the
psychiatrists, not without a touch of humor, that they reflect on the conceivable

scientificity of their knowledge, making use of the model furnished by Lacan for the case of Freud's teachings.[12]

One can understand why, at the time he published his plan, Henri Ey was attacked on all fronts. By the psychoanalysts of the SPP, on one side, who, like Nacht, Misès, or Green, accused him of wanting to liquidate psychoanalysis, and by old Professor Heuyer on the other, who reproached him, on the contrary, with being too favorable to it.[13] In point of fact, it was the entire edifice of organo-dynamism that was declaring its bankruptcy. When he contributed his conclusion to the *Livre blanc* "days," Henri Ey was thus reversing direction and renouncing his unitary projects, which were being contradicted both by institutional reality and by a doctrinal split. "My international contacts," he declared, "have shown me that a tendency I believe to be irresistible is moving toward a practical separation of the two disciplines (psychiatry and neurology). I personally have deeply regretted this and still deplore it, since I am well aware of what danger threatens psychiatry when it allows itself to be dragged out of its orbit to the infinite horizons of a kind of general semantics of human situations and relations, in which, losing its object, it runs the risk of losing its existence. But since we are not yet at that stage, despite the threats facing it, through the very excess of the interpretations which risk dissolving its concepts and its effectiveness, it may reasonably be thought that this tendency to the dissolution of psychiatric reality may also be a reaction against its mechanization through the assimilation of mental illnesses to purely neurological disturbances. I think the moment has come for me to affirm that *psychiatry exists,* and that, existing, it has a right to an *autonomy* which is the very one that most psychiatrists in the world claim for it, even if they are occasionally imprudent enough to confuse it with a purely 'anthropological' conception, with the human condition in general, and to want it independent only in order to dissolve it." [14]

The reform process initiated with the *Livre blanc* was accelerated by the events of May. Thanks to student protests, hospital psychiatrists obtained the desired transformations. Psychiatry was separated from neurology and awarded teaching chairs, while the 1838 law was officially acknowledged to be outdated without for all that being modified. In addition, a national union of French psychiatrists was founded. As for sectorization, it was reinforced by the application of the decrees of March 1972. These gave concrete reality to the extension of psychiatry's authority over society as a whole: The madman no longer went to an asylum, but the geographic grid allowed psychiatrists to detect madness even before its symptoms disturbed the public peace. The era of preventive normalization was thus succeeding that of the "alienated" subject. Lacan did not say anything different when he spoke of the "subject of science."

The reform process was thus twofold. Freed from the tutelary authority of neurology, psychiatry could also take its distance from psychoanalytic practice and seek alliances with other domains, as it could now demonstrate a scientificity no longer conferred by its former affiliation with neurology. Now that process of distancing in relation to psychoanalysis was occurring at a time when, through an opposite and short-lived effect, psychiatrists were continuing to flow toward analytic couches and succeeding in their claim that the human sciences should have a place in their own discipline. In that new configuration, psychiatric science "dissolved," even though the institutional autonomy of psychiatry had just been affirmed. The creation of different "branches" within a domain that no longer had any homogeneity was merely a sign of the liquidation of the field of psychiatry and of the splintering of its doctrine into cloistered locales established by corporatist interests. In October 1972, government authorities thus established an academic option called "pedopsychiatry." The decision was strenuously fought by the psychiatrists' union and by Bonnafé, Ey, and Daumézon, who denounced its absurdity.

A year later, upon leaving the position of editor-in-chief of *Évolution psychiatrique* to a younger generation, Ey submitted his last balance sheet after twenty-seven years of activity as head of affairs. He noted the general tendency toward the isolation of groups and schools within the discipline and the accentuation of a corporatist or guild mentality. Then he announced that the journal was in decline and that its research had grown somnolent. Finally, he emphasized that psychiatrists were deserting EP, even though their number had doubled nationally. "Is this not an opportune time for our society," he asked, "to attempt to clarify and elevate the debate, in order to try for the present crisis of psychiatry to express all the fruitful potentialities it bears within and not to evolve toward the misery and discredit of psychiatry?"[15] The elevation of the debate would not materialize; the dynamic movement was teetering at the brink of its own grave.

On the eve of the 1980s, the door was thus open in France to an orientation (which was already quite powerful in the United States) tending, on the one hand, to ally psychiatry with biology and the "neurosciences," in order to make it scientific, and, on the other, to liquidate the Freudo-Bleulerian nosology and replace them with a behaviorist classification based on information theory and on exclusively pharmacological aims. The definitive liquidation of the dynamic tendency, which had allowed for the implantation of psychoanalysis, occurred in 1983 with the French translation of the *Diagnostic and Statistical Manual of Mental Disturbances,* better known in French as *DSM III.* That year, at the World Congress of Psychiatry, which took place in Vienna in July, rather odd homage was paid Freud by a German therapist who announced that the historic role of psychoanalysis had now come to an end. "*DMS III,*" wrote Marc Lander after the congress, "is not a challenge; it's an undeclared war against Europe and the extraordinary invention it made through the voice, pen, and flesh of the representative of one of its countries of highest culture, the Austro-Hungarian Empire, dismantled during Freud's lifetime. That invention, psychoanalysis, to the highest degree respectful of man, of his quality and his specificity, has always been perversely misused by America, from which one does well to recall that Freud expected nothing."[16] It would be hard to find better words. . . .

Henri Ey was not wrong to call the famous *Livre blanc* a "black book," and the time was distant when he could write: "What psychiatry owes to psychoanalysis is having, thanks to Freud, rediscovered the meaning of its own existence . . . , that of man restored to his imaginary nature."[17]

Threatened "on the right" by new alliances and by splintering, the dynamic legacy was equally troubled "on the left" by antipsychiatric protest, whose effects began to be felt with the May revolt.

Already in 1961, *L'Histoire de la folie* had sounded the death knell of the modern epic of the psychiatric discipline by denouncing the illusions of Enlightenment humanism and the notion of "progress." "This book," Foucault wrote, "has not wanted to write the history of the mad alongside reasonable men, or facing them, nor the history of reason in its opposition to madness. It was a matter of writing the history of their incessant but perpetually shifting division. . . . It was not medicine which defined the limits between reason and madness, but, since the nineteenth century, physicians who were charged with keeping watch over the frontier and standing guard over it. There they marked 'mental illness,' an indication with the force of banishment." [18]

As soon as the book appeared, Henri Ey got the message, and for several years, he meditated on what he called its exercise in "psychiatricide." He was not wrong: Michael Foucault was declaring war on the foundations of a discipline to which Ey had devoted his life. It was something terrible for him. Ey remained above all a clinical practitioner, a leader of men, an organizer, and the head of a school. He was neither an historian nor a theorist in the strict sense, and his "Thomism" took the form of an adhesion to the natural order of things. He favored a far too continualist conception of history, close to Ellenberger's, and that was why Foucault's endeavor was a direct affront to his sense of psychiatry. For Ey, history was to be thought of in terms of evolution. There were no breaks, recastings, rearticulations or dark continents, but a constant progress. For him, the history of psychiatry did not begin with Pinel; it fused with the gradual adventure of a painstaking extrication of "natural" mental illness from the domain of magical thought.

Aware of the importance of the philosopher's enterprise, he decided to devote an EP colloquium to the "ideological conception of *Histoire de la folie.*" The meeting took place in Toulouse in December 1969. Michel Foucault did not attend. "We are faced here," Ey declared, "with a psychiatricidal stance so laden with consequences for the very idea of man that we would have very much wished for the presence of Michel Foucault among us. Both to present to him the fitting homage of our admiration for the systematic achievements of his thought and to contest that 'mental illness' can be considered as the marvelous manifestation of madness or more exceptionally as the very spark of poetic genius, for it is something other than a cultural phenomenon. If some of us, distressed by the vulnerability of their own positions or lured by M. Foucault's brilliant paradoxes, did not desire a debate, for my part, I regret the absence of a 'face-to-face' encounter. Michel Foucault, whom I invited, regrets it as much as we do, as he wrote me, apologizing for his inability to be in Toulouse these days. We will thus proceed as though he were here. In an intellectual debate, the physical presence of those who, precisely, confront each other only through their ideas is of little importance." [19]

The calling into question of the notion of "mental" illness and the critique of a psychiatry judged to be pathogenic were also the objectives of the antipsychiatry movement, whose adventure began in England around 1959 with the clinical experiments of Ronald Laing, Aaron Esterson, and David Cooper. Here too, as for Freud with the discovery of hysteria, or for Lacan in the case of paranoia, a woman played the role occupied by Anna O. at the end of the last century and by Aimée during the 1930s. Her name was Mary Barnes and she was a nurse. She was about forty years old when she met the team of British antipsychiatrists. Thanks to them, she would be cured of a case of schizophrenia judged to be incurable, would write the book of her "voyage," and would become a recognized painter.[20]

In the eyes of the three refractory psychiatrists, madness had a history because it "was" a history: the history of a voyage, a passage, a situation, and not an illness. The critique of the notion of mental illness began for them with the rejection of the Bleulerian legacy and thus with a new definition of the status of schizophrenia. It was no accident that experiments in antipsychiatry developed differently in the United Kingdom and in California, on the one hand, and in Italy, on the other. On those three fronts the contesting of psychiatry occupied the place taken in France by the enlightened dynamism of Henri Ey, by institutional psychotherapy, and by the Lacanian renewal. Antipsychiatry movements found their entry in countries where medical and orthodox psychoanalysis had become the accepted norm and where dynamic psychiatry had developed in a manner even more rigid than that. The protesters were all marked by an itinerary that went from the struggle against colonialism to transculturalism, by way of a political commitment. Gregory Bateson was an anthropologist, David Cooper was born in South Africa and had fought apartheid, and Franco Basaglia was a militant of the Italian Communist Party. As for Ronald Laing, his trajectory was somewhat different, but it too had been marked by the saga of a "voyage." Born in Glasgow and analyzed by Winnicott, he became a psychoanalyst around 1957. Then, in 1961, he entered the Tavistock Clinic. Within the British Society, he was part of the celebrated group of independents, who were in a minority in relation to the tendencies represented by Anna Freud and Melanie Klein. He had been a psychiatrist in the British army, and Gandhi's India constituted a privileged point of reference for him.

Gregory Bateson was the first to study families of schizophrenics, by way of an experiment conducted in New Guinea in the 1930s. He had observed that the natives made use of particular techniques to protect the internal equilibrium of their community. Thus in order to neutralize a rival in love, they would have recourse to sexual transvestism. But missionaries and white men sought to ban such practices with the result that the indigenous culture ran the double risk of being destroyed from without and of suffering wrongs from within. In 1956, on the basis of that observation, Bateson invented the notion of the "double bind" to designate the dilemma in which a schizophrenic finds himself enclosed when he is forced to respond to two contradictory messages that forbid him from formulating a symbolic judgment or finding his bearings. In that perspective, the notion of mental illness, as validated by the discourse of psychiatry, is shattered to the advantage of a definition of a *being schizophrenic* conceived in terms of situations. Thus schizophrenia was no longer a psychotic structure and even less an illness, but an unconscious strategy taking the form of an insane response to a situation of familial or social alienation.[21]

The word "antipsychiatry" was not invented by Bateson, but by Cooper, who was inspired, like Laing, by theses of Sartre, and more generally by existential phenomenology, in theorizing his clinical experience. In 1962, he founded Pavilion 21 in a huge psychiatric hospital to the northwest of London and began an adventure that would bring him to a radical rejection of Bleulerian psychiatry, on the one hand, and institutional psychotherapy on the other. For both did indeed retain the nodal point of mental illness as psychotic structure and as the explanation of madness. If madness were not an illness, but a *metanoia,* as Laing called it, that is a "passage," why treat it rather than allow it to express itself? With that question, Cooper began to ask the personnel of Pavilion 21 to stop doing anything. He then said to one of the patients: "I give you this thing called Largactil to calm you down a little, so we can concern ourselves with more pressing matters." Finally, he allowed refuse to accumulate in the corridors and rooms of the establishment. Dishes were no longer washed and tables remained dirty. Gradually, the patients were able to descend into hell, regress, play with their excrement, rediscover a kind of lost archaic existence and then reascend to the world of the living. At the beginning, the therapeutic staff resisted and sought to return a community gone mad to proper ways. But soon Cooper proposed that the formerly ill become caregivers and that inmates be accorded the right to a sexual life. Despite terrible conflicts and setbacks, the experiment succeeded: Homes were created outside the hospital, and antipsychiatry, as the negation of psychiatry, was born. Its history would be rather short—it came to an end in 1970—but eight years on the English scene demonstrated something unprecedented: In certain specific conditions, schizophrenia can be cured, whereas it had always been considered untreatable, hereditary, organic, and unapproachable.[22]

Parallel to that experiment, Cooper joined Laing in writing a book entitled *Reason and Violence,* in which Sartre's theses on the subjects of totalization, dialectic, and the relation to the other were analyzed and used. The two friends sent their work to the philosopher, who supported their undertaking, saying he was convinced the English effort would give psychiatry a more human face. Thus at a time when the French intellectual scene was rejecting Sartrean philosophy in favor of a tendentially antihumanist structuralism, the British psychiatric movement drew inspiration from it in rejecting a structural tradition which had reigned during the glory days of humanist psychiatry. And to top off the paradox, it was not by way of Sartre that antipsychiatry would become known in France in 1967, but rather through a Lacanian channel.[23]

In 1965, Cooper, along with Laing and Esterson, founded the Philadelphia Association. Financed through the generosity of American philanthropists, it announced a libertarian program whose objective was to free madness, not only from the asylum, which was already done, but from psychiatry itself, and thus from illness. In order to receive the newly unshackled entity, specific welcome sites were to be created in all corners of the globe. As opposed to psychiatry, antipsychiatry was not intent on being "sectorized," but on allowing the mad to live out their madness. The same year, in London, Kingsley Hall opened its doors. Situated in a working-class neighborhood, the two-story brown brick edifice was formerly the site of research and social activities. Gandhi had stayed there in 1931 at the time he was negotiating the independence of India with the British government. Ronald Laing was to be found there thirty-three years later, with his friends, giving shelter to schizophrenics. Before long Kingsley Hall became the symbol of a genuine antipsychiatric revolution. Aside from its welcoming function, the house was a site of transition in which various seminars were held. Weaving, yoga, and Indian dancing were practiced there. Plays were acted and films shown. Soon visitors began arriving from all over the world and learned to share in the life of the community; at the same time they were initiated into the voyage of schizophrenics.[24]

Two years after the creation of Kingsley Hall, the antipsychiatrists organized an international congress on dialectic and liberation, intended to reveal the manner in which hell was progressing in the world. The colloquium lasted sixteen days and inscribed the movement in the framework of the libertarian adventure. It brought together American blacks, Amsterdam "provos," students from West Berlin, and representatives of all the Third World movements. Gregory Bateson, Stokeley Carmichael, and Herbert Marcuse participated in the discussions. Madness unshackled thus offered a new banner for all the world's oppressed to rally to. All that was missing was to add Soviet dissidence to the movement for the whole edifice of classical psychiatry to begin tottering. That addition took place in 1971, at a time when the Kingsley Hall experiment was already over and Vladimir Bukovsky's book, *A New Mental Illness in the U.S.S.R.: Opposition,* appeared simultaneously in several languages.[25]

The antipsychiatric movement did not take root as such in France, but it intersected with the history of psychiatry and psychoanalysis by way of Lacanianism. In 1967, Maud Mannoni decided to devote "study days" to child psychosis. Accompanied by Ginette Raimbault, who was equally familiar with the British situation, she visited Donald Winnicott to invite him to participate in the colloquium. Lacan was quite eager for the visit of the distinguished English therapist, who had once presided over the first commission of inquest sent by the IPA. Relations between the two men had always been complicated because of their respective positions concerning the IPA.

On Jones's advice in 1923, Winnicott ended up spending ten years on James Strachey's couch before undertaking a second analysis with Joan Rivière. During the interwar years, he had observed the quarrel pitting Kleinians against Anna-Freudians on the subject of child analysis. Refusing to choose sides, he developed in the margins his own clinical experiment, centered on play, the "false self," and the "transitional object." In the face of the dogmatism reigning in the two groups, he always insisted on an independence that earned him a reputation as a nonconformist. As a result, he had been denied any honorific position within the British Society. Since no split occurred in England, Winnicott agreed to submit "officially" to the accepted rules even though his clinical practice did not conform to the imposed criteria. In Great Britain, "formal" compliance counted more than an admission of insubordination. Which was why in 1953, even though he grasped the significance of Dolto's work, Winnicott played the game of normalization: He reproached his interlocutor with the "charismatic" aspect of the role she had taken on.

Although he "officially" disavowed the alleged "charisma" of the masters, within his own society Winnicott became the leader of a school. Very early on, he became interested in Lacan's work, and the latter reciprocated his interest. There was a common concern linking their respective work which bore on object relations: the Englishman's "transitional object" and the Frenchman's "objet a." Nevertheless, Winnicott remained perplexed by Lacan's prose, which he could not understand. In August of 1967, he conveyed to him his uncertainties concerning an article in *La Psychanalyse* on Jones's symbolism. On that occasion, he invited him to come to London, but the visit was delayed because of the Amsterdam colloquium on female sexuality and the meeting at Bonneval. A short time later the Turquet commission began its interrogations.[26]

When Ginette Raimbault and Maud Mannoni arrived in London, the 1963 split had wreaked its disastrous effects on communications between the members of the IPA and the Lacanians. Already old and sick, Winnicott had just been named, for the first time in his life, president of the British Society. The distinction was important in his eyes since it conferred on his work an "official" recognition that was far from negligible. It would not be long before his writings would be translated into French and would have a considerable impact within the three societies: the EFP, the SPP, and the APF. Winnicott thus received the two women with great warmth, but he declined their offer (to which he had initially been inclined to respond favorably). In his position as president, he did not want to run the risk of appearing to endorse, through his physical presence, a movement rejected by the IPA: as respect for forms demanded. . . . [27] Nonetheless, he agreed to contribute a text that might be read at the colloquium and constitute a testimonial. Shrewdly, he proposed that his visitors contact his young students in the Society and particularly Ronald Laing. It was thus that Maud Mannoni went to Kingsley Hall and met Mary Barnes at a time when she was covering the walls of her room with excrement. She would long remember an astonishing comment by Laing, referring to the fecal exhibition: "It's rather beautiful, but somewhat lacking in color." Mannoni did a control with Winnicott and became friends with Laing.[28]

The colloquium on childhood psychoses took place in Paris in October of 1967. Winnicott sent the promised text on schizophrenia and announced in writing that he had been "obliged" to modify his initial decision to be present at the meeting. François Tosquelles, Laing, and Cooper were the only lecturers who were not from the house of Lacan, and it was with the latter two that a first confrontation occurred pitting the French structural view against the existential conceptions of the English. All the internal tendencies of Lacanianism were represented: Françoise Dolto, Jenny Aubry, Rosine Lefort, Ginette Raimbault, René Tostain, Anne-Lise Stern, and Maud Mannoni for child analysis as well as Ginette Michaud and Jean Oury for the institutional psychotherapy of the Château de La Borde. The papers were published under the title *Enfance aliénée* in two volumes of the journal *Recherches*. They would be reissued after successive printings were sold out.

Although none of the stars of the non-Lacanian societies participated in the meetings, they enjoyed considerable success with young therapists of all tendencies. They discovered antipsychiatry on that occasion and vented their malaise concerning psychiatry. The gathering served as something of a prelude to the protests of May.

It was during those days that Françoise Dolto presented the twelve therapeutic sessions of a fourteen-year-old child. Taking the opposite tack from the case of "little Hans," who was analyzed by Freud through his father's words, Françoise reported the words and sentences of Dominique with great precision. The case would become famous. The child was phobic. He was afraid of bicycles and merry-go-rounds. He spoke in a mannered or nasal voice, never laughed in the presence of others, and had no knowledge of masturbation. His mother, raised in Africa by nuns in a colonialist spirit, was unaware of the existence of such practices. She allowed her son to sleep in her bed for a long time. As for the father, a business man, he traveled a great deal. He was of the opinion that surgery would be preferable to psychotherapy for solving Dominique's problems. Extremely awkward, weighed down by failure at school, the child was unable to count. He was afraid of multiplication tables—he could "count on no one." He related his story with the help of a fantasied bestiary in which dogs, cows, oxen, fish, and goats were mixed together.

Although she did not employ an antipsychiatric approach, Françoise Dolto, from the very first session, acknowledged Dominique's right to be "nuts." She told him he was being illogical because he was afraid of being scolded. To his family, she issued a diagnosis of psychosis, using the word madness. The mother was relieved. No doctor had dared to pronounce that word. What they evoked was generally retarded growth, with assurances that "things would work out." Over the course of a year, there developed between the doctor and the child a fabulous dialogue in which sexuality, transference, the Oedipus complex, and identifications were symbolized in a language of images. During the fourth session, Dominique explained that the cow dreamed of being an ox and the ox it dreamed of itself dreamed of being a cow. Françoise then asked her patient if he knew the difference between oxen and bulls. According to him, bulls were "nastier" and the cow was a "cow who thought herself to be a sacred ox." Françoise replied without hesitation: "I think that the sacred ox or the sacred cow is perhaps there because of a crush you have on Madame Dolto; you want to make her sacred." Dominique blushed deeply and added: "Yes . . . That yes."

During the eighth session, the child began to be able to count; Françoise spoke to him of breasts, "cocks," "pricks," and penises. Gradually, Dominique's stories became less insane. The child succeeded in evoking the racist ideals of his maternal family, then in rediscovering his right to aggressive behavior. His backwardness at school began to disappear. But during the eleventh session, the father refused to continue the treatment and wanted to resort to surgery. Even though the child wanted to pursue his therapy, he obeyed, with Dolto's agreement. He announced his intention to return when he would be big and able to pay for his treatment. "Dominique was cured only of his psychotic regression," Françoise emphasized. "A delayed elaboration of the components of his Oedipus complex is underway. His sexuality has been rehabilitated for his narcissism, as has his body, in its humanity, as well. His critical sense is now finding expression. He has affective relations with others. He has regained confidence in his future. He is taking charge of his desire for freedom, for which he confesses he is willing (angrily) to put things off in the name of his father's authority." [29]

For the final session of the colloquium, Lacan delivered one of the sublime addresses for which he was gifted. Taking up anew the theme of his October proposal, he spoke of segregation and freedom. In passing, he offered stirring homage to his old friend Henri Ey: "To start out from that well-centered object," he said, "I would like you to experience its unity by way of a few sentences I uttered twenty years ago at a meeting with our friend Henri Ey, of whom you are aware that he was within the field of psychiatry in France what we call a civilizer. He posed the question of what mental illness might be in such a way that it may be said that at the least it awakened the body of psychiatrists in France to the gravest question as to what that body itself represented." [30] Then, as when speaking of racism and religion, he announced the entry of an entire world into a segregationist universe. Wherein the themes of the "camps" and the "subject of science" could be detected.

It will be easily understood why the Lacanian tendency was alone among all those in France to be receptive to the antipsychiatrists' message, without for all that sharing their convictions. Lacanianism occupied a position of contestation in the country which made it an ideological equivalent of antipsychiatry. But paradoxically its implantation served both as a filter and an obstacle to antipsychiatry to the extent that it did not abandon the "structural order" of dynamic psychiatry. The 1967 confrontation showed, moreover, that structural theses and existential conceptions could intersect without melding; they said the same things through different channels and confirmed the validity of the position taken a quarter of a century earlier by Georges Canguilhem on the basis of work by Kurt Goldstein: Illness is not a deviation in relation to a norm but a displacement of the norm. It brings with it a new order by perturbing a structure that is itself in a situation of permanent disturbance. In that sense, antipsychiatry was the existential reverse of dynamic psychiatry. It replaced the prestige of psychiatry with the prestige of madness and thus participated in the historical decline of dynamism. For Lacan, that decline announced the "subject of science" and the return of a process of segregation. Freed from the asylum by dynamic psychiatry, then from dynamic psychiatry by antipsychiatry, the madman had every chance of finding himself alienated by a medical science all the more powerful in that it would have besieged the mental realm in the name of biological or behaviorist rationality.

The conceptions of antipsychiatry were broadly disseminated in France with the translation of the principal works of Laing, Cooper, Basaglia, and Thomas Szasz. In 1970, Maud Mannoni published *Psychiatrie et Antipsychiatrie* in the "Champ freudian" series. It would be the only book emanating from that tendency to appear in a psychoanalytic collection. Maud Mannoni was also the only person in France to set up an institution inspired by the English model of antipsychiatry. Her shelter took the name the Experimental School of Bonneuil-sur-Marne. It functioned as an association under the jurisdiction of the law of 1901, outside the purview of institutions controlled by the Social Security bureaucracy. As a result its status was that of a private school. After six years of bitter struggle and difficulties in attaining financing, Maud Mannoni obtained the recognition of the Social Security Administration, with the risk that the school might become an "ordinary" institution.

At the start, the experiment worked thanks to the benevolence of most of the caregivers. It was animated by Maud Mannoni and Robert Lefort and received the support of Françoise Dolto, Jean Ayme, Rosine Lefort, and Pierre Fedida, a member of the APF. Although similar to an antipsychiatric institution and attracting a clientele excluded from the sectorized circuits, the school did not draw on the existentialist references promoted by the Anglo-Saxons.[31] Maud Mannoni invoked the antipsychiatrist's experiments and not their theses. Her inspiration was to be found in the tradition stemming from Makarenko and Freinet, to which were added Lacan and Melanie Klein. Instead of privileging the imaginary relation to the other—that is, situation as opposed to structure—Maud Mannoni took into account the symbolic order allowing the law to be embodied, and the Winnicottian notion of crisis allowing caregivers and inmates to formulate their malaise verbally. The Bonneuil school was concerned with children and adolescents, not adults. In that sense, it was more like Bruno Bettelheim's Orthogenic School than Kingsley Hall. In addition, it was interested in psychosis in general, without according priority to autism or schizophrenia.

While the English experiment stopped at the time that antipsychiatry was becoming radicalized, the Bonneuil school pursued its activities. In 1975, it became a day hospital and lost the innovative aspect that had made it something unique in France. In that respect, it may be said that the greatness of this kind of experiment lay in its ephemeral character, as though the freshness of madness unshackled could not survive the ills of old age. For the fourth psychoanalytic generation of the EFP, the Bonneuil adventure remained, until 1975, a considerable event. It gave to Lacanianism one of its most attractive faces. Thanks to that genuine struggle, Maud Mannoni leaves the ardent imprint of her courageous clinical militantism on the French history of psychoanalysis. The Fleming with the Corsican name was intent on being simultaneously a Leninist without Lenin, pro-Chinese without Mao Zedong, and a feminist without the women's movement. With her proud, clear face, crowned by strong brunette hair, and her musical voice, she was able to direct her personnel effectively. She knew her craft, as the expression goes: a cross between a prim suffragette and a victorious Communarde.

The antipsychiatric and Reichian thematic received its most brilliant French synthesis in 1972 in a book that obtained a considerable success as soon as it was published: L'anti-Oedipe.[32] It was around September 1969 that the philosopher Gilles Deleuze, already known for his works on Spinoza, Nietzsche, Sacher-Masoch, and Bergson, met Félix Guattari, a therapist come from Lacan's couch and the internal opposition within the Communist Party, who had been part of the team at La Borde since 1953. Each had the impression that the other was way ahead of him. Both had phenomenal respect for the work and person of Lacan. One was already dreaming of "desiring machines," while the other regarded psychoanalysis as miserable. "I said to myself," Deleuze emphasized, "that things would be better still if we found adequate concepts instead of using notions which are not even those of Lacan in his creative phase, but those of an orthodoxy that formed around him. It was Lacan who said: Nobody is helping me. We were going to help him schizophrenically. And we owe all the more to Lacan in that we renounced such notions as structure, symbolic, or signifier, which are poor and which Lacan, for his part, always managed to flip over to reveal their underside." [33]

The philosopher and the therapist decided to work together. They read mounds of books, exchanged letters and concepts, and thus wove their great work over a period of two and a half years. Concurrently, Deleuze gave a seminar on "Anti-Oedipus" in a small room of the department of philosophy of the new university of Vincennes–Paris VIII. Students piled into the room from every direction. They divided their time between courses in which structuralism was studied, texts of the journal *Tel quel,* articles by Derrida, and seminars in which the Lacanian return to Freud was taught. Serge Leclaire had in fact just founded a department of psychoanalysis at Paris VIII, and its office adjoined that of the department of philosophy. In the same building, Chomskyan linguistics was flourishing and crossing swords with the structuralist tradition. Like a tightrope walker with intense gaze, Deleuze each week faced an audience so compact that the little room where he spoke seemed drowned in the vapors of some Turkish bath. Febrile, exalted, and always tolerant, he formulated his thoughts in the manner of some singing madman who would have chosen his melodies from Debussy and his libretto from Charles Trenet: an opera for one voice.

Enthralled by the spectacle, the students listened with a kind of tenderness in which curiosity for an innovative discourse fused with attraction to a singular style. After each seminar, Deleuze opened the floor to his audience, responding point by point, half-serious, half-jocular, to questions raised. They were numerous, since for the first time, Freudianism and Lacanianism were being "grilled" together at the very edge of their most significant innovations. Occasionally the hardcore Maoists of the group led by Alain Badiou, formerly of the ENS, would show up, commando-style, to proclaim their hostility to the King of Thebes, anti-Oedipus, capitalism, and schizophrenia: These were the days of the red front. . . . [34]

At its publication in 1972, *Anti-Oedipe* was presented by its authors as the first volume of a larger work entitled *Capitalisme et schizophrénie.* A second part was promised and was to be entitled *Schizo-analyse.* It never appeared, but was replaced by a different book, *Milles plateaux,* published in 1980,[35] at a time when contesting psychoanalysis would be of interest to neither the intelligentsia nor the psychoanalysts themselves, who had fallen prey to crises internal to their movement. "With this first volume, *Anti-Oedipe,*" Maurice de Gandillac wrote, "one is submerged beneath an impressive flood of readings and experiences in which ethnology, linguistics, and economy are conjugated together, while philosophy in the classical sense, and even literature and the visual arts—despite the occasional references to Descartes's *Cogito* and Kant's Critique, despite a Nietzschean presence that surfaces at several points and subtends the investigation, and however numerous and significant the quotations from Beckett, Michaux, Miller, or Artaud—somehow retreat to the background." [36] The commentary captures rather well the general impression one derives from the book, whose principal theses are astonishing in their simple-mindedness. Drawing comically on the *Histoire de la folie,* the authors claimed to rethink the universal history of societies on the basis of a single and ungrounded postulate: Capitalism, tyranny, or despotism would discover their own limits in the desiring machines of a "successful" schizophrenia, that is in the nets of a madness that would not be shackled by the dominant discourse, be it named "alienism" or psychiatry. For Deleuze and Guattari, Freudian Oedipalism was the completed form of a normative encoding to the extent that it reduced the plural libido of madness to a familialist framework. To extricate oneself from it and rediscover the schizophrenic essence of true desire, one must replace all the structural, symbolic, and signifying theories emergent from psychoanalysis with a plurivalent conceptuality capable of translating the "machinelike" and plural essence of desire. To the imperialism of the sole signifier as to the totalizing Oedipal complex, the two partners opposed a *schizo-analysis* based on a "materialist" psychiatry whose first spokesman, against Freud and Bleuler, would have been Reich, followed closely by the antipsychiatrists.

If one restricts oneself to its theses, *Anti-Oedipe* is a work filled with crude formulations, errors, and gross oversights. But the book should not be reduced to its explicit content. For to do so would be to err on the subject of the book as much as a reader of *A la recherche du temps perdu* who would want to transform the Proustian saga into a story of maternal kisses and rosewater. *Anti-Oedipe* is a great book, not through the ideas it conveys but through the form it bestows on them, through its style and tone: in brief, through that febrile syntax in which—with breath held and like a Rimbaldian drunken boat—the forgotten furor of a language of rupture and unreason comes to be couched. Published at a time when the impasse of the structuralist movement was becoming clear, *Anti-Oedipe* anarchically drew to itself all the hopes of an aborted revolution. At the same time, and because it effected a specifically French synthesis of all the ideals of liberation (from Freudo-Marxism to terrorism, and from the quest for a lost paradise to the cult of drugs), it took psychoanalytic conformism as its principal target, noisily designating the degeneration of Lacanianism into a dogma. Beyond the all too frivolous debate over the "imperialism of the signifier" and the defense of a utopian figure of schizophrenia, there was a ferocious and genuine critique of all Freudian "catechisms." Whence the book's well-deserved success. Whence as well the formidable impact it had on a fragile intelligentsia which thought that thanks to it (and at minimal cost) it could now laugh off the Viennese doctrine, pointing out that the Lacano-Freudian "plague" no longer caused anyone to tremble. The problem with the whole business was that there would very quickly be a "catechism" of schizo-analysis.

As much as the antipsychiatric experiments, like those at Bonneuil, proved innovative, just so much did the practices appealed to in *Anti-Oedipe* remain traditional. Deleuze and Guattari delivered themselves of a formidable panegyric of the methods used by Jean Oury's team at the Château de La Borde. But they were in no way comparable to the innovations stemming from Kingsley Hall, Pavilion 21, and even the Orthogenic School. Emerging in 1953 from the Saint-Alban adventure, the La Borde experiment was part of the field of institutional psychotherapy. As such, it possessed that field's characteristic features: community life, the absence of white smocks, humanizing of the patient, a maintenance of classical diagnostic categories and a plurality of treatments—from electroshock to psychotherapy. To that tradition was added a Lacanian perspective, in the person of Jean Oury, a rather dogmatic disciple of the master and the inseparable companion of Guattari, who was himself a "libertarian" Lacanian of the following generation. There was thus a huge gap between the liberationist, antipsychiatric, and schizophilic theories recommended by *Anti-Oedipe* and the institutional realities those theories were said to be inspired by. The book's ambiguity lay in that gap and it would not be long before it would be denounced by former *stagiaires* and residents of the Château, exasperated at the publicity surrounding an enterprise that ended up appearing to be something it had never been.[37]

None of which prevented, in the context of the 1970s, institutions not conforming to the spirit of sectorization—and such was the case for La Borde—from being subject to the adverse aftereffects of the new organization of the field of psychiatry. In 1973, the National Insurance Administration denounced the agreement signed ten years earlier with Oury's clinic. On the eve of its twentieth anniversary, the clinic was thus threatened with extinction since patients admitted ran the risk of no longer being insured. The motivations invoked were more than suspicious. The Château was reproached for its *gauchiste* orientation, the excessive length of therapeutic stays, and, naturally, the high cost of the enterprise.[38]

The threat came—and not by accident—a month after the publication of a special issue of the journal *Recherches* dedicated to homosexualities and entitled *Trois milliards de pervers* ["Three billion perverts"]. It listed a number of prestigious collaborators: The names of Gilles Deleuze and Félix Guattari appeared alongside those of Michel Foucault, Jean Genet, Jean-Paul Sartre, Jean-Jacques Lebel, Georges Lapassade, and many others. The issue told "who our Berber lovers are," what went on at the public urinals of the Tuileries, how vice imposes itself on children, what in the world two women can do together in bed, how to care for bruised anuses, and how to have done with old-fashioned homosexuality. In the editors' collective statement, the tone was given: "A parenthetical clause for the deaf: No more than the schizo is the homosexual as such a revolutionary, the revolutionary of modern times! We simply say that, along with several others, he can be or become the locus of a major libidinal rupture in society, one of the points of emergence of that revolutionary desiring energy from which classical militantism remains disconnected. We do not for all that lose sight of the fact that there exists an infinitely unhappy asylum-type madness or an infinitely shameful and miserable Oedipal homosexuality! And yet we should be attentive even to those extreme cases of repression. May 1968 taught us to read the walls, and since then there have begun to be efforts to decipher graffiti in prisons, asylums, and today public urinals. An entire new scientific spirit remains to be elaborated." [39]

The affair was given much publicity and the issue of *Recherches* censored. As for the La Borde clinic, it would not be closed. The three institutions linked with the Lacanian current—La Borde, Bonneuil, and the Chailles Clinic, directed by Claude Jeangirard, a third generation student of the master's, were still alive in 1985. But their durability shows that, unlike the antipsychiatry experiments, they adapted to the institutional situation of their day. To that extent, they became "ordinary." What remains to be seen is what will happen when their founders retire. . . .

At the EFP congress of November 1973, the anti-Oedipal theories made their way, midst great commotion, into the Lacanian citadel and thus made the breakup of the school into divergent tendencies even more obvious. On that subject, a long polemic erupted between the team from La Borde, represented by Guattari, Oury, and Michaud, and Jenny Aubry. The "Labordians" accused Aubry of having herself contributed to the liquidation of her own experiment at the Hôpital des Enfants-Malades and of not having been able to prevent the dismissal and dispersion of her staff. But that experiment could not have continued since it was coming up against the natural limit imposed by the mandatory retirement of its principal instigator. Being a hospital physician, Jenny Aubry could not avoid her experiment's being interrupted as soon as a new "boss" arrived. And it was true that her staff had a hard time accepting her successor. In Montpellier, she defended herself as best she could, but the debate was turning to the advantage of the anti-Oedipals, who were then at the height of their triumph. Jean Oury and Félix Guattari were nonetheless more prudent than their epigones.[40]

In 1976, the authors of *Anti-Oedipe* announced: "We no longer speak much about psychoanalysis, and yet we still talk too much, far too much about it. Nothing is going on there anymore. We were profoundly tired of it, but unable to stop all at once. Psychoanalysts, and above all psychoanalysands, are just too boring. All that material, which was holding us back, had to be precipitated (without our harboring any illusions as to the objective import of such an operation). We had to subject it to an artificial acceleration capable of bringing it to a breaking point, making it crack open for us. That is over now; we will no longer talk about psychoanalysis after this book. No one will suffer, neither they nor us."[41] After that fine declaration, Félix Guattari would nevertheless continue to practice psychoanalysis and to exercise his functions as a therapist at the Château de La Borde.

At the same time as there developed in France, before and after May 1968, a (libertarian, Althusserian, and Maoist) movement to renew Marxism, an opposition current emerged in the Soviet Union. That tendency became known in the West around 1969, and in very little time led to a transformation of the revolutionary ideals of the Marxist left. In the face of the revelations coming from the East, the French intelligentsia—the very one that had pressed contestation to the limit—would make the transition to an advocacy of the principles of "dissidence."

Around 1958, a parallel body of writing was organized with the appearance of one of the first *Samizdat* periodicals created by the writer Alexander Ginzburg. Eight years later, the word was officialized. It served to parody the term *Gosizdat,* meaning "state publication" and might be translated as "self-publication." *Samizdat* was not long in being denounced by Soviet authorities as an "agent of Western imperialism"; the dissident movement had been born. It was soon transformed into a veritable resistance, on the occasion of various (parodies of) trials against opponents of the regime held between 1966 and 1968. In April 1968, there appeared in Moscow a clandestine periodical, the *Chronicle of Current Events,* in which the gamut of opposition tendencies found expression, from ultra-Stalinism to the classical right. It revealed new forms of repression that had been used for more than ten years. These consisted of interning adversaries in special psychiatric hospitals under the jurisdiction of the Minister of the Interior and controlled by the KGB.

The most spectacular case of arbitrary internment was that of General Grigorenko. Born in 1906 and graduated from the Frunze military academy, where he taught after World War II, Grigorenko was already a general when he began his gradual entry into dissidence. In February 1964, he was arrested on suspicion of anti-Soviet activities, and the KGB had him certified "psychically irresponsible for his own deeds" by the Institute of Forensic Psychiatry in Moscow. There, for more than fourteen months, he was interned, then excluded from the Communist Party and stripped of his rank.

The legal texts resorted to by the Serbsky Institute in Moscow were those of the penal code of the Socialist Republic of Russia. In a first series of provisions, it was stated that any activity of agitation, slander, opposition, or distribution of tracts or untrue assertions aimed at the regime was punishable by deprivation of freedom or fines. Plainly, this meant that any kind of political opposition to the regime was forbidden and punishable by law. The second series of legal texts resorted to by the experts corresponded more or less to Article 64 of the French penal code and the law of 1838. It defined the status of juridical irresponsibility for one's acts and the modalities of internment. These provisions stipulated that the penal responsibility of a subject may be withdrawn if he is recognized as not responsible for his acts by reason of a mental disturbance. In such cases, he can be subjected to forced or voluntary treatment in a special psychiatric hospital. The first provisions were in flagrant contradiction with the Soviet constitution, which guaranteed the democratic freedoms of its citizens.

The expert evaluation performed at the Serbsky Institute made use of the penal procedure concerning irresponsibility to arrive at a double diagnosis for General Grigorenko of paranoia and arteriosclerosis. The accused, in such a case, was no longer vulnerable to prosecution for anti-Soviet activity, but he was judged to be "insane" for both psychical and organic reasons. He thus had to be "treated." In March 1965, Grigorenko was again examined, this time in a Leningrad hospital. The commission confirmed the Moscow diagnosis, but only to declare forthwith that the general was "cured," not only of the sclerosis of his brain, which was absurd if the sclerosis actually existed, but also of his "paranoid" state. Grigorenko was released but placed under the surveillance of a dispensary near his home.

As soon as he was freed, he continued writing, reproducing, and disseminating documents denigrating the political regime. Since he was "cured" of his paranoia and arteriosclerosis, he was again vulnerable to prosecution according to the provisions of the penal code. In March 1966, he participated in a silent demonstration against the rehabilitation of Stalin. A few weeks later, he distributed to the voters of his district a letter explaining why he would not vote for Kossigin in the forthcoming elections. In January 1968, he circulated a petition demanding that Ginzburg's trial be public, as required by law. Then, in November of the same year, he delivered a resounding address at the funeral of an old Bolshevik and companion of Lenin, Kosterin. Finally, in March 1969, he distributed a tract calling for the withdrawal of Soviet troops from Czechoslovakia.

A few weeks later, he left for Tashkent to defend the Tartars of Crimea. As soon as he arrived, he was arrested by the KGB. In August, he was subjected to a new evaluation at the psychiatric clinic of Tashkent. It was at that point that things turned dramatic. The evaluation performed by the physicians at the clinic invalidated that of the Serbsky Institute, but the Leningrad diagnosis was confirmed. Grigorenko was thus judged to be fully responsible for his acts. The evaluation stipulated that he was in perfect physical health, that he showed no signs of paranoia, and that his relentlessness in wanting his ideas to triumph was indicative of his strength and originality of character. The physicians at Tashkent added this sentence, "It is not out of the question that Grigorenko, under the influence of the unpleasant psychological situation in which he found himself placed in 1964, given his original character traits, had an unhealthy reaction, judged at the Serbsky Institute to be a paranoid development." [42]

Acknowledged to be responsible for his acts, Grigorenko was thus still vulnerable to the courts. It was for that reason that in October 1969, precisely at the time a psychiatrist named Semion F. Glouzman was circulating a counter-opinion on his case similar to the Tashkent one, he was again transferred to the Serbsky Institute. A month later, he came before the evaluation team because of "doubts" concerning his state of health. That third evaluation invalidated the preceding one and moved matters back to square one. "Grigorenko," it read, "is suffering from a mental illness: a paranoid evolution of the personality underscored by the existence of reformist ideas characterized by his psychopathic personality traits and the appearance of phenomena of arteriosclerosis in the blood vessels of the brain." [43] With a diagnosis like that, the experts of the Serbsky Institute could have sent all the founding fathers of the Soviet Union, starting with Lenin, to the asylum. . . . In order to give more weight to their psychiatric argument, they explained an unprecedented phenomenon: In their opinion, the examiners at the Tashkent clinic were unable to detect the modifications in Grigorenko's psyche because the latter's *external behavior had remained normal*. His declarations had remained "to all appearances logical" and his ability to retain acquired knowledge had not suffered. The Moscow experts added that such "normality" was characteristic of pathological development. At the conclusion of the report, the question of the status of madness in the Soviet Union was thus raised. To be sure, the dissidents were unaware of the works of Michel Foucault, Freud, Lacan, and the antipsychiatrists.

And yet, during the fall of 1971, the young dissident Vladimir Bukovsky, himself the victim of arbitrary internments, raised the question in a book entitled *A New Mental Illness in the U.S.S.R.: Opposition*. The work was published in several languages. It related several tales of internment and specifically that of a former Communist, Victor Feinberg, declared "schizophrenic" by an investigatory commission after having participated in several activities of the opposition. In an open letter, Bukovsky requested Western psychiatrists to offer their opinion of the evaluations of their Soviet colleagues. "Do they contain enough data," he wrote, "that is sufficiently sustained not only to establish the existence of the mental problems those very opinions define, but further still, to conclude the necessity of isolating those persons from society? I would be very happy if you could interest your colleagues in this question and if you would deem it possible to submit it to discussion during the next world congress of psychiatry."[44]

Through that letter and that publication, Bukovsky thus addressed himself to the World Psychiatric Association (WPA), whose next congress was to open in Mexico on November 28, 1971. It will be recalled that the WPA was set up in 1950 by Henri Ey. During the congresses that followed those of Paris and took place from Zurich to Madrid, by way of Montreal, Ey remained the organization's permanent secretary. The organization itself was officially created in 1961 and took the name of WPA. In 1950, its first congress allotted time to every dynamic tendency: Freudian, non-Freudian, and neo-Freudian. The second, organized by Manfred Bleuler, was characterized by the emergence of existential and Jungian tendencies, with the personal participation of Jung and Binswanger. As for the third, it took on an exclusively psychiatric and American orientation that was no longer suited to Ey's initial project. The advance of pharmacology and the return to a narrowly conceived organicism began to produce their effects.

Ey consequently resigned in the course of the Madrid congress of 1966, where the All Union-Society, which banded together Soviet psychiatrists, was officially integrated into the organization. By the time Bukovsky sent his letter to the West, the WPA had become a veritable dinosaur, a bit like the IPA. The members of affiliated societies revealed themselves to be more concerned with tourism than brilliant theoretical exchanges, as had been the case in 1950. Four French societies were represented: Évolution psychiatrique, the Société psychanalytique de Paris, the Société médico-psychologique, and finally, the Société française de psychopathologie de l'expression.

Bukovsky's revelations could only be a source of embarrassment to the member societies of the IPA. For the evaluations performed by the Soviet psychiatrists could have been written word for word and in the same style by their colleagues in the Western democracies had they been obliged to examine Grigorenko. One finds in the documents produced by Bukovsky a language and contradictions which have been those of forensic psychiatry for as long as it has existed. Every criminal matter in the last hundred years has always turned on a battle in which expert evaluations have been as senseless as the counter-evaluations pitted against them. If one examines the world history of expert psychiatric opinion, one is forced to admit that psychiatric discourse has been as abusive in the West as in the East. In other words, Bukovsky's revelations concerned less the perversion of psychiatry in the Soviet Union than the status of a science capable of authorizing the existence of such a perversion.

In the Western democracies in which the great movements of "alienism," then dynamism flourished, psychiatry waged against official justice a battle aimed at defining the borders between reason and unreason. At stake, among other things, was protecting the criminally insane from prison and the death penalty. In France, since 1810, Article 64 allowed for the insane to be "treated" rather than "punished." But at the same time, it dehumanized the criminal by making him *irresponsible* for his acts: "There is neither crime nor misdemeanor if the accused was in a demented state at the time of the deed or if he was constrained by a force he was unable to resist." [45] Although it allowed for genuine protection of criminals, the provision was absurd since it annulled the act at the same time as the crime, whence the notion of irresponsibility.

The artisans of the dynamic reinterpretation affirmed that the madman could rediscover his place in society only if he were acknowledged to be sick. But with the crisis of dynamism, which surfaced around the years 1960–65, the question of the status of madness was posed differently. To recognize an individual to be sick was first of all to admit he was a subject. On that score, Freudian and Lacanian structural analyses converged with the existential theses of the antipsychiatrists: Everyone—mad or not—ought to be recognized as a *subject in principle*. Once that is granted, Article 64 falls under the weight of its own absurdity, since it does not recognize crime as the truth of madness. [46]

The documents produced by Bukovsky demonstrate the limits of a "science" no longer able to designate its own object. In that sense, the terminology employed by the Soviets was no different from that used by Western experts. In the one case as in the other, knowledge of madness was defined by the way in which the endless border was established between reason and unreason. There followed from the delineation of that border a system of surveillance, treatment, and repression that was based on the relations entertained by justice with psychiatry. Starting with the 1960s, the entirety of that system was forcefully condemned in the Western democracies by all the partisans of unshackling madness. From their point of view, the question of knowing whether psychiatry was abusive was no longer worth asking, since psychiatry was *in itself* an abuse of power.

And yet, if one studies the specific aspects of the history of psychiatry, according to the various modes of its establishment, the question raised by Bukovsky exceeds the problem of the definition of the status of madness. In the democracies, where the dynamic movement developed, no tribunal of experts would have had to pass judgment on the Grigorenko case. For under such regimes, only *criminal acts* are the object of psychiatric evaluations, and since political opposition is considered neither a mental illness nor a crime, no evaluation would be performed, except in cases of terrorism, physical violence, or material destruction. In democratic nations, political opposition belongs to the world of reason: It is expressed through labor unions, parties, publications, etc. In the Soviet Union, on the contrary, the Penal Code recognizes as infractions acts which, in the democracies, belong to the world of reason. As infractions, those acts can then be the object of psychiatric evaluation, following which the accused may be sent from prison to an asylum, from "responsibility" to "irresponsibility."

If one examines the situation of Soviet psychiatry from the time of the triumph of "Michurinian Pavlovianism," one can understand how a movement moving in the opposite direction from that of the democracies could develop, even as it reflected back to them the image of their own segregative modalities.

The generalized abuse of techniques of psychiatric evaluation was contemporaneous with the process of de-Stalinization and the gradual transition from a policy of massive deportation to more subtle forms of repression. It was made possible by the existence of psychiatric special hospitals and by the maintenance of a

Pavlovian standard at the heart of psychiatric "science." Finally, it was theorized by Professor Andrei Vladimirovitch Snezhnevsky, who had become director of the Institute of Psychiatric Research of the Academy of Medicine. A veteran of the Pavlovian battle, he was the founder of a new theory of "torpid" or "remittent" schizophrenia which allowed—in the name of organicism—all the symptoms connected with dissidence to be categorized under the rubric of insanity. That invention, moreover, was contemporaneous with the birth of the dissident movement—it was psychiatry's political response to a new situation. But it drew support from an old configuration linked to the Pavlovian standard, on the basis of which madness was defined according to a permanent oscillation between organic and societal references. At times the madman would be treated "scientifically," at others he would be "rehabilitated" according to the norms of Soviet society. In both cases, an evaluation might be performed, since acts of political opposition were defined as matters for either psychiatry or the courts.

Although the teaching of psychiatry in the Soviet Union was dominated by that conception of insanity, a majority of psychiatrists remained hostile to apprehending dissidence in such terms, which was why political adversaries of the regime were treated and evaluated in special hospitals. The Grigorenko affair showed that even in such hospitals, diagnoses tended to be contradictory. The generalization of psychiatric evaluations thus affected only a small minority of the therapeutic population, but that marginality was a function of the overall psychiatric situation.

In order to counter any resistance from the medical world, the Presidium of the Supreme Soviet passed, in March 1971, a decree defining the Hippocratic Oath of the Soviet physician, and obliging all therapists to base their practices on the principles of Communist morality. From then on, any psychiatrist who failed to consider dissidence as a form of insanity would himself be vulnerable to legal—or expert psychiatric—action.

The most notorious place for evaluating dissidents was the Serbsky Institute in Moscow. From 1950 on, that special hospital had been directed by Daniil Romanovich Luntz, a Jewish therapist and colonel in the KGB. In all its centers, inmates were treated simultaneously like prisoners of the last century and madmen of the contemporary era. They were subjected to corporal punishment and forced to swallow an impressive quantity of neuroleptics, sedatives, and antidepressants. With such treatment, they could pass for insane in the Soviet Union as well as in Western democracies, which also use the same medication. It thus became difficult for the member societies of the WPA, themselves undergoing a pharmacological invasion at the time, to discern whether Grigorenko was crazier than Snezhnevsky.

A few weeks before Bukovsky's book appeared, Henri Ey sent the leaders of the four French societies affiliated with the WPA the draft of a resolution denouncing both the dangers of the antipsychiatric campaign and the abusive exploitation of psychiatry for political ends. He asked them to have the motion submitted to a vote at the congress in Mexico City. He then sent the text off to the secretary general of the WPA. Already diminished by heart disease, Ey was unable to make the trip. His motion was aimed not only at the Soviet Union, but at all dictatorial regimes in which psychiatry was made to serve the interests of power (notably South Africa).[47]

However courageous, the motion contained a serious flaw. No doubt it should be ascribed to the exasperation of an old man seeing the values for which he had fought collapse around him. Ey's error was in situating at the same level antipsychiatry and the abuses found in dictatorships. Although the antipsychiatry movement contested the notion of mental illness, and thus the dynamic legacy, its experiments were in no way comparable to the episodes of police repression coming from the East and elsewhere. Henri Ey knew as much, since he did not hesitate to devote an issue of *Évolution psychiatrique* to the Anglo-Saxon theses. On that occasion, moreover, he invited several French representatives of the movement, who chose not to participate. In the course of discussions related to the issue, he revealed great prudence and tolerance: He criticized antipsychiatry harshly but did not "condemn" it. Why, then, did he offer that misguided motion?[48]

To be sure, in Mexico, the members of the affiliated societies were not concerned with such problems. The WPA had long resembled a travel agency more than a scientific association. No group was willing to take responsibility for eventually finding itself prohibited from traveling in the Soviet Union. That argument was all the more absurd in that a vote of condemnation would not have prevented scientific exchanges. On the contrary! The Soviets were no fools. Nonetheless, the congress board invoked statutory reasons for avoiding any discussion of the abuses. Despite the opposition of the Soviet delegation, an ethics commission was set up to elaborate universal principles for doctor-patient relations and the status of therapeutic treatment. Before long it would produce a text known as the *Hawaii Declaration*.[49]

The dissidents had invested great hope in a favorable reaction in the West. Before and after the congress they enjoyed something of a reprieve within their country. But the Munich-like attitude of the WPA had the result of immediately intensifying repression within the Soviet Union. The Mexico decision did not impede the establishment of national committees in various countries. In May 1972, a "Committee of French Psychiatrists Against the Use of Psychiatry for Political Ends" was created. It brought together representatives of EP, the National Union of Private Psychiatrists, the Union of Hospital Psychiatrists, and the Union of French Psychiatrists. Among its members were to be found Gaston Ferdière, Jean Ayme, Jean-Paul Descombey, Charles Brisset, Cyrille Koupernik, and Gérard Blès. Of those four groups, only EP was a member society of the WPA. The committee thus ran the risk not only of not being represented in future congresses, but also of finding itself in flagrant contradiction with the exceedingly moderate positions of the other groups represented. After four years of struggles waged alongside the League of the Rights of Man and Amnesty International, the committee sent a letter to the four French psychoanalytic societies. It requested financial, moral, and political support from them to the end of seeing the next congress of the WPA issue a condemnation of the abuses of psychiatry in the Soviet Union and in other dictatorships. The four societies responded favorably and each took initiatives. The EFP favored struggle in Latin-America, where Lacanianism was taking root, while the APF organized a welcome committee for refugees. The SPP, for its part, sent a text to General Videla, asking him to account for the fate of the "disappeared." Whereafter it reaffirmed its hostility to the special asylums in the Soviet Union.[50]

During that period, the Royal College of Psychiatrists of Great Britain invited the WPA to take a position on the abusive internments occurring in the Soviet Union. It was followed in this shortly thereafter by the Royal College of Psychiatrists of New Zealand, which proposed a broader motion concerning all dictatorial regimes. Finally, the powerful American Psychiatric Association presented the WPA with a third motion intended to institute an investigatory commission concerning psychiatric abuse. All these motions were strictly technical in character and the question of the status of madness in the modern era was never broached. In point of fact, dynamic psychiatry no longer had any historical existence. As for the antipsychiatric protest, it too had been forgotten. Nevertheless, the battle the dissidents had lost in Mexico City had a good chance of being won in Honolulu, where the next congress was to be held in August 1977. Over a period of six years, the repression had intensified and new testimony on the violation of human rights was piling up in the offices of every psychiatric society, affiliated or not with the WPA. The struggle had become political, and the dissidents were considered—and rightly so—political adversaries. But that transition from one struggle to another allowed for an elimination of any theoretical discussion of the status of madness. The associations of the Western democracies could then extricate themselves on the cheap by brandishing the star spangled banner of freedom against fascism and Stalinism. The best known dissidents had emigrated to the West. They would be present at the congress at the end of August 1977, which would be presided over by a Frenchman, Professor Pierre Pichot, the future relentless defender of *DSM III*.

On December 18, 1976, the Soviet Union and Chile exchanged, at the Zurich airport, two political prisoners: Vladimir Bukovsky and Luis Corvalan. The former was thirty-four years old. He had spent more than ten years in camps and had been a victim of the notorious psychiatric evaluations. The latter was a hoary Communist, and also the victim of bloody repression. He was sixty years old. Originally, the exchange had been proposed by General Pinochet. It was then approved by Andrei Sakharov and implemented through the good graces of the United States. After he was freed, Corvalan was welcomed in the Kremlin by Leonid Brezhnev. But Bukovsky was careful not to emigrate to Chile. He realized that for the first time, the Soviet Union had recognized *de facto* that opponents of the regime were not madmen but political prisoners. The dissident thus commented on the exchange with a wryness worthy of Freud facing the Gestapo.[51] In so doing, he gave a splendid definition of madness in the modern era: "They ought," he said, "to exchange Brezhnev for Pinochet." The member societies of the WPA would forget that line.

A few months later, Bukovsky addressed an official appeal to those attending the congress: "On the position you take in Honolulu will depend the fate of hundreds of individuals as well, in the last analysis, as the destiny of Soviet psychiatry."[52]

On Wednesday, August 30, in Honolulu, the French committee, through its spokesmen Jean Ayme and Gérard Blès, came down very hard on the Soviets. The first, who had spent nineteen years on Lacan's couch and waged daily battle in the hospitals for institutional psychotherapy, explained that only free speech could be a source of true speech. Then he added that what was not expressed in the symbolic came back in the real. After him, Gérard Blès defended the independence of the profession. Finally, Professor Kammerer recalled the value of the Hippocratic oath. On August 31, Professor Snezhnevsky, accompanied by his delegation and supported by his minister, recalled that he was defending "psychiatric science" and that in the name of that science, politics ought to be banned. He then referred to the declarations by Leonid Pliouchtch two days earlier as an "hysterical show." Finally, Morozov stated that that scholar was suffering from "schizophrenia" and that his illness consisted in a paranoid personality. Pliouchtch, in the eyes of his compatriots, was thus a strange scientific animal indeed: at once hysterical, schizophrenic, and paranoid. As for Bukovsky, who had just been exchanged, he was simply accused of being guilty of criminal acts against the Soviet Union.

On August 31, the New Zealanders' motion was passed with a slim majority of two votes and eight abstentions. The victory of the advocates of condemnation had thus been barely won, and the vote bore witness to the desire of the member societies to save at any cost the alleged neutrality of a psychiatry that no longer had anything at its disposal except pharmacology. "I support the resolution with a heavy heart," declared the president of the American Psychiatric Association. "I would have liked to say to the Soviets that our hearts went out to them and that we do not condemn the totality of their psychiatric community. . . . It was a proud as well as a sad moment for the association. . . . None of us is infallible. . . . What we need is a consensus and to formulate universal psychiatric definitions, valid for different cultures and not legalistic machinations." [53]

The universal definitions called for by the American Psychiatric Association would not be long in unfurling over the WPA, and the generalized recourse to *DSM III* would be one of the responses to the problem of the abuse of psychiatry. Out of ten votes in the French delegation, two supported the motion, two others were against (including Professor Pichot), and eight remained undecided. Jean-Marc Alby, a delegate from the SPP, abstained in the name of "psychoanalytic neutrality." Upon his return to France, Gérard Blès told *Le Monde* that the French vote was not representative of the actual opinion of psychiatrists in the country and that what France lacked was a major association more innovative in its aspirations.[54] Six years later, in a bitter report on the Vienna Congress, at which the adoption of *DSM III* effected the "normalization" of relations among all the member societies of the WPA, he wrote this sentence, worthy of Freud and Bukovsky: "When will we have an investigatory commission on the abuse of politics to psychiatric ends?" [55]

II. Women Problems

In a paper entitled "The Early Phase in the Development of Female Sexuality" and presented in 1927 to the Innsbruck congress, Ernest Jones summarized the heart of a debate dividing the international psychoanalytic community. It concerned the apprehension of female sexuality.[56] Since 1905, the "Viennese" tendency, strictly Freudian in inspiration, supported the thesis of *sexual monism* and an essentially "male" human libido. It was represented by three masterly women and a princess: Jeanne Lampl de Groot, Hélène Deutsch, Ruth Mack-Brunswick, and Marie Bonaparte.[57] The thesis derived from a clinical observation made by Freud of infantile sexual theories. Its aim was neither to delineate sexual difference on the basis of anatomy nor to resolve the question of the condition of women in social history. It dealt with the problem of sexuality from the perspective of its psychical organization, that is, its unconscious representations. From the point of view of monism and a single libido, Freud showed that in early childhood girls are unaware of the existence of the vagina and assign to the clitoris a role parallel to that of the penis. Boys, as far as they are concerned, also recognize the penis as the erectile organ *par excellence*. Girls thus have the impression of bearing a castrated organ.

As a result of that dissymmetry, evolving around a single pole, the castration complex is not organized the same way for both sexes. The fate of each is different not only because of anatomy but because of the ideational representations attached to that anatomy. In puberty, the vagina appears for both sexes: Boys see in penetration an aim for their sexuality, and girls repress their clitoral sexuality. But prior to that, when they perceive that girls are not like them, boys interpret the absence of a penis in girls as a threat of castration against themselves. At the time of the Oedipus complex, they take their distance from their mothers and choose an object of the same sex: The masculine Oedipus complex is thus a *primary* formation.

As opposed to boys, girls do not fear being castrated since they can see that they already *are*. Nevertheless, their sexuality will be organized around the phallus: They want to be boys. At the time of the Oedipus complex, they want a child from their father, and that new object is invested with phallic value. As opposed to boys, girls must take their distance from an object of the same sex, the mother, for an other of a different sex. The male Oedipus complex and its female counterpart are thus not parallel: One is a primary formation, the other a secondary one. Nevertheless, a symmetry does exist, since for both sexes, an attachment to the mother is the shared initial element. Although Freud was an advocate of sexual monism and a theory of a single libido, he considered any argument based on the instinctual "nature" of sexuality to be an error. The child's desire, he thought, was organized phallically, but there was no such thing as a "maternal instinct" or a feminine "nature" or "race." Procreation was one thing, and desire a very different one.[58]

The existence of a single form of libido did not exclude that of bisexuality. From the Freudian point of view, no individual possessed a "pure" male or female identity. While libido was phallic and sexual monism prevailed in unconscious representations, bisexuality, which was the corollary of that situation, affected both sexes. Not only does the attraction of one sex for the other not stem from any complementary order, but bisexuality destroys the very idea of such an order: Both sexes are stricken with a "disorder." And that disorder can impel a girl to remain fixated to her mother and thus to make a homosexual choice, or lead a boy down an identical path through a denial of maternal castration.

This modern romance of sexuality was elaborated by Freud between 1905 and 1932. It shows how a chaste, solidly bourgeois, and occasionally misogynistic man of science managed to disengage the content of female sexuality from all ideals of race, inegalitarianism, and naturalism. In that respect, the "phallic" theory of female sexuality was situated within the general framework of a new conception of human sexuality whose epic I have described in a preceding volume. With that theory, Freud opened the way to a renewed debate over the question of the difference between the sexes. Its existence was no longer to be sanctioned by biology, nor governed by instinct, nor constrained by race. It was organized from the perspective of the unconscious, around desire and its ideational representations. Although anatomy was destiny, not every destiny was anatomical. Similarly, man and woman were not the complementary entities of a natural order of things.

Because of its radical novelty, that theory of sexuality posed several problems. First of all, it was largely indebted to a male representation of the problems of femaleness. This was inevitable. For other "female" ideals to appear, women would first have to be able to articulate them and thus to speak of a theory of sexuality. And for that, it was first of all necessary that a man like Freud give them the possibility to do so. A remarkable vicious circle . . . And then that theory was contradicted by clinical practice, as Freud's adversaries did not fail to object. One must indeed be endowed with a formidable imagination to dare to say, against all evidence, that the sense of a vagina does not exist in girls: Empirical observation proves the opposite. Finally, that theory, through its residual biological basis, undeniably privileged an overly positive aspect of the male Oedipus complex. Freud realized this, since in his last lecture on the subject, he acknowledged that his doctrine was in some respects inadequate and referred his readers to poetry or the science of the future.

It is remarkable to observe that the slow elaboration of the Freudian theory of sexuality was contemporaneous with the broad deployment of the feminist movement, which led, via the suffragette cause, to the political and juridical emancipation of women.[59] That movement contested the thematics of race and inequality to the extent that those themes had contributed, through the nineteenth century, to the theorization of the soundness of female oppression, grounded in an alleged biological superiority of one sex over the other. Now Freud, through his teaching, also fought those ideologies. And yet the construction he proposed remained foreign to the debate over women's liberation. It was as though, in order to construct his doctrine, Freud had been obliged to remove himself from—and indeed even reject—the egalitarian aspirations borne by the struggles of feminism. That distancing may be explained by the fact that psychoanalysis did not oppose an "egalitarianism" to an "inegalitarianism." It constructed a theory of sexuality, which, even as it delivered man from the weight of his instincts, did not free him from the chains of his desire. Freudian doctrine was not a liberation theology; it would be, rather, a proof of the shackles the human condition inflicts on itself. And yet it delineated a kind of freedom based on the recognition of an interdiction. In that sense, it remains one of the principal loci of all struggles for the liberation of the oppressed. As the historical conditions of its implantation in each country where it took refuge bears witness. Everywhere it took root against the dominant ideals, but never did it succeed in flourishing or in forming a movement where freedom of thought had disappeared.

Opposed to the Viennese tendency, which supported the thesis of monism and a single libido, was the so-called British school, represented essentially by Jones, Melanie Klein, and Josine Müller. Its partisans did not contest the entirety of the

Viennese theory; they delved into its impasses and implausibilities. While retaining the primacy of an unconscious organization of sexuality, they maintained the existence of a specifically feminine libido and thus of an "innateness" of bisexuality. In that perspective, the feeling of a vagina would exist in the girl at an early stage, as clinical practice attests. Penis envy would be secondary and the decline of the phallic phase would be the moment when a repressed femininity would surface. Drawing on the works of Melanie Klein, Jones thus recentralized anatomy the better to underscore its instinctual aspect. In his view there existed a veritable complementarity of the feminine and masculine poles, in conformity with the natural order of things. As for the threat of castration, it would be identical in both sexes and take the form of a fear of the disappearance of sexuality (aphanisis). Jones noted, moreover, that psychoanalytic theories served less to illuminate the issue than to sexualize the problem: Men underestimated female organs and women flaunted their preference for the phallic apparatus.

Associated with the British school, Karen Horney was the first to intervene in the great debate of the interwar years, well before her departure for Chicago and her break with the IPA. She went further than Jones in her critique of Freudian theory. Starting in 1926, she psychologized the question, which was a way of nullifying it. In her eyes, psychoanalysis was the work of a male genius; its ideas had been developed by men; and men understood masculine psychology better than female sexuality. Karen Horney, however, did not restrict herself to such tautologies. Like Jones, she maintained that the phallic phase was secondary, that the alleged ignorance of the vagina was the result of a repression, and that attachment to the clitoris served defensive ends.

If one restricts oneself to the surface, the theses of the British school have an appearance of modernity alongside which Freudian phallocentrism looks like some dusty family portrait. In the "real" world, it is, after all, not possible to contest the existence of woman's full and complete femininity, be she mother, prostitute, courtesan, or virgin. Anatomy proves it; biology demonstrates it; and common sense proclaims it: Woman exists. She is not man and the vagina is not a penis. The Freudian point of view has the disadvantage of being exceedingly opposed to factual reality. Against it, the British school has the merit of showing that clinical reality is refractory to that doctrine. Its critique of Freud proved all the more justified in that the introduction of the maternal and the archaic, by way of the works of the Kleinians, demonstrated the prevalence of a series of identity-related phenomena that invalidated the dogma of primary phallicism. The only problem with all this was that clinical evidence is always a bit like Flaubert's Monsieur Homais. If science were entirely dependent on it, science would still believe the Earth was the center of the universe and hysteria a matter of uteruses.

The strength of Freud's theory lay in its renunciation of appearances. It constructed a general system of sexuality in which the female and male poles were opposed to each other in a logically articulated, but asymmetrical, relation. Despite its phallocentrism, which was a function of the fact that Freud was not able to avoid a vocabulary imbued with the paternalist ideal, that theory was far more innovative than that of the British school. But since every innovation presupposes a certain loss, it had the fault of unduly neglecting the reality value attached to the myths of femininity.

It should nonetheless be observed that the historical evolution of the feminist movement has turned out to be rather supportive of Freud. No sooner did women acquire rights making them men's equals than they revealed the prodigious phallicism they harbored. As a result, the femininity of males was also liberated. In 1938, Lacan called this phenomenon the "decline of paternal imagos." It may, of course, always be objected that this phallicism is cultural and that women's "virile" protest bears witness to their identification with the ideals of a male society. This is true, but it is no less the case that such phallicism has authorized women to demand equality. Freud was thus not as misogynistic as he appeared, and perhaps a certain dose of misogyny was necessary for the elaboration of a doctrine of female sexuality which, in discounting appearances, has given women one of the major weapons of their freedom.

Given the declared primacy of the phallic, the British doctrine had the shortcomings of its strengths. In limiting itself to clinical evidence, it produced proof, by way of the early relation with the mother, that a feeling for the vagina was not as absent as Freud believed. In his demonstration, Jones invoked cases of homosexuality in which an infantile fixation on the mother played a preponderant role. Everything inclined one to the belief that Freud had erred on that score. In his role as founding father and listener to hysteria, he privileged the phallic character of female sexuality. He had, moreover, managed to surround himself with women more eager to bear his coat of arms than to delve into the mysteries of their vaginal feelings. Marie Bonaparte's horrendous therapy offers proof. The theses she elaborated during her long and impassioned relation with Freud and the surgical practices on herself to which she resorted[60] sketch out a kind of caricatural reverse side of Freud's failure to think through the question of female sexuality. How could he not have prevented Marie from seeking in the depths of biologism an answer to the mythical idea of femininity according to which the orgasmic capacity of the clitoris might be transmitted to the vagina? If Freud was unable to do anything, might it not be the case that his theory was unsatisfactory? Moreover, he had the honesty to say as much.

But neither was clinical reality all powerful. Thus, when the British school pitted itself against the Viennese doctrine, it did not escape a naturalist prejudice consisting of reimmersing femininity back into the reservoir of mythologies of the feminine. In Jones's perspective, woman has been woman for all eternity. The ancestral role assigned her was that of resplendent goddess, and it cannot be said that that role was particularly propitious to the egalitarian ideas that gave the school its premises.[61]

The matter was all the more complicated in that the discussion of the problem occurred within the IPA at a time when the domination of the Anglo-American sphere over the old world of Mitteleuropa, of the victorious West over a defeated East, was beginning to be imposed. Now the ideals traversing the British theses should be related to the stunning success of the feminist movement in a puritanical country of Victorian traditions. In Great Britain as in the United States, women achieved emancipation far more rapidly than in Latin countries, and in a different way. Englishwomen obtained the right to vote in 1918, and ten years later they became full-fledged electors. As for the women of America, their movement was connected to the antislavery effort, and their right to vote was also acquired after World War I. In other words, the valorization of the omnipotence of femininity in Jones's theses was not merely the result of an internal debate within the IPA on the Kleinian question of vaginal precociousness. It also bore witness to an ideological situation in which female phallicism was related to the appearance of the Eternal Feminine. An identical mechanism was at work in the way in which Karen Horney's theses were able to take root so auspiciously in American soil.

In France things transpired differently. Not only did the suffrage movement of the interwar years remain a pale copy of its Anglo-American counterpart and fail to inspire any debate on the nature of female sexuality, but the psychoanalytic movement, because of its general backwardness, misconstrued the discussion going on between London and Vienna. None of the major texts of the period was translated in the *RFP* between 1927 and 1939. In addition, there was no way for the debate to occur with any serenity, since Marie Bonaparte functioned as sole possessor of a Freudian truth which was, as it happened, completely distorted. The phallicism she invoked and demonstrated was more in the order of a mental disorder than a theory. Opposed to her, Édouard Pichon embodied an equally extravagant set of values. Although he understood the phallicism at work in the feminist movement (which he called "hoministe"), he defended the Maurrassian ideals of marriage, the family, virginity, and patriarchy in terms that were completely ludicrous. The SPP thus served as a fortress for a contest pitting a general in skirts against an inquisitor from the Dark Ages. Since the general was intent on being Freudian and the inquisitor was defending, against Vienna, the principles of Frenchness, no one had the freedom, in the course of the crusade, to grasp the meaning of the Anglo-Austrian debate. It was thus not by chance that the question of female sexuality was broached in the pages of the *RFP* at times through studies of homosexuality, and at others through articles on criminology. In point of fact, the founders of the SPP apprehended female sexuality more through its "excesses" than through its "normality." With that bias, they contributed to the edification of the exacerbated figure of femininity whose preponderance we have seen both in Lacan's first texts and in the works of Jouve and the Surrealists. The discussion of female sexuality was thus not totally absent from France during the interwar years, but it took place on terms limited by the specific conditions of the implantation of Freudian discourse in the country.

In such a context, the first coherent book to take female sexuality for its subject could not have been written by a member of the French psychoanalytic community—it was the work of a woman novelist and philosopher. When Simone de Beauvoir published *The Second Sex* in June 1949, she announced from the outset that feminism was a story that had come to its end. And perhaps she was not wrong to end the discussion in that way. For to be able to discuss female sexuality on the morrow of a war that had allowed French women to obtain voting rights, one certainly had to take one's distance from a movement which itself had contributed so little to an elucidation of the enigma. Simone de Beauvoir may not have known that she was proceeding in the manner of Freud, who opted to misconstrue one reality in order to discover another. But she was even more unaware that her book would be at the origin—first in America, then in France—of a radical transformation of the ideals of feminism. She was so unaware of it that in 1968 she would climb onto the bandwagon and give her support to that "radical feminism" whose first inspiration had been *The Second Sex*. From the time of its initial appearance, the work was a source of scandal as well as the recipient of considerable commercial success. Beauvoir was treated to rounds of insults worthy of those that were showered on Freud during the 1920s: She dared to unveil the mysteries of the notorious vaginal feeling and for that reason was called "frigid," a "nymphomaniac," a "Lesbian," or "in need of a good lay." A charming country, France!

During the entire first half of the century, the women's movement as such had kept its distance from Freudian investigations into female sexuality. Conversely, the psychoanalytic community stayed at a remove from the great themes of emancipation. And yet, as we have seen, that absence of links did not mean that the two areas had remained impermeable to each other. In that respect, and for France, Simone de Beauvoir was the first to connect the sexual question with that of emancipation. That was why she took the internal quarrels of the psychoanalytic movement into account. She proved, in fact, to be so attentive to the problem that a year before publishing her book, she telephoned Jacques Lacan to ask his advice. Flattered, he told her they would need five or six years of discussion to clarify the issue. Simone was not inclined to spend that much time listening to Lacan for a work that was already fully documented. She proposed a set of four interviews. He refused.[62]

In affirming the existence of a "second sex," Beauvoir came down on the side of the British school. She reproached Freud for modeling woman's destiny on a barely modified version of the male's. But she also took her distance from the British point of view, since she drew on Sartrean existentialism to denounce the naturalist prejudice. "One is not born a woman," she said, "one becomes one." Beauvoir thus applied to the elucidation of female sexuality a nonstructural perspective that would be used by the antipsychiatrists in relation to insanity. Just as for Sartre anti-Semitism was not a Jewish problem, for Beauvoir, the feminist question was a male matter since women were culturally in bondage to masculine ideals. That argument, to be sure, did not provide a solution to either the Jewish question or the woman's issue, but Beauvoir, for the first time in France, informed people of the pre-War debate. It skirted the Viennese point of view and the English position and redirected the entire question of sexual identity onto cultural ground. She "sexualized" feminism. In the French context of the 1950s, three positions were thus advanced: Freudian phallicism, Jonesian naturalism, and Beauvoirian culturalism. Where then was the specific sexual identity of women to be found?

For a period of ten years, the French psychoanalytic community remained as deaf to Beauvoir's argument as to the prewar Anglo-Viennese debate. In 1958, Jacques Lacan was the first to break that silence, on the occasion of an annual seminar of the SFP devoted to the examination of psychoanalytic theories of female sexuality. The decision to put that question on the agenda had been taken collectively, so intensely was the need felt to finally discuss the famous controversy. It should be said that with the expansion of the movement, the number of woman therapists had been growing constantly. And just as Jones had introduced a differential factor into the apprehension of the phenomenon in 1927, in France, during the 1960s, the increase in the number of women in the profession was not unrelated to the reexamination of female sexual identity. Once in analysis, women in training spoke differently of their sexuality than mere "patients": Not only did they theorize, but they could not but find bizarre the Freudian dogma of the absence of any sense of the vagina.

The ground was thus prepared for the renewal of a debate in which, once again, clinical reality was at odds with official doctrine. In addition, the personal temperament of the principal representatives of the SFP played a role in that renewal. Most of the men in the movement had a rather idiosyncratic relation with women in training and with their own femininity, linked to the mothering role Lacan had played with his male disciples. With men, the master acted as an abusive mother and with women as a Don Juan or a protective father. With all concerned, he flaunted his femininity. The spread of Françoise Dolto's teaching on childhood sexuality also encouraged inquiries into the archaic levels of sexual identity. In other words, in the perspective on female sexuality maintained by the Lacanians, there intervened a problematic similar to the one that had earlier made the debate between London and Vienna possible.

The project thus surfaced, within the ranks of the SFP, to organize an international colloquium on female sexuality outside the auspices of the IPA. Contacts were initiated between the French group and the Dutch with the aim of securing the participation of several liberals of the empire, such as Franz Alexander, who was then eighty years old. The meeting took place in Amsterdam in 1960. When Lacan saw the man whose theses he had criticized ten years earlier, he exclaimed, in Granoff's presence, "When one is afire with a true flame, one never ages." [63]

Two years before that date, the stars of the movement had begun to study the subject of female sexuality. Lacan sketched matters out in his *Propos directifs pour un congrès sur la sexualité féminine* ["Guidelines for a congress on female sexuality"]. "You are perhaps aware," he wrote to Winnicott, "that we are holding a small congress in Amsterdam this year on female sexuality. That's another subject that has been neglected since the days of Jones and which I have felt obliged to put on our agenda. I will abstain this time from delivering a paper. I shall open the congress and will be less interested in intervening myself than in seeing what those whom I have trained contribute." [64] Lagache, for his part, also wrote up organizational remarks before composing an article of five pages, entitled "Dialectique phallocentrique et sexualité féminine," whose typescript would be lost. As for Granoff and Perrier, they worked together on a text on female perversion, while Françoise Dolto took it upon herself to report on what she had gleaned from her experience with child analysis. Finally, Camille Laurin, a psychoanalyst from Quebec, offered an historical discussion of the debate. [65]

In the French manner of situating the female question, it is possible to see how the great debate of the interwar years, displaced and delayed, finally was joined. On the French scene of the SFP, Lacan occupied the position of a Freud who would have integrated the teachings of the British school into his doctrine without establishing any complementarity between the contradictory poles of the two tendencies. Lacan constructed an edifice in which lacunae were more important than symmetries, thus leaving the way open for both ways of apprehending the problem. He never corrected the impasses of theory with the answers of clinical evidence or the inadequacies of clinical reality with the coherence of theory. He showed rather that both domains were heterogeneous and cohabited together by virtue of their very incompatibility. While retaining the primordial character of the phallic, he proposed both to introduce the archaic relation with the mother (under the rubric of *maternal desire*) and to strip Freudian terminology of its paternalocentric ambiguity. He thus presented his customary orthodox reelaboration, without rejecting—a single time does not a rule make—the revisions to which Freudianism had been subjected. But those revisions were themselves reinterpreted in the light of the Lacanian trio of the symbolic, the imaginary, and the real. Lacan made the phallus the central object of libidinal economy on the condition that it be extricated from its complicity with the biological penis. The phallus thus became an *insignia*, the pure signifier of a vital force shared equally between the two sexes. If the phallus was no one's organ, no male libido dominated the female condition. Phallic power was no longer articulated with anatomy but with desire, which structures sexual identity without any kind of privilege.

In that perspective, Freud's theory, on the one hand, and the English theses, on the other, could be translated into a common ternary algebra. In the primordial relation with the mother, the child is *the desire of the maternal desire*. He may identify with the mother, the phallus, the mother as bearer of the phallus, or present himself as endowed with a phallus. With the Oedipus complex, one enters into a different order: The father intervenes as he who deprives the child of the object of his desire and the mother of her phallic object. Finally, in a third phase, corresponding to the decline of the Oedipus complex, the father intervenes to make himself preferred in favor of the mother, embodying for the child the phallic signifier. The boy emerges from the Oedipus complex by way of castration insofar as the latter is not real but signified by the phallus, while the girl enters into it by the same path, forgoing having the phallus in order to receive it as a signifier.

Whereas that language-oriented rereading of Freudian phallocentrism consisted in not establishing a complementarity between clinical discourse and theoretical formulation, Françoise Dolto occupied a rather different place on the SFP scene. Françoise was not in search of the solution to an enigma. She produced theory spontaneously on the basis of clinical experience. Her position was rather like that of a Melanie Klein who would have accepted the primary character of the phallic without for all that renouncing the Jonesian ideals of femininity. Dolto articulated female sexuality with anatomy by showing that the constitution of one's being-a-woman rested on a girl's acceptance of her sexual specificity. If the girl reacts with narcissistic disappointment to the discovery of her sex, she can also accept her sexual identity to the extent that she is certain of having been desired by her father, on the model of her mother.

As opposed to the Lacan/Dolto duo, the two juniors of the SFP broached the question of female sexuality through the diagonal channel of its overflow as perversion. The paper presented at Amsterdam by Granoff and Perrier was dazzling. It skirted, the better to interpret them, the commonplaces of the mythology of femininity. Even as they appealed to a phallicism revised and corrected from the Lacanian perspective, the two authors took a stand as opposed to Dolto's anatomism as to Jonesian naturalism. And it was for that reason, no doubt, that their prose seemed to espouse the very contours of that inexpressible vaginal pleasure concerning which Lacan emphasized, after Freud, that it was constitutive of a *supplement of femininity.* That supplement rests on the principle of a dissymmetry: It is not bound to a *masculine complement.* In brief, the authors showed that the clinical study of female perversion offers proof of the existence of a *phallicism of dissymmetry* and a *nonnatural supplementarity* of femininity. Perversion in the strict sense does not exist in women, since its sexual manifestations, and particularly fetishism, are not to be found in such cases. Nevertheless, the absence of the phenomenon does not exclude the hypothesis of a specific perversion resulting in a woman's becoming her own fetish. Its dimension is elucidated by the mother-child relation, which can swing toward the extreme pole of erotomania: an "I am everything for him" surfacing in place of sublimation. In that perspective and on the basis of perversion, phallocentrism becomes necessary for the generic explanation of human desire without sufficing in any elucidation of its concrete reality.

Most of the French papers presented at the Amsterdam colloquium were published four years later in the penultimate issue of *La Psychanalyse.* In addition, and for the first time, the texts of the great historic debate were translated. Irène Roublef undertook the transcription of Helene Deutsch's article on the psychology of women as well as Jones's on early development. Victor Smirnoff, for his part, translated two other texts, one by Jones and another by Joan Rivière.

At the time the issue of *La Psychanalyse* was published, the SFP had already broken up and Lacan was conducting his seminar at the ENS. Now, at the same time, at the SPP, women were beginning to inquire into the famous controversy. But since the two groups scarcely had any contact with each other, the therapists of the SPP were completely unaware of the papers presented at the Amsterdam colloquium. Although their investigations were not the same as those of the Lacanians, the reasons for which the question surfaced were frequently identical. At the SPP, as at the SFP, the number of women in training was constantly rising. In addition, with the death of the princess and the waning of Nacht's authority, the "virile" imagos of the venerable IPA-affiliated society had suddenly begun to seem rather old.

A first article published in June 1959 in the *RFP* acknowledged the historic debate in the course of a study of female masochism.[66] But it was in February 1964 that the affair took concrete shape on the occasion of a paper by Janine Chasseguet-Smirgel, an analysand of Grunberger's, on female guilt and certain aspects of the female Oedipus complex. Four months later a colloquium was organized by the SPP on the theme of female homosexuality. Joyce MacDougall, a student of Grunberger's originally from New Zealand, attended and spoke brilliantly; her talk was followed by a discussion, as was that of Chasseguet-Smirgel.[67]

After those two meetings, Janine Chasseguet-Smirgel decided to publish with Payot a collection entitled *Nouvelles recherches sur la sexualité féminine* with articles by Bela Grunberger, Christian David, J. Mac Dougall, Maria Torok, and C.-J. Luquet-Parat. She included her own presentation and wrote an excellent preface in which she introduced the Anglo-Viennese quarrel. To be sure, she knew nothing of the Amsterdam colloquium and was unaware that an issue of *La Psychanalyse,* which had been out since the previous January, was devoted to the same subject. And yet she decided to interest herself in the matter of female sexuality for two essential reasons, one of which was not unrelated to Lacan's reelaboration. For a long while already, she had observed that reading Marie Bonaparte's articles had the effect of depressing her female patients. But in addition she thought that her colleagues "influenced" by Lacanianism, Stein and Green, were adopting phallocentric and conservative positions in relation to women. She thus felt that the time had come to launch an attack against the Viennese catechism and to begin speaking differently about female sexuality.[68]

The *Nouvelles recherches* produced by the SPP kept their promise. All the texts made clear the inadequacies of the doctrine from Vienna the better to rectify them with the work of the English. The authors retained Freudian phallocentrism while specifying that it would have to be stripped of any reference to the biological penis. For them the phallus was not a signifier but the designatory site of the ideals attached to it and referring to the position occupied by the male organ. Thus the British hypotheses about the innateness of femininity were eliminated from the theory without being cast out of clinical reality. That was why the authors of *Nouvelles recherches* proposed an operation completely opposed to the Lacanian reelaboration, of which they were unaware. Rather than leave open the contradiction between the two schools and deduce a supplementarity, they attempted to move beyond both Vienna and London in order to render the two hypotheses complementary: One would be the clinical truth all therapists should refer to, and the other a theoretical necessity whose teaching was by no means to be turned into a dogma. The adoption of such an attitude was in keeping with the evolution of the international psychoanalytic movement since the IPA-members had divided the empire with Kleinians on the one side and Anna-Freudians on the other. For the SPP of the 1960s it thus gave substance to the arrival of Anglo-Saxon clinical practice into a region previously occupied by the theses of Nacht, Bouvet, and Marie Bonaparte. The introduction of that clinical reality also appeared as the SPP's spontaneous response to a triumphant Lacanianism and to the former French theses, which by then were archaic.

The *Nouvelles recherches* enjoyed great commercial success. The book was translated in the United States and England, where it was first published by a feminist press. In France it provoked a polemic in the journal *Planning Familial,* where Geneviève Texier accused it of expressing a position hostile to feminists. Janine Chasseguet-Smirgel responded with a good deal of common sense. "If one believes," she said, "that woman's situation in the world and the conflict between the sexes have their roots in the unconscious, how can one minimize, from that perspective, the research of psychoanalysts such as Jones, who, resolutely contradicting certain views of Freud, conclude, following extremely elaborate clinical observation and theoretical reflection, that a woman is not a failed man, and who show how and why the profound conflicts between the sexes can have made such a view of women so powerful?" [69]

With the May 1968 rebellion, French feminism became radicalized and, in its majority, beholden to Beauvoir, even though, unlike its American counterpart, it had not drawn inspiration from Beauvoir's thought until then. There thus occurred, thanks to the barricades, a fusion between the struggle for sexual liberation, which was the objective of *The Second Sex,* and a political battle, which was more Marxist than it had previously been, for absolute egalitarianism. At that time, Simone de Beauvoir became the principal reference of French feminism, both in her person and her symbolic position. In turn, she committed herself to a militant struggle which had not been hers before.

"Radical" post-May feminism was thus distinguished from the earlier reformist variety in that it drew on a *doctrine* of female sexuality and not merely on the political principles of egalitarianism. Moreover, one of the principal issues of contemporary feminism revolved around the question of women's "bodies": the right to abortion, contraception, and the separation of sexuality from procreation. Through that struggle, the whole question raised by *The Second Sex* in 1949 and by psychoanalysis since the beginning of the century surfaced "spontaneously" in the public discourse of women. And with that, Freudian phallocentrism was held up to obloquy in the most virulent manner without any of the debates internal to psychoanalysis, which had already called it into question, having been broached. Such phallocentrism was thereafter to be called *phallocratisme,* normally translated "male chauvinism." The result was that psychoanalysts at that point rejected what they perceived to be the excesses of feminism, which simply gave new currency, in negative terms, to a thematic of sexuality that had already been debated throughout the history of Freudianism. If the radical feminists were Beauvorian when they affirmed that one "becomes a woman," they were also Jonesian when they maintained the innate character of a second libido. It will thus be seen that beyond its theoretical and political divergences, post-May feminism supported a theory of sexuality that oscillated between Beauvoirian culturalism and Jonesian naturalism. This demonstrated the existence of a narrow meshing, impossible to deny, between the history of feminism and that of the psychoanalytic doctrines regarding sexuality. In their apprehension of the problem, the militant women were no more advanced than the practitioners of the unconscious, even if they claimed the reverse. And yet, over a ten-year period, the existence of the women's movement would serve to implant— over an extremely widespread area—the doctrines of female sexuality born of Freud's discovery.

Around 1970, the acronym MLF was popularized by the mass media to designate the women's liberation movement stemming from the May revolt. A year before that, May 8 had officially become International Women's Day. Between that date, when the major themes of the antisexist battle emerged, and the moment when Simone Veil got Parliament to vote through a law authorizing voluntary abortion, there were six years of struggle in the course of which the MLF split into numerous tendencies, as violent toward each other as many a *gauchiste* group. Then, in 1975, a more reflective tendency won out over the drive to action at all costs even as International Women's Day was being celebrated. From then on, feminism began to reflect on its own history, although it continued to find in Beauvoirism the most accomplished form of its regained modernity. Numerous books were published, dealing as much with past and contemporary struggles as with the sexual theories coursing through them.

Although Beauvoirism dominated the post-May French scene, it was also contested from within the women's movement. It was, in any event, not the only channel through which the debate over female sexuality progressed. At the center of the springtime flareup, there emerged a minority current hostile to the word feminism. The term seemed linked to the American "Women's Lib" and a negative idealization of the male sex. In the beginning, this tendency in no way wanted to be feminist: it rejected the word and took on the name, "Mouvement de libération des femmes," whence its subsequent conflicts over the attribution of the acronym. Against Beauvoirian existentialism, judged to be summary, pre-Freudian, and past-oriented, this movement drew on the structuralist configuration of the 1960s and a libertarian Marxism. It was founded in 1968 by three women: Antoinette Fouque, Monique Wittig, and Josiane Chanel. Very early on, internal conflict emerged to the extent that Wittig was a Marcusean and Antoinette Fouque was intent on being a Lacanian.

On the political level, the movement was represented by the Psychanalyse et Politique group, which functioned on the model of the informal rap groups, characterized by the phenomenon of *prise de parole*—speaking out—that emerged from May. It was a matter of bringing women together in neighborhoods so that they might speak of their sexuality and of their positions as subjects of the unconscious and of history. In point of fact, the group was composed of multiple groups divided into several subgroups throughout France. These were charged with distributing information and bringing together female lycée students, working women, and women intellectuals. Within the subgroups, no therapy occurred, but psychoanalytic terminology was widely used in rather exalted and uncontrolled ways. Freudian discourse played the role of dominant cultural reference, although it was infused with a Reichian and libertarian thematic.

Born in 1937, in one of the poorest neighborhoods of Marseille, Antoinette Grugnardi was the daughter of a Corsican syndicalist who had been part of the Communist struggle since the time of the split in Tours. Very early on, she listened to Thorez's speeches and was initiated to the saga of the insurgents of the Black Sea. Later she chose a teaching career, married René Fouque, and became interested, like him, in Latin culture and Italian literature. Together they participated in the work of the literary journal *Cahiers du Sud*. Montaigne was the favorite author of the young cosmopolitan with the warm voice, who spoke a true southern French in which was blended the fragrance of olive trees and the triviality of a seaport dialect.

As an adult, Antoinette learned that she was stricken with a congenital and incurable disease that would gradually deprive her of the use of her legs. But instead of morbid resignation, she derived from her infirmity a taste for travel and an intellectual energy which allowed her to hear the very nature of all differences. Made a woman by history and anatomy, she was molded in the dialect of island dwellers, shepherds, sailors, or terrorists, but she spoke the noble language of the libertines of the eighteenth century. She thus affirmed the innate homosexuality of women without masking her hostility toward the "transvestites" of feminism: "The infantile malady of MLF," she said, "less the masculinity and the maschismo." [70]

For her, to think through the continent of femininity meant to displace the question onto the ground of women's *homosexuated* sex, defined as a second libido and induced by way of a relation with the mother. Antoinette reproached Beauvoir with having uttered the most foolish pronouncement of the century. For her, one did not become a woman; one *was* a woman. But one also rediscovered oneself as a woman by moving beyond the phallic, or feminist, phase of a sexuality conceived in the image of the paternal phallus. It was then that access to a genital phase of reunion with "homosexuation" loomed. The doctrine remained structural: It was based on the Lacanian notion of the supplement, and the Derridean one of difference. Beauvoir was rectified by Freud, Freud by Lacan, and Lacan by the advance of a postphallicism taking the form of a "homosexuated" symbolic pitted against the language of the male.

Intuitively, Antoinette Fouque was not very far from Dolto's theses or the British doctrine, with the exception that she rechanneled the naturalist prejudice in the direction of a declared primacy of innate homosexuality. The founder and leader of a band, she was a rebel without a pen: She has no written work. No treatise, no essay, no novel, no theory, no articles bound in a sacred volume. Whence the historian's difficulty in evaluating the actual primacy of her oral discourse and in grasping its true impact on the post-May intellectual scene. For the whole art of MLF induced by Antoinette lay in an idiosyncratic way of allowing the signifiers of structuralism, Freudianism, and Lacanianism to resonate, of provoking the eruption of a plural inscription through a multitude of tracts, slogans, posters, and mimeographed sheets of every sort. In sum, the movement implemented, within the configuration of the 1970s, a new mythology of the feminine articulated with a doctrine of sexuality. It did not propose merely to fight for emancipation or to collect the archives of a dark continent; it sought to write, translate, and interpret the history of female sexuality by way of an *écriture* that was itself marked by sexual difference. And it was in order to arouse the trace of that second libido, inscribed in the uterus, that Antoinette and her group created Éditions Des femmes in 1974. That enterprise was destined to publish books capable of bearing witness to the emergence of such gendered writing. As for the business side, it was initially financed by an heiress of the Schlumberger family. The reference is perhaps not unimportant since that family name was already inscribed in the history of psychoanalysis as signifier of a special place accorded to women. It was Marc Schlumberger who had affirmed that the future of psychoanalysis rested on the shoulders of women.

That emergence of a gendered conception of writing could not take place without a break with Beauvoirian existentialism and without a renewal of the Freudian debate. Now that renewal and that break were made possible before May 1968 by Lacan's reelaborations, on the one hand, and by Derridean deconstruction on the other. It may thus be seen how the philosophical battles internal to structuralism were reinscribed within the history of the women's movement. Between 1965 and 1969, Antoinette Fouque was a reader of Italian manuscripts for Éditions du Seuil. Through François Wahl, who urged her to work, she read Lacan without knowing Freud and became acquainted with the work of the journal *Tel Quel*. She even considered writing a thesis on the subject and discovered in 1967 *L'écriture et la différence*. At the same time, she was writing articles for *La Quinzaine littéraire* and seeing Blanche Reverchon and Pierre Jean Jouve. After the publication of the *Écrits,* she thought of undergoing therapy, hesitated between Leclaire and Lacan, and finally found herself on the latter's couch after attending his seminar since 1969. At the same time, she entered into analysis with Luce Irigaray, who had herself been analyzed by Leclaire and influenced by Derrida's teaching.[71]

The doctrine of female sexuality subtending the actions and reflections of the Psychanalyse et Politique group was thus elaborated collectively, over several years, under the impetus of a woman in the "grip" of psychoanalysis. The tendency she represented was, moreover, the only one to actually interrogate Freudian discourse without rejecting it from the outset as male chauvinist pure and simple. That is why, more than others, it established privileged links with the psychoanalytic community, and specifically with the Lacanians. Not only did the women of the group spend time in analysis, but female analysts felt challenged by a discourse that spoke to their own position in the history of the community. . . . When they did not simply become feminists, they proclaimed the emergence of a specifically feminine discourse or *écriture*. There emerged from all this a multitude of meetings, conflicts, homosexual loves, and publications of all sorts. Never had there been so much trafficking with the lexicon of femininity as during that period from 1970 to 1975, when the egalitarian measures demanded by the old feminism were finally passed into law.[72]

It was in the heat of that theoretical climate, marked by the readoption of structuralist themes in literary journals and women's collectives, that a renewal of the historic debate within the Lacanian tendency occurred.

Analyzed by Lacan, in control with Dolto, Michèle Montrelay entertained relations with Lacan redolent of courtly love. She was beautiful, rich, delightful, and intelligent, and could only alienate the envious, particularly in so far as she enjoyed the master's favors. She had earned a living as a graphologist, then as a model. She was also fascinated by astrology, and a serious clinical practitioner in addition to all the rest. A splendid figure in the grand Lacanian adventure. In June 1965, she broached the feminist question, during a presentation at Lacan's seminar on Marguerite Duras's novel, *Le ravissement de Lol V. Stein,* which had been published a year earlier.[73]

The book enjoyed a remarkable success with psychoanalysts, and particularly among Lacanians. When Marguerite Duras wrote it, she was unaware that it would become something of a fetish object. Nor did she know that the whole of her work would be apprehended from the perspective of a literary feminism as emblematic of an *écriture* of the female body. "Lol V. Stein," she said in 1979, "was someone who insisted that others speak for her since she was without a voice. It was about her that I spoke the most and her that I knew the least. When Lol V. Stein shouted, I realized it was I who was shouting. I can show Lol V. Stein only if I am hidden, like a dead dog on the beach."[74]

The return to currency of Duras's thematic in post-May feminist literary discourse is not surprising since the author was a woman and female characters played a particular role in her work. Plunged into lives of infernal leisure, Duras's heroines are damned, mad, or accursed. They are always captured at a moment of crisis bearing witness to the extreme confinement of their world. In addition, they are often Jewish, and that Judaic dimension gives them a melancholic identity—expressed in horror, emptiness, or nothingness. As such, they become the "negative" female bearers of a century of oppression, true unaccomplished symbols of sexual frenzy and death. The male characters in her novels are confronted with this devastated circuit of femininity.[75] Which is why the feminine mythology stemming from Duras's work can be pitted against the Beauvoirian figure of a militant, triumphant, and phallic feminism: on the one side, the "supplement," lived in madness and ecstasy; on the other, an egalitarian liberation, replete with its cortege of culturalist and naturalist prejudices.

The *Ravissement* tells the story of a Jewish woman, Lola Valérie Stein, and is situated in an unspecified nightmarish country. The night of the ball celebrating her engagement, Lola finds herself abandoned for another woman, Anne-Marie Stretter. Her fiancé, Michael Richardson, dances with Anne-Marie. Lola observes the couple. As soon as she sees the other woman, she no longer loves Michael. The day after that episode, she sinks into prostration and goes mad. She then takes on the name Lol V. Stein, as if to indicate the amputation she has undergone. Then she marries and leaves S. Tahla, her native city. The story of her abandonment is forgotten. But ten years later, she returns to S. Tahla. There she meets up with Tatiana Karl, a childhood friend who had stayed with her the night of the ball. She also meets Jacques Hold, the narrator, who becomes Tatiana's lover. Lying in a field of rye, she observes the couple embrace in the Hôtel des Bois. She watches, but does not see. Nevertheless, the episode from the time of her engagement resurfaces in her memory. She remembers, speaks, and relives the crisis. She makes love with Jacques Hold at the very spot where the ball had been held. Her pain disappears. But when the lover returns to Tatiana in the Hôtel des Bois, Lol finds herself already in the rye field, asleep and exhausted by the trip. She is "ravished," perhaps mad, and "dead" in her sleep. The narration tells us nothing more. It is written in short sentences, in the manner of a dream. It contains no clinical descriptions or psychological explications: It espouses the contours of a circulating gaze.

In 1965, Michèle Montrelay was not yet speaking about a style of writing that might resemble erotic ecstasy or a woman's body. But she noted that Lol was the very image of a degradation hidden in the shadows, that she was a fragment without which the unconscious could not exist. "Henceforth," she wrote, "for lovers to be able to love each other, this thing 'Lol,' interspersed with rye, will have to stare at them with her wide-open eyes."[76]

Such a narrative could not fail to interest Lacan. Without being the story of a clinical case (like Breton's *Nadja*), it restored, in terms of nothingness, horror, or the "blank page," that dimension of female insanity which was at work in the story of Aimée. But unlike the Surrealists, Marguerite Duras did not draw on any Freudian or psychiatric sources. She was totally unaware of the range of "clinical" discourses on madness, and it was perhaps for that reason that the psychoanalysts of the 1960s were so pleased with the tale and with the strange proximity of a text that managed to evoke madness become female without the slightest allusion to any diagnostic categories.

Michèle Montrelay gave Lacan the book to read, and he was overwhelmed; he thought that he was rediscovering the substance of his own teaching. Since Marguerite Duras was not a philosopher and there was little risk in any event that she would "steal His Majesty's ideas," Lacan rushed to a telephone and invited her to a midnight rendezvous in the basement of a café on the rue Bernard-Palissy. For two hours, he spoke unforgettably to her about Lol, wanting to know still more. The bill he would foot as a result would be considerable. Marguerite Duras answered him that she did not know where she got Lol from. He should have expected as much, he who had so magisterially observed that women are unable to say anything about their sexual enjoyment. Nevertheless, four months later, he published "Hommage fait à Marguerite Duras du 'Ravissement de Lol V. Stein.'" The article was not in the best taste: Lacan was content to formulate a number of glaring commonplaces. He first recalled that artists had preceded Freud in the discovery of the unconscious, and that Duras had similarly preceded Lacan in the Lola business. He then emphasized that the figure *three* plays an important role in the story, affirming finally that Lola was not a *voyeur:* She looks without seeing, being thus "realized" through the circuit of the gaze. Lacan's text is studded with a multitude of compliments and pointless indulgences in flattery.[77]

Although she found the master's nighttime comments unforgettable, Duras responded to him sixteen years later in a "feminist" mode. "It doesn't interest me," she told Suzanne Lamy, "when Lacan says, 'She knows, the woman knows. . . .' I don't know what his exact words were. . . . Those are a man's words, a master's words. . . . All the same, they are the words of a man of power, it's clear. The reference is himself. 'What I teach,' she, that little female, she knows. It's a formidable act of homage, but it is homage that ricochets back to himself. He might have said: What is taught in general she knows from the outset, but what counts is what *I* teach."[78]

In 1967, Montrelay was dazzled by the paper presented seven years earlier by Granoff and Perrier in Amsterdam. Upon reading the volume *Nouvelles recherches,* she decided, on the basis of that book, to draw up a balance sheet herself on the question of femininity. She wrote a long article. During the time she was working on it, she was victim of a horrendous automobile accident that cost her her sight in one eye and disfigured her. In spite of that, she still remained beautiful, perhaps even more so because of her greater vulnerability. She wanted to get her text published and sent it to *Les Temps modernes.* Pontalis called her in, proceeded to lecture her, and asked her to rewrite the whole piece. Finally, he told her he could not accept it because it was too explosive. Lacan then advised Michèle to speak to Sollers, who refused it because it did not suit his strategies at the time. Finally, Jacques Derrida accepted it for *Critique*. It appeared in 1970.

Montrelay explained that the authors, members of the SPP, made clear the impasses of Freudian phallocentrism and attempted to rectify it with the help of Anglo-Saxon clinical evidence. She then took up anew the entire debate over non-complementarity on the basis of Lacanian positions. Her article was commented on by François Perrier, then by Moustapha Safouan, who in 1976 offered a broad perspective on the state of the problem, confusing a number of tendencies in the process.[79] In the position taken by Montrelay, a reading of Duras's work and a return to prominence of the thematic of *écriture féminine* play a central role. The author did not restrict herself to answering the question of Freudian phallocentrism with Lacan's reelaboration of matters; she moved toward a literary "feminism" consisting of transforming female erotic pleasure into a form of writing. There thus emerged a point of view that exceeded the Lacanian perspective. Through it, femininity was defined as a *shadow,* a *primary feminine,* an *ineffable* dimension repressed by psychoanalysis. In the search for their femaleness, men and women would have to inscribe the name of that shadow. Montrelay thus contributed a new element to the Lacanian edifice.

In the introductory statement of the second issue of *Scilicet,* Lacan paid homage to her in a statement redolent with nostalgia for the Amsterdam congress: "All of which may be gauged from the advantage derived by Michèle Montrelay, an analyst of the École (new formula), from a work belonging to a totally different field. May what is original dispensed therein 'à propos' be appreciated. A propos of the work whose merit is underscored by that critique. . . . It is not unworthy bias to demonstrate the thaw that a work emergent from our training has brought to the problem of female sexuality, which has remained blocked since Jones's objections to Freud. The complaint I keep repeating that I am misread more often than anticipated is disarmed in this case. Not without my receiving a nostalgic echo to the effect that a certain congress in Amsterdam, for which I had proposed the subject, unfortunately preferred there to seize the opportunity to return to the fold." [80]

As soon as the article appeared in *Critique,* it caught Antoinette Fouque's attention. She had read *Nouvelles recherches,* and without rejecting Freud's discovery, she had no qualms about attacking phallocentrism throughout her analysis with Lacan. Shortly thereafter, she lunched with Michèle Montrelay. A relationship between the two was struck up, which resulted in the publication of a dialogue in *La Quinzaine littéraire.* Antoinette Fouque spoke for a second libido and homosexuation, while Michèle Montrelay asked her how the "thing" took place between women, since the penis was absent. Antoinette did not reply to that essential question, and Michèle displaced the debate onto the more sturdy ground of the desire of females for each other. Whereupon her interlocutor evoked the "numerous bodies, with dense, deep, voluminous and fluid, gnarled, supple, and fragmented odors, touches, and tastes at last definitively detached from their (until now) censored and censoring origin." [81] At which, one can imagine the partisans of the British school rejoicing and a tremor passing through the ranks of the Viennese clan.

Lacan, during that period, was also caught up in the feminist blaze. By 1970, he had announced that sexual identification did not consist in believing oneself to be a man or a woman, that woman was the truth of man, that there was no sexual relation since that relation was speech itself, and finally that "Woman" did not exist. The following year, in the framework of his second hyperlogical reelaboration, he developed "formulas of sexuation," then, during the year 1972–73, devoted the whole of his seminar to reopening the debate. He called it *Encore,* thus indicating that he was still present, he the *maître,* and that women seemed to want still more: "All you have to do is go to Rome and look at the Bernini statue to understand immediately that she is in sexual ecstasy, Saint Theresa, no doubt about it. And what is it she is being ravished by? It is plain that the essential testimony of the mystics is precisely to say that they experience it, but know nothing about it." [82] The seminar is stupefying. It reveals the final return to the French scene of the great baroque Lacan of his Roman maturity and failed visit to the pope. But it is also an act of homage to the Bataille of *Madame Edwarda,* to the absolute figure of the hatred and love of God. It was a considerable exploit indeed to have resorted to a female mystic at the very time women were demanding their liberation, and to have done so without the slightest whiff of piety!

On the theoretical level, Lacan did not renounce a single element of his prior doctrine. But the tone of his discourse was different. He had heard Antoinette's message, and although he had taken up none of her affirmations, he showed himself to be sensitive to the new rhetoric of *écriture féminine.* He reaffirmed the primacy of phallocentrism, defined supplementarity once again, and denounced the error of the naturalist prejudice: *La femme*—woman—existed only if the *la* were barred. In other words, there were *des femmes*—women—and a specifically female mode of sexual bliss whose impossibility to be articulated was revealed by the mystics. But *woman does not exist* since her nature was not her generic end, and anatomy was not her destiny. Similarly, the sexual relation was not a relation, but the *non-relation* between two monologues. There was thus no sexual relation. The two formulas would cause much ink to flow, and Lacan recounted how, in Italy, the ambiguity of his words provoked a misunderstanding: "I had given this absolutely insane title for a lecture to the Milanese, who had never heard of all this, *Psychoanalysis in Its Reference to the Sexual Relation.* They're quite intelligent. They understood things so well that that very evening one could read in the paper, 'For Dr. Lacan, women, *le donne,* don't exist!' It's true, what do you expect, if the sexual relation doesn't exist, there are no women. There was . . . a lady from the MLF there. She was really . . . I told her, 'Come tomorrow morning, I'll explain to you what it's all about.' " [83]

In 1974, Luce Irigaray published a book entitled *Speculum, de l'autre femme* ["Speculum: of the other woman"], which would attract a good deal of attention.[84] It effected a fusion between the egalitarian thematic of Beauvoirian feminism and that of the liberation of an *écriture feminine.* The latter was defined as gender-specific; it would be capable, according to the author, of subverting the oppressive language of men. Irigaray's work is shot through and through with sparks emergent from MLF. But unlike Antoinette, who was her immediate inspiration, Luce rejected Lacan's teaching and criticized it from a Derridean perspective. She assimilated

Freudian phallocentrism to a logocentrism and proposed a "deconstructive" reading of the dark continent: Through the emergence of her repressed, *la femme*—Woman—becomes *une*—one—and thus gives birth to her radical alterity. "What is at stake in the situation we are living at present," Luce declared, "is the language refused to our female body."[85]

A year later, Hélène Cixous and Catherine Clément published a two-headed work, *La jeune née* [*Newly Born Woman*], which moved in the same direction and enjoyed considerable success. One opposed an *écriture* of being-a-woman to "phallocentric" language, while the other evoked witches, hysterics, and the various Freudian images of seduction.[86]

All this effervescence resulted in the publication, under the leadership of Catherine Clément, of two special issues of the journal *L'Arc*, the first of which was dedicated to Jacques Lacan,[87] and the second to Simone de Beauvoir.[88] Now the volume paying homage to Lacan was written exclusively by women: "The idea for this issue," wrote Catherine Clément, "is due to what is called chance; one might also say an event, acting-out, in the course of an analysis, an encounter. Which is to announce its function as *real,* if it be true that encounters are those 'radical points in the real' discussed by Lacan in *Séminaire XI*. First a fantasy—and what if we did a Lacan issue with only women?—which returned to us as the subject of a joke. . . . The principle being to demonstrate that Lacan has resulted in effects of cultural reorganization sufficiently important to affect the status of the publication of women's writing."[89]

Naturally, the idea pleased Lacan a great deal. When Clément told him of the project, he burst out laughing. Not only would he be celebrated by women, but—something still more important in his eyes—he would be the first French master of psychoanalysis to figure in the prestigious portrait gallery of one of the leading journals of the French intellectual scene. Before him, Freud was the first psychoanalyst to be paid homage by *L'Arc*, and, following Freud, Lacan himself would now be received in the Pantheon; he would be the equal of Bataille, Sartre, Merleau-Ponty, Deleuze, et al. He was as such already a consecrated value in the worlds of philosophy and literature. Subsequently, Winnicott, Groddeck, and Reich would in turn be celebrated by the journal, then Françoise Dolto. . . . A delightful revenge for the "excommunicated."

The issue of *L'Arc* assembled contributions from women who were for the most part members of the EFP. It featured the names of Maud Mannoni, Luce Irigaray, Michèle Montrelay, et al. To these were added an article by Jacqueline Rousseau-Dujardin, who had resigned from the SPP, and another by Shoshana Felman. "Lacan's writing," she wrote, "so close to Mallarmé's, assumes its irreducibly literary dimension, that of a blindness informing dazzling instances of insight and clairvoyance."[90] The collective homage began with a text entitled "Aimée." At the request of Catherine Clément, who had long been interested in female paranoia, Lacan had agreed to republish the part of his thesis concerning the attack against the actress Huguette Duflos and the anamnesis of the case. A year later, the thesis was republished by Éditions du Seuil. But already the issue of *L'Arc* was restoring currency to a youthful Lacan, who was not a structuralist, one completely unknown to the reading public of the 1970s. If the issue opened with the evocation of that figure of female paranoia, which had prompted so many reactions among the Surrealists, it revealed—to the point of ridicule—the illusions specific to the women's movement. For no female *écriture* emerged from this touching act of homage to His Phallocentric Majesty. The women invited to participate wrote of their subjects in a style no different from that of their male counterparts. And each of their texts demonstrated that writing cannot be captured in the meshwork of any "sexuation" whatever—be it differential, egalitarian, or supplementary. Might the written per se be phallic, or is its libido of the second variety? In order to penetrate that particular enigma (which in fact is none at all, but which enjoyed a certain good fortune), the scholarly reader is invited to pick up the Orient Express in Vienna, headed for London. While awaiting the results of that new inquiry, Lacan, one takes it, must be rubbing his hands with pleasure in his grave, where he has renewed contact with Bernini's Saint Theresa.

III. Red Front and Years of Embers

We have seen how the gradual implantation of Freudian theses within academic literary criticism had modified the configuration of the years prior to the 1960s. The polemic triggered by Roland Barthes's *Sur Racine* had immediate repercussions both on the way in which the psychoanalytic community broached literary texts and on the role played by journals in their apprehension of psychoanalysis. The literary reviews came in turn to reflect on structuralism. And as a result, "modern" writers, as had previously been the case with the Surrealists, appropriated Freudian theses in their attempt to define, through them, a new theory of writing. Created in 1960 by a few bourgeois aesthetes, the journal *Tel Quel* would occupy a central place in the emergence of the notion of "textual practice." Until 1962, it was above all interested in the *nouveau roman*. Then, under the impetus of Philippe Sollers, and with the incorporation into the collective of Marcelin Pleynet, Denis Roche, and Jean-Louis Baudry, a transformation occurred. It centered on the defense of a poetic *écriture* that had been neglected by the *nouveau roman*. The inquiry into the status of writing emerged from the importance assumed by the human sciences in the field of literary criticism, specifically, linguistics and psychoanalysis. But it also stemmed from writing itself and its permanent condition of crisis. In 1964, *Tel Quel* declared itself to be an avant-garde journal. For the first time in France, it published (in a translation by Todorov) certain major texts of the Russian formalists.[91]

In order to differentiate itself from its Surrealist ancestors, the journal sought models among the dissidents: Bataille and Artaud were invoked as the vanguard representatives of a radical anti-Surrealism—one because of his Nietzscheism, his mystical atheism, and his cult of eroticism, and the other for his experience of a monumental prose of madness. Beyond those references, Dante, Lautréamont, Sade, and Mallarmé also appeared as the prophets of a permanent revolution inscribed at the heart of Western writing.[92]

In 1963, the review paid ringing tribute to Georges Bataille, and a year later, a first text was published by Michel de M'Uzan, a psychoanalyst of the SPP and a student of Bouvet's, on "Freud and Literary Creation." [93] But very soon thereafter, the classic terrain of literature per se was abandoned in favor of the theses of Barthes, Lacan, Derrida, and Benveniste. They were incorporated into a "revolutionary theory of Western textuality." Philippe Sollers and Marcelin Pleynet were the artisans of this projected cleaning out of the stables of literature. Sollers was a writer of prose and Pleynet a poet. The former was a child of the bourgeoisie, educated by Jesuits, and the latter a self-taught son of the people. They were in no way similar, but understood each other perfectly in their desire to wage guerrilla war against existent institutions and to charm the leading intellectual figures of the day.

In May 1966, a young Bulgarian, Julia Kristeva, joined the clan and provided it with its academic impetus. A linguist and a polyglot, she had arrived in Paris a year earlier with a study grant. "Having come to France thanks to de Gaulle's dream of a 'single Europe from the Atlantic to the Urals,'" she wrote, "I had the impression of discovering in that territory which went from the Éditions du Seuil to the École pratique des hautes études a cosmopolitanism transcending the socialist and European region and which in fact corresponded to the finest moments of the universalist legend of Paris." [94] Julia Kristeva prepared her "third cycle" thesis with Lucien Goldmann and attended Roland Barthes's seminar. In Paris she met her compatriot Tzvetan Todorov, who had preceded her in the voyage to the West. Soon, through Gérard Genette, she met Philippe Sollers, before becoming the friend of Émile Benveniste. In the spring of 1967, she was accused of being a Soviet spy by the newspaper *Minute,* and the brawl began. . . . Its framework was Éditions du Seuil; its focus intellectual control of the PCF; and its point of reference structuralism.

In 1966, *Tel Quel* published Jacques Derrida's paper "Freud and the Scene of Writing." From the perspective of a surfacing of the "trace," Lacan's reelaboration also aroused a great deal of interest, and particularly his theory of the division of the subject. Through it, the writers of *Tel Quel* could become Freudians; they read Freud in the light of Lacan, Lacan under the banner of Derrida, and Derrida according to a guerrilla-like strategy of the written. It mattered little that those endeavors were opposed to each other; they still seemed to be speaking the same language: signifiers, texts, and inscriptions.

Philippe Sollers met Jacques Lacan for the first time in 1965. Through him, he was in search of the shadow of Georges Bataille. The two lunched together in the company of François Wahl. On that occasion, Lacan was in a particularly exalted mood. He announced to Sollers that he had just conquered his "pack" of Normaliens and begun to implement his project of renewal. Sollers was already attending Lacan's seminar, and the latter took him for a student. He asked him what he was writing his thesis on. Shortly thereafter, he would invite him to speak to his group, and then to come spend a few days in Venice. Sollers refused. He had no desire to commit himself to any formal allegiance. In 1966, the master sent him a copy of the *Écrits* dedicated: "To P. S., we are not, in brief, as alone as we thought." [95]

Lacan was enthralled with the extremely talented, playful, and libertine writer. But he understood before long that the latter was not in search of a master, and that his interests were literary or strategic, and never psychoanalytic. Now Lacan was interested neither in literature as such, nor in writers, whom he wanted to turn into his adepts. He thought of himself as a philosopher, a logician, and the leader of a school, and if he wielded the pen of a genuine writer, he always used literary works to illustrate the soundness of his doctrine. Never did Lacan derive from literature an occasion for authentic and autonomous enjoyment. He made use of it as an adornment. In that sense, the criticism addressed to him by Duras, on the one hand, and Derrida, on the other, was justified. In the *maître*'s entourage that attitude was imitated. As opposed to the psychoanalysts of the other camp, like de M'Uzan, Pontalis, and Anzieu, on the subject of literature, the Lacanians were incapable of producing anything but confirmations of their doctrinal positions. Most spoke on the subject with fascination, but only to rediscover in it what they already knew. Despite that, Lacan remained a producer of literature. His texts are written like fictions, short stories or parables. But his relations with writers suffered as a result.

Sollers, for his part, was a great professional of literature, an adept of the pleasure principle. He was aware that Lacan's work entertained a relation with the notions of "letter" and "signifier" that was essential for "textual practice." Superbly intelligent, lavish in his expenditures, sensitive to every form of femininity, he excelled in cultivating the art of making himself loved or hated, losing himself occasionally in his adversary's desire. Gifted with a splendid ear for the unconscious, he delighted in others infinitely, his senses always alert to the shifting winds of the day. But his cult of success frequently led him to elaborate global strategies which he alone believed to have any foundation. Lacan saw this quite well. He would not have been averse to reigning over the Telquelian Armada, but he did not enjoy divided territories, and remained on his guard. He knew that the journal accorded as much importance, if not more, to the theses of Barthes and Derrida as to his own.

The article published by Jean-Louis Baudry in the winter of 1968 under the title "Freud et la création littéraire," [96] made it clear, moreover, just how much more nourishing Derridean deconstruction was for certain of the group's writers than Lacan's reelaborations. In that text, the author explained Freud's positions on literature by drawing exclusively on Derrida's teaching. He resorted endlessly to the notions of trace, fraying, and effraction, and did not quote Lacan's name a single time. *Tel Quel*'s interest in Lacanianism was significant, to be sure, but it varied according to the political situation of the moment. At the outset, Derridean theses dominated the work of the Telquelians and Derrida, moreover, published part of his work in the journal and with Éditions du Seuil. Sollers had relations of true friendship with him. But caught up in his own strategies, he played a difficult game, wavering between Lacan and Derrida, that would end up with a magisterial failure with one and a breaking off of relations with the other. In that story, personal feelings fused with conceptual concerns.

The displacement of the structuralist configuration onto the avant-garde literary scene began in the fall of 1967 with the publication in *Tel Quel* of a flamboyant manifesto rife with intellectual terrorism. It was called "Programme," and was written by Philippe Sollers. The text reveals an art of verbal inflation reminiscent of *Proletkult* and characteristic of the period preceding the May 1968 explosion. The themes broached were identical to those that had produced literary feminism. Sollers put together a skillful amalgamation with the help of concepts elaborated during the structuralist years. From Foucault he borrowed the pair reason/madness, making of it the site at which a "textual rupture" was emerging. From Derrida he took the idea of a "proto-trace," transforming it into the possibility of a "repressed" *écriture*. In Lacan he was able to find essentially a way of integrating Freudian discourse into the entirety of his project. And finally, through Althusser, he was able to tinker with the Bachelardian notion of an epistemological break, which allowed him to situate the history of textuality within dialectical materialism. On the basis of that mix, which was intended to be explosive, the history of literature was thought through as a series of textual ruptures, which could be grasped in the works of Sade, Bataille, Artaud, et al. These defined a discontinuity in textual practice, from which the notion of an author was swept away (as "bourgeois" and "sacralizing") and superseded by that of the "science of the subject." Writing was not an object of study since the theory charged with thinking it through was already in practice *écriture*. Every revolution thus passes through a convulsion of writing, that is, through an "overall theory" elaborated as a practice of writing. Thanks to which, Telquelism was able to think of itself as the very movement of a proletarian vanguard. For several years, it would thus impose a particular reading of structuralism, drawing along in its wake not only the theorists it had solicited but a number of university academics in search of a new "scientificity" in their approach to texts. After May, a university department in the sciences of texts and documents would be founded, in which Julia Kristeva would teach.

For the joint history of literature and psychoanalysis, the *Tel Quel* adventure had neither the innovative force nor the impact of Surrealism, whose nether side it was intent on being. In its convulsive phase, it did not entertain the same relation as Surrealism with dynamic psychiatry. It was deployed at a time when dynamism was on the wane, and in which the fertile soil that had allowed psychoanalysis to take root was already eroded. As much as the Surrealist writers had been influenced by dynamism and well informed on clinical matters, Telquelism remained—to a similar extent—alien to that tradition. The Surrealists fabricated poems, fiction, and collages on the basis of clinical reality. Telquelism was in search of a scientificity stripped of any reference to diagnostic categories. For that reason, the writers of the group did not produce any work directly inspired by Freud's discovery. Their apprehension of psychoanalysis remained purely theoretical. It was pursued through intellectual commentary on the status of writing and never resulted in a literary or poetic creation. In addition, matters transpired as though the structuralist renewal had already occupied, in France, the place of a new Surrealism. And in those circumstances, the *Tel Quel* experiment took on the appearance of a mimeshow; it repeated the saga of a reelaboration that had already taken place. It thus gave birth to a formalist red front, in which were revealed, in the form of a repetitive carnival, the mythology of the memorable days of the revolution (as well as the pallid fervor of its mornings after).

When the Surrealists joined the Communist Party at the beginning of the 1930s, they dreamed of a Bolshevism which had already ceased to exist. Their fantasies were of Lenin, the taking of the Winter Palace, or a new conspiracy in Red

Square, and they were faced with the follies of Stalinism. So they each withdrew—quietly, violently, or suicidally. But when the *Tel Quel* writers approached the same party, forty years later, the game had already been played out twice over. Not only was October dead and buried, but with it the entire saga of the *avant-garde*. Surrealism staged a dream, and Telquelism helped lay that same dream to rest. Whence the exalted switch to Maoism, conceived as the ultimate form of a revolution that had disappeared, followed by a reconversion to the Christian ideals of a somewhat antiquated Europe. "At a time when a Latin American Marxist revolution threatens at the gates of the United States," wrote Julia Kristeva in 1983, "I feel closer to the truth and to freedom in the space of that contested giant who is perhaps about to turn into a David in the face of the growing Goliath of the Third World. I dream that our children will prefer to join that David, its errors and its impasses, armed with our own wanderings, linked to ideas, to Logos, to Form: in brief, to old Europe." [97]

Telquelism thus drew its strength from three sources. On the one hand, it traversed the history of the PCF and its cultural journals at a time of particular effervescence; on the other, it was supported by three masters of the structuralist renewal, Barthes, Derrida, and Foucault; and finally, it served as a platform for restoring currency to the quarrel over the role of an *avant-garde*. To these should be added the publishing power linked to the group's being firmly ensconced at Éditions du Seuil.

In their relation to Freud's discovery, the theses of Surrealism had been productive of works of literature, whereas those of *Tel Quel* were not. Although the group rediscovered an art of "convulsion," which had formerly been Breton's in his imitation of hysteria, it did not give birth to works of significance. Those were the accomplishments of writers who, as individuals, might at a given time share the journal's positions or reject them. Telquelism was thus permeated by a more general situation of literary modernity, which flourished over twenty years, between 1960 and 1980, and allowed a thematic present in Lacanian theory to surface in a number of works. The fact that Lacan fed on that thematic, by way of structuralism, or that modernity did without realizing as much is of little import in the face of the phenomenon itself. Beyond Telquelism, the literature of the period was concerned with the inscription of a divided subject, of desire, of the "object," and of the "real as impossible," in a manner that found its conceptual realization in Lacanian doctrine. And no doubt Lacan had to be blind to that modernity, as Freud was to Surrealism, for the fusion (at a distance) of the finest phase of a theoretical advance and the best moments of a literary modernity traversed by it to occur. In that respect, the political and ideological history of the *Tel Quel* venture, in its specific relation to psychoanalysis, should be distinguished from the history of the works produced during that period and of which the *Tel Quel* venture would have been only the imitative or playful expression.

A few major works bear witness to the emergence of a Lacanian thematic in literature between 1962 and 1981: *La Veille* ["The vigil"], by Roger Laporte, in which the narrator, following the example of Maurice Blanchot, takes an impossible *écriture* as the object of his narrative; *Compact,* by Maurice Roche, which gives raw

expression to the division of a subject distributed into six meshing "scores";
L'homme qui dort ["The man who sleeps"], by Georges Pérec, in which the author
speaks in the second person to a hero absent from himself, sleeping his way through
life as in an analysis; *Éden, Éden, Éden,* by Pierre Guyotat, exploring the outer
reaches of a language of sex; *Louve basse,* by Denis Roche, which describes the
corpse of a narrator reduced to the delectation of his infantile wastes; and finally
Paradis, by Philippe Sollers, an interminable text without punctuation, constructed
as the soliloquy of a writing for which only an oral reading might awaken the full
range of signifying associations. Between the unfurling of those literary productions
and the theoretical impact enabling their emergence was to be found the French
afterlife of the Freudian discovery, as revised and corrected by Lacan through the
grid of a structuralism that was itself exceeded on all sides by its signifying effects.[98]

Since 1956 and following the publication of Louis Althusser's article, the
attitude of Communist intellectuals toward psychoanalysis had undergone a quiet
change without resulting in any in-depth critique of past errors. The arguments of a
number of psychiatrists who had joined the party, their devotion to the dynamic
tendency and to public service, as well as the policy of alliance practiced by Henri
Ey through his unfailing friendship with Lucien Bonnafé allowed for the disastrous
events of the Zhdanov period to fade from memory. Young Communist therapists
were taking increasingly to analysis without any knowledge of the past. They adhered to a "new" party, and discovered a Freudian psychoanalysis contemporaneous
with their own inquiries. In 1964, Althusser's article did not provoke any immediate
reactions, and Althusserianism itself was criticized because of its theoretical antihumanism. But gradually, that major text became the point of departure for a partial
meditation on the past, and particularly on "concrete psychology." Althusser
showed that Lacan's reelaboration allowed for a critique of both American revisionism and Zhdanovian ideology. Now, by 1953, Lacan had anticipated that his doctrine might well be understood within the ranks of the party. He was not wrong. He
had paid homage to Politzer on several occasions, and his presence at the ENS had
brought new life to debates over Marxism. To be sure, Lacan did not join in any
political or electoral battle, and his family circle was on the whole marked by a left-
wing hostility to the PCF. Against the Communist line, Laurence had participated
in the assistance network of the FLN during the Algerian War. As for Jacques-Alain
and Judith, in 1968 they had joined the ranks of Gauche prolétarienne, which had
embarked on a struggle to the death against revisionism. In that context, Lacan had
no more sympathy for the *gauchiste* version of militant struggle than for the party
apparatus. Nevertheless, the PCF was a powerful institution, and the old master
revealed himself to be quite attentive to the transformations it was undergoing and
the manner in which his thought was received. His severity toward the American
model and his sympathy for Politzer's "errors" led him to write in 1964, "We thus
find justified the hostility psychoanalysis has encountered in the East. It was up to
psychoanalysis not to deserve it."[99]

After the meeting of the Central Committee at Argenteuil in 1966, the way
was open both for a critical reassessment of Politzer's theses and for a more thor-

ough rejection of Zhdanovism. That opening was deployed in several ways within the party ranks, where the apprehension of Lacan's doctrine served the rediscovery of an authentic Freudianism. The "literary people" were not interested in the same Freud or the same Lacan as the philosophers and psychiatrists. For the former, Lacan's theses were understood in the context of a debate over linguistics and the status of writing. In this, the relations established between *Tel Quel* and *La Nouvelle Critique* in November 1967 played an energizing role. For the philosophers, Lacan's theses were the subject of a different kind of discussion to the extent that they took root by way of Althusserian antihumanism. They thus occupied an important position within a framework in which Althusserianism had been invoked as a means to criticize the various branches of psychology. At the time, a student of Althusser's, Michel Pêcheux, decided to wage a battle against psychology within its own university or party bastions, on the basis of an Althussero-Lacanian position capable of integrating the works of Canguilhem and of modern linguistics. He published several articles to that end in *Cahiers pour l'analyse,* under the pseudonym Thomas Herbert. Pêcheux drew a few friends in his wake, notably two researchers at the CNRS [National Center of Scientific Research], Paul Henry and Michel Plon. The former was interested in logic and linguistics, and the latter in politics and game theory.[100] Lacan would write to them or propose that they speak at his seminar.

During this period, Althusserianism was being criticized within the party by the champions of a humanist tendency, drawing, on the contrary, on psychology and Politzer's legacy. Discussion on those grounds was initiated by the publication of Lucien Sève's monumental work, *Marxisme et théorie de la personnalité,* which was published in several languages.[101]

Finally, the psychiatrists were reading a different Lacan, even as they too oscillated between a Politzerian humanism and a theoretical antihumanism. At the beginning of 1967, they met in the framework of the Centre d'études et de recherches marxistes (CERM) with philosophers and psychologists to work collectively on the general theme of "Marxism and Psychoanalysis." The participants in the discussions were not Lacanians, but Lacan's doctrine served as a constant point of reference for their debates on Freudianism. The lecture series ended late in 1968 with a confrontation with Lacan, who agreed enthusiastically to speak at CERM. Two years later, the texts were gathered and published in five mimeographed booklets entitled *Marxisme et Psychanalyse.* They contained several articles, two of which were entirely devoted to the notion of the decentering of the subject in Lacan's work. It was a matter of demonstrating that that work had brought new life to the evaluation of the notion of human personality. For some, the subject of language was the effect of a process in which man was ex-centered from his history; for others it was to be articulated with an anthropology grounded in Marxism. Jean Ayme participated in the proceedings with a presentation on institutional psychotherapy. The entire project was of high theoretical caliber.[102]

For the history of the implantation of psychoanalysis within the Communist movement after 1956, Lucien Sève occupies a place comparable to that of Lagache for the psychoanalytic community. Born in 1926, a student of the ENS after the war, he received the *agrégation* in 1949 and joined the party the following year. Disappointed by the psychology taught in the universities, he inquired into the notions of "person" and "personality" while reading Politzer's work: "With what Politzer demolished, as well as with what he seemed to announce, I was in agreement. Psychoanalysis, in that respect, although it seemed to contain an important core of truth, interested me less than the neglected work of Janet, who, despite his numerous limitations, aroused my enthusiasm through his sense of psychological activity and the historico-social character of personality." [103]

In 1952, Lucien Sève publicly registered his disagreement with the use being made of Pavlovianism in *La Raison*. And in that perspective, he continued his research on the notion of personality, which was to serve as the basis of a renewal of Politzer's project. Thus when the publication of Althusser's works presented a critique of Politzer's position diametrically opposed to his own endeavor, Sève opposed theoretical antihumanism with a concrete psychology of Marxist inspiration that he hoped would be able to account for the essence of human personality. Through Politzer, he continued to opt for Janet against Freud, the "person" against the "subject." The debate over Freudianism in the party at that point took on the appearance of a quarrel about humanism and psychology. For the Sèvian current, the concrete psychology of the person was to be articulated jointly with an historical materialism in the framework of a liberal program of scientific socialism, whereas in the Althusserian perspective, the renewal of Marxism needed to pass by way of a radical struggle against all forms of psychology and thus by way of a Lacanian assessment of Freudianism. The opposition deployed between the two tendencies transposed onto Communist terrain certain divisions already at work within the French psychoanalytic situation. In that respect, the cleavage between Sève's positions and Althusser's theses was a displacement, under the rubric of a "Politzerian standard," of the doctrinal opposition between Lagache and Lacan.

On both sides of the divide, the debate over the relations between Marxism and psychoanalysis was reopened without giving birth to a Freudo-Marxism, that option having been seized by the *gauchiste* movement and given currency through *L'anti-Oedipe*. Nor did it result in a critique of Soviet psychiatry. As for the lines of demarcation indicating the borders between the two tendencies within the party, they were rarely in view and were not experienced as such by the mass of Communist intellectuals. There were many who saw themselves as simultaneously Sèvian, Althusserian, Lacanian, Telquelian, and feminist as the alliances or publishing demands of the day demanded. The effervescence within the PCF was so intense between the Argenteuil congress and the election in 1974 of Giscard d'Estaing to the presidency of the republic that fusions were as important as divisions or reciprocal hostilities. All the militants of the Communist intelligentsia published their articles in the organs of the party, from *Lettres françaises* to *Humanité*, by way of *La Nouvelle Critique, France Nouvelle,* or *La Pensée*. They would all meet in September at the annual outdoor festival in the park at La Courneuve and then in March at the Marxist Book Fair. They participated in numerous colloquiums, and various meetings and commissions in which each pursued his dream of changing the world with the help of the great proletarian fortress.

Despite the tendential disappearance of rifts, two political lines were pitted against each other at the center of the cultural debate. Althusserianism led to a critique of revisionism and ended in a Chinese dream of Leninist revolution, while the theses of Lucien Sève adapted to the new alliance envisaged in 1972 with the signing of the Common Program, which supported the project of an eventual flourishing of individual selves or persons within an "advanced democracy."

In that context, Catherine Clément, who was a member of the EFP, joined the party in the fall of 1968. An *agrégée* and a student of the École normale supérieure, she had long attended Lacan's seminar and participated in the rise of *Cahiers pour l'analyse*. Having embarked on the adventure of *La Nouvelle Critique* (NC), she was charged with organizing debates and public discussions on the theme of "psychoanalysis and politics." She had connections with every tendency: the women's movement, *Tel quel*, Lacanianism, and personality theory. In addition, she knew psychoanalysts of every stripe. In 1970, she organized a panel that brought together Serge Leclaire, André Green, and Lucien Sève.[104] Antoine Casanova, the editor-in-chief of *NC* and Bernard Muldworf, a Communist psychotherapist hostile to Lacanianism, participated in the discussion. It was a matter of simultaneously dispelling the clouds of the Zhdanov period and of bringing the intellectual attainments of Marxism to bear on an assessment of Freudianism. The confrontation ended in total confusion. As an ardent Politzerian, Lucien Sève asked the psychoanalysts to admit that Freudianism was shot through with sociologism and biologism. André Green, for his part, reminded the Communists of their shameful past and explained that psychoanalysis had succeeded in imposing its core of hard truth against them. Then, as a provocation, he proposed that Marx's biography might be the subject of a psychoanalytic study, replete with marriage, Oedipus complex, and complicated paternity. Finally, Serge Leclaire attempted to speak about various registers of erotic pleasure in psychoanalysis. As for the others, each played his assigned role in the conversation. The tone was one of good humor and cordiality, but the theoretical level was rather mediocre.[105]

That discussion revealed that the Communist intellectuals of the 1970s were as ignorant of their own history as the psychoanalysts. And yet both sides brandished the notorious article of 1949 on "reactionary ideology" without being able to situate it in the complex adventure of past relations between the PCF and the psychoanalytic movement. In brief, they made the text function as an imaginary springboard, one side in order to affirm that the party had indeed changed, without any understanding of how or why, and the other in order to forget that the article was the result of a conflictual compromise between its signatories and the party leadership and that, as such, it was much less "Zhdanovian" than appeared. In fact, Louis Althusser was the first Communist intellectual to reopen, in 1964, discussion of a painful past that the party, having neither the theoretical tools nor the political means to understand it in the Stalinist context, had preferred quietly to forget. Now Althusser showed that Lacan's reelaboration allowed for both a critique of the 1949 article and a justification of its contents. In so doing, he was not acting as an historian, but as a philosopher concerned with theoretical interpretation: He sided with Freud against Politzer.

When the *Nouvelle Critique* colloquium on the theme of "Marxism and Psychoanalysis" was held, the various discussants were less interested in reassessing the past than in avoiding it in order to speak of the present. For the psychoanalysts, the discussion meant an opening toward new networks of patients and influence, and for the representatives of the official line of the PCF, it authorized the continuation of the struggle—on psychoanalytic ground—against an Althusserianism deemed to be out of step with the prevailing advocacy of an alliance with social democracy. Under those circumstances, the struggle against theoretical antihumanism proved to be more important in the discussions than the actual assessment of relations between Marxism and psychoanalysis. In order for Lacanianism to offer a Freudianism that would be acceptable in the context of the Politzerian renewal, it would have had to be stripped of all connection with Althusserianism and theoretical antihumanism. Discussions in the 1970s on Marxism and psychoanalysis were thus destined to end in confusion, since their aim was to efface a Zhdanovian past which was still not understood and to neutralize the Althusserian representation of Freudianism.

And yet, since an event never remains buried once it has become an issue in a battle over establishment, those discussions also allowed the Communists and the psychoanalysts to have access, in however deformed a way, to the history of a shared past. The famous debate over psychoanalysis and Marxism, which failed to take place in the 1930s, then again in the 1950s, thus occurred with considerable delay during the period 1965–75, under specific political circumstances. It did not evolve, as in the Soviet Union, under the banner of Pavlov, but rather under a Politzerian standard. There is nothing surprising in that once one is aware of the role played by Politzer's work and person in the joint history of French psychoanalysis and the Communist movement. The first Politzer was the artisan of a concrete psychology; the second the impassioned adversary of a "French psychoanalysis," and the third became the impassioned artisan of an anti-Freudian Marxism. Through those three modalities of the Politzerian standard, three possible paths for the implantation of psychoanalysis in the French Communist movement were formulated. The first took the form of a Pavlovianism blind to itself, the second of a concrete psychology revised and corrected by Marxist anthropology, and the third, of a theoretical antihumanism hostile to all forms of psychological integration. Each of those paths could have become dominant according to the historical situation of the time. Through its antipsychologism, the third path was plainly the most auspicious for Lacan's reelaboration. It is thus that the existence of the Althussero-Lacanian configuration is to be explained in the contemporary history of Marxism and psychoanalysis.

Two years after the *Nouvelle Critique* debate and thanks to the signing of the Common Program, Lucien Sève, who had become the director of Éditions sociales, decided to publish a collective volume on the subject and thus to officialize the research that had emerged from the Communist efforts. For that editorial undertaking, he requested the collaboration of Catherine Clément and Pierre Bruno, a psychologist from Toulouse then in a training analysis with Maud Mannoni. The collective work was thus put together by two authors of Lacanian conviction and by Lucien Sève, who authored an overall positive evaluation of Politzer's legacy. The work bore an implausible title: *Pour une critique marxiste de la théorie psychana-*

lytique ["Toward a marxist critique of psychoanalytic theory"].[106] Catherine Clément opened the volume with a lengthy scholarly study of the history of psychoanalysis from the discovery of the unconscious to Lacan's reelaboration. Pierre Bruno then attacked the question of anthropology and the theory of the subject, and was overtly critical of Althusser in a sybilline note devoted to his 1964 article. As for Lucien Sève, he used Althusser's remarks to turn them into their opposite and thus justify, against antihumanism, the concrete psychology of the first Politzer. He thus rejected (without explaining them) the anti-Freudian "lucubractions" of the last Politzer and the strayings of the 1949 text. "Thus amended," he emphasized, "Politzer's position concerning psychoanalysis seems to us to be essentially invulnerable. The fundamental error of Freud and most psychoanalysts after him, in the general conception of human reality they presuppose, is indeed, as Politzer admirably revealed more than forty years ago, to believe that one can explain history by psychology and not psychology by history, and that because they take cognizance of only a specific aspect of the psyche. . . . That is why it seems extremely debatable to establish a parallel between Marx and Freud as having both equally dissipated the illusion of the human subject, the former through his ex-centered conception of history, the latter through his ex-centered conception of the psyche." [107] The collective work, published by Éditions sociales, benefited from a mass promotion effort, and thus passed as "official doctrine." It was quickly translated in most of the Socialist countries, with a preface adapted to each national context.

Two years before the debate over Marxism and psychoanalysis, the *Tel Quel* group was producing a literary representation of Freudianism and Lacanianism that would intersect, according to circumstances, the Sèvian or Althusserian tendency, only to eventually take its definitive distance from communism itself. The mix of ingredients specific to that red front would become explosive as the illusions and disavowals stemming from the events of May played themselves out.

In November of 1967, a first meeting took place between *Tel Quel* and *La Nouvelle Critique*. A member of the party and a cofounder of the journal *Promesse*, Jean-Louis Houdebine was the instigator of that encounter. At the time, Sollers was closer to Maoism than the PCF, and it was Marcelin Pleynet who directed the Telquelian line toward the proletarian fortress. Sollers, moreover, was supported by Aragon, who, along with Mauriac, had been enthusiastic about his first novel. A series of discussions were set up between party intellectuals (Christine Buci-Glucksmann, Houdebine, Casanova, and André Gisselbrecht) and writers of *Tel Quel* (including Jean-Louis Baudry, Marcelin Pleynet, Philippe Sollers, and Jean-Pierre Faye). Faye himself soon left the group to found his own journal, *Change,* in the summer of 1968. It too assembled a number of avant-garde writers, including Jacques Roubaud, Philippe Boyer, and Jean-Claude Montel, along with the young Chomskyan linguist Mitsou Ronat. The struggle between the two journals was violent and pivoted on the imaginary conquest of the proletarian fortress.

For the Telquelians caught up in the Communist adventure, the science of writing was to allow for the definition of a single proletarian line in matters of literary creation. Now for the adversaries of that Telquelism, the acknowledgment of a plurality of aesthetic forms was to have priority over the notion of a single line, which was deemed to be Zhdanovian. In September 1968, the journal *Action poétique* entered the fray. Created in Marseille during the 1950s, it was directed by Henri Deluy and published mainly poets, such as Jacques Roubaud, Pierre Lartigue, Paul Louis Rossi, or Maurice Regnaut. It was distinguished by its work on the problem of translation, by an original rereading of the medieval heritage and the works of the troubadours in particular, and by an overall meditation on the question of the avant-garde. Just prior to the events of May, Mitsou Ronat joined the group and I myself published a number of texts on literature and psychoanalysis in the journal.[108] For that journal, there was no "science of textuality" possible, and any idea of a "single line" in matters literary was to be dismissed. According to circumstances, tactical alliances were formed against *Tel Quel* between *Change* and *Action poétique*.

In the spring of 1968, *La Nouvelle Critique* organized a colloquium on linguistics in the Cluny cloisters, and invited writers from *Tel Quel*, the linguistics section of CERM, and the Vaugirard Interdisciplinary Study Group to participate. The discussions were impassioned and the discourse as rambling as might be wished. Julia Kristeva spoke on the structural analysis of texts, Philippe Sollers on "metaplasms," Jean-Louis Baudry on the "structuration" of writing, and Marcelin Pleynet on structure and signification in Borges's work. At the end of the series of talks, the mayor of Cluny spoke in praise of his municipality. "This city, as you know, was once great," he said. "Great in its religious, intellectual, artistic and—in a word—human influence. So much so that it was often called a second Rome." [109]

Two months later, under the name of "La révolution ici et maintenant [Revolution here and now]," Sollers announced the creation of a "Theoretical Study Group," meeting once a week in a room on the rue de Rennes, facing the church of Saint-Germain-des-Prés. At stake was the project of constructing a "general theory" rooted in psychoanalysis, linguistics, semiology, and Marxism-Leninism.[110] For a period of a year, the group drew crowds. The whole of the Parisian intelligentsia squeezed in among students to hear about the science of the unconscious, "*différance*," the death of the author, and revolution by writing. Barthes, Derrida, Klossowski, and many others participated in the rather theatrical sessions. Lacan too would make a rather tottering appearance at the edge of the crowded auditorium.

While delighting at the success enjoyed by his operation, Sollers was preparing the publication of a collective volume entitled *Théorie d'ensemble*, which illustrated the history of *Tel Quel* by way of texts by its principal collaborators. Foucault, who had already published in the journal, contributed his support to the joyous exercise in "agit-prop" by publishing an article of homage to Sollers. Barthes contributed a text that had already appeared in *Critique* devoted to *Drame*. As for Derrida, he was represented by a lecture, "La différance," delivered a few months earlier at the Société française de philosophie.

During the winter of 1969, a rather heated polemic pitted *Tel Quel* against Jean-Pierre Faye in the pages of *Humanité*. Between the lines of an article entitled "Camarade Mallarmé," Faye attacked Derrida's theses on the degradation of writing and compared them to the discourse of the German extreme right wing. In a clarification requested by the newspaper, Faye elucidated his thought[111] as well as its relation to Derrida's position. The latter avoided participating in the polemic. Nevertheless, he observed the amalgamations *Tel Quel* was making with his work and kept his silence. For that reason he opted to advance no further on the party's battleground under such conditions. He would not participate in the second Cluny colloquium, in the spring of 1970, on the theme of "Literatures and Ideologies."

Meanwhile, an affair intervened that would provoke a shift in the "planetary" alliances within *Tel Quel*'s red front. In March 1969, Lacan received from Robert Flacelière, director of the ENS, a letter informing him that the Salle Dussane would no longer be available to him and that he would not be able to hold his seminar there the following year. Flacelière offered no motive for the expulsion, but invoked the reorganization of studies at the ENS and the recent Faure law on educational reform. Flacelière, a specialist on pedophilia and Greek love, thought that Lacan's discourse was unduly "worldly" and not in keeping with academic propriety. In addition, he complained of constantly hearing of phalluses while having to put up with an incredible number of luxury automobiles parked on his sidewalk during the lunch hour that the seminar was held.

Lacan kept the letter of exclusion to himself and waited until June 26, the day of the final session of the seminar, to make it public. On that day, he read it to his audience, then had copies of it distributed. He accompanied his reading with some rather nasty commentaries in which he made fun of the director's name. The latter was called "Flatulencière," etc.[112] In point of fact, Lacan was furious, wounded, ashamed, and humiliated, so great was the importance he attached to his academic recognition. Entry into the ENS in 1964 had represented a formidable act of revenge, and for six years, the conquest of that bastion had ensured the renewal of his teaching and allowed him to become famous. And with a single blow, through an idiotic letter, he was again plunged into the dark days of his "excommunication." Again he was treated like a black sheep and expelled from a powerful institution in which he had succeeded in being appreciated. Through the expulsion, he was like a kind of Socrates, accused of debauching his country's youth at the very time a process of normalization was being effected in the university. In this case, public opinion was not favorable to him. The previous year, Flacelière had already wanted to expel him, but under pressure from Althusser and Derrida, he was forced to delay his decision. In January 1969, the linguist Georges Mounin added fuel to the fire by publishing an article against Lacan in the *NRF*. "His style," he wrote, "does not promote a healthy curiosity for linguistics. In this respect, it may be deplored that the École normale, where above all a high-quality linguistic *aggiornamento* should have taken place, has lost, in part because of Lacan, some ten or fifteen years that will be quite difficult to make up at present." [113]

No sooner had Lacan finished reading his letter of expulsion than the crowd at his seminar rose and decided to occupy Robert Flacelière's office. Among the first to arrive were Jean-Jacques Lebel, Antoinette Fouque, Laurence Bataille, Philippe Sollers, Julia Kristeva, and many others. For two hours they stayed on the premises peacefully, before being expelled by the police. The press got wind of the affair and revealed itself to be lukewarm toward Lacan. Nevertheless, a petition was signed on his behalf by numerous intellectuals. When François Wahl asked Claude Lévi-Strauss to add his name, the latter refused, emphasizing that a person invited to a living room ought not to cause a row. Pierre Daix, for his part, went to the rue de Lille to bring Lacan witness of the solidarity of Aragon and *Lettres françaises.* Questioned by *Le Monde,* the "administration" of the ENS answered that Lacan's seminar was a social event and hardly scientific. The following day, under pressure from Derrida and Althusser, who threatened to go public, Flacelière called the "administration's" alleged remarks a provocation. Then he added: "If that declaration was completely false, what is nonetheless true is that M. Lacan's auditors, who occupied my office Wednesday, behaved in a manner ill befitting such a master since they scribbled obscene graffiti and committed a number of thefts." [114]

That week, the Salon of Young Painters opened its doors to the public. A visitor could see there an immense realist painting whose title left nothing to the imagination: "Louis Althusser Hesitating to Go into Claude Lévi-Strauss's Dacha Where Jacques Lacan, Michel Foucault, and Roland Barthes Are Gathered at the Moment the Radio Announces the Students Have Decided Joyfully to Abandon Their Past." In the catalogue, the dacha is described as a "permanent secondary residence, where, in a particularly *recherché* decor, the plenitude of an exceptional nature favors the elaboration of structures."

Lacan felt extremely isolated. He was convinced a "plot" had been organized against him and suggested to Sollers that Derrida and Althusser had not stopped Flacelière from acting. He knew the decision was irrevocable. Every day, he would meet with Sollers to review the situation, resorting to any means possible to get people to talk about him. At the offices of the periodical *L'Express,* he lunched in the company of Françoise Giroud with Sollers and Antonella Guaraldi, a young and quite beautiful Italian philosopher who accompanied him everywhere. He asked Giroud to write an article about his expulsion. She did and reported the courageous statement of Gilles Deleuze. "Dr. Lacan," he said, "is one of the masters of contemporary thought. It would be extremely regrettable and disquieting if he were to be deprived a place to pursue his public instruction." [115] After the meal at *L'Express,* Lacan told Sollers, "The university, you understand, one mustn't play the game." [116]

Yet he would continue to play it. In his own way . . . After several initiatives, he obtained an amphitheater at the Law School, near the Pantheon, in which to continue his seminar in the framework of the École pratique des hautes études. The place was huge, and from the time of the first session, the crowds started pouring in, denser still than at the ENS. The seminar of that year of emigration, moreover, was devoted to *L'envers de la psychanalyse,* that is, the place occupied by academic university discourse between psychoanalysis, the master, and the hysteric: in all, four discourses layered in as many mathemes. In his inaugural lecture, Lacan announced his intention to descend on the university campus at Vincennes, in order to perform four impromptus there; he had been invited by the department of philosophy. Once again, he had transformed a defeat into a triumph, installing his audience in a far larger space and proposing to bring his struggle to the heart of the most contentious academic bastion in France.

The second Cluny colloquium was held in the spring of 1970. For three days, between the walls of the old ecclesiastical property and amid a great number of academics, who had simply come to talk about literature, the polemic between *Tel Quel* and its adversaries proceeded full blast. Only a single presentation, by Catherine Clément, was actually devoted to a reading of Freud and Lacan in a Marxist perspective. Beyond that, skirmishes occurred between *Tel Quel* and *Action poétique*. Mitsou Ronat challenged Julia Kristeva's use of linguistics, while Henri Deluy attacked the avant-garde, Telquelian cult of revolution. Finally, the theses of Derrida were vigorously attacked by the present author, my purpose being to show that they were dependent on a Heideggerian vision of the archaic and were incompatible with Lacan's.[117]

The second day, under pressure from Sollers, who threatened to withdraw his troops from the colloquium, the directors of *NC* decided to censure Mitsou Ronat for her excessively violent polemic against Julia Kristeva. It would be eliminated from the publication, but from then on the directors of *NC* had decided to break off relations with *Tel Quel*. Discussions to that effect went on between Antoine Casanova and *Action poétique*. Nevertheless, the evenings, nights, and meals proceeded in a feverish atmosphere. At times a friendship would collapse under the influence of a fine Macon vintage or the theoretical meanderings of one participant or another. In the wings, then on the podium, the actors of the red front had the impression of destroying and then reconstructing the world thanks to the victorious advance of a phantom proletariat. To be sure, the factory population was not there for the rendezvous. Verbal terrorism and wooden prose dominated the exchanges as the Telquelians already began dreaming of a more crimson East.

The colloquium had the effect of provoking a double break between the PCF and *Tel Quel*, on the one hand, and between *Tel Quel* and Derrida on the other. Because of the 1969 expulsion, Sollers had become much closer to Lacan. The latter had given him a text for the journal, then withdrawn it out of impatience. Sollers had sensed Lacan to be extremely lonely in the midst of a family dispersed by its political commitments. He still had hopes of drawing him into *his* revolution. Derrida, for his part, was invited by the journal *Promesse* to respond to the attacks at Cluny. He accepted. Jean-Louis Houdebine and Guy Scarpetta conducted the interview, which took place on June 17, 1971. Letters were exchanged in the course of the summer, and Derrida decided to add a long footnote in which, for the first time, he clarified his position on Lacan, as he had previously in the cases of Foucault and Lévi-Strauss. He addressed essentially three reproaches to Lacan's undertaking: adhesion to a *telos* of full speech, itself identified with truth; massive recourse to Hegelian conceptuality; and a somewhat frivolous use of Saussurean authority. In passing, he confirmed that he had done all he could to prevent Lacan's teaching at the ENS from being interrupted.[118]

Six months after that interview, at a lecture at the Johns Hopkins University, Jacques Derrida explained still further his position on Lacan's work, taking on the *Seminar on "The Purloined Letter."* That presentation was published in France in 1975 under the title "Le facteur de la vérité."[119] Working on the major seminar opening the *Écrits* and emblematizing the very essence of Lacan's reelaboration,

Derrida labored with a diligence worthy of a Benedictine virtuoso. He produced an authentic textual analysis of Lacan's writing, and as such his critique was something of an act of homage, not to a master's doctrine, which came in for a rather harsh philosophical judgment, but to his particular way of interpreting a fiction so as to situate himself in the story. Derrida observed that Lacan used literature to illustrate the truth of his doctrine, that is, a truth exterior to the text. In so doing, he was resorting to the practice of applied psychoanalysis, even though he formally condemned it.

Aside from that contradiction, Derrida also underscored the fact that Lacan was quite familiar with Marie Bonaparte's commentary on the Poe tale and that he only pretended to dismiss it by referring to the Princess as the "cook" without mentioning her name. Lacan had nevertheless drawn inspiration from her work. Marie had in fact been first to note that the letter purloined by the minister had been slipped into a tray hanging from "a copper knob beneath the middle of the fireplace." In proposing that reading the Princess was rectifying Baudelaire's translation, which had used the word "above." Then she compared the letter to a symbol of the maternal penis suspended above a cloaca represented by the hearth of the fireplace. Based on that parallel between the two commentaries, Derrida then situated the position Lacan sought to occupy *against* Marie Bonaparte in her relation to Freud. For Lacan, he said, the Princess resembled the minister of the Poe story. She was the French delegate of Freud's authority, and thanks to that status she diverted his teaching—that is, she pilfered his letter. As opposed to her, Lacan thought of himself as the representative of the authentic or "undeviating" doctrine. He identified with Dupin. "His desire," wrote Derrida, "with the emotional outburst whose signs we have observed, is to rediscover the direction, rectify, redress, and restore to its proper path what has been 'in sufferance,'" namely, the analytic community in so far as it is organized like a "'general delivery,' maintaining under seal the threatening force of a heritage." [120]

Derrida might have added, but he did not, that Lacan would have the illusion, ten years after the publication of his famous seminar, of being able to prevent his own doctrine from being subject to deviations. Although the master thought of himself as the sole possessor of the "right" Freudian truth, he was not secure from alterations affecting his writing. At the tale's end, Auguste Dupin tells the narrator how he had played a nasty trick on the minister. In place of the letter, which had been regained and restored to the queen, he slipped another one in which he had copied in his own hand a tirade borrowed from Crébillon's *Atrée:* ". . . so infamous a design [*dessein*] / If not worthy of Atreus, is worthy of Thyestes." Since the minister was acquainted with Dupin's handwriting, he would be able to discover the author of the trick. Dupin thus signed his deed, affixing his mark to his "design." In sum, he traced a name on the solution to the mystery. Now Derrida observed that on two out of three occasions, Lacan uses the word *destin* [destiny] instead of *dessein*.[121] This was probably a printer's error. In the first published version in *La Psychanalyse,* Lacan had written *dessein* once and *destin* once. The error was subsequently reproduced in the *Écrits.* But in the version delivered orally by Lacan and transcribed two years after the publication of "Le facteur de la vérité," Jacques-

Alain Miller wrote *dessein* and not *destin*. In that lecture, Lacan evoked the Crébillon quotation only once.[122] To underscore the fact that Lacan "forced *dessein* into
destin on two out of three occasions," Derrida drew on the preface of the paperback
edition of *Écrits*, in which the author returned to the purloined letter and spoke of
"so infamous a destiny," committing this time an alteration which could not have
been a misprint.[123] Derrida deduced from this that Lacan had transformed Poe's tale
in order to impose on it an alien truth according to which a letter must always arrive
at its destination. In other words, he showed that in Lacan's very prose a fictional
operation was being staged in which the author addressed to himself the indivisibil-
ity of the letter, that is, the "whole" or "oneness" of his doctrine.

From all this it is possible to see how deconstruction proceeds. Derrida brings
to light fissures and displacements in the text itself. Above all, in this case, he put
his finger on an essential point in Lacanian teaching, which becomes crucial for the
rest of our story and which touches on the *destiny* or fate of the whole of the seminars: Did they constitute a "totality," a "nontotality," a legacy, a letter finally arrived
at its destination, a "fleeting" message, or an integral transmission? In 1975, Derrida's article did not receive any commentary from the Lacanians. But two years
later the debate was opened anew, after the publication of François Roustang's book,
Un destin si funeste [*Dire Mastery: Discipleship from Freud to Lacan*].[124] That same
year, in the United States, it served as the focus of a discussion of psychoanalysis
and literature at Yale University.[125]

At the time the writers of the journal *Promesse* were interviewing Derrida,
they themselves had joined in *Tel Quel*'s break with the party. Since the battle of
Cluny, it became clear that *La Nouvelle Critique* refused the notion of a single line
in matters literary. In that respect, the hegemonic ambitions of Telquelism seemed
downright Zhdanovian and hardly compatible with the pluralism delineated at the
Argenteuil congress. Sollers, for his part, was evolving toward Maoism. In June
1971, he led the members of *Promesse*, who were Communists, to break with the
party. *Tel Quel* then published a manifesto hostile to the "dogmatico-revisionism"
of the PCF. The party was thrown into the same sack as the bourgeoisie, while Freud
served as a new beacon guiding a dream of the red East dominated by the figure of
the Great Helmsman. The imaginary revolution moved from the place du Colonel-
Fabien, party headquarters, to the Middle Empire: "We have never believed and we
have never pretended to believe that one could dispense with Freud in the development of a Marxist science, or with Marx in the development of a Freudian science.
That division delineates and transforms every political disposition. And the economy of the subjects participating in it cannot fail to be that of analysis. An analysis
of which it is well known that it is never without its costs."[126] In that perspective,
what was at stake was articulating the subject of the unconscious with a Maoist-
inspired Marxism. Derridean deconstruction began losing ground at that point to
the benefit of a Lacanian subject of science. Now Derrida had just criticized Lacan
on the subject of the signifier and at the same time agreed to meet with Antoine
Casanova in order to dispel the lingering ill feelings of Cluny. The break with *Tel
Quel* was thus inevitable. With the publication of his interview in *Promesse*, the
bridges were definitively burned.

The new Telquelian orientation was announced before the June 1971 shift in a collective manifesto on Surrealism.[127] Breton's movement was accused of collusion with the forces of obscurantism, Trotskyism, and Jungianism. In an article entitled "Méconnaissance de la psychanalyse dans le discours surréaliste [Misprision of psychoanalysis in Surrealist discourse]," Jean-Louis Houdebine played Lacan off against Breton, condemning the "deviations" specific to Surrealism. Janet, Myers, Flournoy, and Breton were all cast into the same waste heap and Surrealism was said to be no more than the locus of a Jungian deviation. Against which Houdebine invoked the *whole* of Lacanianism, from the 1932 thesis to the *Écrits*. He made Lacan into a materialist and scientific antidote to Breton's adventure, eliminating not only the young Lacan's links with Surrealism, but Crevel and Dali's reception of the Aimée case. Only Nizan's article was evoked with approbation.

After the break with Derrida and the rejection of "dogmatico-revisionism," *Tel Quel*'s red front drifted toward the world of psychoanalysis in Italy, where changes had been occurring as a result of the beginning of Lacanianism's establishment in countries of Latin culture and Catholic religion.

As of 1967, several Italian intellectuals were beginning to become acquainted with Lacan's work and to be analyzed on his couch. This was the case, notably, for Giacomo Contri and Armando Verdiglione. In 1972, Contri created an autonomous group, "la Scuola freudiana," which became, a year later, an association with a training program. He translated part of the *Écrits*. At the same time, Verdiglione participated in a collective which took on the name of "Semiotica e psicanalisi," whose secretary he became in 1973. In 1974 a "Cosa freudiana" came into existence. The word "cosa" meant "thing," but phonetically evoked "cause." The statutes of that association were close to those of the EFP, but its presidency was collegial, and the *passe* was effected by psychoanalysts rather than a jury. The directorate was composed of two members from Milan (Verdiglione and Contri) and one from Palermo (Giuseppe Musotto). Lacan issued directives for his Italian students to form a "tripod," and Muriel Drazien moved to Rome at that point to represent the master. But before long disputes erupted. The founders reproached each other for their differences and rivalries. Only Musotto and Contri became members of the EFP, along with Sergio Finzi and Virginia Finzi-Ghisi, who led a Marxist-leaning group in Milan named "Pratica freudiana." [128]

Catholicism and Marxism were thus the two ingredients out of which was created a curious Italian Lacanianism, both sectarian and picturesque, rooted in the margins of an official psychoanalytic society in crisis. That Lacanianism was deployed within an ideological framework that had long been dominated by Jungianism and the Roman Catholic Church. It was contested by various antipsychiatry movements and received as "Parisian" by the whole of the Italian intellectual community.

Armando Verdiglione was fortunately not the only representative of the Lacanian movement in Italy. But he was the shadiest and most paradoxically Parisian figure among them. Born in 1940, the strange *professore* was of Calabrese origin. Raised by Jesuits, then a student at the university of Father Gemelli, he became a "Maoist" around 1968, between sessions on Lacan's couch. The man seemed half

Jehovah's Witness, half comic-opera "godfather." He took himself for Dante, dreamed of founding a new Freudian Esperanto and ran furious campaigns against the two "demons" he regarded as troubling the modern world: Jungianism and Marxism. He thus tended to see KGB agents and Opus Dei spies everywhere. Verdiglione spoke a kind of idiolect in which the glossolalia of true literary madmen combined with the pompous verbiage of esoteric sects. During the ten years of a reign that lasted from 1973 to 1983, he built in Italy a fabulous publishing empire composed of numerous groups and journals. He attracted to his orbit the great names of literature, philosophy, and psychoanalysis, with sumptuous colloquiums— all expenses paid—held in New York and Tokyo, Milan and Paris. Verdiglione wanted to bring the plague to the universe. To be sure the celebrities brought to his colloquiums were unaware of where the money was coming from. It did not concern them. And then Verdiglione translated their books, published their presentations, paid for expenses, all in exchange for a vigorous dose of publicity in the Parisian press.

The resistible rise of Armando Verdiglione began in Milan, during a colloquium in December 1973 on the subject "Psychoanalysis and Politics," attended by the *Tel Quel* group with Sollers and Kristeva, the representatives of *L'anti-Oedipe* with Guattari and Oury, Serge Leclaire and several Italians, including Sergio Finzi, Elvio Fachinelli, and Gian Franco Minguzzi. A young French therapist, Marie-Claire Boons, a student of the SPP, also participated in the meeting. She belonged to the "Yenan" tendency,[129] orchestrated by Alain Badiou. She simultaneously rejected Lacanianism, Deleuzianism, and Telquelism. Octave and Maud Mannoni did not make the trip, but sent a written contribution. As for Lacan, he announced his arrival, but at the last moment canceled out; he wanted neither to disavow nor to support this dubious operation, in which the children of Marx, Mao, and His Majesty were to meet. He thus decided to stay in Paris. He would always adopt that attitude of nondisavowal and nonsupport toward Verdiglione—who would be violently rejected by the EFP without ever being a member—as well as toward the enterprises of the Telquelians and the Maoists.

In Milan, the proceedings were comical, rambling, insane, or sectarian. Each defended his own merchandise while pretending he was rebuilding the world or piercing Stalinism, fascism, and totalitarianism to the quick. Sollers revealed himself to be the best performer in the sinister farce and Leclaire its most biting spectator. One had a ball and the other laughed at the other's highjinks. Félix Guattari called down imprecations on the "micropolitics of desire" and lashed out at Nazism and neo-Marxism, announcing that the armies of Castro, Mao, and Trotsky all crystallized a fascist desire. Marie-Claire Boons denounced the "honeyed co-optation of Lacanianism by revisionism." As for Verdiglione, he spoke of "zerofication," "encoding," and the "nonsemiotizable." Before his presentation, Sollers pointed to a painting representing Samson and Dalilah, "head cut off, phallus-lady with a sword, gaze between the legs, the whole thing facing a bust of Leonardo erected on high over the benches for church canons at a colloquium." When the denunciation of Soviet psychiatry failed to retain the audience's attention, he started acting out and stuck a hat on Leonardo's head and eyeglasses on his nose. The audience found all this in bad taste and jeered the speaker. In all the surrounding restaurants, the participants in the colloquium continued to attack each other on the subjects of antipsychiatry, the La Borde experiment, desiring desire and the subject of language. They had ten years of the Calabrian's torment in the offing.[130]

Upon returning to Paris, Sollers continued his march toward the red East. Always quite professional in his short-lived alliances, he took an active role in preparing the trip to China of several of Le Seuil's authors: Roland Barthes, Julia Kristeva, Marcelin Pleynet, and François Wahl. The idea came from Maria Macciocchi, who had just published a book on the subject. Lacan was quite taken with it all; he found the lady "stupefying" and immediately decided to resume Chinese lessons. Sollers took care of the formalities. His hope was to disrupt things for the PCF. In his view, if Lacan went to China, "the objective alliance of Lacanianism and revisionism" would at last be broken. Lacan did not expect as much. His first concern was obtaining a passport for his lady companion. He also wanted to know if the Chinese had an unconscious, and perhaps he wanted to discuss the matter personally with Mao Zedong, as he once had with the pope. Shortly thereafter the Chinese refused to accept Macciocchi. As for Sollers, he took care of the world revolution with his friends in the embassy. From his office on the rue Jacob, he directed an ardent campaign against the thought of Confucius: exactly what was going on in Peking.

One morning a delegation from the embassy arrived at Lacan's home with an official car and a red flag. It brought the requested passport along with a salute from the Great Helmsman himself. In exchange, Lacan presented the group with a dedicated copy of the *Écrits,* which would be deposited at the Institute of Sciences in Peking.[131] Sollers felt he had brought off his initiative—"Lacan *chez* Mao," a headline he had dreamed of—while waiting to find out whether the Chinese had an unconscious. Three days later, His Majesty went to the embassy and canceled his trip; his lady friend did not want to go. There would be no red East for Dr. Lacan. "He was to come with us to China," a statement from *Tel Quel* announced. "It's a pity that, as he himself put it in his apology, he did not have time to work up enough Chinese, before his departure, for that. We would have liked to see Lacan discuss things, unprepared, with the population. The experience would have been interesting. It is true that Lacan had begun to have concerns about the campaign against Confucius and the fact that the latter was being presented as the ideologue of slavery in China. But could a critique of the 'will of heaven,' 'innate knowledge,' and 'moderation in order to return to rites' shock an established psychoanalyst? Perhaps." [132] Upon their return, neither Roland Barthes nor François Wahl would speak in praise of China: a further defeat for Sollers.

The Chinese junket was the beginning for Julia Kristeva of a return to official psychoanalysis. She thus began her studies with the SPP: "Lacan, whose seminar I attended until 1974 and whose baroque genius overwhelms me every time like an actual psychoanalytic session, had not been able to extricate himself from the constraints imposed on him by his entourage in order to accompany us as he had wished to China. From that period on, I had the impression of detecting signs of old age in him and of imposture in his school. I thus avoided following him in his painful end." [133]

While Lacan decided to annul his trip to China, Verdiglione, with the support of *Tel Quel,* pursued his feverish mobilization of the Parisian intelligentsia. Each year, the colloquiums were bigger, more sumptuous, and more insane. Sex and language, culture and the unconscious, hallucinations, madness, art, the plague and bluff—the emperor could resist nothing, and nothing resisted him. He traveled throughout the world, endlessly telephoning his various offices in Milan, suffering from homesickness and the absence of pasta. One day, he decided to slim down, signed himself into a clinic, and emerged a new man, seventy pounds lighter. Then, still with Sollers's backing, he put on weight again and resumed his activity. Around 1980, he established a branch of his empire in Paris following an awful colloquium dedicated to "Truth." In April 1981, he bought an entire page in *Le Monde,* in which he published short notices devoted to his work and his person. They were written by an illustrious assemblage of psychoanalysts, writers, and celebrities of the day, among them Philippe Sollers, François Perrier, Octave Mannoni, Jean Oury, Philippe Nemo, Marek Halter, and Alain de Benoist. All praised his merits.[134] But Verdiglione, for his advertisement, had made use of personal letters and bits of criticism, which were reproduced in *Le Monde* without the authorization of their authors. The result was a number of lawsuits. . . .

This did not prevent him from becoming a stockholder of the periodical *La Quinzaine littéraire,* whose finances were in sorry shape. Intoxicated by his power, he began pressuring the editors to publish puff-material favorable to his person and his endeavors. When they refused categorically to do so, Verdiglione threatened to ruin the journal by dumping his shares. Finally, the *Quinzaine* was saved from bankruptcy by a new bond issue—at which point the prophet appeared for what he was. He was disavowed by the Parisian intelligentsia, abandoned by Sollers, deserted by his friends. After twelve years of intense hullabaloo, his empire collapsed for good. In July 1985, the Italian press related the tragicomic epic of this *mafioso* of culture. His foundation was the subject of a police investigation for misappropriation of funds. A schizophrenic, in analysis with one of the *professore*'s collaborators, had given the Verdiglione Foundation two hundred million lire, in several checks, certain of which had been returned to the signer's family for lack of funds. The family filed suit, and the prosecuting attorney examined Verdiglione's books and had his house searched. Then, as the lawsuits proliferated, the matter became criminal.[135] At his July congress, Verdiglione staged a veritable *happening.* He no longer took himself for Dante, but for Captain Dreyfus, accusing all of Italy of being racist. The French press did not carry the story. Attention at the time was rather on the Greenpeace affair. The red front by then had long been forgotten. Two months later, in an article in *L'Express* by Jacques Derogy and Jean-Marie Pontaur, it was reported that the French Secret Service agent Dominique Prieur was reading Catherine Clément's *Les fils de Freud sont fatigués* ["The sons of Freud are tired"] in his prison cell in Auckland. This time, the story was in fact planetary in dimension and the spy a real one.[136]

10 Kingdoms Asunder

I. Psychoanalysis in the University

Starting in October 1968, the channels through which psychoanalysis gained ground in the universities were restructured. Two experiments were conducted. One took place at the heart of Daniel Lagache's shattered legacy, in the context of the University of Paris VII, and the other, which was entirely new, fostered the penetration of psychoanalysis into the university world outside of any psychological rubric. Sponsored by Serge Leclaire, that second experiment opened a new outlet for Freudianism and Lacanianism at the University of Paris VIII, whose buildings were erected quite rapidly during the summer of 1968 in the Vincennes forest, on military land returned by the Ministry of Defense to the City of Paris. That "experimental" university welcomed students without the baccalaureate and created programs of instruction in the arts, theater, city planning, education, and the human sciences. The innovative spirit which enlivened it offered a particular channel for the implantation of structuralism, in the fields of both psychoanalysis and linguistics. In linguistics, it allowed an opening for Chomsky's work. Four years after the creation of Paris VIII, a retroactive agreement was signed stipulating that at the end of ten years the university would be constrained to return the premises to the City and move its operations to Saint-Denis.[1]

Before 1968, the universities were administered by a dean. He was assisted by a secretary general, in charge of administrative matters, and a council consisting of tenured professors. The other members of the teaching staff, who were a majority, had no voting rights nor did the administrative personnel and the students.

The "orientation" law of November 12, 1969, implemented by Edgar Faure, demolished that edifice and established new bases for university institutions. It dissolved the old structures and retained only teaching personnel invited to meet around the pedagogical project and to form "Teaching and Research Units" (UERs). Once they existed, the UERs were authorized by the overseeing ministry to federate and form universities. The universities thus created, under the aegis of each academy, enjoyed administrative, pedagogical, and financial autonomy. They were multidisciplinary and based on the principle of user participation in their administration. In that framework, it was the teachers, students, and administrative personnel that elected university councils by way of a federated union. Through that law, "democracy" made its entry into territory dominated until then by the reign of mandarins. To be sure, this in no way stopped the mandarins from remaining mandarins and from reigning as they used to over their assistants, students, and disciples.

For the May protesters, the orientation law was Gaullism's "reformist" response to the barricades of the rue Gay-Lussac. But for the progressive-minded Left, from the Socialists to the Communists, it opened the way to a genuine democratization of teaching. As of the fall of 1968, the UERs were federating into universities,

547

which were identified by numerals: from Paris I to Paris VII for the former Parisian centers and from Paris VIII to Paris XIII for the suburban ones. Within that framework, Paris VII was the most multidisciplinary, which explains why it was more open to the human sciences and to a redefinition of clinical psychology. In the office of Maurice Couve de Murville and under the direction of Edgar Faure, Michel Alliot assumed total responsibility for the orientation law, both for its conceptions and its application. A specialist in African law, he would be the first president of Paris VII. In addition, Didier Anzieu was charged by the ministry with the mission of elaborating a new status for psychologists. The National Syndicate of Practicing Psychologists became a National Syndicate of Psychoanalysts, and it was with the support of that body that Anzieu authored a proposal that would be discussed throughout France. De Gaulle's resignation in 1969 put an end to the proposal, but the matter would resurface again ten years later.

Between 1945 and 1968, psychoanalysis had been present in the universities, having arrived through the channels opened by Lagache. It was taught under the rubric of psychology and in keeping with a tradition that owed more to Janet than to Freud. Within that context, Lagache's students already occupied the leading positions, however much the unity of psychology might remain a pure fiction. The experimentalists and the partisans of social psychology waged a relentless battle against clinical psychology, which continued not to exist. That conflict frequently took the form of violent institutional struggle.

In 1955, a year before the publication of Georges Canguilhem's famous article, Lagache began assuming the functions of the incumbent of the chair of pathological psychology, which had been created for him at the Sorbonne. Juliette Favez-Boutonier took his place and occupied the chair of general psychology. But her aspiration was to break out of that field, which she thought sclerotic, to achieve a true clinical psychology whose reality continues to be elusive. She gave a slightly different definition of the field than Lagache. Hostile to "psychological examinations," which she judged to be too medical, she put the accent on the personality's "evolution." In other words, the clinical practitioner should not be satisfied with examining his patient; he should follow him over a period of months and years. Unlike the psychoanalyst, the clinical psychologist works with neither transference nor couch, and restricts himself to an institutional framework: CMPP, IMP, etc. Against medicine, Lagache was aiming at the unity of psychology; Boutonier fought the world of medicine by favoring clinical psychology without any pretense of unity. In both cases, psychoanalysis as an autonomous doctrine was given short shrift, even though the artisans of clinical psychology had received psychoanalytic training and practiced that profession within their societies. From a Freudian point of view, such a position was untenable.

While Favez-Boutonier was searching for a status for clinical psychology, Paul Fraisse, an experimentalist and a former lecturer at the Catholic universities of Lyon, was preparing his state doctorate. Working in the general current of Christian Democracy, he was one of those whom Emmanuel Mounier had won over to the cause of the journal *Esprit* before the war. In 1939, he founded a personalist bookstore on the rue Monsieur-le-Prince, then became one of the group's active proconsuls, playing a central role in it.[2] Appointed professor of experimental psychology at the Sorbonne in 1957, he succeeded Lagache four years later as director of the Institute de psychologie. As soon as he was appointed, he began an active fight against the clinicians, creating his own Laboratory of Comparative Social Psychology in space that Juliette Favez-Boutonier had hoped to use for her own purposes. Her fury was of little avail, however; she obtained little more from Étienne Souriau, who was dean, than a pigeon-ridden garret, where she nonetheless succeeded in setting up a Laboratory of Clinical Psychology. She was thus obliged to wait for Fraisse to decide to move in order to work in more pleasant surroundings. In 1958, she requested the creation of a position in clinical psychology, which was refused her, since that discipline had no existence. She thus had to make do with a post in psychology *tout court*.

Paul Fraisse, for his part, continued to do fierce battle with the students of Lagache. Around 1963, Didier Anzieu offered his candidacy for a second position in general psychology at the Sorbonne, which had been requested by Boutonier because of the mounting number of students. In order to eliminate Anzieu, Fraisse solicited the application of another psychologist, a former student of the ENS and a specialist in animal psychology. The latter was appointed in 1964, and Anzieu migrated to the Faculté de Nanterre, where his teaching was free to follow a more psychoanalytic bent. In October 1967, Lagache, after trying in vain to get elected to the French Academy, made his last public appearance at the Sorbonne. He refused to orient the choice of his successor toward psychoanalysis and arranged for the position to be given to Henri Faure, a disciple of Janet who was hostile to Freudianism. As a result the bastion could no longer be taken over by Jean Laplanche, who, once his thesis was completed, should, in all propriety, have been received by the Sorbonne with open arms.

Meanwhile, Juliette relinquished the chair of general psychology to create an "optional certificate in clinical psychology" in the framework of the *licence* in psychology. In 1966, she installed her laboratory at Censier, outside the walls of the mother institution, in buildings forming an annex to the Sorbonne. She was enthusiastically received there by the administration, but the certificate in clinical psychology remained a fiction, since that discipline existed only in the minds of its advocates: Either the clinical practice was psychological and had to disappear, or it was medical, in which case it had to be joined to the study of medicine. As a result, Anne-Marie Rocheblave, an analysand of Lagache's, who was not a physician, was refused a position.

Furious, Juliette went to see Professor Delay and requested his support. Naturally, he refused to give his approval to such a project and even added that the Ordre des médecins, the medical guild, would not fail to file a lawsuit if clinical procedures were taught without medical supervision. Despite the threat, Juliette defied him and began accepting student enrollments. At the time, she was flanked by four assistants: Claude Prévost, Jacques Gagey, Pierre Fédida, and Anne-Marie Rocheblave. The first was an extremely amiable instructor in the great tradition of the Third Republic. He was the only one whose credentials posed no problem since he was not a psychoanalyst but a clinical psychologist working from a Janetian perspective. The three others were psychoanalysts. Gagey was a philosopher. He had been trained at the SPP. As for Fédida, he came from Georges Favez's couch and the ranks of the APF.[3]

Just prior to the barricades, Lagache's heirs thus found themselves in a paradoxical position. The path opened up for psychoanalysis under the rubric of psychology was becoming a path for the establishment of clinical psychology, in which psychoanalysis occupied only a marginal position. Because clinical psychology had had no theoretical existence ever since Janet had lost his way in its thickets, the Freudianism it nonetheless pretended to be inspired by also resembled something of a fiction.

It was the student rebellion which finally enabled it to take root in the universities as a teachable subject, if not as a theory. "My idea," Jacques Gagey emphasized, "was that psychology *is* clinical psychology and nothing else, with psychoanalysis behind it. . . . Psychopathological clinical practice is a field of rational inquiry. It was plain before May that the unity of psychology did not exist and that what it was teaching was of no use to students cast into the therapeutic marketplace. Psychology was about to explode. . . . I also had the feeling that the psychoanalytic societies could no longer resolve the problem of the increasing number of therapists. One had to step outside the psychoanalytic societies and run psychoanalysis, through clinical psychology, in the framework of contemporary society." [4]

In that respect, the implantation of psychoanalysis in the university system, which took place in the context of the "orientation" law, was not the same sort as formerly. It was indeed laid in an earlier mold, but it did not obey the same constraints. In the immediate postwar period, psychoanalysis had to achieve a status for itself through its own institutional movement, whereas in 1968, it was, on the contrary, a matter of psychoanalysts seeking refuge from societies that had become overgrown, dogmatic, or sclerotic.

In May, encouraged by the ambient agitation, several hundred students demonstrated in favor of a reform of the study of psychology. Juliette Favez-Boutonier, Pierre Fédida, and Jacques Gagey took advantage of the unease to request the formation of a UER in clinical psychology. Prévost proposed that the word "psychology" be replaced by "anthropology." [5] Finally, they sent the project to Edgar Faure. At the time he received it, however, he was considering another request from a group of Rodgerians, represented by Paul Arbousse-Bastide, André Lévy, and Ophélia Avron, a therapist from the SPP. That group requested the constitution of a UER in clinical social psychology. Poorly acquainted with the psychologists' differing orientations, the minister amalgamated them, and created a UER in clinical social psychology, which was entered under that name in the *Journal officiel* of December 1968. After several hesitations, the UER decided to become part of Paris VII. The word "psychoanalysis" did not appear in its syllabus, but Freudian clinical practice was scheduled to be taught under the notorious banner of clinical psychology.

Very early on, conflicts cropped up between the two groups, first over the distribution of positions, then with Paris V, where two UERs were created, one under the name of "Institut de psychologie," the other simply of "psychologie." The first was essentially concerned with practical training and welcomed students already holding a master's degree. Founded by Gratiot-Alphandéry, Roland Doron, and Daniel Widlöcher, it taught the psychology of work, ergonomics, and pathology. The second was created by Paul Fraisse, along with Colette Chiland, a therapist from the SPP. Experimentalist in inspiration, that UER did not dispense any serious instruction in psychoanalysis. It was the result of a compromise between the ultra-medical tendency of the SPP and an experimentalist orientation. Jean Laplanche meanwhile attempted to join the linguist Antoine Culioli in the creation of an experimental university to be named "Mathematics and Human Sciences." The project never reached fruition, and in March 1969, Laplanche joined the experimental UER in clinical human sciences.[6]

Despite difficulties, that UER managed to exist and dispensed its teaching to hundreds of students. The psychoanalysts clung to the Oedipus complex, while the partisans of social psychology concerned themselves with "roles." All formed groups: some "groups with tasks," others "groups without tasks." Paul Arbousse-Bastide was the first director of the UER, followed by Laplanche, who resigned several months later. After him, Jacques Gagey would be elected director which he remained for eight years starting in 1971. With little interest in clinical psychology, Laplanche was the first officially to introduce the word "psychoanalysis" into the experiment, creating during the academic year 1969–70 a Laboratory of Psychoanalysis and Psychopathology whose program was divided into four research divisions: psychoanalytic psychopathology, applied psychoanalysis, the theory of psychoanalysis, the history of psychoanalysis and Freudian practice. His own teaching consisted in reading and commenting on Freud's work in a manner tending to systematize its original conceptuality. That copious labor is a direct offshoot of the *Vocabulaire*. Until the retirement of Juliette Favez-Boutonier, clinical psychology cohabited for better or for worse with psychoanalysis, but then new conflicts surfaced between Jean Laplanche and his colleagues, who ended up rallying to his position. The Laboratory served as a Freudian emblem of the entire experiment.

Upon Lagache's death, Laplanche took over the directorship of the "Bibliothèque de psychanalyse" series at the Presses universitaires de France. With that same publisher, he would bring out his complete lectures in five volumes under the title *Problématiques*. In 1975, he created the journal *Psychanalyse à l'université*, which was quite well named, and in which he published his seminar and articles of his collaborators. The collective was composed of academics from Censier and members of the APF. The cover design is a reproduction of a drawing by the painter Valerio Adami, sketched from a photo of Freud. The journal appears quarterly. Over the years it has presented unpublished texts by Tausk, Freud, and Melanie Klein, as well as articles by Fédida, Rosolato, Anzieu, Widlöcher, et al. According to the wishes of its founder, its intent was to allow all to appropriate their own individual UER. In point of fact, it functions as an annex of Censier and the APF.

At the time the cohabitation of psychoanalysis and clinical psychology was still difficult. On the one hand, the Laboratory represented only psychoanalysis; on the other, the teaching staff in clinical psychology taught Freudianism by way of psychology. Conflicts cropped up with the establishment of diplomas for advanced study (DEA). In 1974, Laplanche created his own DEA of "clinical psychopathology and psychoanalysis," defending a policy of decentering psychoanalysis within multi-disciplinarity. "Psychoanalysis," he said, "ought not to be at the center of a training experience." Laplanche maintained a position identical to that of the university and the APF, which was based on psychoanalysis's extraterritoriality. In the institution, personal analysis should be shielded from any notion of preselection for didactic or training purposes, and in the university the teaching of Freudianism should remain extrinsic to other fields: the opposite of the option of the clinical psychologists.

During a first phase, the DEA was attacked by the full range of psychoanalytic societies. Then, six years later, at the time of the second certification, when it took on the name of a "doctorate in psychoanalysis," it was again challenged by the conservative and medically oriented wing of the SPP. In October 1980, the acting president of that society wrote Laplanche to convey his concern about using the term "doctorate." According to him, it might result in confusion. To which Laplanche quite properly responded that the word "doctorate" referred to theoretical research and not medicine or any criteria for certifying practitioners. "Beyond the minor issue of terminology," he wrote, "what is the *substance* of what we are talking about? The substance is that this certification of a doctorate in psychoanalysis comes as the culmination of something entirely new in France and perhaps in the world: the presence of a team of analysts speaking as such—not under the cover of another discipline, psychology, literature, or philosophy—about analysis, in an authorized manner, within the university." [7]

The DEA in psychoanalysis was defined in the following manner: It was to be completed in a year's time, had no professional value, and constituted the first stage in a third-cycle doctorate in psychoanalysis. Nor was that doctorate a professional diploma; it in no way certified its holder for practice as a psychoanalyst or a psychologist. Only candidacies for careers in teaching or research could legitimately invoke the third-cycle doctorate as a credential. In other words, students wanting to become clinical psychologists were referred to the program for a Diploma of Specialized Higher Studies (DESS) as providing access to therapeutic institutions, while those who preferred psychoanalysis were directed toward one or another couch. For the year 1983–84, the UER in human clinical sciences dispensed instruction to about 2,500 students. It included 160 *chargés de cours,* 13 assistants, 9 professors and lecturers, and 2 honorary professors. Among those four last categories, only four instructors had never been analyzed.[8] The Laboratory was subsequently renamed "Centre de recherche pour la psychanalyse et la psychopathologie."

In 1979, Laplanche added another part to his publishing kingdom, creating the collection "Voies nouvelles pour la psychanalyse." There he has published theses he has directed and books by his students. Finally, it is to him, along with André Bourguignon and Pierre Cottet, that the task of unifying Freudian concepts in French for the much awaited complete works has fallen: a magnificent career for a student who rejected the mandarin lures of his two *maîtres.*

The experiment at Vincennes-Paris VIII was in no way like that at Censier. For the contemporary history of Freudian France, it is far richer in events, theatrical turns, and innovations. In addition, it established for the first time in a French university a psychoanalytic teaching stripped of any debt to medicine or psychology. Just as the UERs of Paris VII and Paris V gathered teaching staff for the most part from the APF and the SPP, the department at Vincennes contained only Lacanians. In that respect it may be said that the universities after May offered terrain for the implantation of the three major tendencies of French psychoanalytic history: the remains of the Lagachian track at Paris VII under the banner of clinical psychology; the medical track at Paris V beneath the standard of experimentalism or a "scientific" psychology; the Lacanian track at Paris VIII.

The experiment was made possible through the efforts of Serge Leclaire, who overcame all obstacles to its realization. In July 1968, he participated in several meetings with the dean of the Sorbonne, Raymond Las Vergnas, to whom Edgar Faure had entrusted the task of creating the experimental center. In order to bring off the difficult undertaking, the dean asked the advice of his friend Hélène Cixous, like himself a specialist in English literature. She then introduced him to Jacques Derrida, who supported Leclaire's candidacy. The informal group became official at the end of the summer, with the appointment of Georges Canguilhem, to whom Derrida had recommended Leclaire, insisting on his medical competence.[9] Michel Foucault participated in the project on behalf of philosophy. Leclaire's idea was to create a space in the university reserved for practitioners of the unconscious, as far removed as possible from psychology. That was why the department of psychoanalysis did not constitute itself as a UER, but joined up with the UER in philosophy, where Gilles Deleuze, François Chatelet, and many others were teaching. Leclaire asked his friends Aulagnier, Valabrega, and Perrier to join him in the adventure, but they refused. Miller, who was teaching at Besançon, was invited both by Leclaire and Foucault to join the experiment. He opted to go to the department of psychoanalysis, whose positions, in any event, were under the control of philosophy. In the spring of 1969, he had joined the GP, whose theoretical objectives included "destroying the university." This did not prevent him from continuing to teach. Unlike Lacan, he was not hostile to the Vincennes experiment. In July, the question of his position was raised, and Leclaire asked him, given his political commitment, to move to philosophy. He wrote a letter to Foucault to that effect. Miller at the time preferred to stay in psychoanalysis.[10]

To be sure, the GP, a clandestine group, had no other weapons than its verbal terrorism. As for its founders, they were in a sense the last Kojèvians of the century, convinced of having discovered in Maoism an issue for the end of history. . . . Once the adventure came to a close, they would pursue careers in journalism, politics, philosophy, publishing, and the universities. Four Lacanians were members of the movement: Jean-Claude Milner and the three Millers:—Judith, Jacques-Alain, and Gérard, who was his brother. Three of this group came from the *Cahiers pour l'analyse*.

Beyond any individual propensities to activism, an overall theoretical interpretation of Lacanian commitment to the GP, in these four cases, may be attempted. Basically, they temporarily "relinquished" one master for another. Now Mao was all the more fascinating a founder in that he, like Lacan, was a rebellious sovereign. The Helmsman spoke of the reactionary (that is, "totalitarian") character of all thought, restricting his own thoughts to a little book of formulas. In that perspective, only the proletariat, as signifying emblem of the class struggle, allowed for a dissolving of the "whole" of thought in action. Such was the program of the GP: to destroy the "whole" of thought through the "whole" of action, with anonymity, a secret society, and a Kojèvian philosophy of the end of history.

The idiosyncratic character of French Maoism fascinated the masters of the previous generation, notably Jean-Paul Sartre and Michel Foucault. Although they did not dream of making a trip to China, they were each taken by the question raised by the GP, which forced them to the very center of their own philosophical— be it humanist or Nietzschean—defiance. Lacan was also challenged in a different way. He had always maintained that thought was a *pas-tout* (a "non-whole"), as was plain from his hyperlogical elaboration, born of a confrontation with the meditations on formal logic in the *Cahiers*. But that *pas-tout* was possible in his eyes only by virtue of the fissure introduced into science by Freudian discourse: divided subject, fallen object, fault, loss or lack. In that context, the entry of the *Cahiers* Lacanians into proletarian Maoism took on a specific valence: how one might dissolve the "whole" of thought, of the theoretical, in the *pas-tout* of psychoanalytic discourse.

Mao offered a response to that philosophical question. However, with the new internal order resulting from the post-May period, it would be necessary to admit that the dissolution of the "whole" could find a solution only in an acceptance of the "non-whole." The Lacanians would thus leave the "dissolved" GP thanks to the "non-whole" formulated by Lacan; they would return in force to academic and social reality. J.-C. Milner would return to linguistics; J.-A. Miller would become a psychoanalyst, then the leader of a school, transcribing the master's doctrine; and Judith would take to journalism. Meanwhile Lacan himself effected a *mathematical recasting* of his doctrine, the third, concerning which we shall see that it attempted to offer an answer to the question of the school and what is teachable. Through it, he modified his judgment on the implantation of psychoanalysis in the university, but also renounced traveling to China. He thus saw neither the revolution of which he disapproved nor its leader, whom he might well have wanted to meet.

At the end of December, 1968, the Centre universitaire de Vincennes-Paris VIII opened its doors in an atmosphere of strident protest. Student meetings, dominated by gauchistes, rejected the electoral procedures needed to set up the various institutions. Before long, the university was occupied, and on January 31, 1969, Raymond Las Vergnas resigned. Inspector General Seïté replaced him but was unable to calm the agitation. The department of psychoanalysis thus began operations under rather troubled circumstances. Following the system then in effect, it distributed *unités de valeur* (UVs; course credits). No curriculum was imposed on students, who could choose their UVs in whatever order they wished. To obtain a *licence,* they were obliged to have a total of thirty UVs, twenty of which had to be in a "major" discipline. Normally, ten UVs were selected from a "submajor" discipline or as free electives. The department was part of the philosophy major, and, as such, dispensed credits as a submajor or as electives. Unlike the UER at Censier, the Vincennes department offered neither diplomas nor clinical training usable for employment. It was supposed to offer theoretical instruction, as part of training that was philosophical or literary. Any ambiguity was thus removed concerning the psychoanalytic curriculum since in no event could a student be certified in psychoanalysis through such a program. Nevertheless, the interest it aroused might attract a number of students to analytic couches, as was the case at Censier. During the first year, the department dispensed ten UVs corresponding to sixteen seminars taught by (among others) Michèle Montrelay, Serge Leclaire, François Baudry, René Tostain, Jacques Nassif, Jean Clavreul, Claude Rabant, Luce Irigaray, Claude Dumézil, Michel de Certeau, and Jacques-Alain Miller. Some were not psychoanalysts, but all were members of the EFP. Several subjects were broached, concerning history, psychoanalytic discourse, the logic of the unconscious, or clinical practice.

At the organization sessions of the EFP, at which the split that would lead to the formation of the Fourth Group became manifest, the Vincennes experiment was unanimously condemned by all those not participating in it. All criticized the notion of "unités de valeur," delighting in bad puns and mimicking *gauchiste* slogans. Despite his evident hostility, Lacan kept his silence. As of March 1969, he knew that he would be expelled from the ENS and gradually he was reaching the decision to torpedo Leclaire's experiment, at times discreetly, at others with violence. Conflict was unavoidable between these two men who had been bound to each other for over twenty-five years. Perpetually in search of adventure, Leclaire was stifling within the walls of the house of Lacan. Without rejecting the procedure of *la passe,* he became less and less interested in it as it came to seem a disaster. By 1968, he was looking for the possibility to open up new horizons for a Lacanianism running the risk of finding itself reduced to sclerosis and dogma. In his eyes, Vincennes was the privileged site for a possible decentering of psychoanalysis, since the system of UVs allowed for the creation of a multidisciplinary field as well as Freudianism's confrontation with something other than itself.

Regarding his disciple's position, Lacan followed a paradoxical course. Even while wanting to establish his reelaboration in new bastions, he could not tolerate the Vincennes experiment, intent as he was on being alone in effecting a decentering toward the outside, by way of his seminar. But he was also aware that the Vincennes experiment had much promise for the expansion of Lacanianism. He thus changed strategy according to the internal evolution of his school or the political situation in France after May.

The adventure of Paris VIII enjoyed its rise at the time the EFP was experiencing its great institutional crisis, with the creation of the Fourth Group and the splintering of the Lacanian movement into several tendencies. In that respect, it may be said that Vincennes was the symptom of a crisis in the Lacanian institution, much as Censier could be seen as been the symptom of a crisis among the followers of Lagache. Those who joined Leclaire were the children of a splintered Lacanianism. For five years, from 1969 to 1974, Lacan adopted in relation to them three different positions. During a first phase, he observed the development of the experiment as a spectator. He thought his procedure of *la passe* would offer a lasting solution to the crisis in the EFP. That was why he favored a policy of concentration around his school, while disavowing Vincennes. He demonstrated his hostility at times in impromptu appearances, at times by silence, at still others by dispatching emissaries to the scene. Lacan at the time felt quite isolated. Since he was effectively "fabricating" a revolution without yielding to the illusions of revolution, he sabotaged the Vincennes experiment even as he abstained from wanting "to destroy the university." In brief he never supported either the *gauchistes* or the Maoists. . . .

During a second phase, between 1970 and 1973, he forced Leclaire to resign and then reigned over the department through his personal guard. At the same time, at the Faculté de Droit, he effected a mathematical reelaboration of his doctrine that gave a theoretical content to his thought on the École. Finally, in a third phase, starting in 1974, he initiated a last attempt at conquest, similar to the one conducted ten years earlier at the ENS. At that point, he drew on the Millerian tendency and the young psychoanalytic generation emergent from the barricades in order to instill new life in the EFP by way of Vincennes. He did not succeed in this. After the dissolution of the GP, Jacques-Alain Miller, supported by Lacan, became the artisan of that last initiative. The political experience acquired with the GP, and the appeal to a hyperlogical conception of Lacanianism, already at work in 1965, allowed that adventure to come into being.

Around March 1969, Leclaire was confronted with numerous problems relating to the assessment of student achievement, the university elections scheduled for June, and Maoist agitation. While the directorate of the EFP reproached him with steering psychoanalysis "off course," the protesters accused him of making an alliance with the reformists and participating in the rise of revisionism. To escape from that trap, he proposed that the department be transformed into an autonomous UER for the purpose of research. He believed he could thus detach psychoanalysis from the philosophy major and promote its contact with other sectors of the university, notably, the UER at Censier and the CNRS.[11]

A month later, accused by Alain Badiou's group of being an agent of the counterrevolution, he faced down his adversaries, answering them wryly: "The true criterion of a psychoanalytic undertaking is a certain kind of impassioned denial that welcomes it. At present, it concerns neither our practice nor our concepts, but our existence. It is nonetheless the case that the situation is the same, to a certain extent, for the 'correct line of thought' presently guiding you. It arouses at least certain resistances, and has received until now only an aristocratic audience. So much the better! It's a sign that it is in contact with a parcel of truth, and that is, for the psychoanalyst I am, sufficient reason for knowing that it is still to you, philosophers, that I feel myself closest." [12]

In June the elections were held in circumstances that were frankly dramatic. The *gauchistes,* who were hostile to participation staged commando operations on the campus, armed with blackjacks and metal bars. Immediately, the advocates of participation reacted, with the support of a team of members from the CGT, [Confédération générale du travail, the Communist labor union]. The GP militants spread the rumor that the Communist Party was about to storm the experimental center. At which point barricades were erected,and the university began looking like an armed camp.

Just prior to vacation, a new administrative council was elected, but as soon as the school year began, disturbances returned, although without interfering with the resumption of teaching. At the end of September, the department was functioning, and Lacan was preparing to announce his arrival at Vincennes for four impromptu appearances. He declined the invitation from the department in order to accept an offer from the UER of philosophy. Leclaire announced in a circular that eight hundred students had attended seminars and that 230 UVs had been distributed. Three new positions were to be created, and 585 students were to be enrolled for the following year.[13]

It was at this juncture that the tragicomic affair of the pirate edition of Leclaire's seminar took place. Between silver covers adorned with crimson letters, a journal called *La Lettre infâme* brought out the transcription of the course given by Leclaire in 1969. It dealt with several subjects: the function of the father, incest, interdiction, the erogenous body, the articulation of the psychoanalytic with other forms of knowledge. The course was interspersed with bits from clinical cases, and a preliminary note specified that the transcription came from tape recordings that had been duly revised and corrected by the author.[14] But Leclaire had not given his approval to what was in fact a pirate edition exploiting his name. He was even quite irritated, since the text contained case analyses intended for a restricted audience. It was not, however, a very serious matter. Lacan's seminars and Freud's unpublished articles also appeared in unauthorized editions, and their readers never complained. But Lacan could not bear the competition Leclaire was involuntarily giving him. Not only was he intent on reigning alone through his discourse, but he also took advantage of the situation to destabilize the Vincennes experiment. At Lacan's urging, the directorate of the EFP summoned Leclaire to appear before it, and accused him of having authorized the publication of his course notes without consulting the institutional apparatus of the EFP.

In the interim, two events made the running of the department even more difficult: Lacan's "impromptu" and the publication by *L'Express* of an interview with Judith Miller. At the beginning of December, Lacan descended on Vincennes, armed with his formidable verbal skill. Always majestic, he arrived with his court at the disorderly campus, where an amphitheatre had been put at his disposal by the Center's administration. The old master was at the height of his reign and was not yet suffering the effects of old age. Superb beneath his shock of white hair, he confronted the contestatory fury of the great Vincennes bazaar like a Venetian doge. The amphitheatre was not packed, but filled with anonymous hecklers, shouting out their disgust for "leaders," cops, and psychoanalysts, and demanding an immediate act of self-criticism from Lacan. Lacan did not yield an inch, and when a young man climbed on the podium and began to undress, insisted that he go further. "Listen, my friend," he said, "I already saw that last night. I was at the Open Theater; there is a guy who did that, but he had a little more nerve than you. He stripped till he was completely naked. Go ahead, I mean why don't you continue! Shit!" Lacan then recalled that he had shown his sympathy for the May movement by stopping his seminar, after which he invoked his Surrealist past: "Contestation makes me think of something that was invented one day, if my memory is right, by my (late) good friend Marcel Duchamp: 'the bachelor prepares his chocolate by himself.'

Watch out lest the demonstrator prepare his chocolate by himself."[15] Finally, he issued an indirect attack against the department of psychoanalysis, mocking the system of course credits.

A few militants then emerged from the crowd to ask Lacan for money; he deposited a large bill in a hat extended for that purpose. Immediately the psychoanalysts imitated him and signed checks for the "revolution" as the master exited from the arena without hesitating to kick away a tape recorder whose presence he found annoying. After the collection, the spectators dispersed.

While the father was disavowing an experiment appealing to his teaching, his daughter agreed to give an interview to Michèle Manceaux and Madeleine Chapsal, who were preparing a book about teachers. Carried away by her Maoist passion, she spoke in praise of the Chinese revolution and mocked the university: "I will do my best," she said, "to make sure it functions worse and worse. The university is a state apparatus, a fragment of capitalist society, and what appears to be a haven of liberalism is not at all one. I don't think it can be shattered without the whole system. All one can say is that one will make it function as little as possible." Then, concerning the content of her teaching, she added that Spinoza and Kant were of no use to her at present and that she was having her students read studies of working conditions in Turin, Marxism-Lenininism in its Maoist variant, and the nature of the socialist countries.[16]

This was no big deal, and any other politicized teacher at the time might have said the same. But in those exceptional circumstances, any error committed by a militant was exploited by the adversary. A few months later, Michèle Manceaux decided to publish her interview with Judith Miller in the press. At the time, the interviewee had no reaction, but by the time she realized that a magazine was not a book, and that the content of her declaration could cost her dearly, it was too late: The weekly was already in press, and the interview would appear as it stood. When Georges Pompidou opened *L'Express* and read the declaration, he immediately asked Olivier Guichard to get rid of "the lady." He did so, and also withdrew certification for degrees in philosophy from Vincennes. He then sent Miller back to secondary school teaching, from which she had enjoyed a leave. She would subsequently be reintegrated into the university system, at the Censier UER, when the Left came to power.

As of January 1970, Serge Leclaire was being attacked from all quarters. Members of the directorate descended on the campus to criticize him in the name of orthodoxy, while Lacan himself put pressure on the Vincennes team to marginalize him. Leclaire resorted to the same policy in relation to the university as he had to the IPA during the glory days of the SFP. He considered the essential thing to allow "Lacanian subversion" to penetrate into the universities while yielding on administrative questions, which he regarded as secondary. That was why he accepted the principle of participation and distributed UVs to the students. His attitude was condemned by the *gauchistes* and by a majority of the Vincennes collective, who submitted to Lacan's directive to sabotage the undertaking.

During the summer, after a second "impromptu," Lacan obtained a reversal of power relations that was favorable to himself. The situation became impossible for Leclaire, who resigned and left his position to Jean Clavreul. A year later, he was elected to the admissions jury of the EFP. For almost four years, a collective would run the department, while obeying orders from the rue de Lille. Lacan kept his silence while affirming that the experiment should continue. In the face of Leclaire's eviction, faculty reacted differently depending on whether they were primarily university academics or members of Lacan's guard. For the young generation of academics, the conflict between Lacan and Leclaire seemed to be a settling of scores internal to the EFP, while for others, supporting Lacan's policies entailed something in the order of submission.[17] Nevertheless, the "line" defined by Leclaire was continued. The department welcomed programs reflecting the splintered situation of the EFP, with all its contradictory tendencies, represented by Montrelay, Roustang, Patrick Guyomard, et al. It remained open to all expressions of Lacanianism; thus, for example, Antoinette Fouque participated in a seminar on female sexuality.

After his expulsion from the ENS, Lacan moved his seminar to the Faculté de Droit [law school]. There, facing the Pantheon, he elaborated over four years a final recasting of his doctrine[18] which would allow him simultaneously to take leave of structuralism (without transcending it) and to move from a rejection of university teaching to its opposite. The hyperlogical reelaboration of 1965 was born of Lacan's discovery of Frege's work and of a confrontation with the theses of *Cahiers pour l'analyse*. It turned on the problematic of the subject of science, of the "suture," and of Gödel's theorem. The reelaboration formulated beginning in November 1969 was its logical consequence. And in that respect, the ENS and the *Cahiers* continued to play an important role: reconquest in 1965, dispersion and expulsion four years later. The last issue of the *Cahiers* appeared at a time when the group had already dissolved because certain of its founders had joined the GP. It dealt with formalization and emphasized the link with logic. It contained a long essay on Ludwig Wittgenstein by Jacques Bouveresse and the translation of texts by Cantor, Boole, Gödel, and Bertrand Russell. In those articles, Frege was no longer the sole reference, and it was the entirety of a problematic linked to logical empiricism and the work of the Vienna Circle that served as a nodal point for a collective meditation conducted by the *Cahiers* group. Psychoanalysis as such was absent from the issue, with the exception of a text by Alain Badiou, who compared Millero-Lacanian logic to a metaphysic.[19]

It was thus no accident if further osmosis occurred, at that late date, between Lacan's teaching and the activities of his "pack" of Normaliens. The first seminar conducted by Lacan at the law school bore the title *L'envers* [the netherside] *de la psychanalyse*. It was traversed in its entirety by a fruitful reading of a major work on the philosophy of language, Wittgenstein's *Tractatus logico-philosophicus*, published in 1921. No doubt Lacan had long been familiar with the name of that other Viennese Jew from the beginning of the century who had played so important a role in the development of logical positivism and Anglo-Saxon analytic philosophy. But before 1969, he had never engaged in a rigorous reading of the *Tractatus* and the name Wittgenstein does not appear in the *Écrits*. Now the discovery of that work was crucial for Lacan in the articulation of his second hyperlogical reelaboration, which may be called his mathematical reelaboration.[20]

The *Tractatus* tests the limits of logic. For Wittgenstein, the sole proper use of language is to express the facts of the world. Given that, philosophy is a language game allowing one to "cure" philosophy through a new use of itself. It is for that reason that Wittgenstein's aphorisms offer an answer to the question: What can be expressed? That answer is summarized in these terms: "Whatever can be said can be said clearly, and whereof one cannot speak one should be silent." Thus, what cannot be said is defined as a residue, and Wittgenstein included the ethical and the aesthetic senses (designated as the ineffable and the indescribable) in that residue. Two domains are incompatible: on the one hand, what can be said, and, on the other, what can be shown. With that incompatibility, philosophy would come to acknowledge the obligation of silence and a kind of *pas-tout* or "non-whole" escaping formalization.

The incompatibility between saying and showing could not fail to interest Lacan, who had drawn on Frege and Gödel in order to elaborate a notion of the subject of science refractory to the "totality" of formalization. Upon reading the *Tractatus* for the first time, independently of its heritage in analytic philosophy, he noted that Wittgenstein had abandoned the idea of metalanguage. Lacan called such metalanguage a *"canaillerie"* [scoundrelry], to the extent that it is defined as someone's *"grand Autre"* [large Other]. Then he again emphasized that Wittgenstein refused to save the truth; his operation would be the flaunting of a detection of philosophical *canaillerie* and thanks to it, the only meaning existent would be that of desire. Finally, Lacan compared that procedure to the psychotic position as defined by Freud: "Not to want to know anything of the recess in which truth is lodged."[21]

The question raised by Lacan starting in 1969–70 with *L'envers de la psychanalyse,* moreover, intersected with the Wittgenstein problematic of the ineffable and the *non-whole,* that is, the extrinsic and intrinsic limits of formalization.

As of 1950, Lacan began including mathematical references in his teaching. In that regard, his meeting of the Catholic mathematician Georges-Th. Guilbaud is essential for understanding the use he made of topological figures. The two men, who resembled each other physically, enjoyed relations of true friendship for thirty years. In 1951, Lacan, Lévi-Strauss, Guilbaud, and Benveniste met to work on structures and establish bridges between the human sciences and mathematics. Each made use of the teaching of the other as one might a topological figure.[22] On the basis of that collective effort, Lacan was not satisfied with empty talk or mere reflections on the history of mathematics. For thirty years, with or without Guilbaud, he engaged in daily mathematical exercises. Occasionally, while traveling, when he came upon a stumbling block, he would telephone his friend to present him with the problem and solve it with him. Guilbaud never went to the seminar, and his relation with Lacan was in the order of a secret garden. Privately, they shared a common taste for mathematical games: strings, inflatable buoys, miniature designs, children's cubes, the art of braiding and cutting, Queneau-like exercises in style. The field of topology retained the whole of Lacan's attention; he never hesitated to blacken reams of paper to teach his audience the elements of his doctrine as transcribed in topological figures.

The *Moebius strip,* with neither front nor back side, offers the image of the subject of the unconscious, just as the *torus* or *air chamber* designates the *hole,* the lack or abyss, that is, a constitutive site, which nonetheless does not exist. To those two figures, Lacan added the *cross-cap,* which allowed one to close the Moebius strip, and the *Klein bottle,* which figured a hollow surface. All those figures were used by him at each stage of the elaboration of his doctrine. But for twenty years topology remained an illustrative tool of Lacan's teaching without resulting in any fertile recasting of his theory.[23] And it was the reading of Wittgenstein, associated with his long-term meditation on mathematics, that would result in 1970 in the creation of a new terminology intended to allow one to think through the status of psychoanalytic discourse in its relation with others, and specifically with the discourse of the university. In order to think through that status, one would have to be able to move from *saying* to *showing*—that is, to incite every member of his audience, and Lacan himself, to perform exercises that were no longer in the order of discourse but of demonstration.

Although Lacan was fascinated by the aphorisms of the *Tractatus,* he did not, like Wittgenstein, conclude with the necessary maintenance of incompatibility. He attempted, on the contrary, to think through the domain of the ineffable by integrating the *non-whole* into it. He was aware that psychoanalytic discourse remained haunted by its origins in hypnosis, and that it still ran the risk of lapsing into a transferential religion—that is, a religion *tout court.* When psychoanalysis is reduced to therapy or transference, it tends toward magic and the unteachable; it becomes a religious practice. But when it evolves toward dogma, it also becomes a religion, a church, or a body of academic knowledge. In that sense, for Lacan, Christianity is the "true" religion, the worst, since the trinity is one in three and there is but one God: Christianity tells the whole of truth. To escape from the dimension of the ineffable, of magic, or religion, without lapsing into the dogma of truth, psychoanalytic discourse must be able to be taught—that is, it must be able to reduce the domain of the ineffable to a minimum. With the constantly present risk in Lacanianism of belief in a single and "undeviating" doctrine. It may thus be said that Lacan's recourse to formalization and mathematics was a final attempt to save psychoanalysis from its hypnotic roots, but also, at the other end of the chain, from schooling, in a society where school tends to replace the church.

Drawing on the notion of a *quaternary group,* and through Guilbaud's teaching on the Latin Middle Ages, Lacan constructed a mathematical object to which he gave the name *quadripodes.* It emerged from two kinds of reversals intended to show the organization of the same within the different, of multiplicity within unity. Lacan, in his home-made algebra, defined four terms: S^1 or the primordial signifier; S^2 or unconscious knowledge; $\$$ or the barred or unspeakable subject; and finally *a,* the object, fissure, quest, residue, or lack. The four terms were placed successively in four positions: the agent or appearance, work or sexual bliss, truth, and surplus enjoyment.

In the first position, a first quadripode defined the "master's discourse" as a reformulation of the Hegelian dialectic of the master and the slave. Lacan added a Marxist reading to this since it was also the discourse of capitalism. S^1 is in the position of agent; S^2 in the position of work; $\mathcal{S}$ in the position of truth; and a in the position of surplus enjoyment. Two successive reversals of the four terms allow for the designation of "hysterical discourse," then "psychoanalytic discourse," with each of the terms occupying the position that had been the other's in the preceding discourse. For *hysterical discourse,* S is in the position of agent, S^1 in that of work, a in that of truth, and S^2 in that of surplus enjoyment: the hysteric "induces" the master so that he produces work, but prevents him from functioning through the truth of a missing object, castration. Lacan placed the *discourse of science* in that of the hysteric, thus rediscovering his subject of science. As for *psychoanalytic discourse,* it may be deduced from that of the hysteric, since the *object a,* once called into question (desire), allows the production of signifiers, while conscious knowledge is in the position of truth.

Until this point, there was nothing much new. In both doctrine and demonstration, Lacan had already expressed the place occupied by each of the discourses. According to the rule of the quaternary group, he deduced his fourth quadripode not from a reversal of psychoanalytic discourse, but from a return to the starting slot. *University discourse* is deduced from the *master's discourse* through a pivoting in the opposite direction; unconscious knowledge then finds itself in the position of agent, a in that of work, S^1 in that of truth, and $\mathcal{S}$ in that of surplus enjoyment. The moral: university discourse produces subjects it addresses as though they were *unités de valeur*—"units of value" or "course credits." It pretends to master truth through technique and conceives of knowledge as a multidisciplinary distribution. In addition, it acts in the name of knowledge itself and not of a master capable of producing knowledge. That last affirmation allowed Lacan to insert the Soviet system into university discourse and to "save" Maoism by placing it on the side of the master's discourse.

The Lacanian analysis of university discourse reflected the evolution of education in a society undergoing radical technological change, in which the function of the master was being replaced by that of a knowledge without words and (why not?) by computers. In his way, and ten years ahead of his time, Lacan announced a radical transformation of the status of knowledge.[24] Now in a first phase, that meditation on schooling led him to refuse absolutely the experiment of "psychoanalysis in the university" and to affirm an incompatibility between university discourse and the others.

One year after Leclaire's resignation, however, which he had himself provoked, Lacan began changing positions, while elaborating the notion of a "matheme." The term does not come from the vocabulary of mathematics.[25] It was probably forged on the model of Claude Lévi-Strauss's *mytheme* and the Greek word *mathêma,* meaning knowledge. Its relation to the field of mathematics was to be deduced, according to Lacan, from Georg Cantor's madness. If that madness, he said in essence, was not motivated by actual instances of persecution, it was linked to mathematical incomprehension itself, that is, to the resistance aroused by a form of knowledge judged to be incomprehensible. And Lacan did not hesitate at that point to compare his own teaching to Cantor's. Was the incomprehension of Lacan a symptom? In other words, how might one adequately transmit a form of knowledge that is to all appearances unteachable? In order to answer that question, whose rudiments he had found in his reading of the *Tractatus,* Lacan invented the term "matheme." Then, between 1972 and 1973, he offered several definitions of it, after having switched from the singular to the plural, then from the plural back to the singular. He articulated his quadripodes with the matheme and defined the latter as the writing of the signifier, the one, the trait, the letter, that is, the writing of what is not sayable but can be transmitted. In other words, Lacan took the opposite tack from Wittgenstein. He avoided concluding the separation of incompatibles and attempted to snatch knowledge from the ineffable in order to give it a fully transmissible form. That form was the matheme, but the matheme was not the site of an integral formalization since it presupposed a residue that permanently escaped it. Thus defined, the matheme included a variety of mathemes—the sum total of the formulas of Lacanian algebra allowing something to be taught. As a result, the discourses are no longer incompatible, and psychoanalysis can be taught in the university, as a matheme, without being reduced to a university discourse.

At the same time, Lacan pursued his mathematical investigations with the help of a veritable mathematical object with which he had become familiar through Georges Guilbaud: the Borromean knot. He spoke publicly of the term for the first time in February 1972.[26] He had just discovered, at a dinner, the existence of the armorial bearings of the Borromeo family, he who had long, in Guilbaud's company, braided and tied knots of all sorts with extreme pleasure. But that evening, something was triggered when Lacan heard the story of the Borromeo family, or at least a few scraps of its story. The armorial bearings of the Milanese dynasty were constituted by three circles in the form of a cloverleaf, symbolizing a triple alliance. If one of the rings is withdrawn, the two others are set free. Each circle evoked the power of one of the three branches of the family. One of its most illustrious representatives, Saint Carlo Borromeo, was a hero of the Counter-reformation. A nephew of Pius IV, he lived in the sixteenth century and, thanks to his function in the Roman Curia, he reformed clerical morals, moving toward a greater discipline. During the plague of 1576, he distinguished himself through his charity, and when he died, Protestantism had retreated from Upper Italy. As for the celebrated Borromean Islands, situated in Lake Como, they were conquered a century later by a Count Borromeo, who gave them his name and made them one of the most famous landscapes in Italy.

Through that encounter with the heraldry of the Borromeo family, Lacan rediscovered the principal signifiers of his intellectual itinerary: the Roman Catholic Church, the Reconquest, the struggle against a "bastardized" psychoanalysis, itself assimilated to a reformism and a "Protestant" sphere of influence, and finally the plague. Why, prior to that date, had he not made the link between the mathematical figure of the Borromean knot and the family's heraldry? We do not know. It was nonetheless the case that he had long been fabricating knots, privately, before naming them publicly "Borromean" and using them in a fertile manner in his doctrine. As opposed to the matheme, the Borromean knot was not a term invented by Lacan.

It has been part of the history of topology since 1892, under the name of *Brunian structure* or *Brunian knot,* named after its inventor. But the term *Borromean rings* is often used to designate a structure in which three rings are linked together without being linked two by two, so that, if one is untied, the others are freed.

Lacan's interest in Borromeanism and in knots in general may be understood. His practice partook first of all of demonstration and of the possibility of being wrong and then pointing to his error and correcting it. Through it, a structure was manipulable in space, bound to language—to what can be said and to the "non-whole" of saying. In addition, Lacan rediscovered there his famous triangulation of the Symbolic, the Imaginary, and the Real, become RSI, a veritable Borromean cloverleaf dominated by the weight of the Real. The knot showed what the matheme conveyed and as a result every discourse had its meaning as a result of another discourse, while Wittgenstein's "whereof one cannot speak" was fused with *little a,* the residue. The matheme was to be taught as the writing of the one, as the teachable snatched from the clutches of the ineffable, and the knot did nothing but show this. In that respect it was also the opposite of the matheme, since it could not be transcribed. It was made the way lace might be woven. It dissolved, brought to light, deconstructed dogmas in an infinite play of loops and openings. It was a metaphor of the fact that everything proceeded from one, but it also served to present that metaphor since no formalization of language was transmissible in the image of that language itself. Starting in 1972, Lacan called Borromean knots "rounds of string." He gradually acquired remarkable dexterity in the manipulation of his pieces of cord, to the extent of constructing a veritable liturgy of demonstration, in the course of which he would all but lose the gift of speech.

If the matheme was situated on the axis of the teachable and allowed psychoanalysis to make its way in the university, the Borromean knot was rather on the side of an act of dissolution. It showed simultaneously that everything proceeded from one and that everything evaporated with the withdrawal of one. In the contours of that knot, Lacan observed himself dying along with his school, and in the figure of the matheme, he postulated, on the contrary, a legacy. It was thus no accident if the designation of a "dauphin" in the person of Jacques-Alain Miller occurred by way of the matheme and the transcription of the seminar, while the death of the sovereign was formulated in a Borromean idiom: nothingness, muteness, silent confinement in a topological monastery.

In 1972, while still a militant in the Gauche prolétarienne, Jacques-Alain Miller conceived the project of transforming the entirety of Lacan's seminars into a series of books. Struck by the success of *L'anti-Oedipe,* whose text stemmed from both oral teaching and joint authorship, he wanted to show that Lacan's work continued to exist and that the criticisms that had been addressed to it had not resulted in its going under. The *Écrits* had become a classic, but the seminars were still unknown to the public at large. In the course of a dinner in June 1972, Miller, in Lacan's presence, criticized the various attempts of others to effect a transcription. He declared that they had done a poor job, to which Lacan shot back, "Prove it." Miller hardly needed as much encouragement to accept the challenge. He opted to work on the seminar of 1963–64, *Les quatre concepts fondamentaux de la psychanalyse* [*The Four Fundamental Concepts of Psycho-Analysis*], which was the first he had attended, the seminar marking Lacan's arrival at the ENS. Miller left for Italy and in the course of a month, working from the stenographer's transcription, prepared a first version of the text. Lacan gave his approval and proposed that they appear as coauthors. Miller refused and evoked the possibility of other transcriptions prepared by others. Lacan replied in the negative, at which point his son-in-law picked up a second gauntlet. "I'll do them all," he said. "I'll call the whole thing *Le Séminaire* and divide it into numbered volumes." [27] The young man had set sail on a terrible voyage.

Lacan had always entertained a curious relation with his oral teaching. For him, the transition from the spoken to the written posed a serious problem. With the exception of his thesis, Lacan never wrote a book. And the strenuous pressure of François Wahl and the publication of Ricoeur's book were needed to convince him to gather his lectures into a volume of writings. When Lacan drafted a text, he conceived of it as a condensed version of his seminar. Most often, he did not improvise and wrote up in advance the lectures he was to deliver. Such was the case, for example, for the interview entitled "Radiophonie" and conducted for Belgian radio by Robert Georgin. It was also the case for the television special entitled *Télévision,* filmed by Benoît Jacquot, in which Miller questioned Lacan. Everything was carefully planned in advance. Most of the articles and lectures were conceived in the same manner. There was thus a radical difference between the words he spoke at his seminar, the occasion of an uncontrolled improvisation, and the fixed language of his writing, either for publication, or for radio or television broadcast.

The words of the seminar were concretized in a variety of ways. There were first of all Lacan's handwritten notes, from which he improvised. Then, there was the *original,* constituted by tape recordings and/or stenographic transcriptions undertaken by stenographers. To the extent that as of 1965–68, tape recording represented the principal testimonial instrument, both for historians and for Lacan's audience, it may be said that the status of the written was profoundly unsettled as a result. For a half-century now, the written no longer has the force of law it once did and oral testimony has itself become the locus of an original inscription. What would de Gaulle's departure for London have been without radio, and what would have become of the Resistance without the coded messages of the BBC?

In that respect, Lacan's seminar did not have the same status as those of Saussure or Kojève. At the time those two thinkers were teaching, recording machines did not yet exist and it was impossible to retain an original. It was thus the notes of their listeners that took on the value of an original: Charles Bally and Albert Sechehaye for Saussure, and Queneau for Kojève. In the case of Lacan, an original inscription exists: in stenographic transcriptions starting in 1953, and in numerous sound tapes after 1968. At the time Miller decided to transcribe the seminar, several individuals were aware of how important it would be to show Lacan in the process of improvising. Philippe Sollers tried in vain to convince a moviemaker working for French television to set up his cameras in the Faculté de Droit. From that same perspective, the Belgians succeeded where the French failed. In 1972, a magnificent document was produced by the television services of that country, based on a lecture given by Lacan at the University of Louvain. The master can be observed in all his freedom, dressed in a Chanel-style shirt, confronting a young *gauchiste* who taunts him with inflammatory declarations. Lacan calms him down gently and continues speaking without looking at his notes. It is the only document showing Lacanian discourse as it was formulated at the seminar.

In the face of those various modalities of inscription, Lacan adopted several different attitudes according to the historical circumstance.

In 1953, he hired a stenographer to transcribe his seminar. The transcriptions were deposited with Granoff, who was in charge of the library, and were generally available to all members of the SFP. Three years later, and until 1959, J.-B. Pontalis, working with Lacan's approval, produced excellent summaries of the seminars on "Object Relations," "Formations of the Unconscious," and "Desire and Its Interpretation," all of which were published in the *Bulletin de psychologie*. During the same period, Solange Faladé offered Lacan the services of her secretary in the interest of a better stenographic transcription. She also envisaged a tape recording, which would in fact occur starting in 1962. Moustapha Safouan, for his part, took it upon himself to transcribe the seminar on "ethics." The results would not be published. In addition Lacan gave stenographic transcriptions of seminars as gifts to certain disciples and women. There thus began to form a veritable cult of the master's sacred words.

At the time of the split, in a gesture of irritation, Lacan himself removed the transcriptions from the SFP library with the intention of depriving disciples who had left him of his teaching. As soon as the EFP was founded, he revealed a distrust of "idea-thiefs." He no longer had a central deposit, but numerous transcriptions circulated among the members of the tribe, who studied them like so many verses of the Talmud. Pirate editions also began to appear in bookstores. Lacan devoted more and more thought to arranging for an authoritative transcription of his teaching. He proposed the exercise to Michèle Montrelay, who quickly saw that she was imposing her own writing style on Lacan's spoken words. She enjoyed it for a while, then gave up. Jacques Nassif also had a go at it, quite officially, and published an abridged version of the seminar on the "Logic of the Phantasm" in *Lettres de l'EFP.*[28] Then in 1968, he undertook the seminar entitled *D'un Autre à l'autre*. The results were profoundly displeasing to Lacan, who became angry. They would not be published.

Again in 1963, a team from La Borde, led by Jean Oury and Ginette Michaud, labored at producing transcriptions on the basis of recordings. They were reproduced in batches of several hundred copies, and in 1971, at the time the EFP's library was being founded, the directorate authorized the team to deposit the stencils with the École. Nicole Cattan, the librarian, took charge of them, entering them into the school's archives, with the assistance of Gérôme Taillandier. They were kept locked up and made inaccessible to the public. Lacan feared that the massive distribution of his seminars outside the École would result in the appearance of defective and uncontrolled versions of them. All these measures did not prevent the proliferation of copies of the seminar.

The displacement of Lacan's teaching toward the Pantheon brought with it a radical transformation in the status of the seminar. Not only was the audience increasingly large, far exceeding the framework of the psychoanalytic community, but dozens of tape recorders began to pop up in the vast amphitheater of the Faculté de Droit. Lacan began by resisting that formidable intrusion, and occasionally asked in anger that the mechanical ears be removed. Eventually, however, he came to tolerate them, without ever mastering the situation. A new stenographer, Maria Pieracos, received an official salary from the EFP for transcribing the seminar amidst extraordinary ritual. She made four copies, which she then transmitted to Solange Faladé, who kept them in her home. As for Maria Pieracos, she did not understand a word of Lacan's oral prose, but was treated like a queen by the crowd: "It was enough for me to arrive in the middle of the crowd and say, 'I'm the stenographer,' and everybody stepped back to make room for me to pass. Nobody wanted the job. There are only about fifty stenographers in all Paris, and everyone said, 'Above all, don't go there; he speaks Chinese. . . .' My role was that of a machine. You understand, I was like a worker on an assembly line; I couldn't have an overview of the whole job, and I was not good at taking orders. Lacan never spoke to me, except once at a congress. Speaking one day about the stenographer, he said: 'the typess.' As for me, all that interested me was the cashier."[29] Such was the world of the seminar at the time Jacques-Alain Miller accepted Lacan's challenge.

That challenge was contemporaneous with Lacan's elaboration of the notion of the "matheme." Now the matheme was already a response to the question of the transition from the oral to the written. It was concerned with the letter, with transmission, inheritance, and the "legalized" fixation of a teaching. In other words, it traced the furrow of a possible posterity for the doctrine, there where improvised words remained the medium of the ineffable.

Miller called the writing he did based on the original the "establishment of the text." He borrowed the term from the tradition of belles-lettres without realizing that it was also a reference to the history of Maoism. "Establishment" was in fact the word used to evoke the move by which a militant "established" himself in a factory and became an *établi*. But a factory *établi* is also the improvised work table on which a worker puts the finishing touches on doors before sending them off for assembly.[30]

In 1972, Miller thus established the text of Lacan's seminar. He removed a number of asperities and ambiguities, regularized the oral inscription, eliminated redundancies, and invented from scratch a system of punctuation. The transcription was fine; it had the disadvantage of suppressing some of the improvisation and the advantage of desacralizing the stenographic record by supplementing it with a written version. In any event, it had the merit of making readable words which until then were not, since their delivery was intended to be listened to and gazed at. But through that "establishment," the seminar's author was no longer quite Lacan, without being completely Miller. In brief, the established text conveys the content of a doctrine which, although Lacanian, bears the trace of Millerism—that is, of a hyperrationalist tendency within Lacanianism.

Séminaire XI was published at the beginning of 1973 with numerous misprints. The printer had forgotten to include corrections made by Lacan of certain diagrams. The master flew into a fury, which may be sensed in the dedication to his old friend Jenny Aubry: "Leave this book to your descendants for the bibliophilic value it will some day have for having revealed the *truly exceptional piece of garbage* a publishing house can make of a manuscript that was the object of the most vigilant attention, not to mention the competence of him whose name follows my own here." [31]

Lacan was thus delighted by the establishment of the text of his seminar and furious at its publication. When *Séminaire XI* appeared, it was welcomed without challenge by the entirety of the Lacanian community. They found it an excellent piece of work, and did not for an instant dream of uttering the slightest public protest. Three volumes were thus published, under the same conditions, during Lacan's lifetime. And it was only after his death, on the subject of *Séminaire III,* on the psychoses,[32] that a polemic would erupt against the transcriber's work. Miller would then be accused by certain disciples of infidelity to the stenographic record, something, moreover, he never denied, since he was inventing a written style, and not copying the work of a stenographer.

The problem raised by Miller's transcription was not that of faithfulness to spoken words or the sacralization of an utterance. It was that of the transmission in writing of an original inscription.

In that respect, Miller and Lacan did not share the same idea concerning the establishment of a text. Their respective positions were formulated in 1973, in a "Postface" and "Notice" at the end of *Séminaire XI.*

Lacan used the word "transcription" and not "establishment" for the work done by his son-in-law: "What you have just read . . . is thus not a written text. A transcription, there's the word I have come up with thanks to the modesty of Jacques-Alain, Miller by name: What is read moves through the writing while remaining unscathed. . . . But I should also credit the author of this work with having convinced me—and having borne witness to it throughout its duration—that what may be read of what I say may be read no less because I have said it." [33]

Lacan was not satisfied with calling a "transcription" what Miller had called an "establishment"; he added that that transcription was not a written text, an *écrit.* If it was not, it was thanks to the modesty of Miller, who authored without signing the work. For Lacan the transcription thus had a clearly defined status—it translated without any loss his oral discourse. It allowed the original inscription to remain unscathed amid the writing transmitting it. Put differently, for Lacan, Miller's transcription resembled a matheme, an integral transcription capable of reducing the share of the ineffable in the spoken. It may be deduced from that "Postface" that Miller's transcription offered Lacan a possible solution—the first in the history of Lacanianism—to the problem of the transition from the oral to the written. For indeed all the other transcriptions were of a different order. They were the precise reproduction of a stenographic record all of whose inexactitudes were merely corrected. Or they were simply summaries or rewritings. It is clear that Miller resolved for Lacan a central problem in his career: the "passage" of an oral teaching into its written translation. For that reason, Lacan underwrote his son-in-law's work and made him the legal owner of the transcription. But at the same time, and perhaps without realizing it, he also designated the tendency to whom it would fall to represent him for the future.

If Miller's transcription offered Lacan a solution to that problem of "passage," it bestowed on Miller something quite different, and of which he was undoubtedly not aware at the time. In the logic of his "establishment," he advanced one step further in his relation to Lacan, by stating that his work *effaced* the original. "Our intent here was to count for nothing," he wrote in the final "notice," "and procure, from Jacques Lacan's spoken work, a transcription in which one could have faith and which, in the future, would stand for the original, which does not exist. For one cannot consider the version furnished by the stenographer—swarming with errors, and in which nothing serves to make up for the absence of intonation and gesture—as such. It is nonetheless a version *sine qua non*, that has been gauged, rectified, word by word—the disposable residue coming to less than three pages." [34]

Miller thus claimed not to count for anything, whereas Lacan had him counting for the entirety of a complete transcription, that is, for a matheme. The author claimed that the original did not exist, whereas Lacan maintained the opposite, by stating that the transcription left his utterance unscathed through a writing that was nonetheless not an *écrit*. Now in order for an utterance to be readable without loss in writing, an oral teaching, all the same, would have to have been pronounced. On that subject, Miller claimed two contradictory things: On the one hand, he affirmed his ability to rectify a version *sine qua non* and, on the other, he denied its existence in the name of stenographic errors. In other words, Miller corrected an original in order to efface its trace.

Having himself wanted to be the commentator of Freud and the "rectifier" of a doctrine "gone astray" or "bastardized," Lacan could not avoid one day finding himself in the situation that was his in 1973. If the historic existence of Lacanianism is to be judged in terms of its preservation and reelaboration of Freudianism, it means that Lacanianism also had to face the hurdle of its own preservation and reelaboration: its fixation, transmission, transcription, etc. In entrusting his son-in-law, and no one else, with the transcription of the seminar, Lacan made a choice that would have numerous consequences for the subsequent history of Lacanianism. He did not efface the original, but consigned the original to inscription by way of the matheme. And as a consequence, the matheme, whose instrument Miller became, would "correct" the whole of Lacan's work in the direction of a reduction of the ineffable and the definition of a "right line." Thus the effacement of the original was the theoretical means through which Millerianism strengthened itself with Lacanianism as the bearer of a "nondeviating" Lacanianism—with the obvious risk of dogmatism.

In July 1974, Serge Leclaire, who had left Vincennes four years earlier, was in search of a new extra-analytic platform for psychoanalysis. Still passionately Lacanian, he directed his efforts toward a "confrontational" format—the word was in the air—organizing a colloquium at the Centre Culturel de Cerisy-la-Salle. "The attempt will be made," he wrote in his draft for a proposal, "to confront psychoanalytic discourse with other forms of discourse: mathematical, scientific, philosophical, political, among others. As opposed to any murky interdisciplinary aim, the confrontation will be predicated on the originality of psychoanalytic discourse and the labor it imposes." The colloquium had a phenomenal success, attracting psychoanalysts of every tendency and from every institution.

While Leclaire favored an ever increasing splintering of what he called the psychoanalytic incestocracy, Miller took an opposite tack in deciding to reorganize the department at the University of Vincennes on new grounds.[35]

In 1971, he had left his position in Besançon to teach regularly, as a *maître assistant,* in the department of psychoanalysis. Around 1974, it was his feeling that the situation was deteriorating and he discussed the matter with two colleagues, formerly of the ENS, Patrick Guyomard and François Baudry. The first was an analysand of Lacan's and the second of Christian Simatos's. Neither of them had been an Althusserian or a Marxist. Miller communicated to them his fears for the future of an experiment that seemed threatened with extinction because of its overextended investment in the contestatory spirit of '68. Certain of the psychoanalysts teaching in the department were content to listen to their students without any concern for the loss of positions, which were tending to be taken over by the psychology section. Since inertia continued to reign, Miller decided to resort to strong-arm tactics for the beginning of the 1974 semester. He proposed to Lacan that he personally undertake a reorganization of the department, arguing that the department after all claimed to be Lacanian. Lacan agreed and wrote to Clavreul, who contacted Miller in order to plan and implement the restructuring. Clavreul volunteered to convince the Vincennes collective to submit to the master's decisions. Lacan had no credentials for directing a university department, but his moral authority was such, and his position of exclusion so unjust, that in appealing to him, Miller was able to become his official delegate at the administrative level. But still, the "base" had to agree if the attempted reconquest was to be legitimate. In September, Clavreul joined Miller in writing a text entitled "Base nouvelle pour un département de psychanalyse," in which the thesis of the matheme was formulated: "If there is a psychoanalytic matheme, something of what analytic experience teaches is effectively transmissible in its entirety. . . . It remains the case that the matheme is still problematic. It can in no way take the form of a manual. . . . The thesis of the matheme thus implies that only effective engagement in an original work pursued within or on the basis of the Freudian field will *henceforth constitute credentials for the exercise of a function in the department.*"[36]

For the second semester of 1973–74, twenty-four UVs, divided among twenty-two members of the faculty, were offered the students. The position of *maître de conférences,* which had been Leclaire's, was "frozen" after his resignation, then finally awarded to a different section because of the negligence prevailing in the department. Four *maître assistant* positions were held by psychoanalysts pursuing their profession elsewhere. Finally seven assistantships were divided among academics who were not yet psychoanalysts but undergoing training on Lacanian couches. Most of the other members of the staff were *chargés de cours,* who were also in analysis and paid hourly wages. The psychoanalysts occupying positions were in fact doing the jobs of *chargés de cours,* since the Ministry did not accord them the title of "associates" allowing them full-time positions. Among the faculty were to be found Claude Rabant, François Baudry, and Patrick Guyomard. Positions as *maîtres assistants–analystes* were held by Clavreul, Dumézil, Tostain, and Conté, all veterans of the master's couch. All these members represented the former legitimacy emerging from Leclaire's experiment, and it was between them and Miller that the contest over control was to be played out. François Roustang also taught in the department.

As a function of the matheme, instructors were called on to send Lacan written projects demonstrating their allegiance to the new line and allowing them access to the UVs. In the interim, all courses were suspended and their resumption was dependent on Lacan's approval—or disapproval—of the proposals submitted to him.

No sooner was the circular distributed than mutterings of revolt could be heard against Lacan's methods, whose abruptness came as a surprise to all concerned. After having asked them to reject university discourse, they were now asked to accept it. Miller left for Italy, and upon returning, decided that Clavreul had been working against the project. In order to shore up his power and accomplish the job more expeditiously, he asked Lacan to appoint Charles Melman. Melman himself could not have asked for anything more; he had always been hostile to the Vincennes experiment and brought his unreserved support to the task of reorganization. A triumvirate was constituted in which Clavreul found himself increasingly obliged to endorse decisions he disapproved of. Between the triumvirate and the teaching staff, two distinct legitimacies confronted each other. One emanated from the rue de Lille and consisted of effecting a fusion between Lacan's doctrine and his person, claiming it was his right to govern a department based on his teaching; and the other emanated from the Vincennes collective and oscillated between a desire to help Lacan and a refusal to pledge allegiance to his person. The master sent the project off to its addressees like a request for love. As a result, the faculty was caught in a dilemma: Either one was with Lacan or one was against him. They would thus end up asking for his advice as doctrinal master of the department (with Miller as his official representative) with the option of subsequently saying they had been the innocent victims of a totalitarian seizure of power.

At the beginning of October, the triumvirate met at the rue de Lille. Lacan proposed that the direction of the department be entrusted to the three partners and that faculty not be readmitted until their projects were approved. In addition, he decided that after two years of operation, a series of days would be devoted to evaluating the experiment. Clavreul, in a fury, objected and left the premises. But the following day, he agreed to a proposal assigning full power to Miller and Melman. Against the collective, he would defend the new line and treat the liberal opposition as so many "impotent and morose beautiful souls." [37] He would wait for Lacan to be dead and buried before setting out publicly the reasons for his submission. In his terms, without his act of servitude, the EFP would have been driven to a split or toward an anti-Lacanian stance: "If I did not, at the time, react more openly, it was only because such a stance would have provoked a split within the school and the analysts who would have followed me would have found themselves embarked on an anti-Lacanian course that would have overwhelmed me. I thus submitted at the time to *raison d'État* because I was convinced that the immense majority of members of the École freudienne had not understood that we had already reached the end of a regime and that all that remained possible were palace revolutions among courtiers intent on securing positions for themselves in the future." [38]

While Clavreul believed he was saving the EFP from dissolution by combatting protesters, a meeting of the opposition took place in the home of Claude Rabant. Miller was invited, but did not go, sending his brother Gérard to attend the discussions, whose contents would be transcribed and forwarded to Lacan. In the course of the proceedings there were violent diatribes against the "Millero-Lacanian dictatorship." François Roustang announced he would not resign for fear of seeming childish. Tostain proposed reproducing five pages of the telephone directory as a project simply to demonstrate how ridiculous the situation had become. As for Luce Irigaray, she joined the protesters as a *chargée de cours,* although she had not taught the previous semester and was not listed on any official faculty list. She emphasized that Lacan had no right to exercise official power in the university, which was perfectly accurate from the administrative point of view. Rabant and Baudry were concerned rather with restoring calm. Shortly thereafter an exchange of letters between Rabant and Miller ensued, in which the two legitimacies confronted each other. "Things are now quite simple," wrote Miller. "Either one accepts that the concern manifested by Dr. Lacan is legitimate and one accepts the orientation he has indicated and the collective intends to implement it in every case, or one contests that legitimacy and appeal is made to the administration of the university. . . . In either case, the result will be the same. The initiative inspired by Lacan will carry the day. In the first case, work will begin (whatever one thinks) in the best conditions. In the second, a commission from Vincennes, after hearing complaints for an hour, will refuse, as it has always done, to take a position on the internal affairs of a department. Those few who have thought they could appeal to that authority against a theorist whom they invoke every day in their teaching and their practice will have to face the consequences. They will be definitively discredited in the eyes of many, including members of the university, and the reopening of the department will not have been delayed a single day. . . . We were originally recruited by Serge Leclaire on grounds that were unambiguous: our reference to Freud and to Lacan. . . . Who would like to play Tartuffe and tell Lacan: 'It's up to you to leave, you who speak as a master. The house belongs to me and I will have it acknowledged.' Perhaps surprise is the reason for a certain reticence. It is now up to all of us to present our projects to Clavreul." [39]

Starting in mid-October, the department's affairs were being conducted by Miller, who undertook, with Lacan's support, to expedite the various projects with all due speed. He quickly drew up statutes to which faculty would have to commit themselves, then asked Tostain, Dumézil, and Conté to relinquish their positions as *maîtres assistants.* Clavreul had already resigned. Miller was then in a position to appoint four nonanalysts favorable to the new line to replace them. And with that he could also reject the projects of four recalcitrant *chargés de cours* and replace them with more submissive candidates (who had themselves recently resigned). On October 13, Baudry, who was worried by the turn events were taking, circulated a letter, sent to Lacan, in which he raised the question of the competence of the newly imposed triumvirate. Three days later he received a withering reply from the master, who promised him explicitly that he would entrust to no one responsibility for the request he had sent to members of the faculty.[40] At the end of the month, twenty-two projects were accepted out of thirty-five submitted. Six instructors who had taught the previous year, all of them *chargés de cours,* were refused and replaced by six new candidates. Four of these occupied the positions of those who had resigned. Miller was thus assured of a comfortable majority.

The EFP congress opened its doors in Rome on October 31, 1974, in the presence of eight hundred individuals packed tight into an auditorium of the Santa Cecilia Conservatory. In his inaugural press conference, Lacan recalled how dear the legendary city was to his heart since the autumn day, twenty years before, when he had delivered his famous "Discourse." Two decades later, his son-in-law would move more quickly still. Always in a rush to act and persuade, the febrile young man wrote in Rome a long intervention that would establish him as His Majesty's heir-apparent. To be sure, he had not yet imposed himself within the rank and file of the École, and in certain respects Lacan distrusted him. For a while, he was only a thirty-year-old philosopher drawing almost exclusively on academics outside the EFP and several members of Lacan's personal guard. But in addition to his general efficiency, he had just added two significant strings to his instrument: the transcription of the seminar and the seizure of power in the university.

Miller was playing a difficult game. Before him, within the École, no one had been able to serve the master as he did, in such manner that publishing or political operations carried out in his name were not disasters. The *passe* procedure was a failure, partly because of Lacan. The projected dictionary was a fiction. *Scilicet* was a catastrophe. The publications, with the brilliant exception of established authors, were not doing well. Written in clunkish prose, they were presenting a disastrous image of Lacanianism. It should also be noted that the "Champ freudien" series, unlike others directed by members of the IPA, did not benefit from the inclusion of texts by Freud. On several occasions, François Wahl and Lacan attempted to bring out unpublished texts of Freud, but they never received a reply from the officers of the archives. In addition, since Lacan had a hard time tolerating the autonomy of his disciples, Serge Leclaire, the most senior of the group, no longer had any desire to second him. He gradually cut off all connection with the EFP. The other members of the third generation adored Lacan, served him poorly, or spent their entire life on his couch without being able to defy him. As for the young generations, at times they dispersed out of a desire to breathe a different air, and at others they evolved toward a terrible sectarianism. In 1974, Miller was thus a second time the man demanded by the situation. He had gained in self-assurance. Not afraid to sully himself with power, he proposed concrete solutions to Lacan, accepted his challenges, and succeeded in convincing him. Lacan was not unhappy, thanks to the young man, to make his disciples pay him their voluntary servitude and their abortive desire to rebel. In addition, he had married Lacan's favorite daughter, for whom

Lacan had a veritable cult. Sustained by the master, Miller was tolerated quite poorly by the Lacanian community, who saw him as something of a Gloucester come to usurp their territory. They would end up hating him for their failure to remove him from power.

In his "Rome Discourse" devoted to the matheme, Miller situated Lacan at the four corners of his quadripodes: as master, analyst, university academic, and hysteric. In addition, he made personal use of the notion of *lalangue*, which Lacan had elaborated in 1971. He gave it a less amorphous and more radical theoretical content, thus confirming Millerianism's contribution to Lacanianism. Lacan had advanced the term, on the basis of a pun on Lalande's *Vocabulaire*, to designate a form of knowledge which knows itself without being aware of it and is revealed by psychoanalysis, then a "far greater thing than language is aware of." [41] Miller advanced the idea that the doctrine of *lalangue* was inseparable from that of the matheme: misunderstanding and ambiguity, on the one hand, integral transmission on the other. He thus saved the Lacanian principle of nontotalization while adding to it the Leibnizian notion of nonambiguity: "While *lalangue* is sustained only through misunderstanding, and thrives on it and lives off it because meanings grow and proliferate out of sounds, the matheme, on the contrary, can be transmitted integrally 'without amphibology or equivocation,' to use Leibniz's terms, because it is made of letters without meaning." [42]

In the Millerian perspective, the matheme is slightly different from Lacan's conception of it. Lacan advanced, on the basis of Wittgenstein, that the nonteachable or ineffable could become a matheme. From which Miller derived a Leibnizian, retroactive, and political conclusion, which allowed him to shore up his reign amid a hostile community. "If there is a psychoanalytic matheme," he said, "individuals other than psychoanalysts can contribute to the discussions of the community sustaining analytic experience. It is because the theory of the matheme is the bedrock of the EFP that from its inception, nonanalysts, among whom myself, those 'not engaged in the analytic act' (as was hurled at me by one of those who are a bit too inclined to confuse analysis with a fixed income) have had their place in the École freudienne since its foundation. And it seems to me they will continue to have it for as long as the École freudienne will be faithful to its orientation." [43] Then Miller announced that he would continue his teaching at Vincennes and, if possible, at the École freudienne. Everything had been said: Symbolically the son-in-law had seized power in the very face of the old guard. It would now be up to the guard to define itself.

That evening, after the Rome Discourse, Lacan had a family dinner along with François Wahl. Quite happy, he congratulated Miller, which did not prevent him, during the following days, from being absolutely furious and telling his intimates that he had the impression that his funeral eulogy had just been pronounced. Nevertheless, his hope was that the Vincennes experiment would stimulate work within the EFP. Around that time, Miller opted to receive analytic training from Charles Melman. The two men, who were quite different, resembled each other in certain ways. Both were Jewish and sons of Polish immigrants; both were influenced by Marxism and its dissident forms; both incarnated the values of an authoritarian, atheistic and rationalist Lacanianism. We will say no more on the subject. The story of that extraordinary analysis would end with a terrible conflict whose deeper meaning belongs to the personal odyssey of each of the participants.

After the congress, events began to accelerate on the Vincennes campus. On November 9, Claude Frioux, the Communist president of the University and a leading specialist of Russian language and literature, asked Lacan to teach a course. "I insist on telling you," he wrote, "how much our university would appreciate your presence among us." [44] Lacan was delighted. Ten years after his triumphant entry in the ENS, and five years after an insulting expulsion, he was a second time becoming part of a university bastion, making his entry through the front door, thanks to the support of a Communist intellectual. He had not been wrong in 1953 to bet simultaneously on the Church and the PCF. He immediately invited Frioux to a memorable meal of caviar and buttered toast, then answered the offer officially by enthroning Miller. "I am very touched by the honor you have bestowed on me through your request," he wrote. "The esteem you show me not only consoles me, it returns me to my work. So much so that I would like to acknowledge my debt at this point. May I ask you, concerning the department presently called 'of psychoanalysis' at Vincennes, to be content with my scientific advice? That, accepting that it is possible only if Jacques-Alain Miller underwrites it, standing in for me as administrative counsel. The arrangement for two years. I am embarrassed, embarrassed toward Paris VIII at not contributing more of my 'presence,' to use your word. The one to which I commit myself will already keep me there sufficiently. No teaching for a period of two years whose competence will not be determined by my evaluation of the practice from which it stems." [45] On November 15, Claude Frioux informed the teaching staff of the department of Miller's official designation as principal administrator of the experiment. What remained was to have the program voted through by a plenary session.

The faculty then declared the procedure illegal and asked to meet with Frioux and Merlin, the vice-president. Miller obtained the right to be present at the meeting, in which François Baudry and Claude Morali participated. In the face of so much divergence of opinion, Frioux proposed a meeting of the department in his presence in order to find out who its true chairman was (Morali had been elected to that position by the opposition). Miller immediately let Morali and Baudry know that he would not make any concession of any sort. Then Baudry sent Lacan a very long letter, which was circulated in the department, in which he recounted Miller's numerous maneuvers. In order to indicate his opposition, he asked that the note he had appended to his project be replaced by these words: "François Baudry did not write the teaching proposal for October 20, but a note broaching the subject of the difficulties of his practice at Vincennes. In the next issue, he will give a presentation of his teaching." [46]

The meeting of the faculty assembly took place on November 26 in Miller's home, with Lacan present. After a discussion, the members of the faculty (some by telephone) signed the Miller-Lacan proposal. Tostain, Clavreul, and Guyomard complied even though they had been violently opposed to Miller. Luce Irigaray and a few others refused to sign while Baudry and Rabant abstained. [47] The trap had

closed on the protesters who had themselves signed on to a procedure they claimed
to disapprove of. Never did the mechanism of voluntary servitude function better
than in the Lacanian community. Jacques Lacan was confirmed in his function as
scientific director, Miller in his role as chief administrator. As for the scientific committee, it was composed of those two, along with Melman and Clavreul. Instruction
in the Vincennes department thus came completely under the domination of the
Lacano-Millerian line. Of the twenty-two members of the teaching staff the previous
year, six were removed and replaced by six newcomers: Catherine Millot, André
Rondepierre, Stuart Schneiderman, Jean-Jacques Gorog, Better Milan, and Alain
Grosrichard. All the university-based members of the opposition were kept on, as
well as Roustang, Clavreul, and Tostain. Of the projects coming from the outside,
six were accepted and seven refused. As soon as the document had been signed,
Miller brought the minutes of the meeting to Claude Frioux, and, as a result, Baudry
and Morali canceled the meeting that had been scheduled with him. It was by then
too late to disavow a commitment subscribed to by a majority. The Lacano-
Millerian operation would have consisted in doing brutally what, under the guise of
democracy, all departments in universities everywhere do.

The affair was further envenomed when Roger-Pol Droit, in a laudatory ar-
Another event would allow Miller to further consolidate his power. By mid-
November, he was being called a "fascist," a "Petainist," and a "Nazi" by certain
members of the opposition. He was reproached for using against his "victims"
purge techniques that Vichy had used for the Jews. Perhaps Miller's adversaries had
forgotten that he himself was Jewish, and no doubt they had also chosen the wrong
dictatorship. If the Vincennes power grab was indeed a *coup de force,* it in no way
resembled a Nazi putsch. No victim had been tortured, threatened, or deported to
concentration camps. There were no deaths, and no one had actually been deprived
of his living. If the victims were unhappy, it behooved them to fight their adversary;
the administrative means were available. "I imagine," Miller wrote to François
Roustang, "that your words exceeded your thought when you told me this afternoon on the telephone, speaking of the department, that it was all Nazism and that
Lacan was using people who were employing Nazi methods." [48]

The affair was further envenomed when Roger-Pol Droit, in a laudatory article on the Rome congress, wrote this sybilline sentence: "In the Paris VIII department, the regaining of control is being called a purge. Without any explicit explanation, faculty members are being excluded. After Rome, Vichy? It's a pity. . . ." [49]
After that article, Gilles Deleuze and Félix Guattari adopted a hostile—but far more
explicitly argued—position against what was transpiring. They observed in a circular that the way the opposition was being treated would rather lead one to think,
keeping in mind the difference in proportion, of a Stalinist operation. They then
emphasized that the excluded had not manifested any strenuous resistance, adding
finally that the history of the psychoanalytic movement was not exempt from "un-
conscious-washing." They noted that Lacan had no right to rule in the university. [50]
And with that they approached Claude Frioux with the request that the university
commission on teaching personnel take a position on the Lacanian *coup.* But Miller
in turn sent out a circular and defended his project, exploiting an article by Robert
Linhart which had appeared in *Libération,* introduced by Serge July, under the title

"Gauchismes à vendre? [Gauchisms for sale?]." The author accused the partisans of the Anti-Oedipal cause, and specifically Félix Guattari, of having sold out to capitalism in order to further their personal endeavors.[51] The moral: Before removing the straw from one's neighbor's eye, it is preferable to measure the beam stuck in one's own. The would-be obliterators of the Lacan-Miller dictatorship would have done well to remember that proverb.

Moving full steam ahead, Miller decided to bring out a department bulletin in order to publish various projects and information concerning the new orientation. Along with Jean-Claude Milner and Alain Grosrichard, he began looking for a name to give to the undertaking. During the Christmas vacation, at Guitrancourt, he was playing a guessing game with his family. Participants were to identify characters with the help of enigmatic definitions. Miller then had the idea of pressing the game to its limit by using as clues his own recollections from primary school: "mais où est donc or ni car?" [—a mnemonic for the French conjunctions]. *Ornicar* thus became the pure signifier of an unfindable individual whom none of the participants could manage to identify. He kept the phrase, turned it into a noun, and retained the question mark. The bulletin would be called *Ornicar?*.[52] Over the years it would become one of the best psychoanalytic journals in France.

The first issue of *Ornicar?* appeared in January 1975, with a text by Lacan announcing the orientation of the department and the list of projects. The cover featured a Hogarth drawing representing a monkey watering to no effect three stalks planted in flower pots. The animal observes the results of his labor through a magnifying glass. Three inscriptions adorn the pots and illustrate the vanity of the monkey's attempt to bring back to life what has long been dead. Hogarth was mocking the aberration of art lovers whose taste for the exotic attracted them to old paintings appreciated essentially for their age. His drawing was thus parodic in intent, its point being to deride pedagogy. As for the monkey, he represented the antiquarian and usurped the place of Grammar, source of all eloquence and knowledge.[53] In other words, Miller was sending the representatives of the old legitimacy off to the junk heap. *Ornicar?*, the unfindable, incarnated the matheme, thumbing its nose [*faisant la nique*] at the old monkeys. The journal bore the subtitle: *Bulletin périodique du Champ freudien*. Lacan wanted the department to take on the name in order to better manifest the meaning of a commitment beyond any mere reference to psychoanalysis. But changing names is not an easy matter and finally Leclaire's title would be retained. The bulletin was initially published by the Société du Graphe and, once it became a true journal, distributed by Le Seuil, with Laurence Bataille as principal editor. *Ornicar?* would subsequently become part of Éditions Navarin, founded by Jacques-Alain Miller, after the street of the same name. With the creation of the journal, the young man again gave proof of his editorial talents. But above all, he was beginning to consolidate his position outside the EFP, from within a bastion of the university that represented for him the wherewithal to negotiate at some future date in the event of a crisis in the EFP.

The Lacanian community would never recover from the Vincennes *coup de force*. And it was more the method used by Lacan than the principle of his presence in the university that was contested. In proceeding in such manner, the master lost the confidence of his organizational base, which had supported him overwhelmingly for the introduction of the *passe* procedure and which would thereafter feel it had been disavowed. As for Miller, he committed a number of blunders linked to his lack of respect for democracy. Confident in his intelligence and his privileged position as son-in-law, he was far too contemptuous of both his potential allies and his adversaries. He had a tendency to silence all concerned with his appeals to a pure and unadulterated Lacanianism that in no way corresponded to the aspirations of the clinical community. In addition, for his entry to the École, he depended on the seraglio and did not open up sufficiently to the base, which might have supported him. But with the exception of Faladé, the seraglio detested him but did not dare to criticize him publicly, either out of theoretical inadequacy or fear of displeasing Lacan (who nonetheless allowed all in his fold to speak). The dignitaries thus kept their peace, but would end up turning against the young man. Ultimately, Miller did not perceive (or did not want to perceive) that in becoming a kind of personal incarnation of Lacan's words, he was destroying the principle of direct monarchy that had been established in 1964. Once the king was gradually deprived of a physical relation with his people, through successive delegations of power, and once the people was deprived of the body of its king through an interpreter, the EFP could no longer function. As a result, Miller was forced to gain in outside influence what the École was losing in unity.

At the Rome congress, Solange Faladé became aware of the crisis wracking the EFP. Her thought was to have Miller intervene within the École rather than act solely on the outside. Closer to the aspirations of the young and the non-Parisians than her colleagues, she requested a general meeting devoted to a broad discussion of the EFP's problems. But the directorate refused. She then suggested that the executive board be graced with a vice-president, an office that was necessary for the organization to be recognized as being of "public utility" as well as for ensuring the spread of Lacanianism throughout France. Denis Vasse was elected. A priest and a physician, he lived in Villeurbanne. Three others also joined the board: Jean-Pierre Bauer for the city of Strasbourg, Pierre Bastin for the Lille region, and Jenny Aubry for the south of France. Solange Faladé, for her part, agitated among the young without ever obtaining the organizational meeting she desired.[54]

In 1976, Miller claimed new turf by creating at Vincennes, with the support of Lacan's guard, a "third-cycle" doctorate in the "Freudian field." Then, when the school year began, he set up a system of permanent psychoanalytic training intended for psychologists, nurses, and social workers. Finally, he got the Council of Paris VIII to approve a "diploma in psychoanalytic clinical practice." This was a title for strictly internal use awarded by a "clinical section of the Freudian field" which had been founded in October 1976. Its purpose was to dispense instruction corresponding to a Lacanian definition of clinical practice. It concerned psychiatrists in training, physicians, and holders of the master's degree, and entailed interviews, courses, and the practice of presenting patients. With that innovation, the Lacano-Millerian tendency attempted to rediscover the tradition of classical psychiatry at a time when dynamism was already on the wane. Through it, and against the heritage of clinical psychology, Lacan again opted for the asylum and his remembrance of the 1930s.

When Henri Ey died, *Ornicar?* paid homage to him by printing an unpublished text of his in praise of Clérambault. While speaking of Ey, that publication was intent on promoting the cult of Lacan, who had been the student of the master of the Special Infirmary.[55]

Lacan, of course, supported the creation of the clinical section, even as he increasingly left administrative matters at Vincennes to his son-in-law. In October, Solange Faladé proposed to Miller that he come work with psychoanalysts in the EFP. She asked him to devote his attention to Lacan's algorithms, and Miller chose the term "matheme." The meeting would be called the "Day of the Mathemes." He himself offered a brilliant discussion on the teaching of the presentation of patients, thus intruding into a field previously restricted to practicing therapists.[56] He delivered harsh criticisms of Maud Mannoni's anitpsychiatric positions, and she was quick to respond that psychoanalysis ran the risk of becoming the crutch of a psychiatry stripped of the support it traditionally derived from neurology. She was not wrong, but the story had already come to a close: both antipsychiatry and classical psychiatry, for which psychoanalysis was no longer of any use. The matheme would not offer any remedy for that historical situation, even if it were to run the risk of fully transmitting—in clinically teachable terms—the language of madness. And while the young Lacanians, trained in the practice of short sessions, made use of the matheme to rewrite the therapies of their patients as equations, Lacan announced that he was looking for the matheme that would be able to offer a substitute solution for psychiatric discourse by allowing the researcher to speak the same language as the madman.

From the "Day of the Mathemes," Miller and Faladé were thinking of continuing to work together in the EFP. Miller proposed a congress on the "tradition" of psychoanalysis. Faladé preferred the word "transmission." She submitted the project to the directorate, and Lacan assented, opting for "transmission." But the members of the directorate, furious that Miller was thus assuming functions within the École, did all they could to sabotage the undertaking. Miller tired of the wrangling and lost interest in the situation and the congress, which would take place without him. Nevertheless, through his other activities, he continued to reinforce his position, and when he returned to business in 1979, he was the first to benefit from his work and from the failures of a directorate and of juries that were by then bankrupt.[57] But he would never be accepted by the rank and file of the EFP and would be obliged to draw on forces outside the kingdom. In the end, even though supported by Lacan, he had the majority of the École against him: whence the horrors of the dissolution.

At present, the department of psychoanalysis is located at Saint-Denis. It is less powerful than the UER in clinical human sciences, but has made no compromise with psychology. It counts one professor, three *maîtres de conférences,* two *maîtres assistants,* three *assistants,* two associate *assistants,* seven certified research directors in the framework of the doctorate in psychoanalysis, thirty-seven *chargé de cours,* and eighteen lecturers. As a result of the *coup* of November 1974, it effaced its origins without being able to change its name. It is still called the "department of psychoanalysis," but in the brochure listing its courses, the following may be read:

"Since its creation by Jacques Lacan, the department of psychoanalysis of Paris VIII has attempted to transmit a body of knowledge about psychoanalysis, etc." [58] Students are thus not aware of the fact that it was Serge Leclaire who initially founded the experiment.

II. The Société Psychanalytique de Paris or Advanced Bureaucracy

While the EFP rapidly grew in size and was already experiencing a grave institutional crisis before May 1968, the SPP seemed to be maintaining itself in a kind of changeless stability. Having opted for post-Freudianism and obedience to the standards of the IPA, it did not entertain the same relations with the literary and philosophical thought of its time as the Lacanian community. Since it had no doctrinal master of any stature, it functioned as something of an oligarchy, without any democratic pretentions. As the masters of the second generation disappeared from the scene, their (third generation) students found themselves pitted against each other in a series of extraordinarily violent conflicts. Having become in turn directors of their society, they continue to produce students who oppose them or attack each other. Starting in 1965, under the pressure of the expansion, the SPP has been the scene of a permanent struggle that continues to exist at present. It pits against each other, first, the heirs of Nacht, Schlumberger, and Bouvet, and then, by ricochet, the students of those heirs. The conflicts are repetitive and cyclical, turning on the question of psychoanalytic training with particular reference to transferential filiations.

The terminology used is not the same as in the Lacanian community. In the SPP, the training analysis and what follows is called the *cursus,* controls are called *supervision,* and the person statutorily authorized to conduct a training analysis is called a *didactician.* Moreover, there is a tendency to gallicize the acronym IPA and call it API (Association psychanalytique internationale), in order to underscore the Society's fullfledged affiliation. The SPP has always been the French "section" of the IPA. Whence this paradox: It has always claimed to be all the more French in that it is beholden to an Anglo-American empire. Its strange relation to its own Frenchness would be the occasion of several institutional disappointments.

It is difficult to pinpoint the various tendencies within the SPP, since its members do not on the whole consider themselves as part of any tendency. They are disposed in general to be post-Freudians, neo-Freudians, and more influenced by the English than by the American school. Their references tend in any event to be to Winnicott, Bion, Melanie Klein, Anna Freud, and Jones, as well as to all trends that did not split from the mother institution. Their conflicts are less theoretical than institutional and have not resulted in any real divergences with the IPA empire concerning the rules of technique, the length of sessions, and the conduct of analyses. From the institutional point of view, there are "liberals" who seek to democratize the Society by reducing the power of the titular members, and "conservatives" who want, on the contrary, to retain the omnipotence of the training analysts. In each camp, there are, in addition, defenders of the ideals of medicine, who are not necessarily hostile to the inclusion of nonphysicians among the titular members. In both camps, there are advocates of a more extensive demedicalization and depsychiatrization. But there are also, among the younger members, those who, not having experienced the split personally, have forgotten its aftereffects and have difficulty understanding their seniors' hostility toward Lacanianism. Finally, there are the Jews and the non-Jews, who are not necessarily opposed to each other but who entertain complex relations with the SPP's Jewish identity. In speaking of tendencies, currents, or identities within the SPP, we should state that these are constructs of the historian. Quite often the participants themselves do not perceive them as such.

There is a considerable difference between the APF and the EFP, on the one hand, and the SPP, on the other. The APF and the EFP had a common institutional and historical origin. Both had to constitute themselves with reference to a choice: Lacan or the IPA, a master or a group. They are thus both profoundly rooted in the history of Lacanianism and its reelaborations. The SPP, on the contrary, never had to make such a choice since it had been "left" in 1953 by a group of rebels. Its relation to the history of Lacanianism is thus not the same as that of its rivals.

As of 1969, the French psychoanalytic community was divided into four major Freudian components: the APF, the EFP, the OPLF (the Fourth Group), and the SPP. The first three had a share in the history of Lacanianism, while the last remained the most alien to it. That does not, of course, mean that the history of Lacanianism is absent from the conflicts in the SPP. But it functions differently there than elsewhere for the simple reason that the transferential relation with Lacan had been broken since 1953. For the fourth and fifth generations of the SPP, trained between the first split and the 1970s, Lacan was not present as a clinical practitioner. There were no members of those recent generations who had been analysed by him, and those of the third generation who had been trained by him were rare indeed. Thus the young generations were not concerned by Lacan's person even if they occasionally attended his seminar. Trained at a remove from active Lacanianism, they envisaged it as one doctrine among others. As a result they remained deeply attached to their own society, which certified their professional competence and identity. In that respect, there is always a formidable *long duration* of bureaucracies which is opposed to the momentary illuminations leading to true theoretical innovations: A revolution is first of all a short session, even if its administration requires centuries.

Since there is no intellectual master of stature promoting a doctrine or an institutional policy, each individual in the community is free to become a petty— and more or less talented—master. Anyone can write without feeling endlessly obliged to situate himself in relation to an omnipresent teaching. The relation to a master's living speech is thus historicized, but there is nothing capable of sustaining a collective psychoanalytic adventure. Members of this type of Freudian collectivity are destined, in such cases, to produce students in accordance with fixed and well-defined criteria. And in so doing, they are obliged to create small transferential baronies around themselves, based not on a direct relation to the person of the sovereign but on an institutional affiliation. Their identification is not with a master and his cause but with the institution conferring an identity on them and administering their ambitions. That identification can become positive or negative according to the relations of power or conflicts of the day. It can even lead to a persecutory relation to institutional reality when the bureaucracy refuses to authentically acknowledge the existence of its minorities.

Within the SPP, after 1953, a split was no longer possible, because the split had *already* occurred, necessitating a choice between Lacanianism and the IPA. The members of the SPP have thus been condemned, for the contemporary period, to live under the same roof—that is, to tear each other apart within a common entity. Any actual break with the mother society would immediately entail a loss of affiliation with the supranational identity considered to be the source of all Freudianism. Now history shows that in order to successfully run the risk of such a loss, one has to be not only a creator but an authentic founder: a sovereign, a political leader, or a legislator. If a break does not lead to a founding act, it results in a return to the empire. One can break with the already-there of an historical foundation only on the condition of founding something else: Such was the sense of the Spinozan gesture with which Lacan reacted to his own exclusion during the difficult winter of 1963. Through that gesture and through it alone, he accepted the risk of being abandoned in turn. Had he been content with being banished or persecuted, he would not have founded anything.

It will thus be understood why neither the APF nor the SPP could tolerate a split. In order to bring one off successfully, a founding gesture would have been needed, and it was for lack of that gesture that the APF returned to the bosom of the empire, having chosen an institution against a man. For identical reasons, the OPLF, without returning to the IPA, remained within the general movement of a sociologized Lacanianism. It founded nothing, but took its distance from a prince in order to grant priority to a group. By virtue of that principle, societies without a "great man" are always surprisingly stable. At times they win over the allegiance of true creators who are not eager to become founders or take their time to do so; at others, they tolerate rebels, who, in the absence of any founding doctrine, play the role of permanent victims. Such has been the case for the SPP. Creators, dissidents, rebels, and antiauthoritarians have had to choose between two attitudes, either returning to the fold and becoming interested in something other than power, or taking power and establishing a new legitimacy. To choose one or the other path, two conditions are necessary: either to have within one a creative work or to be able to govern. In either case, one has to be able, at the right moment, to accept the risk of exile—inner exile if one retreats to one's writings or practice; political exile if one loses the battle for power.

In this respect, the SPP is at present composed of three categories of individual: bureaucrats who always act in the name of an IPA-based legitimacy and who, strong with that power, always emerge victorious; petty masters—authentic practitioners or creators—who always end up accepting the bureaucratic order because they know they have no other choice; and rebels of every stripe, who, if they are unable to break away at the right time or reconcile themselves, are condemned to the role of permanent victims. Because of its bureaucratic structure, the SPP is thus a stable society, without any major doctrinal renewal, resembling at times a local section of a comintern and at others a branch of a multinational corporation. Its stability is commensurate with its hidden conflicts. On the inside, there are fratricidal fights fought through the mediation of transferential filiations, but on the outside, in opposition to the Lacanian tumult, a mask of illusory calm is maintained.

In order to grasp the crisis that gripped the SPP as of 1967–68, one should recall that the creation of the Institut de psychanalyse in 1952 changed the face of the Société psychanalytique de Paris. What is customarily called the SPP or the Institute is in fact a two-headed organization consisting of two associations governed by the law of 1901: the SPP on the one hand, and the Institute on the other. The former has an administrative function, and the latter a teaching function. Despite that division, any member of one is automatically a member of the other. To facilitate matters, we will refer to the juridical entity formed by the SPP as the Société, the society called the Institut de psychanalyse as the Institute, and the joint movement characterizing the tendency represented by both associations as the SPP (it being understood that that tendency can have a variety of aspects.)

Since 1952, the Société has been composed of three kinds of members: *titular members, adhering members,* and *corresponding-affiliate members* (belonging to other societies). Only titular members have full deliberating powers and are authorized to conduct training analyses. Their appointment occurs through election by the titular members. Adhering members are psychoanalysts whose practice has been certified by the Société after they have written a long paper. In December 1966, in order to counter the problem of the society's swelling ranks, the decision was made to introduce the category of affiliates in addition to that of corresponding members. Through that modification, the affiliate becomes a fullfledged member once his training has been declared complete by the Institute's commission on instruction. In March 1967, the change was ratified by vote, and seventy affiliates were elected in a single swoop. The SPP is thus presently in the process of undergoing a quantitative transformation.

The Société, unlike the EFP, does not accept mere members or nonanalyst members. It concedes no rights to students of the Institute, who pay for their training and have no juridical status. It is administered by an administrative college composed of titular and adhering members elected by the titular members. That college elects new adhering members after hearing from an ad hoc admissions commission. Each year it also elects a board composed of five titular members and three adhering members who function as advisors. As a result the Société is governed exclusively by the titular members.

Until 1953, the Institute was run on the model of the Société. It was administered by an administrative council theoretically composed by the Société's titular members. That council was recruited through a process of cooptation submitted to a general meeting in which only titular members had the right to vote. The administrative council elected a board presided over by a director and took the name of "comission on instruction." Administrative power thus merged with the teaching function. Members of the commission were called *commissaires.*[59] The teaching function was delineated by study regulations which determined the modalities of the *cursus.* In order to apply to be a student at the Institute, a candidate had to submit a written request for enrollment accompanied by a curriculum vitae and copies of his university records and any publications. He would pledge not to claim to be a student until relieved of that vow by the commission on instruction. The commission would investigate the candidate's personality, then, after deliberating, let him know if there were a major objection to his being a student of the Institute. This procedure was called *preselection* and led to "command analyses."

If the candidate were preselected, he was authorized to select his psychoanalyst from a list of titular members who alone were certified to conduct training analyses. He thus committed himself to a personal analysis that was not shielded from administrative control. He had to inform the commission of the date of the beginning of his therapy and the name of his training analyst, who was to supply the commission with the same information. The candidate would then become a student of the Institute. In choosing his supervisors, he would follow an identical procedure. Two controls were necessary, one of which was collective, with two titular members other than the training analyst. With that the *cursus* was complete, and the student could cross the various hurdles ranging from affiliation to titular membership. In order to protect personal analyses, in a system in which everything was controlled in advance, Nacht had an article appended to the modalities of the *cursus* stipulating that the training analyst was not to intervene in the commission's deliberations concerning his own student and that, reciprocally, the commission was not to take a position concerning the length or end of that analysis. At the time of the creation of the new category of affiliate, this selective mode of training began to be seriously challenged by most members of the SPP. A further provision was added concerning the *cursus,* in addition to Nacht's, aimed at reducing the "advance" status of the command analysis. It stipulated that a personal analysis can become a training analysis after the fact, at the time of actual practice, the candidate's acceptance for supervision then coinciding with the beginning of training.

In a May 1967 presentation, Jean Favreau effectively grasped the malaise reigning at the Institute a year before the barricades, because of a system that was becoming archaic. "I wonder," he said, "whether a note delivered to candidates proposing that they contact a few wise and experienced analysts (masked training analysts) would not be preferable. Each of those among us chosen by a candidate would proceed as he thought best. The time gained in commission meetings would be devoted to exchanges about the technique of each individual. . . . This measure would not be a panacea, but a preparation for the most essential thing: a personal psychoanalysis." [60]

Fourteen years after the departure of the founders of the SPP, the honorable society had still not devoted serious thought to the training problems that had brought on the first split. Despite a few accommodations, it still found itself in the situation that Lagache and Lacan had denounced at the time. In that respect the conflicts between "liberals," who were hostile to preselection, and "conservatives," who were favorable to the status quo, had existed since the decline of the Nachtian era. But it would not be until the explosion of May 1968 that a true battle would erupt over the problem inside the SPP.

In 1965, the SPP was thus, along with the EFP, the most powerful Freudian society in France. Although it did not occupy in any striking manner the great bastions of modern thought, it was sturdily rooted in the university, in therapeutic centers, and in all psychiatric services. It counted 83 members: 35 titular, 39 adhering, and 9 corresponding-affiliates (old formula). If one includes students, who were not counted as members, it may be said that the society was slightly larger than its principal rival. But not for long. Twenty-five women were fullfledged members, including 17 adhering and 5 titular members: Denise Braunsweig, C.-J. Luquet-Parat, Joyce MacDougall, Janine Chasseguet-Smirgel, and Evelyne Kestemberg. The last three were not physicians. As of that time, the SPP, like the EFP, began to suffer from the strain of excessive size. In 1981, it counted 297 members: 61 titular, 59 adhering, and 177 affiliates. If one adds the students, the figures are close to those of the EFP. In both societies the increase in the number of women was equally important, although slightly higher in the SPP. But positions of leadership were not distributed in the same way. In the EFP, women were present at every level of the hierarchy (ME, AP, AME, AE), whereas in the SPP, they crowded the ranks of the affiliates. The higher one climbed in the hierarchy, the fewer women one found: 140 in all in 1981, with only 17 titular members, among whom 5 were nonphysicians. At the time, the SPP thus remained the most medical society in France. And that medicalization has had its effect on the access of the female population to positions of power, which explains why, in institutional conflicts, the women have tended to gather beneath the conservative banner. In the tradition of Marie Bonaparte, they are all the more submissive to medical ideals in that they are not physicians.[61]

In the realm of publishing, the SPP was powerful without being at the forefront of contemporary culture. It still had only one official journal, *La Revue française de psychanalyse,* which would never change (despite a few efforts in that direction). On the eve of the student revolt, it was moribund. Its publisher had lost interest in it, and members of the group were reading it less and less. It barely had any readership outside the SPP. Nevertheless, between 1965 and 1968, changes began to occur in response to pressures. At the Presses universitaires de France, aside from the series created by Nacht in 1956, was "Le Fil rouge," founded in 1972 and directed by Michel de M'Uzan, Serge Lebovici, René Diatkine, Serge Viderman, and J. de Ajuriaguerra. At Payot, there was Gérard Mendel, who since 1962 had been in charge of "La Petite Bibliothèque" and the "Sciences de l'homme" series. At Denoël, two series were founded by liberals, one by Conrad Stein in 1970, "La psychanalyse dans le monde contemporain," and the other by Jacqueline Rousseau-Dujardin, "Freud et son temps." The latter ceased to exist in 1980. Finally several other members of the SPP established themselves in more marginal publishing bastions: Bela Grunberger and J. Chasseguet-Smirgel at Tchou in 1977, with the series "Grandes découvertes de la psychanalyse," and Alain de Mijolla at Belles Lettres, run by his brother, with a series entitled "Confluents psychanalytiques."

The scientific activities of the SPP are numerous. Aside from colloquia organized by the titular members and numerous seminars for students, each year the Société runs the Congress of Psychoanalysts in the Romance Languages and participates in the major meetings of the IPA. Although the near totality of its titular members are Parisians, it has tended to decentralize without becoming quite as successful in the provinces as the EFP. The SPP possesses a prodigious private library as well as a center for psychoanalytic consultation and treatment where state-reimbursed therapy is practiced. It is a veritable Parisian empire, lucky to count among its members, moreover, two of the most prestigious individuals in French psychoanalytic culture this century, the writer Marthe Robert and Professor Georges Devereux, whose works of ethnopsychoanalysis are recognized the world over without having enjoyed the reception they deserve in France.[62]

In May 1968, rebellion was threatening in the ranks of the SPP. To the stupefaction of all concerned, an immense plenary session succeeded in gathering the totality of the society's members. In response to pressure from the young generations, numerous transhierarchical commissions were created. They took upon themselves the task of thinking through a democratic modification of the society's statutes and a radical transformation of training principles. The rebels demanded all together a democratization of the administration of the society's affairs, the elimination of preselection, and the abolition of any cleavage between training and therapeutic analyses. There thus recurred a revolt of the base identical to the one that had provoked the split of 1953. Titular, adhering, and affiliate members together participated in those commissions, which bore such names as "Cursus and Hierarchy," "Selection and Training," "Cursus and Selection," "Problems of Instruction," etc. All worked with considerable ardor for a year, and numerous reports were written, mostly by members of the fourth generation.

In March 1969, Jean-Luc Donnet, a student of Viderman's, produced a synthesis of demands, to which he added a proposal for reform. There followed extensive discussion in which a cleavage between a progressive and a conservative tendency among the titular members became further manifest. Whereas in 1952, discord among the masters had preceded the revolt of the base, in 1968 it was the insurrection of the young which divided the upper reaches of the hierarchy. In its fundamental structure, the conflict was nonetheless identical with the exception that Lacan's practice no longer functioned as an index of crisis. "Internal protest," wrote Donnet, "has resulted in the establishment of working commissions *to the extent that the crisis provoking that protest encountered a situation of internal malaise.* That crisis thus constituted a privileged opportunity to ponder quite concretely the function of an analytic society for the analyst since precisely so large a number of them have turned to it." [63]

To his considerable stupefaction, Donnet received in March from Lacan a letter of praise for himself and of mockery for the SPP. The master was visibly astonished to see history repeat itself with so comic an insistence. "I have been brought your fifty-four pages," he wrote, "which should be taken in terms of the limited distribution intended for them. But as such, they gave me much pleasure. And even, upon rereading them, amusement. There is, however, an unresolved question: What in the world impelled you to sign your name to it? The suggestion of May? Unbelievable but improbable. I am thus writing to tell you as the signatory of these lines the pleasure I took in seeing the accent placed precisely on what Freud foretold of psychoanalysis. Let us say as a didactic *contribution.* . . . I skip the other delights I gleaned in passing. As for your 'solution,' it comes seventeen years late; I can prove it to you if you like. It is in keeping with the comedy of May that this point eludes you. Don't think you have been disqualified as a result though. You escape that comedy, on the other hand, through the quality of your text, overwhelming for whoever would read it, which is an improbability in our circle. I wanted to testify for you to the fact that it could happen." [64]

Starting in the spring, the Donnet report was discussed at length by members of the SPP, and specifically by such adhering members as Jacqueline Rousseau-Dujardin, Nata Minor, and Jean-Claude Sempé, and by such titular members as Robert Barande and Janine Chasseguet-Smirgel. The latter produced a rather severe attack against the report's positions and proposed that the existent system be retained: "Having reflected and pondered the situation at length, it has seemed to me that the existence of an anonymous and even bureaucratic third party, with all the disadvantages it brings with it—society, commission, institute—tends more to divert all that risks interfering with the development of the analyst-analysand relation in therapy than to alter its process, just as the rigid framework of therapy, the regularity of sessions, their fixed duration, the single place in which they occur, the payment, far from inhibiting the freedom of association, allow on the contrary for the crystallization of the anal dimension of reality upon that frame and free up the capacity for narcissistic regression by thus helping the analytic relation to be established, as Grunberger has shown." [65] Donnet was not about to be diverted from his course and responded to Chasseguet-Smirgel with a good deal of self-assurance, supported in that by Robert Barande, who in turn wrote a reformist text entitled "Application de la théorie psychanalytique à l'institution destinée à s'en porter garante (essai sur la crise de la psychanalyse contemporaine) [Application of psychoanalytic theory to the institution underwriting it (essay on the contemporary crisis in psychoanalysis)]." [66]

At the time the "contemporary crisis" was not merely French. At the IPA congress, which was held in July in Rome, students from all the societies, supported by liberal titular members, met in the margins of the official proceedings to contest the established order. The Italian press immediately called that overflow a "counter-congress." In order to contain the revolt, a European Federation of Psychoanalysis (FEP) was then set up on the model of the APA. The FEP proved ineffective and would not allow for any resolution of the problems of the IPA-based societies of Europe. In the case of France, it would serve to establish a dialogue between the SPP and the APF. Those two societies envisaged the possibility of merging in a federation, but the project was quickly abandoned, being judged too precarious for the respective identities of the two groups. Originally, the idea for an FEP emanated from Raymond de Saussure, who was intent on creating a counterweight to American power on the old continent. In 1971, Daniel Widlöcher became the secretary of the federation and militated for its establishment in France, becoming friends with Serge Lebovici in the process. The two had in common splendid hospital careers and they were both men of power, convinced of the rightness of the IPA line on the subject of training. A hospital *assistant* since 1962, Widlöcher returned to medical teaching after May 1968. First an associate professor, then the holder of a chair, at age fifty, he became director of the hospital group of Pitié-Salpêtrière.

In the fall of 1968, the contours of the split between the SPP's base, supported by a few titular members including Barande, Stein, and Viderman, and the conservative majority, led by Serge Lebovici, became clearer. The "Cursus and Hierarchy Commission" at that time asked that the Donnet report be published in the *RFP*, whose editor was Pierre Marty. Without any explanation, Marty refused, thus revealing the orientation of the leadership. Barande, for his part, also asked for the publication of his text so that the work of the commissions might be made public. He was no more successful in his efforts. In the winter of 1969, both presentations were published in the journal *Études freudiennes,* created by Conrad Stein at Éditions Denoël, with Lucien Covello as editorial secretary. The creation of that journal and of the collection which was to follow it in short order signified the first time in the history of the SPP that a handful of titular members had explicitly entered into dissidence. None of them would tender his resignation from the mother institution.

For the adhering members, who had fewer prerogatives and privileges to lose, things transpired differently. Three attitudes were to be found between 1970 and 1977. Some refused promotion to titular status, like Jean Cournut; others, like Nata Minor, Jacqueline Rousseau-Dujardin, and Jean-Claude Sempé, gradually moved toward resignation from the society; and still others, like Donnet, accepted the conflictual situation in their society, choosing to continue the struggle while becoming titular members. In the end, they grew weary and retreated to their fields of specialization. As for the students, several of them resigned. Among them was Alice Cherki, a likable Jewish Algerian who had fought colonialism in the ranks of the FLN and worked with Frantz Fanon in the hospital at Blida. Serge Lebovici had backed her in her studies during the time of her arrival in France. She entered the EFP in 1975.[67]

At a colloquium in May 1971, in the presence of the titular and adhering members, Serge Lebovici reaffirmed his support for the traditional hierarchy and the classical curriculum in the name of a hostility to all forms of transgression: "I believe that we are dealing with a case of massive transgressions facilitated by the sociocultural situation of psychoanalysis and by what is everywhere being purveyed in the name of psychoanalysis. And you are not unaware of the fact that I am among those who support the role of the institution against transgression, in order to favor precisely the severity and unyielding character of psychoanalysis. And it is for that reason that I would like to conclude by recalling that the institution should be judged in relation to the desire for transgression."[68]

The debate was continued by Green, Barande, Favreau, Donnet, Evelyne Kestemberg, and Janine Chasseguet-Smirgel. To illustrate the current situation, Donnet humorously recounted the extraordinary tribulations of one of his patients afflicted with a "neurosis of fate."

One day, wanting to become an analyst, the patient in question made his request to the Institute and was given the answer that his therapy had no juridical existence. If he wanted his project to succeed, he would have to speak to a training analyst and establish a record for himself. Confirmed in his negative opinion of the IPA bureaucracy, he then went to the EFP, where he was received by Christian Simatos, who had been Donnet's friend during their internship together. He was invited by him to continue his therapy on the same couch, while being authorized to undertake his controls at the EFP. But when he asked a leading Lacanian to accept him for a control, she turned him down, saying he would have to change analysts and engage in a period of therapy at the EFP. She too knew Donnet. In the meanwhile, encouraged by Simatos's reception, the patient contacted a female academic who was a member of the APF, in the hope of preparing a thesis at Paris VII. She asked him for the name of his analyst and realized that she knew Donnet, having previously worked with him. "Since it's Donnet who has sent you," she said, "I will be delighted to sponsor you and personally to take charge of you." The patient did not dare say that his analyst had nothing to do with his initiative, but he fictionalized it by applying for a medico-pedagogical internship directed by a Lacanian with whom Donnet had also had a chance to work. The Lacanian explained to him that a psychoanalyst "authorizes himself" and the patient was promptly hired as a child therapist. In order to control his analyses, he soon spoke to a therapist of the Fourth Group while making sure to tell his analyst it was only for child analyses. Some time later, he read the Donnet report in *Études freudiennes* and returned to the Institute, where a commission had been created for individuals in his situation. He was advised both to apply to the board of supervised analyses and to take a house seminar. Whereupon he contacted a seminar leader only to be sent away with the explanation that he could not attend any courses without first having been accepted for supervision. . . . [69]

This splendid tale offers a precise reflection of the situation of psychoanalysis in France during the 1970s.

After four years of discussion, André Green was elected director of the Institut de psychanalyse, with René Major as his secretary. At his behest, the directorial committee drew up new statutes and submitted them to a vote by the administrative council, which consisted of the titular members. They were accepted. The statutory changes concerned the administration and functioning of the association as well as the provision defining the modalities for modifying statutes. The revised version of Article 9 introduced a democratic reform in the running of the Institute. It stipulated that plenary sessions were henceforth to be composed of all categories of members: affiliates, adhering members, and titular members. Article 10 was smilarly modified: The administrative council was to include a council of representatives comprising all categories of members and functioning as an organ of exchange under the aegis of a directorial committee.

Despite that change, the association was still administered exclusively by titular members and the administrative council was not elected at a meeting of the whole. Given the changes implemented in 1967, the Institute in 1972 was composed proportionately of a majority of affiliates, with adhering and titular groups each holding a fourth of the seats. This meant that the titulars were plainly a minority in the SPP-IP complex. And yet they were supposed to remain the masters. To counterbalance the principle of a sovereign meeting of the whole, which might turn them into a minority, the directorial committee arranged for the passage of Article 15, which stipulated that any modification of the statutes had to occur at a plenary session called by the director, the administrative council, or members of the association. In the last case, the number of requests had to be a simple majority of two colleges out of three. That modification consisted of dividing the plenary session into three colleges, each of which would enjoy equal representation, despite a quantitative inequality. The sovereignty of the plenary session was thus broken. A clause added that in order to vote through a change in the statutes a majority of two-thirds of the members of each college had to be obtained.[70]

Without perceiving it, the Institute's directorial committee had drawn up statutes which were truly crazy. In order to face down the demographic growth of affiliates, it had made it impossible to change its own statutes. Given the relation of forces in the association, it was out of the question that a majority of two-thirds in each college could be assembled in the event the problem of modifying the statutes should present itself. The reciprocal positions of the three colleges prevented the existence of such a consensus from the outset. There would always be one college out of three opposed to the two others or the necessary votes lacking in one of the three.

That year the *cursus* underwent several changes. Visits were no longer obligatory, but "desirable." Files were no longer opened prior to entry into analysis and preselection disappeared. But the principle of the list of certified titular members remained, and they alone were in fact authorized to conduct "training" analyses, which were nevertheless now called "personal" analyses. Article 9 legalized the notion of "deferred action," which had already been introduced during a previous modification. It stipulated that when a desire for training arose following an analysis undertaken without consideration of any such project and conducted by a nontitular member, the candidate could ask, exceptionally, for his situation to be examined.[71] To all appearances, that article seemed to solve the problem of the list, but in fact, it could function as an incitement to lying since it allowed candidates to bypass the law and to choose in advance nontitular members and then subsequently have their analyses approved. The Institute was there facing the insoluble problem to which Lacan alone attempted to supply an answer, in his opposition to the standards of the IPA: either an analysis is necessarily a personal analysis, and the patient effects a first transition toward training by authorizing himself, then a second one by transmitting the content of that passage, or an analysis is authorized as didactic by commissions either before or after the fact and is not an analysis. The fact that that proposition is theoretically true does not prevent authentic analyses from taking place in virtually any institutional setting. In that respect, the catechism of "authorizing oneself on one's own authority" was as disastrous as the gospel of the commissions.

At the beginning of 1973, protest had thus given rise to reform.

If the SPP was traversed by barricades, those barricades divided the SPP in a rather singular manner. In March 1969, Bela Grunberger and Janine Chasseguet-Smirgel published—under the pseudonym André Stéphane—a fearsome book entitled *L'univers contestationnaire* and subtitled *Les nouveaux Chrétiens.*[72] The title itself deserves to be anthologized. It implied, and the accusation was serious, that contestation resembled a (Stalinist or Nazi) concentration camp. As for the subtitle, it was even more serious since it meant that the "concentration camps" of contestation would have been fabricated by "new Christians." This amounted to saying that in the eyes of the two titular members of the SPP, the madmen of May were either adepts of Nazism or agents of the KGB. André Stéphane openly declared his intellectual debt to Raymond Aron and Sigmund Freud in affirming, without the slightest hesitation, that contestation itself was suffering from a poorly resolved Oedipal complex. The poor thing was stuck at an anal stage, and that was why it was trying to slay dear old bourgeois democracy, the source of all paternal values. Our authors thus strayed onto the path of a pseudo-Freudian interpretation of social reality. Like Bouvard and Pécuchet, they observed from the height of their eminence the failings of their century.

The book produced some surprising results. One learned, for example, that the film director Jean-Luc Godard had not "succeeded in integrating his identifications into his global ego," and it was for that reason that he needed to refer to illustrious models in his films, particularly Fritz Lang.[73] Karl Marx is treated in passing as an anti-Semite without the two authors taking care to distinguish between Marx's Judaeophobia and modern anti-Semitism. Finally, left-wing intellectuals are characterized according to a strange typology. Being similarly fixated at the anal stage, they appear as so many poor devils hoping to help the humiliated Arabs avenge themselves against glorious Israel. To these astonishing bits of logic, André Stéphane added a powerful meditation on the unconscious roots of protest movements. Not only are rebels compared to Hitlerians or Stalinists, without the difference between the Soviet state and National Socialism ever being stated, but they are called Christians in the name of a "good" Freudianism.

The authors announced their colors at the very outset. They envisaged Christianity as a schism in relation to Judaism in order thereafter to see in Christianity the prototype of every form of dissidence. Jungianism and Lacanianism are absorbed into the process: one because it emanated from a Protestant, the other because it was founded by a Catholic. But what then is one to do with Freud's Jewish dissidents: Adler, Ferenczi, Rank, Reich, et al.? What is one to do with Spinoza and the founders of ego psychology? André Stéphane took care not to answer that question. And without realizing that Marcuse was Jewish he consigned contestatory revisionism to the trashcan of Christian schisms. Proceeding according to the same reasoning, he offered an interpretation of the alleged structure of the "Christian protester." According to Stéphane, Christians would have been less talented than Jews in treating their neuroses to the extent that their religion, founded on the son's schism, would have forbidden them from resolving their Oedipal conflict. Because of that affiliation, they would have remained prisoners of an "anal revolt" leading them to contest the father. They would thus have been doubly guilty: of their anality, which resulted from their contestatory spirit, and of their anti-Semitism, which sprang from their Christianity.

Several pages were devoted to Daniel Cohn-Bendit, the uncontested leader of the "*universe* contestationnaire." On this point, André Stéphane was an enlightened thinker. He observed that the lad was Jewish. But since he wanted to demonstrate that all rebellion derives from a Christian schism, he also explained that Cohn-Bendit was an anarchist before he was a Jew. He thus became a bad Jew, that is, a good Christian, with an anal-contestatory structure. The proof was that he was intent on destroying everything in order to be his own father, his own end, his own beginning.[74] Strengthened by that reasoning, the two-headed author then recalled that Cohn-Bendit had opted for German citizenship and that students had demonstrated on his behalf to cries of "We are all German Jews." That would tend to prove they were not anti-Semites. But not at all! Since there was a "contestatory structure," that structure could not be changed by a mere slogan. The rebels were thus no less anti-Semitic when crying, "We are all German Jews." Indeed, in their unconscious, they contested the father, and since the Jew is the prototype of the father, they were thus contesting the Jew. As a result, they were anti-Semites. "We are all German Jews" is nothing else, according to Stéphane, than an act of defiance of the father.[75] That affirmation allowed the author to efface the principal symbol through which the May rebellion identified with a foreigner, the status of exiled Jewry, and the ideal of the Diaspora. Brecht once joked that a parliament no longer wanted by the people ought to dissolve the people. André Stéphane understood the lesson. He dissolved all facts refractory to his argument.

Exiled in London, Freud hesitated to publish his *Moses*. Then he decided to. We have seen how that work retraces the family romance of the Jewish people and the manner in which that people had taken itself for God's chosen ones as soon as they persisted, in the face of Christian accusations of deicide, in denying the murder of the father.[76] Now Freud also defined his own Jewishness in relation to a discovery that he wanted to de-Judaize in order to make it universal. If there were no chosen people, psychoanalysis could become universal, since its object, the unconscious, is universal. Renouncing circumcision, that is, the physical trace of a difference, means assuming a symbolic of castration according to which there is no superiority or inferiority of one culture in relation to others since all men are subject to the same law despite their differences.

L'univers contestationnaire reverses that move, making of psychoanalysis a kind of "Jewish science" reserved for the elect. In the name of genocide, the two titular members of the SPP took the liberty of transforming protesters into Christians, Christians into anti-Semites, and bad Jews into nasty Freudians. They Judaized Freudianism, making it function on the model of the chosen people and then reinscribed it within an inegalitarian ideal. Through that move, they turned their own Jewishness into an instrument for the persecution of every affiliation, Jewish or non-Jewish.

The work was unique in the annals of psychoanalysis in France.[77] No one else in the country ever dared insinuate that only Jews could be true artisans of Freudian thought, in opposition to anal Christian "schismatics." And that is all to the good, for had it been otherwise, there would have been scant difference between the old adversaries of "German science" and the modern protectors of the "chosen science." Lacan was not wrong in wanting the Jewish question to be studied by members of his École: In 1969, it was present within the SPP in a form of which *L'univers contestationnaire* was no more than a caricatural symptom.

As soon as it was published, the book provoked the indignation of nearly all the members of the SPP. Some nicknamed it "*L'univers con* [dumb] *et stationnaire*." But since the authors were established titular members, no action was taken; there was no open debate about the book and it was not reviewed in the *RFP*. During a colloquium organized by the Société suisse de psychanalyse in February 1972, N. Nicolaïdis questioned Jean-Luc Donnet on the subject, calling the book a scandal. Without responding on the Jewish question, Donnet was concerned principally with the work's reactionary and pseudo-Freudian aspect. He recalled that the SPP had not uttered a word about it. "It may have been thought," he said, "that the book was not the SPP's concern. But in fact it was of the utmost concern to the society, and outside of analytic circles I have heard it said that the book in fact represented the spirit of the SPP since it had been written by two of its more prominent titular members." [78] Nicolaïdis also observed that through its silence the SPP had hoped to shield its two members.

The left-wing press reacted violently to the publication of *L'univers contestationnaire*. In the *Nouvel observateur*, Anne-Lise Stern published a letter entitled "Un lapsus de SS". "How can I express my revulsion, my disgust," she wrote, "my feeling of impotence. . . . Many of my psychoanalytic colleagues, and not the least of them, share my feelings but have decided not to utter them, for excellent reasons. I cannot and should not." Anne-Lise did not sign with a pseudonym, but at the bottom of her letter inscribed a triangle followed by her deportation number: 78,765. On the opposite page, Michel de Certeau spoke of his identity as a Christian between the lines, and treated the book ironically: "An incredible psychoanalytic dialect," he wrote, "has decked out the imbecilities of the small-minded in true Molièresque garb. The result is a book in which the gravity of the actors is the source of the comedy. Molière's purges and bleedings have merely been replaced by anality and the avoidance of the father. . . . It is truly a marvelous thing to be a psychoanalyst." [79] In *La Quinzaine litteraire,* Roger Dadoun did not beat around the bush. "Out of naïveté or ignorance," he wrote, "the authors pretend to see in Christianity nothing other than its evangelical side. The fact that that religion, after centuries of evolution, has become coextensive with bourgeois thought and synonymous with the ideologies of alienation and mystification . . . appears not to concern them in the slightest. . . . Nothing strikes us more than the hatred or the terror of adolescence emptied in this case of all its determinations." [80] Finally, in *Les Temps modernes,* Alain Didier-Weill, a Jewish student of the Institute, voiced his indignation. He condemned only the reactionary nature of the book without attending to the use made of the Jewish question. He signed Alain Didier, having not yet assumed the name of Weill, which his father had dropped during the Nazi occupation. But as a sign of protest, he resigned from the program, left Jean Kestemberg's couch, and became an analysand of Lacan's. [81]

The publication of the book, and above all the silence with which it was greeted by the titular members of the SPP, would have catastrophic consequences later on, and specifically for the Jewish and non-Jewish students of Bela Grunberger, who could not but feel aggressed by such a confession of hatred toward Christians, the young, and "bad" Jews. The work would function as an index of the juridico-administrative crises befalling the Institute. Grunberger and Chasseguet-Smirgel were Jews and conservatives, and convinced that only Judaism could serve as the medium of a proper Freudian orthodoxy. In that respect, they considered Lacanianism to be a Christian dissidence opposed to an IPA orthodoxy reinterpreted in terms of its Judaic superiority. We have seen that Lacan's "dissidence" was an "orthodox reelaboration of Freudianism" joining a universalism in which psychoanalysis was neither Jewish nor Christian, since it united all identities.

In 1969, the SPP was no longer as strongly characterized as previously by its Jewish identity. All persuasions coexisted in fullfledged affiliation. The confession of feelings of Jewish superiority on the part of two titular members was thus bound to provoke conscious or unconscious reactions of Judaeophobia. These reactions were all the more intense in that Grunberger himself had "contested" Nacht's authority and the Jewish conservatives of the titular group had refrained from criticizing the work publicly.

In January 1973, the institutional crisis surfaced anew with the election of René Major as director of the Institute. He belonged to the fourth French psychoanalytic generation. Bilingual and a native of Quebec, he had been raised in the Catholic tradition, which he subsequently left to become an atheist.

Around 1959, upon completing medical school in Montreal, he had a choice of undergoing training in England, France, or the United States. Feeling himself to be more French, he wrote to representatives of the SFP and the SPP, Serge Leclaire and Michel Fain, asking under what conditions he might embark on the adventure of psychoanalysis. His plan was to spend a year in Paris thanks to an exchange of interns between the two countries. It was thus that he found himself in the psychiatric service of Jean Delay. He took his equivalency exams. The reply from the Institute seemed more encouraging to him than that of the SFP. He thus selected a couch on the rue Saint-Jacques without writing off the possibility of participating in the activities of the rival house. At the Bonneval Colloquium, he followed the proceedings with great interest, took numerous notes, and had the impression of discovering a new Enlightenment. He became friends with Conrad Stein, then did his training analysis with Grunberger, whose persona at the time was that of a "liberal." A classical curriculum led him to controls with Pasche, Marty, and Luquet-Parat. An adhering member in 1967, he was elected a titular member in 1971 without having participated in the rebellion of the base. Elected secretary of the Institute the following year, he worked with Green on modifying the statutes and felt that further democratization was called for. It was for that reason that when he became director, he sought to implement a new change intended to grant the three colleges equality of representation. But in order for such a change to pass, according to Article 15, a majority of two-thirds of each college would be needed. And as we have seen, such a majority was not to be found.

René Major was not a theorist of psychoanalysis, but a true democrat, fond of making legitimate use of executive rules to induce reforms. Having chosen the SPP in order not to have to confront the power of a master, he placed all his ambition in the service of his reformist ideal. Courageous, impertinent, lavish in his generosity toward friends, he would nonetheless come up against the omnipotence of the IPA bureaucracy without ever succeeding in reforming it. He first experienced the disaster of an institutional crisis, only to encounter the persecutory effects of that disaster later on. He thus became a remarkable source of agitation within the Société. The role was splendidly suited to his gamesman's temperament.

As soon as he was elected, he reduced budgetary expenses, proposed that dues be cut in half, and dismissed a few secretaries paid to mark time. He subjected the Institute to the constraints of an efficiency expert. Soon, however, an incident would change the course of events. A secretary submitted a list of members of the new directorial committee to the Prefecture de Police, adding in pencil, beneath Major's name, the words "foreign national." [82] Five months later, a Prefecture employee sent an official notice to the Institute asking it to regularize the association's situation. According to Article 26 of Title IV of the Law of 1901, a French association cannot be administered by an individual of foreign nationality. [83] The problem had already been raised concerning the assumption of the position of scientific secretary by the New Zealander Joyce Mac Dougall in 1971. The juridical council of the SPP, questioned by Serge Lebovici, had not objected to the presence of a foreign administrator. Such was not the case in May 1973 with the new director. Three weeks earlier, Major had applied for naturalization at the Ministry of Population and informed his titular colleagues of his initiative. On May 17, the Police Prefecture gave him a certificate of impending naturalization. [84] Through its attorney, Aimé Jacquin, the ministry indicated that the decree would be issued in June 1973. This turned out to be, however, not at all the case, and for ten years Major would be the object of administrative harassment by the State. Ah! the country of the rights of man . . .

Realizing that he might be obliged to resign, and declaring that he was prepared to do so, Major opted to situate the debate at a juridical level. Instead of submitting to the imperfections of French law, the Institute would do better, he felt, to confront them and make a decision allowing the delicate problem to be resolved once and for all. The question, after all, might be raised again, given the number of *émigré* members of the SPP who might someday be elected to direct the Institute. He thus asked a lawyer to study the entire battery of laws relating to French and foreign associations. Before long, the attorney's answer was conveyed to a commission charged with studying the problem and advising the administrative council.

At the conclusion of an extremely technical study, the lawyer showed that the law was open to several interpretations. It was possible, for example, to consider as "foreign" any society having either a foreign administrator or a fourth of its members foreigners. As a result two solutions might be envisaged: one amounting to transforming the Institute into a foreign association, the other to keeping it French. The first would consist of requesting of the Ministry of the Interior authorization to function, in accordance with the law of April 1939, with the risk of being subject— unlike French societies—to administrative control. The second would require the association, on the contrary, to be directed exclusively by French members. Now Article 5 of the statutes of the Institute stipulated that the association was administered by a council consisting legally of the titular members. In other words, in order to remain French, the Institute would have to modify its Article 5 so as to prevent foreign titular members from being on the administrative council. The Institute in 1973 was *de facto* in violation of the law of 1901, since it declared itself a French association whereas it allowed foreign members the opportunity to serve as administrators. Article 26 was xenophobic and would in fact be abrogated by the Socialists on October 9, 1981.

In 1973, the Institute thus found itself in an absurd situation: Either it remained French in defiance of its own Article 5 or it became a foreign association with the risk of government control. At the time, all psychoanalytic societies were governed by the law of 1901, but with the exception of the SPP none of them had been caught in the imbroglio connected with Article 26. And a single case—René Major's—was enough for the bureaucratic crisis visited on the Institute to take on a chauvinistic air. It is comical to see the imbroglio descend on a French branch of the IPA originally founded by an Alsatian, two Jewish immigrants, two Swiss nationals, a princess, and a member of the Action Française. That last founder, Édouard Pichon, had succeeded in having an article included in the statutes of the SPP stipulating that French was the official language of the Société. It was later eliminated. It is equally comical to note that the Institute at the center of the imbroglio caused by the presence of a native of Quebec had been created by a Romanian Jewish immigrant.

On November 30, 1973, during a session of the administrative council, the members of the commission charged with examining the statutes met in a particularly stormy session. The discussion became mired in a juridico-administrative chaos from which three tendencies surfaced. The conservatives, represented by Lebovici, Diatkine, and Chasseguet-Smirgel, did not dare openly espouse the cause of gallicization, but refused to vote for changing into a foreign society. They revealed a vivid fear of a police descent on the rue Saint-Jacques should the Institute pass under the administrative control of the Ministry. They thus proposed a timid compromise between a French and a foreign identity. The second tendency, which was liberal, supported a motion by Michel de M'Uzan requesting a transition to the status of a foreign society. Finally, the third consisted of a murky attitude unable to choose between the others. Michel de M'Uzan made a remarkable intervention, raising the discussion to its highest level. He recalled that psychoanalysis knew neither homeland nor borders and that all its practitioners would do well to invoke a celebrated slogan: "We are all foreign psychoanalysts." He then emphasized that the SPP had been founded by Loewenstein and Saussure, affirming finally that the Psychoanalytic Association of Berlin had been obliged to pay dearly for the execution of its Jews. The occasion was charged with emotion, and the secret-ballot vote yielded ambiguous results: 19 favorable to de M'Uzan's motion, 11 against, with 8 abstentions. Under such circumstances the director's opinion would normally carry the day. But Major refused to invoke that right and thus allowed the scales to tip in favor of the conservatives.[85] After the meeting, at a dinner at Jo Goldenberg's restaurant, he was voted "honorary Jew" by his friends.[86]

Three solutions were proposed in a meeting on January 22, 1974. The first consisted in modifying Article 5 in the direction of a purely French identity for the Institute. The second recommended a compromise allowing for an exceptional request to be made to the Ministry each time an administrative position would be occupied by a foreigner. The third repeated de M'Uzan's terms.[87] After much discussion, the second was adopted since it simultaneously allowed for no change in the statutes and for the elimination of any fear of the police. It thus obtained a crushing majority: 37 votes out of 44 cast. The third option received six votes. Aware of the chauvinistic nature of the first option, Evelyne Kestemberg requested that it not be submitted to a vote. She declared her sympathy for the second choice, along with Lebovici, Chasseguet-Smirgel, and Green. Joyce Mac Dougall, who was directly affected by the issue, chose not to attend the meeting. As for de M'Uzan, he insisted that the minutes record his firm and definitive support for the third proposal. No doubt his thoughts were on history's judgment, and no doubt he was right. He would have been the first and the last to refuse any compromise with any form of xenophobia, whatever the consequences. It is the historian's duty to salute his courage and his intransigence.[88]

While the Société was busy lacerating itself, Serge Lebovici was actively preparing the Twenty-Eighth International Congress of the IPA, which was to be held in Paris in July. He himself had proposed the French capital. Before long a meeting was arranged between the SPP and the APF, and a majority of the titular members of both societies were in favor of the choice. Lebovici then asked Widlöcher to serve as his secretary for the organizational committee. Flattered at being selected, he accepted and shared the function with René Major. André Green was in charge of the material organization of scientific papers, Misès of relations with government agencies, and Rosolato of public relations. Evelyne Kestemberg and J.-B. Pontalis assisted Lebovici on the organizational committee. The SPP and the APF were thus equally represented in planning for the congress, which was to symbolize, in the face of a triumphant Lacanianism, the rediscovered unity of the two French components of the IPA. In an excellent and much commented on paper, Pontalis celebrated the origins of psychoanalysis in France, recalling the encounter of October 1886.[89] At the end of the proceedings, Serve Lebovici was elected president of the IPA, succeeding Leo Rangell as head of the prestigious institution. He proposed Widlöcher for the key position of secretary. Delighted, he accepted once again, and promptly resigned as secretary of the Fédération européenne de psychanalyse, where he was replaced by Pontalis. The men changed and the institutions remained identical. Two years later, at the London congress, Lebovici's term was renewed until the Jerusalem congress of 1977, at which time he was succeeded by Edward Joseph.

In 1973, Freudian France was at the zenith of its power—with its enormous Lacanian component in the process of going international by way of South America and its no less enormous IPA-affiliated component entering into a phase of advanced bureaucratization. The time of manifold dissidence had not yet arrived, and it would not be until 1975–77 that the Hundred Flowers of a large-scale anti-institutional insurgence could be observed. For the while, couches of every analytic stripe were packed tight and patient networks firmly established. The therapists of the four groups could, if they wanted, pursue their activities in total ignorance of the institutional conflicts of their respective societies. They were never obliged to attend commission meetings or plenary sessions and some would learn their history only when the crises became public.

Two months before his election as director of the Institute, René Major attended a meeting of the Société in the course of which an adhering member, speaking on behalf of the board, made a bizarre declaration on the subject of an affiliate applying for promotion to the rank of adhering member. If he were free to reveal a certain "secret," he said in substance, everyone would be in agreement in rejecting the candidate, but the "secret" would not be revealed. After consultation, a negative vote was recorded. Now the candidate was not just anybody. His name was Nicolas Abraham. A philosopher and a therapist, he was already known on the French psychoanalytic scene for his writings and his practice.[90]

A Jew of Hungarian origin, Nicolas Abraham was born in Kecskemét to a family of printers and publishers trained in Talmudic tradition and respectful of religious orthodoxy. Forced to emigrate in 1938 because of religious discrimination, he continued his studies for a while in Paris, already endowed with considerable cultural baggage. He was a philosopher who spoke German, Hebrew, Greek, and French. The Nazi occupation drove him into the "Free Zone" with papers made out in the name of Aubry. Abraham refused to bear the yellow star. Having taken refuge in Toulouse, he wrote essays for the general instruction of his brothers who had emigrated from Palestine. The texts would be lost. In 1942, he went into hiding, then returned to Paris to celebrate the festivities surrounding the Liberation. He learned shortly thereafter that his family had been decimated by the genocide.

Early on, he entered the aesthetics division of the CNRS, where his enthusiasm for three masters—Husserl, Freud, and Ferenczi—continued unabated. He read them exclusively in their native languages. In 1950, he made the acquaintance of Maria Torok, a Jewish woman who had come from Budapest after the war. Her family had also been destroyed. She became his companion. She was interested in Rorschach tests and worked with maladjusted children in nursery schools. They spoke Hungarian together and remained attached to their country's literature.

Around that time, Abraham began to translate and comment on *The Book of Jonah*, a poem written in a few weeks by Mihaly Babits after he learned he was suffering from an incurable illness.[91] A lyrical autobiography, Babits's text followed rather closely the Biblical story of the prophet refractory to God's will. A pacifist, an anti-Nazi, and a victim of terror under the Horthy dictatorship, Babits was obsessed by the parable of Jonah, which symbolized the place of the poet in the city. Abraham would meditate on it throughout his intellectual odyssey.

About the same time, Abraham organized at his home on the rue Vézelay seminars in phenomenological psychology, centered on a reinterpretation of the works of Husserl. In that respect, the path he took was unique in the French history of psychoanalysis. It was "alien" in all senses of the word to French phenomenology. That was why Abraham, even though attending certain seminars of the SFP, did not follow that orientation. He cultivated an ignorance of Lacan's work, and when he discovered the master's discourse at Sainte-Anne, he was repelled by the hypnotic nature of Lacan's relation to his students. In brief, he did not regard Lacan's reelaborations as central to psychoanalysis.[92] At times he rejected the effects of the fascination linked to an individual, at others he rejected on theoretical grounds the structuralism of his written work. He was also sensitive to the fact that Lacan was not interested in literature as such. Nevertheless, he acknowledged a single great attribute in the man: that of having brought his disciples to read Freud in the original.

He decided to undergo training at the SPP. After a first period of therapy, he

began a personal analysis on the couch of another Hungarian *émigré*, Bela Grunberger. Maria Torok chose the same institution. In 1959, at a colloquium at Cerisy,
he met Jacques Derrida and became his loyal friend.[93] Both shared a similar interest
in Husserlian philosophy and in literature, as well as a certain critical apprehension
of structuralism. But there was something else that bound them: a marginal position
in relation to the dominant philosophical discourse of the day, and an almost identical syntax. Both viewed the reading of texts in terms of a kind of polymorphous
and fractured production of signifiers, shot through with ambiguities of every sort.
While Derrida confronted that structuralist renewal and Lacan's work, Abraham
elaborated an idiosyncratic reading of Freud's discovery centered on several key
terms: transphenomenology, symbol, anasemy, incorporation, the rind, the core, and
the phantom.[94]

Starting with the notion of trauma, which he borrowed from Ferenczi, and
that of introjection, Abraham deduced a typology of primal symbols that he called
transphenomenology. He restored to currency in terms of language what Ferenczi
had situated in terms of biology. Traumas are preverbal, and the traumatic scene is
"encrypted" according to a signifying symbolic whose content psychoanalysis must
"translate" without reducing it to a univocal meaning. It must thus be a traversal of
appearances and attain the "antisemanticism" of the unconscious core.

In 1968, in an article devoted to the *Vocabulaire de la psychanalyse*,[95] Abraham delineated his method with greater precision. By wrenching words from their
ordinary meaning, Freud effected a return to a linguistic source. In Abraham's view,
the exegetical enterprise had to be read as the formulation of an "anasemic" discourse in which meaning disappeared and was reduced to the core of its contradictions and its lacunae. In that perspective, no reelaboration of Freudianism was possible, since any recasting would merge with the ascent toward that primordial
anasemy out of which the discovery of the unconscious emerged. It was with the
Verbier de l'homme au loup [*The Wolf-Man's Wordbook*], published in 1976, that
Nicolas Abraham and Maria Torok best succeeded in defining the anasemic method,
while adding a new topographical model to the Freudian corpus. Abraham gave the
name of *rind* to that agency of the ego defined by Freud in his second topographical
model, and which was constrained to do battle on two fronts: that of the outside
world and that of the internal demands of the drives. But the subject is also the site
of another topographical reality: the crypt. This functions within the split ego as the
eruption of a false unconscious filled with phantoms—to wit, fossilized words, live
corpses, and foreign bodies. That introduction of a new topography allowed Abraham and Torok to undertake—in the case of the Wolf Man—a fabulous exercise in
cryptonymy.

In 1971, there appeared in New York under the editorship of Muriel Gardiner a marvelous book entitled *The Wolfman by the Wolfman*.[96] It recounted the
psychoanalytic itinerary of Serge Constantinovich Pankejeff, the Wolf Man, analyzed first by Freud, then by Ruth Mack-Brunswick and Muriel Gardiner. The story
is unique in the annals of psychoanalytic literature since Pankejeff was the only one
of Freud's famous five patients to have written his memoires and commented on his
analysis after the fact. He thus agreed to assume the role attributed to him by the

Freudian saga. His story is so fascinating that it has always been commented on with great emotion in the psychoanalytic literature. In France it was by way of Freud's commentary on Pankejeff's therapy that Lacan advanced the concept of "foreclosure" and that Deleuze and Guattari opposed the multiplicity of desiring-desire to the univocity of the Oedipus complex.

But Abraham and Torok were the first in France to take into account the case history of the Wolf Man in all of its multiple facets: from Freud's couch to Muriel Gardiner's. They brought to light the polyglottism inherent in the case and demonstrated the existence of several languages in the patient's odyssey: Russian, the mother tongue; German, the language of therapy; and English, the language of the nurse who raised the patient as a child. To these they added a fourth language, "French," which authorized the translation of the labyrinthine communications between the other three. In so doing, they constructed the Wolf Man's crypt, retreating toward "anasemy": a crypt buried in the split ego and ciphered as a network of signifiers meshing with each other in a series of delusional incorporations.

Le verbier de l'homme aux loups appeared with a long preface by Derrida a year after Abraham's unexpected death. The semiposthumous character of the work added a dimension of strangeness to the theory of the crypt. It was as though the book had exhumed a mythology of secrecy specific to the psychoanalytic community and whose living symbol and first phantom the Wolf Man would have been. As for the preface, it further enhanced the enigma of the method since it was written in a syntax almost identical to that of the text whose commentary it pretended to be. A fifth language in a relation of osmosis with the others.

The work enjoyed a remarkable success, specifically with certain Lacanians who were fascinated by this baroque crypt so near and so removed from their own daily lexicon. Lacan himself was astonished. And feeling aggressed at the fact that his own turf was being trod upon, he misinterpreted the efforts of the authors and the prefacer. In his seminar, he commented on the work, forgetting that Abraham had been dead for a year and claiming that Derrida was undoubtedly in analysis with the authors since he had coupled them together. A few insidious auditors broke out laughing, convinced that the interpretation was right.[97] The comment would augment the book's sales still further, but it would be eliminated from publication in *Ornicar?*, where Lacan restricted himself once again to taking himself for the owner of ideas that were common property: "There is something that surprises me still more than the well-known spread of what is called my teaching, in that thing that goes about under the name of an institute of psychoanalysis and which is the other extreme of psychoanalytic groups. What surprises me still more is that one Jacques Derrida supplied this lexicon with a fervent and enthusiastic preface. . . . It does not seem to me, despite the fact that it was I who put matters on this track, that either the book or the preface are in very good taste. In the genre of insanity, this is an extreme. And I fear that I may be more or less responsible for having opened the floodgates."[98] That the *Verbier* may be insane is possible, but why should insanity be excluded from psychoanalytic discourse in the name of "good taste"?

After the notorious meeting of the Société, Nicolas Abraham told René Major that if he had been refused the rank of adhering member, it was because a letter on the subject must have been sent to the commission on instruction by his own analyst. Abraham thus had an intuition of a truth capable of explaining the manner in which he was being treated. He believed that Bela Grunberger had intervened against him previously in flagrant violation of the article introduced by Nacht. Intrigued by the remark and the rigorous logic it betrayed, Major wanted to have a clear conscience on the matter. When he became director of the Institute, he consulted the archives and came upon two letters confirming Abraham's suspicion. The first, typewritten, was not signed, although it was easily attributable. It was dated December 15, 1958, and addressed to the president of the commission on instruction. The author explained that his patient's "structure" was incapacitating for any exercise of the profession of psychoanalysis and that he thus declined to validate his therapy for training purposes. The second was dated May 9, 1959. It was handwritten, signed, and written on personal stationery. It concerned the same matter. At the time, the commission on instruction had not taken the two warnings into account since Abraham had been elected an affiliate—that is, approved for the practice of psychanalysis. Nevertheless, the mythology of the secret had played its role in the negative vote of December 1972, when an adhering member invoked a "secret" that would have to remain so. In any event, Abraham had seen the truth. And since Major perceived that the existence of the alleged message was having adverse effects on his behavior, he decided to tell him the truth and reveal his discovery to him. Abraham immediately felt relieved: His intuition had not been a delusion.[99]

Major did not want to let this shocking matter, bearing eloquent witness to the bureaucratic madness of the system, pass unnoticed. Upon Abraham's death, in a volume of tribute to him brought out by *Études freudiennes,* he published a coded text entitled "La lettre sous le manteau [The letter under wrap]." In it he related the whole story, by way of an associative network linking Edgar Allan Poe, the Wolf Man, the "Seminar on the Purloined Letter" and the "Purveyor of Truth," ending up with the crypt and the phantom. Theory thus served to illustrate the persecutory and psychotic function of the psychoanalytic institution. Major delivered the secret of a "police lexicon." He spoke of Inspector Desieux, of his boss Delouis, of the rues Saint-Jacques and Claude-Bernard, in sum of a panopticon with eyes and ears situated between the Institute's impasse and the byways of the EFP. To all this he added "passwords," quoted passages from the two letters and situated himself as narrator in the position of Dupin defending the lady held hostage by the minister; he called her "Anna-Lyse."[100]

As years passed and the bureaucratic crisis in the SPP deepened, the Abraham affair became increasingly well known and was added on to the rest. Toward the end of 1976, Nata Minor and Jacqueline Rousseau-Dujardin decided to leave the organization as a protest against the entire situation. On November 30, Nata Minor sent Janine Chasseguet-Smirgel, president of the Société, her letter of resignation, asking for her decision to be announced publicly in the SPP house bulletin. She received an unambiguous reply. But when she saw that her name had simply been dropped from the list of adhering members, she sent an open letter to all the members of the Société denouncing the use of secrecy in the institution: "The silence about my resignation and Mme Smirgel's best wishes for my 'career' make me skeptical as to when and how this information will reach you. For that reason, I consider myself authorized to inform you myself, provoked as well to offer a few explanations. . . . Why is a resignation treated as information to be quarantined? Had it been a matter of an expulsion or a death, I believe you would have been informed. Why is it that in the life of psychoanalytic societies there are items which are neither secrets nor confidential in nature and which nonetheless are kept hidden and under wrap by those officially responsible for transmitting them? Why is it, paradoxically, that what ought to be secret and demands silence is used for personal and political ends, as was the case in 1972 for the election to the rank of adhering member of one of our colleagues, without any indignation or denunciation of such an abuse on the part of the majority? . . . I know just how violent this letter is; at least I haven't adorned it with my best wishes." [101]

Whatever the—no doubt valid—reasons leading a therapist of Bela Grunberger's stature to intervene in the progress of a career, then the members of the council to keep secret what everyone in fact knew, this rather sinister affair provoked a good deal of reflection on the state of the honorable French affiliate of the IPA. When one spends some of one's time writing a barbarous book under a pseudonym in which every act of rebellion is dismissed as anal transgression, and the rest of one's time stifling every effort at reform, it is perhaps to be expected that a considerable blaze may erupt in the cellar of the family house. On the one hand, a personal letter existed, without the principal interested party being aware of it; on the other, an official letter was kept secret against the wishes of its author, and said to have disappeared without further commentary. In both cases, a fragment of history was effaced, as in propaganda films in which a suspect hero or a landscape not quite in keeping with the proper cause is eliminated from the print. True cases of insanity, as is known, never have objective causes, even when they attach themselves to material details. In the case of the Institute, the system itself was insane.

Around 1975, the Institute's curriculum was not faring any better than its statutes. For which reason an effort was made to change it. Serge Viderman took it upon himself to write up a Curriculum (or *cursus*) B intended to offset the effects of Curriculum A, which was defended by Lebovici and the conservatives. At stake was support for a federative notion through which minority theses might be represented alongside majority ones in order to avoid a split. Viderman put two conditions on the writing of his proposal. He wanted to be totally independent and not to represent any group. He did not contest the existence of Curriculum A and considered his undertaking in terms of an experimental differentiation. "What had to be found," he wrote, "was the proper distance between one curriculum and the other, that meaningful gap capable of bringing to light the originality of both endeavors. That distance should be a source of stimulation and not conflict. It should be established in such manner that the two curricula remain related and open to articulation in terms of each other. Neither one should be locked into frozen positions in which members would regard the curriculum they had opted for as absolutely superior to the other." [102]

Serge Viderman drew simultaneously on the Donnet model of 1969 and the theoretical positions he had elaborated in his book *La construction de l'espace analytique*.[103] His proposal aimed at a complete elimination of the difference between a personal analysis and a training analysis by voiding the notion of selection. It thus restored to candidates an authentic possibility for *après-coup* or deferred discovery. In addition, it transformed the status of supervision in the direction of greater freedom of choice. In order to avoid conflict with IPA-imposed regulations, Viderman was careful to compare the French situation with that of other countries which, within the framework of those rules, had introduced various curricular modalities. Unfortunately, the system of the dual curriculum would never be implemented.

Along with the efforts of the commission on curricular matters, the statutes of the Institute were also contested. At the plenary session of April 1974, with René Major presiding, eight members, including Joyce Mac Dougall, Robert Barande, and Michel de M'Uzan proposed a motion that was revolutionary in the history of the Institute, but quite normal in terms of the functioning of an association. The motion was known by the name of its principal instigator, de M'Uzan. It called for a reduction in the number of members of the administrative council, the separation of that council from the commission on instruction, and its election at a meeting of the whole. In order to obtain that modification of Article 5, it was necessary to call an extraordinary plenary session to decide on statutory matters as stipulated by the notorious Article 15. Now it was well known that in such a case, it was impossible to obtain a majority of two-thirds of the three colleges. On April 23, de M'Uzan's motion was adopted by a majority of the two colleges of the affiliates and the adhering members. The titular members, however, refused by a vote of 27 to 17.[104] It will be recalled that according to Article 15, a simple majority of two colleges was sufficient grounds for convening an extraordinary meeting of the whole. That session was scheduled for May 15.

But in the interim, Major was stripped of his functions for having unduly favored the democratization of the Institute and fomented disorder through the commotion he had stirred up. A motion of nonconfidence against him was signed by twenty-six titular members. Barande and Green then offered their candidacies for the directorship of the Institute. The former subsequently withdrew his own, and Green was elected by a majority of thirty-three votes: a victory for the conservatives, who had elected a liberal willing to implement their policy.[105] De M'Uzan then painted a rather somber tableau of the situation in the SPP and notably on the subject of the disaffection felt by the affiliates and adhering members toward their institute. A week later, the administrative council adopted a compromise position: It rejected de M'Uzan's motion and recommended that Lebovici draw up a motion taking into account the reformers' point of view. Drawn up on May 15, that motion retained the principle of the election of the council by the three colleges, but rejected any separation between the council and the commission. Naturally, given the existence of Article 15, de M'Uzan's motion was rejected at the extraordinary plenary session of May 15. The adhering members closed ranks with the titular members and only the college of affiliates voted in favor of the motion. In absolute number of votes, it received a comfortable majority.[106] For that reason a commission representative of all three colleges was charged with drafting a proposal for reforming the statutes with the assistance of a competent jurist. The reform effort had reconfirmed the status quo.

During a meeting of the administrative council in June 1974, the conflicts became embittered. Evelyne Kestemberg expressed her concern about the anonymous denunciation of Major for an allegedly illegal practice of medicine. He did not practice it, and had had his degrees validated. But he was still a "foreigner" and thus subject to every conceivable type of harassment. A sure source had told him that the denunciation had come from a member of the SPP. Green and Lebovici immediately demanded that the denouncer be identified or the accusation withdrawn. After a murky discussion (in the worst taste), Lebovici asked Major to secretly confide the name of his denouncer to the director of the Institute. Naturally, Major obstinately refused to become a denouncer himself by identifying his own denouncer. Moreover, he did not know who it was. The council then voted an implausible motion to the effect that any denouncer would be excluded from the organization if his act of denunciation could be proved.[107]

During all this time, Lacan was busy with his matheme.

In the course of the year 1973–74, a working group led by Major met on the premises of the Institute. Its participants were invited to speak of contemporary French or foreign psychoanalytic texts and to discuss their contribution to Freudian thought. The following year, the seminar adopted the name "Confrontations." It was again led by Major as well as by Dominique Geahchan. The two men were hardly in keeping with the ideal of the "non-anal-and-not-Christian-good-Jew" recommended by the authors of *L'univers contestationnaire*. One was a libertarian in the process of being naturalized, and the other a practicing Catholic of Lebanese origin. It is not clear whether they had successfully or unsuccessfully resolved their respective Oedipus complexes. Whatever the case, the two men created a rather "unChristian" form of dissidence that year within an institute run by conservatives. They invited some of the most interesting writers on psychoanalysis in France to speak of their work: among them, Guy Rosolato, Michel Neyraut, Michel de M'Uzan, Nicholas Abraham, and Maria Torok. "Confrontations" was conceived in the singular, but written in the plural because of a typographical error. The idea was in the air, but the name would subsequently enter history. It had been discovered in the course of a collective discussion.

During the first year, only one participant from outside the SPP was invited, but the year after the veterans of the troika met each other there after a lengthy period of eclipse. Serge Leclaire was the first Lacanian to support the venture. And thus it was that he met his friends of former years in the rooms of the rue Saint-Jacques: Pontalis, Aulagnier, Smirnoff, and many more. Soon the crowds started coming, bolts began to spring, orthodoxies of every stripe were contested, but—and this was something new—everyone remained a member of his or her original society. Confrontations was neither a group, nor an association, nor a school, but an open space in which representatives of different varieties of Freudianism came to speak of their dramas, conflicts, and works without having to initiate a split. An island where one could breathe freely, the place was originally internal to the SPP and frequented by the APF, but in 1976, it benefited from the wave of Lacanians distressed by the matheme and disappointed by the new Lacano-Millerian orientation. Arriving there for a variety of reasons, they learned of their own past and how no longer to regard as "traitors" their seniors who had left the master. Alert to new voices, they discovered the saga of the golden age, the Atlantis emergent from the sands of bureaucracy and the heroines of years past stripped of the adornments in which official histories of the movement had draped them. It was at Confrontation (in the singular) that the author of the present work would come to envision the possibility of bringing that rediscovered past back to life. For the members of the SPP, there was an identical movement: They too learned how not to misconstrue the epic of their neighbors. Major and Geahchan had reason to be proud that year. They had erected a splendid utopia bearing a name of tolerance and freedom. It would contribute to a transformation of the whole of the French psychoanalytic community.

In April 1976, Major and Geahchan received from the director of the Institute a letter similar to the one Robert Flacelière had sent to Jacques Lacan: "It has recently come to my attention that the seminar you have organized under the name of 'Confrontations' in the context and on the premises of the Institute is being attended by an audience much larger than the number beyond which, as you know, our insurance company can no longer shield us from civil and criminal responsibility, for reasons concerning the resistance capacity of the floor of the large auditorium." [108] The letter added that because of the installation of new shelving in the library, the room was restricted to a maximum capacity of eighty persons. Given the situation, Major and Geahchan, who had themselves cited an attendance figure of 140, were asked to find some other solution. Sometime thereafter, since they had not proposed anything, they were simply asked to leave the premises.

That eviction was providential for Confrontations, which changed its appearance, encountered a still greater audience, and transformed the spelling of its name. No longer having a home base, the islet became a symbolic space and shifted from the plural to the singular, spelling its name "Confrontation." After an extremely successful colloquium in May, Major moved his troops to the Maison des arts et métiers, to a room rented for that purpose. He took advantage of the occasion to announce that Confrontation had been placed on the Index by the Institut de Psychanalyse. A year later the enterprise was at the height of its success. Major was no longer satisfied with inviting only psychoanalysts; he brought in writers, linguists, and philosophers, imitating in the most salutary fashion the Lacanian principle of decentering. François Roustang, Jean-Michel Rey, Jean Baudrillard, Julia Kristeva, Catherine Clément, Jean-Luc Nancy, and Philippe Lacoue-Labarthe were invited, each on a Wednesday, over a period of six months, to confront their readers. In each session, the bureaucracy of psychoanalysis was placed in the docket in conflictual debates in which members of the audience gave free reign, in the presence of an author, to their hostility to the reigning dogmatism.

René Major had met Jacques Derrida at the home of Nicholas Abraham. He admired the man and his work. Between the two there developed a complicity that soon gave Confrontation the appearance of a kind of "Derridean school of psycho-analysis," as though the path opened up ten years earlier by the philosopher found there, thanks to a remarkable dissident, a mode of splintered implantation conforming to the doctrine of margins, edges, contours, dissemination, and deconstruction. In November 1977, concerning *Glas*,[109] Derrida spoke of a "suburban network of psychoanalysis" in the societies and defined the "Confrontation effect" as a lifting of barriers: "The confrontation effect is a function of the deconstruction of the 'psychoanalytic' institution. It is revealed (and this is even its most manifest characteristic) by the fact that the barrier of allegiances to the four French groups no longer quite holds sway. It is no longer in any way water-tight, water-tight and without air, as was previously the case."[110]

In 1974, Antoinette Fouque met Serge Leclaire to discuss a possible analysis. The analysis did not take place. Fascinated by the woman's passion, Leclaire asked her to work with him. "Are you my political ally?" she immediately asked, with that assurance of a leader that characterized her. Leclaire thus went to work with the Psychanalyse et Politique group, in the country and in the city. He and Antoinette became inseparable.

The idea of "confronting" had occurred to Leclaire for a Cerisy colloquium. He was thus delighted when Major suggested that he organize the colloquium of May 1977 however he pleased. In March, on the occasion of the preparation of a special issue of *Scilicet* devoted to Lacan, which would never be published, he sent Lacan a rather beautiful letter. It sounded the death knell of a dazzling relationship that had lasted almost thirty years: "Today," wrote Leclaire, "you grasp with both hands string and gut in order to construct knots for ends other than strangling voices. It is overwhelming to see you trying to lend voice to innards, body to words, still harnessed to the task of producing psychoanalysis. But instead of perception, what reigns is misunderstanding. . . . Go on . . . I embrace you."[111]

For the May days, Leclaire came up with a very "Antoinette-like" idea: to have a colloquium without texts, allowing the youngest representatives of the fifth French psychoanalytic generation to improvise. They were thirty-three years old, were born with the collapse of the Nazi army. Their mothers had given birth to the sound of the tanks of a different Leclerc, the general of noble bearing. The colloquium would be called "Dites 33 [Speak up, 33]." It would take place in May at Bataclan and at the Orsay Theater, before an excited crowd. Leclaire made a concession to Major by allowing some of the texts to be printed.

He wanted to go further and implant confrontation at the very heart of the EFP, beneath the banner of Antoinette. His project had been welcomed by Simatos, who transmitted the request to Lacan. But in September 1977, the blade fell without any sign of emotion. "My dear," wrote Lacan, "it is out of the question that you conduct the seminar Simatos mentioned to me in the École freudienne de Paris."[112] Lacan had resolutely opted for the path of order and no doubt he was not wrong. At the time, and given the state of his school, he no longer had any other choice. Since the Vincennes *coup,* the game was over.

Confrontation was a fine adventure that had the aesthetic qualities of its principal instigator. But like all enterprises of "deconstruction," it was caught up in admiration of the ephemeral beauty of its youth. It was the Directorate before the Consulate, with its dandified *incroyables* and *merveilleuses;* it was a moment of freedom snatched between two reigns. It was thus a simulacrum of revolution. It would not survive the collapse of the EFP and would cease to exist (without being formally dissolved) in 1983.

In the interim, the future seemed radiant. A month after the May colloquium, Confrontation became an association governed by the Law of 1901. Its purpose was psychoanalytic research outside any training program. In that respect, it was the first of its kind in the history of psychoanalysis in France, since its members could either retain their affiliation with their respective societies or not be part of any other group. Founded by Chantal Talagrand, Major's wife, and Dominique Geahchan, it was a French association. The name of its principal initiator did not appear in its statutes.[113] Major was still awaiting his naturalization and had no reason to create a foreign society which would then be obliged to become French again for lack of foreign members. It defined itself as a different place offering an alternative to discourse encoded with the transferential effects inherent to psychoanalytic institutions. A true scientific society, Confrontation would become, over the years, a kind of free university with numerous seminars, international colloquiums, and celebrations.

In 1977, Major created at Éditions Aubier-Montaigne a splendid series called "La psychanalyse prise au mot." It obeyed the principle of Confrontation—"to open the analytic text, and displace its bearing; to inscribe the irreducibility of its margin and welcome the risk of psychoanalysis: to take it at its word." Major published his first book there, *Rêver l'autre* ["To dream the other"], as well as several works by Lacanians, members of the SPP, and of the APF. In 1979, he brought out the first issue of a lavish journal, *Cahiers Confrontations,* the cover of whose issues would be designed by Valerio Adami. It collected the articles or presentations of those participating in the group's activities. It was illustrated with a great deal of care by Françoise de Gruson, who joined Major in selecting excellent reproductions of modern paintings and lithographs. Finally, in 1980, Chantal Talagrand became the publisher of a "Green and Black" Confrontation, in which several volumes of texts or colloquiums appeared.

Although he did not take any public position against the "Confrontation effect," Lacan was fearful of the enterprise. To be sure, he did not forbid any of his fold from speaking at that theater of deconstruction, but he quite rightly feared that the adventure might destabilize his school. Since it was not a bureaucratic society, the EFP was far more fragile than the dinosaurs of the IPA. If traversed simultaneously by the spirit of contestation and that of order, it might simply disband. That is why, paradoxically, Confrontation had a stronger disorganizing effect on the EFP than on the SPP, even though it was initially created to unsettle the internal order of the Institute by allowing an "alien" discourse to be spoken in its precincts.

After Lacan's letter refusing him the right to hold a seminar with Antoinette, Leclaire understood that the game was over and that nothing would be "confronted" in the EFP. "By November 1977," he has written, "it was clear to me that there was a threat of a palace revolution within the École freudienne de Paris. In that institution, which had become like every other, the issue of power had already become the central factor, although cloaked by the noble project of saving psychoanalysts from the peril of deviationist heresies."[114] Seven months later, in an interview with the local press during a stay in Rio de Janeiro, he declared a dissolution of the EFP desirable. "In the last analysis," he said, "to remain consistent with his own genius, I think Lacan should dissolve the institution, the École freudienne, so that it might be taken up anew in a different manner, with his continued presence. But this is merely my fantasy."[115] Leclaire would have been the only disciple to join Lacan in writing the statutes in 1964 and the first to recommend a dissolution of the EFP. At the time, no one was yet considering such an act.

While Confrontation continued its brilliant career, Major did not lower his guard within the SPP. But the titular members of the honorable French section began to tire of the exhausting quarrel over statutes, which yielded no results. Gradually, the combatants deserted the cause to return to their writings or their practice. Only the most relentless continued the struggle, having the majority forces of the affiliates and a part of the adhering members on their side.

In October 1974, in the course of an extraordinary plenary session, a proposal for modifying the statutes in conformity with the desires of the majority of May 15 was offered. It called for the election of the administrative council by all the members, a council reduced in membership, and the separation of teaching from administration. The meeting did not succeed in marshalling a quorum, and the proposal was thus juridically unacceptable. Return to square one. In order to conform to its own statutes, the Société would have to call a new meeting within a one-month period. It was then that a certain reticence became apparent among the representatives of the affiliates on the reform commission. There began to be talk of a dissolution of the Institute, consisting of a merger with the Société.[116] Since 1973 the Société no longer had the same statutes as the Institute, as modifications could not be applied from one association to the other. The Société still functioned according to the old system, without representation of the affiliate and adhering colleges. But as a result, it was easier to govern, since its Articles 12 and 14 on statutory revision and dissolution stipulated merely a majority vote of three-fourths of the titular members. That mobility would be a further instrument of the conservatives, who could play the Société off against the Institute in cases of conflict. For that reason, the liberals were opposed to any fusion that might constitute a step backward in relation to what had been secured in 1973.

A new proposal for reforming the statutes of the Institute was elaborated by the commission and was quite close to the October one. In February, a titular member from Lyon conveyed his grave concern to André Green, the outgoing director. The text was dense and offered a perfect reflection of the state of mind prevalent at the SPP. In leaden language characteristic of the orthodox idiom, the author compared the degradation of his society to a "chronic pregenital conflictualization of interpersonal relations and of the living experience of the institution." Without mentioning Lacan or the 1953 split, he emphasized that this was not a cancer stemming from the electroshock of the barricades, but a "process of failed reproduction" harkening back to an emotionally charged separation, which had in turn produced, subsequently, the APF in similarly painful circumstances. Then he requested that the history of a crisis that had lasted more than twenty years be calmly compiled. Finally, he condemned the dualism existing between the Société and the Institute, and observed that the psychotic mechanism of the good and bad object was functioning in the institution as a morbid logic in the case of each member.[117]

That view was shared by a majority of the members, but the warning would not be of any help: The machine had already taken off, and was beyond individual control. At the meeting of March 4, the proposed statutes received 120 favorable votes with 34 against, but 4 votes from the titular college were lacking and the proposal was not adopted. Given the insistence of the majority, a "functional agreement" was reached, providing for the application of the proposed statutes for a period of two years, with an administrative council composed of the three categories of members. That agreement was to lead to an evaluation, in 1977, of the new functioning of the association.[118] Three weeks later, the case against René Major for illegal practice of medicine was definitively dropped. Naturally, the formerly accused continued not to practice medicine. Although a physician, he is still not authorized to exercise that profession, which he never will. . . . There would be no denunciation of the denouncer and all expenses were assumed by the court.[119]

The status quo had resulted in a second status quo.

After Articles 5 and 15 of the statutes, it was now around Articles 4 and 8 that the titular members would split into two camps, each interpreting the law in accordance with his own interests. Article 4 stated that membership in the association would be terminated because of resignation, expulsion for serious reason, actions contrary to the statutes, or nonpayment of dues. It stipulated that the affected party must first be called upon to furnish an explanation before a meeting of the titular members. If he were an affiliate, expulsion would have to be ratified by the colleges of adhering members and affiliates; if an adhering member by the college of adhering members; if a titular member, by the college of titular members. Of course, it was still imperative that those to be excluded succeed in obtaining a hearing on the subject of their reasons for going against the regulations. Article 8 provided that in major cases the administrative council had to request approval from a meeting of the entire society.

Now as of 1975, the working agreement implementing the new statutes on a trial basis was renewed without any meeting of the society as a whole. It was for that reason that at the end of 1976, Conrad Stein, René Major, and Serge Viderman stopped paying their dues to the Institute. In June 1977, the Société's council modified Article 4 of the statutes. A clause was added providing for automatic expulsion for nonpayment of dues.[120] Thus a member of the Société could be excluded without receiving a hearing on the reasons for his act. The addition of that clause did not resolve any problem concerning the Institute, since in that association, Article 4 remained the same as it had been. Now Stein, Viderman, and Major were no longer paying their dues to the Institute in the thought that that was the only way to manifest their opposition. In order to exclude them, they would thus have to be brought before a meeting of the titular members. As a result, (revised) Article 4 of the Société would be used for the purpose of voting through a revision of its counterpart in the Institute.

In October 1979, a plenary session was called which transpired in conditions that were lamentable for every tendency, provoking an overwhelming sense of fatigue on the part of the members of the SPP. At the end of that meeting the working agreement was not renewed. As a result, the administrative council annulled the provisional steps taken in March 1974. The return to the 1973 statutes was legal since no revision had taken place, only a working agreement. And yet, in the eyes of the protesters, that legality was only superficial, for the commission had pledged to have a vote on reform measures on the grounds stipulated by the agreement, which was a *de facto* abrogation of the prior statutes. Barande, Stein, Viderman, Geahchan, and Major thus contested that reversion—which they judged illegal—to the previous situation.

The matter resurfaced during a meeting of the administrative council on June 10, 1980. In order to be able to exclude adversaries without giving them a hearing, the council, which had "legally reelected itself," decided to revise Article 4 of the statutes of the Institute on the model of its counterpart in the Société: automatic expulsion for nonpayment of dues. It had the right to do so since in October 1979 it had annulled the measures provided by the working agreement. In the face of this new assault by the conservative group, eight titular members of the opposition brought the Institute to court in order to annul the vote of June 10. Among them: Stein, Viderman, Major, Geahchan, Neyraut, and Barande. At Major's urging, they took on Roland Dumas as a lawyer; he was, at the same time, defending Lacan's interests in the dissolution of the EFP. At the time, the two most powerful psychoanalytic communities in France were lacerating themselves before the country's courts, offering the world a disastrous image of themselves. And yet, as always, the affairs of the SPP remained more secret than those of the EFP, which were widely commented on in the press.

Since it had been sued, the Institute, as part of the same trial, decided to countersue Stein, Major, and Viderman for nonpayment of dues. But before the case came to trial, the Institute agreed to withdraw the revisions proposed for Article 4. For their part, Stein and Viderman, who were fatigued with the whole matter, regularized their situation and paid their back dues. Major remained the only one in the ring for the final round. On June 17, 1981, the court delivered its verdict and dismissed sued and suers alike.[121] It stipulated, on the one hand, that the documents produced by Major and his friends did not prove that the Institute had knowingly violated its own statutes, and that, on the other, the Institute's request was unacceptable as it stood because the procedures listed in its statutes had not been applied. In brief, the court showed itself to be just: It rejected the demands for damages of both parties. With a wisdom worthy of King Solomon, it called on them to come to an agreement in conformity with the spirit of association provided for by the law of 1901. The suit and countersuit were like a sword plunged into water or (if one likes) the triggering of a nuclear war for possession of the rock of Monaco.

The second status quo resulted in a restoration.

Naturally, René Major continued not paying his dues and asked to be heard on the subject in accordance with Article 4. For its part, the Institute continued to want a revision of Article 4 so that it could exclude him without granting him an opportunity to explain the reasons for his act.

On November 3, 1980, a "Collège de psychanalystes" was founded by twenty-nine individuals meeting in the home of François Roustang. The initiative was interesting and bore witness to the shattered condition of the French psychoanalytic community: proposed dissolution at the EFP and bureaucratic conflict at the SPP. The association had as founders three titular members who had not resigned from the honorable society (Stein, Geahchan, and Viderman) but who had taken their institute to court, and two members of an EFP about to disappear from the scene, François Roustang and Anne Levallois, who had signed legal papers against Jacques Lacan nine months before.

They were joined by a psychoanalyst who did not belong to any constituted group, Jacques Sédat. A former student of the Jesuits, he had been trained by François Perrier, then supervised in the ranks of the OPLF and the EFP. He was inclined to invoke Raymond Aron and de Tocqueville. Maintaining both a classically liberal and a conservative position, he reincarnated within the "Collège" an eminently "French" component of psychoanalysis, which had disappeared with the death of Pichon. Fascinated by the corporatism and the intergroup ethos of the 1970s, he implemented a program for the defense of the profession against governmentally imposed fiscal restraints. He had a good knowledge of every aspect of the psychoanalytic movement and was not hostile to any of them. He would thus gradually become a member of numerous groups issuing from the crisis in the SPP and the dissolution of the EFP, tending rather toward a position of active anti-Millerianism.

After participating in the preparatory meetings, Serge Leclaire, Michèle Montrelay, René Major, and Maria Torok refused (for a variety of reasons) to be founders of the College. The new group partook of the same deconstructive trend as Confrontation, but constituted itself as a true society and was not based on any libertarian disposition. It closed what Confrontation had opened and was symptomatic of the first return to order of the whole of a psychoanalytic community that had been coming apart on the one side and bureaucratized on the other. The College was thus a circumstantial association, characterized by its competence and reasonableness, neither of which would prevent its founders from tearing each other apart before the first year was over. Its principal innovation consisted in accepting members belonging to other groups. It had no institute and functioned by cooptation. Founded initially for a period of five years, the association would subsequently have its term renewed indefinitely. It was composed of active and associate members. The first were practitioners, who alone had the right to determine the group's orientations. The second were individuals capable of assisting it. Admission of active members required recommendation by three members of the association entitled to perform in that capacity. Ten years of practice were required in order to be certified as an active member by a cooptation board consisting of all members authorized for that function.[122]

A year after the creation of the College, Dominique Geahchan began publishing an association bulletin entitled *Psychanalystes,* with Jean Cornut and Monique

Schneider on the editorial board. Two years later, in April 1983, he died of a heart attack, exhausted by his numerous activities. The funeral mass was celebrated at the Church of the Immaculate Conception of Boulogne-Billancourt. Around that time, Major decided to put a halt to the Confrontation experiment, while waiting for better days. He continued to direct the journal and the series at Éditions Aubier-Montaigne. In the meanwhile, he had finally obtained French citizenship.[123] Shortly thereafter he would be authorized to register as a psychiatrist with the Ordre des médecins. In brief, at the end of 1983, after ten years of xenophobic harassment, he was at last a free man: Canadian by birth, French by sentiment, naturalized by decree, a "foreigner" in his own society, a physician by his diplomas, internationalist in culture, and "Third World" by ideological choice.

The wheel turned and the IPA remained the same as ever, only increasingly bureaucratic. At its Helsinki congress, in July 1981, its leadership ordered a "visiting committee" to inquire into the difficulties of the seemingly pathological French section. The SPP thus found itself in a situation analogous to that of the old SFP, except for the fact that the society this time had not itself requested an intrusion into its own internal affairs. Judging that the Société and the Institute had not succeeded in producing needed reforms, the committee proposed a moratorium of six months for the elaboration of new statutes.[124]

In the long run, it was a matter of disbanding the Institute, incorporating training into a single association, and eliminating Clause 9 of the house rules about retroactive or deferred decisions, which were judged to be out of line with IPA standards. Despite a few protests, the surveillance was carried out, allowing for neither a reduction of malaise nor a change in statutes nor a modification of the revisions provided by Clause 9. In the meanwhile, the "Major case" remained problematic. He was not paying his dues, and was invoking Article 4 of the Institute's statutes in order to get a hearing from the titular college.

Instead of inviting him to give an explanation, the administrative council called an extraordinary plenary session in order to revise Article 4 of the Institute and bring it into line with its counterpart in the Société. The introduction of a new clause was intended to distinguish between expulsion because of a serious infraction, in which case a hearing was mandatory, and simple exclusion for reason of nonpayment of dues, which did not necessitate any additional procedure. In other words, if the vote swung in favor of that revision, Major could be expelled from the two associations without being heard as to the reasons for his revolt. But since it was impossible to modify the statutes, the results of the operation were known in advance. In brief, Major wanted to be excluded according to the rules, and the Institute wanted to introduce a rule allowing for his exclusion according to a new set of regulations.

Whence the crazy compromise for a society apparently gone mad; Major would be listened to without being formally "heard," not according to the rules, but before a plenary session, which was not called in order to give him a hearing but in order to modify an Article 4 which was impossible to revise.[125]

On February 28, 1984, René Major, in the course of that plenary session, delivered a diatribe aimed at the conservative titular members of the SPP. He accused them of violating all the democratic rules of their association over a ten-year period and asked the plenary session not to vote through the revision of Article 4, since, as it stood, it constituted a final recourse for any member intent on explaining his conduct. Then Major proceeded to recount all the harassment he had been victim of on the part of his colleagues and the French government. He compared the SPP to a society of apparatchiks and, in the name of the rights of man, denounced its totalitarian cast. Finally he admonished his colleagues, evoking both the past and the present: "That psychoanalysis has reinvented associative constraints is already extremely telling. From there to a transformation of free speech into forced confession or a denunciatory technique is only a step. It is no surprise that it has already been taken. That it was taken only yesterday, under the pretext of saving psychoanalysis in Germany; that the German society excluded from its association all members who were Jewish. There was only a single non-Jewish analyst to say no to 'psychoanalysis with the Nazis.' He resigned from the German society. History will have retained his name: Bernard Kamm. What precisely was that German society preserving if not the repression that would establish a rule of silence lasting several generations? Only today is there beginning to be talk in Germany about the serious consequences of that event for a number of generations. And I am not sure that those consequences have occurred only in Germany. It's part of the history we all share in common. A question, How indeed can one psychoanalyze after Auschwitz?, should be in the thoughts of every analyst. Today one finds in Latin America that while some psychoanalysts were imprisoned for not having betrayed professional rules of confidentiality, others have been active or passive accomplices in the torture practiced by a regime that has no use for freedom of thought. All this to say that one cannot compromise on principles when one knows the gravity of the consequences they will have sooner or later.[126]

After the reading of that indictment, three Jewish titular members, Janine Chasseguet-Smirgel, André Green, and Serge Lebovici spoke against Major, stating that they would not stand for being called Nazis. Chasseguet-Smirgel was the most violent. Then, another Jewish titular member, Conrad Stein, responded that the psychoanalysts in the German society were not Nazis but good *petits bourgeois* "like us." Despite the accuracy of that remark, the three titular members continued to feel they had been called Nazis. They had not reacted in that manner when confronted with the same declaration by Michel de M'Uzan eleven years earlier. The vote that followed turned out, as always, to be against any revision of the statutes. Only the titular college proved favorable to adopting the new clause. But the bureaucratic trap was closing on both Major and his adversaries. The latter listened to him at the plenary session and felt defeated at having to summon him in accordance with regulations. He may have been able to deliver himself of an explanation, but the hearing had not transpired as it should have. It resulted neither in his exclusion, nor in his having to pay dues. Major was not expelled, since the clause was not passed. But in the form it had, Article 4 no longer served any function at all. To this day, it is suspected of being unenforceable. The situation had become grotesque and all were exhausted.

And yet this was a serious matter. The Jewish conservatives in the titular college, many of whom had been victims either of genocide (through their families) or of anti-Semitic persecution, felt attacked by this indictment being read by a non-Jew analyzed by one of the authors of *L'univers contestationnaire.* Major had never been a victim of fascism in France. But he had encountered administrative harassment and the horrors of the IPA bureaucracy. Nothing prevented him—in view of the uselessness of any attempt at reform—from no longer combatting his adversaries in the name of an illusory justice. One does not sue a machine; one abandons it. And yet had the titular members of the society wanted to avoid being called Nazis, it was up to them not to deserve the indictment that had come their way. It was up to them to reject, in 1973, a xenophobic law. Michel de M'Uzan, moreover, had warned them of the danger they were slating for themselves. It was up to them to publicly disavow *L'univers contestationnaire,* a book shot through with inegalitarianism and unworthy of the great saga of the Jews.

Three months after delivering that diatribe, without publishing it, Major brought out for the first time in France an anthology of documents by Germans on the situation of psychoanalysis on the other side of the Rhine. The work was entitled *Les années brunes* ["The brown years"][127] and removed the repression affecting a difficult and crucial period in the world history of psychoanalysis. In the meanwhile, the leadership of the IPA continued to keep official watch over its French branch, judged to be suffering from bureaucratic pathology. In a letter of May 1984, Adam Limentani, the new president of the empire, revealed his concerns about the carelessness reigning in the land of Voltaire. He observed that the Société could not find a president, since no one was willing to bear the burden of that impossible responsibility. He added that no agreement had been reached on the subject of dues payment. The two-headed structure was proving to be disastrous; business meetings were deserted and there had been an overproduction of therapists. Finally, he made official the fact that the association was under surveillance and announced the Institute's obligation to transfer all its training activities to the Société. Daniel Widlöcher was placed on the surveillance committee.[128]

The same Limentani, moreover, offered a bizarre interpretation of the situation of psychoanalysis throughout the world. In April 1984, during a meeting in Taunton, England, and after a lecture by Jacques-Alain Miller at the Tavistock Clinic, he said he was convinced that Lacan's son-in-law was intent on grabbing control of Europe as well as dear old London. Imagine! He added that the creation of a Lacanian International would allow the IPA to solve its problems and its members to remain faithful: "We ought to take into account all that Lacan has written, but the 'return to Freud' is an extremely subtle and dangerous question since it is a matter of returning to Freud according to Lacan with all the repercussions on technique that Lacan recommended. Lacan's son-in-law is extremely active and it is his intention to take control of a good portion of Europe, including London and in particular the Tavistock Clinic. The Lacanians intend to create their own international association which would be, in fact, entirely welcome to the IPA: We would then know where we stand and all those who are critical of the IPA in our own ranks would be able to see the real problems and remain loyal to the IPA and, let us hope, act as we have been trying to recommend for quite some time now. The more of an international Lacanian association there is, the better it will be for us, if we allow it to do a bit of publicity for us." [129] And let amateurs take care!

In July, Janine Chasseguet-Smirgel informed the members of the SPP that the next congress of the IPA would be held in Hamburg, following a decision made seven years before at the Jerusalem congress. For the first time since the advent of Nazism, an IPA congress would be held in Germany. Hamburg had been chosen in preference to Berlin. After much negotiation it was decided that the "brown years" would not be discussed without having first been filtered through a "psychoanalytic interpretation": "The program committee was thus faced with a difficult task. It chose not to favor any collective denial, wagering that such a subject could be treated most scientifically in the light of our discipline. A day has thus been devoted to the application of the general theme of the congress to the study of the Nazi phenomenon from a strictly clinical point of view. But Germany was not only a place of persecution and death for psychoanalysts and psychoanalysis. For psychoanalysis was born and developed within German-language culture. A plenary session will thus be devoted to the influence of that culture on Freud's thought." [130]

The organization of the congress had already aroused hostile reactions in January from the Psychoanalytisches Seminar of Zurich, whose members momentarily considered holding a counter-congress. But they renounced that plan for fear of appearing anti-German. Nevertheless a colloquium did take place in May, with the participation of René Major. The Zurich members emphasized that the specific structure of the IPA eliminated the possibility of any serious reflection on the notions of banishment, exile, and persecution, and particularly on the "brown years," concerning which silence had reigned for some forty years. At the Hamburg congress, the participants followed the IPA directives. In order not to compromise a *rapprochement* with the Germans, they avoided speaking about the situation in 1933–44, and restricted themselves to analyzing Nazism through clinical cases of patients who had escaped the camps. An exhibition was devoted to past history, with a splendid catalogue, in which the principal actors in the collaboration with Göring were presented "neutrally" as so many continuers of Freudian thought in a totalitarian regime.[131]

At the meeting of the administrative college of the SPP, in February 1985, the new president, who had finally been found, encouraged members not to allow the reform effort to wane: "It appears we no longer have any choice," he said. "We should remember that the society is presently described as being under surveillance in the first pages of the *Roster,* that is, that it remains an object of particular concern for the visiting committee from the IPA. This situation is certainly not dishonorable, but one is hard put to regard it as glorious or comfortable." [132] Eighteen months later, through a vote of the three colleges, the disbanding of the Institute was obtained by a fusion of the two societies. The new statutes allowed for the election of the administrative council at a plenary session as well as the possibility of reforms concerning which only time will tell whether or not they will be able to change the bureaucratic character of the SPP.

III. The Association Psychanalytique de France:
The Identification of a Group

Founded in secret a month before the EFP and in the heat of a battle for affiliation, the Association psychanalytique de France resembles neither a Lacanian institution nor an ordinary IPA-affiliated society. Its history is that of a collective of individuals each of whom has followed a different itinerary. Its members are not constituted as "clans," as in the SPP, nor do they have a master, as at the EFP, nor are they situated within a Lacanian "tendency" in the same manner as the OPLF. The APF is a group whose identity must be defined on the basis of the career of each of its members. Although calling itself "of France," it is essentially Parisian and without extension in the provinces. As opposed to its two giant sisters, it is indeed an association and not a society or a school. In 1964, it brought together heterogeneous elements: on the one hand, former "seniors" of the SFP, who were divided among themselves; on the other, the various "movers," who differed in personality, but were bound by a pact to abandon the father. At the center of the fray, they agreed to banish Lacan and at the same time they disavowed a practice that had made competent training analysts of them. Whence a determination that would only become more pronounced with time to shield personal analyses from any bureaucratic intrusion. To the group of movers may be added Didier Anzieu and Wladimir Granoff, two men who respected each other but had nothing in common. They had broken with Lacan in circumstances different from the others. One embodied the traditional values of the French university; the other was a cosmopolite without institutional attachments. For reasons having to do with their personal styles and histories, they would never be presidents of the APF, which would always end up being led from its "center" by former movers. Nevertheless, Granoff and Anzieu would retain important teaching functions within the group.

The identity crisis affecting the Association from the time of its birth has been endlessly commented upon by its founders, who have made public confession of their conflicts or failings without masking them, as is the case in the SPP. In that respect, the APF is a healthy society, able to look at itself in a mirror and take stock of its history, even if it has never managed to publish any of its traces. "One thing strikes me as remarkable," Laplanche noted in 1980, "this association is intent on not knowing its identity; and the most categorical way of not taking cognizance of one's identity is to repress one's history. . . . The association has never collected and published the documents concerning its founding, that is, the split of 1963–64. It has allowed a totally tendentious history to be accredited both by the Lacanians (the "excommunication") and by a book such as Barande's. A second example: Most of our members, above all the associates and students, are unaware—even in outline—of what was played out on the subject of training during the years 1969–71, resulting in our present curriculum. Here too, that ignorance has resulted in the accreditation of the idea that our way of training is not essentially different from that of the SPP (Barande), or rather that we situate ourselves as a golden mean between the SPP and the École freudienne." [133]

At its founding, on May 25, 1964, the APF counted twenty-six members. In its initial statutes, it included three categories of membership: titular members, associates, and honorary members. That last category would always be empty. As a result it is the titular and associate members who effectively run the society. The training institute is part of it and consists of two sections: A *selection committee*, consisting of eight members, is responsible for selecting candidates for training while a *teaching committee* provides them with direction and controls the organization of seminars. The institute is directed either by the president of the Association or by a director chosen by the council of titular members. The administrative council is composed of five to seven members, elected by majority vote at a plenary session of all members. Students are not members of the Association, which is thus far less democratic than the EFP was but far more liberal than the SPP. Its statutes stipulate that the administrative council is to be composed of members, without specifying their category. In theory, then, an associate might also be part of it. The election of any new member, however, whether associate or titular member, is solely the prerogative of the titular members. It is thus they who effectively hold power in the Association as opposed to the associates. The curriculum was standardized according to the IPA model: A candidate accepted for training chose his analyst from a fixed list of training analysts. There was thus a preselection and a training phase distinct from one's personal analysis. That system would subsequently be abolished.[134]

In 1964, out of twenty-six members, ten were titular members—that is, authorized to train candidates. Four years later, the APF counted thirty-four members and had absorbed into its titular ranks all the former members of the SFP. At that time, the society fell under the sway of the former "movers," who would replace each other as president. Lagache and Favez, the first two presidents, began to see their influence wane—one because he was ill and had no analytic descendents, the other because he had neither students nor written work.[135] By 1968 then, the APF belonged to the "brothers" of the third generation. The events of May served to confirm that development. Since the Association was not initially able to carry off a majority of the students of the SFP (who had regrouped in the GEP) in its wake, and since, over the years, it had to conserve the fragile equilibrium that reigned among the brothers of the tribe, it was threatened not with overexpansion but extinction. The same individuals succeeded each other in the same slots in ritual manner. That is why the APF was gradually abandoned by its associates, who had to await retirement age before becoming titular members, and by its students, who were occasionally over forty years old. Before very long, it began resembling an extremely elegant private club, in which old friends coexisted politely together for failure to come up with a solution for their advancing gerontocracy. In 1972, the phantom of a slow death began to hover over the most scholarly, distinguished, and elitist society in France. During the plenary session of June, Pontalis evoked the phenomenon on the occasion of the group's move to new quarters on the place Dauphine: "Is the only thing we want to grow old together?" he exclaimed.[136]

Threatened with extinction, the APF is also marked by a propensity to feudal baronies and to masculinity. The founding brothers were men who chose the group against the father. They left Lacan for the IPA because they refused the Caesarism of a master and the merging of his doctrine with his person. They wanted plurality, democracy, fraternity, and comfort without risk. Now they had made that choice because they were already, each in his field, the most brilliant subjects of that saga. In refusing the initiatic function of the master, they had thought they were founding a true collective whereas they had set up a "school of chiefs," each exercising his chiefdom outside the group: a hospital career for Widlöcher, university careers for Laplanche and Anzieu, a publishing career for Pontalis, and so forth. Reigning each in his way beyond the reach of their common roof, they could agree within not to become each other's tyrants. The principal bastions they controlled on the French intellectual scene satisfied their appetites sufficiently for them not to need any supreme chief. Through that effect of collective chiefdom, the APF is a man's school in the same sense that the OPLF is a woman's school. It had emerged from Lacan's womb, just as the Fourth Group had emerged from Leclaire's: one masculine progeny and one feminine.

Women have not enjoyed professional or creative eminence within this manly society, where they are represented solely as spouses. Juliette Favez-Boutonier acquired a certain distinction outside her marriage, but only Marie Moscovici founded a journal, entitled *Écrit du temps*.[137] Other women might have a certain role in the society, but the role has always been secondary in relation to that of the men. None has ever been elected president. In 1964, the APF counted 6 women out of 26 members, and in 1983, 19 out of 50. They are plainly more numerous among the associates than among the titular members. Nonetheless, the distribution is more equitable than in the SPP, where the female population overwhelmingly swells the ranks of the affiliates. In addition, the APF is the least "medical" of the four French components, both in number of physicians and in the academic ethos dominating it.

The history of this group, both calm and agitated, began before the legal existence of the APF. As of January 1964, the SFP was split into two components.[138] The majority, grouped around Lagache and Granoff, directed affairs, but they were a minority in the rank and file, where the Lacanians had gradually consolidated their positions through the GEP. The troika no longer existed, and Granoff, the only one of the three to have shifted to the IPA camp, joined Lagache in taking charge of the secret negotiations that resulted first in the creation of the French Study Group (FSG), then in affiliation a year later. The majority still remained subject to the consulting committee that represented them in their dealings with the Executive, while the Lacanians at that point felt free of any hierarchical subservience. They would soon win their French campaign, and Lacan's teaching would be absorbed by the country's intellectual youth, who rejected both so-called "American" psychoanalysis and the imperialism of the same name. Under those conditions, the partisans of the IPA were considered the "hostages of Chicago," serving a cause whose bureaucratic and political ideals were rejected. The Lacanians of the time were in no way chauvinistic, but hostile to the America of the IPA and ego psychology. Against it, they invoked a universalist and French autonomous psychoanalytic culture that owed nothing to the IPA empire.

Now the IPA's negotiators, Gitelson, Pearl King, Van der Leuw, and even

Turquet, did not take that cultural situation into account. In their eyes, it mattered little whether Lacanianism triumphed in France as Lacanianism was not representative of what they considered to be authentic psychoanalysis. From the moment they excluded Lacan from training, they sought to constitute a second IPA bastion in France, which would conform to its standards and be capable of getting along with the SPP. They were thus in no rush to score points against Lacanianism. Concerned with norms and respecting legality, they held absolute power over the group through the committee. And through it, they dictated their decisions, imposed their rules, and threatened to withdraw their recognition if the group did not yield to their stated demands. Given that situation, and for more than a year, Granoff attempted in vain to make them understand that with their bureaucratic slowness and niggling manner they were in the process of losing the battle against Lacanianism.

In his new role as lone warrior, Granoff resembled Churchill trying to convince Roosevelt that de Gaulle was the embodiment of resistance on the French gameboard. Only Granoff was not Churchill since he had chosen to ally himself with Giraud and was trying to explain to Roosevelt how to defeat de Gaulle. The situation was inextricable. As for Giraud, he existed on his own, but already considered himself defeated by history even as he continued to pretend that his ally of the day had formerly used him for the benefit of his rival. In other words, on the eve of the creation of the APF, Lagache was not aware that he had served as the troika's shield in a grand maneuver seeking to make Lacan acceptable to the IPA. But now he was Granoff's ally—Granoff who remained the empire's best interlocutor in a negotiation conducted toward ends opposite those of the Edinburgh one. It would henceforth be a matter of bringing into existence a collective having neither a master nor an identity against another one that was triumphantly Lacanian.

On May 10, 1964, the group became the FSG, and two weeks later, the FSG became the APF. But for the IPA, it remained a study group and, as such, subject to the committee, which presided over its decisions and did not grant it the right either to train analysts or to recruit new members. According to the statutory stages, a study group first became a provisional society before being granted the status of a member society. Since decisions were taken at congresses, which were held every two years, at least four years would be needed to make the transition from "study group" to "member society." By that calculation, the APF would have a chance of affiliation in 1967, when its members would be over forty years old, and Lacanianism would have gleaned the laurels of its finest victory. In 1964, the battle for affiliation was thus far from having been won, and the APF resembled a prematurely born child awaiting its incubator.

Aware of the precariousness of the situation, Granoff begged Turquet to transform the trench warfare into mobile combat so as to defeat the GEP on its own territory and impose the legal existence of the APF on the SPP. In order to accomplish that, he asked the leadership of the IPA to publish in the pages of the *RFP* an official announcement of Lacan's ejection and the creation of the APF. The text would be rendered null by the creation of the EFP in June. [139]

In July, Granoff alerted Van der Leuw as to the reality of the French situation. He put him on guard against Lacanian "subversion," which was gaining ground while the committee delayed giving any new guarantees to the APF. "I am certain," he said, "that recognition of our group at the Amsterdam congress will not be enough to prevent the subversion, but I'm sure it will raise the dike a few inches, which is, believe me, about all that can be hoped for at present. Moreover, I am not sure that the water behind the dike will continue to rise after Lacan's death." [140]

Four days later, he again conveyed his impressions and manifested his impatience: "I have long been interested in the history of the psychoanalytic movement. . . . and I can affirm that psychoanalysis is here and now facing a major challenge, a new force, which it has not known until now (because of the idiosyncrasies of the French scene). . . . My opinion is that the IPA does not have in its pantry either the recipes, the ingredients, or the effectiveness to pull things off. . . . I suggest that those in charge. . . . not lose any time in realizing that exceptional circumstances call for exceptional procedures." [141] In September, Granoff warned Gitelson that the situation in the SPP was in the process of shifting, that Lacanianism had aroused the interest of all the younger students, and that Nacht's authority had been seriously compromised. He announced that problems were inevitable in the future and recommended an immediate alliance with the APF and the best elements of the SPP in order to create a movement able to compete with Lacanianism. [142] All to no avail.

His arguments were of little interest to the directors of the IPA. For as much as Granoff tried to promote the emergence of a third force, which might accept certain elements of Lacan's teaching, the empire wanted nothing other than the establishment of its bureaucratic power. In November, Turquet sent Lagache, who was president of the APF, a complete list of the demands to be fulfilled in order to secure affiliation. His tone was characteristic; it was a matter of applying as much balm as needed to the French in order to bring them into line. Turquet recalled that the demands were not being imposed out of a taste for dogmatism, but out of a duty toward the rules governing the IPA. He then insisted forcefully on the necessity of standards. Finally, he added that the committee would vouch for the loyalty of the French before the Executive. The essential portion of the document concerned the veterans of Lacan's couch, who found themselves obliged to undergo a new phase of analysis on an approved couch in order to be accepted as training analysts: "We must be quite clear without entering into detail. Lacan's candidates, if they want to be accepted as future analysts, will have to undergo a new personal analysis with a different analyst."

Turquet did not enter into detail, nor did he specify whether he meant the most recent candidates or the founders of an APF not yet certified to train therapists. Several titular and associate members of the APF would nonetheless undergo a new analysis. Turquet then explained at length the committee's grievances against Lacan, specifying that the IPA did not want to eliminate the thinker but the training analyst: "For the committee in July 1963, there were three insurmountable objections to Lacan: (1) Training analyses are not supposed to indoctrinate. But Lacan deliberately used them for that purpose. (2) For training analyses, certain norms have been established to avoid the exploitation of analysands. Lacan does not recognize those basic norms and, despite certain promises, refuses to recognize and apply them. In violating those basic norms, he raises the suspicion that he is exploiting his candidates both materially and psychically. (3) Despite repeated promises, Lacan has never been able to convince us of his sincerity. Similarly, his students, through their tergiversations, have not served his cause. . . . We have not sought to judge Lacan as a thinker but as a training analyst. The two aspects are so tightly connected that his exclusion as a training analyst has led him to exclude himself from the IPA. We never asked for his total exclusion from the SFP; if it happened, it's his responsibility." Finally, after having issued orders, Turquet emphasized that the sins of the parents would not be visited on the children and that time would tell whether the APF would be capable of producing training analysts.[143]

At that stage of its history, the APF thus found itself in a critical situation. It was obliged to de-Lacanize itself in order to obtain its affiliation. But how was one to de-Lacanize oneself when one had been trained for so many years on the benches of a Lacanianism that was itself about to become a major force on the French gameboard? Intent on obtaining that affiliation at whatever cost, Granoff attempted to surmount the juridical obstacles inherent in the IPA statutes. He demonstrated to Turquet that the APF was living on credit, that its members might soon tire of the whole business, and that the hierarchical distinction between a provisional society and a member society did not make any sense in France. Lagache, for his part, wrote a memorandum emphasizing that the IPA statutes had changed several times and that the delay in awarding affiliation concerned the SFP and Lacan rather than the APF. As a result, he proposed a direct transition from the status of study group to that of member society. A discussion ensued and Pearl King insisted on the necessity of respecting the rules. Turquet, on the contrary, ardently defended the French point of view and was himself beginning to have had enough of the IPA bureaucracy.

It was at this point that conflicts arose in the French group. Members of the French group, and specifically Favez and Laplanche, refused to bend to the imposed rules and were accepting candidates that might be judged "dubious" by the committee. In addition, several members continued to work freely, as at the SFP, without heeding considerations of accountability concerning number of analytic or control sessions per week. Some went so far as to take under supervision therapists from the EFP. A terrible confusion was the result, and it ran the risk of undermining the affiliation process.[144] On the selection committee, Granoff played the disciplinarian and encouraged Lagache to combat any laxness. The English, moreover, proved quite severe when it came to the policy of the APF concerning the provinces, notably the Strasbourg and Marseille regions.

On the eve of the Amsterdam congress, the APF had already lost its battle for establishment because of the IPA bureaucracy. From that date on it was threatened with extinction. And the way in which Lagache arranged for his own successor did not help matters any. In 1965, two men seemed in line to run the group's affairs: Granoff, the secretary, and Favez, the vice-president. Lagache felt that Granoff was better placed to assume the presidency. He thus designated him in a letter as his successor.[145] At the time, Granoff had a good chance to obtain a majority, since most of the "movers" were not yet sufficiently along in their careers to fill such a position. Now he wanted to be president because he felt himself to be the father of that association of brothers on whose behalf he had committed a terrible deed: Lacan's banishment written in his own hand. And yet he would let himself be deceived by Lagache in the same manner that he himself had once duped him. After which, it would be too late for him.

Stricken with heart disease, Lagache underwent a serious operation in July which prevented him from attending the congress. He thus commissioned Granoff, through an official letter, to represent him before the Central Executive. He asked the leadership of the IPA not to receive the vice-president in his role as member of the council without the presence of the secretary of the APF. He invoked the fact that Favez was incapable of following a conversation in English and had not been a participant in the negotiation.[146] But at the same time he asked the Favezes to represent him before the Executive without informing them of his other initiative.[147] At bottom, he distrusted Granoff, whom he needed for the negotiation, and wanted to win on all fronts by making sure that each adversary kept watch over the other. When the couple arrived in Amsterdam, Granoff had already taken the affairs of the APF in hand. To celebrate the affiliation, he organized a sumptuous reception at the Hilton, which was attended by dignitaries of the regime. Irritated, the Favezes went there to organize a small official meeting at their hotel. Thus at the time the APF was receiving the laurels of the empire, it was becoming a place of open conflict over Lagache's succession. As for Turquet, disheartened by the bureaucracy, he walked out of the congress slamming the door before the closing ceremony in which, as the folklore of the place required, members donned wooden shoes and blue aprons to salute the herring merchants of the port of Amsterdam.

Already hostile to Granoff, the Favezes would become still angrier upon discovering the notorious letter forgotten by Leclaire. Thanks to it, they symbolically held their adversary in a web he was completely unaware of. Once he learned the truth, he would lose all interest in the presidency. Lagache, for his part, would never know that the Favezes possessed the compromising letter, but he arranged matters, after Amsterdam, to keep Granoff at a distance from power. Granoff himself, moreover, gave him the opportunity simply by behaving in character. For the IPA, he represented a sure and valued source of information. He had the history of psychoanalysis at his finger tips, and Van der Leuw asked him to serve as an advisor on French affairs. But after Amsterdam, Granoff was no longer aligned with the new internal order. At the reception in the Hilton, Holms suggested to him that he give up his position. The battle was over and the peace required more serene leaders, not warriors. The veteran of the troika thus allowed himself to be politely dismissed by those he had served. Appalled by the closing ceremony in wooden shoes and blue aprons, he returned to Paris quite depressed and wrote to Lagache announcing his decision to withdraw from affairs: "Through a series of complications too long to recount," he wrote, "and ultimately with the help of God, I have brought this ship to safe port. . . . To safe port and without having sustained any damage. I deliver it over to you now. There is still much to be done. . . . I will inform the council when the year begins. Be good enough now to allow me a long rest. When I return, we can discuss the ways and opportunities I may have to be of service, if needed, to the association."[148]

During his presidential address of October 1965, Lagache acknowledged Granoff's position. He announced that Granoff was interested in nothing else than becoming involved with a Europe-wide organization, a perfect choice for the deployment of his talents as a diplomat. He dished out praise to all the society's leaders and issued a stirring eulogy of Georges Favez, a solid, lucid, well-meaning and taciturn man, and a good peasant of the Vaud canton to boot.[149] The following year, Favez became president of the APF.

Farewell Volodia! Your role thereafter would be that of the samurai, contemplating the victorious village in bitterness or parody. . . .

While Lagache was more or less consciously arranging his academic succession against Laplanche and his psychoanalytic succession against Granoff, J.-B. Pontalis—for a second time—chose his independence. After leaving Lacan during the split, he took leave of Sartre when the philosopher began supporting the Gauche prolétarienne and selling copies of La Cause du peuple. But before that break, he consolidated his position at the heart of the Gallimard fortress by creating the most prestigious psychoanalytic series on the French scene: "Connaissance de l'inconscient." The series was initiated in 1966 at the time of the publication of the Écrits. It would publish the great classics, from Freud's correspondence to the works of Winnicott and including Bruno Bettelheim's The Empty Fortress, which would sell more than 100,000 copies. "Connaissance de l'inconscient [Knowledge of the unconscious]," wrote Pontalis, "the paradoxical union of those terms itself bespeaks the daring of an undertaking which Freud's genius was able to bring off, if not to completion, since by the very nature of its object, it is perpetually to be taken up anew." [150]

Three years later the affair of the "tape-recorder man" erupted. Opposed to structuralism, an adversary of Lacan and Foucault, Sartre continued to settle his difficult score with Freudianism, which had always fascinated him. Against the ideals of the end of man, he defended a humanism of the rediscovered subject. It was in that context that a member of the editorial board of Les Temps modernes received in the mail a strange manuscript entitled Dialogue psychanalytique. It was the transcription by an anonymous party of an analytic session in which a patient rebelled against his therapist and attempted to impose the presence of a tape recorder on him. The document was clearly inspired by Sartre's play Les Séquestrés d'Altona [The Condemned of Altona], but had no publishing interest. Nevertheless, Sartre decided to print it and to write an introduction himself. That day, Pontalis was not present at the meeting of the editorial board, but, supporting Bernard Pingaud, he opposed its publication. Sartre proceeded with his plan nevertheless, and the issue appeared, accompanied by the commentaries of the three protagonists.

"A.'s text divided us deeply," wrote Sartre. "And then we reached a peaceful compromise that I hope will last. . . . I am not a "false friend" of psychoanalysis but a critical fellow traveler. I have no desire—and no means, moreover—to ridicule it. This dialogue will provoke smiles: It's always amusing to watch Punch beat up the policeman. Personally, I don't find it funny." [151] In fact, Sartre maintained that the dialogue revealed the eruption of the subject in the psychoanalyst's office, thus reversing the univocal relation of subject to object. In his reply, Pontalis preferred to address the philosopher rather than issue a commentary on the document. With his customary wiliness, he noted that Sartre recognized himself in the deforming mirror of the contestatory exploit through which a subject rose up against his oppressor. "One day the story should be written," he added, "of the ambigous relation, comprised of an equally deep attraction and reticence, that Sartre has entertained for some thirty years with psychoanalysis, and perhaps his entire work should be reread in that perspective." [152]

Pontalis would not recount that story. But fifteen years later, after Sartre's death, he published in his series *The Freud Scenario,* along with a lengthy commentary in which he explained that the philosopher had not written on Freud but fabricated for himself a "Freud scenario". . . . He had not expected the text to be as beautiful, as well-documented, and as moving.

After the affair of the tape-recorder man, Sartre adopted the positions of the Gauche prolétarienne on "destroying the university." Pontalis at that time decided to withdraw from *Les Temps modernes.* As of May 1970, his name no longer appeared on the editorial masthead. [153] But in leaving the house of Sartre, he did not lose his position. Already well established at Gallimard, he created in 1970 his own journal and gave it a quite significant title: *Nouvelle Revue de psychanalyse* (NRP). A condensation of the *Nouvelle Revue française* and the *Revue française de psychanalyse,* it was a sequel to the internal bulletin of the APF, which at the same time took on the name of *Documents et Débats,* continuing to serve as an internal publishing organ for the Association. The *NRP* was first of all a Gallimard journal before being a psychoanalytic journal, and also a Pontalis product before being a school publication. Nevertheless, it appeared twice annually with the discreet collaboration of the APF.

For its first issue, *Incidences de la psychanalyse,* the journal was endowed with a homebred editorial board: Guy Rosolato, Didier Anzieu, and Victor Smirnoff. To these were added two Gallimard authors, Jean Starobinski and Jean Pouillon; an English co-editor, M. Masud Khan, who was a member of the British society; and a "Lacanian" from the SPP, André Green. All were celebrities in their fields. As for their texts, which were often excellent, they were sufficiently moderate not to disturb the prevailing psychoanalytic order. As a result, as opposed to the wooden language of *Scilicet,* the rather musty style of the *RFP,* and the various convulsive manifestations that followed May '68, the *NRP* appeared as a reasonable, distinguished, and rather erudite space which shone through its very lack of agitation and flamboyance.

The *NRP* continues to administer in exemplary fashion the interests of Freudian culture, past and present, without ever yielding to the extravagances of the day. Its only competitors in terms of sales and impact outside the analytic villages are *Ornicar?* and the *Cahiers Confrontation.* To be sure, the journal publishes articles breaking with the psychoanalytic order, but on condition that they adopt the elegant style of place Dauphine and the rue Sébastien-Bottin: neither too Lacanian nor too anti-Lacanian, neither Marxist nor anti-Marxist, neither feminist nor antifeminist, neither structuralist nor antistructuralist, etc. In brief, it may be said that

Gallimard, Pontalis, and the APF were born to grow old and die together. In the catalogue it distributes to booksellers, the *NRP* presents itself as free of any affiliation with a psychoanalytic or academic institution or of allegiance to the words of any master. It is intent on respecting a single requirement: "making apparent, without effacing it, making intelligible, without pretending to master it, the work of the unconscious. Its wish is that its readers recognize in the intellectual moves it manifests something of the supple and decisive grace that belonged, that still belongs to *Gradiva.*" [154]

The journal's contents and the titles it adopted were well attuned to that will to suppleness and moderation: neither newly stamped concepts nor overbearing theories. The *NRP* has taken as its rule never to select as a theme for reflection a notion already having a defined status in psychoanalytic theory. Whence the idea of taking words of ordinary language as thematic titles for each issue: objects of fetishism, powers, bodily parts, effects and forms of illusion, etc. After several years, Pontalis brought two assistants onto the editorial board, François Gantheret, a member of the APF, and Michel Schneider, an author in the series who had frequented the byways of *L'Ordinaire du psychanalyste.*

In 1977, Pontalis decided to take an interest in history. To that end, he created a subseries entitled "La psychanalyse dans son histoire." There he published important documents devoted to the Freudian saga and, among them, the famous minutes (in three volumes) of the Vienna Psychoanalytic Society. In his presentation, he offered a conception of history that perfectly reflects the identity crisis specific to the APF. The time has not come, he said, for writing a history of psychoanalysis, because that history is secret and no one knows why a split takes place or is avoided. Pontalis announced, nevertheless, his intention to open up that domain to researchers, adding that that initiative had no equivalent at other publishing houses. Indeed. Then, in early 1980, he published in Gallimard's "Collection blanche" a novel in the style of Paul Bourget in which he recounted the loves of his youth. He was consecrated as a writer by the press. [155]

That same year, he founded a very serious annual review, *Le Temps de la réflexion,* intended as an organ for Gallimard and *NRP* authors, with Jean-Pierre Vernant and Michel Deguy added to the editorial board. Each volume was to have four sections: reflection, research, criticism, readings. It was (and continues to be) open to the exact sciences as well as to book reviews. On that score, it was intent on avoiding any air of mutual indulgence on the part of friends or colleagues. Unfortunately, already in its first volume, it was unable to escape the laws of the genre. Of eight French works commented on, eight were by extremely well-established authors, four were published by Gallimard, and two others, published elsewhere, came either from a house author or from a series directed by one of the members of the editorial board. In his (quite intelligent) presentation, Pontalis for once adopted a polemical tone. He denounced what the APF and the "movers" had always denounced, the dictatorial propensities of masters among the French intelligentsia, to which he opposed the associative spirit of his own society: an equitable division of knowledge among representatives of different disciplines. [156]

Four years later, in the "History" subseries, Pontalis published the work of a young English philosopher, *Le langage aux origines de la psychanalyse*. The field was thus declared open to the young and to researchers of the present period. The author, John Forrester, had translated certain of Lacan's seminars. But in his book, which was, all the same, devoted to Freud, the French master's name was not mentioned. That deliberate omission of a name that functioned as the work's hidden mainspring was explained by the author in his conclusion, where he referred to the "heady prose" and "ineffable ambiguities" of Lacan's analyses. Then he added: "The present work may be regarded as a series of prolegomena to a more direct approach to the Lacanian analytic school, which, in the 1950s, referred to a reading of Freud parallel to the one I have expounded in these pages. . . . Put differently, if we read Freud the way I have here, that reading can help us understand how Lacan could construct his theory by placing it under the sign of a return to Freud."[157]

On the back cover, the publisher specified the book's intentions and those of the "history" series as well. "In France," he wrote, "any reflection on the relations between language and psychoanalysis is immediately and quite rightly associated with the name of Lacan. What was needed no doubt was a view as distant and as singularly perspicacious as that of John Forrester, a young Anglo-Saxon academic, to approach the question as a researcher and not an epigone. If a debt to Lacan, to whom scant reference has deliberately been made in these pages, is not concealed, it is not a mere allegiance to a few formulas." This was a curious manner indeed for Pontalis to broach for the first time the subject of Lacan and his history in a series devoted to history: speaking of him without speaking of him, from England, since to speak of him in France would mean running the risk of manifesting an allegiance or passing for an epigone. What an obsession! There is an extraordinary analogy between the conception of history running through Pontalis's entire editorial enterprise and the very history of the APF, which has never stopped repressing its history while confessing to its worries about a master it had banished. Reciprocally, there was an astonishing contiguity between the conception of history present at the EFP, in which Lacan was seen as a great helmsman betrayed by "evil" sons, and the omnipresent place of a master haunted by a thematics of abandonment. Through those mirror-like figures two different ways of writing history may be intuited. In one case it is repressed, even as it is confessed so it may be forgiven; in the other, it is reinvented in the form of legend.

In 1985, after fifteen years of glory uninterrupted by shifts in the French intellectual landscape, the *NRP* decided to continue its triumphant march toward tranquillity. In an issue devoted to "Destin [Fate]," it awarded itself—in lines by Pontalis—a certificate of good conduct for the past and good luck for the future: "A thirtieth issue, fifteen years of life: and if the time had come for a reflective pause? Not a detailed retrospective or a tally sheet, just a brief period of halt, as this collection devoted to fate invites. . . . When I worry about the future, I hear voices here and there whispering to me in friendly (?) tones: the *NRP*, but it's become an institution! Which, as everyone knows, is a capital sin. I personally have nothing against institutions, so long as they fulfill their functions, neither more nor less. . . . Should the moment come when the *NRP* is no longer moved by the exigency—that is, the desire—to think through the effects of analytic practice, we will put an end to it. That moment has not yet come." [158]

Even as the founders of the APF have shared the prime academic, clinical, and editorial territories of Freudian France, they have never ceased lamenting collectively over their history. In that respect, the addresses delivered each year to plenary sessions by the brother-presidents are true masterpieces.[159] Occasionally they praise the successful functioning of the institution, its numerous students, splendid activities, and the prestigious writings of its members; occasionally they regret that the same institution is too poorly known because of its lack of dynamism, its sclerosis, and its inability to call itself into question. Such is the permanent identity of the APF; a narcissistic group haunted by the ghost of Hamlet.

And yet the institutional adventure of that association exists beyond the words of its partners. On the eve of the May events, the Association was only four years old and the thirty-four members composing it had almost all come from the former SFP. Only its students were new. In that context, protest came not from the base but from the titular members themselves, who were aware of the unduly rigid character of their training procedures. In April 1968, Berge and Anzieu, who were president and secretary, distributed a proposal relative to the selection of training analysts. They proposed eliminating preselection and considering as a personal analysis, for a period of two years, any analysis authorized by the selection committee, with that analysis open to being validated after the fact: "Before knowing whether a candidate is suited for becoming an analyst, one must know if he is suited for undergoing his own analysis. Something which cannot be illuminated unless he is subjected to the ordeal of the couch." [160] The authors also proposed the elimination of any list of training analysts, it being understood that only titular members were authorized to undertake training analyses. Finally, they insisted on maintaining, during a transition period, the category of training analysts, who had two functions to fulfill: ensuring controls of the first therapies conducted by their students, and judging acceptability for control on the selection committee. That proposal kept the APF of 1964 as it was, while introducing a reform that attempted to give concrete form to a mode of functioning that was already in fact in practice.

When the May events erupted, the principal stars of the APF had, on the whole, opinions leaning toward the Left. Widlöcher was a Socialist and unwilling to make concessions to *gauchisme*. Pontalis was still part of the *Temps Modernes* family, but refrained from any extravagant stands. Laplanche dreamed of revolution while recalling his Trotskyist youth, and Anzieu was intent on writing a book on contestation.[161] As for Granoff, he was afire with enthusiasm for the heroes of the student rebellion, in memory of his grandfather and ancestors, who had been deported to Siberia. He felt all the more a Slav in that he had never touched the soil of the motherland. What he had in mind was the failed revolution of his parents, who were Socialists of old Russia, that Russia that had been reinvented in a fantasy of emigration.

Wladimir was bored at the APF. He was nostalgic for the golden age, the troika, and feverish weekends in London. He missed Lacan. He thus envisaged a final comeback that would have the savor of a Renaissance banquet. Thanks to the financial assistance of an American philanthropist, he disposed of sufficient funds to create a society to be called "Association pour l'étude des sciences humaines" and which could serve as a locale for the APF. He had prospected various properties in Neuilly and bought a particularly decrepit townhouse which he proposed to transform for the use of an intellectual community—with a central atrium, a gymnasium, a swimming pool, and a library. He had in mind a collective organization of a libertarian or convivial cast. Before long, he began gathering his friends in the available rooms, and each spoke of his work. Then, in June, he issued invitations, erected a podium, bought fans, and organized a party with huge racks of lamb grilled on a spit. Dressed entirely in white, he greeted his guests in the manner of a slightly withdrawn host. Students were invited. In the course of the discussion, Pujol was questioned on the subject of the confidentiality of files. Applicants wanted to know why they had been accepted or rejected and what the rationale was behind the rule of silence. At summer's end, Granoff renounced his dream of donating a building to the APF and modifying it in accordance with his desires. The fireworks would remain engraved in the memories of those present; it recalled receptions at Guitrancourt. Whence a certain distrust aroused by the veteran of the troika, who was suspected of wanting to seize power and manufacture a miniature Vincennes.[162]

The Berge-Anzieu reform proposal had been buried, but numerous discussions occurred in the atmosphere of May. Groups were formed; relations were opened between members of the APF and the commission led by Jean-Luc Donnet. All opinions converged on the conclusion that serious reforms had to be introduced into the training curricula of the two French components of the IPA. Rebellion was threatening in all corners of the empire—in Sweden, in Holland, in Austria. . . .

As of 1969, Jean Laplanche took charge of a reform project compatible with his own teaching of psychoanalysis in the university. He was intent on giving the APF that institutional identity which it lacked in relation to the École freudienne and the SPP. According to Laplanche, those two groups made personal analysis dependent on adherence to the ideals of the institution. In order to establish a distance from that mode of functioning, he proposed to implement an extraterritoriality of therapy, conforming to the collegial spirit reigning at the APF. The project thus consisted of abolishing the preselection system in order to preserve personal analyses, which would have to be validated after the fact as constituting training without any intervention by the institution. The institution's authority would then come to bear on the control, which remained the only way of selecting candidates. A proposal thus oriented was drawn up and distributed to members. After a lengthy investigation and numerous discussions, it was rejected by a majority of the members. The institutional malaise was nonetheless gaining ground and the colleagues were for a while considering closing shop or initiating a split. Two years later, at Pontalis's behest, the proposal was again presented and was this time approved at the plenary session of June 1972.[163]

Three titular members, and they were not the most negligible, were opposed even though they submitted to the majority decision: Widlöcher, Anzieu, and Granoff. The first, who was close to the powers of the IPA, remained a partisan of the classical system; the second feared an excessive laxness; and the third rejected the prospect of the society becoming too solemn and academic an association. "We are going," he wrote, "after introducing subjects to analysis in the way that seems to us the least onerous, to attempt to replace the intrusion of arbitrariness in their lives, and thus in ours. And to do so, rather, I should say, than augment the weight of an association which has never been, and it's a good thing, anything but the parody of an institution (and only its parody was burdensome); we are going to attempt to truly create an institution. We no longer want to be jokers. But is it certain that we're right?" [164]

A few months after the vote, Granoff vented his bitterness in a contemptuous letter to Georges Favez on the subject of the Vaucresson Discussions and a colloquium at the PLM Hotel: "So you were very careful to make sure the APF wasn't eaten up by the little piggies (not quite ex-Lacanians, skillful in dangerous ruses). . . . That APF guarded by you against tempters whose weight you can now assess . . . is now going to start humming its accompaniment to the tune of its older and true sister, the SPP. The mini-congress at the PLM, in its postwar style, will be a worthy prelude to the international congress. . . . As for me, since my last attempt, which definitively opened my eyes as to what truly interests me in that group, so well prepared to shield itself from any dangerous contamination, I have returned to my precious studies." [165] Granoff by then knew what the others knew of him and did not want to know during the negotiation: Juliette had returned the letter to him. . . . After all that time spent at war and then in a parody of war, he undertook an immense seminar on the history of psychoanalysis, thus joining up with the romance of his origins: "I would like to be the one of whom it is said, 'He's the one who tells stories.' A story. One's own story. Does one ever tell anything other than one's story?" Out of that far-ranging discourse would come a book, *Filiations*, then another, *La pensée et le féminin*.[166]

The reform allowed the APF to bestow on itself a juridico-administrative identity conforming to its individualist and elitist ideals. The statutes, entirely conceived and written by Jean Laplanche, are attuned to the idiosyncrasies of the Association. They are the most copious in the entire history of psychoanalysis in France: thirty-seven articles for juridical administration, fifty-four for house rules. A true Benedictine's labor. In 1972, the APF thus became statutorily what it had always been: a nonexpansive, barely bureaucratic society, without excessive pathology, and semidemocratic. In brief it resembled a school of leaders—brothers and old friends.

It was composed thereafter of four categories of members, only two of which had a real existence: the titular and associate members. The affiliates and honorary members existed juridically, but no quorum of individuals ever gave them concrete presence within the group. Students had the same position as in the SPP or the OPLF: They paid dues, but were not members and had no status. The APF was directed by an administrative council elected at a plenary session and composed of six necessarily titular members. Plenary sessions thus had real weight, but the equality between the two categories of members stopped where the exercise of power began. The associates had no other right than to vote. Only titular members could sit on the council, distributing positions of leadership among themselves. Moreover, it befell them to elect new titular members from a pool of associates who were also elected by them. The associates thus had no power over the conduct of the institution outside plenary sessions.

The training institute was incorporated into the Association but enjoyed a certain autonomy in relation to the society, which delegated authority to it. It was directed either by the president of the APF or by a director chosen by the council. It consisted of two sections: the *institute committee,* which was in charge of teaching, seminars, lectures, or scientific meetings, and the *training committee,* which replaced the former selection committee. It administered the selection of candidates and their access to different stages of the curriculum. It was composed of nine members elected at a plenary session from among the titular members on a slate of analysts which was itself prepared by the titular members. Among those therapists associates were included. And *there* was the statutory innovation: A candidate could freely choose his couch from a list of associate or titular members registered with the training institute. But he could also apply for supervision after having been trained by a psychoanalyst belonging to another society. His training would be validated after the fact.

The notions of *didacticien* [training analyst] and *preselection* were dropped. The applicant interested in being trained at the APF is to submit a written request to the secretary of the training committee. The latter then advises the candidate to meet with three members of the committee whom the candidate chooses. At the conclusion of a report, three recommendations are possible: authorization to undertake a supervised analysis, to attend courses, and to participate in scientific activities; rejection of the application; delay of decision. Refusals are not accompanied by any commentary. If the candidate is accepted, he selects his supervisor from a list of analysts practicing at the training institute. Control sessions are individual and weekly and must involve the analysis of an adult neurotic.

The first control lasts about three years, in the course of which a personal analysis may or may not be continued. It is then validated by a commission of three analysts designated by the training committee. These receive the evaluation of the supervisor and meet with the candidate if they deem it useful. The commission then validates the first control, which functions as an acceptance for a second control performed under identical conditions. Then, after the writing of a short thesis, the candidate can apply for the rank of associate. The system has the advantage of preserving the personal analysis from any institutional intrusion and of bringing the weight of selection to bear at the level of controls. It eliminates the horrid notion of the "special case," which wreaked so much havoc in the SPP, and does away with any notion of "command therapy." It also has the advantage of preventing the pathological development of a mythology of a perpetually violated confidentiality. But it has the drawback, because the statutes are insufficiently democratic, of infantilizing therapists by maintaining them in a student role until a rather advanced age. It is thus poorly suited to check the process of "gerontocrization" which has affected the APF from its inception.

Given the years necessary for an analysis, then for the successive validation of two controls and a short thesis, no candidate can hope to become an associate before age forty or a titular member before about fifty. In reforming itself so as to prevent any risk of laxness, glaring incompetence, or expansion, the APF has thus potentially become a society of the old. In that sense, it is ahead of its time, since it will only be around the year 2000 that France will know a reign of retirees. Even before the adoption of the reforms, in May 1972, Victor Smirnoff observed that the average age of candidates for training had increased considerably. "Ought we to conclude that the image of the APF," he asked, "has drawn to us an aged and almost marginal clientele that is frequently removed from clinical practice? Is this a general development in France as a whole?" [167]

In the following years, the reforms did not bring any solution to that thorny problem. It was for that reason that in the face of the gerontocracy of one group and the bureaucracy of the other, the young preferred to choose their couches within the Lacanian movement: EFP or OPLF. But as Donnet emphasized, their tendency was above all to wander among all the societies—one's analysis here, supervision there, a second analysis still elsewhere, etc. Whence the emergence, among the fifth French psychoanalytic generation, of a hostility toward *all* constituted societies, a reaction from which Confrontation would benefit. "The success enjoyed by extra-institutional manifestations (such as Confrontation, for example)," Smirnoff emphasized in 1977, "bears witness to a dissatisfaction, not to say a disgruntlement, on the part of a large portion of analysts in training. That relative decathexis of the institution by a growing number of its members cannot augur anything encouraging, in our view, and even less anything to be envied." [168]

In 1976, despite intense scientific and publishing activities, the APF could still not succeed in putting a halt to its crisis of stagnation. It was suffering from the ill it had always wanted to cure itself of, being an appendix between two giants, without any precise identity. In June, the president observed a growing absenteeism on the part of its members and a tendency to a certain autodidacticism. Before long a minor crisis revealed the drawbacks of self-sufficiency as a functional principle. A woman candidate whose training had been validated was not accepted as an associate because of a negative vote from the titular college. In opposition to that decision, eight furious members stormed out of the meeting in protest. Thereafter any internal nominations would become impossible. A year later, the president noted with bitterness that the APF had not registered any promotions in the course of the year. He again brandished the threat of old age and extinction, compared the habits of the association to the reshuffling of government cabinet members and explained that the group was functioning according to the slogan: We take the same and begin all over again. In order to put an end to the blockage, he asked that the administrative council be representative of the various currents and theoretical tendencies cohabiting in the society. He also requested that a certain continuity be assured at times when the council was being renewed so that members familiar with matters previously under discussion would continue to be present. [169]

The following year, the APF adopted a statutory modification intended to make the election of associates less rigid and to accord them a bit more leverage in training activities. Thereafter a required quorum would be two-thirds (instead of three-fourths) for the election of associate and titular members. A distinction was introduced between the election of associates and that of titular members. For the former, an absolute majority sufficed, whereas for the latter a two-thirds majority was needed. If a quorum was not obtained, elections would take place no matter what the number of those present.[170] Two changes were made in the rules governing the training committee. One concerned the validation of prior activities and the other dispositions to be taken in the event of a candidate's failure. For validation of a candidate's prior curriculum, a vote by the titular college would not be required if the reporting member's evaluation was not formally contradicted. That evaluation would be valid as admission. In the contrary case, a two-thirds majority vote would be necessary. In the event of a candidate's failing, a complicated system was established allowing for the creation of a category of "guests." Under certain conditions, these could be allowed to participate in the activities of the Association.

All those measures were quite excellent but insufficient to stem the tide of history. At the beginning of the 1980s, the situation of the APF had not substantially changed. It still resembled nothing so much as itself, its prestigious journal, its camaraderie, a club or a private university.

At the conclusion of this extended analysis of the institutional functioning of the four major components of the contemporary French psychoanalytic movement, a remark should be made concerning the period from 1964 to 1980. Only the EFP, the APF, and the Fourth Group attempted a genuine Freudian adventure in the matter of the training of analysts. All three, in different ways, succeeded in placing the institution in the service of psychoanalysis, and not the reverse. All three laid the grounds for a true preservation of the personal analysis and abolished any form of intrusion by a bureaucratic power on the couch. All three eliminated the notion of the "command psychoanalysis," concerning which it was acknowledged that it had nothing to do with an exploration of the unconscious. As opposed to those three components, the SPP half reformed itself. It is today, even in the eyes of the IPA, a society suffering from its clans. It is under surveillance, unable to conduct its own affairs. The only society in France to have broken off all organic links with the Lacanian epic, it is the only one not to have benefited directly from the teaching of a man whose presence profoundly transformed the psychoanalytic landscape of the country, as much through his innovations in training as through his theoretical position. After breaking that connection, the SPP gradually became "pathological." Alongside it, the three other components bear the indelible trace of the Lacanian saga. All three owe their innovative thoughts on training procedures to the history of Lacanianism. They owe them to it because they *are* that history in its very brilliance.

11 The École Freudienne de Paris: The Collapse

I. Last Song

In certain circumstances, a book may reveal itself to be the vehicle of the anxieties and follies of a *milieu*. Such was the case of *Un destin si funeste*, published in December 1976.[1] At the time, the author was still unknown, but he was about to be consecrated as a thinker by the Parisian press. François Roustang owed all his training to the EFP. During the events at Vincennes, he made clear his opposition to the new line. He was not the only one in the École to denounce the institutional dogmatism of psychoanalytic societies, but he was the first in France to revive the hypnotic symptom in a deliberate and concerted manner. Roustang took up (without correcting it) the Crébillon line of verse quoted by Lacan and forced *dessein* [design] into *destin* [fate] to produce one of the most celebrated successes of the psychoanalytic literature of the period.

The book appeared at a key juncture in the history of Lacanianism. In its iconoclasm it cast a glaring light on the bankruptcy of the great structuralist breakthrough, whose impact was no longer proving fertile. The theoretical antihumanism of Lacan, Foucault, and Althusser would thereafter be criticized as though it were a practical antihumanism responsible for a totalitarian vision of the world in which the individual no longer had any rights other than those of a narrow determinism. At the same time the notion of "man" was revalorized in the name of the responsibility of the conscious subject, while any system of a symbolic order was rejected in favor of an exaltation of the ideals of freedom. Without the slightest effort to think things through, the Parisian intelligentsia began declaring that Lacanianism was the most accomplished version of a Gulag of the mind.

Drawing on that rediscovered humanism, François Roustang recharged the batteries of social psychology in order to situate Freudian theory midway between science and delirium. Reduced to a process of subjective rape, it was evaluated by the standard of a pure transferential relationship. Any doctrine was thus the weapon of a form of madness intended to drive the other mad. As a result, the position of the student in the face of a *maître* consisted in a specific alienation which allowed the latter to spare himself the risks of a true confrontation with madness. Roustang reduced theoretical creativity to the primacy of a transference that would never be dissolved and could be conceived on the model of hypnosis. In his book, he accused Lacanianism of all the defects of religion, an opium for—or art of—manipulating crowds. He denounced the idolatrous aspects of the *milieu* in order to promote, in the name of a consoled ego, a genuine calling into question of all organized systems. The book in part renewed the critique formulated in *L'anti-Oedipe*. But instead of the libertarian path trod by Deleuze and Guattari, it was deliberately channeled in the direction of a solemn return to moral order: the individual against society, the profession against adventure, man against thought, itself judged to be the source of every dictatorship. *Un destin si funeste* provoked a considerable commotion on the scene of the EFP, by way of Confrontation, where its author scored an impressive triumph. It should be stated that the book gave concrete reality to a crisis that was already there and had been prepared for by the advent of the matheme.

In *Ornicar?*, Charles Melman declared war on what he vulgarly called a "festin peu honnete" [a barely honest feast]. He accused the author of having depended on a typographical error in the *Écrits* in order to turn *dessein* [design] into *destin* [fate]. "The book," he wrote, "draws up what pretends to be a tonic assessment of the life of psychoanalytic societies, reduced to a study of mores. Curiously, the clinical point of view, from which current fashion would shield the psychopath because of the reification it would mortify him with, becomes ideal when turned against those who have made use of it." [2]

Jacques Derrida, in turn, commented on the affair during a long session of Confrontation devoted to *Glas*. He noted that Roustang had not noted the transition from *dessein* to *destin* in Lacan's text and that Charles Melman simply accepted the typographical error without inquiring into its meaning. He then called the latter a *facteur* (mailman): "In the English language," he wrote, "which, from its base in Poe's tale, directs all these comings and goings, not without itself being somewhat surprised or overtaken in the process, *facteur* is *mailman*. An ear alive to the word I just pronounced will not translate it as "male man," a tautology, or—confusing languages—as a "man who *mêle tout* [mixes everything up]" or as "mail *qui ment*" [that lies], French-style, but as *facteur*. Mailman is the common word for *facteur*; it's a composite word, a divisible signifier, as in *air mail*, when a dispatch is urgent, or *mail box*." [3] Finally, Derrida recounted a strange rumor circulating in the United States at the time Lacan was lecturing there. It pretended that Derrida had for ten years, in America, been Rudolph Loewenstein's analyst. Thus, after having been dispatched by Lacan to Abraham's couch, he was placed by rumor in a curious chair indeed: as analyst of Lacan's analyst and thus "prototrace" of the French psychoanalytic movement, experienced as a legend. Seen from America, the structuralism of the 1960s was lapsing into madness. Seen from France, it became the baleful fate—*destin funeste*—of a Lacanianism reduced to its puns and its cryptic language.

Three months after the publication of *Un destin si funeste*, a tragic event provoked the downfall of the *passe* within the EFP. In March 1977, a young psychoanalyst in the École, Juliette Labin, committed suicide in a mountain chalet by swallowing a fatal dose of medication which she had carefully prepared. Analyzed by Abdoucheli, close to Lacan, Dolto, and Clavreul, she belonged to that fifth psychoanalytic generation which had known its finest days at the École. She had been recognized as an analyst with the rank of AME. An excellent therapist, she had an enormous number of patients from the barricades. And she was not an ordinary analyst. Neither neurotic, nor "normalized," she had invested her whole life in the Lacanian adventure, for which she had true passion. She had always felt violently persecuted by institutions. For her friends, she was a symbol, and although she did not care for banners, she represented the best of what Lacanianism had produced: the risk of a genuine attentiveness to the unconscious.

Around 1976, she began to suffer seriously from the effects of the reigning dogmatism, the fatigue of the barons, and a sense of twilight approaching with undue haste. She thus gave herself over to the ordeal of the *passe* as a veritable act of defiance. She asked to be "judged" by the seniors whose competence she barely acknowledged, but by whom she was nevertheless intent on being heard. She would be the victim of the inconsistencies of the institutional machine. According to the rules, she had the right to come before the jury, being already an AME. However, in those conditions, she would have to bear witness to a "passage" that had already taken place and whose status no one was able to specify with precision. According to the circular of February 1969, which had no legal bearing, she was to be authorized by her analyst to undergo the *passe*. But since she was no longer in analysis, there was no one who could give her that authorization. This mattered little, since the jury did not know whether it was to act on the legal procedure or according to the February circular, which had never been incorporated into the statutes. As a result, Juliette Labin gave herself over to the ordeal although she was precisely the kind of candidate whose "real" request or demand should have been heard before authorizing her to embark on such an adventure. And of course, the ordeal went poorly for her. Overwhelmed by candidates who had never been admitted, the jury members lingered a full year before giving her a reply. She could not bear the wait. On January 27, 1977, she was received by Claude Conté, who conveyed to her the jury's negative decision. On March 4, in a state of depression, she killed herself.[4]

Suicides by both patients and analysts exist in all psychoanalytic societies. In that respect there were as many at the EFP as at the APF, the Fourth Group, or the SPP. But the sole difference between the École freudienne and the others was a function of the public character of the Lacanian adventure. It had always had the merit of not keeping its failings secret nor hiding its skeletons in the closet. Rumor, moreover, had it that Jacques Lacan had had more (future) suicides on his couch than other analysts. That item is both true and false. It is true, if one takes into account the extremely large number of analysands that Lacan accepted for treatment during his career. It is also true if one realizes that he had the courage not to reject the truly suicidal cases that others had refused. But it is false, if it is transformed into an accusation intended to prove that Lacan's technique may have been more murderous than those of his colleagues in other groups. All therapists are confronted with this question, and if they are honest, they all realize that certain suicides are unpreventable, with or without therapy. The real problem is that of deciding who dares—or does not dare—to accept for analysis suicidal cases. Now Lacan had that daring quite often, while others preferred not to run the risk.

If Juliette Labin did not commit suicide because of the *passe*, that ordeal was nonetheless for her the motivating factor in a process that led to her death. Since that act occurred at a time of particular crisis for the EFP, it was itself anticipatory of the school's swan song. Juliette visited ruin on the adventure that had nourished her and the adventure would not survive her. With that suicide the École entered into the first phase of its death throes, and it was women who initiated the battle.

On March 12, a first open letter was sent to the jury, phrased as follows: "Juliette Labin's case is a *passe*-related suicide. . . . The *passe* is an infernal machine and the implacable instrument of a madness for power. . . . Perhaps Juliette would have committed suicide without the *passe,* but that would have been her business, instead of which you have furthered her disintegration." [5]

Following that letter, each of the jury members in turn took a position. Mathis, Conté, Safouan, Clavreul, and Ginette Raimbault stubbornly refused to hear the truth of the case, and maintained that it was less a function of the *passe* than of the candidate's psychical structure. But unable to account for the death which had ensued in the course of the procedure, they preferred to dodge the issue. Only Lacan and Leclaire accepted the idea that the *passe* might in itself harbor a risk. "I declared," wrote Lacan, "that the psychoanalyst derives his authority only from himself. That is undeniable, but carries a risk with it. I add that that risk, in the *passe,* is one he is not obliged to run. He gives himself over to it deliberately." [6]

The affair became public with Jeanne Favret-Saada's letter of resignation, which was published in *Les Temps modernes.*[7] A psychoanalyst and a specialist on witchcraft, she had refused for a year to be Juliette Labin's *passeuse. Her* open letter was more interesting than the previous one. She was still more critical of the glaring incompetence of the jury members: "The recent suicide of Juliette Labin," she wrote, "shortly after she had gone through the *passe,* the silence or merely defensive reactions her death has aroused on the part of jury members, and the spectacle of a psychoanalytic institution stubbornly maintaining your decision rather than accepting the risk of questioning it, all those reasons lead me to leave the École freudienne de Paris and to ask you to acknowledge that fact. I have taken this decision in near solitude, without asking anyone to follow me and without having the intention of joining any other psychoanalytic society. For I believe that at present all the psychoanalytic institutions are bad, although certain of them are worse than others; and that if one hopes to sustain an analytic discourse, one is better off doing without the illusory guarantees constituted by psychoanalytic schools, groups, and associations.

Jeanne Favret-Saada explained that the reflections exchanged by the members of the jury were worthy of the tabloid *France-Dimanche* and that the *passe,* under cover of the most far-reaching analytic experiment, was in fact instituting a space beyond analysis. Whereupon she emphasized that the jury remained invariably silent when confronted with Lacan, concluding: "That the institution of the *passe* is enjoying so great a success may be understood: The *passeurs* finish their analysis on the cheap (such was probably my case), the *passants* manage to dispense with having any at all, and the jury derives pleasure—although with a measure of perplexity—from the scraps of life that are served up to it. That on top of everything else a title is awarded, and the most prestigious of all, needless to say, does not spoil things in the slightest."

A second *passeuse,* Anne Levallois, who had been analyzed by Serge Leclaire, also spoke of her experience in a lecture at the Oceanographic Institute, organized by a member of the directorate, Irène Roubleff. Her text had been prepared before Labin's suicide, but that death conferred on it an exceptional gravity. The secretary of the EFP tried in vain to prevent the lecture so as to stem the growing chaos, but he was not successful. Gradually, testimony of all sorts relating to experiences of the *passe* would abound, resulting in a total destabilization of the EFP. "What remains is that the *passe* continues to fascinate," Anne Levallois noted, "fascinates to such an extent that it may be wondered whether Lacan's desire to delve further into the transition from analysand to analyst has not provoked in the École freudienne the phantasm of a charnel house from which all extremes of sexual pleasure derive, making the *passe* into a Sirens' rock and bringing onto the institutional scene what, to all appearances, does not take place in the analysis of analysts." [8] After that presentation, Anne Levallois did not leave the École, but resigned from her function as *passeuse*.

The destabilization of the EFP worked to the benefit of the Millerian tendency and its allies. The procedure had in fact been implemented by Lacan's fellow travelers and had aroused a rather lively interest on the part of most clinicians in the École. The equilibrium of the École was dependent on the success of the *passe*, in opposition to the Vincennes experiment, which was regarded as dogmatic, extrapsychoanalytic, and academic. And now, all at once, the jury members began to appear as incompetents. They had not produced any serious written work concerning an activity that had been going on for ten years, and they were now being disavowed from within the fortress itself. Against the defeated clinicians, Jacques-Alain Miller could thus shore up his power and situate himself as the savior of a Lacanianism facing imminent ruin. It was for that reason that—precisely when it was decided to hold an organizational meeting devoted to the problem—he published a special issue of *Ornicar?* on the *passe*, in which he shrewdly came down on both sides of the issue. In his article entitled "Introduction aux paradoxes de la passe," he avoided mentioning Labin's suicide, but referred the reader to Jeanne Favret-Saada's text. Then he declared his colors: "Ten years is enough already—for evaluating the results of the 'proposition of October 9, 1967, on psychoanalysts of the École.' In addition, an emotion has imposed itself and settled upon the said school concerning the subject of the *passe* and it is sufficiently strong to warrant the calling of an organizational meeting. . . . I will not beat around the bush in saying that in so far as the jury is concerned, the proposal's promise has not been kept." [9]

Charles Melman, who had not been favorable to the procedure, gave Miller his support by criticizing Anne Levallois's lecture. He took advantage of the occasion to recall that those who had split in 1969 were incapable of opposing the *passe* with any genuine project. Then he took a hard line in denouncing the complaints and blustering of the opposition. Finally he called the letters addressed to the jury on the occasion of Labin's death slanderous. [10]

The study "days" devoted to the *passe* took place at Deauville during the month of January 1978. They took on the statutory character of an organizational meeting of the École. Extremely silent, Jacques Lacan listened attentively to the interventions. Occasionally he would prick up his ears and ask a speaker to raise his voice. At times he seemed plunged in his own thoughts. At others, he would break out in anger. Still majestic, the old doge would thereafter be confronted with the failure of his school and the violence of a crisis that would bring it to its dissolution. The time was tragic: All began to speak openly about the master's death.

Moustapha Safouan was first to enter the arena, with thoughts about the October proposal—ten years later. But instead of stating what had been expected of him and criticizing the inconsistencies and failings of the jury, he launched into an apologetic reconstruction of the procedure. The discussion which followed was dramatic. Michèle Montrelay asked Safouan why he had not seen fit to ask that he be replaced on the jury in the course of ten years, and Lacan answered for him, believing the question had been addressed to him. The discussion bogged down. After Safouan, Ginette Raimbault came to speak on behalf of the jury, agreeing to speak at greater length on the conduct of the *passe*. She explained first of all that several imaginary uses of the *passe* were possible. Some consisted of offering a presentation illustrating Lacanian theory, whereas others sought to contradict it. Then, she commented on the silence of the jury and the kind of response given, indicating the totalizing place occupied by Lacan in the jury's discussions. "The weight and the presence of Lacan among them is beyond doubt," she said, "and all the greater in that for the majority he was and remains their analyst. Lacan addresses the jury, occasionally, as elsewhere, speaking as a master, although he has said, 'If I dared inaugurate this experiment, it was not so that I might intervene in it.' That he speaks there as a master, however, is a fact; it is perhaps to be deplored, but it is a fact. This does not suffice to explain the silence of the jury members among themselves. Each distinguishes himself only scantily from the others. Each attempts to say in his own name what he thinks, but always ends up more or less referring to prior texts of Lacan." [11] Then Ginette Raimbault observed that the jury had discovered that a number of AMEs were not analysts, although they were being endorsed by the École, and that ae a result the functioning of the admissions jury was being questioned. She underscored this unprecedented fact: During the procedure, the candidate-*passants* did not speak of either their private lives or their sexuality. Finally, she raised the central question encountered by the jury: "Can one be a neurotic and a psychoanalyst? What can a psychoanalyst hear and understand according to his own psychical structure? . . . Can one be a homosexual and a psychoanalyst? Can one be mad and a psychoanalyst? And why not, after all, raise the question: Can one be a woman and a psychoanalyst? For women, this is tantamount to raising the question of the legitimacy of the social function of women, since, to be sure, it has never occurred to psychoanalysts to ask themselves: Can one be a man and a psychoanalyst?" [12]

That talk was the best given on the subject of the *passe* as the procedure had evolved over ten years at the EFP. And it was no doubt not by chance that it was given by a woman, the only one, after Françoise Dolto, to have sat on a promotions jury. It was, in fact, more often the women than the men in the École who played the role of challengers of the system. For that reason they were often called "hysterical," as though they had something in common with the "madwomen" of the Salpêtrière. And yet there was in that women's movement within the EFP a certain justice, since it was Lacan who had been the first in France to lay the grounds for a new meditation on female sexuality.

In January 1978, given the state of the crisis in the EFP, Ginette Raimbault's report was nevertheless quite inadequate. It presented certain facts, but in no way raised the veil concealing the criteria retained by the jury in deciding what precisely constituted an AE and, more generally, a psychoanalyst. The *passe* thus revealed itself to be a failure. Instead of conveying an understanding of what a "passage" consisted in or showing the nature of a teaching stemming from the analytic couch, it revealed the limits an institution can bestow on itself in constructing the criteria on which it bases its selection. Having become an infernal machine, the *passe* was a vehicle of madness and the institution was going through its motions to no clear end at all.

After Ginette Raimbault, Serge Leclaire intervened in turn by way of a fiction. He spoke of UFOs, of unidentified subjects, and of the death of the unknown soldier. In the discussion, he was asked why, after having made those comments, he was still a member of the promotions jury. He did not reply. He had done his time and in July would cease all official activity at the École. Following him the candidate-*passants* intervened one after the other. Nicole Pépin recounted her experience: "I was bursting [*j'en crevais*], I mean bursting; I'm not saying 'dying,' because it was unanalyzed and I didn't know what the deterioration was. I was no longer in analysis and as a result I didn't have anywhere else to talk about it." [13] Finally, Irène Diamantis, who had been analyzed by Leclaire, related her story: "On October 28, Ginette Raimbault asked me to ask Safouan (who was absent on February 9, listening to my *passeurs*) to give me a hearing and decide. I ask the promotions jury to acknowledge my refusal. That tardy demand made of a single member of the jury misconstrues the fact that one of the effects of the *passe* is precisely to step out of the circuit of requests. I am alarmed that a member of the jury would be sufficiently frivolous to impel a candidate nine months later to make a request. That attitude and the general embarrassment demonstrate that defending my refusal here would still be too much." [14]

Jean Clavreul then intervened to announce that the promotions jury had no intention of discussing its criteria: "I am well aware," he said, "that the jury is expected to offer the fruits of its experience, which is already so many years old, in the form of a masterable theory of the *passe*. But on that score you are also surely aware that you can only be disappointed and, moreover, are quite prepared to conclude that the promotions jury is not fulfilling its function." [15] Four years later, he would add this: "It is more important for us to acknowledge what our silence meant, that is, our acquiescence, our complicity in the face of the increasingly burdensome silence of Lacan, not only in his seminar, but also at meetings of the directorate and the juries." [16]

As a conclusion, Lacan exclaimed, "To be sure, it's a total failure, this *passe* business." [17] Thus did he himself disavow the promotions jury over which he had presided for ten years. The path of power was thereafter open to a different Lacanian youth and its most established representative in the seraglio: Jacques-Alain Miller. In the interim, at the plenary session in July, Michèle Montrelay and Françoise Dolto were elected to the jury in place of Leclaire and Conté. During the next twelve months, they attempted to transform the way the procedure worked.

During the autumn of that same year, Lacan traveled to Guitrancourt by car, escorted by the young mathematician Pierre Soury, who accompanied him in the tying of his Borromean knots. On the Paris beltway, the car swerved off the road before coming to a stop on the shoulder. Lacan was not hurt, but after that minor accident, he seemed diminished. He prepared his seminar for the new school year on topology and time. At the opening session, for the first time, in the presence of a silent and stunned audience, he lost his capacity to speak. Everyone stared at the old man, deprived of the sublime voice that had held Freudian France breathless for thirty years. "It doesn't matter," the audience responded, "we still love you." That day, on the podium, Lacan had erred in the equations he scribbled on the blackboard. "He turned to us," Catherine David has written, "quite slowly, he spoke of the mistaken detail and then adjourned the session. It was then that the shout of love came." [18]

In February 1979, a sumptuous masked ball was held in the apartment of Michèle Montrelay, on the rue Guynemer. The last spark of a movement on the wane, it brought together for one long night several figures in this history, somewhere between Confrontation and the École freudienne. The Enlightenment had been specially favored by the guests, as though all could sense the arrival, during this last libertine exercise, of the end of a regime and the advent of an as yet unknown order. Dressed as a matron of the *belle époque,* the hostess seemed to be staging a brief revival of the Guermantes salon, precisely at that moment when the narrator's rediscovery of History can be intuited. Amidst the wax museum, all in gold and purple, were Claude Rabant and René Tostain in the silken garb of two marquis. They were handsome and well built. In his Harlequin's costume, befitting the coloration of his shifting moods, François Roustang attempted a *pas de deux;* he had taken lessons in anticipation of the ball. Costumed as an ancient Greek, Christian Simatos rediscovered his ethnic identity and seemed to have learned his role from Richard Burton at Pompeii. As for Serge Leclaire, he was alone in having dared to cross-dress, flaunting the flounces of a Marquise de Pompadour. His wife, Geneviève, accompanied him, dressed as a sailor. Late in the evening, sporting a black hat, René Major joined the guests. That evening Jacques Lacan did not show up. He had promised to come, but had canceled at the last minute. His Majesty would not inaugurate the twilight ball. . . . [19]

Over the summer, and in the face of the waning of the great structuralist thematic of the 1960s, the antiegalitarian ideals of Maurrassian wisdom resurfaced in rather striking fashion with the media-spawned sensation of a tendency dubbed the "new right," whose values had lain dormant since the genocide. Drawing on a book by a dinosaur of anti-Freudianism, Pierre Debray-Ritzen, published in 1972 under the title *La scholastique freudienne,*[20] the philosopher Alain de Benoist reinvented the old polemic against "Kraut"—or *boche*—science and translated into a theoretical discourse what had been merely the arsenal of an organicism fallen into disuse. Now in the context of the decline of dynamic psychiatry, the reemergence of an antiegalitarian thematic took on the appearance of a pseudoscientific debate aimed at defining the conditions of an antiuniversalism in which Freudianism would be reinterpreted as a cultural regionalism. As such, it appeared as a shameful science bearing with it all the defects attributed to a Judeo-Christianity which was itself opposed to an alleged Nietzschean paganism. Already in 1977, Alain de Benoist had latched onto Debray-Ritzen's theses in order to combine them with those of Marthe

Robert and turn Freud into the Jewish inventor of a Jewish doctrine.[21] But in order to take his distance from the sources of Maurrassian doctrine and not appear to want to save themes specific to Action française from going under, Benoist opted for *Kultur* as opposed to *civilisation,* philosophical Germany as opposed to positivist France, and cultural difference as opposed to French universalism.[22] All in order to affirm that every paradigm of human culture bears witness to an innate inequality among races: whence the necessity for the West of producing elites, thanks to the progress of biology.

The argument was old, but it received new inspiration. During the entire summer, three hundred articles in the media and several radio programs were devoted to the theses of the new right, either to denounce the political danger they represented or to establish their existence in public opinion. To be sure, the tendency did not take root in the psychoanalytic movement since the ideals of race were no longer represented there. But the existence of such a thematic, outside the movement, revived for the first time in France the old quarrel of heredity-degeneration, of "Jewish science" and "Kraut science." Moreover, the opening of that field of speculation was not long in bearing fruit with the publication, six years later, of a monumental work on Freud in which one could read: "Dominating the whole, my anal character is not to be doubted. I had a grandmother from Saint-Flour. Jews and Auvergnats are rivals, as everyone knows, when it comes to avarice, and it should be no surprise if I have seen in the Jew Freud a rival skinflint."[23] That would be enough to horrify even the late Pichon, who, despite belonging to Action française, never stooped quite that low.

After the New Right, the New Left joined the fray. At the beginning of the fall, a book came out by a young professor of philosophy: *L'effet 'yau de poele.*[24] In it, the author spoke of Lacan and the Lacanians with a mixture of humor and ferocity. He denounced the mores of a milieu in the throes of its greatest crisis, suffering from its esotericism and its wooden prose. François George did not shine through his talents as a raconteur nor his capacities as a theorist. What he sought were easy effects, memorable cracks, attaching himself to the surface of things like some satirist right out of the Verdurin salon. But the book hurt because it presented itself as a demystification at a time when the new philosophical order was settling its scores with an aging structuralism accused of fostering a "Gulag." In a sense, *L'effet 'yau de poele* was a comic counterpart of *Un destin si funeste.* It treated Lacanianism as a fraud, Lacan as a guru, and his students as charlatans. In a word, the master was compared to Dr. Mabuse, that is, a Nazi hypnotist, and fifty years of a teaching of the highest rigor were annulled and submerged in the murkiest mud of occultism. The book sold thousands of copies and scored a true triumph with the Lacanians, as though the disciples were rediscovering, in that caricature of themselves pressed to an extreme, the evening song of a disappointed hope.

In *Le Monde* of September 21, the day the leftist intelligentsia was demonstrating in the streets of Paris against the murderers of Pierre Goldmann, the journalist Roland Jaccard shot off a "Salve contre Lacan [Volley against Lacan]," in an article of dithyrambic praise devoted to François George's book: "Lacan," he wrote, "whose seminar for a long time attracted gulls and snobs, who were all the more impressed by the master's enigmatic discourse in that they understood nothing of it. On the pretext of a return to Freud, Jacques Lacan, excluded from the IPA, founded in 1964 his own school. . . . Wishing to save psychoanalysis from the medicalization attending it and the mediocrity in which it was stagnating, he succeeded in a few years in the *tour de force* of effecting its loss of prestige on both the clinical level—with the suicidal practice of sessions reduced to a few minutes—and the intellectual one. In that respect, he might be compared with another 'savior,' Ayatollah Khomeini, who succeeded in a few months in discrediting the Islamic revolution." Jaccard then added, "One does not fire at an ambulance."[25] That horrible sentence would cause many intellectuals, sensitive to the climate of racial hatred descending on France at the time with the ideas of the New Right, to blanch.

The very next day, the newspaper was submerged by an avalanche of letters coming less from Lacanians than former friends of the master or psychiatrists shocked by the tone of the article. Always where the action beckoned, Wladimir Granoff sent André Fontaine a long letter of testimony in which he spoke of fascism, Vichy, and the collapse of June 1940. Jean-Michel Rey, Marie Moscovici, and Robert Pujol, for their part, recalled that the gulls and snobs attending Lacan's seminar were named Hyppolite, Jakobson, and Merleau-Ponty.[26] Embarrassed, the editors of Le Monde decided to print only a few responses stripped of any violence that might call into question the honorability of their journalist. While Gérard Mendel congratulated François George, going as far as to say that future generations would know the name of Lacan only through his work of demystification, Conrad Stein took the master's defense, emphasizing that the return to Freud had allowed France to know the work from Vienna. As for Guy Benoit, a psychiatrist independent of any school, he wrote the following: "One simply does not caricature things to that extent and those who, for example, have seen Lacan present cases and have been able to appreciate the tact and intelligence he brought to them, those who have suddenly grasped the new expressiveness he allowed to whoever it was that was speaking to him, will be able to consign François George's miserable gossip to the fate it deserves."[27]

During this period, a true hypnotizer was unwittingly displacing the stakes of the French psychoanalytic movement toward the East. Of Russian Jewish origin, Léon Chertok had been trained before 1953 on Lacan's couch, then supervised by Bouvet and Schlumberger. He never became a member of any psychoanalytic society; his principal merit was having been an authentic hero in the anti-Nazi struggle during the war. When Gilles Perrault met him for the first time, on the occasion of his extensive study of Leopold Trepper, he expected to find an old bearded gentleman in tinted glasses. To his great surprise he encountered a hardy fellow brimming with energy, endowed with the physique of a rugby player, a sparkle in his eye, and a raucous laugh.[28] Léon Chertok devoted all his energy to promoting the technique of hypnosis in the treatment of psychosomatic illnesses. Having long remained at a remove from the Freudian movement, he appeared on the psychoanalytic scene as the phenomenon of the hypnotic symptom regained currency because of the crisis of Lacanianism.

Around 1975, the Georgian psychologist, Serge Tzuladzei, who had studied psychiatry in Paris and been trained by a French analyst, took the initiative of organizing a colloquium on the unconscious in the Soviet Union. An heir of the school of psychology represented by the works of Dimitri Uznadzei, he managed to surround himself with liberals opposed to repressive psychiatry and eager to establish links with psychoanalysis in the West. Tzuladzei died before the accomplishment of his project, which was taken up by Léon Chertok in France and by Professor Philippe Bassine, the author of a book on the problem of the unconscious (published in French in 1973), in the Soviet Union. Bassine's central thesis was characteristic of the post-Pavlovian era following the Zhdanov period. It was a matter of "politically" rehabilitating the Freudian unconscious in order to criticize or refute it in the name of the accomplishments of psychology. In that respect, Bassine took into account the works of Lacan in order to show the extent to which linguistics, cybernetics, and logic allowed one to take one's distance from a Freudianism deemed to be nefarious: a quite surprising and quite "Soviet" use of Lacanianism.[29]

After many complications and the unabating opposition of the fearsome Snezhnevsky, the symposium took place in Georgia, from October 1 to 5, 1979. To be sure, at a time when the psychologists were attempting to rehabilitate an unconscious that was less Freudian than genetic or behaviorist, psychoanalysis was still officially banned in the Soviet Union and Freud's works were not reprinted. As for the abusive internments, they had been condemned at the Honolulu congress under conditions that have been set forth above. The question thus presenting itself to would-be participants was whether or not to boycott a symposium whose organizers represented a tendency hostile to the abuse of psychiatry, but unable—and for good reason—to express its opinions publicly. Three responses were offered in accordance with individual choices and issues linked to the situation of psychoanalysis in France. The first consisted in refusing any participation in a Soviet congress so as not to endorse the system itself by one's presence. The second amounted to accepting the rules of "scientific" debate, as determined by the organizers. The third opted for participation in the congress either by condemning the internments on the spot or by rejecting the imposed rules of the debate. That third path was the one chosen by a majority of the French present at the occasion.

Before the symposium was held, three volumes of the participants' contributions were published. Some were in fact suppressed to avoid displeasing government authorities, specifically those raising problems relating to Judaism or Jews. There were numerous texts by French representatives: Didier Anzieu, Jean-Paul Valabrega, Daniel Widlöcher, André Green, Pierre Bruno, Serge Leclaire, Bernard Müldworf, and Louis Althusser.[30] The two most famous Russians of our saga, Wladimir Granoff and Victor Smirnoff, rejected the very idea of such a congress, although without any dramatic declarations.

In June 1978, the symposium was announced in the French press. In an article in *Le Figaro,* Janine Chasseguet-Smirgel took the organizers to task, while invoking the case of abusive internments: "Nearly the entire membership of the FEP," she wrote, "has sent a letter to the Soviet authorities expressing their reservations about this congress and protesting, to the extent that psychoanalysts feel it is their business, against the abuses of psychiatry to political ends. Ultimately, is it reasonable to imagine that that deeply desocialized space constituted by a session of psychoanalysis, requiring a total absence of control by third parties, can exist in the U.S.S.R.? So why is this congress being held?[31] To which René Major responded in *Liberation,* after traveling to Tbilisi: "Nothing prevents official societies of psychoanalysis from existing in those countries of Latin America where military dictatorships imprison or torture political dissidents, even if certain psychoanalysts pay for it with their exile. Nor does anything prevent a situation in that association of psychoanalysts in the democracies—of which I am, by the way, a full-fledged member—in which I have been for years now forbidden to speak. It is true, of course, that I can choose my place of exile. I felt more free at that symposium at Tbilisi, I dare say, than at a congress of the International Psychoanalytic Association."[32]

Thus was the tone established. Those who publicly condemned the symposium were frequently representatives of IPA conservatism. The congress thus served as a tribunal from which the French could air the crises of their respective societies. All this to the surprise of the Soviets and Léon Chertok. They knew nothing of the quarrels ravaging the two principal French groups and had expected the arrival on Georgian soil of a delegation of scientists familiar with the conventions of dialogue, much like the Americans invited to the symposium. Léon Chertok had proposed to Lacan that he come to Tbilisi[33] and the Frenchman responded with a pun on *cher toc* [dear fake] and *bassine* [preserving pan]. Henry Ey should have been present, but he had died three years before the meeting. A few weeks after the symposium, Afghanistan would be invaded by Soviet troops, following which the Moscow Olympics would be boycotted by the Western powers.

At the end of 1976, there was an incident provoked by the article Louis Althusser had sent to Léon Chertok. In June, the philosopher had hastily written his paper, and made the error of sending it off as it was to the organizers. It was called "La découverte du docteur Freud" and paid ringing tribute to Lacan, even as it criticized certain aspects of his doctrine, specifically his reformulations in terms of formal logic. The slapdash aspect of the text resulted from Althusser's misunderstanding of the meaning of several Freudian concepts. In the case of a beginner, the errors would not have been serious, but for the author of the 1964 article, higher standards were in order. Althusser saw that his text was shoddy and sent it off to three friends: Jacques Nassif, Michel Pêcheux, and myself, asking them to make any corrections needed. "Here is my first cast for the Tbilisi congress," he wrote to one. "*Alea jacta est.* I don't know whether the congress will take place. That matters little. But I am writing to ask you a large favor: Read my (hasty, slapdash) project line by line and note down whatever isn't right with supporting evidence alongside."[34] The friends immediately went to work and their conclusions agreed. They emphasized the text's inadequacy and advised Althusser to rewrite it. The author thus asked to withdraw his draft and replace it with a new article, which was rather mediocre but without any flagrant errors. The second text pleased the Soviets less to the extent that it was not crudely "anti-Freudian" or "pro-Lacanian." Nevertheless, Léon Chertok had it published, although he kept the first version for himself. He then accused Althusser of having allowed himself to be "manipulated" by his entourage, thus projecting onto others his own hypnotic conception of interpersonal relations. The affair caused a certain stir, and three years later, Althusser decided not to go to Georgia.

In the meanwhile, the leading figures of the French psychoanalytic movement reconsidered and decided to boycott the congress. The only ones still in the running for France were Serge Leclaire, René Major, André Bourguignon, Pierre Bruno, Jenny Aubry, Jacques Nassif, Gérard Mendel, Catherine Clément, and myself. Invited at the last minute, Armando Verdiglione feigned an attack of "dissidence" just prior to rushing off to catch a plane back to his offices in Milan. Catherine David covered the event for the *Nouvel Observateur,* Nadine Nimier for "France-Culture," Jacques Nobécourt for *Le Monde,* and Catherine Clément, invited twice over, for *Le Matin.* All were excellent journalists, competent on the subject of psychoanalysis. Most of the French group consisted of Lacanians, certain of whom were former members of the French Communist Party. The PCF, moreover, was the principal absent party at the symposium, since Lucien Sève, on the one hand, and Louis Althusser, on the other, did not attend. Edward Joseph, the president of the IPA, canceled at the last moment, but on the second day of the congress, Anna Freud sent a telegram of good wishes. Arriving from the United States, Roman Jakobson made a triumphant entrance before crowds assembled at the Chess Palace, delivering his communication in the Georgian language. Before leaving, René Major asked Amnesty International to turn over to him the Georgian file on abusive internments, pledging to demand publicly the release of any who might be dissidents. But Amnesty International did not possess any names of prisoners of that category. In an agreement with an opposition group from Tbilisi, the decision was collectively taken not to disturb the course of the congress by any useless declarations that risked playing into the hands of the advocates of political repression. Thereafter it would be a matter of finding a different way to break with the status quo.

During the very first afternoon, conflict erupted openly after a presentation by Serge Leclaire, who, along with René Major, played the role of gadfly, in the style of Confrontation. In order to avoid any risk of censorship, he had his text translated by his friend Granoff, and the official translator only had to read it. Now Leclaire offered a history of the Lacanian movement, ending with a statement of its institutional impasses. He then explained to the audience that Antoinette Fouque's woman's movement had taken over where Lacanianism had left off, in something of a return to the origins of psychoanalysis.[35] Naturally, neither the Soviets nor the Americans nor the scientists of various nationalities who had gathered at Tbilisi knew the "Psychanalyse et Politique" group. They had come to discuss neurons and cortexes, behavior, hypnosis, and the transference, and here they were being served the women's movement. The words "dream," "sexuality," "desire," and so forth were brutally pronounced even though they had been banned from the congress's proceedings. Understanding nothing of Leclaire's discourse, they did not react to its substance. But when, as soon as his talk was done, Leclaire suggested that an informal group gather to discuss things "as we wish," the authorities no longer knew which way to turn. A "free" meeting had not been anticipated in the ground rules. Following Leclaire, Major also broke with expectations by declaring that the unconscious existed only by virtue of a political decision capable of making it exist.[36] He read his text slowly, in a provocative manner, and the chairman of the session reminded him that he had gone beyond his allotted time. Major then turned to his audience and asked authorization to continue. Exasperated by that appeal to a different legitimacy, the chairman allowed the speaker to continue his remarks.

The following day, at four o'clock, the French delegation found the doors to the congress closed. There was not a single Soviet present. Only Bassine was there, explaining that the committee had not yet met to decide on the request for an open discussion. The next day, at the time the French group was scheduled to present its communication, the doors were again locked. Finally, on the third day, the authorities loosened their hold and allowed a seminar on the theory and practice of psychoanalysis to be held. It was a huge success.[37] The participants from Georgia, who were all quite young, learned concretely, for the first time, how an analysis evolves. They knew nothing of the reality of the couch. At the plenary session, my own communication (which had been delayed because of its contents) on the extinction of psychoanalysis in the Soviet Union was finally presented.[38]

The Tbilisi symposium was not limited to the commotion caused by a majority of the French participants in the corridors and plenary sessions of the Chess Palace. The stir did not stop the concerned countries and certain others of the French from confronting their divergent conceptions of the unconscious. But it is improbable that the symposium, however broad and open, allowed the slightest reimplantation of Freudianism in the Soviet Union. For in order for such a penetration to occur, it would have been necessary for the practice of psychoanalysis not to be forbidden, nor its works to be banned. Seen from France, the congress allowed a displacement into Georgian folklore of the institutional chaos affecting the country's psychoanalytic societies. That a hypnotist, a hero of the anti-Nazi struggle, and a veteran of Lacan's couch should have been the intermediary for this *panem et circenses* is one of the most striking paradoxes of the entire affair.

The leftist press had a rather positive reaction to the trip, but the participants were attacked on all sides for not having boycotted the symposium or denounced the abusive internments. All this was combined with conflicts specific to the Parisian scene and linked to the waning of the ideals of May 1968. Toward the end of October, while the EFP was entering the first phase of its final collapse, Confrontation and the "Psychanalyse et Politique" group organized a huge meeting at the Hotel PLM Saint-Jacques on the subjects of Tbilisi, the Freudian revolution, and women's liberation. Antoinette Fouque's troops had just taken on the acronym MLF, which had been *a contrario* the symbol of feminism. As a result, representatives of the other groups invaded the auditorium challenging the alleged banner-snatchers, whom they accused of a variety of infamies. A thousand persons participated in the crepuscular skirmish, among whom there were an impressive number of members of the EFP. Hostile to Fouque, Catherine Clément and Jacques Nassif refused to attend. As for René Major, as a sign of opposition, he refused to speak. Alone with a woman from the MLF, Serge Leclaire faced down the chaotic protest against contestation. He noted that it was hysterics who had invented psychoanalysis and that, once the reserve of their hostage bodies had been exhausted, the MLF had taken over from what had become the psychoanalytic nonmovement. At the end of that interminable fray, with its volley of insults, Victor Feinberg violently condemned the participants at Tbilisi for the support they had given the Gulag, emphasizing that the KGB had been exemplary in its loyalty toward women since it interned women on an equal footing with men.[39]

II. Dissolution

Founded on the principle of direct monarchy and governed by the rules of Athenian democracy, the EFP could not survive once the master's word had been delegated to others. Lacan reduced to silence, Lacan assassinated by the press, Lacan defeated by the errors of his reign was no longer the flamboyant sovereign of years past. Slowly dying beneath the weight of his embattled persona, choked by the trans-formations of a society fallen prey to a media revolution, a hatred for language, and a trivilization of thought, the Lacan of this psychoanalytic Waterloo no longer ex-isted except as a shadow of himself. At times he was lucid and affable, but at others, he would stare at his intimates fixedly without recognizing them. On such occasions an infinite suffering would traverse his handsome, aged face. The commentators, students, loyalists, epigones, and enemies knew it, or pretended not to notice. Lin-gering at the palace gates, they awaited the eulogy that would carry off the "tyrant" for some, the beloved for others.

Ever since 1974, the disorder in the universities had gradually shredded the pact binding the body of the one to the body of all, and the unity of the kingdom had come apart over the failure of the *passe*. When the shipwreck finally came, in colors worthy of Géricault, an oligarchy had already succeeded the monarchy. On the one side, the Vincennes faction, still a minority, but dynamic and with the future seemingly on its side, supported by (far from negligible) members of the guard; on the other, the shattered mass of the turbulent scions of Lacanianism, in part demol-ished by the *passe,* in part displaced by Confrontation, and no longer knowing to which school they belonged. And then another pact was becoming unraveled, the one which had always bound the great dragon to the lesser one: Jacques Lacan to Françoise Dolto. Expelled from the IPA because of their clinical genius, they had become, over the course of fifteen years, the most prestigious parental couple of the entire saga. Now, on the eve of the collapse, and after a year spent with Michèle Montrelay on the promotions jury, Françoise Dolto had removed her stakes from the board and was speaking loudly and clearly about what was not going well in the École. Without any intention of seizing power, she drew to her side, sponta-neously, all those who had attended her courses and no longer found any words emanating from the founding father. With that, the École destroyed itself, and three tendencies internal to Lacanianism divided the resultant territory.

The first, which was Millerian, youthful and intent on conquest, revealed itself eager to bury the old world, that symbol of failure and laxness. It called for a purified Lacanianism, capable of rekindling the flame and confronting the techno-logical tempest of the 1980s. It acted in the name of a Lacan declared to be more alive than ever, the great helmsman of the final victory, the Lacan of years past, as he shone in the shadows of the Salle Dussane. The second tendency was composed of the barons of Lacanianism, worn down by fifteen years of power and surrounded by their students. They represented a world gone bankrupt, but embodied a clinical tradition of Lacanianism. In a first phase, a majority of them would support Miller in the name of loyalty to Lacan. They had the hope of dividing the kingdom among themselves and of leaving the administration of editorial and university-academic concerns to the son-in-law. Then, as the master consumed himself in silence and sickness, one after the other, they disavowed the man they had supported, accusing him of confiscating all power for his own benefit and of falsifying the founding texts of the new cause.

Finally, a third tendency was composed of the authentic adversaries of the Lacano-Millerian line. Since the Vincennes affair, they had been hostile to the Lacanianism of the matheme, and in any event laid claim to a more liberal clinical tradition than that of the barons who had taken power. Against the advance of the Millerian tendency, they wanted to safeguard the existence of a school whose proprietors and perpetuators they felt themselves to be. They were thus caught in a contradiction that was a function of the very structure of the EFP. After fifteen years of accepting the principles of direct monarchy, they suddenly perceived the fact that the École was alleged to be governed "democratically" by the law of 1901. And with that, in order to manifest their hostility to a power whose decisions they rejected, they based their actions on a new legitimacy, which was no longer transferential but juridical. They countered the rule of a single individual with the statutory regulations, thus functioning—but once does not a habit make—like the other constituents of French Freudianism. They played the right of association against that of the royal prerogative and unwittingly became the first regicides in the history of Lacanianism—minus the guillotine, to be sure.

Since one cannot dethrone a king without simultaneously destroying the order he incarnates, they would lose their school for having wanted to preserve it according to the rules. However democratic it may have been in its statutes, it rested symbolically on the power of a single individual, able through his dictates to annihilate it with a single stroke since that power had been democratically accepted by all at the outset. If Lacan said, "I dissolve my school; the administration will follow," the school was of necessity dissolved by virtue of that performative verb. What would then remain would be to respect the rules of juridical liquidation. If, on the contrary, a member of the EFP said, "I dissolve my school; the administration will follow," he would be taken for a lunatic and nothing would be dissolved. And yet, if he mobilized his troops, the administration might follow and a meeting of the whole might pronounce a juridical dissolution against the wishes of the founder. In that case, the people would gently have deposed the sovereign. The charter allowed it, since it was democratic. In the contrary case, in which the founder uttered his performative sentence, the meeting of the whole might reject a juridical dissolution. In that case, it would be abolishing the monarchy in a quite different manner, and the master would have a choice between exile and an impossible cohabitation with a people itself intent on not changing the old order.

It will thus be understood why, in December 1979, no member of the EFP dreamed of uttering the word of dissolution, which would have branded him a madman. And when Leclaire had thought of it a year earlier, he knew what he was saying, that such an initiative fell to Lacan and Lacan alone because Lacan had inscribed on the tablets of the law a principle accepted by all: "I alone found, etc." If he alone had founded, symbolically, it was his alone to be able to dissolve. Such was the symbolic—and not juridical—law of a school like no other.

Given those circumstances, the question of deciding *who* precisely emitted such words or signed such a statement took on central importance, in relation to which the question of the juridical dissolution was no more than a drop in the bucket. And it was not by chance that that question became a fundamental issue in the conflicts traversing the Lacanian community on the threshold of its final collapse. Ever since the incident at the inaugural session of the seminar of 1978, it was a matter of common knowledge at the École, at the seminar, and in the press, that Lacan was speaking very little and writing less and less. Now that silence and that withdrawal were the very image of the degradation that had settled over the common house, since that house had been structured around the words of a master and his privileged relation with each subject. If Lacan was no longer speaking and was now delegating his power to a board or an interpreter, the École was no longer the École. It became a normal society, similar to the other psychoanalytic groups, with clans and individuals opposing each other in an atmosphere of extreme violence, according to the alliances of the moment. In September 1979, the École of the reconquest had already been dissolved by history. What remained to be determined was who would embody the law of that dissolution in the eyes of history: Lacan or his seraglio? Lacan alone? Lacan with his seraglio? The seraglio without Lacan? I will not answer that question, but will show, through the testimony of the principal protagonists of the drama, how the very movement of history answered it with sufficient complexity for that history never to be tempted to lapse into Manicheanism, hatred, or vulgar prejudice.[40]

In February 1979, the Millerian faction muscled its way into the power structure of the École with the creation of an association called the "Fondation du Champ freudien," whose board consisted of Lacan and his daughter Judith, then of a "department of cartels" directed by Jacques-Alain Miller and Eric Laurent, a young analyst and student of the master as well as a veteran of Deleuze's seminar, who seemed destined for a brilliant career thanks to the support of Solange Faladé. Until then the cartels were not part of any department and functioned in a libertarian spirit. Thereafter they would be maneuvered from above with a rather solid line of command. In July, Miller organized an important *Ornicar?* colloquium at UNESCO with the idea of introducing a Trojan horse into the EFP so as to be able to reorganize it from within on the basis of an alternative position. That day he was able to draw together a large number of young Lacanians either from Vincennes or favorable to the new line of the matheme (and knots): Michel Silvestre, Jean Allouch, Philippe Julien, Érik Porge, and Guy Le Gaufrey. Charles Melman and Solange Faladé supported the initiative. The conditions of participation were positively Draconian and each speaker was instructed not to speak for more than fifteen minutes—a contrast with former habits in which speakers stretched their comments out for hours.[41] On the same occasion, Miller and Laurent entered the directorate.

During the same period, Denis Vasse, who was vice-president of the EFP, joined Michèle Montrelay in days at Confrontation devoted to the theme "Le corps et le politique." Without realizing it, he was to provoke a formidable storm, for Lacan, who had never taken a public position on the participation of his followers in the forum initiated by Major, took offense at Denis Vasse's appearance and informed him of his decision to remove him from the vice-presidency. During a meeting of the administrative council, Françoise Dolto rose to his defense, reading a letter he had sent. She noted that a number of the École's barons had gone to Confrontation without being the object of official invective. To which Melman replied that it behooved Vasse to display more reserve in view of his office. Françoise ridiculed her interlocutor, claiming that titles did not interest her and that in a society of analysts no one ought to have to ask daddy for authorization to act as he wanted. In a fury, Lacan rose and left the room without saying a word.[42]

Shortly thereafter, Michèle Montrelay took a stand against the decision aimed at Denis Vasse. She then asked the secretary of the EFP for a room in which to hold a meeting on male sexuality. At the directorate, Lacan, seconded by Melman, refused categorically. Nobody flinched, but Miller was quite astonished. Aware of the impending breakup of the École, he thought that the conflicts ought to be expressed.[43] Melman, on the other hand, wanted to take the opposition from behind, believing he could thus avoid the École's becoming "anti-Lacanian."

On September 30, 1979, while other Lacanians were taking their Aeroflot plane to Georgia, the crisis in the École became a public affair. An extraordinary plenary session was called to modify the charter and thus expand the administrative council from seventeen to twenty-five members. Traveling in the United States, where she was giving a series of lectures, Montrelay entrusted Dolto with a letter to be read at a plenary session, in which she protested against the strictures imposed on her seminar as well as the deposing of Denis Vasse. Prior to the meeting, which all felt was going to be decisive, Simatos and Clavreul advised Dolto not to read the letter lest the crisis assume even broader proportions.[44] But before long, within the auditorium, invectives began to fly. Lacan was called a tyrant. He kept his silence. Simatos then asked Dolto to read the letter. Two votes were to be held, the first to ratify the statutory revision and the second to elect a new slate for the council. But the organizers of the meeting were so unaccustomed to their own juridical rules that they managed to have the second point voted on as part of the first. The procedure was thus unparliamentary and the protest very quickly attained riotous proportions. Naturally, the results of the votes reflected the disgruntled and splintered situation prevailing within the EFP. Two hundred four individuals out of 350 approved the ethics report which implicitly included a statement of Vasse's removal, and 213 out of 354 elected a new slate, whereas a majority of two-thirds was required.[45]

On December 13, Miller and Laurent gave a joint lecture at the Institut océanographique on the theme of "Where then is Lacan's teaching to be found in the EFP?" Miller declared that new things had to be said in new words, accused the analysts of playing at being "anarlysts," and affirmed that Lacan classified their writings alongside the works of the madmen of literature, whereas he considered his own as being written under the sign of the Enlightenment. The opposition was thus called obscurantist in the name of Millerian rationalism.[46] Eric Laurent, for his part, defined who precisely was no longer a Lacanian. Invoking the categories of the Real, the Imaginary, and the Symbolic, he indicated the "deviations" ensuing from the slippage that occurred when one or another was privileged.[47]

The next day, there was a reshuffling of members of the directorate. Laurent replaced Simatos in the key position of secretary; Irène Roublef left the teaching department to join Conté in publications; and Melman was put in charge of teaching, with Simatos as his deputy. The hard-line tendency was reinforced. At the same time, the department of cartels brought out a bulletin, *Plus-Un*, expressing the positions of the party of order. An ally of Miller, Charles Melman was most virulently opposed to what he considered feminist, obscurantist, or religious. In his account of the September meeting, he clearly designated the adversaries: "The vote," he wrote, "expresses the fundamental opposition of a large group to Lacan's teaching. That refusal, moreover, is perfectly explicit. It is to be found in certain works by F. Dolto which, taking up some of her radio broadcasts or dealing with religion, distorts psychoanalysis into a new version of 'good tidings.' In Audouard, whose last book aims at a transcendence of psychoanalysis. In S. Leclaire or M. Montrelay, whose infatuation with feminism is at odds with the ethic of our teaching." [48]

On December 16, Michèle Montrelay informed the members of the EFP in a circular that she was renewing her request to Jacques Lacan and his collaborators for a room in which to hold her seminar on male sexuality. She called for an open discussion of the crisis in the École.[49] As soon as she sent her letter, she went with Claude Rabant to consult a lawyer, showed him the statutes and asked him if she had the right to demand a new meeting of the whole to deliberate on the violation of the rules in the September vote. The mere fact that she took that initiative plainly shows that no member of the school had ever worried about juridical procedure, so great had the impact of the direct monarchy been. The lawyer's answer must have been positive since the statutes of the EFP were those of a classical association. Montrelay then addressed a letter not to Lacan but to the director of the École. She denounced both the bans and the illegal voting procedure. The juridical battle had begun. . . . Contacted so they might sign the letter, Ginette Raimbault and Jean Clavreul refused, while Michel de Certeau and Alain Manier, a former student of the ENS as well as of Roustang, agreed.[50] With that text, the statutory legitimacy of the École was for the first time pitted against the authority of a prince become silent and represented by his seraglio.

During this period, there emerged in Lacan's immediate circle a decision to dissolve the EFP, the only possible response to the existent split. On this point, the testimony of the two protagonists of the story diverges. For that reason, we shall allow them to speak for themselves:

Jacques-Alain Miller: "The difficulties that the directorate had made for Solange and myself, during the Congress on Transmission, which had all the same been entrusted to us by Lacan, had convinced me to take some distance. I was losing interest in the École. It was at the precise time that I organized the first *Ornicar?* colloquium (June 1979) that Lacan brought me back into the institution by appointing me, along with Eric Laurent, to the directorate. Once there, what was to be done? (1) Contain Melman's brutal sectarianism. (2) Upset Simatos's propensity to immobility. (3) Unravel the invisible web that Clavreul was busy weaving. (4) Re-awaken the energies and enthusiasms of 1964. But it was too late. The point of no return had been passed, as the plenary session of September 30 demonstrated. After that one had either to let things continue—or kick over the gaming table. On the Sunday following that meeting, the word dissolution was mentioned for the first time between Lacan and myself. I explained to him that from my point of view, given the way things were going, he would soon have no other choice than to resign or dissolve. His resignation? 'It is out of the question,' he answered me. Dissolving? He laughed: 'There's still something to be tried before that.' Had he already thought of it? What remained was to manage to get the grievances stated openly and as soon as possible, then to sort them out, and finally to reform or even invent, while channeling the ambitions of those concerned. The following semester was quite busy: my first trip to Latin America, where the international meeting of 1980 was conceived with Diana Rabinovitch; upon my return, the invention of L'Ane; the holding of the "afternoon for cartels"; the creation of Plus-Un; in December, the "Tous Lacaniens!" lecture; finally, the growing dissension between Melman and Simatos allowed for the replacement of the latter by Laurent as secretary of the École. But it was late, too late. The 'pervasive feebleness' was spreading as far as could be seen. The moment for concluding arrived for Lacan at the end of the Christmas vacation. It was on January 6, at Guitrancourt, that he gave me the text of the letter of dissolution, to be distributed the following day. On Tuesday morning, I stopped by at the rue de Lille: The telephone didn't stop ringing; Serge Leclaire telephoned an affectionate embrace; Lacan made a few corrections in the text of his letter before going to the Seminar."

Solange Faladé: "By September 30, 1979, the question was being raised of what had to be done. Dissolution was in the air between Lacan, Miller, and myself. I spent Christmas at Guitrancourt. The final decision was taken without enthusiasm by Lacan at Miller's home a few hours before the children were given their presents. One had to move quickly in order to create something while there was still time. Lacan could no longer write. It was decided that Miller would compose the letter and Lacan would correct it. He eliminated passages that were not to his liking. I did not return to Guitrancourt, but during the first weekend of the new year, Miller telephoned me to say the letter was typed up and ready to be sent out."[51]

The two reports agree on three points:
1. Lacan decided to dissolve his school in the course of discussions and with hesitation.
2. He was perfectly lucid when he made his decision.
3. He corrected the letter.

Consequently, the act of dissolution would appear to have been authentically Lacanian, whoever the author of the letter was.

On Tuesday, at the customary time of his seminar, the master read the letter putting an end to the adventure of his school. He added that the document was signed with his own hand. Several persons present that day, including Laurence Bataille, remembered that sentence and that dramatic moment.[52] At the same time, all members of the EFP received the text in the form of a circular dated January 5 and written at Guitrancourt. In his typescript, Lacan spoke in the first person. He emphasized that the departure of a single one was sufficient for all to be dispersed. The letter added that the juridical dissolution would be executed according to the rules established by the charter, in the course of an extraordinary meeting of the entire membership. It also stated that the master "persevered" and that he was calling on all those eager to avoid the deviations and compromises fueled by the EFP to follow him within ten days. Finally, in the name of the matheme, it criticized religion while affirming that Lacan did not need many and that there were many whom he did not need.

That letter short-circuited Michèle Montrelay's proposal that a meeting of the whole be called to rectify the anomalies of the previous year. Moreover, the document signed by her and her partners was dated January 7. It had been written before the fifth, then expanded, after the circular of dissolution had been received, to include a note observing that only a meeting of the whole was sovereign in the EFP.

The press did not make any mistake about it. All the journalists announced in short order that Lacan had dissolved his school. They thus revealed that they attached far greater weight to the symbolic power of a master (however much he may have been called a tyrant) than to the statutes of his school.

If, in the climate of resurgent racism, the France of the 1980s rediscovered its old demons and made of Lacanianism a "plague" identical to the "Kraut—or boche—science" of years past, it was a sign that Lacanianism had taken root in the country and become the most accomplished French form of Freudianism. For resistance to the doctrine, linked to the acceptance of the performative utterances of a master, was but the symptom of the effective progress of Lacanianism's implantation in French soil. Once again, on the threshold of death and at the most horrendous moment of his suffering, Lacan achieved his greatest victory: He entered posterity. The future would offer its ultimate judgment in assessing the accounts.

During the weeks and months following the deed of January 5, the major organs of the leftist press, *Libération, Le Monde, Le Nouvel Observateur,* and *Le Matin,* published testimony by the principal protagonists of the Lacanian scene. For the first time a major crisis of the movement was taken into account by the media to the extent of conducting opinion polls, studies of all sorts, and a vast exercise in "immediate" history on the place of psychoanalysis in France. Amidst the clamor, to be sure, François George, become king for a day, gave his opinion on matters in the analytic world, taking himself for the gravedigger of the greatest fraud of the century: "The crisis of the astonishing system of control established by Jacques Lacan," he wrote, "had been acute for several months. My book, *L'Effet 'yau de poêle,* after François Roustang's, had served to reveal as much. Everyone observed that the only response of the so-called Freudian school was silence. . . . I might add that certain eminent members of the Lacanian institution assured me of their sympathy, going so far as to salute my courage. . . . It will be increasingly clear that all this has only a very distant relation to Freud. Lacan's fraud in claiming to be his heir lasted quite some time." [53]

During this period, the militants of a purified hard-line Lacanianism confronted (both in the media and at the EFP) the defenders of a statutory legitimacy who were trying to save their school from dissolution. From the one side, Charles Melman accused Françoise Dolto of all the sins of the Catholic faith, announcing, "The lukewarm I shall vomit from my mouth," and, from the other, Claude Rabant wrote the "director" of the École to let him know that the École had in no way been dissolved.[54] As for Jacques-Alain Miller, who was still allied with Melman, he denounced Dolto's "lamentable pieties." At that point she was received by Lacan, who immediately asked her to follow him. She refused, saying that she had no desire to come to a place where Melman was attacking her so violently. "As for Miller," she added, "he's a loser, and that is not where psychoanalysis is to be found." Lacan replied, "A loser, you can certainly say that again." Françoise could sense the effects of old age in her own family. Boris, her lifelong companion, would write his final book before lapsing into a state similar to Lacan's. He died in July of 1981.[55]

Attacked by Miller as much as Dolto and accused of cowardice and hypocrisy for having maintained his membership in the EFP after *L'anti-Oedipe,* Félix Guattari responded: "I considered that the diversity of tendencies present there tended to make of that association a place of free inquiry and research. I was aware that the bureaucrats who had taken it over a few years before were intent on a purge. I would have given myself over to such a ploy only if constrained and forced, on the condition that they formulate in a public debate the practical, political, and theoretical reasons for my excommunication. This never happened. Jacques-Alain Miller continued 'hypocritically' to accept my dues. The purge of groups will take other paths. The discussion needed will not gain anything in the process." [56]

Before long, the EFP was divided into two entrenched camps, each of which was split into several factions. On the side of the opponents of dissolution, there emerged a plan to defend to the end the existence of the École and to respond to the reality of an act with the reality of another act. Aware of the fact that for the moment the Millerian faction could not be dissociated from the position—however silent—of Lacan, Michèle Montrelay decided to ask for a court-appointed administrator who might allow problems to be settled otherwise. That act was intended to force the other side to play the game of statutory legitimacy in order to preserve a "liberal" current, which was a minority but nonetheless significant.

Among the advocates of a symbolic dissolution, moves were beginning to be made in the direction of securing a vote for juridical dissolution along the lines indicated in the letter of January 5. Each camp knew that the decision would be a matter of a few votes. At that phase of the fray, there was no third force emerging to allow the members of the EFP to dissociate Lacan's person, the Millerian faction, and the party of the barons. And yet, among the rank and file, that third force existed: There were numerous members of the École who, although favorable to the act of January 5, did not want either a Millerian society or the maintenance of a school which no longer had a *raison d'être.* But everything transpired during an initial phase as though alliances had been sealed on each side, one with the thought of securing a juridical dissolution at whatever cost in order to start up a new group, the other with the aim of voiding the symbolic dissolution.

That nonappearance of a third path stemmed from the fact that none of the barons of Lacanianism wanted to prevent the dissolution. Serge Leclaire, who would have been well placed to represent some middle course, had no reason to lend himself to such a plan. He thought that the future was on the side of the Millerian group, and well before the events of the winter of 1979, he had recommended dissolution. In addition he had no desire to become a leader of a tendency, since the Lacanianism he defended no longer passed by way of institutions insofar as he was concerned, but rather through an ever broader diffusion of psychoanalysis, commensurate with new means of communication. As for Jean Clavreul, who also could have opened up that channel, he felt that the time had not yet come to act. His thought was that the new group emergent from the dissolution would be able to marginalize Miller in the university and retain control of clinical practice and the training of analysts. He published an excellent article in *Le Monde* to that effect, but it would have no immediate effect. "Miller," he wrote, "is an excellent academic and he has placed his talent in Lacan's service by becoming the curator of the seminars. He deserves our respect and he had a place in the École freudienne, but he drags the university with him wherever he steps. . . . He's the one who is in the minority. When he says that Lacan has always been ideologically in the minority in his school, he's wrong." [57]

On the morning of January 17, two court officers arrived at the home of Jacques Lacan bearing a writ of summons signed by twenty-eight members of the EFP. Gloria Gonzalez received them and signed the document in her position as secretary. The old man was summoned on January 21 to the two o'clock session of the court presided over by Mme Rozes.[58] He would not go. His attorney, Maître Roland Dumas, argued on his behalf, accompanied by Jacques-Alain Miller. The subpoena invoked all the failures in the accomplishment of administrative formalities since the creation of the EFP. They were quite numerous but utterly without importance for the authentic history of the school. And yet that document itself allowed the opposition to mobilize its troops in the face of an extremely well-organized majority sustained by Lacan's presence. Among the signatories were to be found the names of Michèle Montrelay, François Roustang, Michel de Certeau, Claude Rabant, Xavier Audouard, Anne Levallois, Thémouraz Abdoucheli, Lucien Mélèse, and Radmila Zygouris: the entire "libertarian" cohort of the EFP. Each of them had played an important role in the École at one moment or another of its history—concerning the *passe,* at Vincennes, at *L'Ordinaire du psychanalyste,* etc. Thereafter they would legally represent the party opposed to dissolution. Nonetheless, they were far from agreement among themselves, and their disunity was evidenced by the presence of two different lawyers in their ranks. Michèle Montrelay, along with the majority of the group, was defended by Maître Claude Crinon, while Claude Rabant and a minority received counsel from Maître Daniel Soulez-Larivière, a friend of Juliette Labin's and the former defense lawyer for Leopold Trepper.

Three days after the subpoena, in the course of a stormy session, the administrative council decided to call for a meeting of the entire membership to consider dissolution. Lacan did not say a word except to read a text and pronounce a celebrated *"Delenda est,"* [from *Delenda Carthago*—Carthage must be destroyed—Cato the Elder], which would serve as the slogan of a brochure circulated by the Millerians. A strange affair indeed! What is to be thought of this master who revived a Hannibalian vision of psychoanalysis, drawing on the Rome of the Reconquest, and who would thereafter place himself beneath the banner of a fearsome Cato demanding the destruction of Carthage, that is a kingdom—his own—as Roman as it was Semitic, as Christian as it was Jewish, as materialist as it was spiritualist, and as Maoist as it was libertarian?

Following that reading, Eric Laurent took the floor as secretary to present a lengthy report on the situation of the École and the old anomalies denounced in the subpoena. The minutes would be transmitted to the lawyers of the opposing party.[59] After Eric Laurent, Miller lashed out violently at Françoise Dolto, who could not understand the hatred she inspired. He sketched a terrifying portrait of the school being run by a court administrator, then reproached Clavreul for his article in *Le Monde*. Jenny Aubry defended Clavreul, but was then accused by Miller of spreading rumors about Lacan's health. . . . A rumor was in fact circulating, which was wrongly ascribed to her, according to which Lacan was about to be interned or operated on for a brain tumor.[60] Jenny denied any responsibility for what she was being accused of and which was, to be sure, a pure fantasy linked to the climate of dissolution. Melman backed up Miller, along with Nassif and Pierre Martin. Against Clavreul, Eric Laurent announced that university discourse was more present in Clavreul's own seminar than in the university itself. To restore a measure of calm, Françoise Dolto asked that a vote of thanks for Simatos be held. Everyone approved. It was the only tension-free moment in the meeting. After which the insults started up with new vigor.[61] Five days later, *Le Monde* published a letter signed by Lacan that disavowed Clavreul while praising Miller, the "at least one" who knew how to read him.[62]

On January 25, the court's decision was made public. Each side congratulated itself on victory. The tribunal in fact accorded the petitioners a court representative, Maître Zecri, to verify the proper functioning of the École, but it did not name a court administrator, who would have disenfranchised the École of its rights. In other words, the court decided the signatories of the suit were right without admitting that their adversaries were wrong.

While the École was tearing itself apart amid horrendous tumult, the conservatives of the SPP lashed out at the old doge, whom they charged with all the world's sins. In *Le Monde* and under the headline "Who will say that the emperor is naked?", Colette Chiland offered her conception of history: "One has to be acquainted with the splits of 1953 and 1963," she wrote, "not only through the documents published by Jacques-Alain Miller, Lacan's son-in-law, but through the abundant testimony of those who lived through them. The essential has not been written, and a historian may regret that those best informed have not violated the duties of discretion and have revealed nothing of the lies, blackmail, and betrayals of principle which do no honor to psychoanalysts and put our ideals to a harsh test." [63] The author of that powerful statement forgot that Jacques-Alain Miller was the first and only one in France to publish documents which the other societies could have brought out, since they were common property. Even if those documents do not account for the whole of that history, they at least have the merit of existing and constituting an introduction to it. [64] As for the historian, she has nothing to regret, since she does not fall short of her duty in reconstituting, through a whole spectrum of testimony, the conflictual, remarkable, and occasionally odious reality of the French psychoanalytic scene. And so much the worse for the ideals of its representatives. Colette Chiland went on in the same tone to denounce Lacan's perverse practice, which she described as a Surrealist farce. Then she evoked the Juliette Labin affair, affirming that suicides were more frequent in the EFP than in other psychoanalytic societies. It was true, of course, that in the other societies, the same suicides were not the subject of public discussion.

After January 5, Lacan received about a thousand letters from individuals wanting to continue with him. Among them, a bit more than three hundred came from members of the EFP. The others came from among the large number of those who had been attending the École's congresses over the years: experts in pedagogy, psychiatric interns, psychologists, etc., who were for the most part in training with Lacanians. Lacan did not want many, he said, and there he was with a crowd at his door. On February 21, those who wrote received a circular: "To the thousand from whom a letter attests to the desire to continue with him, Jacques Lacan announces that he is founding, this February 21, the *Cause freudienne*. A future letter will apprise of the work he asks of those placing themselves under those auspices." [65] To which the petitioners in the lawsuit replied that an association cannot be founded on the basis of a single proper name. The letter to the thousand was soon dubbed "Mille-errent" ["A thousand err"; pronounced "Miller" in French] by the opposition, who were themselves referred to by their adversaries as "référendards" [or court-injunctionists] and "known forgers." Eric Laurent began circulating a petition against the signatories of the lawsuit, which received three hundred signatures. Certain analysts pressured their patients to add their name to the list and defend Lacan's cause. A plenary session was called for March 16 by Maître Zecri in order to vote on the statutory revision that had been mishandled on September 30.

In September 1964, Lacan had sent to the Prefecture the statutes of the EFP, which he had founded in June. He had taken care to specify the composition of the administrative council, to be presided over by himself, and to announce the calling of a sovereign meeting of the entire membership in a year's time to elect the members of that same administrative council. With the statutory revision of 1969, ratified in 1971, the EFP became a democratic organization in which Lacan continued to exercise all powers by the consent of all. Elected by the plenary session of all members, the council administered the École and chose a board composed of a president, a vice-president, a treasurer, and a secretary. The directorate was composed of the administrative council's board and department heads appointed by the president and ratified at a meeting of the whole. One could join the École with the approval of two members of the directorate and the consent of the administrative council. As for rank, it was defined by internal regulations. The council "administered" and the directorate "directed," but the two instances functioned in perfect juridical harmony, reflecting the principle of direct monarchy that characterized the École.

The statutes of the Cause freudienne, drafted in haste and with only provisional status, defined a mode of power radically opposed to that of the EFP.[66] The association was directed by Jacques Lacan, who was assisted by his personal secretary, Gloria Gonzalez, who until then had not exercised any official function in the Lacanian movement. The director presided over the association, assisted by a council chosen by himself and elected for a term of two years at a plenary session of which nothing further was said. The same director was to be elected at the plenary session for a duration of five years. He could choose the council, but not be a member of it. As for the board, it was elected at the plenary session for five years, once presented by the director. It was invested with supreme responsibility. It contained the secretariat without it being possible to determine whether it was (or was not) an emanation of the council. But it held all power and was to solicit the council, which had no precise role other than to assist the director. It contained, moreover, no other member than Gloria Gonzalez for a duration of one year, after which a meeting of the entire membership was to meet and deliberate. Consequently, the Cause freudienne was administered by a board composed of a secretary who had none of the credentials needed to represent a psychoanalytic society. The director was everywhere present, but he might also be everywhere absent—from the council of which he was not necessarily a member, and from the board for the same reasons. Moreover, applications for membership were to be presented to the director and decided on by him. But he could only secure their ratification through his secretariat. In addition, since no category of member was to be defined during the one-year period envisaged for the constitution of a set of internal regulations, it was not clear who could be a member, and under what circumstances.

In February 1980, the new school founded by Lacan and administered by his personal secretary was thus the most considerable juridical mutant ever imagined in the entire history of psychoanalysis in France. It legitimized rule by arbitrary whim and anonymity. No doubt it was a sign of the slow transformation induced by the work of dissolution within the Lacanian movement.

On March 15 there was held at the Onyx Room of the Hotel PLM Saint-Jacques a meeting to which the members of the EFP in favor of dissolution were invited. Three hundred eight participants showed up, each with an invitation. At the entrance, security was tight and undesirables were vigorously shunted off. For five francs, one could purchase the temporary bulletin of the EFP, entitled *Delenda,* in which fantastic testimony concerning the signatories of the legal writ against Lacan was reproduced. They were accused of plotting to steal the École's name.

Suddenly, in the middle of the crowd, a man tried to force his way in. His back hunched over, his gait a bit heavy, he chomped on a rolled cigarette while speaking in a solemn and faltering voice. His eyes, a Vermeer shade of blue, illuminated a high forehead beneath silver hair. He seemed proud, the old teacher who had brought Lacan into the ENS, but the watchdogs planted outside the Onyx Room did not recognize him. They were too ignorant to realize they were blocking

Louis Althusser's way. When asked for his invitation, he shot back abruptly: "I've been summoned by the libido and the Holy Ghost. And everyone has known for a long time that the Holy Ghost is the libido. So I say to you in truth, the Holy Ghost has nothing to do with the whole thing." Whereupon the philosopher made his way into the meeting and sat in the first row. He looked around, listened to what the speakers were saying, and then noticed Jacques-Alain Miller at the back of the room. He went over and joked with him.[67] Standing at the center of the podium, in a white shirt and a silk jacket, Jacques Lacan read a welcome speech to his partisans: "Hello, my good friends, so here you are at our rendezvous. The *école* is coming to the end of its course. You are still here with me. I left because it was dead and didn't realize it."[68] Then he announced that he had become a signifier—"le 'label Lacan,'" [that is, the "Lacan trademark"]—but "la belle Lacan" could only give what she had. He continued with other puns in the same vein.

When his speech was over, Louis Althusser advanced to the central aisle, slowly emptied his pipe against the heel of his shoe, filled it, and went to shake Lacan's hand. Then he began to speak. He described the master as a magnificent and pitiful Harlequin, delivering his single-string message. He noted that analysts tended to bog down in confused speeches, like a woman attempting to sift out lentils while war was breaking out. He added that the Lacanians were as disturbed by the present situation as the militants of the party by Georges Marchais's declarations in support of the Soviet intervention in Afghanistan. Finally, he recalled that the ones who were forgotten in the whole affair were the analysands. He called those attending the meeting fearful. From the podium, Anne-Lise Stern asked him which couch he was coming from to speak in those terms.[69]

In *Delenda,* Érik Porge commented on the event while "speaking Lacanian" in the manner of Bouvard and Pécuchet: "Our *colleagues* of the law suit," he wrote, "have this in common with Althusser, in that they confuse thought with what is said [*le dit*]. That is why they can't understand that what was said on January 5 was an analytic act and that it cannot be compared—Althusser *dixit*—to a performance by Monsieur Marchais on television. We know where thought that indulges itself tends: toward the paunch [*où penche la pensée qui s'épanche: vers la panse*]. Whereas there ex-sists in relation to the said [*le dit*] a saying [*dire*]. Lacan has described very well how *dit-solution* came to him: as a pun and from which a cascade of verbal transformations—among which dissolution—followed. Dissolution is a thought; not *dit-solution.*"[70]

At the general meeting of March 16, the statutory revision was not adopted. The opponents represented about two hundred members and the partisans of dissolution more than two hundred fifty. The latter were from then on in the majority. The symbolic dissolution was a given, but the juridical position continued to resist. Maître Zécri called a new meeting of the membership for April 27. The opposition then published a bulletin, *Entre-temps,* which situated itself opposite *Delenda* and welcomed the testimony of the leaders of the effort to preserve the École. In the course of a meeting at the Hotel Lutétia, attended by Serge Leclaire, Françoise Dolto announced that she would be a candidate for the administrative council on the opposition slate and that she would not vote for dissolution. She nevertheless acknowledged the authenticity of the act of January 5: "Lacan's withdrawal is a good thing for him," she said. "His 'I dissolve the school' is a desire of his, which, were we to respond to it in reality, would mean that we were abandoning the continuation of his work inscribed in that reality, that of our own personal history and that of psychoanalysis at its most alive."[71]

The plenary session of April 27 marked an important date in the history of the EFP. For the first time there were two slates opposing each other for election to the administrative council. Even before the vote, the majority party was aware that it had won. A simple majority was in fact enough to elect the slate backed by Lacan. The discussion was stormy. A member of the administrative council on the majority list, Louis Beirnaert, explained that the document of January 5 was liberating and that its adversaries were perhaps even more bound by a transference with Lacan than the partisans of dissolution. Then he added: "I will support the work as it was begun, without cursing anyone. . . . One more item. On the subject of Moses saved from the waters, Freud wrote: 'The means of getting rid of the child is transformed into a way of saving him.' Lacan's act dooms us as members of the École only to save ourselves as analysts together. We have an opportunity; it's up to us to use it."[72] Louis Beirnaert also evoked a question that had been asked of him by the opposition, "Do you pledge that if you are elected no member will be admitted before the plenary session on dissolution?" He answered that the question did not even arise for himself. The opposition in fact feared that new members would be hastily admitted by the administrative council in order to obtain the votes lacking for dissolution. This would not at all be the case. On January 22, Simatos and Laurent communicated to Maître Soulez-Larivière the list of the seven last individuals accepted into the EFP during the plenary session of September 30. They were added to the members named since 1977, whose names were partially mentioned in the new 1980 roster, which would never be made public.[73] At the time the dissolution process was initiated, the EFP counted 609 members. In two years, it had thus been augmented by sixty-five persons. Such unbridled growth was not unrelated to its breakup.

On behalf of the opposition, Françoise Dolto called on members to vote against the "commandos" who had placed themselves in the master's service. She then added that she had never identified the EFP with Lacan, whose friend she continued to be. Finally, she emphasized that the school could continue without him, referring strictly to his work.

On the evening of April 27, the EFP ceased to exist. The symbolics of dissolution had introduced a *de facto* split within its ranks. Thereafter, the situation would be identical to that of the winter of 1964 for the SFP. On the one side, the majority held the reins of power, still united for a few months; on the other, the members of the minority tended to be busy saving the furniture, despite the division settling into their ranks. Two more meetings of the entire membership would be needed to secure the juridical dissolution of the EFP. As soon as the meeting was over, Jacques-Alain Miller assumed charge of a "department of dissolution" that would hold its first meeting a month later. As for Eric Laurent, he vented his satisfaction in a circular: "The administrative council is delighted that the juridical debate has come to an end. The mission of the court agent has been accomplished. The administrative council is in place. Its election was achieved under circumstances that are beyond challenge. . . . Under those conditions, there can be no solution other than separation. It ought to be possible on friendly terms, on terms that are clear, without undue acrimony. . . . We propose that each of the two groups share the school's holdings on a pro rata basis according to the number of members belonging to it and that each renounce a name which henceforth belongs to the past, indeed to history."[74]

At that stage of their joint collapse, it was in the interest of the members of the majority to settle things amicably. They knew that the juridical dissolution would be difficult to secure and that the increasingly heavy silence of Lacan might make them seem the representatives of a faction cut off from the master's will. Moreover, they were alone in having founded a group that could receive the holdings of the defunct École. The minority members, on the contrary, had an interest in being as opposed as possible to an amicable settlement. In delaying things, they could get organized and benefit from whatever disarray might erupt in the adversary camp.

During the month of May, several efforts at working in concert all ended in failure. The majority group then decided to shut down the premises on the rue Claude-Bernard and transfer the office of the secretariat to the home of Eric Laurent.

At the beginning of June, *Delenda* organized "Dissolution Mondays" intended to implement the principle of a split. The evenings were led by those who were from then on the effective directors of the Cause freudienne: Jacques-Alain Miller, Eric Laurent, Michel Silvestre, Colette Soler. They were between thirty-five and forty years old and represented a severely intellectual mode of Lacanianism, intent on conquest. Michel Silvestre was a former student of the Institute, who was much appreciated by the young, and Colette Soler, a likable *agrégeé* in philosophy who had been analyzed by Lacan. Among the opposition they were known as the gang of four.

The objective of the Mondays was to demonstrate that the minority group were advocates of a practice that substituted the "rock of narcissism" for the "rock of castration" and preferred the ineffable and religion to science. Against them, their adversaries called them; "mutants" capable of changing skin on command and anonymously. The Mondays did not enjoy the success that had been anticipated, and before long the majority group announced its intention of moving the Lacanian scene to Latin America, where, since 1974, numerous "Freudian schools" had been constituted. In November 1979, the decision was taken to hold a colloquium, in Jacques Lacan's presence, in Caracas. At that time, Miller went to Venezuela for a series of lectures. Officially, that country had been preferred to Argentina because of its nondictatorial regime.[75] But there was a different reason motivating the selection: Venezuela was "virgin" territory for Lacanianism compared to Argentina, and thus easier to control from Paris. The Fondation du Champ freudien, created for that reason, thus began to play its true role, which was to sponsor international exchanges beyond the activities of the École and the Cause. Through it, the organization of relations with foreign countries escaped the classical mode of institutional control, and as a result, an authentic Lacanian empire began to be set up, capable of competing with an Anglo-American IPA in lands hostile to the imperialism of the same name.

At the same time that the colloquium was announced, a general assembly of the EFP was called for July 5 to vote on the dissolution.[76] In a circular written on stationery of the Cause freudienne, Lacan announced that he was "inaugurating his last seminar, the first correspondence of the said cause awaited by a thousand and more."[77] Lacan would no longer speak publicly thereafter, even to read texts. Thus ended thirty years of flamboyant and almost weekly discourse.

At the meeting of July 5, Michèle Montrelay called on the opposition to maintain their no to dissolution until the end. She quoted a line from Lacan's last letter about "bringing things to an end" [venir à bout]: "What desire to destroy must gnaw at the person who expresses himself thus? We are not questioning his right to found elsewhere, or to disavow whomever he wants. That's his right and we respect it. But why can't Jacques Lacan bear that what he removes himself from should continue to live?"[78] That day the two-thirds majority was not achieved. Twenty blank ballots were cast. Out of 466 votes cast, 294 were favorable to dissolution and 145 opposed. The École continued to pretend it existed thanks to the abstentions. The minority was losing ground. Fatigue and internal division haunted both camps.

In Caracas, quite tired from his trip in a Concorde, Lacan called on the "Lacan-Americans" to group around him: "I come here to launch my Freudian cause. You can see that the adjective is important for me. You are free to be Lacanians if you like. As for me, I'm a Freudian."[79] Despite that manifestation of his might, the seraglio was already beginning to come apart. Solange Faladé did not make the trip. "As of May," she said, "Lacan was no longer interested in what was going on, and everything had to be discussed with Miller."[80]

In the camp of the partisans of dissolution, the opposition to Miller had not yet manifested itself. Elected in order to dissolve the École and intent on remaining faithful to the act of January 5, the members of the administrative council did not succeed in dissociating the Millerian faction from Lacan's person. If they did so, they would disavow the authenticity of the act of dissolution desired by Lacan and would run the risk of helping the cause of the adversary camp. It was for that reason that until September 27, the date of the extraordinary plenary session called to determine the school's future, they formed a block with the Millerians. Nevertheless, on the day of the vote, Solange Faladé momentarily considered ceasing her support for Miller and opening the meeting with a disavowal. She abstained.[81] On the opposition side, fissures were beginning to be felt, notably in the ranks of those who had joined in the lawsuit. Claude Rabant began to jump ship, while Michèle Montrelay wanted to keep up the fight to preserve the École. Between the two parties, which were already divided beneath the surface, misunderstanding turned into a dialogue of the deaf. Negotiations were conducted by Roland Dumas and Daniel Soulez-Larivière to arrange an amicable separation. They ended in failure.[82] The partisans of dissolution wanted it to take place by consensus, while the adversaries asked for a sharing of holdings without dissolution and the departure of those who so desired. On September 26, Claude Rabant switched sides. He let Lacan know that he would vote for dissolution and asked to join the Cause freudienne. Since until then he had carried with him a goodly portion of the opposition votes, his voluntary submission was a harsh blow for the minority. On the evening of September 27, the dissolution was voted through by a small majority. Solange Faladé and René Bailly were appointed liquidators.[83]

At a victory reception at the Maison de l'Amérique latine, Miller came to inform Lacan of the result of the vote. "Lacan," wrote Claude Dorgeuille, "with a vague smile, apparently indifferent, gave no sign of satisfaction upon receiving the news. He seemed far off, mechanically clasping the hands stretched out to him, not appearing always to recognize those approaching him. A short session of the administrative council, its last, was held on the second floor, where an official announcement that the EFP no longer existed was written up. Lacan left without saying a word. The Cause freudienne had the field free to itself."[84]

Even before the dissolution had been secured, Lacan's entourage was aware that he was stricken with a colon cancer and that he refused to be operated on. The École was dissolved and the master's body was now suffering from the same disease as had Freud's. The last phase of the collapse would turn horrendous.

That month of October marked the shipwreck of a whole era of French thought. Already Roland Barthes had suffered a violent death. A few years later, he would be joined by Michel Foucault, felled by the new disease of the century. An accident and homosexuality for some, madness for another, stony silence for a fourth. Theoretical antihumanism and the logic of the signifier were undoubtedly modernity's most "human" doctrines. Who would dare claim that the body was absent from them, that passions were not unbridled in them, that they had evacuated man?

In October, Louis Althusser chained his final fate to a declining psychiatry and a dying psychoanalysis whose patient, witness, victim, hero, and theoretician, over a period of thirty years of mental illness, he had been. The entire press announced his own act of dissolution: the strangling of his wife Hélène. And to make things still more paradoxical, he benefited from Article 64, which had fallen into disuse and which alone still shielded the insane from criminal court or the guillotine. Irresponsibility: what an insane word for a philosopher, the most "visionary" of all, who placed his thought in the service of an impossible revolution! Since the event occurred at a time when the comedian Coluche, with the support of a handful of intellectuals, was deciding to offer his candidacy in the French presidential election, the press did not fail to comment on the disaster of the structuralist years. "One said to oneself, there are a few left," wrote Hervé Algarrondo. "Barthes let himself die at Pitié-Salpêtrière, Poulantzas jumped out of a window; Althusser killed his old lady; Lacan smashed his toy, the École; but Deleuze, Bourdieu, Guattari—they at least have held fast. And then their names at the bottom of a text. They support Nicoud for election as president, no, not Nicoud, Coluche. . . . What a disaster! May 1968 has given birth to a pair of overalls! Subversion by suspenders. The intellectual masters of the Left falling into homicide or derision. . . . It would all be laughable if while our champions withdrew, the intellectuals of the Right were not raising their eyes and occupying terrain."[85]

Four years later, Althusser would make his first comeback on the French intellectual scene—on the subject of psychoanalysis. In April 1984, in fact, Léon Chertok, with total scorn for editorial propriety and without the slightest hesitation, published the notorious first draft withdrawn from the Proceedings of the Symposium at Tbilisi. He did not inform the interested party, whom everyone believed to be dead and buried. Althusser nonetheless voiced his opinion in a moving letter sent to *Le Monde:* "Personally in charge of liaison work between the French and the Soviets, thus perfectly well informed about all the details of this incident, Dr. Chertok has, on his own initiative, violated every rule of propriety as well as the provisions of the law, and published my first text, both in his journal and his book. I assume that he felt he could speculate on my retirement and thus make do without my authorization. And yet he was sufficiently well informed to be persuaded that I would no more give it to him today than seven years ago." [86]

On October 22, 1980, the new statutes of the Cause freudienne were sent to the Prefecture. That dispatch would be the subject of much commentary. At the end of the month, the movement's organizational structure was in place. A meeting of the directorate was set for November 6 and a second one, billed as "extraordinary," for the twenty-second. In private, Solange Faladé let Miller know of her disagreements with him. She reproached him for not wanting to allow the Cause freudienne to absorb the debts of the EFP. She also thought that the general meeting of the new association should have been expanded to include all those who paid their dues and not just a small number. Solange was wrong to refrain from any public objection.

The EFP's debts amounted to some 140,000 francs. Miller maintained that the Cause freudienne was in no way obliged to pay such a sum. He thus proposed that the new organization officially acquire the assets of the EFP so as to help the liquidators make up the deficit. A business discussion took place in which each party defended his point of view. Disagreeing with Miller, the liquidators reproached him for wanting to retrieve the assets of the EFP for a ludicrous sum. They were not wrong, but instead of exposing their divergences publicly, they preferred to keep them secret in order subsequently to accuse their adversary of not honoring his commitments.

In a mailing of October 30, Miller, secretary of the directorate, announced additionally that the Cause freudienne had petitioned René Bailly, administrator of the SCI [realty corporation] of the rue Claude-Bernard, to lease the building that had been rented to the EFP. That site, it will be recalled, had been bought by about 120 members of the EFP, who had constituted themselves as an SCI, thus placing at the disposition of all, for a rental fee, the building whose owners they were. Among the principal shareholders: Lacan (50), Melman (50), Dolto (25), Bailly (25), Clavreul (12), Aubry, Martin, Safouan, Simatos, Oury, and Roublef (10 each).

Melman committed a serious error in this affair. He would acknowledge it later on. He advised Miller to request a lease. In order to second his effort, Melman got himself named coadministrator of the SCI, along with Bailly. He was, moreover, with Lacan, the principal shareholder. Now once the dissolution was pronounced, the shareholders who were hostile to it had no reason (even if they were in a minority) to agree to rent their building to a cause whose orientations they did not share. The only foreseeable solution at that point was a simple sale of the building, with restitution of the capital to each. But things did not transpire thus. Melman and Bailly, who were themselves committed to the Cause freudienne, approved in principle that absurd rental. They supported the petition without concern for the minority opinion of shareholders hostile to the Cause freudienne and favorable to an immediate sale. That was why, during the first general meeting of the SCI, on November 14, the members of the majority, committed to the Cause, massively endorsed the principle of a rental which in any event should not have had to be envisaged.[87]

During that period, in the course of two meetings of the directorate, conflicts about the EFP's liabilities grew embittered. Nevertheless, they were not made public, and all discussions bore on the setting up of the Cause freudienne's organizational structure. Miller explained statutory dispositions which he proposed on the basis of summary indications by Lacan, who, he said, wanted the following: to hold the presidency of the Cause without having to administer its activities, to make its administration a more open affair without endangering its continuation, to establish an underlying structure allowing for change of administration without affecting the general orientation, and finally to make of general meetings an occasion for reasoned exchange and not confusion. Miller then presented the plan envisioned for the various divisions of the association. He added that the statutes were not intended to define in any detail the functioning of the society. They were there to establish a "framework."

At the extraordinary meeting of November 22, held in the Magnan Amphitheater, the directorate's report was presented to an assembly composed of former members of the EFP. Claude Conté explained that Lacan "expected everything from the functioning of the organization and nothing from individuals," a notion which contradicted all the principles of Lacanianism, based, on the contrary, on a master's privileged relations with his subjects. Miller then explained how the organization would be run, and Marcel Ritter how exchanges with the provinces would be handled. Eric Laurent spoke of the cartels and Michel Silvestre of the library. Charles Melman then took the floor and informed the meeting of the creation of an "École de la cause" internal to the association and intended to receive testimony concerning the *passe*. A lively discussion followed and the announcement was made that in a year's time, an administrative assembly would be held, and that that assembly could elect itself on the basis of those present on November 22.[88]

The principle of a rental being agreed upon, Miller proposed to Melman, on November 24, that a lease be written up. He acted in his role as "Lacan's secretary." The contract contained clauses that were quite debatable. It was stated, for example, that the lease could be revoked solely by the tenant. The rent was to be fixed by an expert and no mention was made of any indexing in relation to inflation. As it stood, the lease was thus unacceptable. But nothing forced Melman and Bailly to sign it. If they were not satisfied with the proposals of the potential tenant, they could modify the contract, reject it, or have a different one written up. They had been charged with that responsibility by the majority shareholders of the SCI. Instead of negotiating, as was customary in this kind of situation, they accused the would-be tenant of trying to cheat them, whereas all he had done was offer an unacceptable contract. At the same time, they confused several problems: the lease, the statutes of the Cause freudienne, and the circulars signed by Lacan after 1980. It was Bailly who urged Melman to act. At which point the latter went further than his colleague had wanted. He accused Miller of using "apocryphal texts" concerning the statutes and circulars and of having wanted to make the two representatives of the SCI sign a contract that would have made them vulnerable to suits for abuse of the social good. But he omitted to specify that nothing obliged the two associates to endorse such a lease. What was at stake for Melman was the breaking off of an alliance and the distribution of power within the new Cause.

At the beginning of December, Melman thus sent three hundred members of the former EFP a letter in which he revealed Lacan's lapses of lucidity (which were apparent to everyone) and the anomalies contained in the lease and in the statutes registered with the Prefecture. "The present situation," he wrote, "merits that an 'oldtimer' take the freedom of saying where things stand. The Cause freudienne was indeed, from the cradle, found to harbor a malformation that has a good chance of either dooming it or turning it into a freak. Why? Because everything is decided and inscribed there in the name of Lacan while it must be acknowledged that Lacan has no part in those measures other than an automatic signature. This is a painful fact. One that is also difficult to perceive, so much is it cloaked by the students' hopes of seeing Lacan establish a new organization they might be proud of. And yet one really should force oneself to grasp that fact: The Cause freudienne is being set up without Lacan, even if we are lucky enough to have him among us. That absence, due to old age and fatigue, thus leaves the field open to whoever disposes of his signature, or even of his voice, and can thus make him endorse—or even articulate—apocryphal texts placed in the service of a cause that is hardly Freudian. It is rather astonishing that the exegetes of Lacan's writings have not noticed, in the course of these last months, the somewhat forced mannerism of the texts disseminated in his name and the cruel lack of any new ideas, with the exception of one or two gleaned from old drafts." Melman added that Lacan had not had a hand in writing the statutes of the Cause freudienne and that he and Solange Faladé were consulted without being allowed any access to him. Finally, he concluded by evoking the situation during the preceding months: "Some of us came back from Caracas physically ill. It cannot be a source of joy to anyone that Lacan is being used as a fetish to stir up crowds. Such circumstances give even the best addresses delivered from the podium the quality of a mascarade." [89]

Three weeks after the sending of that letter, a meeting of the shareholders in the building was held to review the vote of November 14. Delegated by Lacan, Miller reiterated his request to rent, having brought with him a new and perfectly standard lease. On December 19, against the majority shareholders whom he had lured down the path of that absurd rental scheme, Melman gave his support to the minority group, which was favorable—and quite properly so—to selling the property. A fraction of the majority thus did an about-face, some without realizing what was going on, and the decision to sell was voted through by a vote of 444 shares to

250 (with 10 abstentions).[90] But with that, the Cause freudienne exploded and Lacan's principal fellow travelers began to jump ship, accusing Miller of fraud and falsification of documents. Their role was not the finest in the affair since they had publicly supported what they would henceforth be denouncing in the most strident terms. In point of fact, since Lacan was moribund, they finally dared say out loud what they had been thinking to themselves. They would be guilty of not having manifested their hostility to Miller at a time when Lacan was sufficiently present to hear them. If they had not done so, it was probably because they were better placed than anyone else to realize that Lacan would have supported Miller against them, or because they hoped to win power in the new Cause, even if they had to leave control of the university and the Foundation to the son-in-law. The price they would pay for all this was considerable.

On December 23, Solange Faladé confirmed Melman's testimony in an open letter to the members of the Cause freudienne. She resorted to a style and tone quite different from Melman's. She had, moreover, refused to sign his letter and advised him, after seeing a first and even more violent version, to rewrite it so as to eliminate any trace of denunciation. "The October revisions of the Cause's statutes," she wrote, "were not approved by its members, at least not by Melman and myself. No account was taken of the reservations I had voiced except for the statute concerning the administrative secretary, who initially was to be remunerated. All discussion was cut short with the words, 'Dr. Lacan signed the statutes,' without it being possible to tell me what he had thought of my criticisms and reservations. . . . I thought I would be able to resume discussion of the statutes in the course of subsequent meetings of the directorate. Which is what I attempted to do during the first directorate, but in vain. . . . Similarly, the right to speak was withdrawn from Melman in short order when he tried to speak about the statutes of the École de la cause. Those statutes were initially supposed to have been discussed with me. Care was taken to make sure this never happened, and Melman was not even told that I was supposed to join him in taking charge of the École de la cause, whose role was to be central in the training of analysts, even though I was said to be one of its directors." [91] After Solange Faladé, Jean Clavreul took a public stand against Miller, writing to Lacan to inform him of the constitution of a GEP and the calling of a meeting of the entire membership of the Cause. He had the feeling he was reliving the events of the winter of 1964 and spoke of a "witch hunt." [92]

Against that avalanche of disavowals, Miller reacted in an anonymous interview, without date, which was recorded and then transcribed by two of his partisans, Maryse Clastres and Gérard Pommier. He emphasized that his adversaries' arguments did not hold up, and that the very fact that the statutes had been discussed during the meeting of the directorate would tend to prove that they had known about them. He added that the first rental contract was a draft and that there had been a reversal of perspectives since the normal situation was for the owner to propose a lease. His argument seems unassailable, although it did not take into account Lacan's lapses and did not say why, under such conditions, the lessee had proposed so unconventional a contract.[93] As far as Melman and Faladé were concerned, it was inconceivable that they had allowed their interventions to be cut off by young Turks while Lacan remained silent. There is something incomprehensible in that scenario about which we have nothing further to say.

All those revelations were a source of panic and consternation in the ranks of the Lacanian community. Everyone was prepared for a fist fight, but no one imagined that an analyst could denounce his student as a forger and a swindler after having spent so many years combining the affairs of the couch and those of the institution. In that respect, Melman's position was unacceptable whatever the arguments he resorted to. Aware of the situation, Serge Leclaire had lunch in January with Miller and told him that he disapproved of the letter of denunciation and that he would not howl with the pack.[94] For his part, Melman stated publicly that his patient's therapy was in no way at stake in this matter. As for Solange Faladé, she received dozens of letters from disoriented practitioners favorable to the creation of a new association. She proposed to found one to be called *La Lettre freudienne*, but her partners reneged and she herself was paralyzed by financial obligations relative to the liquidation of the assets of the EFP.[95] She would fulfill that task with all the honesty it demanded.

On January 5, Moustapha Safouan, who had voted in favor of dissolution without getting involved in any of the seraglio infighting, received a handwritten letter from Lacan brought to him by Miller before a meeting of *Delenda*. In it, Lacan recommended that his addressee help Miller, because he deserved it. Safouan is certain that the letter was indeed in Lacan's hand and an emanation of his will.[96]

The underlying reason for this new splintering had its source in statutes written up in October. On the formal level, they contained a single anomaly. They mentioned that revisions had been made in the course of a general meeting held on October 19. Now there is no trace of such a meeting in any archive. If it took place, it brought together only the two founders of the association: Jacques Lacan and Gloria Gonzalez. Which is to say that the general meeting on revisions could not properly be qualified as one.

For the rest, the statutes offered a perfect reflection of the situation of the Lacanian community at the dawn of the new year. They bore witness in particular to the mutation that had occurred during eight months in the history of Lacanianism thanks to the labor of dissolution. With them, Millerianism found its first form of institutionalization on French soil. The Cause freudienne association was intent on being a counter-experiment in relation to the mother society and that it indeed was. The February mutant had produced a veritable organizational instrument, one radically the opposite of the former EFP. The words were often the same; the ranks awarded were identical; and the procedures for the exercise of power were similar. Everything had the same aspect, but nothing was as it had been.

The Cause was composed of four principal concentrations of power: a directorate, a statutory council, an annual administrative assembly, and a biannual congress. The supreme organ of the edifice was the council, which was accorded virtually total power. Its members were to be recruited through elections, without it being specified who precisely could vote. It was composed of a four-member board, plus a treasurer and a president concerning whom it was not clear whether they were selected by vote or by self-appointment. Alongside the council, the directorate held office for two years. It was composed of a significant number of members concerning whom it was not specified by whom they were elected. No member of the directorate could sit on the council, whereas a delegate of the council was *ex officio* a member of the directorate. The directorate included a member of the school and an administrative secretary concerning whom it was not known how they were to be recruited. Five individuals were sufficient for it to function, each assisted by a deputy: a director; a secretary of the directorate; a secretary for exchanges (overseeing Paris-province relations through a commission); a secretary for cartels, who presided over the promotions commission; and a library secretary. The deputies were nominated by the commissions and appointed by the council after ratification by a general meeting concerning which we will see later what power it held. The deputy director was appointed by the council according to the same ratification procedure. As a result, the directorate was dominated by the council, which supervised it relentlessly through the deputies and the delegate. The power of the members of the directorate was thus diluted thanks to the system of deputies and secretaries. As seen from above, the directorate was the site of a centralizing power. Through the secretary for exchanges, it administered problems in the provinces from Paris, thus avoiding the possible formation of local insurgencies, as could have existed in the EFP. Thanks also to the secretary for cartels, it exercised power over them: It controlled promotions and the creation of new cartels.

As far as the base was concerned, the Cause was composed of two other organisms without any sovereignty: the administrative assembly and the congress. The first elected its members, who thus became *assembly members,* a category distinct from other categories of membership. It was convened annually by the council. It ratified nominations proposed by the council and heard and approved decisions of the directorate. It was represented by a board composed of a member of the directorate, another from the council, and a third from the assembly without it being stipulated how the board was to be elected. In any event, the assembly had only limited power: plainly, it could not "overthrow the government." In addition, its decisions were to be by hand vote, which, in the event of opposition, allowed the council and the directorate to identify potential protesters. As for the congress, it was organized on the same model as the assembly. It too was represented by a board, composed of a member of the council, a member of the directorate, and a member of the assembly. It could only be convened by the council, whose decisions it was called on to approve. Similarly, it could be convened in an extraordinary session to dissolve the association or revise its statutes. Its decisions were to be taken by hand vote. The congress was thus sovereign only exceptionally and always by decision of the leadership.

The members of the association were to be recruited through the decision of the directorate and with the endorsement of the council. The procedure was logical. But the establishment of five categories of membership resulted in an excessive degree of hierarchization, over and above the nondemocratic mode of selection. Those categories were distinct from the two ranks of AE and AME, which were to be awarded by an École de la cause, internal to the Cause and functioning on the model of a training institute. Through its statutes and the creation of the school, the Cause freudienne began to resemble in part a classical IPA institution.

If one examines now the list of the members of the directorate and the council board sent to the Prefecture on October 22, one sees that among the ten members of the first, six belonged to the Millerian faction, two were veterans of the previous generation, and two others provincials, both from Strasbourg. They controlled the secretaryship for exchanges. Alongside Claude Conté, who was director, Colette Soler was deputy director. Eric Laurent held the key position of secretary for cartels, Jacques-Alain Miller that of secretary of the directorate, and Michel Silvestre that of deputy for the library. As a result, with the exception of the exchange division, the directorate came under the control of the Millerian faction, either through deputies or directorial positions. With regard to the council board, the situation was identical. On it were Miller and Laurent, who held two positions and controlled a majority with Lacan as president and Gonzalez treasurer. Opposed to them, Melman and Faladé were a minority. Now since the council was the cornerstone of the association and the directorate was partially subordinated to it, the Millerian group had effective control of the society, in which any potential opposition would find it hard to achieve expression at the base.

Whether or not Lacan drew up the statutes of the Cause freudienne in his own hand matters little, since starting in 1974 he was unceasing in his support of Miller—in entrusting the transcription of his seminar to him, in installing him at the university of Vincennes, and in responding favorably to his proposals. Consequently, if one truly wants to criticize the Millerian line, one would have to deal as well with the teaching and conception of power of the last Lacan. The osmosis between the master and his son-in-law was so strong as of 1974 that the latter appeared increasingly as the former's interpreter. And it was for not having been able to dissociate the two in time that a majority of senior members found itself in the impossible situation of supporting the latter in the name of the former and then of disavowing him for the same reason.

The Cause freudienne was indeed a "counter-experiment" in relation to the EFP. It dropped the mix of direct monarchy and democracy which grounded the École's existence in 1964 and privileged the anonymity of a functioning apparatus at the expense of a master's relations with his subjects. In addition, it banned in advance any disturbances such as those of 1969 or 1979, as well as the constitution of any oligarchies. On that score it bore no resemblance to an IPA-affiliated society and maintained Lacanianism's opposition to any form of organized "barony." It transformed a school into a party, a doctrine into a cause, and a master into a great man already passed into posterity. It became Millerian while saying it was Freudian at the very moment it wanted to be Lacanian. It thus belonged to the history of the break-up of Lacanianism the way Lacanianism belonged to the history of the break-up of Freudianism. For the 1980s, it was symptomatic of the first emergence in France of a large-scale neo-Lacanian movement. The fact that it drew in part on a model borrowed from the Chinese revolution should not surprise once one recalls the role played by the eruption of Maoism in the formation of Millerian Lacanianism. In that respect, it took into account Lacan's person, for he had always been a rebellious master: Spinozan when he assumed his banishment, de-Gaullian when he founded his school, and Maoist when he supported his red guards against his old friends in a concerted practice of divisiveness.[97]

Starting in January 1981, an avalanche of resignations would provoke the fall of the Cause freudienne, which had barely had the time to exist. Among the members of the directorate, Jean-Pierre Bauer, Marcel Ritter, and Claude Conté remained in office for a while. Given the hemorrhage of the barons and a portion of the members, the Cause directorate decided not to move to collect dues and to create instead an École de la cause freudienne (ECF), which would be juridically independent of the preceding association.[98] That school was for the most part to take over the statutes of the defunct Cause, absorbing into them more specific provisions concerning the administrative assembly, the commissions of the directorate, and the new mode of appointment of AEs and AMEs. Lest he be accused to concealing the founding texts, Claude Conté mailed members copies of the ECF statutes registered with the Prefecture on January 19. "The present statutes," he wrote, "have been reviewed in the course of two plenary sessions of those constituting the directorate of the Cause freudienne (with a single exception) and who now constitute that of the École de la cause. These statutes have been completed according to Lacan's indications: a double commission for the *passe* consisting of two cartels working independently and including *passeurs;* a certification commission; no single individual in charge of the department of instruction, each person teaching at his own risk. This text thus offers a framework in which analytic work can resume at its different levels: cartels, teaching, certification, and *passe.*"[99]

The ECF's statutes[100] were far more interesting than those of the Cause. They clearly delineated the nature of the enterprise and defined the meaning of its power apparatus. This was still without democracy at the base, and it still banned both contestation and the constitution of oligarchies. The statutory revisions concerned the functioning of the directorate, the council, and the administrative assembly. The deputy secretaries were to be elected by the assembly, which was itself composed of delegates, at the behest of the directorate. The deputy director continued to be appointed by the council, but no delegate figured among its members. At the end of their terms, the director and secretaries were to be replaced by their deputies. Whence a rotational system allowing the directorate to be elected by the assembly. Nevertheless, the council retained control over the directorate through its appointment of a deputy director destined to become director. In addition, the assembly was never sovereign since it was represented by delegates at a proportion of one per ten members if the association were to have fewer than four hundred and one per fifteen if it were to exceed that figure. Ultimately, since the ECF would not have more than three hundred members, each delegate would be chosen to represent five members. A nondelegate member could thus not sit in the assembly. It was not specified whether a quorum of delegates was needed in the event that a significant number of members should reject the principle of delegation. Similarly, nothing was said of each member's obligation to participate in the selection of delegates.

The directorate was assisted by four commissions corresponding to the four secretaryships. Each was to meet once each trimester at the summons of the concerned secretary or his deputy. The director was *ex officio* part of each commission, each of which included eight members: four chosen by the assembly, that is, by the delegates, and four named by the directorate. Each secretary could summon from his commission any members whose presence he deemed useful. The directorate was thus all-powerful, but at the same time it was not, since its possibilities for making decisions were diluted by the existence of four secretaryships assisted by four commissions with a consultative role. In brief, the directorate controlled an assembly whose advice it was to hear, even as it itself was diluted by commissions and controlled by the council.

As for the council, it no longer had a board. The length of its term was unspecified, except for the president's, which was fixed at twelve months. It disposed of powers which were not reserved for the directorate, the assembly, or the congress. Its decisions had to be taken by majority vote. In the event it could not come to a decision in the course of a year, the assembly would be called on to decide for it. Since no means of election has been envisaged for the council during the coming years, and the council is to be designated by the president after nomination by the director, it is hard to imagine how an opposition might manifest itself, at least in an initial phase. The nonsovereign assembly would thus have nothing to decide. The self-designated council would receive proposals from the members of the association and eventually propose them to a vote by the congress. This amounts to the council disposing of absolute control over the functioning of the association.

The congress was to be the sole instance at which all members would be present: corresponding members, honorary members, members, and members of the statutory council. The category of member of the administrative assembly had been eliminated since that body would no longer be sovereign and since, in the congress, each member would represent himself. The congress was to meet every two years when convened by the council, or in extraordinary session, through the same procedure, in the event the council should want to have a vote on dissolution or a revision of the statutes. As in the assembly, voting would be by hand. Thus the secrecy of the ballot box would have no existence in this school organized like a panopticon. The congress, the only sovereign assembly, would have no other power than to accept or reject dissolution or a revision of the statutes. Concerning ordinary meetings, nothing was said about the congress's actual power except that it was to hear scheduled scientific and ethical reports and debate all questions on the agenda. Given such a system, it may be understood why the jurist Pierre Legendre, who had been in favor of dissolution, could mock the ECF, saying that with the exception of a few rare religious congregations, he had never seen anything like it.[101]

The means of attaining the ranks of AME, AE, and AP were incorporated into the statutes without any additional internal regulations except for the proposal of October 1967. The word *jury* was replaced by that of *commission*. The certification commission awarded the rank of AME. It was led by the director and composed of six members. The first commission would be appointed by the president for a term of three years. Thereafter, it was to renew itself at a rhythm of two members each year. In an initial phase, members would be selected randomly at a session of the council. Once the rotation was established, renewal would take place through seniority of appointment. Each year one of the two entering members would be chosen by the commission from within itself, the other to be chosen by the council. In itself the system was not bad, although the commission remained too dominated by the council and the director, who was himself an emanation of the council. Since there were no stipulations concerning the status and rank of members selected in the course of renewal, it could have meant that anyone could serve on a commission: AEs, AMEs, or other members who were arbitrarily chosen and never elected.

The procedure of the *passe* was to be implemented through a *double commission,* which was to bear that name. Instead of a single jury of eminent members elected at a meeting of the entire association, two cartels were to function independently of each other, hearing and appointing candidate-*passants*. Each cartel was to be composed of five members: three psychoanalysts, including at least one AE; and two *passeurs*. Each cartel was to be replenished alternately every two years according to the following modality: The AE was to be replaced by another one to be selected randomly. The same concerning the *passeurs*. One of the two psychoanalysts was to be renewed for two years while the other was to be named by the president. Once the rotational system was implemented, replenishment was to take place according to seniority of appointment. There were no specifications concerning that seniority.

Aside from the incorporation of *passeurs* into cartels, two interesting innovations were introduced in relation to the system in effect at the EFP. The rank of AE was to be temporary, valid for only three years. A secretariat for the *passe* was created, composed of four exiting members from the cartel about to be replenished. Its charge was to examine candidacies, to assign them to each cartel, to establish the list of *passeurs* selected by the AMEs and AEs, to draw their names at random and if need be, to add other *passeurs* drawn at random. The secretariat could enter into discussion with the analysts who had designated them.

That system for the *passe* was conceived as an unabashed disavowal of the procedure that had been in effect at the EFP. The orientation of candidates by the secretariat was intended to avoid the extraordinary vagueness which had led the École to its downfall. As for the appointment of AEs on a temporary basis, it was the reflection of a mode of power intent on banning the formation of any oligarchies. It had the advantage of emphasizing the role of a teaching function perpetually called into question. Finally, it avoided the constitution of a group of titular members named for life. If the association had functioned on democratic bases, such a procedure would have been quite interesting.

The publication of the statutes of the ECF had the effect of provoking the resignation of former AEs from the EFP, who had been called on to assure the functioning of the double commission for the *passe*. Among them were Jean Allouch, Marie Albertini, André Espaze, and Guy Sapriel. Before long the ECF would be nicknamed the *école-cause,* an allusion to Soviet jargon. On January 25, twenty-two psychoanalysts, some of whom had never stirred before, denounced the enterprise. Among them were such former fellow travelers as Louis Beirnaert, Maud and

Octave Mannoni, Christian Simatos, Thérèse Parisot, and Claude Dumézil. Almost all were AEs and the most famous would subsequently found a psychoanalytic society. They would be joined by Charles Melman, Solange Faladé, and Jean Clavreul; they would all become heads of schools. "A thousand and more wrote to Lacan," they said, "wanting to continue with him. We certify the fact that those in charge of the cause and its substitute, the school, have acted in such manner as to break the pact. . . . By inaugurating an organization that is authoritarian in its principle and manipulative in its behavior, incompatible with the ethics of analysis. In making of the Freudian domain a marketplace in which positions and functions could be traded in exchange for submission. By manifesting the primacy of a thirst for power at the cost of the degradation of Lacan's teaching. By exploiting Lacan's authority on behalf of activities alien to his method. By attempting to impose statutes that are unacceptable for reason of the contempt they display toward the members, something apparent even to the uninitiated." [102] Melman and Clavreul daring to give Miller lessons in democracy in the name of the ethics of analysis: as surreal a situation as might be imagined!

The following day, in an open letter bearing his signature, Lacan announced that he had broken his ties to everything except his practice. He continued with an appeal to his students' love and proposed the convening of an École "forum" in which all could be debated. In order to prepare for it, he designated eight advisors, including Robert Lefort, Paul Lemoine, Lucien Israël, Pierre Martin, Jacques-Alain Miller, Moustapha Safouan, and Colette Soler. Two days later, they accepted the mission. Safouan had a statement added to the reply saying that no one had the right to pretend to be Lacan's representative.

The situation was explosive. Israël and Safouan in fact thought that the forum should be independent of the École, since its objective was to discuss the statutes of that organization. They thus obtained agreement that the preparatory text would be written on stationery without letterhead, but their anger exploded when they saw that the announcement of the meeting had been sent in envelopes of the ECF. They nevertheless established the first week in March as a deadline for the submission of proposals and projects. In opposition to that attitude, Robert Lefort reacted by affirming that the maintenance of the ECF was a prerequisite for the existence of the forum. He wanted to exclude protesters from it. "My support is accorded wholeheartedly," he said, "to propositions without compromise, which is to say that the participation in the forum of those wanting the dissolution of the ECF appears to me not at all desirable, since they will not live within it." [103]

Maud and Octave Mannoni, for their part, asked the eight advisors to dissolve the ECF or to resign from their positions. [104] During the preparatory efforts, the eight advisors did not succeed in cooperating with any degree of calm. This was why, after having addressed Lacan personally, Safouan wrote to Conté to ask him whether the forum should be aimed at a debate of the ECF or a debate allowing for the creation of a new school. [105] Two days later, Bauer and Ritter resigned from the directorate in order to let the advisors organize the forum. But before long other members of the directorate, who were favorable to Miller, let it be known that the holding of the forum was not incompatible with the maintenance of the ECF. Immediately, Claude Conté resigned out of solidarity with Bauer and Ritter. He was the last to leave the ship after having traversed the storm. Thereafter, the ECF would pass entirely under the control of the Millerian faction. One last time, Safouan addressed Lacan—in vain—to beg him either to dissolve the ECF or relieve him of his function. That same day, Israël resigned from the same council. Conté, for his part, took a stand against the forum.

On the eve of the meeting, almost all Lacan's former companions had broken with a community which had become Millerian in the disposition of its statutes and the composition of its base. Only a few individuals remained on the side of the new leadership: the Thises, the Leforts, the Lemoines, and Pierre Martin. By the beginning of April, the dissolution of the EFP was actually complete and the ECF became the first Freudian component of post-Lacanianism. The master did not show up at the forum, which was held without him and in his name. "This enterprise and this forum," Serge Leclaire declared, "are in fact Miller's, whether he wants it or not. He is in a position to be the leader of this new school. If he withdraws, it won't continue. It's thus his affair, since Lacan delegated it to him. It will be a cultural enterprise of very high caliber, with transmission through the university and publishing activity. It will be quite an interesting thing, as the magazine *L'Ane* testifies. But it's a cultural project. The analytic will have a hard time finding a home there. Proof of this is offered, symptomatically, by the massive withdrawal of those that are called psychoanalysts. They don't feel comfortable. It is the cultural aspect which dominates in this quest and that quest is in the process of succeeding. The real difficulty will be finding the current problems of psychoanalysis in it." [106]

During this period, those who had resigned from the ECF continued to meet, bound by their violent opposition to Miller's institutional politics. There was no unity possible among those different tendencies within Lacanianism represented either by oldtimers or by the younger generations. The first initiative to found a group emanated from a cartel composed of clinicians having gone through the experience of the *passe*. It brought together Diane Chauvelot, Christian Simatos, Claude Dumézil, Jean Allouch, and André Rondepierre, who would soon be joined by Claude Conté. On February 1, they sent out an open letter [107] calling for the creation of "Constituent Cartels." The initiative's interest lay in showing that only a collective organization was possible, following the break, in which no one could invoke the position of a master. That was why the term *cartel* was preferred to those of association, school, or society. The group thus took up an important element in the Lacanian notion of the social bond. That creation also had the advantage of not being a hasty anti-Millerian fabrication.

As opposed to that initiative, Melman, Clavreul, and Faladé reacted quite differently by founding, on March 7, a "Centre d'études et de recherches freudiennes" (CERF), which would break up a year later since it had been conceived largely in order to settle scores with Miller. Out of that unnatural alliance joining three barons incapable of getting along with each other would emerge three distinct associations, each with its central personality and regrouping a portion of his or her students: Charles Melman's "Association Freudienne," Solange Faladé's "École freudienne," and Jean Clavreul's "Convention psychanalytique" (in which he was joined by Moustapha Safouan and several other cofounders).

While the various tendencies issuing from the Cause continued to splinter, the ECF did not lose any time. On the publishing level, Miller's enterprise took on the aspect of an expanding power established on a family-based administration: the three Millers—Judith, Jacques-Alain, and Gérard—were its undisputed leaders, even though the notion of individual power had been excluded in favor of those of a "cause" or "network." In April a superb magazine appeared, the first of its type, whose objective was to put psychoanalytic interpretation to the test in the domain of media-dominated culture, to consider contemporaneity in a new light, from the perspective of a deciphering of its signifiers. The magazine was named *L'Ane* [Donkey], and its name was based on a pun: "*l'ane à listes*" [the donkey with lists, also: the analyst]. Gérard and Judith bore the lion's share of responsibility for the affair and revealed an astonishing journalistic talent. In the very first issue, under the title "Ephémérides," Catherine Clément explained how she conceived of her intervention in the magazine. Originally, in fact, the idea was Jean Laplanche's and the column was to appear in *Psychanalyse a l'université*. But when the editorial board of that journal specified that they wanted it to deal above all with the work of its own group, Clément transferred the experiment to the pages of *L'Ane,* while reversing its perspective. She would write a chronicle of all the activities of the psychoanalytic world with the exception of those connected with the ECF and its representatives.[108]

With that initiative, Jacques-Alain Miller and his partisans found themselves at the head of an empire oriented according to four axes: implantation in the publishing world, psychoanalytic society, academic bastion, and international organization. On the eve of his death, Jacques Lacan would thus gradually have established the formidable instrument of his greatest revenge against those who had banished and humiliated him. But the price to be paid was high, once one recalls the fate of imperial pretensions in the history of psychoanalysis. Millerian Lacanianism had broken the pact with what had been the splendor of the EFP from 1964 to 1974: unity in diversity, democracy at the base, direct monarchy, respect for individuals and identities. That splendor came after ten years of a magnificent golden age, punctuated by the disaster of the split in 1963. Its fate was to be ephemeral like all such adventures. With the massive departure of its senior membership, the ECF was deprived of two major elements needed for its proper functioning: on the one hand, democracy, and on the other, clinical training. Every psychoanalytic society, in order to train therapists and transmit a doctrine, needs at least two generations of practitioners: the seniors trained by their "fathers," and the juniors trained by the seniors. But the ECF did not have them. Its members were consequently obliged to reinvent everything, that is, to analyze each other among themselves, notably for second phases of analysis, and to supervise each other and live self-sufficiently within the intricate machinery of an apparatus without being able to appeal to the experience of masters living among them. Which was tantamount to their having been orphaned twice over—by the ancestor who was no longer there to guide them, and by the sons of that ancestor, who disavowed them after having trained, analyzed, and sustained them. That lack of a heritage had something tragic about it, just as the removal of a link in the history of any genealogy is tragic. And it was no doubt not by chance that the ECF's first slogan, two months after the master's death, was situated under the sign of a grand return to clinical practice, presented as a formidable disavowal of the preceding generation and as the glorification of a Lacan eternalized in the practice of each member.[109]

Despite its triumphalism and its absence of democracy, the ECF was, from its inception, a poignant institution in which young brothers—who were intransigent but also high-spirited and ready to take on the world—directed their juniors who knew nothing of the old EFP except the horrors of the dissolution. Those "juniors" were dismayed witnesses to the stampede of the barons without understanding the reasons for their flight. Having not been members of the former school, they knew nothing of its history. But for them, the elder brothers appeared as the true possessors of a Lacanian teaching, which, in becoming Millerian, was also easier to transmit, less baroque, less equivocal, less encumbered by the opulence of its rebirth. In five years, the ECF would reconstitute the link that had been lost with the departure of the seniors. As a result, Miller would occupy in the eyes of the young who had never known the master in his splendid maturity, the place previously occupied by him for other generations. He would be the rationalist incarnation of the discourse of the deceased ancestor. There was a logic to the process, since Lacan, before lapsing into silence, had wanted Miller to be the transcriber of his oral work.

If the ECF was galloping toward omnipotence, the constituent cartels were not long in suffering dislocation. With the creation of the journal *Littoral*, whose first issue appeared at the same time as *L'Ane*,[110] a young group of former members of the EFP began to be constituted around Jean Allouch, Philippe Julien, Guy Le Gaufey, and Érik Porge. They were more interested in the last Lacan of the Borromean knot than in that of the matheme. Their journal, which would be followed by a collection, bore witness to a serious doctrinal effort. After a year of discussion, they would leave the cartel movement in order subsequently to found their own society, the "École lacanienne de psychanalyse," the first to be so named. As for the Constituent Cartels, they would become a genuine association in January 1983: "Cartels constituants de l'analyse freudienne" (CCAF).

At Lacan's death in September 1981, four components of the Lacanian movement were sharing among themselves the terrain occupied by the former Cause freudienne: an expanding ECF, the journal *Littoral* in search of an institutional identity, the "Cartels constitutants" in the process of splintering, and the CERF, about to break apart. The first two were the youngest.

Epilogue

Aimée died, in the Christian faith, on June 15, 1981, at the age of eighty-nine. Lacan survived her by barely two months. At the end of the summer, vacationing at Guitrancourt, alone with Gloria, he suffered bleeding. The abdominal tumor provoked a series of occlusions and an operation became indispensable. The master was hospitalized on an emergency basis at the Hartmann clinic in Neuilly, where his mother had died thirty-three years earlier from complications following surgery. In order to avoid unwanted rumors, and meddling, the family decided not to list the name of the patient on the admissions register. Lacan thus settled into his last residence under the name of the physician treating him. That name had been retained for reasons of convenience. He feared injections, found it hard to bear nurses, and awaited the date of his operation. The operation itself went normally. Upon awakening the body was whole and without infirmity. But a few days later, Lacan lapsed into a coma as a result of kidney failure. On Wednesday, September 9, late in the evening, he died after pronouncing the words: "I am stubborn. . . . I am disappearing." Dead under an assumed name—such was the fate of this great artisan of the symbolic function.[1]

The following morning radio and television announced the news. Among Lacanians, the wildest rumors were rife. Some, albeit few in number, believed that Lacan's enemies had succeeded in infiltrating the air waves so as to make people believe he had died. Others attempted to conceal as much as possible the sad reality. On Europe 1, the master of ceremonies announced that there was no end to the bad news: "Lacan has died and clouds are drifting in from the west." That evening on Antenne 2, a few fragments of Lacan's Louvain lecture gave an incomprehensible view of the thinker. Only the written press and "France-Culture" would manage to offer a coherent version of things.

That same day, the body was transported to Miller's home, where Lacan had resided during the last months of his life. There he was laid on a bed and prepared for his funeral; a few militants from the ECF were allowed to pay their respects. The date of the funeral was not announced publicly and the place would be known only after the event through the obituary page of *Le Monde*.[2] On Friday, having just celebrated the fiftieth anniversary of his entrance into a religious order, Marc-François Lacan traveled to Paris to celebrate a mass in memory of his deceased brother. The ceremony took place in the church of Saint-François-de-Sales, in the presence of the children of Marie-Louise Blondin. The other part of the family did not appear. Nor did the body. Lacan was an atheist. And yet, once, out of bravado, he had dreamed of an elaborate Catholic funeral.[3]

On Saturday, about thirty persons accompanied the funeral procession along the narrow village road leading to the country cemetery of Guitrancourt. Among the intimates, friends of Sylvia: Michel and Louise Leiris, Suzanne Merleau-Ponty.

As for the entourage, there was a simple delegation come from the ECF. No former companions, no personal friends, no eminent personalities from the Freudian saga. Marc-François chose not to come to that lay farewell at which the members of the family were assembled in their entirety: Laurence Bataille, Judith and Jacques-Alain Miller, Thibaut and Sybille Lacan. Before the coffin, Thibaut delivered a brief eulogy of his father while Judith, quite pale, confirmed that the man being buried was indeed her father. A journalist from Mantes-la-Jolie took a few photos. Sandra, Laurence's daughter, broke into sobs. Slowly the procession climbed toward the cemetery where a gray tombstone was to cover forever over the fifty years of a fabulous history. Each person threw a last flower and dispersed in silence. On the gravestone facing the hill and dominating the village, simple words were inscribed in letters of gold: Jacques Lacan, April 13, 1901–September 9, 1981.

Libération and Humanité were the only dailies to devote their entire first page to the master's death. Along with Jacques Lang, the minister of culture, Georges Marchais was the only leader of a political party to send the family a telegram of condolence. "With him," he wrote, "a great contemporary thinker has disappeared. His name remains connected to advances in the theory of the unconscious. His works, which influenced an entire generation of intellectuals, have thus favored a veritable resurgence of that discipline in our country and more generally have left their mark on the very movement of ideas. Beyond the controversies it provoked, there remains the contribution of a work that has added to the renown of French thought. I salute for that reason the memory of Jacques Lacan." [4] In the materials published by L'Humanité, Lucien Bonnafé paid homage to Lacan who had been a precious interlocutor for him after the Liberation. Jean-Pierre Léonardini, for his part, compared Lacan's style to Mallarmé's and mentioned the name of Louis Althusser in the context of the episode at the Hôtel PLM Saint-Jacques.

While the newspaper of the PCF offered grandiose praise of this man who had never been favorable to their politics, Libération composed an explosive special issue. The headline was Lacanian to order, admirable in it humor and dash of journalistic genius: "Tout fou Lacan." Beneath that slogan adapted to the 1980s, a photograph showed the master in profile, his chin encased in the palm of his hand. He seemed to be pondering with some curiosity the commotion of a major demonstration. On the inside, numerous chroniclers recalled the Surrealist adventure, the splits, Vincennes, and May 1968. A series of puns punctuated the coverage: Lacan n'est plus, que Lacan même . . . Lacan n'est plus, que Lacan m'aime . . . Lacan n'est plus, que là quand meme." [Lacan is no longer, anything but himself . . . may he love me . . . anywhere but right here.] There was mention of Gloria Gonzalez, psychoanalysis, and Pierre Goldmann. [5] Libération was far and away the only newspaper to offer an account of the baroque character of the man, his doctrine and his unique school in French intellectual life. In 1981, the extreme Left emerging from the barricades was thus Lacanian: in its language, its style, its puns, and a certain uncontrolled way of seizing the signifiers of media-transmitted events. The children of Maoism recognized themselves in the figure of the master so intractable to the illusions of revolution.

Without being composed in Lacanian style, the material assembled by *Le Matin* was none the less remarkable, thanks to Catherine Clément, who had been the master's student. "He was an individual concerned about his own representation," she wrote, "careful about staging his own appearances. His seminar, first at Sainte-Anne, then at the ENS, and finally in one of the largest amphitheaters of the University of Paris I, near the Pantheon, assembled around his name hundreds of individuals, as Bergson had done in years past at the Collège de France. He was a power, an occasionally whimsical person, a generous man with unpredictable generosities, often a terror, and finally a psychoanalyst with a superb capacity for listening, but the force of his words and his thought imposed themselves, and imposed respect, as the saying goes, on all." Catherine Clément did not forget the women's movement and asked Antoinette Fouque and Hélène Cixous for their thoughts. "Lacan was a practitioner," wrote Antoinette, "and I bear within me, as an unforgettable privilege, the benefit I derived from analytic work done with him. In every moment of cultural aridity, I refer to it as an oasis, a source of life." 6

The report published by *Le Figaro,* on the cover of its fourth section, was quite different. Alongside a confused article by Bernard This on knots, the columnist Bernard Bonilauri presented Lacan as a sadist treating his patients with immense cruelty.8 The *Quotidien,* for its part, showed itself to be objective. Pierre Daix recalled Lacan's battles against conformism, and Georges-Marc Benamou, quoting Bernard-Henri Levy, underscored the bond uniting the master to the Gauche prolétarienne.8 In *Le Monde,* Roland Jaccard abstained from writing, and it was Christian Delacampagne who assumed responsibility for a positive account of Lacan's thought. André Green and Octave Mannoni each published an obituary that had been prepared in advance. One was critical and the other laudatory. The whole of the coverage ended up as neutral and somewhat colorless. It nevertheless rectified the "blunders" of the fall of 1979.9 In order to remain still more neutral and dispassionate, the paper published, four days after the event, two pieces of testimony, one "pro" the other "contra." One was by Alain Didier-Weill and the other by Colette Chiland, who did not deprive herself of the opportunity to take pot shots at her perpetual enemy: "Lacan's very idiosyncratic practice was a perversion of psychoanalysis through seduction, manipulation of the transference, and lying. . . . With Lacan, psychoanalytic theory became a discourse about psychoanalysis. The great absent figure in the *Écrits* is the patient." 10

The weeklies reported Lacan's death in the same way as the dailies. With the exception of *Révolution,* an organ of Communist intellectuals, none devoted its cover page to the event. Nevertheless, the densest and best organized coverage emanated from the left-wing press and the so-called cultural press. Aside from *Révolution, Le Nouvel Observateur* and *Les Nouvelles littéraires* were the most prolix and assembled the most interesting texts, with testimony from Serge Leclaire and Françoise Dolto. In *L'Express,* on the contrary, it was the philosopher Marcel Gauchet who took it upon himself to bury the master in simplistic and vengeful terms. In the socialist France of the post-May 1981 period, he thus sounded the note of the broad swerve to conservatism which would flourish four years later with the antistructuralist pieces produced by the adepts of a neo-positivism *à la francaise.*11 Gauchet's

Lacan resembled an esoteric thinker purveying a dubious Heideggerianism, which was itself assimilated to a pejoratively dubbed "German" philosophy. In passing, he was compared to an insatiable pick-up artist when it came to patients, half-Stalinist, half-Maoist, fitting for the Pantheon of Jaurès and Moulin—a species nearing extinction.

In 1939, on the eve of the war, Freud's death was celebrated in the French press with an assortment of nonsense. Only Marie Bonaparte, the official representative of psychoanalysis for public opinion, defended the memory of the Jewish and Austrian scientist persecuted by the Nazis.[12] By the time of Lacan's death, forty-two years later, the situation had reversed itself. France had become Freudian through its Left, its literature, its Communism, and its *gauchisme*. At the same time, it had become Lacanian. The assortment of nonsense emanated less from the written press than from an intelligentsia become anti-Freudian anew or from psychoanalysts intent on destroying Lacanianism. Generally speaking, the journalists did their job properly. On the other hand, and with only a few exceptions, the testimony of intellectuals and therapists was painful in the extreme. The great—third generation— names of the saga shone through their absence, the epigones through their fanaticism, the "new-thinkers" through their simple-mindedness, and the perpetual adversaries through their vociferations. As evidence, if it be needed, there was the bewildering response given by Paul Racamier, then president of the SPP, to a journalist from *Libération:* "The president cannot be disturbed. One does not treat psychoanalysts the way one does garage mechanics—even for the death of Lacan." [13]

Seen from the United States, the event occupied a few lines in the *New York Times.* On the morrow of Lacan's death, Lacanianism had thus won its battle for an implantation of Freudianism in France. What remained was for it to conquer the world.

A Hundred Years of Psychoanalysis: An Inventory

It is still too early to historicize the situation of psychoanalysis in France between 1981 and 1985. Nevertheless, a hundred years after the meeting of Freud and Charcot, and four years after the death of Lacan, an observation should be made: Freudian doctrine is flourishing within the nation's boundaries. That prosperity has been accompanied by a temporary crisis, since the proliferation of schools and therapists has led to a different distribution of requests for therapy which has resulted in the impression that such requests are diminishing. With 418 members, the SPP is the largest IPA-affiliated society in the world. It has grown at a rate that some have found worrisome and has been placed under surveillance. The APF, on the other hand, is threatened, if not with extinction, at least with a certain stagnation. It is, however, rather healthy from the administrative point of view. France in 1985 counted 478 psychoanalysts recognized by the IPA, to which hundreds of students, who were not included in the list, may be added. For Lacanians, who are more numerous, and non-Lacanians outside the IPA empire, the figure is probably around 1,600, to which a number of unregistered individuals can be added.

That flourishing condition has been accompanied by certain losses. In becoming more and more institutionalized, psychoanalysis has become detached from the great cultural adventures which had given it such strength in former times. It no longer interests literary vanguards, and fuels theoretical discussion somewhat less. In brief, it has tended once again to become a mere therapeutic technique for human suffering. Whence the malaise affecting some of its representatives, concerned with preserving its noble—and only incidentally guildlike—image. Jacques Lacan was alone in France in having restored that aspect to the discovery from Vienna. He owed that role to his personal genius, but also to the Surrealist and Kojèvien facets of his youth. The structuralist "revolution" would do the rest. His former students or partisans are at present the finest representatives of that intellectual Freudianism whose emergence he was responsible for: Jean Laplanche, Didier Anzieu, Wladimir Granoff, J.-B. Pontalis, Serge Leclaire. All broke with him, for one reason or another, but all have remained marked—either positively or negatively—by his position and his teaching. After them, in the 1980s, it is the Millerian Lacanians who have occupied, in their own way, the bastions of the resurgence of such an adventure. For them, that adventure is not individual but collective. It is to be articulated with the media revolution and issue in the constitution of an international network capable of competing with an IPA which for all its power has lost its doctrinal urgency. That expansive network is above all concerned with preventing the IPA from appropriating the doctrine of a deceased master whose teaching it rejected while he was alive—a magnificent revenge for the humiliations of 1963. Lacanianism owes it to Jacques-Alain Miller, who since 1980 has implemented that strategy of reconquest.

For the IPA leadership, as is evidenced by the unbelievable declaration of Adam Limentani in 1984, the Lacanian expansion throughout the world is all the more dangerous in that it is now spreading to the Anglo-American sphere, in which Lacan's seminars are being brought out in translation by Norton, the company that has also published Freud. Miller does not have to gain control of Europe or London in order for that expansion to prosper. The Fondation du Champ freudien, which is independent of the ECF, is sufficient for that. Thirty-four groups throughout the world are affiliated with it.[1] The most complex, active, and expanding situation is that of the Latin Americans, who at times belong to the Fondation, at others reject Miller's "colonialism" without for all that returning to the fold of the IPA, whose leadership has compromised itself with the dictatorships, notably in the person of certain local practitioners. On that continent, Lacanianism (of all stripes) is better rooted than the neo-Freudian empire.

It would be a mistake to think that Lacanian internationalism might some day resemble the IPA. Not only is there no real symmetry between the two empires currently confronting each other on the international scene, but there probably never will be. The IPA remains at present a bureaucratic and centralized comintern owing its unity to the imposition of a certain number of standard rules and a precise juridical system that has emptied Freudianism of its substance. That internationale derives its power from its history: It was created by Freud and with his support, even though Freud never took command of it. The Lacanian internationale is something quite different; it was not the work of the master, but of his family and heirs. During Lacan's lifetime, several groups were created in countries of Latin culture in the form of local "Freudian schools," which were occasionally directly affiliated with the person of the master. Those groups became affiliated with the Fondation du Champ freudien only in 1980–81, at the time Lacan was dying. The Fondation does not impose any standard rule for analytic practice or the training of therapists. It recognizes "networks" or favors their creation. It is based on adherence to a doctrine and not on respect for technocratic rules. It is thus more flexible than the IPA, even if a priori it rejects eclecticism. As a result its propensity to imperialism will always be threatened by internal divisions and splits, which have been inherent to the splintered history of Lacanianism.

Being first of all a Millerian enterprise, the Lacanian internationale will of necessity be more contested than the IPA, which was legitimated for thirty years by the physical presence of Freud. Paradoxically, the Fondation du Champ freudien owes its present strength to its fragility. The more a colossus rests on feet of clay, the more it can move or be transformed along with history even as it continues to expand in different directions. The future will tell whether that foundation will be able to accept the autonomy of the groups founded on Lacanianism and rallying to it or if, on the contrary, it will favor a policy centered on a Jacobin catechism. For the while, it is essentially the catechism which dominates Miller's enterprises.

In the face of the formidable expansion of Lacanianism, spontaneous impulses toward a reconquest have been felt at the heart of the IPA, as evidenced by the creation in 1985, by nonphysicians in New York, of an International Freudian Foundation for New Perspectives in Psychoanalytic Research. That foundation is attempting to draw together various Freudian tendencies throughout the world, including Lacanians of various stripes. Established in France with a member of the SPP, Alain de Mijolla, as its European coordinator, it organized its first clinical symposium in Paris in June 1986. It thus drew together members of all societies: Joyce Mac Dougall, André Green, and Michel de M'Uzan for the SPP, J.-B. Pontalis for the APF, François Roustang for the Collège des psychoanalystes, and finally Maud Mannoni for her own school. At the end of the proceedings a prize was awarded for the best clinical case presented. Perhaps the day is not far off when we will see Oscars and Prix Goncourt for psychoanalysis. Whatever the case, through that foundation, a battlefront has been opened in France for a new division of zones of influence among the various groups emerging from the dissolution of the EFP. What is at stake is nothing less than Millerian Lacanianism. The Lacanians of other tendencies will have to choose among three approaches: a return to a more "liberal" empire, now open to the doctrine of a master who is no longer a burden; neutrality without any organized international dimension; or a "critical" alliance with a Millerianism disposing of its own worldwide network.

Parallel to the venture in cultural resurgence that has developed in the EFP, the Confrontation experiment, which stemmed from dissidence within the SPP, has attempted an identical course with the works of Jacques Derrida and Nicolas Abraham as poles of reference. The experiment has ceased to exist, but its publications continue and René Major's activities at the Collège international de philosophie will prolong the spirit of Confrontation in years to come. In that connection as well, Latin America has played a role. Several groups hostile to the IPA have based their appeal on the spirit of Confrontation—that is, an anti-imperialist form of noninstitutionalized psychoanalysis of libertarian inspiration.

The flourishing of guildlike organizations is the logical consequence of a history which was deployed for fifty years around the figure of Jacques Lacan. For that reason, his death in September 1981, four months after the arrival of the Left in power, caused a tremor of true panic in the ranks of the French psychoanalytic community.

Dispersed, feeling isolated, and already orphaned of a father by whom they felt dispossessed, the Lacanians were the first, even before the master's death, to brandish the scarecrow of the [legal] "status of psychoanalysis." Then toward October 1981, they were imitated by their colleagues from other institutions, who imagined that the Socialist government was about to devour them by concocting an official mode of recognition necessitating membership in an association and the holding of diplomas. The presence in the government of a Communist minister of health, the transformation of the situation of psychiatrists, and the problems linked to the obligatory payment of the TVA [value-added tax] for therapists who were neither physicians nor psychologists quickly fueled an extravagant rumor which had everyone expecting to see a Bolshevik policeman at his door, bearing a statute between his teeth. It is presently possible to fix the origin of that rumor and to describe its agitated course.

It took concrete form in January 1981, with a letter sent by Charles Melman to Claude Conté. "Do you approve, for example, of the present negotiations with Lebovici," he wrote, "a request for support having been made to a politician (with the Institute and the APF laughing it off) to set up a statute for psychoanalysts—that is, the first effort of the State to lay its hands on training and certification? Is this the new Lacanianism?" [2]

During the months that followed, the rumor enjoyed extraordinary circulation. In November 1981, Jean Cournut grabbed the ball and ran with it in an introductory text to a discussion in the first issue of the journal *Psychanalystes*. "A rumor, a stray report," he wrote, "disquietude and fascination: The world of analysts, in doubt but on the whole against, is wondering about the statute in whose sauce, risking to find itself accommodated, it already sees itself devoured. There had been talk of it for several years, once the old regime, sniffing out the fiscal possibility, began subjecting nonphysician nonpsychologists to the TVA and exercising intensive control over the others. More recently, it has been wondered whether a Socialist government might not take to heart, and as a matter of priority, the task of moralizing an exercise whose reputation has it that in being too liberal, it might become 'wild,' as well as associations concerning which the same gossips claim that in the midst of hurling anathemas at each other, they might have forgotten to verify that their functioning was truly . . . what was the word? . . . democratic." [3]

During that period, and although the Socialist government had other fish to fry, the rumor took on new intensity on the occasion of an astonishing practical joke in which Jean-Paul Moreigne played a role, having sent five diverse figures in the movement (including Valabrega, Donnet, Sédat, and Major) a document he had written. He was seeking to alert the analytic world of the statist danger. Now the text was sufficiently ambiguous to allow the possibility that negotiations were already under way between its author and hypothetical "governmental authorities," with the aim of establishing the notorious statute. Since Moreigne was a member of the radical faction of the Socialist Party, everyone thought that the Socialo-Communists wanted to seize control of the Freudian societies. The document contained four parts: a letter of introduction, the draft of a legislative bill concerning psychoanalysis in France, a projected decree concerning a "higher council for psychoanalysis," which, of course, had no existence, and a questionnaire to be filled out by the associations in their request for ministerial endorsement. [4]

Moreigne sent the document out in January 1982, at the time Claude Dorgeuille's book, *La seconde mort de Jacques Lacan*—which contained Melman's letter—was appearing. Rumor was at that point at its height and began to obsess individuals in the manner of Captain Ahab's white whale. A confusion occurred between genuine fiscal problems and hallucinatory phenomena. That confusion, moreover, risked impelling the psychoanalytic associations to anticipate the imaginary requests of a state identified as an ogre and to demand the officialization of a statute themselves. It is in fact not uncommon to see the puppet Guignol provoke the policeman as best he can while the policeman has no desire to beat Guignol.

Matters were at that point when a proposal, which was quite real, surfaced. In March 1982, Jean-Pierre Chevènement, the minister in charge of research and technology, entrusted Maurice Godelier, a Marxist ethnologist, with the task of compiling a study of the human sciences. Gérard Mendel, a member of the CERES and the SPP, was responsible for the section on psychoanalysis. At stake were structural reforms concerning a possible introduction of psychoanalytic research in the CNRS. Three divisions were envisaged. The first had the aim of establishing institutions for psychotics; the second concerned the university; and the third, which was more amorphous, would ultimately be intended to finance research pertaining to psychoanalytic associations. That proposal had nothing to do with any official status, but it did imply, *de facto,* a recognition by the state of certain groups, judged to be more solid, at the expense of others. As a result, the white whale leaped out of the ocean once again, and the proposal was seen by all as the state's attempt to gain control of psychoanalysis. Nevertheless, debate was initiated in an atmosphere of greater calm, and the various interested parties met to discuss the matter. As of 1986, there were no precise results.[5]

Although that attempt showed that the state was not pondering any official status (and concomitant regulation), the French psychoanalytic community continued to brandish its favorite scarecrow for another two years. In May 1984, the journal *Le Débat* devoted several pages to the practice of psychoanalysis in France. At the hand of Robert Castel, the white whale surfaced again. Without drawing on any documents or supplying the slightest evidence, the author announced that "government authorities" were in the process of concocting the notorious statute. He did not say which "government authority" but declared himself delighted at the initiative. Then he sketched an apocalyptic picture of the situation of the movement in France, composed, in his view, of "groupies," the unemployed, and numerous free-floating or fly-by-night therapists, whose elimination and replacement by fully certified individuals (preferably non-Lacanian) he advocated.

Castel ascribed the malaise he observed to professional or sociological causes without realizing that it was temporary and a function of the new division of territory resulting from the break-up of the EFP. The journal invited the principal parties involved to give their views. Lebovici seized the opportunity to denounce the practices of the Lacanians, even as he refused the very principle of any official regulatory statute. Jacques-Alain Miller, for his part, claimed the whole affair was a "chimera." He observed that psychoanalysis was doing well and that it was recognized in all quarters. "Its problem," he wrote, "is not with the government, but with society. I ask myself the question, How ought one to proceed so that psychoanalysis will be recognized not by the state, but by the people?"[6]

The spread of the rumor about an official status for psychoanalysts was contemporaneous with the establishment of the various societies emergent from the dissolution of the EFP. It began with the crisis of the Cause freudienne and ended at the beginning of 1985 when the post-Lacanian groups rediscovered a situation of relative stability. During that period, the *milieu* was suffering from a combination of malaise and agitation. By 1986, the dominant note was rather a return to a balance of power with a division of territory between those intent on remaining strictly Lacanian and those effecting a breakthrough to other components of the movement, more prepared to hear them since the master's death.

Beyond the three "classical" associations (SPP, APF, OPLF), there are ten societies functioning. Some have the aim of training analysts; others merely regroup them through a process of cooptation. Nine of these emerged from the dissolution: either directly, through a split from the ECF, or through the breakup of the CERF. In chronological order, in addition to the Collège de psychanalystes and the ECF, there are the Association freudienne (AF), founded by Charles Melman in June 1982; the Centre de formation et de recherches psychanalytiques (CFRP), created by Maud Mannoni and Patrick Guyomard a month later; the Cartels constituants de l'analyse freudienne (CCAF), legalized in January 1983 around former AEs of the fourth generation; the École freudienne (EF), founded that same year by Solange Faladé; the Fédération Espaces psychanalytiques (FEP), which arose from the bulletin *Entre-temps* and initially regrouped the former partners in the legal action, who had joined in an Association des ateliers de psychanalyse (AAP) and a Collectif Evénement psychanalyse (CEP); the Convention psychanalytique (CP), created in May 1983 with Jean Clavreul and Moustapha Safouan as its leading members; Errata, founded in July of the same year by former members of the CERF; and finally the École lacanienne de psychanalyse (ELP), the last in date (March 1985) and the first of its name.[7] With Jean Allouch as president, it regrouped the founders of the journal *Littoral* and the tendency associated with it.

To those ten societies may be added three others that also emerged from the dissolution and which are more like study groups than associations: the Cercle freudien, with its journal *Patio*, the Coût freudien, and the Groupe régional de psychanalyse (GRP). The first two are miniscule and essentially Parisian. The third, in Marseille, constitutes the first initiative of its type, since it is in no way dependent on the capital. It is the work of such former members of the EFP as Jean-Paul Ricoeur, Geneviève Baurand, and Paul Alérini. Alongside the ECF, which is well organized in the region, the GRP represents a significant force. In the face of those two Lacanian organizations, the APF and the SPP are virtually without an audience on the shores of the Mediterranean, with the exception of a few local personalities.

If one counts the thirteen groups resulting from the generalized crisis of 1980–81, and adds the three "classical" components, one reaches a sum of sixteen Freudian institutions in France. That figure is no doubt not exhaustive, but the period of proliferation is now over. Certain eminent Lacanians, such as Françoise Dolto, Serge Leclaire, or Pierre Legendre, no longer belong to any society. While Leclaire is above all interested in the possibilities of psychoanalysis in television, Dolto is actively involved in a center, the Maison verte, which receives children younger than three along with their parents. In addition, she dispenses her teaching through her books, which have sold thousands of copies and been translated in all major languages except English.

Most of the former AEs of the EFP have founded their own groups. But a second element is characteristic of the situation in the 1980s. Since Confrontation and the creation of the Collège, psychoanalysts have tended to become members of several institutions at once. As a result it is not easy to calculate the actual membership of each group. There are presently two tendencies. In general, the members of the CF live in a state of self-sufficiency. They do not mingle with their colleagues from other associations, either for colloquia or for training, supervision, and therapy. The other groups issuing from the dissolution, however, are more permeable to their neighbors. They barely frequent the meetings of the SPP or the APF, which remain closed societies. But the members of those societies have begun taking prudent steps in their direction. That situation has had an effect on the practice of all concerned. The Millerians have tended to take up Lacan's technique as their own: short sessions, active intervention, mixing of registers. Nevertheless, no rule has been decreed to that effect, and each is free to proceed as he believes best. In the other groups, the tendency is different. The absence of self-sufficiency has led to a coexistence of the full range of technical modalities, from the very short session, practiced in certain cases or by certain individuals, to sessions of very long—and above all very variable—length. In general, the therapists of those groups give appointments every half hour, whereas the Millerians give theirs every fifteen minutes and occasionally function without appointments.

At the time this history draws to a close, the ECF is the only institution whose present history can be sketched. Three axes may be intuited for that history: an internal conflict, with a significant resignation, Laurence Bataille's; a process of internationalization, of which we have already spoken; and the emergence of a polemic concerning Jacques-Alain Miller's transcription of Lacan's seminar.

Volume 3 of the seminar, devoted to the psychoses, was published two months after the death of Lacan. As had been his habit since 1973, Miller had worked zealously at establishing the text. But the job was more difficult than it had previously been. Not having had Lacan's reply to queries about certain ambiguities, he decided to leave a few passages in quotation marks with suspension points.[8] In addition, for the first time, he appended a note, observing that the revision of the text was an ongoing labor and that readers wishing to suggest possibilities to him could write to him. At the time the seminar appeared, Miller had become, by a notarized document dated November 13, 1980, the appointed executor of the oral and written work of Jacques Lacan. He was no longer the transcriber recognized by a living master, but the legitimate heir, recognized by the law. Since at the time of Lacan's death, a large part of his oral work remained unpublished, the will bestowed complete authority on Miller to transcribe it or have it reproduced however he wished.

That new situation provoked certain transformations within the Lacanian community. The "originals" (recordings, stenographic records, etc.) that were already in existence could continue to circulate freely, and be read, commented on, deposited in the libraries of psychoanalytic institutions. No policeman would come seize them if they were not published or sold commercially. All were thus free to consult them. But as far as publication was concerned, everything would now have to pass through Miller's hands. Only his transcriptions had the right to official existence, and it was his duty to have them appear at a rate that would not allow his adversaries to accuse him of abusing his moral right. Five volumes of seminars have already appeared; another nineteen remain to be prepared. Upon becoming the leader of a school, following Lacan's death, Miller has worked somewhat less than previously. No seminar appeared between 1981 and 1986. Two are currently in preparation. Miller's transcription is the only one that can legally be published, unless the executor were to authorize others to perform the task. It was Miller's version that had been chosen by Lacan, who preferred it to that of others. It was a writing of spoken words, and even if it presented itself as "functioning as an equivalent of the original," it never claimed to be the exact reflection of those spoken words. Moreover, it would have been more satisfying had the transcriber prepared a name index and a few bibliographical references.

With Lacan's death and the constitution of numerous Lacanian groups, that transcription became the issue in a struggle through which the anti-Millerians attempted to define themselves as more "Lacanian" than their adversaries, without being willing to admit that the history of Lacanianism had already become that of the breakup of Lacanianism into a variety of currents and tendencies. The fact that Miller was the official possessor of a right did not imply that the Millerian tendency was more "Lacanian" than the others, and vice versa. Through the matheme, as we saw, Lacan had the illusion that he might preserve his doctrine from any deviation. The facts reveal that he was wrong; the history of a doctrine is always that of its recastings, revisions, and undoings. And it was no doubt because he made Miller's transcription into something of a matheme that Lacan led his heirs—legitimate or not—to tear each other apart over the subject of his written work.

The problem posed by that transcription is neither that of its faithfulness nor of its quality. Miller's text is a worthy restitution of Lacan's discourse. It demanded a colossal amount of work from its author. If its quality is one day to be called into question, criticism will have to be on a level as high as that of the work criticized: solid, pertinent, precise, and without idiotic hatred. This is not the case at present. If the anti-Millerians have lashed out at the transcription, it is because they have fetishized the master's discourse to the point of believing either that it could not be put into writing, or that only an allegedly faithful writing could recapture it. Moreover, they waited for Lacan's death before launching their polemic. Between 1973 and 1981, four seminars were "established" by Miller and published by Éditions du Seuil. No one in the EFP ever sounded the slightest public protest against the work of Lacan's son-in-law. On the contrary, Miller's work was glorified by those who are at present its fiercest adversaries. Had true criticisms surfaced earlier, the situation at present would have been different. Once again, as in the case of other activities, the currents opposed to the Millerian reading of Lacan's work were never able to impose themselves in the face of the master's decisions.

The seminar on the psychoses was published at the time the ECF was rapidly expanding and the other groups resulting from the crisis, on the contrary, had not yet constituted themselves as institutions. In that context, the polemics became wild, and Miller was accused of falsifying the whole of Lacan's work. And yet, with the exception of a few admitted details, the method used for *Séminaire III* had not varied at all from that previously employed. What had changed was that the anti-Millerian struggle was now taking the form of a fight against a transcription that had been accepted by all for seven years.

The first challenge emanated from a journal created by Charles Melman in October 1981, *Le Discours psychanalytique*. In its seventh issue, in June 1983, there appeared an anonymous article in the form of a letter from Elie Hirsch to his brother

Hyacinthe. Venomously, the author listed several typographical errors and a few questionable turns of phrase, but he did not hesitate to say that Miller's transcription was to be considered a "summary" or an "elimination" of the original stenographer's record. The article contained several superfluous insults.[9] Nine months later, Maud Mannoni published a review by one of her partisans of a book devoted to a bibliography of Lacan's works. She stated that the book mentioned the presentations made by former associates of Lacan's at the seminar, but not retained by Miller. But she omitted to say that although the transcriber did not publish all those presentations, he rarely forgot to mention their existence in his edition, and even left a blank at times to remind the reader of their omission. Maud Mannoni added that fortunately recordings of Lacan's oral teaching had escaped "destruction" and "censorship."[10] She thus implied that Miller might have consigned to the flames work that was reproduced in tens of copies and that anyone is free to procure should he so desire.

The tone of the special issue of *Littoral* devoted to the subject in June 1984 was quite different. It contained several well-documented articles on the dual question of the translation of Freud and the transcription of Lacan. Jean Allouch made several justifiable remarks on Miller's choice of titles for the seminars. But above all, he attempted to situate the interventions of the stenographer and the transcriber on the same level, showing that in both cases there was an intervention by a third party. Then he added that in his lifetime, Lacan undoubtedly did not verify his son-in-law's work in detail. "Evidence of this is provided by the transcriber," he wrote, "when he relates that Lacan had suggested to him that they cosign the seminars. He adds that he refused to do so, which does not dispel the question of determining why Lacan accepted that refusal and withdrew his proposition. That proposition in itself, however, remains instructive: Lacan did not consider himself the sole author of what he allowed to be published under his name."[11]

One is hard put to follow Allouch in his claim. It is not possible to situate the stenographer's intervention and Miller's on the same level. The first offers a precise reflection of speech—with errors in typing, spelling, and punctuation—whereas the second was an exercise in writing. Moreover, there is no evidence that Lacan did not verify the transcription. His fury on the occasion of the publication of the first seminar would tend to demonstrate the opposite. Finally, the fact that he proposed to Miller that they be cosigners of the transcription does not necessarily imply that he did not consider himself to be the sole author of the seminar. If such were the case, he would have said as much in his preface of 1973. . . . But at that time, he opted to emphasize that Miller's transcription conveyed *without loss* the essence of his teaching.

In reality, the Millerian transcription confirms the existence of a current of the same name in the history of psychoanalysis in France. We have seen in what conditions it was born between the years 1964 and 1966, through an osmosis between the master's teaching and his disciple's commentary. Commentary enjoys a strange status in the Lacanian saga. It was established in a direct line moving from Kojève, the reader of Hegel, to Lacan, the reader of Freud, to Miller, the interpreter of Lacan. Each of the three owes his position to a specific relationship to the work of another. But Miller's is distinguished, at least for now, by not having separated from its root to become an independent body of work. Initially it derived its strength from a hyperlogical rectification. Then, starting in 1973, it drew it from the existence of an *écriture* that succeeded in turning an oral work into an established doctrine. Finally, after Lacan's death, the established doctrine tended to be imposed as an official doctrine. As a result, Miller lost the freedom enjoyed by Lacan of effecting a "return" to a work. How indeed could he since he stands as the guarantor of an original assumed to be a matheme? Thus situated, he enjoys only the freedom of administering a doctrine and governing an empire in its name. Time will tell whether Miller's personal teaching will succeed in becoming a body of work capable of sufficient detachment from the Lacanian corpus as to constitute itself as a theoretically innovative commentary on it.

It was around the journal *Littoral,* in 1983, that an association for the transcription of Lacan's seminars was formed. It was called "Après [After]," and produced a bulletin *Stécriture,* in which several sessions of the seminar on the transference (1960–61) were published. The word *strécriture* was forged from a term borrowed from Lacan. The founders of the association were quite understandably concerned by the interruption in Miller's work after 1981. The transcription published by *Stécriture* was an improved stenographic version of the seminar. It had the advantage of being more faithful than Miller's, but the problem of being less "written." It treated the master's spoken words as sacred and accompanied them with commentaries on his thought. It might have circulated serenely within the ranks of the psychoanalytic community if the authors had asked Miller for authorization to work on Lacan's seminar, even if he had refused, or if they had not violated the law by selling their text commercially in the hope of being reimbursed for their costs. Miller, armed with his legitimate claim, did not hesitate to sue them for infringement of his rights. After two court hearings and much conflicting testimony, the Lacanian community was once again tearing itself apart in a trial which recalled—in reverse—the suit brought against Lacan in February 1980.

At the end of 1985, Miller won his trial, but he was far from having the support of all the members of his school. His error in the affair was in exploiting his legitimacy as a means of imposing interdictions. A question as important as that of the existence of a plurality of transcriptions cannot, after all, be resolved in a court of law. As for his adversaries, they were defended in court by a garrulous attorney who ended up ridiculing their work by pretending it was the original achievement of a group and not the transcription of a seminar.[12] The entire press discussed the case, turning the polemic into a question open for the future. In keeping with his strategy at the time, Sollers defended the cause of *Stécriture* brilliantly, while Roland Dumas took up the cause of the legitimate heirs. Laurence Bataille, for her part, testified in favor of *Stécriture* without criticizing Miller's transcription.

At the time Miller was beginning to be attacked from all quarters by those who had never said a word while Lacan was alive, the ECF proceeded with the final revision of its statutes. This took place in May 1982.[13] The principal modification consisted in replacing the category of corresponding member with that of associate member, and eliminating the category of member of the statutory council. In addition, it improved the functioning of the *passe,* which would be activated a year later. There was no effort at democratization, but that absence was compensated for by the fact that every member had the right to teach at the ECF. The statutes recommended that that risk be assumed, and there were no regulations envisaged to forbid it.

As soon as the first roster appeared, a malaise was felt, which would lead to a significant resignation: that of Laurence Bataille. In 1982, Lacan's step-daughter sent Colette Soler, Jacques-Alain Miller, Pierre Martin, and Paul Lemoine a letter in which she objected to the appearance, as official documents, of texts signed by Lacan after 1980, and their presence alongside those written earlier. The roster did indeed situate on the same level the founding act of the EFP, the proposal of October 1967, the letter of dissolution, and a group of circulars, signed by the master and concerning the events of February 1980 and March 1981. "The utilization of texts signed by Lacan starting in 1980," wrote Laurence, "may have been useful at one time. It is being perpetuated by their publication in the roster. Would those who receive their training from the École have been incapable of sustaining themselves without that comfort? If so, they would be incapable of facing up to the demands of being an analyst—a Lacanian one, I mean. This is a contradiction I am no longer able to take on. I would no longer be able to occupy the position of an analyst if I continued to accept it. That is why I am resigning from the École de la cause freudienne." [14] The meaning of that resignation would barely be perceived in the ranks of the ECF, but in 1985, the roster and the statutory texts would be published without the inclusion of any text by Lacan: neither the old ones, nor those from after 1980.

Despite its internal malaise, echoed in that letter, the ECF remains at present the premier French component of a splintered Lacanianism. Thanks to the action of the three Millers and their friends, that component is the most powerful in the world of publishing and the universities, as well as in its internationalist dynamic. For its congresses and meetings, it mobilizes some two thousand participants. It is the only group emergent from the dissolution to have absorbed a considerable number of former members of the EFP's anonymous base: 90 out of a total membership of 273. Some are at present leaders in their school. This would tend to demonstrate that the Millerian current had proved more attractive at the time of the final crisis than the other groups, which quickly splintered and have at present in their ranks about 130 diverse members of the former EFP. Generally speaking, one does not find in the ten societies emergent from the dissolution that many members of the EFP. Of the 609 members composing it in 1980, about 250 were registered in the various extant groups. The rest—that is, the majority of the members of the EFP— wanted neither a Millerian school nor a school of barons. As a result, more than a third of the members of each of the Lacanian groups at present is new.

Opposing the ECF and in fierce rivalry with it, the CFRP is the second major component of the Lacanianism of the 1980s. Created in June 1982 by Maud Mannoni, Octave Mannoni, and Patrick Guyomard, it consists of about 390 members,[15] a majority of whom pay dues without having the right to vote. To all appearances, the CFRP is a more liberal group than the ECF, but in terms of its internal mechanisms, it is somewhat less so. That fact would tend to show that the extreme democracy that reigned at the EFP and that, in certain respects, brought about its fall, has been abandoned by the two most powerful groups in favor of a vast antidemocratic reaction linked to the disappearance of the system of direct monarchy. Powerful in its membership, the CFRP is poor in its publishing, academic, and internationalist activities. It has a collection published by Éditions Denoël, which is going well, but the question of doctrinal renewal has not yet been resolved. Nevertheless, thanks to the exemplary professionalism of Maud Mannoni, it occupies a place of choice within French Freudianism, as much for its numerous activities as for its openness to non-Lacanian currents.

The statutes elaborated by Maud Mannoni give an adequate image of the orientations of the CFRP. With the exception of massive references to doctrine, the Centre has retained nothing of Lacan's contribution to the question of training analysts. Hostile to the *passe* as early as 1967, Mannoni did not carry it over when she founded her group. The association is composed of six categories of members: founders, honorary members, benefactors, psychoanalysts, adhering members, and auditors.[16] The category of psychoanalysts is subdivided into two groups: *active members* and *associate members*. The first correspond to the former AEs of the EFP or the titular members of the IPA-affiliated societies. They are engaged in doctrinal work. The second resemble rather the AMEs of the EFP and the associate members of the IPA-affiliates. They are recognized as analysts by the Centre. Only the active and associate members (that is, the psychoanalysts) have voting rights. They form a community of 59 members, of whom 31 were formerly in the EFP. Consequently, the mass of adhering members and auditors (331 members) pay dues without having any right to influence the conduct of the association. Those members thus resemble the affiliates of the SPP, but with even less power. In this respect, the CFRP is the least democratic psychoanalytic society in Freudian France. As for the benefactors, it is not stipulated in the statutes whether they have any other right than that of paying the institution at least ten times the dues of the active members.

Concerning the training of therapists, the CFRP has recycled a classical model: The brunt of selection is brought to bear on the control. The personal analysis is preserved. On this question, Patrick Guyomard has adopted a position close to that of Jean Laplanche: The Centre must construct an ethic of the institution in which analysis is shielded from having to serve the institution. "For this," he has written, "we had to do away with the *passe*. Not as a concept, but as an institutional procedure. One of Lacan's strengths was to assume the antinomies which he himself had denounced. He wanted to be an analyst and the leader of a school. . . . The *passe* did not elude that law. In its procedure, it wanted simultaneously to interrogate analysis beyond and, in a sense, against the institution and its repressive effects, and to enlist that act and that discourse in the service of the institution in order to strengthen it."[17]

The CFRP is administered by an administrative council exclusively composed of active and associate members. The Centre recognizes analysts, but never training analysts as such. Acceptance to the rank of adhering member has to be ratified by the administrative council. The candidate comes before an admissions committee, which solicits the opinion of the supervisors and can, in certain circumstances, ask an analyst whether the candidate has indeed embarked on an analysis. That clause is rather curious and unique in our history. It demonstrates that the institution can refuse in advance to believe a candidate without however choosing to solicit the opinion of the psychoanalyst who trained him. To become an associate, an adhering member has to have spent a year in the CFRP and have undergone at least two controls. He then forms a *jury of association* consisting of four psychoanalysts: Two are chosen by him from among the active members of the CFRP (with one of the two selectable from outside the society with the agreement of the administrative council). The two others are chosen at random from the list of active members. The jury's (and candidate's) work deals with the field opened by the latter's training: his practice, his writings, his interventions, etc.

The associate becomes an active member in accordance with curricular considerations shared by the classical psychoanalytic societies. After three years in the ranks of the CFRP, he comes before a teaching commission. His appointment is ratified by the administrative council, after the candidate presents work to a seminar of the active members.

In its regulations and statutes, the CFRP has reinstituted a mode of functioning, appointment, and training modeled on the liberal procedures adopted by the APF in 1968 and the Fourth Group in 1969. It plainly bears the imprint of the Lacanian heritage, but has radically taken its distance from that legacy's more innovative aspects concerning psychoanalytic training. It constitutes at present a perfectly acceptable institution for the three other components of French Freudianism, only two of which were marked by the history of Lacanianism. Moreover, the CFRP is the only group resulting from the dissolution to have established significant organic links with the APF, the OPLF, and the SPP. Through the mediation of Jacques Sédat, who is a member of its administrative council, it is also connected with the Collège de psychanalystes. In the short term, and as a result of those alliances, it could readily come under the influence of the IPA in the context of the struggle against Millerian Lacanianism. Following the split of 1963, Maud Mannoni remained a member of the IPA through her membership in the Société belge de psychanalyse.

The situation of the other societies that emerged from the dissolution is quite different, since they continue to appeal to Lacan's legislation on the subject of training—that is, to the procedure of the *passe*. These societies are the Cartels constituants de l'analyse freudienne (CCAF), the Convention psychanalytique (CP), the Association freudienne (AF), the École freudienne (EF), and the École lacanienne de psychanalyse (ELP).

The CCAF and the CP are quite similar. They possess ultrademocratic charters, with a sovereign general assembly consisting of a single category of member, charged with electing the administrative and training bodies. Surprisingly, both have the same number of members, 212, with 29 veterans of the EFP for the CCAF and 40 for the CP. In addition, like the CFRP they have the same number of former AEs of the EFP: five for each of the three as opposed to four for the ECF and two for the ELP. The CCAF has already set up operations[18] whereas the CP, in 1986, was still becoming established, its statutes not yet complete. That society is remarkably well rooted in the provinces and has established its main offices in Besançon—ninety-three of its members do not reside in Paris. The democratic character of the two groups appears not to have spared them the internal problems that are linked to the constitution of inevitable clans and local accretions of power. Nevertheless, they have attracted some of the most competent clinicians of the Lacanian movement. They are not actively involved in publishing, contenting themselves with bringing out a bulletin for internal use. There has been no remarkable writing emerging from the groups between 1981 and 1985.

In its inaugural text of September 1982, the AF announced its intention of reviving the training procedures in effect at the EFP: self-designated rank (AP); certification (analyst member of the association, AMA); and *passe* (analyst of the association, AA).[19] Nevertheless, since that statement no organs have been set up to realize that intention. The AF appears to function through cooptation, without hierarchy or nomination.[20] Its statutes do not stipulate its mode of functioning. The society is composed of 123 members of whom 18 were formerly in the EFP, a sign that Charles Melman had hardly been heeded in his denunciation of Miller. He is himself, in his organization, the only former AE of the EFP. The group is characterized by intense activity in the order of colloquia, self-publication, and relations with nonanalysts. Thanks to the teaching of Marcel Czermak, who resigned from the clinical section of the Cause freudienne and has an adjunct appointment at the Hôpital Henri-Rousselle, the AF enjoys considerable recognition among interns in psychiatry. It also has a sizable audience in the Montpellier region and in Belgium, where it publishes a bulletin. Four (self-published) journals are directly connected with it: *Le Discours psychanalytique, Nodal, Mi-dit,* and *La Psychanalyse de l'enfant.*

Founded by Solange Faladé, the EF is an institution deprived of all democracy, at least for the while. Its director has assumed all powers for a transitional period to end in 1988, at which time a revision of its statutes will be undertaken. The École is also to reflect on the procedure of the *passe* and gather to it young therapists disoriented by the new division of the territory. It comprises three categories of members: members, associates, and auditors. The first choose from among themselves a director, who selects a directorate and a board. The general assembly is composed of members and associates, who elect an admissions jury upon nomination by the director. That jury selects members. Auditors have no power.

The ELP is far and away—with the ECF—the most interesting institution to emerge from the breakup of the Lacanian movement. And it was not by chance that certain of its founders found themselves facing Jacques-Alain Miller, in court, defending *their* transcription of the seminar. Most of them, Jean Allouch, Philippe Julien, Danièle Arnoux, et al., had been analyzed by Lacan and felt dispossessed of their theoretical legacy by a legitimate heir who did not come from the master's couch. They are the same age as he and are equally dynamic, although without expansionist ambitions. They are haunted by an incredible passion for the words of Lacan, which is also a true passion for psychoanalysis. They have thus transformed their love for the person of the master into a cult of his work, which explains the painstaking ardor they have brought to their labor on his texts. They have produced extremely interesting and personal works centered on a permanent return to Lacan's oeuvre. They prefer the Borromean knots to the matheme and the clinical reality of paranoia to that of hysteria.[21] In the history of psychoanalysis in France, they did something unprecedented by calling their school "Lacanian." The choice of such a name derives from a theoretical option that may be found in the discourse of Jean Allouch. Lacan, he maintained, is no longer Freudian, and in order to draw the consequences of the master's break with the ancestor's corpus, his disciples should confess to being Lacanians, even if they then reread Freud and even reinterpret him with the help of Lacanian concepts.

Initially grouped around the journal *Littoral,* these Lacanians have since united in a small school of forty-five members, which has enjoyed such marked success that it will surely grow. Its self-published works are significant and original, and its colloquiums quite well attended. As for its statutes, they are perfectly democratic: a sovereign general assembly composed of a single-category membership elects an administrative council. An admissions cartel is selected randomly from among the members. The *passe* was about to be established on the basis of a proposal of November 17, 1985, considered to be a transposition of that of October 1967.[22]

Among the institutions of Lacanianism existing after its breakup, space should be accorded to two quite different endeavors which did not recycle the *passe* procedure. One is a small group, part of the fallout from the dislocation of the CERF, which took on the name of "Errata," as a reference to the notion of "corrections in the margin." It is composed of several former AMEs of the EFP and functions through cooptation. The second endeavor has united veterans of the *Ordinaire du psychanalyste,* certain of whom were part of the court action of February 1980, then worked briefly on the bulletin *Entre-temps.* It is called the Fédérations Espaces psychanalytiques, which has regrouped three other collectives: the Association ateliers de psychanalyse, the Collectif Evénement psychanalyse, and the Collectif Journal. The federation is intent on being open to other groups that might join it. It has no training ambition and functions in a libertarian spirit.[23] The nonactive members of the AAP do not have voting rights, but neither do they pay dues.

The implantation of French Freudianism in the world of publishing is quite interesting to observe. In general, when a new group becomes autonomous, it begins by creating a bulletin or a journal to express its options. Then, when it becomes powerful, it either starts up a self-publishing project or is taken in by a publishing house, which may welcome a review, a collection, or a series of books. In this respect, there is an editorial logic to psychoanalysis reflecting the logic of its expansion and its mode of dividing up the turf. Three major French publishers—Gallimard, Presses universitaires de France, and Payot—share publication of Freud's work, even as they are dominated by IPA-affiliated societies: the APF for Gallimard, the SPP for Payot, and the two together for the Presses universitaires de France, which is also the home of *Topique,* the journal of the Fourth Group. Between 1965 and 1981, on the contrary, Lacanianism flourished exclusively at Éditions du Seuil with the "Champ freudien" series, then the distribution of Navarin. Seuil's aspect changed,

moreover, following Lacan's death and the breakup of the EFP, since Miller inherited
the "Champ freudien" series. Authors of that house who did not share his orientation tended to disperse. While Moustapha Safouan and Françoise Dolto have continued to publish their works under the same roof, Maud Mannoni has left it. At
present she directs a series—"Espace analytique"—for Denoël, representing her
own school, and as a result she publishes her own texts there. If it is common to
find several authors of different opinion cohabiting under the same roof, it is rare,
on the other hand, to find several rival schools living together within the same walls.
According to this logic, the IPA-affiliated societies have had their own houses, distinct from the Lacanian bases, and the Lacanians have tended to disperse among
several publishing houses as they have endured successive splits. To be sure, within
that expansive implantation, a distinction should be made between "official" series,
representing a group, and unofficial ones, which might be founded by individual
members of a society. But here too a logic is at work, and the different Freudian
tendencies have spontaneously shared their territories.

If Seuil has retained a Lacano-Millerian image, and Gallimard, the Presses
universitaires de France, and Payot an IPA-oriented aspect, the Éditions de Minuit
has been characterized by a spirit of dissidence. That house has always welcomed
voices of protest from every quarter, who thus take their distance from their group
even as they retain affiliation. Minuit does not have a psychoanalytic series, which
has allowed it to shelter authors on an individual basis and outside of any rivalry
between schools. Today, with the proliferation of groups, the phenomenon of self-
publishing has tended to grow, and the dispersion of authors into different sectors
of the publishing world has become increasingly massive.

There is another element characterizing the situation of psychoanalysis in
France in 1985: the domain of history has been opened. Interest in it began between
1975 and 1980, at the time the crises of the institutions were becoming acute. The
first book to appear was that of Ilse and Robert Barande, which no one regards as
serious at present. During the same period, Wladimir Granoff published *Filiations*,
thus returning to history as a witness of and actor in events. Professor André Bourguignon, for his part, has been interested in the pioneers of the French movement
and directed numerous theses on the subject, which I made use of in my earlier
volume. Bourguignon also was responsible for the publication in 1977 of the correspondence between Freud and Laforgue, and conducted a polemic against the
"official historians," the Barandes. The domain was also opened, the same year, by
J.-B. Pontalis, who remained silent on the subject of France and devoted his efforts
to origins and situations in other lands. In 1976, Jacques-Alain Miller was the first
to publish documents concerning the splits. But one would have to await Lacan's
death and the breakup of the EFP to see an authentic work of history emerge. The
simultaneous appearance in 1982 of Célia Bertin's biography of Marie Bonaparte,
two volumes of essays edited by Roland Jaccard, and my earlier book marked the
definitive opening of the field.[24]

Publications were apparently no longer sufficient, since two historical societies emerged after 1981 that were intended to collect archives and favor the holding
of colloquiums and the conduct of research. Created at the instigation of Jacques

Postel and Michel Collée, the first took on the name of "Société internationale d'histoire de la psychiatrie et de la psychanalyse" in 1981. It had the advantage of not being attached to any psychoanalytic institution and of attracting members of all tendencies: psychiatrists, psychoanalysts, or academics. René Major was its new president and would undoubtedly bestow on it a liberal aspect in the face of the various empires. The second, the "Association internationale d'histoire de la psychanalyse," was founded in June 1985 by Alain de Mijolla, who himself was a member of the SPP. Although that society maintained a certain façade of autonomy and tended to recruit—in accordance with a political trend characteristic of the post-Lacanian era—members not belonging to the IPA empire, it remained completely subordinate to it. It thus ran the risk of producing, in both its publications and its style, texts partaking of an "official history". . . . As evidenced, for example, by this declaration by its president: "I would like to conclude by adding that, although this association would like not to be a direct emanation of the IPA (any more than of any other group) so as to be able to recruit historians of all tendencies and all forms of training, we nonetheless would like to establish a privileged and durable relation with the IPA, which for more than seventy-five years has made and continues to make the history of psychoanalysis, which it symbolizes throughout the world, as proved at the Hamburg congress." [25] When one recalls how the Nazi question was treated at that congress, one has reason to worry about the future of an association which is so quick to declare its happiness with the methods of the IPA when it comes to history.

Still two more associations bear witness to the transformation linked to the end of the Lacanian saga. These are the "École propédeutique à la connaissance de l'inconscient" (EPCI), founded by Gérard Bonnet, a member of the APF, and "Expérience freudienne et recherche scientifique" (EFERS), created by Jean-Michel Louka. Both have teaching vocations and function beyond the pale of the official institutions. They bear witness to a movement of decentralization and a mood of dissidence specific to the situation of the 1980s.

Paris, March 1986. In his last—and posthumous—book, Fernand Braudel seems to be surprised by an obvious piece of evidence: Division reigns in the house of France. The unity of the kingdom is no more than an envelope or a wager. The history of this country, so slow to unite its peoples and territories, is that of a Dreyfus Affair perpetually started afresh. Communards against partisans of Versailles, Protestants against Catholics, blues against reds, anti-Surrealists against Surrealists . . . The battle outside is thus a battle within, and nothing illustrates that cliché better than the situation of psychoanalysis in France. Sects or quarrels between schools, clans or rivalries among individuals, intellectual master or anti-Caesarism, rationalism or obscurantism? Certainly not, except in appearance. But a divided identity, to be sure. Were Freud to take today, for one last excursion, the place of the traveler of 1925, or were he to become again, for a moment, the anxious pilgrim of October 1885, he would observe the reality of what he had intuited concerning the specific resistance to his doctrine in the house of France. But he would be the first to be astonished, he who so admired the pacifism of Romain Rolland, at seeing that the battle within remains the surest means to perpetuate the energy of the battle without.

Observing quite cynically the homage paid to the Vienna of years past, the cradle of every implosion, the birthplace simultaneously of the unconscious, the renewal of logic, Zionism, and the most pernicious forms of anti-Semitism and Jewish self-hatred, he would undoubtedly remember a certain thesis sent his way by a young stranger whose name and address he could not recall: Jacques Lacan. Regretting he had given him short shrift, in a few lines befitting the courtesy of kings, he would go stand beneath the mist before the grey tombstone in a somnolent village cemetery. There he would meditate on the divided destiny of this country, so refractory to his discovery and, now, so populated with adepts. He would observe the flourishing of the cult of his person, would be frightened by the lunatic formalism attached to every word of his work, every gesture of his life, reinterpreted amidst a proliferation of texts and soon to be digested by the computers of our managerial societies. Perhaps he would then go, in a last pilgrimage, to the place of his first encounter with French intelligence, the residence of Jean-Martin Charcot, now the Maison de l'Amérique latine. At the end of his voyage and the "time for understanding," he would send to Vienna a telegram of his invention, intended for history: "Thanks to all. Start everything over again."

Appendixes

A page from *The Interpretation of Dreams* translated by Moustapha Safouan

والآن أعثر لأول مرة على خبرة الحداثة التى ظلت تعرب إلى اليوم عن سلطانها فى كل هاته الانفعالات والأحلام . ربما كنت فى العاشرة أو فى الحادية عشرة من عمرى حين بدأ والدى يصطحبنى فى نزهاته ويكاشفنى فى أحاديثه بنظراته فى أمور هذا العالم الذى نحيا فيه . وهكذا حدثنى مرة بالقصة الآتية لكى يرينى كم تفضل الأيامُ التى ولدتُ بها أيامه . قال : كنت وأنا شاب أتنزه فى يوم سبت فى شوارع البلد الذى ولدتَ به وقد لبست لباساً حسناً ووضعت على رأسى قلنسوة من الفراء وإذا مسيحى يقبل فيضرب بقبعتى فى الوحل . صائحاً : أيها اليهودى انزل عن الرصيف ! فسألت والدى : وماذا فعلت ؟ فأجابنى فى هدوء : نزلت إلى عرض الطريق والتقطت القلنسوة . لقد بدا لى ذلك مسلكاً مجرداً من البطولة إذ يصدر عن الرجل الضخم القوى الذى كان يقودنى ممسكاً بيدى — أنا الولد الصغير . وقارنت هذا الموقف الذى لم يرضى بآخر أكثر تلاؤماً ومشاعرى . قارنته بالمشهد الذى فيه يستحلف هاميلكار باركاس[1] — أمام مذبح العائلة — ابنه هانيبال إلا أن يأخذن بالثأر من الرومان . ومنذ ذلك الحين وهانيبال يحتل مكاناً بين تخايلى .

وأظنى قادراً بعد على تأثر هذه الحماسة للقائد القرطاجنى إلى عهد أقدم من عهد طفولتى ؛ بحيث لا يخرج الأمر هنا أيضاً عن أن يكون تحويلا إلى حامل [أى موضوع] جديد لعلاقة عاطفية متكونة من قبل . فقد كان من أوائل الكتب التى وضعت بين يدى وأنا طفل حديث العهد بالقراءة كتاب تيير « تاريخ القنصلية والإمبراطورية » . وما زلت أذكر كيف ألصقت بالظهور المسطحة لجنودى الخشبية قصاصات من الورق تحمل أسماء القواد الإمبراطوريين . وأذكر أن ماسينا (باليهودية : منشا) كان بطلى المفضل إذ ذاك[2] . (وهو تفضيل يفسر أيضاً من غير شك بكونى قد ولدت فى ذات التاريخ ، قرناً بعده) . [3] ونابليون خليفة هانيبال ؛ لعبوره جبال الألب . وربما أمكن أن أتتبع نشأة هذا المثل الأعلى الحربى إلى زمن أقدم من طفولتى : إلى علاقتى فى خلال السنوات الثلاث الأولى من حياتى بولد يكبرنى بعام واحد ، وإلى المشاعر التى لا بد قد أثارتها فى نفس أضعف الرفيقين تلك العلاقة التى كانت طوراً صداقة وطوراً حرباً[4] .

وكلما تعمق المرء تحليل أحد الأحلام ؛ زاد عثوره على آثار خبرات الطفولة التى كان لها نصيبها بين مصادر المحتوى الكامن لهذا الحلم .

(١) [١٩٠٩] جاء هذا الاسم فى الطبعة الأولى على تلك الصورة : هاسدروبال . وهو خطأ عجيب فسرته فى كتابى : سيكوباثولوجية الحياة اليومية (١٩٠١ ب ، الفصل العاشر) .

(٢) [١٩٣٠ :] وأثير عرضا إلى أن الأصل اليهودى لهذا القائد موضع شك .

(٣) [أضيفت هذه الجملة عام ١٩١٤] .

(٤) [سيتحدث فرويد عن هذه العلاقة كثيراً فيما بعد] .

Texts slated for an English edition of works by members of the SFP

S U M M A R Y

- . Acnowledgements, by W. Granoff.
- . Preface, by M. Balint.
- . Introduction.

- Function and Field of Speech and Language in Psychoanalysis, by J. Lacan.
- On a Preliminary Issue to any possible Treatment of Psychosis, by J. Lacan.
- Psychoanalysis and the Structure of Personality, by D. Lagache.
- A new Hypothesis on the so-called Jealousy Reactions on the birth of a younger sibling, by F. Dolto-Marette.
- Phobias and Anxiety Hysteria, by F. Perrier.
- Desire for Children, Children's Desire, by W. Granoff.
- The obsessional-neurotic and his Desire, by S. Leclaire.
- Psycho-analytical Anthropology, by J.-P. Valabrega.
- On Contention, by G. Favez.
- The Unconscious - A psychoanalytic study, by J. Laplanche et S. Leclaire.

École freudienne de Paris: 1964–1980 Comparative Development

1965   134 members, 85 physicians, 49 non-physicians, 46 women
          \ 24 AEs, 35 AMEs /
       without possibility of holding two titles

       58 recognized psychoanalysts

SFP (1962)	*SPP* (1965)	*APF* (1964)
182 members	83 members	26 members
	25 women	6 women

January 1967:   Height of 200 members

January 1969:   Split→ creation of the Fourth Group (OPLF)

1971   276 members, 150 physicians, 126 non-physicians
       introduction of the category of AP

       28 AEs: 3 AEs not AMEs + 25 AEs-AMEs

       109 AMEs→81 non-AEs

       4 departures and 2 deaths—6 *passes,* 5 appointments as AE without *passe*

       109 recognized psychoanalysts

1975   401 members: increase of 125 over 1971,
                of 267 over 1965

       30 AEs: 2AEs not AMEs + 28 AEs-AMEs

       130 AMEs→ 102 non-AEs

       1 death, 4 *passes*

       132 recognized psychoanalysts

1977   544 members

       34 AEs: 4 AEs not AMEs + 30 AEs-AMEs

       153 AMEs→123 non-AEs

       4 *passes*

       157 recognized psychoanalysts

École freudienne de Paris: 1964–1980 Comparative Development (*continued*)

1980   609 members (December 1979):

increase of 468 over 1965

no new member admitted in 1980; no promotions

January 5: Lacan's dissolution

September 27: juridical dissolution

38 AEs: 5 AEs not AMEs + 33 AEs-AMEs

170 AMEs→ 137 non-AEs

4 *passes*

175 recognized psychoanalysts

SPP (1981)	*APF* (1981)	*OPLF* (1981)
297 members	50 members	25 subscribing members
61 titular members	24 titular members	
59 adhering members	26 associate members	
177 affiliates		

IPA, France: 347 recognized psychoanalysts

Members of the four components: 949

Progress in Female Membership in the Four French Freudian Groups: 1964–1983

1964–1965	Members	Women	Percentage
EFP	134	46	34%
APF	26	6	27%
SPP	83	25	30%

1978–1983	Members	Women	Percentage
EFP	570	242	42%
APF	50	19	40%
SPP	297	142	48%
OPLF	25	15	60%

These figures do not include students or "contributors" for the SPP, APF, OPLF.

Psychoanalysts listed in *Who's Who in France,* 1982–1983: Didier Anzieu, Jean Laplanche, Serge Leclaire, Jacques Lacan, Françoise Dolto, Philippe Marette, Gérard Mendel, Serge Lebovici, Daniel Widlöcher, André Green, Jean Ayme, André Bourguignon

Groups Affiliated With the International Meetings of the "Champ Freudien"

Argentina
  Ateneo Freudiano de Mendoza
  Ateneo Psicoanalítico de Córdoba
  Centro de Estudios Psicoanalíticos Sigmund Freud de Tucumán
  Escuela Argentina de Psicoanálisis (Buenos Aires)
  Escuela Freudiana de Buenos Aires
  Escuela de Psicoanálisis Sigmund Freud (Rosario)
  Espacio Psicoanalítico (Rosario)
  Mayéutica (Buenos Aires)
  Seminario Lacaniano (Buenos Aires)
  Simposio del Campo Freudiano (Buenos Aires)

Belgum
  École de la Cause freudienne en Belgique

Brazil
  Biblioteca Freudiana Brasileira (Sao Paulo)
  Clinica Freudiana (Bahia)
  Grupo Psicoanalitico de Curitiba
  Letra Freudiana (Rio de Janeiro)
  Mayeutica—Porto Alegre

France
  École de la Cause freudienne

Great Britain
  Cultural Center for Freudian Studies and Research (London)

Italy
  Agalma. Centro Studi de Psicanalisi (Turin)
  Centro Studi de Clinica Psicanalitica (Milan)
  Circolo Psicanalitico di Bologna

Japan
  Psychoanalytic Research Society of Tokyo

Mexico
  Fundacion Mexicana de Asistencia Psicoterapeutica (Mexico City)

Peru
  Centro Freudiano de Lima

Spain
  Ambito Madrileno de Psicoanálisis (Madrid)
  Asociacion de Psicoanalisis (Barcelona)
  Biblioteca de Estudios Freudianos de Bilbao
  Biblioteca Freudiana de Malaga
  Biblioteca Galega de Estudios Freudianos (Vigo)
  Pacto Psicoanalítico de Barcelona

United States
  New York Lacan Study Group

Groups Affiliated With the International Meetings of the "Champ Freudien" (*continued*)

Uruguay
  Escuela Freudiana de Montevideo

Venezuela
  Escuela del Campo Freudiano de Caracas

Yugoslavia
  Society for Theoretical Psychoanalysis in Yugoslavia (Ljubljana)

IPA: Congresses and Presidents

Year	Place	President
1908	Salzburg, Austria	Informal Meeting
1910	Nuremberg, Germany	Carl Jung
1911	Weimar, Germany	Carl Jung
1913	Munich, Germany	Carl Jung

1914–1918: World War I

Year	Place	President
1918	Budapest, Hungary	Karl Abraham
1920	The Hague, Holland	Ernest Jones (Prov. Pres.)
1922	Berlin, Germany	Ernest Jones
1924	Salzburg, Austria	Ernest Jones
1925	Bad Homburg, Germany	Karl Abraham
1927	Innsbruck, Austria	Max Eitingon
1929	Oxford, England	Max Eitingon
1932	Wiesbaden, Germany	Max Eitingon
1934	Lucerne, Switzerland	Ernest Jones
1936	Marienbad, Czechoslovakia	Ernest Jones
1938	Paris, France	Ernest Jones

1939–1945: World War II

Year	Place	President
1949	Zurich, Switzerland	Ernest Jones
1951	Amsterdam, Holland	Leo Bartemeier
1953	London, England	Heinz Hartmann
1955	Geneva, Switzerland	Heinz Hartmann
1957	Paris, France	Heinz Hartmann
1959	Copenhagen, Denmark	William Gillespie
1961	Edinburgh, Scotland	William Gillespie
1963	Stockholm, Sweden	Maxwell Gitelson
1965	Amsterdam, Holland	William Gillespie, Phyllis Greenacre
1967	Copenhagen, Denmark	P. J. Van der Leeuw
1969	Rome, Italy	P. J. Van der Leeuw
1971	Vienna, Austria	Leo Rangell
1973	Paris, France	Leo Rangell
1975	London, England	Serge Lebovici
1977	Jerusalem, Israel	Serge Lebovici
1979	New York, U.S.A.	Edward D. Joseph
1981	Helsinki, Finland	Edward D. Jospeh
1983	Madrid, Spain	Adam Limentani

IPA: 1985 Global Distribution

	Regional Societies	Members
United States	American Psychoanalytic Association 35 affiliated societies 4 study groups 27 institutes	2,100
Canada	*Member Societies* Canadian Psychoanalytic Society 6 Branches: CPS, Montreal, Toronto, Ottawa, Alberta, Ontario	270
Mexico	Asociacion Psicoanalitica Mexicana	124
Argentina	Asociacion Psicoanalitica Argentina Asociacion Psicoanalitica de Buenos Aires Asociacion Psicoanalitica de Mendoza	420 160 12
Brazil	Sociedade Brasileira de Psicanalise do Rio de Janeiro Sociedade Psicanalitica do Rio de Janeiro (under obser- vation) Sociedade Brasileira de Psicanalise de Sao Paolo Sociedade Psicanalitica de Porto Alegre	 150 140 200 30
Chile	Asociacion Psicoanalitica chilena	30
Colombia	Sociedad Colombiana de Psicoanalisis	45
Uruguay	Asociacion Psicoanalitica del Uruguay	46
Venezuela	Asociacion Venezolana de Psicoanalisis (under observa- tion)	 64
Belgium	Belgische Vereniging voor Psychoanalyse	50
Great Britain	British Psychoanalytical Society	378
Denmark	Dansk Psykoanalytisk Selskat	26
Holland	Nederlandse Vereniging voor Psychoanalyse	164
Finland	Suomen Psykoanalyyttinen Yhdistys Finlands Psyko- analytiska Förening	 84
France	Association psychanalytique de France Société psychanalytique de Paris, Institut de psych- analyse (under evaluation)	 50 418
Germany (Federal Republic)	Deutsche Psychoanalytische Vereinigung 12 Institutes	 390
Italy	Società Psicoanalitica Italiana 8 Branches: Rome (2),	

	Milan, Bologna, Florence, Palermo, Naples, Venice 3 Institutes	300
Spain	Asociacion Psicoanalitica de Madrid Sociedad Espanola de Psicoanalisis	30 23
Norway	Norsk Psykoanalytisk Forening	38
Sweden	Svenska Psykoanalytiska Föreningen	114
Portugal	Sociedade Portuguesa de Psicanalise	23
Switzerland	Schweizerische Geselleshaft für Psychoanalyse	120
Austria	Wiener Psychoanalytische Vereinigung	25
India	Indian Psychoanalytical Society	36
Israel	"Hahevra Hap- sychoanalitite Be-Israel	70
Japan	Nippon Seishin-Bunseki Kyokai	22
Australia	Australian Psychoanalytical Society (under evaluation)	35
Hungary	*Provisional Societies* Ideiglenes Magyar Pzichoanalitikus Tarasag	23

Study Groups
Grupo de Estudios Psicoanaliticos de Cordoba
Hellenic Psychoanalytical Study Group
Grupo de Estudios Psicoanaliticos de Monterrey
Grupo de Estudios Psicoanaliticos del Peru

Abbreviations

AAAP	American Association for the Advancement of Psychoanalysis
AAGP	Allgemeine Ärztliche Gesellschaft für Psychotherapie
AAP	Association des ateliers de psychanalyse
AF	Association freudienne
AE	Analyste de l'École (EFP)
AIHP	Association internationale d'histoire de la psychanalyse
AMAR	Association médico-psychologique d'aide aux religieux
AME	Analyste membre de l'École (EFP)
AP	Analyste practicien (EFP)
APA	American Psychoanalytic Association
APF	Association psychanalytique de France
API	Association psychanalytique internationale (Gallicized version of IPA as used by the SPP)
CCAF	Cartels constituants de l'analyse freudienne
CEP	Collectif Événement psychanalyse
CERF	Centre d'études et de recherches freudiennes
CERM	Centre d'études et de recherches marxistes
CFRP	Centre de formation et de recherches psychanalytiques
CHU	Centres hospitalo-universitaires
CMPP	Centre médico-psycho-pédagogique
CNRS	Centre national de la recherche scientifique
CP	Convention psychanalytique
DEA	Diplôme pour étude avancée (Diploma for advanced study)
DPG	Deutsche Psychoanalytische Gesellschaft
DPV	Deutsche Psychoanalytische Vereinigung
DSM III	*Diagnostic and Statistical Manual of Mental Disturbances (APA)*
ECF	École de la cause freudienne
EF	École freudienne
EFERS	Expérience freudienne et recherche scientifique
EFP	École freudienne de Paris
ELP	École lacanienne de psychanalyse
EMP	Externat medico-pedagogique
ENS	École normale superieure
EP	Évolution psychiatrique (Group)
EP	*Évolution psychiatrique* (Journal)
EPCI	École propédeutique à la connaissance de l'inconscient
ESI	Éditions sociales internationales
FEP	Fédération européenne de psychanalyse
GEP	Groupe d'études de la psychanalyse (Study Group)
GP	Gauche prolétarienne
GRP	Groupe régional de psychanalyse
IJP	*International Journal of Psychoanalysis*

IMP	Internat médico-pedagogique
IP	Institut de psychanalyse
IPA	International Psychoanalytical Association
ME	Membre de l'École (EFP)
MLF	Mouvement de libération des femmes
NC	*Nouvelle Critique*
NRF	*Nouvelle Revue française*
NRP	*Nouvelle Revue de psychanalyse*
OPLF	Organisation psychanalytique de langue française (Fourth Group)
PCF	Parti communiste français
RFP	*Revue française de psychanalyse*
RHLF	*Revue d'histoire littéraire de la France*
SASDLR	*Le Surréalisme au service de la révolution*
SBP	Société belge de psychanalyse
SFP	Société française de psychanalyse
SHC	Sciences humaines cliniques
SIHPP	Société internationale d'histoire de la psychiatrie et de la psychanalyse
SPP	Société psychanalytique de Paris
TM	*Temps modernes*
TQ	*Tel Quel*
UEC	Union des étudiants communistes
UER	Unité d'enseignement de recherche (Teaching and Research Unit)
UJCML	Union des jeunesses communistes et marxistes-léninistes
UV	Unité de valeur (Course credit)
WPA	World Psychiatric Association
WPS	Washington Psychoanalytic Society

Principal Archives

E.R.	Elisabeth Roudinesco
J.A.	Jenny Aubry
J.-A.M.	Jacques-Alain Miller
J.-L.D.	Jean-Luc Donnet
R.E.	Renée Ey
R.M.	René Major
S.L.	Serge Leclaire
W.G.	Wladimir Granoff
X.A.	Xavier Audouard

Notes

Chapter 1. Surrealism in the Service of Psychoanalysis

1. Pierre Daix, *Aragon, une vie à changer* (Paris: Seuil, 1975), p. 167; *Tracts surréalistes et déclarations collectives*, edited by José Pierre (Paris: Losfeld, 1980), pp. 41–49; Nicole Racine, "Une revue d'intellectuels communistes dans les années vingt: 'Clarté'" in *Revue française de sciences politiques*, vol. 17, June 1967, p. 509; Maurice Nadeau, *Histoire du surréalisme* (Paris: Seuil, 1964), p. 83. See also special issue of *NRF*, dedicated to André Breton, 172, April 1967.

2. Elisabeth Roudinesco, *La bataille de cent ans: Histoire de la psychoanalyse en France*, vol. 1 (Paris: Ramsay, 1982), part 3, chap. 1. Hereafter cited as *Bataille* I.

3. Michel Winock, *Histoire politique de la revue "Esprit"* (Paris: Seuil, 1975).

4. See *Bataille* I, part 2, chap. 2.

5. *Révolution surréaliste*, 9–10, 1927, pp. 25–31; republished by J.-M. Place (Paris, 1980).

6. Ibid., 10, March 1928, pp. 20–22.

7. Concerning Codet and Laforgue's article on Charcot, see *Bataille* I, part 1, chap. 2.

8. *Révolution surréaliste*, 3, April 1925, p. 29. The text of Desnos's first draft is reproduced in *Les Nouvelles-Hébrides et autres textes* (Paris: Gallimard, 1978), pp. 518–519. See also *Tracts et déclarations*, p. 388.

9. Concerning the history and definition of dynamic psychiatry, see *Bataille* I, part 3, chap. 1.

10. *EP*, I, 1925; Sarane Alexandrian, *Le surréalisme et le rêve* (Paris: Gallimard, 1974), p. 63.

11. Jean Frois-Wittman, *Révolution surréaliste*, 12, December 1929, pp. 41–44, and "Le mot d'esprit" in *SASDLR*, October 1930; republished by J.-M. Place, pp. 26–29.

12. L. A. M. Hesnard, *Freud dans la société d'après guerre* (Geneva, Lausanne: Mont Blanc, 1946), p. 118.

13. *SASDLR*, 5, May 1933, pp. 2–3.

14. H. Ey, "La psychiatrie devant le surréalisme," in *EP*, XIII, 4, pp. 3–52. See also *EP*, I, XLIV, 1979, special issue, "Surréalisme et psychiatrie."

15. S. Alexandrian, *Le surréalisme et le rêve.*

16. See *Bataille*, I, part 2, chap. 2.

17. Thomas Mann;, *Freud et la pensée moderne* (Paris: Aubier-Flammarion, 1970). On the (marginal) creation of the first Jungian group in France in 1928, see *Le Temps: Cahiers de psychologie jungienne*, September 1978.

18. André Breton and Philippe Soupault, *Les champs magnétiques* (Paris: Au Sans-Pareil, 1920); republished by Poésie-Gallimard (Paris, 1976).

19. Tristan Tzara, *Oeuvres complètes* (Paris: Flammarion, 1975), vol. 1, p. 364; M. Sanouillet, *Dada à Paris* (Paris: Pauvert, 1965).

20. René Crevel, "Le patriotisme de l'inconscient," in *SASDLR*, 4, December 1931.

21. *Révolution surréaliste*, 1, December 1924, p. 2.

22. Pierre Drieu La Rochelle, *Le feu follet* (Paris: Gallimard, 1963), p. 81; André Breton, *Anthologie de l'humour noir* (Paris: Sagittaire, 1950).

23. André Breton, *Point du jour* (Paris: Idées-Gallimard, 1970), p. 81.

24. Max Schur, *Freud: Living and Dying* (New York: International University Press, 1972) [in French, *La mort dans la vie de Freud* (Paris: Gallimard, 1975), p. 394]. On the subject of the death drive, see also *Bataille* I, part 4, chap. 2.

25. See part 2, this volume.

26. Julien Gracq, *André Breton* (Paris: José Corti, 1948).

27. *Tracts et déclarations*, p. 156.

28. *Révolution surréaliste*, 11, March 1928, pp. 32–40.

29. Ibid., p. 33.

30. Ibid., p. 38.

31. Ibid., p. 40.

32. J.-M. Fitère, *Violette Nozière* (Paris: Presses de la Cité, 1975).

33. At the time, the name was written "Nozières." *Fascicule* (Brussels: Nicolas Flamel, 1933), partially reprinted in *Tracts et Déclarations*, pp. 247, 483.

34. Ibid., p. 486.

35. Georges Bataille, *Madame Edwarda*, published between 1941 and 1945 under the pseudonym Pierre Angélique; reprinted by Pauvert (Paris, 1956). For the importance of the paranoid woman for Lacan, see Catherine Clément, *The Lives and Legends of Jacques Lacan* (New York: Columbia Univ. Press, 1983).

36. H. Ellenberger, *The Discovery of the Unconscious* (New York: Basic Books, 1970) [in French, *A la découverte de l'inconscient* (Villeurbanne: Simep, 1974)].

37. A. Breton, *Nadja* (Paris: Gallimard, 1962), p. 44.

38. A. Breton, *Entretiens* (Paris: Gallimard, 1969), p. 38.

39. A. Breton, *Les pas perdus* (Paris: Idées-Gallimard, 1969), p. 99. See also S. Alexandrian, *Le surréalisme et le rêve*, and Marguerite Bonnet, *André Breton: Naissance de l'aventure surréaliste* (Paris: Corti, 1975).

40. Louis Aragon, *Traité du style* (Paris: Gallimard, 1980), pp. 146, 149.

41. Quoted from the unpublished seminar of Pierre Macherey (1980–1982) on the "Introduction of Hegelianism in France: From Victor Cousin to Alexandre Kojève."

42. See chap. 3, this volume.

43. Concerning T. Flournoy, see *Bataille* I, part 2, chap. 1.

44. A. Breton, "Entrée des médiums" (1922), in *Point du jour*, p. 127.

45. See "Le message automatique," ibid.

46. Ibid., p. 171.

47. From Macherey's seminar, "Introduction of Hegelianism in France."

48. *L'Arc*, 34, 1968, p. 95. See also H. Deluy, *Anthologie arbitraire d'une nouvelle poésie* (Paris: Flammarion, 1983).

49. A. Breton, *Nadja*, p. 7.

50. Ibid., p. 133.

51. Ibid., p. 155.

52. A. Breton, "La médecine mentale devant le surréalisme," in *Point du jour*, p. 89.

53. Ibid., pp. 92–93.

54. André Breton, *Manifestes du surréalisme* (Paris: Idées-Gallimard, 1979), p. 78.

55. See B. Caburet, *Raymond Roussel* (Paris: Seghers, 1968); E. Roudinesco, *L'inconscient et ses lettres* (Paris: Mame, 1975); *L'Arc*, 68, 1977; Michel Leiris, "Conception et réalité chez Raymond Roussel" in *Critique*, 89, October 1954; Michel Foucault, *Raymond Roussel* (Paris: Gallimard, 1963).

56. *Revue hebdomadaire*, December 23, 1922, reprinted in *Bizarre*, 34–35, II, 1964, p. 54.

57. R. Roussel, *Comment j'ai écrit certains de mes livres* (Paris: Pauvert, 1962), pp. 127–132.

58. Pierre Janet, *De l'angoisse à l'extase* (Paris: Alcan, 1928), vol. 1, pp. 132–137. See commentary in Claude Prévost, *La psycho-philosophie de Pierre Janet* (Paris: Payot, 1973), pp. 313–319.

59. See *Bataille* I, part 4, chap. 1.

60. Ernest Jones, *The Life and Work of Sigmund Freud* (New York: Basic Books, 1953) [in French, *La vie et l'oeuvre de Sigmund Freud* (Paris: PUF, 1961), vol. 2].

61. M. Leiris, "Conception et réalité chez Raymond Roussel."

62. André Breton, *Les vases communicants* (Paris: Idées-Gallimard, 1977), p. 18.

63. Ibid., p. 176.

64. Quoted by P. Macherey in his seminar, "Introduction of Hegelianism in France."

65. A. Breton, *Entretiens*, pp. 153–154.

66. *Tracts et déclarations*, p. 143.

67. J. Gracq, *André Breton*, p. 142.

68. A. Breton, "Trajectoire du rêve," *Cahiers G. L. M.* (Paris, 1938), p. 4.

69. Sigmund Freud, *Correspondance 1873–1939* (Paris: Gallimard, 1967), p. 490 [in English, *Letters of Sigmund Freud* (New York: McGraw-Hill, 1964), p. 449. Note: Unless otherwise indicated, I have translated excerpts from Freud's writings from the French.— Trans.]

Chapter 2. Marxism, Psychoanalysis, Psychology

1. Léon Trotski, *Ma vie* (Paris: Gallimard, 1973), pp. 263–264 [in English, Trotsky, *My Life: An Attempt at Autobiography* (New York: Scribners, 1930]; "Lettres nouvelles," in *Littérature et révolution* (Paris: Julliard, 1964), pp. 303–305, preface by M. Nadeau.

2. I. P. Pavlov, *Les réflexes conditionnels* (Paris: Alcan, 1927) [*Conditioned Reflexes* (London: Oxford, 1927)].

3. P. Janet, "Les sentiments d'emprise et la phase ultra-paradoxale," *Journal de psychologie*, 9–10, 1933.

4. Joseph Wortis, *La psychiatrie soviétique* (Paris: PUF, 1953).

5. See *Bataille* I, part 3, chap. 2.

6. J. Wortis, *La psychiatrie soviétique*, p. 50. See also E. Astarian, *I. Pavlov* (Moscow, 1953), p. 29.

7. Ibid., p. 51. See also chap. 5, this volume.

8. Concerning the discussions in philosophy, see René Zapata, *Luttes philosophiques en URSS* (Paris: PUF, 1983); F. Champarnaud, *Révolution et contre-révolution culturelle en URSS, de Lénine à Jdanov* (Paris: Anthropos, 1975).

9. Roy Medvedev, *On Stalin and Stalinism* (New York: Oxford Univ. Press, 1979).

10. The history of psychoanalysis in the Soviet Union remains to be written. For the principal references, see Jean Marti, "La psychanalyse en Russie" in *Critique*, 346, March 1976; J. Wortis, *La psychiatrie soviétique;* W. Reich, *La révolution sexuelle* (Paris: Plon, 1968); A.-M. Costa, *La Psychologie soviétique* (Paris: Payot, 1972); A. Kollontaï, *Marxisme et révolution sexuelle* (Paris: Maspero, 1973); J.-M. Palmier, "La psychanalyse en URSS," in *Histoire de la psychanalyse*, ed. R. Jaccard (Paris: Hachette, 1982); Mikhäel Stern, *La vie sexuelle en URSS* (Paris: Albin Michel, 1979). Concerning Freud's relations with Marxism and Bolshevism, see *Civilization and Its Discontents* (New York: Norton, 1962); *New Introductory Lectures on Psychoanalysis* (New York: Norton, 1965); P. Roazen, *Freud's Political and Social Thought* (New York: Knopf, 1968); P. Cabestan, "Freud et les communistes," *Cahiers Confrontation*, 7, 1982; E. Roudinesco, *Un discours au réel* (Paris: Mame, 1973);

Cyrille Koupernik, "La psychiatrie russe avant la révolution de 1917," *Perspectives psychiatriques,* 11, 96, 1984.

11. According to J. Marti, Vera Schmidt was the wife of Otto Schmidt.

12. *T.M.,* March 1969. See also the account by Reich in *La révolution sexuelle,* pp. 279–285; V. Schmidt and W. Reich, *Pulsions sexuelles et éducation du corps* (Paris: 10/18, 1979).

13. See *Bataille* I, part 2, chap. 2.

14. See R. Zapata, *Luttes philosophiques en URSS.*

15. See Bykhovski, "Fondements méthodologiques de la théorie psychanalytique de Freud," in *Sous la bannière du marxisme,* 12 (Moscow, 1923); B. D. Fridman, "Les grandes vues psychologiques de Freud et la théorie du matérialisme historique," in *Psychologie et marxisme,* ed. Kornilov (Moscow, 1925); A. R. Luria, "La psychanalyse en tant que système de psychologie moniste," ibid.; Zalkind, "Freudisme et marxisme," in *Rouges semailles,* 4 (Moscow, 1924); V. Jurinetz, "Freudisme et marxisme," in *Sous la bannière du marxisme,* 8–9 (Moscow, 1927); M. Bakhtine, *Le freudisme* (Lausanne: Age d'homme, 1980), trans. Guy Verret. In his introduction Verret attributes Voloshinov's articles to Bakhtin, whereas in the Italian translation they are attributed to the author. See Valentin N. Volochinov, *Freudismo* (Bari: Dedalo Libri, 1977). [Note: Bakhtin and Voloshinov are the English spellings.—Trans.]

16. See chap. 5, this volume; Makarenko, *Poeme pédagogique,* 3 vols. (Moscow). See also Lidia Bogdanovitch, *Carnet d'une psychiatre soviétique* (Paris: Editeurs français réunis, 1963) and *Recherches psychologiques en URSS* (Moscow, 1966).

17. Ernest Jones, *La vie et l'oeuvre de Sigmund Freud* (Paris: PUF, 1961), vol. 3, p. 18, and P. Cabestan, "Freud et les communistes," p. 171.

18. S. Freud, *Malaise dans la civilisation* [*Civilization and Its Discontents*], pp. 66–67.

19. S. Freud, *Nouvelles conférences* [*New Introductory Lectures*], p. 247.

20. For the resonances in German of the word *Kultur,* see *Bataille* I, part 4, chap. 1.

21. S. Freud, *Nouvelles conférences,* pp. 245–246.

22. Lou Andreas-Salomé, *Correspondance avec Sigmund Freud* (Paris: Gallimard, 1970), p. 216.

23. For Reich's biography, see Ilse Ollendorf-Reich, *Wilhelm Reich* (Paris: Belfond, 1970), and *W. Reich, L'Arc,* 83, 1982.

24. W. Reich, *La fonction de l'orgasme* (Paris: L'Arche, 1952); *L'analyse caractérielle* (Paris: Payot, 1973).

25. The first French publication of the text was by Éditions sociales internationales (PCF) in an anthology entitled *La crise sexuelle.* After the first German edition, it reappeared in 1934, in German, with additional notes and a new text: "Toward the Application of Psychoanalysis to Historical Research." The new collection was translated into French in 1970 for Éditions de la pensée molle.

26. See W. Reich, *La révolution sexuelle.*

27. W. Reich, *Reich parle de Freud* (Paris: Payot, 1972), pp. 264–265.

28. *RFP,* 7, 2, 1934, pp. 378–387.

29. See chap. 6, this volume.

30. André Thirion, *Révolutionnaires sans révolution* (Paris: Laffont, 1972). And M. Nadeau, preface to Trotski, *Littérature et révolution,* p. 146; Herbert Lottman, *The Left Bank* (Boston: Houghton Mifflin, 1982); J.-P.-A. Bernard, *Le parti communiste français et la question littéraire (1921–1929)* (Grenoble: Press universitaires, 1972); David Caute, *Le communisme et les intellectuels français: 1914–1966* (Paris: Gallimard, 1967).

31. See P. Robrieux, *Histoire intérieure du PCF,* vol. 1: 1920–1945 (Paris: Fayard,

1980); Danielle Tartakowsky, *Les premiers Communistes français* (Paris: Presses de la Fondation des sciences politiques, 1980).

32. D. Tartakowsky, "Le marxisme et les intellectuels de 1920 à 1935," *La Pensée,* 205, June 1979.

33. *A la lumière du marxisme* (Paris: Éditions sociales internationales, 1935–36), preface by Henri Wallon.

34. Interview with Victor Fay, who was unable to inform me as to the identity of Manet.

35. *A la lumière du marxisme,* p. xiii.

36. R. Zapata, *Lutte philosophiques en URSS.* For an unexpurgated version of the text, see Éditions de la pensée molle (1970).

37. I. Sapir, in *La crise sexuelle,* p. 194.

38. Ibid., p. 229. In 1929, the break between Freud and Reich had not yet occurred, but Sapir was able to intuit from Reich's text the latter's opposition to Freud.

39. Reproduced in G. Politzer, *Écrits 2: Les fondements de la psychologie* (Paris: Éditions sociales, 1969), pp. 252–281.

40. Concerning Souvarine, see *La critique sociale,* republished by Éd. de la Différence (Paris, 1983).

41. Jean Audard, "Le caractère matérialiste de la psychanalayse" in *Cahiers du sud,* 2d series, September 1933.

42. G. Politzer, *Écrits 2,* pp. 282–302.

43. *Psychologie de masse du fascisme* (Paris: Payot, 1972).

44. G. Politzer, *Écrits 2,* p. 300. For an account of the relations between Jung and the Nazis, see *Bataille* I, part 2, chap. 1.

45. The totality of Reich's works would be translated between 1968 and 1975.

46. René Crevel, *Le clavecin de Diderot* (Paris: Pauvert, 1966), pp. 163–164.

47. *SASDLR, 5,* May 1933, p. 51.

48. Ibid., p. 52.

49. R. Crevel, *Mon corps et moi* (Paris: Pauvert, 1974), p. 95.

50. Conversations with H. Lefebvre. I have also made use of the work of Bernard Daubigney, *La psychanalyse et les lettres françaises: 1919–1929,* doctoral thesis supervised by Y. Brès, Paris VII, 1983. See H. Lefebvre, *La somme et le reste,* 2 vols. (Paris: La Nef, 1959).

51. Henri Daniel-Rops, *Notre inquiétude* (Paris: Perrin, 1927).

52. See *Bataille* I, part 2, chap. 1.

53. Michel Winock, *Histoire politique de la revue "Esprit"* (Paris: Seuil, 1975); J. Maritain, *Humanisme intégral* (Paris: Aubier, 1936).

54. See *Bataille* I, part 4, chap. 2.

55. Jacques Petit, "Un non-conformiste des années vingt: Jules Monchanin," in *Cahiers d'histoire,* 26, 1981.

56. Quoted by M. Winock, *Histoire politique de la revue "Esprit,"* p. 53. See René Rémond, *Les catholiques, le communisme, et les crises (1929–1939)* (Paris: Colin, 1960).

57. H. Lefebvre, *La somme et le reste,* p. 387.

58. Presently Oradea.

59. G. Politzer's two texts have been republished in *Écrits 2.*

60. H. Lefebvre, *La somme et le reste,* p. 425.

61. André Breton alludes to the event in the *Second Surrealist Manifesto.*

62. H. Lefebvre, *La somme et le reste.* Victor Fay contests the episode. See D. Tartakowsky, "Le marxisme et les intellectuels de 1920 à 1935."

63. Paris: Rieder, 1928 and Paris: PUF, 1968. Concerning Politzer, see Laurent Alexandre, "Freud et Politzer" in *Europe*, special issue on Freud, 539, March 1974; *Politzer, cahiers de l'IRM*, February 1982; Henri Lefebvre, "G. Politzer et la psychanalyse" in *La Raison*, 18, 1957.

64. Such is the position of Lefebvre and of Pascal Ory in *Nizan* (Paris: Ramsay, 1980).

65. Georges Politzer, "L'obscurantisme au XXᵉ siècle" in *La Pensée libre*, I, February 1941, republished in *Écrits 1*, ed. J. Debouzy (Paris: Éditions sociales, 1969).

66. Georges Politzer, "La fin de la psychanalyse" in *La Pensée*, 3, October–November 1939, author listed as Th. Morris. Republished in *Écrits 2*.

67. "Race, nation, people," in *Écrits 1*, p. 75.

68. See *Bataille* I. Lowenstein wrote a positive review of *La critique des fondements de la psychologie* in the *RFP*.

69. See *Bataille* I, part 4, chap. 1.

70. *Écrits 2*, p. 199.

71. Jacques Lacan, *Propos sur la causalité psychique* in *Écrits* (Paris: Seuil, 1966), p. 161.

72. Most of Wallon's texts on psychoanalysis have been reprinted by Émile Jalley in his *Wallon, lecteur de Freud et de Piaget* (Paris: Éditions sociales, 1981). I largely follow Jalley's argument here. See also the special issue of *EP* (27, I, 1962) dedicated to Wallon as well as René Zazzo, "Méditations" in *Psychologie et marxisme* (Paris: Denoël-Gonthier, 1975).

73. See chap. 6, this volume; Henri Wallon, "Pavlovisme et psychologie" in *La Nouvelle Critique*, July–August 1955; *Psychologie et matérialisme dialectique* (Societa, 1951), republished in *L'École et la Nation*, 31, VIII–IX, 1954. See as well Y. Galifret, "Le biologique dans la psychobiologie de Wallon," *Enfance*, 5, 1976.

74. Text published in 1920 in *Journal de psychologie*, reproduced in E. Jalley, *Wallon, lecteur de Freud et de Piaget*, p. 393.

75. Ibid., p. 416.

76. Henri Wallon, "Comment se développe chez l'enfant la notion de corps propre," *Journal de psychologie*, November–December 1931, pp. 705–748; reprinted in *Enfance*, 1963. This text was brought to my attention by E. Jalley. See also *Les origines du caractère chez l'enfant* (Paris: PUF, 1973) (first edition, Paris: Bovin, 1934).

77. H. Wallon, "Comment se développe," pp. 147–148.

Chapter 3. Writers, Literati, Dream-Devourers

1. See *Bataille* I, part 4, chap. 1.

2. B. Daubigney's dissertation, *La psychanalyse et les lettres françaises: 1919–1929*, doctoral thesis supervised by Y. Brès, Paris VII, 1983.

3. Ibid. See also Robert de Traz, "Visite à Freud" in *Les Nouvelles littéraires*, March 24, 1923; J.-P. Meylan, *La revue de Genève: Miroir des lettres européennes* (Geneva: Droz, 1969).

4. For a listing of journals, see B. Daubigney's dissertation.

5. J. Dandieu, "Le freudisme," in *L'Information universitaire*, no. 138, March 7, 1925.

6. *Disque vert*, special issue, 2d year, 3d series, Paris-Brussels, 1924. See also Franz Hellens, *Documents secrets* (Brussels and Maestricht: Stols, 1932), p. 52.

7. *Disque vert*, special issue, p. 13.

8. Ibid., pp. 92–93.

9. André Gide, *Journal*, June 28, 1924 (Paris: Gallimard, 1958), p. 785.

10. Concerning O. Gross, see *Bataille* I, part 2, chap. 1.

11. See David Steel, "Les débuts de la psychanalyse dans les lettres françaises," in *Revue d'histoire littéraire de la France,* I, 1979; M. Poupon, *Apollinaire et Cendrars* (Paris: Minard, 1969).

12. Blaise Cendrars, *L'homme foudroyé* (Paris Denoël, 1960), p. 313.

13. D. Steel, "Les débuts de la psychanalyse dans les lettres françaises," and S. Sarkany, *Paul Morand et le cosmopolitisme littéraire* (Paris: Klincksieck, 1968), p. 208.

14. Guillaume Apollinaire, "Monsieur Paul Bourget et les aliénés," *Mercure de France,* 16, December 1913, quoted by D. Steel in "Les débuts de la psychanalyse dans les lettres françaises."

15. Paul Bourget, *Némésis* (Paris: Plon-Nourrit, 1918), pp. 198–199.

16. Henri Daniel-Rops, *Notre inquiétude* (Paris: Perrin, 1927), pp. 95–96.

17. P. Bourget, "La maison de Saint-Cloud" in *Anomalies* (Paris: Plon, 1920), p. 9.

18. See *Bataille* I, part 4, chap. 1.

19. H.-R. Lenormand, *Les confessions d'un auteur dramatique* (Paris: Albin Michel, 1949).

20. H.-R. Lenormand, *Le Mangeur de rêves* (Paris Crès, 1922).

21. See the material assembled by Mireille Cifali in *Bloc-notes de psychanalyse,* 2 (Geneva, 1982).

22. Ibid., p. 138.

23. Ibid., p. 141.

24. See J. Nobécourt and M. Guibal, *Sabina Spielrein entre Freud et Jung* (Paris: Aubier, 1981).

25. F. Mauriac, *La Revue hebdomadaire,* February 1922, quoted by D. Steel in "Les débuts de la psychanalyse dans les lettres françaises," p. 96.

26. F. Lefèvre, "Une heure avec" in *NRF,* 1924. Interview with Jacques Rivière, December 1, 1923, vol. 3, p. 96.

27. H.-R. Lenormand, "Dadaïsme et psychologie," *Comedia,* March 23, 1920. A. Breton, "Pour dada," *NRF,* August 1920, vol. 14, p. 213; F. Picabia, *Écrits* (Paris: Belfond, 1975), vol. 1, p. 216.

28. H.-R. Lenormand, *Les confessions,* vol. 1, pp. 270–271.

29. S. Freud, *Correspondence* (1873–1939) (Paris: Gallimard, 1967), p. 372 [*Letters,* p. 341].

30. Rolland's letters to Freud have been reprinted in Colette Cornubert's thesis, *Essai sur la découverte de la pensée psychanalytique par les écrivains français,* Faculté de Médecine, March 1966; Roger Dadoun, "Rolland, Freud, et la sensation océanique," *RHLF,* 1976.

31. S. Freud, *Correspondence,* p. 395 [*Letters,* p. 341].

32. Ibid.

33. C. Cornubert, *Essai sur la découverte de la pensée psychanalytique,* letter of May 6, 1926.

34. T. Reik, *Trente ans avec Freud* (Brussels: Complexe, PUF, 1975), p. 106.

35. C. Cornubert, *Essai sur la découverte de la pensée psychanalytique.*

36. S. Freud, *Correspondence,* p. 424 [*Letters,* p. 388].

37. C. Cornubert, *Essai.*

38. Romain Rolland, *Essai sur la mystique et l'action de l'Inde vivante,* 2 vols. (Paris: Stock, 1930).

39. S. Freud, *Correspondence,* p. 424 [*Letters,* p. 388].

40. S. Freud, *Malaise dans la civilisation,* p. 6 [*Civilization and Its Discontents,* trans. J. Strachey (New York: Norton, 1961), p. 12].

41. *Malaise*, p. 15 [*Civilization*, p. 20].

42. C. Cornubert, *Essai.*

43. S. Freud, *Correspondance*, p. 428 [*Letters*, p. 392].

44. Ibid.

45. C. Cornubert, *Essai.*

46. Ibid.

47. S. Freud, *Correspondance*, p. 443 [*Letters*, p. 406].

48. *L'éphémère* (Paris: Ed. de la Fondation Maeght, 1967), trans. Marthe Robert. For an analysis of this text, see *Bataille* I.

49. See *Bataille* I.

50. C. Cornubert, *Essai.*

51. See Jacques Brenner, materials on the 1930s assembled in *Le Matin*, August 24–30, 1981; H. Lottman, *The Left Bank* (Boston: Houghton Mifflin, 1982); A. Anglès, *André Gide et le groupe de la NRF* (Paris: Gallimard, 1978); B. Grasset, *La chose littéraire* (Paris: Gallimard, 1929).

52. Ernest Jones, *La vie et l'oeuvre de Sigmund Freud* (Paris: PUF, 1961), vol. 3, p. 88 [*The Life and Work of Sigmund Freud*]; D. Steel, "Gide et Freud," *RHLF*, January–February 1977, 1, pp. 48–74.

53. André Lang, *Voyage en zig-zag dans la république des lettres* (Paris: La Renaissance du livre, 1922), pp. 266–267.

54. See *Bataille* I, part 2, chap. 2.

55. "Correspondance Gide-Bussy" in *Cahiers André Gide*, 9, vol. 1 (Paris: Gallimard, 1979), p. 252.

56. Ibid., pp. 254–255.

57. D. Steel, "Les débuts de la psychanalyse," p. 75 and n. 52 (my emphasis).

58. "Correspondance Gide-Bussy," p. 258.

59. When consulted on this subject, M. Jean Lambert, who initiated the publication of this correspondence, affirmed the letter had been destroyed. See Bernard Daubigney, *La psychanalyse et les lettres françaises: 1919–1929,* doctoral thesis supervised by Y. Brès, Paris VII, 1983.

60. Marcel Proust, *A la recherche du temps perdu* (Paris: Gallimard, 1922), illustrated by Van Dongen.

61. See Claude Lorin, *Le jeune Ferenczi: 1899–1906* (Paris: Aubier, 1983).

62. For current reflection on this topic, see Robert Stoller, *Recherches sur l'identité sexuelle* (Paris: Gallimard, 1968); *NRP,* 7: *Bisexualité et différence des sexes,* Spring 1973; Cathering Millot, *Horsexe: Essai sur le transexualisme* (Paris: Point hors ligne, 1983). The term "uranism," which was used by Freud, Gide, and the "alienists," was introduced in 1860 in a novel written by a magistrate writing under the pen name Numa Numantis. It comes from the goddess of pure love, Aphrodite urana (= celestial). The word subsequently fell into disuse. See also Janice Raymond, *L'empire transsexuel* (Paris: Seuil, 1981).

63. Claude Francis and Fernande Gontier, *Marcel Proust et les siens* (Paris: Plon, 1981).

64. *Cahiers d'occident*, 4, 1926, "Deuxieme conférence," January 17, 1924, p. 23.

65. Ramon Fernandez, "Note sur Freud," *NRF,* 20, September 1922, pp. 337–340.

66. A. Gide, *Corydon* (Paris: Gallimard, 1981), pp. 8–9.

67. Albert Thibaudet, "Réflexion sur la littérature, psychanalyse, et critique littéraire," *NRF,* April 1921, 16, pp. 468–481; Jules Romains, *NRF,* 18, 1922, pp. 5–20. See also B. Daubigney's dissertation, and François Gautrey, *Sigmund Freud, la France et la littérature:*

Contribution à l'histoire du mouvement psychanalytique, dissertation in psychiatry written under supervision of A. Bourguignon, Créteil, 1980.

68. See *Bataille* I as well as M. Gourevitch, "Eugénie Sokolnicka, pionnier de la psychanalyse et inspiratrice d'André Gide" in *Médecine de France,* 1971, pp. 17–22; Jean Delay, *La jeunesse d'André Gide,* 2 vols. (Paris: Gallimard, 1956); *Correspondance 1913–1934* (Paris: Gallimard, 1968), introduction by J. Delay.

69. For commentary on this case, see *Bataille* I. French translation by M. Gourevitch and commentary by D. Widlöcher, *Revue de neuropsychiatrie infantile,* 16, 5–6, May–June 1968.

70. The sentence is Jacques Martins's in *Gide par lui-même* (Paris: Seuil, 1963), p. 149.

71. M. Gourevitch, "Eugénie Sokolnicka," and A. Gide, *Journal des faux-monnayeurs* (Paris: Gallimard, 1927), appendix, p. iii.

72. See *Bataille* I, part 4, chap. 1.

73. J. Lacan;, *Écrits* (Paris: Seuil, 1966), pp. 741 and 744.

74. Pierre Jean Jouve, *En miroir, journal sans date* (Paris: Mercure de France, 1970), p. 47; Daniel Leuwers, *Jouve avant Jouve* (Paris: Klincksieck, 1984).

75. Ibid., p. 32.

76. Ibid., p. 42. See also D. Leuwers, "Jouve, Breton, et la psychanalyse" in *NRF,* 323, 1979, p. 101.

77. Special issue of *Cahiers de l'Herne* dedicated to Jouve (Paris: 1972), pp. 114 and 409.

78. Ibid.

79. Conversations with Olivier Jouve, Daniel Leuwers, and Martine Broda.

80. Concerning the prose works prior to this date, see D. Leuwers, *Jouve avant Jouve.*

81. P. J. Jouve, *Vagadu* (Paris: Mercure de France, 1963), p. 12.

82. See Jean Starobinski, "La traversée du désir," preface to *Noces* and *Sueur de sang* (Paris: Poésie-Gallimard, 1981); see also "Entretien avec Laurent Cossé" in *Le Quotidien de Paris,* January 18, 1983.

83. René Spitz, *"Vagadu",* RFP, 3, 7, p. 550.

84. P. J. Jouve, *En miroir,* p. 69; M. Broda, *Jouve; Cahiers Cistre* (Lausanne: Age d'homme, 1981).

85. P. J. Jouve, *En miroir,* p. 75.

86. P. J. Jouve, *Noces,* p. 143; see also Marcelin Pleynet, *Poésie et psychanalyse* (Les Roches de Clermont: Actuels, 1984).

87. Concerning Jouve's prosody, see Jacques Roubaud, *La Vieillesse d'Alexandre* (Paris: Maspero, 1978).

88. P. J. Jouve and B. Reverchon-Jouve, "Moments d'une analyse," *NRF,* 15, March 1933.

89. Ibid., p. 371.

Chapter 4. Jacques Lacan: A Novel of His Youth

1. Jacques Lacan, *De la psychose paranoïaque dans ses rapports avec la personnalité* (Paris: Le François, 1932); republished by Le Seuil (Paris, 1975).

2. See special issue of *Actualités psychiatriques* (2, 1981) devoted to the situation of psychiatry in 1930 as well as "Hommage à Pierre Mâle" in *RFP,* 4, 40, July–August 1976.

3. J. Lacan, "Exposé général de nos travaux scientifiques," republished in *De la psychose paranoïaque.*

4. Jacques Lacan, *Écrits* (Paris: Seuil, 1966).

5. Ibid., p. 69.

6. Ibid., p. 71.

7. Individual interviews with Marc-François Lacan, Madeleine Lacan-Houlon, Julien Rouart.

8. Ibid.

9. See Élisabeth Renard, *Le docteur G. G. de Clérambault, sa vie, son oeuvre,* doctoral thesis in medicine (Paris: Le François, 1942); Guy Rosolato, "Clérambault et les délires passionnels," and André Green, "Passions et destins de passions" in *NRP,* 21, Spring 1980; G. G. de Clérambault, *Oeuvre psychiatriques,* 2 vols. (Paris: PUF, 1942). Consult as well Y. Papetti, F. Valier, B. de Fréminville, and S. Tisseron, *La passion des étoffes chez un psychiatre* (Paris: Solin, 1980); Guy Rosolato's unpublished lecture at the APF of June 14, 1980. For a discussion of the positions of Henri Claude, see *Bataille* I, part 4, chap. 1.

10. E. Renard, *Le docteur G. G. de Clérambault,* p. 26.

11. G. Rosolato, unpublished lecture.

12. S. Tisseron;, *La passion des étoffes,* p. 83.

13. Separate interviews with M.-F. Lacan and J. Rouart.

14. Jacques Lacan, *Télévision* (Paris: Seuil, 1973), pp. 66–67; concerning Lucien Sebag's suicide, see chap. 5, this volume.

15. *Semaine des hôpitaux,* July 7, 1931, pp. 437–445.

16. Separate interviews with J. Rouart, Lucien Bonnafé, Renée Ey.

17. Presentation to the Société médico-psychologique of November 12, 1931, published in *Annales médico-psychologiques,* 11, 1931, reprinted in J. Lacan;, *De la psychose paranoïaque,* pp. 365–382.

18. Ibid., p. 379.

19. Dominique Desanti, *Drieu La Rochelle* (Paris: Flammarion, 1978), p. 272.

20. Salvador Dali, "L'âne pourri," *SASDLR,* 1, July 1930; see Patrice Schmitt, "Dali et Lacan dans leurs rapports à la psychose paranoïaque" in *Cahiers Confrontation,* 4, Fall 1980 (Aubier), pp. 129–135.

21. S. Dali, "L'âne pourri," p. 10.

22. Salvador Dali, "Interprétation paranoïaque-critique de l'image obsédante: *L'angélus* de Millet" in *Le Minotaure,* I, 1933; republished by Skira, vol. 1, p. 10.

23. On "rationalizing disorders," see *Bataille* I, part 3, chap. 2.

24. See Jacques-Alain Miller, "Clinique psychanalytique, enseignements de la présentation de malades" in *Ornicar?,* 10, 1976, pp. 13–24.

25. Concerning the genesis of the concept of "foreclosure," see *Bataille* I, part 4, chap. 1.

26. J. Lacan, *De la psychose paranoïaque,* p. 153.

27. Ibid., p. 253.

28. See *Bataille* I, part 2, chap. 1.

29. Jean Bernier, "Compte rendu de lecture" in *La critique sociale* (Paris: Ed. de la Différence, 1983), pp. 139–140 (my emphasis).

30. Paul Nizan, *L'humanité,* February 10, 1933 (my emphasis); for Crevel's article, see chap. 2, this volume.

31. J. Lacan, *De la psychose paranoïaque,* p. 301.

32. See *Bataille* I, part 4, chap. 3.

33. See *Bataille* I, part 4, chap. 2.

34. Marie Bonaparte's affair with R. Loewenstein was made public by Célia Bertin, *La dernière Bonaparte* (Paris: Librairie académique Perrin, 1982) [*Marie Bonaparte: A Life*

(Harcourt Brace Jovanovich, 1982; reprinted by Yale University Press, 1987]. See also E. Roudinesco, interview with P. Sollers, *L'Infini*, 2 (Paris: Denoël, 1983).

35. See *Bataille* I, part 4, chap. 2.

36. Conversation with Didier Anzieu. See also D. Anzieu, *Une peau pour les pensées* (Paris: Clancier-Guénaud, 1986).

37. R. Loewenstein, "Un cas de jalousie pathologique" in *RFP*, 5, 1932, pp. 554–585; "D'un mécanisme autopunitif," ibid., pp. 141–151; "La psychanalyse et la notion de constitution" in *EP*, 4, 1932, pp. 57–65.

38. R. Loewenstein, "La psychanalyse et les troubles de la puissance sexuelle" in *RFP*, 8, 1935, pp. 538–600.

39. *RFP*, 4, 1938, pp. 799–760; concerning Loewenstein, see also S. Lebovici's note on his death in *RFP*, 4, 1976.

40. See *Bataille* I, part 4, chap. 2.

41. J. Lacan, "De l'impulsion au complexe" in *RFP*, 1, 1939, pp. 137–141.

42. C. Bertin, *La dernière Bonaparte*, pp. 382 and 329.

43. Reprinted in the reedition of the thesis.

44. For all the materials in the Papin case, see Francis Dupré, *La solution du passage à l'acte* (Toulouse: Érès, 1984); Paulette Houdyer, *Le diable dans la peau* (Paris: Julliard, 1966).

45. See *Revue des grands procès*, vol. 39, 1933, pp. 558–614; Michel Coddens, "La colère rouge: Le procès des soeurs Papin" in *Revue interdisciplinaire d'études jurdiques*, 9, Brussels, 1982.

46. *SASDLR*, 1, July 1930, p. 28.

47. F. Pottecher, *Les grands procès de l'histoire* (Paris: Fayard, 1981).

48. Text reprinted in the reedition of the thesis, p. 389.

49. Ibid.

50. See *Bataille* I, part 3, chap. 1.

51. Written by Lacan, but prepared in collaboration with Michel Cénac, *Écrits*, p. 125.

52. Ibid., p. 142.

53. *RFP*, vol. 8, 4, 1935, pp. 688–696.

54. Conversation with M.-F. Lacan.

55. Concerning H. Ey's positions in the EP group, see *Bataille* I, part 4, chap. 3.

56. Conversations with R. Ey, Charles Durand, Andrée Bonnier-Lespiaut; see also *Hommage à H. Ey*, Société EP (Toulouse: Privat, 1977).

57. Paris: Alcan, 1934.

58. *EP*, I, 1935, pp. 87–91.

59. H. Ey and J. Rouart, *Essai d'application des principes de Jackson à une conception dynamique de la neuropsychiatrie* (Paris: Monographe de l'Encéphale, 1938).

60. H. Ey, "Ce que la psychiatrie doit à la psychanalyse" in *Les Études philosophiques*, 4, October–December 1956 (Paris: PUF); "Médecine et psychanalyse" in *La Revue du practicien*, April 1970.

61. J. Lacan, *Écrits*; "La psychiatrie anglaise et la guerre," *EP*, 1, 1947, pp. 293–338. Lacan's text on the family was republished under the title *Les complexes familiaux dans la formation de l'individu* (Paris: Navarin, 1984).

62. See F. Ansermet, "Entretien avec J.-A. Miller" In *Bloc-notes de la psychanalyse*, 4, 1984; republished by Navarin (Paris, 1985).

63. See Vincent Descombes, *Le même et l'autre* (Paris: Minuit, 1979); P. Macherey, "Queneau scribe et lecteur de Kojève" in *Europe*, June–July 1983; A. Kojève, *Introduction à*

la lecture de Hegel (Queneau's seminar notes) (Paris: Gallimard, 1947); G. Bataille, *Oeuvres complètes,* vol. 6 (Paris: Gallimrd, 1973), note p. 146.

64. Raymond Aron, *Mémoires* (Paris: Julliard, 1983), pp. 94–100.

65. Interview with Nina Ivanova, Kojève's companion; see also A. Kojève, "Entretien" in *Quinzaine littéraire,* 53, 1968.

66. Unpublished seminar of Pierre Macherey (1980–1982) on the "Introduction of Hegelianism in France: From Victor Cousin to Alexandre Kojève."

67. Ibid.

68. Hegel, *La phénomonologie de l'esprit,* 2 vols. (Paris: Aubier-Montaigne, 1939); Georges Canguilhem, "Hegel en France," *Revue d'histoire et de philosophie religieuses* (Strasbourg, 1948–1949); A. Koyré, "État des études hégeliennes en France," postface to *Études de la pensée philosophique* (Paris: Colin, 1961); M. Merleau-Ponty, *Sens et non-sens* (Paris: Nagel, 1966), p. 109. Concerning Mallarmé as a reader of Hegel, see J. L. Austin, *Mallarmé et le rêve du livre* (Paris: Mercure de France, 1953).

69. G. Canguilhem, "Hegel en France."

70. Macherey's unpublished seminar, "Introduction of Hegelianism in France," and "Le leurre hégélien" in *Bloc-notes de la psychanalyse,* 5, 1985.

71. See Philippe Monti, *Introduction à la lecture de Kojève,* dissertation supervised by J.-T. Desanti (Paris, 1981).

72. Macherey's unpublished seminar, "Introduction of Hegelianism in France."

73. Jacques Lacan, *Scilicet,* 1 (Paris: Seuil, 1986), p. 33.

74. See *Bataille* I, part 2, chap. 1.

75. Conversation with N. Ivanova.

76. Concerning *La vie mentale,* see the introduction by E. Jalley; J. Lacan, *Les complexes familiaux.*

77. In J. Lacan, *Écrits.*

78. See chap. 2, this volume.

79. J. Lacan. *Écrits,* p. 151.

80. Ibid., p. 181.

81. Ibid., p. 93.

82. See J. Laplanche and J.-B. Pontalis, *Vocabulaire de la psychanalyse* (Paris: PUF, 1967) [*The Language of Psychoanalysis* (New York: Norton, 1973)].

83. See *Bataille* I, part 4, chap. 2.

84. Ibid.

85. Separate interviews with Thibaut Lacan and Célia Bertin.

86. Interview with Sylvia Lacan.

Chapter 5. The Situation of Psychoanalysis at Midcentury

1. See J. Le Ridder, "La psychanalyse en Allemagne" in *Histoire de la psychanalyse,* ed. R. Jaccard (Paris: Hachette, 1982), vol. 2, p. 138; Harald Schultz-Henke, "La psychothérapie et la psychanalyse en Allemagne," *TM* 46–47, August–September 1949; see also *Bataille* I and J.-L. Evrard's introduction to and translation of texts of German history, *Les années brunes* (Paris: Éd. Controntation, series "Vert et noir," 1984).

2. Quoted in *Les années brunes,* p. 69.

3. See Regine Lockot, *Errinern und Durcharbeiten* (Fischer, 1985).

4. See *Bataille* I, part 4, chap. 2.

5. A. de Mijolla, "La psychanalyse en France," in *Histoire de la psychanalyse,* ed. R. Jaccard.

6. See *Bataille* I, part 4, chap. 1.

7. Célia Bertin, *La dernière Bonaparte* (Paris: Librairie académique Perrin, 1982).

8. Interview with Janine Chasseguet-Smirgel.

9. "Hommage à Georges Favez" in *Documents et Débats,* March 1982.

10. See *RFP,* 16, 3, 1952.

11. Interview with Françoise Dolto.

12. Françoise Dolto, *Psychanalyse et pédiatrie* (Paris: Seuil, 1971).

13. This was *L'échec de Baudelaire,* which would be published in French in 1964 (Geneva: Éd. du Mont-Blanc).

14. Letter of February 23, 1939. All the letters quoted are from the Koblentz Bundesarchiv. They were communicated to me by Regine Lockot and I have published them in *Cahiers confrontation,* October 1986.

15. Letter from Göring to Laforgue, November 9, 1940.

16. Testimony by Captain Brun (July 6, 1945) at the purge trial. Archive René Laforgue, released to me by D. Clauzel-Laforgue. Published in part in *Cahiers Confrontation.*

17. Interview with Charles Durand, who had been present at the meeting.

18. Testimony of Jean Jostand. Archive René Laforgue.

19. Letter from Knapp to Göring (November 17, 1940).

20. Letter from Laforgue to Göring (December 9, 1940).

21. Undated document.

22. Letter from Göring to Laforgue (December 19, 1940).

23. Letter from Göring to Laforgue (February 26, 1941).

24. Letter from Laforgue to Göring (March 11, 1941).

25. This was *La psychopathologie de l'échec* (Geneva: Éd. du Mont-Blanc, 1963); see *Bataille* I.

26. Letter from Laforgue to Göring (July 3, 1941).

27. Letter from Dillenburger to Göring (July 6, 1941).

28. Letter from Laforgue to Göring (July 20, 1941).

29. Letter from Dillenburger to Göring, date undecipherable.

30. Official letter to Göring (December 31, 1941).

31. Offical letter to Göring (December 16, 1941).

32. Written depositions of René Valentini, member of the Resistance (March 1, 1945), Louis Cauvin, Socialist councillor from La Roquebrussane (August 5, 1945), and B. Steele (May 19, 1946). Archive René Laforgue.

33. Copy of Laforgue's letter to Göring, received November 17, 1942.

34. Letter from Göring to Knapp (November 17, 1942).

35. Letter from Laforgue to Göring (December 15, 1942).

36. Henri Stern,"Observation sur la psychologie collective dans les camps de 'personnes déplacées,'" *Psyché,* 21–22, Paris, 1949.

37. John Leuba's letter to H. Stern, communicated to me by A.-L. Stern.

38. See Robert Aron, *Histoire de l'épuration,* 4 vols. (Paris: Fayard, 1967–1975); Peter Novick, *L'épuration française* (Paris: Balland, 1985).

39. Testimony of Henri Stern.

40. Separate interviews with F. Dolto and A. Berge.

41. Letter of April 21, 1946. C. Bertin, *La dernière Bonaparte,* p. 357.

42. Published by Martine Lilamand in her thesis on Laforgue (see *Bataille* I).

43. I. and R. Barande, *Histoire de la psychanalyse en France* (Toulouse: Privat, 1975), p. 49; Paul Denis, "La psychanalyse en France" in *Les écoles psychanalytiques* (Paris: Tchou, 1981), p. 189; A. de Mijolla, in R. Jaccard, ed., *Histoire de la psychanalyse,* vol. 2, p. 38.

44. On the history of psychoanalysis in the United States, see Clarence P. Oberndorf,

A History of Psychoanalysis in America (New York: Harper & Row, 1953); the volume edited by Jacques M. Quen, M.D., and Eric T. Carlson, M.D., *American Psychoanalysis: Origins and Development* (New York: Brunner-Mazel, 1978); and Robert Castel, *La société psychiatrique avancée* (Paris: Grasset, 1979).

45. J.-P. Sartre, *Le scénario Freud* (Paris: Gallimard, 1984). Interview with Sartre in *Jugements et témoignages* (Paris: PUF, 1976); Robert Benayoun, *John Huston* (Paris: Lherminier, 1985).

46. Anna Freud, *Le moi et les mécanismes de défense* (Paris: PUF, 1949); H. Hartmann, *La psychologie du moi et le problème de l'adaptation* (Paris: PUF, 1968); "Commentaires sur la théorie psychanalytique du moi. Implications techniques de la psychologie du moi et du ça dans le développement. Notes sur le principe de réalité" in *RFP*, 31, 3, 1967; H. Hartmann and R. Loewenstein, "Notes sur le surmoi," *RFP*, 28, 5–6, 1966; *Essays on Ego Psychology* (New York: New York International Univ. Press, 1958 [1938]); David Rapaport, "La théorie de l'autonomie du moi" in *RFP*, 28, 3, 1964; H. Hartmann and R. Loewenstein, "Notes sur le surmoi" in *RFP*, 28, 5–6, 1966; H. Hartmann, E. Kris, and R. Loewenstein, "Rapport sur la psychologie psychanalytique" in *RFP*, 30, 5–6, 1966; E. Kris, "Ego Psychology and Interpretation" in *Psychoanalytic Therapy, The Psychoanalytic Quarterly*, vol. 20, I, 1951; reviewed by D. Lagache in *RFP*, 16, 4, 1952; criticized by J. Lacan in *Écrits* (Paris: Seuil, 1966), p. 381; Erik Erikson, "The Problem of Ego Identity" in *Journal of the American Psychoanalytic Association*, 14, 1956; Jeanne Lampl de Groot, "On the Development of the Ego and Superego" in *International Journal of Psychoanalysis*, 18, 1947; Paul Roazen, *Freud and His Followers* (New York: Penguin, 1975); Jacques Adam, "Heinz Hartmann" in *Ornicar?*, 29, Summer 1984 (Paris: Navarin).

47. See *Bataille* I, part 2, chap. 1.

48. D. Rapaport, "La théorie de l'autonomie du moi."

49. On the English psychoanalytic movement, see C. Girard in R. Jaccard, ed., *Histoire de la psychanalyse*, vol. 2.

50. See S. Lebovici and A. Solnit, *La formation du psychanalyste* (Paris: PUF, Monographies de l'IPA, 1982). The statutes of the IPA are published in the annual *Roster* of members of the IPA.

51. Karen Horney, *La psychologie de la femme* (Paris: Petite Bibliothèque Payot, 1981); J.-B. Pontalis, *Après Freud* (Paris: Gallimard, 1968); Moustapha Safouan, *La sexualité féminine* (Paris: Seuil, 1976). See chap. 9, this volume.

52. See *Bataille* I, part 2, chap. 2.

53. First World Congress of Psychiatry, vol. 8, *Actes généraux* (Paris: Hermann, 1952).

54. J. Favez-Boutonier, *Documents et Débats*, 14, March 1978.

55. First World Congress of Psychiatry, section 5, *Psychothérapie, psychanalyse, médecine psychosomatique*, in *Actes généraux*, p. 13.

56. Ibid., p. 32.

57. Ibid., p. 136.

58. Ibid., p. 113.

59. Ibid., p. 104.

60. Concerning Raymond de Saussure, see *Bataille* I.

61. First Congress, section 5, *Actes généraux*, p. 173.

62. J. Lacan, *Écrits*, p. 403.

63. See A. de Mijolla in *Histoire de la psychanalyse*, ed. R. Jaccard.

64. C. G. Jung, *Ma vie* (Paris: Gallimard, 1970), p. 183.

65. A. Bogdanov, *La science, l'art, et la classe ouvrière,* introduction by H. Deluy and D. Lecourt (Paris: Maspero, 1977).

66. A. Jdanov [Zhdanov], "Discours au Iᵉʳ Congrès des écrivains soviétiques (1934)" in *Action poétique,* 43, 1970.

67. A. Jdanov [Zhdanov], *Sur la littérature, l'art, et la musique* (1948) (Paris: Nouvelle Critique, 1950).

68. Jaures Medvedev, *Grandeur et chute de Lyssenko* (Paris: Gallimard, 1971); Dominique Lecourt, *Lyssenko, histoire réelle d'une science prolétarienne* (Paris: Maspero, 1976).

69. See Y. Mignot, F. Gadet, J.-M. Gayman, E. Roudinesco, *Les maîtres de la langue* (Paris: Maspero, 1979); Régine Robin, *L'amour du yiddish* (Paris: Sorbier, 1984).

70. *L'Humanité* (January 27, 1949). See also Serge Moscovici, *La psychanalyse, son image, et son public* (Paris: PUF, 1976).

71. "Autocritique: la psychanalyse, idéologie réactionnaire" in *La Nouvelle Critique,* 7, June 1949, pp. 52–73; republished by J.-A. Miller, *La scission de 1953,* supplement to *Ornicar?,* no. 7, 1976 (abbreviated as *Sc. 53*).

72. Separate interviews with L. Bonnafé and V. Leduc.

73. Interview with Serge Lebovici.

74. *RFP,* 15, 1, 1951, pp. 131–132.

75. *L'Humanité* (June 9, 1949), my emphasis.

76. *La Raison,* 1, January 1951, p. 117.

77. Ibid., 3, November 1951, pp. 97–98.

78. Ibid., 9–10, December 1954.

79. S. Follin, "Bilan de la psychanalyse," *La Nouvelle Critique,* 27, June 1951, p. 43.

80. *La Nouvelle Critique,* 45, April–May 1953, pp. 220 and 227.

81. *La Raison,* II, 1956.

82. 2 vols. (Paris: PUF, 1956).

83. *La Raison,* I, 1957.

84. *Revue de psychothérapie institutionnelle,* 6, 1968, p. 98.

85. G. Bermann would subsequently write a book on mental health in China (Paris: Maspero, 1973).

86. Interview with W. Granoff.

87. Interview with L. Bonnafé.

88. Lecture reprinted in *EP,* 1947.

89. Separate interviews with F. Tosquelles and L. Bonnafé. See as well F. Tosquelles, *Éducation et psychothérapie institutionnelle* (Paris: Hiatus, 1984) and *L'Ane,* 13, November–December 1983; Paul Balvet, "Asile psychiatrique, expérience d'un établissement rural," Congrès des aliénistes et neurologistes français (Paris: Masson, 1943); Georges Daumézon, "La psychothérapie institutionnelle française contemporaine," *Anaïs portugueses de psiquiatria,* 4, December 1952; Robert Castel, *Le psychanalysme,* (Paris: Maspero, 1973).

90. Interview with G. Canguilhem.

91. Claude Quétel and Jacques Postel, eds., *Nouvelle histoire de la psychiatrie* (Toulouse: Privat, 1983).

92. Concerning the experiment at La Borde, see chap. 9, this volume.

93. Marc Oraison, *Tête dure* (Paris: Seuil, 1969); *Au point où j'en suis* (Paris: Seuil, 1978).

94. *Critique,* special issue on Trieste, 435–436, 1983.

95. Michel David, *La psicoanalisi nella cultura italiana* (Turin: Boringheri, 1966).

96. A. Manoil, *La psychologie expérimentale en Italie* (Paris: Alcan, 1938).

97. Decree of the Holy Office in *La documentation catholique,* 1048, July 31, 1949, pp. 961–966.

98. Alain Woodrow, *Les Jésuites, histoire de pouvoirs* (Paris: Lattès, 1983).

99. "La question juive et le sionisme," *La documentation catholique,* 1047, July 17, 1949, p. 937.

100. "Condamnation des écrits de Sartre," *La documentation catholique,* 1033, January 2, 1949, p. 6. In August 1956, the works of Simone de Beauvoir were also placed on the Index.

101. "Condamnation des écrits de Gide," *La documentation catholique,* 1125, July 13, 1952, p. 851.

102. Quoted by M. David, *La psicoanalisi nella cultura italiana,* p. 125.

103. Père Gemelli, "Le psychologue devant les problèmes de la psychiatrie" in *Psyché,* 51–52, 1951; M. Choisy, "La psychanalyse et le catholicisme," ibid., 1950.

104. *Le Monde,* April 11, 1952.

105. Ibid., September 18, 1952.

106. *La documentation catholique,* 1146, May 3, 1953.

107. Marc Oraison, *Vie chrétienne et problème de la sexualité,* preface by Père Tesson (Paris: Lethielleux, 1950); republished by Fayard (Paris, 1970) with an introduction by Louis Beirnaert.

108. Interview with L. Beirnaert.

109. See M. Oraison, *Tête dure,* and interview with Albert Plé. See also A. Plé, "L'église et l'idée qu'on s'en fait" in *Supplément,* 142, September 1982 (Paris: Cerf), pp. 295–301.

110. *La documentation catholique,* 1191, January 23, 1955, p. 81, and 1194, March 6, 1955, p. 288.

111. L. A. M. Hesnard, *Morale sans péché* (Paris: PUF, 1953).

112. *Recherches et débats,* II, March 1955.

113. In *Vita e pensiero,* October 1955, reprinted in *La documentation catholique,* 1219, February 19, 1956, p. 217.

114. Ibid., pp. 201 and 204.

115. *Sedes Sapientiae,* internal document, from the Latin, Rome, 1957, pp. 57–58.

116. Numerous documents on the subject have been published in *La vocation, éveil et formation* (Paris: Cerf, 1975); *Mariage et célibat,* ibid.

117. Interview with A. Plé.

118. *Mariage et célibat,* in *La vocation, éveil et formation.*

119. "Investigation psychologique des candidats au sacerdoce" in *Expérience chrétienne et psychologie* (Paris: Epi, 1964).

120. *La documentation catholique,* 1357, August 6, 1961, p. 1000.

121. Ibid., 1373, April 1, 1962, p. 449.

122. Grégoire Lemercier and Françoise Verny, *Dialogues avec le Christ* (Paris: Grasset, 1966).

123. Henri Fesquet, *Journal du Concile* (Forcalquier: Robert Morel, 1966), p. 74.

124. Ibid., p. 895.

125. Ibid., p. 1085.

126. *Le Monde,* June 29, 1969.

127. Ibid., November 11, 1973.

128. *La documentation catholique,* 1477, September 4, 1966, p. 1535.

129. François Roustang, "Le troisième homme" in *Christus,* 52, vol. 13, October 1966.

130. Denise Saada, *Sacha Nacht* (Paris: Payot, 1972).

131. Sacha Nacht, *Contribution à l'étude de l'anatomie pathologique des myélites syphilitiques en général et de leur forme progressive en particulier,* thesis (Paris: Legrand, 1926).

132. Letter communicated to me by Marc Nacht.

133. Ibid.

134. Sacha Nacht, *Le masochisme, étude historique, clinique, psychogénétique et thérapeutique* (Paris: Denoël, 1938); republished by Payot (Paris, 1965).

135. Official document communicated to me by M. Nacht.

136. Ibid.

137. See Pierre Stévenin, "Exercice illégal de la médecine," *Psyché,* 81–82, pp. 382–390.

138. *Le Monde* (December 12, 1951; December 19, 1951; and April 2, 1953).

139. C. Bertin, *La dernière Bonaparte,* p. 374.

140. Judicial opinions published in their entirety by *Psyché,* 81–82; Raphaël Brossart, "Le psychanalyste non autorisé, *Charlatan,* 4, (Paris: Collectif Événement psychanalyse, 1985).

141. *Sc. 53,* p. 33; published in *RFP* in 1949.

142. *Le Monde* (July 3, 1952).

143. *Le Monde* (November 9, 1953).

144. *Sc. 53,* p. 32.

145. Interview with Marcel Bleustein-Blanchet.

146. Interview with Élisabeth Lagache.

147. Lagache has recounted his life in *Œuvres complètes,* 5 vols., vol 1 (Paris: PUF, 1977); "La psychanalyse comme science exacte" in *Psychanalysis, A General Psychology: Essays in Honor of H. Hartmann* (French translation by R. and M. Pages), *Psychologie française,* 19, 4, 1974, pp. 217–246.

148. D. Lagache, *Oeuvres complètes,* vol. 1.

149. Ibid.

150. Ibid., p. 238.

151. Ibid., pp. 241–242.

152. Ibid., pp. 242–243.

153. See D. Anzieu, "Daniel Lagache" in *Bulletin de psychologie,* 305, XXVI, 10–12, 1972–1973.

154. Interview with G. Canguilhem. See Kurt Goldstein, *La structure de l'organisme* (Paris: Gallimard, 1983); G. Canguilhem, *Le normal et le pathologique* (1943); republished Paris, 1966.

155. Sigmund Freud, *Naissance de la psychanalyse* (Paris: PUF, 1969), p. 244 [*The Origins of Psychoanalysis* (New York: Basic Books, 1954), p. 274].

156. D. Lagache, *Oeuvres complètes,* vol. 2, p. 82.

157. Ibid., vol. 1, p. 413.

158. Daniel Lagache, *La jalousie amoureuse* (Paris: PUF, 1947).

159. Daniel Lagache, *L'unité de la psychologie* (Paris: PUF, 1983).

160. Georges Canguilhem, in *Études d'histoire et de philosophie des sciences* (Paris: Vrin, 1968).

161. Interview with Jean Laplanche.

Chapter 6. The Great Divide

1. J.-A. Miller, *La scission de 1953,* supplement to *Ornicar?,* no. 7, 1976 (abbreviated as *Sc. 53*), and *RFP,* 13, 3, 1949, p. 436.

2. Ibid.

3. *Sc. 53*, p. 36.

4. *RFP,* 13, 4, 1949, p. 572.

5. See *Bataille* I and Paul Roazen, *Freud and His Followers* (New York: Penguin, 1975).

6. Announcement of the lecture "Dialectical Psychoanalysis?" in *IJP,* vol. 35, part 3. Meeting of the administrative council on February 3, 1953, *Analytica,* 7 (Paris: Navarin, 1978), p. 10; J. Favez-Boutonier, *Documents et Débats,* 11, May 1975, p. 60.

7. Separate interviews with D. Anzieu, X. Audouard, R. Pujol, J.-P. Valabrega, O. Mannoni, A.-L. Stern, and R. Lefort. For the analyses of Nadia and the Wolf Child, see below as well as R. Lefort, *Naissance de l'Autre* (Paris: Seuil, 1980). See also Didier Anzieu, *Une peau pour les pensées* (Paris: Clancier-Guénaud, 1986).

8. Célia Bertin, *La dernière Bonaparte* (Paris: Librairie académique Perrin, 1982), p. 351.

9. "Mémorandum Lagache," in *Sc. 53,* p. 107.

10. Lacan's letter to Loewenstein, ibid., p. 123.

11. Ibid., p. 121.

12. Ibid., p. 42.

13. Ibid., pp. 104 and 121.

14. *Analytica,* 7, p. 8.

15. *Sc. 53*, p. 52.

16. Ibid., p. 56.

17. Ibid., p. 64; *Analytica,* 7, p. 10; A. de Mijolla, in *Histoire de la psychanalyse,* ed. R. Jaccard, p. 56.

18. Certificate signed by Darquier de Pellepoix, April 29, 1943.

19. See *Bataille* I, part 4, chap. 3.

20. Interview with Jenny Aubry. See *Enfance abandonnée,* republished by Scarabée/Métaillé (Paris, 1983).

21. *Sc. 53*, p. 73.

22. Ibid., p. 67.

23. *Analytica,* 7, p. 15.

24. Ibid., p. 15.

25. Ibid., pp. 4 and 5.

26. Written testimony of J. Favez-Boutonier, July 1984.

27. Letter from S. Lebovici to the author, August 1984.

28. *Sc. 53*, pp. 109–110.

29. Ibid., p. 82.

30. Pierre Marty, *Cahier noir,* minutes of the meeting of June 2, archives of the SPP-IP, private sources.

31. Interview with Jenny Aubry.

32. P. Marty, *Cahier noir.*

33. "Mémorandum Lagache," in *Sc. 53,* p. 110.

34. *Sc. 53*, p. 129. Lacan and Lagache noted Pasche's remark, but not Marty.

35. "Mémorandum Lagache," p. 111. Marty noted the anomalies without however speaking about Article 35.

36. See J. Favez-Boutonier, *Documents et Débats,* p. 62.

37. J. Aubry, "Là où les chemins divergent" in *Ornicar?,* 9, April 1977.

38. *Sc. 53*, p. 88.

39. Ibid., p. 89.

40. P. Marty, *Cahier noir*, interview with J. Favez-Boutonier; *Sc. 53*, pp. 90–91.

41. *Sc. 53*, p. 99.

42. C. Bertin, *La dernière Bonaparte*, pp. 384–385.

43. Ibid.

44. *Sc. 53*, p. 96.

45. Ibid., pp. 136–137.

46. Ibid., p. 138.

47. Unpublished lecture by Lacan.

48. Jacques Lacan, *Écrits* (Paris: Seuil, 1966), p. 218.

49. Ibid., p. 197; the fable of the prisoners is taken up again in *Séminaire II* (Paris: Seuil, 1978), pp. 332–336.

50. The first version of the *Rome Discourse* appeared in the journal *La Psychanalyse*, 1 (Paris: PUF, 1956). A slightly different version appeared in *Écrits*, p. 237; there is also a different (and mimeographed) original version extant.

51. *Écrits*, p. 315.

52. Sigmund Freud, *Cinq psychanalyses* (Paris: PUF, 1954), p. 356.

53. *Écrits*, p. 257.

54. *Sc. 53*, p. 145.

55. Interview with L. Bonnafé.

56. Letter dated September 1953 from the Archives of M.-F. Lacan.

57. See *Bataille* I.

58. "Actes du Congrès de Rome" in *La Psychanalyse*, 1, p. 255.

59. Ibid., p. 211.

60. Ibid., p. 213.

61. Ibid., p. 220.

62. Ibid., p. 222.

63. *RFP*, 13, 4, 1949, pp. 566–574; republished in *Au jeu du désir* (Paris: Seuil, 1981).

64. *La Psychanalyse*, 1, p. 230.

65. Ibid., pp. 229 and 231.

66. Ibid., pp. 251–252.

67. Ibid.

68. Ibid., p. 255.

69. Interview with André Green; *RFP*, 24, 6, 1960, issue dedicated to M. Bouvet.

70. M. Bouvet, "La cure-type," *Encyclopédie médico-chirurgicale, Psychiatrie 2* 1955, 37812, A10, A30, A40; J. Lacan, "Variantes de la cure-type," ibid., C10, republished in revised form in *Écrits*.

71. The Strachey translation is: "Where id was shall ego be" [trans.], see *Bataille* I, part 4, chap. 2.

72. *Écrits*, p. 323.

73. *Encyclopédie médico-chirurgicale*, 37812, C10, p. 7. Concerning defenses and resistance, see also *Séminaire I* (Paris: Seuil, 1975), pp. 27–49.

74. Jacques Lacan, *Encyclopédie médico-chirurgicale*, p. 11.

75. Ibid., article by M. Bouvet, vol. 1, pp. 41–121.

76. J. Lacan, unpublished seminar. See also *Séminaire I*, pp. 227–245.

77. Interview with A. Green and *RFP*, 24, 6, 1960.

Chapter 7. Life and Death of the Société Française de Psychanalyse

1. See Katia Granoff, *Oeuvres complètes* (Paris: Bourgois, 1980).

2. Interview with Wladimir Granoff.

3. W. Granoff and J. Lacan, "Fetishism: The Symbolic, the Imaginary, and the Real" in *Perversions: Psychodynamics and Therapy* (New York: Random House, 1956); French translation in *L'Objet en psychanalyse* (Paris: Denoël, 1986).

4. Interview with W. Granoff.

5. *La Psychanalyse,* 1 (Paris: PUF, 1956), p. 233.

6. Ibid.

7. Interview with Serge Leclaire. See also interview in the journal *Synapse,* 1985.

8. Martial Perrier, *L'adieu à Don Juan* (Paris: Grasset, 1929).

9. François Perrier, *La chaussée d'Antin* (Paris: 10/18, 1978), vol. 1, back cover, and vol. 2, p. 13.

10. François Perrier, *L'alcool au singulier* (Paris: Inter-Éditions, 1982), p. 186.

11. Interview with F. Perrier.

12. F. Perrier, *L'alcool,* pp. 92–93.

13. François Perrier, *Les corps malades du signifiant* (Paris: Inter-Éditions, 1984), p. 12.

14. Interview with Moustapha Safouan.

15. Interview with Jean Laplanche.

16. *TM,* 1, October 1945 and 1948.

17. *TM,* 41, March 1949.

18. *TM,* 50, December 1949.

19. *TM,* 98, January 1954.

20. *TM,* 104, July 1954.

21. *Bulletin de psychologie,* vol. 10, 1956–1957, 7, pp. 426–430; 10, pp. 602–605; 12, pp. 742–743; 14, pp. 851–854; vol. 11, 1957–1958, 1, pp. 32–34; 4–5, pp. 293–296; vol. 12, 1958–1959, 2–3, pp. 182–192; 4, pp. 250–256; vol. 13, 1959–1960, 5, pp. 263–272; 6, pp. 329–335.

22. *TM,* 215, April 1964.

23. Interview with J.-B. Pontalis.

24. See *Bataille* I, part 4, chap. 1.

25. *La Psychanalyse,* 1, p. vi.

26. Concerning French translations of Freud before 1940, see *Bataille* I. By 1985, all Freud's work was available in French, although not yet collected in an edition of complete works.

27. A. and O. Bourguignon, "Singularité d'une histoire," *RFP,* 6, December 1983.

28. Gisela Pankow, letter of resignation (October 21, 1959).

29. G. Pankow, *Vingt-cinq années de psycho-thérapie analytique des psychoses* (Paris: Aubier, 1984). See also from the same publisher, her *L'être-là du schizophrène,* 1982; *Structure familiale et Psychose,* 1983; *L'homme et sa psychose,* 1983.

30. J. Lacan, letter to Winnicott, *Ornicar?,* 33, Summer 1985, p. 10.

31. See chap. 7, this volume.

32. Interview with Kostas Axelos. There are several different versions of this episode.

33. See Gérard Almaleh, "Logique de la philosophie et psychanalyse" in *Sept études sur Éric Weil* (Presses Universitaires de Lille, 1982).

34. Interview with K. Axelos and special issue of *Cahiers de l'Herne* devoted to Heidegger (1983). See Jean-Pierre Cotten, *Heidegger* (Paris: Seuil, series "Écrivains de toujours," 1974).

35. Interview with Sylvia Lacan.

36. Maurice Merleau-Ponty, *Éloge de la philosophie* (Paris: Gallimard, 1953), pp. 74–75.

37. Vincent Descombes, *Le même et l'autre* (Paris: Minuit, 1979), p. 89.

38. Jacques Lacan, *Séminaire XI* (Paris: Seuil, 1973), p. 65; Merleau-Ponty, *TM*, 184, 185, 245, 254.

39. Jacques Lacan, *Écrits* (Paris: Seuil, 1966), pp. 363–367, 369–399; *Séminaire I* (Paris: Seuil, 1975), p. 63.

40. Macherey, "Le leurre hégélien," in *Bloc-notes de la psychanalyse*, 5, 1985.

41. Jacques Lacan, *Séminaire II* (Paris: Seuil, 1978), p. 207.

42. J. Lacan, *Séminaire I*, p. 186.

43. See *Bataille* I, part 4, chap. 1.

44. J. Lacan, *Écrits*, p. 809.

45. J. Lacan, *Séminaire II*, p. 207.

46. E. Poe, *Tales*, translated into French as *Histoires extraordinaires* by Charles Baudelaire.

47. J. Lacan, *Séminaire II*, p. 231.

48. Republished in *Écrits*.

49. See *Bataille* I, part 2, chap. 1.

50. Bertrand Ogilvie, unpublished seminar.

51. *Écrits*, p. 799.

52. Roman Jakobson, *Cahiers Cistre*, 5 (Lausanne: Age d'homme, 1978); *Dialogues avec K. Pomorska* (Paris: Flammarion, 1980).

53. Reprinted in R. Jakobson, *Essais de linguistique générale* (Paris: Minuit, 1964).

54. J. Lacan, *Écrits*, p. 517. See also J.-L. Nancy and P. Lacoue-Labarthe, *Le titre de la lettre* (Paris: Galilée, 1973).

55. J. Lacan, *Écrits*, p. 800. Concerning Pichon's article on negation, see *Bataille* I, part 4, chap. 1.

56. Individual testimony of several participants.

57. *VIᵉ Colloque de Bonneval: L'inconscient* (Paris: Desclée de Brouwer, 1966).

58. Michel Foucault, *Histoire de la folie à l'âge classique* (Paris: Plon, 1961), republished by Gallimard in 1972 [*Madness and Civilization: A History of Insanity in the Age of Reason*, trans. R. Howard (New York: Plume, 1971)].

59. Interview with S. Leclaire.

60. *VIᵉ Colloque*, p. 107.

61. Jacques Derrida, "La pharmacie de Platon" in *Tel Quel*, Winter–Spring 1968, pp. 32–33.

62. Serge Leclaire, *Psychanalyser* (Paris: Seuil, 1968).

63. Written testimony of November 1984.

64. J. Lacan, *Écrits*, p. 829; *VIᵉ Colloque*.

65. J. Lacan, *Écrits*, p. 833.

66. *VIᵉ Colloque*, p. 95.

67. J. Lacan, "La Science et la vérité" in *Écrits*, p. 855.

68. A. Lemaire, *Jacques Lacan* (Mardaga), republished in Brussels in 1977.

69. "Radiophonie," interview conducted by Rosine and Robert Georgin, in *Scilicet*, 2–3.

70. Separate interviews with A. Green and G. Rosolato.

71. Interview with A. Green.

72. Interview with F. Dolto.

73. "Autocritique: La Psychanalyse, idéologie réactionnaire" in *La Nouvelle Critique,* 7, June 1949, pp. 52–73; republished by J.-A. Miller, *La scission de 1953,* supplement to *Ornicar?,* no. 7, 1976 (abbreviated as *Sc. 53*).

74. Letter from Hartmann to Lagache (December 21, 1954), arch. W.G.

75. Letter from Lagache to Hartmann (January 6, 1955), arch. W.G.

76. Letter from Hartmann to Lagache (March 5, 1955), arch. W.G.

77. Letter from J. Favez-Boutonier to Hartmann (June 4, 1956), arch. W.G.

78. Letter from Hartmann to J. Favez-Boutonier (January 27, 1957), arch. W.G.

79. Documents from *L'excommunication* (abbreviation: *Ex.*), edited by J.-A. Miller, supplement to *Ornicar?,* 8, 1977. For the other documents, we have depended essentially on the personal archives of S. Leclaire and W. Granoff.

80. Letter from P. King to Lagache (July 11, 1959) and from Lagache to Leclaire (August 3, 1959), arch. S.L.

81. *Memorandum* kept daily by W. Granoff, arch. W.G.

82. Interview with D. Widlöcher.

83. Separate interviews with J. Favez-Boutonier and Xavier Audouard.

84. Interview with Jenny Aubry.

85. Written testimony of Didier Anzieu.

86. Interview with Ginette Raimbault.

87. Interview with J. Laplanche.

88. W. Granoff, *Mémorandum.*

89. Ibid.

90. Ibid.

91. Letter from Lacan to Granoff (July 24, 1961), arch. W.G.

92. Interview with W. Granoff.

93. *Ex.,* pp. 19–21.

94. Célia Bertin, *La dernière Bonaparte* (Paris: Librairie académique Perrin, 1982), p. 408.

95. *Ex.,* p. 18.

96. Interview with W. Granoff.

97. Letter from Lagache to Granoff (August 7, 1961); letter from L. Beirnaert to the Executive (September 20, 1961), arch. W.G.; interview with L. Beirnaert.

98. *Ex.,* pp. 20 and 25.

99. Arch. W.G., undated.

100. Letter from Granoff to Leclaire, undated, arch. W.G.

101. See E. Joseph and D. Widlöcher, *L'identité du psychanalyste* (Paris: PUF, 1979).

102. Letter from Leclaire to Turquet (October 20, 1961), arch. W.G.

103. Ibid.

104. *Analytica,* 7, 1978, p. 17.

105. Ibid., p. 19.

106. Letter from Lacan to Leclaire, arch. S.L.

107. Letter from Leclaire to Turquet (September 29, 1962), arch. S.L.

108. Letter from Turquet to Leclaire (November 1, 1962), arch. S.L.

109. Official letter from the troika (December 14, 1962), arch. S.L.

110. Letter from Lacan to Leclaire (January 7, 1963), arch. S.L.

111. Letter from Valabrega to Leclaire (January 11, 1963), arch. S.L.

112. Separate interviews with Piera Aulagnier, J. Favez-Boutonier, Moustapha Safouan, and Robert Pujol.

113. Letter from Widlöcher to Leclaire (January 17, 1963), arch. S.L.

114. Letter from Pujol to Leclaire (January 19, 1963), arch. S.L.

115. Arch. S.L. (January 19, 1963).

116. Letter from J. Favez-Boutonier to Leclaire (January 20, 1963), arch. S.L.

117. *Ex.*, p. 39.

118. Undated report, arch. S.L.

119. *Ex.*, p. 41.

120. J. Lacan, "Conférences et entretiens dans les universités américaines," *Scilicet* 6–7, 1976, p. 9.

121. Name of D. omitted by E. Roudinesco. Letter from Leclaire to Turquet (May 29, 1963), arch. S.L. Concerning the May meeting, see W. Granoff, *Mémorandum.*

122. W. Granoff, *Mémorandum* on meetings of June 22 and 23 at Hotel Westminster.

123. Letter from Leclaire to Lacan, transmitted to Granoff (June 24, 1963), arch. S.L. and W.G.

124. Letter from Lacan to Leclaire (June 24, 1963), arch. S.L.

125. Letter from Lacan to Paula Heimann, unsent (June 27, 1963), arch. S.L.

126. Letter from Leclaire to Lacan (July 2, 1963), arch. S.L.; *Ex.*, p. 73.

127. Letter from Turquet to Leclaire (July 12, 1963), arch. S.L.

128. Lettre from Leclaire to Turquet (July 15, 1963), arch. S.L.

129. *Ex.*, p. 79.

130. Testimony of D. Anzieu.

131. Letter from Leclaire to Lagache (July 20, 1963), arch. S.L.

132. Letter from Lebovici to J. Favez-Boutonier and from J. Favez-Boutonier to Leclaire (July 21, 1963), arch. S.L.

133. Interview with Solange Faladé.

134. *Ex.*, p. 82.

135. Interview with S. Leclaire.

136. Letter from Audouard to Lacan (September 17, 1963), arch. X.A.

137. Notes taken by Audouard and confirmed by the arch. S.L.

138. Ibid., (September 23, 1963), arch. X.A.

139. See Charles François, *Le mouvement de l'hygiène mentale en Belgique et la Formation des psychothérapeutes* (Univ. de Liège, 1978–1979).

140. Undated letter from Leclaire to Maud Mannoni and Valabrega's public letter of September 23, 1963, arch. S.L.

141. Letter from Widlöcher to Leclaire (October 12, 1963), arch. S.L.

142. Letter from Lagache to Leclaire (October 11, 1963), arch. S.L. Leclaire did not yet know of P. Aulagnier's defection.

143. *Ex.*, p. 87.

144. Undated letter from J. Favez-Boutonier, arch. S.L.

145. Undated letter from Granoff to Leclaire, arch. S.L.

146. Letter from E. Amado-Valensi (November 7, 1963), arch. S.L.

147. Official document by L. Beirnaert (October 14, 1963), arch. S.L.

148. Letters from Leclaire to Turquet and Turquet to Leclaire (November 22, 1963 and November 25, 1963), arch. S.L.

149. See *Ex.*, pp. 106–107.

150. Ibid., p. 91.

151. Ibid., p. 97.

152. Interview with D. Widlöcher.

153. *Ex.*, p. 111.

154. Interview with Jean Clavreul.

155. *Ex.,* pp. 123–124.

156. Letter from J.-L. Lang to Leclaire (January 20, 1964), arch. S.L.

157. Interview with W. Granoff; see appendices.

158. J. Lacan, *Séminaire XI,* p. 8.

159. C. Lévi-Strauss, "Entretien avec J.-A. Miller and A. Grosrichard" in *L'Ane,* 20, January–February 1985.

160. J. Lacan, *Séminaire XI,* p. 8.

161. Yirmiahu Yovel, "Marranisme et dissidence" in *Cahiers Spinoza,* 3, (Paris: Réplique, 1980); interview with P.-F. Moreau on the excommunication of Spinoza.

162. H. Méchoulan, "L'excommunication de Spinoza," *Cahiers Spinoza,* 3, p. 133.

163. Ibid., pp. 127–128.

164. Letter from J.-P. Valabrega to J. Favez-Boutonier (February 26, 1964), arch. S.L.

165. Introductory note corrected by J.-B. Pontalis, *La Psychanalyse,* 8, 1964.

166. Letter from Granoff to Turquet (January 29, 1964), arch. W.G. For the history of the APF's affiliation with the IPA, see below: chap. 10.

167. W. Granoff, *Filiations* (Paris: Minuit, 1975).

168. *Ex.,* p. 168; interview with D. Widlöcher.

169. *Ex.,* pp. 129–130.

170. Ibid., p. 135.

171. Ibid., p. 161.

Chapter 8. The École Freudienne de Paris: The Reconquest

1. Michel Foucault, *Quinzaine littéraire* (May 15, 1966).

2. Dominique Desanti, *Les clés d'Elsa* (Paris: Ramsay, 1983); interview with Louis Althusser; see also S. Karsz, *Théorie et politique: Louis Althusser* (Paris: Fayard, 1974).

3. Interview with Louis Althusser.

4. Louis Althusser, *Pour Marx* (Paris: Maspero, 1965), p. 12.

5. Ibid., p. 16.

6. Ibid., pp. 16–17.

7. Interview with J. Rancière and course notes of E. Balibar.

8. Louis Althusser, *Revue de l'enseignement philosophique,* XIII, 5, July 1963.

9. Interview with L. Althusser.

10. Interview with Michel Tort.

11. Course notes of E. Balibar.

12. F. Ansermet, "Entretien avec J.-A. Miller," in *Bloc-notes de la psychanalyse,* 4, 1984; republished by Navarin (Paris, 1985), p. 21.

13. Course notes of E. Balibar.

14. Louis Althusser, "Freud et Lacan," republished in *Positions* (Paris: Éditions sociales, 1976), p. 13.

15. Ibid., pp. 19–20.

16. J. Rancière, *La Leçon d'Althusser* (Paris: Gallimard, 1974), p. 91.

17. Waldeck Rochet, *Le marxisme et les chemins de l'avenir* (Paris: Éditions sociales, 1966); D. Caute, *Le communisme et les intellectuels français: 1914–1966* (Paris: Gallimard, 1967), pp. 930–933.

18. Interview with M. Tort.

19. Course notes of E. Balibar.

20. Lucien Sebag, *Marxisme et structuralisme* (Paris: Petite Bibliothèque Payot, 1967), p. 7; see also M.-C. Boons and J.-P. Boons, *TM,* 226, March 1965.

21. Separate interviews with M.-C. Boons and L. Althusser.

22. L. Sebag, *Marxisme et structuralisme.*

23. Jacques Derrida, *De la grammatologie* (Paris: Minuit, 1967) [*Of Grammatology,* trans. G. Spivak (Baltimore: Johns Hopkins Univ. Press, 1976)].

24. Interview with J. Derrdia.

25. Jacques Derrida, "Cogito et histoire de la folie" in *L'écriture et la différence* (Paris: Seuil, 1967) [*Writing and Difference,* trans. A. Bass (Chicago: Univ. of Chicago Press, 1980)]. For M. Foucault's reply, see the definitive edition of *Histoire de la folie* (Paris: Plon, 1961; republished by Gallimard, 1972) [in English, in *Oxford Literary Review* 4, 1979, pp. 5–28].

26. J. Derrida, *De la grammatologie,* p. 32.

27. J. Derrida, *L'écriture et la différence,* p. 296.

28. Sigmund Freud, *Esquisse* in *Naissance de la psychanalyse* (Paris: PUF, 1969) ["*Project for a Scientific Psychology,*" in *The Origins of Psychoanalysis,* pp. 347–445].

29. Laplanche and Pontalis, *Voc. de la psychanalyse,* op. cit.

30. S. Freud, *Wunderblock* in *Résultats, idées, problèmes,* vol. 2 (Paris: PUF, 1985) ["A Note upon the Mystic Writing Pad" in Freud, *General Psychological Theory* (New York: Collier, 1963), pp. 207–212].

31. J. Derrida, *L'écriture et la différence,* p. 326.

32. Ibid., p. 340.

33. Jean Laplanche, *Hölderlin et la question du père* (Paris: PUF, 1961).

34. C. Baudouin, *Psychanalyse de Victor Hugo* (Geneva: Mont-Blanc, 1943); republished by A. Colin (Paris, 1972).

35. C. Mauron, *Des métaphores obsédantes au mythe personne: Introduction à la psychocritique* (Paris: José Corti, 1962).

36. Roland Barthes, *Le degré zero de l'écriture* (Paris: Seuil, 1953) [*Writing Degree Zero,* trans. A. Lavers and Colin Smith (Boston: Beacon, 1970)]; *Sur Racine* (Paris: Seuil, 1963) [*On Racine,* trans. R. Howard (New York: Hill and Wang, 1964)].

37. R. Barthes, *Sur Racine,* p. 10.

38. *Le Monde* of March 14, 1964.

39. Raymond Picard, *Nouvelle critique ou nouvelle imposture* (Paris: Pauvert, 1965).

40. Roland Barthes, *Critique et Vérité* (Paris: Seuil, 1966), p. 27.

41. See *Bataille* I, part 2, chap. 1.

42. Paul Ricoeur, *La symbolique du mal* (Paris: Aubier, 1960) [*The Symbolism of Evil* (Boston: Beacon, 1967)].

43. Paul Ricoeur, *De l'interprétation: Essai sur Freud* (Paris: Seuil, 1965) [*Freud and Philosophy: An Essay on Interpretation,* trans. D. Savage (New Haven: Yale Univ. Press, 1970)].

44. Paul Ricoeur, "Le conscient et l'inconscient" in *VIᵉ Colloque de Bonneval: L'inconscient* (Paris: Desclée de Brouwer, 1966), p. 422.

45. Separate interviews with Paul and Jean-Paul Ricoeur. Correspondence with Charles Reagan, the American biographer of Paul Ricoeur.

46. Interview with Paul Ricoeur.

47. Jacques Lacan, *Écrits* (Paris: Seuil, 1966), p. 851.

48. *La Sfida Semiologica* (Rome: Armando Armando, 1974), pp. 356–359.

49. P. Ricoeur, *De l'interprétation,* pp. 358–359; Charles Reagan, "Psychoanalysis as Hermeneutics" in *Studies in the Philosophy of Paul Ricoeur* (Columbus: Ohio Univ. Press, 1979).

50. See Stuart Schneiderman, *Jacques Lacan: The Death of an Intellectual Hero* (Cambridge: Harvard Univ. Press, 1983), p. 29; French translation (Paris: PUF, 1986).

51. *Critique*, 224, January 1966, p. 70.

52. See also J.-L. Scherer, *Critique*, 223, December 1965.

53. *Critique*, 225, May 1966, p. 186.

54. Michel Tort, *TM*, 237, February 1966.

55. Interview with M. Tort.

56. M. Tort, *TM*, 237, February 1966, p. 1472.

57. Information transmitted to me by J.-P. Valabrega and confirmed by P. Ricoeur; see Renée Remond, *La règle et le consentement* (Paris: Fayard, 1979).

58. Reprinted by Société du Graphe, 1–2 (Paris: Seuil, 1969).

59. Ibid.

60. Unpublished seminar.

61. Lecture on N. Chomsky in *Problèmes cruciaux pour la psychanalyse* (unpublished); "La science et la vérité" in *L'objet de la psychanalyse* (unpublished); reproduced in *Cahiers pour l'analyse* and *Écrits*. Y. Duroux, "Logique et psychologie" and J.-A. Miller, "La suture, éléments de la logique du signifiant" in *Problèmes cruciaux* . . . , session of February 24, 1965, introduced with comments by J. Lacan. Miller's article in the *Cahiers* was a completely revised version of the lecture. Duroux's article was reproduced as it stood.

62. The book's subtitle was *The Language of Pure Thought Conceived on the Model of the Formulas of Arithmetic* (unpublished in French). Concerning logic, interview with Paul Henry.

63. Gottlob Frege, *Les fondements de l'arithmétique* (Paris: Seuil, 1969), p. 12 [*The Foundations of Arithmetic*, trans. J. L. Austin (New York: Philosophical Library, 1950), p. 10].

64. Noam Chomsky, *Structures syntaxiques* (Paris: Seuil, 1969) [*Syntactic Structures* (Gravenhage: Mouton, 1957)].

65. See Nicolas Ruwet, *Introduction à la grammaire générative* (Paris: Plon, 1965).

66. N. Chomsky, *Structures syntaxiques*, p. 17 [*Syntactic Structures*, p. 15].

67. See F. Gadet and M. Pêcheux, *La langue introuvable* (Paris: Maspero, 1980).

68. Roman Jakobson, *Essais de linguistique générale* (Paris: Minuit, 1964), p. 206.

69. J. Lacan;, *Problèmes cruciaux*, session of December 2, 1964.

70. J.-A. Miller, "La suture," p. 39.

71. Piera Aulagnier, "Remarques sur la structure psychotique," in *La Psychanalyse*, 8.

72. Interview with J.-A. Miller.

73. J. Lacan, *Problèmes cruciaux pour la psychanalyse*, session of March 24, reproduced in *Cahiers pour l'analyse*, pp. 52–54.

74. See *Bataille* I.

75. Michel Foucault, *Les mots et les choses* (Paris: Gallimard, 1966) [*The Order of Things* (New York: Pantheon, 1970)].

76. Jacques Derrida, "Nature, culture, écriture" in *Cahiers pour l'analyse*, 4, 1969; letter from C. Lévi-Strauss, *Cahiers* 8, SER (Paris: Société du Graphe, 1967).

77. Reprinted in *L'écriture et la différence* [*Writing and Difference*]; proceedings of the Baltimore symposium, unavailable in French, *The Structuralist Controversy: The Languages of Criticism and the Sciences of Man*, ed. R. Macksey and E. Donato (Baltimore and London: Johns Hopkins Univ. Press, 1970).

78. Interview with J. Derrida. See also *The Structuralist Controversy*, p. 21.

79. Ibid.

80. J. Lacan, "La méprise du sujet supposé savior" in *Scilicet*, 1, 1968, p. 35.

81. Maria Ruegg, "The End(s) of French Style: Structuralism and Post-Structuralism

in the American Context" in *Criticism, a Quarterly for Literature and the Arts,* vol. 21, 3, Summer 1979.

82. A. Wilden, *The Language of the Self: The Function of Language* in *Psycho-Analysis* (Baltimore: Johns Hopkins Univ. Press, 1968).

83. *The Structuralist Controversy,* p. 186.

84. Ibid., pp. 189 and 197.

85. Interview with François Wahl.

86. *Écrits,* p. 67.

87. Ibid., p. 894.

88. Statistics established by F. Wahl.

89. Jacques Brosse, *Arts* (December 14, 1966).

90. Jean-François Revel, *L'Express* (December 18–25, 1966).

91. André Robinet, *Nouvelles littéraires* (February 9, 1967); Didier Anzieu, Charles Melman, *Quinzaine littéraire* (November 15, 1966).

92. Pierre Daix, *Lettres françaises* (December 1–7, 1966); Gilles Lapouge, *Figaro littéraire* (December 1, 1966).

93. *Lettres françaises,* cover page.

94. *L'Arc,* 30 (November 4, 1966); Sartre responded on p. 92.

95. Jacques Lacan, *Figaro littéraire* (December 29, 1966), p. 4.

96. J. Lacan, "Acte de fondation" in *Annuaire de l'EFP,* 1965; "Adjoining Note" written in September 1964; "Preamble" not dated. The original text of the founding act, written along with Serge Leclaire, arch. S.L. See also *Ex.,* op. cit., p. 149 and the documents published in *Lettres de l'EFP,* 7, March 1970. The address delivered by Lacan on June 21 was different from the written document.

97. Interviews with F. Hofstein, Gérard Pommier, Antoinette Fouque, Roland Castro, Danièle Arnoux, Jean-Michel Ribettes, and Colette Soler.

98. *Annuaire de l'EFP,* p. 7.

99. Undated drafts, transcribed by Renée Boulay.

100. Interview with Bela Grunberger.

101. *Annuaire de l'EFP,* p. 2.

102. Ibid., p. 3.

103. Aubry, Dolto, Reverchon-Jouve, Hesnard, Lacan, Leclaire, Gessain, Perrier, Safouan.

104. Arch. J.A.; *Lettres de l'EFP, Analytica.*

105. Interview with Charles Melman.

106. Ibid.

107. *Le désir et la perversion* (Paris: Seuil, 1967). The other book is Maud Mannoni's *L'enfant arriéré et sa mère.*

108. *Analytica,* 7, p. 34.

109. *Lettres de l'EFP,* p. 176.

110. *Analytica,* 7, p. 42.

111. Circular of January 31, 1967, arch. J.A.; *Lettres de l'EFP,* pp. 177–178.

112. Unpublished letter, quoted in J. Aubry, "Là où les chemins divergent," in *Ornicar?,* 9, April 1977.

113. *Analytica,* 7, pp. 31–40.

114. J. Lacan;,"Proposition du 9 octobre," first version, in *Analytica,* 8; supplement to *Ornicar?,* 15, April 1978, p. 5.

115. Ibid., p. 8.

116. Concerning the end of analysis, see S. Freud, "L'Analyse avec fin et l'Analyse

sans fin" in *Résultats, idées, problèmes;* S. Ferenczi, "Le processus de la formation psychanalytique, le problème de la fin de l'analyse" in *Oeuvres complètes* (Paris: Payot, 1982), pp.
43–52 and 229–245. Anna Freud, "Sur l'analyse de formation" in *L'Enfant dans la psychanalyse* (Paris: Gallimard, 1976); Michael Balint, *Amour primaire et technique psychanalytique*
(Paris: Payot, 1972). See chaps. 5 and 6, this volume.

117. J. Lacan, "Situation de la psychanalyse en 1956" in *Écrits.*

118. *Analytica,* 8, pp. 22–23.

119. See *Bataille* I, part 2, chap. 2.

120. *Analytica,* 8, p. 23.

121. "Proposition du 9 octobre," second version (the first to be published) in *Scilicet*
1, pp. 14–15.

122. Interview with S. Leclaire.

123. J.-A. Miller, "Introduction aux paradoxes de la passe" in *Ornicar?,* 12–13, December 1977, p. 103.

124. Notes taken by J. Aubry at the request of J. Lacan to assess the number of his
adversaries.

125. Arch. J.A. and *Lettres de l'EFP,* 7, p. 186.

126. *Analytica,* 7, pp. 147–151.

127. Interview with G. Rosolato.

128. Interview with P. Aulagnier.

129. J. Clavreul, undated text, arch. J.A.

130. First version, arch. J.A.; second version, *Scilicet* 2–3, accompanied by a commentary.

131. Circular of March 21, 1969, arch. J.A.

132. *Analytica,* 7, pp. 53–54.

133. Letter from J. Clavreul, ibid., pp. 58–60.

134. The position of M. Safouan, ibid.

135. Interview with Michèle Bargues.

136. Unpublished seminar, session of May 15, 1968.

137. "Principes concernant l'accession au titre de psychanalyste dans l'EFP" in *Scilicet,* 2–3, pp. 30–33.

138. Undated response by M. Mannoni, *Analytica,* 7.

139. J. Oury, *Scilicet,* 2–3, pp. 47–48.

140. Interview with T. Abdoucheli; letter from Pierre Benoit, arch. J.A.

141. Project B, *Scilicet,* 2–3, p. 39; interviews with Francis Hofstein and Lucien
Mélèse.

142. Testimony from members of the Lander group.

143. *Scilicet,* 2–3, pp. 34–50.

144. Ibid., p. 51.

145. Ibid., pp. 51–52.

146. Ibid., p. 52 and circular of the EFP, arch. J.A.

147. Circular of February 9, 1969, arch. Anne Levallois.

148. Interview with Laurence Bataille.

149. See the statistics in the appendixes.

150. On this subject, Moustapha Safouan's book—*Jacques Lacan et la question de la
formation des analystes* (Paris: Seuil, 1982)—is insufficient.

151. See *Lettres de l'EFP,* 8, January 1971, p. 135.

152. *Scilicet,* 1, p. 3.

153. Ibid., p. 11 (my emphasis).

154. See François Wahl et al., *Qu'est-ce que le structuralisme?* (Paris: Seuil, 1968).

155. Undated proposal for a dictionary. See also *Lettres de l'EFP*, 15, presentation by Charles Melman, June 1975, pp. 194–211.

156. Interview with J.-A. Miller.

157. *L'Ordinaire du psychanalyste*, 11, November 1977, "Sigismond," p. 163.

158. Interview with F. Hofstein.

159. *L'ordinaire du psychanalyste*, 12, April 1978.

160. Pierre Legendre, *L'amour du censeur* (Paris: Seuil, 1974).

161. E. Ortigues, *Oedipe africain* (Paris: Plon, 1966); H. Collomb, *La relation thérapeutique interculturelle*, Sixth International Colloquium on Medical Psychiatry, Tours, September 27–29, 1983; M.-C. Ortigues worked in the clinic of J. Aubry.

162. Letter from Jean-Paul Moreigne, arch. J.A.; counterproposal, arch. J.-P. Moreigne.

163. Robert Castel, *Le psychanalysme* (Paris: Maspero, 1973).

164. *Topique*, 1, Paris, PUF, 47, reprinted in *La formation du psychanalyste* (Paris: Belfond, 1979), pp. 55–86. Aulagnier's and Perrier's articles were published in *Topique*, 1. See as well their texts in *L'inconscient*, 8, and *Topique*, 2.

165. *La formation du psychanalyste.*

166. *Topique*, 1, p. 60.

167. Ibid., p. 65.

168. See *Topique*, 6, 1971, pp. 131–138. The texts in issues 1 and 6 were dubbed the "blue book" ["Cahier bleu"] by the founders.

169. See chap. 3.

170. François Perrier, *Voyages extraordinaires en Translacanie* (Paris: Lieu commun, 1985), p. 68.

171. For the mathème, see chap. 3.

172. J.-P. Valabrega, *La formation du psychanalyste*, p. 133; M.-C. Celerier, "Compte rendu de la journée scientifique du 2–12–76, l'analyse quatrième," in *Topique*, 19, 1977, pp. 19–24; J.-P. Moreigne, "L'exercice de l'analyse entre technique et pratique, entre ascèse et poésie?" in *RFP*, 5, 1982.

173. *Topique*, 32, 1983, p. 154. See also A. Gasquères, "La formation psychanalytique au IVᵉ Groupe" in *Psychanalystes* (bulletin of the Collége de psychanalystes), 3–4, 1982. Micheline Enriquez, "Analyse possible ou impossible" in *Topique*, 18, 1977, pp. 48–62; "On forme un analyste" in *NRP*, 20, 1979.

Chapter 9. Sunset Boulevard

1. See the journal *Autrement: 68–78, dix années sacrilèges*, 12, 1978.

2. Jacques Lacan, *Télévision* (Paris: Seuil, 1973), p. 54.

3. The letter is dated November 7, 1977, the day of Ey's death.

4. Jacques Lacan, *La scission de 1953*, supplement to *Ornicar?*, no. 7, 1976 (abbreviated as *Sc. 53*), p. 4.

5. See chap. 2, this volume.

6. *Arguments*, reprinted in 2 volumes (Toulouse: Privat, 1983), vol. 1.

7. *Arguments*, vol. 2, pp. 1–59.

8. Both books were published in the "Arguments" collection of Éditions de Minuit; see J.-A. Cohen, *Marcuse* (Paris: Éditions Universitaires, "Psychotheque," 1974).

9. Claude Quétel and Jacques Postel, eds., *Nouvelle histoire de la psychiatrie* (Toulouse: Privat, 1983).

10. *Livre blanc de la psychiatrie française* (Toulouse: Privat, 1967).

11. H. Ey, *Plan d'organisation du champ de la psychiatrie* (Toulouse: Privat, 1966).

12. *Livre blanc,* vol. 2, pp. 147–202.

13. Letters shown me by Renée Ey.

14. *Livre blanc,* vol. 3, p. 106.

15. *EP,* 4, 1974, p. 24.

16. *DSM III* (Paris: Masson, 1983); M. Leclerc, "1984 DSM-III ou la novlangue" in *Psychiatries,* 61, 1984, p. 64; see also the summary by M. Cadoret in *Psychanalystes,* 8, July 1983, p. 55.

17. See C. Koupernik, *Confrontations psychiatriques,* 16, 1978; H. Ey, *Les études philosophiques,* 4, October–December 1956, p. 619.

18. Michel Foucault, *Histoire de la folie à l'âge classique* (Paris: Plon, 1961), republished by Gallimard in 1972, back cover.

19. *EP,* vol. 36, 2, April–June 1971, p. 226.

20. Mary Barnes and John Berke, *Mary Barnes: Un voyage à travers la folie* (Paris: Seuil, 1973).

21. G. Bateson's works have been published in French by Éditions du Seuil. See also G. Bateson, D. Jackson, J. Haley, and J. Weakland, "Toward a Theory of Schizophrenia" in *Behavior Science,* I, 251, 1956; Ronald Laing, *La politique de l'expérience* (Paris: Stock, 1972).

22. D. Cooper, *Psychiatrie et antipsychiatrie* (Paris: Seuil, 1970), p. 134; see also R. Laing, *Le moi divisé* (Paris: Stock, 1970) [*The Divided Self* (Chicago: Quadrangle, 1960)]; and R. Laing and A. Esterson, *L'équilibre mental, la famille, et la folie* (Paris: Maspero, 1971).

23. *Raison et violence,* letter from J.-P. Sartre (November 9, 1963), (Paris: Petite Bibliothèque Payot, 1976), p. 5.

24. See O. Mannoni, "Le(s) mouvement(s) antipsychiatrique(s)" in *Revue internationale de sciences sociales,* XXV, 4, 1973, pp. 538–552; and Chantal Bosseur, *Clefs pour l'antipsychiatrie* (Paris: Seghers, 1976).

25. W. Boukovski, *Une nouvelle maladie mentale en URSS: L'opposition* (Paris: Seuil, 1971).

26. Winnicott's works have been published in French by Gallimard and Payot. See as well *L'Arc,* 1977, and *La Psychanalyse,* 5, 1959; letter from Lacan to Winnicott in *Ornicar?,* 33, 1985.

27. Interview with G. Raimbault.

28. Interview with M. Mannoni. See *L'enfant, sa maladie et les autres* (Paris: Seuil, 1967).

29. Françoise Dolto, *Les cas Dominique* (Paris: Seuil, 1971). It was on the advice of Paul Flamand that F. Dolto wrote up the case as a book which appeared in the "Champ freudien" collection. Her thesis was republished separately the same year. See also *Enfance aliénée,* two issues of *Recherches,* September and December 1967; republished by 10/18 in 1967 and Denoël in 1984.

30. Ibid., Denoël, p. 257.

31. M. Mannoni, *Éducation impossible* (Paris: Seuil, 1973); *Un lieu pour vivre* (Paris: Seuil, 1976).

32. Gilles Deleuze and Félix Guattari, *L'anti-Oedipe,* the first volume of a work entitled *Capitalisme et schizophrénie* (Paris: Minuit, 1972).

33. Interview with Catherine Clément; *L'Arc,* 49, 1972, p. 47.

34. Starting with this date, I personally participated in most of the events recounted. I shall draw on personal memories.

35. Gilles Deleuze and Félix Guattari, *Mille Plateaux* (Paris: Minuit, 1980).

36. Maurice de Gandillac, *L'Arc,* 49, 1972, p. 56.

37. See *Garde-fous,* 10, special issue devoted to the La Borde clinic, 1976.

38. *Le Nouvel Observateur,* May 7, 1973, article by M. Righini.

39. *Recherches,* March 1973, p. 3.

40. *Lettres de l'EFP,* 17, 1956, pp. 234–255.

41. Gilles Deleuze and Félix Guattari, *Rhizome* (Paris: Minuit, 1976), p. 8.

42. See W. Boukovski, *Une nouvelle maladie;* E. Antébi, *Droits d'asile en URSS* (Paris: Julliard, 1977); *Esprit,* 11, November 1969; *Psychiatrie aujourd'hui,* 24–25, 1975.

43. W. Boukovski, *Une nouvelle maladie,* p. 97.

44. Ibid., p. 24.

45. See *Bataille* I and chap. 4, this volume.

46. For the challenge to Article 64, see special issue of *Actes, Psychiatrie et Justice,* 39, 1983; Michel Landry, *Le psychiatre au tribunal* (Toulouse: Privat, 1983); *Psychiatrie française,* June–August 1977, May–June 1983, and February 1985; Serge Ferraton, *Ferraton le fou l'assassin* (Paris: Solin, 1978).

47. Motion reprinted in *EP,* 4, 1971, p. 181.

48. *EP,* 1, 1972, and 1, 1974.

49. *Psychiatries,* 37, 1979, p. 50 (materials on the Mexico City and Honolulu Congresses). General Videla's junta took power on March 24, 1976.

50. Ibid., p. 59.

51. On Freud and the Gestapo, see *Bataille* I, part 2, chap. 2.

52. *Psychiatries,* 37, 1979, p. 61; declaration dated August 8, 1977.

53. Ibid., p. 47.

54. *Le Monde* (September 9, 1977).

55. *Psychiatries,* 56, 1983, p. 6.

56. See *La Psychanalyse,* 7, 1964, p. 239.

57. See *Bataille* I, part 4, chap. 1.

58. S. Freud, *Three Essays on the Theory of Sexuality* (New York: Basic Books, 1962); *La vie sexuelle* (Paris: PUF, 1969); Élisabeth Badinter, *L'amour en plus* (Paris: Flammarion, 1979).

59. Maïté Albistur and Daniel Armogathe, *Histoire du féminisme français* (Paris: Des femmes, 1977).

60. See *Bataille* I; Célia Bertin, *La dernière Bonaparte* (Paris: Librairie académique Perrin, 1982); *L'Infini,* 2.

61. "La phase phallique et la portée subjective du complexe de castration" in *Scilicet,* 1, p. 61.

62. Jacques Lacan, *Le savoir du psychanalyste,* unpublished lecture series at the Sainte-Anne Hospital.

63. Interview with W. Granoff.

64. J. Lacan, "Letter to Winnicott" p. 9.

65. *La Psychanalyse,* 7. W. Granoff and F. Perrier, *Le désir et le féminin* (Paris: Aubier-Montaigne, 1979). D. Lagache: the first text remains unpublished and the second one has been lost; see *Oeuvres complètes,* 5 vols. (Paris: PUF, 1977), bibliography; F. Dolto, "La libido génitale et son destin féminin" in *La Psychanalyse,* 7, and expanded in *Sexualité féminine* (Paris: Scarabée/Métailié, 1983); J. Lacan, *Écrits* (Paris: Seuil, 1966); W. Granoff, *La pensée et le féminin* (Paris: Minuit, 1976).

66. C.-J. Luquet, "La place du mouvement masochiste dans l'évolution de la femme," *RFP,* 23, 3, 1959.

67. In *La séxualité féminine: Nouvelles recherches* (Paris: Payot, 1964); republished in Petite Bibliothèque Payot, 1982; discussions in *RFP*, 29, 4, 1965.

68. Interview with J. Chasseguet-Smirgel.

69. Letter provided by J. Chasseguet-Smirgel. See also A. Michel and G. Texier, *La condition de la Française aujourd'hui* (Paris: Gonthier, 1964).

70. Antoinette Fouque, "Féminisme et/ou mouvement des femmes" in *Images de femmes* (Paris: CEFUP, 1982), p. 179; also interview with A. Fouque.

71. See A. Fouque, comments on her analysis with Lacan in chap. 1 of this volume.

72. On the women's movement in general: Louisette Blanquart, *Femmes: L'âge politique* (Paris: Éditions sociales, 1974); Gisèle Halimi, *La cause des femmes* (Paris: Grasset, 1973); F. d'Eaubonne, *Le féminisme ou la mort* (Paris: Horay, 1974); Jean Maudit, *La révolte des femmes* (Paris: Fayard, 1971); M. A. Macciocchi, *Les femmes et leurs maîtres* (Paris: Bourgois, 1979). Journals: *Sorcières, Le Torchon brûle*, the "ordinary sexism" section of *TM*. "Le mouvement des femmes" in *Mouvements sociaux d'aujourd'hui*, ed. A. Touraine, Cerisy Colloquium of 1979; Warren Montag, "Lacan and Feminine Sexuality" in *Quarterly Review of Film Studies*, vol. 9, 4, Fall 1984.

73. Marguerite Duras, *Le ravissement de Lol V. Stein* (Paris: Gallimard, 1976).

74. *Art Press International*, January 1979, p. 4.

75. *Marguerite Duras à Montreal* (Monteal: Spirale, 1981). See as well Marcelle Marini, *Territoires du féminin* (Paris: Minuit, 1977).

76. Michèle Montrelay, *L'ombre et le nom* (Paris: Minuit, 1977).

77. Jacques Lacan, "Hommage fait à Marguerite Duras du 'Ravissement de Lol. V. Stein'" in *Cahiers Renaud-Barrault*, 52, December 1965. Reprinted in *Marguerite Duras* (Paris: Albatros, 1974 and 1979).

78. In *Marguerite Duras à Montreal*, p. 61.

79. The article in *Critique* is reprinted in M. Montrelay, *L'ombre et le nom*. See also François Perrier, *La chaussée d'antin* (Paris: Inter-Éditions, 1982), and Moustapha Safouan, *La sexualité féminine* (Paris: Seuil, 1976).

80. *Scilicet*, 2–3, pp. 5–6.

81. *Quinzaine littéraire*, August 1–31, 1975.

82. Jacques Lacan, *D'un discours qui ne serait pas du semblant*, 1970–1971, unpublished; *Ou pire*, 1971–1972, unpublished; *Seminaire XX, Encore* (Paris: Seuil, 1975), p. 54.

83. J. Lacan, *Séminaire XX*, ibid.

84. Luce Irigaray, *Speculum: De l'autre femme* (Paris: Minuit, 1974).

85. *Libération* (November 26, 1974).

86. Catherine Clément and Hélène Cixous, *La jeune née* (Paris, 10/18, 1975).

87. *L'Arc*, 58, 1974.

88. *L'Arc*, 61, 1975.

89. *L'Arc*, 58, 1974, Introduction, p. i.

90. Ibid., p. 45.

91. Tzvetan Todorov, *Théorie de la littérature: Textes des formalistes russes* (Paris: Seuil, 1966).

92. Marcelin Pleynet, *Lautréamont* (Paris: Seuil, 1967).

93. *TQ*, 19, 1964.

94. Julia Kristeva, "Mémoire" in *L'Infini*, 1, Winter 1983, p. 41.

95. Interview with Philippe Sollers.

96. *TQ*, 32, 1968.

97. J. Kristeva, *L'Infini*, 1. See P. Sollers, *Logiques* (Paris: Seuil, 1968).

98. Roger Laporte, *La veille* (Paris: Gallimard, 1963); Maurice Roche, *Compact* (Paris: Seuil, 1966); Georges Pérec, *L'homme qui dort* (Paris: Denoël, 1967); Pierre Guyotat,

Éden, Éden, Éden (Paris: Gallimard, 1970); Denis Roche, *Louve basse* (Paris: Seuil, 1976); Philippe Sollers, *Paradis* (Paris: Seuil, 1981). Between 1971 and 1975, Georges Pérec was in analysis with a member of the APF. See *Penser/Classer* (Paris: Hachette, 1985). As in the case of writers in the interwar period, a distinction should be made between the experience of personal therapy, on the one hand, and the role of a Freudian problematic in a writer's works, on the other.

99. J. Lacan, *Écrits*, p. 833.

100. Michel Plon, *La théorie des jeux: Une politique imaginaire* (Paris: Maspero, 1977); Paul Henry, *Le mauvais outil* (Paris: Klincksieck, 1977).

101. Lucien Sève, *Marxisme et théorie de la personnalité* (Paris: Éditions sociales, 1969), in three successive editions.

102. *Cahiers du CERM*, 5 vols., 81–85, 1970. R. Roelens, "Problèmes de structure et de décentrement du sujet dans l'oeuvre de Lacan"; T. Goldberg, "Notes et reflexions sur Jacques Lacan."

103. *Marxisme et théorie de la personnalité*, p. 7.

104. André Green had just published *Un oeil en trop* (Paris: Minuit, 1969), and Serge Leclaire, *Psychanalyser* (Paris: Seuil, 1968).

105. *NC*, 37, October 1970, pp. 22–34; see also Catherine Clément, "Les beaux jours," *Magazine littéraire*, 166, November 1980, p. 19.

106. *Pour une critique de la théorie psychanalytique* (Paris: Éditions sociales, 1973); see also *Europe*, special issue on Freud.

107. *Pour une critique*, p. 264. See also *Une psychiatrie différente, dites-vous?*, *NC*, supplement to no. 63; J.-P. Rumen, *Psychiatries questions actuelles*, supplement to no. 83, 1975.

108. *Action poétique*, 41–42, 1968.

109. *NC*, special issue on *Linguistique et littérature*, undated, p. 176.

110. *TQ*, 34, Summer 1970, pp. 3–4; *Théorie d'ensemble* (Paris: Seuil, 1968).

111. *L'Humanité* (September 12 and October 12, 1969); *TQ*, 39 and 40, 1969 and 1970.

112. J. Lacan, *D'un Autre à l'autre*, 1968–1969, unpublished, session of June 26, 1969.

113. Quoted by P. Daix, *Lettres françaises* (July 2, 1969).

114. Ibid.

115. *L'Express* (July 14–20, 1969).

116. Interview with P. Sollers.

117. Elisabeth Roudinesco, reprinted in *Un discours au réel* (Paris: Mame, 1973).

118. *Promesse*, 30–31, Fall–Winter 1971, reprinted in *Positions* (Paris: Minuit, 1972).

119. Jacques Derrida, *Poétique*, 21, 1975, reprinted in *La carte postale* (Paris: Aubier-Flammarion, 1980).

120. J. Derrida, *La carte postale*, pp. 474 and 484.

121. J. Lacan, *Écrits*, pp. 14 and 40.

122. Jacques Lacan, *Séminaire II* (Paris: Seuil, 1978), p. 239.

123. Jacques Lacan, *Écrits* (Paris: Points-Seuil, 1969), p. 8.

124. François Roustang, *Un destin si funeste* (Paris: Minuit, 1976) [*Dire Mastery: Discipleship from Freud to Lacan*, trans. N. Lukacher (Baltimore: Johns Hopkins Univ. Press, 1985)].

125. Barbara Johnson, "The Frame of Reference: Poe, Lacan, Derrida" in *Yale French Studies*, 1977.

126. *TQ*, 53, 1973.

127. *TQ*, 46, 1971.

128. See Michel David, *La psicoanalisi nella cultura italiana* (Turin: Boringheri, 1966); *Lettres de l'EFP*, 15, 1975; *Ornicar?*, 16, 1978.

129. See *Marxisme-léninisme et psychanalyse, Cahiers Yenan*, 1 (Paris: Maspero, 1975).

130. *Psychanalyse et politique* (Paris: Seuil, 1974) (Proceedings of the Milan Colloquium, 1973).

131. Interview with P. Sollers; *Lettre mensuelle de l'ECF*, 40, June 1985, p. 29.

132. *TQ*, 59, 1974, p. 7; P. Sollers, *Femmes* (Paris: Gallimard, 1983), pp. 87–89.

133. Julia Kristeva, *L'infini*, 1, p. 53.

134. *Le Monde* (April 3, 1981).

135. Materials from the Italian press (July 29–August 10, 1985).

136. *L'Express* (November 1–7, 1985).

Chapter 10. Kingdoms Asunder

1. Pierre Merlin, *L'université assassinée* (Paris: Ramsay, 1980); René Réymond, *La règle et le consentement* (Paris: Fayard, 1979).

2. See M. Winock, *Histoire politique de la revue "Esprit"* (Paris: Seuil, 1975).

3. Interview with J. Favez-Boutonier.

4. Interview with Jacques Gagey.

5. Interview with Claude Prévost.

6. Interview with J. Laplanche.

7. J. Laplanche, *Psychanalyse à l'université*, vol. 6, 24, September 1981, p. 559; letter from R. Cahn to Laplanche (October 28, 1980); arch. J. Laplanche.

8. Arch. of the UER of the SHC, transmitted by C. Prévost.

9. Interview with J. Derrida.

10. Letter from Leclaire to Miller (July 9, 1969) and from Leclaire to Foucault, arch. J.-A.M. and S.L.

11. Circular of March 26, 1969, arch. S.L.

12. General meeting of philosophy section (April 18, 1969), arch. S.L.

13. Circulars of September 20, 1969, and November 13, 1969, arch. S.L.

14. "Vincennes, psychanalyse, Leclaire," in *La Lettre infâme* (Paris: F. Gruyer, September 1969); interview with S. Leclaire.

15. *Magazine littéraire*, special issue devoted to Lacan, 121, February 1977, p. 23.

16. *Les professeurs pour quoi faire?* (Paris: Seuil, 1970); interview conducted in November 1969, *L'Express* March 16–22, 1970.

17. Interview with Patrick Guyomard; see also J. Clavreul, "Les élèves de Lacan," *Tertulia*, January 1982.

18. The concepts elaborated for this recasting may be found in the following seminars: *L'envers de la psychanalyse*, 1969–1970, unpublished; *D'un discours qui ne serait pas du semblant*, 1970–1971, unpublished; *Le savoir du psychanalyste*, Sainte-Anne seminar, 1971–1972, unpublished; *Ou pire*, 1971–1972, unpublished; *Les non-dupes errent*, 1973–1974, unpublished; *Séminaire XX, Encore* (Paris: Seuil, 1975); "L'Étourdit" in *Scilicet*, 4, 1973. See also seminar fragments published in *Ornicar?* starting in 1975.

19. *Cahiers pour l'analyse*, 1969.

20. Concerning Wittgenstein, see *Bataille* I; *Tractatus* (Paris: Gallimard, 1961), French translation by P. Klossowski [in English, *Tractatus Logico-Philosophicus* (London and New York: Routledge & Kegan Paul, 1981), translated from the German by C. K. Ogden]; D. Lecourt, *L'ordre et les jeux* (Paris: Grasset, 1981); Antonia Soulez, *Manifeste du cercle de*

Vienne (Paris: PUF, 1985); Jacques Bouveresse, *La parole malheureuse* (Paris: Minuit, 1971); R. Jaccard, *Freud: Jugements et témoignages* (Paris: PUF, 1976).

21. J. Lacan, *L'envers de la psychanalyse.*

22. Interview with G.-Th. Guilbaud.

23. Concerning topology, see J.-C. Pont, *La topologie algébrique* (Paris: PUF); F. Tingry, *Recherches logiques et linguistiques pour la psychanalyse: Nom propre et topologie des surfaces,* thesis (UER of SHC), 1983; *Littoral,* May 5–6, 1982, *Abords topologiques;* G.-Th. Guilbaud, *Leçons d'à peu près* (Paris: Bourgois, 1985); J.-C. Milner, *Les noms indistincts* (Paris: Seuil, 1984); E. Roudinesco, interview with J.-C. Milner, *Action poétique,* 72, December, 1977.

24. See J.-C. Milner, *De l'école* (Paris: Seuil, 1985).

25. J. Lacan, *Le Savoir du psychanalyste,* session of November 21, 1971.

26. J. Lacan, *Ou pire,* session of February 9, 1972.

27. Interview with J.-A. Miller.

28. *Lettres de l'EFP,* 1–5, 1967–1968.

29. *Stécriture,* 1984, house bulletin. For a chronology of the unpublished seminars, see Marcelle Marini, *Lacan* (Paris: Belfond, 1986).

30. See Robert Linhart, *L'établi* (Paris: Minuit, 1978).

31. Dedication by Lacan, copy shown me by J. Aubry.

32. J. Lacan, *Séminaire III* (Paris: Seuil, 1981).

33. J. Lacan, *Séminaire XI* (Paris: Seuil, 1973), p. 251.

34. Ibid., p. 249.

35. For this period, I have made use of the personal archives of J.-A. Miller, P. Guyomard, and F. Baudry, supplemented by separate interviews with each of them.

36. Circular of September 1974, arch. P. Guyomard.

37. Letter from Clavreul to Morali (October 15, 1974), arch. J.-A.M.

38. J. Clavreul, *Bulletin de la Convention psychanalytique,* 8, January 1986, p. 38; see also *Tertulia,* January 1982.

39. Letter from Miller to Rabant (October 15, 1974).

40. Letter from Baudry to Lacan (October 13, 1974) and Lacan's reply (October 16, 1974), arch. Baudry.

41. J. Lacan, *Le savoir du psychanalyste,* session of November 4, 1971, and *Seminaire XX.*

42. *Ornicar?,* 1, 1975, p. 33.

43. Ibid., p. 34.

44. Letter from Frioux to Lacan (November 9, 1974), arch. J.-A.M.

45. Letter from Lacan to Frioux (November 10, 1974), arch. J.-A.M.

46. Letter from Baudry to Lacan (November 26, 1974), arch. P. Guyomard.

47. Minutes of November 26, 1974, arch. J.-A.M.

48. Letter from Miller to Roustang (November 17, 1974), arch. J.-A.M.

49. Roger-Pol Droit, *Le Monde* (November 15, 1974).

50. Undated circular, arch. J.-A.M.

51. *Libération* (December 7, 1974).

52. Interview with J.-A. Miller.

53. *Ornicar?,* March 2, 1975, p. 81.

54. Interview with S. Faladé.

55. *Ornicar?,* 12–13, December 1977, p. 199.

56. *Lettres de l'EFP,* 21, August 1977.

57. Interview with S. Faladé; "Congress on Transmission," *Lettres de l'EFP,* 25, 1979.

58. Booklet published by Navarin; see also *Analytica,* 39, 1984; statistics on the department conveyed to me by G. Miller.

59. Statutes from before 1973, arch. SPP-IP, private sources. See also *Psychiatrie aujourd'hui?,* 1972; chap. 6 in this volume.

60. J. Favreau, comments on the training of psychoanalysts, May 27–28, 1967, arch. J.-L.D.

61. See statistics in the appendixes.

62. Georges Devereux died in 1985, and at the time of this writing Marthe Robert was a member of the Médicis Prize jury.

63. *Études freudiennes,* November 1–2, 1969 (Denoël), p. 174.

64. Letter from Lacan to Donnet (March 17, 1969), arch. J.-L.D.

65. Meeting of March 31, 1969, arch. J.-L.D.

66. Published in *Études freudiennes,* 1–2.

67. Interview with Alice Cherki.

68. Serge Lebovici, Colloquium of May 1971, arch. J.-L.D.

69. J.-L. Donnet, "A propos de l'analyse a visée didactique," presentation of May 18, 1971, arch. J.-L.D.

70. Statutes of the Institut de psychanalyse, arch. IP, private sources; interview with André Green; statutory modification of January 23, 1973.

71. Rules of the Institut de psychanalyse, internal document.

72. André Stéphane, *L'univers contestationnaire* (Paris: Petite Bibliothèque Payot, 1969).

73. Ibid., p. 38.

74. Ibid., p. 28.

75. Ibid., p. 69.

76. See *Bataille* I, part 2, chap. 2.

77. Other books have been published by psychoanalysts on the subject, but they have nothing in common with that volume.

78. Minutes of the Société suisse de psychanalyse, February 22–27, 1972, pp. 85–86, arch. J.-L.D.

79. *Le Nouvel Observateur* (June 3, 1969).

80. *Quinzaine littéraire* (June 1–15, 1969).

81. Alain Didier, "La psychanalyse triste" in *TM,* 277–278, August 1969.

82. Fragment of the deliberations of the administrative council, arch. IP, private sources.

83. Letter of May 9, 1973, arch. IP, private sources.

84. Official documents conveyed to me by René Major.

85. Minutes of November 30, 1973, arch. IP, private sources.

86. Interview with R. Major.

87. Circular of January 16, 1974, arch. IP, private sources.

88. Minutes of the administrative council, January 22, 1974, arch. IP, private sources.

89. See *Bataille* I, part 1, chap. 1.

90. Meeting of December 7, 1972; interview with R. Major.

91. Nicolas Abraham, *Jonas* (Paris: Aubier-Flammarion, 1981).

92. Interview with Maria Torok and Nicholas Rand.

93. N. Abraham, in *Structure et morphogenèse* (Paris: Mouton, 1965).

94. N. Abraham, *Rhythmes* (Paris: Flammarion, 1985).

95. N. Abraham, in *Critique,* 249, February 1968, reprinted in *L'écorce et le noyau* (Paris: Aubier-Flammarion, 1978).

96. N. Abraham and M. Torok, *Le verbier de l'hommer aux loups* (Paris: Aubier-Flammarion, 1976); *The Wolfman by the Wolfman* (New York: Basic Books, 1971); French edition by Gallimard (Paris, 1981); Karin Hobholzer, *Entretien avec l'homme aux loups* (Paris: Gallimard, 1981).

97. Interview with J. Derrida, who listened to the tape and transcribed its contents.

98. *Ornicar?*, 14, 1978, pp. 8–9.

99. Interview with R. Major.

100. *Études freudiennes*, 13–14, 1978; reprinted in *L'agonie du jour* (Paris: Aubier-Montaigne, 1979).

101. Letters shown me by Nata Minor.

102. Serge Viderman, "Préambule à un projet de cursus" in *La formation du psychanalyste* (Monographics de l'IPA), p. 287.

103. S. Viderman, *La construction de l'espace analytique* (Paris: Denoël, 1970).

104. Minutes of May 6, 1974, arch. IP, private sources.

105. Minutes of May 7, 1974, ibid.

106. Extraordinary meeting of May 15, 1974, ibid.

107. Minutes of June 11, 1974, ibid.

108. Letter of April 30, 1976, arch. R.M.

109. Jacques Derrida, *Glas* (Paris: Galilée, 1974).

110. Jacques Derrida, *La carte postale* (Paris: Aubier-Flammarion, 1980), pp. 536 and 538.

111. Serge Leclaire, *Rompre les charmes* (Paris: Inter-Éditions, 1981), p. 26.

112. Ibid., p. 198.

113. Statutes registered June 13, 1977, arch. R.M.

114. S. Leclaire, *Rompre les charmes,* p. 201.

115. Ibid., pp. 202–203.

116. Circular of January 9, 1975, arch. IP, private sources.

117. Circular letter to André Green, arch. IP, private sources.

118. Minutes of March 4, 1975, ibid.

119. Paris court document (*Tribunal de grande instance*), March 22, 1975, arch. R.M.

120. Statutes of the SPP of June 1977, arch. SPP.

121. Verdict of the Paris Court, Fifth Chamber, First Section, June 17, 1981, arch. R.M.

122. Archives of the Collège de psychanalystes, J. Sédat. See also *Tribune* (Bulletin of the Cartels constituants de l'analyse freudienne), 1, *L'institution en question* (Paris, 1985).

123. Decree of February 22, 1982, arch. R.M.

124. Circular letter of the IPA, October 1981, arc. SPP-IP, private sources.

125. Circular of December 14, 1983, arch. SPP-IP, private sources.

126. Unpublished document conveyed to me by R. Major.

127. J.-L. Evrard, *Les années brunes* (Paris: Éd. Confrontation, series "Vert et noir," 1984).

128. Letter from Limentani (May 21, 1984), arch. SPP-IP, private sources.

129. IPA Monograph Series, 4, *Les changements intervenus chez les analystes et dans leur formation,* published under the direction of R. Wallerstein, M.D., 1985.

130. Circular of July 3, 1984, arch. SPP-IP, private sources.

131. Documents of the Zurich Seminar; J. Rousseau-Dujardin, "Sauver la psychanalyse au cours des années brunes" in *Psychanalystes*, 11, 1985. See also *Hier geht das Leben auf eine sehr merkwürdige Weise weiter* (Verlag Michaël Kellner, 1985), exhibit catalogue.

See also the article on the IPA Congress by Rainer Appel, "Weh dem der Enkel ist" in *Frankfurter Allgemeine,* July 8, 1985.

132. Meetings of the Administrative Council, February 5, 1985, arch. SPP-IP. The *Roster* is the IPA's directory.

133. *Documents et Débats* (internal bulletin of the APF), April 1980.

134. Statutes of 1964, arch. W.G.

135. Georges Favez, *Être psychanalyste* (Paris: Dunod, 1976).

136. *Documents et Débats,* 6, September 1972.

137. *L'écrit du temps* (Paris, Minuit).

138. See chap. 7, this volume.

139. Letter from Granoff to Turquet (May 31, 1964), arch. W.G.

140. Letter from Granoff to Van der Leuw (July 17, 1964), arch. W.G.

141. Ibid. (July 21, 1964).

142. Letter from Granoff to Gitelson (October 18, 1964), arch. W.G.

143. Letter from Turquet to Lagache (November 3, 1964), arch. W.G.

144. Correspondence between Lagache, Turquet, Granoff, and Laplanche, February 1965, arch. W.G.

145. Letter from Lagache to Granoff (March 25, 1965), arch. W.G.

146. Letter from Lagache to the Executive (July 24, 1965), arch. W.G.

147. Interview with J. Favez-Boutonier.

148. Letter from Granoff to Lagache (August 3, 1965), arch. W.G. Concerning the "letter to Serge," see chap. 7, this volume.

149. D. Lagache, Presidential Address of October 23, 1965, arch. W.G.

150. On back cover of volumes of the collection.

151. *TM,* 274, April 1969, p. 1813.

152. Ibid., p. 1820.

153. Interview with J.-B. Pontalis.

154. Catalogue of the *NRP* (Paris: Gallimard, 1985).

155. J.-B. Pontalis, *Loin* (Paris: Gallimard, 1980).

156. *Le Temps de la réflexion* (Paris: Gallimard, 1980), p. 16.

157. John Forrester, *Le langage aux origines de la psychanalyse* (Paris: Gallimard, 1984), p. 313 [*Language and the Origins of Psychoanalysis* (New York: Columbia Univ. Press, 1980)].

158. *NRP,* 30, Fall 1984, p. 12.

159. All these remarks are faithfully reproduced in *Documents et Débats.*

160. *Documents et Débats,* 3, March 1971.

161. Épistemon (Didier Anzieu), *Ces idées qui ont ébranlé la France* (Paris: Fayard, 1968).

162. Separate interviews with R. Pujol and W. Granoff.

163. *Documents et Débats,* 6, September 1972.

164. W. Granoff, "Lettre ouverte aux collègues de l'APF," March 14, 1972, arch. W.G.

165. Letter from Granoff to G. Favez (November 8, 1972), arch. W.G.

166. Wladimir Granoff, *Filiations* (Paris: Minuit, 1975); *La Pensée et le Féminin* (Paris: Minuit, 1976).

167. *Documents et Débats,* 6, 1972. Statutes published in *Documents et Débats,* 10, July 1974.

168. *Documents et Débats,* April 1977.

169. *Documents et Débats,* 14, March 1978.

170. Change of statutes voted through on January 30, 1978. See *Documents et Débats,* 18, May 1978.

Chapter 11. The École freudienne de Paris: The Collapse

1. François Roustang, *Un destin si funeste* (Paris: Minuit, 1977). See E. Roudinesco, review in *La psychanalyse mère et chienne* (Paris: 10/18, 1979).

2. *Ornicar?,* 10, 1977, p. 56.

3. Jacques Derrida, *La carte postale* (Paris: Aubier-Flammarion, 1980), p. 543.

4. Letter from C. Conté to E. Roudinesco (March 18, 1977), arch. E.R.

5. Open letter from myself (March 12, 1977).

6. Letter from J. Lacan to me (March 14, 1977).

7. Letter sent March 22, 1977, published under the title "Excusez-moi, je ne fais que passer" in *TM,* 371, June 1977.

8. Spoken May 12, 1977, in *Ornicar?,* December 12–13, 1977.

9. *Ornicar?,* ibid., p. 105.

10. Ibid., p. 191.

11. *Lettres de l'EPF,* 23, p. 27.

12. Ibid., p. 31.

13. Ibid., p. 100.

14. Ibid., p. 125.

15. Ibid., p. 167.

16. *Tertulia,* January 1982.

17. *Lettres de l'EFP,* 23, p. 181.

18. *Le Nouvel Observateur* (October 12, 1981).

19. Photographic documents, Michèle Montrelay; separate interviews with Michèle Montrelay and R. Major.

20. *La scholastique freudienne* (Paris: Fayard, 1972). See also B. Schuster, *L'argumentation antipsychanalytique en France depuis 1945,* doctoral thesis in medicine, Paris VI, April 1977.

21. Alain de Benoist, *Vu de droite* (Paris: Copernic, 1977).

22. See *Bataille* I, the debate concerning Pichon.

23. Gérard Zwang, *La statue de Freud* (Paris: Laffont, 1985), p. 26.

24. François George, *L'effet 'yau de poele* (Paris: Hachette-Essai, 1979).

25. *Le Monde* (September 21, 1979).

26. Letter and testimony of September 24, 1979, arch. W.G.

27. *Le Monde* (October 2, 1979).

28. Gilles Perrault, *L'orchestre rouge* (Paris: Fayard, 1976), p. 293.

29. See Philippe Bassine, *Le problème de l'inconscient.*

30. *The Unconscious* (Tbilisi: Metsniereba, 1981), 3 vols., ed. by Bassine, Sherozia, Prangishvili.

31. *Le Figaro* (June 19, 1978).

32. *Libération* (October 19, 1979).

33. Interview with Léon Chertok.

34. Letter from L. Althusser to me (June 30, 1976).

35. Presentation published in *Des femmes hebdo,* I, 9–16, November 1979; reprinted in Serge Leclaire, *Rompre les charmes,* (Paris: Inter-Éditions, 1981).

36. Presentation published in *Libération* and reprinted in *Cahiers Confrontation,* 3, Spring 1980.

37. See Gérard Mendel, *Vendredi,* October 26–November 8, 1979; J. Nobécourt, *Le Monde* (November 11, 1979).

38. Published in *La Quinzaine littéraire,* November 1, 1979.

39. Recording by Martine Bacherich-Granoff. I too was present on the podium.

40. Sources used for the chronicle of the dissolution: archives of the EFP assembled by J. Aubry and E. Roudinesco: approximately 800 circulars; archives of the Cause freudienne and the École de la cause freudienne; *Delenda, Entre-temps* (bulletins); personal archives of J.-A. Miller; documents published in *L'Ane,* 1, April-May 1981, reprinted in *Almanach de la dissolution* (Paris: Navarin, 1986); separate interviews with M. Montrelay, F. Dolto, C. Melman, S. Faladé, J.-A. Miller, J. Aubry, A. Cherki; documents furnished by D. Soulez-Larivière; A. Cherki, "Pour mémoire" in *Retour à Jacques Lacan* (Paris: Fayard, 1981); Claude Dorgeuille, *La seconde mort de Jacques Lacan* (Paris: Actualité freudienne, 1981); examination of the French press during the period; diary of J. Aubry, member of the EFP administrative council.

41. *Ornicar?* documents, arch. J.-A.M.

42. Separate interviews with C. Melman and F. Dolto.

43. Separate interviews with J.-A. Miller and S. Faladé.

44. Interview with F. Dolto.

45. EFP circular, October 1979.

46. *L'Ane,* 1, reprinted under the title "Tous lacaniens!", p. 28.

47. Notes taken by A. Cherki.

48. C. Melman, *Plus-Un,* December 1, 1979.

49. Circular of December 16, 1979.

50. Letter dated January 7, 1980.

51. Since the authenticity of the letter of dissolution has been strenuously contested, I asked the principal protagonists, whose positions are quite different at present, Miller, Faladé, and Melman, to give me their testimony. All three agreed. But at the last moment, Charles Melman imposed unacceptable conditions for giving me his version: He wanted to read Miller's before producing his own. Given those conditions, I preferred to do without his opinion. The authenticity of the circulars signed by Lacan after January 5 has been contested more forcefully still than the letter of dissolution. Nothing proves that those circulars were written by Lacan, but nothing proves that they were not. All the documents written by those contesting the circulars and attributing them to J.-A. Miller are published in Claude Dorgeuille's book, *La seconde mort de Jacques Lacan.*

52. The letter of dissolution was reproduced throughout the press.

53. *Libération* (January 11, 1980).

54. *Libération* (January 10, 1980) and *Le Matin* (January 15, 1980).

55. Interview with F. Dolto; see Boris Dolto, *Le corps entre les mains* (Paris: Hermann, 1976) and *Traité de podologie* (Paris: Maloine, 1981).

56. *Libération* (January 11, 1980).

57. J. Clavreul, *Le Monde* (January 19, 1980).

58. Official document conveyed to me by Daniel Soulez-Larivière.

59. Minutes of January 19, 1980.

60. See *L'Ane,* 1, p. 25.

61. Diary of Jenny Aubry.

62. *Le Monde* (January 24, 1980).

63. *Le Monde* (February 9, 1980).

64. The two volumes published by *Ornicar?: La scission de 1953* and *L'excommunication;* see chap. 7, this volume.

65. Archives of the EFP, reproduced in *L'Ane,* 1, p. 25.

66. Statutes registered with the Prefecture (February 21, 1980).

67. Interview with L. Althusser.

68. *Le Matin* (March 18, 1980).

69. Article by Catherine Clément in *Le Matin* (March 17, 1980). There are several extant versions of Althusser's intervention. I have chosen that of the protagonist.

70. *Delenda,* 2 (March 25, 1980), p. 4.

71. *Entre-temps,* April 1980.

72. Documents and archives of the EFP.

73. 1980 *Roster,* arch. J.-A.M.; letter from Simatos and Laurent to D. Soulez-Larivière. With the assistance of C. Simatos I have been able to reconstitute the complete list of members of the EFP.

74. Circular of April 27, 1980.

75. *L'Ane,* 1, p. 32.

76. Circular of June 16, 1980.

77. Circular of June 29, 1980.

78. *Entre-temps information,* circular.

79. *L'Ane,* 1, p. 30.

80. Interview with S. Faladé.

81. Ibid.

82. Circular of September 22, 1980, signed by Montrelay, Rabant, Brochier, and circular of September 23, 1980, from the directorate of the EFP.

83. Circular of the EFP, September 27, 1980.

84. C. Dorgeuille, *La Seconde Mort,* p. 26.

85. *Le Matin* of October 24, 1980. Article 31 of the new Penal Code elaborated by Robert Badinter's team is to replace the former Article 64, no longer nullifying the performance of deeds. Mention is made of nonpunishable—rather than nonresponsible—subjects: "Whoever, at the time of his actions, suffers from a psychic or neuropsychic disturbance abolishing his judgment or the control of his deeds cannot be prosecuted."

86. *Le Monde* (May 11, 1984); *Dialogue franco-soviétique sur la psychanalyse* (Toulouse: Privat, 1984).

87. Concerning the vote of November 14, 1980, see arch. J.-A.M.

88. Session of November 6, 1980; circular of October 30, 1980; report of the directorate of the CF; circular of November 22, 1980.

89. C. Dorgeuille, *La Seconde Mort,* pp. 28–29.

90. Vote of December 19, documents of the SCI, arch. J.A.

91. C. Dorgeuille, *La Seconde Mort,* p. 49.

92. Ibid., p. 50.

93. Document distributed to members of the Cause freudienne and conveyed to me by J.-A. Miller.

94. Separate interviews with J.-A. Miller and S. Leclaire.

95. Interview with S. Faladé.

96. Interview with M. Safouan.

97. Statutes of the Cause freudienne, published in C. Dorgeuille, *La Seconde Mort.* See also Bernard Sichère, *Le moment lacanien* (Paris: Grasset, 1983).

98. Claude Conté, circular of January 3, 1981.

99. *Courrier de l'ECF* (January 19, 1981).

100. First statutes of the ECF, published in C. Dorgeuille, *La Seconde Mort.*

101. Public meeting of January 22, 1981.

102. C. Dorgeuille, *La Seconde Mort,* p. 87.

103. Circulars of January 26, 1981, and January 28, 1981.

104. Circular of January 27, 1981.

105. Letter of February 11, 1981, C. Dorgeuille, *La Seconde Mort,* p. 125.

106. *Le Matin* (March 27, 1981).

107. See *Tribune* (bulletin of the CCAF), 1, Paris, 1985.

108. *L'Ane,* 1, p. 16.

109. See the ECF "day" of November 1981. Proceedings published in February 1985 (Paris: Navarin).

110. *Littoral,* 1, *Blasons de la phobie* (Toulouse: Érès, 1981).

Epilogue

1. Private sources.

2. *Le Monde* (September 15, 1981).

3. Testimony of J. Aubry.

4. *Humanité* (September 11, 1981).

5. *Libération* (September 11, 1981).

6. *Le Matin* (September 11, 1981).

7. *Le Figaro* (September 11, 1981).

8. *Le Quotidien* (September 11, 1981).

9. *Le Monde* (September 11, 1981).

10. *Le Monde* (September 16, 1981).

11. *L'Express* of September 18–24, 1981; see also A. Renaut and L. Ferry, *La Pensée 68* (Paris: Gallimard, 1985).

12. See Epilogue to *Bataille* I and R. Major, *Le Monde* (October 28, 1981).

13. *Libération* (September 11, 1981).

A Hundred Years of Psychoanalysis: An Inventory

1. See Appendixes.

2. Claude Dorgeuille, *La Seconde Mort* (Paris: Actualité freudienne, 1981), p. 55.

3. *Psychanalystes,* 1, November 1981. The same issue contains materials concerning the TVA organized by Anne Levallois.

4. Document conveyed to me by J.-P. Moreigne.

5. See the materials assembled in *L'Ane,* May-June 1982; *Psychanalystes,* 2, March 1982.

6. *Le Débat,* Paris, Gallimard, 30, May 1984, and the continuation in 32, November 1984.

7. There is an "École lacanienne de psychosomatique" whose founders were not members of any other group previously.

8. See F. Ansermet, "Entretien avec J.-A. Miller" (Paris: Navarin, 1985).

9. *Le Discours psychanalytique,* June 1983.

10. Joël Dor, *Bibliographie des travaux de Jacques Lacan* (Paris: Inter-Éditions, 1984); Maud Mannoni, *Quinzaine littéraire,* 412, March 1–15, 1984.

11. *Littoral,* 13, 1984, p. 110. For the question of the transcription of the seminars, see chap. 10, this volume.

12. Documents on the trial conveyed to me by Danièle Arnoux; verdict published by *Ornicar?,* 35, Winter 1985–1986.

13. Roster and statutes of the ECF, 1982.

14. Laurence Bataille, letter to Colette Soler (November 25, 1982), arch. Laurence Bataille. Laurence Bataille read and corrected the manuscript before her death.

15. Actual figures not transmitted.

16. CFRP, *Administration, statuts, règlement interieur,* internal bulletin, 1986.

17. Ibid., p. 4.

18. See *Tribune* (bulletin of the CCAF), 1.

19. Internal document of the AF, September 1982.

20. Interview with Contardo Calligaris.

21. See Jean Allouch, *Lettre pour lettre* (Toulouse: Érès, 1984); F. Dupré, *La solution du passage à l'acte;* P. Julien, *Le retour à Freud de Jacques Lacan* (Toulouse: Érès, 1985).

22. ELP, internal bulletin, 1986.

23. AAP, bulletin, 0, 1986.

24. Reference has already been made to all these works.

25. Association psychanalytique internationale, *Lettre d'information,* vol. 18, 1, January 1986, internal circular, p. 7.

Index